ISBN 978-0-483-13579-6
PIBN 10783338

LONDON.
NIALL AND COCKSHAW, PRINTERS, 4, HORSE-SHOE-COURT, LUDGATE-HILL.

LONDON .
BEALL AND COCKSHAW, PRINTERS, 4, HORSE-SHOE-COURT, LUDGATE-HILL.

THE

# Eclectic Review.

---

## JANUARY, 1851.

---

ART. I.—1. *Aids to Reflection.* By Samuel Taylor Coleridge. Edited by Henry Nelson Coleridge. 2 vols. Pickering. 1848.

2. *Essays on his own Times; forming a Second Series of the Friend.* By Samuel Taylor Coleridge. Edited by his Daughter. 3 vols. Pickering. 1850.

3. *Notes and Lectures upon Shakespeare, with other Literary Remains of S. T. Coleridge.* Edited by Mrs. H. N. Coleridge. 2 vols. Pickering. 1849.

4. *Confessions of an Inquiring Spirit; and some Miscellaneous Pieces.* By Samuel Taylor Coleridge. Edited by H. N. Coleridge, Esq., M.A. Pickering. 1849.

5. *Biographia Literaria; or, Biographical Sketches of my Literary Life and Opinions.* By Samuel Taylor Coleridge. Edited by H. N. Coleridge, and his Widow. 2 vols. Pickering. 1847.

6. *General Introduction to the Encyclopædia Metropolitana; or, a Preliminary Treatise on Method.* By Samuel Taylor Coleridge. Third Edition. Griffin.

ALL human things are subject to one absolutely universal law— that of *change.* Religion itself, the highest of the affairs of man, is not exempted from its operation. There are various proofs that this is the fact; thus, in our personal religious experience we begin by trusting in Jesus as the Saviour of sinners, and thence advance to child-like confidence towards God in Him,

and, beyond this, by Him attain to that state, which apostles
have described as Christ living in us, the participation of the
Divine nature, being children of God.    The accuracy with
which the 'Pilgrim's Progress' depicts the soul's life of a Christian, and the help which it has ever afforded to its development,
would alone be sufficient to show that in this aspect religion is
subject to change.    The comparison of the manifestations of the
religious life in different ages,—as, for example, that of patri-
archs with that of prophets, and the psalmists' with the apostles',
—conducts us to the same conclusion.    But it is much more
evident in the intellectual aspect of religion; and the whole history of doctrines is one continuous and incontrovertible proof of
this extent of the reign of change.    For the want of attention
to such considerations, the opinion has become widely prevalent,
that Christianity, unlike all else that concerns man, is immutable.
With many this opinion has sprung from the *feeling* that religion
has to do with eternal truths, and must, therefore, like them, be
unchangeable.    But with others the source is very different.    All
who have adopted as their formula of faith the creed or system
of any Church or theologian of former days, are obliged to hold
that, whatever modifications the expression of gospel truth may
have been subject to before the date of their formula, it can
know none after it.    They are obliged to hold this, or else to
renounce for their creed that which has most especially recommended it for their adoption.    And they who have embraced
the philosophy of the day as a religion, are also obliged to maintain the unchangeableness of Christianity, or else they would
not be able to boast of the superiority of their invention to it,
in its fitness for men of the present age.

    This opinion widely prevails; and meanwhile, on every side
in society are indications of the imminence of a great change both
in the intellectual and vital aspects of the gospel, commencing,
most probably, in the former, but assuredly extending to, and
terminating in the latter.    Works of every variety of calibre,
indigenous and imported, passionately proclaim it.    The premature and too confident triumph of those that 'seek after wisdom'
over Christianity, and the timid conservatism of those to whom
the kingdom of God is more in word than in power, alike
bespeak its approach.    But a surer sign is the hopefulness which
possesses those who, whether in years so or not, are young in
heart, and which impels them to lay hold of every help time
brings for the nurture of the spiritual life within them; for dis-
encumbering their faith of the traditional beliefs which have
weighed upon it so heavily; for manifesting their knowledge and
love of the truth in the clearest and completest manner; and for
expressing it in such a way as to lead themselves and others

onwards to a more full and satisfactory experience of all that is given to man in Jesus Christ.

It is scarcely needful to say, that we heartily sympathize with those that thus strive and hope. And if what we have already said does not justify us, we might make our appeal to those who hold by the past, in preference to the present or coming aspects of the gospel. The most resolute in orthodoxy do not shape Christian truth into the same doctrines that they did whose names they employ as watchwords; and if they employ the same terms, the explanations they give of their meaning are vastly different. Father Newman, in his ' Essay on Development,' has gone far beyond the canons and decrees of the Romish Church; and the evangelical views of Mr. Gorham are not those of the Puritan divines whose ground he professes to maintain. Nor is it possible for them to do otherwise. The world has moved on during these last three hundred years; and it is with mankind as it is with individuals, who proceed from the first crude imaginings of childhood to the maturer, though still imperfect, opinions which beseem men of riper years; the cheerful docility of infancy is all that can or ought to be preserved. It would be as wise to insist that the Bible should never be printed, because it was originally preserved by writing alone; or that it should not be translated into modern languages, because first of all composed in Hebrew and Greek. The Church of Rome itself, in allowing the printing of modern translations, has admitted in effect what is sufficient to overthrow her claim of infallibility in the embodiment of Christian truth in her creeds of former ages.

The worst enemies of the truth are those that oppose themselves to these changes. They attempt impossibilities. Men must for ever up and on; and if hindered in attaining new and wider apprehensions and manifestations of truth, will attain new and fatal apprehensions and manifestations of falsehood, all the more fatal because mistaken for truth. The complaints uttered against the restlessness and mobility of young and active minds have less than no weight and value. If such minds move not, which will? It was so at the Reformation, when one of the favourite declamations against the Reformers was grounded on the youth of their adherents. Nay, it was so when the gospel was first preached amongst men. Every morbid stupidity that is ridiculed or condemned by these, is a reflection on the wisdom and faithfulness of their elders. The part the elders should have taken was that of preparing for the change, and guiding, and even leading on to it. Or, supposing that so much as this was impossible, and that settled and habitual modes of looking at the great things concerned could not be so altered or modified as to lead to such labours; at least, there should have been so

much knowledge as to allow them to see, that what has proved
in every way suitable and sufficient for themselves must not of
necessity be suitable and sufficient for others belonging to a later
and more advanced age.   And when they complain that these
aspirants condemn them retrospectively, they should not forget
their own unfairer judgment, which has condemned beforehand
that which is sought from the 'treasures of wisdom and knowledge' hidden in Jesus Christ.   There is a grand word in
'Locke's Journal,' which they who ponder the characteristics of
these times would do well to keep in mind:—'It is a duty we
owe to God, as the fountain and author of all truth, who is truth
itself; and it is a duty also we owe our own selves, if we will
deal candidly and sincerely with other souls, to have our minds
constantly disposed to entertain and receive truth wheresoever
we meet with it, or under whatever appearance of plain or
ordinary, strange, new, or perhaps displeasing, it may come in
our way.'   This thought we commend to those of whom we
speak, and address ourselves to the task before us.

   We have placed at the head of this article the titles of several
of the works of our distinguished philosopher and poet, Samuel
Taylor Coleridge, for the purpose of recommending the study of
his writings to those of our readers who are desirous of obtaining
a sure standing-place, whence they may look upon the religious
controversies that are now proceeding, and discern whither they
are tending; and whence, too, they may set forth, with some
assurance of success, in the arduous and noble endeavour after
genuine Christian life and knowledge.   This recommendation
we wish especially to impress upon our younger readers, remembering how this study furnished to ourselves the means of
gaining such a confidence in the gospel, that not only were we
placed out of the reach of the old objections to it, but forefended
also from the misery of feeling ourselves beset with difficulties
unknown before, which we could not dispose of, and which
would have left us no alternative but to renounce what we
heartily believed, or to hold by it without a reason that could
satisfy the heart.   Many beside ourselves ascribe to Coleridge
such service as this; and most surely, at no time was such
service needed as at the present, when the truth is assailed with
weapons, apparently from her own armoury, and by men whom
we might well believe to be willing to die for her sake; and
when she is defended in a manner that leaves us little ground
for expecting an ultimate triumph, save the eternal life which is
hers as the offspring of God.

   But we must narrow our field, for it would be too large a
task on this occasion to show the bearing of our author's principles upon all the theological questions which are now under

discussion; and the position taken by him in respect of one at least, the connexion of the Church with the State, is such, that though Dissenters cannot agree with it, they could find more in it than Churchmen to approve. We shall confine our remarks, therefore, to the relation of Philosophy to Theology, which will include the Method, or *Organon*, of theological inquiry, and the relation of Theology to Religion, excluding specific notice of the sources of theological knowledge, of the doctrines of theology, and of all which is associated with ecclesiastical matters. And we shall adopt this course, both because these subjects are well suited to our pages, and also because in them are involved some of the points of the greatest moment, respecting which definite and available principles need now to be obtained. Something we must say of the questions themselves first, and then we shall endeavour to show what aid Coleridge can afford to an honest and intelligent inquirer.

The question of the relation of Philosophy to Theology appears to us to be the primary one of our day, and, indeed, of every day; for according to the conclusion arrived at upon it, almost every other question is answered, and it is one upon which shallow and most unsafe opinions may be easily formed, and such as shall seem to be incontrovertible whilst they are utterly baseless. It must be remembered that this is a subject of a purely scientific character, for theology is truly a science, inasmuch as it is knowledge reduced to method and organic order, although that knowledge is of such a kind as to make the system constructed, in every case, in no small degree individual. A Christian man alone can apply scientific method to that knowledge which is the material of theology, since he alone possesses it; but any man of philosophical insight and education can teach the scientific method by which a theology can be formed, since it is only the method common to all sciences. Excepting those good simple souls, who mean nothing but the service of truth, though they often do it great disservice, who are not sufficiently cultivated to avoid the confusion of theology with religion, of the science with the knowledge which it methodizes, the relation of philosophy to religion is denied only by such as will allow no philosophy to be true but their own, and who, not always knowing exactly what that is, fear that, if they admit such a relation generally, their own theology will not be able to stand its ground. And yet it is evident that, as a man's philosophy is, so, if he be a Christian man, must his theology be; that is, a Christian man must needs ' interpret' (as Lord Bacon says) the facts of his religious life by the help of those views and principles, whatever they may be, that form his philosophy. We do not speak of theologies taken at second-hand from the works of professed divines, which may, or may not, represent a man's own knowledge, but of that which, however defective or erroneous, he has consciously, or it may be even unconsciously, framed for himself, and which he has by him, not like a book upon a shelf, but like a thought in his mind, part of his very self. It cannot be doubted that a disciple of the school of Locke would construct a wonderfully different system of theology from one of the school of Hegel; and the outcry against the study of German philosophy, so common and so loud now in some quarters, is an acknowledgment of this fact. What is needed is the clear perception of the necessity of this relation; and that whatever system of theology any one may have formed, or honestly adopted, necessarily involves the philosophical principles of its constructor, and without them could not have been.

When this is perceived, it will be seen of what moment it is that our philosophy should not ignore any of the great facts of human consciousness, or grovel and maunder about sensations or suggestions, as if in them all the secret of the universe was hidden, while the lofty themes of spiritual knowledge, and freedom, and truth, invite its attention and research. Systems of philosophy are for philosophers, but their influence spreads far and wide beyond this select band. As years roll on, the thoughts which sprang into being in the mind of the solitary thinker, and the very terms in which he embodied them, become the common property and market-language of human-kind. The philosophy of Hobbes, expounded by Locke and Paley, until very lately, when an opposite system began to make its influence felt, has given a peculiar character to the entire English mind, both here and in the New World; and Cooper could make his famous 'Leather-stocking' speak of his 'idees,' in a way that would have horrified both Plato and Aristotle, although it was with the exact signification assigned to the word by the sensational school. No attentive student of the history of the great French Revolution can fail to discern in it the influence of the same philosophy, as it was expounded by Condillac. And now, both in the United States and in our own country, the thoughts and the terms which Kant, first of all in these later times, gave currency to, are beginning to show themselves in a similar manner. And it is thus that the philosophical spirit of an age is formed; and this, just as with the individual, determines the character of the theological systems that prevail. An illustration in proof, of a very remarkable character, is afforded us by the history of doctrines during the last two hundred years. The forms of belief that truly represented the religious life and knowledge of the sixteenth and seventeenth centuries, by degrees ceased to hold this relationship, and grew to be mere forms, animated by no living faith. During the hundred years that followed the Puritan Revolution, the philosophy which Locke taught spread in England, and, as a necessary consequence, appeared that cold and dreary Unitarianism which overran this land at the commencement of the last century. And then Whitfield and Wesley arose, and summoned back some spirit of life into the old doctrines, rekindling the piety which had almost expired with their fervent breath; but they were both men of their own age alone, and in neither dwelt the power which could shape, or bring on, the coming age; they held by the doctrines of the Reformation and the philosophy of Locke, welding, but not fusing, them into one by their mighty zeal. It could not but result from this that, when years had passed, and men of lesser mark in inward devoutness entered upon their labours, and knowledge and arts had imparted their impulse to the world, the life should shrink from out the old forms again, and men should anxiously look about them for new forms by which to shield and nourish their faith. But now a new spirit of philosophy had arisen, not such as grew out of the teaching of Locke, a spiritual philosophy; and we see to-day in Germany, in America, and in our own country, a species of Pantheism eagerly adopted as the theology of the age, just as when, a hundred years ago, a new theology was needed, and a sensational philosophy prevailed, Unitarianism was embraced as the system most accordant with such life as the age could boast. This illustration reveals much of the relation of Theology to Religion also, as will appear when we have treated of that question; and in both respects it is full of most concerning instruction for teachers at the present time.

Theology being a science, it not only follows that it should be affected by every change in philosophy, in the manner we have noted, but also, as every science is, by the extension of human knowledge generally; questions continually rising respecting what was formerly received without hesitation, and much that was considered to be indissolubly connected with it being removed to other departments of science, and investigated and classified by means of their laws. And this, which at first awakens the liveliest alarm and hostility, is afterwards discovered to be right; as has been the case with astronomy and geology, and metaphysics, all of which, by the Schoolmen, and by others of later date than they, were included in the domain of this Queen of the Sciences. But especially is Theology affected by every advance towards what Bacon designates *philosophia prima;* which in our days is called *method.* Aristotelian Logic was, and by a few still is, considered the legitimate *organon* of inquiry;

but as theological science, like every other, is based upon facts,
and ought to be cultivated so as to bear the soundest and most
abundant fruitage (to employ Bacon's metaphor), and this method
can neither discover, nor invent, nor apply, but only develop
and prove, though it were faultless, it must be as inadequate to
explain the facts, and to direct the practice that should be
grounded on them, in this science, as it is by all men known to
be in physics ; and the employment of it must be as unwise.
The splendid *organon* of Lord Bacon, cleared of the obscurities
which his own imperfect apprehension and incomplete treatment
of it have occasioned, and corrected and rendered applicable by
the aid of more recent labourers in the same wealthy field—this,
by which every science that now adorns and blesses human life
has been constructed, must be resorted to; and then Theology,
which has hitherto produced little beside thorns and contentions
in all our ways, shall fill her proper sphere, and, through her,
Philosophy shall (as her great teacher prayed) bestow ' a largess
of new alms upon the family of mankind.'

The relation of Theology to Religion ranks only next in interest, at the present time, to the question we have discussed, and
outstrips it in importance.   Perhaps the reason for the common
denial of any relation of Philosophy to Theology arises from the
circumstance that the latter is so frequently confounded with
Religion.   Now it is of the utmost moment that the distinction
between them should be seen ; and it is so obvious that when
seen it appears most wonderful that it should ever have been
necessary to point it out.   We have already, in effect, done so ;
but we repeat it that we may show how the confusion has arisen,
and also more clearly exhibit the true relation of the one to the
other.   Religion, in such phrases as ' the Christian religion,' has
a signification near akin to Theology, being a little wider, as it
includes the outward observances of devotion, &c. ; and in those
communities in which outward profession and observance is
valued for its own sake, as in the Church of Rome, it signifies
those observances, and nothing more ; but when so used, there is
a tacit assumption that there *is* nothing else to be so entitled—
that in these things the whole relation of man to God is fulfilled.
We know, however, that these are of the smallest possible value
in the fulfilment of that relation ; and that it is by the allegiance
and love of the heart spontaneously and truthfully rendered to
God, by the aspiration after such oneness of spirit and will with
him as may realize the being a child of God, that man takes his
proper place in his sight; and to this aspiration and confidence
and love we give the name Religion.   Constituted as man is,
such a spiritual state cannot exist without being shared, according
to its capability, by the intellect ; for religion is the self-devotion

of the whole man to God; and hence it arises that he is not only able, but constrained, to construct a systematic representation of the knowledge and experience which lead to, and follow from, this self-devotion; and such a representation is Theology. Religion, thus, is the material, Philosophy supplies the form and method, and the science Theology is the result; in it Philosophy and Religion are wedded. But this is not the whole of the relation of which we now speak. All human science, worthy of the name, not only methodizes what is already known by man, but also furnishes him with the means of making new acquisitions in knowledge, and especially directs him in the practical application of it; theological science must needs have this scope, as a science; and it has, moreover, from its peculiar character—its facts being those of the inner life—a most powerful influence in keeping that life at the level it represents, and of producing harmony and consistency in its various manifestations and modes of activity. Herein lies the unspeakable worth, or the deadly danger, of Theology. If it do not embrace all the phenomena or facts of a man's religion, what is left out is in great danger of being overlooked, and the life of becoming, in consequence, unsymmetrical and imperfect. If it do not give to any of these facts its proper rank; if it exalt what is subordinate, and depress what ought to have pre-eminence; there is the danger that, in the life, henceforward, the same inversion should be displayed. If it do not aim at practice, there is the danger that, practically, religion should be divorced from the life, and become a mere speculation, or, worse still, a fanaticism, powerful only for ill. Such are the consequences, on the one hand, of the relation of Theology to Religion; those, on the other, are the harmonious culture, and constant advancement, and progressive development, of all that enters into this spiritual and inward life, accompanied by such manifestations of it, not only in devotional observances, but in all that makes up man's life in time, as shall attest its character and source, and give to it a higher completeness, and fit the subject of it in ever loftier services here to help forward the accomplishment of God's great purpose respecting the world, as 'a living epistle of Christ, known and read of all men.'

These are the questions respecting which we purpose to exhibit the kind of assistance that all who desire to become acquainted with matters of such infinite concern as are agitated now, and to find a means of safety and defence in these times of conflict and peril, and especially beginners in theological inquiry, may find in the writings of Coleridge. Our efforts have been directed simply to setting them, as questions, before our readers; for our space and our scope alike forbade the attempt at complete

discussion of them ; and we have so treated of them as, if possible, to awaken reflection respecting them, and thus to lead
away the thought from the subjects of lighter moment to these,
upon which, if true conclusions are reached, there will be little
difficulty, comparatively, in attaining the truth respecting the
others.   They have, in fact, been already proposed in Mr.
Morell's 'Philosophy of Religion ;' but will, we fear, have to be
repeatedly urged upon both teachers and taught, and brought
forward in various forms, before they receive the attention they
deserve ; and by this consideration, as well as by those we have
mentioned before, we have been moved in our selection of them
for our present purpose.

It is not our intention on this occasion to speak of the Biography of Coleridge, rich though it is with profound and varied
instruction.   Nor shall we regard him in his ' many-sidedness,'
but simply as a Philosopher and a Theologian.   Neither can we
stay to notice all that has been or can be said to his disadvantage.
Much of it is irrelevant.   The charge of plagiarism, one of the
most vexatious attacks upon his name, has been well met, in the
later editions of his works, by a minute and careful reference of
all that even seems to be borrowed to the primary sources ; the
editor has shown her appreciation of the original wealth of her
father's mind, by thus acknowledging the full amount of what
he appears to be indebted to others for ; and we think that this
accusation is effectually silenced.   And much cancels itself, being
self-destructive.   Thus, if one party in the Church of England
holds him to be the guilty source of John Sterling's ' infidelity,'
others, whose opinions are quite as weighty, regard him as the
' father of the Puseyites.'   The fact respecting his writings is,
that he declares great truths and principles with sufficient boldness and clearness, but often fails completely in his deductions
from them, and in his applications of them ; as Bacon himself
has failed in the practical illustration of his *novum organon ;* and
so it has fallen out, that men of most opposite schools and creeds,
dwelling on the principles, or on the conclusions, and overlooking the others, have claimed him as belonging to them.   This
we hold to be one excellence of his works for the purpose we
have in view, which is not to enforce ready-made opinions, but
to discipline the mind so that it may be able to form them for
itself.

For the same reason we consider it to be a great advantage
that Coleridge does not in any of his works formally expound a
system either of philosophy or of theology.   That he had such
systems every attentive reader of his writings can perceive, but
the whole habit of his mind forbade his undertaking the task of
' the practical architect, by whose skill a temple of faith, or a

school for wisdom, should be reared.' He is rather, as a transatlantic writer has said of him, 'an inspired poet, an enthusiastic
prophet of a spiritual philosophy;' or, more truly, treasures
both of wisdom and faith lie dispersed through his books, like
the wealth of nature in mine and mountain, in forest and plain,
seemingly without plan or order, yet all really placed by the
operation of secret laws of most exquisite order, which reveal
themselves only to the earnest student. We shall not attempt
to develop his systems, for we do not recommend him as a
master whose *ipse dixit* is to put an end to all controversy, and
whose modes of thought are to be implicitly received and followed; but as a teacher of the art of reflection, whose ability is
all the greater from this seeming desultoriness.

We shall confine our extracts, as far as possible, to the illustration of the two questions we have stated, but we must premise
that we cannot always strictly do so. And we shall endeavour
to prevent any passage from losing its force by appearing as a
mere fragment, though, in general, no precaution of this kind
will be required; his best work, as we esteem it, the 'Aids to
Reflection,' from which we shall borrow most largely, being
wholly of a fragmentary character, and his most thoroughly com-
pacted writings consisting of series of essays, the connexion of
which appears at times rather arbitrary. Much in these extracts,
and in his philosophical and theological works, may not seem to
throw any light directly on the matters now most eagerly controverted; yet we know, from experience, that the principles and
elements of truth to be learned from them, and the habits of
thought cultivated by them, can and will lead to the discovery
of what does most satisfactorily illuminate the darkest of these
questions. It ought also to be mentioned, that very many of his
thoughts have passed into general circulation, and, therefore, not
all even of what we quote must be expected to wear an air of
novelty.

One other remark we feel bound to make—but a few years
back it was quite customary, even amongst thinking men, to
speak of Coleridge's metaphysics as deep and mysterious, as
being, in their sense of the word, 'transcendental;' but a total
change has passed over this subject, and now what was so high
and unearthly as to be deemed fit only for cloud-land, is pronounced shallow, elementary, and fit only for boys at school.
The truth, as ever, lies between these extremes; not *elementary*,
as his present critics use the term, his philosophy most assuredly is;
but at the same time not dark and mysterious and verging upon
the inane. The men who have been most ready in the outset
of their studies to acknowledge their obligations to his works,
have, when they had gained a deeper and wider acquaintance

with their great themes, wondered a little that they should ever
have been able to think of them, as they well remember that
they did.  For Coleridge, as we have said, teaches no system,
not even his own, and hence he cannot be such a constant companion, nor, for so long a time, the guide of those who are
aiming at the loftiest heights of wisdom, as if he had done so,
and driven his readers' minds along his own line of reflection,
instead of inspiring them with the will and the power to construct and to move along lines of their own.  All that he has
written may, in short, be regarded as *propaideutick* to the larger
study of philosophy and theology, and as such alone we recommend it now.

By way of confirming the opinions we have expressed respecting the value of Coleridge's works, we refer our readers to the
'Preliminary Essay,' which is contained in the second volume of
the 'Aids to Reflection,' written by the late Mr. James Marsh,
President of the University of Vermont, in the United States;
and subjoin the opinions of two other philosophical writers of
the same country, which we happen to have lying before us.
Kaufman, in the preface to his translation of Bockshammer's
'Treatise on the Will,' says,—'Coleridge's writings afford the
best introduction to the study of German philosophy.  He had
much of the German spirit, and often employs German terms.
Yet he was by no means bound to the Germans; for instead of
translating their works, or retailing their speculations, he drew
his thoughts from the depths and fulness of his own exhaustless
mind.'  And Ripley, in his 'Introductory Notice' of Victor
Cousin's writings, observes, that the works of our author are
'exceedingly valuable to two classes of persons: to those on
whom the light of spiritual truth is beginning to dawn, who are
just awakened to the consciousness of the inward power of their
nature, and who need to have the sentiment of religion quickened into more vital activity; and to those who have obtained,
as the fruit of their own reflections, a living system of spiritual
faith.  The former will find the elements of congenial truth
profusely scattered over his pages; and the latter may construct
out of their own experience a systematic whole with the massive
fragments that are almost buried beneath the magnificent confusion of his style.  But he cannot satisfy the mind whose
primary want is philosophical clearness and precision.'  The
grateful dedication prefixed by Archdeacon Hare to his 'Mission
of the Comforter,' will be fresh in our readers' memories, and
may stand as the representative of the feelings with which his
name is cherished by those in his own country who have proved
themselves the best able to appreciate his worth.

The 'Aids to Reflection' consists of a copious selection of

passages from English theological writers of the sixteenth and seventeenth centuries, and principally from Leighton, with comments, and so arranged as ' to establish the distinct characters of prudence, morality, and religion;' 'to substantiate and set forth at large the momentous distinction between reason and understanding;' and with this framework to afford, what Mr. Marsh designates, ' a philosophical statement and vindication of the distinctively spiritual and peculiar doctrines of the Christian system.' It would have been more satisfactory, had our space permitted it, to have shown how, in the principles laid down in this work, a safeguard from the errors of our day may be found, and a reply to the most prodigious of its false assertions. We are obliged, however, to restrict our employment of it to quotations, which can only show the kind of assistance in reflection it can afford; and perhaps, also, which is of more moment, how, practically, philosophy subserves the great interests of religion through its bearing on theology. The distinction between reason and understanding, of which Coleridge says: ' Not only is it innocent in its possible influences on the religious character, but it is an indispensable preliminary to the removal of the most formidable obstacles to an intelligent belief of the peculiar doctrines of the gospel, of the characteristic articles of the Christian faith, with which the advocates of the truth in Christ have to contend, the evil heart of unbelief alone excepted ' (*Aids*, vol. i. p. 196)—this distinction, which will appear clearly enough in some passages, must be borne in mind in reading them all, or the author's meaning will not appear.

Take this, from the ' Notes on the Pilgrim's Progress,' as embodying his view of the influence of philosophy on religion, through theology :—

' If by metaphysics we mean those truths of the pure reason which always transcend, and not seldom appear to contradict, the understanding; or (in the words of the great apostle), spiritual verities which can only be spiritually discerned—and this is the true and legitimate meaning of *metaphysics;* then I affirm that this very controversy between the Arminians and the Calvinists, in which both are partially right in what they affirm, and both wholly wrong in what they deny, is a proof that without metaphysics there can be no light of faith.'—*Lit. Rem.* vol. iii. p. 403.

Elsewhere he says :—

' A hunger-bitten and idea-less philosophy naturally produces a starveling and comfortless religion.'—*Statesm. Man.* p. 230.

And—

' To the immense majority of men, even in civilized countries, speculative philosophy has ever been, and must ever remain, a *terra incognita.*

Yet it is not the less true, that all the epoch-forming revolutions of the Christian world, the revolutions of religion, and with them the civil, social, and domestic habits of the nations concerned, have coincided with the rise and fall of metaphysical systems.'—*Ib.* p. 215.

In another remark he touches a deeper point in the relation between the subjects of which we speak :—

' The same principle, which in its application to the whole of our being becomes religion, considered speculatively, is the basis of metaphysical science; that, namely, which requires an evidence beyond that of sensible concretes.'—*Friend*, vol. iii. pp. 97, 98.

And thus he states the scope of his writings :—

' This has been my object, and this alone can be my defence, . . . the unquenched desire, not without the consciousness of having earnestly endeavoured, to kindle young minds, and to guard them against the temptations of scorners, by showing that the scheme of Christianity, . . . . though not discoverable by human reason, is yet in accordance with it; that link follows link by necessary consequence; that Religion passes out of the ken of Reason only where the eye of Reason has reached its own horizon; and that Faith is then but its continuation: even as the day softens away into the sweet twilight, and twilight, hushed and breathless, steals into the darkness.'— *Biog. Lit.* vol. ii. pp. 308, 309.

But we may, before we take up the ' Aids to Reflection,' spare our readers some thought by giving the following eloquent passages, in which the most distinctive characteristics of Coleridge's philosophy are clearly indicated :—

' *God created man in his own image. To be the image of his own eternity* created he man ! Of eternity and self-existence what other likeness is possible, but immortality and moral self-determination ? In addition to sensation, perception, and practical judgment—instinctive or acquirable—concerning the notices furnished by the organs of perception, all which, in kind at least, the dog possesses in common with his master; in addition to these, God gave us reason, and with reason he gave us reflective self-consciousness ; gave us principles, distinguished from the maxims and generalizations of outward experience by their absolute and essential universality and necessity ; and, above all, by superadding to reason the mysterious faculty of free-will and consequent personal amenability, he gave us conscience—that law of conscience, which in the power, and as the indwelling word, of a holy and omnipotent legislator, commands us, from among the numerous ideas, mathematical and philosophical, which the reason, by the necessity of its own excellence, creates for itself—unconditionally commands us to attribute reality and actual existence to those ideas, and to those only, without which the conscience itself would be baseless and contradictory, to the ideas of soul, of free-will, of immortality, and of God. To God, as the reality of the conscience, and the source of all obligation ; to free-will, as the power of the human being to maintain its obedience which God, through the conscience, has commanded, against all the might of nature; and to the immortality of the soul, as a state in which the weal and woe of man shall be proportioned to his moral worth. With this faith all nature,

"All the mighty world of eye and ear,"

presents itself to us, now as the aggregated material of duty, and now as a vision of the Most High, revealing to us the mode, the time, and particular instance, of applying and realizing that universal rule pre-established in the heart of our reason.'—*Friend*, vol. i. pp. 146—148.

And this, which is of a more strictly scientific tone :—

' The spirit of man, or the spiritual part of our being, is the intelligent will; or (to speak less abstractly), it is the capability with which the Father of spirits hath endowed man, of being determined to action by the ultimate ends which the reason alone can present. The understanding, which derives all its materials from the senses, can dictate purposes only; that is, such ends as are in their turn means to other ends. The ultimate ends, by which the will is to be determined, and by which alone the will, not corrupted, *the spirit made perfect*, would be determined, are called, in relation to the reason, moral ideas. Such are the ideas of the eternal, the good, the true, the holy, the idea of God as the absoluteness and reality (or real ground) of all these, or as the Supreme Spirit in which all these substantially are, and are one; lastly, the idea of the responsible will itself—of duty, of guilt, or evil in itself without reference to its outward and separable consequences.'—*Ch. and State*, pp. 133, 134.

In the following extracts the student will find material for thought, not merely respecting the general relations of Philosophy to Theology and Religion, but specifically respecting the *method* he should pursue in his investigation. How these views are connected with, and spring from, a spiritual philosophy, will appear, if the passage quoted last but one be attentively re-perused.

Our author, in his discussion of the doctrine of election, says :—

' The following may, I think, be taken as a safe and useful rule in religious inquiries. Ideas, that derive their origin and substance from the moral being, and to the reception of which as true objectively (that is, as corresponding to a reality out of the human mind), we are determined by a practical interest exclusively, may not, like theoretical positions, be pressed onward into all their logical consequences. The law of conscience, and not the canons of discursive reasoning, must decide in such cases; at least, the latter have no validity which the single *veto* of the former is not sufficient to nullify. The most pious conclusion is here the most legitimate.

' It is too seldom considered, though most worthy of consideration, how far those ideas or theories of pure speculation, which bear the same name with the objects of religious faith, are indeed the same. Out of the principles necessarily presumed in all discursive thinking, and which being in the first place universal, and secondly, antecedent to every particular exercise of the understanding, are therefore referred to the reason,—the human mind (wherever its powers are sufficiently developed, and its attention strongly directed to speculative or theoretical inquiries) forms certain essences, to which, for its own purposes, it gives a sort of notional subsistence.'—*Aids*, vol. i. pp. 124, 125.

After various illustrations of the need of attention to the danger pointed out in the last paragraph, Coleridge re-states his view of the part to be taken by human reason, for the purpose of providing ' a safety-lamp for religious inquirers.'

' This,' he says, ' I find in the principle, that all revealed truths are to be judged of by us, so far only as they are possible subjects of human conception, or grounds of practice, or in some way connected with our moral and spiritual interests. In order to have a reason for forming a judgment on any given article, we must be sure that we possess a reason by, and according to which, such a judgment may be formed. Now in respect of all truths to which a real independent existence is assigned, and which yet are not contained in, or to be imagined under, any form of space or time, it is strictly demonstrable that the human reason, considered abstractly as the source of positive science and theoretical insight, is not such a reason. At the utmost, it has only a negative voice. In other words, nothing can be allowed as true for the human mind which directly contradicts this reason. But even here, before we admit the existence of any such contradiction, we must be careful to ascertain that there is no equivocation in play, that two different subjects are not confounded under one and the same word.'   .   .   . ' But if not the abstract or speculative reason, and yet a reason there must be in order to a rational* belief, then it must be the practical reason of man, comprehending the will, the conscience, the moral being, with its inseparable interests and affections ; that reason, namely, which is the organ of wisdom, and, as far as man is concerned, the source of living and actual truths.'—*Ib.* pp. 132, 133.

Illustrations of the position, that every doctrine is to be interpreted in reference to those who know, or might know it, follow ; and the essay concludes thus :—

' Do I then utterly exclude the speculative reason from theology ? No. It is its office and rightful privilege to determine on the negative truth of whatever we are required to believe. The doctrine must not contradict any universal principle, for this would be a doctrine that

---

* We append one of the earliest aphorisms in the ' Aids to Reflection,' to prevent any mistake respecting Coleridge's use of this word. ' The word *rational* has been strangely abused of late times. This must not, however, disincline us to the weighty consideration, that thoughtfulness, and a desire to bottom all our convictions on grounds of right reason, are inseparable from the character of a Christian.'—*Aph.* xvi. p. 9.

contradicted itself. Or philosophy? No. It may be, and has been, the servant and pioneer of faith, by convincing the mind that a doctrine is cogitable, that the soul can present the idea to itself, and that, if we determine to contemplate, or think of, the subject at all, so, and in no other form, can this be effected. So far are both logic and philosophy to be received and trusted. But the duty, and in some cases, and for some persons, even the right, of thinking on subjects beyond the bounds of sensible experience, the ground of real truth, the life, the substance, the hope, the love, in one word, the faith; these are derivatives from the practical, moral, and spiritual nature and being of man.'—*Ib.* p. 142.

Amongst the ' Notes on Leighton,' not contained in the ' Aids to Reflection,' is one upon the consequences logically deducible from his Calvinistic doctrines, and which are so frequently regarded as conclusive against the reception of those doctrines. In it, some of the thoughts we have seen in the preceding passages are thus expressed :—

' The consequences appear to me, in point of logic, legitimately concluded from the terms of the premises. What shall we say then? Where lies the fault? In the original doctrines expressed in the premises? God forbid. In the particular deductions, logically considered? But these we have found legitimate. Where then? I answer, in deducing any consequences by such a process, and according to such rules. The rules are alien and inapplicable; the process presumptuous, yea, preposterous. The error lies in the false assumption of a logical deducibility at all in this instance. First, because the terms from which the conclusion must be drawn are accommodations, and not scientific. . . . Secondly, because the truths in question are transcendant, and have their evidence, if any, in the ideas themselves, and for the reason; and do not, and cannot, derive it from the conceptions of the understanding, which cannot comprehend the truths, but is to be comprehended in and by them. Lastly, and chiefly. because these truths, as they do not originate in the intellective faculty of man, so neither are they addressed primarily to our intellect, but are substantiated for us by their correspondence to the wants, cravings, and interests of the moral being, for which they were given, and without which they would be devoid of all meaning. The only conclusions, therefore, that can be drawn from them, must be such as are implied in the origin and purpose of their revelation; and the legitimacy of all conclusions must be tried by their consistency with those moral interests, those spiritual necessities, which are the proper final cause of the truths, and of our faith therein. For some of the faithful these truths have, I doubt not, an evidence of reason; but for the whole household of faith their certainty is in their working.' —*Lit. Rem.* vol. iv. pp. 158, 159.

For the development of the method by which Coleridge would construct his theology, we must refer the reader to his ' Essay on the Science of Method.' which was written as the general introduction to the ' Encyclopædia Metropolitana,' and is republished as a separate volume, in the edition of that costly work now in progress; or to the third volume of the 'Friend,' in which most of the matter of that essay will be found, with other illustrations and applications. Of it we can only say, that he preceded Whewell in the representation of the Baconian system of induction, which forms the groundwork of that writer's 'Philosophy of the Inductive Sciences.'

In the last extract may be discerned Coleridge's view of the Evidences of Christianity; and on this subject, which is so intimately connected with his philosophy, and is of such moment in its relation to existing controversies, we would that we had space for the insertion of some of his fuller statements of the position he took up. Here is one, however, which, though brief, is complete, and which expresses a fear that has, in fact, been realized, though not exactly in the way which he expected.

'I more than fear the prevailing taste for books of natural theology, physico-theology, demonstrations of God from nature, evidences of Christianity, and the like. Evidences of Christianity! I am weary of the word. Make a man feel the want of it; rouse him, if you can, to the self knowledge of his need of it; and you may safely trust it to its own evidence—remembering only the express declaration of Christ himself, *No man cometh to me unless the Father leadeth him.* Whatever more is desirable—I speak now with reference to Christians generally, and not to professed students of theology—may, in my judgment, be far more safely and profitably taught, without controversy or the supposition of infidel antagonists, in the form of ecclesiastical history.' —*Aids*, vol. i. pp. 333, 334.

After the paragraph containing our author's statement of the 'tenets peculiar to Christianity,' he supposes the questions, 'How can I comprehend this? How is this to be proved?' to be asked, and replies in this manner:—

'To the first question I answer: Christianity is not a theory, or a speculation, but a life; not a philosophy of life, but a life and a living process. To the second, TRY IT. It has been eighteen hundred years in existence, and has one individual left a record like the following?—" I tried it, and it did not answer." . . . . Have you, in your own experience, met with any one in whose words you could place full confidence, and who has seriously affirmed, " I have given Christianity a fair trial. . . . Yet my assurance of its truth has received no increase. Its promises have not been fulfilled, and I repent of my delusion?" If neither your own experience, nor the history of almost two thousand years, has presented a single testimony to this purport; and if you have heard and read of many who have lived and died bearing witness to the contrary; and if you have yourself met with some one, in whom on any other point you would place unqualified trust, who has on his own experience made report to you that he is faithful who promised, and what he promised he has proved himself able to perform: is it bigotry, if I fear that the unbelief which prejudges and prevents the experiment, has its source elsewhere than in the uncorrupted judgment—that not the strong free mind, but the enslaved will, is the true original infidel in this instance?'—*Ib.* pp. 157, 158.

Between this and our next quotation is the essay on 'The Difference in Kind between Reason and Understanding,' which, to such as are yet unacquainted with the fundamental proposition of the new and spiritual philosophy, is as good an introduction to it as may be found, and is not wholly without value to others. The following occurs in the 'Reflections,' by which the aphorism and its comment, discussing the doctrine of ' Original Sin,' are introduced :—

' The practical inquirer hath already placed his foot on the rock, if he have satisfied himself that whoever needs not a Redeemer is more than human.   Remove from him the difficulties and objections that oppose or perplex his belief of a crucified Saviour ; convince him of the reality of sin, which is impossible without a knowledge of its true nature and inevitable consequences ; and then satisfy him as to the fact historically, and as to the truth spiritually, of a redemption therefrom by Christ ; do this for him, and there is little fear that he will permit either logical quirks or metaphysical puzzles to contravene the plain dictate of his common sense, that the sinless One who redeemed mankind from sin must have been more than man, and that He who brought light and immortality into the world could not, in his own nature, have been an inheritor of death and darkness.   It is morally impossible that a man with these convictions should suffer the objection of incomprehensibility, and this on a subject of faith, to overbalance the manifest absurdity and contradiction in the notion of a Mediator between God and the human race, at the same infinite distance from God as the race for whom he mediates.'—*Ib.* pp. 201, 202.

This passage has an immediate bearing upon some of the most thorny and fruitless speculations which now occasion such distress to those who would fain be firmly grounded in the truth.   How many would have been kept from wandering in the trackless desert of doubt, where the only hope is a mirage, and the sand-storms ever threaten to overwhelm, had they received such guidance as it can afford, at the time when they first discovered that the broad, beaten path, they had pursued, could not lead them to the goal they desired !   Although in appearance somewhat dogmatically, because it but indicates the line of thought to be taken, it supplies an exact reply to one of Mr. Newman's dicta.   He says, in his ' Phases of Faith,' pp. 199, 200 :—' It is with hundreds or thousands a favourite idea, that " they have an inward witness of the truth of (*the historical and outward facts of*) Christianity."   Perhaps the statement would bring its own refutation to them if they would express it clearly.   .   .   .   But for the ambiguity of the word

c 2

*doctrine,* probably such confusion of thought would have been impossible. " Doctrines" are either spiritual truths, or are statements of external history.  Of the former we may have an inward witness—that is their proper evidence—but the latter must depend upon adequate testimony and logical criticism.' It is the portion of truth contained in such representations that makes the injury done by them the greater.  As soon as it is seen to be but a *fragment* of truth, no danger is to be apprehended from them, and this may be seen in the present instance, we think, if the extract from Coleridge be attentively considered in connexion with it.

The essays on ' Original Sin' and ' Redemption,' in the ' Aids to Reflection,' are too long for quotation, and we could not do them justice, either by abstracts or extracts.  We can only point them out, and particularly the latter, to our readers, as deserving most careful study, and as calculated, not merely to correct, but still more cogently to preclude the possibility of falling into such bewildering errors as we know not a few in these times, with the very best intentions of discovering and holding only the truth, have been deluded by.  And respecting these essays, and, indeed, respecting Coleridge's theological writings generally, the fact that he, who was intimately familiar with the philosophy whence the objections that are deemed most weighty have arisen, and with the divines of the best ages of our English school,—and who, moreover, though a Churchman, was by no means enslaved to the prejudices of the Church, for he did not shrink from the investigation of the most daring speculations respecting the faith, and he spoke with honest admiration of Cromwell and Bunyan, and with as honest reprobation of Charles and Laud,—the fact that Coleridge treats with such reverence, and avows with such heartiness his belief in, the truths that are now so pertinaciously impugned, ought to influence the feelings, though not the judgment, of any who are devoutly seeking a well-founded assurance respecting the Gospel of Christ.

We have not thought it needful to say a word in vindication of any proposition, either in philosophy or theology, which we have quoted, or which we know Coleridge to have laid down, for we have not recommended him as any other than a teacher of the art of thinking to good purpose on the great themes which he discusses ; and any introduction of polemical disquisition would have detracted from the force of that recommendation. It will be an augury of the highest hope and promise, that men shall be able to do as Locke counselled in the passage from his Journal we have given above ; and shall thankfully welcome, and diligently use, help from any hand in their arduous quest of truth; but suffer no hand, under the pretext of giving help, to lay fetters upon their souls, or to stop them in their high undertaking.

One of the characteristic features of our days appears to be this,—that the discussion of religious, or rather of theological questions, is so much in the hands of non-professional men. Coleridge was not a cleric. The audacious assumptions of authority were revived in the Anglican Church by a 'layman'; and they who have broached the most audacious denials in the name of reason, have been unconnected with any ministry. We do not undervalue a *theological* training; but we are deeply persuaded that both theology and religion have suffered from the *professional* cast of the minds that have hitherto been most forward in teaching and vindicating them. The world is so much larger than the cloistered student wots of, and the interests of every-day life are so varied, and far-reaching, and complicated, that it is no wonder if truths, in themselves the most momentous, and which ought of all to be the most universally influential, when treated of by such as know nothing of these common human affairs, should seem to be mere impertinences, and come to be regarded as having no relation whatever to the engagements that claim the greatest part both of the time and the thoughts of practical men. That non-professional minds should be directed to these matters, is surely a hopeful sign. The impulse given to physical and moral studies by the *educated common sense* of those who have joined in the pursuit of them, none can deny; and the stagnant and chaotic condition of the two great branches of knowledge, which, having been ranked with theology as 'professions,' have not shared this impulse— medicine and law—alike declare to us the vast benefits which may be expected, in the end, from these voluntary labours, and one cause, at least, of the present condition of the noblest of all sciences. Many a year may come and go before all we long to see accomplished will be brought to pass; but not bating 'a jot of heart or hope,' we will watch for and hail every token that the time draws near, and strive, as now, to enlist the hearts and minds of those who best can aid in such services as must effectually hasten the advent of the reign of God's truth alone amongst men.

Amongst the works we have enumerated at the head of this article are two which we could not refer to in connexion with our theme. The 'Notes and Lectures upon Shakspeare, and some of the old Poets and Dramatists,' is a republication, in a more commodious and cheaper form, of the substance of the first two volumes of Coleridge's 'Literary Remains,' which have been long out of print. They will be welcomed by all who know the value of the criticisms and critical principles of our philosopher; and to all who desire to become acquainted with those glories of our national literature, we can heartily recommend them, as containing some of the very best helps that are to be found in our language. There are other 'literary remains' included in these volumes, some of which have not before appeared in any collection of our author's writings, which greatly increase their worth. The 'Essays on his own Times' are a reprint of Coleridge's contributions to political journals, commencing with the papers published in his own 'Watchman,' the story of which he has told with such effect in his 'Biographia Literaria.' They are said to form 'a second series of the Friend,' and they are not unworthy of ranking with that work. But they have an independent value from their relation to the eventful period in which they were written. And, whether we agree with the writer's politics or not, now that the personal feelings that were associated with the movements of those days have died out, we can profitably avail ourselves of them as *mémoires pour servir*, in constructing, for our own satisfaction, some outline of the history of the first decade of this century. Added to this, is the biographical interest they possess, for they afford as clear an explanation of the process of change which Coleridge's political views underwent, as his other writings do respecting his religious opinions; and for such a man, these 'Remains' are the best and truest account of his 'life' that could be given to the world.

---

ART. II.—*Lays of the Kirk and Covenant.* By Mrs. A. Stuart Menteath. Edinburgh: Johnstone and Hunter. 1850.

THE volume before us is a rich and beautiful quarto. Bound in ultramarine and gold, the paper is thick and fine, the printing is excellent, the margins are ample, the blank pages are neither few nor far between, and the whole affair is suggestive, to the poor reviewer, of drawing-room tables, white sofas, painted recesses and other unattainable particulars of the Paradise of this life. Never was a little book ushered into the world with more of the pomp and circumstance of publication. It is a pity. If the contents be naught, it is always pitiful to see nothing pretending to be something. If they be good, it is a sad thing to see them consecrated to the rich and withheld from the poor in so very absolute and needless a manner.

There is a certain sacredness in poetry. There is an especial sacredness in religious poetry. The true reader demands that it be first-rate of its kind, otherwise he rejects it quite. Properly speaking there is no such thing as second or third-rate poetry. Its secondary or tertiary character at once thrusts it out of the poetic sphere. Such versification is simply bad prose. It therefore becomes every new aspirant to be very modest in the offering of his first fruits. Ostentation and outward splendour will even help to defeat his dearest wish. Let him, then, come before the public humbly and meekly, and yet with all befitting comeliness and decency. 'Great is the art, great be the manners of the bard.' If his book be a soul of beauty and not a mere body of show, the world cannot afford to let it die, and therefore it is sure to live. If eclipsed or unnoticed for a time, its day of honour is certain. Future publishers will array it in the glories of their art. Congenial artists will illustrate its undying features. Critics will descant upon it as a text. A thousand kindred readers will bless the soul from which it came.

We wish these lays had come out in the form of a neat, clear, compact little volume; and at as low a price as possible. As it is, they will never be sold in the only way which can please an author, namely, by the spontaneous purchase of a satisfied public. Being not only religious, but also Protestant and evangelical in their spirit, these poems will be bought only by the pious lady-friends of the author's own circle, whereas they should have been made accessible to the thousands in Scotland, and in England too, whom they are capable of delighting, of refreshing, of uplifting and of permanently edifying.

To speak still more plainly, it would have been for Mrs. Menteath's interest, in another way, to have appeared in a more lowly guise. It is only the most correct writing that can bear these large types, wide spaces and broad phylacteries. Now the punctuation of the 'Lays of the Kirk and Covenant' is vicious from the beginning to the end of the book; and punctuation is the most important of the arts of grammar. The author has no conception of the respective values, whether in point of time or in point of logical separation, of the full stop, the colon, the semicolon and the comma. She cuts her nominatives off from their verbs by means of the most impertinent commas. She uses and abuses the black dash, an illegitimate point which no Englishman should acknowledge, without discrimination and without effect. Here is the first stanza of the introductory poem.

'SCOTLAND! hallowed in thy story—
   Who would trace thine annals right—
One peculiar page of glory,
   Ever brightens on his sight!

> Not the honours—far descended—
> Of thine ancient hero kings—
> Not thy bulwarks—blood defended—
> These are but thy meaner things !'

Let us examine it a little from this the lowest of all the points of view in which literature can be considered.  What do the words ' hallowed in thy story ' belong to ?  Are they adjective to SCOTLAND or to ' One peculiar page of glory'?  The punctuation does not inform us, and we shall therefore suppose them to relate to the third line.  What is the meaning of the black dashes at the ends of the first and second lines ?  They certainly do not indicate a parenthesis, which is the only tolerable use of such dashes in any circumstances in our opinion.  Neither do they indicate that sort of falling pause, for which they are employed by some good writers :—along with one or other of the classical points, as we have just done in this sentence for the purpose of showing what we mean.  Then what is the use of the comma after ' glory'?  There is no parenthesis or interjection of any sort to divide the ' page of glory ' from its poor verb !  The dashes which isolate ' far descended ' are defensible as the substitutes for those honest old brackets which are used in the English classics to shut in a parenthesis ; but a parenthesis is quite unnecessary in so short a sentence.  The same remark is applicable to the dashes before and after ' blood defended ' ; and the solitary one after ' kings ' signifies we know not what.  To conclude our animadversions on this specimen-stanza, ' far descended ' and ' hero kings ' may be suffered as uncoupled words : but ' blood defended ' are wholly without a meaning unless they be printed as one compound word.  In short, the stanza should have been printed as follows ; and still the relation between the first three lines is obscure.

> ' SCOTLAND ! hallowed in thy story,
>     Who would trace thine annals right,
> One peculiar page of glory
>     Ever brightens on his sight.
> Not the honours, far-descended,
>     Of thine ancient hero-kings ;
> Not thy bulwarks, blood-defended :
>     These are but thy meaner things. '

The reader may think us punctilious. . Some authors will condemn this sort of criticism as trifling and trashy.  The author of the Lays will, perhaps, think it beneath her contempt.  But, whether it be insignificant or important, it is just.  Here is a woman of fine intelligence printing poems so ungrammatically that a practised eye finds a comma where there ought to be none, two interjectional points instead of plain full stops, and seven ugly black dashes, all within the space of two brief sentences. It is surely desirable that she should be kindly and authoritatively told to study the difficult art of punctuation; and that not only because it is beautiful in itself, but because it is essential to the lucidity of every kind of literary expression.

It is an art villanously neglected in the present day. It is very much left to the printer's care. It has even grown difficult to get a manuscript printed as it is written in this respect. For our own parts, we never let a paper out of our hands without first inditing a petition to the compositor on the frontispiece, imploring him to punctuate according to the author and not according to his private experience. This usurpation of one of the most delicate of an author's duties by the man of types, however, has been brought about by the negligence and the ignorance of literary people themselves. The majority of the articles, which pass through our hands to the press, can hardly be said to be punctuated at all. The printer has just to dust in his commas the best way he can. The author seldom complains, the public never. In truth, readers have lost the sense of punctuation; and it glimmers in the vast proportion of writers as a shadowy notion of mechanical division and subdivision. The most distinguished of our contemporary penmen have grown somewhat careless in this respect. It were impossible to deduce a coherent theory of punctuation from the works of our most popular writers, they differ so much from one another in their practices. There is therefore no wonder that an inexperienced craftswoman, like the author now under censure, should be so incorrect. It is, accordingly, with charity and consideration that we beg her to acquire this minor but important part of authorship.

This is not the place to discourse upon the laws and rules of punctuation; but there is one hint, which we should like to give in connection with the present poet. She must understand that there are two schemes of punctuation. One of these should never appear upon the printed page at all. It should remain invisible. The writer of a book has nothing whatever to do with it. Neither has the reader, unless he be reading aloud. It is that scheme of punctuation according to which a good reader will speak a passage. Doubtless it has its laws, but hitherto it has been always left to the taste or the genius of the reader. It is quite independent of the punctuation on the visible page. It often contradicts the latter indeed. For example, it will sometimes separate a nominative from its verb although not a word comes between them. It is a punctuation for the ear, and it is æsthetical in its foundations.

The other scheme is the grammatical one. It alone, indeed,

is usually called by the name of punctuation; although the
' actor's stops ' are well known to playgoers. The visible points,
which are employed in this fine art, have their regular musical
values; but the use of these signs is an art wholly dependent on
the perception of the logical relations subsisting between the
members of a sentence, between sentences, between paragraphs,
and so forth. It is therefore quite distinct and very different
from the punctuation of the spokesman. They have nothing in
common. Yet it may be safely averred that the principal cause
of the degeneracy of the punctuation of the writer is nothing else
than the confounding of it with that of the reader on the part
of authors. Examples of this confusion may be found in almost
every page of almost every book that is published in these days.

> ' One peculiar page of glory,
> Ever brightens on his sight.'

There is an instance of it. The reader places a pause after
glory. The rythm, the very feeling of the passage demand
it. The writer, however, had no business to put a comma there.
The logical law and the rule of grammar unite to forbid it. Yet
such is the punctuation all through this beautiful work. It is
almost universal in the literature of 1850. The writer points
his writing as he wishes it to be read aloud instead of pointing
it as it ought to be thought. We deliver this protest against the
prevalent incorrectness all the more feelingly that we cannot
escape from it ourselves; while there is little doubt but the
printers will do all that is in their power to hinder us from
doing so.

Alien to this trifling yet important defect (for it disappears
from them when they are said or sung, instead of being read by
the eye) there is another vice in the bodily structure of these
printed Lays. There is an inadequate mastery of the craft of
rythmical cadence. The sense of measure is yet feeble in the
poet. Her lines are often weak, not infrequently awkward, and
sometimes far worse than prosaic.

> ' And they'll burn young Hamilton.
> *    *    *    *    *
> Oh! young Hamilton—from beyond the sea
> *    *    *    *    *
> Still " Convert ? " " Convert ! " roared the black friar,
> *    *    *    *    *
> With Patrick Hamilton.
> *    *    *    *    *
> The dove died too—as if of its heartchill.
> *    *    *    *    *
> Struggling with love—unspeakable ! '
> *    *    *    *    *

. Such are half a dozen of the kind of verses now objected to. A little care could soon weed them all out of a soil they have no natural right to. Mrs. Menteath's numbers are never inharmonious when she is deeply moved. She is truly poetical by nature. It is only rhetorical talent she wants. Sedulous culture will supply her deficiency. Let her compare Macaulay's 'Lays of the Roundheads,' and 'Lays of Ancient Rome' with these too inartificial canticles of hers. All that varied talent, multifarious study and immense painstaking can do for English verse is visible in those celebrated pieces. Even Aytoun's 'Lays of the Scottish Cavaliers,' though belonging to the region of mimetic rather than that of creative art, are very superior in these respects. They show how much can be accomplished by fair talent, great conversancy with similar works and remarkable powers of imitation. Macaulay and Aytoun are rarely if ever wrong in their rythmical measurements; yet not a line of their poems, it must be confessed, is deeply and essentially musical. Not a line sings in the imagination or the heart of the reader long after he has read it. Not a verse lingers in his ear, refusing to be put away. In one word, there is no essential poetry in the versified works of the historian, any more than in those of the lecturer on Rhetoric in the college of Edinburgh. They are works of rare and noble eloquence perhaps; they are hardly poems.

Should an immature poet, then, studiously acquire the art of these masters of the (artificial) shell? Most assuredly; for even in the lyrical effusions of his spirit there will occur lines requiring its skilful hand. Although he be a poet born, not made, he cannot be perfect in a year. Immense experience and prolonged poetic life are necessary. In the meantime he must eke out his inspiration here and there by conscious art, in order to hinder his imperfect works from being also offensive. For this purpose he must learn the external art of poetry by common and diligent study. He must peruse the best works of the true masters with an intelligent view to the discovery of their methods. When he reads, he must observe; when he reflects on his readings, he must generalize. This process of study, however, must not be carried too far; for it has its perils. He must not write when engaged in it. He must first give the fruits of such labour time to die and be changed in his mind; otherwise the dead letter of the poetic law may overmaster him and kill the spirit of poetry by which he is possessed.

The sooner he has done with this part of his education the better, so it have been thorough in its time and place. Let him rather hasten forwards to a sympathetic contact with as much of the vast body of poetry, divine and human, as he can reach. Let him enter into poetic communion with every one of the poets if he can. Let him move to the music of them all. Let him drink into their rythms. Let him run over all Parnassus with tinkling feet, with the airs of heaven murmuring through his hair, with melting eyes, with ever-opening ear music-mad and drunk with the spirit of beauty which haunts the vocal hill. It appears to us that the immense reading of perfect poetry, without any other purpose than the instinctive longing for poetical delight, is the most effectual part of the outward cultivation of an aspirant.

If there be one rule more important than another however, for the help of the student of poetic art, it is this. Let him clearly understand, and never for an instant forget, that he must not pen a line in verse which could possibly be written in prose. That which he sings must be musical by its own inalienable nature. His rythmical cadence must be the ebb and flow of the soul, not of the intellect. That is no poetry in which there is no indwelling necessity that it be chaunted or sung, using these verbs with a latitude of meaning inclusive of the rythmical speech of the ancient rhapsodist and the modern actor. In one word, thought which does not fall to singing of its own accord, and whether the thinker will or no, is not poetic thought. All impassioned oratory is rythmical. Listen to the man of true eloquence, and whenever his spirit is deeply moved his utterance heaves and swells away to the music of an unwritten score. But the orator is not and cannot be a poet. He has an audience before him and he knows it. He is there to agitate his people. But the poet knows no people. He stands before no audience. He is alone and impersonal. His world is self-contained and he is singing to himself. Such is the idea of the poet. It is doubtless rarely realized. There is no perfect poet in this sense, but such is the mood in which the masters of the sounding lyre uttered all those portions of their imperfect works which keep them immortal. In proportion as the poet remembers his audience does he become an orator; just as it is possible for the man of eloquence to forget his hearers, for a blessed moment, and become transfigured into a poet. The two terms are not convertible. Poet and orator are for ever discrete in their essence. The vast majority of poetical aspirants, however, are only orators in disguise. Nay, they are orators in a state of enchantment. They have submitted themselves to the bondage of the rules of verse. They move in fetters of their own forging, instead of standing up in freedom before the public and speaking like honest men, obedient to the law which sways the irregular movement of oral discourse.

Is the author of the impassioned Lays now under review

a poet in this high and exclusive sense? Is she so at any time? Yes, reader, she is; else all these preliminary remarks might have been spared. It is solely because she often forgets herself, and because she at times forgets her audience, that we have dwelt so fondly on her shortcomings. It is because she is manifestly capable of possession by her subject, and not merely possessed of its details and points, that we bid her welcome to this breathing world and wish her godspeed. Religious poetry, we mean English religious poetry, is the very rarest, as it is the very richest of all human creations; this pen-woman appears to know the secrets of that life of Christ which is hid with God by experience; and it is therefore within the bounds of possibility that she may one day approve herself the poet of that life in these unholy days. Psalms and spiritual songs may haply yet fall from her lips. With the exception of Herbert in some parts and pendicles of ' The Temple,' of some of Cowper's breathings, and of James Montgomery's hymns, there is scarcely such a thing as religious poetry in the literature of Great Britain. The energetic and magnificent race which has produced the Plays of Shakspeare, the 'Paradise Lost' and 'Regained' of Milton, the Love-songs of Burns, has not yet given utterance to a single immortal psalm. James Martineau confesses and laments, in the preface to a hymn-book prepared for the use of his congregation at Liverpool, that Unitarianism has not brought forth anything like a psalmody worthy of the name. He has recourse to the fervid, if all unclassical, spiritual music of Doctor Watts in these ungenial circumstances. It is a terrible fact for the sect he represents. But is not almost as much implied in our far larger confession for all England? Is it not a sign that we are a theological more than we are a religious people after all? Does it not suggest the painful suspicion that, at the very least, we are not religious with all our strength and might and heart and soul?

We also rejoice that our present poet is a woman. Woman is now free of the commonwealth at last. She may think, she may speak, she may sing as she lists. Her comparatively open, disinterested, affectionate, inseeing, spiritual nature is allowed its scope of action in society to a wonderful extent. Not that she is yet all that she deserves to be, all she ought to be, or all she behoves to be for the good of society; but she is free, inasmuch as she has at length attained to the power and also to the liberty of speech. Hannah More, Joanna Bailie, Felicia Hemans, Mary Sommerville, Harriet Martineau, Margaret Fuller, Elizabeth Barrett Browning can never be put to silence again. They may not always speak wisely, any more than their elder brothers; but we are not afraid of their total effect. On the contrary, we hail it. It is for good. It will neutralize the excessive mannishness of all our works, institutions, manners, practices and theories. It is therefore with peculiar pleasure that we descry, in the author of our Lays, a woman whom we infer from the music she makes to be gentle yet stern, sympathetic yet strong, pious yet thoughtful, intelligent yet meek, and every inch a woman. If this portrait be untrue, nobody will know it so well as herself; and it may serve her as a motive.

This exalted praise reminds us that the reader of these pages may now be longing to peruse some specimens of the lyrist, who has given rise to such tantalizing criticism. Here are a few. What could be more sweetly thought and expressed than the following stanza in the threnody of James Melville over his infant child?

> ' My blessed master saved me from repining,
>   So tenderly He sued me for his own :
>   So beautiful He made my babe's declining,
>   Its dying blessed me as its birth had done.'

Two white doves had played about the sacred death-cradle of the darling :—

> ' So tame they grew that, to his cradle flying,
>   Full oft they cooed him to his noontide rest ;
>   And, to the murmur of his sleep replying,
>   Crept gently in and nestled in his breast.'

When the little innocent gave up the ghost, his timid and tender guardians departed too :—

> ' 'Twas my first hansel and propine to heaven ;
>   And so I laid my darling 'neath the sod.
>   Precious His comforts :—once an infant given,
>   Now offered with two turtle-doves to God.

It reminds us of a Christian father whom we once accompanied to the grave with the body of his child. The funeral company was very small. We were only four, including the mourner himself. He held the tiny coffin in his arms :—' Ah !' said he, ' I am about to take the infeftment of my portion in the world to come.'

But Mrs. Menteath's spirit never reaches the top of its bent until the persecution of God's people in old covenanting Scotland, and the refuge they found from the bloody hand of man in the arms of nature, come before it :—

> ' For still the greenwood's quivering screen
>   A very Bethel oft hath been,
>   Where Scotland's peasant-saints have found
>   That all God's earth is holy ground.
>   \*         \*         \*

' O ! Arthur's seat gave back the shout of that assembled crowd,
As one bare forth the mighty bond, and many wept aloud :
They spread it on a tombstone-head ; (a martyr slept beneath,)
And some subscribed it with their blood, and added ' Until death.'

\*　　\*　　\*　　\*　　\*

' O ! green and fresh upon his soul, those early haunts arise ;
His kirk, his home, his wild wood-walk, with all their memories ;
The very rushing of the burn by which so oft he trod,
The while on eagle-wings of faith his spirit met its God.

\*　　\*　　\*　　\*　　\*

' The years, the years when Scotland groaned beneath her tyrant's hand,
And it was not for the heather she was called the purple land ;
And it was not for their loveliness her children blessed their God,—
For the secret places of the hills and the mountain heights untrod.

\*　　\*　　\*　　\*　　\*

' They will not cease, they will not sleep, those voices of the wave,
Forever—ever whispering above the martyr's grave :
'Tis heard at night, 'tis heard at noon, the same low-wailing song,
In murmur loud, in cadence low, ' How long, O Lord, how long !' '

\*　　\*　　\*　　\*　　\*

These scattered fragments, gathered at random from the book, are examples of our lady-covenanter's best manner. There is pathos, tenderness, delicacy, truth and a certain wild expressiveness in the pieces from which they are taken. Their full effectiveness, however, cannot be felt in this detached state. They need the story to sustain them. They are not pure poetry, but they are touched with the pure spirit of poetry. The poems themselves are far from perfect; but, with a few exceptions, they touch the heart. They owe much to their subject-matter certainly; but they owe still more to the noble love with which they are set to music by the Northern ' Fair Saint,' who now places them before the public of Great Britain. Let her cultivate her gift then with sedulity and care. Let her give over the comic vein, which she essays in ' Young Sanct Geil,' for heaven has denied her the gift of humour. Let her hold by her peculiar inspiration and abandon herself to its movement with free obedience. Let her dwell much with the beauty of holiness; and her surfeited heart will surely give it forth, to the great easing of her sweet pains and the melting (that is the refining) of her pious reader. Let her dwell apart; apart from the society of her condition in life, apart from sectarian influences, apart from her own personalities and private tastes. Let her, in fine, live the sincere, single-hearted, self-denying, industrious, austere, yet serene and untroubled life of the progressive poet ; and she will not be long in transcending the limits of her present poetical development ;—truly excellent as is her

### PEDEN AT THE GRAVE OF CAMERON.

\*      \*      \*      \*      \*

' There came a worn and weary man to Cameron's place of rest,
He cast him down upon the sod, he smote upon his breast;
He wept as only strong men weep, when weep they must or die ;
And, ' Oh! to be wi' thee, Ritchie !' was still his bitter cry !

' ' My brother! O my brother! thou hast passed before thy time,
And thy blood it cries for vengeance, from this purple land of crime.
Who now shall break the bread of life unto the faithful band,
Who now upraise the standard that is shattered in thine hand ?

' Alas! alas! for Scotland the once beloved of heaven!
The crown is fallen from her head, her holy garment riven,
The ashes of her covenant are scattered far and near,
And the voice speaks loud in judgment—which in love she would
    not hear !

' Alas! alas! for Scotland! for her mighty ones are gone,
Thou, brother, thou art taken—I am left almost alone;
And my heart is faint within me, and my strength is dried and lost,
A feeble and an aged man—alone against a host !

' " O pleasant was it, Ritchie, when we two could counsel take,
And strengthen one another to be valiant for His sake ;
Now seems it as the sap were dried, from the old blasted tree,
And the homeless, and the friendless, would fain lie down with thee !"

' It was an hour of weakness—as the old man bowed his head,
And a bitter anguish rent him, as he communed with the dead ;
It was an hour of conflict, and he groaned beneath the rod,
But the burthen rolled from off him as he communed with his God !

' " My Father! O my Father! shall I pray the Tishbite's prayer,
And weary in the wilderness while Thou wouldst keep me there !
And shall I fear the coward fear, of standing all alone,
To testify for Zion's King, and the glory of His throne !

' " O Jesus! blessed Jesus! I am poor, and frail, and weak,
Let me not utter of mine own—for idle words I speak—
But give me grace to wrestle now, and prompt my faltering tongue,
And breathe Thy name into my soul, and so I shall be strong !

' " I bless Thee for the quiet rest thy servant taketh now,
I bless Thee for his blessedness, and for his crowned brow,
For every weary step he trod in faithful following Thee,
And for the good fight foughten well, and closed right valiantly !

\*      \*      \*      \*      \*

' " The glory! O the glory! it is bursting on my sight,
Lord! thy poor vessel is too frail for all this blinding light!
Now let Thy good word be fulfilled, and let Thy kingdom come,
And, Lord, even in thine own best time, take thy poor servant home !"

' Upon the wild and lone Airsmoss, down sank the twilight grey,
In storm and cloud the evening closed upon that cheerless day ;
But Peden went his way refreshed, for peace and joy were given—
And Cameron's grave had proved to him the very gate of heaven !'

ART. III.—*Discourses and Sayings of our Lord Jesus Christ. Illustrated in a Series of Expositions.* By JOHN BROWN, D.D., Professor of Exegetical Theology to the United Presbyterian Church. 3 vols. 8vo. Edinburgh: Oliphant and Sons. 1850.

THESE volumes add fresh lustre to Dr. Brown's well-deserved reputation as a Biblical scholar and practical theologian. They bear the impress of keen critical sagacity—of a calm, comprehensive, and independent judgment—of extensive research—of the operation of sound exegetical principles, and of the most devout and loving reverence for Him whose ' sayings ' they are intended to ' illustrate.' They are dedicated to James Douglas, Esq., of Cavers. In this there is singular beauty and appropriateness. The Church of Christ is not a little indebted to Mr. Douglas. By his example and writings he has done much to urge on its members the duty of vigorously pursuing the highest enterprises of Christian philanthropy. We know not how a more felicitous selection could have been made than that which Dr. Brown has made. The name of Mr. Douglas on the fly-leaf of the first volume is an indication of the character of the whole work—the key-note to the flowing harmony that follows.

The preface is—what every preface ought to be—the natural history of the production. From it we learn that these volumes are the result of Dr. Brown's growing conviction that the interests of vital godliness can be better served by promoting ' an intimate personal acquaintance and friendship with our Lord Jesus Christ,' than by interminable logomachies and subtle speculations respecting his person and work.

' The very life of Christianity [he says] consists in loving, confiding in, obeying *him*, and God *in him;* and he plainly can be loved, confided in, and obeyed, only in the degree in which he is known. Speculation about the person and work of Christ, however correct, is not the " excellent knowledge " in comparison with which the apostles counted all things loss ; assent to abstract propositions, however true, is not Christian faith ; conformity to ethical rules, however good, is not Christian obedience.

' Dr. Owen did good service to the cause of Christianity two hundred years ago, by showing the pre-eminent place the person of Christ holds in that religion, in opposition to the British rationalists of that age, who had almost lost sight of him in speculation about evidences and dogmas and ethics ; and Schleiermacher, and his noble followers, Neander and Tholuck, have done similar service in opposition to the German rationalists of our times. A personal Deity is the soul of natural religion ; a personal Saviour—the real, living Christ—is the soul of revealed religion. How strange that it should not be impossible

—how sad that, through a perverted ingenuity, it should not be uncommon, in reference to both of these, to convert that into a veil which
was intended to be a revelation!'—*Preface,* p. vi.

These are weighty words which speculative theologians will
do well to ponder.  We do not, nor does Dr. Brown, mean that
no attention should be given by the guides and members of the
British Churches to the mass of facts—psychological and historical
—which justify our faith in the integrity, authenticity, genuineness, and inspiration of the Scriptures ; neither do we decry the
examination and enforcement of the teaching of the sacred books
respecting the constitution of the person of the Redeemer, or the
'extent' of his atonement ;  but we entirely concur with Dr.
Brown in thinking that these topics may be so projected as to
obscure, or completely shut out, considerations of more immediate import.   An army may successfully defend, or do battle to
the death to save, a country in which it has no inheritance—
a garrison may be so 'divided against itself' as to allow the
fortress to be captured and its treasures borne away ; so likewise,
in our headstrong zeal to repulse the attacks of Rationalism,
there is an unmistakeable tendency manifested by the Church
to overlook the primary necessity of a *real* union to the 'living
Christ,' and, on the other hand, to split itself into factions, by
bitter, fruitless discussions as to whether many or few will be
saved, so as to waste its strength, and render it almost, if not
altogether, incapable of fulfilling its mission.   Apologists for this
state of things—and there are such—may say or write as they
please, the fact is indisputable, that while theologians have been
thus engaged, the masses of the British people have been permitted to remain in ignorance of the gospel—sunk in the mire
of the grossest forms of vice and infidelity—baptized heathens—
a prey for Mormonism or Romanism, or any other 'ism' that
exhibited the slightest inclination to come to their rescue or
to compassionate their condition.   Well did Jeremy Taylor
say :—' Disputation cures no vice, but kindles against it
many, and makes passion evaporate into sin ; and though men
esteem it learning, yet it is the most useless learning in the
world.'*

Let us not be misunderstood ; we speak in no uncharitable
mood.  We have no sympathy with those who are mere accusers
of the brethren.  We know that fault-finding is the easiest thing
imaginable : that it is no proof of wisdom or of piety to bring
against Christians sweeping charges of defection.  We repudiate
the one-sidedness that sees evil, and only evil, in all things
ecclesiastical ; on the contrary, we behold much that is good,

---

* Heber's Ed., vol. vi. p. 374.

and are thankful for it. But while we would not, for a moment, ignore the generous, self-denying, and vigorous efforts made, in numerous instances, to preach the gospel to the poor, and to ameliorate their physical circumstances—while we endorse with pleasure much that the firmest friends of the Bible, Tract, Home Missionary, Christian Instruction, and other kindred societies, have said of the vastness and value of their labours—and, in addition, believe that there is much doing in the right spirit and the right direction, of which the world knows little, if anything, we are, nevertheless, obliged to give utterance to our conviction—a conviction to which we are irresistibly impelled by an appalling array of facts—that the religious condition of the country is a disgrace to Protestant Christianity, goes far to substantiate what many of its enemies have affirmed respecting the width of the gulph that separates its profession from its practice, and should fill the churches with 'shame and confusion of face.'

Some, perhaps, may imagine that our opportunities of forming a correct judgment on this matter are limited, or that the sources of information accessible to us are not reliable. Would that it were so! But it is not. The thing is patent to every thoughtful man in the land. To many, the 'Commissioners' of the 'Morning Chronicle' revealed a world of misery and wickedness, of the existence of which they had no previous conception. But not so to us, or to any pastor, or other intelligent Christian in town or in the provinces, who cares about the moral welfare of the people. Were it needful, we might fill page after page with extracts from 'Blue-books,' from the reports of gaol chaplains and governors, from charges given to the grand juries of the various circuits by the judges, and from well-authenticated statements of town missionaries and ministers of nearly all denominations, in support of what we have advanced. Unhappily, there is no lack of evidence. Go where we may, we find it in abundance. At the last meeting of the Congregational Union, for instance, when speaking in support of 'British Missions,' the Rev. T. Adkins said,—that 'if his auditors were to proceed forth through the metropolis of this country, and thence down to the towns and hamlets of the land, they would behold such fearful scenes, brutal in manners, vicious in morals, and heart-rending in woe, as would stimulate every true lover of his country and of their common Christianity to energetic action to provide a remedy. He did not caricature the moral condition of the land, when he declared that there were millions within its precincts who, in all that affected the destination of beings hastening to eternity, were as ignorant as the aboriginal inhabitants of some dark region which no commercial enterprise had ever opened up, no missionary had ever visited!' This was affirmed in the presence of a large number of men, well informed as to the actual condition of the population in all parts of the country —many of them, directly and indirectly, connected with the press—most of them pastors and influential members of metropolitan and provincial churches—delegates from the densely-populated towns of Lancashire and Yorkshire, as well as from the quiet and secluded villages of Wilts and Devon. If, then, Mr. Adkins had been guilty of exaggeration, he stood in the midst of the very persons who would not have hesitated to tell him so. But they did not. They accepted his statement as a correct portraiture of an existing and appalling state of things. And, consequently, we quote and regard his words not as the opinion of an individual, but as the deliberate and solemn conviction of one of the most observant bodies of religious men in the kingdom! There is one man, a member of the 'Union,' who has spoken out upon this topic, and whose testimony we commend to the serious attention of our readers. We refer to Mr. James, of Birmingham. He says,—

'The town in which I live contains, with its suburbs, nearly two hundred and ten thousand inhabitants, and of these, perhaps not more than forty thousand, above twelve years of age, are ever at public worship at the same time. Take from these all Roman Catholics, Unitarians, and other denominations who do not hold evangelical sentiments, and what a small portion remains out of the whole population who are enjoying those soul-converting means of grace which stand so intimately connected with eternal salvation. Where are the bulk of the remainder, and what is their state and character as regards eternity? This is but a specimen of other large towns, and of the state of the metropolis. . . . The moral, or rather demoralized, condition of a large proportion of the people of this country is beyond the conception of those who have not been inquisitive upon the subject. All persons know the prevalence of drunkenness and sensuality, and most are impressed vaguely with the idea that there is a great deal of infidelity at work ; but the depths of iniquity, the stagnant, pestiferous sinks of vice, which are ever sending forth their destructive miasma into the moral atmosphere, and poisoning the souls of the people of these realms, are neither known nor conjectured by those who are ignorant of the statistics of the kingdom of darkness.'*

Now this is true, or it is not. If not, how are we to account for the fact, that so many persons, and from so many different stand-points, have, after the most careful survey, arrived at precisely the same conclusion? If it be true—if not a single shade has been given to it, to make it more horrible than it really is— if, moreover, it be ascertained that nearly thirty millions of

---

* The Church in Earnest, 3rd Ed., pp. 93, 94.

copies of antichristian and filthy publications appear annually in London\* alone, and are, for the most part, circulated among the operative classes of this country—how, we ask, can the apathetic conduct of British churches in the face of this monster evil be accounted for on any other hypothesis than that they have failed to recognise the chief purpose of their organization, or, recognising it, are indifferent to its attainment? Has the salt lost its savour? We hope not.

That contemplative minds, noting the recent developments of our higher-class literature, marking the organized, skilful, and successive assaults which have been made by gifted and accomplished disciples of the 'new philosophy' upon what they deem the bulwarks of Christianity, and satisfied that a fiery ordeal, similar to that which they have been subjected to in Germany, awaits the Scriptures in this country—that such minds should gird themselves for the conflict, and use their best exertions to direct whatever moral force the Churches possess to this point of attack, we can readily comprehend. We do not underrate the danger which they perceive. We admit to the full the urgent need of the preparation which they advocate. It is no time for ignorance or idleness. Both abroad and at home we have been within the enemy's lines, and we know something of the determined spirit there exhibited to raze, if possible, the foundations of the Christian faith, and to blot out the Christian name. But we think we have indicated the existence of a danger more alarming, because more formidable, than that which threatens us from pantheistic speculation or bewildered criticism. While deliberating how to turn the course of the rivulet, the tide is upon us! Our faith is unknown or despised by myriads of our countrymen. They are uninfluenced by scriptural ideas; and not only so, they are ready to help on any enterprise set on foot for the complete destruction of Christian institutions. If, therefore, we be imperilled by the importation of Teutonic philosophy, is it not owing to the public mind being in a state of readiness to receive it, whoever may be the ministering spirits? The spark is powerful for evil only because of the explosive elements to which it is near. Change their character, and it is harmless. Let, then, the unclean spirit be cast out of the heart of the nation by the inflow of the 'glorious gospel'—let the people be instructed and well grounded in the practical as well as the doctrinal—let them thoroughly understand *why* we accept the Bible as the word of the Most High, and as the only infallible guide in faith and practice—to this end let the Churches 'examine themselves,' and be humbled before God—purge

---

\* The Power of the Press, p. 15.

themselves of their mammon-worship—cease their bitter controversies—determine to break down the barriers that separate them
from each other, and bound together by fraternal affection, and
animated by compassion for their perishing brethren, and by the
self-denying principles of the truth—let them descend into the
rugged and dusty ways of life, and there address themselves to
the work given them to do : and then, when our Christianity is
what it ought to be, the reproduction of the sympathy and love
of the Redeemer, we may laugh to scorn all the efforts of Popery,
and all the attempts of an infidel philosophy to poison or mis-
guide the public mind.

In the evangelization of the people, we shall find the best
protection against the baleful influence of a spurious spiritualism.
They are our strength or weakness. Neglect them much longer
and we are defenceless. We may multiply ecclesiastical edifices,
endow colleges, create scholarships, send forth from our divinity
halls a race of highly-educated men, call into existence journals
of every kind and degree, and peripatetic associations without
number, but all will be in vain if the churches do not become
the incarnation of Christ. This left undone all the rest will be
abortive. Wave after wave will surge around us until the light
is quenched. What produced the ' dark ages ' can re-produce
them. God has nowhere promised to preserve any who are
faithless to their trust. In our anxiety about ' evidences' it
seems to be almost forgotten that *a Christ-like Church* could not
be accounted for, except by admitting all that we demand on
behalf of the New Testament. This is a sort of proof that could
not be easily disposed of. It silenced philosophy in Greece and
Rome. It caused the grass to grow in the temples of idolatry.
It dispelled the black night of Paganism, and led the nations to
confess that ' Jesus Christ was Lord to the glory of God the
Father.' It has lost none of its power. Let us put it to the
test. Reason and experience warrant our faith in its efficiency.

With these views we hail the appearance of Dr. Brown's
' Illustrations' with unfeigned satisfaction. By directing attention to the ' Discourses and Sayings of our Lord,' they are
calculated to lead back the Churches into the path from which
they have strayed; to re-awaken the Christian consciousness ; to
revivify the Christian life. The world needs a manifested
Christianity—a church, not of lawn-sleeved dignitaries, or idle
ecclesiastics, or popularity-hunting preachers, or wrangling
sects. Of these the human heart is weary. But such a Church
the world will never see until the words of Christ are more
constantly and seriously pondered, his authority regarded with
more devoted and unswerving allegiance, and his example more
closely and cheerfully imitated by those who call themselves his

followers. It is equally evident, that before anything like this can take place in England, the character of the current popular theological teaching must undergo a complete change. If the ancient church-life is to be restored, there must be a return to the ancient church practice of expounding the Scriptures in the assemblies of the people. We need not inform our readers that the discourses of the teachers of the apostolic churches—like those delivered by the apostles themselves—were, as Origen terms them, 'Explanations of the Lessons,' or chapters, read. Respecting the manner in which those ' Explanations' were given we lack no information. From Justin Martyr, from Tertullian, and from the notices and remains of the popular religious teaching of the first, second, and third centuries, that have come down to us, we are as familiar with it as with anything of yesterday. It was very similar to, but not so elaborate as, the expository lectures which occupy such a prominent place in the public teaching of the churches of Scotland, of which the volumes before us are a splendid specimen.* The want of the churches at this hour is, a universal adoption of this primitive practice of expository teaching. There are shoals of preachers, but few competent expositors. We are not unaware that it would necessitate a more extensive and profound acquaintance with every department of biblical science than the majority of our church-teachers either have attained or aspire to. Nothing can be more erroneous than the popular notion that any dolt can ' expound,' but that it requires genius and high culture to ' preach' well. The reverse is much nearer the truth. But the very fact that it would demand the elevation of the standard of biblical scholarship should give it favour in our eyes. Certain it is, that the mode of teaching that at present obtains in our pulpits can never induct the persons taught into the meaning of the word of God, and consequently cannot prepare them to give an intelligent ' reason for the hope that is in them,' to detect the sophisms of infidelity or of Jesuitism, or to scout the impostors who affirm that they are divinely commissioned to lead men to the New Jerusalem at Nauvoo or California. What is the ordinary plan of pulpit instruction? A morsel of Scripture is taken—a striking sentence—often used as a ' motto,' and generally wrenched from its connexion; this is made the basis of a discourse—a discourse, we admit, that may be full of truth and distinguished by sound doctrinal statement, careful reasoning, and eloquent and persuasive appeals;

---

* Bernh. Eschenburg, Religionsvorträge in der Griech. und lat. Kirche. pp. 84—87.
Justin Martyr, Apol. 11. Tertullian, Apol. 39.
Rheinwaldt und Vogt, Homiliarium Patristicum.

but which, when finished, leaves the audience in complete ignorance of the meaning of the book, or section of the book of
Scripture from which the 'text' was extracted. Against the
continuance of this abuse of ' the work of the ministry,' and of
the sacred writings, we record our protest. God's word was
never intended to be treated after this fashion. Had the same
plan been pursued with any other book, under the pretence of
rendering the people familiar with its character, claims, and
contents, it would, long ago, have been denounced as a mere
subterfuge to hide the ' gross ignorance of the teacher.' By its
fruits we know it. If it behoves us to be thoroughly acquainted
with any volume, it is with that on which our eternal hopes are
built, and which we call upon others to believe and obey under
the penalty of everlasting exclusion from God. But has this
plan aided us in forming such an acquaintance? Is it likely to
do so? We think not. It may stultify, it cannot educate.

The age, moreover, demands that the pulpit should be freed
from the bonds of scholasticism. In it we behold united the
anti-biblical characteristics of the sixteenth and eighteenth
centuries. The battles fought by our fathers must be re-fought
by us, with this difference, that the enemies we have to cope
with are better equipped and disciplined than those with whom
Luther and Melancthon had to struggle, or who were put to flight
by Butler's ' Analogy,' or Lardner's ' Credibility.' We need learning and power in the pulpit, but not that they may remain there.
Both are required that the Bible may be ' expounded' to the
people who assemble in our places of worship, so that it may
be better understood and be more highly appreciated. Let the
ministry burn their ' Skeletons of Sermons,' and ' Pulpit Helps,'
and ' National Preachers,' and betake themselves to the study
of works similar to Davidson's invaluable ' Introduction,' and
Kitto's ' Cyclopædia,' and cast their discourses into the mould
of Dr. Brown's exquisite and exhaustive expositions of the
words of our Lord. Then we shall hear fewer complaints of
the lack of freshness, or variety, or force in the modern pulpit,
and shall have no fears in regard to the boldest sorties of
Popery or Rationalism. But let this be left undone—let our
popular theological instruction continue to be manacled by the
*method* of Duns Scotus or Thomas Aquinas, or fashioned after the
well-divided bewilderments of our Puritan fathers, and the result
is easily forescen.

ART. IV.—*Journal de St. Petersbourg de* 1849 *et* 1850.

FOR several generations Russia has been silently advancing her frontier towards the South and East; subjugating one rude nation after another, and gathering through intrigue and imposture the fruits of victory. The countries, however, over which she has thus extended her sceptre are, for the most part, so little known in Europe, that they appear almost to belong to a fabulous system of geography. The circle of our studies seldom includes the steppes of Central Asia, peopled by races savage or semi-barbarous, scarcely capable of comprehending what civilized nations understand by the word conquest or annexation. But if we are negligent in this respect, Russia by no means shares our apathy, but keeps up an immense establishment of agents and emissaries, whose sole duty it is to examine the countries contiguous to her borders, in order to discover the best means of bringing them within the limits of her empire.

Political considerations of the highest importance should induce us to follow her example, in part at least, if not altogether. The pastoral tribes and herds encamped on the vast table-lands of Asia constitute a species of moral barrier between Russia and India; and it is extremely interesting to us to calculate the amount of resistance they are likely to offer to the realizing of ambitious schemes from the West. It is true the materials of knowledge on this subject are scanty. Few travellers have visited those countries; and of these scarcely any have been competent to write fairly on the investigation most interesting to the communities of the West. What is usually called science, they may sometimes have been able to promote; but we look vainly to their pages for any information calculated to excite or mitigate our anxiety respecting the proximate destiny of the East. Accepting, therefore, the materials they supply, we must endeavour to examine for ourselves the circumstances of the case; and, having patiently done so, to concentrate, if possible, the attention of our readers on the result.

There is, perhaps, no part of the world that exhibits more extraordinary features than the high plateau of the Asiatic continent, in some beautiful nook of which the human race is supposed to have been first planted. Interminable plains alternate with inland seas, and ridges of rocky or snowy mountains run from East to West or from South to North, sometimes intersecting the central table-lands extending from the back-bone of the world to the Polar circle. Here the seasons follow each other with monotonous regularity. Spring covers the earth with verdure,

which having flourished for a brief space, is withered by the devouring heats of summer, these render saline the earth's crust,
and reduce the fertile surface of the soil to a fine powder, blown
in every direction by the winds.    To them succeeds the autumn,
as short-lived as the spring ;  and then follow the horrors of a
protracted winter, abounding with storms and tempests, frosts,
sleet, hail, and snow, which sometimes covers those mighty
plains to the depth of many feet, and borne hither and thither
by the whirlwind, brings death to man and beast.

But though such are the great features of the year in the more
Northern parts of Central Asia, the monotony of the scene is
broken by accidental circumstances, by the occurrence within a
limited range of beautiful hills and valleys, lakes, ponds, and
rivers, and whatever else nature can hold forth to tempt man to
substitute a stationary for a wandering life, and patiently to
cultivate the ground from which he was taken.    These, nature,
poetry, and romance, have invested with singular power—the
charms of association and tradition.    It is man, however transitory he may be, that communicates an everlasting interest
to the spots on which he makes his home, where he toils and
loves, and builds up for his body and mind superb physical
structures, with moral and political institutions adapted more or
less to his necessities.

These cultivated portions of Central Asia, which may almost
be regarded as so many oases, since they are surrounded by
sandy steppes or plains devoted solely to pastorage, present an
interesting spectacle to the eye of the political investigator.
Society, under the influence of peculiar circumstances, has there
put on extraordinary forms.    Khiva, Bokhara, Merve, Balk,
Samerkand, have at various epochs formed the *nuclei* of so many
small states, which, having attained a certain degree of civilization,
have dwindled suddenly, and retrograded towards barbarism.    In
some instances, as in the case of Timùr, the sovereign of one of
these petty communities has risen to great power, subjugated his
neighbours, enlisted the wandering hordes in his service, and,
by the aid of their indomitable valour, has carried his standards
over a large portion of the world.    But the fabric, thus erected,
has been of brief duration.    After the death of Amir Timùr,
the circle created by his genius diminished rapidly ; the forces
of the desert ebbed back into their original bed ; and, save
what we find in history, there is now little to remind us of that
mighty conqueror but his tomb of green jaspar in a mosque at
Samerkand.

The effects produced by the victory of Jenghis Khan were
of a more durable character.    He arose among the pastoral tribes,
whom he seduced to follow him in his career of conquest and

slaughter, by dazzling their imaginations with the idea of the subjugation of the world. He did not achieve this, human life being too transitory to develop so vast a scheme; but he shed oceans of blood, converted flourishing cities into ruinous heaps, and devastated all the countries which had the misfortune to be contiguous to Tartary and Turkistân. His sons and grandsons followed steadily in his footsteps. Nearly the whole of Central Asia, with China and its dependencies, was reduced under the sceptre of the Mongols who some centuries later traversed the lofty barrier of the Hindoo Koosh, and founded that superb empire in India whose power and grandeur have now passed into the hands of England.

For many centuries ambition seems to have forsaken the pastoral tribes, who, content with a humble subsistence, and therefore aiming at nothing beyond, cultivate few or none of those arts which lead to empire. The care of their flocks and herds, their droves of horses and camels, constitutes their chief occupation, though they devote a portion of the year to that sort of rude commerce which can be carried on by men with ideas, manners, and pursuits, so primitive. Such among them as inhabit the steppes bordering on the Russian frontier drive their cattle, sheep, and horses to Renburgh, where they receive in exchange the merchandise of Europe. Others who pitch their tents in the vicinity of the great wall recognise for commercial purposes the sovereignty of the Chinese Emperor, who allows them an access to his dominions without submitting to any of those government restrictions which interfere with the needy operations of 'outside barbarians.' The tribes inhabiting the centre and southern portion of the plateau, carry on a profitable intercourse with Persia, Affghanistan, and India, which they supply with a variety of articles, formerly including great numbers of horses, and receive in exchange the hard-ware and printed calicos of England, the shawls and muslins of India, and the odoriferous gums, and spices of the Indian Archipelago.

From what has been said some idea may be formed of the obstacles lying in the way of Russian conquest in that direction, but the Czar and his subjects are not easily drawn from any plan which they have formed, whether for good or for evil. While the present order of things exists, the conquest of India and China, both projected by the Court of St. Petersburgh, must obviously be all but impossible ; and therefore a system of policy has been organized, and with incredible perseverance pursued, having for its object the annexation to the Russian dominions of all the adjacent steppes. Most of our readers are, perhaps, acquainted with the plan of subjugation pursued by the Dutch in Insular Asia, where, through craft and intrigue, they have established an extensive empire. It is their practice to present themselves with the external tokens of weakness and humility before some native prince, and petition him for leave to trade with his subjects, promising, of course, the introduction of mountains of wealth into his territories. The prince is dazzled by this pleasant prospect, and, yielding to their solicitations and his own cupidity, consents to enter into a treaty with these specious and submissive foreigners. In good time the document is drawn up in the language of the natives as well as in that of the Netherlands. With extreme adroitness and dexterity, concealing their real meaning beneath a cloud of words, the negociators introduce clauses which, without the chiefs perceiving it, place them completely at their mercy. To those in their own language they gave still greater extension, so as to justify, in the eyes of European nations, any course of policy they may think proper to pursue. As might be easily forseen, bickerings and quarrels arise—the chief with Asiatic impetuosity rushes to arms, is attacked by European discipline and beaten, when he discovers that what he imagined to be a commercial treaty was in reality a political instrument, reducing him to dependence. In such cases he sinks quietly into slavery, or escapes from it by suicide or exile.

This, merely changing the scene, is a correct picture of what the Russians have attempted in Central Asia. Voltaire's friend, Frederic II. of Prussia, suggested many years ago a comparison between the Dutch and the Russians, who, in several points of character, strongly resemble each other, both being stolid, heavy, apathetic, though amazingly active where money is concerned. It is quite natural, therefore, to suppose that they would be equally dishonest in politics, and make use of much the same arts in developing their principles of imposture. And this we find to be much the case in fact. The Russians never sparing money when more is to be gained by its outlay, have long been in the habit of trading in the Asiatic steppes, and have converted that circumstance into a preliminary of subjugation. Frequently, engineering officers are sent disguised as merchants, to examine the steppes, follow the caravan routes, calculate distances, lay down wells—in one word, to construct maps of the country which may enable a Russian force to traverse it with the least possible obstruction. When real merchants are engaged in carrying on this trade, they are enjoined by their government to pursue much the same course as its military agent, and thus numerous reports, more or less valuable, have been treasured up in the archives at Renburgh. If these were published or placed in the hands of an honest and able compiler, we might possibly obtain something like a correct knowledge of the regions of Central Asia. But the Court of St. Petersburgh is too jealous and exclusive to permit the execution of any such plan, so that we are left to depend almost entirely on reports authorized by the government, and therefore false; or on a few isolated facts which creep accidentally into the journals of St. Petersburgh, and are sometimes copied into the newspapers of the West.

Besides, the enormous mass of documents at Okenburgh is often totally neglected by those commissioned to take charge of it. Damp, mildew, and moths, attack the perishable instruments of ambition, so that at length, when the desire to consult them seizes upon some subaltern servant of the government, they frequently, like the apples of Sodom, turn to ashes in his hand. Still, considerable additions to the information we possess on those countries, have from time to time been made by the agents of the Russian government, who, beginning with the shores of the Black Sea, have published descriptions of the Caucasus, and the plains of the Kubans and Circassia, Georgia, Mungrelia, and Armenia, of Persia, and the country of the Turkomans of Khiva and Bokhara, of the steppe of the Kirghiz Kazuks, and of the immense plains of Mongolia, touching southwards on the limits of Thibet, and stretching away eastwards to the grazing grounds of the Mantchu Tartars.

It would be extremely useful to possess a compendious abstract of all that is useful to be found in these works. But, besides that the task of making such an abstract would be highly laborious, it might be doubted whether the taste of the public would afford sufficient encouragement to any one disposed to undertake it. Our object, accordingly, is very different. We only desire to awaken the curiosity of our readers, and induce them to study for themselves the character, dimensions, and bearings, of that great battle-field, on which England and Russia may hereafter have to decide, which is to take the lead in the civilized world? Of course when we first bestow attention on the subject, several circumstances are encountered calculated to repel investigation. The names of tribes and things are barbarous and uncouth. There is a want of precision in all the accounts laid before us. Each author seems to have a different idea of the nomenclature of nations and class, and the absence of natural barriers gives rise to much indistinctness and uncertainty in geography.

Still, in spite of all these obstructions, we may, by the exercise of patience and industry, obtain some insight into the organization of society in that part of the world. One of the first features that strikes us is the readiness with which many tribes succumb to nominal dependence, while their reluctance to

submit to real servitude is insurmountable.  Besides, it may be
questioned whether they comprehend what is meant by political
dependence.  Russia, for example, offers them certain advantages, which, according to the forms of reasoning adopted by
civilized communities, imply subjection; and the nomadic
hordes, no way versed in this system of logic, accept the
benefits without at all foreseeing that they must, at the same
time, accept also all the disadvantages of the compact.  Thus
the Nogais and the Kalmuks were tempted, many generations
back, to encamp within the Russian frontier, where they were
promised a complete immunity from all vexations, on the apparently easy condition of making slight presents, from time to
time, to the Russian court.  In the East, no one approaches
another without a gift in his hand; and the Nogais and Kalmuks, familiar with this practice, little suspected that the offerings they made, in conformity with Asiatic custom, would be
regarded as tribute, and be appealed to as unequivocal proof
of servitude.

Nor was the unpleasant truth pressed upon them all at once.
They were suffered to become accustomed to their new pastur-
ages, to experience all the force of local attachment, to connect
pleasant associations with the place of their abode, to conse-
crate the earth, by making it the birth-place of their children
and the receptacle of the ashes of their parents.  Then
Russia began to develop her real designs : agents visited the
tribes, suggested the prudence of acquiring favour at court by
more numerous and costly gifts, spoke of the honours and
emoluments certain to flow from military service under the
emperor, of the benefits of intermarriage and constant habits of
traffic; until, by degrees, the deluded Nomadees discovered that
they were regarded as Russian serfs, and must thenceforth reckon
on being treated accordingly.  The indignation they felt can
scarcely be conceived by persons tamed down by civilization.
Scarcely elevated above the condition of the savage, they experienced all a savage's rage; and, in the first burst of their fury,
were ready to attack the forces of the Czar, which were for
the first time perceived to be encamped in their vicinity.
Barbarians, however, though their passions may be fierce, are
not always destitute of policy.  The Kalmuks—for it is of them
we principally speak—comparing their own numbers with those
of the enemy, saw clearly that a contest would be hopeless.
Yet, to continue in servitude, was a thing not to be thought of.
They therefore conceived a design which has few precedents in
history, and accomplished it with a courage and constancy never
surpassed.  Collecting their flocks and herds, their parents, their
wives, and their little ones, they struck their tents, turned

their faces eastward, and resolved to fight their way through the heart of Asia till they should find some peaceful grazing-grounds far beyond the reach of Russian despotism.

The number of the Kalmuks who undertook this glorious enterprise has been variously estimated from 700,000 to 1,000,000. For the convenience of pasturage, they advanced in an immense hollow column, the flanks of which were the distance of three days' journey apart; and, alternately fighting, and terrifying the inhabitants into flight, they intrepidly continued their march for several thousand miles, till at length they found a home in the precincts of the Great Wall. Many of them, of course, fell by the way, so that the graves of the Kalmuks may be said to sanctify a broad belt through the whole interior of Asia; many stragglers were made captive and sold into slavery; and, consequently, numerous families have had to transmit from father to son sad reminiscences of that mighty expedition. But national liberty was achieved, they had escaped the fangs of Russia, and had, moreover, inspired all the nomadic hordes, whether hostile or friendly, with dread of the treacherous Muscovite, who never smiles but to enslave.

What the Kalmuks accomplished on a grand scale, the Nogais effected in part; for while a large portion of the tribe, with tame effeminacy, sank into hopeless serfdom, a thousand heroic families resolved to prefer all difficulties and dangers to servitude, and, cutting their way across the frontier, took refuge in the territories of Bokhara. These facts, we are aware, have been often referred to by political writers on the affairs of Russia, though they have never, perhaps, been estimated at their true value.

Another circumstance must not be overlooked in our attempt to form some idea of the character of the military tribes encamped along the Asiatic frontiers of the Russian empire. It has been remarked by Russian authors, that among the social phenomena observable in Central Asia, none are more extraordinary than the periodical disappearance of tribes, which seem to vanish as if by magic from the face of the country, and to be no more heard of. In the neighbourhood of the Kirghiz Kazaks, of whom we shall have occasion to speak presently, there was formerly encamped a powerful tribe, which, under the name of the Karakalpaks, long maintained a gallant struggle for political independence. Suddenly, we are told, the chiefs came to a singular resolution: they dispersed their people, retreated from before their enemies, and melting into the neighbouring tribes, all trace of their separate existence was completely lost. Similar phenomena, it is affirmed, occur from time to time, though not frequently. The circumstance, as the journals would express it, is extremely strange if true; and, speaking generally, we do not possess the means of testing the statements of the Russian. But, in the particular case of the Karakalpaks, we are able to throw some light on what, in itself, appears so much out of the common order of things. Nearly all the details of the transaction have escaped notice, or, at least, have not been publicly recorded; but, from what we have learnt, the vanishing of the tribe in question may be accounted for something after the following manner.

Actuated by feelings different from those of the Nogais and Kalmuks, the Karakalpaks determined to effect by stratagem what the others had accomplished by the sword. Having concerted their measures, the loose materials of their social fabric appeared, all at once, to lose the principle of cohesion; each separate family resolved to shift for itself, the great encampment was broken up, the horde dissolved, and the scattered fragments were swept away into the desert by some mighty influence operating like a whirlwind. At this point of time they were lost both to the Russians and to the Kirghiz. But did they perish? or, were they, as the Muscovites affirm, transmuted into other hordes? Quite the contrary. Reassembling in the solitude of the vast steppes, they followed the route traced out for them by the Nogais, and, marching into Turkistân, placed themselves under the protection of the Amir of Bokhara, in whose territories the Karakalpaks are still enumerated among the most powerful of the pastoral tribes.

Among the most singular tribes found in the elevated table lands of Asia, must be reckoned the Kirghiz Kazaks, whose country extends from the forty-fifth to the fifty-second degree of north latitude, and from the sixty-second to the hundred-and-third of east longitude. This immense steppe Russian history represents as having been indissolubly annexed to the empire as far back as the year 1730. But numerous circumstances, commonly overlooked by the partisan of the Czar, prove this account to be fabulous. First, it is not attempted to be denied, that one great division of the tribe under the name of the Kara (or the black) Kirghiz, have resisted equally the arms and arts of Russia, and continue up to the present hour in perfect independence. Their manners are said to be gross and uncouth, and their character to be distinguished by immitigable ferocity. But we may reasonably distrust our authorities, if it is meant that in point of manners the black Kirghiz are inferior to their neighbours. In the warlike virtues they are unquestionably their superiors, cultivating with assiduity the use of arms, and scrupulously retaining that article in the creed of their ancestors which includes the worship of the sword.

With respect to the Kirghiz themselves, we must also accept

with reservation the account given by Russian authors, who represent them as more intent on smoking and taking snuff than on the cultivation of warlike habits, though on these exclusively depends their existence as a separate people. Could we accept this as a true picture, we should be at no loss for the means of explaining to ourselves the flexibility with which the Kirghiz Kazaks yield to the force of circumstances. But the agents of despotism are in the habit of libelling those whom they have failed to entice into servitude, so that, in a moral and political point of view, we may not unfairly presume the Kirghiz horde to be better than they are said to be by the Russians.

Still there are several facts in their history from which it may be inferred that they are willing enough to ward off present calamity by calculating on the chances of the future, and will consent to act the part of dependents, rather than entrench themselves habitually behind the sword. But these facts, while they prove the absence of a high sense of honour among the Kirghiz, make with equal force against the pretensions of Russia to their Steppe. If there was anything like annexation, it is admitted to have taken place in 1730. But the same historians, who allude with so much complacency to what happened then, proceed immediately afterwards to narrate occurrences totally incompatible with any degree of belief in their previous statements. Twenty-six years after the pretended annexation, an army of Mongols, under the command of Chinese generals, having traversed the great plains of Central Asia, approached the Kirghiz Steppe. It does not appear that any threatening message was sent to the chiefs of the tribes, the exclusive object of the Mongol expedition being to reduce to subjection two or three refractory tribes who had thrown off their allegiance to the court of Pekin.

But the neighbourhood of an army considerable enough to justify the hopes of driving a profitable trade with it, was a temptation which the Kirghiz could not resist; and, accordingly, their chiefs, having assembled and consulted together, determined to send presents, and make submission to the Chinese, not in the slightest degree imagining that this empty formality would afterwards be construed into annexation to the Manchu empire. Nor was it. The Celestials perfectly understood the value of such proceedings, and no more thought of including the Steppe of the Kirghiz Kazaks in the map of their country, than we do of introducing Thibet into a map of Great Britain, because our picquets in the Himmalaya may have exchanged civilities with those of the Chinese.

We have already observed that, under pretence of advancing the interests of scientific geography, the Russian Government

has, from time to time, despatched numerous emissaries into the
Steppes to collect the fullest particulars respecting the facilities
and obstacles to the passage of a disciplined army, and by the
way to glean mere geographical information for the amusement
of the harmless part of mankind.  If we may rely on the reports thus obtained, all that part of Asia bears evident marks
of having been, at some period or other, submerged beneath
the ocean ; not when, at the conclusion of the reign of
Chaos, it emerged with the rest of the habitable globe
from beneath the waters, but at some epoch far more recent, and after animal and vegetable life had been developed
on the surface of our globe.  In the midst of petrified shells,
and flints of various colours, Baron Meyendorf found a shark's
tooth, and, scattered over the soil, are innumerable trunks of
trees, petrified like those which occur in that elevated chain of
mountains that borders the valley of the Nile.  Coal, too, exists,
which may give birth to other reflections.

The growth of the soil on the eastern shore of the Caspian,
exactly in the manner witnessed on the coast of Borneo, Celebes,
and other islands of the Indian Archipelago, may probably excite in the reader's mind an idea not undeserving of consideration.  Is not the Caspian a remnant of that ocean by which the
Steppes were submerged, rather by some depression, effected
through the agency of forces in the interior of the earth,
than by rising in the general bed of the waters, which would
be inexplicable on any known principle of science?  No power
with which we are acquainted would suffice for the second purpose, whereas the former is altogether in conformity with experience.  The north of Asia seems to resemble, in this respect, the
north of Australia, now visibly rising from the ocean's bed, perhaps, in this case, for the first time.  But all the countries
north of the Himmalaya were probably submerged, after being
peopled, cultivated, and civilized, and after remaining in this
state for ages, are again, through the operation of volcanic agency,
upheaved and rendered fit for the abode of man.

Since that period, many changes have taken place in the fortunes of that portion of Asia, chronicled by no history, and not
susceptible of explanation by any knowledge we possess.  In
several parts of the Kirghiz Steppes, we discover mines, some of
which were worked with skill and science by a race unknown to
us, but whose tombs lie scattered over the face of the country,
and contain vases and other relics of singular beauty.  The
traveller likewise meets with Lamaic pagodas of great antiquity,
sometimes contiguous to mosques, erected, to all appearance,
about the time when the first apostles of El-Islam spread themselves over the eastern world.

With such inducements as these to investigation and research, antiquarians, whether Russians or not, might be excused for feeling some degree of curiosity to examine the plateaus of Central Asia; yet no comprehensive plan of study has been pursued, nor has any encouragement apparently been given, to such inquiries by civilized governments. This, however, may be accounted for; but how it has happened that we have displayed equal indifference to other and more useful investigations, is a circumstance which may be allowed to perplex reflecting statesmen and politicians. History has revealed to us the truth that these nomadic hordes have, at various periods, risen suddenly to greatness by passionate appeals to the use of arms; have been seized by the thirst for conquest; have sent forth vast bodies of warriors; and swept irresistibly, like a torrent, over every contiguous part of Asia, from the Yellow Sea to the Mediterranean.

At present, if the Russian agents may be credited, nothing can be ruder than the military weapons and practices of the nomadic tribes, who possess so little ingenuity, that they are unable to manufacture even the bows and arrows, in the production of which the rudest savages excel. To collect materials for aiding us to form a sound opinion on these points, would be worth the consideration of an adventurous traveller. The belief passes current, at least in Russia, that the Kirghiz procure their bows from the Chinese—their swords and muskets from Turkistàn. No weapon is indigenous but the chapan: a battle-axe with a long handle, which they wield with great dexterity, and generally inflict with it a mortal wound. Their foreign muskets are said to be of the rudest and most primitive construction, having no lock, but merely a touch-hole, to which the match is applied. Entering into a groove in the stock is a rest, which, by touching a spring, is suffered to drop down to enable the combatant to take aim. Consequently, every time they discharge their pieces, the Kirghiz cavalry are transformed into infantry, since they cannot fire on horseback. Might it not be worth while for two or three enthusiasts from India to make a pilgrimage into Central Asia, to instruct these rude men in their favourite science? Those Russians who send reports to their government observe, with much satisfaction, that such troops would be obviously unable to obstruct the progress of a regular army possessing all the advantages of discipline, and accompanied by artillery.

We cannot, however, fail to have remarked, that in war events do not invariably shape themselves in conformity with the theories of military or political speculators. Forces deemed invincible have been dispersed, or destroyed, by troops previously regarded with contempt—discipline has fled before enthusiastic ignorance; and countries, to enter which it was supposed was to subdue them, have successfully resisted every attempt at conquest, and remain independent to this hour. For instance, the English in India imagined, many years ago, that the Nepaulese, a mere handful of ragged mountaineers, would not be able to stand before a British force, and, accordingly, sent a number of regiments to reduce them to obedience. The result was unexpected, and not flattering to those who had conceived the design. Our expedition proved abortive, we were defeated in almost every encounter, and, after much loss and humiliation, retreated into the provinces without having effected anything worth mentioning.

What happened in Affghanistan makes neither for nor against the opinion we are here urging. European courage and discipline proved triumphant there; so that it was through no want of military power we relinquished the country. It had been effectually subdued; all the forces in the land were at our feet; we possessed every pass, every stronghold, and, chief of all, those fertile plains which supply the inhabitants with the means of subsistence. It was through an ignorant and mistaken policy that we retreated into Hindostan, and relinquished the incalculable advantages we might have secured to ourselves by retaining the Acropolis of Asia.

Russia felt the value of our acquisition, and so vehemently envied us the possession of it, that it made a foolish and spasmodic effort to neutralize the consequences of our Affghan victories. We allude, it will be perceived, to the expedition of General Petrowski against Khiva, undertaken under the weakest of all pretexts. It was then, however, constantly repeated at St.Petersburgh that the Uzbek cavalry, like that of the Kirghiz Kazaks, were so wretchedly armed and accoutred, so wanting in discipline, and, perhaps, even in courage, that, so far from being able to resist the march of a well-appointed army, it would be altogether incapable of throwing any serious impediment in its way. Under this impression, Petrowski marched from Orenburg, with infantry, artillery, and a body of what was regarded as brilliant cavalry, which, it was supposed, would ride down the desert horsemen on their own Steppes. All the journals in Europe were filled with the details of the expedition, with accounts of its vast trains of camels, its abundant *materiel*, its contrivances for obtaining water, its provisions, and, above all, its discipline. Even they who knew the Uzbeks and Turkomans began to fear lest they would give way, at least for a time, and retreat so far into the desert, that the Russians, strengthened by rumour, and by the panic terror of their adversaries, might advance to the foot of the Affghan mountains.

The Uzbeks of Khiva experienced none of these apprehensions. Wherever they obtained their arms, they felt fully confident they could make good use of them. To them the libels of the Russian scribes were subjects of merriment. They accordingly awaited till Petrowski and his thirty thousand men, dreaming of nothing but victory, and already, in imagination, on the banks of the Indus, had advanced sufficiently far to feel the rays of the desert's sun. Turn their eyes on which side they pleased, nothing was visible but glittering sand, feeling, to the touch, like the ashes of a furnace, while the heavens poured down a scorching heat, which inflamed the very air they breathed. The phlegmatic soldiers of the North now began, like Pope's mouse, to find that this *desert* was not so pleasant. Fevers, agues, dysenteries, and, above all, depression of mind, at once seized upon them. Deserted by their guides, they could not find the wells; their throats were parched for want of water; their heads dizzy from the eternal glare; their spirit of enterprise was quenched by despondency. Then, suddenly, from behind the sand-hills, emerged the fiery squadrons of Uzbek horse, fierce as lions, whose lair has been invaded. Without allowing them time to form, or even to reflect on their position, they burst upon the bewildered Muscovites, and cooled the desert sands with their blood. The rout was instantaneous and complete, and back pell-mell towards Orenburg were the Russians driven. Those of them who escaped death are now, probably, of opinion that the cavalry of the desert was not quite so despicable as they had been taught to believe, and the probability is that not one man engaged in that expedition will again enter the Steppes in a hostile character. He would rather perish by the knout, or in Siberia, than by the Uzbek swords, after having been reduced to a despairing skeleton by the heats and pestilential winds of the desert.

But supposing the Khanat of Khiva passed, would a Russian army be in much better plight? Let those answer who have heard of the horsemen or Turkistân, inspired at once by the fiercest love of independence and of slaughter. These men, whose boast it is, that they have never taken shelter under a tree or a king, and who say they should not know their father or mother in the desert, would, with their collective force, be able to deal with a very considerable army of Russians. We are apt to represent their tribes to ourselves as a few handfuls of marauders, scattered over a boundless waste, and, therefore, incapable, however brave personally, of opposing any resistance to the forces of an empire. We may learn to correct our notions when we reflect that the single state of Bokhara employs fifteen thousand camels in carrying on its foreign trade, of which six thousand are engaged in the commerce with

Russia. If we consider this fact, and, at the same time, remember that an extremely small proportion of the inhabitants of Bokhara engage in commerce, that the wandering tribes subsist chiefly, we might almost say entirely, by the breeding of sheep, cattle, and horses, we shall be able to form some slight conception of the vast cavalry of the Steppes, which at present might be entirely directed against Russia.

But we should not neglect the records of history, a diligent study of which might probably lead to the conclusion that were a Timur or a Jenghis Khan now to arise, and to succeed in uniting the scattered forces of the Steppes, he would be equal to the conquest of the entire Russian empire. The want of discipline is an evil of short duration. Every day's march would assist in imparting it to his troops, the plunder of every town and camp would supply fresh incitement to their valour, and they would precipitate themselves over the Wolga upon the rabble of serfs, termed soldiers, like wild beasts into a cattle enclosure. That this will actually happen, we cannot undertake to foretel; but, that it may happen, the whole tenor of Asiatic history convinces us. No armies have been so numerous, or so irresistible, as those that have poured down upon the lowlands of Asia, from the mighty table-land of which we have been speaking. Thus the Uzbeks, the tribes of Turkistân, the Tartars, the Kirghiz, the Mongols, with their innumerable divisions, with the hardy mountaineers, whose countries skirt the northern foot of the Himmalaya and the Caucasus, have always lent themselves joyfully to accomplish the designs of any great conqueror who has arisen among them; and as nature may yet produce such a man, or a succession of such men, we see no reason for thinking it impossible that the fabric of the Russian empire may yet be shattered by a blow from Central Asia.

At all events, we trust that the facts we have laid before our readers, will suffice to convince them that the wandering hordes of Central Asia possess sufficient power to render impossible the march of a Russian army across their territories, without their consent. It should rest with the government of India to indispose them to grant it. We should cultivate commercial relations with those vast and numerous tribes, which, if we properly consult their taste, would consume great quantities of our manufactured goods, and acquire, while doing so, a predilection for their producers. Hitherto we have almost entirely neglected this great market, which the possession of Affghanistan would have placed under our influence. Even now we are not excluded, for, besides the narrow and difficult passage from Ladak, we may still command the use of the roads through Affghanistan, though obviously with much less effect than formerly. The chief obstacle to the development of our trade in that part of the world is our ignorance, which we have now endeavoured to point out rather than dissipate. Our object, however, is not to be effected at once; we must return to the subject again and again. The press must take it up—the public must be made to study for itself, and in the end correct notions will obtain respecting those extraordinary countries and races over which we have thus cast a hasty glance.

---

ART. V.—*Game Birds and Wild Fowl: their Friends and their Foes.* By A. E. Knox, M.A., F.L.S. 12mo. Pp. 264. London: John Van Voorst.

WE are no sportsmen. Many things prevent our being so. A town residence affords few opportunities for the indulgence of such a taste, even if we had it; but to tell the truth, there are other and graver considerations which would always, and in every situation, prevent our doing much in this line. We have no sympathy either with Mr. Cumming, ' the lion-hunter of South Africa'; with our old acquaintance Walton, whose name is on the lip of every sciolist in the art of angling; or with the hundred-and-one sportsmen who, with gun in hand, or horse at gallop, pursue the pastimes of the field with an ardour and a relish due only to the higher interests of life. There are aspects of these things which move us to sympathy, but a moment's reflection checks the current of our feeling, and gives rise to queries which shade the bright and attractive picture.

On the other hand, we are far from joining in the hue-and-cry raised in some quarters against field-sports, or from attributing to those who find pleasure in them, the worldliness and inhumanity with which they are frequently charged. The language held on this subject by some religious people betrays much want of discrimination and intelligent thought. They condemn without consideration, erecting their own prejudices into the standard of appeal, and including under one category characters the most opposite, and pursuits which have nothing in common, save a name. There is much of this, unhappily, amongst religious people, and we know not a better service that can be rendered to the truth than its correction. Any man can use strong words, can call hard names. No intellect is required to confound things which differ, though some of their outward expressions may be similar. A fool may do this as easily, and will do it much oftener, than a wise man, and we ought, therefore, to be on our guard against being led astray by vague and general epithets, which are readily employed, but not so easily explained.

In the matter before us it is better to discriminate than to condemn, and he who does so will probably find that there are vast differences, of which note must be taken, if we would rightly estimate the morality of acts. We have no notion, for instance—to illustrate our meaning—of pleasure being found in animal suffering by the majority of sportsmen. Indeed, very few are, in our judgment, open to a charge of this kind. We have known many humane men—not mere sentimentalists, but men of healthy and robust humanity—who have taken much pleasure in such pursuits. We have conversed with them on the subject, and have occasionally watched their movements in the field, and can have no hesitation in saying, that on the point in question they must have an acquittal. Their excitement may, or may not, be disproportionate and unhealthy; other and higher vocations may be sacrificed to the favourite sport; they may be confounded, by their pursuits, with men of a totally different character and spirit; but they seek no pleasure, and they have none, in animal suffering. The supposition is absurd, and every feature of their character proclaims it false. Few men would charge the late Sir Thomas Fowell Buxton with inhumanity, and yet he is well known to have entered with great zest into the sports of the field. We are aware that some refer to this as his weakness, but we are not sure that such engagements did not contribute to the masculine vigor he displayed on some critical occasions.

These remarks, which we must not extend, have been suggested by the title of Mr. Knox's volume. Its contents are ' chiefly derived from the observations and experiences of the author, in reference to those birds which are usually the objects of pursuit with the British sportsman; and to certain other animals which, either justly or erroneously, are supposed to be injurious to their welfare and increase.' Mr. Knox is already well known to the lovers of natural history by his ' Ornithological Rambles in Sussex'—a charming book, evincing genuine love of nature in connexion with a keen relish of field-sports. His powers of observation are considerable, his patience is unwearied, and his faculty of tracing facts to their origin, and of referring effects to their causes, gives a fascination to this work of which similar productions are mostly destitute. He needs, therefore, no introduction on the present occasion, and we shall proceed at once, to lay before our readers some of his observations on the habits and adventures of the 'game birds and wild fowl,' of which his volume treats.

The partridge and pheasant are, of all the birds named by Mr. Knox, the most familiar to the inhabitants of towns. They are daily seen in large numbers, and constitute an article of merchandise to a much greater extent than any other birds. Indeed, it is somewhat surprising that their numbers are maintained, considering the casualties to which they are exposed, and the slaughter practised on them. However, so it is, and no fear of the extinction of the breed need yet be entertained. Other wild fowl retire before the advance of cultivation. The ptarmigan finds a home on the most inaccessible peaks of mountains; the black-cock flourishes in the swamp or glen; the red grouse haunts the moor and barren heath; and the quail evidently prefers the partial culture, which betokens a slovenly and unproductive husbandry. 'But the partridge is, *par excellence*, the game of the farm; and, *cæteris paribus*, the finer the crops of cereal grain, and the higher the turnips, the larger and more numerous will be the coveys found in such districts.' Mr. Knox contends that the partridge is a friend to the farmer, in consequence of the great quantity of noxious weeds and insects which it devours. During the summer months, the bird is well known to feed on insects; and if its crop be examined in winter or spring, 'it will be found,' he says, 'to contain chiefly grasses, grubs, and minute coleopterous insects, which in the larva state are, in a greater or less degree, injurious to vegetation.' The peculiar mode of roosting adopted by the partridge greatly facilitates the success of many of its foes. The whole covey usually squat, in a circle, with their heads turned outwards; and the following is one of the many modes in which they are trepanned :—

' Two or three poachers, disguised in respectable attire, travel about the country in a gig or dog-cart, accompanied by a single pointer or setter. One of the party alights at the outskirts of a village or country town, and proceeding to the public room of the nearest tavern, soon falls into conversation with some of the unsuspecting inhabitants; and passing himself off as " an intelligent traveller," or keen sportsman, about to pay a visit to the neighbouring squire, soon obtains sufficient local information for his purpose. The other " gentlemen " have in the meantime put up their horse and gig at an inn in a different quarter, and, while discussing their brandy-and-water at the bar, have " pumped " the landlord of all the news likely to prove useful to the fraternity. At a certain hour in the evening the trio meet by appointment at some pre-arranged spot outside the village, and commence operations. After comparing notes, the most promising ground is selected. A dark night and rough weather are all in their favour. The steady old pointer, with a lantern round its neck, is turned into a stubble-field, and a net of fine texture, but tough materials, is produced from a bag in which it has hitherto been closely packed.   The light passes quickly across the field—now here, now there, like a ' Will-o'-the-Wisp '—as the sagacious dog quarters the ground rapidly, yet with as much care and precision as if he were working for a legitimate sportsman in open day. Suddenly, it ceases to move, then advances slowly, stops, moves once more, and at last becomes stationary.   Two of the men then take the net, and making a circuit until they arrive in front of the dog, shake out the meshes and place it in a proper position on the ground.   Then, standing opposite to each other, and holding either end of the string, they draw it slowly and noiselessly over their quadruped ally—whose exact position is indicated by the lantern—frequently capturing at the same time an unsuspecting covey huddled together within a few inches of his nose.   When this operation is carried on by experienced hands, an entire manor may be effectually stripped of partridges in an incredibly short space of time.'—Pp. 7, 8.

The pheasant is a shy bird, as is well known to every sportsman.   Though many centuries have passed since his introduction to our island, he is really an exotic, and no pains have sufficed to reconcile him to the restraints of the farm-yard.   Much has been attempted in this way, but the degree of success achieved is not very encouraging.   Our author's observations on the hatching and rearing of young pheasants are worthy of attention.   They are the result of considerable personal experience, and bespeak both practical sagacity and deep interest in the pursuit.   We commend his remarks to all who have the opportunity and inclination to reduce them to practice, and, in the meantime, content ourselves with the following extract, in which an untoward accident is shown to have been productive of the best results :—

' All my pheasants having escaped on the night of the accident, I was obliged to commence operations *de novo*, and, to avoid the expense of netting, I pinioned fifteen tame-bred poults,—eleven hens and four cocks,—with which the kindness of a neighbouring friend supplied me, and turned them all into the enclosures.   The operation of pinioning consists in amputating the forehand or pinion of one wing at the carpal joint.   The bird is never able afterwards to ascend in flight more than two or three feet from the ground, and therefore escape from an enclosure such as I have described would be impossible.*   The wounds soon healed, the birds enjoyed excellent health through the winter, and in the following March, when the males began to exhibit the usual symptoms of pugnacity, I was preparing to locate them in their respective compartments for the season, when I was unexpectedly obliged to leave home, and directed that the pheasantry should remain

---

* Birds thus pinioned are of course unfit for subsequent liberation in the covers.

in *statu quo* during my absence. On my return, how changed was the state of affairs! Love and war had been running riot within its once peaceful precincts. Three of the four cock-birds were completely *hors de combat*. One of them, indeed, was dying, two were severely lacerated, but the fourth, who, like the surviving Horatius in the combat with the Curiatii, had probably vanquished all his rivals in detail, appeared, like his classical prototype, perfectly uninjured, and strutted in all the pomp and pride of a conqueror among a crowd of hens, who seemed to regard matters with perfect equanimity, passing with contemptuous indifference their unfortunate knights-errant, as they sat moping on the ground with their heads buried in the friendly shelter of the bushes, but following obediently in the wake of the victor, and evidently disposed to admit to the full extent that " none but the brave deserve the fair."

' I should have mentioned that the grounds in the neighbourhood of the enclosure were stocked with wild pheasants, most of which had once been "tame-bred birds," and—although always exhibiting the innate timidity of the species on any sudden alarm—evinced an attachment to the place in which they had been reared, and continued to haunt the garden and evergreens during the greater part of the year. As I had now no opportunity of procuring any pinioned male pheasants to supply the place of the three discomfited heroes, I allowed matters to take their chance, fully prepared to find that most of my eggs would prove unproductive, and almost inclined to break up the pheasantry altogether, but my half-formed intention was suddenly arrested by a new turn in the aspect of affairs. On entering the enclosure one morning, I was surprised to see a fine old cock-pheasant, with a tail of portentous length, take wing from among the midst of the hens, and, with a protracted crow of triumph, fly over the fence into the evergreens beyond. But where was Horatius? Alas! his days were numbered. He had found his match at last. After a long search, I discovered him squatted in a corner, his once brilliant plumage torn and covered with blood. One eye was closed; the other was completely extinguished. His neck entirely plucked, and as bare as a vulture's. His crimson cheeks were sadly lacerated. His head was absolutely scalped, and where a pair of purple egrets had lately been so proudly erected, a bare skull was now alone visible. Poor fellow! he died the same evening. The rest may be briefly told. Day after day did the conqueror visit his newly-acquired territory, and many a youthful rival, too prudent to come into close quarters with the long-spurred tyrant, would pay a stolen visit to his seraglio during his absence and win the favours of his fickle fair ones. I obtained an immense number of eggs during that season, which proved unusually productive. No further care was necessary than to provide the birds with a sufficiency of food and to remove the eggs every day—which, by the way, were never deposited in a nest, but dropped here and there in different parts of the enclosure. Thus, from what I regarded at the time as a succession of untoward accidents, I became acquainted with the most effectual, because the most natural way of keeping hen-pheasants with a view to obtaining a constant and ample supply of prolific eggs during the

breeding-season. Every gamekeeper's cottage in the heart of a preserve must possess in its neighbourhood much greater facilities for the
undertaking than were within my own reach.'—Pp. 95—98.

Before leaving the pheasant we must quote our author's sketch
of ' an asylum' for them, which he inspected at Walton Hall,
the seat of Mr. Waterton, and which, as he remarks, ' appeared
to be the very *beau ideal* of everything that could be wished for
in that way.' In this spot, with ordinary discretion on their own
part, they might evidently laugh to scorn the cat, the stoat, the
fox, and the poacher :—

' This paradise for pheasants is situated in an open part of the park,
not far from the lake. A thick hedge of holly surrounds a clump of
yew trees, in an oval form, and is rendered still more secure by a ditch
which encircles it externally. This holly hedge is regularly clipped
and quite impenetrable from top to bottom ; being in fact an evergreen
wall, and the only entrance is by a small gate, which is carefully locked.
Within, a narrow space intervenes between it and the yew trees, which
being also constantly cut on the top and underneath, have so spread
and interwoven their lateral branches as to form a dense verdant
canopy overhead, through which not a single ray of light can penetrate. To enter this evergreen grotto it is necessary to stoop very low
through a little archway cut in the thick foliage, but when once arrived
at the interior a man may stand almost upright. Then, and not until
then, the advantages of the place as an asylum for pheasants become
evident. There is no under cover or brushwood, and, therefore, no
inducement to the birds to sleep on the ground, where they too frequently, in less favoured spots, become the prey of nocturnal four-
footed vermin; while the horizontal branches of the yew trees afford
everything desirable in a roosting place. Even during the day it would
be difficult to perceive a pheasant when perched among them. If, notwithstanding all these obstacles to the ingress of an unwelcome visitor,
one should succeed in reaching the centre of the clump and alarm the
pheasants, they would drop quietly from the branches of the yews
upon the smooth ground, and running through the hollow space below
towards the exterior, arrive at once in the narrow passage between
them and the holly hedge, where there is sufficient room to enable
them to start from the ground, and their first appearance from the outside would be just as they topped the summit in a rapid flight to
another place of security. Such a spot is of course secure from the
depredations of the night shooter ; and the impenetrable nature of the
hollies, through which even the pheasants themselves cannot force a
passage, baffles at the same time the machinations of the wirer and
trapper.'—Pp. 184, 185.

' The noble science of falconry ' is little known in these
degenerate days. It was the favourite pastime of our ancestors,
affording to ' gentle ladies' and ' noble lords' an exciting and
healthy occupation. Various causes have contributed to its
decay, into the history and operation of which we shall not stop

to inquire. We confess for ourselves that, of all field sports, this would be to us the most attractive. We have, however, now to do with the habits of the bird formerly used so extensively by the gentry, rather than with the sport in which they took such deep and passionate interest. The wide distribution of the peregrine has long been noticed by naturalists, and is strikingly illustrated by the fact that, 'there is no nest of this falcon on the face of the earth, however remote or isolated, where, in the event of the death of one of the proprietors, the survivor will not succeed, generally within twenty-four hours, in finding a helpmate of the opposite sex, even when none but the original pair had, up to that moment, perhaps, ever been observed in the neighbourhood.'

Mr. Knox had frequent opportunities of noticing the habits of this bird, and his record of them is full of interest. Their sudden appearance, rapid flight, promptitude, and courage, are depicted with genuine earnestness, so as to carry along the reader, notwithstanding that he may just have risen from a perusal of the reports of the Society for the Prevention of Cruelty to Animals. There is nothing over-strained in his descriptions. The charm of his picture is its truthfulness. A few simple strokes constitute its outline, while its coloring is so disposed as to render the whole scene familiar and attractive. The author does not write for effect—at least, the intention is not visible. He recounts his adventures with the enthusiasm of a genuine sportsman, and seems never troubled with a doubt as to the recital being as interesting to others. The following sketch, descriptive of what was witnessed on the banks of the Brosna, in Ireland, may serve as a specimen :—

'Despatching a light-footed native, who was well acquainted with all the favourite resorts of wild fowl among the labyrinthian recesses of a distant bog, through which the river meandered in its earlier course, I directed him to flush them from these haunts, while I resumed the post which I had occupied on the preceding day. For the first half-hour I was almost in despair; for the falcon was absent from her accustomed station, and I thought it not improbable that the operations of my coadjutor might have attracted her attention, and that she was perhaps at that very moment in full enjoyment of a chase which I was fated not to witness; but on looking up a few moments afterwards, there she sat, bolt upright as usual, and now every minute appeared an hour, as I strained my eyes continually in the direction from which I expected the arrival of the first detachment of ducks. Presently a cluster of dark spots appeared against the distant sky, gradually becoming more distinct, and sinking lower and lower as they neared the river, and at last keeping close to its surface, until they scudded by within a few yards of the commanding position of their enemy; who, probably from her reluctance to strike so large a quarry as a wild duck, which she could not have clutched and carried off with ease across the water, suffered them to pass unmolested. Next came two or three wigeons, which also ran the gauntlet with impunity. I now began to fancy that the appetite of the hawk must have been satisfied by some recent prey, or that perhaps the bird which I had seen her strike two days before might remain still undigested. Just at that moment, however, a whistling of wings reached my ear; and I perceived a party of five or six wild ducks and a few teal approaching from a different direction, and nearly at right angles to the course of the river, which they would apparently have reached at a point about thirty yards distant from the falcon's position. But she had no intention of allowing them such an advantage. In an instant she was on the wing, and had cut them off from their retreat. For a few seconds it seemed doubtful which was to be the victim, but one of the mallards having made a bolder dash at the stream than his companions, she seemed to mark him at once for destruction, while on his part he endeavoured to mount above his pursuer, and strained every nerve to accomplish this object by ascending spirally. In the meantime his comrades, availing themselves of this diversion in their favour, scudded down to the water and dashed at once into the friendly shelter of the sedges. Almost at the same instant the falcon made a swoop, but missing her quarry, she suddenly appeared a considerable distance below him, and now it seemed doubtful whether she could recover the advantage which she had lost by this unexpected failure. While she struggled upwards again in circular gyrations, and the mallard also made the best of his time to attain a higher elevation by executing a similar movement, but in a much wider curve, the two birds frequently seemed to be flying in opposite directions. The superior ease and rapidity, however, with which this manœuvre was performed by the peregrine, soon convinced me that the result of the chase could not be doubtful; for the drake was now far from his favourite element, and as each successive evolution brought his enemy nearer and nearer, he seemed to relax in his efforts to ascend any higher, and at length turning his tail to the wind, away he went towards the bog of Killeen, trusting for escape to the rapidity of his flight, and closely pursued by the falcon. I felt that not a moment was to be lost if I wished to witness the *dénouement;* so, scrambling to the top of the bank, I was just in time to see the mallard tumbling headlong to the earth, while the falcon checking her downward career for a moment, as if to satisfy herself of the success of the stroke, dropped to the spot where he had fallen in the middle of a wide marsh.'—Pp. 28—31.

Ornithologists have differed in opinion respecting the manner in which the falcon strikes its prey. Some assert it to be by the foot, while others attribute it to the breastbone, which is supposed to be protected by strong pectoral muscles. Our author agrees with Colonel Bonham in regarding the hind talons as the weapon employed. 'If,' he tells us, 'a grouse, a duck, or a woodcock, that has been thus suddenly killed by a peregrine, be examined, it will generally be found that the loins and shoulders are deeply scored, the back of the neck much torn, and even the scull sometimes penetrated by this formidable weapon. Now as the stroke is almost always delivered obliquely, that is, in a slanting, downward direction from behind, this laceration could not be effected by any of the talons of the front toes; nor would the severest possible blow from the breast of the falcon produce such an effect.'

There is sometimes great danger of losing the falcon by the eagerness with which it follows its prey. When the woodcock, for instance, which is a bird of great vigor and rapidity of flight, after ascending to a considerable height, strikes off in a direct line, the falcon will pursue for many miles, until all traces of its starting-point are lost. A remarkable instance of this occurred to Colonel Bonham, which Mr. Knox thus records :—

'When hawking for woodcocks in Rossmore Park, in the county of Monaghan, Ireland, with the Hon. R. Westenra, a woodcock, after a short chace, "took the air," closely pursued by the falcon—the property of the latter gentleman—who had her bells and "varvels" on, with the name and address of the owner engraved upon them. In a short time both birds had attained such an elevation that it was only by lying down on their backs, and placing their hands above their eyes, so as to screen them from the rays of the sun, and at the same time contract the field of vision, that the spectators could keep them within view. At last, just as they had become almost like specks in the sky, they were observed to pass rapidly towards the north-east, under the influence of a strong south-west wind ; and were soon completely out of sight. Some days elapsed without any tidings of the truant falcon; but before the week had expired, a parcel arrived at Rossmore Park, accompanied by a letter bearing a Scotch postmark. The first contained the dead body of the falcon : the latter the closing chapter of her history from the hand of her destroyer, a farmer who resided within ten miles of Aberdeen. He was walking through his grounds when his attention was attracted by the appearance of a large hawk which had just dashed among his pigeons, and was then in the act of carrying one of them off. Running into the house he returned presently with a loaded gun, and found the robber coolly devouring her prey on the top of a wheat-stack. The next moment the poor falcon's wanderings were at an end ; but it was not until he had seen the bells on her feet that he discovered the value of his victim, and upon a more careful examination perceived the name and address of her owner ; and while affording him the only reparation in his power by sending him her remains and the account of her fate, he unconsciously rendered the story worthy of record in a sporting and an ornithological point of view; for, upon a subsequent comparison of dates, it was found that she had been shot near Aberdeen, on the eastern coast of Scotland, within forty-eight hours after she had been flown at the woodcock in a central part of the province of Ulster in Ireland.'—Pp. 171—173.

Before hastening to other matters, we must extract another passage, which discloses a feature of the falcon's character not commonly appreciated. We are so accustomed to regard the hawk as a bird of prey, that many will probably be surprised to learn that he is susceptible of the more kindly emotions.

'A friend of Colonel Bonham—the late Colonel Johnson, of the Rifle Brigade—was ordered to Canada with his battalion, in which he was then a captain, and being very fond of falconry, to which he had devoted much time and expense, he took with him two of his favourite peregrines, as his companions, across the Atlantic.

'It was his constant habit during the voyage to allow them to fly every day, after "feeding them up" that they might not be induced to rake off after a passing sea-gull, or wander out of sight of the vessel. Sometimes their rambles were very wide and protracted. At others they would ascend to such a height as to be almost lost to the view of the passengers, who soon found them an effectual means of relieving the tedium of a long sea voyage, and naturally took a lively interest in their welfare; but as they were in the habit of returning regularly to the ship, no uneasiness was felt during their occasional absence. At last, one evening, after a longer flight than usual, one of the falcons returned alone. The other—the prime favourite—was missing. Day after day passed away, and, however much he may have continued to regret his loss, Captain Johnson had at length fully made up his mind. that it was irretrievable, and that he should never see her again. Soon after the arrival of the regiment in America, on casting his eyes over a Halifax newspaper, he was struck by a paragraph announcing that the captain of an American schooner had at that moment in his possession a fine hawk, which had suddenly made its appearance on board his ship during his late passage from Liverpool. The idea at once occurred to Captain Johnson that this could be no other than his much-prized falcon, so having obtained immediate leave of absence he set out for Halifax, a journey of some days. On arriving there he lost no time in waiting on the commander of the schooner, announcing the object of his journey, and requesting that he might be allowed to see the bird; but Jonathan had no idea of relinquishing his prize so easily, and stoutly refused to admit of the interview, "guessing" that it was very easy for an Englisher to lay claim to another man's property, but "calculating" that it was a "tarnation sight" harder for him to get possession of it; and concluded by asserting, in unqualified terms, his entire disbelief in the whole story. Captain Johnson's object, however, being rather to recover his falcon than to pick a quarrel with the truculent Yankee, he had fortunately sufficient self-command to curb his indignation, and proposed that his claim to the ownership of the bird should be at once put to the test by an experiment, which several Americans who were present admitted to be perfectly reasonable, and in which their countryman was at last persuaded to acquiesce. It was this. Captain Johnson was to be admitted to an interview with the hawk—who, by the way, had as yet shown no partiality for any person since her arrival in the New World, but, on the contrary, had rather repelled all attempts at familiarity—and if at this meeting she should not only exhibit such unequivocal signs of attachment and recognition as should induce the majority of the bystanders to believe that he really was her original master, but especially if she should play with the buttons of his coat, then the American was at once to waive all claim to her. The trial was immediately made. The Yankee went up stairs, and shortly returned with the falcon; but the door was hardly opened before she darted from his fist and perched at once on the shoulder of her beloved and long-lost protector, evincing, by every means in her power, her delight and affection, rubbing her head against his cheek, and taking hold of the buttons of his coat and champing them playfully between her mandibles, one after another. This was enough. The jury were unanimous. A verdict for the plaintiff was pronounced: even the obdurate heart of the sea-captain was melted, and the falcon was at once restored to the arms of her rightful owner.'—Pp. 177—180.

We are glad to find our author entering a protest against the exterminating war waged against the badger, ' the last representative of the *ursidæ* (bears) in the British islands.' There is nothing certainly prepossessing in its appearance, but its habits are innocuous, and the hostility it encounters is as senseless as that to which the poor toad is exposed. Though occasionally devouring small quadrupeds, its food consists principally of vegetables and insects. ' Chestnuts, roots of all kinds, blackberries, beech-mast, and all manner of beetles, with the larvæ of wasps and wild bees, furnish his ordinary supplies; while even frogs and snakes contribute to vary his dietary during the summer and autumn. It is therefore difficult to palliate the senseless persecution which, in these islands, has already doomed the species to a gradual but certain destruction.'

The hedgehog, on the contrary, is admitted to be a great transgressor, while the weasel is stoutly defended against all comers. Of the former, Mr. Knox says :—

' No one was ever more reluctant than myself, for many a day, to credit the evil reports that continually reached me, touching his robbery of pheasants' nests—and even now I am satisfied that his destruction of worms, insects, mice, and snakes, fully atones—in a general sense—for his poaching offences; but as an egg-devourer he stands pre-eminent among British quadrupeds. To a superficial observer his structure would appear to be rather of a defensive than an offensive character, but "facts are stubborn things." I speak from personal experience when I say that if a steel trap be set over night in any wood where hedgehogs are known to exist, and baited with an egg, the capture of one of those animals will, in nine cases out of ten, be the result.'—Pp. 257, 258.

Our author happily ranks amongst the defenders of the squirrel, one of the most elegant, as well as agile, inhabitants of

our woods.  Though its habits are inoffensive, and such as ought
to secure it immunity from the game preserver, it is pursued
with unrelenting hostility on many estates.  A violent prejudice exists  against it, strange tales are told of its destructive
qualities, and the mandate has in consequence gone forth to
harass and slay it.  We shall be glad to find that a more
correct knowledge of facts stays the exterminating process, and
for this  purpose  recommend  the attentive perusal of Mr.
Knox's vindication.  His volume is specially, though not exclusively, interesting to the sportsman.  It contains a good deal of
sound advice, mingled with, and indeed based upon, a large
personal experience.  The extracts given will suffice to attract
our readers to the volume itself; and we are greatly mistaken, if their prevalent impression on closing its perusal be
not one of regret at its dimensions being so limited.  Unlike
many volumes, it awakens a strong desire to receive something
more from the same author.

ART. VI.—*Tracts on Christian Socialism.*  1. *Dialogue between Somebody (a person of respectability), and Nobody (the writer).*  2. *History of the Working Tailors' Association, 34, Great Castle-street.*
3. *An Address to the Clergy, by a Clergyman.*  4. *The Working
Associations of Paris.*  5. *The Society for Promoting Working
Men's Associations.*  London: George Bell.

THERE is some ground for hope that the appalling facts lately
published, in illustration of the privations and sufferings of the
labouring classes, have not fallen coldly on the public ear.  The
revelations of newspaper 'commissioners,' in spite of the gross
materialism of the age, and its intense mammon-worship, have
stirred up some feeling of compassion in the breast of Dives.
For half a century has Capital, successor to Feudalism, been
regarding unpropertied human flesh and bones as its proper
machinery and vested right for money-getting; and now, when
it is found that the machine has been urged by the maximum
pressure almost to the rending point, the world is full of astonishment, and asks, 'Can such things be?'  It does not say much for
our intelligence or prudence that the discovery has only in these
years of social peril been made that we have been sitting quietly
over an unstirred volcano.  Thanks to the European revolutions,

if they had done no other good for mankind, they were fraught with blessings in leading the respectability of England to behold, in all its ghastliness, a social depression darker and more destructive than the serfage and slavery of the darkest age of modern history.

Contrast the state of the serf of the eleventh century as exhibited in the Colloquium of Alfric, with the condition of our free slaves of the nineteenth, as discovered by the 'Morning Chronicle.' What says the serf?—

'My lord, I labour excessively. I go out at dawn of day, driving my oxen to the field, and yoke them to the plough. There is no weather so severe that I dare rest at home, for fear of my lord; but having yoked my oxen, and fastened the share and coulter to the plough, every day I must plough a whole field or more.'

'Hast thou any companion?' asks the sympathizing priest.

'I have a boy who urges the oxen with a goad, and who is now hoarse with cold and shouting.'

'What more doest thou in the day?'

'Truly still I do more; I must fill the mangers of the oxen with hay, and water them, and carry out their litter.'

'Oh, oh! it is a great tribulation.'

'Yea, it is great tribulation, because I am not free.'

Eight centuries have rolled on, and the toiler is a free man. The law declares that no man can hold property in human blood and bones; yet in happy England are there millions of bondmen—serfs in body and soul to the grinding oppression of unrequited toil or starvation and death. Is the social lot of the English needle-woman or tailor better than that of the poor Saxon theow? The slave labouring in the fields had air and blessed sunshine and the sympathy of a kindly clergy; for our toilers in the garret and the sweating-den, there is neither sunshine to glad the eye nor cheer the heart. Verily is their lot a great tribulation, because they are not free.

And how are we to get rid of this black spot of serfage? All England is in an enthusiasm of benevolence. The French noblesse of the first National Assembly on the memorable fourth of August were not more generous in zeal for social freedom, than are our privileged orders in their new-born benevolence. Respectability has shut up his gig, and called in the social doctors to a consultation. Vast is the amount of prescription and nostrum planning; the only fear is that they may doctor away the flickering remnant of vitality. Air exercise, freedom, a small wholesome dietary counsel—above all, strict avoidance of the sentimental doctor's stuff, and there is some hope for the patient, desperate though his case may seem.

In the philosophy of history there is one great axiomatic truth everywhere written, which receives little regard in sentimental aspirations after progress. Self-dependence has been the mainspring of all social improvement. The history of mankind everywhere shows it; the history of man, the toiler, imperfectly as that has been written, is nevertheless plain with proofs. The English workman has grown from serfage to the theoretic dignity of free man by the might alone of that principle. Trace his career through the Saxon age from the time when he came to our island the war captive of a Teuton master, and his attainments in humanity and culture were not inconsiderable, his progress was his own achievement. Norman oppression cast him down to the level of the brutes, and self-exertion, painful and toilsome, but sure, again gave to the villain the feelings and the name of man. What was the origin of that mighty proletarian movement of the fourteenth century—much talked of, but little understood? Follow it from the atrocious Jacquerie wars of France—the Wat Tyler tumults of England—the peasant wars of Hungary in the fifteenth and of Germany in the sixteenth centuries, which deluged lords and serfs in oceans of blood; everywhere is it plainly written in the bold red hand of strife that it was the rising of a serf-race strong in self-knowledge from a new-born consciousness of power. The peasants had learned that they were men with the same rights and the same eternal responsibilities as their task-masters. By association they developed their power; but too soon they taught tyrants, ignorant as themselves, how much the very existence of the mighty ones of the earth depends on the hewers of wood and the drawers of water. But half the battle of emancipation was won, when the despised peasant had struck terror into his lordly master's soul.

It is not to strengthen the unhappy feeling of class antagonism, nor as precedents to justify the ' sacred right of insurrection ' by an oppressed people, that we cite these terrible facts, but as lessons of history beyond price for the governing and the governed —teaching the one the exceeding great power of justice in keeping the masses of men in contentment; for the other showing the mighty strength which in them lies, and the fearful results of an abuse thereof. The history of Wat Tyler has yet to be written, but not as men place scarecrows in the fields to frighten the multitude; it is full of great political instruction, and requires the pen of a philosopher. These bold men were not, as scarecrow penmen would have us believe, a horde of savage barbarians. They had caught some of the blessed light of religious freedom which John Wickliffe was then diffusing throughout the land. No one can palliate the excesses they committed, though the tyranny of their oppressors may account for them. They had discovered the rights of men, though they asked, in clamorous chorus,

> 'When Adam delved and Eve span,
> Who was then a gentleman?'

In seeking for primal equality, they had, unfortunately, over-looked the history of man in the next generation from Adam. If the rhyme is homely, and the conclusion illogical, the moral of the history is wholesome even for an enlightened age, which has not discovered the distinction between the equality which con-sists of equal laws, and the so-called social equality which, granting the possibility of its establishment, would reduce men to the capacity of oxen. The peasant champions erred, in that they went too fast, and would outstrip the laws of progress, as slow in their development as they are certain in their result.

Much does humanity owe to the fourteenth century. Its master-spirit left a priceless bequest to the poor man. Intole-rance in dishonouring his bones only paid homage to his great-ness. The Council of Constance outraged all that was mortal of the first reformer, and the ashes of his bones were cast into the brook Swift. 'Thus,' as old Fuller quaintly expresses it, 'this brook has conveyed his ashes into Avon, Avon into Severn, Severn into the narrow seas, then into the main ocean; and thus the ashes of Wickliffe are the emblem of his doctrine, which now is dispersed all the world over.' Alas! we have hardly got be-yond the recognition of his doctrines; the practical morality of Christianity has yet to be learned. Toiling millions sigh for the coming of a second Wickliffe.

Strange that economical doctrines, which all money-seeking men so conscientiously worship, should not have taught juster notions of social rights and duties. But economical science is only emerging from the barbarian period when might is right. Is there, however, no moral instruction to be derived from our idolatry of materialism? Is there no philosophy in the history of our canals, our railways, our docks, the leviathan works which are to testify our greatness to posterity? It would not be unprofitable meditation, were we at times to think a little of what posterity may have to say of our greatness. In the gymnasia of the Cannibal Islands, in anno MMDCCCL., the archæological catechizing, freely rendered from the classic Can-nibalee, may run thus:—

'*Professor.* What are the most probable conjectures as to the use of these Britannic remains?

'*Scholasticus.* From the report of the commission of inquiry sent by the Lyceum of Timbuctoo early in the last century, when the Cossacks were planting the deserted island with corn for the supply of the manu-

facturing districts of Tartary, it appeared that these tracts were the remains of water-courses and pathways used for terrestrial transport by
the barbarians, many centuries before animal-magnetic locomotion was
discovered.   In the President's library at the North Pole there is a
small collection of documents, preserved from the terrible conflagration
when the Russian republicans set fire to the Thames in the twenty-first
century.   From these fragments, the learned suppose that the works
were executed by a high caste of the nineteenth century, who were called
Capitalists.
  ' *Prof.* What is known of these Capitalists ?
  ' *Scho.* Little but the name ; derived from a word in their language
signifying chief or head man, because they were rich in slaves ; a fact
deduced from a lyric fragment called the " Song of the Shirt," attributed to Moses and Son, a great popular poet of that age.   They were
the priests of the religion of the islanders, who worshipped a god called
Money.   The name of one Hudson has been preserved as a great
capitalist, whence some conclude that he was chief priest, or, according
to the native tongue, Archbishop of Canterbury ; others say that he
was the principal deity of the Anglican mythology.'

  The great fact that man is a co-operative animal—at least from
the hunting period of savage life—has been used only by those
who benefit by the subjection of one class to another.   This has
been long a recognised truth in political economy, when the
interests of money capital were alone concerned.   Men have
heretofore, at times, proved it for evil ; it is now time that they
should learn to use it for good.
  One of the most seeming practical plans in the many schemes
lately proposed for improving the condition of the labouring
classes is based to some extent on this principle.   The movement has originated in the metropolis, and is denominated
' Christian Socialism.'   In the last week of 1849, as we learn
from the interesting ' history of the working tailors' association,'
ten persons, amongst whom were two of the metropolitan clergy,
a member of Parliament, and two working men, met together in
the house of one of their number.   The commissioner of the
' Morning Chronicle' for the metropolitan districts had just published his letters on the condition of the tailors and needle-women
of London.   The disclosures of these letters had sunk deep into
the breast of every man who was present that evening.   ' Ragged-
schools, soup-kitchens, model lodging-houses, baths and wash-
houses, had, for the moment, lost all interest in their eyes ; all
good, that was as yet struggling to make itself felt, seemed but
as a tiny brook pouring its devoted healthiness into the Thames
at Bermondsey.'   Before they separated, they resolved that they
should at once endeavour to establish associations of work-people
in the trades which were most beaten down, which should work

for mutual profit 'in places and under conditions befitting men and women in the nineteenth century of Christianity.'

These were practical men; they did not lose the opportunity of doing good in idle talk. But let the historian speak—

'The next meeting of the promoters (as I shall now call the persons whose doings I am describing) was held on the 8th of January, 1850, at the house of one of the clergymen, and by that time something had been done. Several other gentlemen had joined their body, and they had all been in constant communication with some of the best of the working men, whom they had known before, and upon whom they could rely as upon themselves. These men were with them on that evening; and, to their honour be it spoken, more than one master tailor also, to whom the promoters cannot be too thankful for the aid then and since so heartily given. At this meeting it was determined to make the first trial with the tailors, and by the help of their working friends and the master tailor, an estimate of the expense was formed, which has since proved singularly accurate. It was determined at once to raise the necessary sum, and to take fitting workshops; and a sub-committee was appointed to frame the conditions upon which the money was to be advanced, and the association set to work.'

In the course of ten days, the promoters had entered into a lease for suitable premises, and all that remained to set the concern afloat was to draw up a set of conditions for the regulation of the community. It was at length resolved that twelve men should commence work on the 11th of February. Nothing remained except to buy stock and to set the cutter to work, the promoters having taken care to give from themselves and friends a sufficient number of orders to afford employment for the first week, at least. On the day in question, the manager and cutter were enabled to set their whole force to work in good earnest.

'I will not enter into the little difficulties which have since arisen, and which have been easily overcome. They have just sufficed to draw the promoters and the associates more closely together, and to convince both parties that their principle is a living one, and cannot fail while they carry it out honestly. Neither will I set out a long statement of the accounts; but I shall here mention, that in the first month sufficient business was done to keep all the men at work nine hours and a half on an average; and that their wages *averaged 1l. a man per week* for that period; that in the second month, the men worked on an average ten hours a day, and obtained average wages of 1*l*. 2*s*. 6*d*. a man. *I think that no fact can prove more clearly that these men at least are fit to govern themselves than this,—that they voluntarily left in the hands of their manager an absolute power of dismissing any of the number during the first three months of their associated life.*'

However much we may rejoice at the success of the experiment, we cannot say much in praise of the wisdom of the course indicated in the *italicised* sentence. This is pure centralizing despotism in humble imitation of modern parliamentary practice. It is making the servant the master. These 'associates' are, or ought to be, partners, or shareholders, who have invested the capital of their labour. Each man's share is his property, and inviolable. We are therefore simply informed that these men have voluntarily empowered their servant to deprive any one of his masters of his property at will! Imagine such a power imposed in the directors of railways. How comfortable would the Hudsons then contrive to make things, when they could so easily dispose of too inquisitive shareholders! We shall have occasion presently to point out some other radical defects in the scheme of organization proposed. In the meantime we would only remark, that the experiment has been successful, not only in demonstrating the possibility of co-operative labour, but the ease with which it may be put into practice.

We learn, from a statement lately published by the association, that during the six months it has been in operation, work has been completed to the amount of 2,500*l.*, yielding, after payment of all expenses, interest on capital, &c., a net profit of 220*l.* The earnings of the association are divided into thirds :— one portion accrues to the 'associates,' divided equally ; one-third goes to repay capital; the remainder falls into trade for extension of stock. 'It would surprise those who know not what we are doing,' says the writer, 'to see a list of our customers. We work for all classes—Bishops, Catholic and Protestant, lords and draymen, marquises and masons, clubs and costermongers, earls and bricklayers, with general satisfaction.' The association then included twenty-two 'associates,' and six 'auxiliaries.' It appears, that since its establishment eight other associations have been formed, including a needlewoman's association, established in Red Lion-square, under the management of a committee of ladies, three associations of shoemakers, and associations of working printers, working bakers, and working builders. A 'central office of the Working Men's Association' has been established for the purpose of affording information and of receiving orders. The movement is now exciting much interest amongst the working classes throughout the country. At a meeting of delegates lately held at Manchester, it was resolved that a congress of working men should be convened to discuss the question of wages, particularly in the relation they bear to the actual deserts of the recipients of wages, and to consider how far co-operative association may be used as the means of securing to the labouring classes the fruits of their labour.

If there is one thing more puzzling at the present day than

another, it is to find out what is precisely meant by the term Socialism. It has as many meanings as orthodoxy itself. 'Christian Socialism' is not an exception. Let us see if we can derive some intelligible notion of its principles from the dialogue between Messieurs Somebody and Nobody:—

'*Somebody*. Christian socialism! I never saw that adjective united to that substantive before. Do you seriously believe that a Socialist can be a Christian, or a Christian a socialist?

'*Nobody*. I seriously believe that Christianity is the only foundation of socialism, and that a true socialism is the necessary result of a sound Christianity.

'*S.* Sound and true! One understands those words very well. True socialism is your socialism, not that of Owen, Fourier, Louis Blanc, or any other Englishman, Frenchman, German. Sound Christianity is your Christianity, not that of any church, sect, school, or divine, hitherto known in Christendom.

'*N.* The socialism I speak of is that of Owen, Fourier, Louis Blanc, and of the Englishmen, Frenchmen, Germans, who have fraternized with them, or produced systems of their own.'

'Somebody' objects that his opponent's socialism is that of a hundred different men at strife with each other. The other replies that they differ *only* about the means of compassing it. Our 'Christian Socialist' objects to the maxim of his infidel brethren, 'that man can be made blessed by a certain set of circumstances, because he is the creature of circumstances;' but he remarks, that all the stoutest asserters of competition agree with him in their worship of circumstances.

'But it is just here that they find the breach with Christianity, which had been continually widening, has become irreconcilable. Christianity evidently contemplates men as something else than the creatures of circumstances. If divines do not perceive that fact, our Owenites, with a much clearer and juster instinct, do perceive it. Therefore they say, "Christianity and our system must be for ever at war till one has either banished the other, or reduced it into a tributary."

'*S.* By what charms do you hope to persuade Socialists to cast aside their favourite dogma and to embrace one the most directly opposed to it?

'*N.* I have no charms for the purpose.'

No, truly. How then do you propose to convert the world to your orthodoxy?

'*N.* I hold that there has been a sound Christianity in the world, and that it has been the power which has kept society from the dissolution with which the competitive principle has been perpetually threatening it. I hold that this Christianity has been sound, because it has not been mine or yours, but has been a Gospel from Heaven concerning the relation in which God stands to his creatures, concerning the true law under which he has constituted them, and concerning the false, selfish tendency in you and me, which is ever rebelling against that law.

' *S.* I have noticed for some time, in a certain class of French Socialists, the remnants or relics, I believe, of the St. Simonian fanatics, a disposition to invent some religious or ecclesiastical cover for their scheme. Socialism *plus* Christianity is not an English novelty, whatever you may think.

' *N.* I rejoice to think that it is not. There is, as you say, a very strong and evident feeling among the most thoughtful and earnest Frenchmen that, if ever co-operation is to establish itself in the world, it must have some spiritual power to influence and direct its movements. There is a conviction more and more strongly, if blindly, working in their minds, and expressing itself in their language, that this spiritual influence must have some very close connexion with that old Christian influence, which at one time they desired to banish altogether.

' *S.* Which said Christian influence must be entirely remodelled and constructed for Socialist uses.'

After a good deal of wandering, N. comes to the declaration of his faith :—

' *N.* I said that I agreed with Owen, Fourier, and Louis Blanc, in holding co-operation to be the social principle, and competition the dividing, destructive principle. I agree with them because I discover an order through all society, which seems to me to have its natural and necessary expression in united work, and its natural and necessary destruction in individual rivalship. The men to whom you allude hope to create such an order—to build the universe upon it. I find it existing, I desire only to bring it to light, to act as if it existed. From this primary difference all others which you have detected between them and me proceed. But surely I am not less a Socialist than they are in consequence of this difference; I am more of one. I assume that to *be* the only possible condition of society which they wish to *make* the condition of it.

' *S.* If that is your notion, I do not see why you should want Christianity, or any other power, as a help or make-weight in your system.'

' S.' presently rallies our sentimentalist on his modest ambition of

' Converting a nation of competing shopkeepers into a family of loving Christians ; a Society of Friends, probably, or a Moravian *Unitas Fratrum.*

' *N.* Not with the least wish to *form* a Society of Friends, or of United Brethren. These experiments have been made, and have, as I conceive, failed, for the same reason which must cause the failure of Owenite and Phalansterian combinations, that they sought to create a new state of things, instead of proclaiming what that state of things is which God has made, and which we are trying to set at naught.'

We are not told how this Christian Utopia is to be established. Is it to be by act of Parliament, or how? Christian Socialism had better remain at home if it has nothing more profound to enunciate than the novel fact, that mankind has not yet learned Christianity. The same fact is, or ought to be, declared in ten thousand parish churches every Sunday morning. But our Christian Socialist has a little pet nostrum of his own, if we may be permitted to draw an inference from his rather mystical speech. Like an amiable nobleman who has undertaken the cure of humanity, he would simply repeal the law of nature: for is it not a direct denunciation of the law of nature, to speak with this sweeping, unqualified censure against the principle of competition, which is only a practical exercise of self-dependence, the first law of progress? Because the law has been abused by human cupidity, are we to conclude that it is radically unsound? This is the fundamental error of Socialism, from the time it was first propounded down to this its latest development, that it deals with men, not as mortals, but as abstractions. Notoriety is easily won now-a-days. Catch a truism or two, dress them up in high-sounding phrase—use equivocal words if possible, rail stoutly at all existing institutions, proclaim an impossibility as the only possible remedy for the ills of humanity—and you are safe for a nine days' immortality in the morning papers. Vanity, or an egregious self-conceit, is the moving cause of three-fourths of the socialism and sentimentalism of the age. To render any of the socialistic schemes with which the world now abounds possible, we must devise some plan by which men and women shall be endowed with mental qualities meet for the fair forms of a Belvidere Apollo, or a Venus de Medicis. When we make mankind the 'concentration of eclectic loveliness' of which a grandiloquent writer speaks, it will be time to order the phalansteries and parallelograms, and to hope for the Christian Utopias, of which our amiable enthusiasts dream. We believe as sincerely as any wanderer in dream-land, that the spirit of Christianity must pervade every social institution, and regulate every action of humanity, ere man can hope for rest in his earthly pilgrimage. But is it not a narrow—nay, a degrading—view of Christianity which such teachers would promulgate, not that it is the great business of human existence as ordained by the Creator of the universe, but a means to an end—success in life? The Christian code is thus reduced to the level of the maxims of good breeding, which Chesterfield declared as necessary to success in society. The scheme is palpably a delusion. It may possibly be a self-delusion; but it looks very much like an organized effort to hide the deformity of Socialism in a graceful robe, to captivate sentimentality.

We do not participate in the dread of Socialism commonly entertained by our countrymen, for the plain reason that we believe it to be impossible. It deals with abstractions, and so long as these touch not the distinction between *meum* and *tuum* they may be regarded with easy indifference. It was well said of Sièyes, the constitution-maker, that his political speculations were so abstractly perfect that they would not work, simply because mankind had not been mentally squared to a mathematical equality. It would, perhaps, be unfair to the superior intelligence of the Abbé to say the same thing of the present favourite speculations of his lively countrymen. Nevertheless, till we get a race of Apollos and Venuses, they may be allowed a place among the commonwealths of fancy. Is there anything more perfect, on paper, than Fourier's Phalanstère? But however eccentric the social flights—Louis Blanc's grand State-banking scheme — Cabet's Wanderings in Icaria, or Robert Owen's matrimonial theory—however inconvenient the present agitation of these topics, in diverting attention from practical measures of political and social improvement, they cannot be without use as regards the future. Extravagance of opinion always produces reaction, and reaction reflection, which is in time attended with the natural fruits of human improvement. We already see symptoms of this. French Socialism, which had proclaimed a war of extermination against Christianity, is now fain to seek aid from Christianity. This social agitation has stirred up men's minds to reflection. While they are thinking of impossibilities, they are learning great truths, to become in time practical verities. Progress is slow, and men will find that it is sure because it is slow.

The principles of this Christian-Socialistic scheme are captivating to the imagination, and they have been hastily caught up by those who are not much accustomed to exercise the reasoning faculty. It is said that some men of considerable talents and educational acquirements, churchmen and laymen, are at the head of the movement. The name of a learned professor connected with the Church of England, well known for the liberality of his theological views, has been named as a leader. So far well; the people have hitherto lacked leaders of enlightenment and education; the influence of well-educated men is never unproductive of some good results. One good result has come from the movement. When all the world had risen from the perusal of the 'Morning Chronicle's' revelations, London Tavern meetings pronounced for rushing straightway to Parliament to interfere between employers and employed. It says something for the intelligence of the working classes that the advice was not followed. They have, at least, learned to lean on a kind of self-reliance. But 'Christian Socialism' steps in to mar the good work by declaring that progress can only be achieved by destroying competition. It has been reiterated by those who now seek to raise their position by association, 'that the system of competition is not only unjust in its principle, but immoral in its tendencies, endangering the public, and robbing the working-man of a just remuneration for his labour.' Had they substituted for 'system,' the words 'abuse or excess of competition,' we might have been able to award a qualified assent to the proposition. As it stands, it is a simple declaration in favour of Communism, which, by tying up the energies of man, will reduce him to the level of the beasts of burden. *Animi imperio, corporis servitio magis utimur, alterum nobis cum diis, alterum cum belluis commune est.* A little reflection —a little self-examination—might convince reasoning men of the utter futility, nay, the impossibility, of establishing such a system on the earth as at present peopled. The 'navigator,' whose skill lies in the sinew of his arms, or the poor hodman, whose greatest industrial achievement is to serve bricks and mortar to the builder, would be on perfect equality with the accomplished artizan who constructs our time-pieces, and with the tasteful chaser who fabricates the ormolu goddess for the boudoir of young beauty. This is the levelling philosophy of famous Jack Straw, who went back to the age of Adam for a theoretical equality, which, could it be effected, would not be maintained for six weeks. The clock-maker and the ormolu-chaser would soar above the ranks of unskilled labour before Utopia was a week old. Competition is, in short, the exercise of the mental gifts with which the Creator has endowed man. It will be as easy to reduce the human countenance to one standard of uniformity as to place mankind on such social equality. The whole course of history proves that man has been enslaved, or kept in slavery, from the want of freedom of energy and freedom of action. But all the sentimental aspirations of Socialism and Communism are directed to this common end, to cramp still further, fetter, and tie up all mental energy and effort in action. The true remedy for suffering humanity will probably soon be found out to consist in giving the largest freedom to the human will.

Take a familiar illustration, within the observation of every working-man. Turn into any one of the fourth-rate streets of the metropolis, where 'chevaline traffic,' to adopt Dr. Dionysius Lardner's pet phrase, is represented by the costermonger's donkey-cart. You may observe one, or perhaps two or three, dingy little shops, where every article of vulgar consumption, from pork ham to a pipe of tobacco, can be procured in exchange for the current coin of the realm. You behold the petty chandler's shop, whence the labouring men procure the few necessaries which serve to sustain struggling nature. In that little emporium of extortion thriftlessness may procure credit; but dearly does it pay—fifteen, twenty, fifty, even cent. per cent. Another ten per cent. to the pawnbroker, for the loan to meet the chandler's demand when the credit is expired, and we may form some notion of one way in which the profits of labour are eaten up, and how chandlers do contrive to drive chaises and sport race-horses. Adjacent to that street there is a public market where the same articles can be procured at little more than prime cost. There the thrifty labourer may save the per centage to the chandler and pawnbroker, and lay by, from the saving, a little money capital to cheer in a rainy day, and perhaps help to break down the barrier between money capital and labour capital. The preference of the one mart for the other is, surely, no insignificant proof of the use of competition materially and morally; materially in enabling the labourer to save one-third or more of his hard-earned money—morally, in showing how, by the mere effort of his own unaided energies, he may resist the evil influences which surround his class, and better his social lot. But Communism and Socialism, for it is hard to discover any real distinction, would tie him to the one source of supply. Provided always, that Communists and their first cousins, and all other sentimental relatives, do not first obtain a repeal of the law of nature, and invent a machine for equalizing the human faculties.

In their efforts after improvement, our working classes in the mass seem very much like children groping in the dark, afraid at every step to be swallowed up by some giant of monstrous shape. They are, for the most part, in utter ignorance of their own capacities and of their own power. They have yet to be honestly taught that they are the real capitalists of England, with wealth far exceeding all the glittering hoards of their masters. The profuseness of California may one day render our money capitalists powerless for want of a suitable representative of wealth; but no California, even should it turn up as auriferous as Pactolus, can ever denude labour of its wealth. It has been truly said by an earnest and able friend of the working classes—and his words cannot be too often repeated:—

‘ Money without labour can do nothing : labour and skill without money may do everything. A hundred men every day unite their money capital to establish a profitable business as a public company. Why cannot a hundred other men unite their capital of skill and labour, without money (or with a merely trifling amount), to do the same? The latter are far the more likely to succeed; and the latter effort is, in every respect, as legitimate as the former. The working men only want confidence in themselves, self-respect, a consciousness of their true position, and a determination to rise above the condition of serfdom, to adopt this course, and to ensure success. It will speedily be found that herein lies the working man's true remedy. It will soon be found that there is nothing to be asked for from Parliament—no true hope to be placed on sentimental philanthropists; that self-reliance is the one true and sure panacea. Here is something tangible, and practical, and immediate; something which depends upon himself. There is no need to wait upon that hope deferred which maketh the heart sick. His own energy, his own skill, his own labour, is the working man's capital. It is a safer capital than the Bank of England can supply. He has only, like a good capitalist, to use it well. The joint-stock principle will be his wisest mode of investment. Let him enter, on that principle, into the fair field of competition. Some of the journeymen tailors are already acting upon this course. Their emancipation is secured.'

Why must this simple, and practical, and obvious expedient, be mixed up with all the Communistic nonsense and the shallow sentimentalism of Socialism, even when dignified with the prenomen of Christian ?  Some shrewd heads amongst the workmen were demonstrating the value of independent association and independent co-operation long before Messrs. Somebody and Nobody measured weapons before the public. We learn from the report of the Manchester Conference, to which we have already alluded, that a valuable and most exemplary working-man's joint-stock company, called the Jersey-street Association Store, has been in active operation for two years. It was established for the purpose of enabling working men to purchase provisions at wholesale prices. They occupy two shops, and sell to the extent of from 60l. to 70l. per week. The best proof of success is the fact that the 20s. shares are now at a premium of 18s. A delegate from Rochdale stated, that in an association with which he is connected—but the object of which does not appear in the report—there are five hundred members, with a capital of 5l. each. They have resolved to take in more members, with every prospect of increasing the number to a thousand. They began humbly with a 12l. shop. Prosperity soon compelled them to take larger premises, and they are now 'doing' from 200l. to 300l. a-week. They rent a corn-mill, and grind their own corn. They also contemplate the establishment of a woollen manufactory, for the employment of their own members when out of work. Societies which deal in provisions only are rapidly extending throughout the neighbourhood. Another delegate stated, that a shirting manufactory and Shirt-making Association has begun business with a capital of 50l. The members receive 6d. per shirt, exactly double what the shopkeepers pay. A delegate from a Working Tailors' Association stated,

that his society commenced business in March last with a clear
capital of three pounds sterling; they had since paid wages to
the extent of 239*l*. A few facts were elicited in discussion which
should be a warning to the crafts to proceed in the work of self-
emancipation. We are told that the stonemasons, organized
throughout England and Wales, pay about 2,000*l*. a-year towards
'tramps.' The letterpress printers have about one-sixth of their
number out of work; of the hand-loom weavers, one-third are
continually out of work, and the average weekly wages are only
8*s*.; and the proportion of unemployed amongst the bakers is
stated at 10 per cent. The case of the glass-cutters is the most
curious. They are in number from 900 to 1,000, and have from
100 to 150 constantly out of work. Their delegates state, that
they pay 6*d*. a-week to the unemployed; and yet they complain
that they cannot make a start to commence manufacturing for
themselves for want of a capital of 1,000*l*. If these men would
only have the resolution to drink water instead of beer at dinner
for twelve months, they would more than accomplish their
purpose. Here are the plain figures for those who may stare at
the seeming extravagance of the assertion. Say that there are
800 beer-drinking men at dinner: a pint at $1\frac{1}{2}d$. gives 1,200*d*.,
or 5*l*. daily = 35*l*. weekly = 1,820*l*. per annum. Capital nearly
sufficient for the establishment of two manufactories, with a
possible saving of a thousand a-year to unemployed workmen
into the bargain!

The ancient guilds were not, as is often erroneously supposed, phalansteries, but mutual protection societies. They did
not destroy the individualism of the workmen by reducing
all to an equality in toil; they protected him against the excess of competition, by determining trade disputes. Employer
and employed were on a better footing of equality, because
there was protection for both. We have long outgrown the
necessity for such institutions; and if the workman sighs for
the equitable system of the ancient guild, let him recollect that
the means is within his own reach—means more in accordance
with the freer spirit of our age. These guilds were voluntary
associations, recognised by the municipal laws of the country;
but they had nothing of communism in their constitution.
Probably, the most perfect remains of these ancient institutions
are our Inns of Court. These are voluntary societies, which
possess the privileges of calling men to the bar, after the payment of certain fees and performance of exercises. These legal
guilds make the advocates, and take cognizance of breaches of
professional decorum; but they do not in any way cramp or
fetter the individual energies of men. Where is there greater
competition than at the English bar? and where are the uses of

competition more strikingly displayed in calling forth the abilities of men ? We cannot now enter into the details of the associative trade efforts which have been made in Paris, and other towns. Tract No. 4, mentioned in the title, will afford the reader desirous of further information, some curious and interesting particulars, and some useful facts, to warn workmen against the high-sounding dogmas of Socialism.

The scheme of organization proposed by the 'Society for promoting Working Men's Associations' in the fifth tract, contains some practical suggestions, valuable if taken as *suggestions*, with not a few points which call for unqualified censure. In the first place, these benevolent persons proceed, not on the sound workmanlike principle that the workmen are to rely on themselves for a start on the path of emancipation, but they are to rely on somebody else for the first effort. This is self-evident on the first glance at the scheme of organization, where we find two classes of persons mixed up with the most admired disregard to the principles of progress. The 'promoters' everywhere take precedence of the 'associates,' that is, of the working-men. Association is not to proceed on the simple principle of self-reliance by men clubbing together their capital of money and labour, but they are to be taught to rely on eleemosynary money-lenders, and start with a borrowed money capital. Only imagine our railway-makers, our joint-stock bankers, or our assurance companies, beginning business with a borrowed capital! As a beginning, in the case of the Working Tailors' Association, it was, perhaps, unavoidable, in order to set the scheme at once afloat, for a good example and for the encouragement of other workmen. As a feature in a general scheme of co-operative labour it is most objectionable, and for reasons so obvious that they need not be enforced. The first effort should be to teach the working classes that the work of emancipation is in their own hands, and that the best reliance is self-reliance. There is a council of promoters with these functions :—

' 1st. To collect and administer all funds contributed or *advanced* to the society, for the promotion of its objects.
' 2nd. To diffuse the principles of co-operation, as the practical application of Christianity to the purposes of trade and industry.'

This is association dependent on private charity, not the association by which labour is to work out its emancipation.

Centralization, most dogmatic and despotic, is another distinguishing feature of the scheme. The plan of government proceeds, not on the every-day notion that men are the best judges how their own affairs should be conducted, but that some other person or persons unknown are better qualified for the task.

Notwithstanding the expressed 'desire of the promoters that the association shall be self-governed,' qualified by the immediate assertion, 'that as much power should be held by the workmen (most gracious liberality, oh, most excellent promoters!) as is consistent with their success,' we have centralization at every step. A 'central board,' and a 'council of promoters,' figure in almost every governing provision.

The political centralization of our government boards and crown commissions is nothing to this model centralization for the regulation of domestic life. Dr. Johnson had a joke about teaching the mysteries of tailoring and shoemaking by means of lectures: it would seem that it is about to be realized by the speculative authors of this model constitution.

We are sorry to be obliged to speak thus severely of a well-meant effort to assist the working classes. But truth and the interests of those classes compel us to speak plainly of a scheme which, if it is to be made on the 'unity of principle and of rules' insisted on by the promoters, cannot prove otherwise than a grand self-delusion. But, with all its defects, want of sound principle and empirical theorizing, we believe that the move-ment will ultimately do good in rousing the minds of the working classes, and stirring up their energies to the work of self-improvement. There may be many failures—it is in the nature of things that such should be—but we believe that a healthy, self-relying system of independent association, may work wonders in a few short years, in the social regeneration of the toiling millions of England.

These remarks may serve to indicate some of the good and bad points in the Associative Labour Movements under the direct influence of the Christian Socialist leaders. It may interest the reader to learn a few facts of another co-operative association, established on the principle of independent asso-ciation, and without any borrowed capital. Some months ago, when the wretchedness of the condition to which the journey-man tailors of London have been reduced, was exciting lively attention, and sentimentalists were propounding their parlia-mentary specifics, one hundred journeymen formed themselves into a 'Working Tailors' Joint-Stock Company." An extract from their modest prospectus is worthy of attention:—

'The above Company consists of a hundred experienced journeymen tailors. They have well considered the position of themselves and of their class, as well as of the artizan in general. They deeply feel that the work of improvement must depend—and can only truly and per-manently depend—upon their own efforts; and that any reliance upon the aid of parliament can only be delusive, while to be content to crave such aid is unworthy of men who have the capital of their own skill

and labour at their command.  They have, therefore, resolved to combine that skill and labour for their own benefit; and with that capital
to ask no external or artificial aid, but to place themselves before the
public in the spirit of an equal and honourable competition.  They are
particular in saying this, that it may not be supposed that they embark
in their undertaking with any spirit of hostility to the present fair-
dealing master tailors.  The Company guarantees that every article
supplied by it shall be made on the premises.'*

The shares consist of £20 each.  The shareholder must be a
*bona fide* journeyman tailor, and can only hold one share.  The
shareholders were desirous of obtaining a legal status, and acting
under the judicious counsel of Mr. Toulmin Smith, the company
was registered under the Joint-Stock Companies' Registration
Act.  This necessitated an expenditure of about £60, and
rendered advisable an increase in the amount of shares from £5
to £20.  The calls have been most punctually paid up, and the
Company, who have carried on business at 314, Oxford-street,
for several months, have not only covered all current expenses,
and given to the partners a fair remuneration for their labour,
but they have realized a considerable profit.  If there is to be
any legislation on the subject, let us have a reduction in the
exorbitant fees charged under the Registration Act.  It is also
a matter worthy of grave consideration whether Parliament may
not materially aid these associations by a revision of the laws
of association, and, perhaps, even an adoption of the principle
of the *société en commandite,* or limited partnership, in those
countries in which the Code Napoleon prevails.

It is the fundamental principle of sentimentalism to pin its
faith to one pet scheme ; and we hear it loudly proclaimed that
association is the one only means of regeneration.  With all our
faith in that great principle, we cannot subscribe to the opinion
that it is the only instrument which is to break the chains of the
social bondsmen of the nineteeth century.  It is only one of
many means.  Not to speak of the moral effects of education,
temperance, frugality, and industry, we would only point to the
barriers which still oppose the progress of industrial freedom,
and which must be removed by legislative enactment.  Foremost
in the ranks is that great social want expressively summed up
in the phrase ' free trade in land.'  In our railroad haste to grow
rich, we are forgetting that the soil, and the good culture of the
soil, form the ground-work of national wealth and happiness.
We must effect a more healthy distribution of the employments
of the population.  It is meet that husbandry should have one-
half of the workers of England.  Man was not made to be the

---

* This meets the great grievance under the 'sweating system.'

slave of the cotton spindle. We must draft off as much of unskilled labour as possible to the tillage of the fields. New views are breaking on men's minds on this subject. We are gradually getting over the prejudices against ' peasant proprietors.' With 60,000,000 of cultivable acres, it is monstrous to say that we have not ability to feed our own population. We make no deductions for the feudal parks and forests of aristocracy and plutocracy, nor are we going to cry out against property. But we must have free trade in land; and, with the example of Ireland before us, the oldest of men need hardly despair of seeing the beginning of the good work.

One of the most pleasing features in Fourierism is the provision made for the alternation of labour. Why should men be doomed to toil and moil over the minute subdivision of modern handicraft? Is there no mode of alternation without the erection of Phalansteries? Where are the suburban colonies of cheerful artisans, which railway enthusiasts once promised the poor man, where he might at times gain new strength by healthy labour in the garden or the field? It is a subject well worthy the attention of those now zealous for human improvement, how far the associated labour of handicraft might be blended with the pleasing toil of husbandry. The same principle of association which animates men to labour for their own profit, will enable them to invest the profits of that labour in the imperishable soil. What nobler reward for honest industry—what better inducement to habits of temperance and frugality?

The present time is one of deep interest and moment in the history of labour. A bright opportunity has opened for men of enlightenment and benevolence to guide their suffering fellows into the ways of progress and prosperity. But the people must be led and guided by the great light which can alone lighten the darkness of our toilsome journey through life; not the speculative Christianity with which schemers clothe their fantastic dreams, but that which is given us as our rule of action, from the day when reason dawns till the closing scene when it cheers with the blessed promises of immortality. Man is not doomed to be for ever the slave of material being.

> '——— would we aught behold of higher worth
> Than that inanimate, cold world allowed
> To the poor, loneless, ever-anxious crowd—
>      Ah! from the soul itself must issue forth
> A light, a glory, a fair luminous cloud,
>      Enveloping the Earth—
> And from the soul itself must there be sent
>      A sweet and potent voice, of its own birth,
> Of all sweet sounds the life and element!'

ART. VII.—*Alton Locke: Tailor and Poet. An Autobiography.* 12mo. 2 vols. London : Chapman and Hall. 1850.

THIS is one of those books which make a reviewer feel at once the difficulty and responsibility of his task. That it will exercise a deep and extensive influence on the public mind may be assumed as certain. That this influence will be healthy in many instances, need not, perhaps, be doubted; but that in many others it will revive decaying errors, and irritate into activity dormant disease, is, we fear, equally unquestionable. It is no easy task to modify such influences as these by the restraining hand of criticism, and, while admitting the power of this book, to divert its impetus from those quarters in which it would be powerful only to desolate and destroy.

Alton Locke is the book of an age. Like most eminent men and eminent books, it is the offspring of the times, which it moulds and informs. It is a kind of concrete thrown up from that vast cauldron of civilization, in which luxury and filth, brutality and art, virtue and intellect, tyranny and wretchedness, seethe tumultuously together. In the infinitude of possibility, there exists one, and one only, element, which can allay this turmoil and re-arrange this dislocation of human destiny. It is the defect of this book, and the misfortune of its author, that of this single sovereign element he has but a confused and erroneous conception.

If the characteristics of Alton Locke could be expressed in one word, that word would be INTENSITY; hence there is a vividness about its delineations which would seem to pertain rather to experience than to fiction. The passionate love of nature it evinces might belong to one who had lived from birth to the grand climacteric of sensibility in a dungeon; and his all-absorbing, all-consuming hate of the tyranny of aristocracy throws over every page a lurid glare, as of a fire that 'burns to the lowest hell.' Hence, too, there is an outspoken, unconcealing boldness in the treatment of delicate and dangerous topics, from which the timidity of some writers and the delicacy of others would recoil. The putrefying sores of society are laid open ; the veil of conventionalism is rent aside ; and the baseness which too often supports commercial prosperity, and the vulgarity which so often constitutes the substratum of rank, and the rottenness of heart not seldom masked beneath the vestments of sacerdotal dignity, are exposed in an unsparing style, from which most authors are withheld by that reverential love of humanity, which would throw a mantle over its nakedness.

The innermost purpose of this book is to reveal a truth of which the aristocracy know but little, the priesthood less, and the squirearchy, as a rule, nothing at all;—namely, that the working classes have claims on the rich, both in respect of their intelligence and their moral sensibilities, of the extent of which the latter are profoundly insensible. That even 'the swinish multitude' read and think, reason and feel; that they are not the mere soil manured with the filth of cities for aristocracy to flourish and blossom in, but rather a foundation of homogeneous material, on whose stability the columns of wealth and the Corinthian capital of rank repose in security together. The 'lower orders' may do as a missile term, and is worthy of the baleful statesman who originated it;—

   ' Sic placuit vano, qui nos distinxit, Othoni!'

but the artificial society of the nineteenth century has yet to be taught the lesson which Alton Locke rehearses, scourge in hand (and may they learn it in time!) That these 'orders' are only accidentally lower; that there are ' village Hampdens,' and 'mute inglorious Miltons;' that their intellects entertain and ponder the same truths; that their hearts are kindled and elevated by the same aspirations; that their natures are subject only to kindred infirmities, while they are born heirs to the same privileges, and conscious inheritors of the same glorious or disastrous destiny.

This, we say, is the much-neglected lesson which Alton Locke essays to teach. His method of tuition, however, we cannot altogether approve. He administers the most salutary truths in poisonous combinations. He alternately confounds the classes he seeks to reconcile, and mutually exacerbates them against each other. He is the Taliacotius of social economists, and seems to think that the moral, like the fleshly surfaces, cannot cohere until both have been excoriated. This may be good surgery, but it is bad politics. The distinction between the rich and the poor is not adventitious, but dependent upon an ultimate law, which results from the very necessity of things. So long as intellectual distinctions shall exist among mankind—so long as knowledge shall be power—so long as industry and indolence, virtue and vice, shall produce their appropriate results, nay, so long as an Omnipotent Providence shall interpose in the affairs of mankind, these disparities in human condition will not be the product of a changeful and precarious conventionality, but the results of an inevitable law. To improve this condition of things to a wise and benevolent end, to practise the virtues which spring out of this permanent arrangement, and which are enjoined by that Divine power which at once recognises and creates it;—this

is the true lesson which has been but confusedly dreamt of in
Alton Locke's philosophy.

The narrative of this fiction, though striking, is, comparatively,
an unimportant portion of it.   Its hero is the child of a widow,
a Baptist, and a high Calvinist, and his early and religious
training are represented in a style which presents at once the
gloomiest, and the most crude and unenlightened view of the
Calvinistic scheme.   The mother does not dare to pray for the
conversion of her children, but she adopts towards them a discipline the most sovereign and severe.   The boy is brought up
in a low suburb in London, in equal ignorance of nature and
society, under the frown of the Ten Commandments, and the
discipline of the rod.   The maternal influence is seconded by
that of a Dissenting minister, whose manners and conversation
are painted with all the false and exaggerated shading which
characterises the entire work.   The youth, who has a rich uncle
and cousin, is apprenticed to a West-end tailor, and shortly grows
to a premature manhood amidst a set of the most depraved
fellow-workmen; the only exception being an intellectual and
imaginative young man, who is an enthusiastic Chartist.   Unhappily, the tree of knowledge is interdicted by the arbitrary
pietism of the parent, who seems to regard learning and heathenism as synonymous, and includes in her Index Expurgatorius,
all books except the Bible, the ' Pilgrim's Progress,' and, oddly
enough for an ultra-Calvinist, some missionary tracts.   An old
book-stall, kept by one Sandy Mackaye, supplies the temptation.
The classics constitute the forbidden fruit, and an angry discussion in the presence of the aforesaid minister, and consequent
upon the detection of the ill-starred student, issues in his summary expulsion from the most uncomfortable Paradise of his
youth.   The old second-hand bookseller, the development of
whose character in his conversation constitutes the masterpiece
of the book, befriends him, and receives him into his house.
Meanwhile, in a holiday visit with his cousin to Dulwich gallery,
he had been condescendingly accosted, while melting over
Guido's ' Martyrdom of St. Sebastian,' by two high-born ladies,
who figure prominently in the subsequent part of the narrative,
the younger of whom first lights up his sensitive soul with a
vague sentiment of impassioned love.   And now the tailor ex-
foliates into the poet, and the generous youth into the enthusiastic
advocate of the political rights of the million.   He produces a
manuscript volume of verse, and on the advice of his quaint old
patron, Sandy Mackaye, makes a pilgrimage to bring them before
the notice of his cousin, who is now an under-graduate of Trinity
College, Cambridge.   Here he had opportunity of acquainting
himself somewhat extensively with the denizens of the uni-

versity; and the impressions which he thus received, as described
by himself, may give the reader his first insight into the character of Alton Locke. He says,—

' I cannot say that my recollections of them were pleasant. A few
of them were very bigoted Tractarians ; some of whom seemed to
fancy that a dilettante admiration for crucifixes and Gothic architecture
was a form of religion, which, by its extreme perfection, made the
virtues of chastity and sobriety quite unnecessary ; and the rest, of a
more ascetic and moral turn, seemed as narrow, bitter, flippant, and
unearnest young men as I had ever met. . . .
' But the great majority of the young men whom I met were even of
a lower stamp. I was utterly shocked and disappointed at the contempt and unbelief with which they seemed to regard everything beyond mere animal enjoyment, and here and there the selfish advantage
of a good degree. They seemed, if one could judge from appearances,
to despise and disbelieve everything generous, enthusiastic, enlarged.
Thoughtfulness was a " bore ; " earnestness, " romance." Above all,
they seemed to despise the university itself. The " Dons " were " idle
fat old humbugs ;" chapel, " a humbug too ;" tutors, " humbugs " too,
who played into the tradesmen's hands, and charged men high fees for
lectures not worth attending; so that any man who wanted to get on
was forced to have a private tutor besides his college one. The university studies were " a humbug"—no use to man in after life. The
masters of arts were " humbugs " too ; for " they knew all the evils, and
clamoured for reform till they became Dons themselves; and then, as
soon as they found the old system pay, they settled down on their lees,
and grew fat on port wine, like those before them." They seemed to
consider themselves in an atmosphere of humbug—living in a lie—out
of which lie element those who chose were very right in making the
most, for the gaining of fame or money. And the tone which they
took about everything—the coarseness, hollowness, Gil-Blas selfishness—was just what might have been expected. Whether they were
right or wrong in their complaints, I of course had no means of accurately knowing. But it did seem strange to me, as it has to others, to
find in the mouths of almost all the gownsmen, those very same
charges against the universities which, when working men dare to
make them, excite outcries of " calumny," " sedition," " vulgar radicalism," " attacks on our time-honoured institutions," &c. &c.'—Vol. i.
pp. 27, 28.

At Cambridge, our hero is thrown in the way of a young
nobleman, for whom he performs some literary labour, and
through this connexion renews his acquaintance with the elder
and graver lady who first accosted him in the Dulwich gallery ;
and, subsequently, with her cousin, the fair phantom of that adventure, who ever since had haunted his sleeping and waking
dreams. Through the young Lord Lynedale, the future husband
of the former lady, the MS. poems of Alton Locke find their
way to the eyes of the dean. This is followed by an interview,

and an invitation to his residence at the cathedral town of D***,
by which Peterborough appears to be intended.   Here Alton
first becomes acquainted with the usages of really good society.
In the genial atmosphere of ecclesiastical luxury, and sunned by
the presence of his goddess Lillian, his democracy experiences a
slight thaw, and he falls into the dread apostasy of suffering his
poems to be emasculated of their ultra-liberalism by the pen of
the dean, and himself to be thus shorn of his glory as a poet of
the people.   His experience of Trinity College and of the
deanery in combination, conclusively fix his opinions touching
the general character and tendency of the Established Church.
If there is any ground on which these volumes deserve to be
read, besides that of the brilliant vivacity with which they are
written, it is their point blank and destructive fire against all
practical shams.   In the present state of the Anglican Church
Alton finds one quite to his mind, and he exposes it in numerous
passages, of which the following may be taken as a sample :—

‘ For the clergy, our professed and salaried teachers, all I can say
is—and there are tens, perhaps hundreds of thousands of workmen
who can re-echo my words—with the exception of the dean and my
cousin, and one who shall be mentioned hereafter, a clergyman never
spoke to me in my life.

‘ Why should he ?   Was I not a Chartist and an Infidel ?   The
truth is, the clergy are afraid of us.   To read the *Dispatch*, is to be
excommunicated.   Young men’s classes ?   Honour to them, however
few they are—however hampered by the restrictions of religious
bigotry and political cowardice.   But the working men, whether
rightly or wrongly, do not trust them ; they do not trust the clergy
who set them on foot ; they do not expect to be taught at them the
things they long to know—to be taught the whole truth in them about
history, politics, science, the Bible.   They suspect them to be mere
tubs to the whale—mere substitutes for education, slowly and late
adopted, in order to stop the mouths of the importunate.   They may
misjudge the clergy ; but whose fault is it if they do ?   Clergymen of
England !—look at the history of your establishment for the last fifty
years, and say, what wonder is it if the artizan mistrust you ?   Every
spiritual reform, since the time of John Wesley, has had to establish
itself in the teeth of insult, calumny, and persecution.   Every ecclesiastical reform comes not from within, but from without your body.
Mr. Horsman, struggling against every kind of temporizing and
trickery, has to do the work which bishops, by virtue of their seat in
the House of Lords, ought to have been doing years ago.   Everywhere
we see the clergy, with a few persecuted exceptions (like Dr. Arnold),
proclaiming themselves the advocates of Toryism, the dogged opponents of our political liberty, living either by the accursed system of
pew-rents, or else by one which depends on the high price of corn ;
chosen exclusively from the classes who crush us down ; prohibiting
all free discussion on religious points ; commanding us to swallow

down, with faith as passive and implicit as that of a Papist, the very
creeds from which their own bad example, and their scandalous
neglect, have, in the last three generations, alienated us; never mixing
with the thoughtful working men, except in the prison, the hospital, or
in extreme old age; betraying, in every tract, in every sermon, an
ignorance of the doubts, the feelings, the very language of the masses,
which would be ludicrous, were it not accursed before God and man.
And then will you show us a few tardy improvements here and there,
and ask us, indignantly, why we distrust you? Oh! gentlemen, if
you cannot see for yourselves the causes of our distrust, it is past
our power to show you. We must leave it to God.'—*Ib.* pp.
286—288.

Still, amongst its other eccentricities, the tendency of Alton
Locke is decidedly Socialist. In illustration of this, as a cardinal
error of the work before us, we will abridge a conversation
between Eleanor (the elder of the two young ladies) and Alton
in the cathedral of D * * *. 'Perhaps,' observes the latter,
' these cathedrals may be true symbols of the superstition which
created them—on the outside offering to enfranchise the soul
and raise it up to heaven, but when the dupes had entered
giving them only a dark prison and a crushing bondage, which
neither we nor our fathers have been able to bear.'

' " You may sneer at them, if you will, Mr. Locke," said Eleanor, in
her severe, abrupt way. " The working classes would have been
badly off without them. They were, in their day, the only democratic
institution in the world; and the only socialist one, too. The only
chance a poor man had of rising by his worth, was by coming to the
monastery. And bitterly the working classes felt the want of them
when they fell. Your own Cobbett can tell you that." . . .

' " If, then," I answered, " in spite of your opinions, you confess the
clergy to be so bad, why are you so angry with men of our opinions, if
we do plot sometimes a little against the Church?"

' I do not think you know what my opinions are, Mr. Locke. Did
you not hear me just now praising the monasteries, because they were
socialist and democratic? But why is the badness of the clergy any
reason for pulling down the Church? That is another of the confused
irrationalities into which you all allow yourselves to fall. What do
you mean by crying shame on a man for being a bad clergyman, if a
good clergyman is not a good thing? If the very idea of a clergyman
was abominable, as your church-destroyers ought to say, you ought to
praise a man for being a bad one, and not acting out this same
abominable idea of priesthood. Your very outcry against the sins of
the clergy shows that, even in your minds, a dim notion lies somewhere that a clergyman's vocation is, in itself, a divine, a holy, a beneficent one." . . .

' " Mark my words, Mr. Locke, till you gain the respect and confidence of the clergy, you will never rise. The day will come when you
will find that the clergy are the only class who can help you. Ah,

you may shake your head.  I warn you of it.  They were the only
bulwark of the poor against the mediæval tyranny of rank; you will
find them the only bulwark against the modern tyranny of Mammon." '
—*Ib.* pp. 255—259.

In this passage, and throughout these volumes, the reader
must understand the term Mammon to designate the middle
classes of society, and with this key he may judge for himself
how far the clergy ever have been, or ever will be, the bulwark
to protect the great masses of the population against any tyranny
of theirs.  It is true, indeed, that in the days of monasteries the
clergy were an intervening estate between the lay aristocracy
and the poor.  But this was for a purpose of their own.  They
only interposed to deliver them from the serfdom of the soil in
order to make them the still more ignorant and abject serfs of
the Church.  The two despotisms were the players, and the
million were the stake.

But the sophism involved in the former part of the above
quotation requires to be exposed, and the more so, because
it is insisted on still more emphatically at the close of the work.

The argument may be thus stated:—' You express especial
disgust at the secularly and false pretensions of the clergy.
Why this very fact indicates that you regard the institution
thus unworthily administered as divine, holy, and beneficent.
The fallacy of this reasoning is obtrusively evident.  It is not
the delinquency of the Anglican clergyman, as such, which is so
repulsively unseemly, but the delinquency of those who profess,
not only to be spiritual men, but to be specially moved by the
Holy Ghost to take upon themselves the cure of souls.  It is the
viciousness of a person supposed to be a Christian that galls our
sense of propriety, and not the worldliness of a man, who,
through any one of the thousand legal and secular avenues,
is thrust, unqualified and unbidden, into the pastoral office.
The want of respect for the clergy indicated by the lower
classes, by no means necessarily implies a want of respect for
religion.

We now resume the thread of the narrative.  Alton Locke
leaves the Cathedral town intoxicated with love for Lillian, and
the almost equally stimulative prospect of literary fame.  He
returns to London and Sandy Mackaye.  His poems are published and lay on the table at the town-house of the Dean, where
Locke is kindly received, and rubs shoulders with the great
literati, and among others with a distinguished foreign ambassador in whom many readers will recognise the Chevalier Bunsen.
He soon finds that his cousin is his successful rival in the affections of the beautiful Lillian, and a bitter hatred accordingly
springs up in his mind, which is only returned by the gay and

triumphant frivolity of the dashing aspirant for clerical promotion.   The latter attends a Chartist meeting over which Alton
Locke is exerting all the powers of his talents and eloquence.
He divulges the secret of Alton's intimacy with the Dean's
family, and of his compromise in the matter of the ultra-liberal
passages in his poems.   His relations to a party utterly unworthy
of him speedily change, he is exposed and abused by the
Chartist press, and driven from the conclave to which he had
attached himself by a storm of vulgar indignation.   Meanwhile
Lord Lynedale inherits his patrimonial title, and Eleanor
becomes Lady Ellerton.   Locke is consoled by the eloquent
wisdom of Sandy Mackaye, expressed in Scotch only inferior to
that of Sir Walter Scott himself; but having been presented
anonymously with a pair of plush breeches as a satire on his
'Flunkeyism,' passionately throws himself back into the gulph
of wild physical-force Chartism, and approves the honesty of
his conversion by volunteering an embassy into the excited
agricultural districts in the neighbourhood of D * * *.   Inflam-
matory speeches are delivered, in which he takes a half-con-
senting half-restraining part.   The infuriated labourers fire an
adjoining farm-yard, in spite of Locke's efforts to withhold them.
On the approach of the yeomanry they fly in all directions.   Our
hero is seized apparently *in flagrante delicto*, is tried in the
presence of Lillian, and sentenced to an extended term of
imprisonment within sight of the hospitable deanery.   Having
at length been liberated, and smarting under his fancied
wrongs, he joins the frenzied few who precipitated their own
ruin on the tenth of April, 1848.   This catastrophe Sandy
Mackaye could not live to see.   The wise but resolute advocate
of popular freedom sank under the disgrace of seeing any members of the party to which he was attached, disgracing and
ruining the common cause by an appeal to that physical force
by which alone the wrongs of the people were perpetuated, and
after an outburst of dying eloquence closed his eyes on the dawn
of that eventful day.

Alton Locke is designated by the 'Times' newspaper as the
autobiography of a Chartist.   Had the writer considered without
prejudice the widely-held principles which that unhappy name
consigns to reprobation, and read dispassionately the pages of
Alton Locke, he would not have adopted this title.   The author
of this book, with all his talents, and with all his accurate outline
of Chartism, has not enough of freedom and comprehensiveness
of mind to grasp this great subject.   Let us listen to his own
words.   The autobiographer and his quondam shopmate, to
whom we have before referred as the enthusiastic Chartist, are
passing the Victoria Theatre at night, and, observing the youthful

and profligate rabble at its doors, 'Would a change in the franchise,' said Alton, ' cure that ? '　His companion replies :—

' " Household Suffrage mightn't—but give us the Charter, and we'll see about it!　Give us the Charter, and we'll send workmen into Parliament that shall soon find out whether something better can't be put in the way of the ten thousand boys and girls in London who live by theft and prostitution, than the tender mercies of the Victoria—a pretty name!　They say the Queen's a good woman—and I don't doubt it.　I wonder often if she knows what her precious namesake here is like? . . .　From that night I was a Chartist, heart and soul—and so were a million and a half more of the best artizans in England —at least, I had no reason to be ashamed of my company.　Yes; I, too, like Crossthwaite, took the upper classes at their word; bowed down to the idol of political institutions, and pinned my hopes of salvation on " the possession of one-ten-thousandth part of a talker in the national palaver." . . .　I had so made up my mind that it was the only method of getting what I wanted, that I neglected, alas! but too often, to try the methods which lay already by me. " If we had but the Charter"—was the excuse for a thousand lazinesses and procrastinations. "If we had but the Charter"—I should be good, and free, and happy. Fool that I was! It was within, rather than without, that I needed reform. . . .　For my part, I seem to have learnt that the only thing to regenerate the world is not more of any system, good or bad, but simply more of the Spirit of God.　About the supposed omnipotence of the Charter I have found out my mistake.　I believe no more in " Morison's-Pill-remedies," as Thomas Carlyle calls them. Talismans are worthless. The age of spirit-compelling spells, whether of parchment or carbuncle, is past—if, indeed, it ever existed.　The Charter will no more make men good, than political economy, or the observance of the Church Calendar—a fact which we working-men, I really believe, have, under the pressure of wholesome defeat and God-sent affliction, found out sooner than our more " enlightened" fellow-idolaters.'—*Ib.* p. 158.

Now all this appears to us to the last degree crude and erroneous.　The writer seems to think that the theory of manhood suffrage was framed to supersede the Christian religion—he fails to see that political and spiritual reformation, though they may be prosecuted from the same motives, contemplate different objects, and pursue them by different means.　There is no necessary connexion between the abolition of the Corn-laws and a religious revival; and, while on the one hand spiritual religion is degraded by being thus coerced into connexion with projects to which it has no natural relation, so it is utterly absurd to set aside a demand for political reforms by urging the duty of personal amendment.　We are not aware that the Municipal Reform Act produced any effect upon the really Christian world; but if it saved a hundred boroughs from long-continued spoliation, and introduced into them a mild and economical administration which allayed the animosities of years—that of itself was a grand advantage. If such measures are not the dew of grace, they are at least the rain that descends on the evil and the good.

Our author's notices of the celebrated 10th of April, equally show him incompetent to write a history of Chartism. A few misguided and unprincipled men undoubtedly sought that occasion as an opportunity for violence and plunder. The thief population of London, which is said to be twenty thousand strong, though without concert in the movement, doubtless hailed it with the highest satisfaction; but the vast numbers who had intended to assemble on that day, prior to the Metropolitan demonstration of resistance, clearly showed that they had none but peaceful intentions. The large majority absented themselves from the meeting, while those who attended it came entirely unarmed. The parturient mountain assuredly gave birth to the mouse, but it was the city that was in labour and not the country. But a few months before a hundred thousand men had marched to the Treasury to make a demonstration against the Navigation Bill, and their exhibition of physical force met with no rebuke. The advocates of Parliamentary Reform felt justified by this fact in attempting a similar demonstration; and the base designs of a few insignificant individuals, occurring coincidentally with the outbreak of Continental revolutions, gave an occasion to the conspiracy, of which, as we cannot but think, the enemies of popular rights basely availed themselves to throw a charge of treason and sedition upon multitudes of British subjects as loyal as the Parliament itself. That sham is now in a great measure exploded, but no thanks to Alton Locke.

The conclusion of this autobiography may be briefly told. The hero has a personal collision with his exulting cousin, in which the latter is, of course, successful, and finds his way in despair to the filthy den in which the wife and children of a quondam fellow-workman are lying dead of an infectious fever. A half-finished coat is thrown over the corpses, and the cousin, who has now married Lillian, dies of the contagion by wearing the garment. Lord Ellerton has been killed by a fall from his horse; and Eleanor, who drops her title, spends her life and fortune as a Sister of Mercy, carrying out the principle of associated labour amongst the poorest and most degraded of her own sex. Alton has caught the fever, and, after the delirious dreaming of a few days, the description of which we consider the most tedious and the only foolish part of the book, finds Eleanor at his bedside. By her conversations he is converted to what the author regards as true religion, quits the country at her expense for a warmer climate, and expires while gazing on the verdant shores of some Eldorado of emigration.

Such is the plot of this singular fiction.  We have already shown that we regard the theology and the politics of the writer as alike defective.  To these great subjects the latter portion of the work is especially devoted, and the enthusiastic Eleanor, and her uncle, the dean, who is represented as having exchanged a genteel and scientific Christianity for true religion, are made the exponents of the author's sentiments.  In their instructions to their gifted convert, there is unquestionably much of truth and beauty; still this elaborate *eclaircissement* of the work only confirms the opinion which we deliberately record respecting it.  We never met with a book, written, as this is, with extraordinary power, which contained within it so strange a mixture of vital truth and pernicious error.

In answer to the dying youth's suggestions, against the miracles of Scripture, the mild dignitary suggests the grandest achievements of moral science, and even the phenomena of mesmerism, as illustrative of his principle, that it is only the customs, and not the laws of nature, which were superseded in the ministry of the Son of God.  In a word, he seeks to show that these inventions, interfering, as they do, with all the old relations of time and space, differ only in degree, and not in kind, with the miracles which attested the divinity of Christ.  Need we expose the fallacy of this argument?  If the difference between the miracles of Christ and the achievements of scientific men by merely a natural one, dependent only on a superior development of those powers by which sagacity and moral excellence ordinarily compel both matter and mind to the service of men, what becomes of the evidence of the divine mission of Christ any more than (if we may speak it with reverence) that of Watt and Wheatstone?  What becomes of the divine condescension of our Lord's appeal : ' If I had not done among you the works which no other man did, ye would not have had sin?'  Nay, what becomes of the whole system of the Christian religion, as divinely and preternaturally revealed?

The arguments by which Lady Ellerton, or, as she is still designated, Eleanor, adapts the truths of Christianity to the bewildered mind of her patient, are of a much less exceptionable kind ; and, could we afford the space, we would gladly extract the impassioned address in which she harmonizes what are called the extreme doctrines of popular rights with the religion of the New Testament.

We have left ourselves no space for further extracts, nor, which we most regret, for the delineation of the character of Sandy Mackaye, which, as we have before intimated, is the masterpiece of the book.  Let the reader suppose Edie Ochiltree retaining all the simplicity of his humour, and all the native

power of his eloquence, through the discipline of an extensive
acquaintance with men and books, and he will have before him
the idea of Sandy Mackaye. We can only represent him in a '
single soliloquy. He and Alton have been hearing an infidel
Chartist lecture on the right-mindness of human nature, and
its consequent capacity for every social and political function.
Our hero was a little captivated with the bold paradoxes and the
wild mock-eloquent declamation he had listened to, whereupon
the old Scotchman thus delivers himself :—

' " An' sae the deevil's dead!" said Sandy, half to himself, as he sat
crooning and smoking that night over the fire. " Gone at last, puir
fallow!—an' he sae little appreciated too! Every gowk laying his
ain sins on Nickie's back. Puir Nickie! verra like that much misunderstood politeecian, Mr. John Cade, as Charles Buller ca'd him in the
Hoose of Commons—an' he to be dead at last! The warld 'll seem
quite unco without his auld farrant phizog on the streets. Aweel,
aweel, aiblins he's but shamming.

> " When pleasant spring came on apace,
>     And showers began to fa' ;
>   John Barleycorn got up again,
>     And sore surprised them a'."

At ony rate, I'd no bury him till he began to smell a wee strong, like.
It's a grewsome thing, is premature interment, Alton, laddie!" '

We venture to predict, that if this author will place himself
under the posthumous instruction of Sandy Mackaye, he will not
write another Alton Locke. We lay the book down with mingled
feelings of admiration and dissatisfaction. It presents us with
the evidences of a fine and cultivated mind, and with many of
the elements of a great and lasting work. But in every grand
system of principles which the author seeks to develop, there is
some cardinal eccentricity which disorders the whole machinery.
His political economy is an impracticable chimera, his zeal for
social reforms is fierce and volcanic, and his theology lacks the
foundation of simple and reverent faith. Still there is something in his very errors suggestive of right; and when he does
enunciate truths which other men only hint and whisper, he
stamps his idea ineffaceably on the memory and the heart of the
reader in ' thoughts which breathe and words that burn.'

Art. VIII.—1. *The Acknowledged Doctrines of the Church of Rome; being an Exposition of Roman Catholic Doctrines, as set forth by esteemed Doctors of the said Church, and confirmed by repeated publication, with the sanction of Bishops and Ministers of her Communion.* By Samuel Capper. London: Gilpin. 1850.

2. *Popery in Power; or, The Spirit of the Vatican, To which is added, Priestcraft; or, the Monarch of the Middle Ages: a Drama.* By Joseph Turnley. Illustrated with Engravings on Wood by eminent artists. London: Effingham Wilson. 1850.

3. *The Trial of Antichrist, otherwise the Man of Sin, for High Treason against the Son of God, tried at the Sessions House of Truth. Taken in Short-hand by a Friend to St. Peter.* Aberdeen: King. London: Ward and Co. 1849.

4. *Antidote to the Popish Articles of Faith, enacted by the Sorbonne,* 1542. By John Calvin. Dundee: Middleton. London: Hamilton, Adams, and Co.; Nisbet and Co. 1846.

5. *The Rise and Fall of the Papacy. Delivered in London, A.D.* 1701, *by Robert Fleming, V.D.M. With an Appendix, containing Extracts on Prophecy from Mede, Owen, Durham, Willison, &c.* Eleventh Thousand. Aberdeen: King. London: Ward and Co. 1849.

6. *Auricular Confession and Popish Nunneries.* By William Hogan, formerly Roman Catholic Priest, and Author of 'Popery, as it was, and as it is.' London: Ward and Co.

7. *The Pope, and his Pretensions.* By Andrew Reed, D.D. London: Ward and Co. 1850.

8. *The Papal Invasion: How to Defeat it. An Appeal to British Protestants.* (Dedicated to Lord John Russell, M.P.) By James Carlile, D.D., Editor of the 'Protestant World.' London: Seeleys; Ward and Co. 1850.

9. *The Present Aspects of Protestantism in Great Britain; Facts, Forebodings, and Hopes, regarding our Fatherland. A Discourse occasioned by the Pope's Bull.* By John Morison, D.D., LL.D. London: W. F. Ramsay.

10. *Lectures on Cardinal Wiseman.—Notes on the Cardinal's Manifesto, in a Letter to the Right Hon. Lord John Russell.* By the Rev. John Cumming, D.D. London · Hall, Virtue, and Co. 1850.

11. *Dissent and the Papal Bull.* ' *No Intolerance,*' *A Response to the Cry of* ' *No Popery.*' By Newman Hall, B.A. London: John Snow. 1850.

12. *Romanism in England Exposed. The Redemptorist's Fathers of St. Mary's Convent, Park-road, Clapham.* By Charles Hastings Collette. Second Edition. Enlarged and Improved. London: Arthur Hall, Virtue, and Co. 1851.

13. *Plain Words to Plain People.* By the Rev. William Forster. London: Ward and Co.

14. *Priest, the Essence of Pope; or, the Lord's Supremacy. An Appeal to the Reason and Candour of the People, on the subject of the True Head of the Church.* By J. B. Brown, A.B. London: Ward and Co.

15. *The Reasons of the Protestant Religion.* By John Pye Smith, D.D., F.R.S. Second Edition, enlarged and adapted to the Popish Aggression of 1850, with some Remarkable Disclosures of Romanist Policy in the Age of the Reformation. London: Jackson and Walford. 1851.

WE are not sorry to begin our labours in this New Series of the ' Eclectic Review' amid the strife of THE GRAND CONTROVERSY. Whatever may be said of the political aspects of Popery in England, or of the wisdom of the way in which our great statesmen deal with it, or in whatever light we may regard its relations to the Queen's supremacy, to the rights of the national Episcopacy, or to the interests of the Established Churches, the time has come for a fair exposition of the doctrines, institutions, and spirit of the Papal church, and for a strong advocacy of the religious principles embodied in the Protestant Reformation. For many years past, British Christians have deeply shared the liberal-mindedness by which the legislature has enlarged the freedom of all religionists; and, while honestly upholding the civil rights of their fellow-citizens without distinction, they have not liked to touch the theological controversies, for fear of reviving the civil animosities of their manly progenitors. Of this feeling Nonconformists have partaken to a greater degree, we believe, than any other Protestant bodies. That they have been prudent as well as generous, wise as well as Catholic, in cherishing this feeling, has long been our opinion, and such is our opinion still. We have an unshaken reliance on the soundness of our principles, and on the power of truth; and it is no small consolation to us that, amid the *perversions* which have troubled the ancient universities, and the clergy of the Church of England, very few—scarcely any—movements towards Rome have ruffled the tranquillity of Protestant Dissenters.

At the same time we cannot be insensible to *the gradual decay of interest* in the questions at issue between the Romanists and ourselves. We have been hurt and sickened, now and then, by the fierce onslaught, the unsparing bitterness, the exaggerated tone of proud audacity, with which zealous Protestants, very good friends of ours, have seized every opportunity for the flourish of platform trumpets, the roll of ' drum ecclesiastic,' the gleam of the theological sabre, against the Papists and their clergy. We have watched such demonstrations of the ' church militant here upon earth,' with more apprehension than hope, and we think we have good authority for saying, that the ' Papists' are rather pleased than otherwise with these exhibitions, as bringing them into notice, placing them in the position of persons attacked, enabling them to ply against the Church Establishment the weapons which are hurled against themselves, and thus, not merely confirming their own people, but increasing the number of their converts.

Not a little of the apathy towards polemical discussions of the pretensions of the Papacy has been occasioned by the impossibility of meddling with them at all without irritating several millions of our fellow-subjects, especially in Ireland. They cannot bear to have their religion attacked. Accustomed to look on that religion as one entire system, identified with all that is true, holy, good, ancient, authoritative, and divine, the less they reason, the more they feel. The intellect slumbers in reverential ease while the passions are awake; and what, in other communities, is quickly responded to as a challenge to discuss, is felt by the Romanists as an insult to be revenged. A similar danger, it must be candidly acknowledged, lies among ourselves. We know something of Orange processions, of toasting ' the pious, glorious, and immortal memory' of the Kentish fire, of No-Popery riots; and we should deprecate, as among the sorest evils, any approach towards the re-appearance of Protestant mobs. Among Dissenters, too, special causes have operated to prevent strong excitement in this direction. They have argued, not unjustly, ' the Church of England has done all she could to *ignore our existence ;* her clergy have looked on us with insolent scorn; her organs of literature have not done justice to the scholarship and genius of men among us, who would have adorned her highest places if they had not been conscientious in their dissent; and the smaller fry of empty but busy curates have gone from house to house denouncing our doctrines as damnable, and maligning our pastors as unauthorized and unfit to teach us, or to conduct our worship. If *they* were consulted—the great body of the Anglican bishops and priests—we should not be even tolerated ; all *our* liberties have been secured, not by the Church, but by the British House of Commons. We hold doctrines which are as really opposed to the Church of England as to the Church of Rome, and we have no mind to fight for either of them against the other. We will not join in the cry, " The Church is in danger," or, " No Popery." We have no need to care for Protestant ascendency or Papal ascendency. We look to Parliament for protection against both. We want no church establishment for ourselves. We would not have it for others.'

We have little hesitation in glancing at what appears to us to be another source of inattention to the profound dispute on which we are dwelling ; we allude to the taste for the rhetorical, the sentimental, or the semi-philosophical, rather than the instructive and the argumentative, in public teaching. It is a great improvement on the cold and formal preaching of the last century, to be regaled with eloquence, to be moved by pathetic touches, to revel in the creations of fancy, or to float away to some dreamy cloud-land of enchantment on the silvery stream of speculation ; but these are not the teachings that are to keep among us the robust faith of our fathers, and to perpetuate the race of bold, earnest, and resolute believers. We hope the age is preparing to demand something higher, more clear, powerful, elevating, dealing more freely with the rudiments of things, better fitted to the onward progress of individual and social energy, less irascible in small matters, yet never shrinking from bold and earnest controversy where essentials are at stake. For frivolous, personal, or purely sectarian wranglings, we have no taste, nor have we any complacency towards those who are fond of indulging in them ; but we have no hope of seeing great truths firmly grasped by any other minds than those which delight in vigorous thought.          •

There are quarters in which, we fear, there is undue reliance on the intellectual and liberal spirit of the age. It seems to be imagined by some that our people are too well educated to be seduced by the trumpery of superstition, or the plausibilities of Jesuitical pretensions ; as if it were not true that large masses of our people are *not* well-educated ; that among the well-educated the greatest number of recent converts have been made in England to the Church of Rome ; that the highest order of education is familiar to an increasing proportion of the agents of that Church ; and that the *training of children in their peculiar tenets* is one of their most successful modes of propagation. Then as to the liberal spirit of the age, the liberality is either theological or political. The theological liberalism of our times has a manifest tendency towards scepticism, a state of mind which is not of a nature to be permanent, and which ends in the subjection of the wearied intellect to the authority of the Church, as often, for what we know, as in a satisfactory conviction of the truth. The political liberals are so extensively open to the imputation of indifference, or of severe aversion, to evangelical truth, that they are naturally regarded as much more the allies than the opponents of the Papal hierarchy. Who have been the most forward advocates of Maynooth grants? By what party has the course been pursued towards Roman Catholics in the colonies, which gives so much the appearance of vindication to the recent pretensions of the Pope? On whose support have statesmen relied, in the prospect of measures for endowing the Roman Catholic priesthood in Ireland?

But, it may be said, 'we rely on the wisdom and sagacity of our rulers. They are bound to take care, and we believe they will take care, that our Protestant liberties and institutions are defended from foreign interference.' Far be it from us to impugn the wisdom, or to doubt the power, of the present Government in this business; yet we have seen enough to convince us that the Government is slow to move unless stimulated, and powerless *for good* unless supported, by the people. What is most wanted is, therefore, that the people be thoroughly enlightened on the question. We have no desire that the Government should assume, in any department, the functions of a teacher; most of all, do we object to such assumption in things pertaining to religion.—It is no matter of regret to us, that for the last few years there has been a strongly expressed desire for the manifestation of Christian unity. Impelled by this desire, Christian professors have been learning to prize the essential points of their agreement greatly more than their lesser grounds of difference, and the spiritual in religion has been gradually superseding the dogmatic. The stern logic, the accurate definition, the refined distinctions, which divided the theological schools of Britain two hundred years ago, and which in some parts of the island were eagerly read, or listened to, by strong-minded and stout-hearted Protestants, have almost disappeared from our pulpits and our books. It is well, in many respects, that it should be so. These things had their day, did their work, and their good effects will probably pervade all coming time. Of late we have been more accustomed to being instructed in the mysteries of the inner life, and summoned, by lucid statements or passionate appeals, to the great philanthropic enterprises of Christian charity. It belongs to the imperfectness of our nature, that, in the midst of the elevating or exciting ministrations of evangelical truth, men have scarcely been calm enough, nor always sufficiently informed, for dealing with the

great vital doctrines in which Christianity consists, and for perceiving how essential the intelligent holding of those doctrines
is to the true spiritualism, and to the proper direction and tone,
of our benevolent confederacies for the welfare of mankind.
Thus it has come to pass, that the real difference between
Popery and the Gospel, and all the evil consequences of every
sort which necessarily follow this ancient and *cumulative* embodiment of errors, have ceased, in a great measure, to occupy
men's thoughts, and for any person to distinguish himself by
unusual attention to such old-fashioned themes, was to bring
upon himself the scorn of the ignorant, or the pity of the accomplished and the liberal.   Now whatever was true in the apostolic
age, or at the epoch of the Reformation, is true still.   The
enemies of that truth are as bitterly opposed to it now as they
were in the days of Paul or of Luther, and, therefore, it is as
important to the life of the Church, and the conversion of men
to Christ, in our time as it was in theirs.   We are willing to
concede, that as the intellectual aspects of this age are not the
same as those of any which have gone before, so the mode of
presenting the fixed and certain truths of the gospel must vary
from former modes; but we are not willing to concede that
these truths are to be merged, or modified, by transient speculations.   Phrase it as you will, there is one truth, and one only,
which concerns man in his highest interests, and the affirmation
or denial of that one truth is the test of belief or disbelief in
Christianity.   If the SOLE MEDIATION OF JESUS CHRIST is, as
we hold, the actual groundwork of Christianity, and if the
apostolic doctrine concerning that mediation is, as we maintain,
the cardinal doctrine of the gospel, it surely behoves us to be
ever on our guard lest something else—that is, something false
—should be substituted for a truth of such Catholic and permanent concern.   The something else—the false instead of the
true—is, in our apprehension, the distinctive essence of the
Roman Catholic theology.   On that theology, whether avowedly
or not, yet with perfect consistency, its hierarchy, its observances, its arrogant assumptions, and its enslaving superstitions,
are strongly built.   Its advocates claim for that theology the
authority of apostolical teaching, of ancient and consentaneous
interpretation, and of universal practical expediency; and on
behalf of these claims they are well prepared by learning, mental
discipline, and the traditionary skill of long experience, to offer
such arguments as many conscientious Protestants have been
unable to resist.   Supposing that a large body of such advocates
can be found in England to-day, and that they are likely to be
strongly reinforced from the Established Church and two of the
universities of England, we ask our readers, how are they to be

met, and by whom? No proceedings of the government, no act of parliament, will avail us here. The national hatred of Popery, and the hereditary Protestantism of the bulk of our population, may be subdued by such means as the Papacy has at its command. Without being either bigots or alarmists, we ask again, how are the devices of this subtle adversary to be overthrown?

We are obliged to remark that there has been a widely-spread incredulity among us, as to the actual spread of Popery in this nation. Though chapels, colleges, monasteries, priests, reviews, newspapers, vicars-apostolic, have been increasing over the land, and proselytes have been rapidly gained from the higher classes, some of us have imagined that all this is unworthy of serious notice, and is easily accounted for by Irish immigration, by the temporary reaction arising from the repeal of the laws against Roman Catholics, and by the weak fancies of a few Churchmen, who spend their lives in colleges, having little knowledge of the world, and less influence on its every-day proceedings.

'A minister of the Establishment,' says Dr. Morison, ' better acquainted, perhaps, with the statistics of his own Church than any other living man, assured me lately that there were at least three thousand of his brethren who sympathized more or less with the Tractarian heresy.* But they all retain their livings snugly, and will, in some dioceses, receive kinder treatment than if they believed with Thomas Scott, or John Newton. What may be the effect upon the English mind of so much adverse teaching, accompanied by all the characteristic zeal of the Romish priesthood, whom the Tractarians closely imitate in dress and manner, it is difficult to determine. But there can be no lack of charity in affirming boldly that such teachers cannot help forward the cause of Protestantism, nor aid the true interests of our dearly-purchased Reformation. . . . . It is a fact, then, that from 1830 to 1850, the Tractarian Era, Roman Catholics, in England alone, built two hundred and thirty-four chapels or cathedrals ; *a number exceeding by one hundred and seventy-five the two best decades they experienced before, from the period of the Reformation.* In fact, the Tractarian reign, from 1830 to 1850, has done more for Popery by far than the thirty years before, of hard Popish labour, had been able to effect. From 1800 to 1810, the Romish chapels built were *sixteen ;* from 1810 to 1820, they were *twenty ;* from 1820 to 1830, they were *thirty-nine.* During the *thirty* years, then, which preceded 1830, there were only *seventy-five* Catholic places of worship erected ; while, in the Tractarian period, from 1830 to 1850, *two hundred and thirty-four* reared their heads in our cities, towns, and villages.†

Now, make what you will of our increasing population, and of any other circumstance you please to name, you cannot account for this

* Our own inquiries on the subject have led us to form the opinion, that the number of such clergymen does not exceed *two* thousand.

† See Catholic Annual Register, p. 7.

remarkable fact in any other way than by admitting the common-sense explanation, THAT TRACTARIANISM HAS BEEN THE BEST FRIEND OF ROME SINCE THE DAYS OF THE REFORMATION. How could it be otherwise ? Think of the respectable accessions which Tractarianism has actually made to the ranks of Romanism. To say nothing of the lords and ladies, and persons of good family, who, by the teaching of Tractarians, have been induced to go over to the Romish Church, what an impulse must it have given to all the movements of that community, to find itself, *in nine short years,** enriched and glorified by the accession of nearly one hundred of the best educated men which Oxford and Cambridge could supply !'— *Morison's Present Aspects*, pp. 10—12.

The absorption of so large a portion of our people in the busy scenes of life is favourable to that disregard for the question of Protestantism against Popery, which we are endeavouring to explain. Even religious men have, in this day of struggle and competition, but little leisure for thought on such matters : they imagine that their scattered fragments of time for reading are too precious to be frittered away in discussions about Popery and the Reformation. It is enough for them to read the Bible and books of practical devotion, and to leave their neighbours to think for themselves, and to adhere to their own churches, what-ever they may be. While we take this view of the feelings of our working and busy men, we are happy in regarding these feelings as essentially Protestant, and we rely on them, not a little, for the defence of our country from the aggressions of the Pope. Our unfeigned respect for these classes of our fellow-Protestants, however, prompts us to offer for their perusal the results of our reading and meditations on subjects which, we are well assured, are more closely connected than appears at first with their liberty to read their Bibles and practical treatises, and to think for themselves in the affairs of salvation. It is to be deeply regretted, for their own sakes personally, and for the sake of their children and of their country, that any circumstances should draw their minds away from the investigation of those religious truths, that, both in theory and in historical fact, lie at the foundation of all the liberties which they so dearly and so justly prize. The truths to which we refer are as noble as they are sacred, as practical as they are sublime ; they elevate man while they honour God ; and the intelligent apprehension of the reasons for believing them is as conducive to the dignified and safe enjoyment of the blessings of the life that now is, as it is to a cheerful preparation for the higher blessings of the life eternal. Besides the vital truths of the gospel, other prin-

* This is the time given in the 'Catholic Annual Register' for the con-versions.

ciples, bearing on the rights of the Christian people, have been utterly subverted by Popery, and but imperfectly restored by the Reformation, which cannot fail to be brought out by a *thorough* handling of the Papal controversy. To these principles we attach a degree of importance which is nearly equal to that which we attach to the gospel itself, because they emanate from the same Infallible Wisdom, are invested with the same authority, are *the only church principles which fully harmonize with the entire gospel*, and are revealed to us in the New Testament for the purpose of preserving the pure gospel from human corruptions, and of spreading it freely through the nations. We do not think that the church principles of the New Testament are less easy to discover than the teaching of that book on any other subject, and we are no more disposed, or at liberty, to submit to human authority, whether civil or ecclesiastical, in the matter of *church government* than in the matter of *church doctrine*. We hold the Church to be, intentionally, a popular institution. Whatever provision is made for order, offices, and discipline, the whole power, under Christ, is in THE PEOPLE, and administered not *over* them, nor *for* them, but *by themselves*, convened in free assembly. Such was, confessedly, the constitution of the earliest Christian churches. So long as this constitution remained, the gospel was preserved in its original freshness. But when the power of the people was usurped, first by philosophizing teachers, and then by ambitious rulers, the ancient simplicity of belief, freedom of worship, and equality of fellowship, were gradually worn away by the proud pretensions which ripened, at length, into the full-grown Papacy. Towards the restoration of the first, best, divine, mode of teaching and of acting, the Reformers made a noble approach. Some of them saw more clearly than others. But *in England* they were the minority; while in Switzerland, in Germany, and in Scotland, they prevailed. The Marian Confessors at Frankfort differed among themselves. The Episcopal party out-manœuvred, or overpowered, the Presbyterian. On the accession of Elizabeth, the controversy was transferred to England. *Puritanism* was the antagonist of the Papal tendencies in the Church of England. Elizabeth *hated the Puritans more than she hated the Papists*. The struggle lasted through the reigns of all the Stuarts; it continues still; it must continue till the Papacy is restored to its palmy state in England, or till all the Papal principles and leanings in the Anglican Church are completely rooted out by a religious and determined people.

With such views as these, we are concerned, and that most deeply, to keep the Papal Controversy, in its widest bearings, and remotest issues, continually before the British public. It is among our strongest convictions, that many of the errors, in belief and in practice, which are now denounced in high quarters, flow from the fair interpretation of acknowledged standards in the Established Church. We are not sorry that there should be so much of the old *doctrinal* Puritanism in that church, as well as out of it: what we long to see is—the faithful carrying out of the evangelical testimony in the acknowledgment of the rights which have been granted by the Supreme Authority to *the whole brotherhood of Christians*. So long as this acknowledgment is delayed, Protestant principles demand it, cannot relinquish it, must secure it; the controversy *will* be prolonged; the cause of the Christian People *will* be pleaded; the press *will* be worked for this purpose; the gatherings of earnest men *will* multiply; parliaments, governments, churches, *will* be urged to confess the truth, and to do the right; the foundations of national freedom will be broadly and strongly laid in the judgment and the affection of an enlightened community; and on those foundations such a structure will be raised as no foreign potentate will venture to attack, or even find an excuse for making the attempt. Then, indeed, will Christianity be revered and loved as the true emancipator of nations, the giver of peace, the bond of amity, the benefactress of the world, shedding her light on every dwelling, and covering all the interests of humanity with her celestial shield.

Besides the general reasons which we have for urging this controversy, there are those arising from the strange and sudden ferment which has spread so rapidly throughout the nation. We do not look upon the present agitation as either unnecessary, unwise, or useless. An attempt has been made to turn a relaxation of statute law, in which statesmen of all parties have concurred, into a plea for pushing the interest of the Papacy in these realms as far as possible. There is no mistake about this: and it is what no sincere Protestant can regard with indifference. Whatever can be done, or *undone*, in the way of strengthening the liberties of *all*, without conferring invidious distinctions on *any*, ought to be done, promptly and firmly, yet with wise deliberation. Too much caution, however, cannot be used, lest the national zeal for Protestantism should infringe the universal and permanent claims of that freedom which is as necessary to Protestantism as it is to any other phase of human dignity. It might be easy enough to prove that certain public measures would be the surest means of preventing the encroachments of Popery; but let such measures be once sanctioned by law, and there are *other* encroachments, as they are deemed by many honest Churchmen, to which it might be thought desirable, and found practicable, to apply them. There is a tone in some of the memorials, sermons, speeches, and pamphlets, that crowd upon us, which suggests the apprehension of danger to the religious liberties of England much nearer than the Vatican, and more terrible than Papal bulls : we mean a determination to push the power of Government as far as it can be pushed in the suppression of errors and superstitions in religion. We cannot but look on the *animus* of such a determination as the very essence of the evil which we denounce as Popery. Without stopping to settle the question of English law, as involved in the doings of Pio Nono and his subordinates, we confess to a jealousy, more intense than we can utter, of *any legal enactments concerning religion.* We have too many enactments of this class already. There is but one to which we could thoroughly assent—a comprehensive act of equality before the law, in sacred as in civil relations, for every subject in the empire.

The only weapons that beseem a warfare so pre-eminently spiritual are not of earth but of heaven ; and, *on a fair field*, we are content to meet the adversaries of our faith and freedom with these alone ; if knowledge, argument, persuasion, holy example, and humble prayer will not bring success, if we be vanquished by wiser, abler, holier, and more devoted men, we deserve to be vanquished, and all the virtuous intelligence in the universe will congratulate us on the defeat. We are saying this with the serene confidence of men who know that in the main substance of their principles they are on the side of truth, and who have learned from the Scriptures, and from the history of nations, that they who abide by these principles, consistently and perseveringly, are sure to triumph at the last.

Now, it is because we leave, for the present, the civil, legal, and political questions involved in the Papal controversy, that we implore the reader's attention to the views which we are giving of the manifold and vital aspects of the same controversy on the heart's core of our religion. It is not necessary, so far as we can see, that the logical form of controversy should be always preserved. We have less and less reliance on polemics. They are seldom carried on with perfect fairness. The very strength of an argument sometimes weakens a cause by producing on antagonists the impression that some fallacy must lurk within it, or it would have been impossible for thinking men to resist it. The heat of disputation is, often, at a temperature which scorches the verdure, and blasts the fruits, of Christian piety. It is extremely difficult to act upon the maxim of hating the principles and loving the men, when the men become the living embodiment of the principles, and our own mortal enemies. We question whether it belongs to human nature—or to any nature, indeed—to hate a mere abstraction of the intellect. It is in *beings* not *notions* that the affections find their objects ; the man thinking, rather than the thought, is what we love on the one hand, or hate on the other ; and if there were no persons to trouble us with their advocacy of any opinions, the opinions themselves, abstractly considered, would give us no concern. Whether this be so or not, we have not often had the good fortune to see the calmness of a truth-loving spirit combined with the keenness or the fervour of controversial champions, so that we can scarcely recommend the method of direct encounter with the defenders of the Papacy as the best method of diffusing what we believe to be the truth.   Occasions there must be, indeed, for doing this, and men, competent to judge of the occasion and to deal with it, are not likely to be wanting ; but it is not our opinion that the style of argument appropriate to a debate, and within the grasp of accomplished and experienced disputants, is best fitted for the ordinary work of popular instruction.   Every public teacher is not qualified for using this style with good effect ; and the general edification would seem to us more likely to be advanced by a more conciliatory and more practical method of instruction.   Let the *right* of private judgment and the DUTY of *using that right* be vigorously exemplified by preachers with all meekness and wisdom, and urged, in like manner, on their hearers ; let the claims of the Bible be explained and advocated with discrimination and impartiality ; let the entire work of the Messiah, in his life and death, his resurrection and ascension, his *royal* as well as sacerdotal glories in heaven, be broadly and boldly set forth ; let the human corruptions of truth and assumptions of authority be devoutly avoided and as devoutly condemned ; let the characteristic privileges of the redeemed church be described by men who are living in the enjoyment of them, mindful of their high origin, jealous of their peculiar sanctity, and earnestly inviting their fellow-men to share them ; let plain and popular speech, familiar, yet serious, earnest without rant, and dignified but not pompous, be used as the vehicle of living thoughts ; let the English people, of all classes, be allowed and encouraged both to hear such discourses and to become acquainted with the men who utter them ;—let all this be done, done always, in all places, heartily and consentaneously, by the 'goodly fellowship' of preachers in every Church, and a power stronger than that of Government, and suitable (which that of Government is not), to the performance of this work, will be at hand through our entire population, and will form such a breastwork of defence as no created force can overthrow.

It is well to remember, amid our confident assertions of the strength of the Protestant interest in England, that not a little of this interest is sheer politics, and that much of it is blind, unreasoning sectarianism.   On such auxiliaries let there be no reliance in the conflicts of believing men for truth. That there are large bodies of well-informed and truly evangelical professors is, indeed, a matter for rejoicing, and for hope. From their hearts, we doubt not, holy and fervent supplications are daily poured out at the throne of mercy, on behalf of that which we conscientiously revere as the cause of God and of humanity. Yet there are among us rudiments of weakness of which it is wise that we take note, for the purpose of exerting our best energy to clear ourselves entirely from them. To dwell on these, at any length, is beyond our present limits. But we shall not lose sight of them.

The absence of visible and practical union is one of these rudiments. Without foregoing our individualism for the sake of a fictitious uniformity, a comprehensive survey of things as they are would dictate a *manifestation* of the oneness which really pervades the communities of Protestant worshippers. To the extent of actual agreement there should be, there ought to be, *avowed co-operation.* This would silence the taunt of Roman Catholics, by showing them that there is something more spiritual and more manly than their vaunted but deceptive unity. It would, also, be a real augmentation of the power of each separate and independent Protestant against the wiles of an enemy, who, however he may flatter one division of ' ' heretics' at the expense of another, aims at the destruction, or absorption, of them all.—As a consequence, in one respect, and, in another respect, as a cause of our disunion, we must advert to what we may call the *pettiness* of some of our distinctions, and the narrow-heartedness which is generated by attaching to them an undue measure of importance. We are not here denying the importance of any of these distinctions, but lamenting that they should be so exclusively or preferentially regarded as to draw towards them those functions of our spiritual and social life which demand a higher order and a wider range of thought. While Protestants are contending about the pattern of the altar, the ornaments of the temple, the details of the glorious dispensation which makes them free, they are in danger of *letting the sacred fire go out,* of leaving the foundations to be sapped, and of losing the very liberty of worshipping in *any* place, with *any* forms, according to their own judgment.

Some readers will be surprised, perhaps, when we enumerate among the weak points—*not of Protestantism,* but—of Protestants, *a defective share of self-reliance.* We cannot be supposed to mean reliance on themselves as opposed to reliance upon God ; but we do mean the reliance of each person on his own judgment, and on the best use of his own faculties as a responsible servant of Christ, instead of leaning on other men's opinions and

activities ; and we also mean, the reliance of Christians, *as*
Christians, on the agencies which are clearly appointed by God
for establishing the kingdom of heaven upon earth.   We do not
look at this pusillanimous dependence on extraneous help as at
all the result of humility.   It is rather a want of manliness,
courage—the ' Virtue ' which an apostle inculcates as the native
product of Christian faith.   Something of this *may* have mingled with feelings which we honour, in some of the recent
memorials to the throne.   If so, let it be ' cast away.'   There is
no harm in looking for the protection of civil interests to rulers ;
but to them we must not look for the promotion of our religious
views.   There can be no harm, either, in sometimes waiting to
see how the most judicious supporters of our own principles are
likely to act on important occasions ; but this waiting ought to
be for equal and spontaneous co-operation rather than for the
mere purpose of swelling the followers of any leader ; and, instead of bringing forth the books of by-gone ages, expecting
the dead to do the work of the living, we would urge the diges-
tion, the condensation, or the amplification of these ancient
thoughts expressed in the popular language, and instinct with
the vitality, of our own time.   In this way, we think, an immense
quantity of literary work will be required, for a long while to
come, in England.

It is in no spirit of censure that we frankly own to the reproach
of a *lack of earnestness* in the general profession of Protestantism
among us.   We covet not the earnestness of partizanship or of
mere proselytism.   We desire the quiet, loving, devout, patient
thoughtfulness which is really *alive*, and which is as different
from the spasmodic fits of general excitement, as the constant
functions of animal life are to the contortions of a galvanized
muscle.   It is the deep, full, ever-flowing stream, and not the
dashing cataract, that carries life within its waters, and bears
fleets upon its bosom : in like manner, the steady working of a
vital principle in the heart, and not the impatience of intellectual
contradiction, or the passionate invective of enraged sectarianism, displays the dignity of Truth, while it diffuses wide her
blessings, and assures us of her final victory.

We must pause.   Our endeavour has been to expound our
views of the Papal Controversy without touching, or but slightly
touching, the differences that so unhappily separate one class of
Protestants from another ; and this we have done in order to
awaken attention to some of the causes which have produced
comparative apathy and weakness in us all.   We shall advert,
ere long, to the strong points, whether of argument or of policy,
on the side of the Roman Hierarchy, and the methods by which
those arguments are to be refuted, and that policy resisted.

We shall continue, from time to time, to notice such publications as bear on either side of this great controversy, being particularly careful not to omit those produced by Nonconformists. For the present, we briefly characterise a few.

Mr. Capper is a member of the Society of Friends. He has done good service by the volume of which the title is prefixed to this article. He presents the doctrinal tenets of the Romish Church in the language of the doctors of the College of Douay, *distinctly marking the alterations which have appeared in the successive editions* of the Douay Bible. He shows what the doctrines are, inviting the reader to judge for himself whether they be true or false. We are much assisted by having the doctrines classified in twenty-seven chapters, on Reading the Scriptures—Knowledge of Scripture—Canonical Books—Errors of the Protestant Version—Atonement of Christ—Trinity—Faith—Prayer—Perfection—Justification by Faith—Election and Reprobation—Baptism—Infants entirely lost without Baptism—Mass and Eucharist—Grace of God and Holy Spirit—Christ's Descent into Hell—Romish Establishment—Authority of Kings and Governments—Pope and Councils—Tradition—No Salvation out of the Romish Church—Heretics and Sectaries—Punishment and Extirpation of Heretics—Virgin Mary—Worship of Saints, &c.—Confession and Remission of Sins—Extraordinary and Miscellaneous. As a faithful compilation and useful hand-book of Roman Catholic doctrines, this is a volume which we have great pleasure in recommending.

'Popery in Power, or the Spirit of the Vatican,' exposes, in a vivid style, the antagonism of Popery with monarchy, with civil power and good government; its dissimulations and importunities; its delusions and infatuations; its monstrous assumptions and relentless cruelties; its forgeries; and its remarkable attitude, at the present time, in regard to England. The work is mainly addressed to the Tractarians. More than a hundred pages of the volume are filled with 'Priestcraft; or, The Monarch of the Middle Ages: a Drama.' The volume is illustrated with numerous engravings on wood, which we have examined with some care; they are very numerous, exhibiting a striking variety, and are all executed with superior power and taste.

Mr. Collette's 'Romanism in England Exposed' consists of letters which appeared in successive numbers of the 'Historic Times,' under the signature of 'A Lay Subscriber,' with some additions and notes. These letters were occasioned by an advertisement in a Roman Catholic journal, the 'Tablet,' of a 'Beautiful Image of St. Joseph, Rosaries, Beads, Crucifixes, Scapulars, AN ACCOUNT OF THE FOUR SCAPULARS; to be sold

at a NEW WAREROOM FOR THE SALE OF ARTICLES OF
CATHOLIC DEVOTION.' On seeing this advertisement, Mr.
Collette wrote to the gentleman advertising, requesting him to
let him know whether the 'accounts' of the scapulars advertised
by him had the sanction of the Roman Catholic clergy in
London; being informed, in reply, that the little book was published under the superintendence of the Redemptorist Fathers
of St.Mary's, Park-road, Clapham. To these Fathers Mr.Collette
then wrote, asking, among other things, whether the scapulars
and publication in question were recognised by Dr.Wiseman and
the Roman Catholic clergy in London. As soon as he obtained
satisfaction on this point, the letters, here re-published and
enlarged, commenced. He deals boldly with Dr.Wiseman, and
Dr. Wiseman's saints—' the angelic St. Thomas,' ' the seraphic
Doctor St. Bonaventura,' and St. Alphonsus Lignuori, of whom
his Eminence says, that while he is ' celebrated throughout the
world for his theological writings, his heroic virtues and extraordinary sanctity prove how close was the connexion between
the wisdom of his understanding and the purity of his heart.'
He takes the writings of these three men, canonized saints of the
modern Church of Rome, and proves them to be superstitious,
idolatrous, blasphemous, debasing, and immoral. He publicly
dares Dr.Wiseman to publish, in English, the ' Moral Theology'
of his Church, particularly the instructions on the subject of the
Confessional. In the Appendix is a leading article from the
' Times ' of November 26, 1839; in which something more than
controversial 'intrepidity' is proved against Dr. Wiseman, in a
controversy with Professor Turton.

We can honestly recommend this little volume as containing,
within a small compass, and in a style of *piquant* interest, an exposure of ' Romanism in England,' which we hope will have a
wide circulation, and will open the eyes of not a few to the
*religious and moral* prospects of this country, so far as they may
be influenced by Cardinal Wiseman, and the system which he is
extending with so much boldness, subtilty, and skill.

Of the smaller publications mentioned at the head of the
present article, we have only space for saying, that we have read
them all with advantage. The Sermon of Dr. Morison is a fair
sample of his lucid and hearty preaching, and suggests many
apprehensions in reference to the religious condition of our
country. Dr. Reed's Discourse is dignified, perspicuous, discriminating, and remarkable for the quiet power of language in
which the preacher is known to excel. Mr. Newman Hall's
Tract is written with much acuteness, and deserves to be read as
a counteractive of impetuous and undiscerning sympathy with
the popular cry of the day.

Dr. Cumming's 'Lectures' and 'Notes' are already too familiar, we presume, to most of our readers to require our special commendation: which, however, we very cordially tender to so popular and experienced a combatant against Popery in all its phases. In the main object of his Lectures, we certainly think he has cut away the ground from beneath the Cardinal's feet.

From the venerable Dr. Pye Smith's enlarged 'Reasons,' we make one extract, which fully expresses the principles on which the Papal Controversy will be carried on in the pages of the 'Eclectic Review':—

'*These*, then, are our REASONS of Protestantism. We reject the authority of the Pope and Church of Rome,—because it is an *usurped* authority;—because its *tendency* is to destroy the very essence of real religion;—because it demands belief in doctrines palpably *absurd*, *unscriptural*, and *pernicious*:—because it is an impious *invasion* of the office of our Lord Jesus Christ, the only Spiritual Lawgiver:—because it is subversive of the *use* and *value* of the Holy Scriptures:—because it promotes the vilest forms of *tyranny*:—and because, while it falsely claims a right of prescription, it is, in fact, an audacious system of *innovation* on the *old, apostolic*, and *primitive* religion of Christ.

'Permit two closing observations.

'1. Under the circumstances of the present crisis, I cannot but think it right and seasonable to remark that the fundamental PRINCIPLES of our DISSENT from the Church of England are the *very same* as those of our PROTEST against the Church of Rome. Those principles are, the sole *supremacy* and *legislative authority* of Christ over the faith and the consciences of men; the unrestricted *use* of the Bible, and its *sufficiency* as the rule of religious belief and obedience; and the *unlawfulness* and *impiety* of human *dictation* in matters purely belonging to religion.

'These are the principles on which Mr. Chillingworth, and all the best defenders of the Reformation, have, with greater or less explicitness, rested their arguments; and the sober and consistent application of these principles appears, to our most serious judgment, to *require* a conscientious separation from the religious establishment of our country. To the civil Government of our country we pay the cheerful obedience, not of mere duty, but of choice and affection, in all civil matters; but "TO GOD we must render the things that are GOD's." We pay respect and honour to the pious and upright members of the Church of England, and are their ready coadjutors, so far as we are able, in the numerous works of patriotic and Christian philanthropy; and at the present time, especially (1850-51), in efforts to repel the audacious aggression of Popery upon our common Protestantism. In this, and every similar work, all true-hearted Protestants are united. O that they would vigorously unite in abolishing unnecessary differences! But it is even a part of the respect and honour due to them, to tell our brethren *why* we are constrained to differ from them. We rejoice that their Church is purified from the grosser errors of the Romish community ; but we lament that she still retains an unscriptural conformity in many points of doctrine, constitution, and worship. We especially lament that her constitution involves a denial, virtually at least, of the three GREAT *principles* of Protestantism ; and that she is so tied and bound with the iron fetters· of a merciless *uniformity*, imposed by the most profligate prince of the arbitrary house of Stuart—so tied and bound with those heavy chains, that improvement and amelioration are doleful and forbidden sounds to her ! We cannot, moreover, be insen‑ sible to the strong fact, that the Church of England rejects ministerial communion with every Protestant Church upon earth, but owns and exercises it with the Church of Rome. Our being Dissenters, then, is nothing but the result of our *consistency* as Protestants.'

---

## Brief Notices.

*The Imperial Cyclopædia.* (Dedicated, by permission, to Her Majesty.) Royal 8vo. Parts I. to V. London : Charles Knight.

IT is impossible to speak too highly of the skill with which Mr. Knight, for some years past, has catered for the public. His successive works are amongst the most valuable of the many contributions, which our day has witnessed, to a sound popular literature, and their circulation has, happily, been proportionably large. His judgment is equal to his enterprise, and the latter has wrought an entire change in an important department of the book-trade. ' The Imperial Cyclopædia,' now before us, is another monument of his zeal and indefatigable indus‑ try, and, like its predecessors, it goes far to supply a national want, and is entitled to national support. It is founded on the vast mass of original materials combined in ' The Penny Cyclopædia,' with such additions as the progress of invention and discovery has since made. The arrangement of the work is entirely different from that of its pre‑ decessors. This, indeed, constitutes its distinctive feature, and will insure it, through a wide circle, a hearty welcome. Instead of the continuously-alphabetical order, it will be divided into nine depart‑ ments, entitled, The Cyclopædia of Geography, Arts and Industry, Science—Mathematical and Physical—Natural History, Biography and History, Science—Metaphysical and Moral, Theology and Biblical Literature, Law and Jurisprudence, Government and Political Economy. Each of these departments will be complete in itself, so that every purchaser may consult his own taste and studies in his selection. He need not buy the whole work in order to have the part he wishes to consult. For obvious reasons the work has commenced with 'The Geography of the British Empire,' which is to form two volumes, and to be completed in twelve monthly parts. Such a work, written with care, and brought up to the information of the day, will be one of the most useful books which a library can contain. 'A Geographical Cyclopædia, at once original, full, accurate, and cheap, is a desideratum for the general public. Such a work is of daily necessity. It addresses itself, as of paramount utility, to the cursory reader and the diligent student.' So far as we have had an opportunity of examining 'The Imperial Cyclopædia,' it appears to be very much what is thus described, and we recommend it accordingly to our readers. A vast amount of useful information is conveyed within narrow limits, and at a very reasonable cost.

We ought to add that 'the getting up,' of the work is in admirable style, befitting its dedication, by express permission, to the Queen. In this respect, at least, there is nothing to desire.

---

*Mornings among the Jesuits at Rome; being Notes of Conversations held with certain Jesuits on the subject of Religion, in the City of Rome.* By Rev. M. Hobart Seymour, M.A. London: Seeleys.

MR. SEYMOUR represents himself as getting access to the gentlemen with whom he held the conversations reported in this volume, from their being under the impression that there was some prospect of making a convert, and he tells us that he had to be very cautious in what he said, lest they should find out their mistake. We do not much admire this way of going to work. We are indebted, however, to the reverend gentleman's *ruse* for a volume of very curious information. The main features of the controversy were discussed, and Mr. Seymour evidently thinks with a uniform success on his part. We should not for a moment dream of questioning a Christian man's honesty, in reporting what he said and how he defeated the enemy; but we may very safely hint, that such easy victories as are here won over professors and dignitaries of all shades, perhaps, assumed a different aspect from the point of view occupied by the said dignitaries. It would be satisfactory to have their impressions of the fight to compare with the reverend gentleman's. From this volume, readers may gather some striking instances of the power of religious association, in making sensible men of cultivated minds (as many of the interlocutors seem to have been), swallow absurdities the most gross. The facts disclosed as to the prevalence of pure Mariolatry in Italy are also valuable, and there is appended an interesting chapter on the Catacombs of Rome— the burial-place of a better generation of Christians than those who now live above them, and use their graves as a store-house from which bones of saints, to any extent, can be supplied to order on the shortest notice.

---

*The Working Classes of Great Britain, &c.* Prize Essay. By Rev. S. G. Green, B.A. London: Snow.

MR. GREEN has brought to his task a thorough sympathy with the class of whom he writes; he thinks vigorously, and writes well—with

beauty sometimes, with power sometimes, with precision and definite-
ness always. But we rise from the book with a strong impression,
that in writing on the condition of the people—the manufacturing
artizans especially—he is not dealing with a subject which his eyes
have seen, so much as with one of which he has thought a good deal,
and read more. We miss anything like the signs of personal familiarity
with the hand-workers of England; and hence, while we have numerous
detached observations such as a sensible man, studying the subject for
this express essay purpose, would be sure to make, either for himself or
by the help of others, we do not find the complete grasp of the case
which only long personal knowledge could give. His facts do not
seem vivified into one whole. The author is not strong, either, in
political economy; and has almost omitted one part of the 'specifica-
tion' which the editor of the 'Standard of Freedom' put forth in
announcing this prize—a part, too, which, whatever we may think of
the wisdom that dictated it, or the advantage of fulfilling it, ought to
have taken a prominent place in the essay, in order to bring it within
the conditions—' 3, *and chiefly*, a well-directed scheme of practical and
practicable remedial measures.' This is almost untouched in the
essay.

We give the author all praise for his volume—as one that shows a
kind heart and a good head, plenty of thought, and plenty of fresh
vigour; but which still is deficient, as we think, in full familiar knowledge of the subject. Mr. Green's next book on working-men will be
better.

---

*The Course of Creation.* By John Anderson, D.D. London: Long-
mans.

WE are glad to receive a volume on geology from a man of Dr.
Anderson's stamp—an acknowledged proficient in the science, who
can wield his pen as effectively as his hammer, and has used the
latter over the length and breadth of England and Scotland before he
took up the former. Not the least pleasant part of this pleasant
volume are the affectionate reminiscences of such wanderings, while
the familiarity with the geology of the island, which is gained by such
a course, gives solid value to the book. The plan of the volume is to
take the geology of Scotland first, describing, not only the various
formations as one might do from specimens in a museum, but giving
them in geographical sequence as well as in the order of antiquity;
beginning, for instance, with Ben Macdhui and the Grampians, as the
types of the primary, and working at once southwards and upwards
till we emerge into daylight in the coal-fields of Midlothian. England
and France are taken next—their points of correspondence and contrast
with the former being carefully noted. The volume closes with an
interesting and full deduction of general principles—another attack
on the 'Vestiges of Creation,' the vestiges of which are nearly gone
now, we hope, and a sensible chapter on the Mosaic record. We are
glad to travel over, or rather under, all this ground, with a gentleman
fully master of his subject, a lover of nature, a keen observer, an

acute reasoner, a pleasing writer, who shows us in his own person that geology and Christianity may live together, and never does violence to either for the sake of the other, but gives all prominence to the manifold manifest harmonies, and waits confidently for the full accordance.

---

*Christianity in harmony with Man's Nature, present and progressive. Lectures preached in Gallowtree-gate Chapel, Leicester.* By George Legge, LL.D. London: Snow.

THIS course of sermons presents considerable freshness and freedom of thought, with more resolute casting off of old garments and more liberal communicating of seeds of thought, than we often find in pulpit addresses. The author has done good service in that field of Christian evidence which the current of modern thinking pronounces the chief—the internal marks of divine authority. He brings out forcibly and well that the gospel is in harmony with man's nature—that every man carries in him a prophecy of Christianity. Thanking him for his book, we should have been more grateful still if he had sobered down the glare and tinsel of his style. We are sorry that in casting away so much that usually goes into the pulpit he has not pitched the wretched seven-leagued-booted words and sentences that bear with some the name of fine preaching after the rest of the trash. He does not need the heavy cotton-velvet robes to disguise his lean thoughts, they are quite strong enough to stand up in simplest dress, and will look best so.

---

*Light in Dark Places; or, Memorials of Christian Life in the Middle Ages.* Translated from the German of Augustus Neander. London: Low.

IT was well said at Neander's funeral, that his whole spirit and labours might be described by the passage,—'Then said the disciple whom Jesus loved, It is the Lord.' The man lived in the Master's love; and that brightened his vision to see in all the darkness of a corrupt Church the faintest sign of his Lord's presence, and of likeness to him. We trust that our readers know enough of his noble work on Church History to recognise this as the guiding thought of it. He goes sounding through the centuries, searching in all forms for the deep-lying life beneath, faithful to the principle—'There are diversities of administration, but the same Spirit.'

We rejoice to see a translation of this second part of his ' Denkwür-digkeiten ;' a work better fitted, perhaps, for the general English public than the more scientific and elaborate history, whilst it is instinct with the same loving spirit, and full of the same profound knowledge. It embraces, 1. The period of the irruptions of the barbarians into the Roman Empire—taking for its subjects, the North-African Church under the Vandals, Severinus in Germany, Cæsarius in France, and Gregory the Great ; 2. The History of Missions in the Middle Ages, including Patrick in Ireland, &c., down to Raymond Lull.

Since we have no history of the Church in English undeformed by the influence of a false point of view, or written with anything like the thorough grasp of the whole field, which is the only means of painting with life and correctness any part of it, we hope that this well-executed translation of the more popular work of the late—alas! that that sad word should have come yet—historian of Christianity will command thankful study.  It will well repay it.

---

*A Manual explanatory of Congregational Principles.*  By George Payne, LL.D.  Second Edition.  London: Snow.

WE need only notice this second edition of Dr. Payne's valuable tract, which is well worthy of the careful perusal of all Congregationalists. Its wide circulation would be an immense benefit.

---

*A Christian Jew on the Old Testament Scriptures.*  By B. Weiss. Dundee: Middleton.

THIS volume is devoted to showing a direct Messianic reference in the principal events and ritual observances of the Pentateuch.  The author seems a good man, but his book is too much coloured by a Talmudical taste, too full of strained, elaborate forcing of gospel into law, to furnish thoughtful readers with either sound principles, or useful examples of typical interpretation.

---

*Thoughts for Home, in Prose and Verse.*  By Mrs. Thomas Geldart. London: Hall, Virtue, and Co.

FULL of simple, touching thoughts, that will, we doubt not, find a response in many a Christian home, all the inmates of which, from oldest to youngest, may read appropriate words here.

---

*The Effects of Civilization on the People in European States.*  By Charles Hall, M.D.  London: Gilpin.  Phœnix Library.

THIS book describes symptoms better than it traces them to the right disease, and does that second stage of a physician's duty still better than the third—prescribing remedies.  In other words, the author, a kind-hearted observer, has seen the evils that exist clearly—has been rather puzzled as to their cause—is inclined to think manufactures the evil-doer—and finds no better cure than to abolish the law of primogeniture, and prohibit ' refined manufactures.'

---

*The Annotated Paragraph Bible.*  Part I.—The Pentateuch.  London: Religious Tract Society.

THIS is a well-printed edition, illustrated with serviceable maps, brief introductions to the books, explanatory notes, which are generally sensible and correct.  Its most valuable part is a copious selection of parallel passages, which seem really such, and not mere verbal similarities, as so many of our authorized version's are.  The work will be completed in six octavo parts.

## Review of the Month.

THE first act of the Papal drama is drawing to a close. Parliament will soon meet, when the Queen's Government must disclose their intentions. In the meantime, all is uncertainty and conjecture. We do not complain of this. The silence maintained is prudent, and may prove useful. A premature divulgement would serve no other purpose than that of fettering Ministers, and of supplying their opponents with an opportunity of turning the exigencies of the public service to their party interests. The Premier's letter to the Bishop of Durham was a sufficient departure from the reserve usually observed on such occasions. Prompted in part by the excitement of the hour, and designed, it is probable, to answer a specific purpose, its end was instantly accomplished. Like all extremes, however, it was significant, to thoughtful men, of reaction; and we were, therefore, not a little amused to find the good citizens of London expecting, on the 10th of December, to receive some distinct intimation of the measures which would be submitted to the legislature on the meeting of Parliament. It would not have accorded with precedents—a binding rule with statesmen—to have given such intimation, and, in the present case, it was least to be expected. In proportion as the Premier, in the first moment of excitement, had spoken with emphatic distinctness, his Administration was likely to preserve unbroken and profound silence afterwards. The torrent of popular indignation might, at the moment—though this is a strange supposition—carry away so phlegmatic and self-commanding a man as Lord John Russell. But this could not last; his natural temperament and position would soon be regained; and the advantages of an equivocal policy would then be sought to counterbalance the more frank, if not more honest, views which had been expressed. The vagueness of the Royal replies to the City and the Universities did not therefore surprise us. It is only what we looked for, and is sufficiently obvious from the comments to which they have given rise. Each party has sought to extract from them its own views and policy; while in the end it is clear, that, like all similar documents, their perfection really consists in hiding the intentions of their framers.

On the other hand, the country has spoken out with a unanimity and earnestness, of which our history furnishes few examples. We have never seen anything like it, save during a brief period when the Reform Bill was supposed to be in danger. Right or wrong, the people of these realms have been stirred most powerfully. Their heart has been deeply moved—agitated by a passion swift and omnipotent as an electric shock. This movement has had its principal scope amongst those who are usually the calmest and most reflecting section of the community. The middle class, with few exceptions, have been its subjects; and where they have not originated opposition, they have zealously crowded about those who have projected it.   The excitement has not, however, been confined to any class.   Though it has prevailed amongst the trading and commercial part of the nation, beyond what is common, it is far from having been limited to them.   Peers and commoners, the clergy and the laity, Churchmen and Dissenters, manufacturers and agriculturists, artizans and farm-laborers, have alike felt its influence, and given utterance, in language appropriate to each, to the intensest indignation of which our nature is capable.   Such unanimity, conjoined with such vehemence, is rarely witnessed.   It occurs only when the passion of a nation is aroused, and becomes an instrument of good or evil according as it is enlightened by wisdom, or misled by folly.   At present, we note the fact simply ; and we do so in all sincerity, aiming neither to exaggerate, nor to diminish its importance.

We need not detail the circumstances which have produced it. Briefly, we may state, that a material alteration has been effected in the organization of the Roman Catholic Church in this kingdom, by the substitution of an archbishop and twelve suffragan bishops, for the eight vicars-apostolic previously existing.   These latter were really bishops with foreign titles, but have now been exchanged for bishops in name with territorial designations derived from some English town or city within their several dioceses.   This change has been effected by a Bull of Pope Pius IX , dated at Rome the 24th September, 1850.

On this simple statement of the case we fail to discover adequate cause for the excitement which has been produced.   There is no proportion between the one and the other.   The effect is not in keeping with its alleged cause ; and we feel assured, therefore, that other elements must be involved, and have had their influence, fairly or otherwise, in the general result.   The excitement is obvious, and has scarcely been paralleled in modern times.   How, then, we naturally ask, is it to be accounted for?   To what must we refer it?   It had some cause. What is it, and where may it be discovered?   These are grave questions ; and to reply to them fully, is to solve much of the difficulty involved in the pending question.

Most of the explanations given are, we confess, unsatisfactory.  They do not, to our minds, at least, bear the test of a rigid scrutiny.   Their apparent force may be considerable, but their real strength is trifling. They break down, like faulty witnesses when subjected to cross-examination, and ought not, therefore, whatever momentary purpose they may answer, to be relied on by the friends of truth.   A few examples will illustrate our meaning.

It is alleged by some that the establishment of a Catholic hierarchy in these realms is an infraction of law.   If it be so, nothing can be easier than to point out the statute in question, and its enforcement will follow as matter of course.   When a nation is stirred so deeply, as is now our case, we shall not hesitate long to avail ourselves of so easy and prompt a method of warding off an apprehended danger.   But we have yet to learn that law has been violated.   We have read much and thought much on the subject, but are free to declare, that the defence of Cardinal Wiseman on this point appears to us to be conclusive ; and we know not that the inquiry promised by the Premier has elicited any refutation.   Should it, however.

turn out otherwise, we are quite sure that the violations of such law have been so numerous and flagrant that no Administration will venture to enforce it.

But the Queen's *supremacy*, it is said, is assailed by the act of the Pope; and hence the indignation felt by her subjects. If by the Queen's supremacy be meant her having supreme power in matters 'ecclesiastical and spiritual,' then it is obvious that, as Dissenters do not cede such authority, they cannot deem this objection valid, and must refuse to be moved powerfully by it. We know that the Royal supremacy in spiritual affairs is now sometimes spoken of by Dissenters as though it were a mere assertion of the subjection of the ecclesiastical to the civil power,—the right of the monarch to enforce on spiritual persons the requirements of law. Were this all it involved, we should not, of course, demur to its admission. But such is not the sense in which the supremacy of the Crown has been hitherto maintained. In popular apprehension, as well as in historic import, the phrase means much more, and the limiting interpretation contended for fails, therefore, to command our confidence. The men who now declaim most loudly about the invasion of the Queen's supremacy were doing their utmost, only yesterday, to array against it the sympathies of the nation.

But the civil supremacy of the Queen is said to be assailed. This is a grave matter, and deserves the gravest attention. If it be so, then there is an end of the dispute, and every Englishman should rally round the throne. This view has been taken by some of the best friends of religious liberty amongst us—men of broad views, of large mental grasp, clear and well-defined principles, and of undoubted attachment to freedom. The respect in which we hold them, has led us to deliberate much on their opinion. We have done our best to place ourselves in their position in order to catch, if possible, their view of this subject; but, after all, we are bound to confess that we see no proof of the 'Civil' Supremacy being touched by the recent enactment of the Pope. To say nothing of the silence of Lord Minto at Rome—of which some explanation must be given on the meeting of Parliament—we have had many Catholic bishops with territorial designations before now, and yet never heard of their creation being regarded as an invasion of the 'Civil' Supremacy of the Crown. Ireland is proof in point, and her bishops have not only been recognised by the authorities, but have been royally honored. It is only a few years since that Galway was erected into a bishopric by the sole authority of the Pope, and yet no remonstrance was heard of. In our colonies it is notorious that the Catholic Hierarchy has been introduced without opposition from the Home Government; nay, that it has been aided by that influence to the serious discomfort of many who deemed Popery a delusion. In Australia, for instance, we have the Archiepiscopal See of Sydney, with suffragans at Maitland, Hobart Town, Adelaide, Perth, Melbourne, and Port Victoria. These Catholic prelates are publicly acknowledged in official documents, and have been salaried by successive Governments.

The same state of things exists in British North America, where the dioceses of Kingston, Toronto, Bytown, and Halifax, have been erected by the Pope, and a similar rule now exists in the West Indies. Such being the case, we are compelled to pronounce a verdict of acquittal on this count of the indictment. Convict the accused we cannot, for Cardinal Wiseman asks triumphantly, ' Was it something so unnatural and monstrous in us to call for what our colonies have received ? or had we any reason to anticipate that the Act would be characterised in the terms which I do not love to repeat ?'

But the Catholic Hierarchy has ignored that of the Protestant Church in these realms.  There is no doubt of the fact.  It lies on the very surface of the documents which have been issued, and is in keeping with the spirit of the Papacy.  ' We have just reason,' says the Archbishop of Canterbury, ' to declare our indignation at the present invasion of our rights, and the assumption on which it is avowedly grounded, that our Protestant communion is unsound, and even heretical.'  The Bishop of London expresses a similar feeling, recording his indignation at the Pope ' treating as mere nonentities the ancient archbishoprics and bishoprics of England.'  This insult— for such it is deemed—has been felt most keenly, and the English clergy, from the primate to the curate, have been unwise enough to give utterance to their feelings.  A little consideration might have prevented this.  It would have been more dignified to be silent, and had they been so, their own sins would not have been recalled to remembrance in their day of trial.  But they have chosen their course, and must abide the consequences.  With the measure that they have meted to others, it is measured to them again.  They have been long accustomed to do to us what the Pope and Cardinal Wiseman are now doing to them, and we shall be glad to find, when their alarm has subsided, that they have learned wisdom by the things they suffer.  We do not glory in their humiliation, but we cannot, of course, be expected to join their outcry or to sympathize with their feelings. If we had to chose between a Protestant and a Catholic hierarchy, we should not hesitate for one moment; but, as we are not reduced to this alternative, we leave the two parties to contend for supremacy, assured that we know ' a more excellent way.'

But the aggression of the Pope is ' insolent and insidious.'  So says the Premier ; and so say hundreds of the clergy, who now gladly re-echo the words of a man whom they have been accustomed to denounce and bitterly oppose.  That the mode of effecting the Papal object has been ' insolent,' we do not deny ; but that it has been ' insidious,' we cannot see.  It has been done openly, has been matter of protracted consideration, has grown out of, and was needful to the completion of, former measures, and was officially notified to the diplomatic envoy of the British Government.  If by 'insidious' be meant, that it is a stepping-stone to something else—that, in accordance with the policy of Rome, it will be appealed to, in coming times, in support of doctrines yet unavowed and claims unstated—that its end is political, though its phraseology is religious, and its object absolute and universal supremacy—then we should not except to such an application of the term. We believe the recent measure to be all this ; and would, therefore, oppose it with all the force which enlightened sense and religious conviction can supply.  This very consideration, however, renders us jealous of the ground we take.  The matter is too serious to be discussed in any other than a grave temper, and on principles .which will bear the strictest scrutiny.  We are threatened by a fearful peril. A monstrous error stares us in the face—one which exceeds all others, and against which the record of history is clear and unequivocal. The subtilty of this error is equalled only by its malignity. It can assume all garbs, can utter all forms of speech, can supplicate or threaten, talk the language of humility or the big-swelling words of pride. Such is the system which Cardinal Wiseman would re-introduce amongst us; and we are deeply anxious that the opposition he encounters, especially from Protestant Dissenters, should be sound in principle, and be based on durable ground.

That there should be differences of opinion amongst us on some points of the case, is not surprising. It has ever been so, and, for aught we see, may be expected to continue. The Papal is not so clearly and simply a question of religious liberty as that of other communities. The head of the Papal Church is a temporal prince, and his influence has often been employed to further his political ends. The priest has not unfrequently been subordinate to the king, while the awful sanctions of religion have been prostituted to mere secular ends. Hence the distinction made between Catholics and others by the earlier advocates of religious liberty; and, though this difference has been overlooked in modern legislation, it has not been wholly lost sight of by the most intelligent and discriminating advocates of freedom. This fact should suffice to make us pause ere we reflect on the consistency or rectitude of those who differ from us. Various views may well obtain amongst men whose intellect is equally unclouded, whose love of freedom is alike intense, and whose religious convictions are of the same masculine and practical character. Above all, it becomes us to abstain from censorious or harsh judgments on those of our friends, who unite to an intelligent and practical voluntaryism, what we deem a defective application of their principles to the Papal question.

Having thus noticed some unsatisfactory explanations of the existing excitement, we hasten very briefly to indicate the view that should be held, and the course taken, by Protestant Dissenters. We do not affect to judge for others. Such is not our vocation, and we have no wish to undertake it. Let each be fully persuaded in his own mind; but, as public journalists, we have a duty to discharge, to which we proceed without timidity or assumption.

In the first place, then, we say. Let Protestant Dissenters discard all reliance on mere legislative devices to meet the case which has arisen. Something will, no doubt, be done by Parliament; for our statesmen have marvellous faith in the wisdom and omnipotence of their decisions. Judging, however, from the prorogation of Parliament to the latest possible day, and from the feelers which have been put out by the ministerial press, we do not expect—notwithstanding the Premier's letter, and the Chancellor's Mansion-house speech—that much will be attempted in this way. To judge from present appearances, we look for little more than an act prohibiting the assumption, on the part of Catholic prelates, of territorial designations. Should it be so, a more ridiculous termination to a great national excitement cannot well be imagined. Our vanity may prevent our feeling the rebuke which such an issue will inflict : but the future historian, in detailing the events of our day, will expose with bitter scorn the folly and the littleness chargeable upon us. To prohibit the use of certain titles may pander to the pride of the Protestant clergy, but it will leave Popery just where it was, or rather it will give its members the advantage of a grievance real or supposed. How Lord John will reconcile such a measure with his declaration of 1846 we cannot imagine. His judgment was then distinct and unhesitating. 'As to preventing persons,' he said, ' assuming particular titles, nothing could be more absurd and puerile than to keep up such a distinction.' We leave his lordship to decide the matter of consistency for himself. Our vocation is to impress on our readers the folly of relying on legislative enactments in such a case. To whatever extent they do so, they will be bitterly disappointed. All history reads an instructive lesson on this point. There are other weapons more congenial to the contest, and to the skilful and vigorous use of these we must address ourselves.

It is scarcely necessary to add that we must be specially careful not to give countenance to the re-enactment of penal statutes. If we are not to rely on legislation for the defence of Protestantism, still less must we permit it to become the agent of persecution to the Catholics. Our principles demand this, and our own interests enforce it. We shall be traitors to the one, and the veriest idiots in creation in reference to the other, if we give the slightest sanction to the revival of a code attaching civil disabilities to religious opinions. We have no fear of any substantive or formal sanction being given by Protestant Dissenters to such a policy; but when we look at the tone which pervades the speeches delivered, and the memorials adopted, at many of the meetings now held, throughout the country, we are jealous of the mere presence of our friends lest their silence should be construed into approval. We have no fear of fines or imprisonment, of the suppression of conventicles, or even of the repeal of the Emancipation Act. We have outgrown all this. But there are other and more subtle forms of persecution, and against these we would have our friends specially to guard. Much as we abhor Popery, and firmly as we are persuaded that it is still the same bitter and persecuting thing it has ever been, we do verily believe that at this precise moment there is more danger ' to the religious and social liberties of Englishmen' from those who are endeavouring, 'to go back a step in the legislation of toleration,' than from the Cardinal and his hierarchy. But, however this may be, let every voluntary be on his guard, not to sanction, even by implication, the intolerant spirit so frequently and so offensively avowed. In perfect consistency with such a course, we may demand— and certainly should do so—that all grants of public money, whether to Maynooth College, or to Colonial ecclesiastics, be withdrawn. We have always protested against these, and may, therefore, fairly take advantage of passing events to reiterate and enforce our objection.

Again, let Protestant Dissenters maintain their own distinctive principles in their opposition to the Papacy. Our Dissenterism is our Protestantism. There is no real difference between them. We cannot hold one in abeyance, and yet act on the other. They stand or fall together. Hence the difficulty—to us, the impossibility—of acting with Churchmen in opposition to Popery. We yield to none in our hostility to it, and are resolved, come what may, to labor hard for its exposure and overthrow. But we must do this in our own way, and on our own principles. The Churchman cannot, in our judgment, fairly grapple with Popery, and in travelling with him, even for an hour, we feel shorn of our strength like Samson before the Philistines. Let each, then, take his own ground, unshackled by compromise, and unrestrained by what may be deemed due to the opinions or the prejudices of an associate. More service will thus be rendered to the common cause, and the consistency and rectitude of each will be best preserved.

Again, we may learn from what has happened, the unaltered temper of the Papal Church. It is of the last importance that Protestant Dissenters should do so, as, in their opposition to intolerance, they have been accustomed to speak of the more liberal policy of the Popedom. Great reliance has been placed on the spread of knowledge. A more tolerant and genuinely catholic spirit has been supposed to prevail. There has been a good deal of foolish talk on this matter. Our words have been expressive of our hopes rather than our knowledge. We have painted a fancy scene, which has been mistaken for reality. The truth, however, is now disclosed. We see facts as they are, and shall be amongst the most infatuated of mortals if we do not profit by them. It is impossible to read the Bull of the Pope, or the Pastoral of the Cardinal, without perceiving that the Papal Church is as arrogant and despotic as in former days, when she made kings tremble, and laid empires under interdict. Hildebrand himself could not claim more proudly ' the power of governing the universal church' than does Pius IX., just restored from exile by the soldiery of France, whilst Cardinal Wiseman, forgetting his policy in his priestly pride, tells us ' Catholic England has been restored to its orbit in the ecclesiastical firmament, from which its light had long vanished, and begins now anew its course of regularly-adjusted action round the centre of unity, the source of jurisdiction, of light and vigour.' Well may we say, ' We thank thee, Jew.' A more conclusive or emphatic disavowal of the hopes we had entertained cannot be imagined, and it will be well for us at once to apprehend the entire case, and to shape our course accordingly. We know that the tone and language of these documents have been vindicated, on the ground of their official character. 'Every official document has its proper forms,' says the Cardinal, referring to the Bull; 'and had those who blame the tenor of this taken any pains to examine those of Papal documents, they would have found nothing new or unusual in this.' We doubt not the fact; but the defence is, in our judgment, more damaging than the charge itself. So high-minded and arrogant is this Papal Church, that she will not bate one jot or tittle of her pretensions, even when her ruler is dependent on foreign bayonets, and the nation for which she assumes to legislate is so thoroughly Protestant as England. We cannot enlarge, for our space is completely exhausted.

In conclusion, we merely urge the counsel given in a former article, to study well, and thoroughly to master, the great controversy, which is evidently destined for some time to come to occupy much of our national attention. Protestant Dissenters have a great duty to perform, for the religious discharge of which, extensive research and profound thought are absolutely needful. May they be equal to the crisis, and be prompt, vigorous, and inflexible in the performance of their trust!

1

6

## Literary Intelligence.

### Just Published.

Popery in Power; or, the Spirit of the Vatican. To which is added, Priestcraft, or the Monarch of the Middle Ages. A Drama. By Joseph Townley.

Some Passages in the Life of a Convert from Anglo-Catholicism to the Truth as it is in Jesus. A Narrative of Facts. By R. C. J.

The Greek Church. A Sketch. By the Author of Proposals for Christian Union.

Game Birds and Wild Fowl; their friends and their foes. By A. E. Knox, M.A., F.L.S., author of Ornithological Rambles in Sussex.

The Imperial Cyclopædia: dedicated by permission to her Majesty; Cyclopædia of Geography. 1. The Geography of the British Empire. Parts 1—5.

Poems. By H. C. Bennett.

The Dynamical Theory of the Formation of the Earth. By Archibald Tucker Ritchie. 2 vols.

The Bards of the Bible. By George Gilfillan.

Conversations of Goethe with Eckermann and Soreh. Translated from the German by John Oxenford. 2 vols.

The Church a Family. Twelve Sermons on the occasional Services of the Prayer Book; preached in the Chapel of Lincoln's-inn. By Frederick Denison Maurice, M.A.

New and Popular History of England. By Robert Ferguson, LL.D. Vol. III.

A Practical Treatise on Musical Composition. By G. W. Röhner. Second Part—Counterpoint.

The Protestant Dissenter's Almanack for 1851.

The Financial Reform Almanack for 1851.

Dissent and the Papal Bull. 'No Intolerance,' a Response to the cry of 'No Popery.' By Newman Hall, B.A.

The Christian Faith no Fable; or, a plain and condensed View of the leading Arguments which prove the Divine Origin of Christianity. By Rev. R. Brown, Superintendent of the Liverpool Town Mission.

Physiology of Human Nature; being an Investigation of the physical and moral Condition of man, in his relation to the Inspired Word of God. By Robert Cross, M.D.

Stories for Summer Days and Winter Nights.

The Mother's Recompense; a Sequel to Home Influence. By Grace Aguilar.

The Family Economist. Vol. III.

The National Cyclopædia of Useful Knowledge. Part XLVII. Tree Cotton—Ural.

The Papal Invasion; how to defeat it. An Appeal to British Protestants. Dedicated to Lord John Russell, M.P. By James Carlile, D.D., Editor of the Protestant World.

The Pope and his Pretensions; a Discourse delivered at Wycliffe Chapel, 17th November, 1850. By Andrew Reed, D.D. Published by request.

Why must we educate the whole People? and what prevents our doing it? By Rev. Foster Barham Zincke, Vicar of Wherstead, near Ipswich.

A Letter to the Rev. E. B. Elliott, A.M., showing that his Exposition of the Seven Seals in his Horæ Apocalypticæ is without any solid foundation. By Rev. R. Gascoyne, A.M.

The Life and Epistles of St. Paul. Part X.

Lectures delivered at the Monthly United Service of the Nonconformist Churches in Nottingham, with other discourses preached on public occasions. By Samuel M'All, Minister of Castlegate Meeting House.

Select English Poetry, designed for the use of Schools, &c. Edited by the late Dr. Allen. Fifth Edition.

Prophetic Studies; or, Lectures on the Book of Daniel. By Rev. John Cumming, D.D.

The British Churches in relation to the British People. By Edward Miall. Second Edition.

The Illustrated Year Book. Second Series.

The Wonders, Events, and Discoveries of 1850. Edited by John Timbs.

Popish Infallibility. Letters to Viscount Fielding on his secession from the Church of England. By Charles Hastings Collette, Author of 'Romanism in England exposed.'

Romanism in England exposed. The Redemptionist Fathers of St. Mary's Convent, Park-road, Clapham. By Charles Hastings Collette. Second Edition.

Notes on the Cardinal's Manifesto, in a Letter to the Right Hon. Lord John Russell, her Majesty's Prime Minister. By Rev. John Cumming, D.D.

Protestant Popery; or, Lessons for the Times. By Henry Christopherson.

Plain Words to Plain People: the Dangers and Duties of the Free Churches of England in the present Crisis; a Discourse delivered in the Congregational Church, Kentish Town. By Rev. William Forster.

An Essay on the Science of Pronunciation. Dedicated to her Majesty.

Public Opinion the Queen of the World. By an Advocate of Consistency.

Voices from Prisons and Penitentiaries, respectfully addressed to the Patrons and Teachers of Sabbath Schools.

Secret Prayer, and its accompanying Exercises. By Rev. James M'Gill. Hightae, Lochmaleen. 3d edition.

Lyrics of the Heart; with other Poems. By Alaric A. Watts.

The Reasons of the Protestant Religion. By John Pye Smith, D.D.

The Ladies of the Covenant. Memoirs of Distinguished Scottish Female Characters, embracing the period of the covenant and the persecution. By Rev. James Anderson.

Family Prayers, adapted to portions of the Holy Writings, and chiefly based on the Commentaries of the Rev. Thomas Scott. 3 vols. By William Burt Whitmarsh.

Missionary Addresses, delivered before the General Assembly of the Church of Scotland in the years 1835, 1837, 1839; with additional papers on Female Education, and the Danish, or earlier Protestant Mission to India. By Alexander Duff, D.D.

Home Organization for Foreign Missions. Being the substance of an Address delivered before the Commission of the General Assembly of the Free Church of Scotland. Nov. 20, 1850. By Alexander Duff, D.D.

# 128 LITERARY INTELLIGENCE.

Sunday Services at Home, for Young Children. By different authors. Edited by the Countess of Ducie.

No Popery: a Course of Eight Sermons Preached at the Episcopal Jews Chapel, Palestine Place, Bethnal Green. By Rev. J. B. Cartwright, M.A.

Pleasant Pages for Young People. Part VI.

Excise Duty on Paper: a Letter to the Right Hon. Lord John Russell, M.P., from a Paper Maker.

The Papal Panic: a Sermon delivered in the Baptist Chapel, Hemel Hempsted, December 1, 1850. By W. S. M. Aitchison.

The Reformer's Almanack and Political Year Book, 1851.

The Duties of Dissenters in the present Crisis: a Lecture delivered at the New Hall, Reading, December 6, 1850. By John Jenkyn Brown.

The Two Rocks, Christ or Peter. By Rev. Alexander M'Caul, D.D.

Why does the Church of Rome hide the Second Commandment from the People? a Tract. By Rev. Alexander M'Caul, D.D.

A Tract of Future Times, for the Reflection of Posterity, on the Excitement, Hypocrisy, and Idolatry, of the 19th Century. By Robert Hovenden.

Instruction for Young Enquirers; being a Series of Addresses intended to explain and enforce the leading Doctrines of the Word of God. By W. Innes, D.D. 7th edition.

The True Church, showing what is the True Church; the Ingathering of the Jews to the Church—in what manner, and when; the Course of the Church; the Past, the Present, and the Future. By James Biden.

The Chronological New Testament, in which the Text of the Authorized Version is new, divided by Paragraphs and Sections, &c.

The Henderson Prize Essay upon the Advantages of the Sabbath, when rightly observed, to literary and professional men. By Peter Young Black, Writer, Glasgow.

The Sunday School Union Magazine. Vol. VII.

The Bible Class Magazine. Vol. III.

A Dictionary of Scripture Proper Names, with their Pronunciations and Explanations.

The Child's Own Book. New Series.

The Juvenile Harmonist: a Selection of Tunes and Pieces for Children, arranged for two trebles and a bass. By Thomas Clark, of Canterbury.

The Sunday School Teacher's Class Register and Diary for 1851.

The Union Spelling and Reading Book, containing Lessons chiefly extracted from the Holy Scriptures, and a Dictionary of Scripture Proper Names.

Notes on the Scripture Lessons for 1850.

Christian Baptism; or, the Baptism of Christ. Do the Christian Churches generally entertain sound Scriptural views respecting it?

Ecclesiastical Pretensions, Romish and English, with the antidote which a Catholic Protestantism supplies. A Tract for the Times: being a Sermon preached in Renshaw-street Chapel, Liverpool, Sunday, November 17, 1850. By John Hamilton Thom.

Memorials of Augustus Neander. Translated from the German by William Farrer, LL.B., late Student in the University of Berlin.

A Plea for Romanizers (so called) in the Anglican Communion; a Letter to the Right Hon. and Right Rev. the Lord Bishop of London. By Rev. Arthur Baker, M.A.

THE

# 𝕰clectic 𝕽eview.

## FEBRUARY, 1851.

Art. I.—*An Inquiry into the Establishment of the Royal Academy of Arts. To which is prefixed a Letter to the Earl of Bute.* By Robert Strange (1775). Edited by William Coningham. London: Olivers. 1850.

Of our social monopolies, the Royal Academy is among the worst. So long as it exists in its present form art must suffer under a degrading oppression. It is a private society, assuming the pretensions of a public body; or it is a public body disdaining responsibility. In either case it appears under a false character. It is neither, by its practice, a national institution for the advancement of art, nor, by its position, a private association established to promote private interests. It is not an academy of art; but a society of artists, arrogating sovereignty over a whole class. As such it exercises only an unjust and injurious influence. From its commencement it has been worse than useless to the country. It was at first formed to flatter a private scheme; its constitution was modelled to suit personal views; and to this day, in the operation of its system, it continues to be a monopoly supported by the many, but advantageous only to the few. That these remarks may not be misconceived, we shall concisely sketch the history and character of the Royal Academy.

Exactly a hundred years ago there existed a small society of artists possessing an academy in St. Martin's Lane. It was an exclusive body, but as a private association had a right to be so, for it attempted to exercise no public influence. At the same time, another society, animated by a more liberal spirit, collected a considerable fund, projected an institution for the promotion of art, and proposed a coalition with the elder body. That company, inspired by a feeling akin to that which animates the present academy, refused any concession which should open its honours to competition. Mediocrity then, as now, feared to compete with genius. At length, however, after ten years' struggle, an exhibition was opened, some young men of talent were introduced before the public, emulation was excited, and the arts promised to revive under the influence of a popular system. All the while, however, a committee of artists was meditating a plan of complete monopoly. The conspiracy flourished; regular advances were made towards despotism, and abuses thickened in the management of the association. At length some liberal members became alarmed, and resolved to protect the arts by procuring a public charter. In January, 1765, the charter was signed, but, being royal, it favoured oligarchy. It granted power, but imposed no responsibility. The association was as despotic as before.

Two years later, a resolution was carried by the society that 'a public academy' should be established. Now, however, private influence interfered. Dalton, the king's librarian, who was treasurer of the association, possessed a building in Pall Mall, where he projected an exhibition of prints. The scheme failed when all the expense was incurred. He applied to the king for relief from the burden. 'His majesty' promised to promote a job for his obsequious servant. The idea of a 'public academy' was set aside, and 'a royal academy' was graciously lodged in the print warehouse, especially for Dalton's profit. Guinea subscriptions were raised. Everything was played into the manager's hands, and the society went on well. A few accidents occurred, with quarrels innumerable among the members, but these were obstacles easily overcome. Ultimately, the association settled into form, a new Draconic code was compiled, and the Royal Academy proclaimed its readiness to govern all the painters and sculptors in the country.

We say painters and sculptors, because engravers were excluded. But why? Because, said the academicians, engravers were servile copiers—men of no genius.* This reason, how-

* Consult the opinions of Albert Durer, Andrea Mantagena, Marc Antonio, Parmigiano, Salvator Rosa, Annibali Caracci, Agostino Caracci, Guido, Guercino, Cantarini da Pesaro, the Siranis, Rubens, Rembrandt, Dorigny, and other eminent artists, who not only *respected*, but *practised*, the art of engraving; Raffaele also esteemed it in the highest degree. We have to choose between the decisions of these illustrious men, and that of the Royal Academy!

ever, was only alleged after they had relinquished two others. The first was because 'they had copied this part of their institution, which regarded the exclusion of engravers, from the Royal Academy of Painting at Paris:' thus pleading guilty to the servile copying they affected to despise. But the engraver Strange was then a member of the academy they copied. The next excuse was, that the Academy of St. Luke at Rome admitted no engravers. The engraver Strange was then a member of it, as well as of the academies of Paris, France, Bologna, and Parma.

The real cause of exclusion was a private hatred entertained by the king and his noble parasites against the engraver Strange. That artist, at a time when his hands were completely full of engagements, had declined to paint, for a paltry sum, two whole-length portraits—the one of 'his Majesty,' the other of the Earl of Bute. This offence was fatal to his career in England. When he travelled on the continent, a low spy was set to track him, to prevent the depositories of ancient art being opened to him, to baulk all his plans, to copy the very pictures he wished to copy, to slander him, and deface his unblemished reputation. Disreputable intrigues were excited against him. Persons high in office condescended to utter falsehoods, to please the king and persecute his victim. The fame of Strange—universal on the continent—was almost shut out of England, or damaged by paid critics, and this able artist was ruined by 'a great patron of art' in his own country.

The Royal Academy, planted under the shade of a palace, obsequiously followed its instructions. It excluded engravers—it made a hecatomb of victims in order to satisfy upon one individual the vindictive feeling of 'Majesty.' But while this persecuted man, whose prospects were blasted by the low malignity of a court, was compelled to look abroad for the encouragement he deserved at home, the Academy opened its arms to a foreign engraver of inferior talent, exhibited his works, and honoured him with its finest pearls of patronage. A body of men, professedly educated, claiming consideration as gentlemen, confident in their own merits, secure in their own distinctions, consented, in order to gratify the malice of a king upon one person, to throw contempt upon a whole class. Was it honourable, was it English, was it civilized? But it was—we hear it said—the act of men living in the barbarous age of George III., when royal influence was powerful in the country. Much may be allowed for the savage state of the times. Is the case, however, improved at the present day?

Six 'associate engravers' are indeed admitted, but on humiliating terms. Insulting distinctions are made between them and the superior members. They are excluded from every

K 2

advantage and honour of the Academy, rendered incapable of reaching the higher degrees, and patronized in terms of supercilious impertinence. Genius, in general, revolts from servility, and by imposing the necessity of it the Academy sought to effect its aim, by excluding great engravers.

Subservient as we, as a nation, are to court fashions, we nevertheless honour and support the engraver. Public taste, in some degree, compensates for the private influence of the Academy. Engraving is the most popular branch of art. It is not servile copying. The artist who can re-produce on a thousand plates the reflection of Raffaele's genius, is himself a man of genius. His art should be encouraged as one which ensures the productions of a master's pencil from altogether perishing by accident; which opens the Vatican ·to all the world, unlocks the cabinet of the Italian connoisseur, and places within reach of every eye, the paintings that adorn the walls of churches in the South. In some manner, indeed, it compensates for that monopoly of the gems of art which must always be enjoyed by the opulent. That it shuts out the engraver, therefore, from the honours to which he has a claim, is an important charge against the Royal Academy. Can a greater anomaly be imagined? An institution, professedly erected to encourage art, endeavours to depreciate and destroy a branch of it.

The society consists of forty 'Academicians.' They are supposed to be the distinguished artists of the day. But if, in her prolific birth of genius, the age were to produce eighty such men, of course, says common sense, they would be admitted. By no means. Neither common sense nor justice has to decide in the matter, but the Academy. By law we are compelled to recognise, publicly, only forty able artists. Among foreigners, as well as among the unsophisticated classes in this country, Peter Smith, R.A., is a great man, while plain Thomas Robinson, without the magical initials, is nobody. The idea is prevalent with many thousands, that any able artist is sure to be admitted as an academician, and some innocent persons actually disdain the productions of all but the mystic forty. Such, indeed, is the general opinion of those who are unacquainted with the details of this enormous monopoly. The injury thus inflicted on art, the injustice perpetrated against artists, is incalculable.

When we reflect on it, it is difficult to conceive why the public has so long tolerated this abuse. Forty men, possessing absolute control over their own body, and owning no responsibility to country, are allowed to appropriate all the recognised nours of art; every artist of distinguished talent, exceeding that number, must be made the victim of this selfish spirit; we confess ourselves so poor that forty painters and sculptors represent all our excellence; persons of the highest genius may be excluded by the votes of a clique; individuals of low capacity may be thrust above their superiors; the public pays for this abuse, and possesses no power of reforming it. Such is a sample of the civilization we are to exhibit this year for the contemplation of ' unsophisticated foreigners.'

'Had the Academy,' says Strange, in the pamphlet in which he records his persecutions, ' comprehended all the arts and all the respectable artists of this country, and attracted distinguished artists from other parts of Europe—had it exhibited annually, and gratis, to all the lovers of the fine arts, the best works of the members only (as in other Academies), and excluded whatever was unworthy of public attention—in that case the exhibition would have been a sight that would have charmed the public, inflamed that affection towards the arts which was rising here, produced rewards and honours to artists, raised their emulation, distinguished this country and these times, and set a lasting and honourable mark on "his Majesty's" reign. (It needed one.) But, alas! all such exalted ideas have been swallowed up in contracted, mean, selfish plans, which in any country of the world, and under any patronage whatever, will as certainly depress the fine arts, as it is certain a great artist will detest whatever is dirty and mean.

' Accordingly, we see annually a Royal Exhibition collecting shillings at the door, in order to raise money, and the Academicians going about the town, beating up, as it were, for recruits, to rake together a sufficient number of pictures to cover their naked walls, forced thereby to admit many performances disgraceful to the place and to the occasion, and instead of exhibiting a few capital pictures by their best hands they have often introduced so many by the same master as to satiate the spectators.'

Forty individuals, therefore, monopolize all the advantages and honours of the Royal Academy. When a vacancy occurs it is supplied from the body of twenty associates. Genius is no claim. It is not the public voice that decides—it is the private choice of a majority among the Academicians themselves. An artist may fill Europe with his fame; may command the admiration of the most distinguished men; may produce pictures which rival those of Rubens and Claude ; but these recommendations are not enough. Another painter may possess wealth, live in a handsome house, enjoy the favour of a few dog-fancying noblemen, flatter the R.A.'s, and ' creep up their sleeves' by those alluring arts which servility is so skilful to employ. He, therefore, is a star of the first magnitude by the side of his honest competitor whose genius is his only claim. This system must continue as long as the mystic number forty is adhered to.

There are, say the laws of the Academy, to be no more than forty distinguished artists. Other institutions, indeed, can receive those whom the Academy rejects ; but the artist who applies to them suffers a species of outlawry. To enjoy a chance of welcome from this insolent corporation, the artist must refuse all other offers of distinction, throw away every opportunity, and meekly await the pleasure of the Royal Academicians. If this be royal patronage of art, literature may well be thankful that it has escaped the pernicious favour.

Thus, this Academy, we repeat, enjoying inviolable privacy within the walls of a public building, arrogates to itself every honourable degree of art, and the man of true genius who has no means of conciliating the Forty Academicians, suffers under neglect. The same plan, on a still more extravagant scale, is pursued with respect to the 'associates,' the corps of reserve from which the Academicians recruit their ranks. Twenty fortunate individuals thus occupy the porch of the Academy, secure of admission, each in his turn. They are the friends, relatives, or protégés of the patrician order, to which the artist class in this country obsequiously submits. Meanwhile the multitude remains without, and once in the course of years a single individual is pulled in by a side door. A more absurd system it is impossible to conceive. At the election which took place on the 4th of November last, there were fifty candidates. They did not, however, represent the number of those who claimed admittance. Many, disgusted by frequent failures, refused to be nominated again. Of those that stood, some were men of exalted genius, and had long enjoyed a high reputation in the country. Others were young artists of promise. One of these was elected, leaving the rest, for the most part, hopeless of ever winning the prize.

The first picture exhibited by this young man, procured for him, we believe, a gold medal. He was thus preferred before men of established reputation, who possessed an undoubted claim to these restricted honours. Why was this? We have been at the pains to discover the reason. It is because a certain princely personage considers that mature talent should take care of itself, and that it is proper to encourage the young.* It may be well to foster the ability of youth ; but it can never be necessary or politic to encourage the young by acting unjustly to their seniors in age, and their superiors in genius. Landscape-paint-

---

* When the Westminster-hall exhibition competitions were first projected, the Academicians repudiated the idea altogether, and were quite indignant at the notion of competing with 'little boys.' A short time after, when Jove had nodded, these very 'little boys,' these untutored tyros, were elected, to the exclusion of all other artists.

ing enjoys no longer the honours of the Royal Academy. The painters of portraits, who contribute so greatly to the attraction of the yearly exhibition, are excluded. Eleven years have passed since one was elected. True art is thrown aside, the talent which has been matured by years of study; the men whose names have become household words among the admirers of genius, are neglected, that juvenile ' history painters '—the gold-medal pets of promise—may be adorned by the favours of these Forty Bishops of Art. A single clever little picture, painted by one of the class which a prince desires to elevate, will crown any young artist with the glories of academic patronage. Honours crowd on him when he has scarcely acquired the use of his palette. Meanwhile the mature artists finish their pictures, exhibit them, and fill the coffers of the society with the shillings paid for a view of their productions.

This is the system of the Forty. But why do they not act like honest men, declare their desire of monopoly, and close their doors entirely. It would be more manly than cajoling the public by an annual election of one out of hundreds. But if we may offer a hint to the artist class, we advise them to repudiate the Academy, as the Academy repudiates them. Let them withdraw altogether from it, refuse to send their pictures, establish a national academy, solicit the patronage of that nobility of genius which is rapidly outrivalling the nobility of birth, and declare themselves independent of the pernicious oligarchy. Let them form a league, petition Parliament for a public charter, and erect an institution of their own. The idea has already been broached. We trust to see it take root. There are men of the first genius, not belonging to the present society, who would at once render illustrious, not a royal, but a national academy. Let them combine, and then let their enemies conspire. We believe we may answer for our readers that they would support the new, and abandon the old institution; for the National Academy would found itself on love of the arts, while the Royal Academy has been established for the benefit of forty artists. Let us concisely sum up its offences against common sense, justice, and the arts it pretends to promote.

This institution, numbering forty members, is the only recognised one in the country. Professing to rely on royal munificence, it levies thousands a year on the public. Existing on these contributions, it monopolizes for its own purposes the power, patronage, and revenue, gained by exhibiting the works of unprivileged artists. It proclaims it an offence to exhibit with any other society. It excludes engravers, although originally composed of historical, landscape, portrait, miniature, enamel, flower, and coach-painters; die engravers, chasers,

architects, sculptors, and a bricklayer to the Board of Ordnance. It occupies a public building, and exercises public functions, but is not subject to public control. Its own members are allowed to retouch and varnish their own pictures before the annual dinner given to foreign favourites, while unprivileged artists are not. It occupies half the room originally intended for the national collection, and makes the public no concessions in return. Above all, it exercises a tyranny over artists, enjoys the power of shutting its gates against genius, and holds out its honours only as the reward of servility.

When the period for the annual exhibition arrives, each of the forty oligarchs erects his crest. The members of the council then walk lords of the ascendant. They possess, with their brethren, the right of exhibiting eight pictures each, all 'on the line.' Their private friends, of course, are accommodated with the 'next best' places, their *protegés* in order; and the vulgar herd wherever there is room for them. Thus we have seen a ragged cur, the work of a notorious animal-painter, displayed in extravagant prominence on 'the line,' while a classical land-scape, enriched by every beauty, has been removed almost beyond reach of sight. The reader must not imagine these things to be the result of accident. On the contrary, private deliberations are held on the subject. The conclave assembles in its private chamber, under the roof, be it remembered, of a public building. This artist is to be favoured by a place near the line, where his five feet square of canvass may glare in the spectator's face, covered, perhaps, with blazes, smoke, walls, towers, armies, and clouds; a second is accommodated midway between roof and ceiling, where all his linear and aerial per-spective are lost to view. Another is triumphantly driven to a dim corner near the ceiling, where the gilt frame is all that can attract the eye. It is true that scores of yards of the painted canvass exhibited could be nowhere better placed than out of sight, but, unfortunately, it is ability which is chiefly persecuted. Genius, we repeat, refuses to be servile, and nothing less is required by this oligarchy of the arts. As the one is an order of despots, so the other is an order either of slaves or outlaws.

When men do evil, it is an old saying, and an obvious truth, that they lack either sense or honesty. We acquit the Acade-micians of folly. There is a deep purpose in their policy. In arranging the pictures for exhibition they fortify their monopoly. The public, visiting the Academy, pays attention to those pro-ductions of art within reach of its hundred eyes. But the public is a lordly power; it will not strain its sight to view pictures perched twenty feet above the floor; consequently, all the critical chit-chat is lavished on the paintings exhibited ' on

the line.' The R. A.'s monopolize all the exclamations of, ' How very fine !' ' Beautiful !' ' Really, beats nature !' ' Talk of the decline of the arts !' with which innocent old gentlemen and young ladies express their admiration of the favoured works. This gossip is circulated, a sort of public opinion is set afloat, and while the R. A.'s become the favourites of the tea-table and the drawing-room-rug, the unprivileged painter attains little of the notice he deserves. His landscape, shaded by the ceiling, is lost in mist; his figures, unless they command attention by their ghastly whiteness and herculean size, are disregarded ; and his ' faces' look all awry from the awkward position in which they are placed. The critics of many among the daily and weekly journals are conquered by the academic plan ; their nobility will not, or cannot, discover the merits of any pictures placed above the level of their eyes, and thus a flagrant injustice is committed against the class of unprivileged artists. Lost in an ocean of gold frames and canvass, some gem is utterly unnoticed, the modest merits of truth and delicacy attract no regard, and the painter, in despair, endeavours to enforce attention by the colossal magnitude of his work. He dazzles the eye with flaming colours and mountains of flesh ; his plan succeeds, his picture attracts the visitor's eye ; his example is followed, and thus, year after year, art degenerates, and artists become the ministers to a corrupt and capricious taste.

This leads us to consider the condition of art in England. A glance at the exhibitions of the Academy displays the result of academic teaching. A majestic tone and a lofty style are confined to the few. Chastity and truth yield to the meretricious attractions of ' effect.' Nature is caricatured into absurdity ; instead of grandeur, we have pomposity ; instead of beauty, *fâde* sentimentality. One great sign of degeneracy is the poverty of invention—the meanness of taste displayed by our modern artists. Year after year a few stock subjects are tortured in eternal repetition. Lear and Cordelia are among the unhappy historical personages doomed to an annual caricature. In one famous representation of Shakspeare's scene, the two elder sisters are depicted dark as the darkest daughters of the South ; while the third, with flaxen ringlets, bleached almost to whiteness, stands in such contrast with them, that by no possibility could the same woman have been the mother of the three.

Elizabeth at Kenilworth is another favourite subject. The Knight of La Mancha, Sancho Panza, and the Duchess, usually meet the eye a score of times. The rueful countenance, the lanthorn jaw, the broad face of the squire, and the lively beauty of her ladyship, are all properly reproduced, according to rule, in precisely the place and the attitude laid down by the laws of

architects, sculptors, and a bricklayer to the Board of Ordnance. It occupies a public building, and exercises public functions, but is not subject to public control. Its own members are allowed to retouch and varnish their own pictures before the annual dinner given to foreign favourites, while unprivileged artists are not. It occupies half the room originally intended for the national collection, and makes the public no concessions in return. Above all, it exercises a tyranny over artists, enjoys the power of shutting its gates against genius, and holds out its honours only as the reward of servility.

When the period for the annual exhibition arrives, each of the forty oligarchs erects his crest. The members of the council then walk lords of the ascendant. They possess, with their brethren, the right of exhibiting eight pictures each, all ' on the line.' Their private friends, of course, are accommodated with the ' next best' places, their *protegés* in order; and the vulgar herd wherever there is room for them. Thus we have seen a ragged cur, the work of a notorious animal-painter, displayed in extravagant prominence on ' the line,' while a classical land-scape, enriched by every beauty, has been removed almost beyond reach of sight. The reader must not imagine these things to be the result of accident. On the contrary, private deliberations are held on the subject. The conclave assembles in its private chamber, under the roof, be it remembered, of a public building. This artist is to be favoured by a place near the line, where his five feet square of canvass may glare in the spectator's face, covered, perhaps, with blazes, smoke, walls, towers, armies, and clouds; a second is accommodated midway between roof and ceiling, where all his linear and aerial per-spective are lost to view. Another is triumphantly driven to a dim corner near the ceiling, where the gilt frame is all that can attract the eye. It is true that scores of yards of the painted canvass exhibited could be nowhere better placed than out of sight, but, unfortunately, it is ability which is chiefly persecuted. Genius, we repeat, refuses to be servile, and nothing less is required by this oligarchy of the arts. As the one is an order of despots, so the other is an order either of slaves or outlaws.

When men do evil, it is an old saying, and an obvious truth, that they lack either sense or honesty. We acquit the Acade-micians of folly. There is a deep purpose in their policy. In arranging the pictures for exhibition they fortify their monopoly. The public, visiting the Academy, pays attention to those pro-ductions of art within reach of its hundred eyes. But the public is a lordly power; it will not strain its sight to view pictures perched twenty feet above the floor; consequently, all the critical chit-chat is lavished on the paintings exhibited ' on

the line.' The R. A.'s monopolize all the exclamations of,. ' How very fine!' 'Beautiful!' 'Really, beats nature!' 'Talk of the decline of the arts!' with which innocent old gentlemen and young ladies express their admiration of the favoured works. This gossip is circulated, a sort of public opinion is set afloat, and while the R. A.'s become the favourites of the tea-table and the drawing-room-rug, the unprivileged painter attains little of the notice he deserves. His landscape, shaded by the ceiling, is lost in mist; his figures, unless they command attention by their ghastly whiteness and herculean size, are disregarded; and his 'faces' look all awry from the awkward position in which they are placed. The critics of many among the daily and weekly journals are conquered by the academic plan; their nobility will not, or cannot, discover the merits of any pictures placed above the level of their eyes, and thus a flagrant injustice is committed against the class of unprivileged artists. Lost in an ocean of gold frames and canvass, some gem is utterly unnoticed, the modest merits of truth and delicacy attract no regard, and the painter, in despair, endeavours to enforce attention by the colossal magnitude of his work. He dazzles the eye with flaming colours and mountains of flesh; his plan succeeds, his picture attracts the visitor's eye; his example is followed, and thus, year after year, art degenerates, and artists become the ministers to a corrupt and capricious taste.

This leads us to consider the condition of art in England. A glance at the exhibitions of the Academy displays the result of academic teaching. A majestic tone and a lofty style are confined to the few. Chastity and truth yield to the meretricious attractions of 'effect.' Nature is caricatured into absurdity; instead of grandeur, we have pomposity; instead of beauty, fâde sentimentality. One great sign of degeneracy is the poverty of invention—the meanness of taste displayed by our modern artists. Year after year a few stock subjects are tortured in eternal repetition. Lear and Cordelia are among the unhappy historical personages doomed to an annual caricature. In one famous representation of Shakspeare's scene, the two elder sisters are depicted dark as the darkest daughters of the South; while the third, with flaxen ringlets, bleached almost to whiteness, stands in such contrast with them, that by no possibility could the same woman have been the mother of the three.

Elizabeth at Kenilworth is another favourite subject. The Knight of La Mancha, Sancho Panza, and the Duchess, usually meet the eye a score of times. The rueful countenance, the lanthorn jaw, the broad face of the squire, and the lively beauty of her ladyship, are all properly reproduced, according to rule, in precisely the place and the attitude laid down by the laws of

architects, sculptors, and a bricklayer to the Board of Ordnance. It occupies a public building, and exercises public functions, but is not subject to public control.   Its own members are allowed to retouch and varnish their own pictures before the annual dinner given to foreign favourites, while unprivileged artists are not.   It occupies half the room originally intended for the national collection, and makes the public no concessions in return.   Above all, it exercises a tyranny over artists, enjoys the power of shutting its gates against genius, and holds out its honours only as the reward of servility.

When the period for the annual exhibition arrives, each of the forty oligarchs erects his crest.   The members of the council then walk lords of the ascendant.   They possess, with their brethren, the right of exhibiting eight pictures each, all 'on the line.'   Their private friends, of course, are accommodated with the 'next best' places, their *protegés* in order; and the vulgar herd wherever there is room for them.   Thus we have seen a ragged cur, the work of a notorious animal-painter, displayed in extravagant prominence on 'the line,' while a classical land-scape, enriched by every beauty, has been removed almost beyond reach of sight.   The reader must not imagine these things to be the result of accident.   On the contrary, private deliberations are held on the subject.   The conclave assembles in its private chamber, under the roof, be it remembered, of a public building.   This artist is to be favoured by a place near the line, where his five feet square of canvass may glare in the spectator's face, covered, perhaps, with blazes, smoke, walls, towers, armies, and clouds; a second is accommodated midway between roof and ceiling, where all his linear and aerial per-spective are lost to view.   Another is triumphantly driven to a dim corner near the ceiling, where the gilt frame is all that can attract the eye.   It is true that scores of yards of the painted canvass exhibited could be nowhere better placed than out of sight, but, unfortunately, it is ability which is chiefly persecuted. Genius, we repeat, refuses to be servile, and nothing less is required by this oligarchy of the arts.   As the one is an order of despots, so the other is an order either of slaves or outlaws.

When men do evil, it is an old saying, and an obvious truth, that they lack either sense or honesty.   We acquit the Acade-micians of folly.   There is a deep purpose in their policy.   In arranging the pictures for exhibition they fortify their monopoly. The public, visiting the Academy, pays attention to those pro-ductions of art within reach of its hundred eyes.   But the public is a lordly power; it will not strain its sight to view pictures perched twenty feet above the floor; consequently, all the critical chit-chat is lavished on the paintings exhibited ' on

the line.' The R. A.'s monopolize all the exclamations of, 'How very fine!' 'Beautiful!' 'Really, beats nature!' 'Talk of the decline of the arts!' with which innocent old gentlemen and young ladies express their admiration of the favoured works. This gossip is circulated, a sort of public opinion is set afloat, and while the R. A.'s become the favourites of the tea-table and the drawing-room-rug, the unprivileged painter attains little of the notice he deserves. His landscape, shaded by the ceiling, is lost in mist; his figures, unless they command attention by their ghastly whiteness and herculean size, are disregarded; and his 'faces' look all awry from the awkward position in which they are placed. The critics of many among the daily and weekly journals are conquered by the academic plan; their nobility will not, or cannot, discover the merits of any pictures placed above the level of their eyes, and thus a flagrant injustice is committed against the class of unprivileged artists. Lost in an ocean of gold frames and canvass, some gem is utterly unnoticed, the modest merits of truth and delicacy attract no regard, and the painter, in despair, endeavours to enforce attention by the colossal magnitude of his work. He dazzles the eye with flaming colours and mountains of flesh; his plan succeeds, his picture attracts the visitor's eye; his example is followed, and thus, year after year, art degenerates, and artists become the ministers to a corrupt and capricious taste.

This leads us to consider the condition of art in England. A glance at the exhibitions of the Academy displays the result of academic teaching. A majestic tone and a lofty style are confined to the few. Chastity and truth yield to the meretricious attractions of 'effect.' Nature is caricatured into absurdity; instead of grandeur, we have pomposity; instead of beauty, *fâde* sentimentality. One great sign of degeneracy is the poverty of invention—the meanness of taste displayed by our modern artists. Year after year a few stock subjects are tortured in eternal repetition. Lear and Cordelia are among the unhappy historical personages doomed to an annual caricature. In one famous representation of Shakspeare's scene, the two elder sisters are depicted dark as the darkest daughters of the South; while the third, with flaxen ringlets, bleached almost to whiteness, stands in such contrast with them, that by no possibility could the same woman have been the mother of the three.

Elizabeth at Kenilworth is another favourite subject. The Knight of La Mancha, Sancho Panza, and the Duchess, usually meet the eye a score of times. The rueful countenance, the lanthorn jaw, the broad face of the squire, and the lively beauty of her ladyship, are all properly reproduced, according to rule, in precisely the place and the attitude laid down by the laws of

custom. From the romance of Spain we take flight to the fables of ancient Greece. Venus and Adonis invariably request the attention of our eyes. The goddess of beauty, sometimes as a southern gipsy, sometimes as an Irish milk-maid, sometimes as a free-and-easy London belle, but very rarely as the embodiment of the Grecian ideal of beauty, wooes Adonis, who usually resembles one of the swains in the 'Gentle Shepherd.' The Lady of the Lake always affords a few scenes; while the Tempest contributes a fantastic Ariel and a Miranda, with hair like dried flax. Lady Macbeth is equally constant in her attention, but under an infinity of aspects. We believe a year never passes without introducing to us Malvolio, 'the trout that must be caught with tickling,' practising behaviour to his own shadow.

Of the humbler description of the Wilkie school the productions are very numerous. Boys sliding, playing marbles on their forms, eating large pies, catching shrimps, ringing doorbells, and making small attempts at the fine arts, are scattered in profusion over the walls. In contrast with these a number of maidens bathing exhibit the eccentric tastes of our artists on the subject of flesh tints. Some delight in skins as white as Dover cliffs; some cause the modest damsel to blush from head to feet, reminding us of the old epigram—

> ' Fabius, you say, is much inclined
>    His cheeks with too much red to fill—
> His pictures only blush to find
>    The painter does his task so ill.'

Others present figures which appear to have been moulded in wax; while a fourth class tinges the flesh with a blue, unhealthy tint, almost approaching the symptoms of cholera morbus. In the colour of the hair we have strange tastes displayed. The hue of brass is now a general favourite. Auburn is out of fashion. The rich golden brown, flushed, as it were, with light, has almost wholly disappeared. That exquisite appearance of floating massy tresses has been replaced by saffron-coloured 'bands' of hair plastered down with pomatum; so that even Pallas Athene and Venus appear to have used ' *bandoline fixature*.' The blue-eyed goddess is generally a mimicry of that conventional allegorical personage, Britannia, who was herself at first a plagiarism of the Grecian mythology. To complete the modern ideal of beauty, we have the sleepy eye of the ' mournful,' the ' broken-hearted,' and the ' lovely,' with the upturned nose and low brows of the ' pensive,' or the ' scornful;' and portraits of ' ladies,' with half-exposed busts, tight-waisted dresses, and all the other indecent and ungraceful appendages of the line.' The R. A.'s monopolize all the exclamations of, ' How very fine !' ' Beautiful !' ' Really, beats nature !' ' Talk of the decline of the arts !' with which innocent old gentlemen and young ladies express their admiration of the favoured works. This gossip is circulated, a sort of public opinion is set afloat, and while the R. A.'s become the favourites of the tea-table and the drawing-room-rug, the unprivileged painter attains little of the notice he deserves. His landscape, shaded by the ceiling, is lost in mist; his figures, unless they command attention by their ghastly whiteness and herculean size, are disregarded; and his ' faces' look all awry from the awkward position in which they are placed. The critics of many among the daily and weekly journals are conquered by the academic plan; their nobility will not, or cannot, discover the merits of any pictures placed above the level of their eyes, and thus a flagrant injustice is committed against the class of unprivileged artists. Lost in an ocean of gold frames and canvass, some gem is utterly unnoticed, the modest merits of truth and delicacy attract no regard, and the painter, in despair, endeavours to enforce attention by the colossal magnitude of his work. He dazzles the eye with flaming colours and mountains of flesh; his plan succeeds, his picture attracts the visitor's eye; his example is followed, and thus, year after year, art degenerates, and artists become the ministers to a corrupt and capricious taste.

This leads us to consider the condition of art in England. A glance at the exhibitions of the Academy displays the result of academic teaching. A majestic tone and a lofty style are confined to the few. Chastity and truth yield to the meretricious attractions of ' effect.' Nature is caricatured into absurdity; instead of grandeur, we have pomposity; instead of beauty, *fâde* sentimentality. One great sign of degeneracy is the poverty of invention—the meanness of taste displayed by our modern artists. Year after year a few stock subjects are tortured in eternal repetition. Lear and Cordelia are among the unhappy historical personages doomed to an annual caricature. In one famous representation of Shakspeare's scene, the two elder sisters are depicted dark as the darkest daughters of the South; while the third, with flaxen ringlets, bleached almost to whiteness, stands in such contrast with them, that by no possibility could the same woman have been the mother of the three.

Elizabeth at Kenilworth is another favourite subject. The Knight of La Mancha, Sancho Panza, and the Duchess, usually meet the eye a score of times. The rueful countenance, the lanthorn jaw, the broad face of the squire, and the lively beauty of her ladyship, are all properly reproduced, according to rule, in precisely the place and the attitude laid down by the laws of

custom. From the romance of Spain we take flight to the fables of ancient Greece. Venus and Adonis invariably request the attention of our eyes. The goddess of beauty, sometimes as a southern gipsy, sometimes as an Irish milk-maid, sometimes as a free-and-easy London belle, but very rarely as the embodiment of the Grecian ideal of beauty, wooes Adonis, who usually resembles one of the swains in the 'Gentle Shepherd.' The Lady of the Lake always affords a few scenes; while the Tempest contributes a fantastic Ariel and a Miranda, with hair like dried flax. Lady Macbeth is equally constant in her attention, but under an infinity of aspects. We believe a year never passes without introducing to us Malvolio, 'the trout that must be caught with tickling,' practising behaviour to his own shadow.

Of the humbler description of the Wilkie school the productions are very numerous. Boys sliding, playing marbles on their forms, eating large pies, catching shrimps, ringing doorbells, and making small attempts at the fine arts, are scattered in profusion over the walls. In contrast with these a number of maidens bathing exhibit the eccentric tastes of our artists on the subject of flesh tints. Some delight in skins as white as Dover cliffs; some cause the modest damsel to blush from head to feet, reminding us of the old epigram—

'Fabius, you say, is much inclined
    His cheeks with too much red to fill—
His pictures only blush to find
    The painter does his task so ill.'

Others present figures which appear to have been moulded in wax; while a fourth class tinges the flesh with a blue, unhealthy tint, almost approaching the symptoms of cholera morbus. In the colour of the hair we have strange tastes displayed. The hue of brass is now a general favourite. Auburn is out of fashion. The rich golden brown, flushed, as it were, with light, has almost wholly disappeared. That exquisite appearance of floating massy tresses has been replaced by saffron-coloured 'bands' of hair plastered down with pomatum; so that even Pallas Athene and Venus appear to have used '*bandoline fixature*.' The blue-eyed goddess is generally a mimicry of that conventional allegorical personage, Britannia, who was herself at first a plagiarism of the Grecian mythology. To complete the modern ideal of beauty, we have the sleepy eye of the 'mournful,' the 'broken-hearted,' and the 'lovely,' with the upturned nose and low brows of the 'pensive,' or the 'scornful;' and portraits of 'ladies,' with half-exposed busts, tight-waisted dresses, and all the other indecent and ungraceful appendages of

modern fashion. When these are the efforts of our favourite
artists, we may excuse the landscape-painter who defaces the
blue and brilliant skies of the south by masses of northern
clouds.

Are we to conclude from this, however, that the Royal Academicians are right, that the country produces only a few men
of ability, and that this society possesses the monopoly of genius?
On the contrary, it has been the opinion of many great artists
that the Royal Academy is the curse of English art. By its
obsequious servility to the taste of certain personages it upholds
a low fashion of painting; by its tyranny over artists it degrades
them; by its ministry to the foppery of the 'higher classes' it
introduces a pernicious style; by its system of instruction it
fosters that degeneracy, and by its general influence on society it
dwarfs and deforms the art of the country. Some of the worst
caricatures exhibited are the performances of the Royal Academicians, and many of the finest are by men not belonging to that
body. Yet when we speak of the Academicians we allude to
the collective body, not to every member of it. For several of
them we have the highest respect. There are many men of unquestionable genius, and some of the most liberal views. But
there are others also whose qualifications are no higher than an
acquaintance with the principles and practice of tuft-hunting.
Secure in their own privileges they fear the competition of
genuine ability, which might put them to the blush.

The nation should be solicitous to preserve the dignity of art,
because it possesses painters and sculptors who would render
illustrious any age and any country. In that chamber of the
National Gallery, where annually

'Sculpture with her rainbow sister vies,'

we find much to redeem our age from the disgrace of degeneracy
in the arts. Baily (himself a Royal Academician) has achieved
an European reputation. Every lover of art must confess admiration of the genius which wrought a block of marble into that
exquisite figure of 'Eve at the Fountain,' which is celebrated
throughout Christendom, and must carry down the artist's name
to all posterity. If the reader would know what we mean by
the perfection of art, we direct him to this superb performance.
There he may see embodied the ideal of womanly beauty and
innocence. The lovely mother of the human race, bending over
the margin of a fountain, beholds her own face in the water.
The innocence of infancy is infused into the countenance of
womanhood. The form is chaste and delicate; the marble
appears to be alive, and there is suffused around the whole a
nameless beauty, which inspires us as we contemplate this work

of the greatest living sculptor. Recently Baily has sculptured
the Three Graces grouped on a rock. When we see such masterpieces of genius we readily believe the witness of history to
the singular influence caused by the arts on the mind of ancient
Greece. We cannot attempt to describe in ' the jargon of the
marble mart' these works of Baily. We

> —————' leave to learned hands
> The artist and his ape, to teach and tell
> How well his connoisseurship understands
> The graceful bend and the voluptuous swell :
> Let these describe the indescribable ;'

and let us proceed with our review of the sculptors of the day.

Writing of sculpture, justice requires a tribute to the memory
of Wyatt (not an R.A.). Years of his life were spent in Rome,
where the wrecks of antiquity are gathered in the Vatican—that
vast mausoleum to the memory of ancient art, enriched by the
munificence of successive Pontiffs with the treasures bequeathed
by ages of genius. The chisel of Wyatt wrought out of marble
forms full of classic grandeur. Under his hand were moulded
creations of beauty more than human. He has left works which
reflect lustre on his name and on his times ; and if he was not a
member of the Royal Academy, his exclusion was no discredit to
himself, but a digrace to that oligarchical body. As he is dead,
we may the more freely describe him as a man whom none could
know without admiring. Perhaps he scorned the Academy ; but
more probably the Academy feared him.

Whatever may have been the case, this much is certain—that
no society of sculptors could have represented the genius of the
age without including R. J. Wyatt. His works are worthy
of a place beside those of Baily and Marshall. William Calder
Marshall* is an artist of high rank, whose reputation increases
with every successive production of his chisel. Macdowell
(R. A.) is another sculptor of great eminence ; Behnes (not an
R. A.) produces works of extraordinary ability ; Davis (not an
R. A.) ; Earle (not an R. A.) ; Miller (not an R. A.) ; Mac-
donald (not an R. A.) ; and A. Brown (not an R. A.), all occupy
prominent positions among our distinguished sculptors. Edgar
Papworth is another of the ' excluded artists,' whose ability
should put to the blush many preferred before him by the
despotic ' forty.' J. Fillans—whose beautiful work, ' Rachel
weeping for her Children,' was exhibited in last year's exhibition,
is another, and in addition there are scores of men to whom
justice owes a tribute. That we do not indicate all their
names is because we cannot, but what we have said may serve

* An associate of the Royal Academy.

to illustrate the truth of our opinion, that there are far more able artists out of the Royal Academy than in it.

From the workers in marble let us turn to the workers on canvass. Linton, Linnel, Fielding, Martin, Cox, Holland, Stark, Prout, Fripp, Cooke, Harding, Kennedy, and others out of the Academy, with Stanfield, Lee, Eastlake, Cope, Ward, Witherington, and others in it, prove that the genius of landscape-painting, once the pride and boast of England, still lives among us. Linton— one of the artists whom Sir Robert Peel most admired—requires no panegyric upon his works. Travelling through the sunny regions of the south, he has become familiar with beauty in her chosen home, has viewed nature under her loveliest aspects, has seen blue skies and brilliant seas, has visited Venice, sailed along the shores of the Adriatic, and viewed the landscapes of immortal Greece. These he has reproduced. In the spirit of an *Eclectic* artist he has, when engaged in the production of an ideal scene, gathered together the beauties of a whole province, and concentrated them on a single spot; while in others, as in 'Mount Ætna and Taormina,' he has taken Nature's portrait and reflected her grandeur. His landscapes are full of light— true, but poetical; instinct with animation, but breathed over by the spirit of repose. There is beauty in every creation of his pencil. The sky seems infinitely deep; the green of the earth appears to grow, the water plays before the sight, and in the evening scenes the shadows seem to lengthen as you look. None that have ever seen Linton's magnificent picture of the 'Darkness coming over Jerusalem,' 'when the veil of the mighty temple was rent, and the dead came out of the graves;' none, we repeat, who have experienced the influence produced on the mind by a view of this sublime picture, will consider that we exaggerate his merits in our eulogium. We recommend such of our readers who appreciate true art to search for Linton's pictures at the exhibition, and justify our remarks by their own observation.

Linnel chooses different scenes and subjects; but many of his landscapes display beauties only to be created by a master's pencil. Many familiar spots in England have been chosen by him for illustration; and one curious picture of his, 'Sandpits,' especially attracted our attention. Linnel, our readers will remember, is not an R.A., though equal to the painters of the 'Great Forty' in everything which constitutes merit in an artist. John Martin is most probably known to all our readers. Those grand pictures of his—the Deluge, Belshazzar's Feast, and the Fall of Nineveh, entitle him to a high place among his contemporaries. The grandeur of his architecture, and the general grouping of the scenes he has represented, are all but unequalled.

Lately, he exhibited an extraordinary scene from that odd poem of Bulwer's—King Arthur. Two of the *dramatis personæ*, Arthur and Ægle, are standing in the Happy Valley. The landscape is magnificent; all its features are beautiful, and blend harmoniously together. Mountains, forests, rocks, lake, sky, moon, and clouds—

> ' The vine on high, the willow branch below,
> Mixed in one mighty scene, with varied beauty glow.'

But a gloomy hue—like Campbell's ' Hurricane Eclipse of the Sun '—a universal indigo colour, spread all over the picture, spoiled it. A moon as red as blood, and its reflection in the water, alone relieved the sight. Of the other painters we have mentioned, some delight in city-scenes, where human life is crowded; some love nature in her lonely moods, where she re-tires among mountains, lakes, and woods ; some choose domestic episodes, to illustrate and give animation to a rural landscape ; others depict the beauties of the sea meeting the shore, in calm or storm. Stanfield is distinguished by pictures of this class. Few can excel him in lighting up a night-scene on the ocean by the rays of a summer moon. His shadows seem to dance on the waters ; the radiance appears to penetrate the surface, and be reflected from it ; the blue of heaven and the blue of the sea, the struggle between day and darkness—all these we have seen delineated on canvass by the pencil of Stanfield, so finely that not a word can be breathed against his enjoyment of all the honours accruing to an Academician. We regret that the distinction ap-pears likely to lose its dignity. The Academy, however, has to blame itself for its own disgrace.

Turner, also, has been crowned with the favour of the Academy. Here is another instance in which we have not a word to say against its choice. Turner deserves his laurels.

> ' He won them well, and may he wear them long.'

We have seen pictures of his, a few inches square, worth acres of exhibited canvass. But if we may offer a word of advice to a veteran artist whom we have always admired, it is to be tender of his reputation. In the vigour of his genius he painted pictures of exquisite beauty ; let him be careful not to suggest comparison between them and the latest productions of his pencil. His recent works have induced us to make this remark. Nor can Etty—now removed from his stage of earthly action—be for-gotten. His genius was eccentric, but it was genius ; and the public favour bestowed on his works reflects credit on the public taste. Creswick, Cooper, the Pickersgills, and also the Landseers, with many other names, especially from among the unprivileged artists, could be introduced to show that Art is still animate among us. It has not lost its vitality; it has still a sanctuary in England. But the Royal Academy is to Art what the Popish Conclave would be to Religion. It is a despotism—degrading and unjust —which elevates the few at the expense of the many, and monopolizes for a small body of these the honours which should be fairly distributed among a large and meritorious class.

Where, however, is the remedy? Shall we look to Parliament—that is, shall we persuade the corrupt to cure corruption? Shall we look to the press? The press, alone, is powerless. It is only as the leader of the people that it is influential. The only hope is from the public. The people and the press, acting by a mutual process on each other, should exert a pressure on parliament, and require the reform of the Royal Academy. It has too long monopolized the honours of art. It has too long benefited by oppressing hundreds, though supported by their efforts, in the degrees of genius, ability, and talent. Eighty-two of the exhibitions have taken place; and thus, during fourscore years, it has exerted its injurious influence.

During this long period, we trust the artists have learned a lesson, which they must thoroughly understand before their position in the country can be what it should be. Art never flourishes as a toy of monarchy, which does not advance art, though it may patronize a few artists. Nor is it a luxury for an aristocracy to enjoy. It is a great and noble thing for the democracy to support. It is to democracy that artists must look. If they will consult history, if they will be guided by reason, they will find that democracy and the arts have flourished and fallen together. Examples of the contrary, no doubt, occur; but a free, wealthy, and enlightened people, refined by civilization and ennobled by religion, look to the beautiful for a portion of their happiness. In the great ancient republic of Greece, the sculptor and the painter ranked among the foremost men of the day; in Rome, honour was given to genius in whatever shape it appeared; and now, in the flourishing democracy of the United States, merit is most closely united to distinction.

A nation completely emancipated from oppression would possess the time, the energy, the means of accumulating the materials of intellectual enjoyment. In a state where public liberty was perfect, patriotism would warm the hearts of the citizens, and they would desire that their age and country should equal, if not outrival, all which preceded it. Thus galleries of modern sculpture and modern painting would be found to treasure up the productions of the age's genius. The fashion of painting for effect would disappear, and true beauty—which exists nowhere without chastity and truth—would be the artist's aim.

Among other things, the result of a higher degree of social enlightenment would be to range the degrees of excellence in their legitimate order. Then we should not see the deer and dog painter preferred before the historical or the landscape painter. We should not see the portrait painter excluded from honour, or the engraver's part stigmatized as mere servile copying. As it is, we are unjust in our terms of praise. To the man who finely draws a dog we award a panegyric greater than to him who embodies the ideal of beauty in a figure of Aphrodite, or excels even the beauty of nature in a landscape. Now the artist who should outrival Myros's famous cow is not to be esteemed in comparison with him who paints some sweet spot on the shores of the Lago Maggiore. Yet, we repeat, this is the fashion. The artist who is perpetually in the kennel or the cow-shed is petted and favoured by the leaders of fashion, while the classical painter—not honoured by a smile from the Royal Academy—is left in comparative neglect. Others would also labour without reward, were it not that the Academy contains some liberal members, and the public many more, who compensate the artist in some degree for the injuries he suffers.

What we at present, however, insist upon chiefly, is the monopoly of honours and advantages enjoyed by the forty members, and the twenty associate members, of the Royal Academy. This is one of the most absurd and extravagant anomalies of our incongruous social system. It imperatively requires reform ; but whether or not it *will* be reformed depends, we believe, on the artists themselves. They must be active, bold, and indefatigable. They must form a league, oppose combinations to conclave, and maintain a perpetual movement. The institution must yield to pressure. It will expand for fear of bursting, and when the monopoly is destroyed, the artists of this country will find, in their own improved condition, an apology for the importance we attach to the subject.

But it is not to artists only we would address ourselves. The general public is no less interested, and should be no less active in this question. Art is for the nation, and the nation derives advantage from it in proportion as it is elevated or debased. In conclusion, then, we appeal to the public to agitate this question. If we are to have an academy at all let it be as a public institution, subject to public control, supported by the nation, regulated by Parliament, open to all and and partial to none.

We ourselves—connected in no way with the arts—view the subject in this light. Mr. Coningham has supplied us with many facts ; but we have drawn largely from other sources also. That gentleman has contributed some useful observations but his ideas seem to centre on one special point.   From him, however, as well as from every other witness, we discover evidence that the Royal Academy is what we have described it to be—a monopoly, exercising only an evil influence on English art.

---

ART. II.—*Memoirs of Sir Andrew Agnew, of Lochnaw, Bart.*  By Thomas McCrie, D.D., LL.D., Author of ' Sketches of Scottish Church History,' &c. &c.   London : Johnstone and Hunter.  8vo. pp. 442.  1850.

IN this beautiful and portly volume, we have the history of a man whose life was devoted to one main object—an object distasteful to many, but to a large section'of the Christian public fraught with deep interest.   Sir Andrew Agnew, for several years the leader of the Sabbath cause in Parliament, possessed many of the requisite qualifications for his office.   He had enthusiasm, untiring devotion, industry, perseverance, and consistency of private character.   But he wanted the powers of intellect and gifts of oratory necessary in a parliamentary leader, as well as the faculty which discerns the practical, and the wisdom which adopts the expedient.   Through a morbid conscientious-ness he was tied to extremes, by which he exposed his cause unnecessarily to hostility and ridicule.

Still these Memoirs will be found both instructive and entertaining.   It is true they do not possess that peculiar, life-like charm which belongs to works in which the great and good become, in a large measure, their own biographers.  Sir Andrew kept no diary ; and, in this respect, Dr. McCrie was placed at a disadvantage.   But, in the preface, he expresses his trust that ' the reader will share with him in the feelings of grateful surprise with which, as he advanced in the history of Sir Andrew's career, he discovered so many features of varied and unexpected incident, and so many points of general and enduring interest.'   These were supplied by an immense accumulation of letters, and by communications from his family and friends.   Sir Andrew was for many years the centre of Sabbath correspon-dence in Scotland, and he never destroyed a letter that he received.   It was no easy task to extract from such a mass of letters the information which the biographer required ; but

Dr. McCrie has done his part with judgment, skill, and taste, and has produced a volume worthy of the subject and of his own reputation as an author.

Sir Andrew Agnew -was often described by those who denounced his Sabbatarian views as an austere, sour Presbyterian, whose mind had been imbued from childhood with the gloomy notions of the Sabbath which prevailed in Scotland; and his rigidity on the subject was attributed to an inborn bigotry. This was a great mistake. He was not a Scotchman, nor a Presbyterian, by birth; he was an Irishman, and grew up to manhood in the Church of England, mingling in society which thought no more of the sanctity of the Lord's-day than the people of France or Italy.

He was born at Kingsale, county Cork, on 21st March, 1793, and was the only child of Lieutenant Andrew Agnew, eldest son of Sir Stair Agnew, the sixth Baronet of Lochnau, and of the Hon. Martha de Courcy, eldest daughter of John, twenty-sixth Lord Kingsale, premier Baron of Ireland. This nobleman was the heir of the famous warrior, Sir John de Courcy, who conquered Ulster in the twelfth century, and became the champion of the King of England in a quarrel with the King of France, when his gigantic bulk and massive strength frightened his antagonist from the field; on which account he obtained the privilege of remaining covered in the Royal presence—a privilege used by his descendant when George IV. visited Ireland. De Courcy was accompanied in Ireland by another Norman, named Agneau, who settled in Larne, and obtained large possessions in the county Antrim. In the reign of David II. the Agnews seem to have removed to Wigtounshire, in Scotland, and settled at Lochnau, then a royal castle; and, from a very early period, the family held the heritable offices of Constable and Sheriff of Wigtounshire. After the Restoration, Sir Andrew Agnew was deprived of his sheriffdom, and fined 6,000*l.*, because he was a Presbyterian, and refused to take a self-contradictory oath, designed to exclude conscientious men from office. He was superseded by the infamous Claverhouse, who was 'sent down to show the Agnews, at the end of 230 years, how to execute the office of sheriff in such times.' Another of Sir Andrew's ancestors was Lieutenant-General Agnew, mentioned by Sir Walter Scott as celebrated in Scottish tradition. It was he that addressed the following laconic exhortation to his soldiers:—'Weel, lads, ye ken yon loons on the hill. If ye dinna kill them, they'll kill you!'

There is an amusing anecdote related of Sir Andrew's grandfather, which does him great credit as a landlord. He let his lands at low rents, required punctual payments, and suffered no arrears. On one occasion, he got his estate valued, but the valuation was much too high for his notions of justice and self-interest; indignantly throwing down the report on the floor, he demanded who had dared to send him such a document. He was told that its author was below, waiting to dine with him. ' Na, na,' exclaimed Sir Stair, ' I canna see him ; he would ruin baith me and my tenants out of home and ha'. Send him awa'—send him awa'—he canna stay here ! '

Sir Andrew's father died in the twenty-sixth year of his age, four months after marriage, when the young widow returned to the paternal roof at Kingsale. The bereavement so affected her health, that it was feared she would not survive her confinement, unless the infant was sacrificed. Lady Kingsale entreated that the operation might be delayed for *five minutes ;* and this request was the means of saving the life of the leader of the Sabbath movement. The birth was safely accomplished, though not without great difficulty. ' No sound was heard when the infant entered this world of sorrow ; and fears were entertained for his life, but by the prompt use of means he was restored to animation. God had work in store for the child ; and the mother lived sufficiently long to discover and appreciate the holy purposes to which the life so wonderfully preserved was afterwards so zealously devoted.'

His early youth was spent in Ireland, generally at Kingsale, under the care of his mother. He was a gentle and amiable boy, without the advantages of religious education, yet scrupulous in acting up to his idea of what was morally *right*, and opposed to everything like deceit. His affections, naturally warm, were drawn out in the genial atmosphere of kindness that surrounded him ; and his relations held him up as a pattern to all those of his age. ' Indeed,' says his biographer, ' if we find in the family of Agnew traces of the firmness and determination which characterised Sir Andrew, it is equally apparent that he was indebted, so far as natural temperament is concerned, for the manliness, affability, and gracefulness with which these sterner virtues were accompanied, to his excellent mother.'

Upon the death of Sir Stair Agnew, his paternal grandfather, in 1809, Sir Andrew, now only sixteen years of age, accompanied by his mother and Lord Kingsale, went to take possession of his estate in Wigtounshire.

' He was not a little disappointed on his first arrival at Lochnau with the grim look of the old castle, and the neglected state of the grounds around it. The trees, long undisturbed, had formed a barricade, through which he could with difficulty make his way on all fours ; and the swamp below, which was once a lake, was now anything but ornamental. The whole was so different from what his imagination had pictured, that his spirit died within him as he surveyed his doleful possessions; and he has confessed to having strongly felt the temptation of becoming an absentee—drawing the rents of the property, and enjoying them in some more favoured spot of the earth. Long and earnestly did he ponder over this idea. No early associations bound him to the seat of his ancestors. The retired and remote neighbourhood of Lochnau was alike unsuited to his social disposition and to his previous mode of life. He felt he had but two alternatives—either to remain and endeavour to alter the whole face of things around him, or to remove and think only of selfish enjoyment. He decided at length for the former.'—P. 24.

He succeeded in converting Lochnau into an 'earthly paradise.' At this time he gave another remarkable proof of his decision. Finding that his education was very imperfect, he spent the winters of 1810 and 1811 at the University of Edinburgh, and studied to some purpose. But he was not insensible to the pleasures and gaieties of the world. 'He was fond of dancing, an exercise in which he excelled. Graceful in his appearance and manners, he was a general favourite among the votaries of fashion. Before he attained his majority, he had passed the ordeal of four winters in the gay world of Edinburgh and London, "the admired of all admirers," his society eagerly courted, and the voice of flattery ever sounding in his ears.' His manly attentions to ladies, especially to those who were aged or infirm, or who seemed neglected, 'were bestowed on all with so much feminine gracefulness and delicacy as to excite general observation.' A still nobler trait in his character was that 'he *never forgot an old friend*, and could not even understand the littleness of those persons who would receive cordially an old acquaintance in one place and would not notice him when in higher company.'

In 1812, he went to Oxford, where he wrote his first letter on *Sunday*, remarking that the University sages, when sitting over their wine and fruit, studiously avoided *books* in their conversation. While at the University, his tutor died very suddenly: a fact which made a deep impression on his mind. It completely stunned and unnerved him, and contributed much to the seriousness that marked his subsequent career.

In 1815, he became acquainted with the family of Lady Carnegie, at Cheltenham, and married her youngest daughter, Madeline, in July 1816. This union proved a very happy one. Lady Agnew sympathized cordially in the public labours of her husband, and fully appreciated his good qualities. Soon after the wedding, Sir Andrew, accompanied by his young wife, visited the continent, where, however, his stay was very short. While at Paris, he happened to be at the Tuilleries on the feast of St. Louis, when he saw 'the king (Louis XVIII.) with a napkin tucked under his chin, *eat profusely of every dish until he became black in the face.*'

Up to this time Sir Andrew had not paid much attention to religion. The first 'gospel sermon' he ever heard was from the Hon. and Rev. Gerard Noel; but he professed to be then no judge of the doctrine. The Astronomical Discourses of Dr. Chalmers produced a powerful impression on his mind, and led to a full and distinct conception of the truth. The 'Evidences,' by the same author, and Bickersteth's 'Help to understand the Scriptures,' secured also much of his attention, and he began, in consequence, to take an interest in religious movements.

Having spent nearly 14,000*l.* in buildings and improvements, and made an abatement to his tenants of 9,000*l.* in consequence of the distress of the times, he was obliged to economize and live in close retirement. This tended to sober down his mind, and to strengthen his character, and prepared him for the great work that lay before him. Had these nine years (from 1821 to 1830) been spent on the continent, his subsequent career might have been very different.

We come now to the period when Sir Andrew changed his views in regard to the Sabbath. He had been accustomed to write letters, pay visits, travel, and amuse himself on that day as freely as on any other, without the least qualm of conscience. Having perused some of the works of the late Dr. M'Crie, he was induced to go to hear that eminent man preach. The text of the preacher was, 'Remember the Sabbath-day to keep it holy.' The curiosity of Sir Andrew was excited; but he felt somewhat staggered at what he regarded as the very extreme views of the preacher. The result, however, was his ultimate adoption of those views.

'The determination formed in the humble Presbyterian meeting-house, says an eloquent writer, led to a struggle whose arena is the British empire, and which, whatever reverses it may experience, is sure of success in the end. In Foster's well-known 'Essay,' there is not a more remarkable instance of decision of character than that which this interesting anecdote furnishes.'—P. 88.

In 1828, Sir Andrew having obtained the office of Vice-Lieutenant of the county, his attention to business won for him the powerful influence of Lord Galloway, who warmly encouraged his pretensions as a candidate for the county representation at the general election, which occurred on the accession of William IV. He gloried in ranking himself as a 'moderate reformer;' and constructed an ingenious map, which was used in the debates in Parliament to show the injustice and absurdity of the old system of representation; still he did not go the whole length of the Reform Bill. He was returned unanimously on the 18th of August, 1830. He entered the house in the autumn of the same year, and contented himself for a while with surveying the state of parties. His first remark on individuals there does not display so much charity as his friends gave him credit for. The H—— and O——, in the following, no doubt, refer to Hume and O'Connell :—

'The House of Commons,' he says, 'is an extraordinary scene. At times it appears inextricable confusion, and then again order and method appear. Messrs. H—— and O—— are most wearisome. If they are not speaking themselves, they are the subjects of the speeches of other people. It can never for a moment be forgotten that these two vulgar men are in the House. They pervade everything; they are indefatigable, warm, but weighty speakers. O—— is the most disagreeable being I ever beheld. His fiendish smile and discordant voice correspond. His incessant "Hear, hear," is the most jarring sound I ever heard.'—P. 107.

On a new Parliament being summoned, Sir Andrew again offered himself to the constituency of Wigtounshire, in May 1831. This was a time of great excitement on the subject of Reform, and his 'moderate' views exposed him to suspicion and misconstruction on both sides. He felt himself in the position of the poet :—

'In moderation placing all my glory,
While Tories call me Whig, and Whigs a Tory.'

He was accordingly opposed by Mr. Hawthorn. There was a severe contest, and great excitement. Sir Andrew won the election only by the single vote of a gentleman who posted from Edinburgh, and arrived just in time. Influenced by a tendency to magnify everything connected with their subject, too common with biographers, Dr. M'Crie remarks :—' Had Mr. M'Kenzie's post-horses been somewhat less expeditious, or had Mr. Blair's been a little less tardy, Sir Andrew's career in Parliament might have terminated with his first session, and the Sabbath might have looked as vainly for its advocate in St. Stephen's, as Mr. Hawthorn for his supporter on the hustings.'

Surely the Lord of the Sabbath could have found instruments elsewhere, and instruments far more powerful, if Sir Andrew had never been born ! God's institutions never lack supporters and defenders when he considers them needed.

Sir Andrew moved as an amendment on the Reform Bill, ' that the boroughs enumerated in Schedule A shall have a share in the election of a member, or members, to serve in Parliament, as hereinafter provided.' Sir Robert Peel strenuously supported this amendment, in the hope of defeating the bill. It was opposed by the Government, as inconsistent with the principle of their measure, and was lost by a majority of 316 to 205.

Sir Andrew Agnew took every opportunity of disclaiming the honour of having originated the Sabbath movement. The Bishop of Calcutta had published seven sermons on the Sabbath in 1827, and had described it as one of the grandest practical topics on which statesmen were called to treat. The Bishop of London also had, in 1830, published a letter to the inhabitants of London and Westminster on ' The Present Neglect of the Lord's-Day,' which excited much attention, and ran quickly through many editions. ' The Society for promoting the due observance of the Lord's-Day ' was formed in the house of Mr. Joseph Wilson, Clapham Common, February 8th, 1831. ' To the Rev. Daniel Wilson, of Islington, afterwards Bishop of Calcutta, whose praise is in all the churches, and to his excellent brother, Joseph Wilson, Esq., there can be no hesitation in ascribing the commencement in good earnest of this great work.' Sir Andrew Agnew himself says,—' In the session of the year 1832, many petitions had been presented to Parliament, and some influential members of the House of Commons had given their opinion that it would be expedient to endeavour to obtain a select committee for the purpose of investigating the manner in which the Lord's-day was observed, *before my attention was called to the subject.*' So little did he think of the leadership, and so little did others think that Providence marked him out for it, that he was appointed one of a deputation to wait on certain members of Parliament, in order to induce some one of them to take up the question. Sir Thomas Baring was first applied to, but declined. They repaired next to Sir Robert Inglis, who likewise refused the honour. They were then obliged to fall back upon Sir Andrew, who assumed the position with great reluctance, being conscious of his deficiency in those brilliant gifts and oratorical accomplishments which enable their possessor to triumph over parliamentary difficulties.

On the 28th of June, 1832, he rose, pursuant to notice, to move for a select committee ' to inquire into the laws and practices relating to the observance of the Lord's-day.' In consequence of the lateness of the hour, the motion was postponed to July 3rd, when Sir Andrew renewed it in a brief speech. Several members manifested considerable suspicion as to the ' practices ' which were to be made the subject of inquiry; which were not lessened when Lord Sandon let fall the too candid remark, that ' the recreations of the rich affect themselves only, while the recreations of the poor affect society in general !'

It was manifest that a measure conceived in such a spirit, and
based on such an assumption, must bring a tempest of popular
indignation on the head of the new leader.  Sir Andrew, in
reply, regretted that the debate should have turned on the amusements of the poor, and said, it was no part of his intention to
confine his inquiries to them.   He stood upon his original
motion, and the committee was appointed accordingly; among
the members were Sir Thomas Baring, Sir Thomas (then Mr.)
Fowell Buxton, Sir Robert Peel, Lord Ashley, Mr. Stanley, Mr.
Goulburn, Lord Morpeth, and Sir George Murray.  It comprised
most of those who were at that period distinguished for their advocacy of religion in its connexion with legislation, and were
generally known as 'religious members.' They were accustomed
to meet for devotion in the rooms of Mr. Andrew Johnstone, then
M.P. for St. Andrews, at Manchester-buildings, near the House
of Parliament.   Sir Andrew, Sir George Sinclair, Mr. Plumptre,
Sir T. F. Buxton, Sir John Dunlop, Mr. J. H. Balfour, and
Mr. Chisholm, were the most constant attendants.

'Having obtained his committee, Sir Agnew lost no time in setting
it to work.   Appointed on the 3rd, it commenced its investigations on
the 6th of July, and the report, with the minutes of evidence, was
ordered to be printed on the 6th of August, 1832.   Few can have
any idea of the amount of personal labour and anxiety incurred by
Sir Andrew in collecting this evidence, and arranging the facts elicited
in the course of the examination.   "In truth," he says at this time,
"I have been worked like a cart-horse for the last few weeks."
There he sat, said his friend, Mr. A. Johnstone, often alone, patiently
taking down and sifting the evidence supplied by our indefatigable
secretary (Mr. Joseph Wilson).   He *loved* the Sabbath, and heartily
pitied those who were deprived of its blessings.   He was clear and
discerning in his inquiries, and the result was the publication of such
a body of facts as greatly roused the country, so that the next session
our hands were full of petitions.'—P. 131.

We transcribe at length Dr. M'Crie's summary of the contents of this important report, which was in itself worth all the
labours devoted to the Sabbath question :—

' To give anything like an abstract of this valuable document, which
extends to 306 pages, would exceed our limits.   Suffice it to say, the
labours of the committee were directed to three grand objects :—*First*,
to disclose the amount of the evil of Sabbath desecration in all its
prevailing forms; *Secondly*, to prove the general desire of persons of
different trades and occupations to obtain for themselves the benefits of
the Sabbath rest; and *Thirdly*, to show the inefficiency of the existing
laws, either to prevent that evil or to secure that benefit.   The first of
these objects was accomplished through the testimony of various witnesses of unimpeachable credit,—clergymen, magistrates, merchants,

and commissioners of police,—all of whom bore witness to the wide-
spread desecration of the Sabbath, with its accompanying mischiefs,
especially in the metropolis.  A more appalling spectacle of human
depravity on a large and systematic scale has seldom been brought to
light.  It was as if a curtain had been lifted up, revealing to the eyes
of the Christian public, as to those of the ancient prophet, the series
of abominations done in the midst of Israel.  Let us imagine whole
districts with open shops, trafficking in all manner of wares as on the
week-day—markets thronged with purchasers through the whole day,
more like fairs than markets—scenes of confusion and uproar, to which
the bustle of any other day in the week was comparative quietude—
Saturday-night " pay-tables," established in public-houses, to tempt
the tradesman to spend his earnings in liquor, " for the good of the
house," while his poor wife, with an infant in her arms, going in search
of him to procure sustenance for the family, finds his means exhausted,
and is fain to drown bitter reflection in the intoxicating cup—whole
rows of gin-shops and public-houses pouring out their lava-streams of
debauchery in the morning at the very hour of divine service—
wretched men, and more wretched women, reeling through the streets
with such horrid looks and disgusting language, that the decent inhabitants durst not take their families to church with them—500 steam-
boats, filled with shoals of gaily-dressed Sabbath-breakers, plying on
the Thames—the parks crowded with fashionable carriages—while on
the roads leading from London, the grand attraction to multitudes on
this day was " to see the gentry going to Newmarket," the said gentry
playing at cards all the way, venting imprecations on the tardy hostlers
and their jaded horses, or, in a fit of passion, scattering the implements
of their unholy pastime on the road.  Besides these gross nuisances,
let us add others less offensive to public decency, though not less productive of evil—that moral dram-shop, the Sunday news-room, the
Sunday newspapers, the Sunday tea-gardens, and concert parties,—
which the hand of legislation cannot reach ; and we have the picture
of a London Sabbath, differing very little from a Parisian.'—Pp. 132
—134.

This report led to an influx of 1061 petitions, signed by
261,706 persons, praying for an amendment of the Sabbath
laws.  But the general feeling in the House towards the Sabbath
movement was far from friendly.  It was suspected by many that
the real design was ' to curtail the innocent enjoyments of the
poor,' and the Government held out little prospect of success.
Sir Andrew, however, began to think of framing a bill on the
subject, in which he had the co-operation of G. Rochefort
Clarke, Esq., of the Middle Temple.  It was not without many
consultations, and much anxious consideration, that he resolved
to bring in such a sweeping measure as that which he finally
adopted.

' At length he resolved to base his bill, first on the *recognition*
of the . *divine commandment*, and secondly, on the principle, that

according to that commandment *all* work on the Lord's-day should be declared unlawful, and that *permissions* for works of necessity and mercy should be held as exceptions. On these principles Sir Andrew took his stand, and from these he never swerved to his dying day.'— P. 114.

And therefore he died without carrying his bill, or getting the legislature to adopt any measure in furtherance of his object. His *first* principle was questioned or denied by the majority of the nation. Among the most learned and the most pious of Christians opinions differed greatly as to the requirements of the divine commandment under the present dispensation. Many who admitted them to their fullest extent under the Mosaic economy, denied that it was the province of a secular legislature to recognise or enforce them, *as divine*. The second principle, that ' all work should be declared unlawful on the Sabbath,' was felt to be utterly impracticable; and the third was equally so. Who was to give 'permission' to do works which were held to be exceptions to the divine law? Who was to determine what works were works of necessity or mercy? What is ' necessity'? and what is 'mercy'? Will not men give a thousand different answers to these questions, according to their habits, customs, prejudices, and interests? A law based upon such principles would have been a violation of the rights of conscience, and, while subjecting social life to an intolerable coercion, would have proved an utter failure in practice.

On the 20th of March, 1833, Sir Andrew moved that ' leave be given to bring in a bill to promote the better observance of the Lord's-day.' Mr. Shaw seconded the motion. The feeling of the House was in favour of the measure. The preamble of the bill began thus:—' Forasmuch as nothing is more acceptable to God than the true and sincere worship of him according to his holy will, and that the holy keeping of the Lord's-day is a principal part of the true service of God,' &c. All this is good and true, and is very proper in its own place ; but what business had it in an Act of Parliament? How could the civil magistrate enforce ' the *true and sincere worship and service of God, according to his holy will ;*' or 'the *holy keeping* of the Lord's-day ?' Yet this preamble assumes that it belongs to the functions of civil government to do so.

After the preamble followed the different clauses, which Dr. M'Crie truly describes as of the ' most *sweeping and unsparing* character.' Sunday-marketing and opening of shops, games and pastimes, drunkenness, stage-coaches, sailing of boats, barges, and ships, corporation meetings, cattle driving, &c., were strictly prohibited, under penalties varying from 10s. to £50.

'The exceptions, referring to works of necessity and mercy, were placed at the end of the bill, and purposely left vague and general, with the view of being more definitely fixed in the Committee. . . . Many, startled at the very outset, read no further than the prohibitory clauses, with their formidable looking penalties—and putting the worst possible construction on the legal phraseology—at all times ungracious in its tone and stringent in its provisions—set themselves to expose the whole measure to public odium.'—P. 152.

Everything betokened a stormy reception for the unfortunate bill. Mr. Beaumont told the House that the petitioners were actuated by 'cant, humbug, and hypocrisy', and he said he would move as an amendment, that it be entitled, ' A Bill to promote Cant.' Cobbett thanked the mover for bringing in a bill so bad that it could never pass. The bishops in the Upper House declared it went too far for them. The 'Times' denounced its author as a 'sour Covenanter,'—'a Scotch fanatic'—a 'modest and benevolent Puritan'—the ' *Draco of devotion*.' The 'Examiner' called the measure ' a bill for the *bitter* observance of the Sabbath.' Only two journals, the ' Record ' and ' Standard,' stood by the bill and its author.

Sir Andrew bore all with the fortitude of a martyr. On the 16th of May, 1833, he moved the second reading. The hour was late, and the moment unpropitious ; for the House had just been excited by a tremendous flagellation inflicted on Cobbett by Sir Robert Peel. Sir Andrew therefore wished to postpone it. The Speaker asked to what day ? and was replied to by cries of ' To *Sunday* next !' However, he proceeded with his motion. The conclusion of his speech betrays a strange confusion of ideas, though his biographer has printed the passage in *italics* as most important. He said he would rather they rejected the whole measure than pass it without the first clause, ' *because*, without recognising *the authority of God in this institution*, the most perfect Sabbath Bill you could construct would prove nothing better than a beautiful edifice without a foundation, a castle in the air—*a statute not binding on the conscience, and therefore inoperative, because it would not be in the power of the magistrate to carry it into execution.*'

We do not wonder that Sir Andrew failed as a legislator. *First*, it is assumed in this passage that God has no power to execute his own law unless the Legislature recognises it. *Secondly*, that the magistrate cannot carry into execution a law which is not based upon the authority of God, though it is admitted that on the point in question that authority was generally disregarded. *Thirdly*, it is alleged that no statute can be *operative* that is not ' *binding on conscience*.' It is much to be regretted that this legislator was not blessed with greater illumina-

tion to distinguish between things human and divine—between
the kingdom of God and the civil government.  He ought to
have learned that the English constitution is not a theocracy ;
and that nobody believed in the infallibility of Parliament.

The motion was seconded by Mr. Plumptre, and several
members spoke warmly in favour of the measure.  But by the
majority it was regarded with the greatest aversion.  It was
charged, and justly, we think, with gross partiality, in not dealing
with the rich, who travel in their own carriages, and employ
their own servants.  Others opposed it on theological grounds.
On a division, the numbers were, Ayes, 73 ; Noes, 79.  Majority
against the second reading, 6.  It would not have signified much
in so thin a house had the numbers been the other way.

Sir Andrew manifested admirable temper, patience, and perseverance, in the midst of the discouragements and odium which
he drew upon himself by his advocacy of *his* question.  In the
press, and in general society, his name was a byword of scorn.
While reading the Psalms on one occasion he found himself the
burden of the song of a drunken ballad-singer under his own
window.  Not unfrequently, when he got up to address the
House, his voice was at first drowned in a discordant chorus of
loud and impatient murmurs.  Yet his spirit was never ruffled,
and he never retaliated in angry words.  Many denounced him
as a hypocrite.  But Mr. Wakley, who is a great phrenologist,
set these uncharitable parties right, and raised a laugh in Parliament, by saying, ' It is just what I should have expected from
the organization of his head.'  And going up to Sir Andrew, in
the House, he said, ' Sir, I once thought you a great hypocrite,
and I heard many attacks upon your character ; but the moment
I saw you I could say, This is an honest man.  You have a large
development of *veneration,* and you cannot help acting as
you do.'

There is no doubt of his honesty, nor that in private life he
carried out his own views of Sabbath observance to a degree of
strictness almost ludicrous.  He arrived at Lochnau late on
Saturday night, and, though great improvements had been going
on in his absence, he took the most scrupulous care on the next
day not to let his eye rest for a moment on any of them.  Mr.
Roebuck taunted him for not carrying out his principle, inasmuch
as he had ' *hot* potatoes on Sunday.'  He thanked the hon. gentleman for the rebuke, and never afterwards suffered potatoes
to form part of his Sabbath meal !

In 1834, Sir Andrew was at his post again, and introduced
his Sabbath Bill.  But great was the surprise and indignation of
honourable members when they found it word for word the same
that had been rejected the year before.  It was submerged in a

flood of ridicule and invective. Mr. E. Lytton Bulwer accused its author of drawing his principles from the ' unerring wisdom of the Habakkuks and Ezekiels, the Faintnots and the Sparenots.' The supporters of the bill found their voices drowned in shouts of. laughter and cries of ' Oh, oh !' On the second reading the bill was rejected by a majority of 36.

In 1835 he presented himself a fourth time to his constituents. There was a sharp contest, but he was elected by a considerable majority. On the 21st of April, 1836, the indefatigable champion again moved in the House of Commons for leave to introduce another bill essentially the same as the former. On this occasion Mr. Gisborne entered into a curious calculation to show the expense the House had been put to by the Sabbath bills. There had, he said, been nine bills, and twelve discussions upon them. Not less than 84,000 sheets of paper had been printed on the subject, at the public expense, and all to no purpose. This bill was lost in a thin house by a majority of 32.

In May 1837, he was emboldened to bring his bill before the House of Commons for the *fourth* time. The first reading was carried by a majority of 146. The grand debate, however, was reserved for June 7th—the day fixed for the second reading. The discussion was opened by Mr. Plumptre. Mr. Roebuck, Mr. Wakley, and others, spoke strongly against it. But at length victory declared for Sir Andrew. The numbers were— for the second reading, 110; against, 66; majority, 44. He was delighted, and wrote to Lady Agnew in devout raptures. Congratulations poured in upon him from all quarters, and he felt himself amply rewarded for his long-enduring toils.

But it was not the will of Providence that he should get his bill passed into law. In the summer of 1837 he lost his seat for Wigtounshire. At the request of his friends, he then offered himself for the *burghs* of Wigtoun, and was rejected. He entered Parliament no more, and was obliged to leave to other hands the work on which he was so much set. A hostile journal then issued this true, though heartless, prediction :— ' The political career of the Knight of Lochnau is thus closed, aye, closed for ever!' It was a severe trial, to be torn away from the arena when victory began to smile upon his efforts, and hope came nearer with her proffered crown! Sir Andrew, however, did not murmur, and, so far from losing his interest in the subject, he lent others all the assistance he could in their parliamentary advocacy.

Nor was he wholly a man of one subject. He took an active part in several religious and philanthropic movements. Though brought up in the Church of England, he attached himself to the Scottish Establishment, where he acted with Dr. Chalmers and the Evangelical party, whom he accompanied at the disruption, and became a member of the Free Church; which proved the strength of his principles and the purity of his motives, since his tendencies were decidedly Conservative. As might be expected, he took an active part in the agitation against opening the Scottish railways on the Sabbath. During the whole of this railway war he had the cordial co-operation and sympathy of the Free Church. He became a member of the Evangelical Alliance, which he liked for its catholicity, but he does not seem to have retained his zeal for it very long.

In 1844, Sir Andrew had a remarkable escape in Glasgow. He was run over by a carriage on turning the corner of a street. How he escaped he was never able to tell. His only recollection was, that when lying on his back, under the cab, with a wheel on each side of him, and the horses' heels in alarming proximity to his head, the thought passed through his mind, ' What a singular position to be in ! '

Though he had now only reached the age of fifty-six, he had symptoms of failing health ; he said, he felt growing old, and found life precarious. To the infection of scarlet fever he had been repeatedly exposed in his own family, yet had never caught it; now, however, without being consciously exposed to any contagion, he took that disease. His last work was looking after the preparation of an article on the Sabbath, which was to appear in the newspapers. Lady Agnew and another member of the family were seized with the same malady. From fear of infection, no one came near the house, and the family was for a while left alone in the midst of the crowded city ; with the exception of the servant and nurse that waited on him, and the doctor's daily visits, Sir Andrew was left to himself. Ten days had thus elapsed ere he was able to visit the sick-room of his lady, who was shocked at his altered and somewhat haggard appearance. Soon after, he had a serious relapse. His lady, who had sufficiently recovered to wait on him, became now his constant and almost sole companion. Having enjoyed a refreshing slumber, a requisition to the Lord Provost to call a meeting against Mr. Locke's Railway Bill was brought to him for signature ; he signed it, and immediately felt ' as if something had given way at the heart.' This was followed by acute suffering. But, ere long, all suffering was at an end, and he was privileged to depart in peace. Lady Agnew has written a most interesting account of his last moments, which were cheered by the faith and hope of the gospel. He died in Edinburgh, on the evening of April 12th, 1849.

' The news of Sir Andrew's death came upon all as an event they had never anticipated. Upon the hearts of all good men they fell

heavily as                                                        ublic
                                                                  cha-
racter, and regret for his loss.
individuals, from societies, and from churches, were kindly addressed
to the bereaved widow and family—all breathing sentiments of the

cherished, his profound sense of the spiritual, or scrupulous
regard to what he deemed duty, his public career did little more
than strengthen the aversion with which the restraints of religion
are regarded.  Right or wrong, we cannot readily conceive of
any person deriving a favorable estimate of religious influence
from the views enunciated or the policy enforced by Sir Andrew.  The whole tenor of what he did was suited to strengthen
the irreligious prejudices of his contemporaries, and this not
simply by virtue of the hostility with which piety is regarded by
worldly men.   There was much in what he said and did to
produce such a result.  It was as though he were concerned to
exaggerate and caricature those features of Christianity which
are specially distasteful to secular minds.  We do not regret his
numerous failures in Parliament.  Had his bill been carried, a
yet more serious injury would have been inflicted on religion.  Its
effect would have been the reverse of what he anticipated, and the
augmented force thus given to impiety must have rebounded on

religion itself.   We have no question with men like Sir Andrew
respecting the end they propose.   It is a noble and divine one;
the poor man's right—the rich man's glory.   The social and religious benefits connected with a devout observance of the 'Lord's
day' cannot be estimated too highly, and he is no friend to our
country who seeks to divert our people from its pure yet exhilarating occupations.   Our controversy with the parties in question
respects the mode of effecting the end contemplated — the
manner in which a religious observance of the day may be best
secured.

Now Sir Andrew and his friends evinced, in our judgment, a
lamentable want of confidence in *the truth*.   They saw no safety
for the Sabbath but in legislation, and were so possessed by this
notion, as not to perceive the impossibility of so gross an agency
effecting so spiritual an object, or the necessarily partial character of any measure they could frame.   The application of law
to the observance of a Sunday is as objectionable, in our view,
as to any other part of religious duty.   Sabbath legislation,
pertains to a system of *forms*, not one of principles; and has
done more to maintain the practical delusion so fearfully prevalent, than any other branch of the state-church theory.
The Sunday measures of Sir Andrew were based on a radically
unsound principle.   They were vicious at the heart; and, had
they been carried, most mischievous results must have ensued.
If our legislators be authorized to enforce one department of
religious duty, why not all?   And, if so, where shall we look
for the sacredness of conscience, or how shall we maintain our
title to serve our Maker according to our own conviction of
what is right ?

There is no safety short of an entire repudiation of state
authority in religious matters.   Let us have faith in the means
devised by God, and we shall find that they are mighty.   A
nation's welfare is bound up with a devout maintenance of Sunday, and all Christian people should therefore unite to secure
that observance.   There are various moral means within their
reach.   Let these be used with diligence, prayer, and faith, and
a thousand-fold more good will be accomplished than by any
statutes which legislators can frame or magistrates enforce.

ART. III.—*Social Aspects.* By John Stores Smith. 12mo. Pp. 258. London : John Chapman.

IT is a remarkable phase of our times, that the great subjects for public discussion have rather a social than a political bearing. The future historian will have occasion to remark, that the great questions of our age are those which are connected with eco- nomics—not with the divine right of kings, nor the extent of prerogative, but with health of towns, the duration of factory- labour, and the condition of the poor. They who have carefully observed how the larger portion of the historic page hitherto has contained the narrative of royal plots and ambitions, of military achievement and priestly intrigue, will remark it as something altogether new in our annals, that at present they must record chiefly domestic and social reforms. Such a fact may be accounted for partly, perhaps, by the long peace which the nation has enjoyed; for in times of war, there is so feverish an excitement in the public mind, that that is most heeded which tells ' how the sounding battle goes.' During peace, however, commerce expands, invention is both happy and constant, facto- ries become more important than barracks, and the public mind seeks more eagerly for works of art, for the increase of manu- factures, and for civil improvements, than for the exploits of the soldier, the capture of cities, and the various atrocities which constitute military glory. In war, nations cripple or destroy each other; in peace, they reform their abuses and increase their resources.

The work which lies before us relates entirely to social matters. The author takes various views of the home-life of England; and such observations as he has made we shall first have to consider, and afterwards we shall examine how accu- rately and philosophically he has discerned the signs of the times. He does not regard the exchange, the market, and the public streets; but he looks, and often with a searching scrutiny, into the sanctuary of domestic life—prying eagerly into the home- habitudes of the people. The volume is divided into ten chap- ters ; and the points of view are numerous. Some of the observations are well made, while of others we can say only that they are obtained, not unfrequently, through distorted *media,* and from incorrect elevations. On the first chapter, which pre- sents the *rationale* of the rise and fall of empires, we cannot dwell; though there is much in it which seems utterly wrong in philosophy, contradictory to the universal teachings of history, and offensive to all who seek Truth at the only legitimate source of it. Much which we have read in our author's first chapter is by no means new to us ; a considerable portion of it is *crambe repetita.* Especially, the sections on the *Rationale of Civiliza-tion* and *The Perfect Man* so much reminded us of Mr. Thomas Carlyle, that we were almost compelled to pause, and see if the printer had not omitted to place among his types the usual marks of quotation ; but there seems no other conclusion possible for us than this—that our author has devoured and but ill-digested the productions of that great thinker. We have often said, if H. R. H. Prince Albert should affect an interesting lisp, we have no doubt that all the loungers and yawners, whom one sees honouring the fashionable promenades by their High Emptinesses' presence, would lisp after the royal fashion ; so that one would hear nothing but muffled sibilations among all the glossy *élite ;* squires would catch the sound polite from peers and county-members—the tradesman would become infected, and the very tailor who gauged us for pantaloons, and the milliner who ex-hibited to our wife the last new Paris bonnet, would alike drawl their most intense obligations—till at length the very cabmen and ' conductors ' would lisp for ' fares.' Now, not less ridiculous has been the Carlyleian form of speech which some of our younger *literati* affect. That Mr. Carlyle's great thoughts are expressed in language rugged as his ' native hills,' is an unfortunate accident to their utterance ; but, that young men, or any men, should studiously imitate his *brusquerie,* is, indeed, most lamentably to ' quote deformities.' It is as if one of our Academicians, study-ing Canova, should also imitate the flaws in his marble. Our author has considerable mental power ; but that he should now and then put forth some waterish *dicta* in the mode of Mr. Car-lyle, and should think them to be very Delphic vaticinations, is an amusing delusion of his own. From the general tendency of this book, we should have thought imitation in any form had been in the teeth of his philosophy, and that, whatever ' golden image ' might be set up on the plains of literature, our author would be a very Shadrach, and would refuse to bend the knee ; but that such a conjecture had been erroneous, the first chapter of the volume clearly proves ; for the whole of that portion of the work—which we think the weakest—is to our disturbed imagina-tion a kind of Olla, wherein one finds floating fragments of Carlyle, a little that is *piquant,* as M. Soyer would say, from Novalis, a few tainted morsels from Emerson, and a few sprigs thrown in of Mr. George Dawson's peculiar cultivation. We write thus, more in sorrow than in anger ;' for, if he will learn self-reliance, he may take far wider surveys than those of our ' social aspects.'

   In the remarks on the *Social and Domestic Tendencies of the*

*Age,* there is much well worthy of close attention. Here one of the glaring evils of our age is pointed out—the endeavour of the lower strata of society to be assimilated to the higher; an evil which was only here and there discernible when Dryden pointed the keen shafts of his satire; when Hogarth and Fielding, each in his own way, rebuked the errors of their times; or, when sturdy Sam. Johnson grunted his condemnation of a fashion or a book, to the awe and instruction of all the Boswells. Perhaps the increased and facilitated locomotion now among us, and the contact perpetually occurring in markets, exchanges, steam-ships, and institutions, between the various classes of our people, have either reduced the higher, or are gradually raising the lower, to a superior level. The first French Revolution effected a remarkable change in the costume of all classes. Before that tremendous upheaving, the murmur of whose tempest is faintly audible to-day, each rank of life had its own style of apparel. The coats of the *comme-il-faut* and entirely courtly nobleman, and of the great bibliographer who surlily waited in his hall, were as different as were the outward show and bearing of these two men. Egalité Orleans and Desmoulins were utterly apart in their attire; and the hot royalism of Attorney Wedderburne, and the calm democracy of Benjamin Franklin, differed not more than did the garments they severally wore. But when the revolutionary armies, maddened by their first draughts at the fountain of liberty, had defeated York and humbled Austria, the civilized world set aside the preposterous custom of class-garments, and from that time he has worn the best broadcloth who has had the most money to procure it. Now, we have oscillated to the other extreme, and imitation is the custom of the time. Thus, to quote from the literature of the Minories, all Englishmen wear, or are tempted to wear, a 'Codrington,' a 'D'Orsay,' or a 'Chesterfield'—garments which, we presume, were first invented or approved by some men of fashion, and then presented by the tailors as the fitting costume for all British citizens. The great tyrant of the day is fashion. Notwithstanding our liberal or even democratic tendencies, and our increasing enlightenment, whatever is fashionable—that is, whatever style or species of garment Lord Vogue or Lady Modish may have worn in public, commands imitation on an immense scale. The boldest man among us dare not wear a hat of his own designing, however convenient his invention might prove itself to be; and he who should plan a coat according to his own imagination, and should wear it in Fleet-street or the Strand—though he had had the philosophy of a Sartor, and the cunning workmen of a Nicoll, or a Moses, to his aid—would be as much an object for wonder and for ridicule as an Ojibbeway or a Bushman. We and our wives

M 2

and children are in utter vassalage to some mysterious personage
who sets the fashions either in London or in Paris, or to the
capricious scissors of a West-end tailor, and to the strange
imaginings of a French milliner.   Another sad aspect of our
social life, remarked in this chapter, is the extravagance of many
among the middle classes in house-furniture and in 'party'-giving.
We have indeed gone a long way from the green rushes and the
straw-carpet of Raleigh's time.   The middle-class family now
possesses carpets and hangings which would have excited general
wonderment even at so recent a period as the American war; and
not a few of our London middle-class tradesmen possess a better
family stock of plate and linen than many a country squire even
of the last generation.   To have showy furniture and a little
plate, is the great ambition of many young housekeepers, who
unfortunately begin where they should end—commencing life
with a glitter and display which would show better in their
home as the result of long years of industry and of successful
trading.   Against this system our author protests with considerable power; and as a reformer of an evil which is not the less
dangerous because it is domestic and of general manifestation,
we wish him complete success.

The education and position of English women—to which
delicate themes a chapter is devoted—have been subjected of
late years to no little discussion.   In proportion to the refinement of any age, is the power of woman's influence; for, after
all, it is not in the crowded congress, nor in the busy mart and
ever-active city, that character receives its great and lasting
impress,—but it is to the mother, the sister, the wife, that a man
must trace many of his tendencies.   On this subject of home-
influence very much has been written which has proved itself to
be ridiculous in theory and impossible in practice—very much
that is unhealthy in sentiment and childish in its aim.   The
subject was by no means exhausted when our author embraced
it, and though he has passed some strong censures upon the
silliness and sickliness of much of that which goes by the name
of female-education, there is still need of considerable reformation in the educational process for the young of both sexes.
We do not want to quote from the volume before us—though
the phraseology, if at all intelligible out of Bedlam or Charenton,
in our judgment partakes more of the dialect of Stamboul or
Teheran, than of Manchester—' the Eve, beguiled by the serpent,' whom ' the outside rosy goldenness of the conventional
apple captivates' [we should like to know the man who grows
this extraordinary fruit]; which apple ' she presses with her
winning blandishments upon the Adam,' who devours the
fruit, ' and the avenging angel forthwith is *there* [?] with

flaming scimetar to drive forth the fallen from the ethereal Eden of spiritualities and truth into the weed-bearing world of etiquette and falsities.' We wish not our English women to be of this species; nor have we an intense desire, as Mr. J. S. Smith seems to have, that any one of our young men, attaining to connubial bliss, should be 'a brave Titanic husband who, after having struggled and laboured in the busy world throughout the day, will have the unresting nobleness to renew the labour and the conflict in his home, by endeavouring to make his wife and the domestic sacraments the solid genuine substantialities they ought to be.' We would not begin our work of reformation by giving young ladies, for their contemplation, such fustian as this: ' That to her, also,' the hard rock, the bleak morass, the fruitful harvest-lands have voices; that to her the sun, rising fresh with *light* [does it ever rise with *darkness* ?] from the presence of the Maker, brings daily lessons, and the moon and stars repeat incessantly their nightly and unvarying tale; that to her in fact the mighty anthems of creation are for ever being sung.' But, still, there is a great want of reform in the education of our young people. That things are as they are—that a mother should be pleased to hear her daughter whisperingly sing a trashy Italian ditty, or jingle dexterously a polka or a waltz, or to see her clever at the chromatic mystery of wool-knittings— and that a father should delight that his son writes ridiculous Pentameters, or quotes fluently the ballads of Schiller or Uhland; and that all this should be mistaken for education, is sad indeed.

A glaring evil among us, is the superficialness of the education given and received. We attribute this evil to two causes—or the one may be a consequent of the other—that the teachers are often quite incompetent to their work, and that the food given for the nurture of the minds of the young people is often only gilded trash. Now, here we wish not to write harsh things, nor do we presume to class all scholastic establishments in one category of condemnation; but we must be allowed to enter our protest against the unfounded assumptions of many who train the young. We do not write without examples at hand, painful instances of scholastic incompetency, nor without considerable knowledge of the subject. How many there are who, after complete or partial failure in their previous pursuits, have presumptuously betaken themselves to school-keeping for a livelihood! We have proof positive that some, who are engaged in the scholastic work, took to it only as a last resource, when they found it impossible to live by any other means. Mr. Charles Dickens has paid considerable attention to, and has much knowledge of, this subject; and our readers may safely believe that

his Salem-House, with its proprietor and its system, is no
caricature.

But we intend our censures should apply to some of the
' Establishments for young ladies.' Many of these, both in
town and country, are conducted by highly-accomplished
women, who are interested in their employment beyond what
it may produce them; but how many have taken such duty
in hand, entirely without ability to discharge it! A few light,
French, German, and Italian works lying on the drawing-
room table—a cushion or a screen worked by the young ladies
for their teacher—a showy painting or two, *not* after Titian or
the' Caracci—and an abundance of frivolous music, attract the
fond parent, and lead him to believe that his daughter—if placed
in the school in whose sanctum these vanities are discoverable—
will have the advantages, ' good easy man, full surely!' of polite
literature and modern accomplishment. Now, we would not
have our children—or any young ladies—ignorant of the better
portion of continental literature; we would have them speak
French as they speak it at Versailles—German, as at Dresden,
and Italian, as at Siena; to be skilful in painting and embroidery,
as these have ever been, from the days of Helen to our own, the
delight of the sex; and to be able to cheer their fathers or husbands, exhausted and depressed by the day's labours either in
the study or in the office, by the all but divine harmonies of
Beethoven and Mendelssohn. But, even if these accomplishments be all gained, which we fear is seldom done, how much is
yet lacking!—how much knowledge is to be learnt of the
world's great story, of the rise and fall of republics and of cities,
of the progressions of man from primal barbarity to the beauty
and glory of civilization, and of those principles which, in every
age, and under every form of society, have been motive to actions
both of good and of evil results! We would not forbid the
acquirement of what is elegant, but we would insist upon the
pursuit of that also which is *useful* and which has some relation
to the domestic economy. As in architecture, so in education,
embellishment is merely accidental to the strength and dignity
of the work. For a young English woman to attain to all that
is elegant and attractive, is well; but, infinitely better that she
should be educated to her position and work in after life; that
she should learn—if indeed it can be learnt—how to preside
with dignity and gentleness over the family circle—to help and
cheer her husband in his life-employ—to minister to all that is
kindest and best in the world's progress; and should she, by the
dispensation of Providence, be left, as a widow, to struggle
against the injustice of the world, to be enabled, by her knowledge, sagacity, and self-reliance, to be equal to her destiny. The

principles and the knowledge necessary for efficient action in so painful an emergency, are to be gained chiefly by a careful and philosophical study of history, so justly styled 'the biography of nations.' It would delight us to know that such a study, based upon the works of the ablest writers, was of highest rank in our private schools.

In the chapter on *The Aristocracy of Mammon and Mammon-worship* there are some excellent sentiments; and the writer takes a very just view of the sad vassalage we are in to the money-god. Everything among us is estimated by its market-price. To some extent, this must always be the standard of estimation among a mercantile people; but the evil is, that this gauge is applied to things which are not marketable, and which, therefore, are not estimable by money's worth. What cannot wealth do among us, and what can it not secure? How sordid and base soever a mortal may be—if he lack honour, that true nobility—if he be utterly vicious and degraded; so that he have but wealth, the country acknowledges him as great—the town buzzes with his fame—and, in many instances, the proud and titled will deem it not beneath them to associate with him. We have had of late more than one proof of a sad fact—a proof painfully conspicuous —that those who boast a Norman ancestry and many a broad acre of demesne, can court the favour of a man whose title to their esteem is the gain of fortunate speculation. The influence of money works universally throughout our system. The great Reform-measure, as it was termed, which had, for more than a quarter of a century, kindled eloquence in the senate, and disturbed the quietude of the country, was formed essentially under this influence; so that, as the law of England now obtains, a man is a citizen, enfranchised and directly interested in the welfare of the republic, not as he is good and skilful—not as he has unlocked for the people the treasures of science, or taught them by his poetry or philosophy—but, as he possesses. If he have the coin, whether he worked for it or not, that does not enter into the question, he votes; if he have it not, he is a very serf. We imagine, if Socrates lived in our day and among us, he had not been an elector; 'divine philosophy' might proceed from his lips, he might eclipse Locke and Reid, Kant and Fichte, but if he had not yearly forty shillings' worth of freehold property, he had no more interest in his Fatherland than the Boor who dwells on the Don. In everything money is the standard. In the army a man buys himself on; so that a peasant, enlisting into any regiment of the line, though he have the military talent of a Turenne, or of a Suchet, unless he have money to open the door to promotion, must be content to manœuvre and to conquer only in his dreams, and to spend his precious days in drilling, in cleaning his fire-lock and bayonet, and amid the brutalities of the barracks. Let us, again, instance the State-Church among us : how many 'mute Miltons' and 'inglorious' Paleys verge the year-long towards starvation on miserable curacies of £80 per annum ; while Lord Noodle's youngest son, the Hon. Mr. Fitzbrains—who never in his life has had an idea unworthy of a lad in a British School; whose biblical lore never extends itself beyond the Diatessaron and the Thirty-nine Articles, excepting, perhaps, to fragments of Jewel, or Hooker, or Jeremy Taylor ; who hunts every season, patronizes the parish cricket-club, is great at billiards, and comes out mightily at bowls, when the shooting season is gone by ; who abhors Dissent and Baptist Noel ; and who buys his weekly sermon of Hatchard or of Darling, or employs some needy Nonconformist to write it for him—this Hon. Mr. Fitzbrains fattens and preaches in a rich living in the fens, which his wealthy father bought for him—no, *the presentation* to which his father bought for him—or which the Lord Chancellor gave him.   Money makes shallow, frivolous Fitzbrains a rotund rector ; the want of it, not mental or spiritual deficiency, keeps good little Mr. Smalltalk a pinched and pitiable curate.   We open the Clergy-list, or we read such reports of ecclesiastical matters as the ' Times ' deigns to furnish ; and we read the names of men who hold a great many letters of the alphabet in fee as the initials of university honours, and who are highly ranked among the ecclesiastical officers of the State, but who have no public fame—have written no books, and edit no serials ; who are known neither as writers nor as preachers, except in their own parishes ; but they had the golden key which unlocks all English difficulties, and they are what they are simply because they are rich, and for no other reason in the world. Money pushed them softly through Cambridge or Oxford—money gave them degrees and livings, and all earthly fat things, and all spiritual indolences and indulgences—money makes them magistrates and magnates—money makes them great in the eyes of bucolical squires and drowsy farmers—and money will very magnificently bury them, by and bye, when their life-work is done, or, rather, when their life-drowsiness passes into the dream-less sleep of the grave.   In no public or social department which we know of has money a more directly evil influence than in the Anglican Church.   From the grand old house at Lambeth down to the humble lodgings of the chaplain to the workhouse, the monetary calculation is universal.   If we meet with a worthy curate, toiling among his schools and his paupers, doing as much good as his ' system ' will permit him; and if we ask him why he, with his thirteen children, is, after thirty years' service, only a curate; the answer we invariably receive is, 'I have been without influence'—that is, being interpreted, 'Neither I nor my family had money.' A sad 'social aspect,' this!

'A truth-seeker,' says our author, 'finds the influence of the prelates derived, not from piety and personal worth, but from the cash and its adjuncts which their ecclesiastical dignity bestows. Take away from a bishop his income, his princely habitation, and his seat in the assembly of the Peers, and the respect, reverence, and adulation he receives, go also with him. Let him be as pious as Paulinus, but rob him of these, and he sinks into quiet obscurity upon the instant. I do not seek to join in the wide-mouthed vulgar cry against bishops; but surely to the sincere Churchman this matter is worthy to be studied.'—P. 139.

The chapter on *Literature* is not without its merits, but there is an extremeness and one-sidedness about the writer's views—qualities which peculiarly distinguish the school of impracticable economists to which he has attached himself. We fear we shall ourselves fall under his censure. In speaking of style, and of an author's reception, in case of freshness of style, by the critics, he delivers himself thus:—

'Let a man speak forth heavenly truths in language natural to him, and we find that little attention awaits him either from reader or reviewer. But let another man string together a collection of respectable extreme-avoiding truisms in laboriously-flowing prose, and the book is largely patronized. Now, what is the end and aim of style in composition? It is that words should be selected the most adapted for adequately expressing the conceptions to be uttered. Style is, therefore, *per se*, nothing.'—P. 187.

We agree with our author, that, when a man writes, he should use the words which are best adapted to express his thoughts; but we find great fault with him for using words which, in their connexion, clumsily and periphrastically convey a simple idea—and for having a set of words and phrases, which he uses over and over again with most ingenious variations. We could quote scores of phrases which are used in his book, in violation of philosophy and philology; but we will only ask, why we have —and some of them many times—such phrases and words as 'a true man,' 'a broad man,' 'conventionalism,' 'hopeable,' 'high-souled,' 'rose-pink,' 'huge religious hearts,' 'a bottomless abyss of bright vacuity,' 'the mighty swoop of intense convictions marching in earnest action,' 'conventional man,' 'Evangel,' &c.? Now, when an author thinks style is not of much importance, and when he endeavours to justify the barbarity of his diction, whether natural or assumed, we beg to remind him that there are not only philosophical and artistic, but also literary, proprieties. It is the *misfortune* of Mr. Carlyle—'the ISAIAH of his

age,' as our author styles him, though we fail to perceive the
justness of the parallelism—that his style is rugged; but it is
evidently our author's *fault*. Why should every dwarf imitate
the limp of the club-footed giant? It may be that we love, in
contradistinction to Mr. J. S. Smith, ' chastity of style ' and
'fluent prose.' We confess to an admiration of, and a great
jealousy for, the proprieties. We should have heard Plato with
pain, had he stammered or lisped.

The chapter entitled *The Spiritual*—making due allowance
for the unhealthy atmosphere in which, as it seems, the writer of
it has sometime breathed—we deem the best in the book. It
will well repay perusal. We make a short quotation :—

' The carriage of my Lord the Bishop rolls through the city, and the
poor are sprinkled with the mud its wheels do scatter. All men are
alike in the eye of God; He knows but the good and evil, they are his
sole distinctions, says Christianity : the practice and the feeling of
social England say, as clearly as action can speak it, A man, as a man,
is nothing; he is, in proportion as he has cash or birth. When you
are smitten, smite not again, says Christianity, for peace is its vital
essence. A peace-man is almost a term of contempt in society ; the
pulpit is the best support of the war-spirit : and bishops bless the
colours that are to be steeped in the blood of man and the tears of
orphanage and widowhood. . . . Humility is another key-note
of Jesus Christ. The wretched Pharisee with his pride ; the Publican
(the social unmoneyed man now-a-days) with his humility ; the degradation of the self-elevated, the promotion of the lowlier-minded;
these are salient features in his evangel. And yet, what is rank and
the arrangements of precedence, and, above all, selectness in society,
but one vast round of the basest, the emptiest of pride ? '—Pp.
210, 211.

We have remarked sufficiently on the style of this writer ;
against his theological sentiments, so few of them as gleam out
from the mass of his work, we must earnestly protest. If he
hold any *credo*, we fear it is that which is most abundant in
negations. A few words from his own pen will explain our
meaning :—

' Let the reader pause a little and reflect upon the leading characteristics in the idiosyncrasies of Job, David, JESUS (!!!), Paul, MA-
HOMET (!!!), Luther, Milton, or Cromwell, and he will have no
difficulty in assenting to the following exposition of the elements of a
True Man.'—P. 25.

None but a wild Rationalist, a follower of such men as Paulus,
Wegscheider, Strauss, &c., or only such men as Messrs. Parker
and Emerson, and their sickly brood, would place the name of
the REDEEMER in such offensive juxta-position. Sad, sad indeed,
must be the health of that man's soul—whatever be his sect or

creed—who can so degrade, by unhallowed association, the name of Him before whom angels bow! Again—and this must be our last example—at pp. 158, 159, our author gives us a little of his philosophy and theology; and the one is as ridiculous as the other is unsound :—

'It is physiologically and religiously true, that were it possible for a man to commit bodily misdeeds of the grossest kind, and at the same time maintain his soul untainted by those misdeeds, he would be a true and blameless man. The character of King David has ever been a stumbling-block to men; they have not been able to understand how he could have been an adulterer, a murderer, a debauchee, and yet the man after God's own heart. . . . David had one of the strongest and most vigorous souls ever sent upon the earth. The consequence was, that when the scum and residue of his fleshy excesses fastened upon his soul, it had strength to rise against them, and cast them away. *The bodily sin had not its corresponding influence upon his powerful soul, and therefore to the God of souls was no sin.*'

Did Mr. Smith never read the Fifty-first Psalm, that model prayer for all the penitent; or Nathan's mission to David? or does he not know the evils which fell on the monarch's posterity in consequence of this very sin, which our author says, 'to the God of souls was no sin?' If he will deign to turn to what his school call 'the Hebrew book,' and read, he will find that David's anguish arose from this fact, that his soul consented to the sin; and, therefore, his earnest prayer was, 'Create in me a clean heart!'

It is no small portion of this volume of which we approve; it contains much 'food for meditation;' the aim of the author was unquestionably to reform many crying evils among us, and we shall have made happy progress, as a nation, when much which he justly condemns is reformed and removed. We beg, with all kindness, to tender our advice to him; for his mind, when restored to the power of healthy conceptions, will be capable of doing much good service for his generation; to prune away ridiculous excrescences—to learn a little of the art of condensing—to believe in names greater and nobler than those of Novalis and Emerson —and to submit himself, as an humble truth-seeker, to the Word of God. Let him not bow down to a meteor or a comet, but to the great Sun, which gives light to all. There is something of truth in the works of Novalis: Mr. Carlyle, with all his eccentricities and impracticabilities, is a glorious thinker, and is sound at heart; and there may be found a few faint rays of truth in the chaotic ponderosities of Emerson; but in that Word, the Everlasting Truth, which shall never pass away, our author will find life and light, truth and joy.

Art. IV.—*Popular Rhymes and Nursery Tales; a Sequel to the Nursery Rhymes of England.* By James Orchard Halliwell, Esq. 24mo, pp. 276. London: John Russell Smith.

HAD a reviewer in former times thought of noticing a book like these 'Popular Rhymes and Nursery Tales,' he would have felt it necessary to commence with a formal apology to his readers, for occupying their attention with a subject so childish—nay, worse, so common-place and vulgar. Thanks to the labours of many professed scholars, above all to Grimm, no apology is needed in the present day for bringing before the reader these fragments of what has been well termed our 'Folk-lore,' and which are to be gleaned, by careful search, from the cottage, the farm-kitchen, the nursery itself; fragments consisting of little more than snatches of old song, of wild, but often singularly constructed stories, of doggrel rhymes, which though lisped by the child, or hummed by the old nurse, are still most useful as forming parts of a once important whole, just as the minute *tesseræ*, and fragments of pottery, wherewith the child may amuse himself, become valuable to the antiquary as indicating the site of some luxurious Roman villa, perhaps of the stately forum.

Truly does Mr. Halliwell say—

'Traces of the simplest stories and most absurd superstitions are often more effectual in proving the affinity of different races, and determining other literary questions, than a host of grander and more imposing monuments. The history of fiction is continually efficacious in discussions of this kind, and the indentities of puerile sayings frequently answer a similar purpose. Both, indeed, are of high value. The humble chap-book is found to be descended not only from mediæval romance, but also not unfrequently from the more ancient mythology, whilst some of our simplest nursery-rhymes are chanted to this day by the children of Germany, Denmark, and Sweden, a fact strikingly exhibiting their great antiquity and remote origin.'—P. 1.

The same may be said of our nursery tales. The story of Whittington's cat—the chief incident relating to the cat, perhaps we should rather say—was told, before Whittington's time, in Italy. The story of Cinderella's slipper, too—not the sweet story of the poor outcast girl, sitting disconsolate in rags and ashes, but watched over by the kind fairy, for that belongs to our northern climes, but the tale of the prince finding the slipper, and sending forth messengers to seek out the owner—had already been told by Herodotus in the story of Rhodope. But there are others which are closely connected with the myths of

the ancient world. 'Jack the Giant Killer is founded on an
Edda;' and 'Jack and the Bean-stalk '—that marvellous bean-
stalk which grew so high that no man could see the top, and
which still, as the boy hurried onward, stretched upward in mid
air, had, doubtless, its origin in the towering ash Yhdrasil.
Indeed the close similarity which Grimm so repeatedly points
out in the genuine nursery literature of Denmark, Sweden,
Germany, England, and Scotland, proves the common origin of
these nations even more forcibly than points of resemblance. in

m afar, and
we suspect they were originally crocodiles. We trace them in
a tale forming part of a series of stories entitled the relations of
Ssidi Kur, extant among the Calmuck Tartars:' and from the
same distant source, Sir Francis Palgrave derives the cap of
darkness, and the shoes of swiftness which aid our old friend
Jack in his exploits against the giants. 'The Bull of Norroway'
we are inclined to place rather among Scotch, than *English* nursery
tales; its similarity to the pretty story of 'Lily and the Lion,' in
the German tales, is, however, very striking, and the rhyme—

'Far hae I sought ye, near am I brought to ye;
Dear Duke o' Norroway, will ye no turn and speak to me?'

has quite the rythm of the remotest old time; although it cannot
compete with poor Lily's poetic adjuration: 'I have followed
thee seven years; I have been to the sun, and the moon, and
the night-wind to seek thee; wilt thou then forget me quite?'
The stories of 'the three questions,' of 'the Princess of
Canterbury,' and such like, closely resemble the German
humorous ones; and although certainly not of equal antiquity

with the foregoing, are yet admissible, inasmuch as they claim a
comparative antiquity, and illustrate the quaint, though often
rude, sort of humour, and the love for practical jokes, which our
Teutonic forefathers delighted in.    But the tale of 'Puss in
Boots,' pleasant though we found it in our childhood, and
pleasant, as involving a moral of gratitude towards the brute
creation, as it certainly does, is inadmissible here; for Perrault,
no more than Madame d'Aulnay—admirable weavers of fictitious
lore as they both were—has right to be heard, when the genius
of long past times, though in the guise of a nursery tale, speaks
out.    Let 'Puss in Boots' take his place with 'Beauty and the
Beast,' and the 'Royal Ram,' and 'the King of the Fortunate
Islands,' but not among these rude, half forgotten tales, which
were the solemn myths of an age long passed into oblivion.
   Among stories of high antiquity, although far from equal
interest with the old fairy-tale, may be placed those which, like
'the House that Jack Built,' tax the breath, as well as the
memory, of the child to get through them.

   'Accumulative tales are of very high antiquity.    The original of
"the House that Jack Built" is well known to be an old Hebrew
hymn in Sepher Haggadah.    It is also found in Danish, but in a somewhat shorter form (See Thiele, Danske Folkesagn, II. iii. 146, *Der
har du det Huus som Jacob bygde*); and the English version is probably
very old, as may be inferred from the mention of "the priest all shaven
and shorn."    A version of the old woman and her sixpence occurs in
the same collection, II. iv. 161, *Konen och Grisen Fick*, the old wife
and her piggy Fick,—"There was once upon a time an old woman who
had a little pig hight Fick, who would never go home late in the
evening, so the old woman said to her stick :—

       'Stick, beat Fick, I say!
       Piggie will not go home to-day!'"

   'This chant-tale is also common in Sweden.    One copy has been
printed by N. Lilja in his Violen en Samling Jullekar, Barnsanger och
Sagor, i. 20, *Gossen och Goten Neppa*, the boy and the goat Neppa,—
"There was once a yeoman who had a goat called Neppa, but Neppa
would never go home from the field.    The yeoman was therefore
forced to promise his daughter in marriage to whoever could get Neppa
home.    Many tried their fortune in vain, but at last a sharp boy
offered to ward the goat.    All the next day he followed Neppa, and
when evening came, he said, ' Now will we homeward go?' but Neppa
answered, ' Pluck me a tuft or so,' " &c.    The story is conducted in an
exactly similar manner in which the *dénouement* is brought about in the
English tale.'—P. 6.

   'Piggie' has indeed a wide popularity, for it is known in
Sweden, and also in Alsace.
   The superstitions connected with animals, and their accompa-
nying rhymes, lead us back to a very high antiquity.    Little are

that when the child sings the rhyme, 'Lady-bird
away home,' he is singing the self-same words
in Sweden, Denmark, and Germany, sings, and
have been handed down from the remotest antiquity.
the lady-bird, or lady-cow, should be a general favou
not surprising, when its harmlessness, and its pleasing appearance are remembered; but it seems difficult to account for the

rather surprising, considering the important station assigned to
the raven among the Teutonic tribes, that so few tales, or old
rhymes, respecting him should be met with; the magpie, indeed,
almost seems to have usurped his place, as indicating good or ill
fortune.   The rustics, however, are not altogether agreed as to
the signs; for while in Lancashire the rhyme assigns 'mirth,'
from the appearance of two, in Yorkshire they are considered as
an undoubted sign of bad luck—indeed, Tim Bobbin expressly
says he would ' as leef o' seen two awd harries.'   One magpie is,
however, considered a sad bringer of misfortune, but this it is
believed can be obviated, ' by pulling off your hat, and making
a very polite bow;' and this, Mr. Halliwell tells us, he has ' more
than once seen quite seriously performed.'
The 'superstition rhymes' and charms form a very curious
chapter, although it is melancholy to think that even in the
present day so many are still religiously believed in by our
peasantry—nor indeed by these alone, but by many townspeople
also.   The efficacy of rhyme, in curative processes, seems to
have obtained from the earliest times; and the mighty
powers assigned to 'the Runic rhyme' are well known to

our readers. That peculiar short jingling verse which is so common in nursery rhymes, is pointed out, we remember, by Sir Francis Palgrave, as greatly resembling those in the Anglo-Saxon metrical psalms; and we have often thought that the pleasing, though rather monotonous chant to which it is sung, might be even a more than *faint* echo of the very music sung by the Trolquind, as she circled the cauldron and threw in the mystic ingredients. Many of the herbs thus used are still dear to superstition. Vervain, of classical celebrity, was in great estimation with our forefathers, and here is an ancient formulary, to be said when gathering it.

'A magical MS. in the Chetham Library at Manchester, of the time of Queen Elizabeth, furnishes us with a poetical prayer used in gathering this herb:

> " All hele, thou holy herb vervin,
> Growing on the ground;
> In the mount of Calvery
> There was thou found;
> Thou helpest many a greife,
> And stanchest many a wound.
> In the name of sweet Jesus,
> I take thee from the ground.
> O Lord, effect the same
> That I doe now go about."

The following lines, according to this authority, were to be said when pulling it:

> " In the name of God, on Mount Olivet
> First I thee found;
> In the name of Jesus
> I pull thee from the ground." '

We can easily perceive the substitution here of the name of our Lord, and of Mount Calvary, for the original names of some god and sacred locality of heathendom. Mr. Kemble, in his most interesting work, to which we lately called the attention of our readers, 'The Saxons in England,' gives, in his appendix, some curious instances of these Christian substitutions, and among them that charm which Mr. Robert Chambers has given as still considered efficacious in dislocated limbs.

> 'Our Lord rade
> The foal slade,' &c.,

in its original Saxon, and in it Thor is represented as the rider, and as performing the cure. The efficacy of the vervain is almost forgotten, but the beneficial influence of the ash is still fully believed in. Warts are supposed to be charmed away by sticking the pin with which the warts have been crossed into an ash tree, and the leaf of the even-ash will indicate to the young woman who bears it in her hand her future husband. The ash-keys are supposed, in Essex and Suffolk, to bring good fortune; and the undoubtedly heathen custom of passing a sick child, for the recovery of its health, through the cleft trunk of a tree, is only efficacious with the ash-tree. We are surprised Mr. Halliwell has not referred to this most singular superstition, which, as we were informed by correspondents to the 'Folk Lore,' which appeared in the 'Athenæum' three years ago, is actually practised both in Gloucestershire and Devonshire. The reason of the high degree of veneration with which the ash is regarded, is evidently derived from the myth of the ash, Ygdrasil, 'the world-tree, from whose boughs fall the bee-feeding dew, and which embraces earth, heaven, and hell.' Ague— that malady so dependent on the nerves, and, therefore, the very ailment to be affected by whatever laid hold on the imagination, —is thought, even in the present day, to be curable by the first branch of the maiden ash being cut off in secrecy and in silence. The following rhyme, alone, is still used in some parts to cure the ague; and if the patient has but faith enough in it, will, doubtless, go far to effect a cure.

> 'Tremble and quake!
> First day shiver and burn:
> Tremble and go!
> Second day shiver and learn:
> Tremble and die!
> Third day never return.'

These rhymes certainly have some meaning, but 'charmers' did not always care even for that, as the following will prove:—

'Reginald Scot relates, that an old woman who cured the diseases of cattle, and who always required a penny and a loaf for her services, used these lines for the purpose:—

> " My loaf in my lap,
> My penny in my purse;
> Thou art never the better,
> And I am never the worse."

'The same writer gives a curious anecdote of a priest who, on one occasion, went out a-nights with his companions, and stole all the eels from a miller's wear. The poor miller made his complaint to the same priest, who desired him to be quiet, for he would so denounce the thief and his confederates by bell, book, and candle, they should have small joy of their fish. Accordingly, on the following Sunday, during the service, he pronounced the following sentences to the congregation:—

> " All you that have stol'n the miller's eels,
> Laudate Dominum de cœlis;
> And all they that have consented thereto,
> Benedicamus Domino."

" So," says he, " there is sauce for your eels, my masters!"

' An " old woman came into an house at a time whenas the maid
was churning of butter, and having laboured long, and could not make
her butter come, the old woman told the maid what was wont to be
done when she was a maid, and also in her mother's young time, that
if it happened their butter would not come readily, they used a charm
to. be said over it whilst yet it was in beating, and it would come
straightways, and that was this :—

> " Come, butter, come,
> Come, butter, come;
> Peter stands at the gate,
> Waiting for a buttered cake;
> Come, butter, come!"

This, said the old woman, being said three times, will make your
butter come, for it was taught my mother by a learned churchman in
Queen Marie's days; whenas churchmen had more cunning, and could
teach people many a trick that our ministers now-a-days know not."
(*Ady's Candle in the Dark*, 1656, p. 59.)'—Pp. 208—210.

Of dairymaids' charms there were, however, plenty; although
we doubt not that the just-mentioned rhyme, which bribed St.
Peter himself with the thoroughly English promise of 'a but-
tered cake,' was considered most efficacious; still the charm that
Master Reginald Scot recommends must have surpassed it, for
he quietly advises the master to look well to the dairymaid, 'that
she neither eat up the cream, nor sell away the butter.'

The chapter on ' Custom Rhymes ' is amusing; but we wish
Mr. Halliwell had collected from a wider range of materials.
While the silly rhymes and usages respecting saints'-days and
so-called ' holy-tides ' may be allowed to pass away, a collection
of the May songs and harvest-home songs, especially with their
*tunes*, would form a very interesting contribution toward the
history of our popular antiquities.

The chapter on ' Nursery Songs,' which concludes this little
volume, is by no means so full as it might have been. The
earliest lullaby songs are those in the Coventry Mysteries, full
a hundred and fifty years earlier than the one Mr. Halliwell has
given, and these the reader will find in Douce. ' Lairde Row-
lande, my son,' is simply an old ballad, whether in its Scotch or
English form, and, therefore, has no place among nursery songs,
any more than ' Chevy Chace,' or ' Fair Elinor.' ' I had a cock,
and he loved me,' with the merry enumeration of all the inhabitants of a farm-yard, and their crowing, and cackling, and
quacking, and grunting, and neighing, is a genuine nursery
song, and we doubt not might be sung with great effect and to
the no small delight of the little people there; ' Jack Sprat '
and ' Cock Robin,' too, legitimately belong to the nursery.
There is also a chapter on ' Game Rhymes,' and a description of

the games, but one of the prettiest known, and we consider it one
of the oldest—

      ' Here we go a ring, a ring,
        As maidens go a maying '—

is not mentioned; indeed, while we have been much pleased with
what Mr. Halliwell has done, we regret to observe marks of
haste, and also that his space is so limited.   Still we thank him
for his little book, which will recall to many a reader the pleasant
days of his boyhood; for sure we are, to use his parting words,
' the universal and absorbing prevalence of one pursuit has not
put to flight all kindly memory of the recreations of a happier
age.'

    ' The sports of childhood's roseate dawn
    Have passed from our hearts like the dew-gems from morn ;
    We have parted with marbles—we own not a ball,
    And are deaf to the hail of a " whoop and a call."
    But there's an old game that we all keep up,
    When we've drank much deeper from life's mixed cup—
    Youth may have vanished, and manhood come round,
    Yet how busy we are on " Tom Tidler's ground,
        Looking for gold and silver ! " '

----

ART. V.—1. *Tenth Report of the Colonial Land and Emigration Com-
    missioners.*   Folio.   1850.

  2. *Britain Redeemed, and Canada Preserved.*   By F. A. Wilson,
    K.L.H., G.S. ;   and Alfred B. Richards, Esq.   8vo.   London :
    Longman and Co.   1850.

BRITISH *emigration* has assumed the character of a great social
movement, in which all Europe is more or less taking part;
whilst British *colonization* lags behind at a pace painfully unequal—its failures fearfully contrasting with its successes.   The
very rapidity in the occasional progress of some of the colonies
sets their generally sluggish condition in dark relief, which betrays
the untoward influences obstructing their natural career.   The
following table of our emigration for twenty years past, shows its
fluctuating distribution in lights deserving the most serious
attention.   The original table in the Colonial Land and Emigration Commissioners' Report begins with 1823, in which year the
earliest large emigration in our time, 14,000, took place.   In the

first few years after the general peace the number was about
5,000 annually.

| YEARS. | North American Colonies. | Australia and New Zealand. | Cape of Good Hope, &c. &c. | United States. | TOTAL. |
|---|---|---|---|---|---|
| 1830 | 30,574 | 1,242 | 204 | 24,887 | 56,907 |
| 1831 | 58,067 | 1,561 | 114 | 23,418 | 83,160 |
| 1832 | 66,339 | 3,733 | 196 | 32,872 | 103,140 |
| 1833 | 28,808 | 4,093 | 517 | 29,109 | 62,527 |
| 1834 | 40,062 | 2,800 | 288 | 33,074 | 76,222 |
| 1835 | 15,573 | 1,860 | 325 | 26,720 | 44,478 |
| 1836 | 34,226 | 3,124 | 293 | 37,774 | 75,417 |
| 1837 | 29,884 | 5,054 | 326 | 36,770 | 72,034 |
| 1838 | 4,577 | 14,021 | 292 | 14,332 | 33,222 |
| 1839 | 12,658 | 15,786 | 227 | 33,536 | 62,207 |
| 1840 | 32,293 | 15,850 | 1,958 | 40,642 | 90,743 |
| 1841 | 38,164 | 32,625 | 2,786 | 45,017 | 118,892 |
| 1842 | 54,123 | 8,534 | 1,835 | 63,882 | 128,344 |
| 1843 | 23,518 | 3,478 | 1,881 | 28,335 | 57,212 |
| 1844 | 22,924 | 2,229 | 1,873 | 43,660 | 70,686 |
| 1845 | 30,803 | 830 | 2,330 | 58,838 | 93,500 |
| 1846 | 43,439 | 2,347 | 1,826 | 82,239 | 129,050 |
| 1847 | 109,680 | 4,949 | 1,487 | 142,154 | 258,270 |
| 1848 | 31,065 | 23,904 | 4,887 | 188,233 | 248,089 |
| 1849 | 41,367 | 32,191 | 6,490 | 219,450 | 299,498 |

There is no official return yet for 1850; but the number is
understood to have fallen, except in one port, Liverpool.
    The original country of the emigrants—England, Ireland, or
Scotland, and their distribution in the colonies, in India, in the
United States, in South America, may be collected from the
Report, and its Appendix. Of those of 1849, about 170,000
were Irish, 120,000 English, and 10,000 Scotch. All the Irish
settled in the North American colonies and the United States,
except *six*, who went to the West Indies. The only adventurers
to the East Indies were 1,202 English and 10 Scots. The
English settlers in Africa were 3,350, and Scots 139. Neither
Scots nor Irish went to California, Vancouver's Island, China,
Port Natal, Van Dieman's Land, Western Australia, the Auckland Islands, or to the Falklands. Englishmen were scattered
everywhere ; even Central and South America received 599 of
them, with 53 Scots. This distribution of our people abroad is,
however, in a great degree probably casual, and not to be traced
to any peculiarities in *national* character. The poor Irish go to
North America only, because the passage is cheap ; and they
prosper there. But the Irish *convicts* in the Australias prosper

equally with those from England and Scotland. The female Irish orphans lately sent to New South Wales are well reported of, and are worthy of a better destination. Let circumstances favour free Irish emigration elsewhere, and it will spread elsewhere with advantage.

The fluctuations in emigration to the colonies, as shown in the preceding table, and which are so injurious to the colonial labour-market, as well as to the progress of the settlements, indicate great errors in our administration. The sudden start in 1840, and especially in 1848 and 1849, in South Africa, is to be traced to the partial correction of those errors, which can indeed be so easily corrected, that, if a good system for all the colonies be not soon introduced by act of parliament, so as to attract emigrants, the colonial legislatures themselves may be expected to make early efforts to form a system for their respective localities.

But the most striking feature of the table is the broad contrast it exhibits between the fluctuations in the resort of emigrants to our colonies, and their steady thronging to the United States. To change this, means must be devised at home, at any cost, to open new fields of colonial enterprise, and so to divert towards prosperous British settlements the hundreds of thousands of valuable men at present annually lost to us.

At the same time, it is to be remarked, that the increase of emigration is not likely to go on at the same enormous rate, unless the stimulus of system be used to give a permanent character to the movement, already beginning to halt. The commissioners notice the great decrease of emigration in the first three months of 1850, compared with that of the same months of 1849; —viz , from 60,000 to 46,000. This decrease, however, allowed for, enough remains to require zealous endeavours to give to emigration the best possible direction; and abundant evidence has been produced in a most interesting chapter of the book quaintly entitled, ' Britain Redeemed, and Canada Preserved,' to prove that fields of emigration, sufficiently extensive for all our needs, are at our doors. They are to be found in Central British America, which Lord Selkirk discovered in vain forty years ago.

The time is now propitious for a minute inquiry into the true character of that region; and colonial reform, already very seriously begun, will, if properly guided, turn our increased emigration into extended colonization ; in which case, Central British America, connected as it is with the New World now opened on the Northern Pacific, offers an inexhaustible resource to our people. Thus *the power reserved in the last charter, granted to the Hudson's Bay Company, to carve colonies out of its territories, may have to be acted upon sooner than was expected.*

Not only does the increase of emigration show a necessity of further colonial reforms, in order that we may colonize as well as emigrate; but ministers seem to have been preparing the way for those reforms, and, in addition to essential facilities given to emigration, to make the foundation of new colonies more and more parts of our public policy.

'Great and increasing importance is attached to the questions *connected* with emigration,' say the Colonial Land and Emigration Commissioners, in opening their valuable Report of 1850; and the observation is the more worthy of attention, as it is the first official hint of what must have been passing in the Cabinet on the subject of *emigration* since the Prime Minister's declaration at the commencement of last session,—not only that several unpopular *colonial* constitutions should be reformed, but also in favour of measures to keep uncurtailed, and even to extend, our colonial empire. The mode of conveying this hint was significant, although characteristically cautious.

The words of these Commissioners have often, in years past, been mere echoes of ministerial deliberations; and such they clearly were on this occasion. In his speech on Colonial Reform, Lord John Russell insisted, that to help emigrants by Treasury grants would damage emigration; this unintelligible paradox is reproduced in the Report, although with studious avoidance of all allusions to the fact, that emigration is less damaged by unwise Treasury help, than the cause of colonization is injured by impolitic colonial government. At the same time, in examining, with all the care the topic demands, the choice between assisting our people to settle in British colonies, and letting them go to the labour-market of the United States, so long as it is sufficient to employ them, the Commissioners do not disguise that there are 'political considerations of great moment connected with the question.'—(*Tenth Report*, p. 3.)

Such, unquestionably, was the opinion of the minister, who did not overlook the bearing of the Commissioners' statistics, proving our positive decline in the 'profitable business' of *colonizing*, whilst they exhibit the enormous advantage to the United States of the increasing emigration of our people thither. This disagreeable contrast, which Lord John Russell was certainly studying in the winter of 1849-50, with results afterwards stated in the Report before him whilst preparing his speech, must have been quite as strong a stimulus to the determination to introduce colonial reform as the succession of parliamentary defeats upon colonial questions which threatened the administration. These simple and convincing statistics, taken out of the tabular form, are as follows :—

From 1830 to 1839, 290,000 only of our people went to the

United States, whilst 320,000 went to our North American colonies.

From 1839 to 1847, 500,000 went to the States, and only 354,000 to those colonies.

But in the last two years, the United States received 400,000 of our emigrants, and our North American colonies got 72,000 only. So that, whilst our emigration itself has increased, with slight fluctuation, for twenty years, more and more of our people have gone every year direct to the United States. But even in the year of its greatest increase, 1849, our North American colonies obtained fewer of these emigrants than they had before received; and besides this positive decline, an extensive emigration is going on from the North American colonies themselves to the United States, with but little from the latter to the former. It is possible that, although in the ten years, from 1829 to 1839, the American colonies received 320,000 out of the whole body of our emigrants, they could not have accommodated the other 292,000, who were consequently compelled, as the Commissioners say, to settle in the United States. But it would be hardly possible that in the next eight years, from 1839 to 1847, the same colonies, with boundless tracts of good land still in command, could accommodate only 354,000 more emigrants, so that the surplus, 500,000, must, *against their wishes*, go to the United States. And, however that might be, it is absolutely incredible, that the last distribution of 72,000 to those colonies in 1848 and 1849, and of 400,000 to the United States, should have taken place without the operation of more potent causes than a short passage to New York, and high wages, relied upon by the Commissioners.

These causes still less satisfactorily account for the fluctuations in the emigration to our respective colonies themselves, during a series of years.

The North American colonies from 1830 to 1849, began with 30,574 emigrants in the first year, and ended with 41,367 in the last, having in the intermediate years run through every degree of variation from 4,577 to 109,600. The Australian colonies and New Zealand, during the same period, began with 1,242 emigrants in the first year, and ended with 32,191 in the last, having in the intermediate years run through still greater variations from 32,625, down to 830; and from 1842 to 1848, emigration to these colonies was almost extinguished. The Cape of Good Hope and other colonies have offered no fluctuations in this period of twenty years, but since the grievous disappointment of 1819 impediments of all sorts have gratuitously prevailed, and emigration to them was so uniformly low until 1849 and 1850, that the reproach due to the former cases for

uncertainty, equally belongs to this for negligence in our
colonial policy. All this time, emigration to the United States
has gone on regularly increasing from 24,887 in 1830, the first
year, to 219,000 in 1849, with the single exception of a
great falling off in 1838, the disturbed year of the Canadian
rebellion.

Lord John Russell must have seen in these facts grounds of
apprehension. They betrayed the incapacity of our colonial
administration, and were startling illustrations of the mischievous
character of the colonial system it has set up in breach of the
best principles of the constitution. It was the ancient, express
duty of the Government to encourage colonies. It has of late
years determined to discourage them. New Zealand and Natal
had become ours in spite of a reluctant Government. The
different destination of Oregon and California, which might
have become British without reproach, affords the Government
a poor vindication from the charge of being ambitious and eager
to cover the earth with British settlements. The dangerous
character of our modern colonial system, to which reform is at
last coming, has received a startling illustration in the unparal-
leled legislative purpose to *annex* the Canadas to the United
States—realizing Franklin's pictorial satire of Britannia quietly
suffering her arms and legs to be lopped off. The late *emigration* of our people by hundreds of thousands to the United
States, furnished with capital estimated at 25,000,000*l.* sterling,
is analogous to *annexation*, and equally discreditable to our
colonial governments ; but chiefly to the colonial administration in Downing-street. Few will be satisfied with the following
feeble reasons which the Commissioners offer as explanatory of
the fact :—

' Such a result,—(say the Commissioners, in reference to the disproportion of 72,432 emigrants to the British Colonies in 1848 and 1849,
to the 407,683 who emigrated to the United States in the same two
years,)—may be considered as, in some measure, the necessary consequence of the vast increase of emigration in late years. So long as the
emigration was comparatively small, the proportion for which the
British American provinces could find employment, and a home, formed
no inconsiderable part of the whole. *But as emigration increased,
without any corresponding increase in the means of employment in British
North America*, the numbers who were compelled to look for a home
in the United States became larger. These again, by sending home
funds to enable their friends and relations to emigrate, assisted to keep
up the stream of emigration to the States. At the same time, other
circumstances, such as the SUPERIOR accommodation on board the
American " liners," and the comparative shortness of the voyage to
New York, conduced to the same end.'—*Tenth Report*, p. 2.

This, we repeat, will satisfy no reasonable mind. Laying

aside, as of little moment, the shortness of the distance,' and the superiority of the ships to New York, this logic of the Commissioners is false. The proper explanation of the fatal figures produced by the Commissioners is, that our emigrants are, on the whole, better off in the United States, voyage and wages all included, than in our colonies; in which condition of things the only question worth discussing is, whether this comes from their unchangeable nature—from soil, or climate, or situation—or whether it is attributable to acts of government which reform can alter. How British emigrants are better off in the United States than in their own colonies, concerns a very large number out of 200,000 to 300,000 souls, who, in all time to come, will every year have to determine the choice of new homes. The solution of the difficulty also concerns the proper expenditure of more than two millions of pounds sterling, annually taken from us by these emigrants; as well as the general interests of the country, which are materially affected, according as this emigration is most profitably directed. The mass of the emigrants shape their course to new homes, just as they can go cheap, and as they can be sure of employment. Now from the improvement in the internal navigation up the St. Lawrence, across the lakes and by our canals, the passage by Quebec to the great fields of settlement in the West is *cheaper* and quicker than that by New York. If the American 'liners' continue to be superior to ours, with this advantage in our favour, the disgrace will belong to the British shipowner. So much for the first head. In regard to the second, *employment*, the Commissioners declare that Canada and the other North American colonies *cannot* offer attractions equal to those of the United States. But this involves the whole subject of monarchical-colonial government compared with republican government; and it will be exceedingly difficult to convince reasonable minds that Upper Canada, and the vast interior beyond to the Pacific, NEED be less attractive than the States lying in the *same* parallels of latitude, and in *less* advantageous conditions for transfer of supplies and produce. A like hesitation will occur in admitting the *necessity* of comparative backwardness in our other colonies, and still less the *necessity* of greater fluctuations in their progress.

The first material distinction between the position of the settler in our colonies and that of the British emigrant to the United States, is, that the colonist sinks at once to an inferior political condition,—the emigrant to the United States becomes a sharer in republican sovereignty. This evil in the British colonies is soon felt in the most important relations of life; and although the reforms that are certain in the constitutions of the Australias and the Cape of Good Hope will do much to lessen it, the change in that respect does not go to the root of the matter. The Canadian constitutions are popular, and quite as good as those now preparing for the eastern colonies ; but, as the Commissioners say, ' *the Canadas are not able to employ the lower class of emigrants thither ; and the prospects of even artizans and mechanics were in* 1848 *less encouraging than in former years. So, from the depressed condition of New Brunswick, nearly all the emigrants of the season in* 1848, *and* 8,000 *of the old inhabitants, went to the United States.*'* Something more, then, is necessary than popular constitutions in the colonies themselves for their steady prosperity, and to make them capable of receiving *our* emigrants: and that something is the reform of the system of the Colonial Office, through the introduction of colonial members into the House of Commons. This would invigorate all our colonial measures, and connect harmoniously the resources and wants of our home and colonial world. Ordinary public works are pronounced to be too dear to be undertaken on parliamentary grants of money ; which, it is insisted, would have the inconvenient effect of stopping the present large remittances from America, to pay the passage of the friends of former years' emigrants to join them.

' Such objections, however, apply in their full force,' say the Commissioners (*Report*, p. 5), ' only to a grant of public money towards emigration generally. They apply with much less force to assistance by loan, or grant, to a special locality, in order to enable it to relieve itself from some temporary congestion of population for which there is no employment. They do not apply at all to assistance in such circumstances from local rates ; in which case the rate-payers have all the knowledge necessary to a just, and all the personal interest necessary to a frugal, application of the funds. In the latter case, judicious assistance can scarcely fail to be as advantageous to the rate-payers as to the emigrants ; and it is to be regretted that, in districts where labour is in excess, the powers in the Poor Law Act, for raising funds for emigration purposes, are so little resorted to.'

The perplexity springing from the want of resources in Canada, which the people at home are unwilling to supply, for the purpose of keeping emigrants within the British boundary, might be removed if that colony were not, in another point, inferior to the United States. That point is, the encouragement of territorial enterprise and aggrandisement, respecting which there is a grand distinction to our disadvantage. Both Governments are equally careless of the rights of the aboriginal occupants of the soil ; but the British adventurer has in practice lost his old constitutional privileges as to newly-acquired lands, which the American pioneer and squatter enjoy. The conse-

_____

* Report, p. 3.

quences of this distinction may be seen in the ruins of such promising enterprises as Lord Selkirk's, on the Red River, in Central British America; Lieutenant Farewell's, at Natal; and in the recent and more deplorable ruin of the New Zealand Company; compared with the slightly-varying success of the United States' settlements along their whole western frontier, from Ohio in 1777 to Oregon, California, Texas, and New Mexico, in our time. The Government of the United States encourages such settlements; ours discourages them. The American *territories*, peopled mainly by squatters, are essentially states; our borders, covered with wanderers of the same classes of men, are scenes of lawlessness or of neglect.

The work of Messrs. Wilson and Richards proposes an effectual remedy for the present want of territorial attractions in the interior, by opening it on a plan of great importance, although sadly encumbered with strange speculations, on the *voluntary* abandonment of its wealth by the Established Church for the good of the poor; on covering central British America with convicts to promote its moral culture; and on the conquest of Japan, for the purpose of spreading civilization in the East; and the like in almost endless profusion.

But the projected line of settlement and cheap railways from Halifax (*eight days' steam from Ireland*), *via* Quebec, due west by Lake Superior, 28,000 miles to Vancouver's Island on the Pacific, which is not perfectly new, is worked out in this volume with great effect. The rigour of winter in this region is clearly shown to be by no means such as its latitude would lead us to suppose; the productiveness of the soil is unquestionably great; the engineering difficulties of the railway line are not insuperable; and its construction would be very cheap.

The first stretch of this gigantic undertaking is from Halifax to Gueva, 400 miles, of which there is little difficulty to prove the practicability and advantage. And, since our authors first speculated on this portion of their gigantic line, it has been begun by a powerful company, with some slight variation of the starting point, which is now in New Brunswick. The second 400 miles cover a region which is thus described:—

'Among other imperfect attempts to take cognizance of these abandoned portions of our British possessions, an exploring expedition was sent out by Sir John Colborne, Governor of Canada, who reported that they have found excellent land. Settlements have since been gradually creeping in upon this central reserve; whilst vast deposits of ore have been discovered on its leading river, the Ottawa; and some of the richest copper in the world on the shores of Lake Superior, with the finest forest trees, such as oak of the best quality, and of great size, prodigious elms, and gigantic walnut-trees.'

For another thousand miles the forests and the plains furnish the thinly-scattered posts of the Hudson's Bay Company with rude plenty, and all the luxuries of nature. At one point is drawn a striking picture of a spot, which the authors compare advantageously with a flourishing Russian settlement in a similar locality. After tracing the proposed British settlements through a rich country well known to the factors of the Hudson's Bay Company, although almost unknown in England, and now a tenantless desert, Messrs. Wilson and Richards close this part of their narrative with a clear and powerful contrast of that desert with the adjacent settlements of the United States, and the parellel settlements of the Russians.

If the conjecture be well founded, that Ministers have been seriously contemplating a great measure of emigration at the public expense, all the colonies will share it according to their respective capacities of receiving and disposing of the emigrants. But it is plainly to the above-described regions that the millions must be sent. The shortness of the voyage thither, and the abundance of its internal resources, determine the choice of this New United Kingdom ; and the success of a national emigration to that place may be secured at the cheap price of great care in every department of this service, of which our vast experience should have furnished system, and the spirit of colonial reform that is abroad will soon supply in that system the essential means of good colonial and emigration administration. A few of those means shall be very briefly mentioned.

The first is *to acquire knowledge of colonial things, colonial men, and colonial interests.* If we go on governing in the dark, as at present, we must go on misgoverning. The acquisition of this knowledge is impossible by official despatches and reports alone, as now used. Therefore, on this account, and still more in order to rule like British statesmen, Canada, and all the other North American colonies, must be incorporated with England, by bringing members from them into parliament. The measure is in harmony with our earliest history ; and its difficulties are trifling, compared with the immense advantages it would confer on the whole empire, to which the principle must be applied.

The Congress at Washington receives such *colonial* members from the American *territories,* and others from the incorporated new states every year, with an increase of strength and of order. The British Parliament has been made more numerous on the same principle already, in the admission of members from almost all our European dominions ; and there are other quarters of the earth want only the declaration of our will and an invitation to make the adoption of this great measure easy.

Complete *publicity* in regard to the chief acts of the Colonial

Office, by reviving the great Lord Somers's yearly reports of all the colonies, as shown on the journals of Parliament, not the present disjointed and almost casual disclosures produced by the explosion of discontents, would shed a flood of purifying light over misdoings in that office.

So *the restitution of the controlling power of the Privy Council* over that office, by permitting all appellants against it to *be heard there*, will work a silent revolution in its policy and character. These things, together with good constitutions for all the colonies, will make us a great people indeed!

On minor points much remains to be done.

The Commissioners say, they have laboured hard to form a corps of capable *emigrant*-ship surgeons: an excellent object, on which their last report contains many prudent remarks. And they would have done a graceful act by declaring the obligations we are all under to the late Mrs. Maury, of Liverpool, the eloquent advocate of the measure of compelling *all* emigrant ships to have surgeons. The great perseverance of that lady overcame the curiously ignorant resistance to the measure, for which our own Government and that of the United States were equally culpable. And both cut an equally sorry figure in the correspondence which she spiritedly carried on and published on the subject. Before her death, she had the satisfaction to know that the measure she had so earnestly called for, after seeing the extreme need of it in her own voyages, was carried.*

*Emigrants' homes* are zealously called for at the great out-ports. At Plymouth one such is formed. It is an establishment, partly, or wholly, founded upon benevolent contributions of money, at which *some* of the passing emigrants can spend the few last days of their stay before sailing, safely, comfortably, and with economy; and where, also, *all* may obtain disinterested and correct information. Of all the out-ports, Liverpool is that in which these emigrants' homes are the most wanted, good as are many of the ordinary lodging-houses for emigrants. Above 166,000 emigrants left Liverpool in 1849; and last year more than 174,000. The mass are Irish; ill provided with money or necessaries. They suffer grievously from the elements, and from the far more pitiless ' *man-catcher*,' a well-known term in this port. The unquestionable fact of the iniquitous conduct these poor people are too often exposed to, has led to the earnest proposal of one emigrants' home on a large scale in Liverpool. Great differences of opinion prevail on the subject; and those differences having prevented the local authorities executing a

---

* See the history of the Emigrants' Surgeons' Bill, in Mrs. Maury's ' Englishwoman in America.' Liverpool. 8vo. 1848.

plan carefully prepared for this object, *a bill is to be brought into Parliament next session to carry out their plan.*  The usual notice has been given ; and a powerful association is already formed to support the measure.

When it is considered that the sum of 600,000*l.* is now spent by emigrants in Liverpool, it is easy to see that the parties interested in its expenditure are not likely to be quiet under the threatened diversion of any part of it.  A similar objection was made to a *Sailors' Home :* one of those admirable institutions which do honour to our time—providing a bank for the imprudent, patronage for the friendless, instruction for the intelligent, and innocent amusement for all.

But, as neither the *Sailors' Homes* nor the Emigrants' Homes pretend to substitute huge charities for the common business of living, both deserve support ; and, perhaps, the greatest advantage to be ultimately derived from both will be, to improve the character of the private establishments for similar objects.  In New York, the '*British Protection Emigrant Society*' has laboured, for six years, to guard the hundreds of thousands of friendless people from 'fraud and imposition of every sort,' by which crowds of unprincipled men in that city feed upon them. How much corresponding societies are wanted at the ports of *departure,* may be inferred from the fact, that *confederates of the rogues are known* to be in the practice of taking their passages in the emigrant ships as a speculation, in which to inveigle the real emigrants to their connexions in America!  Mr. Labouchere's Act will exceedingly improve the character of the passenger service, along with that of the merchant service at large ; and the Emigration Commissioners have done much to improve the discipline and comfort of emigrant ships.  But all that is done, falls far short of what ought to be accomplished.  Exact calculations may be made as to all the reasonable wants of emigrants on shipboard ; and those wants, with a proper provision on arrival, must by all means be satisfied from various sources under compulsion of law at setting out.  The most extravagant outlay possible in such a case for *necessaries,* is economy compared with letting our colonial lands lie waste, our people be idle at home, or sent miserably out.  A more brilliant accompaniment of the Exhibition of 1851 could not be conceived, than the promulgation of a wise and beneficent plan of emigration, which should send our multitudinous visitors from the wildest regions, back with news of successive swarms being about to come from our full hive to help to fill the earth, and to share in advancing the civilization of its inhabitants.

ART. VI.—*A Lecture on the 'Genius of Pope.' Delivered at the Leeds Mechanic Institution.* By Lord Carlisle.

'THERE shall be no Popes,' is at present the cry' of Britain. 'Yes,' interjects Lord Carlisle, ' there shall be one—Pope Alexander—the Alpha and the Omega of poetry, the infallible High-priest of all the Nine.' And some two thousand men of Leeds have shouted a loud Amen to his words.

We were not fortunate enough to hear Lord Carlisle's lecture on Pope. But his appearance on a lecturing platform is a sign of the times, too important to be overlooked, and his lecture itself is sufficiently able to entitle it to notice. Besides, it furnishes us with a peg for a candid review of Pope as a writer, which seems a desideratum in the criticism of the age.

In what various aspects and attitudes, besides those of legislation, have the lords of the British Parliament contrived to exhibit themselves! We have had lords fighting, drinking, gaming, embezzling, presiding at Bible and Missionary meetings, publishing travels, horse-racing, building telescopes, endowing colleges, poetizing, running away with other people's wives, doing, in short, a thousand wise or foolish, good or bad, actions, with characteristic energy and independence; but a lord lecturing is almost a new thing under the sun. *It* is an action at once bold and good, at once startling and wise; it is the stooping of a noble nature; it proclaims a proper sense of what the age demands from those who have a hereditary stance upon its high places, this, namely, that they not only rule but teach—not only present a living example, but utter a powerful precept, that they be guides, as well as governors, to the lower classes of the community. A lord, indeed, can lecture more gracefully, and more effectively, than any other man. A recluse student, however profound, is a mere bear in a lecture-room. A man of genius becomes an awkward compound of the prophet and the play-actor. Even around those best qualified for that peculiar arena, who unite grace and gravity, depth, and the elegant *dishabille* of its expression ; who can, at one and the same time, realize their *subject* and their *audience,* there hangs often a certain paid and professional air. In one word, lecturing is, in general, a vulgar and a false medium between the higher and the less instructed minds of the community; it is not a spontaneous and beautiful rain, like that from a summer-tree, dropping irresistibly upon the soil below. But when an intelli-

gent and kind-hearted scion of the nobility appears on the platform, it is as if—

> ' Like Maia's son he stood,
> And shook his plumes.'

He is a volunteer in the cause.   He has come, uninvited, not to
attend, but to give a feast.   He is presumed to be superior to
all doubtful motives, whether of interest or vanity.   If he
wanted praise, it would be that of his peers.   The cheers of
2,000 humble men cannot brighten the lustre of his riband, or
add to the glory of his star.   He can, therefore, ' speak with
authority.'   He can take his place at once as one of the natural
guides, the born counsellors, the unhired advocates, the friends—
fathers of the people, who has come down from the vantage-
ground of his rank to instruct and comfort his inferiors, and who
wears the proud plumage of his high degree only to enhance the
beauty and dignity of that message which he bears, and which
is more than worthy to be carried on ' feathers covered with
silver, and with yellow gold.'

All this we hold to be true of Lord Carlisle's late visit and
lectures to the West Riding.   Indeed, if anything could revive
the ancient spirit of loyalty to the nobility of the land—if anything could redeem them from the aversion which bespatters
them, go where they may ; or, if anything, on the other hand,
could elevate the lecture-platform from its present false, low,
and fast-lowering position ; it were the frequent renewal of such
advents as that of this noble and accomplished lord.

We heard him give the second of his two lectures—that on
America—and were profoundly impressed by the scene presented.   Standing up, as in a shrine, and receiving the sincere
and heart-steaming incense of two thousand human beings, Lord
Carlisle preserved his equanimity, dignity, and meekness ; and,
without the slightest vestige of even concealed vanity, began to
speak as if he had been alone by the side of Lake Huron.  The object
of his lecture was, manifestly, to give as much information in
a short compass as he *intelligibly* and *gracefully* could ; and this
object was accomplished.   We learned more of America from
his two hours' lecture, than from Dickens's two volumes of
' Notes.'   Omitting all useless details, leaving a thousand things
to be elegantly understood, touching minor points with a slight
and masterly finger, and never or seldom aspiring either to the
profound in thought or poetical in language, his descriptions of
nature were free, graphic, and rapid ; his sketches of character
were discriminating and candid ; his statement of facts was clear
and full ; and his glance at contested questions was quiet and
quick, yet never failed to give us precisely the impression he

wished to convey. The most masterly passage of the lecture was one in which he stated, *seriatim*, the advantages and disadvantages, the merits and defects, of America, the country, and of the American character. No summing up was attempted; and to us, at least, no summing up was needed. The balance was left in that exact equipoise in which Providence has at present left it. America, the Country of the Future, must *depend* on the Future for its complexion, and cannot give it to the Future. The influences which shall make or mar it, must, we think, come from the East.

Lord Carlisle read one or two pieces of poetry, composed by himself, which were much applauded. They seemed prose vigorously rocked into the appearance of poetry. His lordship is not possessed of the *mens divinior*—the 'vision and the faculty divine.' But under two subjects, especially, he broke down—Daniel Webster and Niagara. From the one, indeed—that black-browed Jupiter Tonans of the West—he ran away, like a boy from a bull, crying out, 'What horns! what a bellow! what a brow!'

But he fairly tried to grapple with the other, and, like everybody else, was overthrown. Niagara remains in her wilderness, visited, painted, panegyrized, but undescribed. Dickens has attempted it—but, as some one has said, would have better succeeded with the 'next pump.' Howison, in an excellent, but, we fear, forgotten, volume of travels, walks and talks 'about it and about it,' and rather drenches us with its spray, and deafens us with its noise, than lets us into its 'secret place of thundering.' Fanny Kemble springs back from it, like a frightened actress from an adder, crying out, in true stage phrase,

'O God! who can describe that sight?'

Lord Carlisle, although he failed in describing Niagara, indicated well the reason why it has not hitherto been described. One must *grow* to grasp its greatness. The first feeling at beholding it is, and must be, that of disappointment. It were the same at the first sight of the sun to one born and brought up, till manhood, in a mine. And this springs—not so much from the indefinite and exaggerated language in which the marvel has been described, and the undue expectations which have thereby been excited—not so much from the *inferiority* of the object to that language and those hopes, as from its *unlikeness* to them. We have been expecting something different from, if not superior to, the reality. Hence a shock of disenchantment. We find a stranger, where we had been looking for an old familiar friend. From a hundred descriptions, we have generalized, painted, framed, suspended in our souls an image of the object, which, when placed beside it, seems a contrasted colour—red instead of green, or orange where we had expected blue. But we are determined to surmount this first shock, and to see the object ' as it is'—whether it be the sun or Niagara—let us *wait*, and the sun will dawn on us at noon, and Niagara will slowly gather glory as it gathers spray around its head, and seem at last to the enthusiast, a thing ' born out of due time,' a belated ' fountain of the great deep,' broken up at the deluge ; or, one of the giant cataracts of Jupiter transferred to our tiny planet, and thundering out an everlasting sense of its disproportion to human scenery and to human souls.

But our proper business is with his lordship on Pope. The ' little Nightingale of Twickenham' was a subject better adapted to his talents and taste than Niagara—the tongue of the world.

He commences his lecture by deploring the fact that ' Pope had sunk in estimation.' And yet, a few sentences after, he tells us that the ' present Commissioners of the Fine Arts' have selected Pope, along with Chaucer, Shakspere, Spenser, Milton, and Dryden, to fill the six vacant places in the New Palace of Westminster. This does not substantiate the assertion that Pope has sunk in estimation. Had he sunk to any great extent, the Commissioners would not have dared to put his name and statue beside those of the acknowledged masters of English poetry. But, apart from this, we do think that Lord Carlisle has exaggerated the ' decline and fall' of the empire of Pope. He is still the most popular poet of the eighteenth century. His ' Essay on Man,' and his ' Eloisa and Abelard' are in every good library, public or private, in England. Can we say as much of Chaucer and Spenser ? Passages and lines of his poems are stamped on the memory of all well-educated men. More terse sayings of Pope are afloat than of any English poet, except Shakspere and Young. Indeed, if frequency of quotation be the principal proof of popularity, Pope, with Shakspere, Young, and Cowper, is one of the four most popular of English poets. In America, too, Lord Carlisle found the most cultivated and literary portion of that great community devoted to Pope.

What more would his lordship desire ? His favourite Pope is, a century after his death, by his own showing, a great and general favorite wherever the English language is spoken. And we are persuaded that there is not a literary man alive but will subscribe, on the whole, to Lord Carlisle's enumeration of the Poet's many exquisite qualities—his terse, and motto-like lines—the elaborate gloss of his mock-heroic vein— the tenderness of his pathos—the point and polished strength of his satire—the force and *vraisemblance* of his descriptions of character—the delicacy and refinement of his compliments ; 'each of which,' says Hazlitt, ' is as good as an house or estate'; and the heights of moral grandeur into which he can at times soar, whenever he has manly indignation, or manly patriotism, or highminded scorn, to express.

Why, then, has Lord Carlisle sought to defend one against whom no charge was brought?  Why make a client out of an acquitted, rewarded, honoured man?  Why create a jury, that he might instruct them by a sham charge, and obtain a needless and belated verdict?  Why has he '*plentifully* declared the *thing as it is ?*'  If his object was to elevate Pope to the rank of a classic, it was a superfluous task ; if it was to justify the Commissioners in placing him on a level with Chaucer, Shakspere, Spenser, and Milton, we hope to show that it was as vain as superfluous.

In endeavouring to fix the rank of a poet, there are, we think, the following elements to be analyzed :—his original genius—his kind and degree of culture—his purpose—his special faculties—the works he has written—and the amount of impression he has made on, and impulse he has given to, his own age and the world.  In other words, what were his native powers, and what has he done *for*, *by*, and *with* them ?

Now that Pope possessed genius, and that of a high order, not even Bowles or Wordsworth have denied. But whether this amounted to creative power—the highest quality of the poet—is a very different question.  That Pope possessed *that* eyesight which sees in the rose a richer red, and in the sky a deeper azure, and in the sea a more dazzling foam, and in the stars a more spiritual gold, than Nature's 'own sweet and cunning hand put on ;' or, that this supreme vision ever lighted him on to form a new and more gorgeous nature—the fresh creation of his own inspired soul—we beg leave distinctly to deny.  In native imagination, Pope was not only inferior to Chaucer, Shakspere, and the rest, with whom Lord Carlisle and the Commissioners have associated his name, but to twenty besides among the poets of Britain: to Young, Thomson, Collins, Burns, Wordsworth, Coleridge, Shelley, Byron, &c.  Pope's native faculty, indeed, seems rather fine than powerful—rather timid than daring, and peeps out rather like the petal of a rose into the summer air than the feather of the wing of a great eagle, dipping into the night-tempest which raves around the inaccessible rock of his birthplace.  In proof of this, many of those fine aphorisms which he has thrown into such perfect shape, and to which he has given such dazzling burnish, are proved by Warton and others to be borrowed.  Shakspere's wisdom, on the other hand, can be traced to Shakspere's brain, and no further.  Who lent Chaucer his pictures, fresh as dew-drops from the womb of the morning?  Spenser's Allegories are as native to him as his dreams.  And as to Milton, if he has now and then carried off a load which belonged to another, it was a load which his arm only could lift, and which he added to a caravan of priceless and hereditary wealth.

The highest order of poets descend upon their sublime sub-jects like Uriel on his sunbeam ; the second, with care, and effort, and circumspection, often with

> ' Labour dire and weary woe,'

reach noble heights, and then wave their hats, and dance in astonishment at their own perseverance and success.  So it is with Pope, in the peroration to the Dunciad, and in many other of the serious and really eloquent passages of his works.  They *are* eloquent—brilliant—in composition faultless ; but their in-tense consciousness, and visible elaboration, prevent them from seeming and from being great. Of Pope you say ' he smells of the midnight lamp '—of Dante boys cried out on the streets, ' Lo ! the man that was in Hell.'  With the first class of poets, artificial objects become natural—the ' rod ' becomes a ' serpent ; ' with Pope, natural objects become artificial—the ' serpent ' becomes a 'rod.'  Wordsworth makes a ' spade ' poetical ; Pope would have made Skiddaw a mass of prose.

A great deal was said, during the famous Bowles and Byron controversy, about the question as to what objects are, or are not, fitted for poetic purposes.  The real gist of this matter lay in a previous inquiry—Is the eye which beholds them a poetical eye, or not ?  For, given a poet's eye, then it matters little on what object that eye be fixed—it becomes straightway poetical, or, more strictly speaking, the poetry already in it comes rushing out to the silent spell.  Now Pope, it appears to us, wants al-most entirely this true second sight.  Take, for instance, the ' lock' in his famous Rape ! What fancy, humour, wit, eloquence, he brings to play around it !  But he never touches it, even *en passant*, with a ray of poetry.  You never could dream of inter-twining it with

> ' The tangles of Neaera's hair,'

far less with the ' golden tresses ' and ' wanton ringlets ' of our primeval parent in the garden of Eden.  Shakspere, on the other hand, would have made it a dropping from the shorn sun, or a mad moonbeam gone astray, or a tress fallen from the hair of the star Venus, as she gazed too intently at her own image in the calm evening sea.  Nor will Pope leave the ' lock ' entire in its beautiful smallness.  He must apply a microscope to it, and stake his fame on idealizing its subdivided single hairs.  The

Sylphs are created by combining the smallness of Ariel with the lively impertinence of the inhabitants of Lilliput.   Yet with what ease, elegance, and lingering love, does he draw his petty Pucks, till, though too tiny for touch, they become palpable to vision !   On the whole, had not the ' Tempest ' and the ' Mid-summer's Night Dream ' existed before the ' Rape of the Lock,' it had proclaimed him a man of creative imagination.   As it is, it proves wonderful activity of fancy.   Shakspere's delicate creations are touched again without crumbling at the touch, clad in new down, fed on a fresh supply of ' honey-dew,' and sent out on minor but aerial errands.   Ariel's ' oak ' becomes a ' vial ; ' ' knotty entrails ' are exchanged for a ' bodkin's eye ; ' the fine dew of the ' Bermoothes ' is degraded into ' an essence ; ' pomatum takes the place of poetry ; an enchanted lock of an enchanted isle, and the transformation of original imagination into ingenious fancy is completed before your eyes.   Let the admirers of Pope, like those of Cæsar, beg not a ' hair,' but a ' lock ' of him, for ' memory ; ' for certainly he is more at home among curls than in any field where he has chosen to exercise his powers.

About Pope, originally, there was a small, stunted, and trivial *something*, which did not promise even the greatness he actually attained.   We do not seek to prop up the nine pin notion by alluding to his small stature, remembering that Napoleon over-threw half the thrones of Europe.   But he possessed, *sana mens in sano corpore*, an erect figure, and was ' every inch a man,' although his inches were few.   While in Pope, both bodily and mentally, there lay a crooked, waspish, and petty nature, which his form but too faithfully reflected.   He was never, from the beginning to the close of his life, a great, broad, genial nature.   There was an unhealthy taint, which partly enfeebled and partly corrupted him.   His self-will—his ambition—his pariah position as a pro-fessed Roman Catholic—the feebleness of his constitution—the uncertainty of his creed—and one or two other circumstances we do not name, combined to create a life-long ulcer in his breast, against which the vigour of his mind, the enthusiasm of his literary tastes, and the warmth of his heart, struggled with much difficulty.   He had not, in short, the basis of a truly great poet, either in imagination or in nature.   Nor with all his incredible industry, tact, and talent, did he ever rise into the ' seventh heaven of invention.'   A splendid Sylph let us call him—a ' Giant Angel' he never was.

His culture, like his genius, was rather elegant than profound. He lived in an age when the knowledge of the classics, with a tincture of the metaphysics of the schools, was thought equiva-lent to learning.   He seems to have glanced over a great variety

of subjects and books with a rapid *recherché* eye, not with a
quiet, deep, longing, lingering, exhaustive look.   He never
'trusted that he could draw up Jordan into his mouth.'   He became thus neither an ill-informed writer—like Goldsmith, whose
ingenuity must make up for his ignorance—nor one of those
*doctorum poetum*, whose works, according to Buchanan, shall
alone obtain the rare and regal palm of immortality.   That his
philosophy was empirical, is proved by the ' Essay on Man,'
which, notwithstanding all its brilliant rhetoric, is the shallow
version of a system of shallow scepticism.   And one may accommodate to him the well-known saying about Lord Brougham,
' who would have made a capital Chancellor if he had had only
a little law;' so Pope was very well qualified, barring his ignorance of Greek, to have translated Homer.   But every page of
his writings proves a wide and diversified knowledge—a knowledge, too, which he has perfectly under his control, which he
can make go a great way, and by which, with admirable skill, he
can subserve, whether his moral or literary purpose.   But the
question now arises, what was his purpose?   Was it worthy of
his powers?   Was it high—one holy and faithfully pursued?
No poet, we venture to say, can be great without a great purpose.   Purpose is the edge and point of character; it is the
stamp and superscription of genius; it is the direction on the
letter of talent.   Character without it, is blunt and torpid; talent
without it, is a letter, which, undirected, goes nowhere.   Genius
without it, is bullion, sluggish, splendid, and uncirculating.   Now
Pope's purpose seems, on the whole, dim and uncertain.   He is
indifferent to destruction, and careless about conserving.   He is
neither an infidel nor a Christian—no Whig, but no very ardent
Tory either.   He seems to wish to support morality, but his
support is stumbling and precarious, although, on the other
hand, he exhibits no desire to overturn or undermine it.   His
bursts of moral feeling are very beautiful, but brief, and seem
the result of momentary moods, rather than the spray of a strong
steady current.   In satire, he has not the indomitable pace and
deep-mouthed bellow of a Juvenal pursuing his object like a
bloodhound, he resembles more a half-angry, half-playful terrier.
To obtain a terse and musical expression for his thought, is his
artistic object, but that of his mind and moral nature is not
so apparent.   Indeed, we are tempted at times to class him with
his own Sylphs in this respect, as well as in the cast of his intellect.   They neither belonged to heaven nor hell, but wavered
between in graceful gyrations.   They laughed at and toyed
with all things, never rising to dangerous heights—never sinking
into profound abysses—fancying a curl a universe, and a universe
only a larger curl—dancing like evening ephemera in the sun-

beam which was to be their sepulchre, and shutting their tiny eyes to all the grave responsibilities, solemn uncertainties, and mysterious destinies of human nature. So too often did their poet.

Pope's special faculties it is not difficult to see and enumerate. Destitute of the highest imagination, and of constructive power (he has produced a number of brilliant parts, but no *great* whole), he is otherwise prodigally endowed. He has a keen, strong intellect, which, if it seldom reach sublimity, always eliminates sense. He has wit of a polished and powerful kind, yet less refined and delicate than Addison's, the very curl of whose lip was crucifixion to his foe. This wit when exasperated into satire, is very formidable, for, like Addison's, it does its work with little noise. Pope whispers poetic perdition—he deals in drops of concentrated bitterness—he stabs with a poisoned bodkin—he touches his enemies into stone, with the light and playful finger of a fairy, and his more elaborate invectives glitter all over with the polish of profound malignity. His knowledge of human nature, particularly of woman's heart, is great, but seems more the result of impish eaves-dropping than of that thorough and genial insight which sympathy produces. He has rather painted manners than men. His power of simulating passion is considerable, but the passion must be mixed with unnatural elements ere he can realize it—his game must be putrid ere he can enjoy its flavour. Humour he has none. It is too much of an unconscious outflow, and partakes too much of the genial and human nature for him. His fancy is lively and copious, but its products resemble rather the forced fruits of a hot-house than those of a natural soil and climate. His description of Sporus, lauded by Byron as a piece of imagination, is a mass of smoked gumflowers. Compare, for mere fancy, the speeches of Mercutio, with the ‘Rape of the Lock,’ if we would see the difference between a spontaneous and an artificial outpouring of images—between a fancy as free as fervid, and one lashing itself into productiveness. His power of describing natural objects is far from first-rate ; he enumerates instead of describing ; he omits nothing in the scene except the one thing needful—the bright poetical haze which ought to have been there. There is the grass, but not the ‘splendour’—the flower, but not the ‘glory.’ In depicting character it is very different. His likenesses of men and women, so far as manners, external features, and the contrasts produced by the accidents of circumstances, and the mutation of affairs, are inimitable. His power of complimenting is superior even to that of Louis XIV. He picks out the one best quality in a man, sets it in gold, and presents it as if he were conferring instead of describing a noble gift.

' Would you be blest, despise low joys, low gains,
*Disdain whatever Cornbury disdains,*
Be virtuous, and be happy for your pains.'

His language seems to have been laboriously formed for his peculiar shape of mind and habits of thought. Compared to all English before him, Pope's English is a new, although a lesser language. He has so cut down, trimmed, and shorn the great old oak of Shakspere's speech, that it seems another tree altogether. Everything is so terse, so clear, so pointed, so elaborately easy, so monotonously brilliant, that you must pause to remember ' these are the very copulatives, diphthongs, and terminations of Hooker, Milton, and Jeremy Taylor.' The change at first is pleasant, but by and bye, you begin to miss their deep organ tones, their gnarled strength, their intricate but intense sweetness, their voluminous music, their linked *chains* of lightning—and to feel the difference between the fabricator of lines and sentences, and the former of great passages and works. In keeping with his style is his versification—the incessant tinkling of a sheep-bell, sweet, small, monotonous, producing perfectly melodious single lines, but no great masses of harmony. The grand gallop of Dryden is exchanged for a quick trot. And there is not even a point of comparison between his sweet singsong, and the wavy snow-like, spirit-like motion of Milton's loftier passages, or the gliding, pausing, fitful, river-like progress of Shakspere's verse, or the ' torrent rapture' of brave old Chapman, in his translation of Homer; or the rich, slow-swimming, long, drawn-out melody of Spenser's ' Faery Queen.'

Our glance at Pope's individual works must necessarily be brief and cursory—the more so, as we have no copy of his works beside us. His ' Ode to Solitude' is the most natural thing he ever wrote—and in it he seems to say to nature, ' Vale, longum, vale.' His ' Windsor Forest' is an elegant accumulation of sweet sounds and pleasant images, but the freshness of the dew is not resting on every bud and blade. Keats could have comprised all its essential poetry into a single sonnet; Thomson, or Wordsworth, into one epithet. The ' Essay upon Criticism' is a wonderful feat for a boy of nineteen, a unique collection of clever and sparkling sentences—displaying the highest powers of talent and assimilation—but hardly a gleam of profound and original insight. Yet would that more of our critics were to write in verse. The music might lessen the malice, and set·off the common-place to advantage. If not ' reason,' there would be at least ' rhyme.' His ' Lines to the Memory of an unfortunate Lady' are too elaborate and artificial for the theme. It is a tale of murder and suicide, set to a musical snuff-box! His 'Rape of the Lock' has been already characterised. It is an ' Iliad in a nutshell'—an Epic of Lilliput, where all the proportions are accurately observed, and where the finishing is so exact and admirable that you fancy the author to have had microscopic eyes. It proves him a pyramid among pigmies, a man-mountain among a race of Tom Thumbs; and contains certainly the most elegant and brilliant badinage, the most graceful raillery, and the most exquisitely managed machinery in the language. His ' Pastorals' have an unnatural and luscious sweetness. He has *sugared* his milk. It is not, as it ought to be, warm from the cow, and fresh as the clover. His ' Eloisa and Abelard' is to us the most untrue and ill-chosen of all his poems. He compels you indeed to weep, but you blame and trample on your tears after they are shed. Pope in this poem, as Shelley in the Cenci, has tried to extract beauty from death, and to glorify moral putrefaction. But who can long love to look at worms, however well painted; or will be disposed to pardon the monstrous choice of a bride for the splendour of her wedding garment? The passion of the Eloisa and that of the Cenci were both indeed facts, but many facts should be veiled statutes in the temple of Truth. To do, however, both Pope and Shelley justice, they touch their painful and shocking themes with extreme delicacy. ' Dryden,' well remarks Campbell, ' would have given but a coarse draught of Eloisa's passion.' His moral satires, epistles, characters, &c., contain much of the most spirited sense, and elegant sarcasm in literature. ' Villars,' and Addison, will occur to the mind of every reader. His Homer is rather an adaptation than a translation—far less a transfusion of the Grecian bard. He does not, indeed, go the length of clothing in a bag, sword, and big-wig, the old blind rhapsodist, but he does all short of this to make him a fine gentleman, and something of a *petit-maître* too. Scott, we think, could have best rendered Homer in his ballad-rhyme. Chapman is Chapman, but he is not Homer. Pope is Pope, and Hobbes is Hobbes, and Sotheby is Sotheby, but none of them is, nor has even thoroughly tried to be, the grand old Greek, whose lines are all simple, plain, but pointed on their edges with fire, like the lances of his warriors, and who we could fancy to have dipped a spear in blood, and to have written with it on the Chian sand the first draught of his immortal poem.

Those who are disposed to stake much of Pope's reputation upon his Homer, should remember this pregnant fact, that the one-half of the Odyssey was translated by such second-rate men as Broome and Fenton, and so well translated, that it was impossible to distinguish their twelve books from his!

' Ha! I think there be *six* Richmonds in the field.'

Imagine three employed about Chapman's Homer! The task of making ten of *his* gigantic lines would have given Broome an asthma, and driven Elijah Fenton to prussic acid!

Two works of Pope's remain to be glanced at. The 'Essay on Man' ought to have been called, an 'Epigram on Man;' or, perhaps, better still, should have been propounded as a riddle, to which the word 'Man' was to supply the solution. But an Antithesis, Epigram, or Riddle, upon Man, of some thousands of lines, is rather long. Especially it seems so, as there is no real or new light cast in it upon man's destiny or nature. In fact, the Essay, or Epigram, on Man, is just the eloquent expansion of two thoughts—the one to be found in Shakspere's 'Hamlet,' and the other in Pascal's 'Pensées.' But such an eloquent and beautiful puzzle as it is! It might have issued from the work-basket of Titania herself. It is another evidence of Pope's greatness—in trifles. How he would have shone in fabricating the staves of the Ark, or the fringes of the Tabernacle!

The 'Dunciad' is, in many respects, the ablest, the most elaborate, and the most characteristic, of all Pope's works. In embalming idiots, preserving fools, impaling cockchaffers, he seems to have found at last his most congenial work. With what sovereign contempt, masterly ease, and judicial gravity, does he set about it! And once his Museum of Dunces is completed, with what dignity, the tyrant mannikin that he was! does he march through it; and with what complacency does he point to his slain and dried Dunces, and say, 'Behold the work of my hands!' It never seems to have occurred to him that his poem was destined to be an everlasting memorial, not only of his enemies, but of the annoyance he had met from them—at once of his strength in crushing, and his weakness in having felt their attacks, and in showing their mummies for money!

That Pope deserves, on the whole, the name of 'Poet,' we are willing to concede. But he was the most artificial of true poets. He had within him a real, though limited vein, but did not trust sufficiently to it, and at once weakened and strengthened it by his peculiar kind of cultivation. He weakened it as a power, but strengthened it as a faculty; he lessened its inward force, but increased the elegance and facility of its outward expression. What he might have attained, had he left his study and trim gardens, and visited the Alps, Snowdon, or the Grampians— had he studied Boileau less, and Dante or Milton or the Bible more—we cannot tell; but he certainly would have left works greater, if not more graceful, behind him; and if he had pleased his own taste, and that of his age, less, he might have touched the chord of the heart of all future time. As it is, his works resemble rather the London Colosseum than Westminster Abbey—

they are exquisite imitations of nature, but we never can apply
to them the beautiful words of the American poet :—

> ' O'er England's abbeys bends the sky,
> As on its friends with kindred eye ;
> For Nature gladly gave them place,
> Adopted them into her race,
> And granted them an equal date
> With Andes and with Ararat.'

*Read,* doubtless, Pope must always be—if not for his poetry
and passion, yet for his elegance, his wit, his satiric force, his
fidelity as a painter of artificial life, and the clear, pellucid
English in which his thoughts are shown.  But his deficiency in
the original or creative faculty (a deficiency very marked in two
of his most lauded poems we have not specified, his ' Messiah '
and ' Temple of Fame '); his lack of profound speculation ; the
poverty of his natural pictures ; the coarse and bitter element
into which his satire often degenerates ; the monotonous glitter
of his verse ; and the want of profound purpose and compact
unity in his writings ; combine to class him in the second, or,
perhaps, third rank, of poets.  And vain are all attempts—such
as those of Lords Byron and Carlisle—to alter the general
verdict.  It is very difficult, after a time, either to raise or to
sink an acknowledged classic.  And Pope, above many of this
rank, has obtained a 'peculiarly defined and strictly apportioned
place upon the shelf.  Once, unduly exalted, he was, in turn,
unduly depressed, and has risen, in fine, to his proper altitude.
He was, unquestionably, the poet of his age.  But his age
was far from being one of a lofty order.  Nay, it was, in many
respects, a low, languid, artificial, and lazily-infidel, age.  It
required to be tickled, and Pope tickled it with the finger of a
master.  It loved to be lulled into semi-sleep ; and the soft and
even monotonies of Pope's versification effected this end.  It
liked to be suspended in a state of demi-doubt, swung to and fro
in agreeable equipoise ; and the ' Essay on Man ' was precisely
such a swing.  It was fond of a mixture of strong English sense
with French graces and charms of manner, and Pope supplied
it.  It was fond of keen, yet artfully-managed satire, and
Pope furnished it in abundance.  It loved nothing that threatened greatly to disturb its equanimity, overmuch to excite or
arouse it, or to weigh in a trembling balance its own destinies ;
and there was nothing of this in Pope.  Had he been a really
great poet of the old Homer and Dante breed, he would have
outshot his age ' till he dwindled in the distance ;' but in lieu of
immediate fame, and of elaborate lectures in the next century to
bolster it up, all generations would have risen up and ' called
him blessed.'

ART. VII.—1. *Royalty and Republicanism in Italy; or Notes and Documents relating to the Lombard Insurrection, and to the Royal War of* 1848. By Joseph Mazzini. London : Gilpin. 1850.

2. *Young Italy.* By Alexander Baillie Cochrane, M.P. London : Parker. 1850.

AMONG the events which have characterised the recent history of Europe, and assisted us to conjecture the future, there is, perhaps, none more significant or remarkable than the rising of the Italian populations. They who from without attempt to judge of this movement, to penetrate into its causes, to comprehend its concomitants, to appreciate those who directed it, and to draw from the whole an augury of what is yet to happen, encounter innumerable obstacles, chief among which is the discrepancy between the testimony of witnesses, whom we might at first be tempted to pronounce competent. As we proceed with our investigations, light breaks in upon us, not exclusively through any one channel, but here a little and there a little, supplied consciously or unconsciously equally by the friends and enemies of the independence and freedom of the Peninsula.

The result, as far as we have been able to arrive at it, is, that Italy, impregnated with noble sentiments, by a race of political apostles, is combating—for the struggle, though under varying conditions, is still going on—for an idea. In this exclusively lies her hope of future emancipation. If her aim were bounded by material advantages, if she sought nothing but the increase of trade, the encouragement of industry, the laying down of railways, the inter-communication of scattered and unsympathizing communities, she might possibly secure these to herself without the turmoil and sacrifices of a revolution. Her object is far higher and nobler. She seeks to become a distinct country, having a centre and frontiers of her own, a peculiar political organization, a language, a literature, a civilization on which she may stamp the impress of her own character; domestic and foreign relations, different from those of her neighbours, and independent of them ; and, above all, a faith which, modified by traditions, by climate, by national feelings and peculiar forms of intellect, may be entirely her own, while it agrees on all essential points with the general system of Christianity.

There is something at once beautiful and refreshing in the contemplation of a people either acquiring a knowledge of its rights for the first time, or recovering it after long ages of indolent indifference. Italy is in the second predicament. Once she stood at the summit of civilization, dispensing the rudiments of instruction and power to the whole of the known world; inviting, almost forcing, other countries to follow her example; flooding them with learning and philosophy, and affording them the strongest incitements to emulation by the example of her heroes and statesmen. Time, at length, however, witnessed her fall, and a long night of superstition and servitude followed in which she lay confounded with the least enlightened regions of the globe. What had once constituted her glory came in the end to constitute her shame; her intellect degenerated into craft; her pride into a base vanity; the energy and genius by which she had excelled in all liberal and useful arts, into mere instruments of luxury and effeminacy. She became a scorn and byword among nations, until the name of her children was synonymous with whatever was ignoble, sordid, selfish, unpatriotic.

Causes, originating in that mental effervescence which for more than three centuries has been gradually diffusing itself over Europe, at length inspired many Italians with the wish to emancipate their country. Having no domestic philosophy, they received the seeds of political regeneration from abroad—a fact which some of the leaders of Young Italy may be anxious to conceal. Dante, Machiavelli, Fra Paolo, and other great Italian writers, formerly no doubt contributed to awaken the political intelligence of Christendom. But to their own countrymen they were mute for centuries, and even now it may be doubted whether in any part of Italy there be more than a very few, who bestow sufficient study on their remains to derive from them any intellectual advantage. It was the example of Great Britain and France, and the shocks of the political earthquake of 1789, that awakened beyond the Alps the passion for independence and liberty. To overlook this, is to be blind to the teaching of history; but Italy need not blush to accept the germs of freedom from the martial north, since we return thus only a small portion of what in former ages she bestowed on us with a broad and liberal hand.

In studying this subject, which has an interest co-extensive with that of social improvement, we are constrained to make some observations which are by no means flattering to our contemporary literature. Strange to say, while the mass of the English people sympathize with the triumphs of liberty throughout the world, there are persons among us, more or less talented and educated, who employ themselves in decrying the efforts of other people to free their country, who labour to sully their noblest displays of patriotism, who heap calumny on their leaders, and thus convert their abilities into the instruments of tyranny, and so constitute them an offence against humanity and justice. Some time ago, we administered chastisement to one of this class of writers, who, limping with malignant impotence through Italy, sought to console himself for his personal sufferings by libelling the warm-hearted and friendly people in whose country he briefly sojourned. With such an individual we are sorry to class Mr. Baillie Cochrane. When confining his efforts to fiction, he writes pleasantly, and is, we dare say, an amiable and respectable man; but though a member of parliament, he seems never to have bestowed a second thought on politics. It would have been well, therefore, when the desire seized him to write something about Italy, if he had managed to gratify his love of authorship without touching on subjects altogether unintelligible to him. He is fond of quoting poetry, good, bad, and indifferent, applicable or inapplicable; we would, therefore, advise him to turn to the Earl of Roscommon's translation of ' De Arte Poetica,' where he will find this piece of advice :—

> ' Often try what weight you can support,
> And what your shoulders are too weak to bear.'

Mr. Cochrane describes very well, and tells a good story, but being entirely without classical learning, he spoils all by striving to appear erudite; he blunders into numerous displays of vanity, which sometimes excite our laughter, sometimes our pity. On approaching the Mediterranean, his self-esteem is inflated to such a pitch, that he imagines himself a second Scipio, and finds his friend Lælius—one of our well-known novelists, we believe—rusticating in grim dignity at Cannes.

In the emasculated literature of the middle of the eighteenth century, we have abundant Læliuses and Scipios, and Atticuses and Ciceros; and among the female entities, endless Delias and Celias, and Amelias and Corinnas, and Chloes and Daphnes. But the brood seems scarcely to have survived the century which gave it birth; and our contemptuous ridicule is excited by finding a fat gentleman, in blue frock-coat, white waistcoat, and trowsers, perking the name of Lælius in our face.

This, however, is a small fault compared with others found in Mr. Cochrane's book. To his opinions, whatever they may be, he is perfectly welcome. He may be a republican or a royalist, a democrat or an oligarch, a malignant or a patriot, just as the humour seizes him; but while he is rejoicing in his own liberty, which is his birthright as an Englishman, we invite him to think more charitably of other men, who, animated by the same passions and desires, covet liberty also in their turn. Mr. Cochrane, through some peculiar perversity of taste, appears to consider it genteel to advocate, in his small way, the cause of despotism. We are aware that nothing is more common than the worship of power. It is the characteristic vice of weak minds. Not comprehending how it is generated, or after what fashion it exists, they look up to it as a marvel and a mystery, and bend their knee before it instinctively. They cannot, however, be altogether ignorant that there exists in the world another class of men, who, through veneration for the dignity of their nature, refuse to become guilty of the idolatry of power. They think that the great thing is to be a man, and to acknowledge no superior but their Maker. Their object in life is to diffuse happiness, to enlighten and elevate their brethren—to take out from their breasts their hearts of clay, and give them hearts warm and full of passion like their own. To suffer and make sacrifices, to endure persecution, to make themselves the butts of calumny, sometimes even to shed their blood in the cause of liberty, is familiar to men like these.' Nor do they thus lose their reward, or. miss tasting the sweets of life. They have within them a treasure which the world knows not of—the conviction that they are promoting the good of mankind; that, long after they shall have passed away from this scene of struggles, the happy fruits of their toils and dangers shall be enjoyed by millions of their fellow-men.

This feeling is the basis on which pure patriotism rests; and taking into consideration the qualities of mind for which our English tourists are usually distinguished, we need not be surprised that they are incapable of sympathizing with it. What, for example, can Mr. Baillie Cochrane have to do with those processes of thought, or courses of action, of which the object is to ensure the happiness of others? He is a dandy, a politician in white waistcoat—a frequenter of fashionable saloons, a lisper of conventional formulas, who would be apprehensive— poor man—lest he should lose caste if he even appeared to desire the tumult of a popular movement. Austria is a great political fact, a thing recognised by pacts and treaties, possessing powerful armies, and equal therefore to the perpetration of enormous mischief. How could an amateur grinder of sentences be expected to emancipate himself from the superstitious reverence naturally engendered among the effeminate by such a political institution?

Properly speaking, there are only two classes among men— those who are formed to receive opinions, and those who are formed to give them. Mr. Baillie Cochrane belongs to the former, Mr. Mazzini to the latter. The one is a mere mental receptacle, in which all the intellectual frippery of past ages is suspended to decay and moulder at its ease; the other is a moving energy, which stedfastly resisting all impressions from without, originates its own ideas, and throws them forth profusely, fresh minted and glowing before the world. It is impossible, therefore, to experience any surprise at the difference we discover in their works. Throughout Mazzini's volume, one great thought seems ever present. His object is to do good to men ; to leave the world better, if possible, than he found it—to breathe once more into decayed and worm-eaten institutions the breath of life—to pull down the dens of superstition, and set up the pure lamp of religion and conscience where previously there was nothing but darkness. The helpless and common-place, the slaves of antiquated forms, the partizans and instruments of the established order of things, will doubtless pronounce him visionary and impracticable ; but all unrealized reforms are visions, and must remain so till they pass from the ideal world, from the region of theory and speculation, into that of stern practice. The world before the creation was a vision in the mind of God. All actions are visions till they are performed ; and that which is now the vision of Italian democracy will hereafter, we cannot doubt, be reckoned among the noblest of political realities, and shed glory and enjoyment over the most beautiful portion of this earth's surface.

Mr. Mazzini contemplates modern society from the right point of view. He perceives distinctly what is coming, and come when it will, must inevitably enjoy the happiness of having hastened its progress. He has thought and toiled for his species, and not in vain. All Italy is pervaded by his mind ; and there are many countries, once provinces of the Roman Republic, with others far beyond the circle described by the shadow -of the Capitol, which have derived incentives to liberty from his writings. Mistaken he may sometimes of course be, but we would almost rather be wrong with him than right with a conventional coxcomb like Mr. Baillie Cochrane.

In this sentimental individual we witness one of the worst effects of journalism. Incapable of forming an independent original opinion, he adopts his notions from his newspaper, of which he is a sort of hollow echo. The little experience he has had, and it is extremely little, has yet sufficed to teach him that among the privileged classes there is nothing so rare as an exalted love of country. He has, consequently, got the idea into his head, in common with thousands of others, that it indicates smartness, and a knowledge of the world, to doubt the sincerity of men's intentions, to throw the taint of suspicion on their noblest endeavours, and if they prove unsuccessful, to account for the triumph of evil in their case, by maintaining that these designs and projects were unworthy of accomplishment.

No achievement is easier than this. You have but to deny a few facts, to invent a few fictions, to deal liberally in aspersions, to refer all actions to false motives, and your work is done: Many, without being absolutely bad, have yet, from innate littleness, an extreme jealousy of whatever is great, and you accordingly delight them when calling in question, with the slightest appearance of probability, the virtues and achievements of public men.

In Mr. Cochrane's case, besides natural hostility to whatever is noble, there is a strong party bias, urging him into the wrong course. He is what is technically called a Conserva·tive, and that, too, of the worst and most crotchety school. Knowing, therefore, that the great body of the people of England, with whatever is liberal among the middle classes and the aristocracy, sympathizes with the heroic efforts made by Italy to emancipate herself from popes and kings, his political prejudices induce him to take part with the aggressors. He does not understand Italian affairs well enough to form an independent opinion on the subject. It must be obvious to the most cursory reader of his work, that he knows comparatively little of the antecedents of Italy; that the history of old Rome is a mystery to him; and that though he may have waded through Gibbon's words—which, however, we very much doubt —he has never certainly rendered himself master of the political wisdom which the work of that great historian is calcu-lated to teach. Doubtless, in flitting up and down the world of letters, he has occasionally caught glimpses of the fact, that there once existed a cluster of republics in Italy, which, however imperfectly they may have been organized, still bequeathed to posterity useful lessons in the art of government. But he has not been led by this marvellous discovery to perceive any unity of sentiment or purpose between the republicans of the present day and their forefathers of the middle ages. He sees, from the Alps to the Faro of Messina, nothing but vulgar agitators and anarchists, aiming at bringing down certain destruction on them-selves and their neighbours.

From motives of charity, we deeply commiserate a man when we find him in such a plight; and if it were not that we owe a duty to the public, should consider it cruel to expose him. But, as there may possibly be found in this country indi-viduals still more ill-informed than himself, we feel it incum-bent on us to warn them against following so blind a guide. One of the points on which he most earnestly insists, is the attachment of the humbler classes of northern Italy to Austria. This is one of the stalest fallacies in the whole armoury of political delusion. When the great revolution broke forth in France, there were not wanting persons in this country, who, with Burke at their head, laboured to propagate the opinion that the masses, together with the army, nobility, and clergy, were altogether sound in their loyalty to the monarchy; and that the confusion they beheld was the work of a few audacious democrats, madly intent on the ruin of their country.    There is nothing too wild for political fanaticism to invent, or for ignorance and preju- dice to believe; but since those days, the schoolmaster has been abroad, which Mr. Baillie Cochrane should have remembered when attempting the resurrection of the fictions and sophisms that bewildered and misled our fathers.

Whoever has been in Italy, and conversed for ever so short a time with the peasantry, must have remarked that they are an extremely cautious race.    When a foreigner presents himself to them, especially if he be fair-haired, and look like an Austrian, they suspect at once that he is some agent of Radetzky, who has no other object than to rob them of their property, and turn them out helpless and hopeless on the world.    Of course, there- fore, they are in self-defence lavish in professions of attach- ment to Austria.    Slavery and fear put a mask on their faces; but let any master of the watchword of the Carbonari sit down with them by their firesides, take one of their children on his knees, and ask them solemnly whether they wish to bequeath to it all the concomitants of the Austrian yoke, and he will elicit a very different answer.    The mother will exclaim, with tears, that she prays nightly for deliverance from the yoke of the foreigner; and the father, with clenched teeth and threat- ening gesture, will point to the place of concealment in the wall, where his musket lies treasured up for the day of vengeance. This Mr. Baillie Cochrane might have known, had he ever ven- tured to stroll among the villages, and ask the humble hos- pitality of the poor.    One sentiment pervades the whole mass of the Lombardo-Venetian population—the sentiment of inex- tinguishable hatred to Austria.    It is impossible it should be otherwise; unless the Italian peasant were degraded and sunk in vice and ignorance below the Kaffir or the Hottentot.

Our readers must be more or less familiar with the events of the last three years, every one of which stamps, with a character of audacious fiction, the assertions made by Mr. Baillie Cochrane in the following passage:—

' It is quite unjust to suppose that Austria is regarded with un- favourable eyes by the population of Lombardy.    Charles Albert found, to his dismay and surprise, that it was far otherwise.    The nobility and the upper classes of the bourgeoisie retain all their ancient here- ditary animosity to the name and habits of the Tedeschi: not so the people—with a happier, although uncultivated, instinct, they perceived that the government which Austria organized at least preserved order, that the returns of their labour were secured to them, and that equal justice was administered; in the towns where many a man is naturally *alieni appetens, sui profusus.* As might be expected, there were sects and clubs which exploited all the possible errors of the Austrian Government for their own advantage; but throughout the provinces there is but one feeling—that the rule of some great power is the only possible means of saving the country from perpetual warfare and all its attendant miseries.'—Pp. 26, 27.

The reader must in this passage be struck by the absence of all logic. The nobility, the middle classes, the inhabitants of the towns, are excluded from the category of contentment in which the people are supposed to stand. But on what is the supposition based? Why, we are told that there exists but one feeling throughout the country, namely, the conviction that the rule of some great power is necessary to preserve order and tranquillity. But what has this conviction to do with its attachment to Austria? What the Northern Italians desire may, for aught Mr. Baillie Cochrane knows, be the rule of some great native democracy, capable of protecting the independence of the country, as well as of securing liberty to the citizen; and this is precisely what Mr. Mazzini supposes. We quote, therefore, from his work a passage indicating a very different state of mind among the Lombards from that which Mr. Cochrane attributes to them. It should be remarked, moreover, that one opinion is that of a man who passes through the country for his pleasure, and writes to gratify his vanity; while the other is that of an earnest politician, ready at any moment to make his life the guarantee of his sincerity, and who has given the world undeniable proofs of his unshaken honesty and veracity.

' The insurrection of Milan and of Venice. invoked by all true Italians, burst forth amongst a people irritated by thirty-four years of slavery, imposed upon Venetian-Lombardy by a foreign government, which was both abhorred and despised. Its immediate provocation arose out of the ferocious conduct of the Austrians, who sought to drown a revolt in blood, and who did not believe in a revolution. It was facilitated by the apostleship and by the influence which they had meritoriously acquired over the people, of a *nucleus* of young men, belonging for the most part to the middle classes, and who were all Republicans, with the single exception of one, who, however, gave himself out for one at the time. It was resolved upon, and this is a solemn boast of the Lombard youth, but too little known, when the abolition of the censorship, and other concessions, had been already published. Venetian-Lombardy asked not for ameliorations; it demanded independence.

' The revolution commenced without being desired or foreseen by the men of the municipalities, or by those who were parleying with

Charles Albert.   The youth of Milan had been fighting for three days, when these were already despairing of success, and regretting, in a proclamation, the abandonment of legal measures and the unforeseen absence of the political authorities, and proposing armistices of fifteen days' duration.   The revolution continued, supported chiefly by men of the people, fighting to the cry of " Viva la Republica," and directed by four men of the Republican party united in a council of war.   Alone it triumphed, costing the enemy 4,000 dead, and amongst that number 395 cannoneers.   These are incontestable facts, henceforth a part of Italian history.   The combat of the people began on the 18th of March. The Piedmontese Government was already extremely disquieted by the news from France, and the extraordinary fermentation which increased each day amongst its own people.'—Pp. 19, 20.

Doubtless, the time is not yet come for judging definitively the acts of Carlo Alberto or Pio Nono ; but a large portion of what the one and the other has done, is already so well known, that we can decide upon it as completely as our posterity of the twentieth century will be able to do.   This is not the case with the part taken by the diplomacy of England in Italian affairs.   Mr. Baillie Cochrane's party-politics naturally lead him to accuse our Government of having fomented disturbances in the Peninsula, with the intention of bringing about a state of revolution and anarchy, and afterwards, when events took a sinister turn, of abandoning the populations it had excited to the consequences óf their own rashness.   This accusation we believe to be unfounded : though it cannot be denied, that the policy we pursued during those two years of trouble was much less consistent and decisive than it ought to have been.   It was in our power to preserve the independence of Northern Italy, and the prolonged existence of the Roman Republic ; but, for reasons which we may possibly conjecture, but cannot as yet appreciate fully, we stood aloof from the agonies of Italy, and beheld her sink without stretching forth a helping hand.   Mr. Cochrane's views, however, on this subject, are so confused, prejudiced, and trivial, that they would scarcely deserve the most transient notice, if he were not a member of Parliament, and in the habit of joining with the wrong-headed among our Commoners to misrepresent the policy of Lord Palmerston.

When this knight-errant of absolutism speaks of the proceedings of the Pope, he falls into blunders and inconsistencies whose very number and enormity preserve them from refutation.   Nearly every sentence is fraught with error, and is calculated to make false impressions by collateral inferences. Nothing can be more contemptuous than his opinion of Pio Nono.   He describes, step by step, the follies and political crimes of which he was guilty ; but when these crimes and follies have resulted in their legitimate consequences, he starts back and accuses, not the author of them, but the individuals who aided the people in bringing their rash and incompetent ruler to reason.

We like a man with a dash of Quixotism in him, whether the windmills he combats be moral or physical, and, therefore, we experience at times a sort of affectionate leaning towards Mr. Cochrane. It matters not at all that we detest the governments he admires; that his heroes are our absolute aversion; and that the gentlemen he most vehemently vituperates enjoy our respect and esteem. We are pleased to see him lay aside his man-milliner habits, his silk and taffeta phrases, and attack our party in right earnest. It would have afforded us greater pleasure to bear testimony to his frankness and equity, had he exhibited anything of the kind in the treatment of his political opponents. But truth compels us to observe that among the most monstrous misrepresentations to which the bitterness of p
birth in our time, we know nothing that surpasses

sacrifice to impartiality, and gained the praise of magnanimity, for yielding to fallen men commendations which would have cost nothing. He seems to be possessed, however, by some dire consciousness that democratic principles have not been extinguished at Rome, though the statesmen who sought to realize them have, for the moment, been put down by overwhelming force, and has indited one of the most offensive rhapsodies against the Roman Republic we ever remember to have seen in print :—

‘ It is of course very difficult to obtain sufficient evidence of assassinations which are committed in the dark; but all that can be said is, that in almost every case in which the circumstances of the case could be investigated, the facts asserted by the party of order have been amply vindicated. The murders of the priests in 1792, at the Abbaye des Carmes, were committed in open day—murder shrank not from raising her livid head ; we know from the ecrou of the prison that the number of priests who were martyred there amounted nearly to one hundred, but under the Roman Republic how can any one pretend to enumerate the list of victims ? Some accounts give the missing priests at one hundred and eighty; others again increase the number to two hundred and fifty; but who can tell what acts of private vengeance were performed, what dastardly blows were given in the dark? All this history cannot record, for the people have never been numbered; but in such a case popular opinion is in general accurate, and those who live among the lower classes can form a pretty just estimate of the number of hearths which have been left desolate; and if mourning be not always a test of sorrow, it is at least an evidence of a loss sustained. On speaking to those who have mixed the most amongst the people, I find that the feeling is quite universal, that the number of murders far exceeded the limit assigned by those who were most hostile to the young Republic; and the reply that there were no public executions only serves to illustrate the cowardly profligacy of those who committed the atrocities.

' There is, however, one apology for the Roman citizens, namely, that the most conspicuous characters throughout the Revolution were foreigners. Of their military men, Garibaldi and Avezzanna, were Genoese; Mezacapa, a Neapolitan; Colonel Mettara, a Bolognese; Manara, a Milanese; Galletti, a Bolognese; Durando, a Piedmontese; Terrari, a Neapolitan; the brigands whom Garibaldi introduced into Rome, from the neighbourhood, could not have been less than two thousand. The sanguinary and ill-disciplined financieri were some three or four hundred, and taken from the frontiers, where they had filled, and duly performed, the triple duties of footpads, bravos, and revenue officers. Of the Romans, properly so called, very few were accused of being implicated in the massacres; and it is generally asserted that the mass of the people were never favourable to the Republican Government. This is a point on which the best informed may err; but, undoubtedly, the popular impression is, that all the demonstrations were organized by foreigners, by those commercial travellers of revolutions who travel about with their trunks full of specimens of constitutions, ready to turn out of hand any order that may be given them. That such was at least the impression of his Holiness, may be gathered from all his *motu proprios*, in which even when insult upon insult had been showered upon him, he still alluded to that pressure from without under which his people were suffering. I have not concealed, and assuredly in no way endeavoured to palliate, the evils of the Papal Government, but the people were well aware that his Holiness had endeavoured to relieve the administration of its abuses. That they behaved most ungratefully we must admit; that they rose against their benefactor is a fact which all history will record to their eternal disgrace; but it is something at least to say in their favour, that they acted under the influence of foreign demagogues, who, after they had satiated themselves with plunder, revelled in anarchy, and committed every atrocity, were the first to flee into the country, and leave their two-fold victims to bear the evil consequences.' —Pp. 117—120.

This long and dreary passage we have given without curtailment, that the reader may be able to follow us in the remarks we are about to make, and fully to recognise their justice. The first thing that must strike is the display of those artifices of rhetoric which even the most vulgar writers have at their command, especially when animated by vindictive prejudice. When a strict logic, however, is applied to these phantoms of argument they vanish from our sight. What have the assassinations in the prisons of Paris to do with the recent events in Rome? And yet we behold our unfortunate countryman laboriously grouping them together for the purpose of bewildering and misleading all who may have the weakness to put their trust in him. He admits that he has no grounds whatever to go upon ; that there are no documents; that there is no sort or form of evidence ; that he interrogated no witnesses ; that he obtained no distinct information, but trusted entirely to those floating and fallacious rumours on which he is silly enough to bestow the name of public opinion. His work, if there were any vitality in it, would be a disgrace to the literature of our age; but a few months, will obliterate it from memory, and consign it to contemptuous oblivion.

The least and meanest of human beings may mimic the malignity of their superiors; and thus we find the libeller of the Romans imitating the conduct charged against Addison in literature, by his great antagonist, who says of him, he was—

‘ Willing to wound, but yet afraid to strike.’

And so with Mr. Cochrane. He has scarcely named the person, and that incidentally only, at whom his blows in the above passage are chiefly aimed. But all Europe is familiar with his illustrious name, and experiences disgust and indignation at the efforts which have been, and are still, made by insignificant men, both here and on the Continent, to tarnish and disfigure it. We of course allude to Giuseppe Mazzini, the man of his age in Italy whose actions history will be proud to record, whose genius and virtue have sufficed to quicken and elevate a whole people, and who is yet destined, we trust, to witness the realization of his noble plans for the regeneration of his beloved country.

But let us proceed with Mr. Cochrane. He asks with much simplicity :—‘ Under the Roman Republic, how can any one pretend to enumerate the list of victims?’ True, but it is first necessary to prove that there were victims, and no evidence has yet been adduced that any individual, except Rossi, lost his life by the dagger for political reasons. That there may have been assassinations, originating in private revenge, is more than probable—such things occur in Italy as well as in other countries —and times of trouble and confusion are naturally chosen by men to wreak vengeance on their enemies. If any priests fell under the stiletto, it may have been by husbands, fathers, or brothers, whose dearest feelings they had outraged in the confessional. The Romans are a jealous people; their passions are fiery, and their memory of injuries enduring. Possibly, therefore, some of the fraternity of Gothland may have suffered their crimes by other crimes; but should this have been the case, we can discover nothing in the circumstance to justify Mr. Baillie Cochrane in directly attacking the Roman Republic, and indirectly Signor Mazzini.

When we fairly examine the accusations of this feeble libeller we feel ashamed of our employment. Criticism should scarcely condescend to deal with such inanities. Besides being utterly ignorant of the courtesies of political life, which forbid men of superior minds to introduce into contests with their equals coarse and unmannerly vituperation, Mr. Cochrane is incapable of comprehending the meaning of the terms he employs. 'On speaking to those,' he says, 'who mixed the most among the people, I find that the feeling is quite *universal*, that the number of murders far exceeded the limit assigned by those who were *most hostile* to the young Republic.' Now what signification is it possible to attach in this passage to the word universal? Does Mr. Cochrane mean to assure us that the great body of the Roman people, unquestionably attached to the Republic, laboured, after its downfal, to create the belief that more murders were perpetrated during its continuance than its worst enemies and detractors gave out? If this be his aim, we know not which he merits most, our scorn, or our pity; for if the malignity be great, the imbecility is still greater.

Mr. Cochrane's ideas of human society are probably peculiar to himself. He thinks it quite possible for a few strangers to arrive on a given day at a city like Rome; to compel the people against their conviction to take up arms and overthrow their Government; to establish other institutions altogether distasteful to themselves; to make immense pecuniary sacrifices; to devote their lives to the new order of things; to fight with heroic valour and constancy in its defence; and, by way of exercise, to assassinate their friends and neighbours, merely to gratify insolent and ferocious foreigners. All this is implied in the following silly sentences :—' Of the Romans, properly so called, very few were accused of being implicated in the massacres. And it is generally asserted, that the mass of the people were never favourable to the Republican government.'

Again, speaking of Pio Nono, this fantastical logician observes :—' That they' (the Roman people) ' behaved most ungratefully we must admit; that they rose against their benefactor, which all history will record to their eternal disgrace.' He then repeats the hackneyed legend about the influence of foreigners, of which our readers will have already disposed. We need not, therefore, point out its absurdity, or expend ridicule on the individual who could repeat or believe it. Let us for the present pause at the word benefactor, and examine what sort of a benefactor to the Roman people his Holiness, according to Mr. Cochrane, really was. It should, perhaps, be premised that the word signifies a man who actually accomplishes good for some-body. To mean well is not to be a benefactor. *Benè facere* implies the actual transmission of benefits from one individual to another, or from one to many. Now how stands the account between Pio Nono and the Roman people? Mr. Cochrane, who never cares to make the end of his commonwealth agree with the beginning, shall answer. Early in his book, he says:—' The Pope commenced his ill-timed, ill-projected, and ill-administered reforms.' Not very complimentary this to the benefactor of his country. But we ought, perhaps, to illustrate the clearness of the writer's conceptions by what he says of Gregory XVI.—' He was, in no sense of the word, a bad man;' but being cowardly, his fear constantly led him into acts of tyranny, and even of injustice; he lavished on profligate favourites the funds de-signed for charity; he winked at the mal-administration of the hospitals, in one of which ninety persons were employed to attend on fifty-six; he bestowed on ladies of rank, and probably of equivocal character, the funds which should have gone to the sustenance of the poor. He rendered his country weak at home, and contemptible abroad—and yet if we are to adopt Mr. Coch-rane's principles of ethics, he was, in no sense of the word, a bad man.

Let us, however, examine Pio Nono's claims to be regarded as the benefactor of his people. Mr. Cochrane himself shall enumerate them:—He speaks of him at the outset as a harmless youth of fifty-six, who did very well as Bishop of Imola, but who, immediately after his elevation to St. Peter's chair, suffered him-self to be made the victim of the vilest flatterers. ' He found,' says our curious panegyrist, ' that he was possessed of qualities, the existence of which he had never imagined'—' that he was a great reformer '—' that he was famous '—' that the fame of his great actions had preceded, not him, but the actions themselves ' —' that from childhood he had been endowed with liberal opinions '—' that he was a statesman, who was a necessity '— ' that he was elected as the regenerator of Italy '—' and the simple episcopal youth listened at first incredulously; but, at last, like the *médecin malgré lui*, or the Irish diplomatist, he ended by believing that he possessed those qualities which others attributed to him.'

Our readers will remember Dogberry's emphatic request to be written down the animal on which Balaam rode. His ingenuous self-appreciation might very well, according to Mr. Cochrane, have suggested to Pio Nono a similar prayer. Yet this is the great patriot and benefactor towards whom, as we are afterwards told, the Roman people, at the instigation of foreigners, behaved ungratefully. Verily the Hibernian compliment once paid to an ancient hero may be applied to Mr. Cochrane—None but himself can be his parallel! He is altogether *sui generis*. He sneers and praises, defames and exalts the same persons, without, in the slightest degree, perceiving what he is at. If the Romans conceived a partiality for their Pope at first, but afterwards grew to detest him, Mr. Cochrane shall explain the phenomenon:— ' Those,' he says, ' who knew Pio Nono first, loved him best ; those who knew him longest, loved him least.' Our author, we dare say, would rather obtain credit for saying a smart thing than for being consistent. We, therefore, beg to inform him, if he has not sagacity enough to perceive it, that he has here blundered into a bitterness of which his friend Lælius would not be ashamed. And the sting of it lies in its truth. It means that Pio Nono was beloved so long as he was misunderstood ; that when he became known he was detested : a fact which we leave Mr. Cochrane to reconcile as he best may with the character of a public benefactor.

The Republicans, in their fiercest manifestos, never delineated the Pope in more offensive colours than Mr. Cochrane, whose intellectual vision is too obtuse to discern his own contradictions. He, therefore, stumbles on through his pages, reeling now on this side, now on that ; sometimes flinging a compliment at the Pope, and sometimes an insult.

Most of our readers will remember the pranks which Mr. Cochrane plays in Parliament, where his attacks on Lord Palmerston forcibly remind us of the fable of the frog and the ox. The little creature, very respectable when croaking in its own bog or quagmire, conscious of its diminutiveness, and aiming at nothing inconsistent with it, becomes an object of unbounded ridicule when, strutting forth on dry land, it puffs and swells, and tries to assume the port and bearing of the largest and most useful of our quadrupeds. Weakness, intellectual or physical, is not contemptible in itself. Mr. Cochrane, therefore, if he could content himself with the place assigned him by nature, would provoke no one's scorn. But when he gets on stilts, and provokes Lord Palmerston or Signor Mazzini to the combat, we really think it time his friends should look after him. We repeat, that if he would become painstaking and diligent, he might - produce fictions which would amuse young ladies at boarding-schools, hypochondriacs, and servant-girls; but that a man, designed by nature for this sort of work, should mistake his destiny, and perversely betake himself to politics, is a thing not to be endured in a civilized country. We ought, perhaps, to ask pardon of M. Mazzini and our readers for bestowing so much time and space on so thorough a literary abortion as Mr. Cochrane's ' Young Italy.'

statesman and philosopher, which an interest in the welfare of the to find a man obtaining the reputation of a hero among his contemporaries, because persons like Giuseppe Mazzini are not common. But this man, through unsullied patriotism and virtue, occupies, in the estimation of Europe, this enviable position, which he has won for himself by years of struggle in exile, by suffering, by privation, and afterwards by heroic action in the face of the world. Doubly fortunate in his misfortunes, he possesses the courage to perform great deeds when time and opportunity permit; and the genius to incite others to the performance of them when the calamities of his country consign him to exile and comparative inaction.

If the brief career of the Roman Republic require a defender, the proper man has been found in Giuseppe Mazzini. But his thoughts are too much absorbed by noble projects for the future to allow him to take anything like a complete retrospect of the past. With all his energy, with all his eloquence, however, he defends Italy from the charges brought against her by the advocates of Austria, whether hired or duped. Where circumstances permit, he supplies irrefragable proofs of the truth of what he advances; and where they do not, we accept his word, as an historical proof of the first value. Every day that passes over us strengthens the faith of Christendom in the probity and rectitude of this distinguished man; and the little book he has now put forward will tend, wherever it is read, to secure for its writer the esteem of those, if any such there be, who have continued, up to this moment, unacquainted with his fame.

Of course, we have no intention of insulting M. Mazzini, by instituting the slightest comparison between him and Mr. Baillie Cochrane. The one we regard as a patriot and a statesman; the other as a mere scribbler, whose testimony, however, may be accepted for infinitely more than it is worth by that section of the British public which has no sympathy but for despotism. Possibly, also, he may, in some cases, be able to mislead the unwary, by the dogmatical manner in which he puts forth his calumnies against the Roman Republic. For the sake of these, we shall extract one or two passages from M. Mazzini's letter to MM. de Tocqueville and Falloux, which must be regarded as

satisfactory and decisive by all who are able to elevate their minds to the level of the writer's character. Much more would we have taken from this admirable volume, of which every page contains something important, but that we persuade ourselves it will find its way into the hands of all readers, its historical interest and literary fascination being quite equal to its political value. M. Mazzini says :—

'The small army concentrated in Rome at the time of the siege was composed of the 1st of the Line, Colonel de Pasqualis; 2nd ditto, Colonel Gaucci Mollara; 3rd ditto, Colonel Marchetti; all these Romans, soldiers and officers. Two light regiments : the first commanded by Masi—the very man whom M. de Corcelles, in his despatch of the 12th of June, puts down as a foreigner—entirely Romans ; the second commanded by Pasi, the same. The Roman Legion, commanded by Galletti ; the Riflemen, commanded by Mellara—since dead of his wounds—all Romans. The small body of the *Reduci*, Romans. The Battalion Bignami, Romans. The regiment called " The Union," Romans. The body of Carabiniers, General Galletti, Romans. The Dragoons, Romans. The body of Engineers, Romans; the Artillery, Romans. All these, all the chiefs I have already named—the Colonels Piana, Amedei, Berti-Pichat, the General-in-Chief, Roselli, the Chief Intendants, first Gaggiotti, and afterwards Salvati, the principal *employés* at the Ministry of War—all Romans represented the indigenous element.

'Where, then, were the foreigners ? Garibaldi and his legion, 800 men ; Arcioni and his legion, 300 men ; Manara, dead for liberty, and his Lombard Riflemen, 500 men ; 200 Poles ; the Foreign Legion, 100 men ; the handful of brave men who defended the Vascello under Medici. Altogether, 2,000 men ; but not really so many, because Arcioni's legion contained, at least, one-third of Romagnoli, because the little knot of cavalry which formed part of Garibaldi's legion, and which was commanded by Masina, of Bologna—dead on the field—were almost all Roman citizens, and because half even of the foot soldiers of Garibaldi belonged to the country.'—Pp. 127, 128.

The reader will have observed, in the dreary passage we extracted from ' Young Italy,' that Mr. Cochrane adduces the Pope's declarations that his people had been misled by foreigners as a convincing proof of the fact, whereas no one can be ignorant that such assertions signify absolutely nothing, but the desire of the person who makes them to produce a false impression. When the affections of a whole people have been alienated, when their fierce passions have been roused, and their feelings insulted, so that in reviewing their own condition nothing appears left to them but insurrection, it has at all times been the common trick of governments to attribute to some designing few what has been palpably the result of their own delinquencies. Such foreigners, again, as sympathize with them will adopt the

same tone, and, therefore, we cannot be surprised that the partisans of reaction in France, and the witless Quixotes of absolutism in England, should babble as they do about the existence of foreign influence at Rome. Let our readers consider the import of the following passage, and compare it with wretched rhapsodies uttered by the enemies of liberty, and they cannot fail to discover on which side truth lies :—

of Rome
to fifteen
hundred men amongst a total of fourteen thousand; for it is well that Italy should know that fourteen thousand men, a young army without traditions, and improvised under the very fire of the enemy, held in check for two months thirty thousand soldiers of France. You knew all this, gentlemen, or you *could* have known it, and, therefore, you *ought* to have done so ; and, nevertheless, you shamelessly gave out to the Assembly the number of foreigners as twenty thousand, as a proof that after all it was not the Roman idea that you had endeavoured to stifle in blood; and upon this cipher of your own invention depends the greater part of your argument. Foreigners! I entreat pardon of my country for having inscribed the word, after you, upon my page. What! Lombards, Tuscans, Italians, foreigners at Rome! And it is by you, Frenchmen, by you—who, in re-establishing the Pontifical throne, have been supported by Austrians and Spaniards—that this reproach is made. A year ago our provinces sent the *élite* of their youth to fight upon the plains of Lombardy, as to a convention of honour; but I do not remember that Radetzky ever called them in his
The absolute denial of Italian nationality
nephew of him who, at St. Helena, uttered these words :—"*Unity of manners, of language, of literature, shows that Italy is destined to form a single country.*" '—Pp. 128, 129.

If we now glance backwards we shall find it results from what has been said that Italy desires to realize for itself unity of existence, a Republican form of government, and a greatly-reformed church. Entire independence from the yoke of foreigners is implied in the idea of unity, because, taken as a whole, it would be altogether impossible to hold the country in thraldom. It might, perhaps, be too much to maintain that the universal sentiment of the Italian people is precisely what it ought to be in a political sense. There is indifference in many parts of the country, as the whole tenor of late events compels us to believe ; since it is in no way credible that want of success would have been within the range of possibility had the whole nation thrown itself into the scale against Austria. But the circumstances of these times, different from any witnessed by former ages, are rapidly combining to give oneness and concentration to the Italian mind ; every day brings about a closer communion between the various sections of the Italian population ; railways will be laid down, literature will exert its force, and the increased flocking of strangers to every portion of the Sub-alpine peninsula, will rouse, quicken, and vivify the desire of freedom.

All practicable pains will, of course, be taken to exclude from the country every book, the tendency of which is liberal. But when once a nation has become persuaded that it requires instruction, writers will be found to supply it openly or clandestinely. What the Italians now want is knowledge; not scientific knowledge, not a knowledge of music or the arts, but a knowledge of politics, of the social condition of mankind, of what can be accomplished by institutions, and of the total impracticability of regenerating a people without giving it a government calculated to meet its wants, which has by industry or accident multiplied its intellectual resources, and conceived the wish to be free. Italy now possesses among her children persons of the highest eminence for virtue and capacity, and of these none is more distinguished than M. Mazzini, all whose thoughts and aspirations bear the impress of grandeur, and are well suited to inspire an oppressed population with an inextinguishable thirst for freedom. He is a man of whom any country might be proud, and all we wish is, that Italy had thousands of such. That he is creating a school of patriots, and that his country is ripe for a moral revolution, we stedfastly believe; but it may, perhaps, be doubted whether the failure of the late insurrection will not postpone for a considerable time the breaking forth of another. Still it is obviously now only a question of time, for the progress of thought and opinion in Italy must have at length convinced all who can reason that her day of final deliverance is at hand.

----

ART. VIII.—*Wuthering Heights and Agnes Grey.* By Ellis and Acton Bell. *A New Edition; with a Biographical Notice of the Authors, a Selection from their Literary Remains, and a Preface.* By Currer Bell. Pp. 504. London: Smith, Elder, and Co.

WE purpose dealing rather with the Biographical Notice prefixed to this volume, than with the two works which it contains. There are various reasons for this. It is sufficient to say that the former interests us deeply, which the latter do not; and that the present is its first appearance, whereas the *Fictions* it prefaces are already somewhat known to the public. Not that we shall wholly omit to record our judgment, more particularly on 'Wuthering Heights'; but our special business is with the 'Notice' now supplied by Currer, rather than with the productions of Ellis and Acton Bell. Our readers are, doubtless, aware of the questions which have been raised respecting the authorship of 'Jane Eyre' and 'Shirley,' with that of their predecessors reprinted in the volume on our table. Whether these works were the productions of a gentleman or a lady, and whether their authorship was single or threefold, have been mooted with considerable interest in some literary circles, and have sometimes been pronounced on with a dogmatism which would have been amusing, had it not indicated a sad lack of modesty and intelligence. Though the internal evidence of the works is strongly favorable to the hypothesis of a female authorship, there is, nevertheless, a certain masculine air about their style, a repudiation of conventionalisms, and a bold, nervous, cast of thought and action, which suggests the presence of the other sex. Slight inaccuracies in some matters of female dress are, moreover, alleged in proof of their being the production of a masculine pen.

These considerations, however, avail little against the general complexion and air of the works in question. It appears to us impossible to read them without feeling that their excellences and faults, their instinctive attachments and occasional exaggerations, the depths of their tenderness and their want of practical judgment, all betoken the authorship of a lady. In their perusal, we are in the company of an intelligent, free-spoken, and hearty woman, who feels deeply, can describe with power, has seen some of the rougher sides of life, and, though capable of strong affection, is probably wanting in the 'sweet attractive grace' which Milton so beautifully ascribes to Eve.

As to the other point which had been mooted, it is marvellous, we confess, that a doubt should ever have existed. That either of the works now before us should be attributed to the same writer as 'Jane Eyre' and 'Shirley,' is one of the strangest blunders of criticism with which we ever met. It is true there is talent in them, and that too of an order—we refer more particularly to 'Wuthering Heights'—similar in its general character to what those works display. Yet the points of distinction are numerous, and of a character which ought to have precluded doubt. But we may now dispense with conjecture, for one of the sisterhood has kindly withdrawn the curtain, and invited us to look upon the *terra incognita* about which we have been contending. The revelation is deeply, yet painfully, interesting. The scene we behold, though partially illumined, is shaded by some deep clouds. We hear sighs and groans, look upon faded forms and weeping eyes, and turn from the spectacle with a painful conviction that sorrow, in some form or other, is the heritage of man. Well, be it so. The mystery of life will soon be disclosed, and we shall then see the intimate connexion that subsists between the afflictions of this world and the higher and nobler interests of the human soul.

About five years since, Currer Bell, and her two sisters—for we doubt not that *Currer* is a lady, though she does not plainly say so—after a long separation were reunited at home. They resided in a remote northern district, and were entirely dependent on each other and on books 'for the enjoyments and occupations of life.' In the autumn of 1845, a volume of poetry in the handwriting of one of the sisters was accidentally discovered, which, being approved, Currer Bell informs us, 'My younger sister quietly produced some of her own compositions, intimating that since Emily's had given me pleasure, I might like to look at hers. I could not but be a partial judge, yet I thought that these verses too had a sweet sincere pathos of their own.' What followed will be best told in the writer's own words:—

'We had very early cherished the dream of one day becoming authors. This dream, never relinquished even when distance divided and absorbing tasks occupied us, now suddenly acquired strength and consistency; it took the character of a resolve. We agreed to arrange a small selection of our poems, and, if possible, get them printed. Averse to personal publicity, we veiled our own names under those of Currer, Ellis, and Acton Bell ; the ambiguous choice being dictated by a sort of conscientious scruple at assuming Christian names positively masculine, while we did not like to declare ourselves women, because—without at that time suspecting that our mode of writing and thinking was not what is called " feminine "—we had a vague impression that authoresses are liable to be looked on with prejudice ; we had noticed how critics sometimes use for their chastisement the weapon of personality, and for their reward, a flattery, which is not true praise.

'The bringing out of our little book was hard work. As was to be expected, neither we nor our poems were at all wanted; but for this we had been prepared at the outset; though inexperienced ourselves, we had read the experience of others. The great puzzle lay in the difficulty of getting answers of any kind from the publishers to whom we applied. Being greatly harassed by this obstacle, I ventured to apply to the Messrs. Chambers, of Edinburgh, for a word of advice ; *they* may have forgotten the circumstance, but *I* have not, for from them I received a brief and business-like, but, civil and sensible reply, on which we acted, and at last made a way.

'The book was printed: it is scarcely known, and all of it that merits to be known are the poems of Ellis Bell. The fixed conviction I held, and hold, of the worth of these poems, has not indeed received the confirmation of much favourable criticism; but I must retain it notwithstanding.'—P. ix.

This is perfectly natural, and we do not find fault with it. Authors profess vast deference to critics and the public, yet contrive to retain a good opinion of their own productions, though the former may condemn, and the latter neglect, them. The ill-success of the sisters did not consequently crush hope. Their effort to succeed had aroused faculties of which they were previously unconscious, and the mere exercise of these faculties ministered delight infinitely superior to the frivolous and evanescent enjoyments of the gay. They resolved, therefore, to persevere, and each set vigorously to work at the production of a prose tale. Ellis Bell wrote 'Wuthering Heights,' Acton Bell 'Agnes Grey,' and Currer a narrative, the title of which is not given. These manuscripts were offered to various publishers, but their usual fate was 'an ignominious and abrupt dismissal.' Still the sisters persevered, and the issue is thus narrated :—.

'At last "Wuthering Heights" and "Agnes Grey" were accepted on terms somewhat impoverishing to the two authors; Currer Bell's book found acceptance nowhere, nor any acknowledgment of merit, so that something like the chill of despair began to invade his heart. As a forlorn hope, he tried one publishing house more—Messrs. Smith and Elder. Ere long, in a much shorter space than that on which experience had taught him to calculate—there came a letter, which he opened in the dreary expectation of finding two hard, hopeless lines, intimating that Messrs. Smith and Elder were not disposed to publish the MS., and, instead, he took out of the envelope a letter of two pages. He read it trembling. It declined, indeed, to publish that tale, for business reasons, but it discussed its merits and demerits so courteously, so considerately, in a spirit so rational, with a discrimination so enlightened, that this very refusal cheered the author better than a vulgarly-expressed acceptance would have done. It was added, that a work in three volumes would meet with careful attention.

'I was then just completing "Jane Eyre," at which I had been working while the one volume tale was plodding its weary round in London : in three weeks I sent it off; friendly and skilful hands took it in. This was in the commencement of September, 1847 ; it came out before the close of October following, while "Wuthering Heights" and "Agnes Grey," my sisters' works, which had already been in the press for months, still lingered under a different management.'—Pp. 10, 11.

'Jane Eyre' was instantaneously popular ; but not so the productions of Ellis and Acton Bell. We are not surprised at this. The fact is easily solved. A single perusal of the three will explain the mystery. The successful work was attractive as well as talented, while 'Wuthering Heights'—we know little of 'Agnes Grey'—is one of the most repellent books we ever read.

Our readers will remember Dogberry's emphatic request to be
written down the animal on which Balaam rode. His ingenuous
self-appreciation might very well, according to Mr. Cochrane,
have suggested to Pio Nono a similar prayer. Yet this is the great
patriot and benefactor towards whom, as we are afterwards told,
the Roman people, at the instigation of foreigners, behaved ungratefully.    Verily the Hibernian compliment once paid to an
ancient hero may be applied to Mr. Cochrane—None but himself
can be his parallel!  He is altogether *sui generis*.   He sneers
and praises, defames and exalts the same persons, without, in the
slightest degree, perceiving what he is at.   If the Romans conceived a partiality for their Pope at first, but afterwards grew
to detest him, Mr. Cochrane shall explain the phenomenon:—
' Those,' he says, ' who knew Pio Nono first, loved him best ;
those who knew him longest, loved him least.'  Our author, we
dare say, would rather obtain credit for saying a smart thing than
for being consistent.  We, therefore, beg to inform him, if he
has not sagacity enough to perceive it, that he has here blundered into a bitterness of which his friend Lælius would not
be ashamed.   And the sting of it lies in its truth.   It means that
Pio Nono was beloved so long as he was misunderstood ; that
when he became known he was detested : a fact which we leave
Mr. Cochrane to reconcile as he best may with the character of
a public benefactor.

The Republicans, in their fiercest manifestos, never delineated
the Pope in more offensive colours than Mr. Cochrane, whose
intellectual vision is too obtuse to discern his own contradictions.
He, therefore, stumbles on through his pages, reeling now on
this side, now on that; sometimes flinging a compliment at the
Pope, and sometimes an insult.

Most of our readers will remember the pranks which
Mr. Cochrane plays in Parliament, where his attacks on Lord
Palmerston forcibly remind us of the fable of the frog and
the ox.   The little creature, very respectable when croaking
in its own bog or quagmire, conscious of its diminutiveness, and
aiming at nothing inconsistent with it, becomes an object of unbounded ridicule when, strutting forth on dry land, it puffs and
swells, and tries to assume the port and bearing of the largest
and most useful of our quadrupeds.   Weakness, intellectual or
physical, is not contemptible in itself.   Mr. Cochrane, therefore,
if he could content himself with the place assigned him by
nature, would provoke no one's scorn.   But when he gets on
stilts, and provokes Lord Palmerston or Signor Mazzini to the
combat, we really think it time his friends should look after him.
We repeat, that if he would become painstaking and diligent, he
might-produce fictions which would amuse young ladies at

boarding-schools, hypochondriacs, and servant-girls; but that a man, designed by nature for this sort of work, should mistake his destiny, and perversely betake himself to politics, is a thing not to be endured in a civilized country. We ought, perhaps, to ask pardon of M. Mazzini and our readers for bestowing so much time and space on so thorough a literary abortion as Mr. Cochrane's 'Young Italy.'

We now turn to the work of a statesman and philosopher, which should be read by all who take an interest in the welfare of the human race. It is not common to find a man obtaining the reputation of a hero among his contemporaries, because persons like Giuseppe Mazzini are not common. But this man, through unsullied patriotism and virtue, occupies, in the estimation of Europe, this enviable position, which he has won for himself by years of struggle in exile, by suffering, by privation, and afterwards by heroic action in the face of the world. Doubly fortunate in his misfortunes, he possesses the courage to perform great deeds when time and opportunity permit; and the genius to incite others to the performance of them when the calamities of his country consign him to exile and comparative inaction.

If the brief career of the Roman Republic require a defender, the proper man has been found in Giuseppe Mazzini. But his thoughts are too much absorbed by noble projects for the future to allow him to take anything like a complete retrospect of the past. With all his energy, with all his eloquence, however, he defends Italy from the charges brought against her by the advocates of Austria, whether hired or duped. Where circumstances permit, he supplies irrefragable proofs of the truth of what he advances; and where they do not, we accept his word, as an historical proof of the first value. Every day that passes over us strengthens the faith of Christendom in the probity and rectitude of this distinguished man; and the little book he has now put forward will tend, wherever it is read, to secure for its writer the esteem of those, if any such there be, who have continued, up to this moment, unacquainted with his fame.

Of course, we have no intention of insulting M. Mazzini, by instituting the slightest comparison between him and Mr. Baillie Cochrane. The one we regard as a patriot and a statesman; the other as a mere scribbler, whose testimony, however, may be accepted for infinitely more than it is worth by that section of the British public which has no sympathy but for despotism. Possibly, also, he may, in some cases, be able to mislead the unwary, by the dogmatical manner in which he puts forth his calumnies against the Roman Republic. For the sake of these, we shall extract one or two passages from M. Mazzini's letter to MM. de Tocqueville and Falloux, which must be regarded as

satisfactory and decisive by all who are able to elevate their minds to the level of the writer's character. Much more would we have taken from this admirable volume, of which every page contains something important, but that we persuade ourselves it will find its way into the hands of all readers, its historical interest and literary fascination being quite equal to its political value. M. Mazzini says :—

'The small army concentrated in Rome at the time of the siege was composed of the 1st of the Line, Colonel de Pasqualis; 2nd ditto, Colonel Gaucci Mollara; 3rd ditto, Colonel Marchetti; all these Romans, soldiers and officers. Two light regiments: the first commanded by Masi—the very man whom M. de Corcelles, in his despatch of the 12th of June, puts down as a foreigner—entirely Romans; the second commanded by Pasi, the same. The Roman Legion, commanded by Galletti; the Riflemen, commanded by Mellara—since dead of his wounds—all Romans. The small body of the *Reduci*, Romans. The Battalion Bignami, Romans. The regiment called " The Union," Romans. The body of Carabiniers, General Galletti, Romans. The Dragoons, Romans. The body of Engineers, Romans; the Artillery, Romans. All these, all the chiefs I have already named—the Colonels Piana, Amedei, Berti-Pichat, the General-in-Chief, Roselli, the Chief Intendants, first Gaggiotti, and afterwards Salvati, the principal *employés* at the Ministry of War—all Romans represented the indigenous element.

'Where, then, were the foreigners? Garibaldi and his legion, 800 men; Arcioni and his legion, 300 men; Manara, dead for liberty, and his Lombard Riflemen, 500 men; 200 Poles; the Foreign Legion, 100 men; the handful of brave men who defended the Vascello under Medici. Altogether, 2,000 men; but not really so many, because Arcioni's legion contained, at least, one-third of Romagnoli, because the little knot of cavalry which formed part of Garibaldi's legion, and which was commanded by Masina, of Bologna—dead on the field— were almost all Roman citizens, and because half even of the foot soldiers of Garibaldi belonged to the country.'—Pp. 127, 128.

The reader will have observed, in the dreary passage we extracted from ' Young Italy,' that Mr. Cochrane adduces the Pope's declarations that his people had been misled by foreigners as a convincing proof of the fact, whereas no one can be ignorant that such assertions signify absolutely nothing, but the desire of the person who makes them to produce a false impression. When the affections of a whole people have been alienated, when their fierce passions have been roused, and their feelings insulted, so that in reviewing their own condition nothing appears left to them but insurrection, it has at all times been the common trick of governments to attribute to some designing few what has been palpably the result of their own delinquencies. Such foreigners, again, as sympathize with them will adopt the

same tone, and, therefore, we cannot be surprised that the partisans of reaction in France, and the witless Quixotes of absolutism in England, should babble as they do about the existence of foreign influence at Rome.   Let our readers consider the import of the following passage, and compare it with wretched rhapsodies uttered by the enemies of liberty, and they cannot fail to discover on which side truth lies :—

'The number of "foreigners" who assisted in the defence of Rome was from fourteen to fifteen hundred men ; from fourteen to fifteen hundred men amongst a total of fourteen thousand ; for it is well that Italy should know that fourteen thousand men, a young army without traditions, and improvised under the very fire of the enemy, held in check for two months thirty thousand soldiers of France.   You knew all this, gentlemen, or you *could* have known it, and, therefore, you *ought* to have done so ; and, nevertheless, you shamelessly gave out to the Assembly the number of foreigners as twenty thousand, as a proof that after all it was not the Roman idea that you had endeavoured to stifle in blood ; and upon this cipher of your own invention depends the greater part of your argument.   Foreigners!   I entreat pardon of my country for having inscribed the word, after you, upon my page.   What ! Lombards, Tuscans, Italians, foreigners at Rome !   And it is by you, Frenchmen, by you—who, in re-establishing the Pontifical throne, have been supported by Austrians and Spaniards—that this reproach is made.   A year ago our provinces sent the *élite* of their youth to fight upon the plains of Lombardy, as to a convention of honour ; but I do not remember that Radetzky ever called them in his proclamations *foreigners*.   The absolute denial of Italian nationality has been reserved for the nephew of him who, at St. Helena, uttered these words :—"*Unity of manners, of language, of literature, shows that Italy is destined to form a single country.*" '—Pp. 128, 129.

If we now glance backwards we shall find it results from what has been said that Italy desires to realize for itself unity of existence, a Republican form of government, and a greatly-reformed church.   Entire independence from the yoke of foreigners is implied in the idea of unity, because, taken as a whole, it would be altogether impossible to hold the country in thraldom.   It might, perhaps, be too much to maintain that the universal sentiment of the Italian people is precisely what it ought to be in a political sense.   There is indifference in many parts of the country, as the whole tenor of late events compels us to believe ; since it is in no way credible that want of success would have been within the range of possibility had the whole nation thrown itself into the scale against Austria.   But the circumstances of these times, different from any witnessed by former ages, are rapidly combining to give oneness and concentration to the Italian mind ; every day brings about a closer communion between the various sections of the Italian population ; railways

Our readers will remember Dogberry's emphatic request to be written down the animal on which Balaam rode. His ingenuous self-appreciation might very well, according to Mr. Cochrane, have suggested to Pio Nono a similar prayer. Yet this is the great patriot and benefactor towards whom, as we are afterwards told, the Roman people, at the instigation of foreigners, behaved ungratefully. Verily the Hibernian compliment once paid to an ancient hero may be applied to Mr. Cochrane—None but himself can be his parallel! He is altogether *sui generis.* He sneers and praises, defames and exalts the same persons, without, in the slightest degree, perceiving what he is at. If the Romans conceived a partiality for their Pope at first, but afterwards grew to detest him, Mr. Cochrane shall explain the phenomenon :— ' Those,' he says, ' who knew Pio Nono first, loved him best ; those who knew him longest, loved him least.' Our author, we dare say, would rather obtain credit for saying a smart thing than for being consistent. We, therefore, beg to inform him, if he has not sagacity enough to perceive it, that he has here blundered into a bitterness of which his friend Lælius would not be ashamed. And the sting of it lies in its truth. It means that Pio Nono was beloved so long as he was misunderstood ; that when he became known he was detested : a fact which we leave Mr. Cochrane to reconcile as he best may with the character of a public benefactor.

The Republicans, in their fiercest manifestos, never delineated the Pope in more offensive colours than Mr. Cochrane, whose intellectual vision is too obtuse to discern his own contradictions. He, therefore, stumbles on through his pages, reeling now on this side, now on that ; sometimes flinging a compliment at the Pope, and sometimes an insult.

Most of our readers will remember the pranks which Mr. Cochrane plays in Parliament, where his attacks on Lord Palmerston forcibly remind us of the fable of the frog and the ox. The little creature, very respectable when croaking in its own bog or quagmire, conscious of its diminutiveness, and aiming at nothing inconsistent with it, becomes an object of unbounded ridicule when, strutting forth on dry land, it puffs and swells, and tries to assume the port and bearing of the largest and most useful of our quadrupeds. Weakness, intellectual or physical, is not contemptible in itself. Mr. Cochrane, therefore, if he could content himself with the place assigned him by nature, would provoke no one's scorn. But when he gets on stilts, and provokes Lord Palmerston or Signor Mazzini to the combat, we really think it time his friends should look after him. We repeat, that if he would become painstaking and diligent, he might-produce fictions which would amuse young ladies at boarding-schools, hypochondriacs, and servant-girls; but that a man, designed by nature for this sort of work, should mistake his destiny, and perversely betake himself to politics, is a thing not to be endured in a civilized country. We ought, perhaps, to ask pardon of M. Mazzini and our readers for bestowing so much time and space on so thorough a literary abortion as Mr. Cochrane's ' Young Italy.'

We now turn to the work of a statesman and philosopher, which should be read by all who take an interest in the welfare of the human race. It is not common to find a man obtaining the reputation of a hero among his contemporaries, because persons like Giuseppe Mazzini are not common. But this man, through unsullied patriotism and virtue, occupies, in the estimation of Europe, this enviable position, which he has won for himself by years of struggle in exile, by suffering, by privation, and afterwards by heroic action in the face of the world. Doubly fortunate in his misfortunes, he possesses the courage to perform great deeds when time and opportunity permit; and the genius to incite others to the performance of them when the calamities of his country consign him to exile and comparative inaction.

If the brief career of the Roman Republic require a defender, the proper man has been found in Giuseppe Mazzini. But his thoughts are too much absorbed by noble projects for the future to allow him to take anything like a complete retrospect of the past. With all his energy, with all his eloquence, however, he defends Italy from the charges brought against her by the advocates of Austria, whether hired or duped. Where circumstances permit, he supplies irrefragable proofs of the truth of what he advances; and where they do not, we accept his word, as an historical proof of the first value. Every day that passes over us strengthens the faith of Christendom in the probity and rectitude of this distinguished man; and the little book he has now put forward will tend, wherever it is read, to secure for its writer the esteem of those, if any such there be, who have continued, up to this moment, unacquainted with his fame.

Of course, we have no intention of insulting M. Mazzini, by instituting the slightest comparison between him and Mr. Baillie Cochrane. The one we regard as a patriot and a statesman; the other as a mere scribbler, whose testimony, however, may be accepted for infinitely more than it is worth by that section of the British public which has no sympathy but for despotism. Possibly, also, he may, in some cases, be able to mislead the unwary, by the dogmatical manner in which he puts forth his calumnies against the Roman Republic. For the sake of these, we shall extract one or two passages from M. Mazzini's letter to MM. de Tocqueville and Falloux, which must be regarded as

satisfactory and decisive by all who are able to elevate their minds to the level of the writer's character. Much more would we have taken from this admirable volume, of which every page contains something important, but that we persuade ourselves it will find its way into the hands of all readers, its historical interest and literary fascination being quite equal to its political value. M. Mazzini says :—

'The small army concentrated in Rome at the time of the siege was composed of the 1st of the Line, Colonel de Pasqualis; 2nd ditto, Colonel Gaucci Mollara; 3rd ditto, Colonel Marchetti; all these Romans, soldiers and officers. Two light regiments : the first commanded by Masi—the very man whom M. de Corcelles, in his despatch of the 12th of June, puts down as a foreigner—entirely Romans ; the second commanded by Pasi, the same. The Roman Legion, commanded by Galletti ; the Riflemen, commanded by Mellara—since dead of his wounds—all Romans. The small body of the *Reduci*, Romans. The Battalion Bignami, Romans. The regiment called " The Union," Romans. The body of Carabiniers, General Galletti, Romans. The Dragoons, Romans. The body of Engineers, Romans ; the Artillery, Romans. All these, all the chiefs I have already named—the Colonels Piana, Amedei, Berti-Pichat, the General-in-Chief, Roselli, the Chief Intendants, first Gaggiotti, and afterwards Salvati, the principal *employés* at the Ministry of War—all Romans represented the indigenous element.

'Where, then, were the foreigners ? Garibaldi and his legion, 800 men ; Arcioni and his legion, 300 men ; Manara, dead for liberty, and his Lombard Riflemen, 500 men ; 200 Poles ; the Foreign Legion, 100 men ; the handful of brave men who defended the Vascello under Medici. Altogether, 2,000 men ; but not really so many, because Arcioni's legion contained, at least, one-third of Romagnoli, because the little knot of cavalry which formed part of Garibaldi's legion, and which was commanded by Masina, of Bologna—dead on the field— were almost all Roman citizens, and because half even of the foot soldiers of Garibaldi belonged to the country.'—Pp. 127, 128.

The reader will have observed, in the dreary passage we extracted from ' Young Italy,' that Mr. Cochrane adduces the Pope's declarations that his people had been misled by foreigners as a convincing proof of the fact, whereas no one can be ignorant that such assertions signify absolutely nothing, but the desire of the person who makes them to produce a false impression. When the affections of a whole people have been alienated, when their fierce passions have been roused, and their feelings insulted, so that in reviewing their own condition nothing appears left to them but insurrection, it has at all times been the common trick of governments to attribute to some designing few what has been palpably the result of their own delinquencies. Such foreigners, again, as sympathize with them will adopt the

same tone, and, therefore, we cannot be surprised that the partisans of reaction in France, and the witless Quixotes of absolutism in England, should babble as they do about the existence
of foreign influence at Rome. Let our readers consider the
import of the following passage, and compare it with wretched
rhapsodies uttered by the enemies of liberty, and they cannot
fail to discover on which side truth lies :—

'The number of "foreigners" who assisted in the defence of Rome
was from fourteen to fifteen hundred men; from fourteen to fifteen
hundred men amongst a total of fourteen thousand; for it is well that
Italy should know that fourteen thousand men, a young army without
traditions, and improvised under the very fire of the enemy, held in
check for two months thirty thousand soldiers of France. You knew
all this, gentlemen, or you *could* have known it, and, therefore, you
*ought* to have done so ; and, nevertheless, you shamelessly gave out to
the Assembly the number of foreigners as twenty thousand, as a proof
that after all it was not the Roman idea that you had endeavoured to
stifle in blood; and upon this cipher of your own invention depends
the greater part of your argument. Foreigners! I entreat pardon
of my country for having inscribed the word, after you, upon my page.
What! Lombards, Tuscans, Italians, foreigners at Rome! And it is
by you, Frenchmen, by you—who, in re-establishing the Pontifical
throne, have been supported by Austrians and Spaniards—that this
reproach is made. A year ago our provinces sent the *élite* of their
youth to fight upon the plains of Lombardy, as to a convention of
honour; but I do not remember that Radetzky ever called them in his
proclamations *foreigners*. The absolute denial of Italian nationality
has been reserved for the nephew of him who, at St. Helena, uttered
these words :—"*Unity of manners, of language, of literature, shows that
Italy is destined to form a single country.*"'—Pp. 128, 129.

If we now glance backwards we shall find it results from what
has been said that Italy desires to realize for itself unity of
existence, a Republican form of government, and a greatly-reformed church. Entire independence from the yoke of foreigners
is implied in the idea of unity, because, taken as a whole, it
would be altogether impossible to hold the country in thraldom.
It might, perhaps, be too much to maintain that the universal
sentiment of the Italian people is precisely what it ought to be
in a political sense. There is indifference in many parts of the
country, as the whole tenor of late events compels us to believe ;
since it is in no way credible that want of success would have
been within the range of possibility had the whole nation thrown
itself into the scale against Austria. But the circumstances of
these times, different from any witnessed by former ages, are
rapidly combining to give oneness and concentration to the
Italian mind ; every day brings about a closer communion
between the various sections of the Italian population ; railways

clouds. We hear sighs and groans, look upon faded forms and weeping eyes, and turn from the spectacle with a painful conviction that sorrow, in some form or other, is the heritage of man. Well, be it so. The mystery of life will soon be disclosed, and we shall then see the intimate connexion that subsists between the afflictions of this world and the higher and nobler interests of the human soul.

About five years since, Currer Bell, and her two sisters—for we doubt not that *Currer* is a lady, though she does not plainly say so—after a long separation were reunited at home. They resided in a remote northern district, and were entirely dependent on each other and on books ' for the enjoyments and occupations of life.' In the autumn of 1845, a volume of poetry in the handwriting of one of the sisters was accidentally discovered, which, being approved, Currer Bell informs us, ' My younger sister quietly produced some of her own compositions, intimating that since Emily's had given me pleasure, I might like to look at hers. I could not but be a partial judge, yet I thought that these verses too had a sweet sincere pathos of their own.' What followed will be best told in the writer's own words:—

' We had very early cherished the dream of one day becoming authors. This dream, never relinquished even when distance divided and absorbing tasks occupied us, now suddenly acquired strength and consistency; it took the character of a resolve. We agreed to arrange a small selection of our poems, and, if possible, get them printed. Averse to personal publicity, we veiled our own names under those of Currer, Ellis, and Acton Bell; the ambiguous choice being dictated by a sort of conscientious scruple at assuming Christian names positively masculine, while we did not like to declare ourselves women, because—without at that time suspecting that our mode of writing and thinking was not what is called " feminine "—we had a vague impression that authoresses are liable to be looked on with prejudice; we had noticed how critics sometimes use for their chastisement the weapon of personality, and for their reward, a flattery, which is not true praise.

' The bringing out of our little book was hard work. As was to be expected, neither we nor our poems were at all wanted; but for this we had been prepared at the outset; though inexperienced ourselves, we had read the experience of others. The great puzzle lay in the difficulty of getting answers of any kind from the publishers to whom we applied. Being greatly harassed by this obstacle, I ventured to apply to the Messrs. Chambers, of Edinburgh, for a word of advice ; *they* may have forgotten the circumstance, but *I* have not, for from them I received a brief and business-like, but, civil and sensible reply, on which we acted, and at last made a way.

' The book was printed: it is scarcely known, and all of it that merits to be known are the poems of Ellis Bell. The fixed conviction I held, and hold, of the worth of these poems, has not indeed received

the confirmation of much
notwithstanding.'—P. ix.

MS., and, instead, he took
He read it trembling.    It
business reasons, but it discussed its merits and demerits so courteously, so considerately, in a spirit so rational, with a discrimination so
enlightened, that this very refusal cheered the author better than a
vulgarly-expressed acceptance would have done.    It was added, that a
work in three volumes would meet with careful attention.

'I was then just completing "Jane Eyre," at which I had been
working while the one volume tale was plodding its weary round in
London: in three weeks I sent it off; friendly and skilful hands took
it in.    This was in the commencement of September, 1847; it came
out before the close of October following, while "Wuthering Heights"
and "Agnes Grey," my sisters' works, which had already been in the
press for months, still lingered under a different management.'—Pp.
10, 11.

'Jane Eyre' was instantaneously popular; but not so the
productions of Ellis and Acton Bell.    We are not surprised at
this.    The fact is easily solved.    A single perusal of the three
will explain the mystery.    The successful work was attractive as
well as talented, while 'Wuthering Heights'—we know little of
'Agnes Grey'—is one of the most repellent books we ever read.

With all its talent—and it has much—we cannot imagine its
being read through from any fascination in the tale itself. The
powers it displays are not only premature, but are misdirected.
The characters sketched are, for the most part, dark and loath-
some, while a gloomy and sombre air rests on the whole scene,
which renders it anything but pleasing. But to our narrative.
'Neither Ellis nor Acton allowed herself, for one moment, to sink
under want of encouragement; energy nerved the one, and
endurance upheld the other. They resolved on another trial—
Hope and the sense of power were yet strong within them.' But
a fearful change was at hand. Their domestic circle was obtruded
on by one whose might they could not resist. In the midst of
labour their strength failed them :—

'My sister Emily,' says Currer Bell, 'first declined. The details
of her illness are deep-branded in my memory, but to dwell on them,
either in thought or narrative, is not in my power. Never in all her
life had she lingered over any task that lay before her, and she did
not linger now. She sank rapidly. She made haste to leave us.
Yet, while physically she perished, mentally, she grew stronger than
we had yet known. Day by day, when I saw with what a front she
met suffering, I looked on her with an anguish of wonder and love.
I have seen nothing like it; but, indeed, I have never seen her
parallel in anything. Stronger than a man, simpler than a child, her
nature stood alone. The awful point was, that, while full of truth
for others, on herself she had no pity; the spirit was inexorable to
the flesh; from the trembling hand, the unnerved limbs, the faded
eyes, the same service was exacted as they had rendered in health.
To stand by and witness this, and not dare to remonstrate, was a pain
no words can render.

'Two cruel months of hope and fear passed painfully by, and the
day came at last when the terrors and pains of death were to be
undergone by this treasure, which had grown dearer and dearer to
our hearts as it wasted before our eyes. Towards the decline of that
day, we had nothing of Emily but her mortal remains as consumption
left them. She died December 19, 1848.

'We thought this enough; but we were utterly and presumptuously
wrong. She was not buried ere Anne fell ill. She had not been committed to the grave a fortnight, before we received distinct intimation
that it was necessary to prepare our minds to see the younger sister go
after the elder. Accordingly, she followed in the same path with
slower step, and with a patience that equalled the other's fortitude. I
have said that she was religious, and it was by leaning on those Christian doctrines in which she firmly believed, that she found support
through her most painful journey. I witnessed their efficacy in her
latest hour and greatest trial, and must bear my testimony to the calm
triumph with which they brought her through. She died May 28,
1849.'—Pp. xiii—xv.

Such, in brief, is the sorrowful tale unfolded in this biographical notice.   It has much literary interest, but to us it is yet far more interesting in the picture it exhibits of domestic harmony and love, broken in upon and shaded by the presence of 'the king of terrors.'   Such scenes are of frequent occurrence, though it rarely happens that a sisterhood is linked by such mental sympathies and literary engagements as distinguished Ellis, Acton, and Currer Bell.   May the survivor combine, with her intellectual occupations, the faith and devotion which stand in intimate connexion with 'joys unspeakable and divine!'

Of ' Wuthering Heights' we must say a word before closing. We have already indicated our opinion ; but it is due to our readers and to ourselves that we should state somewhat more fully the grounds of our judgment.   That the work has considerable merit we admit.   The scenery is laid in the North, the bleak, moorish, wild, character of which is admirably preserved.   Ellis Bell was evidently attached to her native hills.  She was at home amongst them ; and there is, therefore, a vividness and graphic power in her sketches which present them actually before us.  So far we prefer no complaint, but the case is different with the *dramatis personæ*.   Such a ·company we never saw grouped before ; and we hope never to meet with its like again.   Heathcliff is a perfect monster, more demon than human.   Hindley Earnshaw is a besotted fool, for whom we scarce feel pity ; while his son Hareton is at once ignorant and brutish, until, as by the wand of an enchanter, he takes polish in the last scene of the tale, and retires a docile and apt scholar.   The two Catherines, mother and daughter, are equally exaggerations, more than questionable in some parts of their procedure, and absurdly unnatural in the leading incidents of their life.   Isabella Linton is one of the silliest and most credulous girls that fancy ever painted ; and the enduring affection and tenderness of her brother Edgar are so exhibited as to produce the impression of a feeble rather than of a virtuous character.   Of the minor personages we need say nothing, save that, with slight exceptions, they are in keeping with their superiors.

As the characters of the tale are unattractive, so the chief incidents are sadly wanting in probability.   They are devoid of truthfulness, are not in harmony with the actual world, and have, therefore, but little more power to move our sympathies than the romances of the middle ages, or the ghost stories which made our granddames tremble.

Art. IX.—1. *Prophetic Studies; or, Lectures on the Book of Daniel.*
By the Rev. John Cumming, D.D. London: Arthur Hall,
Virtue, and Co. 1850.

2. *No Popery! A Course of Eight Sermons, preached at the Episcopal
Jews' Chapel, Palestine-place, Bethnal-green.* By the Rev. J.
B. Cartwright, M.A. London: Wertheim and Macintosh.
1850.

3. *Lectures on the Principles and Institutions of the Roman Catholic
Religion; with an Appendix, containing Critical and Historical
Illustrations.* By the late Rev. Joseph Fletcher, D.D. Fifth
Edition. Edited by the Rev. Joseph Fletcher, of Christchurch.
London: William Kent and Co. 1851.

4. *Letter to Cardinal Wiseman, in answer to his 'Remarks on Lady
Morgan's Statements regarding St. Peter's Chair.'* By Sidney
Lady Morgan. London: Charles Westerton. 1851.

5. *The Heavenly Supremacy; or, the Position and Duty, at the present
Crisis, of those who hold that Christ is the only Head of the
Church.* By the Rev. Thomas Stratten. London: J. Snow.
1851.

6. *Village Lectures on Popery.* By the Rev. W. Ellis. London:
Ward and Co. 1851.

7. *Protestantism for 1850. A Sermon on the recent Papal Movement.*
Preached in Belgrave Chapel, Leeds, on Sunday Evening, Nov.
10, 1850. By the Rev. G. W. Conder. London: Simpkin,
Marshall, and Co.

It must be obvious to all our readers, even the most superficial,
that the great system of belief and worship over which the Pope
of Rome presides, is an actual POWER in the world. This power
is the boast of its adherents, and the dread of its adversaries. It
has grown up in the heart of civilized Europe. It has subordinated to itself, at one time or other, and with more. or less
appearance of ease, the great forces of mankind, whether intellectual, social, or political. It has gained the reverence and the
love of millions in nearly every land. It has covered the
brightest regions of Europe with its trophies; and its missionaries
have followed man in all his wanderings. Every form of humanity has done homage to this system, from the slave to the
emperor, from the lowest criminal to the most ascetic 'saint.'
It has leagued itself with every variety of government, flourishing

amid the forced tranquillity of absolute monarchy, the feuds of haughty oligarchies, the jealousies of old or young Republics, and the dignified and ever-growing freedom of our own peculiar institutions. In all seasons of national vicissitude, this great power has appeared, for good or for evil, ruling the spirits of men, controlling the councils of governments, moulding the institutions of ages, and casting the light of its splendour, or spreading the clouds of its adversity, on the shifting landscapes of modern history. For the docile it has traditionary creeds; over the superstitious it wields the terrors of the world to come. It addresses the devout in the accents of piety. To the lover of solitude, or the heart-sick victim of society, it opens the asylum of retirement. The bold are summoned to hard enterprize, and the zealous to self-denying toil. The scholar is enticed by leisure, libraries, and patrons; the artist, by the rarest means of culture, and the amplest opportunities of employment; the lover of art, by the blending of the art he loves with the services of Him whom he professes to adore; the orator, by the picturesque variety of themes for eloquence, and by the priestly authority with which he denounces the sinner, or consoles the penitent; the poet, by the grandeur of historical associations, the breadth of geographical extent, and the rich colouring and moving phantasms with which the past, the future, the earthly and the unseen, are mingled in the vast fields of imagination; the philanthropist, by the sacred ministries through which his bounty is to flow, not only to the wretched sufferers of this world, but to the more wretched inhabitants of the doleful regions which, according to his creed, are peopled by innumerable outcasts, depending on the charity of the faithful for deliverance from woe, and admittance to the fellowship of the blessed; the young, by the promise of gentle guidance, and by the perpetual presence of a revered authority; and the aged and the dying, by symbols which have been the companions of a chequered life, and by sympathies which are believed to be uttered by holiest lips in the darkest hour of sorrow.

The Roman Catholic religion is thus remarkable for its *many-sidedness*. It combines within itself nearly all the elements of human potency, and it combines these with so much skill that it is as impossible to define the limits of each, or to separate any one element from any other, as it would be to mark the boundaries, or to dissolve the union, of the rivers of the globe in the great ocean. And this wonderful combination of several agencies is *all-pervading*. In a sense which is easily understood, it is an elastic circle of human influences which may be said to move around the papal chair as its axis; yet the real power lies in the circumference more than in the centre, and the sustaining pressure is

from without rather than from within: unless we ought to compare
it to the attraction of the particles of matter, where every atom is
acted on by every other atom, with a double motion,—*towards* a
common point, and *from* it. Not only is the power of 'the
church' thus distributed in the actual relations of the members
towards each other, and especially towards their priests, but it
is believed to extend beyond the grave ; it is thought, felt, or
imagined, to comprehend all the conditions and the abodes of
the human family ; the sinners on earth are supposed to be bene-
fitted by the intercession of the saints in heaven; while the saints
who are yet in the body are expected to perform similar functions of Christian love on behalf of their brethren, whose imperfect sanctity has failed to secure the felicity of heaven, though
they are not doomed to hell; and in these functions the prayers
and alms of the laity have their appropriate value, as well as the
more solemn and official ministrations of the priests.

To deny this power of Romanism, would be to evince the
most stupid ignorance. Not to care for it is inexcusable apathy.
To bow before it is unreasoning superstition. To understand it
is wisdom. To deal with it wisely, is to do the duty of a
man. To oppose it successfully requires a large combination of
intelligence, devotion, and firmness, the compactness of unbroken
unity, the earnestness of the most elevated faith, and energy
which comes from God alone in answer to enlightened prayer.

We propose, in the present brief disquisition, to lay bare to the
eye of every reader the *real element* of this power—its heart's
core, its vital principle, its essential and characterizing spirit ;
and, having laid bare this *element*, to trace its development and
progressive outworking in the broad light of history. If the
analysis which brings out the element of Romanism should exhibit that same element in other religious organizations which
are popularly regarded, and devoutly cherished, as the antagonists of Romanism, we are prepared to undertake the responsibility of bringing the light of truth to bear steadily upon them :
not seeking to offend, yet not shrinking from our testimony as
disciples of the truth, because of the alarm, the suspicion, or the
animosity, which may follow the *self-applications* of our argument,
be they where they may.

That which appears to us to be the Central Force, the Living
Spirit of Romanism, is *the substitution of the human for the
Divine* in the spiritual affairs of men. The simple gospel teaches
us that Jesus Christ is the Instructor of mankind in all that pertains to the relations of sinful men to God. The same gospel
teaches that this same Jesus is the 'one mediator between God
and man'—'the *way*, the *truth*, and the *life*'—who says of
himself ' no man cometh unto the Father but by ME,' and of

whom his commissioned messengers bear witness in the most copious variety of plain assertions, and in the richest drapery of imaginative illustrations, that, through his sacerdotal sacrifice and intercession, and in no other way, can man, the sinner, worship God. The entire strain of evangelical teaching in the original documents of Christianity goes to show that the worship thus presented to God, in the name of His Son, is spiritual worship—the homage of man's spirit to his gracious Father, under the quickening and comforting guidance of the indwelling 'Spirit of life,' and producing the surrender of every sentiment and purpose to the reverential loving, obedient, and constant service of the 'Blessed God.' The ministry of the gospel, in all its departments, was designed, pre-eminently, to make known the great facts in which these truths are incorporated, to expound both the facts and the principles involved in them, and, by all the natural arts of human persuasion, accompanied with faith in the presence of the Saviour, and reliance on the promise of his Spirit, to beseech men to repent and believe, and, as the fruits of their penitence and faith, to enjoy the blessings of a free redemption, and to live a life of holy fellowship with Christ. The teaching, whether oral or written, of the first preachers of the gospel was symbolized by significant acts of personal and social worship, and the simplest modes of association for exemplifying the gospel and spreading it abroad were provided in the formation and the discipline of the early churches. United in the same faith, and in equal communion with their unseen *Lord*, these churches had their centre above the skies; their 'citizenship' was 'in heaven'; their Head was 'at the right hand of the Majesty on high'; their brotherhood included all the blessed who had been conducted to rest by the same leader though in the feeble light of earlier dispensations, and all 'that should hereafter believe on him unto life eternal.' This is the Divine idea, the human reality, of the Catholic Church. As a body of human beings, taught by men, ruled by men, and in many ways helped by men, whom they loved, and chose, and trusted as their teachers and guides, according to the revealed will of their common Master, they were exposed to danger from opposite extremes. In one extreme was the tendency to an exaggerated individualism, a morbid sentimentality, a neglect of order, of regard for the body of believers as a whole, and of the practical duties towards the Lord and towards the nations, which were binding alike, though in subordinate degrees, on every member of the spiritual family; in the other extreme, was the tendency to exalt the official, and imperceptibly to place the servants in the Master's room, to cover the unseen with the veil of earthly adornments, to lose the sense of the supreme authority and sole mediatorship of Christ in the deference paid to human teaching, and in the reliance felt on human ministrations.

We are not forgetful of the evils that arose at the beginning, and that have been perpetuated or revived ever since, from the former of these tendencies, in schisms, heresies, enthusiasms, and sectarian extravagancies; but our concern, in this place, is with the opposite extreme, as manifested in the pith and power of the great system which we are endeavouring to expound.

The proneness of man being to excess, we are not surprised that teachers of a revealed truth should be tempted to graft upon that truth their own opinions, yielding to the prejudices of their education and of their function, and claiming for the *human conception of the Truth* the authority which belongs to the truth itself; neither are we surprised that the officials of the churches should so far forget the proper *ministerial* character as to imagine that they stood nearer to God than their fellow-worshippers, and to liken themselves, or permit themselves to be likened by their brethren, to those priests whom they had seen at heathen altars, or in the Jewish temple, offering sacrifice, and interceding on behalf of the common people. Ancient indeed is this notion, embodied in institutions, of a human mediation visibly acting with God for man. But the true and only mediation between man *as* man, and God *as* God, in the worship which the holy God receives from sinning man, was already exhibited in 'The Great High Priest' of the human race. The apostles trusted HIM, and they preached HIM, as the only sacrificer, the only advocate; but when the apostles fell asleep, there were men whose coming they had foretold, who, instead of preaching Christ, assumed his office, established a fearful mimicry of his awful work, and professedly became to the people *that* which it is not possible for any but Jesus Christ to be. And so it continues to this day. It is believed by many millions of men called Christians, that these ministers are authoritative teachers, standing in a special relation to God, which is more sacred than their own, empowered to take cognizance of their spiritual successes, to pronounce absolution of their sins, to offer a real sacrifice for those sins, to administer 'grace' through appointed channels of which they have the exclusive charge, and to transmit these tremendous powers from hand to hand by the mysteries of orders and succession.

Herein lies *the power* of Romanism,—*the belief of the people.* Let the people cease to believe that the priests have their power from God, and in that moment it vanishes as spectres of the night depart at break of day, and as other phantasies of ignorance melt into thin air and nothingness before the blaze of truth. Our own sympathies, as 'Eclectic' reviewers, are with the people, of

England chiefly, and of all the lands in which our stout and hearty tongue is spoken; but not to Englishmen and their descendants only: our party is mankind. It is a serious mission. We feel it to be as sublime as it is serious, as benevolent as it is sublime, as mighty as it is benevolent, and as sure of success as truth and Providence can make it. In the Church of Christ, there is but one supremacy, but one sacrifice, but one priest; and he who believes this ancient, apostolic, Catholic, unchangeable tradition, is 'free of the universe,' calls no man master in religion, and spurns away from him, calmly and courteously, yet with bold and brave determination, any man that would stand between him and his Redeemer in the solemnities of his worship, and in the communion of his soul with God. But while men are so ignorant, so timid, so slavish, so slow of heart to receive the pure and entire truth of the gospel, as to listen to human teachings instead of the divine, and to prize the benediction of a fellow-sinner instead of cleaving to the Lord with purpose of heart, Romanism *will* have power, and there is no combination of human forces that can destroy it.

The united and never-relaxing assiduities of *the sacerdotal order* are directed to the maintenance of this power. With this view they keep the written revelation of Christ from the people when they can, and, when they cannot, they translate it and interpret it to serve the same object: not that we mean to affirm that this is done consciously and wittingly in every case; but it is the system, it is Romanism, it is essential to its life. With the same view, the same persons are ever descanting on the feebleness of the human reason, taking up exaggerated pictures of the mischiefs of unbridled inquiry and unfettered action in religion, dreading nothing so much as the free communion of each man with the light of heaven and with the Son of God. With the same view, whether confessedly even to themselves or not, the priests, who are clothed in the garb of humility, are ever winding their way into the hearts of men, *and of women* especially, rendering themselves and their offices necessary to mental repose and to spiritual satisfaction in a world where temptation is so rife, and where transgressions, alas! are so easy and so common. To uphold the priestly power, the theory of sacraments—than which nothing could be invented more revolting to reason, more opposed to Scripture, or more degrading to humanity—is not taught merely, but daily and hourly *acted out* so as to be made an indispensable part of human life. For this, the silly fiction of purgatory—a fiction closely intertwined with the passions and weaknesses of our nature—is perpetually wrought into the habitual thinkings of men who dare not reason. The Holy Text is tortured to give out the appearance of support to the most childish superstitions, to assumptions the most arrogant, and to doctrines the most pernicious.   There is not a dogma peculiar to ' The Holy Roman Church,' or a rite, or a formulary, or a tradition, or a symbol, or an embellishment, which does not centre in this grand anti-Christian delusion, this iniquitous mystery of the ROMAN PRIESTHOOD.

We resume our notice of some of the almost innumerable publications that continue to pour forth on this absorbing theme. Each of these publications has local claims, and does good, we doubt not, in the circles where the writers are well-known.  We do not complain that they are too numerous.  In most of them we have a healthy spirit of Protestantism, which cannot be too strongly cherished, and which it is the object of these publications to regulate as well as cherish.

Dr. Cumming's volume is distinguished by the same characteristics with his previous ' Prophetic Studies.'  The arrangement of the Discourses is highly popular, and a large amount of information is drawn from writers of established reputation, and presented in a lively oratorical style.  The great doctrines of the gospel are glowingly exhibited, and many practical principles of religion are pressed home with affectionate faithfulness.   The lecture on ' The Papacy' (xvi.) is, as might be supposed, a compendium of arguments with which long practice has made him familiar.  We are glad to find the lecturer insisting so plainly on the ever-momentous truth :—

' We are strong, not by possession of the Bible as a book, but by the embodiment of the Bible as a living, plastic, regulating faith.  It is God's truth *within* us, not God's truth *without* us, that is the strength of Christians, the safety of the saints of God.  Show, then, to the Church of Rome—show to the world at large, that we have a succession that never fails—the succession of the sons of God; that we have a religion which is ever beautiful, and mighty to make us holy and to make us happy—a religion that is not meat nor drink, but righteousness, and peace, and joy in the Holy Ghost.'

In p. 259, we find these remarkable words :—' *I do not believe that the Man of Sin shall* (will) *re-assert his ancient political supremacy in this land.*'  How does Dr. Cumming understand the recent aggressions of ' the Man of Sin ?'  Do they *re-assert* political authority, or not ?  The whole of the lecture in which these words occur is to us very far from being satisfactory.  The exposition of ' the Ancient of Days' strikes us as harsh, constrained, and too manifestly adapted to views which not a few conceive to have been gathered from other sources than the Scriptures.  We are sorry to observe a large abundance of the blemishes in style which usually disfigure Dr. Cumming's pages — hastiness, superficiality, straining after rhetorical effort —

flippant mode of reiterating in prefaces, and everywhere else, the cardinal truths of Christianity—a dogmatical and one-sided dealing with difficult questions, which our judgment seriously condemns in books of any kind, and most of all in books entitled 'Prophetic *Studies*.' More '*studies*' would, we think, inspire the author with greater caution in reaching his conclusions, and greater deliberation in committing them to the press. It is not always a good thing for an author's reputation or usefulness that his works should be in great demand. The most popular writings are not invariably the best, or the most likely to imbue the many with the love of the truth. Popularity sometimes arises from circumstances so entirely adventitious, and is sustained by peculiar means so assiduously plied, as to lessen, instead of increasing, the worth of his instructions, even when they are unquestionably good. We purpose to go at length into the large question of prophetical interpretation at a future time. There is scarcely any other which, as we apprehend, has so frequently been handled with rashness, prejudice, and a painful oversight of the laws of language as developed in the Scriptures, and of the principles which characterise the Christian dispensation.

Lady Morgan's pamphlet is one of the most spirited, witty, and truly learned *brochures* of the day. The story to which it relates has been repeated by most of the London and provincial newspapers. It is, in brief, that the supposed 'chair of St. Peter' was examined by 'the sacrilegious curiosity' of the French when they invaded Rome.

'They actually removed its superb casket, and discovered the relic. Upon its mouldering and dusty surface were traced carvings which bore the appearance of letters. The chair was quickly brought into a better light, the dust and cobwebs removed, and the inscription (for an inscription it was) faithfully copied. The writing was in Arabic characters, and is the well-known confession of the Mahomedan faith, "*There is but one God. and Mahomet is his prophet.*" It is supposed that this chair had been among the spoils of the crusaders, offered to the Church at a time when taste for antiquarian lore and the deciphering of inscriptions was not yet in fashion. This story has been since hushed up, and the chair replaced, none but the profane believe it, and none but the audacious repeat it. Yet such there are even at Rome.'—*Lady Morgan's* '*Italy.*' *Vol. II.*

Now, Dr. Wiseman has *never seen this chair*, yet he gives an elaborate description of it—in George Robins's style—and brings forward sundry witnesses to prove that it is the chair given by Pudens, the Christian senator, to Saint Peter, when he laid the foundation of the Roman Church in that senator's house! Lady Morgan significantly hints, and we agree with her ladyship, that

'a more compendious course would be, perhaps, to remove the
cover, and show the chair.'   It is evident that Dr. Wiseman was
exceedingly angry with this heretical lady when he wrote his
' Remarks;' and we do not envy him the severe, but refined
and womanly, castigation with which she has replied to his coarse
and ill-tempered invective.   We need not say that the whole
story about this ' ricketty ' old chair is a most paltry piece of
business, and that, in our sober judgment, it *does* record against
the ' hierarchy of a religion professed by millions of Christians,'
what the Cardinal calls ' a weighty charge of hypocrisy and
imposture.'

Mr. Stratten's Discourse on the ' Heavenly Supremacy ' is designed to show—that the central place or seat of government to
the Church is heaven; that the law of this government is the
word of Christ; and that Christ is the *only Head* of the Church.
His arguments for this exclusiveness of the heavenly supremacy
are—1. The fitness, coherence, and beauty of the few and simple
terms employed to describe it; 2. The divine perfectness of the
heavenly Head; 3. The responsibility of the individual conscience to Christ; 4. The ultimate purpose of the Head of the
Church towards each particular member.   Each of these arguments is ingeniously and ably urged, though in language which,
as critics, we should like better if it were simpler and less encumbered with the drapery of rhetoric.   The English ecclesiastical supremacy is declared to be ' renounced ' by the monarch so
far as we (Dissenters) are concerned.   Then who gives the churchwardens power to distrain our goods ?   Are Dissenters not
amenable to the authority of the spiritual courts, and is not the
last appeal, in those courts, to her Majesty in Council?   We
cannot but accord with the sentiment expressed by Mr. Stratten,
in page 25 of his ' Discourse :'  ' The present truth, then, the
voice of which should be heard in our streets, and in all places
of concourse is, that the great moral remedy for the dangers
of our country, and the *only remedy* which, in the long run,
can be effectual, is to awaken every man's conscience to the
vigilant exercise of the functions divinely assigned to it.'   In
page 31, the ' Martyrs of Papal Rome ' are apostrophised:
the Author means, we surmise, the witnesses for the truth
against Rome, her *victims*, not her martyrs.   In the Appendix,
the writer refers to some local and personal matters.   He
demands a ' *legal repression* of the hierarchy created by the
Papal bull '; and rests his demand, especially as addressed to
Protestant Nonconformists, on the ground that religious liberty
is staked on the issue.   Mr. Stratten regards the prohibition of
the Cardinal's ' red stockings ' with more seriousness than we
should have advised.   ' If the Cardinal succeed in parading his

red stockings over the Protestant soil' (Protestant *soil!*) 'of England, he becomes the hero of the day, and will command hero worship. If he cannot tread the soil of England without putting the offence from his feet, or if he have *to walk back in them* to Rome' (Cardinals *ride,* we believe), 'they become the symbols of his disgrace, and show the colour of his shame.'—There is no other *political* suggestion in the pamphlet. We scarcely think that the prohibition of 'red stockings,' or the declaration (from Dissenters, too !) that 'the soil' of England is Protestant, or the banishment of Cardinal Wiseman would do much towards keeping 'the citadel of (our) country's power and glory free from the curse of a Romish hierarchy, and so make it the vantage-ground from which, wisely and seasonably, to conduct such operations as the general cause of scriptural religion may require.' With the *end* which the propounders of such measures have in view, we sympathize as heartily as they can desire; but, as to the *means,* we ask, first of all, are we temporising because, in common with a large portion of the British community, we doubt, even while we abominate, the Papal hierarchy, whether it be a case for legal enactment and, secondly, whether we are not honouring our Protestantism, by guarding against every approach to the use of that order of agency in its support, which has already done more than the aggressions of Popery to confine its sphere, and to impede its progress in the European nations? We appeal to the history of all the Protestant establishments in Europe. It is because we yield to none in all that is meant by Protestantism, that we will not lend ourselves to any legislation which claims 'the soil' of England for any religious party. We should greatly rejoice to see a law so large and free in its principles as to forbid the ecclesiastics of Rome, or any other ecclesiastics, claiming, as such, territorial dignity in England, by virtue of their office in the hierarchy. We hope that the civil law of this ancient realm will ever protect our free citizens from the canon law of Rome. We address the English *people,* whether Roman Catholics or Protestants, and we invite them to help us in propagating the undying principles of evangelical truth and righteousness, well knowing, as we do, that these principles, deeply rooted in men's minds, are sure to overturn all the priesthoods which have deceived and enslaved the nations, and thus destroy effectually and for ever one of the most deadly curses that sin has brought upon our race.

Mr. Ellis is well known and much loved by a large circle of friends, in various parts of the world, as a devoted missionary, and as the secretary and historian of the London Missionary Society. In these lectures he has judiciously availed himself of his extensive reading, and of his personal observation in many lands, including Italy and Rome. Having delivered them to a village congregation in Hertfordshire, we think he has done wisely to commit them to the press. They are remarkable for their simple and explanatory character; and they seem to us to be more suitable to the mass of readers who need to be taught what Popery is, and by what arguments it can be confuted, than any of the countless publications with which the press is now teeming. We honestly commend them to readers of every grade.

The drift of Mr. Conder's able and spirited discourse is to show that ' the germs and elements of all that marks the Romish Church' are ' within a so-called Protestant community '; that the real ground for apprehension lies not in the advances of Rome towards us so much as in that tendency towards Rome which is in the midst of us. Mr. Conder has gone very much into the core of the great question. Speaking of the English Church, he says, with much simplicity and force :—

' Against what, then, does it chiefly object? Will it not be true to reply—Against details, and not against principles; against particular forms and practices, and not against the root from which they spring? It has no objection to a temporal Head of the Church; but it has an objection to a Pope as Head of the Church. It does not condemn the appointment of priests, but objects to the mode of their appointment and the functions they are to perform. It does not object to rites and ceremonies which have no spiritual origin, but to what those rites and ceremonies shall be. It says that the kingdom of God *may* be a visible, secular thing; i. e., may be joined with, aided and protected by, secular power and honour—even by jails and policemen, and laws of laymen; but its quarrel is with the form which this kingdom shall assume, and the character of its connexion with secular power. It protests against details, and not against principles. It will not have images, and real presence, and extreme unction, and purgatory, and cardinals, and a Pope, and confessionals; but it will keep holy orders, and priestly absolution, and baptismal regeneration, and a sovereign head, and a hierarchy, with exclusive right to the Christian service. In form and practice then, it is in opposition, in principle, it is at *one*, with what it opposes.'

We are glad to welcome a new and cheap edition of the late Dr. Joseph Fletcher's ' Lectures on the Roman Catholic Church.' They excited much attention at the time of their first publication in 1817, and numerous proofs of their general acceptance and great usefulness are given by Mr. Fletcher in the preface to this edition. There is that pervading dignity of thought and diction which characterised all the writer's productions; the tone is eminently serious, devout, and spiritual; the arguments are faithfully condensed, and clearly expressed; while there is a healthy

pulse of tol(      ) not always found in controversies with Roman
Catholics.

Mr. Cartwright's ' No P(      ' )   a fair      ple          :t
protesting which the late P.          r          s pro\
of the Episcopalian pulpits.   It      not cha              by
*strength* of any kind.   Per]   t    tame          p   es
compositions are the best th       t      u:   s (   .d prodt
or their auditors receive—a \   '   ble
either Popery from without )r

---

# Brief Notices.

*Additional Annotations, Critical, Philological, and Explanatory, on the
New Testament ; being a Supplementary Volume to the Greek Testament with English Notes, in two volumes.* By the Rev. S. T. Bloomfield, D.D.   8vo.   London : Longman and Co.   1850.

Dr. BLOOMFIELD has, in this volume, fulfilled the promise made eleven
years since, of completing a body of critical, philological, and exegetical notes on the New Testament. He refers, in his preface, to the colla-
tion of numerous MSS., before ' either wholly unknown, or but little
known, and only partially examined,' and critical editions of no ordinary
scale, and of no little pretension (as those of Lachmann and Tischendorf), and states that he has again revised the whole of the text of
the New Testament.   The result of this revision is, in general, that
he differs almost *in toto* from Lachmann, and, in a great measure, from
Tischendorf.

The philological and exegetical notes will be appreciated by biblical
students, especially by ministers of the gospel.   In several instances
they are brief dissertations rather than passing notes.   The additional
matter in the present volume exhibits very great attention to the
Gospel of St. John, and the Acts ; while the whole text of the Apocalypse has been completely revised—à work indispensable to the right
interpretation of a book for which so much remains to be done in the
way of interpretation.   We congratulate the venerable author on the
completion of his sacred engagement, and most heartily sympathize in the prayer that ' his various labours in the service of the sanctuary, carried on for a period of far more than a quarter of a century,
may be blessed to the right understanding of those Holy Scriptures,
which are alone—as the *only* source of pure religious knowledge, the
only ground of faith, and rule of duty—able to make us wise unto
salvation, through faith which is in Christ Jesus.'   In the great struggle which has begun to call forth the powers of every intelligent
Protestant, we need scarcely say no man is so well equipped as he who

is 'mighty in the Scriptures;' and we do not know of a more safe
and useful compendium of well-sifted interpretations than the New
Testament here published. No reader expects us to endorse every
explanation. We speak in general terms, and with a marked reference
to the studied accuracy which is so unspeakably valuable in a work of
this description.

———

*Lyrics of the Heart: with other Poems.* By Alaric A. Watts. With
Forty-one Engravings on Steel. London: Longman and Co.

THIS is a beautiful volume, and will prove an acceptable present to a
large class. It is fitted alike for the drawing-room and the library. In
the one case, it will be admired for its tasteful exterior, graceful verses,
and rich embellishments; while in the other it will be prized for the
deeper sympathies it indicates with what is tender and beautiful. Mr.
Watts's name has been before the public too long, and the characteristics of his poetry are too well known, to require either introduction or
comment from us. He was engaged for many years in editing some of
the most popular of our Annuals. His services to illustrated literature
have been conspicuous. Few men have done more in this direction, or
possess higher claims on the esteem and gratitude of artists. That
such a man should have been aided, in the production of a beautifully-
illustrated edition of his own poems, by some of the most distinguished
members of the profession he had served, is alike honorable to all
parties. Their joint production is now before us, and we receive it as
a graceful tribute to the merits of the poet. 'It is not improbable,'
says Mr. Watts, with genuine modesty, 'that I may have rendered myself liable to an imputation which I do not deserve, for having embellished, in an expensive manner, a series of trifles of so little real
importance. My explanation is a very simple one. For upwards
of fourteen years I was intimately associated with many of our
most eminent artists in the production of a series of illustrated works,
and the agreeable nature of that intercourse led to a desire on my part
to connect myself with them in some volume which should be composed
wholly of my own writings. Hence the decorative form which these
pages have assumed.'

Mr. Watts's poetry is graceful and pleasing, and for the most part is
conversant, as the motto on his title-page indicates, with

> 'Familiar matter of to-day;
> Some natural sorrow, loss, or pain,
> That hath been, and may be again.'

It partakes occasionally of a sickly sentimentalism—a fault almost
universal amongst the poets of our Annuals. In his more healthful
moods, however, this fault is avoided, and a cheerful, hopeful tone is
assumed. Many of the pieces reprinted here are great favorites with
the public, and some of them we can never read without admiration
and pleasure. 'Ten Years Ago'; 'He never said he loved me'; 'My
own Fireside'; and 'The Death of the First-born'; are of this number.
There is no pretension in Mr. Watts's poetry to subtility of intellect, or
to those marvellous creations in which the genius of Shakespere and

Milton delight. The flow of his verse is soft and musical, and the impression it generally makes partakes more of the nature of pleasure than of admiration.

The *Illustrations*—forty-one in number—are happily conceived, and their execution does great credit to the skill of the engraver. They bear the names of some of our most distinguished artists; and though we might, in a few cases, make exceptions, the doing so would be ungrateful to our feelings, and our readers would scarcely receive the impression we are desirous of conveying. We shall be glad to learn—what the volume richly merits—that it finds much favor with the public.

---

*The Chronological New Testament, in which the Text of the Authorized Version is newly divided into Paragraphs and Sections, with the dates and places of transactions marked, the Marginal Renderings of the Translations, many Parallel Illustrative Passages printed at length, Brief Introductions to each Book, and a Running Analysis of the Epistles.* London: R. B. Blackader; S. Bagster and Sons. 1851.

We cheerfully recommend this remarkably beautiful and useful edition of the New Testament. It has been carefully prepared, under the guidance of eminent biblical scholars. As the editor projects an edition of the Old Testament on the same plan, we take the earliest opportunity of expressing our satisfaction with this fruit of his labours, and our hope that he will be encouraged by readers of the Bible generally, and especially by students of theology and Christian ministers, to persevere. By an arrangement which we believe has been suggested by former editions of the New Testament, the reader is perpetually reminded of his *personal* interest in what he reads, and aided in the practical application of the truth to his own spiritual state. We are glad to learn that, in order to a large circulation, the price of the volume has been reduced to seven shillings and sixpence.

---

*Bertha. A Romance of the Dark Ages.* By William Bernard M'Cabe, Author of ' A Catholic History of England.' Three Vols. 12mo. London : T. C. Newby.

WIDELY as we differ from Mr. M'Cabe on the principles of historic evidence, we readily do justice to the diligence with which he has drawn forth, from musty tomes, the records of monks and other Papal chroniclers. Of his history we have formerly spoken freely. It may be advantageously consulted in connexion with the labors of Mackintosh, Hallam, and others, but is wanting in those qualities which would render it a safe and intelligent guide to the youthful student. The present work, which claims a lighter and more attractive character, is open to the same exception. As a work of art it is deficient in an exhibition of the minor or secondary qualities of the parties described, some of its conversations are sadly wanting in sprightliness and force, and a few of the scenes described are simply ridiculous. The general manners of the times, however, are accurately drawn. Light is thrown over an obscure page of

242

European history, and many of the characters sketched, stand out in bold relief, and obtain much of the reader's sympathy. The beautiful Beatrice, the pilgrim, her noble grandfather, Gretchen, the Saxon maid, the two Dedis, father and son, and Bernhard, the forester of Aschaffenburgh, are amongst this number. The appearance of the elder Dedi before the Frankfort Parliament, as the advocate and defender of Otho of Bavaria, is one of the finest passages in the work. It is conceived and executed in the author's best style. The heroism of the Saxons in resisting the sanguinary despotism of Henry is also portrayed with admirable effect, so as to bring out the character of individuals and the general complexion of the national struggle. The radical defect of the tale is the false light in which it exhibits the leading personages of the day. This will be instantly understood when we say that it is written in the blind and undiscriminating spirit of the Guelphs of the middle age. We are no admirers of Henry IV. of Germany, nor do we wholly reprobate the memory of his great antagonist, Hildebrand. Neither, however, was what Mr. M'Cabe sketches. Henry was not a perfect monster; nor was Hildebrand a faultless and heroic saint. We admit the fearful vices of the former; but there were some redeeming points in his character, and the force that was early put on his person—of which the Archbishop of Cologne was the prime agent—and the methods employed to corrupt and enfeeble his boyhood ought, in all fairness, to have been considered in the sketch drawn by our author. This, however, is not the case, and the natural consequence follows—an untruthful and erring portraiture of a man, whose vices constituted the strength of his opponent. Henry was naturally brave and generous, and but for the Archbishop Anno and his associates, might have been a temperate man and a righteous sovereign. Unhappily, he proved far otherwise; but there is a manifest violation of justice in canonizing Anno, as the Papal church has done, and anathematizing Henry. We regret to find that a writer of the nineteenth century can so unscrupulously adopt the distorted views and false judgments of the dark ages.

---

*The Journal of Sacred Literature.* No. XIII. January, 1851. Edited by John Kitto, D.D., F.S.A. London: Simpkin, Marshall, and Co.

In this number, Dr. Kitto commences the *seventh* volume of his Journal. The contents are varied and interesting, embracing Dissertations on Nineveh; the Jansenists and their Remnant in Holland; the Septuagint; the Theory of Human Progression; Letter and Spirit in the Old Testament; John Calvin; First Lessons in Biblical Criticism; on the Interpretation of 1 Cor. vii. 25—40; our Lord's Discourses and Sayings; Annotations on the New Testament; together with sundry matters of Correspondence; Biblical Intelligence; and Quarterly List of English and Foreign Works in Sacred Literature. We are glad to find it announced that the learned Editor has received a grant of £100 a-year from her Majesty's Civil List, on account of his useful and meritorious literary works.

*The Congregational Year-Book for* 1850 ; *with an Almanack for* 1851. 8vo. Pp. 244. London : Jackson and Walford.

THIS is a marvellously cheap publication, and ought to have a proportionably large circulation. Nothing short of a sale of many thousands can reimburse the expense of its production, and we shall be glad to find that the Congregationalists of the kingdom are sufficiently alive to their own interests to secure such a sale. The preparation of the volume has been a work of immense labour, and we attach great value to its contents. In addition to an Almanack for the current year, it contains :—' The Proceedings of the Congregational Union of England and Wales—Selections from the published Proceedings of the Congregational Board, and of other Associations of Independents—Lists of recognised Ministers in England and Wales, with the Colleges in which they were educated ; and of Churches in the Denomination within the same bounds, with their Pastors—Lists of Ordinations and Settlements within the year, and also of openings of Chapels newly built, or after material enlargements—Notices of the Deaths of Pastors, or brethren otherwise eminent, within the year, with Brief Biographical Minutes—Lists of Publications during the year, by Members of the Congregational Body—Accounts of the Colleges, Missions, Schools, and other Institutions of the Independents in England and Wales—Notices of the Congregational interest in other parts of the World.' The value of such a collection of statistics can be duly estimated only by those who have engaged in historical compositions. We strongly recommend it to our readers, and shall be glad to find all other religious bodies supplying equally full and accurate information.

---

*Chronology of Prophecy, tracing the Courses of Divine Providence from the Flood to the End of Time, in the light as well of National Annals as of Scriptural Predictions.* By Adam Thom. London : Longman and Co.

MR. THOM has a fixed idea on the subject of Chronology of a rather extraordinary kind. He holds that the periods occurring in several prophecies, such as 1,290 years, 1,260 years, 391 years (the hour, day, month, and year of the sixth trumpet) are found to be of perpetual recurrence in the chain of Divine Providence. They are not merely the measures of the duration of the events with which they stand connected in the prophecies; they are also the measures of the periods of all the greatest incidents in the history of the world, in conformity with which the whole of chronology may be marshalled off into regular periods. But the author finding it somewhat difficult to get all the events of the world's history at the right distances from each other, tortures these unfortunate numbers in all sorts of ways; mercilessly cuts them up into halves, quarters, eighths; throws aside remainders without compunction; draws them out a year or two where it is necessary, and, in a word, resorts to all the shifts which honest men bent on twisting one or two coincidences into a grand universal law must adopt. We may give a part of one of Mr. Thom's tabular summaries, taken at random, as an illustration of his conjuror's style of tossing about numbers.

We must just explain that the object is to show that 391 years (the duration of the sixth trumpet) is a constantly-recurring period. At the very outset the author stumbles. He seeks for a number contained in 391 sufficiently small to allow of several instances of its recurrence to be found, and for this purpose he divides 391 into twenty-nine thirteens and one fourteen! and forthwith proceeds to find events which have happened at distances of 13 years from each other, all of which he sets down as instances of the prevalence of the period of 391 years, thinking it quite unnecessary to notice that 13 is not a division of 391 at all :—

| | A.D. | | A D |
|---|---|---|---|
| Mohammrdan Invasion of Spain | 710 + | (3 × 13) | = 749 Accession of Abbassides. |
| Accession of Abbassides........ | 749 + | (25 × 13 + 14) | = 1062 Passage of Euphrates by Turks. |
| Passage of Euphrates ........ | 1062 + | 13 | = 1075 Capture of Jerusalem. |
| Capture of Jerusalem ......... | 1075 + | (13 × 13 + 14) | = 1258 Overthrow of Caliphate of Bagdad |

And so he runs on, taking one thirteen or twenty-five thirteens wherever it suits, and throwing in a fourteen here and there; and then, having thus arbitrarily treated his materials, brings out and holds up, conjuror-like, the wonderful results. But the above fragment of a table is one of the most sober in the volume. In one table, having 430 for its key number, we find the half of 430 set down three times; once as 215, once as 214, once as 216; a sixth of 430 as 71! two-thirds as 286; one-third as 144! one (430) as 427, 428, 430, 431; a quarter as 108, 107; two and a half as 1,074. And these are absolutely all the dates in that table.

We wonder if it never occurred to Mr. Thom that in a world with 800,000,000 of men on it, it is possible that on *whatever* year of its existence he pitched, he might find that something had been done—worthy of going into history.

---

*The Illustrated Year Book.* Second Series.
*The Wonders, Events, and Discoveries of* 1850. Edited by John Timbs.
London: Arthur Hall, Virtue, & Co.

THE success of the ' Illustrated Year Book ' for 1850 has naturally led to the appearance of this volume, the character and claims of which are much the same as those of its predecessor. The volume eschews politics, and is altogether of an informing and entertaining character. The subjects of which it treats will sufficiently indicate its nature. These are ' The Hippopotamus in England,' ' Ocean Steamers,' ' Miss Burdett Coutts's Church,' ' The " Koh-I-Noor," or Mountain of Light,' ' Tornado in the Bahamas,' ' The Submarine Electric Telegraph,' ' The Nepaulese Embassy,' ' Paronomania,' ' Colossal Statue of Bavaria,' ' A Lion Hunt in Algeria,' ' Journey to the Mountains of the Moon,' ' The British Museum,' and ' The Exhibition of 1851.' Such a volume supplies much interesting reading, and may be taken up with advantage at any leisure half-hour. We counsel the editor, however, to be somewhat more careful in selecting his topics for future volumes. With every disposition to do justice to his labors, we cannot see on what principle the erection of a church, a lion-hunt in Algeria, or the two panoramas described, are classed under 'The Wonders, Events, and Discoveries of 1850.'

---

*The Year-Book of the Country.* By William Howitt. London: Colburn.

As the title imports, this new volume of an old friend is a sort of calendar of country life, divided into monthly sections, each of which opens with a sketch of the aspects of nature at that particular season. These sketches are conceived in the purest, sweetest tone, and come to us pent-up town-folk with a strangely-blended pain and pleasure, like the fragrance of fresh flowers in crowded streets. They comprise some of the most genial prose pictures of our English country life that we have,—revealing in every line a loving student of Nature's varying aspects, a true and gentle poet spirit. That is the William Howitt whom we knew long ago, and always rejoice to hear. But there is another and darker spirit dwelling in him—a political demon—who breaks out every now and then with an effort, as if a dove were to start up a dragon, or Goldsmith were to be possessed by a legion of Cobbetts. We confess, that, though agreeing in most of the things that are said when that *æstus* is on our author, we do not love nor like him half so well, denouncing woe on speculators in corn as being 'ghouls and afreets,' or thundering about political corruption, as we do when we get him in his other aspect. He will do more, he may rest assured, for his country's good by wooing us in his own pure way to the love of beauty and of God's world, than by declaiming on education and the suffrage. Plenty of us can do that: our voices are cracked at the best, and will not spoil by stump-oratory; but do not let him strain his sweet notes in such a way. As good Dr. Watts might tell him, the birds are to sing and agree; it is bears and lions whose high prerogative it is to growl and fight. These remarks are suggested by the frequent recurrence of digressions which strike us as blots in this otherwise loveable book. Apart from such *escapades*, it is full of beauty, and love for all things in earth and air; whilst the occasional hasty glimpses of out-of-the-way nooks both of place and character, and the sweet, graceful snatches of verse (true old Howittish) interspersed, make it—to use a word which for its richness of sound and sense deserves a better fate than its hacknied repetition promises— *delightful.* There are many exquisitely true and tender veins of thought and feeling running through it, part of which we should gladly transfer; but, failing space, we commend the volume itself, with a hearty word of welcome, as the work of a genuine, though not a giant, child of song.

---

*Peeps at Nature; or, God's Works and Man's Wants.*
*Nature's Wonders; or, God's Care over all his Works.* By the Author of 'Peeps at Nature.' London: Tract Society.

Two admirable little books, conveying much useful information, in a form well suited to engage the attention of young readers.

*The Museum of Classical Antiquities : a Quarterly Journal of Archi-*
*tecture and the Sister Branches of Classical Art.*  No. I.  January,
1851.  London: John W. Parker.

THIS new journal, with a title partially resembling another, which has
ceased, is a very elegant publication.  It purposes to draw attention to
the vestiges of classic antiquity, making architecture the *basis* of the
researches to be carried on, and, in connexion with this main subject,
selecting such studies as improve the taste rather than promote speculation.  While appealing to classical scholars for help in clearing up
the doubts and difficulties occasioned by the descriptions of monuments
which abound in ancient authors, the editors say, ' We shall also render
it our particular object to strive to interest the *public*, by selecting such
themes as will prove agreeable and profitable to the general reader,
being convinced that invention, progress, and perfection in art do not
originate so much from the studio of the artist, or the patronage of the
great, as from the cultivated mind of the *people*.'  This first number
treats of the advantage of the study of antiquity and excellence in art ;
the rapid destruction of ancient monuments ; the polychromy (many
colours) of Greek architecture ; description of one of the city gates of
Pæstum ; communication from Professor Schoenborn, of Posen, relative to an important monument recently discovered by him in Lycia ;
on the paintings, by Polygnotus, in the Lesche at Delphi, Part I., with
folding plate, representing the painting on the right-hand wall, by
W. Watkiss Lloyd, Esq. ; on the plan and disposition of the Greek
Lesche, with illustrations by the EDITOR; on some Egyptian-Doric
columns at Thebes, with illustrations, by Edward Falkener, Esq. ;
Archæographia Literaria ; and notices of new publications.

*The Core of Creeds ; or, St. Peter's Keys.*  By Rev. David Thomas.
London : Ward and Co.

THIS is one of the best specimens we have seen lately of pulpit
addresses.  There is strong, hard thinking in it—not ' dry,' but vigorous
and manlike, and conveyed in a style which, if not laying claim to
finery, is unmistakeably direct.  We rejoice in the growth of this kind
of ' earnest ministry' amongst us, composed as it is of men sympathizing with, and moulded by, the pressure of the time, and
consequently speaking the language of this living century, and not of
dead ones; likely, therefore, to speak to purpose.  We heartily recommend this little volume as the work of a thoughtful Christian man,
who has already done good service, and will do more.

*A Compendium of Universal History.*  Translated from the German.
By C. T. Stafford.  London : Longman and Co.

A VERY admirable manual, compiled with diligence, and translated
with accuracy.  Popular as a school book in Germany, it would be
advantageously used in the same way here.  We recommend it to our
readers who may need it for such a purpose.

*South Africa Delineated.* By Rev. Thornley Smith. London: Mason.

WE happened to take up this little volume immediately after laying down Mr. Gordon Cumming's. They embrace a great deal of the same ground; but there the resemblance ends, inasmuch as Mr. Smith's is about men instead of beasts, contains a large amount of information as to the native inhabitants of the district, is undeniably true, and a little tedious. It is, however, worth reading, both for what it says of the different tribes of South Africa and for its compendious sketch of missionary operations there.

---

*Hints for the Earnest Student.* Compiled by Mrs. William Fison. London: Seeleys.

A GREAT collection of wise sayings, which may be read with advantage; or (if we may venture to say it of the production of a lady, with evident sincerity of purpose and Christian principle), may be left unread without any very conspicuous detriment,—the hints being so very true that they become truisms, and the advices so very obvious that any one who does not read them here will be pretty certain to do so somewhere else.

---

# Review of the Month.

---

THE Papal is still *the* question of the day. There is no sign of diminished interest in it. Popular feeling certainly has not evaporated. Every county has, we believe, recorded its judgment, while cities, boroughs, and parishes innumerable, have spoken with unwonted unanimity and zeal. So far, the facts of the case are undoubted. The national mind has unquestionably been aroused to an unusual extent, and has spoken with a vehemence which, if not always wise, has, at least, disclosed its deep and impassioned earnestness. The lull which now occurs is apparent rather than real. The fifth of November returns only once a year; and the counties and boroughs of England, having held their meetings and pronounced their judgment, now wait the assembling of parliament to see how our legislature will deal with the crisis which has arisen.

We are glad that the meeting of Parliament has been deferred till February. It was a wise resolution on the part of her Majesty's Government, and its good fruits will be seen in the more sober and statesman-like views which will be broached. Had our senators met immediately after the publication of the Papal bull, there would have been serious ground for apprehension. The passions of the platform would have been transferred to the floor of St. Stephen's, and the indiscretion of the Premier's letter—for such, to use the mildest term, we deem it—might have been expected to characterise the ministerial measure.   As it is, all parties have had time for reflection.   The popular mind has thrown off much of what was questionable in the effervescence of its zeal; the friends of religious liberty have reviewed their position and principles ; while the Cabinet has had ample opportunity for weighing the various and complicated bearings of the case. The result, we doubt not, will be advantageous to a sound and healthy Protestantism.   Many foolish things will, no doubt, still be said; the ghost of an *effete* intolerance will be invoked; the memory of departed days, when political protestantism was rampant, will be revived; and bills of pains and penalties, it may be, will be called for.   But we have no fear.   There has been time for consideration, and our senators will not be allowed to go far wrong.

To a certain extent, a small reaction is taking place.   It is natural that it should be so.   Where a people have been strongly and generally moved, something of this kind commonly happens, and our only wonder is, that it has not gone further.   The Town Council of Leeds furnishes an example of what we mean, and we have no desire that it should be followed.   It would pain us to believe that the indifference expressed by some of its members pertained to our countrymen generally.   The meeting of the Dissenters of Leeds was a vastly different affair, and betokened the immense advantage accruing from the delay which had occurred.   Calm, clear, and earnest, it recorded an unmistakable protest against the Papacy, at the same time that it refused to involve itself in the responsibility of questionable measures against it.

Since the publication of our last number, three Dissenting bodies of considerable prominence have pronounced their judgment on the Papal question.   We refer to the London Deputies, the London Board of Baptist Ministers, and the General Body of the Three Denominations of Protestant Dissenting Ministers.   The first of these is an exclusively lay body, and the other two are ministerial.   The resolutions adopted by all three agree in spirit, and are substantially similar to those which have been passed throughout the country by the more considerate and reflecting opponents of the Papal procedure.   The resolutions of the Three Denominations are the most important, and will be embodied in an address to the Throne.   The protest, which they record at considerable length, has respect to Popery itself, rather than to the recent procedure of the Pontiff.   In our judgment, this might have been spared, as the Protestantism of the body is beyond question.   It might, however, have been thought—and we admit there is force in the consideration—that it was important *just now* to place before the sovereign, and the country, the strong views entertained respecting Popery, and the reprobation with which its principles and spirit are regarded by the Evangelical Dissenters of England.   In this point of view there is significance in the protest, which is strengthened by the statement of the resolvers, that it was adopted 'not under the sudden impulse of feeling, which they shared in common with others when the obnoxious measure was first announced, but after time has been allowed for a calm and deliberate judgment to be formed upon it.'   We should have been glad to concur wholly in the resolutions of such a body, but we cannot do so, as they affirm things which are not, as we think, proven, about some of which we have doubts, and respecting others our judgment is positively adverse. The recent measure of the Pope is said to be *illegal*, of which we wait for evidence. If it be so, let the violated statute be specified by competent authority, and let proceedings be taken against the transgressors. It is affirmed, moreover, to be an interference 'with the prerogatives of the British sovereign,' which we deny, as those prerogatives are conferred by law, and no law bestows on the Crown the right of creating other than the bishops of the Protestant endowed Church. The creation of Catholic bishops—whether, on other ground, right or wrong—is no more an invasion of the royal prerogative than the creation of Moravian bishops, or those of the Episcopal Church in Scotland. The recent measure, moreover, it is affirmed, in terms too general and sweeping to command our approval, 'ought to be disallowed and annulled.' Now these words may mean much or little. There is a sense in which we should not much object to them, though they are clearly susceptible of another interpretation, from which we should dissent. We are glad to find the body recording unmistakably its determination, 'to be no parties to any legislative enactment by which their Roman Catholic fellow-subjects should be deprived of the same measure of civil and religious liberty which they claim for themselves.'

The present condition of public feeling remains, in our opinion, much as it was. It is gradually working itself clear from alloy, but there is nothing in its aspect to embolden the policy or to revive the hopes of Rome. What, then, is to be done? Parliament will meet in a few days. A bitter and stormy session will probably ensue, and some legislative measure will undoubtedly be proposed to meet the case which has arisen. What will that measure be? Many rumours are afloat. Every man, probably, has his expectation, yet each differs somewhat from his neighbour. The past declarations of the Premier, the policy of the Viceregal Court at Dublin, and the dictatorship assumed by the Colonial Office 'in matters ecclesiastical,' will render it impossible, without manifest inconsistency, for the Government to meet the expectations of the nation. The Prime Minister, however, has committed himself by his celebrated *Letter*, and the result will perhaps be a compromise unsatisfactory to all parties, and discreditable to the Ministry by which it is proposed. Amongst the many schemes attributed to Government, none appears to us more ridiculous than that adverted to in the ' Daily News,' of January 20th. ' The project of Ministers,' reports that journal ' is said to be to prevent any Roman Catholic prelates in England assuming territorial titles *in futuro*, leaving the present dignitaries in full blow, and in possession of those titles and splendour which they carried by storm.' Should anything of this kind be submitted to the legislature, we cannot doubt its meeting with the contemptuous rejection which it will richly merit. Though not rating the wisdom of our legislators as highly as some, we believe there is enough of common sense and of common honesty amongst them to laugh derisively at such a proposition.

But, leaving the region of conjecture—waiting patiently the hour of revelation—what ought to be the measure adopted? How should the case be met? How far and in what direction may the friends of religious liberty—we dislike the word *toleration*—go with the Government or the majority of the legislature in the measures they frame? These are serious questions. We have pondered them deeply—have given attention to what has been advanced on every side, and have sought, to the best of our ability, to bring the conflicting opinions hazarded to the test of those principles which we deem axioms. We have formed our own conclusion, and are not disposed to shrink from the responsibility of its avowal. The obligation which rests upon us as public journalists is increased tenfold in the case which has now arisen.

Our readers need not be told that we have no confidence in the suppression of territorial titles. As we remarked last month, 'It will leave Popery just where it was ; or rather, it will give its members the advantage of a grievance real or supposed.' Such an enactment would be, we think, as faulty in its logic, as it would be out of keeping with the practice of successive administrations. It would only delude the British people, and might ultimately serve some of the worst designs of the Popedom.

Our answer, then, to the inquiries put above must depend mainly on the view entertained of the Papal bull. If it be designed for spiritual ends only, then it must be met by similar means; and to invoke against it the authority of the State, is to forfeit our title to the character we assume, and to be recreant to the principles professed. Whatever our estimate of Popery may be, yet, as a *religious* system, it is amenable only to moral agencies. Its members are as entitled to regard the Pope as their head, as our Churchmen are to designate the Queen as such. It may be matter of regret that they should so view a foreign pontiff, but this has nothing to do with their right or title. They *do* so regard the Bishop of Rome, and in all matters *purely spiritual* they are entitled to receive from him instruction and command. To prohibit this would be, in our judgment, incompatible with the toleration which has been conceded.

But is the Papal bull a purely religious instrument? This is a grave question, and considering the complex character of the Pope, taking into account the testimony of history, and looking at the terms and spirit of the document itself, we feel that a thoughtful man will pause before replying in the affirmative. The more we ponder it, the deeper becomes our conviction that it cannot be so regarded, and the freer we consequently feel to deal with it through the medium of our legislators. There is force in the distinction drawn by the editor of the ' Scottish Congregational Magazine,' between the Roman Catholic religion and the Papacy, though we should not go to the extent he does, as some of his positions require explanation before we could commit ourselves to them. Now there is more of the latter than of the former in the Pope's bull. It is throughout conceived in the worst spirit of the Papacy; it savors of the age of Hildebrand rather than of the nineteenth century ; and arrogates, with offensive pride, an

authority and power in this country which is so manifestly opposed
to the existing state of things, as to create a strong impression that
the *future* rather than the *present* was contemplated by its framers.
Considering, moreover, the impression which the document is evidently
designed. to make on other nations we cannot but deem its reception
unadvised and pernicious. ' Up to this year,' to quote the language
of our contemporary, ' England was viewed by the Pope only as a missionary field : hence he appointed to it only such bishops as he sends
to such parts of the world, viz., vicars-apostolic, consecrated titular
bishops of some diocese, formerly in the hands of the Christians, now
in the hands of the infidels. England formed no part of the Papal
ecclesiastical territory, and, therefore, the Pope had no claim over
it territorially; in short, he could exercise authority and appoint
bishops only over the Romanist portion of its inhabitants. But it is
no longer so. The Pope now divides England into territorial dioceses,
over which he appoints bishops, who take their title from some
important place in these dioceses. The Pope, therefore, *has now done
in England what, by his own law, he can do only in countries wholly
subject to his sway.* He has thus, in the most public and authoritative
manner, declared that England, as a country, is no longer a mere
missionary field for Romanism, but is become a Roman Catholic
country, in which the Pope's authority is re-established as before the
Reformation.'* This representation is borne out by the pastoral
letter of Cardinal Wiseman, by the language of Father Newman, and
by the views unhesitatingly broached by the least cautious of the
Popish journals throughout Europe.

Taking all things into account, we come, somewhat reluctantly, yet
without hesitation, to the conclusion that the Papal bull ought not to
be admitted. We would say to our Roman Catholic fellow-citizens,
' Entertain of the Pope what estimate you please, revere him as your
father, receive at his hands the law of your religious service, trace up
your spiritual orders to him, and recognise as your teachers only such
as are invested with his authority and speak in his name. All this
you are entitled to do ; and any interference, on the part of prince or
priest, will find in us as strenuous opponents as in yourselves. But if
you go beyond this, and report the reunion of *England* to the Papal
see, and arrogate an authority repudiated by our fathers, and unknown
to our constitution, then, we say, you step beyond the province of
religion, and nullify your appeal to her protection. While you keep
within the limits of the spiritual we are with you, but the moment
you exceed these, we admit the propriety of legislative interference.
Against such a bull, therefore, as was given at Rome, on the 24th of
September last, we protest, while we most earnestly contend for your
right to receive, by way of bull or rescript—call it what you please—
the decisions and counsels of your spiritual head in all purely religious
matters.'

As to the canon law, which Dr. Wiseman tells us ' is inapplicable
under vicars-apostolic,' we would not on any account allow of its intro-

* The Scottish Congregational Magazine, Jan. 1851, p. 24.

duction. It is the very essence of spiritual domination and wickedness, and ought to be abjured by every people who prize and would perpetuate their liberty. What, then, it may be asked, would you have Parliament do? We reply in few and simple words :—

1. We would have the bull of September the 24th disallowed, and its reception into this country prohibited, it being at the same time distinctly notified that no interference is contemplated with the appointment of purely ecclesiastical officers of whatever grade.

2. All appointments under such bull should be forthwith cancelled.

3. Public officers should be appointed to inspect and report on religious houses, in order to guard against parties being retained in them contrary to their will.

4. All grants of public money, whether to Maynooth College, or to colonial ecclesiastics, should be immediately and for ever withdrawn.

Such, in brief, are our views, and we wait to see how far they will be embodied in the measure of Government. We cannot say we are sanguine. Lord John Russell has failed on various occasions to realize our notion of a sagacious and high-minded statesman. We fear that he will do so again. Public rumor alleges that the Queen is dissatisfied with the reference to this absorbing topic which her ministers propose to insert in the royal speech. There is no improbability in this; but should it be so, there is a power greater than that of the Premier, which we do not want to see further aroused, lest its vehemence should outstep the bounds of principle and right. In the meantime, let the friends of religious liberty be wakeful and active. Let them think well before committing themselves to any specific measure, lest in meeting a present evil they incur future ones of greater magnitude. But we must turn to other topics. Necessity is laid upon us, and we yield.

The approach of the Parliamentary Session has brought on the Chancellor of the Exchequer numerous applications for a share in his anticipated surplus. Amongst these the Window Tax, the Paper Tax, and the Malt Tax, have been the most clamorous, and we are glad to find that the first is likely to gain the favor of the State financier. The Window-tax, one of the most odious imposts ever imposed, is, we believe, to be abolished, and a House-tax, about one-third in amount, is to be substituted for it. Such, at least, is the project of Ministers, if credit is to be given to the opinion of the best-informed circles. It remains for the country, or rather for our senators—practically a very different thing—to say whether such a substitution shall be permitted. If the expression of an adverse judgment be sufficiently general and earnest, the window-tax will probably be abolished without the substitute of a house-tax. Let those, therefore, who feel strongly on the point, be prompt and vigorous in their actions.

From public matters we turn to others of a somewhat more private character.

The Rev. Algernon Wells, minister of the Congregational Church at Clapton, and Secretary of the Congregational Union of England and Wales, has been removed from his labours after a protracted illness. Few men were ever loved, admired, and trusted, by so large a body of friends. Five and thirty years ago he was received into Hoxton College, and, by earnest study till the end of life, he acquired an amount of theological and general knowledge rarely equalled by men of earlier advantages and ampler leisure. His lovely temper, tender spirit, and deep and ardent piety, were gracefully harmonized with the most fascinating charms of conversation, and with a power of transacting public business with singular felicity. We sympathize very cordially with the denomination of which he has been so distinguished an ornament, in the sorrow which such a bereavement has brought upon them. Happy and honoured, indeed, will that man be who may be found worthy of succeeding him. Such a man, we earnestly hope, will not be wanting to guide the proceedings of the important confederacy of Free Churches to which the wisdom and urbanity of its departed Secretary imparted so much unity and power.

Mr. Robert Norris, of Bristol, though a vastly different man, was equally beloved in his circle. The pertinacity with which he clung to what he deemed right, offended some; while his disregard of many of the conventionalisms of social and religious life, awakened prejudice and rendered him an object of suspicion. For the last two or three years, however, he had been gaining rapidly on the respect and confidence of his fellow-citizens. Those who saw Mr. Norris only at a distance or infrequently, knew little of his character. He united qualities rarely found together—the earnestness and zeal of a reformer with the tenderness of a sister; a scrupulous adherence to principle with a large-hearted candor in interpreting the actions of others; the simplicity of a child with the acuteness and wisdom of a cultivated intellect; entire exemption from vanity with a conscientiousness which compelled him occasionally to occupy positions from which his modesty shrunk; a speculative cast of mind with deep reverence for Christian truth; a devout reception of the Redeemer without any particle of intolerance or bitterness towards those whom he deemed in serious error. One who knew him well tells us, and we subscribe to the statement, 'A truer form of humanity, a gentler, lovelier, more guileless spirit, has seldom trodden our earth.' The last time we saw him was at the Convention of the Anti-state-church Association. May our next be in a better world, where our departed friend and fellow-labourer is now enjoying the happiness which flows from a devout consecration to the service of the Lord.

Another crisis has happened in France. Few observant men will be surprised at this. The tendency of events, for some time past, has betokened it, and now that it has happened, it awakens little concern, and is regarded with ominous indifference. This is to be deplored, but it is the natural result of what we have witnessed. Our experience of French revolutions does not strengthen our faith in the integrity of the public men of France, or in the political sagacity of her people. The idol of to-day is cast down and trampled on to-morrow. So it was at the close of the last century, and so it has been since February 1848. Louis Napoleon, and the nation over which he presides, are now reaping according as they have sown. The harvest is what the seed-time prognosticated, and no one pities their perplexities, or cares one whit about their party criminations and struggles. The immediate occasion of the present crisis is the dismissal of General Changarnier, whom the President had learnt to mistrust and dread. This soldier of fortune, in whom the whole military power of the Republic centred, had shown himself less tractable than Louis Napoleon desired. A short time since he was the most supple of courtiers, and the vain and treacherous Louis imagined that he might be relied on in the working out of his schemes. In this he was disappointed, not from the patriotism of the soldier, but from other passions which had been engendered by his elevation to power. For a time no minister could be found sufficiently bold to append his name to the dismissal of the General, and when at length one did so, the opportunity was seized by various parties hostile to the Government, to carry a vote in the Assembly expressing want of confidence in the ministry. The juncture of parties was singular. Monarchists and Republicans, adherents of the elder and of the younger Bourbon branch, Constitutional and Red Republicans, traders in politics, and young deputies breathing patriotism, were united for the moment. Their majority against ministers was considerable, and the Cabinet in consequence resigned.

One good, however, has been accomplished. A charlatan has been removed; one less appears on a stage unhappily crowded with such; and the sooner M. Thiers, and others like him, are dismissed from public life the better. There is a sad want of new blood, of healthy, virtuous life in the political society of Paris. In the meantime, the President is endeavoring to ride out the storm. Many of his efforts have failed, but the *Daily News* of this morning (27th), reports that he has at length formed ' a ministry of transition.' We wait the result. If Louis Napoleon be teachable—which we doubt—he will learn the folly of pursuing his reactionary policy any further. Let him fairly administer the constitution which he has sworn to maintain, and France will rally to his aid, with a unanimity and heartiness which will insure the easy attainment of every object of a just ambition.

The Schleswig-Holstein contest is, at length, terminated, so far at least as the sword and battle-field are concerned. Such a result was to be anticipated immediately that Prussia resolved on succumbing to Austrian dictation. There was no other course open to the Duchies than to accept the propositions submitted by these powers. To have done otherwise would have been to bring on themselves certain and speedy destruction, as no force which they could arm would have the slightest chance of resisting the armies arrayed against them. Thus far the strong have overborne the weak; reactionary policy has gained another triumph; and the monarchs of Austria and Russia, with their constrained ally of Prussia, will probably be encouraged to take some other backward step. In the meantime, Europe is learning a most important lesson, and we shall see whether the pen cannot accomplish what the sword has failed in. Intellect is at work, and we have strong faith in its power. The end is not yet.

# Literary Intelligence.

## Just Published.

Biblical Commentary on the Gospels and on the Acts of the Apostles. By Hermann Olshausen, D.D. Translated from the German, with additional Notes. By Rev. J. Gill Nithan; Rev. R. Garvey, A.M.; and (on the Acts) by Rev. W. Lindsay, D.D. Vol. IV.

Memoirs of the Dukes of Urbino; illustrating the arms, arts, and literature of Italy, from 1440 to 1630. By James Dennistoun, of Dennistoun. 3 vols.

Bertha; a Romance of the Dark Ages. By W. Bernard McCabe, Author of a Catholic History of England. 3 vols.

Voyage of the Prince Albert in search of Sir John Franklin. A Narrative of every-day Life in the Arctic Seas. By W. Parker. Snow.

Table Talk; to which are added, imaginary Conversations of Pope and Swift. By Leigh Hunt.

Wuthering Heights and Agnes Grey. By Ellis and Acton Bell. A New Edition, revised, with a Biographical Notice of the Authors, a Selection from their Literary Remains, and a Preface. By Currer Bell.

A Shilling's-worth about our State-Church.

The Bishop's Wife. A Tale of the Papacy. Translated from the German of Leopold Schefer, with a Historical Notice of the Life and Times of Hildebrand (Pope Gregory VII.), to which it relates. By Mrs. J. R. Stodart.

The Contrast. Two Sermons, preached in Union Chapel, New Road, Chelsea. By Rev. Thomas Bayfield. Nov. 24th, 1850. Contrasting the Errors of Romanism with the Truths of Bible Christianity.

An Examination of the Claim of the Papal Supremacy on the Faith of Christians, by Reason and by the Principles of the Church of Christ, acknowledged in all times; in which it is demonstrated to be an unwarrantable and anti-Christian assumption.

Historical Sketches and Personal Recollections of Manchester. Intended to illustrate the progress of public opinion from 1792 to 1832. By Archibald Prentice.

Remains of the Rev. Robert Shirrer Linkton, Kirkcaldy. With a Memoir, by John B. Johnson, Kirkcaldy.

The Imperial Cyclopædia. Part VI. Cornwall—Dorsetshire.

The Museum of Classical Antiquities. A Quarterly Journal of Architecture, and the sister branches of the Classic Art. No. I. January, 1851.

Lectures on the Principles and Institution of the Roman Catholic Religion. With an Appendix, containing critical and historic Illustrations. By the late Rev. Joseph Fletcher, D.D. Fifth Edition. Edited by Rev. Joseph Fletcher, of Christchurch.

The Earthly Resting-places of the Just. By Rev. Erskine Neale, M.A.

Peeps at Nature; or, God's Works and Man's Wants.

Nature's Wonders, or God's Care over all his Works. By the Author of 'Peeps at Nature.'

The Looker-on. No. I., Vol. II. A Literary Miscellany. Edited by Fritz and Liolett.

The Papal Aggression and Popery Contemplated Religiously. A Pastoral Address to his Flock. By J. A. James.

The Best Means of Protestantizing the Church of England. Being a Letter to the Right Hon. Lord Ashley, M P., and 'The Protest' made by an ancestor of H.R.H. Prince Albert, and others, from whence the title of Protestant is taken; with Northhouse on Church Rates.

Journal of Sacred Literature. No. XIII. By John Kitto, D.D.

The Signs of the Times; or, the Popery of Protestantism.

An Historical Inquiry, concerning the Age, Authorship, and Authenticity of the Old Testament. By Rev. Dr. Giles.

The Core of Creeds; or, St. Peter's Keys. By Rev. D. Thomas.

The Weekly Sabbath no Part of the Ceremonial Law, &c. A Discourse delivered in the Kneesworth-street Chapel, Royston. By A. C. Wright.

Divine Providence considered and illustrated. By Charles Hargreaves.

The Congregational Year Book for 1850.

Protestant Priestism. A Lecture on Christianity without a Priest. By Henry More.

Dealings with the Inquisition; or, Papal Rome, her Priests and her Jesuits. With Important Disclosures. By Rev. Giacinto Achilli, D.D.

Encyclopædia Metropolitana. A System of Universal Knowledge on a Methodical Plan. Projected by Samuel Taylor Coleridge. Second Edition, revised. First division,—Pure Sciences, Moral and Metaphysical Philosophy.

Wandering Sketches of People and Things, in South America, Polynesia, California, and other places, visited during a cruise on board of the U.S. ships 'Levant,' 'Portsmouth,' and 'Savannah.' By W. Maxwell Wood, M.D., Surgeon U.S. Navy.

The Royal Pardon vindicated, in a Review of the Case between Mr. W. H. Barber and the Incorporated Law Society. By Sir G. Stephen.

Social Statistics; or, the Conditions essential to Human Happiness specified, and the first of them developed. By Herbert Spencer.

Euphranor. A Dialogue on Youth.

Midnight Harmonies; or, Thoughts for the Season of Solitude and Sorrow. By Octavius Winslow, M.A.

The Modern Judea compared with Ancient Prophecy. With Notes illustrative of Biblical Subjects. By Rev. J. Aitken Wylie. New Edition.

The Idol Demolished by Its own Priest. An Answer to Cardinal Wiseman's Lectures on Transubstantiation. By J. Sheridan Knowles.

Our State Church. I. In England. II. In Ireland. III. In Scotland. IV. In Wales.

The Kickleburys on the Rhine. By M. A. Titmarsh.

The King of the Golden River; or, the Black Brothers. A Legend of Styria.

Papa's and Mamma's Easy Lessons in Geography. By Anna Maria Sargeant.

The Believer's Assurance of Salvation. Is it attainable? By Rev. W. Davis, Minister of Croft Chapel, Hastings.

The Duty of England. A Protestant Layman's Reply to Cardinal Wiseman's Appeal.

Lectures on Social Science and the Organization of Labour. By James Hole.

Cosmos. Sketch of a Physical Description of the Universe. By Alex. Von Humboldt. Vol. III. Part I.

The History of Greece, from the Earliest Period to the Roman Conquest, with a Sketch of its Modern History to the Present Time. Adapted for schools and families. By Miss Corner.

THE

# Eclecti Review.

## MARCH, 1851.

ART. I.—*Memoirs of the Du*
James Dennlstoun, of Do
and Co.

WE know none of all the m
are more instructive to the aillg      ident    i to    or t
Italian nations, both of earlier and or later tim      At a remote
period, Italy was at once the centre of civilization, and the cradle
of the arts. Enthroned upon her seven hills, mighty in her
legions, inexhaustible in her resources, and boundless in her
sway, Rome, whether republican or imperial, exercised immense
influence on the whole civilized world. Honoured in Greece,
and feared in her colonies, her arms had penetrated to very
remote regions. The Parthian had seen the glitter of her
cohorts, and had retreated farther and farther to his wilds, unequal, at least for many ages, to successful warfare with men
brave by nature and irresistible by discipline. The German
found it well to retire to his primæval forests before the terror
of the Italian forces; and our rude fathers, long undisturbed
and secure in their insular position, discovered at length that
even the fury and the terror of the deep were no barriers to
Cæsar and his hosts. But at the early period to which we
allude—that is, down to the decline and fall of the Roman
empire—Italy governed the world no less by the excellence of
her economical institutions than by the force of her arms. The
people, who were invincible in war, cultivated perhaps with

greater, certainly with more enduring success, the arts of peace; and, even to this day, the great Roman jurists, in no small degree, influence the social institutions of mankind. So that, look where we will—at our law-courts, at our political and social organizations—we see much which reminds us that the ancient Italian jurist, 'being dead, yet speaketh,' and that his influence underlies many of our political arrangements. The swarms of barbarians emerging from the forests of Northern Europe, and who, in their successive invasions of Italy, hurled from its base the gigantic Roman power, did not, nevertheless, break the thread which connected Italy with the rest of the world. When the imperial power was overthrown, the ecclesiastical domination succeeded; and during the dark ages, the iron feudal times, Italy still ruled the European world. The crozier had taken the place of the sword in the ruling hand, and craftiest policy and intrigue effected results which, ages before, were attained by military violence alone. Through all those dim years, as we look at them with such faint light as history affords, how often do we see in the plots of the crafty, in the deeds of the cruel, on gory battle-fields, and in kings' palaces, the ever-active Italian priests, repressing freedom of opinion, deepening the existing mental darkness, and stained with many crimes. Still, in our nineteenth century, how great an influence does the present evil genius of that sunny land exert upon all countries and societies of men; with what an iron grip does it hold down the advances of large portions of mankind! In political developments and convulsions, there is ever a trace of Italian intrigue; and indeed, among ourselves, to its direct interference, we may attribute certainly one of the angriest agitations of our own time. It is possible that, amid the various changes which political events may effect, and from the extension either of French or of Austrian power, the ultramontane influence may become almost as powerful as it was when our own Henry resisted its encroachment. Indeed, late events lead us directly to the conclusion, that this influence is increasing from day to day. What political intrigue cannot effect, force readily accomplishes, as in the invasion of Rome by the troops of the French republic: a procedure which contrasts badly with the liberal professions so vauntingly made by the chief of that government. If we are not greatly mistaken, it is just to counteract this Italian intrigue, ingenious and consummate in its audacity, that the efforts of all free government must be more and more directed; for that intrigue has ever worked to subvert liberal institutions, and to hinder the progress of mankind towards light and truth. We have seen, in our own day, how ultramontane craft and daring have excited almost to sedition Rhenish Prussia; evincing, as they did, that priestly intolerance and ambition have lost none of their offensiveness since the Tridentine conclave. It has been patent to the world how Jesuitism has worked its dreadful work in the policy of Metternich, and, more recently, in the judicial slaughterings in Hungary, and in the great endeavour to destroy liberalism throughout Germany by the strengthening everywhere of the autocratic element: a result which we may reasonably expect to follow from the Manteuffel and Schwartzenberg conferences at Dresden. In Ireland, notwithstanding the gross wrongs of the Protestant establishment, the absenteeism of the large holders, the almost boundless pauperism of the lower orders, and the many political and social injustices which are constant there, no one can doubt that Italian policy is the leaven which ferments in the Protean forms of its agitation, and that the very best intentions of the English government, in the administration of Irish affairs, as in the instance of the priestly agitation against the new colleges, have been baffled and counterworked by the bold and offensive policy of the Papal cabinet. The Italian ecclesiastical domination is, perhaps, the reproduction, under a new form, of that ancient republican and imperial rule which held sway over the world. Constantine merely gave the imperial jurisdiction an ecclesiastical aspect and *nomenclature ;* and since his day, the very air of Rome has generated and fostered the desire in its chief to rule the world, and that through the Church. So, it is clear, for more than two thousand years, Italy has exercised no small influence on the affairs of the world.

The work before us, embracing a very important portion of Italian history, cannot fail to be highly interesting at the present time, when the attention of the greater portion of our people is eagerly directed towards political and ecclesiastical proceedings in Italy ; and though the subject-matter of the work is not directly connected, or at least not entirely, with Papal ambition, cruelty, and wrong, yet there is, of necessity, so much reference thereto, that we are persuaded, among intelligent readers, this work will be greatly esteemed. The three volumes into which Mr. Dennistoun has extended his narrative are indeed worthy to appear at the beginning of this year, in which the rarest and choicest specimens of the world's art and manufacture are to be assembled in London, for they are beautiful in the choicest style of the craft both of the artist and the printer. Mr. Dennistoun has spent many years in Italy, and is perfectly conversant with the language and habits, as well as with the history, of its people ; and though this work is the result of immense reading, and thus, of course, to some extent, of laborious compilation, we find abundant proof that the author is quite at his ease in

narrating his lengthy, but most instructive, story. He seems to
have been at great pains to search such libraries as the liberality
of the monks and the courtesy of gentlemen placed at his disposal; and all his authorities—and we dare not attempt their
mere enumeration—from Giovanni Sanzi to the late work of
Signor Mariotti, are judiciously, perhaps sometimes copiously,
used, and their errors philosophically discriminated and corrected. The volumes are dedicated to Lord Lindsay, whose
work on the Progress and Development of Christian Art, and,
subsequently, on the 'Lives of the Lindsays,' will be fresh in
the recollection of our readers; and Mr. Dennistoun, enamoured,
as it would seem, not merely of the balmy air, but also of the
great handiworks, of the sweet South, has written his work from
a wish to introduce to his countrymen the progress of reviving
art, particularly in religious painting; and, as he himself states,
' to render accessible some details of the political and social condition of that bright land, in its golden age, hitherto unpublished,
or scattered in volumes rarely met with.' With this intention,
our author has entered—a little too late, perhaps—into the field
of literature; for, if we mistake not, the check which the clamour
against the Papal agitation in this country will undoubtedly give
to the Tractarian tendencies of the younger clergy, will also put
a stop to the partial revival of mediæval style and sculpture in
our ecclesiastical erections. We trace this partial revival to the
Puseyite movement of the last ten years; and we know not, in
our entire lack of *dilettanti-penchant*, to predicate whether a return to the style of the monastic architecture in our public
buildings is for good or for evil. There has been, we doubt not,
an expression of much sickly sentimentality on this subject. We
go readily to extremes. Moderation does not satisfy us. We
must be entirely imitative, according to our modern custom, of
all that to which the judges of artistic taste and skill among us
have set their seal. All classes of society have been, more or
less, infected by the morbid desire for imitating whatever the
sun shone upon during the middle ages. In churches, school-
rooms, railway-stations, institutions—in whatever the cunning
workmen put their hands to—we see continually the monastic
idea, till we almost wonder that the ' chambers of the East' have
not an oriel-window for the sun to shine through at his rising.
Now, we do not find fault with Mr. Dennistoun for enlightening
his countrymen, through the pages of his beautiful work now
before us, on so fascinating a subject as the history of Religious
Art; nor are we blind to the exquisite beauty of much which
the middle ages have bequeathed to us. The ' Romish' temples
of the South, the grand columns, the fretted roofs, the tesselated
pavements, and, above all, the glowing canvass of immortal

limners—these will always command the admiration and reverence of men of taste; but we are quite tired of the present
extensive imitation of these things. He who desires to acquire
information, carefully collected, and well presented, on the
Religious Art, will find much in these volumes which will fully
and satisfactorily instruct him. Such a study will always amply
repay him who pursues it, by not only refining the taste, but by
indirectly teaching the domestic progress of a people; for, perhaps, the public and private buildings of a nation, in the gradual
improvement of them, are more instructive than its written
annals of its growth from barbarism and nomadic habits towards
the refinement and the elegancies of a true civilization. Peculiarly is this the case in the private buildings, the homes of the
people. In a rude or half-barbarous age, men live gregariously,
or if in societies, closely, as the prairie-dogs; their dwellings are
raised but little above the earth—close, ill-ventilated, confined.
In a civilized age, they build loftily and extensively; their dwellings are detached and roomy, and light and oxygen are in high
estimation. By way of example, we might contrast the houses
of Mayfair, where refinement is at the highest, with the close
and unhealthy Syrian huts so graphically pictured by Aubrey
de Vere, in his inimitable volumes on Eastern travel. But, it
may be asked, why, then, is a barbarous age so productive of
cathedrals, of churches, and of works of religious art? We
reply: These were designed and built by men who were above
the surrounding barbarism; the men who had at their command
libraries and manuscripts, and to whom we are immensely indebted, as the conservators of science and art, that the works of
the glorious past have come down to us—the works of poets and
orators, the stars of that wondrous past, which we would not
willingly let perish. These were the men, dark-stoled and
ascetical, and by their high profession ever in warfare with the
evils of the gross physical and degraded spiritual, who were, in
many instances, our mediæval architects and builders, and who
made even the structures of their Church the symbols of divine
realities; for, in their gorgeous tracery and groining, their
elaborate carving and decoration, and in their

' Storied windows richly dight,'

they embodied their grand religious ideas. We cannot attempt
to solve the often-perplexing enigma of chancel, porch, and altar-
piece; but, as we have said, the lovers of antique religious art
will find very much to gratify them in these volumes; to which
we will now proceed to give more particular attention.

Urbino is a town in the Papal States, built on that projection
of the Apennines which extends into the valley of the Metauro,

about twenty miles from the coast of the Adriatic.  At present, its chief importance arises from the fact of its being the repository of some antique and rare inscriptions and sculptures ; but, for more than two hundred years, this town was the seat of government for the duchy of the same name.  At the close of the fourteenth century, the family of Montefeltro became *entitled* to the duchy ; and in their little capital its dukes long held a small but brilliant court, to which were invited the men most conspicuous in their time for scientific attainment.  Finding there a calm and not undignified retreat from the vicissitudes, the passions, and the tumults of the world, as if under the ægis of a divinity favouring their genius, they cultivated those delightful pursuits, and wrought those imperishable works, which make even the Italy of to-day, prostrate as she is from the pedestal of her ancient fame, to be still great and reverend among the nations, as the nursery of the humanizing arts, and the birth-place of poetry and song.  In that dim time, when the twilight of the middle ages was slowly merging into the morning of civilization, it was well that learning and art, too much confined to the monks and to the sombre atmosphere of the religious houses, the cloisters, whose sickly air nurtured not freedom, should have also a laical extension, and that for them there should be a place and home of repose for whom the confusion of camps, the circle of the tournament, and the din of war, had no charms.  Much, indeed, are we indebted to those who lived, in some instances, afar from the ecclesiastical seclusions ; to those unprofessional men who, at the dawn of civilization, retired from the busy haunts of men, and from military association, to their tranquil studies, and to those parchments which have now such a wondrous value in our eyes ; and who, comparatively unmolested, excavated for us from amid the confusion and rubbish of monastic libraries, the works of the great masters of the perished classic world.  One cannot without gratitude look at their surviving manuscripts, carefully and beautifully written.  Like the rough-handed sons of toil, in our own day, unknown and unhonoured by the nation, who hollow out tunnels, raise aerial bridges, and construct our vast modern works—so these, in their secluded homes, or under the fostering care of some enlightened potentate, first opened the long-hidden mines of knowledge, that we, who follow them, might easily arrive at the golden ore beneath.  Great works are, for the most part, quietly wrought ; the chisel and the pencil, producing matchless beauty, toil noiselessly ; their progress frets not the public ear.  They who, of old time, laboured among the rocky Andes for those precious metals which, circulating through Europe, have, these many years, decorated nobility and beauty, or which have been current money with the merchant, are most of them unknown. So the men of marvellous labour, who toiled over the ancient scrolls in copying for us those manuscripts either of classic or of scholastic lore which we now so highly value, are generally unknown. They worked their life-work, and when, at last, that calm sleep came, which we call death, no kind hand chronicled their departure; but their handiwork alone silently testifies to their incessant toil. These were they who found in the little court of Urbino a happy retreat and home. Here they copied chronicles of times earlier than their own, or recorded the events of their own day, or awakened the muse to song. A brighter spot we have not in all these times, than this duchy; and it is refreshing to see how the arts of peace flourished amid constant hostilities, just as in the desert the weary pilgrim is gladdened to find, among the inhospitable sand-wastes, herbage and a fountain.

It may be interesting, perhaps, to our readers that we should take a hasty view of the state of society in Italy at the time (1444) when the gallant Frederigo was elevated to the dukedom of Urbino. Ignorance and superstition had long hung, like heavy mists, over the ultramontane peninsula, and over Europe; but, here and there, the dawn of civilization was beginning faintly to appear. The political condition of the people was miserable in the extreme. As laborious and useful machines, they tilled the fields, and wrought for their imperious lords; or, when these fell out among themselves—and wars are frequent, or otherwise, as a nation is barbarous or not—they fought and bled in defence of his banner under whose dominion they were born. Society was everywhere out of joint. Surrounded by the relics of a former grandeur, the people murmured against their oppressors as men murmur in dreams. Commerce was strangled by the rough hand of war. On the Arno and the Po there was but scanty traffic. The interchange of commodities was rare and rude. A few persons wove that tapestry which a later age far surpassed in design and in execution. The precious metals circulated on a barbarous system. The implements of husbandry, and of domestic use generally, betokened an uncivilized period; but the kindly earth, almost unsought, poured from her bounteous bosom enough to supply the needs of the present; and they who were reckless of plenty in hand, had but little anxiety and showed but little prudential care for the future. The cities and larger towns were walled and garrisoned. Defence was necessary for safety. It were scarcely an exaggeration, in describing the society of the time, to say that each man's hand was against his fellow. The villages and hamlets were often a prey to the forays of successive freebooters. Fuller information than we can afford on this subject may be obtained from the pages of Sismondi and Raumer, how the rival factions of Guelphs and Guibelines agitated the entire peninsula—factions which were the embodiments of contradictory political doctrines, appearing and re-appearing more or less in all ages and in all states—the antagonism of the aristocratic and democratic elements ;—and from the work before us much information may be gained of that wretched condottiere-system, the most decided proof we can discover of the extreme degradation and barbarism of the times, of ever-recurring hostilities, and of the insecurity of all private property and private interests.  By this system our author writes—' Any bold baron or experienced captain, having formed round his banner a corps of tried and daring spirits, leased his services and their own for a stipulated term and price.  Their whole arrangements being avowedly mercenary, they had no patriotism, no preference for standards or watchwords.  The highest offer secured them, and when their engagement expired, or their pay fell into arrear, they were free to pass over to the enemy, or seek any other master.  But, besides their fixed stipend, they had perquisites from the hazards of war ; the ransom of rich prisoners accrued to the leaders, while the soldiery were glutted by the occasional booty of a sacked city.' (Pp. 12, 13.)  Unhappy land, ever subject to the feverish excitement of war—the prey of savage hordes, distracted by cruel factions, lying passive beneath the iron heel of the spoiler, forgetful of olden glory, and fired to no heroic resistance by the speaking memorials of her former fame, scattered everywhere among her people ;—how little differs the groaning Italy of mediæval time from the same fair land in our own day, the prey of Austrian, of Pontiff, and of that relentless tyrant whose banners still drip with Sicilian carnage!

A single glance at these facts will show the utter impossibility of a flourishing commerce or a true civilization in a society in which the volcano of war was continually eruptive; for the sword and the ploughshare are ever antagonistic, and the sweet notes of peace are hushed by the tocsin of political discord. But the spirit of the age was utterly martial.  A man was estimated as his lance had won the guerdon in the tournament, or as his pennon had been conspicuous where the press of battle was closest and the strife was fiercest on well-foughten fields.  Thus, the worst passions which can injure and disgrace mankind were in the ascendant, and ferocity ruled where, otherwise, humanity had smiled.  At this period, too, the whole south of Europe was in anxiety, if not in terror, at the constant advances of the Ottoman arms.  A tribe of barbarians, emerging from the wastes of Arabia, had already overrun the north of Africa, and had for a long period held the fairest province of Spain, till their name had become a terror even to princes whose lands were far removed from the presence of the Mahomedan sword. In the East, converting the nomad tribes and the half-civilized towns to the faith of the Koran, or else exterminating their unwilling people, they had occupied Syria, and the lands which the Bosphorus only divided from Europe. Successive crusades had been undertaken, to drive back to their wastes the hosts of the infidel. The banner of the Teuton and the Gaul had fluttered side by side with the St. George's red-cross flag before Acre and Ascalon, and the battle-axe of the royal Lion-heart had been the terror of the Paynim host; but, after the expenditure of immense treasure and the slaughter of thousands of Europe's chivalry, the martial flower of the age, the crescent still glittered where the true cross was raised, and the ancient but dishonoured Salem remained a stronghold for the Arabian creed. Every year, the Ottoman forces advanced towards Europe, till already the Osmanlis seemed to have tainted the very breezes of the South. There had been various combinations of republics and of princes to stem this torrent of infidel invasion; but still the crescent overcame the cross, and the turbaned warriors threw a haughty and a frequent defiance at the European chivalry, Oddantonio, the first Duke of Urbino, had already slept with his fathers, and Frederigo had for some time held the government of the duchy, when Mahomet II., advancing step by step, laid siege to Constantinople. To quote from the work before us :—

'Europe was now startled by an event which exposed Italy to peculiar peril. The Eastern Empire had long been falling into feeble senility, and in proportion as her vigour relaxed and her frontier receded, the crescent extended its domination, and menaced the Bosphorus. The Greeks appealed for aid to Western Christendom : but men's enthusiasm had become selfishness ; the crusading spirit was extinct, and the cry echoed unheeded along the Mediterranean shores. The siege of Constantinople by Mahomet II., a barbarian endowed with qualities which would have shone in any sphere, might have been prevented or raised by very moderate efforts of the Italian powers ; and it was not until the loss of that great capital that they perceived the folly of their neglect, which had sacrificed the best bulwark of Europe against Ottoman aggression. But, besides this general consternation, the maritime republics staggered beneath the blow, for it annihilated that trade with the Archipelago and the Euxine which had crowded their ports and filled their coffers ; and when Constantinople fell, many wealthy Christian merchants, there resident, were stripped of their property, and passed into menial slavery.'—Vol. i. p. 100.

Thus fell that magnificent city, which had been founded in an age when many fondly hoped the time was near at hand wherein men should no more draw the sword against each other—for not a few had dreamed then that the glorious prediction of Hebrew

prophets should be accomplished to the very letter of its symbo-
lical expression; and that men, universally, should beat their
' swords into ploughshares,' and their ' spears into pruning-
hooks.' But the ancient faith, in which that city had been reared,
was to be driven out by the sword; and the descendants of those
fiery children of the desert, who had already conquered all the
southern and eastern shore of the Mediterranean, won by their
scimitars, and have since held, that city of profuse magnificence.

Frederigo was accepted as the successor to duke Oddantonio
in 1444, at a remarkable period, but to be followed by one still
more remarkable; for, in the next half century, Christopher
Columbus opened the gates of the new world to the horrors of
Spanish conquest, and to the murky light of Spanish civilization.
Early connected with the Sforza family, and, as we learn from
his laudatory poets, Sanzi and Porcellio, a knight of our English
order of the Garter, with which he was invested by our Edward IV., Frederigo ruled his duchy during almost forty years.
Illustrious by military successes, and skilful in diplomatic intrigue, he was also the patron of learned men and of the liberal
arts.   From the meagre account of him by Baldi, we are inclined to believe that the duke was one of the most popular men
of his age; and while his court was a model for princely magnificence, his people were well cared for.   His city—attractive
to European literati, and, in after years, a residence for some
time of the ill-starred Chevalier de St. George—he beautified by
a palace which, with its spire-capped tower, catches and fixes
the eye of the tourist as he journeys from Tuscany to Urbino—
a building which even the magnificent Lorenzo de' Medici
deigned to imitate.   We have to notice the character of Frederigo chiefly as that of a collector of the rarest and most valuable
manuscript: a pursuit which, in that age, was impeded by
obstacles neither few nor trifling.   Of the best works there were
but few copies, and these were scattered in the gloomy recesses
of convent-libraries throughout Christendom.   When printing
was rare, and books were few, manuscripts would be tedious in
preparation, and costly to procure; but Frederigo was not a man
to be easily daunted or baffled by any difficulties.   Availing himself of that catalogue which Thomas of Sarzana, afterwards
Nicholas V., and the founder of the Vatican, had prepared, he
had already collected, after fourteen years of labour and expenditure, and in the constant employ of more than thirty transcribers
the choicest classical works, the writings of Fathers, controver-
sialists, and schoolmen, and of the chief Italian poets, whose
names are venerated by all lovers of the true and the beautiful.
He spent thirty thousand ducats in the formation and binding of
this library; and, indeed, in the binding and decorations of the

volumes he showed great taste, as we gather from the chronicles of a gossiping agent employed in this work, who narrates that the duke ordered every book to be bound in crimson decorated with silver. Particularly must we mention his magnificent copy of the Vulgate with arabesque ornaments, brilliantly illuminated by Perugino, and which is now one of the treasured beauties of the Vatican Library; and the Hebrew Bible from the Urbino collection, also in the Vatican, executed in the thirteenth century, and for which Philip II. offered twenty thousand scudi. All writers of literary history speak highly of the intelligence and liberality of this duke. Accustomed, as their equal, to discuss with his courtiers the theological and philosophical subjects of the day, he became the idol, as he was the patron, of literary men. Bringing fugitive Greeks to his court, that there they might teach their honied tongue, and handsomely rewarding all who excelled as painters and sculptors, he made his court an asylum for the gifted and the learned whom political troubles or other adversities had driven from their homes. Thus, though engaged, according to the fashion of the times, in frequent wars, he cultivated the arts of peace; and, through all his long reign, he was honoured and beloved by those in whose esteem thought was stronger than armies, and by whom learning and art were higher ranked than victories and military spoils. He died of fever, in 1482.—But it is not our purpose to follow the course of Italian history, and to trace the influence of the duchy upon other states, nor to specify the various causes which contributed to the repose of Italy until the death of Lorenzo de' Medici. We refer our readers to the volumes before us for that satisfactory information on this portion of Italian history, which our present limits do not permit us to present.

It were impossible for the historian of the Italian states, when recording the events of the fifteenth and sixteenth centuries, to forget the great influence which literature and art exerted during those periods. When the night of the dark ages was gradually receding before the dawn of civilization, men awoke to great mental activity; and, like pioneers, who form roads over morasses and through forests, the benefit of which subsequent ages inherit and enjoy; so athletic minds toiled for us in the grey morning-time of awakening knowledge and of reviving art, constructing the crude forms of lexicon and glossary which a future age used and improved. The fourteenth and fifteenth centuries produced much scholastic philosophy and much fruitless discussion, based on the ancient Aristotelian method; but they gave birth to but few, comparatively, whom we can designate as strong in thought and rich in creative faculty. Ancient art, wearied by its endless productiveness, lay down to a long repose when the barbarian

invasions desolated the Ausonian lands, and struck down for
ever the eagle of the Cæsars; but after that long and feverish
night, in which even the cross in the hands of the priests had a
sharp edge, and when feudalism restrained commerce and ignored the rights of man, art arose, as in the freshness of youth;
and the impartial historian certainly must record that she was
fostered and flourished as much under the care of tyrannous
kings as of factious republics.   Florence and Venice, in the days
of their prowess and glory, shed a cheering light upon literature
and art; and even in courts where popular freedom, as we now
understand those words, either was unknown or was reprobated;
the courts of Urbino and of the Sforza, of Malatesta and Gon-
zaga; that kindly patronage was liberally bestowed on scientific
men which was denied them in the republics of Lucca and
Genoa.   With the exception of the Venetian commonwealth,
conspicuous not more for her martial distinction than for her
tender care of manuscript and sculpture, perhaps science developed itself more fully and speedily in the autocratic than in
the republican states.   For when these republics were rent by
intestine discords, or engaged in barbarous hostilities with each
other—those wars, which have ever dwarfed freedom, curtailed
of 'her fair proportion';—Frederigo of Urbino, as we have seen,
and Lorenzo and Cosmo de' Medici, formed libraries at immense
cost, collected the treasured scrolls of the wondrous past, and
opened their palaces as havens for expatriated or unfriended
genius.   Even Dante, the tones of whose harp still vibrate
through his sorrowing fatherland, fled away from Florentine faction, and sought refuge where popular clamour could not assail,
nor popular fickleness grieve him.   Classical literature, which,
at the revival of letters, was the subject of almost universal
study, speedily effected a great change in the thought and
style of all literary men.   Plato and Aristotle became the watchwords of rival schools.   A pedantic use of their phraseologies
was common in those schools; and men thought and spoke in the
very form of words which had been used in the days of Athenian
glory and magnificence.   Philology grew slowly into a science;
and grammars gradually were constructed by those mediæval
Titans who delved and built from the ruins of a perished world.
The lords of Urbino were active and zealous in the new pursuit.   They foresaw its immense results; and there lived not a
few in their duchy whose names are great among the thinkers,
and whose works rank high among the artists, of the world.   The
typographic art had been introduced into Urbino in 1480; Francesco Venturini, an inhabitant of that town, was the first who
wrote a complete Latin grammar.   Raffaele and Michael Angelo
were his pupils.   Polydoro di Vergilio, archdeacon of Wells,

was also born at Urbino. We introduce him to our readers, because, at the command of Henry VII., he wrote a Latin history of England, the manuscript of which is preserved in the Vatican. The names of two eminent men at the court of Urbino are still remembered by the learned, and are still highly esteemed: Castiglione, the Chesterfield of Italy; and Bembo, the historian, poet, and rhetorician, sometime secretary to Leo, and raised by him to the rank of cardinal. His style has been severely criticised; his pedantry has been often rebuked; and Lipsius points out many errors in his letters, which evince but a partial acquaintance with the purities of the masters of classical literature. Bembo made Cicero his constant study; his model, indeed; and he carried his study of that orator and philosopher to so great an extent, that he came at length to be the most exclusive Ciceronian of his age; so much so, that, when alluding to ecclesiastical topics, he adapted heathen phraseologies to Christian doctrines and to ecclesiastical usage and ceremonial. Elegance in Bembo degenerated into fastidious purity of style. He arranged his sentences and set his adjectives like a literary drill-serjeant.

We have neither time nor space to allude to the Urbino poets; for the critic cannot justly do otherwise than censure the pedantic sonnets, as the moralist must condemn their obscene authors, who either placed their muse at the feet of the reigning power, or wedded it to lust and vice. We must, however, bring to notice the mediæval religious art, so far chiefly it was developed in Urbino. During the dark ages, the limners exercised their art principally on religious subjects; taking their idea either from Scripture history, or from those pages in which it was written how a martyr had preferred the truth to his life, and had chosen death rather than belie his conscience and deny his God; or how a holy woman had quenched the passions of her sex within her, and had given herself, by an oath of perpetual virginity, to the offices of a life-long charity and to the service of the Church. Not as yet, or but rarely, had the painter turned from the annals of his Church, or from those ancient traditionary memorials in which it was told how martyrs and confessors had died for their faith, to study the wondrous volume of nature; not as yet had men, in whom genius lived, mused thoughtfully on the far-drawn glories of the setting sun, the tinting of the summer evening, nor had that genius looked inquiringly at the thickly-studded glories of the nightly sky revolving in their everlasting anthem to the Highest; and not as yet had artist-men pondered by the wild sea, and learnt to picture forth its calm or its storm, the beauty of its repose, and the sweep of its agitated billows. But the masters of the Umbrian and Sienese schools aimed only at a Christian ideal. Their fancy roamed not to

waving harvest-fields and quiet dales, not to roaring torrents
and deep-shadowed boscage, nor to white-walled towns whose
spires showed ruddily in the glowing eventide; but they drew
their conceptions from the cold cavern where the rigid saint
dwelt in perpetual winter, hoping to win God's heaven by
making a hell of God's earth; from the lonely cell where pious
eremite prayed and pined; or from the chilly dungeon where
the holy were in chains, or from the arena where they died.
Sometimes, their genius fed its flame from the lamp of the
Everlasting Word, and then the artist's pencil showed how the
woman of Magdala wept penitentially at His feet who had
'power on earth to forgive sin'; how a widow begged Him, by
whom no second entreaty was required, to give her back from
the gates of death her only child, the darling of her lonely life,
and the hope and solace of her declining years; how Peter, in
his passionate love for the Nazarene, as He found a safe pathway
on the crested waters of the inland sea, essayed to equal Him
whose ready hand rescued the fisherman from death; or sometimes
that genius imaged forth the agony and the conquest at Calvary,
the darkened sky, the bloody cross, and the dying LORD; or showed
how He, 'who robbed the grave of victory,' broke away from
the captivity of death, because it was not possible that he could
be holden of its chain; brought life and immortality to light; and
opening, in his triumph, the 'gates of mercy to mankind,'

'Pointed to brighter worlds, and led the way.'

Sometimes, too, the rapt fancy of the artist pictured, to a wondering age, upon his glowing canvass, the home and the employ of
the blest—a calm and constant joy, of which ancient song had
never warbled when it told the heathen good of Happy Western
Isles—and showed how, around the sapphire-throne, the blissful
martyrs rested from their labours; and how, their fiery trial
past, the holy Twelve dwelt with their loved Master in those
'many mansions,' from which they shall go forth no more for
ever.   These were the subjects those mediæval limners, faithful
children of their Church, loved to portray on abbey-walls and
on high altars.   In many cases, the hand of the artist never
touched his colours till he had invoked more than mortal aid,
and till a hallowed feeling ruled his soul.   Even when sublime
conceptions were begotten within him, he dared not body them
forth as his genius might prompt him; for the Holy Office,
during the sixteenth century, exercised the strictest censorship
over all works of religious art, and all, however exquisitely
wrought, which in the least contradicted the traditions, or
offended against the canons, of the Church, were ruthlessly destroyed.  For the tyrannous priests of the Italian hierarchy—who

once threw Galileo into prison because he said the world moved, though the Church, ever infallible, had decreed otherwise—fearful lest a picture should teach a new truth to the people, put even genius in chains. The art of teaching by pictures had been early known, and had long been used : a mode of instruction, perhaps, not unsuited to convey great truths to the ignorant and simple, and which was no slight addition to the various sources of instruction the Church possessed. But the mystic or religious ideal ceased to satisfy the artist when civilization dawned upon the world; and not only were portraits painted, but especially, under the fostering patronage of the Medici, the strictly-devotional painting gave place to works produced on the models of classical antiquity. The great genius of Michael Angelo was devoted to this 'new manner,' as it was termed ; showing, as he did, that there is no reason à priori why art should be consecrated to devotion, or to the high service of religion; but that while he takes them as the subjects for his study, the artist may learn much from the grand remains of a vanished mythology. It was among the Umbrian Hills that religious art wrought and reigned, till Raffaele brought it to its perfection. Of late, the Germans have done much to revive the love for religious art, which had grown cold in the earlier part of this practical and utilitarian century ; and they have clearly shown the power of the Umbrian school in that art, tracing its growth and greatness, from the primal anchorite-sketchings to the glorious conceptions of Raffaele. In the second volume of these Urbino Memoirs the reader will find—and Mr. Dennistoun seems to have gone to his æsthetical task *con amore*—clear and satisfactory accounts of these wondrous men, who never touched the pallet till they had offered up 'orisons for divine influence,' whose pencils 'embodied the language of prayer,' and who, in the words of Michael Angelo, 'must have studied in heaven the faces which they depicted on earth.' It was in Urbino, and under the patronage of the Montefeltrian dukes, that these immortal limners executed their conceptions. Giotto and Gentile da Fabriano laboured there ; and while Francisco di Giorgio beautified the ducal home with pencil and chisel, his fertile mind suggested military improvements, and designed fortresses on a greatly-improved system. To Giovanni Sanzi, the epic poet, we have already alluded; but we have to refer to him as an artist also, and whom, perhaps, we ought to class among the Umbrian school. His artistic education seems to have been deficient, though true genius depends not on adventitious circumstances. He has left behind him no mean specimens of correct conception and skilful delineation. His expression does not want grace ; his forms are slender ; the hands and feet in his pictures are exquisitely delicate; but his outlines are occasionally too rigid, and his tints too sombre and heavy.

We pass to his son, Raffaele, who was born at Urbino, in 1483. Various writers have corrupted the orthography of this master's name. The English fashion of writing it Raffaelle is, it would seem, an error originated by Sir Joshua Reynolds. There were but a few works of the older masters in the duchy which could appropriately form a school for young Sanzi's study; but from his father he received instruction in at least the rudiments of art. Soon, however, losing him, he was sent to Perugia to study under Vannucci, known as Perugino. After some time very profitably spent in Perugino's study, and when he had already laid the foundation of his fame by various youthful efforts, Raffaele was engaged by the Oddi family, at Perugia, to paint, as an altar-piece, the Coronation of the Madonna, which is now among the treasures of the Vatican. Repairing to Florence, the cradle and school of perfect art, the young painter associated with others, spirits kindred to his own, who were at that time rapidly attaining, or who had already reached, fame. Leonardo da Vinci, Michael Angelo, and Ridolfo, were producing their matchless works; and for more than three years, the young artist of Urbino dwelt with these, and lit his torch at their undying lamp. Invited, subsequently, to Perugia, he designed and finished his grand altar-pieces; one of which decorates Blenheim, and the other is a glory of the Borghese Collection. Perhaps at this time, that is, from 1504-6, Raffaele executed his 'Christ in the Garden,' 'St. George Slaying the Dragon,' some small 'Madonnas,' and 'The Holy Family.' In 1508, Raffaele repaired to Rome, where Julius II. was engaged in building the metropolitan church of the Catholic world, and which was designed to be the pride of Christendom and the wonder of the age. He invited the genius and skill of Europe to his aid; and while Michael Angelo and Bramante consecrated their talent to its adornment, Raffaele also went thither to leave the glories of his art in that magnificent shrine—those marvellous works, before which we feel as if in some august presence, or our hearts are lifted up as when we have stood among 'the everlasting hills,' where Nature is enthroned in an awful grandeur, by the rushing waterfall, or among the icy crags. Here, in mural paintings, and in the tapestry-cartoons possessed by this country, the great artist won his fame; for when the Pope, who had summoned him to Rome, had passed to the tomb, his successor fully occupied the fertile genius of Raffaele. He was appointed curator of the antiquities of the city, and the general superintendence of the building of St. Peter's was committed to him. He continued at Rome till 1520, the darling of the Pope, and all but worshipped for his transcendent genius. His last work was the decoration of what is now the Farnese Villa, but which was at that time the abode of Chigi, the banker. An attack of fever, brought on by attending to consult with the Pope in a cold saloon, carried off ' the most gentle and most eminent painter ' from the scene of his toils and glories. Nothing was ever produced from his pencil offensive to religious feeling. He laboured for the defence of his faith. His genius was, from its dawn to its setting hour, consecrated to the highest service. A ' bright particular star,' he shines with no borrowed light. The age in which he lived was not remarkable for purity of morals ; his associates were more vicious than virtuous, for the public morality was universally lax. Discarding the ridiculous, and perhaps malicious, stories of his ill-fame, but admitting the probability of his occasional frailty, since even the sun has obscurations ; we may say of him, than whom Urbino produced never a man greater or nobler, nor Italy an artist more conspicuous among all her gifted children, that he left

' No work which, dying, he would wish to blot.'

The great genius and fame of Raffaele had attracted to a permanent residence in Rome multitudes of artists from the Catholic countries, who became there eager and successful students, forming what we may, perhaps not improperly, style the Raffaele School. The remarkable sweetness of that great man's disposition, and his constant affability, linked these inferior spirits to him by no fragile bonds. But, as ' the fashion of this world passeth away,' so this delightful society of those whom genius made kindred was destined speedily and for ever to be dissolved. This harmony of brother-souls was unbroken while the great master lived, and his life, as we have seen, came hastily and sadly to an end. Soon after his departure, a dark cloud, charged with tempest, ' a sable cloud of war,' lowered over Northern Italy ; and in the bursting of this tempest-darkness, the constable Bourbon, at the head of twenty-six thousand greedy ruffians, invaded the Papal States and swooped upon Rome. The seven-hilled city, incapable of vigorous resistance, made a few palsied movements in her own defence ; but the furious invaders, when the traitor Bourbon had fallen in the assault by the hand, it is said, of Benvenuto Cellini, burst into the city, which a few thousand Swiss troops, had they not departed in disgust from the Papal service, might easily and successfully have defended. The Imperialists, whose sole aim was plunder, enraged at the death of Bourbon, and knowing that the army of the League and the Duke of Urbino were at no great distance, forced their way along those ancient streets ; and easily beating the timid Italian levies, and dispersing such citizens as dared still to resist, their forces, battalion after battalion, passed the ill-guarded walls, marching, we may imagine, to their battle-song :—

> ' Up, up, with the lily,
> And down with the keys ;
> In old Rome, the seven-hilly,
> We'll revel at ease.
> Her streets shall be gory,
> Her Tiber all red,
> And her temples so hoary
> Shall clang with our tread.'

The Pontiff and his Cardinals, soldiers and citizens, a mingled mass of fugitives, rushed to the Castle of St. Angelo ; and the unhappy city saw deeds of blood and of shame done within her walls, which had scarcely been equalled by the merciless barbarians in the days of her ancient conquest and fall.

' The delight of these sacrilegious villains, especially of the German Lutherans, was to outrage everything holy. The churches and chapels, including the now blood-stained St. Peter's, were desecrated into stables, taverns, or brothels ; and the choirs, whence no sounds had breathed but the elevating chant of prayer and praise, rang with base ribaldry and blasphemous imprecations. The grand creations of religious art were wantonly insulted or damaged ; the reliquaries and miraculous images were pillaged or defaced. Nay, a poor priest was inhumanly murdered for his firm refusal to administer the blessed sacrament to an ass. Nor was any respect paid to persons or party feelings. The subjects of the Emperor who happened to be in Rome, the adherents of the Colonna and other Ghibelline leaders, were all involved in the general fate. Four Cardinals attached to that faction had declined entering St. Angelo, calculating that they would not only

> " Guide the whirlwind and direct the storm,"

but, peradventure, promote their own interests in the melée. They were, however, miserably mistaken, for they, too, were held to ransom; and one of them (Araceli), after being often led through the streets tied on a donkey, behind a common soldier, was carried to church with mock funereal rites, when the office of the dead was read over his living body, and an oration pronounced, wherein, for eulogy, were loathsomely related all the real or alleged immoralities of his past life. Another outrage in especial repute with the Germans, was a ribald procession; in which some low buffoon in sacred vestments was borne shoulder-high, scattering mock benedictions among the mob, amid shouts of " Long live Luther." '—[Admitting many of the gross details, it is clear to what sources our author has been for his information.]—Vol. iii. pp. 15, 16.

This fearful sack of the Papal city dispersed ' the goodly company of painters,' and scattered far and wide the members of

Raffaele's school. But the reputation of Urbino, as a nursery for art, was speedily revived and continued by the brothers Zuccaro, Fran. Baroccio, and Carlo Ridolfi. It is interesting to observe the fostering care which the Dukes of Urbino bestowed on Michael Angelo Buonarotti, Titian, and others, whose 'pencils, pregnant with celestial hues,' have bequeathed to their sunny Southern land beauties glowing as its own unclouded sky. It were a pleasing task, to show how illustrious this little Urbino duchy has been rendered by its association with the great men of our modern world, whose handiworks are the glory of our common humanity, and whose thought has given a healthful impulse to all societies of men. Not seldom does Nature, rarely prodigal of her higher gifts, cast her noblest children forth upon the wild ; not seldom are the early days of poets, philosophers, and artists spent in poverty and sorrow; and not seldom, indeed, has cruel Might driven forth to a hopeless exile those whose thaumaturgic thought can better serve the true interests of all thrones, than the sword and the lance, the army and the fleet. Such men never in vain sought shelter from the Montefeltrian dukes. Venice, Genoa, and Lucca, might close their gates against the fugitive children of painting and of song ; but the humble Urbino sheltered them from the vengeance of the pursuer, and was ever a city of refuge, during the two centuries of her splendid prosperity, for those sons of science and of art, whom magnates feared and republics banned. While the duchy produced such men as Comandino, Paciotti, Baldi, and Bonaventura, it could also boast of giving a kindly shelter to Ariosto and Tasso.—Our limits have permitted but an occasional reference to the political history of Urbino. A few words will suffice to tell of its declining glory under its last duke, till, after ' this little state had enjoyed two hundred and twenty years of a prosperity unknown to the neighbouring communities,' her rulers, beloved by their people, and respected by European potentates generally ; the people themselves tranquil, contented, and happy ; the metropolis, the home of art, the Athens of Italy ; the duchy became merged in the Papal States, and, since that sad devolution, genius has been blighted in her towns, freedom has withered by her hearths, and contentment has fled from her people.

We congratulate Mr. Dennistoun on the happy execution of his labour, and on the publication of his beautiful volumes, which are worthy the attention of all lovers of art, and of those, too, who are interested in the now oft-changing lights and shadows of the mourning Italian lands. These Memoirs cannot be read but with pleasure and profit. Our author is, perhaps, sometimes too one-sided ; and, occasionally, he allows his disgust

at the late proceedings of a few among the Italian patriots almost
to blind his perception to the detestable enormities of the Papal
system, past and present, and which we proclaim the foe alike
of God and man. We would heartily commend these Urbino
Memoirs to the attention of all to whom religious art in particular,
and Italian history in general, are attractive themes.

---

ART. II.—1. *Œuvres de Bourdaloue.*   3 vols. royal 8vo.   Paris : Didot.
2. *Œuvres Complètes de Massillon.*   6 vols.   Idem.

BEFORE Bourdaloue had raised the pulpit eloquence of his
country to that perfection which it attained during his lifetime,
France possessed in this branch of literature but a few scattered
fragments, more remarkable for vigour of thought than for purity
of style or learned and logical arrangement of argument and
proof.   If, at the present day, the preachers of France, with two
or three brilliant exceptions, seem to take pleasure in quenching,
under the scrupulously correct but icy forms of a cold and
inanimate art, the electrical effusions of genius and the high-
soaring flights of imagination; if too much occupied with the
harmony of their periods, they restrict their ministry to a certain
intoxication of the ear, and never seek to project the light of
gospel truth into those dark and noisome abysses, wherein the
uncontrolled vices and passions of their frivolous fellow-countrymen hold riotous company; on the other hand, the pulpit orators
of the latter part of the sixteenth, and beginning of the seventeenth, centuries, took not sufficient thought of the legitimate
requirements of a sound and healthy literature.   A more severely
correct taste was all that the terrible haranguers of the League
required, in order to attain to the loftiest summits of sacred
eloquence.   But at a period, like that stormy epoch of French
history, when the tongue was a two-edged sword, men thought
rather of striking at once and forcibly the mark they aimed at, than
of carefully disposing the means which would lead them thereto, by
slower, though not less certain, gradations.   Besides, the general
excitement and exaltation of the auditors exempted the orator
from the necessity of employing those thousand industrious precautions, the use of which cannot be neglected when he is in
presence of a less passionate congregation.   But for what pur-

pose, we may ask, would rules have served in a discourse addressed to a Leaguer congregation? The arguments and circumlocutions of rhetoric would only have fretted and provoked an excited populace, which awaited but the signal to rush into the heat of the fray.

The popular orators and preachers of the League succeeded in their aim, through the aid of volcanic eruptions of eloquence, ever mingled, it is true, with ashes and smoke, yet, for all that, possessing a marvellous power of quickly and surely inflaming all hearts and all imaginations. Let the student of French history, if he entertain any doubt as to the truth of our statement, but turn, for an instant, to the few sermons of the sixteenth century which have escaped oblivion, and he will be convinced that we have characterised them justly. Their end was less to demonstrate the truths of Christianity than to impel to the hatred and extinction of Protestantism; and, as about the same period, Greek and Latin letters enjoyed a high degree of vogue in France, we find the introduction of a certain ostentatious erudition occasionally abating the orator's bursts of passion, and subduing, in some measure, the thunders of his eloquence; while some few brilliant sentences would, at intervals, it is true, sparkle forth from out this strange heterogeneous mass of quotations, in which sacred and profane history were jumbled together in the most grotesque and inextricable confusion. This pedantic garb gave place, on several occasions, to a more severe and healthy style of oratory, during which periods, the preacher, having divested himself of his harlequin's jacket of fragments borrowed from Greece, Rome, and Judea, and being freed from all extraneous ornament, would proceed towards his end with a rapid and assured step.

An impassioned and seductive, though impure and incorrect style, and a monstrous abuse of erudition, are the two principal characteristics of the French pulpit eloquence of the sixteenth century; transferred to the street and market-place, it reflected all their disordered oscillations, without ever succeeding in thoroughly divesting itself of its classical reminiscences. It was, as it were, an amalgamation of newly-forged murderous weapons, and of antique javelins, which, by their rusty state, piqued the curiosity, without, in any way, contributing towards the issue of the fight. But when men's minds had grown calmer, and religious dissensions no longer found a voice from the pulpit, the preachers were obliged to seek out new means of triumph; they, accordingly, applied themselves to the task of better arranging their arguments, and to the adornment of their discourses with the treasures of language.

But erudition, though employed with more discernment and sobriety, still maintained a foremost place in the discourses of the time ; prolix and entangled theological arguments discouraged even the most attentive auditor.  In place of limiting himself to the interpretation of the broad truths of Christianity comprehensible to all, the preacher would ever wander from his direct road into the by-ways of obscure and subtle theories, the mysteries of which he would endeavour to expound in a language bristling with scholastic terms.  Art and inspiration were gradually tending towards a fruitful alliance, but previous to their giving birth to the works which are, at the present day, deservedly worthy of our admiration, pulpit eloquence was obliged to feel its way carefully, slowly, and circumspectly, towards its definite object.  We do not certainly mean to affirm by this that Bourdaloue, who so greatly contributed towards the present improved style of French pulpit oratory, is, in all respects, a perfect model ; he seems to us to shine by a skilful amalgamation of the different qualities of the orator, rather than by those traits of genius which open to the astonished eyes of a congregation new and boundless prospects.  The light which he casts upon his subject is propagated with a certain degree of deliberation, which permits him to penetrate its most secret recesses ; but we look in vain for those sudden and brilliant illuminations which, in Bossuet, seem to snatch us up at once from earth, and bear us into the very midst of the celestial choir.  Bourdaloue climbs slowly and painfully the steep and rugged path which leads to the sublime.  Bossuet, on the contrary, attains his end at a single bound : the first shows us all the accidents and chances of the route he pursues ; the second, like nature, accomplishes marvels while shrouding his creative powers in the most profound mystery.  Bourdaloue's view, though penetrating and sure, pauses on a thousand details before daring to embrace the whole ; Bossuet, standing erect upon the ruins of empires delights to interrogate the infinite prospects of eternity. The one teaches, the other commands.  In reading the sermons of Bourdaloue we seem as though we recollected the thoughts we are yet perusing for the first time, the writer appears to make an appeal to our memory ; Bossuet, on the contrary, gives us new worlds to contemplate ; one might say that, like Moses, he brought forth in profusion a crowd of unknown truths from this desert, through which we are painfully journeying towards the promised land.

But if the sublime and magnificent thoughts which we discover in the writings of Bossuet do not, in the sermons of Bourdaloue, gush forth in such liberal profusion, on the other hand, no orator can better mould them into the required form, or display them in all their varieties. He enchases them in language at once concise and abundant, luminous and substantial. A large exposition of subject followed by simple divisions, at once places the preacher in perfect sympathy of intelligence with his congregation; the reader perceives without effort the end he proposes to attain, and, though vast and almost numberless are the means he employs, they are retained in the mind without ever being confounded, so happily are the various transitions brought about, so firmly and solidly established the foundation and order of the discourse. In general, the sermons of Bourdaloue are but commentaries upon the particular texts of Scripture to which they are allied, and that frequently by the slenderest possible relationship; or else paraphrases of the best thoughts of the Fathers of the Church. After Bossuet, that great master of French pulpit-eloquence, Bourdaloue is unquestionably the one who has best succeeded in catching the inspiration of the Fathers, and of appropriating it to the end he had in view; but we must, above all things, beware of confounding the admirable fecundity of Bourdaloue with that sterile procedure of the early Christians, which consisted in submerging a simple thought beneath a perfect deluge of words. It is not by the aid of vain and empty sentences that he lengthens out the thoughts gleaned from the writings of the firmest supporters of the Christian faith—he adds many new and ingenious views to those which serve as a pivot for his arguments; from a single ray he draws a splendid galaxy of light, leaving nothing exposed to its influence in the shade. Point out to him in some old and apparently exhausted mine of theological lore, one slender vein only of true metal from which merely a few superficial layers have been raised to the surface, he will dig there with unceasing perseverance, and from the depths below you will behold, ere long, arise a continuous succession of unexpected treasures.

Bourdaloue takes the elements of his discourses from the common reservoir of evangelical dogmas, and contents himself with displaying them to the view of his readers surrounded with all the light they are capable of receiving. Though a consummate theologian, he never displays his learning with fatiguing ostentation; far from pitching the tone of his discourse in the lofty, but frequently cloud-capped, regions of science, he places it within reach of all capacities. How wonderful are the resources he displays in the application of Gospel truths to the various circumstances of actual life! If the theologian be occasionally effaced by the orator, nevertheless we feel, even when our heart alone is touched by Bourdaloue, what profound study

was required to give him such a perfect mastery over the
mysteries of the religion he professed; the illustrations he
draws therefrom denote the deep thinker, and his discourses
will ever be considered as luminous developments of the principles of Christianity, as well as a vast repertory of secondary
propositions corroborating essential truths. But it must be
allowed that Bourdaloue aimed less at convincing the mind,
than at animating and revivifying the heart; in his time faith
predominated; the scepticism and infidelity so unhappily prevalent throughout France during the eighteenth century, had
not as yet succeeded in totally eradicating that firm belief in
Christianity which had animated European society during fourteen centuries. Noble precepts might, it is true, be eluded in
practice, but, amid mundane pre-occupations, sensual gratifica-
tions, and the intoxication of the passions, the people still clung
stedfastly to the religion of their forefathers. What was then
required in a preacher was rather the art of leading souls to
the altar, than of demonstrating truths which none contested.
And certainly we do not fear being accused of exaggeration
when we affirm that never was man better fitted than Bourdaloue
to fulfil this difficult ministry.

Born at Bourges, in 1632, of one of the first families of the
city, he could, while still a youth, form some tolerably exact
ideas of the world from personal experience; for if, while we
are children, we but too frequently restrict ourselves to sensation,
later, when retracing the course of our earlier years, we succeed
in drawing energetic conclusions from those first vague impressions which seemed for a time lost. It is by no means
improbable that the preacher who depicted with so much
force and truth the ravages of ambition, and the fatal consequences of vice — outwardly so attractive, yet within so
full of corruption and ruin — had derived the principal
features of more than one sketch from the powerfully awakened
recollections of his youth. Childhood is the period during
which the development of the moral faculties is accomplished
in some sort in an occult manner. The sap circulates not in
the bark; it works secretly and noiselessly, and when the
elaboration is complete, it breaks forth in odorous flowers and
luscious fruits. The superficial eye notes merely the instant
in which all these marvels are brought to light, but the
philosophical observer, who has deeply meditated on the
evolution of nature's laws, occupies his mind far more in the
study of the mysterious labour which has preceded the triumphant outbreak of this vital sap, enriched successively with
the juices of the earth, and the treasures of celestial dew.
The experiences of youth were the faint principle of those

fruitful impulsions which the genius of Bourdaloue was destined from all sides to receive.

Having, at the early age of fifteen, entered the society of the Jesuits, he drew from the resources open to him in this celebrated company, the precepts and examples of elegant literature, as well as the habit of contemplating simply the positive face of things, and of judging men only according as circumstances had made them what they were. While a philosopher in the calm solitude of meditation may content himself with abstract ideas upon our inclinations and infirmities, the preacher has need of acquiring knowledge easy of application; he must not merely be well acquainted with the general tendencies of the human heart, he must also be able to track its many by-ways and mysterious turnings, while mere outward appearances, above all, must never be permitted to warp his judgment or lead him into error.

Bourdaloue exhibited, from his very outset, all the advantages acquired from an attentive and detailed study of human nature. There is not one of his memorable sermons from which we could not detach maxims as profound, and as well expressed, as those of La Rochefoucauld; and it must be said that, although he had completed with much distinction his course of literature, philosophy, and theology, in the schools, it was in the pulpit only that the grandeur of this marvellous intellect shone forth in all its brilliancy. Not until after a period of eighteen years, entirely given up to his own instruction and that of others, did he resolve, with the assent of his superiors, to devote himself to the Pulpit. He was more than thirty years of age when one of the princesses of the blood-royal accidentally heard him preach in the city of Eu, and at once conceived for him the most lively admiration. The provinces knew and appreciated his talents long before Paris had even so much as heard of his name. Bourdaloue, after having sufficiently 'tried the strength of his youth' before a congregation less formidable than the fastidious auditories of the capital, was summoned to exercise his ministry upon that vast arena wherein he was destined to achieve so signal a triumph. Undoubtedly, he was a man who could have had no difficulty in adapting his discourse to the humblest capacity; the true orator is enabled to mould his language to suit all circumstances, as well as all classes of society; and no one will be disposed to deny to Bourdaloue the gift of convincing; but pictures of the world, and reflections upon the thousand stratagems which our passions make use of in order to conceal their tortuous march, all those large developments wherein are displayed such a profound knowledge of mankind, would be,

perhaps, but 'leather and prunella' to simple minds, which calculate neither the sacrifices prescribed by virtue, nor the fleeting
advantages of vice and crime; it is amid the tumult of populous
cities that the Chrysostoms and Bourdaloues can launch forth
the thunders of their eloquence without fearing lest their blows
may fall on souls already prostrate in the dust. All the fires of
sacred eloquence scarcely suffice to purify hearts already stained
with impurity. The discourse from the minister must issue
from the pulpit in burning words in order to penetrate the
all but impregnable coat of mail beneath which our evil thoughts
lie sheltered. The villager rarely resists the paternal warnings
of his pastor; he yields to the voice of the apostle of the
fields, and if he does sin it is almost always either through
ignorance, or when seduced in an unguarded moment by some
fatal combination of circumstances. There is a species of inge-
nuousness observable in a rural population, even in its widest
deviations from the path of rectitude; one might almost suppose
that in these primitive organizations the senses wandered as it
were unknown to the drowsy intellect, buried, so to speak,
beneath the superincumbent weight of matter. But with the
inhabitants of the city it is far otherwise; they exhaust
all the resources of the intellect in the machination of their
iniquities; when they wallow in the mire of sin and corruption they do their best to stifle within their hearts the
consciousness of their degradation, and it is by dint of perversity
alone that they succeed in quenching that inward light which
would otherwise point out to them the straight path of rectitude.

Not only must the preacher when dealing with such people
be enabled to impress salutary terrors on their minds, he must
also have at instant command a reply for every sophism and
miserable subtlety they may call to their service. Even
among the privileged of this earth who joyfully accept the glad
tidings of the gospel, how many do we see who torment themselves in vain endeavours to escape the practice of those
duties which that very gospel they profess inculcates! Like
certain lawyers, who seek, by captious interpretations, to
endue a bad cause with a false varnish of justice, they
torture the letter while losing sight of the spirit. It is necessary to have deeply studied the human heart in order to
unravel and expose the specious arguments and false logic
of such persons; and it is in this sense that we ought to
'·ke the famous axiom of antiquity: that orators are formed by
ti    . In fact, independently of the literary qualities which
go towards the formation of a discourse—whether delivered
from the pulpit or the platform—there is required a certain

knowledge of men and things which is the rule and foundation of the public speaker. Now this knowledge is never acquired from books; it is imperatively necessary to have breathed the very atmosphere of worldly passions and interests in order to be enabled to seize upon their various and diverse complications. Vague generalities serve at best but for the amplification of common-places, of which the most complaisant auditory cannot fail of soon becoming heartily weary.

In perusing at the present day the sermons of Bourdaloue we are amazed at the force, truth, and delicacy of his observations. When he does not shed an entirely new light upon the mysteries of the human heart, he illuminates them in a manner so complete that we willingly attribute to him all the honour of having been their first exponent. While pursuing the track already cleared by other hardy pioneers of the gospel, we feel convinced that his piercing glance will, ere long, discover points of view which had escaped the perspicacity of his predecessors; and when he takes possession of a subject, he circumscribes its limits with such exactitude, he turns it so well in all senses, that it would seem impossible to add anything to the riches he draws therefrom. Bourdaloue was endowed with two qualities which, in ordinary natures, impede each other's progress, but which in organizations above the common stamp mutually fortify and enrich each other: to the promptitude of glance which divines, he joined the gift of never permitting himself to be dazzled by a first impression of the truth upon his mind. He was well aware that false lights very frequently exercise the same degree of illusion as do true ones, and that above all if we pause too long to collect the rays which have at first shone forth we incur considerable risk of possessing but a very incomplete view of things. By subduing the natural vivacity of his temperament he succeeded not only in mastering his passions, but in moderating the sallies of his intellect. We thus discover in this great man the most opposite and antagonistic faculties harmonizing together for the creation of prodigies; and, in our opinion, it is chiefly this mutual accord of all the moral powers which distinguishes Bourdaloue.

Respectful and polished towards the great and powerful of the land, among whom he reckoned numerous friends and admirers; affable and tender-hearted with persons of more humble condition of life; tolerant, kind, and indulgent, in the ' salons' of the seventeenth century; austere in his habits of life; ever anxious to solace the afflictions of the unhappy—hastening from the confessional to the bed of death, and afterwards ascending the pulpit to distribute to all that bread of life which he so well knew how to apportion to each; isolating himself by the effort of meditation in the midst of the most tumultuous assemblies, and nevertheless possessing in the highest degree the gift of a conversation enriched by reading and study, and a consummate experience of the things of this life; Bourdaloue devoted himself entirely to the strict performance of his various duties, and knew no other joys save those which spring from a mind at peace with itself and the world, and a consciousness of having sought to do his duty in that sphere of life in which Providence had placed him. He was cloistered, so to speak, in the daily circle of his religious occupations, and no one could ever reproach him with nourishing in his breast any of those mundane passions which have but too frequently animated the company of which he was a member. His death, which took place in 1704, inspired throughout France a universal feeling of regret, of which there still remain many authentic testimonies in the memoirs and letters of the time.

To Bourdaloue belongs incontestably the honour of having given to the sermon the peculiar form best suited to an advanced state of civilization. A profound theologian, he was enabled to place within reach of his hearers the truths of holy writ by translating them into a clear and logical language, divested of the pedantic rubbish of the schools. To the luminous exposition of Christian truths, he allied the most subtle and penetrating analysis of human nature; as a moralist, he successfully contends, in precision, vigour, and perspicacity, with Pascal and La Rochefoucauld; in the many and faithful pictures which he draws of our passions, we discover details which have escaped the author of the ' Maxims,' and above all that of the ' Thoughts,' who almost always seeks to compress vast generalities into the concisest possible phrases. An orator cannot proceed by aphorisms; he has need of constantly varying the development of his ideas, in order to render them intelligible to all capacities. A sententious laconism of style, while it would utterly destroy all the eloquence and fire of his discourse, would altogether isolate him from the mass of his public, and would, in point of fact, be incomprehensible save to a select few. It is difficult to surpass Bourdaloue in the art of skilfully anatomizing a thought, and of divesting it of all the coverings by which its sense or beauty is obscured; inspiration never seduces him from the path he has traced out for himself. In his most passionate movements he curbs himself without effort; and if the waves of his eloquence occasionally rear their crests to the sky, they soon fall back into their accustomed channel, and pursue the first impulsion without ever overflowing their boundaries. Such are the incontestable merits of that genius, born to dispose, according to a symmetrical plan, the riches which abound in the Scriptures, in

successor of Bourdaloue in the pulpit, he profited by the improvements introduced by his predecessor into the pulpit-eloquence of
his country, while wholly rejecting the yoke of a servile
imitation ; it was, in point of fact, the only means by
which he could hope to equal the wonders accomplished by the
illustrious Jesuit.   The human mind tires of contemplating the
same prospects, how beautiful soever they may be ; even the
ocean fatigues by its monotonous grandeur — after having
gazed for a time upon its illimitable expanse, we love the
repose afforded by other and more broken horizons.   The loud
and sonorous tones of Bourdaloue would, doubtless, in course of
time have fallen on jaded ears.   It was necessary that other
oratorical qualities should be developed, to find favour with the
masses, and entice a fickle and worldly population to the house
of God.   Thus, among the elements of success which men of
genius turn to their advantage, the novelty of their works is not
one of the weakest instruments of their popularity.   But let not
the reader imagine that they can innovate at will ; they are restricted to the necessity of seeking their means of action in the
human atmosphere by which they are surrounded.   If they do

not wish to see their thoughts shine in the void, they must seek
to place them in affinity with the social medium wherein they set
them forth, as a flame destined to spread, at the same time, light
and heat.   Orators, whose influence may not be indefinitely adjourned, like that of philosophers, who write almost always with
posterity in view, cannot dispense with the necessity of making a
deep and searching study of the land upon which they are about
to venture.   If their speech has not the magic power of captivating the public, it will meet with the derisive echoes of
empty courts; for eloquence increases by violent opposition as
well as enthusiastic applause.   A discourse is but a heavy and
ambitious piece of declamation when regarded as a monologue;
to be successful, it must be the ardent interpretation of the
orator's own sentiments, which sentiments he must be enabled to
make his audience thoroughly partake.   If the entire assembly
is not thus placed, as it were, in communication with its interpreter by means of a species of magnetic fluid, you may safely affirm
that the sounds which strike your ear, harmonious though they
be, no longer possess aught save an insignificant value.

Massillon understood very well, that, in order to obtain triumphs after Bourdaloue, it was essential that he should bring
forward into the light what his rival had left in the shade.
Having the same ground to cultivate, and rigorously enclosed
within the theological circle, he could alter only as far as regarded
the form and accessory ideas.   The epoch in which he entered
upon his career was singularly fitted for the development of his
faculties.   The reign of Louis XIV. was rapidly declining from
its former magnificence.   The great men who had illustrated
this golden age of French history had disappeared one after the
other, leaving their places to be filled by a host of mediocrities,
who in the way of services could boast only of the exploits of
the bedchamber or the negotiations of the boudoir.

The discernment of the great king—for great, despite all his
vanities and weaknesses, he surely was—was impaired by the
empire of subaltern influences; and that firmness of character
which had formerly, in many a trying emergency, shone forth
so conspicuously when supported by the voices of such men as
Colbert, Louvois, or Turenne, had now degenerated into the
pig-headed obstinacy which maintained, in the hands of a Villeroi,
the dishonoured baton of Marshal of France.   The bulletins
from the frontier announced a succession of disastrous defeats,
or victories furiously contested by a formidable league of
enemies bent on the ruin of France.   The line of fortifica-
tions, so skilfully drawn by the genius of Vauban, seemed
no longer able to withstand that onward and triumphant pressure
of an inimical force, so sad a spectacle in the eyes of the veterans

of Lens and Rocroy. In vain did the French troops perform prodigies of valour; the long-suppressed vengeance of Europe burst forth in a torrent, whose force no power could withstand. The exhausted nation had no longer either blood, or food, or money to give; crushed to the earth, beneath the weight of many reverses, it had nothing better than its own lifeless corpse to oppose to the advance of the conquering allies.

It was then that threatening murmurs began to arise from all parts of the kingdom against a despotism which the *prestige* of glory no longer saved from the lash of bitter and well-deserved censure. In that vigorous unity which tended to level all classes, as well as to suppress the barriers of the provinces, men saw a heavy chain, which encircled and compressed in its iron embrace all parts of the social body, to make it act for the profit of a single individual. From a blind and excessive admiration of royalty, amounting almost to worship, the people passed at once to the most outrageous explosions of intense hatred. Of all the good that had been done, they attributed the merit to the powerful auxiliaries which Louis XIV. had found in that little band of men of genius grouped around his throne, while they accused him alone as the author of all the evils to which the country seemed irremediably devoted. In the minds of the people, kings were now detested as insatiable vampires. The eloquent discourses against the ambition of princes, with which the pages of Fenelon's ' Telemaque ' is filled, were greeted with frantic enthusiasm; in short, men were sick of that imposing uniformity which sacrificed with so much facility all the resources of the nation, and which, after having placed it for an instant on the perilous summit of the European pyramid, was on the eve of excavating for it a vast tomb beneath the foundations of this monstrous pedestal.

Such are the terrible reprisals of the masses against those who have abused their confidence for the purpose of enticing them into crooked paths wherein nought but ruin is to be expected. In face of such calamities, what course, it may be asked, was the preacher to pursue? To make Christian truths palatable to a congregation so completely pre-occupied with the stirring events of the day, it was necessary that he should, along with the warnings addressed to his flock in general, introduce some harsh but necessary truths for kings. To hearts ulcerated by the spectacle of their country's abasement, it was not altogether un-profitable to offer some of those consolations which the enlarged spirit of the Christian religion does not condemn. Thus, although the ' Grands Sermons ' of the rival of Bourdaloue be, in our opinion, the most solid foundation of his fame in the eyes of posterity, his ' Petit Carême,' preached before the youthful

Louis XV., was his principal title to the high degree of popularity he enjoyed among his contemporaries. It is this abridged course of morality for the use of princes which acquired for Massillon the favour of the entire philosophical school of the eighteenth century. It cannot be denied that the political doctrines of Voltaire, and even of Rousseau, approached, in many points, those of the Bishop of Clermont ; and when we compare the most vigorous passages of Bourdaloue upon the ambition of the great with some of those of Massillon, we might readily imagine that an abyss of several centuries separated these two illustrious preachers. The first restricts himself to general reflections, whose end is rather to ameliorate the lot of individuals than to change the bases of society ; he depicts, in the most striking terms, the ravages which the unbridled lust of wealth and honours produces in the human heart. The most jealous despotism, however, could give in a free adhesion to the sentiments of Bourdaloue without in anywise being deeply moved by them ; the duties of governors towards their subjects are but lightly and vaguely touched on, while, on the other hand, purely moral subjects are treated with depth and plenitude. He always carefully eludes those social questions which in the following century so seriously occupied men's minds. Massillon, equally with Fenelon, is one of the links connecting two memorable epochs, between which, though in appearance so hostile, it would be possible to trace many mysterious affinities. Sincerely attached to the Christian belief, he follows its precepts with scrupulous exactness ; he never yields in any way to the anti-religious influence of his times ; and we find him deploring the progress of scepticism and infidelity in accents of sadness we might imagine borrowed from Bossuet. To raise the slightest doubt upon the sincerity of Massillon would be to calumniate his memory ; in that point he belonged wholly to the seventeenth century, to that century wherein theological discussions excited so lively an interest even among the most worldly-minded ; but he was irresistibly drawn towards those doctrines of civil liberty and religious tolerance which Fenelon so thoroughly understood, and to the support of which a powerful phalanx of philosophers were destined to lend the charms of eloquence and the evidence of reason.

If we have, in the foregoing pages, clearly expressed our thoughts, the reader will now be enabled to comprehend the two, if not diametrically opposite, at least different, tendencies, by which the genius of Massillon was swayed ; he can also form a just idea of the innovations which were introduced by him into the general plan and arrangement of his sermons. Intimately acquainted with the most secret recesses of the human heart, he could, like Bourdaloue, confine himself to the vast field of the moral virtues, and certainly he has given more than one striking proof of the incontestable superiority he possessed in unmasking the passions, and laying bare their most deceptive artifices. He evidently did not seek to dwell on political considerations in order to appeal to the known sympathies of his congregation; by so doing he would have lowered the sacred ministry with which he was invested to the coarse combinations of a mundane rhetoric.

respect to the false delicacy
of divine truths he should
necessary, their most susceptible propensities.
of com-
manding respect
words — how
unpalatable soever
t fall from his
lips. He has no
turnings and
windings of a lab
order to sur-
as it were,
by means of

and minutely studied in the schools of Greece. Above before all things, the minister of God, with the Bible of truth in his hand, and the word of truth on his lips, should proceed directly to the end he has in view; undeterred by a false delicacy for the worldly ideas and prejudices of his congregation, he should not recoil before the obligation—a sacred one confided to him,—of severely condemning the violations of that holy law of which he is at once the minister and the expounder.

Massillon quailed not before this task; unwittingly, perhaps, he expressed the ideas which circulated in the atmosphere of his time. In clothing these ideas in a religious garb, he imagined he but performed his duty. Thus the impression experienced therefrom had that character of depth and profundity which constitutes the conviction of the orator. Massillon followed the torrent of his country in politics, while strenuously opposing the sceptical and anti-religious feeling which was now beginning to gain head in France. The unrelenting adversary of the Oriental despotism so energetically prescribed by Louis XIV., it was with profound disgust that he was a witness of the degrading and shameless excesses of the short, but most inglorious Regency. As a Christian, also, he could not but shudder at the aspect of unbridled licentiousness which, like some impure inundation, swept over the whole of France during the deplorable reign of Louis XV.—that king who may truly be said to have passed his life in the mire of sensuality. Provoked by the monstrous abuses, as well as the utter and open disregard of Christianity—its outward forms and mummeries only excepted

—which on every side met his eye, the great soul of Massillon overflowed with sublime anger; and more than once
did the sweet-toned and harmonious voice of the orator rise to
the inspired accents of the ancient prophets, when, scandalized at
the idolatries of the Israelites, they poured forth in words of fire
the denunciations of an offended God.    There were here certainly new and striking elements to introduce into the pulpit-
eloquence of the day, and the admirers of Bourdaloue could not
fail of being astonished at the promulgation of doctrines as yet
so new to them.    But the Bishop of Clermont possessed, in
addition, qualities which his predecessor had but timidly
developed, though successfully cultivated by certain Fathers of
the Church.    Born in Provence, he was, like almost all its inhabitants, endowed with one of those lively and fertile imaginations which impart the richest colours to objects, in appearance
the dullest and least attractive.    A profound study of the Scriptures, the exquisite poetry of which had made a deep and lasting
impression on his mind, had also contributed, in a great measure,
to favour the growth of this faculty, which in him possessed a
prodigious natural power.

It must, however, be remarked that the *Folle du logis,* as
quaint old Montaigne styles the imaginative portion of our
human organization, subjected itself, with a very good grace, to
the sound good sense of this admirable orator ; so that, far from
destroying the logical evolution of ideas, it showed them all the
brighter, from the illumination it cast upon them ; it enriched
the discourse without destroying the majestic whole.    The gems
and precious metals which it, as it were, wove into the learned
tissue of the argument, refreshed, but never misled, the attention
of the congregation; the regularity of the edifice never disappeared beneath the magnificence of the ornaments with which
it had been so ingeniously decked.    It was a parterre studded
with a profusion of the most variously-tinted flowers, but whose
clearly-defined limits ever presented a harmonious symmetry to
the spectator's eye.

To adorn the thought is not to paint it, but, on the contrary,
to illumine and better display it under its various aspects.    We
are ready to admit that an image, *per se,* brilliant and pompous
though it be, is nothing better than vain phosphorescence, if
it serve neither to explain nor embellish an idea.    To multiply
useless comparisons, for the mere purpose of dazzling his reader,
is, at best, but a coquetry of art, the sterile advantages of
which no serious writer should, for an instant, be ambitious of
possessing.    Let us leave kaleidoscopes to children ; the only
playthings fitted for men are, the plough which turns the
earth, the compass which guides the mariner on his ocean-

path, and the pen which consigns to immortality useful thoughts or ennobling sentiments. We altogether condemn those species of literary fireworks, which, though they may dazzle for the moment, leave behind them only a cloud of empty, and not infrequently noisome, smoke, while serving but to exhaust, for no good end, the most precious faculties of the mind. But, on the other hand, to the mathematicians who would reduce literary style to the dryness of algebraic formulæ, we have one reply to make: we defy them to write three consecutive phrases without a recurrence to metaphors—old or new—in order to render their idea comprehensible to their readers. Were we perfectly pure spirits, it is very probable that an entirely abstract language would suffice us; but we are, unfortunately, so overlaid with matter that we grasp with ease only what we can touch and see. Our intellect promptly and surely fulfils its functions only when aided by the concurrence of the organs. So true is this, that many superior men have considered that the best methods of instruction were those which bestowed a tangible form even upon metaphysical ideas. Without adopting these exaggerated theories, the offspring of the spirit of system, we yet believe and maintain that it is impossible either to think, write, or speak, without the aid of images. We have occupied ourselves hitherto with the philosophical side of the question only; if we look at the literary side we shall find a thousand arguments to justify the employment of metaphor. But though many similes have fallen into disrepute, and while others, in these stirring and troublous times, would be considered childish and paltry, the effect of brilliant metaphor skilfully employed, observable in the works of several modern writers, clearly proves that it is not the imagination which is discredited by the prosaic utilitarianism of the age, but certain images either too common-place or else too frequently repeated.

In perusing the writings of Massillon we are, above all, struck with the happy abundance of images which we find interlaced round profound truths, like graceful flowers twining round the knotty trunk of the oak. Rarely do the comparisons which he makes use of fail of that clearness and purity which the severe taste of the seventeenth century, above all things, imperiously exacted. The figures employed by him may be considered as ingenious similitudes of thoughts embellished with all the riches of elocution. He never seeks to produce artificial effects by a puerile contrast of words; it is the ideas which, in his fruitful brain, are attracted by common affinities, and thus give birth to views at once the most just, clear, and brilliant. Very different from the writers and poets of his time, who, for the most part, contented themselves with merely turning over the surface

of things in search of hidden treasure, Massillon went straight
to the heart of the questions he had to treat; he submitted
them to a patient and searching analysis, and when he had
thoroughly decomposed their most tenacious particles, he collected them into a body as solid as it was majestic.   Like a
skilful sculptor he would carefully reduce the marble he had
to elaborate, and the lines of the statue, once designed with
methodical exactness, he would smooth away all angles, and
endow with grace and expression the hitherto mute and shape-
less block.   In a word, Massillon never moved the imagination
of his auditors until he had first of all fertilized their intellect.
He reasoned first; his energetic picture seemed but as a framework for larger discussions; while a close and convincing logic
was crowned with the most harmonious ideas.   In this respect,
Massillon is incontestably superior to Bourdaloue.

In the writings of the Fathers of the Christian Church we find a
poetry quite as rich, if not richer, than that with which the Bishop
of Clermont ornamented his gravest dissertations.   St. Chrysos-
tom has shed over his style all the splendours of the East ;
Massillon himself never displayed a more magnificent profusion
of graceful and powerful images.   There is, however, one point
on which he had no equal : none could like him touch the more
delicate fibres of the heart; he moves and persuades even when
apparently one would suppose he sought but· to convince ; he
inspires sympathy as well as admiration ; and, on laying down
the book, we often ask ourselves if we have yielded to the irresistible evidence of reason, or to the burning effusions of deep
sensibility.

The Christian minister must not truckle to the passions of his
hearers, neither can he make any concessions to their weaknesses
or deviations.   The interpreter of divine truth would strangely
misunderstand his duty, were he to make use of the time-serving
arms and figures which the political or forensic orator is permitted to employ; firm and immovable in his convictions, he
must ' speak the truth with all boldness,' heedless of the angry
words or bitter speeches to which his discourse may give rise;
yet, without relaxing anything of the severity of his mission, it
is in his power to lead back many lost sheep to the fold by the
employment of those gentle and persuasive means which seldom
fail to induce all hearts to draw near in praise and prayer to their
Lord and Maker.   Gentleness is a secret power which at once
disarms and attracts the most refractory, and which moderates
their opposition even when it does not altogether triumph over
their will.   Now Massillon united these two qualities in an
eminent degree :—while, on the one hand, the thunders of his
eloquence, when threatening the wrath of God on the impeni-

tent, struck terror to the hearts of the most hardened, nothing, on the other, could equal the irresistible sweetness of his voice when it modulated tenderer sentiments—when it sought to bless, and not to curse, to reassure, and not to affright. The tenderest mother could not find in her heart words more kind, more sweet, more persuasive, than those which then flowed from the lips of Massillon. He was incontestably the most pathetic of the pulpit-orators of the day. The true Evangelical sweetness and gentleness seemed to have passed into his discourse, imparting to it an invincible charm which none could resist. All the faculties in this beautiful organization concurred harmoniously to the same end; the ideas were in accord with the sentiments, while the heart, in its most unexpected movements, obeyed the wise direction of the mind.*

Born at Hyères, in Provence, Massillon, early in life, entered the congregation of the Oratory, and soon devoted himself entirely to pulpit oratory. His ' Grands Sermons,' his ' Petit Carême,' his ' Paraphrases sur les Psaumes,' and his ' Conferences,' are finished models of style, which will ever be perused with delight by every admirer of what is really good in French literature. Appointed Bishop of Clermont, he gave himself up entirely to the performance of his episcopal duties with a truly Christian humility. The recollection of several examples of his benevolence of character have been preserved, which prove that he knew how to preach by example as well as by word of mouth—by practice as well as by precept. He died in 1742, at the age of seventy-nine, universally regretted both by rich and poor.

One word, in conclusion, upon the respective merits of the two eminent men whose lives and works we have been considering.

In the seventeenth century, Bourdaloue was generally considered the first preacher of France; the critics opposed to him

* As illustrative of the wonderful power exercised by Massillon upon his congregation, Voltaire relates, that during the delivery of his celebrated sermon upon the *Small Number of the Elect*, a sort of transport seemed, as it were, to seize upon the congregation, and almost every one in the church half rose by a sort of involuntary impulse; the movement of acclamation and surprise was so marked, that it seriously disturbed the preacher; and this evident nervousness served but to augment the pathos of the discourse. Rollin relates, that having taken some of the students of the College of Beauvais to hear one of Massillon's sermons, they returned so profoundly touched that, during several weeks, reflection replaced amusement throughout the whole school; not a duty was neglected, not a single fault committed, nor was there a dispute raised even among the most undisciplined. To touch deeply a youthful heart is not difficult; but to produce upon it a lasting impression, is an achievement only to be attained by the most penetrating and persuasive eloquence—such was the eloquence of Massillon.

neither Bossuet, nor Fenelon, who extemporized with wonderful
facility and penetrating unction, nor even Massillon, his successor in the public favour. The eagle of Meaux, as Bossuet was
termed, said of him, ' *Il est notre maître à tous ;*' and competent
judges have ever maintained him in the elevated rank assigned
him by his contemporaries. Even those who allowed themselves
to be captivated by the more harmonious forms of Massillon's
eloquence, scarcely dared to place the latter above his rival.
It has been said of Bourdaloue that, although he represents,
by the correctness of his proportions, the beauty of his arrangement, and the exactitude of his development, the perfection of
the highest class of the pulpit eloquence of his country, yet,
when read at the present day, with all his healthy, solid
qualities, he wearies. To this we cannot altogether agree. It
is true that Bourdaloue may be wanting in invention of detail
and richness of expression, yet if we take the trouble to study
him deeply and closely, we shall discover in his writings the
highest merits; pure, lofty, and ennobling thoughts expressed
in language at once correct and elegant, never overladen with
vain epithets, nor false though sparkling brilliancies; are the attributes of his discourses. We shall not certainly find even in his
best pages that lofty audacity of Bossuet which despotically
moulded the idiom of his native tongue to the sometimes
arbitrary exigencies of his genius; it was rather upon the
groundwork of his subject than upon the form in which he could
best place it before his hearers, that Bourdaloue loved to dwell;
he occupied himself with the ordinance and grandeur of the
*idea* more than with the beauty of the *expression*. If Bourdaloue
is not one of the authors who have contributed most towards
the enrichment of the idiom of his native language, on the other
hand he is one of those who have the least outraged it. His
simple, modest, and unaffected eloquence scarcely ever sins
through those glaring defects so frequently perceptible in the
best pages of Bossuet and La Bruyere—writers whose originality
but ill accommodated itself to the least rigorous rules of grammar.
He accepts without difficulty the results of the philological labours
of his time, and thus composes for himself a language which,
though astonishing often by magnificent alliances of words, and
by oppositions and comparisons the most unexpected, rarely if
ever wounds either good taste or syntax. We admit that the
writings of Bourdaloue are much less read in France at the present day than those of his great rival, the Bishop of Clermont,
but this is easily accounted for. To the generality of readers
Massillon is a more captivating writer than Bourdaloue, simply
from the possession of those qualities already described, which
find so ready a response in almost every breast; he addresses

the feelings rather than the understanding, the heart rather than the head, and hence his success.   The diction of Massillon is in general pure, elegant, and harmonious, sometimes even to a fault; he has been reproached for a too frequent repetition of the same thought under different forms; yet this defect, if defect it be—an assertion we are rather inclined to doubt—is less to be condemned in an orator than in a writer, and we must bear in mind that it was for pulpit delivery, rather than for closet perusal, that Massillon's sermons were composed.   An audience, however enlightened it may be, requires an idea to be fully developed in order to its being thoroughly understood.   Even when the idea has been clearly comprehended, it likes to have it represented under a new aspect; by these means it is more deeply engraven in the mind, while possessing, moreover, the further advantage of better demonstrating the general connexion of the discourse.

Here we bring our task to a close.   We have endeavoured in the foregoing pages to lay before our readers a brief sketch of the lives and writings of the two greatest ornaments of the French pulpit in the seventeenth century.   A severe critic of the French language might, it is true, discover flaws in the style and language of both these eminent preachers, but it is far from our purpose to descend to such criticism; in so doing we should but parade the vain glory of the self-sufficient pedant.

---

ART. III.—*Poems, by Elizabeth Barrett Browning.*   New Edition, in Two Vols.   London: Chapman and Hall.   1850.

MRS. BROWNING has presented us with her collected poems, in two compact and yet handsome volumes, so that we have all her productions at once before us in a very convenient and inexpensive form.   We are thus enabled to compare her writings at all points of her progress, and to take a comprehensive view of their lights and shadows, and of the real character and strength of her genius. The result, as a whole, is highly favourable; and we are glad to be in possession of a work of a living authoress, which abounds so with splendid poetry, with evidences of profound thought, and with a pervading spirit so pure and so womanly. At the same time, we do not mean to represent this collection as faultless; it would have been much the better for a degree of

stern selection.   There are various poems which are of comparatively little merit, which are written on trivial subjects, and only
tend to dilute the collection as a whole ; and, what was least to be
expected, these are chiefly met with in the last volume.   Such
poems as ' The Deserted Garden ;' 'Hector in the Garden ;' ' A
Lay of the Early Rose ;' 'A Flower in a Letter ;' and ' The Pet
Name ;' would do very well for an annual ; but we pass them
over impatiently amongst such things as 'Lady Geraldine's Courtship ;' ' The Rhyme of the Duchess May ;' ' The Cry of the
Children ;' ' The Cry of the Human ;' or the fine ' Drama of
Exile.'   Many of these poems that we speak of are drawn out to
a most unconscionable length, totally disproportionate to the
value of the subject or the amount of thought expended upon it.
' The Lost Bower,' for instance, consists of no less than seventy-
four stanzas ; the whole burthen being, that the authoress, going
into a wood, finds a sort of natural bower under a lime-tree, and
never can find it again.

We note these as defects in the volumes, but by no means such
as to prevent the whole being a very noble and delightful one ;
yet, at the same time, tending to lower that idea of the authoress's
greatness which would have followed a more exclusive perusal
of such truly masterly productions as those we have alluded to.
While we are looking on the shadow side of Mrs. Browning's
genius, we must, in strict justice, also, note that affected quaint-
ness which disfigures a great number of her best performances,
and often induces her to use terms which are utter nonsense.   In
' The Lost Bower' occur such stanzas as these :—

> ' As I entered, mosses hushing,
>    Stole all noises from my foot ;
>    And a green elastic cushion,
>    Clasped within the linden's root,
> Took me in a chair of silence, very rare and *absolute*.'

Why so *absolute* a chair ?   Because it is quaint, and rhymes.
Again, in ' The Vision of Poets,' we are treated to such stanzas
as these, as descriptive of particular poets :—

> ' And Burns, with *pungent passionings*
>    Set in his eyes.   Deep lyric springs
>    Are of the *fire-mount's issuings*.

> ' And Shelley, in his *white ideal*,
>    All statue blind : and Keats, the real
>    *Adonis*, with the hymeneal

> ' Fresh, vernal buds half-sunk between
>    His youthful curls, kissed straight and sheen
>    *In his Rome-grave, by Venus queen*.

> ' And poor, proud Byron,—sad as grave,
>   And salt as life ; forlornly brave,
>   And quivering with the dart he drave.

> ' And visionary Coleridge, who
>   Did sweep his thoughts as angels do
>   Their wings, *with cadence up the Blue.*'—Vol. i. p. 220.

Angels ' sweeping their wings *with cadence* up' the Blue,' must be pronounced more fantastically visionary than Coleridge himself. These passages, here and there, betray rather a straining after the sublime, which does not succeed, than a reliance on the simple power which Mrs. Browning really possesses. It must strike the reader, too, that in one portion of these volumes she has been deeply infected by that imitation of Tennyson—perhaps unconsciously—which has spread itself so provokingly amongst our younger poets. ' The Lost Bower' is full of it. ' The Vision of Poets' is still more so ; and ' The Romaunt of Margaret' is of the same borrowed character. We are delighted with the music of Tennyson's own poetry, but we would wish it to remain his ; writers of real genius who echo it, do it to their loss ; and we rejoice to perceive that, as Mrs. Browning proceeds, she gradually regains her own character. That character is one of peculiar beauty and earnestness. It is full of tenderest pathos, the most graceful fancy, and an imagination capable of reaching the heights and depths of the profoundest thought. ' The Drama of Exile,' or the banishment of Adam and Eve, shows Mrs. Browning to possess dramatic talent of the highest stamp. After Milton and Byron, the attempt was a bold one ; but it is amply justified by its originality, by the masculine vigour of intellect, and the grave mastership of the language ; while the character of Eve, drawn by a woman's hand, is pre-eminently beautiful. There is none of the impiety of Byron, nor of the recriminating spirit in the fallen pair which we have in Milton ; they are fallen, but not so low as to weaken their love and trust in each other. There is something fantastic in the spirits of the zodiac presenting themselves in the way of the flying pair, but again the spirits of the earth, whom their transgression has plunged into trouble and dissonance, opposing and accusing them, and having no pity on them, till softened by the appearance and tender sentiments of the Saviour—has something very fine and original in it :—

> "*Eve*— ' They wail, beloved !  They speak of glory and God,
>     And they wail—wail !  That burden of the song
>     Drops from it like its fruit, and heavily falls
>     Into the lap of silence !'

> '*Adam*—
>     ' Hark again !'

' *First Spirit*—
  ' I was so beautiful, so beautiful !
    My joy stood up within me bold and glad,
  To answer God—and when his work was full,
    To " very good," responded " very glad !"
  Filtered through roses, did the light enclose me,
  And bunches of the grape swam blue across me—
                Yet I wail !'

' *Second Spirit.*—
  ' I bounded with my panthers ! I rejoiced
    In my young tumbling lions rolled together !
  My stag—the river at his fetlocks—poised,
    Then dipped his antlers through the golden weather.
  In the same ripple which the alligator
  Left in his joyous tumbling of the water—
                Yet I wail !

' *First Spirit.*—
  ' O my deep waters, cataract and flood,—
    What wordless triumph did your voices render !
  O mountain-summits, where the angels stood
    And shook from head and wing thick dews of splendour !
  How with a holy quiet did your earthy
  Accept the heavenly—knowing ye were worthy !
                Yet I wail.

' *Second Spirit.*—
  ' O my wild wood-dogs, with your listening eyes !
    My horses—my ground-eagles, for swift fleeing !
  My birds with viewless wings of harmonies—
    My calm, cold fishes of a silver being,—
  How happy were ye, living and possessing
  O fair half-souls, capacious of full blessing.
                Yet I wail !

' *First Spirit.*—
  ' I wail, I wail !   Now hear my charge to-day
    Thou man, thou woman, marked as the misdoers,
  By God's sword at your backs !   I lent my clay
    To make your bodies, which had grown more flowers :
  And now in change for what I lent, ye give me
  The thorn to vex, the tempest fire to cleave me—
                And I wail !  '—Vol. i. p. 44.

The  translation of the ' Prometheus Bound ' of Æschylus, in
the same volume, is a noble achievement from the hand of a
lady, and, indeed, the evidences of a solid classical scholarship
abound in these volumes.   But we turn from proofs of learning,
however honourable, to the proofs of native genius, and that
dedicated to the highest purposes, with a satisfaction the more
profound because they are here pre-eminently noble.   First, we
would call the reader's attention to two superb sonnets, addressed
to that eccentric and, from the splendour of her talents, unfortu-

nately, very mischievous, writer, Madame Dudevant, and which
so favourably contrast the English female authoress with the
French one.

### 'To George Sand.
#### (*A Desire.*)

'Thou large-brained woman, and large-hearted man,
  Self-called George Sand! whose soul, amid the lions
Of thy tumultuous senses, moans defiance,
  And answers roar for roar, as spirits can:
I would some wild miraculous thunder ran
  Above the applauded circus, in appliance
Of thine own noble nature's strength and science,—
  Drawing two pinions, white as wings of swan,
From thy strong shoulders, to amaze the place
  With holier light!   That thou to woman's claim
And man's, might join besides the angel's grace
  Of a pure genius sanctified from blame;
Till child and maiden pressed to thy embrace,
  To kiss upon thy lips a stainless fame.

### 'To George Sand.
#### (*A Recognition.*)

' True genius, but true woman! dost deny
  Thy woman's nature with a manly scorn,
And break away the guards and armlets worn
  By weaker woman in captivity?
Ah, vain denial! that revolted cry
  Is sobbed in by a woman's voice forlorn :—
Thy woman's hair, my sister, all unshorn,
  Flouts back dishevelled strength in agony,
Disproving thy man's name : and while before
  The world, thou burnest in a poet-fire,
We see thy woman-heart beat evermore
  Through the large flame.   Beat purer heart, and higher,
Till God unsex thee on the heavenly shore,
  Where unincarnate spirits purely aspire.'—Vol. i. p. 346.

'The Romaunt of the Page,' 'The Lay of the Brown
Rosary,' and ' The Rhyme of the Duchess May,' with which
the second volume of these poems opens, are all poetic romances
of the middle ages, told with singular power and harmony of
diction ; but this volume is, indeed, amazingly rich in its contents,
and the next piece, ' Bertha in the Lane,' a tribute to the noble
disinterestedness of woman, is unrivalled in its pathetic beauty.
A betrothed damsel, while wandering in the summer lanes, over-
hears her betrothed lover confessing to her sister Bertha, that she
it is that he really loves—his betrothed ' has all his esteem.' The
triumph of the poem is the exquisite manner, so simple, and so

full of feeling, in which it describes the triumph of the heart
which has made this woful discovery over all its own wishes,
and the heroic strength with which it secures the sister's happiness at the risk of its own life.   The very next poem, 'Lady
Geraldine's Courtship,' is a triumph of another sort.   It has evidently been suggested by Tennyson's 'Locksley Hall,' it is no
imitation however, but a rivalry.   It attempts to describe a noble
woman, as Tennyson has described, a weak one, yielding to conventional convenience.   The hero in this case is a poet of
peasant origin, and the heroine, a lady, not only of high beauty
and accomplishment, but of very elevated rank.

'There's a lady—an earl's daughter; she is proud and she is noble,
 And she treads the crimson carpet, and she breathes the perfumed air;
And a kingly blood sends glances up her princely eye to trouble,
 And the shadow of a monarch's crown is softened in her hair.

'She has halls and she has castles, and the resonant steam-eagles
 Follow far on the direction of her little dove-like hand—
Trailing on a thunderous vapour underneath the starry vigils,
 So to mark upon the blasted heaven, the measure of her land.

'There are none of England's daughters who can show a prouder
     presence;
 Upon princely suitors suing, she has looked in her disdain:
She was sprung of English nobles, I was born of English peasants;
 What was *I* that I should love her—save for feeling of the pain?

'I was only a poor poet, made for singing at her casement,
 As the finches or the thrushes, while she thought of other things.
Oh she walked so high above me, she appeared, to my abasement
 In her lovely silken manner, like an angel clad in wings!

'Many vassals bow before her, as her chariot sweeps their door-ways;
 She hath blessed their little children—as a priest or queen were she!
Far too tender, or too cruel far, her smile upon the poor was,
 For I thought it was the same smile which she used to smile on *me*.

'She has voters in the Commons, she has lovers in the palace,
 And of all the fair court-ladies, few have jewels half as fine;
Even the prince has named her beauty, 'twixt the red wine and the
     chalice;
 Oh, and what was *I* to love her? my beloved, my Geraldine!

'Yet I could not choose but love her; I was born to poet-uses—
 To love all set above me, all of good and all of fair.
Nymphs of the mountain, not of valley, we are wont to call the Muses,
 And in nympholeptic climbing, poets pass from mount to star.

'And because I was a poet, and because the public praised me,
 With their critical deductions, for the modern writer's fault,
I could sit at rich men's tables, though the courtesies that raised me,
 Still suggested clear between us, the pale spectrum of the salt.

'And they praised me in her presence—" Will your book appear this
summer ?"
Then returning to each other—" Yes, our plans are for the moors ;"
Then with whisper dropped behind me—" There he is ! the last
new-comer !
Oh, she only likes his verses        is o'    she    (

' Quite low-born! self-educated !  ᵢ    ,   t gif              by nature—
And we make a point of ask      ɴᵢɪ  -  b   g
You may speak, he does not he     ,     ;         ne               —
These new charmers who keep  ʙ      ,s nave      anti(   ᵢ
resigned."

' I grew scornfuller, grew cold    as I stood up there among them—
Till as frost intense will b      you, the cold scorning scorched my
brow;
When a sudden silver speakin    ɪ
And a sudden silken stirrin          my

' I looked upward and beheld l      With a   ᵢ ᵢ   'e|
Slowly round she swept her e      ᵢ        :
" Have you such superfluous h      ,    ᵢ
You will come down, Mr. B٤      ᵢ                          '.
—᷾      p.

So writes the poet from Wycombe Hall to a friend. The
visit there, the description of the place, with its grand old
rooms, its gardens, its woods, its fountains and lakes—the
aristocratic company, and the way in which the time was passed—
wandering in the grounds, or seated in the library with talk of
poetry and poets, of life and of books, while the more jovial
were out after the hounds—the flocking round the lady hostess
of proud suitors, the poor poet's passion, his outburst of indignation when he thinks that his feelings have been sported with by
the noble fair one—and the charming *denouement* which this produces—are all sketched with a brave hand, and form one of the
most charming and finely-elaborated poems in the language.
There is such a noble nature in the noble and beautiful woman,
and the author has left you so uncertain of the turn which things
will take till the last moment—whether we are to have a
fascinating intellectual syren, or a true-hearted maiden—that the
effect is indescribably delightful.

But fine as this is, there are poems following still finer.
They are steeped in the strongest and tenderest sympathies of
humanity. They are called all warm from the heart by the
miseries that haunt the daily walks of life—the deeds of base
oppression—the lash and manacle of the tyrant—the grinding of
the bones and sinews of children to make us bread. 'The
Runaway Slave at Pilgrim's Point' is a passionate and trenchant
denunciation of American slavery. The author seizes on the

antithesis of the landing of the Pilgrim Fathers to make the
wrongs of the captive negro-women tell with terrible effect.

'I stand on the mark beside the shore
    Of the first white pilgrim's bended knee,
Where exile turned to ancestor,
    And God was thanked for liberty.
I have run through the night, my skin is dark,
I bend my knee down on this mark—
    I look on sea and sky.

'O pilgrim-souls I speak to you !
    I see you come out proud and slow
From the land of the spirits pale as dew—
    And round and round me ye go !
O pilgrims! I have gasped and run
All night long from the whips of one
    Who, in your names, works sin and woe.

'And thus I thought that I would come
    And kneel here where I knelt before,
And feel your souls around me hum
    In undertone to the ocean's roar ;
And lift my black face, my black hand,
Here, in your names, to curse this land,
    Ye blessed in freedom's evermore.

'I am black, I am black ;
    And yet God made me, they say.
But if He did so, smiling back,
    He must have cast his work away
Under the feet of his white creatures,
With a look of scorn—that the dusky features
    Might be trodden again to clay.

'And yet He has made dark things
    To be glad and merry as light.
There's a little blackbird, sits and sings ;
    There's a dark stream ripples out of sight ;
And the dark frogs chant in the safe morass,
And the sweetest stars are made to pass
    O'er the face of the darkest night.

'But *we* who are dark, we are dark !
    Ah, God, we have no stars !
About our souls in care and cark
    Our blackness shuts like prison-bars ;
The poor souls crouch so far behind,
That never a comfort can they find
    By reaching through the prison-bars.'—Vol. ii. p. 129.

But we must not indulge in further witness of the wild grief
of the unhappy black woman; our space reminds us that we
must draw to a close, which we do with regret.

Whatever may be the eccentricities of style in which Mrs. Browning indulges, or the colours and tones which she may catch from others in passing, she never departs from the sacred sense of her mission. With her, poetry is a high art exercised for a high purpose—the soothing and encouraging of afflicted humanity. This pervades all her writings. Their ideal is not more lofty than their moral character. Though residing in Italy her spirit is essentially English. There is not a touch of foreign sentiment, nor a trace of foreign manner. Her verses might be composed in an English library or under the green oaks of an English park. If we may judge by the tone and spirit of Mr. Browning's last work, her influence is as much felt and as persuasively operative in its deep religious tone by her own hearth as in her published volumes. Of these we trust that we shall yet receive many more, for we can point to none of our female writers who, combining solemn purpose with large intellect and the same intensity of imagination, are more fitted to make a truly beneficial impression on their age, while they are delighting it by the beauty of their thoughts and the music of their numbers.

---

ART. IV.—*History of Ancient Art among the Greeks. Translated from the German of John Winckelmann.* 8vo. By G. H. Lodge. London: John Chapman.

AMONG the nations of antiquity, the Greeks were not only the most refined and civilized, but also the most reflective and learned. They occupied the most exalted position in every branch of art and science. They were great as philosophers and legislators, poets and moralists, and were unsurpassed as orators, and as admirers and cultivators of whatever is sublime and beautiful. If ancient Greece boasted of the most eminent statesmen, philosophers, and poets, it boasted no less of its artists—sculptors in particular. With this gifted people, sculpture, as, indeed, art generally, was something more than a mere mechanical pursuit. It was here, but chiefly in sculpture, that the Greek conceptions of sublime and glowing fancies were embodied in the productions of what may justly be termed a race of inspired artists. Whatever were the causes which favoured the display of the wonderful genius of the ancient Greek sculptors—whether their superiority was owing to a fine and brilliant climate, as Winckelmann and others assert, or to the prevalence of beautiful forms; or, finally, to the various public exercises that were so general in ancient Greece—it is an undisputed fact, that as for heroic and dramatic poetry, philosophy, and oratory, so also for sculpture, they are unrivalled. Nevertheless, it would be wrong to suppose that whatever is excellent and beautiful in Greek sculpture was purely owing to the accidents just enumerated, as we shall endeavour to show presently. The perfection of Greek sculpture was owing, in a very great measure, to a totally different circumstance. They made Nature, in her fairest and most perfect forms, their model, and acting on the knowledge thus obtained, their productions were similar to their great exemplar. In this circumstance we discover the secret of the superiority of their schools. While the Persians, the Egyptians, the Etruscans, and even the Romans, were confined within a very limited circle, the Greeks attained the utmost excellency possible to human knowledge. While sculpture in Egypt was no better than monstrous ideas made visible in monstrous forms, that of Greece was an embodiment of whatever was sublime, beautiful, and noble. But even in Etruscan and Roman art, how much is owing to Greek influence—to a connexion which at one time or other existed between Etruria, Rome, and Greece? Little originality and beauty of conception may be traced in either of the former. Indeed, it may safely be said, that both the Romans and the Etruscans were, to a considerable extent, mere imitators of the Greeks, and altogether indebted to them for the possession of a knowledge of this art. Hence art with them never advanced beyond certain limits. Their art, like that of the ancient Persians, is a mere inanimate and lifeless representation of objects, without that elevation of sentiment which distinguishes and spreads an indescribable charm over Hellenic art. For, inasmuch as it rose in Greece, superior to all those prejudices which restricted its advancement elsewhere, it became something more than a merely mechanical pursuit.

We have said, that the secret of the superiority of the schools of Greece consisted in the Greeks making Nature their model. So true is this, that they had a law, we are told, which subjected artists to a fine if their works were inferior in beauty to the objects which they professed to imitate.* Nor were the habits of the Greek people, as has justly been said, less favourable to this natural sensibility to the charms of beautiful forms. Institutions of various kinds, in which the youthful mind was trained alike to scientific pursuits and the pleasures of life, were frequented by all classes, who were thus in the habit of seeing the

* S. Lessing, Laocoon, vol. ii. p. 12. Tren. De Pict., vol. ii. p. 4, and elsewhere.

human form in its various aspects and phases, draped or naked, in repose or in action.   So that while the disciple of art—the sculptor as well as the painter—was storing his mind with ideas of the beauty and capabilities of the human figure, the mere spectator was acquiring the knowledge which enabled him to become a competent judge of imitative art, whenever he met with it in the course of life.

Among the favourite institutions in Greece were the Gymnasia, in which young men were trained to take part in the public games, such as racing, fighting, wrestling, and so on. Great importance was attached to distinction in these games, and the education of the youth was, therefore, very strict and careful. No means were neglected to increase the elegance, strength, suppleness, and active powers of the body.   Now the artist, or, to speak more definitely, the sculptor, who, frequenting these institutions, had before him the finest forms which discipline and judicious training could produce, naturally benefited by such an exhibition.   The small head, thick neck, deep and spacious chest, the broad shoulders, and the sinewy and well-knit frame, of the wrestler, suggested the elements of a Hercules ; the clean legs, small, well-knit joints, and light proportions, of the victor in the foot-race, furnished the form of Hermes, or Mercury ; while the union of strength and agility in the athletæ formed the primary foundation of the statues of gods, demigods, and heroes, in which Greek history as well as mythology abounds.

The same rule also applies to the embodiment of female beauty ;  not that ancient Greece was favoured before other nations in this respect.   It would be easy to prove that this was not the case ; but wherever female beauty *was* found, it was sure to form the material for the sculptor's inspiration.

Having thus access to the best models, the Greek sculptor inquired into their moral character, and by a union of the two, was enabled to embody those *ideal* beauties, which up to the present day constitute the main charm of Greek sculpture.   If to this be added the high purpose to which sculpture was applied in Greece, and the general interest that was felt in its productions —for, be it remembered, that that classic land had her critics as well as her philosophers and statesmen—we then shall understand the success with which this art was practised.   The mind of the sculptor was enlarged by reflection on the great objects of his labours.   Praise or profit was not found among the motives by which he was actuated.   ' He felt, and truly felt,' it is said, ' that his art, properly practised and rightly understood, was capable of producing great moral effects upon those who were to contemplate them, and, consequently, in the best period of Greek art, the appeal was always made to the higher feelings rather than the

mere senses.    The artist did not produce his works to gratify a·
patron—however different the case might have been in Rome—
but to improve a people ; and, whether they were destined for
the temple, the grove, the portico, or the place in which the
public games were celebrated ; whether, like the Jupiter of
Olympus, they were intended to excite religious impressions of
the majesty of the gods ; or, as in the *icones*, *i. e.* portrait statues,
in Altis, to stimulate the energy of the youths of Greece to
gain distinction in the public games—the sculptor .felt, and he
acquired power as he was impressed with the ennobling idea,
that he was contributing to a great end.    This is the principle
of the success of the arts in Greece; and in the presence or
absence of this recognition of the public utility of art, may be
discovered the causes of its comparative success or failure in the
other nations and in later times.'    It was this public expression
of its utility which gave rise to a Phidias, Praxiteles, Glaucias,
Onatas, Myron, Polycletus, Ageladas, and a host of other
immortal names, whose admirable creations have descended, in a
more or less perfect state, to posterity.

The foregoing remarks have been called forth by the nature
of the book before us, which is neither more nor less than a
*history of ancient art among the Greeks ;* and is, therefore,
something like a novelty, especially in these our days.    If to
this be added that the work is from the pen of one of the
greatest antiquarians and scholars of the age, it will be readily
concluded that it must be of no common order.    And so it is, in
spite of the peculiar view the author seems to take of Greece,
its inhabitants, form of mind and disposition, legislative institutions, &c.    However, as some of our readers may, perchance, be
unacquainted with the history and character of the writer, we
subjoin a brief account of his life, which we do the more willingly as it will form an illustration of the peculiar views expressed in the work under consideration ; and show, further,
how genius, although labouring under the most unfavourable
circumstances, will overcome every difficulty, and break in upon
the world in all its strength and beauty when least expected.

Johann Joachim Winckelmann, a native of Stendal, in
Prussia, was born in the year 1717.    Being of poor parentage,
his desire to study, for which he had early displayed an extraordinary disposition, could not be satisfied.    He was placed in the
Free-school of his native town, where he laboured with such
zeal, that in a very short time he rose to the top of the
school, and attracted the notice of his teachers, and, among the
rest, of the rector, or head-master, who, in consequence, took
him into his house, where he remained until 1735, when he
went to Berlin, and was admitted student of the Köllnische

Gymnasium.  Having spent two years in this place, he returned to Stendal, whence, in a short time, he set out for Halle, with the intention of devoting himself to the study of divinity.  Finding, however, that theology did not suit his inquiring and classical spirit, he entered, in the year 1741, on the situation of tutor in a private family, which he exchanged twelvemonths afterwards, for one at a place called Heimersleben, near Halberstadt, where he devoted himself to the study of universal history.  Owing to his great learning he was very soon appointed co-rector, or second head master of the school at Seehausen.  During the whole of this period, his biographers tell us, he seldom went to bed, as he was used to sleep on a bench, wrapped in a fur cloak (in which we often find him represented), devoting what time he could spare from four in the morning until twelve at night to the study of history and ancient literature.  Tired, however, of the miserable life he here led, he applied to Bünau, a German nobleman, who made him secretary of his library, at his seat, called Nöthenitz, near Dresden, with the munificent salary of twelve pounds sterling per annum: a situation which he gladly accepted, although he felt at the time that he was fitted for better things than reaching books from the shelves to some stray visitor, or writing for the librarian and his noble master.

Living thus in the neighbourhood of the capital of Saxony, and being attracted by its great and splendid picture-gallery, he frequently visited this place, grew acquainted with some of the leading artists of the day, and determined to become one himself.  Finding it, however, too late to apply practically to any of the arts, he resolved to devote himself to the study of their theory and history: a resolution to which he adhered most conscientiously; and which, in due season, bore most excellent fruits.  It was about this time that he made the acquaintance of a Monsignore Archinto, the Pope's Nuncio, who for some time resided at Nöthenitz, and, being struck with Winckelmann's great learning and universal acquirements, offered to procure him a situation in the Vatican library, or, at least, a pension, which would enable him to pursue his studies at Rome, provided he would renounce the faith of his fathers, and embrace the Romish creed.  This he did in 1754, in which year also he gave up his situation at Nöthenitz.  Of the *morale* of this recantation there can be no question.  It was of the lowest possible order, and exhibits Winckelmann in any other than a reputable light.

As the promised pension, without which he could not set out for Rome, was not forthcoming, he took up in the meantime his abode at Dresden, where he prosecuted his new studies with redoubled ardour, and the immediate result was a treatise entitled, 'Gedanken über die Nachahmung der Griechischen Kuntstwerke'; *i. e.* Reflections upon the Imitation of Greek works of Art; which he published in 1755. About this time the promised pension arrived from Rome, which, together with one granted him by the Elector of Saxony for two years, enabled him to set out for the Eternal City. Here he was presented to the Pope, Benedict XIV., and, in consequence, he soon became known to the leading members of the literary and scientific world at Rome, as well as to the most celebrated virtuosi of that place. About a year after his arrival in Rome, he published a new edition of the treatise above mentioned, together with others. He next undertook a journey to Naples, for the purpose of examining the remains of Herculaneum, Pompeii, and Pæstum, which then excited a general interest among the learned. It was about this time that he was engaged by Archinto, to arrange his library, who, with true Italian liberality, gave him for his trouble *free apartments,* but *no* salary. Soon afterwards he made a catalogue of the cabinet· of cameos and coins formerly belonging to a Baron Stosch, which was published under the title ' Description des Pierres gravées du feu Baron de Stosch': a task, which he executed at Florence. Cardinal Albani, a man of literary attainments and considerable eminence, now engaged him as librarian, and custos of his gallery of antiquities, with apartments free, and a monthly salary of ten scudi: a situation exactly suited to Winckelmann's tastes and habits, and which, with his pension from Dresden, enabled him to live comfortably in the pursuit of his interesting studies.

In 1763, he was appointed Antiquario della Camera Apostolica, with a monthly pay of fifteen scudi, and this, together with the fifty scudi allowed him per annum, by Cardinal Albani, as a retaining salary for the first vacancy in the Vatican library, was at that time considered a handsome income for a single person. The year previously he published his 'Anmerkungen über die Baukunst der Alten'; *i.e.* Remarks on the Architecture of the Ancients. It had been for some time his favourite wish to publish a history of ancient art, but his comparative poverty prevented him from doing so. Under existing circumstances, however, this wish of his was realized; so that there appeared at length his 'Geschichte der Kunst des Alterthums'; *i.e.* History of Ancient Art, which produced at the time a profound sensation. It made him known throughout Europe, and caused him to be elected member of most foreign, literary, and scientific societies. Together with this work he published his ' Sendschreiben über die Herculanischen Alterthümer'; *i.e.* A Letter on the Antiquities of Herculaneum; and ' Nachrichten von den neuesten

Herculanischen Entdeckungen,' Accounts of the most recent Discoveries made at Herculaneum. Two years later, there appeared his ' Monumenti Antichi Inediti,' with very numerous and most beautiful plates; and in 1767, his ' Anmerkungen zur Geschichte der Kunst'; *i. e.* Notes to the History of Art; which is a kind of supplement to his ' History of Ancient Art.'

After an absence of twelve years, he undertook a journey to his fatherland, in the course of which he lost his life in a tragical manner.   He had no sooner arrived in Germany, than finding, or fancying, that its climate did not agree with his health, he determined on an immediate return to his adopted country.   He was received with open arms and the utmost distinction, wherever he went, and the most advantageous overtures were made to him as an inducement to remain, but nothing could change his resolution; and he left Germany for Italy, arriving at Trieste in the beginning of June, 1768.   He was accompanied by an Italian of the name of Francesco Archangeli, formerly cook to the Count Cataldo, in Vienna. This fellow perceiving the simplicity of Winckelmann's character, gradually gained his confidence, and in an evil hour was shown a gold medal and other valuable presents which he had received during his brief stay in Germany. At Trieste, Winckelmann had to wait for a vessel which was to take him to Ancona.   Francesco Archangeli, however, anxious to possess the valuable things shown him by his unsuspecting companion, now came apparently to take leave, saying that urgent business called him to the Venetian States, and requesting of him, at the same time, as a particular favour, to show him once more the gold medal he had received in the capital of Austria. Winckelmann of course complied.   But while he was so doing, the Italian struck him with a knife in the belly, inflicting several wounds, in consequence of which he died in a few hours.   The assassin was immediately arrested.   But, although he paid with his life for the murder, this could not retrieve the irreparable loss sustained by Art.

Several editions of Winckelmann's complete works have been published under the superintendence of the most able men in Germany.   Some of them have been translated into the French, Italian, Russian, English, and other languages.

Let us now turn for a while to the volume before us, which the translator has chosen, ' because it treats,' he tells us, ' of *Greek* art, the monuments of which are far more numerous and interesting than those of any other nation, and because it presents a systematic exposition of the principles by which the author supposed the Greek artists to have been governed in the conception and conformation of those works which still stand the noblest creations of artistic genius, and about which the students and the lovers of beauty, grace, and majesty, still gather with admiration and reverence.'    (Translator's Preface.)

It is almost impossible to pass an opinion on the merits of this work, inasmuch as it is professedly a mere fragment, and a very small one too, of Winckelmann's 'History of Ancient Art,' which, besides the Greek art, embraces that of the Egyptians, Phœnicians, Etruscans, and other nations.    However, what little we have to say, we will say it in a candid and unbiassed manner.

That Winckelmann was well fitted for the task of writing a History of Ancient Art, no one will deny, who is acquainted with his profound learning and genius.    He was richly endowed with all the powers and elements which an undertaking of this kind requires.    Though not destined to be an artist himself, he undoubtedly possessed, in the highest degree, the power of appreciating artistic skill wherever it was met with, but never more so than when seen in the garb of antiquity.    We have seen how, at an early period of life, he made himself acquainted with the history and literature of Greece, so that his mind, long before he thought of devoting his life to the study of ancient art, had acquired a classical and antique cast, which, when surrounded by her glorious works, made him feel, think, and speak like a Greek.    Hence proceeded the contempt he cherished for modern art; as, in his opinion, distinguished for nothing but exaggeration, fantastic conceit, and affectation; features which never appear in a worse light than when compared with the simplicity, purity, and truth of the creations of antiquity.

But, we venture to say, in spite of all this, that what Winckelmann chooses to call his 'History of Ancient Art,' is anything but it: being in reality neither more nor less than an enumeration and critical examination of the merits of ancient works of art, and the causes to which they owe their existence.    To speak with the translator, Winckelmann ' is not contented with presenting to view the most beautiful monuments of human genius, but he investigates and exhibits the sources of their beauty, the characteristics of their style, and the reasons why they still command the admiration of the world, even as they did in those distant ages when, like Minerva, they came into being, radiant with wisdom and beauty.'

Hence that part of the work before us, which in some degree partakes of the nature of *history*, is almost exclusively confined to the first chapter of the first part; whilst the remainder is pure criticism, or something akin to it. Now, in this chapter assertions are made, and causes are assigned for the success of Greek art, which, we think, are not borne out by facts; as, for example, where the author speaks of the ·influence the climate exercised ·in the production of the masterpieces of ancient Greece.

' The influence of climate,' he says, ' must vivify the seed from which art is to be produced ; and for this seed Greece was the chosen soil. The talent for philosophy was believed by Epicurus to be exclusively Greek; but this pre-eminence might be claimed more correctly for art. The Greeks acknowledged and prized the happy clime under which they lived, though it did not extend to them the enjoyment of a perennial spring ; for, on the night when the revolt against the Spartan government broke out in Thebes, it snowed so violently as to confine every one to the house. Moderateness of temperature constituted its superiority, and is to be regarded as one of the more remote causes of that excellence which art attained among the Greeks. The climate gave birth to a joyousness of disposition; this, in its turn, invented games and festivals; and both together fostered art, which had already reached its highest pinnacle at a period when that which we call learning was utterly unknown to the Greeks. At this time they attached a peculiar signification to the honourable title of author, who before was regarded with a certain degree of contempt; and Plato makes Socrates say, that distinguished men, in Greek cities, had not drawn up or left behind them any writings, for fear of being numbered among the sophists.

' Much that might seem ideal to us was natural among them. Nature, after having passed step by step through cold and heat, established herself in Greece. Here, where a temperature prevails which is balanced between winter and summer, she chose her central point; and the higher she approaches the more genial and joyous does she become, and the more general is her influence in producing conformations full of spirit and wit, and features strongly marked and rich in promise.'—§§ v. and vi. pp 4, 5.

All this, no doubt, appears at first sight very plausible and very true. But, while we admit the former proposition, we very much question the soundness of the latter, which, certainly, is contradicted by some of the ablest and most trustworthy writers of antiquity. It is a fact, that none of those states in which the arts of design and sculpture most flourished, were in this respect peculiarly favoured beyond others. The climate of Attica, for example, it is allowed on all hands, was very unequal; and though vegetation appeared in the greatest luxuriance in some spots, in others the soil was barren and naked; resembling more the Russian steppes of the present day, than the lovely spots so much extolled by some writers. So much for the beautiful climate of ancient Greece.

Nor can we go all lengths with our author, who so eloquently expatiates on the corporeal beauty of the ancient Greeks. In the same place, from which we have just quoted, Winckelmann says :—

' Where clouds and heavy mists rarely prevail, but nature acts in a serene and gladsome atmosphere, such as Euripides describes the Athenian, she imparts an earlier maturity to the body; she is distinguished for vigorous development, especially of the female form; and it is reasonable to suppose that in Greece she perfected man to the highest degree—for what the scholiasts assert respecting the long heads or long faces of the inhabitants of the island of Eubœa is an absurd dream, devised for the sole purpose of finding the derivation of the name of a people there, called Μάκρωνες.'—§ vi. p. 5.

Now, so far from this being the case, there is much reason to believe, that the Athenians, who most excelled in the fine arts, were by no means distinguished above other Grecians for this quality. Cicero, speaking of the crowd of young men whom he saw at Athens, says that *there were few who were really handsome.* But, what is no less curious, is the fact that of all the women whose celebrity for beauty has reached us, not one appears to support, in this respect, the honour of Athens. The celebrated Phryne, for example, was a native of Thebes; Aspasia was born at Miletus; and so it is with the rest, not one of whom claimed Athens as her native place. And when Zeuxis, the great painter, desired to procure the most beautiful models for his Venus, it is said he produced his masterpiece from the study of seven virgins of Crotona. We do not, of course, mean to deny the existence of beautiful forms amongst the Athenians; all we wish to show is, that it is not to this that their success in the imitative arts can with justice be ascribed. The admiration of beauty amongst the Lacedemonians is admitted; but the fine arts, as is well known, were not permitted to be practised in Sparta. In other parts of Greece, also, personal beauty conferred a title to distinction; but no school of art arose out of this which at any period equalled, or attempted to equal, that of Athens.

The constitution and form of government, too, of which the author speaks in such glowing terms, can scarcely be said to have affected Greek art. With respect to this, Winckelmann says :—

' The independence of Greece is to be regarded as the most prominent of the causes, originating in its constitution and government, of its superiority in art. Liberty had always held her seat in this country, even near the throne of kings—whose rule was paternal—before the increasing light of reason had shown to its inhabitants the blessings of entire freedom. Thus, Homer calls Agamemnon a shepherd of his people, to signify his love for them, and his solicitude for their welfare. Although tyrants afterwards succeeded in establishing themselves, still they did so in their territories alone ; the nation, as a whole, never recognised a common ruler; and, prior to the conquest of Naxos by the Athenians, no free state in Greece had ever subjugated another. Hence, no individual possessed the sole prerogative of greatness in his own country, and the power of gaining immortality for himself to the exclusion of all others.'—§ xii.; p. 10.

Whatever may have been the nature and form of the Greek constitutions and governments—and the report concerning either is rather vague—this much we know, that the arts flourished where the most different, and not seldom arbitrary, forms existed.  Corinth held a secondary rank among the cities of art, while Athens and Sicyon were in the first.  Neither had wealth, pomp, or luxury, the slightest effect on Grecian art.  Indeed, if either of them had been necessary, or alone favourable for its success, it would have been exhibited among many of the splendid communities of Asia, and not been left to its comparatively tardy development in the small, scattered, and often disturbed, states of Greece.

There is a great deal more of truth in what the writer says respecting the honour and respect in which the Greek artists were held :—

'A wise man,' he says, 'was the most highly honoured; he was known in every city, as the richest is among us ; just as the younger Scipio was, who brought the statue of Cybele to Rome.  The artist also could attain to this respect.  Socrates, indeed, pronounced the artists the only true wise, as being actually, not apparently so ; it was probably from this conviction that Æsop constantly associated with sculptors and architects.  At a much later period, Diognetus, the painter, was one of those who taught Marcus Aurelius philosophy. This emperor acknowledged that he had learned of him to distinguish truth from falsehood, and not to regard follies as merits.  The artist could become a lawgiver, for all the lawgivers were common citizens, as Aristotle testifies.  He could command an army like Lamarchus, one of the neediest citizens of Athens, and see his statue placed besides those of Miltiades and Themistocles, and even near those of the gods themselves.  Thus, Xenophilus and Strabo placed statues of themselves, in a sitting posture, close to the statues of Æsculapius and Hygeia, at Argos ; Chirisophus, the sculptor of the Apollo at Tegen, stood in marble near his work ; the figure of Alcamenes was wrought in relief on the summit of the temple of Eleusis ; and Parrhasius and Silanian, in their picture of Theseus, were honoured together with the hero himself.  Other artists put their names upon their works—as Phidias, for example, at the feet of the Olympian Jupiter.  The names of the artists also appeared on different statues of the victors at Elis ; and on the chariot with four bronze horses, which Dinomenes erected to his father Hiero, king of Syracuse, was an inscription in two lines, to the effect that Onatas was the artist.  Still, however, this custom was not so general, that the absence of the artist's name upon admira-

Nor can we go all lengths with our author, who so eloquently expatiates on the corporeal beauty of the ancient Greeks. In the same place, from which we have just quoted, Winckelmann says :—

'Where clouds and heavy mists rarely prevail, but nature acts in a serene and gladsome atmosphere, such as Euripides describes the Athenian, she imparts an earlier maturity to the body; she is distinguished for vigorous development, especially of the female form; and it is reasonable to suppose that in Greece she perfected man to the highest degree—for what the scholiasts assert respecting the long heads or long faces of the inhabitants of the island of Euboea is an absurd dream, devised for the sole purpose of finding the derivation of the name of a people there, called Μάκρωνες.'—§ vi. p. 5.

Now, so far from this being the case, there is much reason to believe, that the Athenians, who most excelled in the fine arts, were by no means distinguished above other Grecians for this quality. Cicero, speaking of the crowd of young men whom he saw at Athens, says that *there were few who were really handsome.* But, what is no less curious, is the fact that of all the women whose celebrity for beauty has reached us, not one appears to support, in this respect, the honour of Athens. The celebrated Phryne, for example, was a native of Thebes; Aspasia was born at Miletus; and so it is with the rest, not one of whom claimed Athens as her native place. And when Zeuxis, the great painter, desired to procure the most beautiful models for his Venus, it is said he produced his masterpiece from the study of seven virgins of Crotona. We do not, of course, mean to deny the existence of beautiful forms amongst the Athenians; all we wish to show is, that it is not to this that their success in the imitative arts can with justice be ascribed. The admiration of beauty amongst the Lacedemonians is admitted; but the fine arts, as is well known, were not permitted to be practised in Sparta. In other parts of Greece, also, personal beauty conferred a title to distinction; but no school of art arose out of this which at any period equalled, or attempted to equal, that of Athens.

The constitution and form of government, too, of which the author speaks in such glowing terms, can scarcely be said to have affected Greek art. With respect to this, Winckelmann says :—

'The independence of Greece is to be regarded as the most prominent of the causes, originating in its constitution and government, of its superiority in art. Liberty had always held her seat in this country, even near the throne of kings—whose rule was paternal—before the increasing light of reason had shown to its inhabitants the blessings of entire freedom. Thus, Homer calls Agamemnon a shepherd of his people, to signify his love for them, and his solicitude for their welfare. Although tyrants afterwards succeeded in establishing themselves, still

ble statues proves them, conclusively, to be works of later times. Such an inference was to be expected only from those who had seen Rome in dreams, or, like young travellers, in one month.

'The reputation and success of artists were not dependent upon the caprice of ignorance and arrogance, nor were their works fashioned to suit the wretched taste or the incompetent eye of a judge set up by flattery and fawning; but the wisest of the whole nation, in the assembly of united Greece, passed judgment upon, and rewarded, them and their works; and at Delphos, as well as at Corinth, contests in painting, for which judges were specially appointed, were instituted in the time of Phidias. The first contest of the kind was between Panænus, the brother, or, as others have it, the nephew of Phidias, and Timagoras of Chalcis, in which the latter won the prize. Before such judges Ætion appeared with his picture of Alexander and Roxana; the presiding judge, named Proxenides, who pronounced the decision, bestowed his daughter in marriage upon the artist. We also see that the judges were not dazzled by a brilliant reputation in other cities, so as to deny to merit its rights; for at Samos, the picture by Timanthes, representing the decision upon the arms of Achilles, was preferred to that of Parrhasius.

'The judges, however, were not unacquainted with the arts; for there was a time in Greece when its youth were taught in the schools of art as well as philosophy; Plato learned drawing at the same time with the higher sciences. The design was, as Aristotle says, that they might acquire a correct knowledge and judgment of beauty.

'Hence the artist wrought for immortality; and the value set upon his works placed him in a position to elevate his art above all mere mercenary considerations. Thus, it is known that Polygnotus gratuitously embellished with paintings the portico at Athens, and also, as it appears, a public edifice at Delphos, in which he represented the taking of Troy. Gratitude for the latter work seems to have induced the Amphictyons, or national council of the Greeks, to award to the noble-minded artist the honour of being entertained at the public expense throughout Greece.'—§§ xxiii.—xxviii. pp. 18—21.

We have endeavoured to point out, as briefly as possible, what we conceive to be the errors under which this learned and indefatigable writer labours when assigning causes for the success of Art among the ancient Greeks. We deeply regret that our limited space will not allow us to dwell longer on so interesting a subject. We refer the reader to the volume itself; a perusal of which, independently of the numerous admirable plates with which it is embellished, will amply repay his trouble. We cannot conclude, however, without saying, that the remarks contained in the remainder of the work on the essential of art—the conformation and beauty of the male deities and heroes—the conformation and beauty of the female deities and heroines—the expression of beauty in features and action—proportion—composition—beauty in individual parts of the body—

&c. &c., are both admirable and true. And we, therefore, fully agree with the able translator, who, in allusion to Winckelmann and his performance, observes, that

'The soundness of his judgment, the acuteness and originality of his observations, and the copiousness of his illustrations, drawn from an intimate familiarity with every extant monument of ancient art, and with everything in ancient classic literature which could elucidate the subject to which he had devoted his life, render him the most trustworthy, instructive, and delightful of the writers on art.'

A careful study of Winckelmann's 'History of Ancient Art,' and a thoughtful consideration of the great principles embodied in it, must necessarily tend to form a pure, correct, and elevated taste, and for this end we commend its early perusal.

---

Art. V.—*Voyage of the 'Prince Albert' in Search of Sir John Franklin. A Narrative of Every-Day Life in the Arctic Regions.* By W. Parker Snow. London: Longman and Co. 1851.

Scarcely any of the mystery in which the fate of Sir John Franklin is enveloped has been cleared away by the inquiries set on foot for that purpose. We are, consequently, left in the same dim uncertainty as to whether, blocked up and surrounded by floes and icebergs, he exists in a strange world of his own, unable either to advance or return; or whether his vessels, overwhelmed by some terrific storm, have sunk in one of those silent seas where the voice of man is seldom heard. No record will, in all probability, ever reach us of the toil and danger he has experienced—of the rare and marvellous things he has beheld—of the startling scenery, magnificent in its strange desolation, he has witnessed—of the new stores he would have added to the wealth of science. What mighty perils he has passed—what glorious triumphs of thought achieved, as guided by an invisible, but certain, instinct, he resolutely steered his vessel into waters never before ruffled by the efforts of man—what alternate feelings of hope and despair have assailed him—we shall, in all probability, never learn. His fate and fortunes are still overshadowed by a mystery which it is left for future time to unravel.

Surmises, therefore, are almost worse than useless; but, in common with all who have ever heard his name, we share the hope that he may, at an hour however distant, reappear before us as the hero of countless adventures, full of extraordinary revelations, worn with years of anxiety and fatigue, but victorious in the success of a mighty undertaking.   And this not less for his own sake, than for her whose touching zeal has excited universal admiration and sympathy.  It is not the province of the reviewer often to touch upon a chord like this; but we cannot take up the volume before us, and think one moment upon its object, without a thrill of admiration of the rare affection which was the means of calling it into existence.

The little vessel in which Mr. Snow journeyed was fitted out by Lady Franklin herself, for the purpose of proceeding on a voyage of discovery, under the command of Captain Forsyth, who generously volunteered his services on the occasion, as did also our enthusiastic and intrepid author.   That less was accomplished by the *Prince Albert* than was originally intended, is indisputable; that she returned after the end of four months, instead of wintering in the Arctic Ocean, and exploring Cape Boothia, is a source of considerable regret to Mr. Snow, as it must be to all who peruse his entertaining work.   What were precisely the causes which contributed to produce the determination to return, instead of waiting the breaking up of the ice, does not appear.   Whether a sudden doubt as to the possibility of the project oppressed them, or a mistrust of the capability of their little bark to undergo the perils of a winter in those rigorous climates arose in the mind of the exploring expedition, cannot be clearly ascertained.   Certain it is, that, although Mr. Snow, from private reasons, into which he has the prudence not to enter, perceived that a journey homeward was necessary, he is constantly found expressing his regret that, after having only just reached the field of their labours, they should return hastily, without in reality making any very important discovery.

The failure of the actual expedition, however, does not detract from the interest awakened by Mr. Snow's narrative.  A mastery over language, the evidences of an active imagination, and considerable powers of observation, conspire to produce the impression that this journal is the production of an educated man, who has travelled much, and made, in every respect, the most of his time.

We cannot linger upon the threshold, but plunge at once with our author into the icy regions through which it has been his fate to travel.  Nothing peculiarly new or interesting to the general reader occurred until they had fairly reached the entrance to the frozen seas.  The vessel was elegant and firmly built; the crew were dauntless and hardy, and, animated by a deep interest in the cause in which they were engaged, and not a little degree of pride was aroused by the reflection that they were about to share the same dangers as he had done who had gone before them—just the spirits, in fact, fit to be entrusted with the mission committed to them.

Much unfavourable weather, and many vexatious delays caused by contrary winds, at first greatly retarded them from entering upon the actual field of their labours; while it unconsciously, perhaps, was also deadening something of the ardent enthusiasm more early awakened. All eyes were on the look-out for the first iceberg which, like the outpost of some mighty city, should denote that they were in reality within the limits of the Frozen Sea. At length, gleaming like an enormous crag sheathed in moonshine, a broken, irregular, jagged, glistening substance, rocked upon the waves, and all on board, as they strained their gaze towards it, knew that they had beheld one of those destructive masses of ice which wander over the surface of the treacherous waters of the Arctic Ocean. Another and another berg rose beyond; and from the dim vapour gradually stealing over rock and wave, these sparkling crags jutted out now and then, while a sheet of almost unbillowed waters ruffled silently along their feet, laving them, as it were, in low-murmuring submission. Imagination, so prone to idealize what the eye has not actually rested upon, has, in its most gorgeous and fertile moods, scarcely perhaps realized the strange and marvellous landscapes into which nature has moulded herself in the Arctic regions. It is as if, over the ruins of fallen cities and whole countries convulsed, a spirit had withdrawn all vitality, and converted their shattered hills and plains and habitations into crystal. Everything reflects and irradiates a white glare, too oppressive to be long dwelt upon by the eye. Vast ridges of mountains, their forms half-curtained by continual fogs, their cloud-capped summits reposing against the leaden sky; while between, white-bosomed valleys, where the snows of many a winter lie unmelted, stretch untrodden and barren, unless perchance in some lofty nook, a little spot is seen where a timid plant trembles into existence, or a mossy stone upon the beach contrasts strangely with the lifeless scenery around. Over the ocean the gaze is bounded by towering bergs which rise one behind the other as far as the eye can reach, disclosing long tortuous channels, and white defiles, diverging like the streets of a great city. Miles of glistening ice stretch far away, and every vista is terminated by the same unchanging scene. No living thing seems to invade the repose. No bird or fish was at first seen. All, from the snow-capped summits of the hills, the ever-shifting bergs, the glistening beds of ice, the unconscious motion of the sea, was silence; and often, as the undarkened night came on, and as, rolling the waters noiselessly from under her keel, the little ship glided

through the spectral channels, where nor sound was heard, nor
motion felt, it seemed, indeed, as if—

> ' They were the first that ever burst
> Into that silent sea.'

The midnight sun, hanging on the verge of the mountains,
with its blood-red glow and rayless circle, imparted a still
stranger aspect to everything; and those who had never before
penetrated into this region were deeply impressed with the
marvellous varieties of the beautiful and strange world in which
they now found themselves.  Every hour imparted fresh food
for wonder and admiration.  Sometimes, in the dead of the
night, a huge mass of snow seemed to wrench itself forcibly
from the mountain-side, and bound and rebound over ledge after
ledge, until, with a roar more grand than heaven's artillery, it
fell into the sea, but, after convulsing the waters for a great
distance, would suddenly emerge and drift over the ocean in
company with the other bergs, into one of which the avalanche
becomes converted.  Sometimes, one of these icebergs is suddenly seen to totter and shake, while, all around, the waters
quiver and tremble as if agitated by an earthquake; then, with
a sound like the roar of cannons, it bursts asunder, and plunges
into the sea, rising again with the cone reversed, and disclosing
a broad, even surface of ice, from which cascades and numerous
*jets d'eau* are often seen to stream.  Every valley re-echoes
with the sound; the sea-bird soars with fluttering wing to some
more peaceful habitation, and nature gradually resumes the
awful silence to which in these regions she appears to have
resigned herself, unless some mighty throe of the pent-up
passions of her own bosom occurs to break it.

Completely within the frozen circle, the crew of the *Albert*
prepared for active contact with the ice.  The ' Crow's Nest,' a
sort of barrel fixed at the mast-head, was hoisted; ice-anchors,
claws, axes, &c., were laid in order; tow-ropes, warps, and
tracking-belts, were brought out; and great caution was observed
in the advance.  The number of the icebergs continually increased; and rugged hammocks rose above the surface, opposing
their progress.

Slowly, amid many difficulties, and considerable variations in
wind and tide, the *Albert* advanced further on her course, the
secret hope that cheered them on making every day's labour
more light.  The storms of a sea possessed of warmth and
vitality, terrific as they may be, are less to be feared than
those unseen and unexpected snares which attend the mariner
bound on a voyage through these treacherous waves.  At every

step the ship seemed to encounter an opposing obstacle grating against the keel, and it was only by observing extreme caution and calling to their aid that scientific skill for which our seamen, above others, are remarkable, that the greatest disasters were avoided. Slowly, then, we say, the little vessel glided through the labyrinth of waters, thickening and congealing each hour, and herself placed in close proximity to those giant bergs, one angry movement of which would have utterly overwhelmed her.

Occasional patches of clear water now seemed to extend in unbroken continuity, but on a nearer approach large drifts would be discovered, or some streams of ice found extending in the worst possible direction. Sometimes, in front, a crescent belt of bergs shaped itself threateningly in view, and round the ice sketched in broad glittering plains eight or nine feet in thickness, only split by rents, through which it seemed impossible to steer the smallest boats. The whole day was frequently expended in manœuvering a passage; sometimes the *Albert* was made to dart down upon a rock of ice and splinter it to atoms with the force of its sudden and impetuous advance; now the effect of heaving her through a narrow path was tried, now the windlass was set to work, then saws were employed, with unwearied patience the men toiled on until with some fortunate stroke of the pole the stubborn mass was sent shivered into the sea, then a loud and cheering huzza broke from the men, quickly responded to by all on board, and, wet through very often by sinking up to their necks in water, they merrily regained the deck, satisfied and proud of their hearty exertions.

Life, though necessarily somewhat monotonous, was anything but disagreeable. The sun uprose and set and brought a round of the same duties, but no discontent or unhappiness made itself visible. Under a kind and worthy commander the men performed their allotted tasks with cheerful alacrity. Oftentimes in the evening when the ship was borne softly over the waves the fiddle was brought upon deck, and there, in the midst of those grand and awful solitudes, the music which has so often cheered our own fireside stole forth and startled the echoes with jigs and dances to which it is more than probable the cliffs and bergs had never before listened. The merry song and hearty laugh went round—the memories of friends crowded upon them, and many a cheer to the absent broke a stillness which had otherwise been ofttimes worse than that of death. When the sun shone forth and imparted mildness to the air, the rigging was garnished with numerous strange decorations, in the shape of every kind of garment brought up from below to have the benefit of an airing. The beds, too, were placed upon deck to dissipate the

close effects of the cabin, and all these things carefully attended
to, conspired to preserve the health of the men, which, with
one exception, appears to have been good throughout the
voyage.

From the Crow's Nest some were continually going and coming,
anxiously reporting upon the condition of the ice ahead, and all
objects there discernible. With much delight an English vessel
had been sighted, and now she was distinctly revealed fastened
to an ice-floe, where she had been bound for three months. It
was the *Felix*, under Sir John Ross. Bound on the same errand,
a deep sympathy necessarily existed between the vessels, but
it deepened now that, after so long an absence from new faces,
the sound of their own tongue floated in a cheerful hail from
deck to deck.

With delight the officers exchanged greetings, and were
speedily on board each other's vessels, reciprocating intelligence
and venturing hopes as to the ultimate termination of their
search. Sir John Ross, ennobled by his many dangerous experiences, and his long sojourn among seas the most treacherous of
any perhaps on the surface of the globe, stood, the hero of a
hundred strange escapes, and engaged the attention of all on
board the *Albert*—he who had passed four years and more in
miserable bondage in a desolation similar to that now extending
around them—who had gazed on the same monotonous scenery
until the soul sickened of existence—who daily rose to the same
round of duties—tracked animals and did not see them—carried
guns and did not fire—watched for the invisible sun and counted
the hours, until the uncurtained night came down and permitted them to shut out all thought of life by going to bed.
All sufferings, all trials, all dangers, all fears, faded into nothing
by comparison with his; and a deeper sense of the importance
of their mission stole into the heart of every one. The old
veteran, whose frame had been battered by many a storm—
whose eye had rested upon scenes of which few may see the like
again, venturing once more through the perilous path of the
frozen sea in search of a brother officer, was a sight to inspire
courage and faith.

It is, of course, impossible to linger long upon each separate
incident of a voyage in every respect interesting. Each day
seemed to present them with a fresh difficulty; now for a little
while, smiling weather and a fair breeze sent them on their way
rejoicing, then a dead stagnation and sickening calm riveted
them to one spot, where, enveloped in dense fogs, the little
vessel seemed perfectly surrounded in these silent seas, incapable
of moving either forward or backward. Day after day the sun
rose and set, and found them still bound in their vast solitudes,

the only sound heard was the grating of the floes against
ip's sides, as they slowly drifted by.  At length a move-
vas discernible in the ice, the breeze sprang up, and yet a
urther the *Albert* made her way.

h interest was every day awakened by the increasing
f and laborious nature of their contests with the ice, which
l to assume a more stubborn and forbidding character at
step.  Now between broad frozen fields a pathway seemed
ad, and instantly the vessel would be turned towards it;
sooner had she reached the mouth of the seeming river,
ie treacherous waters closed again abruptly, not only pre-
g their advance, but placing them in positions of consider-
anger, from which it required all their daring tact and
' to extricate them.  Eager, however, in the cause in
they were engaged, no one on board felt inclined to suffer
it insurmountable obstacles to delay them.  As often as
ss and energy would disentangle them from their difficulty,
ut it in practice, and rarely waited the disappearance of
of its own accord.  Men descended in boats, and with
d chisel patiently attacked the opposing barrier.  Many
were frequently occupied in this manner, the perspiration
ing down their faces in spite of the coldness of the atmo-
, and their bodies often up to the waist in water.  They
lly succeeded in making way through the point they had
l, though occasionally compelled to desist and seek another
l, by retracing their steps, or tacking to and fro until
iscovered some opening.

ength, much to the joy of all on board, they came up with
n Austin's vessels, which were just preparing to start
d, after having been bound for a short time to an ice-floe.
eamer immediately offered to take the *Felix* and *Albert* in
hich offer was gladly accepted, since it promised them
iundred miles advance on their journey with comparatively
lifficulty.  The ropes were accordingly fixed, and those
iping bergs and frowning mountains looked down upon as
e a scene as perhaps ever was enacted.  There, in desola-
rand and awful, in seas where billows are almost un-
ied, the English vessels proceeded in a long line perfectly
ic in their quiet progress.  At the rate of four miles an
hey were proceeding, when they came upon an opposing
:, in the shape of a 'nip,' as it is technically termed.  To
his by boldly dashing through it with the steamer was at
ied, but finding this endeavour unsuccessful, a still grander
of destroying the obstacle was resolved upon.  A con-
ile quantity of powder was sunk and ignited.  No sound
vement at first took place, but presently, the enormous

masses of ice were seen agitated by a convulsive quiver along
the whole extent, and then, suddenly rending in twain, piece
after piece, rose into the air, and fell with a mighty splash
into the sea.   Considerable time and labour were expended in
forcing the passage, but the task was at length accomplished,
and, late in the afternoon, one by one, the vessels threaded
through the channel, and cast anchor in a smooth piece of water
on the other side.   After this busy and exciting scene, the
evening sank with peculiar stillness, and the silence—at all times
deep in those seas—seemed doubly so.   Then, as night came on,
no actual darkness accompanied it; the shadows of the long line
of ships slanted athwart the placid, glistening waters, and the
smooth surface of the passing floes of ice.   A chain of mountains stretched to the right; in front, and on all sides, the tall
form of icebergs rose, towering from the sparkling surface, and
on the hummocks thickly dispersed around rested numerous
seals, the only living things then to be seen.   The sun, gilding
midnight with his soft and mellowed beams, was soaring through
the polar sky at the back of Melville Cape, already on his
way to  commence another day's journey.   The only sound
heard was the regular working of the steamer.   No stars or
moon shining in the heavens, the sky above expanded like a
leaden arch, save where the faint rays of the sun struggled
through the curtain of haze already beginning to rest upon hill
and berg.
    The opening into Melville's Bay was soon reached, and it was
reported that some men were observed moving about the ice
ahead.   Immediate communication with the Esquimaux, for such
they were, was resolved upon, and, accordingly, starting in a
boat with the captain, Mr. Snow made for land.   Several of
them afterwards came to the ship for the purpose of receiving the
letters with which they were to be entrusted.   Few could, perhaps,
conceive the dreariness of that region where these tribes of men
make to themselves habitations, derive a varying and uncertain existence from the chase of animals, and brave the greatest
hardship.   Ridges of enormous glaciers rise in the back ground
of their scenery, from between fissures in which stream absolute
torrents of snow.   Perpetual winter unrelieved by the shortest
summer, seems to have settled there; no vegetation is beheld,
yet here, upon one of the farthest points of northern land on
which the foot of civilized man has rested, dwell a portion
of the Esquimaux race.   They take, in their daily round of
life, the sun for their guide, and rise ofttimes with him, and
when fatigued seek their bed.   If hunger is felt, they taste of
food; and if thirst, then, with difficulty and tedious labour,
they melt down the ice or snow and drink of it.   A cursory

glance at such a life may to civilized man realize nothing of the ideas of happiness which in his artificial state he has learnt to form, nor does it suggest any of the concomitants of comfort which are become necessary to him, and the condition of the being destitute of these is not by any means to be envied. But the Esquimaux, unconscious of any other state of existence, is cheerful and contented in his ice-bound solitude, and finds a rude protection from every description of weather.

At this interview they were found to be conversible in the extreme, and willing to afford every information in their power. Little satisfactory intelligence was, however, obtained. Sir John Ross had on board of the *Felix* an Esquimaux by the name of Adams, who belonged to a tribe professing some different traits of habits and language. This man held a long conversation with the natives, the nature of which seemed to perplex and overpower him with gloom; but the origin did not appear until some days afterwards; when, perplexed and harassed by the jokes of the men about his melancholy, he, as it will be seen, related as much as he could of what he had heard. It was intended to leave despatches with the natives, who faithfully performed the office entrusted to them, and during the time of their preparations the ice-plains were converted into the theatre for the enactment of an amusing and novel scene. The sledge in which the Esquimaux postmen had neared the ship was flying about in all directions. Lieut. O'Donnell had harnessed himself, Lieut. M'Clintoch thrown himself across it, and away they went over the smooth surface of congealed water, all by turns sharing in an amusement perfectly new and delightful to those accustomed to seek entertainment here at home by a much easier method. The crews of the ships were no less active. Rigging, mast, and deck were deserted, and leap-frog and running-races took the place of the customary occupations. The solitude and majestic silence of the Arctic regions was broken by peals of laughter—honest English laughter—while the natives stood grinning around amazed and delighted at the strange antics they beheld. Various presents were distributed among them, including some dolls dressed in the most gaudy manner. One habited like a showy girl awoke the deepest surprise and admiration in the heart of the untutored inhabitant of these wild districts; he gazed at it again and again, gave it a most lengthened examination, then wrapped it in a piece of paper given him, and put it carefully away in his seal-skin dress, with the object, doubtless, of carrying it home to excite great wonder among his wife and children. It was amusing to see the bewildered stare of astonishment with which one of the young Esquimaux danced about the ship and examined the machinery of the steamer, the construction of which excited his wonder and unspeakable surprise. The lever was for an instant placed in his hand, by which the whole engine was set in sudden motion. No sooner did it begin to move than he dropped the handle and turned on his heels with a sort of half comic grin, which in their countenances expresses both fear and laughter. Every possible information having been obtained, the natives were sent on shore, and the steamer and vessel once more pursued their way.

For many days after their interview with the Esquimaux, it was observed that Adams, who could only utter a few words of English, was restless and uncomfortable, avoiding every opportunity of conversing with strangers. The steward of the *Albert*, from his long stay in the Hudson's Bay Company's service, was better able to understand him than any one else, and accordingly, by dint of his examination and that of Mr. Snow, it was discovered that he had heard a tale from the Esquimaux, which, if true, would have for ever set at rest all surmise as to the fate of Sir John Franklin and his crew.

'By his account he had been told by the natives, when on shore, conversing with them in the morning, that in 1846 (I could not make out whether the early or the latter part of the year), two vessels, with officers having gold bands on their caps and other insignia of the naval uniform, had been, in some way or another, destroyed at some place to the northward of us; that the crews were ultimately much enfeebled, and, after great hardship and suffering, encamping by themselves in tents, and not communicating much with the natives, were all brutally massacred. This was the substance and the pith of the long and tedious statement that was elicited from him.'—P. 207.

The whole fleet now moving about these seas was in commotion, and the most searching investigation set on foot. A dim, but horrible fear possessed the minds of all, and thoughts they dared not utter crowded swiftly upon their minds. Communication with every ship took place, the officers met, consultations took place, another interview with the natives was decided upon. This was accordingly done, and it was discovered, by questioning and cross-questioning, that the whole foundation for the story lay in their having told the man that the *North Star* had wintered at Wolstenholme Sound the past winter, and that one one had been killed by a fall from the cliffs. Some time had been lost by investigating the details of their story, and the vessels now prepared to regain it by redoubled exertions. The ships parted company, and the *Albert* went on her way alone. The weather became so hazy that it was necessary to have the gong kept beating continually to give notice to any other vessels or persons that might happen to be in the way; little by little the fog gradually cleared, and the vicinity of land was announced by shoals of eider ducks and other birds. While those engaged in the boats were still longing for the disappearance of the mist, the curtain of vapour was suddenly lifted up, as if by magic, and the sun streamed down upon the range of the Byam Martin mountains, which almost pierced the clouds with their snowy peaks. Every one was now upon the look-out for an object of extreme interest—the spot where the provisions and coals sent out by Lady Franklin, in 1849, were deposited. As usual on such occasions, many mistaken surmises were made. Captain Forsyth imagined he had found the place, and it was impossible then to pause and examine it. Subsequently, however, Mr. Snow landed on one of the Wollaston islands where some cairns were erected. Here they deemed it probable the provisions were deposited, and searched carefully around, but discovered nothing save a lonely grave underneath a ledge of rock jutting out like an oblong peninsula into the sea, underneath which the waves continually sounded a hoarse music; some moss and mould clung over the oblong-shaped resting-place, a few bones were scattered near, but no word or sign to tell who rested there. Regaining the ship, away they steered, a dense fog obscuring the land and rendering their progress slow and uncertain. Their hearts beat anxiously; they were in reality, as it seemed, approaching the commencement of their labours in a spot unknown to all. How little they at that moment foresaw that, in less than a fortnight, they would be retracing their steps and making for home without accomplishing one half their proposed work. Nothing of this feeling, however, dimmed the joy they experienced, when, after many days and nights of anxious look-out, they found themselves in Barrow's Straits, within sight of Leopold island, for whose harbour they now rapidly steered. The gutta-percha boat was lowered and made for the shore; a strange sail coming rapidly towards them, giving a double spur to their endeavours to be first on land. With some hard work they forced her along through the ice and got her up to the extreme end of Whale Point. Every eye was fixed upon the little home standing there, in the awful grandeur of these scenes, an untenanted dwelling, waiting for him who may never pass that way, to welcome him with everything which imagination could suggest. The idea of erecting their storehouse on that extreme point of the Arctic region was a grand and beautiful one. It was deemed not improbable that the vessels of Sir John Franklin might, after emerging from their imprisonment, wherever it was, come upon this point, worn and harassed with privations which no one sitting here at home could foresee, and scarcely daring to hope that the scanty remains of their provisions could endure more than a day.

Should this unhappily prove to be the case, how difficult it is to realize the joy that must be awakened by this unexpected oasis, teeming with everything that could rejoice his heart after his long and dreary absence from his native home. We scarcely dare to penetrate, in imagination even, into the sacred gladness of his heart when he knows whose hand has guided and caused their deposit there. There stood the home, well built of canvass, and amply stored with everything that could conduce to comfort. Ropes, iron gear, blankets, stoves, &c., &c., were scattered about in a confused medley; outside, and nearer the beach, were piles of soup and bouilli canisters, and tins of preserved meat, with labels diversified and numerous, preserved mutton, ox-cheek soup, concentrated gravy, green peas, roast beef, mixed vegetables, carrots, besides casks of beef, pork, chocolate, flour, navy bread, sugar, pickles, lime-juice, and various other articles suitable for a lengthened residence in that region. There were bags of coal and coke, and then the steam launch, with every help for launching. The men gazed with swelling hearts on all these provisions, and not a little melancholy feeling stole over them, as, when the time came for departure the thought rushed into their minds, perhaps they will never, never be required.

A little more travelling and they reached Prince Regent's Inlet, and here, where they were in hopes of being so actively engaged, nothing but disappointment met them. No sign or hope of egress; all before them was a dense mass of ice, around on every side the same blockade, and a dreary expanse of heavy hummocky sea extended. Not a channel for the vessel was seen: in vain was the opinion of mate and second-mate requested. All agreed that there was no chance of making way, and a silent gloom settled upon the hearts of every one on board. All was now to be abandoned—there, on the threshold of their labours, they were to turn the prow of their ship homeward, quit the scenes in which they had come to labour with so proud and hopeful a spirit. Some clung to the secret anticipation of wintering there, and being able to proceed in the spring. But no sooner was the return home determined upon, than everything conspired to make it seem necessary. Some anticipations were entertained that unless they did so, the ice would gradually enclose them altogether, and leave them no room to move. So, with heavy hearts, did our mariners, after receiving the order to return, in perfect silence, prepare to fulfil their duties.

As their determination was not known when they had passed Cape Leopold, some fresh notice was needed, and this Mr. Snow again requested he might be allowed to deposit in the gutta-percha boat, which was accorded to him, and about half-past nine he quitted the ship, with a few provisions in readiness. He kept a sharp look-out along the land as they neared it in the uncertain light. But, gradually, as they left their ship behind, midnight thickened around them, and they found themselves in their little boat alone upon the wild waste of waters; the wind rushing down the declivities on land, and the even-timed splash of the oar, were the only sounds to be heard. A mournful silence pervaded the crew, the hopes that cheered them through so many perils were gone, and they gradually advanced forcing their way through the floating ice and small bergs. In the far East a sudden brightness made day visible, and they knew that the sun was coming up above the sea. This inspired fresh courage, and by three o'clock the little party found themselves off a deep valley or ravine, close to Cape Seppings, and the ice began to appear in greater masses. Creeping close in shore, they avoided the drifts as much as possible, but soon discovered themselves fronting a dense pack of heavy ice, which intercepted their progress. No egress was possible, save by the way they had entered, and, in doubt and uncertainty, they paused and consulted how to meet the opposing difficulty. A dense fog was rising from the sea, and rapidly covering the rocky hills; the ice was in quick motion, and carried to seaward by a strong current, and, by the circular movement it was making, it was certain soon to enclose them altogether. The *Albert* was completely lost to view, and a few moments only were allowed for deliberation, when it was resolved to take to the ice and haul up the boat. This was a task of no small difficulty; indeed, one perfectly inconceivable to those not on the spot. No one thought of self, but sprang from pieces of ice and settled the hook, working every now and then half way under water. Every foot of ground gained was a triumph, with intense labour. At length, with a wild hurrah! and joyous shout, the boat was launched once more into her proper element. Then no further difficulty was experienced in landing. The house was found in precisely the same condition as when they had left it; the document Mr. Snow had brought was placed in the cylinder, and then the little party lighted their fire, and prepared for as romantic a morning's meal as was ever tasted beneath the rising sun. Water was obtained from a little pool of melted snow near the beach. A plank was cleared of some ropes at one end, and two or three large stones, with a small keg, brought out for seats. The plank served for a table, and upon it were spread salt pork and biscuit, the teapot, and an oblong mug, which served alike for all. There the four sat, like brigands round a fire, laughing merrily, discussing now one subject, now another, and all joining in a hope that the vessel would proceed on her homeward journey and leave them there. After their meal was over, tired of the night's exertions, one by one, the men dropped off asleep, and then awoke again to hope that in that spot they might winter and proceed on a dangerous and early voyage in the spring. Wandering about the place, taking a last look at objects and scenes he never might again witness, Mr. Snow lighted upon a scrap of our friend 'Punch,' who had found his way into these Arctic regions and been dropped there. About two in the afternoon they quitted their position, bade a long adieu to Sir John Ross's home, breathed a deep and earnest prayer that its stores might not be left to decay unused, and plunged once again into the ice-bound waters.

Little of moment occurred on the journey homeward. A few gales were experienced, some dangerous, others not; but the bark reached England, ultimately, in safety, after an absence of four months, on, as it proved, a fruitless undertaking.

---

ART. VI.—*A Practical Treatise on Musical Composition.* By G. W. Rohner. 2 vols. London: Longman and Co.

MUSIC is an art, not a science. It is, however, otherwise treated, not only in common discourse, but in didactic works which profess to inquire into its principles and lay down its rules. We not only hear, every day, people talking about 'musical science,' 'scientific composers,' and even 'scientific performers' on the pianoforte, or the violin, but we meet with 'Systems of Harmony,' and 'Treatises on Composition,' in which it is attempted to deduce the principles of music, and the practice of composition, from the physical phenomena of sound. This misconception of the nature of music, by involving it in an obscurity which does not belong to it, has thrown serious difficulties in the way of its acquirement. The student has been either repelled by the arid prospect of pages bristling with arithmetical calculations and mathematical diagrams, or has been rewarded for his perseverance by the attainment of a quantity of lore, which he finds wholly unavailing for any practical purpose.

Such has been the prevalent manner of teaching the principles of music almost down to the present time; and, though sounder views are now adopted, yet the older impressions are by no means obliterated. Within the time of our own student-days,

music was universally taught according to the famous system of
Rameau, which then formed the foundation of every treatise, not
only on what was called the theory of the science, but on the
practice of composition.

Rameau was a celebrated composer of operas in the middle of
the last century; but his fame, as the founder of a system, grew
and spread long after his operas were forgotten. He came to be
regarded throughout Europe as a kind of Newton; a philosopher
who had resolved the principles of music into a law of nature,
grand, simple, and comprehensive as the law of gravitation. He
himself, as it happened, did not possess the gift of lucid explanation, and his book was so obscure that his system would never
have been heard of but for the aid of D'Alembert, who digested
and illustrated it in a work so concise, methodical, and luminous,
that it was every where received as a model of scientific investigation, and used as the text-book of teachers and the *vade-mecum*
of students.

Rameau based his superstructure on the foundation of a physical fact which he had discovered, or, at least, was the first to
point out. If a deep sound is produced by striking a bass string
of the pianoforte, the harp, or the violoncello, and attentively
listened to it as it dies away, two high notes will be heard
along with it; the octave of the fifth, and the double octave of
the major third. Hence he concluded that the ' perfect chord,'
or the principal chord in harmony, composed of the fundamental
sound with its major third and its fifth, is given by nature itself.
He next observed that, if two other sounds are taken, the one
a fifth above, and the other a fifth below, the first fundamental
sound (for example, C, with G its fifth above, and F its fifth
below), these three sounds, each being accompanied, by nature,
with its perfect chord, will give all the notes of the natural scale.
And he showed that each note of the scale, being a third or a
fifth above one or other of those three sounds, would have one
of them for its fundamental bass. Thus is *concord* derived from
nature; as to *discord* (of which harmony largely consists) he
made it a factitious invention, the harshness of discordant sounds
being used to give poignancy to harmony which would otherwise be too sweet and luscious. From this principle he deduced
the maxim, that, as the discordant note produces pain to the ear,
it is necessary that it be previously heard as a concord, and still
more necessary that it should be followed by, or melt into a
concord; or, in technical phrase, that a discord must be generally *prepared*, and always *resolved*.

The utter insufficiency of these ' scientific' principles to explain
the practice even of the most ordinary harmony used in his own
day was apparent from the beginning, and pointed out by

numerous contemporary critics.  Admitting, it was said, that
nature furnished the harmony of the major mode, what became
of the *minor* mode, as beautiful, as expressive, and as commonly
used, as the major—a mode, too, which prevails in the sweetest
and most pathetic strains dictated by nature to the songsters and
minstrels of rude and uncultivated tribes.  A sounding body
generates its *major third ;* but whence comes the *minor third ?*
To this question there is no answer, and it strikes at the very
root of the system.  Then Rameau laid it down, as a consequence of his theory, that the ' fundamental bass' must always
proceed by fifths either upwards or downwards: for example,
that a chord whose fundamental note is C must be followed,
either by G the fifth above, or F the fifth below. One or two other
progressions he was constrained to admit because he found them
in practice, but he got rid of the difficulty by describing them
as *licenses ;* although, even in his own day, they occurred in
every line of music, and were essential to the production of
good harmony.   Others, which he absolutely excluded, are now
in constant use ; and so completely is his rule exploded, that the
fundamental bass may now move upwards or downwards, through
every degree of the scale.   It is the same thing with discords ;
the rules for their *preparation* and *resolution* are so much relaxed
that they can scarcely be said to exist.

Rameau and his followers claim credit for the principle of the
' fundamental bass' as a great scientific discovery.   One of them,
M. de la Borde, in his voluminous history of music, published
in 1780, says :—' Music, since the revival of the arts. was
abandoned to the ear, caprice, and conjecture of composers, and
was equally in want of unerring rules in theory and in practice.
Rameau appeared, and Chaos was no more!  He was at once
Descartes and Newton, having been of as much use to music as
both those great men were to philosophy.'   On this high flown
passage Dr. Burney makes the following just comment :—

' But were Corelli, Geminiani, Handel, Bach, the Scarlattis, Leo,
Caldara, Durante, Jomelli, Perez, &c., such incorrect harmonists as to
merit annihilation because they never heard of Rameau or his system ?
Indeed, it may be further asked, what good music has been composed
even in France, in consequence of Rameau giving a new name to the
bass of a common chord or chord of the seventh?   The Italians still
call the lowest sound of music in parts, the *bass*, whether fundamental
or derivative ; but do the French imagine that the great composers
above-mentioned, and the little composers who need not be mentioned,
were ignorant whence every supposed bass was derived?  The great
harmonists of the sixteenth century seldom used any other than fundamental basses.   And the fundamental bass to the hexachords has
always been the key-note and the fifth above and the fifth below, just
as Rameau has given it in his theoretic tracts.'

Instead of good music having been composed, in France or anywhere else, in consequence of Rameau's system, the very opposite effect has been produced by it.   Its narrow code of laws—its restrictions and prohibitions—its ungracious permission, on the footing of licenses, of the most beautiful and essential progressions of harmony—were so many stumbling-blocks to the student's progress, so many fetters on the composer's imagination; and there are musicians, even to this day, who have never been able to shake off the trammels of Rameau's system.

Besides Rameau's system, there have been various others, chiefly modifications of his, in which it is attempted to deduce, from some general law, a body of fixed and immutable rules of harmony.   They are all liable to the same objection: the rules are so narrow and so inapplicable to the actual practice of the art, that they are nullified by a host of exceptions and licenses.

The investigation of the phenomena of sound, like that of the phenomena of light, forms a curious and interesting branch of physical science.   But the musician has no more concern with acoustics than the painter has with optics.   No artist ever derived the slightest benefit from either; and the greatest artists have never found it worth while to waste their time and labour upon studies to them utterly unprofitable.   'Most teachers of musical composition,' says Gottfried Weber (the author of one of the last and best works on the subject), ' imagine that the theory of musical composition must necessarily be founded on harmonic acoustics, and on this account commence their books of instruction with arithmetical and algebraical problems and formulas.   But this seems to me nothing else than an unseasonable display of pedantry; for one may be the most profound musical composer, the greatest contrapuntist—a Mozart or a Haydn, a Bach or a Palestrina—without knowing anything of the matter.'   The rules of music, in fact, have never, in any case, been the result of scientific investigation; they have uniformly been deduced from the *practice* of musicians.   All that science has done—or rather attempted to do—has been to apply mathematical or physical principles to the explanation of rules already existing and acted upon; and in this attempt, as we have seen, science has signally failed.

Music, in some form or another, is doubtless coeval with the world.   Wherever we find human beings, we find musical sounds; and we find all over the world such a general similarity in the arrangement of the sounds which please the ear and move the feelings—or, in other words, such a general analogy in the musical scale—that we are warranted in concluding the musical scale, in its simplest form, to be dictated by nature, however much it may have been refined and extended by art.   We

believe that there always have been, in ancient as well as modern
times, two kinds of music : the one consisting of the simple
effusions of untutored feeling—melodies such as are described
by Duke Orsino in ' Twelfth Night '—

> ' Mark it, Cesario—it is old and plain ;
> The spinners and the knitters in the sun,
> And the free maids that weave their thread with bones,
> Do use to chaunt it : '

the other, the lofty and complex superstructure raised upon this
simple foundation, by the successive labours of a long line of
artists. Both kinds were certainly possessed by the most civilized
nations of antiquity.   The *artistic* music of the Greeks was of
the most refined and artificial description, but this is all that we
know of it.  Every trace of it has vanished, and all the researches
of historians only show an ignorance so complete, that no one
has even been able to ascertain whether the Greeks were acquainted with *harmony*, or the combination of simultaneous
sounds.   The modern art of music has been reared, from its very
foundation, since the middle ages, and cannot be regarded as,
at the utmost, more than four or five centuries old.   The discovery of harmony seems to have followed the invention of the
organ, for it was impossible to possess an instrument with keys
without stumbling upon the agreeable effects produced by
sounding two or three notes at the same time.   But the first
attempts at harmony were as rude as the original form of the
instrument that suggested them, and sounds were combined in
a manner intolerable to modern ears.   From that beginning,
down to the present day, the art of harmony has been extended
and developed by the trials and experiments of an unbroken
line of musicians.   The art, consequently, has been in a state of
ceaseless change ; new combinations, dictated by pure taste and
the sense of the beautiful, have been generally and permanently
adopted ; others, resulting from caprice and the desire of innovation, have had their temporary vogue, and been displaced by
others equally arbitrary.   To this course of change there is no
prospect of termination.   It seems, on the contrary, to move
with accelerated speed ; and the century to come will probably
make greater changes in the aspect of music than any century
which is past.

It follows from all this, that a systematic treatise on musical
composition ought to be a body of rules adapted to the state of
the art as it exists.   Each rule ought to be a generalized expression of the concurrent practice of the great masters, whose works
are regarded as pure and classical models.   In this process of
generalizing, two dangers must be avoided.   In attempting to

make the rules broad and comprehensive, they may be clogged with such a multitude of exceptions as to be no rules at all.   In endeavouring to prevent their being liable to exceptions, they may be made so narrow in their application, and consequently so multitudinous, as to be in a great measure useless.   In these respects, as in many others, the rules of music are analogous to the rules of grammar.

Such is our notion of what a didactic musical work ought to be, though we cannot say that we have found it realized in any work that has come under our observation.   The lumber of scientific pedantry, indeed, has been generally thrown aside, and the rules of music are deduced from the practice of musicians; but every treatise with which we are acquainted is liable, more or less, to the objections already mentioned.   In the first place, the authors of new works borrow much of their materials from the labours of their predecessors, and consequently retain rules and restrictions no longer applicable to the actual practice of the art.   We find the antiquated doctrines of Fux and Marpurg gravely laid down in treatises of the nineteenth century; and, moreover, they err, either in excessive generalization or the reverse.   The works of Albrechtsberger, of Reicha, of Cherubini, valuable as they are upon the whole, are seriously injured in different ways by these faults.   The ' Treatise on Musical Composition,' by Gottfried Weber (already mentioned), recognised in Germany as the standard book on the subject, is, taken altogether, the most satisfactory.*   The author is an acute and original thinker, ' nullius addictus jurare in verba magistri.'   He applies the test of reason to the rules of the art, and exposes, with unsparing ridicule, the fallacies which have so long passed current; but his anxiety to avoid the error of excessive generalization has led to a multiplicity of rules and a minuteness of particulars, which render his treatise a more laborious study than it might have been.   But there is no royal road to music; and those who apply themselves seriously to the pages of Gottfried Weber will assuredly profit by their labour.

The work before us, without any novelty of plan, is a useful compilation.   Mr. Rohner has aimed at conciseness; and, though his work is by no means a small one (consisting of two goodly quarto volumes, with the promise of a third), yet we have nowhere found the same quantity of matter in a smaller space.   The first volume treats of the scales and their component intervals; of the different consonant and dissonant chords; of rhythm; and of the rules of harmony in two or more parts.   The second

---

* There is an excellent English translation of this work, by Mr. Warner, published at Boston in the United States, and reprinted at London.

volume is occupied with the various species of counterpoint; and a third is announced, which is to explain the rules of Fugue and Canon. Much good may be obtained from this work, especially when used as a manual to assist the teacher; for, while its examples are copious and excellent, its rules and explanations often lack completeness and precision, and their looseness of expression may perplex the solitary student. The complicated diagrams on pages 6 and 7, and on pages 12 and 13 of the first volume, are more calculated to puzzle than to enlighten; and what is said, on page 9, about the ' enharmonic series,' will only mislead the learner, by inducing him to suppose that there is an actual scale of sounds proceeding by enharmonic degrees, in the same manner as there is a scale proceeding by chromatic degrees. But there is no analogy between the two things. While there is a real chromatic scale in constant use, there is no such thing as an enharmonic scale in existence. ' Music,' says Mr. Rohner, ' is not written in keys which require more than seven sharps or seven flats.' This, again, is calculated to mislead; for, though we do not find more than seven sharps or seven flats placed as the *signature* of a piece of music, yet it is quite common, in pieces of considerable length, to find passages written in keys of eight, nine, or even more sharps or flats.

Our greatest objection to this treatise is one already alluded to; the retention of antiquated matter, not applicable to the present state of the art. In treating of counterpoint, the author, following some of the old German treatises, has preserved the obsolete and absurd distinction of the *strict* and the *free* styles. Under the head of each species of counterpoint, he has given, first a set of rules belonging to the *strict* style, and then another set of rules belonging to the *free* style; the latter rules being contradictory of the former. He first lays down a number of restrictions and prohibitions as belonging to the one style, and then informs the student that they are disregarded in the other. Mr. Rohner, and the modern authors whom he has followed, seem to have considered the strict style and the free style as two different musical dialects, both of which are in present use; while the truth is, that what is now called the strict style was, while in actual use, the *only* style; and that the free style, having been gradually formed, in the progress of the art, by the removal of narrow rules and restrictions, is in reality the *only* style *now* employed by musicians. Teaching our students to write music both in the free and the strict style is, in effect, teaching them to write, not only in the style of the nineteenth, but of the sixteenth century. What would be thought of a school, in these days of Queen Victoria, in which boys and girls were taught the English language, not only as it is written and spoken now, but as it was written and spoken in the days of Queen Bess. As a good deal of misconception still exists on this subject, we shall strengthen our own view of it by the authority of Gottfried Weber.

' Since,' he ' the expressions *allowed* or *forbidden* in this or that style meet us at every glance into the theoretical books hitherto published, I will here take occasion to explain myself once for all on this irst place, then, as respects the distinction between style, I will here confess that I think but little of this whole distinction, and least of all of those technical theories which subject this thing for that is forbidden in the strict style but allowed in the steel and Vhatever sounds positively ill, theory should forbid everywhere; but that which sounds well cannot rationally be forbidden anywhere. Accordingly, if a prohibition is really well founded, that style only is good which avoids what is forbidden; and every other which, less scrupulous, violates that principle — steps over that forbidden ground—is necessarily a faulty style. The so-called *free style* is in that case a style contrary to good rule, and, of course, a bad style, or, at least, a worse style than the other. In regard to the secular or profane, and the church or sacred style, I have much too high an opinion of the latter to regard it as essentially dependent upon such prohibitions. Woe to the dignity of the church style, if its distinction from the profane is to be sought in its being prohibited the use of this or that technical material!'

Had Mr. Rohner viewed the matter in this light—and we are convinced it is the true one—at least one-third part of his second volume would never have been written.

With these qualifications, however, we repeat that Mr. Rohner's work is calculated to be useful, especially in the hands of an experienced teacher. The art of musical composition, indeed, cannot be acquired by any course of self-instruction or solitary study. The student will find, at every step, obstacles which can be removed only as they present themselves, by the ever ready hand of a master.

---

ART. VII.—*Foreign Reminiscences of Henry Richard Lord Holland.* Edited by his Son, Henry Richard Lord Holland. Pp. 362. London : Longman and Co.

NOTHING is more natural than that the literary members of political parties should be overrated by their associates. It has been so at all times, and by men of every grade and variety of opinion. It is not needful to look far for its explanation. The solution of the problem is easy, and lies on the surface. It is resolvable, in fact, into the common element of our nature which leads us to take pride in what exalts ourselves, or is accepted by others as *our* distinction. It is common with the writers of a certain school to represent this over-estimate of the literary talents of their members as the special weakness of the Whig party. We believe nothing of the kind. That it has been evinced by the Whigs we freely admit; but it has only been in common with others, and in conformity with a law to which all political parties have yielded obedience. If their history has exhibited more numerous instances of it than that of their opponents, the simple, and certainly not discreditable, reason has been, that the Whig leaders have been more distinguished by attachment to literature, and eminence in its walks, than the Tories. That such has been the case cannot well be doubted; and the *Eclectic*, though far in advance of mere Whiggery, will not scruple to do them honor on this account.

The late Lord Holland was a distinguished member of the Whig party, to which he attached himself in early life with a sincerity and earnestness to be expected from the nephew of Charles James Fox. He succeeded to the peerage when an infant, and had not, in consequence, the advantage of early training in the Commons. His talents, however, were worthy of his house; and the consistency with which he maintained, throughout an extended life, the principles of his party, insured their confidence, and won for him universal respect. We knew him as the advocate of religious liberty, and feel no hesitation in saying that, with his views as a Churchman, his public course on this great subject indicated a large, generous, and catholic mind, capable of appreciating an unpopular principle, and of laboring honestly in its service. We hold his memory in great honor, as an intelligent, sincere, clear-sighted, tolerant, and earnest man, in days of political profligacy and of rampant-churchmanship. The munificent hospitality of Holland House was celebrated throughout Europe. Wherever literature was cultivated, wherever the votaries of a sound philosophy dwelt, or the amenities of life were known, the name of the English peer was held in repute. One who knew his lordship well, a member of the same political party, himself a distinguished ornament of the republic of letters, has painted, in his own fascinating and graphic style, the scene frequently exhibited at Holland House. 'They will remember,' says Mr. Macaulay, anticipating the emotions of the last survivors of those who partook of his lordship's hospitality, 'how the last debate was discussed in one corner, and the last comedy of Scribe in another; while Wilkie gazed with modest admiration on Reynolds's Baretti; while Mackintosh turned over Thomas Acquinas, to verify a quotation ; while Talleyrand related his conversations with Barras at the Luxembourg, or his ride with Lannes over the field of Austerlitz.    They will remember, above all, the grace— and the kindness, far more admirable than grace—with which the princely hospitality of that ancient mansion was dispensed.' Such were the habits and position of the man whose ' Foreign Reminiscences' are now before us.    The volume is likely to meet with the fate which might have been anticipated.    On the one hand, it is unduly praised ; and, on the other, most ungenerously depreciated.    The truth lies between the two.    Neither Whig nor Tory report is to be received.    Lord Holland was superior to his uncle in private worth, but certainly not his equal in talent.    We would much rather trust to his guidance ; but it is sheer folly to attribute to his sketches of public men, the profound sagacity and marvellous eloquence which distinguished the great opponent of Pitt.    His volume is one of the most readable books we have met with for a long time past.    Its style is unaffected and clear ; its views of men and events are fresh and honest, not hastily gathered, but formed from personal knowledge or from the report of eye-witnesses whom his lordship deemed worthy of confidence.    The personages introduced are the leading political characters of the first French Revolution, and of the earlier part of the present century ; and the light thrown on their character and policy, though not distinguished by any special brilliancy, discloses some traits not fully apprehended, and thus aids toward the solution of problems which have long perplexed inquiring men.

In some cases Lord Holland's judgment is opposed to the conclusions of powerful parties amongst us.    The worshippers of Burke, those at least whose adoration extends beyond his deep searching philosophy, will be scandalized at the opinions expressed respecting Marie Antoinette.    A furious outcry has already been raised on this point ; and the case is only an illustration of what occurs in other passages of the book, and in reference to other personages than the French queen.    We only refer, at present, to his lordship's statement of the grounds on which his judgments were formed.    He was no democrat, though the opinions of his party on the great drama then being acted in France should in all fairness be taken into account.    ' I can only vouch,' he says, ' for the anecdotes I record, by assuring my readers that I believe them : I repeat them as they were received and understood by me from what appeared sufficient authority ; and I delineate the characters either as the result of my own impressions, or of the opinions conveyed to me by those who were most capable of drawing them correctly.'

Lord Holland's first visit to Paris was in 1791, when not

quite eighteen years old.  His judgment was, of course, immature, and slight value would attach to the opinions he then formed, did we not know that those opinions were reviewed at a more advanced age, and various notes appended to the record of them, in confirmation of their general correctness.  Mirabeau, Carlyle's 'herculean man,' had just departed from the stirring scene, which he had done more than any other mortal to invoke. His purpose to stay the progress of revolution, had long been suspected, and a counter-plot was formed, between which and his policy a deadly struggle would have ensued.  But he died in the prime of manhood, and with him the hope of royalty expired.  Lord Holland's sketch of this great and bad man is far from favorable.  He tells us—

'The solicitude of the people during his illness was unabated, and stories almost incredible of the attention of the populace, in preventing the slightest disturbance in the street where he was lying ill, were related in all societies with that delight and admiration which dramatic displays of sentiment never fail to excite in Paris.  The shops and quays were crowded with his portraits and busts.  A stranger could discern in his physiognomy nothing but visible marks of debauch, vanity, presumption, and artifice, which were strong ingredients in his composition ;  but the Parisians, yet, stunned by his eloquence, and dazzled by his splendid talents, seemed to dwell on the representation of his large features, pock-fretted face, and frizzed hair, with fond complacency mingled with regret.  He was certainly an extraordinary man. That his powers would have been equal, as has often been suggested, either to check or to guide the subsequent course of the French Revolution, may nevertheless be very questionable.  He was thought to be, and probably was, very corrupt ; but an exemption from that vice was the solitary virtue which gave individuals, and Robespierre in particular, any ascendency in the latter and more stormy seasons of that frightful period.  Mirabeau had the talent, or at least the trick and contrivance, of appropriating the ideas and labours of other men to his purposes in a very extraordinary degree.  I have been assured by one who knew him intimately, and acted for a short time as his secretary, that not only the reports he made, but the speeches he delivered, were often written by others, and read by him in the morning, or even run through and adopted by him (as I have seen briefs by our lawyers) while he was actually speaking.  The various imprisonments and embarrassments to which his disorderly life and licentious pen had exposed him are well known.'—Pp. 3, 4.

After the king's attempted flight many demanded his deposition and the establishment of a republic.  This, however, was opposed by Lafayette, and other distinguished members of the popular party.  Their course, though chivalrous, was mistaken.  Few yet dreamt of a republic.  It was the idea of a small class, not the passion of a generation.  Lafayette expressed to Lord Holland, in 1826, his surprise at the most violent of the revolutionists concurring in the preservation of the monarchy. At a meeting held immediately after the arrest of Louis, all, with two exceptions, agreed that it must be maintained, at least for a season, so little faith had they in the prevalence of republican notions. We may now see the error of this conclusion. It is easy to pronounce judgment after the issue of events has been ascertained. Neither political sagacity, nor large experience of human life, is required for this. It is different, however, with the actors in a scene. Their decision, in many cases, must be prompt and final. They have to act at the moment, amid the strife of contending parties, and in the face of possible revelations, which might greatly modify their views.

' The notion,' says Lord Holland, ' that Louis XVI. could become a constitutional king, disposed to weaken rather than strengthen his own authority, after his intended flight, and with the queen for his consort and adviser, was chimerical and puerile in the extreme. He had justified his deposal by his flight. It was imprudent in Constitutionalists, it was madness in Republicans, not to insist on it. Above all, it was, as the event proved, very mistaken mercy. Lafayette and others, however, from very generous motives, were averse to seizing such a moment for the subversion of monarchy; and they were actively instrumental·in discouraging all harshness, severity, or insolence to the king and his family.'

His lordship was much in the company of General Lafayette, and became strongly attached to him. He avows this partiality, and explains by it his faith in the attachment of the king to the new constitution. This partiality, however, does not blind him to the minor defects of the French patriot, as the following brief sketch will show. It does ample justice to a man who, with all his foibles, was intent on bringing the monarchy into harmonious working with popular freedom.

' He was loud in condemning the brutality of Petion, whose cold and offensive replies to the questions of the royal prisoners on their journey back from Varennes were very currently reported ; and he was in his professions, and I believe in his heart, much more confident of the sincerity of the King than common prudence should have allowed him to be, or than was justified either by the character of Lewis himself, or by the truth as disclosed by subsequent events. Lafayette was, however, then, as always, a pure disinterested man, full of private affection and public virtue, and not devoid of such talents as firmness of purpose, sense of honour, and earnestness of zeal, will, on great occasions, supply. He was indeed accessible to flattery, somewhat too credulous, and apt to mistake the forms, or, if I may so phrase it, the pedantry of liberty for the substance, as if men could not enjoy any freedom without subscribing to certain abstract principles and arbitrary tests, or as if the profession and subscription, nay, the technical observance of such tests and principles, were not, on the other hand, often compatible with practical oppression and tyranny. These strictures, however, on his blemishes are less applicable to the period to which I am now referring than to most others of his public life ; for, with all his love of popularity, he was then knowingly sacrificing it for the purpose of rescuing a court from contumely and injury, and, though a republican in principle, was active in preserving the name and perhaps too much of the authority of a King in the new constitution.'— Pp. 11—13.

The believers in Burke's splendid panegyric on Marie Antoinette will be grossly offended at the opinions expressed by Lord Holland respecting her. That much of what occurred is imputable to her influence, we have never doubted, since we looked closely into the history of these times. The dark tragedy which followed grew out of prior events, many of which would never have happened if the Austrian princess had not exercised a disastrous power over her feeble, changeful, and untruthful husband. The following anecdote will sufficiently explain our meaning :—

' M. de Calonne told me that when he had ascertained that the Queen and her coterie were hostile to the plans he had prepared, he waited on the King, respectfully and delicately lamented the Queen's reported disapprobation of his project, earnestly conjuring his Majesty, if not resolved to go through with the plan and to silence all opposition or cavil at it within the Court, to allow him to suppress it in time ; but if, on the other hand, his Majesty was determined to persevere, suggesting the propriety of impressing on the Queen his earnest desire and wishes that nothing should escape her lips which could sanction a doubt of the excellence of the measures themselves, and still less of the determination of the Court to adopt and enforce them. Lewis at first scouted the notion of the Queen (*une femme,* as he called her,) forming or hazarding any opinion about it. But when M. de Calonne assured him that she spoke of the project in terms of disparagement and censure, the King rang the bell, sent for her Majesty to the apartment, and after sternly and even coarsely rebuking her for meddling with matters, *auxquelles les femmes n'ont rien à faire,* he, to the dismay of De Calonne, took her by the shoulders, and fairly turned her out of the room like a naughty child. "*Me voilà perdu,*" said De Calonne to himself ; and he was accordingly dismissed, and his scheme abandoned in the course of a few days.'—Pp. 16, 17.

Her personal attachment to the King was more than doubtful, though, in the judgment of some partizans, it is heresy of the worst kind to say so. Some chivalrous writers have undertaken the defence of Mary of Scotland, and so, in our own day, men are found to attach the vilest epithets to those who refuse to subscribe to the domestic purity of the French Queen. ' Lord Holland is one of these, and we fear that his incredulity is not without good proof. Passing over this topic, however, we extract a brief passage, descriptive of the Queen as she appeared to her youthful observer :—

' As I was not presented at Court, I never saw the Queen but at the play-house. She was then in affliction, and her countenance was, no doubt, disfigured by long suffering and resentment. I should not, however, suppose that the habitual expression of it, even in happier seasons, had ever been very agreeable. Her beauty, however extolled, consisted, I suspect, exclusively in a fair skin, a straight person, and a stately air, which her admirers termed dignity, and her enemies pride and disdain. Her total want of judgment and temper no doubt contributed to the disasters of the Royal Family, but there was no member of it to whom the public was uniformly so harsh and unjust, and her trial and death were among the most revolting parts of the whole catastrophe. She was, indeed, insensible when led to the scaffold ; but the previous persecution which she underwent was base, unmanly, cruel, and ungenerous to the last degree.'—Pp. 19, 20.

The Duke of Orleans, father of Louis Philippe, acted, as is well known, a prominent part in the Parisian drama, and his name has been handed down as a synonyme for intrigue and selfish ambition. No epithets have been too harsh or degrading in the judgment of royalist scribes to denote his baseness. He is described as at once feeble, vain, restless, and unprincipled—reckless of the ruin of others, and intent only on the advancement of his own criminal designs. Lord Holland's sketch is much more favorable, and the considerations he advances are, to say the least, entitled to weight. ' I believe,' says his lordship, ' that no man has lived in my time whose character has been more calumniated, or will be more misrepresented to posterity.' We have our misgivings on this point, and can neither concur in the lenient decision of his lordship, nor in the harsh judgment given by the enemies of the Duke. He perished in the storm which he had aided to raise, and both jacobin and royalist exulted in his fate.

Lord Holland's introduction to M. Talleyrand occurred in 1791, and this acquaintance was continued through all the strange vicissitudes of the Frenchman's life. At the period of his residence with his uncle, the Archbishop of Rheims, 1782, he entertained William Pitt, who visited that town, in company with the late Mr. Wilberforce, for the purpose of learning French. The English minister, however, found it convenient, subsequently, to forget the obligation when Talleyrand was an exile from the land of his fathers. He ' was initiated into public affairs under M. de Calonne, and learnt from that lively

minister the happy facility of transacting business without effort
and without ceremony in the corner of a drawing-room, or in
the recess of a window.  In the exercise of that talent, he
equalled the readiness and surpassed the wit of his model, but
he brought to his work some commodities, which the latter
could never supply; viz. great veracity, discretion, and foresight.  He displayed little or no talent for public speaking in
the National Assembly.  His reports and papers, especially one
on education, procured him some celebrity, but were, I suspect,
the composition of other men.  His abilities were, however,
acknowledged, for they were undeniable, and his future success
foreseen.'

‘ For thirty or forty years, the bon-mots of M. de Talleyrand were
more frequently repeated, and more generally admired, than those of
any living man.  The reason was obvious.  Few men uttered so many,
and yet fewer any equally good.  By a happy combination of neatness
in language and ease and suavity of manner, with archness and sagacity
of thought, his sarcasms assumed a garb at once so courtly and so
careless, that they often diverted almost as much as they could mortify
even their immediate objects.  His humorous reproof to a gentleman
vaunting with self-complacency the extreme beauty of his mother, and
apparently implying that it might account for advantages in person in
her descendants, is well known :—“C'était donc,” said he, “ Monsieur
votre père qui n'était pas si bien.”  The following is more recent, but
the humour of it hardly less arch or less refined.  The celebrity of M.
de Chateaubriand, the vainest of mortals, was on the wane.  About the
same time, it happened to be casually mentioned in conversation that
Chateaubriand was affected with deafness, and complained bitterly of
that infirmity.  “Je comprends,” said Talleyrand; “depuis qu'on a
cessé de parler de lui il se croit sourd.” '—Pp. 39, 40, note.

Of another prominent actor, Fouché, to whom Lord Holland
was introduced, we are told that his ‘countenance, manner, and
conversation exhibited at that time the profligacy and ferocity,
the energy and restlessness, which one might well expect to find
blended in the character of a revolutionist, and which, though
more carefully concealed when he became a courtier, were the
chief ingredients in the composition of that vain and unprincipled tool of the Republic, the Consul, and the Bourbons.'
The summer and autumn of the following year, 1792, were
spent in Denmark and Prussia, in both which countries Lord
Holland remarked a universal persuasion that France would be
subdued by her invaders, and the prevalence of extreme dissatisfaction at the prospect of such a result.  ‘Military men, politicians, and all who were styled good company, treated any resistance to regular German armies by French troops, much more by
National Guards, raw levies, volunteers or peasantry, as an utter

impossibility. The art of war, said they, was reduced to a certainty; the notion of valour, enthusiasm, or numbers defeating disciplined troops commanded by an experienced captain like the Duke of Brunswick, was as chimerical as an attempt to confute a problem in mathematics by metaphor, fancy, or ingenuity.'

We may well smile at such a persuasion, but let us not despise the men who entertained it. Nothing had yet occurred to test the vast power of the enthusiasm of a nation when thoroughly roused and rendered half frantic. Not only was the tide of invasion thrown back, but the Italian campaign of the first Consul established, in fact, the European ascendency of France. At the time of his lordship's visit to Denmark, the Crown Prince, afterwards Frederick VI., was the ostensible head of the government. We know few satires on monarchy more bitter or cutting than an anecdote of the Court of Copenhagen, thus recorded by our author :—

'The incapacity of his father was acknowledged, and though he continued to sign the edicts and public instruments, he was not permitted to take any part in the deliberation upon them, nor were any of his acts deemed valid, unless countersigned by his son, whom the council had in truth invested with all the functions of royal authority. In fact, the royal signature was preserved as a medical rather than political expedient. The object was to humour and soothe the feelings of the deposed monarch, not to give any validity to acts which without reference to such formality were recognised by the courts of justice, and obeyed by the people. When first set aside, he had bitterly wept at being no longer a king, and adduced as a proof of the misfortune which had misfallen him, that he had no longer any papers to sign. To satisfy him, they were afterwards offered him for signature, and he never declined annexing his name to all that were presented to him, from a fear of losing that, his sole remaining, but, in his view, distinctive prerogative of royalty. It happened, once or twice, from some motive of convenience or accident, that the Crown Prince put his name to an instrument before it was sent to his royal father for his signature; the jealous old Monarch perceived it, and when the next paper was brought, he, to the surprise and consternation of the courtiers, signed " Christian and Co^nia," maliciously observing, that he was once sole proprietor of his firm, but he found it was now a partnership, and would spare his associates the trouble of adding their names.'— Pp. 50, 51.

Of the Prussian Court we shall say but little, as the sketch given of its morals is most repulsive. For the honor of the parties concerned, we hope it is overcharged. By-the-bye, at page forty-seven, his lordship's visit to Prussia is said to have been in 1792, whereas at page fifty-eight its chronology is recorded as 1791. The latter, we presume, is a typographical error.

In 1798, Lord Holland visited Spain, and returned thither on two subsequent occasions. He mastered the language, attained considerable knowledge of its literature, and, by the access granted him, obtained an insight into the character and policy of the Court. His sketch is proportionably extended, but its features are so dark and disgusting that we readily pass it over. The character of Ferdinand VII. was unredeemed by a single generous or virtuous trait. 'The hideous uniformity of his base, cowardly, and perfidious career,' gives him an execrable pre-eminence amongst the most perfidious wearers of a crown..

The latter part of the volume, extending from page 187 to 320, is devoted to Napoleon, ' the greatest prodigy,' says Lord Holland, ' of the times to which my notices refer.' The sketch given is, in our judgment, much too favorable. Every extenuating circumstance which the utmost partiality could suggest, is advanced on his behalf, while the worst features of his policy, and its terrible effects, are kept wholly out of sight. His lordship writes more as a friend than a judge, and the portraiture he gives fails, therefore, to convey any accurate notion of the French emperor. We regret these faults. They constitute, in our judgment, a serious offence, and, to whatever extent they have influence, will strengthen mere brute force, apart from the consideration of the manner in which it is employed. We are happily getting out of the iron age, and are learning to estimate men's merits, not by the slaughter they have perpetrated, the hearths they have rendered desolate, the widows and the orphans they have created, but by the higher, nobler, more divine qualities of which our nature is susceptible. We readily admit the vast powers of Napoleon—his gigantic intellect, his sagacity, his unwearied diligence, and marvellous military skill ; but his career is to us, we confess, one of the most painful exhibitions which history-supplies, and the manner in which Lord Holland adverts to it, is adapted to foster rather than to correct the evil passions out of which it grew. But it is not our purpose to discuss the character and policy of Buonaparte. We shall, therefore, content ourselves with laying before our readers his lordship's report on one or two of the more prominent points of his history.

The following is the account given of the manner in which he obtained the resources needed in order to his assuming the command of the army of Italy. It is strikingly characteristic of his decision and promptitude.

' On his first nomination to the army of Italy, the Directory is said . to have been unable or unwilling to supply him with the money necessary for the journey of himself and his aide-de-camps to the spot, and their suitable appearance at the head-quarters of a considerable force.

In this emergency, after collecting all that his resources, the contribution of his friends, and his credit could muster, he is reported to have applied to Junot, a young officer whom he knew to be in the habit of frequenting the gaming-tables, and confiding to him all the money he had been able to raise, in itself no great sum, to have directed him either to lose the whole, or to increase it to a considerable amount before the morning, as on his success that night at play depended the possibility of his taking the command of the army and appointing Junot his aide-de-camp. Junot, after succeeding beyond his expectations in winning to an amount in his judgment equal to the exigencies of his employer, hastened to inform General Buonaparte, but he was not satisfied, and resolving to try his fortune to the utmost, bade his friend return, risk all that he had gained, and not quit the table till he had lost the last penny, or doubled the sum he had brought back to him. In this also, after some fluctuation, the chances favoured him; and Napoleon set out to his head-quarters furnished with sufficient to take upon him the command with no little personal splendour and *éclat*.'— Pp. 217, 218.

No light is thrown on the murder of the Duke of Enghien, one of the darkest tragedies of the reign of Napoleon, but every extenuating plea which can diminish the horror awakened by so infamous an event is set forth. It is probable, as Lord Holland suggests, that the Duke was mistaken for Pichegru; but,-if so, what shall we think of the recklessness which could thus trifle with life, or of the policy which could employ the forms of investigation, in order to overrule the requirements of justice? Of his mental habits, and prodigious powers of application, we are told :—

' Great as was his appetite for knowledge, his memory in retaining, and his quickness in applying it, his labour both in acquiring and using it was equal to them. In application to business he could wear out the men most inured to study. In the deliberations on the Code Civil, many of which lasted ten, twelve, or fifteen hours without intermission, he was always the last whose attention flagged; and he was so little disposed to spare himself trouble, that even in the Moscow campaign he sent regularly to every branch of administration in Paris directions in detail, which in every government but his would, both from usage and convenience, have been left to the discretion of the superintending minister, or to the common routine of business. This and other instances of his diligence are more wonderful than praiseworthy. . . . Yet with all this industry, and with the multiplicity of topics which engaged his intention, he found time for private and various reading. His librarian was employed for some time every morning in replacing maps and books which his unwearied and insatiable curiosity had consulted before breakfast. He read all letters whatever addressed to himself, whether in his private or public capacity; and it must, I believe, be acknowledged that he often took the same liberty with those directed to other people. He had indulged in that unjustifiable practice before his elevation ; and such was his impatience to open both parcels and letters that, however employed, he could seldom defer the gratification of his curiosity an instant after either came under his notice or his reach.  Josephine, and others well acquainted with his habits, very pardonably took some advantage of this propensity. Matters which she feared to mention to him were written and directed to her, and the letters unopened left in his way.  He often complied with wishes which he thought he had detected by an artifice, more readily than had they been presented in the form of claim, petition, or request.  He liked to know everything ; but he liked all he did to have the appearance of springing entirely from himself, feeling, like many others in power, an unwillingness to encourage even those they love in an opinion that they have an influence over them, or that there is any certain channel to their favour. . . .  With the temper and habits I have described, he was not likely to be scrupulous in furnishing his police with much vexatious authority.  It was accordingly most active and most odious ; but such has always been, and is still, the practice in France.  Napoleon's agents were for the most part restored emigrants, ex-nobles, and pretended royalists. Many after the restoration were indiscreet enough to acknowledge, or at least to prove by their complaints of the niggardly boons which they received from Lewis XVIII., that the profit derived from betraying the cause of legitimacy under the Usurper had exceeded what they earned by their support of it under a Bourbon prince.'—Pp. 277—281.

The extracts we have given will enable our readers to judge of the character and merits of this volume.  We have read it with considerable interest, and, though we cannot say it has greatly enlarged our knowledge, yet we are free to confess that it has given a freshness and definite form to many notions which had previously floated loosely in our mind.

---

ART. VIII.—1. *The Letters Apostolical of Pope Pius IX., considered with Reference to the Law of England and the Law of Europe.* By Travers Twiss, D.C.L., of Doctors' Commons, Fellow of University College, Oxford;  and Commissary General of the Diocese of Canterbury.  London : Longman and Co.  1851.

2. *The Queen or the Pope?  The Question considered in its Political, Legal, and Religious Aspects.  In a Letter to Spencer H. Walpole, Esq., Q.C., M.P.* By Samuel Warren, Esq., F.R.S.  Fifth Edition.  With a Note concerning Ireland.  London and Edinburgh : Blackwood and Sons.  1851.

3. *The Duty of England. A Protestant Layman's Reply to Cardinal Wiseman's 'Appeal.'* London : John Chapman. 1851.

4. *Reflexions arising out of the Popish Aggression ; for the Consideration of the Church, Laity, and Parliament. With Comments on the Dispute between the Rev. W. J. E. Bennett, of Saint Barnabas, Pimlico, and the Bishop of London.* By a Simple Protestant. London : Kendal. 1851.

5. *Cautions for the Times. Addressed to the Parishioners of a Parish in England.* By their former Rector. To be published occasionally. No. 1. London : Parker.

6. *The Papal Aggression and Popery contemplated Religiously. A Pastoral Address to his Flock.* By J. A. James. London : Hamilton, Adams, and Co. 1851.

7. *The Protestant Reformation. A Lecture.* By the Rev. George Smith. Second Edition. London : John Snow. 1851.—*The Right of Private Judgment. A Lecture.* By the Rev. George Smith, of Trinity Chapel, Poplar. London : Gorbell, Wertheim, and Macintosh. 1851.

8. *A Voice from an Outpost. Two Discourses on the Papal Aggression.* By W. Urwick, D.D. Dublin : Robertson. London : Simpkin and Marshall. 1851.

9. *Roman Catholicism and Protestant Christianity contrasted. A Tract for the Times.* By John Rogers, Author of 'Am I a Christian?' &c. Second Edition, revised. London : John Snow. 1851.

10. *A Tract for the Times. Not the Church, not the Pope, but the Bible.* By William Thwaites, Author of 'Facts and Opinions for Churchmen and Dissenters.' London : Houlston. 1851.

DR. TWISS's elaborate consideration of the Letters Apostolic of Pope Pius IX. is, what it professes to be, a discussion of a purely *legal and political* character. To some of our readers such a discussion may be destitute of interest ; to others, we apprehend, it may prove, as in our own case, remarkably attractive ; and, for their sakes, we shall give as full and luminous a report as we are able of the learned writer's production.

He shows that the document of the date of 29th September, 1850, with the signature of Cardinal Lambruschini attached to it, is not what is technically termed a papal bull. A bull consists of letters patent issued from the Roman Chancery, with a leaden seal (*bulla*) attached to them (*sub plombo*). ' Letters apostolical' are in the form of a brief, given under the Fisherman's Ring (a

seal on which an image of St. Peter is engraved), and subscribed
by the Secretary of Briefs. The document in question belongs
to the latter class of instruments—a brief, not a bull. Its title
is—' Sanctissimi nostri Domini Pii Divina Providentia Papæ IX.
*Litteræ Apostolicæ* quibus Hierarchia Episcopalis in Anglia
restituitur. Romæ Types Sacræ Congregationis de Propaganda
Fide M DCCC L :' which, being interpreted in English, is—
Letters apostolic of our most holy lord Pius IX. by Divine Providence Pope, by which the Episcopal Hierarchy is restored
in England. The difference between a brief and a bull consists
in something more than the mere forms. A brief *may* be, and
*has* been, *suppressed ;* it may be cancelled by a second brief; it
is mostly of a more limited application than a bull. A bull may
*not* be suppressed ; it can be cancelled only by a bull which must
pass through the Roman Chancery. It is, not infrequently,
binding on the entire communion of the Church of Rome. The
brief which has lately appeared in England does not deal with
Roman Catholics alone, but the *territories* of England, appointing persons to *govern* them *with ordinary jurisdiction*. The
country is recognised as Catholic England. This brief was expounded in the pastoral letter in which Nicholas, Archbishop of
Westminster, Cardinal Priest of the Church of St. Pudenziana
in Rome, and Administrator Apostolic of the diocese of Southwark in England, enjoined that the said pastoral letter should be
publicly read in all the churches and chapels of the arch-diocese
of Westminster, and the diocese of Southwark, on the Sunday
after its being received.

After these explanations, Dr. Twiss examines patiently, courteously, and with characteristic acumen, Mr. Bowyer's pamphlet,
published ' by authority,' and Cardinal Wiseman's ' Appeal to
the English people.' The latter publication is described as
' more rhetorical' than Mr. Bowyer's in its mode of treating the
subject, and as ' replete with irony and sarcasm.' To the arguments of both these writers the answers of Dr. Twiss appear to
us to be as exactly just in reasoning as they are calm and dignified
in temper. From this part of the volume, which it would not be
easy to condense, we glean a few statements of fact which it is of
some importance that our readers should know, as naturally
guiding them in judging of this legal question :—

' The Protestant Episcopalian Church in Scotland is maintained by
the law of the land, under the spiritual authority of bishops exercising
episcopal functions within given districts, but *without any fixed sees
or tithes recognised by law* . . . The system of vicars apostolic is *not a
system confined to heathen countries*, but is *the recognised* mode of
administering the spiritual affairs of the Roman Catholic body in such
European States as are *not in ecclesiastical communion*, or at least under

As far as the Roman

its peculiar constitution,
been favoured with an exemption from many of the provisions of the
Canon Law which *were at variance with the institutions of the country.*
They now become subject to it in its .locality; and a legal writer, a
Roman Catholic member of the 'House of Commons, has already

'If the desire to possess this power—to have a hierarchy—through
which alone it can be given, "is," as Dr. Wiseman states, "essentially
a Catholic purpose and a Catholic object," then Catholic objects and
Catholic purposes are not those which the law of the land can be
expected to further; and Catholic organization, in the manner in which
it is provided for by the Letters Apostolic, and in the sense in which it
is intended, according to Dr. Wiseman's own avowal, to be carried into
execution in England, becomes inconsistent with the safety of the
state, for it saps the foundations of the pillars of obedience to the law
of the land, upon which the safety of the State rests.'

Dr. Twiss opposes to Dr. Wiseman's references to Belgium a
large collection of facts, which show that the Government of that
country has entertained very considerable fear to the State, from
*the ecclesiastical encroachments* of the Roman Catholic bishops
upon the law of the land. Only in 1845, the Belgian government was under the necessity of putting down an attempt of
the bishops, by means of *secret conventions* with the communal
authorities, to fetter them in discharging the duties imposed on
them by the civil power.

'A further observation may be added upon the attitude of the Roman
Catholic Church in Belgium. It is well known that the Belgian clergy

gave in their adherence *en masse*, with a very few exceptions, to the famous Encyclical Letter of Gregory XVI. (18 Sept., 1832.) That Encyclical Letter condemned, in the most absolute manner, " that absurd and erroneous maxim, or rather wild notion, that *liberty of conscience* ought to be assured and guaranteed to every person."* Whether the Pope on this occasion adopted a sound view, it boots not to inquire; but this at least may be said, that it would ill become those who deny liberty of conscience to others, to demand, under the plea of liberty of conscience, an impunity in infringing the solemn sanctions of the law of the land.'

The pains and penalties attaching by statute law to the exercise of the Roman Catholic religion in England were removed by Act of Parliament in 1791. The Relief Act of 1829, an act of the *Imperial* Parliament, bestowed on the laity of the United Kingdom a *political status*, but made no change in their religious or ecclesiastical condition. The Toleration Act of 1791 permitted the Roman Catholics to have ' ministers of any higher rank or order than priests.' To this permission the Relief Act added nothing. Neither the one act nor the other contemplated an *episcopate*—a hierarchy—a capacity in which the bishops of the Roman Catholic Church were refused to be recognised long ago by the Empress Maria Theresa, and, so lately as the year 1845, by the existing Belgian government. The more recent laws of England relating to Roman Catholics—

' Have not made *lawful* anything in respect of the supremacy of the Pope as claimed, used, or usurped, within this realm before the reign of Queen Elizabeth.' . . . ' It is still against the law of the land for a subject of her Majesty to *maintain* or *defend* the spiritual or ecclesiastical supremacy of the Pope, as *heretofore claimed or used* by him, within this realm, or to put in use or execute anything for the maintenance or defence of it. On the other hand, the Roman Catholic subjects of her Majesty have been relieved from the necessity of making any *positive renunciation* of the Pope's spiritual authority as a *condition of enjoying their full civil rights.* Whilst their religion is thus completely tolerated, and they are not called upon to do or declare anything against their religious convictions, they are, on the other hand, restricted from putting into use or execution the complete ecclesiastical system of their Church. The contrary position cannot be reasonably maintained in the face of the provision and declaration of the statute just recited.'

One of the arguments relied on with much confidence, both by Mr. Bowyer and by Dr. Wiseman, is, that the Relief (or

---

* ' Atque ex hoc putidissimo *in differentismi* fonte absurda illa fluit ac erronea sententia, seu potius deliramentum asserandam esse ac vindicandam cuilibet *libertatem* conscientiæ.'—*Epistola Encyclica Gregorii Divina Providentia Papæ XVI.*

Emancipation) Act, ' by forbidding any one from assuming or using the style or title of any archbishopric or bishopric of the Established Church, *virtually allows* Roman Catholics to assume *any others.*' Now, in that statute, it is *assumed* that *it is an offence* at common law to use them unless *authorized by law.* But, even if we admitted that Mr. Bowyer and Dr. Wiseman have interpreted rightly the law referred to, the brief is illegal, and offensive, *on their own showing,* for it constitutes a bishop of St. David's—an act which *these gentlemen* tell us is ' forbidden,' but which Dr. Twiss, with more legal accuracy, *proves* to be an ' offence, not created by any enactment of this statute ; on the contrary, the assumption and use of the style and title, without lawful authority, is dealt with penally.'

'Now the style and title of *Episcopus Menevensis,* or *Bishop of St. David's,* cannot be assumed by the nominee of the Holy See without a direct violation of the statute 10 Geo. IV. c. 7, s. 24 ; and the consequent forfeiture on each occasion of one hundred pounds of good and lawful money of the Queen. This may have been an oversight on the part of the Holy See, unless it is to be considered in the light *of a farther experiment upon the elasticity* of the statute law of England.'

There appears to have been much popular misunderstanding, in which we acknowledge our participation, respecting the recognition, by Government, of the claims of the Irish bishops. It is clearly shown by Dr. Twiss that on no occasion has the assumption and use of the *name, style,* or *title* of archbishop of any province, or bishop of any bishopric, by the Roman Catholic prelates in Ireland, been recognised, directly or indirectly, as lawful. Their episcopal order has been recognised, and social rank has been conceded to them. *Territorial* titles are not accorded. At the same time, Dr. Twiss admits that—

' It is to be regretted that greater care has not been taken with the phraseology of several documents of a public nature in which *spiritual jurisdiction* is spoken of, where *spiritual authority* would have been the more appropriate and less ambiguous phrase, as *jurisdiction* properly implies a *forum externum, authority* need only refer to the *forum conscientiæ.*'

A similar explanation applies to the colonies. In 1835, her Majesty's Government acceded to a proposal that Dr.Polding, who went to Australia as a simple chaplain to the Roman Catholic population, should be allowed to exercise *episcopal authority.* After an absence for awhile from the colony he returned with the title of Archbishop of Sydney, whereas, previously, he had the title of Bishop of Hiero-Cæsarea, and executed episcopal functions as vicar-apostolic. But her Majesty's Government has hitherto never recognised any *archiepiscopal* see of Sydney.

Dr. Twiss, who has gone thoroughly and impartially into the whole question, says, most explicitly :—

' It may therefore be safely said, that her Majesty's Government has carefully declined to recognise the *territorial* titles assumed by the Roman Catholic bishops from sees assigned to them from their Church within the Australian colonies. And so far from no remonstrance having ever been made, as Dr. Wiseman asserts, in consequence of the creation of the Papal sees, and the assumption of the style and title of the Australian bishops of the English Church, the printed correspondence on the subject laid before the House of Commons in 1849 and 1850 supplies very full evidence to the contrary. From this printed correspondence, which we have examined critically, we find that the rule laid down by her Majesty's Secretary of State for the Colonies on this question is,—" That the Roman Catholic prelates are *not* to be recognised by the local government under *the titles assigned to them by* their own Church." ' . . .

' Dr. Wiseman complains that old and long dormant statutes should be wakened up, and obsolete legislation should be turned against himself and his colleagues. But the Pope himself has awakened up *a long dormant hierarchy, and has turned against England an obsolete code of law.* Surely, if the spectre of Popery once more stalks at large on the banks of the Thames, and casts the shadow of its gaunt form before it; if the Pope has disinterred what were believed to be dry bones, and they have come together at his bidding, and he has sought to breathe life into them; shall Dr. Wiseman, with reason, complain that the guardians of the temple of the laws of England rouse themselves up to confront their ancient foe ? But the statute law has not been mute since the reign of Elizabeth ; it was heard to speak forth in clear and distinct tones in 1846, when it expressly declared the laws of Queen Victoria to continue in this respect the same as those of Queen Elizabeth.'

As to Cardinal Wiseman's own liability, let us look at the facts of the case, and to the precedents in the history of England. We learn, on the authority of public newspapers, that the brief of the Pope was read aloud in the congregation assembled, with open doors, at the enthronement of the Cardinal. *This was a violation of the statute law of England.* Cardinal Wolsey committed the same offence, and the Judges of the Court of King's Bench held that it was ' a contempt of the King and the Crown, and contrary to the statute.' Wolsey, accordingly, was *convicted.* Subsequently to the ' Reformation,' we learn from Howell's State Trials, and from Sir John Davies's Reports, that Robert Lalor was convicted by a jury of the city of Dublin of exercising episcopal *jurisdiction* by virtue of a bull or a brief procured from Rome.

It is well known that Dr. Wiseman, in his ' Appeal,' relies on the assumed analogy between the recent brief of the Pope, in

d by

xercise his functions within that realm, subject to certain laws.
n Protestant Saxony, where the King is a Roman Catholic, his
Majesty's confessor is accustomed to receive the title of a bishop
n partibus, with the authority of vicar-apostolic. Thus it
ppears that the practice of countries in which the ecclesiastical
upremacy of the Roman see is not acknowledged, as also the
ractice of the Roman see in relation to such countries, has

bishops of
VI. to omit the
to their peculiar circumstances as

actice and usage in such matters, or there
e or usage. Thus much, at least, ultra-
Rome must admit that from the earliest
ntiff has exercised any authority in the
bishops in foreign lands, he has exercised
piritual or ecclesiastical, with the assent
sovereign. That practice originated when
It was observed invariably by

him for three centuries, during which he possessed no temporal power.
It has continued to be the rule, with very rare exceptions, in such
matters, since the Popes separated themselves from, and became independent of, the princes of Constantinople, down to the Reformation,
in all countries which have acknowledged the spiritual supremacy of
the patriarch of the Western Church; whilst, subsequently to the
Reformation, we find that no contrary practice has grown up in regard
to either those states which have continued in ecclesiastical communion
with the Holy See, or those which have renounced such communion.
It is difficult to understand how a principle of such importance, if it
involved a spiritual question, should never have been asserted by the
Pope in his relations with sovereign princes, who have professedly
acknowledged and recognised the supremacy of the Holy See, and
that meanwhile a use and a practice should have intervened which has
shifted the matter altogether from its foundations on abstract principle,
The necessity of protection at the hands of the territorial sovereign
has introduced the right of consent on his part, and the PRACTICE OF
EUROPE HAS ESTABLISHED IT.'

The case of Ireland is admitted by Dr. Twiss, and with
melancholy truth, to be that of ' a land of anomalies.'

' In Ireland there has always been a Roman Catholic Church; in

A A 2

The Pope may give a bishop *mission—i.e.*, may authorize him to go forth as the spiritual ambassador of the Holy See—but that the Pope should establish a territorial *seat* for his bishop in the realm of a sovereign power without its consent, would be to usurp an attribute of local sovereignty, and to take possession of the land for ecclesiastical purposes.  For it matters not that the possession is only formal and figurative, for such is, also, for the most part, the character of civil occupation.  *Words* are for such purposes taken to represent *things*. But the Pope has not been content merely to declare his will to erect sees—he has gone further.  He has sent *his subject*, a prince of his court, to take effective possession of his see, and to execute such acts as serve to mark his ecclesiastical occupation of the land.  All that is now required to establish an irrefragable title is, that the sovereign of the land should *acquiesce* in *the* settlement of the cardinal.'

An instrument of government is issued by one of the powers recognised in Europe, dated from his capital, and subscribed by his Minister.  Such an instrument of foreign government would not be allowed in any state of Europe.  In the sixteenth century, the borough of Bresse, in Savoy, was made a city and the see of a bishop by Pope Leo X.; but because the King of France had not consented to it, the Pope's diploma to that effect was recalled. It was *on condition of being received by the English nation* that Pope Gregory agreed to make Augustine a bishop.  It was not the Pope, but the English monarch, who assigned to him the city of Canterbury as his see.  It was the successor of Alfred, Edward the Elder, who erected five new sees, which royal act was confirmed by Pope Formosus.  It was with the consent of William the Norman that Archbishop Lanfranc established episcopal sees in Chester, Salisbury, and Chichester.  Eadmer, Matthew Paris, and Matthew of Westminster, the Church annalists of their times, most amply illustrate the rule that no new bishop could be instituted to a see without the consent of the King.  The Pope's confirmation was required; but the territorial sovereignty of the British Crown was never abdicated.

Of Protestant states, there are some which have, and others which have not, diplomatic relations with the see of Rome.  The Netherlands is still considered as a *mission in partibus infidelium*, under the superintendence of vicars-apostolic; ' and it is not unworthy of remark that the bishop *in partibus* designed by the Pope to reside in Amsterdam, as vicar, has not, as yet, ventured to take possession of the building allowed to him for a residence, in the presence of the difficulties raised in his way by the Protestant communions in Holland.'

In Prussia, and in Hanover, the King must be consulted before Roman Catholic sees can be assigned.  In Denmark there is no Roman Catholic bishop, but a vicar-apostolic. In Schleswig and Holstein, there is bare *toleration*.  In Sweden there is a vi.... .p.....lic authorized by royal diploma to exercise his functions within that realm, subject to certain laws. In Protestant Saxony, where the King is a Roman Catholic, his Majesty's confessor is accustomed to receive the title of a bishop *in partibus*, with the authority of vicar-apostolic. Thus it appears that the practice of countries in which the ecclesiastical supremacy of the Roman see is not acknowledged, as also the practice of the Roman see in relation to such countries, has been uniformly based on the principle of recognising the local sovereignty in the constitution of episcopal sees. When Catherine II., the Empress of Russia, consented to the erection of the archiepiscopal see of Mohilow, but objected to the oath, as *at variance with the law of the country*, that oath—or rather the famous clause, ' hæreticos persequar et impugnabo '—was cancelled, and, *on this prece*    , the Roman Catholic bishops of Ireland obtained permission trom Pope Pius VI. to omit the clause, in accommodation to their peculiar circumstances as British subjects.

' Either there has been a practice and usage in such matters, or there has not been any such practice or usage. Thus much, at least, ultramontanists of the Church of Rome must admit that from the earliest period since the Roman Pontiff has exercised any authority in the business of erecting sees for bishops in foreign lands, he has exercised such authority, be it either spiritual or ecclesiastical, with the assent and consent of the territorial sovereign. That practice originated when the Pope was not a sovereign prince. It was observed invariably by him for three centuries, during which he possessed no temporal power. It has continued to be the rule, with very rare exceptions, in such matters, since the Popes separated themselves from, and became independent of, the princes of Constantinople, down to the Reformation, in all countries which have acknowledged the spiritual supremacy of the patriarch of the Western Church ; whilst, subsequently to the Reformation, we find that no contrary practice has grown up in regard to either those states which have continued in ecclesiastical communion with the Holy See, or those which have renounced such communion. It is difficult to understand how a principle of such importance, if it involved a spiritual question, should never have been asserted by the Pope in his relations with sovereign princes, who have professedly acknowledged and recognised the supremacy of the Holy See, and that meanwhile a use and a practice should have intervened which has shifted the matter altogether from its foundations on abstract principle. The necessity of protection at the hands of the territorial sovereign has introduced the right of consent on his part, and the PRACTICE OF EUROPE HAS ESTABLISHED IT.'

The case of Ireland is admitted by Dr. Twiss, and with melancholy truth, to be that of ' a land of anomalies.'

' In Ireland there has always been a Roman Catholic Church ; in

England there has been ever since the Reformation a Roman Catholic Mission. In Ireland there have always been local Roman Catholic bishops; in England there have been no local bishops, but vicars-apostolic. In Ireland, the Pope has always appointed to the *ancient* sees; in England he has established *new* sees. In Ireland the Canon Law has always been in force among the Roman Catholics; in England it has been introduced by the brief of Pope Pius IX.'

Dr. Twiss proceeds to show that the judges of the land cannot refuse to take cognizance of the law, if its violation should be raised in Westminster Hall. In England the established custom has been in accordance with the law. In Ireland the statute law is practically a dead letter. In this view of the facts of the case, the writer calmly examines the notions both of Roman Catholics and of Protestants as to *ignoring* the violation of the law in England, or repealing the laws which are thus systematically broken. He then fairly sums up the whole question now before the public and the Parliament of Great Britain in these words:—'The point of the Papal wedge has been inserted; and the brief may drive it home, and the *laws of England will then be scattered to the winds.*'

Mr. Warren's pamphlet is a more earnest expression of Protestant judgment and feeling than the larger work of Dr. Twiss. We need say no more of it than that it is well suited to the occasion on which it is written, and worthy of the writer's reputation. We are glad that *he* recognises 'our dissenting brethren,' and we thankfully accept the agreeable morsel which he has extracted for our special consolation, from Count le Maistre's treatise, entitled 'The Pope.'

'As the putrefaction of large organized bodies produces innumerable *sects* of many reptiles, national religions, *when putrefied*, produce, in like manner, a *multitude of religious insects*, which drag out, on the same soil, the remains of a divided, imperfect, and disgusting existence. This may be observed on all sides; and by this may England and Russia particularly account for the number and inexhaustible fecundity of the sects which pullulate within their immense territories. *These sects are born of the putrefaction of a great body.* Such is the order of nature!'

With the deepest seriousness of mind we sympathize with the beliefs and the emotions of this noble passage.

'If so unworthy a person as myself might presume to offer a word of entreaty to my earnest brother Protestants, it would be this: to keep our eyes fixed upon, and continually direct those of others to, the *cardinal points of distinction* between us and the Romish Church. One of them is a truth blazing above us in the gospel firmament, like a sun: I mean the awful and self-supporting doctrine of *the all-sufficient and exclusive priesthood of Jesus Christ.* Let this glorious and consolatory truth, with its kindred truths, especially the *royalty* of that priesthood, that of a priest *upon his throne*, be constantly mingled with the thinkings of our innermost souls, and all the deadly exhalations of Romish corruption will melt away from us for ever.'

We have occupied so much space with Dr. Twiss's volume, that we have left room for no more than a most cursory, yet respectful, reference to the smaller publications now before us. The 'Protestant Layman' writes as an advocate of toleration and of reason. He has no sympathy with evangelical doctrines, whether in the Church of Rome, or elsewhere. He denounces the ambition of Rome. He demands the abolition of all tests and creeds. He has faith in human progress. He sees nothing in the aggressions of the Papacy that can be met by law. His confidence is in employing ' all the efforts of reason, and all the powers of mind, setting them free from clog, impediment, and restraint, so that, dispelling ignorance and counteracting superstition, they may lead the world, through the paths of knowledge, to the unclouded perception and soul-forming recognition of Truth.' We do not believe that this writer means by ' Truth' the same thing that the apostles meant by ' THE *Truth*.' He seems to have looked at this grave practical question with the calmness of one who has no perception of the kind of danger with which our land is threatened ; or who, perhaps, regards the cool, and learned, and impartial men of all parties who do see that danger, as persons unhappily destitute of reason.—The 'Simple Protestant' treats his readers to a rambling comment on sundry things in which we now feel no special interest, and in a manner which, however *simple*, does not touch us with any sense of either intelligence or power.

' Cautions for the Times ' is the commencement of a series of tracts, bearing evident marks of the presence of a master mind. The writer is no novice, no bigot ; but, we presume, a practised and liberal observer of the working of parties in this nation. The tone is so moderate and Christian, that we shall be glad to see the series prolonged.

In Mr. James's 'Pastoral Address,' all the good qualities of the experienced and esteemed writer are advantageously displayed. While urging on ' his flock ' the *religious* view of the question, he advocates the spirit of inquiry, and boldly, yet kindly, reminds ' our Church-of-England friends,' that the principle which renders Popery so dangerous is ' that which she holds in common with every Protestant secular establishment of religion —THE UNION OF CHURCH AND STATE. We must, therefore, stand forth against the Popery of Protestantism as well as of Rome.' In the same manly tone of Christian discrimination, he guards his people against uncharitableness, divisions, and the neglect of public duties, while he presses on them the spirit of prayer, the study of Popery, the diffusion of fair Protestant principles, and the closer union of all evangelical denominations. We sincerely congratulate both the 'flock' and the 'pastor' on the appearance of so vigorous and Christian an address, which needs from us no words of commendation.

Mr. Smith's 'Lectures' are both seasonable, expressing sound doctrines, and conveying valuable information, in nervous and popular language.

Dr. Urwick's 'Two Discourses' contemplate 'the Pope's measure, *First*, in its immediate references to our sovereign, to the Church of England, to the Roman Catholic Church, and to scriptural Protestantism. *Secondly*, in reference to the facts which it has made apparent—that the Papacy claims the same prerogatives as formerly, and is prepared to exercise them when a fitting opportunity is presented; that Romanizing influences have been, to a considerable extent, leavening the population of England; yet, that the average heart of Great Britain is sound against the Papacy. *Thirdly*, as naturally, if not necessarily, bringing under discussion such topics as,—the Papacy itself, the *hierarchical system of church polity*, the nature of Christian piety, and the *connexion* between religion and the State. *Fourthly*, as devolving upon the Protestants of Great Britain certain obligations. In enforcing these obligations, Dr. Urwick finely suggests the amazement which would be excited if 'the Queen, as sovereign of the United Kingdom, simply and throughout, took the conduct of the Pope, as sovereign of his Italian realm, for her rule; our sovereign giving to Roman Catholics in London, and other parts of our empire, just that measure of civil and religious liberty which *the Pope gives to Protestants of all kinds* in Rome and Italy, *and no more!*' Of course, *he* does not counsel such reprisals. He calls on statesmen and senators to secure for the royal position and prerogative all the vindication that the case demands, and whatever further may be necessary for guaranteeing *full civil and religious freedom to every loyal subject*, in discharging his conscience towards God *without trenching upon the civil rights of his neighbours;* and he exhorts all Protestants to redoubled vigilance and energy in the use of scriptural means for evangelizing the *masses and the aristocracy* of the empire, to rid themselves of whatever now, in their fellowship or its order, affords countenance or facility to the tenets or aims of the Church of Rome, to cordial good-will towards each other in the brotherhood of the Gospel, and simply, steadfastly, and increasingly to make their great God and Saviour their entire and constant trust, and hope, and joy.

We do not know that we have seen the entire question so completely and skilfully handled as in these Discourses.

Of Mr. Rogers's interesting pamphlet we have only space for saying that we have read it with much admiration of the intelligence, discrimination, broad humanity, and hearty piety with which he contrasts Roman Catholicism and Protestant Christianity in their most vital and obvious features.

Mr. Thwaites's ' Tract for the Times—not the Church, not the Pope, but the Bible,' is, as may be inferred from the title, an argument for the word of God as the sole rule of faith. He gives a brief sketch of the Primitive Churches for the purpose of showing how absurd it would be to go to the Romans, the Corinthians, Galatians, Ephesians, Philippians, Colossians, or Thessalonians, or any other early communities, as infallible *standards* of Christian truth. It is an ingenious and novel, but sound and judicious, method of demonstrating the truth which must be at the foundation of every argument on behalf of any doctrine of ' the faith once delivered to the saints.'

We sum up our review of these various publications by frankly observing that those persons appear to us to be greatly in error—*far behind* in their intelligence and in their love of religious freedom—who, on the one hand, treat ' the Great Controversy ' of our day as one of slight moment, or of mere party rivalry; or who, on the other hand, expect that the truth of the gospel is to be *defended by acts of Parliament.* The pretensions of the Papacy are partly such as relate to religion, and partly such as relate to *political power.* The former pretensions *we* propose to deal with, unceasingly, in the use of moral and spiritual means alone: for the latter—the ULTRAMONTANE POLICY—the Papal as distinguished from the Roman Catholic—*power as distinguished from opinion*—can be dealt with only in one way, and that is, by *wise laws impartially and vigorously enforced, as the will of an enlightened, free, strong, and resolute nation.* We shall see whether the Imperial Parliament is prepared for *this.*

ART. IX.—1. *The Case of the Authors as regards the Paper Duty.* By Charles Knight. Second Edition. London. 1851.

2. *Excise Duty on Paper considered as affecting the Employment of the Poor, the Grievances of the Manufacturer, and the Injury to the Consumer.* By J. B. Crompton, Farnworth Mills, Bolton, Lancashire.

3. *The 'Morning Post,'* January 23rd, January 31st, February 4th, 1851.

WHILE grave objections lie against all indirect methods of raising revenue, there are some of a special kind which apply to those duties that affect the manufacture and circulation of books, and other appliances for the transmission of opinion and the spread of knowledge. These interests the Lord J. Russell Government affect to hold pre-eminently dear, and for them have made a sacrifice of some principles which, in our opinion, they were bound to have held still dearer. In pressing their favourite measure for national education, they greatly depreciated both the desire for education prevailing among the lower classes, and the amount of it which actually exists; while, to serve their purpose, they either ignored or repudiated statistical evidence, alike comprehensive and unimpeachable. Yet with all this appearance of zeal, they perpetuate a tax upon the most necessary article, and, so to speak, the raw material of education, operating in many cases as a prohibition, and in all cases as a grievance, the extent of which will, we think, surprise those of our readers who have not specially directed their attention to this subject.

It would be superfluous, we trust, to insist upon the superior importance of moral and intellectual over mere material progress. It is a sufficiently-established principle in the creed of all thoughtful persons, that the statistics, by which we estimate national power and greatness, are but the indexes upon a dial, while the essential mechanism is unseen because it is internal, and incapable of numerical definition because it is spiritual. None, therefore, but the superficial statesman and the unskilful financier will be misled by the specious appearance of immediate productiveness, and dam up the very fountain of production, while drawing his resources from the stream. It is by this short-sighted and semi-barbarous policy, that all those taxes are maintained which tend to restrain the moral and intellectual advancement of the people. Let us see to what extent the taxes on knowledge, and pre-eminently the paper-duty, produce this effect.

In a former article * we presented, at length, the statement of Mr. Charles Knight (the stout-hearted man who first volunteered to lead the forlorn hope of cheap literature), touching the financial history of the 'Penny Cyclopædia': a work, than which, no other published in our days, was entitled to a wider circulation, or adapted to more extensive usefulness. Of this we will briefly recapitulate the results. The production of this work, burdened with toil and anxiety a period of thirteen or fourteen years. It was entirely original, and upon it Mr. Knight expended the sum of forty-two thousand pounds; yet, with all his intelligence, resources, and enterprise, as a publisher, and with all the intrinsic attractions of the work itself, backed by the *prestige* of the Society for the Diffusion of Useful Knowledge, it has not been remunerative. Does the reader inquire the reason? He paid to Government, for paper-duty, no less than sixteen thousand five hundred pounds, *directly*, and indirectly the enormous amount of twenty-nine thousand pounds. 'Had the duty,' he said, 'not been reduced by one-half at the end of 1836, I could not, by any possibility, have carried on the work. As it was, I struggled to the end.'

Our next illustration shall be drawn from the business transactions of the Messrs. Chambers, of Edinburgh, than whom, as the energetic circulators of useful literature, in a popular and accessible form, no men deserve better of their country, or have a stronger claim upon the consideration of the Government. 'At a recent meeting, one of the Messrs. Chambers stated that, in making their calculations as to the paying of the cheap publications, the amount of composition is never taken into account; even the price paid to authors is comparatively trifling. When 50,000 copies of a cheap work are issued, the cost of authorship is not more than fifteen or twenty guineas, and bears no proportion to the whole expenditure. The total quantity of paper used in his establishment is 18,000 reams, or 8,640,000 sheets per annum, the cost of which is 13,000*l.*, and this pays duty to the Government to the amount of 3,000*l.*'

The same firm commenced the publication of a popular and instructive work, entitled, 'The Miscellany of Tracts,' which reached a steady sale of 80,000, but, even with this large circulation, they were compelled to discontinue it, because they found that the Government had received what ought to have been the publishers' profit, not less than 6,200*l.* for that single work.

---

* Eclectic Review, vol. **xxvii.** pp. 433, 434.

'On striking the balance of the account,' says Mr. Chambers, ' it
was found that the Government had got all.   After having toiled for
three years, and employed a great number of printers and literary men,
and having spent 18,000*l.* a year on the work, they, the publishers,
got nothing; and therefore they discontinued the publication.   But it
might be asked, why they had not raised the price of the work a penny
or a half-penny?   Had they done so, they would have reduced the
circulation from 80,000 to 20,000 copies; and then the question of
composition, of authorship, and other expenses, would have become
important.   They (the Messrs. Chambers) started another publication,
a halfpenny dearer in price, and the circulation was at present from
20,000 to 30,000 copies.   On this they expended about 12,000*l.* per
annum, and the duty paid to the Government from it was 800*l.* per
annum—the same amount that was paid as a remuneration to authors.
This publication paid its expenses, and a little over; but, on the whole,
it was not worth the expense of carrying on.   Last week, they announced its discontinuance, the Government having taken near 2,000*l.*
from it.   They had had communications from Boston, in the United
States, with orders to discontinue furnishing copies of the work, as
the publishers in America were about there to print it on paper that
paid no duty—the Americans thus getting all the authorship for
nothing, and circulating the work on untaxed paper throughout the
States, and even in our British possessions on the other side the
Atlantic.'

From such statements as these the reader will deduce this
important conclusion, that the paper-duty chiefly operates to
suppress cheap literature,—that is, to prevent the circulation of
useful knowledge among the great mass of the people; and how
nearly this impost amounts in such cases to a prohibition, may
be learned from the fact, that one of the most sagacious men
of business in the book-trade was obliged to give up a penny
publication, with a regular sale of 80,000, solely because the
profits of the work accrued to the excise instead of the proprietor.

And this leads us to expose a very short-sighted argument,
which has frequently been used to justify the maintenance of
this pernicious impost.   'Only weigh these volumes,' says the
lounging and beardless legislator, placing his hand upon Lady
Blessington's ' Country Quarters,' ' they cost half-a-guinea
a-piece, and only pay a duty of three halfpence a pound.   Why,
if it were a bishop's theology, instead of the wit of the charming
Countess, it would not weigh more than two pounds; so that
this much-abused tax is just three-pence in a guinea.'   Let us
weigh the logic of the ingenuous youth in the balance of the following table, which strikingly exhibits the contrast which prevails
throughout our financial system, between the imposts levied upon
the luxuries of the rich and on the necessaries of the poor :—

What fractional expression would designate the
e of some of the works included under the first head

 duty,
amidst
period
was contracted, is now, after thirty-five years of nearly uninterrupted peace, obstinately maintained by a government whose
Premier fought in the van of the ' Society for the Diffusion of
USEFUL KNOWLEDGE!'

But, perhaps, we shall show the mischievous incidence of
this tax in a clearer light if we exhibit another table, constructed
by Mr. Charles Knight, and published in his pamphlet, entitled,
' The Case of the Authors,' &c. In this diagram the author
shows the cost of the production of a large octavo volume,
arranging the expenses under two heads, those that are divisible
and those that are recurrent. By the divisible, it will be perceived that Mr. Knight intends those charges which are incurred
by the production of a single copy, and which become less and
less per copy in proportion to the number sold ; while the recurrent changes remain the same upon every copy, and, consequently, multiply in exact proportion to the amount of the
circulation. Here is Mr. Knight's diagram—

The *Divisible* Charges are exhibited in the descending scale. The greater the number printed the less onerous are the first expenses of a book upon the individual purchasers. This is the *rationale* of the union of goodness and cheapness in a Book. The *Recurrent* Charges are precisely the same, whatever number be printed. Of these charges the Paper Duty is an eighth. Upon an impression of 1,000 copies the Authorship represents 20s. of the cost per copy, the Paper-duty 6¼d. Upon an impression of 40,000 copies the Authorship is reduced to 6d. per copy—the Paper-duty requires its unyielding 6¼d. Upon the entire impression the Authorship remains at £1,000—the Paper-tax mounts up to £1,040.

## 1. DIVISIBLE CHARGES.

| | |
|---|---:|
| Authorship . . . . . . | £1,000 |
| Composition, 66 sheets . . . . | 330 |
| Stereotyping . . . . . | 180 |
| Advertising . . . . . . | 200 |
| | £1,710 |

| | s. d. | | |
|---|---|---|---:|
| For 1,000 copies, per copy . . . | 34 2 | | 4 1¾ |
| „ 2,000 „ | 17 1 | | 4 1¾ |
| „ 3,000 „ | 11 4½ | | 4 1½ |
| „ 4,000 „ | 8 6½ | | 4 1½ |
| „ 5,000 „ | 6 10 | | 1 |
| „ 10,000 „ | 3 5 | | 4 1½ |
| „ 20,000 „ | 1 8¾ | | 4 1 |
| „ 40,000 „ | 0 10½ | | 4 1¼ |

## 2. RECURRENT CHARGES, *per 1,000 copies.*

| | | |
|---|---:|---|
| Paper, without duty . . . | £100 | |
| Paper-duty . . . . . | 26 | Per copy, |
| Presswork . . . . . | 40 | 4s. 1¼d. |
| Binding . . . . . | 40 | |
| | £206 | |

The argument which Mr. Knight founds upon these facts is this :—With the craving for extreme cheapness amidst the great body of book-buyers, and with the growing appreciation of what is really excellent in literature—of what is clear, condensed, imaginative, earnest, benevolent—what prevents our having the noblest popular literature in the world ? The inroads upon the labour-fund out of which the best authorship is to be supported. The state which enacts a paper-duty, and thus robs the capital which would otherwise go to the remuneration of literary industry, is the power which denies the popular writer his maintenance, or abridges his profits and limits his fame. The diagram develops this principle—that the authorship is the only item amongst the original expenses of a book of which the rate of payment may greatly vary. The paper-duty is the only item of the recurrent expenses which is capable of being saved without lowering the quality or limiting the sale of a book. The authorship and the paper-duty are, therefore, essentially antagonistic. The case which it is the design of Mr. Knight's pamphlet to-make out is the following :—

' 1. That the tax presses most unequally upon the fund for the remuneration of those who are labouring for the instruction and amusement of the people.

' 2. That this tax, which in its effects upon cheap literature is excessive, operates against the extension of the best English authorship, and interferes with the improvement of all the productions of the press.

' 3. That it diminishes the author's profit to the lowest point ; and substitutes for useful English works invasions of foreign copyrights, or encourages the production of inferior and injurious works by unskilled labourers in literature.'

This last proposition leads us to the refutation of another argument urged in favour of the paper-duty, namely, that it operates as a check on the lowest and most pernicious class of publications. It is easy to demonstrate that, so far from this, it tends to foster them, while it protects them from that competition by which they would inevitably be defeated. If a work could be produced without the expense of authorship, pictorial illustration, and advertisement, it could just afford to pay the paper-duty and retain a profit sufficient to justify its continuance. The combined pressure of these expenses, however, with the tax, is the destruction of all literature that is at once cheap and valuable. But what is its effect upon the lowest class of publications? They require nothing that deserves the name of authorship. Such translations from French novels as they contain might be made by a nursemaid or a journeyman. A dead wall would publish the advertisement without the duty ; and the youngest apprentice of

a wood-cutter would supply the illustrations for a sum upon
which he might twice a-week luxuriate in the gallery of a minor
theatre. Thus the lowest publications can afford not only to pay
the duty, but even to suffer an occasional confiscation of their
stock; while a higher class of publications, unable to compete
with them, retire from the market, and leave them to the full
enjoyment of their fetid monopoly.

Our observations, hitherto, have only exhibited the effect upon
publishers, authors, and readers. We will now view it in its
financial aspect, and in its bearing upon the paper manufacture.
Paper is not so much a finished article as it is a material of
manufacture; and, next to the almost worthless canvass and pig-
ments which fetch their thousands of pounds in the form of a
Titian or a Correggio, there is no better instance than paper of
the value with which the human mind can invest the lowest forms
of matter. It has now become the professed policy of our fiscal
administration to leave the materials of manufacture free from
taxation. It is many years since the committee of the House of
Commons, of which Sir Henry Parnell was the chairman, in this
wise spirit recommended for immediate abolition the taxes on
leather, paper, and glass. The first and last of these have been
emancipated from their restrictions. The most important of them
all still groans under the tyranny of the Board of Excise. If
anything more-than general principles, and the public experience
of the effect of the remission of duties on other articles of general
consumption, were necessary, we might find it in the financial
history of paper itself. In the year 1836 the duty on paper was
reduced from threepence to three-halfpence per pound; and the
consequence of this alteration was an increased consumption of
the article amounting to no less than eighty per cent. What,
then, might not be expected in increased production, and, consequently, increased employment, circulation of money, and consumption of exciseable articles, to say nothing of the diminution
of pauperism and poor-rates, if this enormous blunder were
altogether corrected?

But if, in other departments of production, it has been the
policy of government to release the raw material from duty, on
the ground that it restricts employment and cripples trade, how
much more urgently does the same motive press the abolition of
the duty on paper. For in other cases, the incidence of the tax
is partly upon labour, and partly upon material; but this impost
is literally upon labour only. For what is the history of this
most important article? It begins in refuse whose only occupation has been gone ever since the lucifer superseded the tinder-
box; it ends in the bank note, the engraving of Landseer, and
the volume that enchants an age or renovates a world. Between

the rags of the wallet, and that panacea which regales the monarch, inspires the student, and gives dignity to destitution, nothing but labour intervenes; *its* magic only effects the miracle; and while effecting it for the highest benefit of man, it is crushed to deformity and torture under the incubus of a barbarous taxation.

It would seem absurd to attribute mere wantonness to the government of such a country as this, or to charge hypocrisy upon our present cabinet in their professions of zeal for the advancement of popular intelligence; but really the facts are almost enough to stagger our candour. The entire amount of revenue derived from paper is only 800,000*l*. The mode in which it is collected involves an expense which we cannot pretend to estimate. The Chancellor of the Exchequer admits it to be 7½ per cent.; but this, we are persuaded, is not even an approximation to the truth. In some of our paper-mills, stands, as they are called, of excisemen, numbering eight to each stand, are employed night and day in watching the process of manufacture on the part of the revenue; while in some no fewer than fourteen are thus engaged. Yet, notwithstanding these precautions, the frauds committed are such as to enrich the smuggler to the ruin of the fair trader, and to stamp the whole system with a character of fatuity. A few firms in Ireland return such an amount of duty compared with the quantity of paper manufactured in that country, as to make it manifest that a large proportion of the commodity produced in Ireland is smuggled into the market without paying any duty at all. Many of the manufactories are situated on the sides of hills; and from these the government spy can be descried long before he enters the mill. This arrangement affords a fine scope for the characteristic cunning of the Irish labourer; to adapt the language of Mr. Burke, 'they augur *taxation* at a distance, and snuff the approach of an *exciseman* in every tainted breeze.'

All the efforts of the principal paper manufacturers in England to obtain a return of the convictions and compromises for the frauds thus committed in the United Kingdom have been fruitless; indeed, the Government dare not disclose them, as such a disclosure would attach to the impost such a demoralizing character that it would be at once swept away by a blast of universal odium. All that we can attempt, therefore, is to arrive at an approximation to the truth.* A document which was published last year, by authority of the House of Commons, contained the names of a considerable number of fraudulent manufacturers, of whom some had been heavily fined, some

---

* See Mr. Crompton's Excise Duty on Paper, &c. &c.

imprisoned, and in other cases compromises had been made, or the offenders had absconded. Opposed to competition such as this, the fair and honest trader has no alternative but absolute ruin, and such are the facilities for fraud arising out of this tax, and the mode in which it is levied, that the temptation to act dishonestly becomes almost irresistible. The excise duty on the lower descriptions of paper amounts, in some cases, to as much as 120 per cent. on the cost of production; and as is well known to every practical manufacturer, the evasion of this duty is so easy that, provided the officer of excise is in collusion with the manufacturer, it amounts almost to impossibility of detection. Nor is the improbability of this collusion so great as may be imagined, even without unnecessarily impugning the general character of the excise officers. Look at the position of one of these men, who, with a net salary of certainly not more than thirty shillings a week, has to be the guardian of the revenue, which, in some individual cases, amounts to 20,000l. a-year, and when a present of 50l. may secure the object and add so much to the resources of each party, it is not difficult to see that such a temptation to a fraud, both upon the revenue and the honest trader, may break down the moral probity of the trader and the excise officer. It is a temptation to which no man ought to be exposed, and which is the greater in this case from the largeness of the gain to be derived, and the facilities for successfully carrying it out.

We are indebted to Mr. Crompton, one of our first paper manufacturers, for the following startling, but unquestionable facts :—

‘ All who were present,’ said he, (we quote the report of his speech at a recent meeting of the trade) ‘ knew that from year to year frauds were increasing. Last year he had with great difficulty procured a document from the Government, telling how many fraudulent traders had been detected from the year 1840 to 1848. He had endeavoured also, but in vain, to get from the Chancellor of the Exchequer a return of the mills at work and closed, but had failed, on the plea that it was not thought desirable to give such a return to any one. What might be the motive of the Board of Excise in refusing that return, he could not say; but the association of paper manufacturers in Lancashire were not afraid of publicity. They said, by all means let us have the return. They paid one-fourth of the whole paper duty, and they had again requested it, but Mr. Wood, the chairman of the board, had made them no reply. He could only suppose that the refusal arose from a conviction that the proportionate amount of convictions for fraud were so great, that the authorities were afraid of horrifying the public with the revelation. He would, however, take the mills in the United Kingdom at 600, and the return he had obtained showed that in England there had been forty-three convictions, in Scotland nine, and in Ireland thirty, which would amount to about fifteen per cent. on the number of mills. How could any trade flourish with such a number of fraudulent men connected with it? The total amount of penalties levied for these frauds was 10,671*l.* The amount received had been, for England—compromises, 444*l.*; full penalties, 3,525*l.*; Scotland—compromises, 16*l.*; penalties, 200*l.* The penalties levied in Ireland were 3,947*l.* The amount of compromises was 72*l.*; the amount received 1,384*l.* He said, if it was nothing else but the morals of the country, a tax which led to such results ought· to be repealed. The tax of 120 per cent. on the cost price was a temptation to the trade. On the value of the raw material employed, in many cases, it was not less than 600 per cent., while the raw material of every other manufacture in the country was free. Sir Robert Peel was of opinion that the tax of five or eight per cent. on raw cotton was so injurious to the manufacturers that he repealed it. To that measure he had no objection, but the paper manufacturers were the scavengers of the cotton mills; they took the refuse of those mills, amounting to perhaps one-fifth of the whole, and while the best portion was free, they were compelled to pay a duty of 300 per cent. on the refuse.'

From Mr. Smith, again, the chairman of a similar meeting, recently held at Leeds, we gain the following facts :—

'He adverted,' says the report, 'to the frauds on the revenue which, notwithstanding the vigilance of the revenue officers, are perpetrated by certain paper-makers in Ireland, who, by collusion with parties to whom they send paper, get back the stamped labels, and use them a second time. These fraudulent parties were frequently found selling paper for less than it cost the honest manufacturer to make it, and they were of course afraid of the duty being repealed. One Irish paper-maker had said he never paid more than half the duty, and before he would do so he would allow his mill to be shut up.—Mr. Crompton said he had it from the Government officers themselves that fourteen policemen and two revenue officers were attending one mill in the neighbourhood of Dublin.'

We pass now from the bearing of this tax upon the Exchequer, and the morals of the manufacturer and his workmen, to the vexation and loss inflicted by the mode of its assessment upon the honest producer, and in doing so we will rely upon the vital importance of the question to excuse a somewhat extended detail of facts. We quote again from that most zealous advocate of the repeal of the taxes on knowledge, Mr. Crompton. We feel that we are almost taxing the faith of our readers in laying before them the facts which Mr. Crompton asserts on the guarantee of his personal experience.

At a conference of gentlemen interested in the abolition of the tax on paper, held at the King's Arms, Palace-yard, Westminster, on the 29th of January last, Mr. Crompton is reported to have made the following observations :—

'He would now briefly narrate some of the difficulties to which the paper-manufacturer was liable. After erecting the necessary premises, he must give notice to the Excise, and enter in a schedule the number of rooms and every particular; he must number every vat and every other article employed in the manufacture. The Government officer then comes down to inspect the whole, and take an exact account of it; and all this being done to the satisfaction of the officer, a license is granted. He must then make up every article, not with such modifications as his judgment or his skill may suggest, but according to the mode described in the Act of Parliament. True, some of these were not much attended to, and evasions were frequent. He himself had told the officer that some of the requirements were so vexatious that he could not abide by them. The officer replied, that he had reported the fact; but the board were so conscious of the unreasonable and arbitrary character of those particulars, that they had shut their eyes, and he had heard nothing more of it. The truth was, he had been forty years in the trade, and the board reasonably assumed that he would not do anything dishonest. To return to his sketch. Having made the paper, the next thing would be to provide a sufficient number of clerks to receive labels, containing an accurate account of the sheets in each parcel, and their weight. Then he must apply to the officer of excise for labels, which, formerly, he was not allowed to affix himself. These labels were small pieces of paper, something like bank notes. These were entrusted to a man employed at 1*l.* a-week for the purpose, and the loss of any of them subjected the paper-maker to a penalty of 10*l.* for each. The paper is now ready to go to the market, but it is detained until the officer has weighed it, and tested the accuracy of the labels. But the Government will not trust its own officer, lest there should be a collusion between him and the manufacturer, and so it has to remain twenty-four hours on the premises until it has been checked by a supervisor. This operation takes up time, and that and other hindrances which frequently occur may make it fifty-eight hours after it is ready before the article can be sent off the premises to the market. Supposing, however, it happens that Sunday intervenes, and the maker not liking his men to be weighing on that day with the supervisor, another twenty-four hours' delay is required, and thus, then, it may be eighty-two hours before the article can leave the premises. But even then it is not free from the surveillance of the Excise, for an open book—open to all the workmen, and by which the officer could, if he chose, hand over all his trade to a rival manufacturer—must be kept in the premises, stating to whom and by what conveyance the goods were sent away; and if any mistake should arise in those statements, the whole is liable to be seized and condemned. These were some of the difficulties under which the poor paper-maker had to labour, and to which no other trade in the kingdom, on which there was no excise, was subject. He must now say a word with respect to the way in which the customers of the paper-maker were affected by this tax, and especially by its inequalities. The consumers of the low qualities, such as wrapping papers, consumed each from 500*l.* to 3,000*l.* worth per annum. Those papers were taxed at from 40 to 50 per cent., and it was marvellous how little the public were aware of it. He asked a gentleman the other day, who took from him 1,000*l.* worth per annum, what he supposed was the amount of taxation on that article. At a guess, he replied, perhaps 5*l.* per cent., and was quite surprised when he demonstrated to him that it was little short of 50 per cent. But worse than that, he had orders sent from the continent for the same identical paper, on which for exportation the tax was remitted in the shape of drawback, to wrap up foreign goods, to be sent into this country, and sold as English, to the great detriment of the home producer.'

By the fifteenth section of the act of 1839, which is now in force, a period of forty-eight, and, in some instances, of eighty-two hours is thus consumed after paper is ready for delivery into the market. This time would be sufficient, Mr. Crompton says, for him to purchase the rags in Manchester, carry them to his mill at Farnworth, manufacture them into paper, and convey the article ready for the market to any part of the kingdom. This could no doubt be done were it not for the excise regulations. We next present a different aspect of the losses and vexations to which the manufacturer of paper is subject, and on this point we will cite the evidence of Mr. Baldwin, of Birmingham :—' It costs me,' he says, ' above 100*l.* per annum to help to charge myself with the duty on paper ; I make about twelve tons a week, and, in consequence of these excise laws, have to weigh every ream four times over, besides taking the number of every ream and writing the name on each.' The Association for the Abolition of the Duty on Paper, have pointed out another inconvenience to which some branches of the trade are subject, and of which Mr. Baldwin furnishes an example. He manufactures, mainly for exportation, an article commonly known as gun-wadding. This is made at his mill, but the excise laws will not permit him to cut it up at the place of manufacture. He is compelled to comply with the Act of Parliament, and keep another establishment at a distance of one mile from his mill, and at an expense of 150*l.* per annum, to prepare it for the market. This regulation is enforced in other instances, especially upon those who manufacture jacquard boards: an article which is now extensively used in the fancy weaving. The makers have to keep separate establishments for making the board and for cutting it up into the sizes ready for use. The price is greatly increased by this absurd regulation. A recent case of extreme hardship, arising out of the restrictions laid upon loom-weavers, deserves to be mentioned, and will be read, we think, with much surprise. Mr. Kèen, of Paisley, resolved to compete in the great Exhibition, now about to be opened, in the article of shawl manufacture, and applied to the Lords of the Treasury for a drawback of the excise duty chargeable on the card boards necessary to be used in the preparation

of his designs.  The cost of these boards, duty included, but
exclusive of the cost of preparation, would be 270*l.*, of which
the duty amounts to no less than 92*l.* 15s., a charge from which
his foreign competitors are entirely exempt.  *His application
was refused.*

We return to the evidence of Mr. Baldwin.  He states that
in the single article of gun-wadding he could export three times
the quantity he is able to do now, were it not for the duty; and
would be able to employ 500 more hands within twelve months
after the repeal shall have taken place.  The paper duty amounts
to 15*l.* per ton, and the greater amount of paper manufactured
sells wholesale for about 35*l.* per ton; so that pretty nearly one
half of the cost is in consequence of the duty.  Mr. Baldwin
gives his own case:—During the last year he manufactured
paper to the value of 24,000*l.*, and paid in duty 9,640*l.*  There
are merchants in Birmingham who use 20 tons of paper annually in wrapping their goods, so that the tax upon them is about
300*l.* per annum.  Then, again, the tax operates as a premium
to foreign manufacturers of paper, and articles made from paper
or pasteboard.  In Paris there are not less than thirty thousand
females employed in the fancy box trade.  Ornamental and
fancy articles are sent into the British ports, and thence into the
British colonies, free of duty, thus superseding the home manufactories, and it has been shown that paper boxes can be imported
from Paris, and after paying the import duty undersell those made
in London.  Take, again, the article of steel pens.  In consequence
of the duty, the paper on which the pens are mounted is more
costly than the article itself.  Of this circumstance the French
avail themselves.  They import the pens, mount them on their
own untaxed paper, and can thus successfully compete with
Birmingham in its own article in the European and Colonial
markets.

The facility with which that paper which pays duty may be
imitated by that which does not, is another aspect of this question which deserves attention, involving, as it must, great loss
and disadvantage to the fair trader.  This was illustrated by
Mr. Cowan, M.P., at a meeting held at the London Tavern, on
the 4th of January.  He exhibited a sample of pasteboard made
from straw, which, from the material having to be made into
pulp, was considered paper.  The cost of the material was 2s.
per cwt., and the duty upon it, when made into paper, was
14s.9d.  He presented another article, very similar to millboard,
but stated his ignorance of the material from which it was manufactured.  It was made *in the dry state*, and was, consequently,
not considered paper.  Hence it was exempt from duty, and had
superseded the article made from straw for all the purposes to

which the former is applicable. Substitutes for paper are continually produced so much like the article itself, that the excise officer cannot detect the difference. Indeed, Mr. Crompton placed two specimens in the hands of the Chancellor of the Exchequer, one of which paid the duty and the other was free, and the minister confessed himself unable to perceive the slightest distinction between them.

From these facts, two inferences, equally condemnatory of this impost, naturally suggest themselves. The first shall be given in the words of the ' Paper-Maker's Letter to Lord John Russell:'

'Another evil,' he says, 'arising from the heavy duty is, that it becomes a matter of no small difficulty, and, indeed, sometimes involves the most ruinous consequences, to attempt any experiments in the way of improving, or of introducing new modes of manufacturing the article. This has lately been sadly realized by a party who started a mill in England some years ago to make paper from *straw*. Well, what was the result? After a few years of anxiety, much ingenious effort, and praiseworthy perseverance, the attempt was given up, the mill closed, and the large capital invested in the business totally lost. Now, the question is, how came this result about, when it is so well known that beautiful papers, fitted for many useful and ornamental purposes, have long been made in France from straw? Surely it will not be said that the skill, the enterprise, or the capital of our English manufacturers are not equal to those of our French neighbours. No; the real solution is obvious. In France there are no heavy duties levied on the article; whereas here, let the article be good or bad as the result of experiment, the heavy duty is levied on all alike; and hence, when an experiment does not fully succeed, the loss in that case in this country becomes very serious. For instance, straw may cost 2*l*. per ton; well, then, a maker may try 100 tons as an experiment, and if it turns out not to be good, his whole risk is on 200*l*. and workmanship; but if, in addition to this, a duty of 15*l*. per ton is charged, the risk is now increased to 1,700*l*. and workmanship—a very different matter indeed, and the difference proved to be a very serious and fatal one, as in the case just alluded to. Depend on it, my lord, manufacturers will not look about them for improved modes of working, or new materials to be worked, so long as to do so involves such fearful risks as the paper duties impose.'—P. 9.

The other inference respects the injury inflicted by this duty on other trading interests. The whole country echoes at this moment with the complaints of the occupiers of land, and her Majesty, in her recent speech, admits their sufferings with expressions of regret. Yet this tax forbids their making a profitable use of the article of straw. The repeal of the duty would occasion a very large demand for that article, and there is no doubt that if the farmer obtained three times its present value for his straw, the manufacturer would still realize a handsome profit.

We come, in conclusion, to consider the injurious effect of this impost on other trades, and on the material interests of society at large. The number of persons engaged, directly or indirectly, in the paper-trade, are greater beyond all proportion than would be conjectured by simply considering the gross returns of that trade. The number of mills in the United Kingdom does not exceed 500, and the total duty paid is 800,000*l.*

'This,' says the paper-maker already quoted, 'may be taken on an average to represent 20 per cent. of the value of the paper as sold by the maker. This, then, gives us the total value of the paper so sold at 4,000,000*l.* Well, here we have, on the one hand, the small amount of 4,000,000*l.* as the total value of that article; and, on the other, the large number of 160,000 people as dependent for their daily bread on that one branch of business, apparently so trifling in its results. Now, how is this? Just from the fact, that the whole sum (with the exception of the duty) is *distributed in labour*—the material in itself being valueless—*wages and profits* absorbing the whole, intrinsic value being nothing.'—P. 10.

After alluding to the large amount of tonnage in constant transit from the mills to the warehouses, and the number of carters, porters, clerks, and seamen, thus furnished with employment, he continues—

'Now it appears clear to me that those considerations show that this branch of trade is of great importance to the country; but perhaps to test this value more clearly, it may be worth while to make a supposition of two different cases. Suppose an edict in council put an end to the paper manufacture in this country—why, the total value in money, as we have seen, is only 4,000,000*l.* a-year —a mere trifle when deducted from the mighty sum of this country's domestic and foreign trade, and such as we might expect, in this view of it, would scarcely be felt—a mere ripple on the surface of the deep; but what, in reality, would be its effects? The forcible ejection of 40,000 people from their labours—the withdrawal in whole or in part of the sustenance of 320,000 of our population—a deep wail of distress from every corner of the country—a fearful augmentation of the poor's-rates in every parish, and a settled gloom in almost every other branch of trade. Suppose, again, an edict in council to put down or to prohibit the goldsmith and precious-stone trade to the extent of 4,000,000*l.* a-year, what, in that case, would be the result in the labour market? Why, three or four London houses do that extent of business annually, and supposing them shut up and prohibited, the amount of labour thrown out of employment would be the merest trifle, not heard of, nor even felt, in the labour market? And why such a difference in the cases? Simply, because *the total money value of the one is all labour* and *no intrinsic value;* and in the other, *the intrinsic value is very large*, and *the labour value almost nothing.*'—P. 11.

To these must be added the trades in connexion with, and dependent on, the paper-trade : stationers, booksellers, and publishers, with all their assistants ; printers, with their multitude of compositors and pressmen ; type-founders, ink-makers, bookbinders, tool-makers, gold-beaters, leather-merchants, &c. &c. ; and, on a moderate calculation, half a million of our countrymen are supported from sources connected with the paper manufacture, and sympathetic with its prosperity or depression. But the question then arises, how many would be employed if the production of paper were unfettered by this oppressive excise ? One or two patent facts will help us to an approximation to this result. First, the reduction of the duty from $3\frac{1}{2}d.$ to $1d.$ per pound, produced an increase in the quantity of paper, on which the duty was charged, of no less than 80 per cent. in twelve years, and how much evaded the duty we have given the reader an opportunity of guessing. Add to this another fact, stated at a recent meeting by Mr. Towle, a large manufacturer. After enumerating by name a number of paper-mills in Oxfordshire, which the proprietors had been compelled to close, he declared that he was the only manufacturer now left in that county, and that he should have been also compelled to give up, but for the possession of an independent fortune.

It will be recollected that this manufacture is chiefly carried on in rural districts, and it is computed that the liberation of this department of industry from the fetters of excise would employ in these districts fifty thousand additional unskilled labourers, while the impetus given to collateral trades would be such as to furnish employment to no fewer than half a million additional hands. It should be remembered that many of these would be women and children, and that those employed in paper-mills would be engaged in a light and healthful occupation, while even old and infirm women are found in such establishments earning five or six shillings a week by sorting rags. The diminution thus occasioned in the amount of poor-rates would be a most seasonable relief to the agricultural interest. The undue pressure of this impost constitutes another powerful reason for its abolition. For example—A ream of brown paper will weigh seventeen pounds, and the duty upon it will amount to $2s.$ $2d.$, while its intrinsic value is only $3s.$ $8d.$, making the excise duty equivalent to 70 per cent. A ream of writing paper weighing the same as the brown, will be charged with the same amount of duty, while its intrinsic cost is $17s.$ $6d.$ ; thus the duty upon the comparative luxury is only 15 per cent., while the tax upon the article of necessity is no less than 70 per cent.

Here we finish our case.  We have exposed, on unquestionable testimony, the various and oppressive evils inseparable from an excise duty on paper, and the still more various benefits which would flow from its removal, and we appeal to every reader whether the obstinate persistance of the Government in maintaining so flagrant a tax for the sake of so insignificant a return, can be attributed to any other cause than that callous insensibility to injustice which alone can account for the recently-expressed determination of the same Government to reimpose the Income-tax, marked, as it is, by all those features of injustice and oppression which render it infamous in the eyes of every honest man.

## Brief Notices.

1. *Our State-church: in England, Ireland, Scotland, and Wales.*
2. *A Model Law.*  London: British Anti-state-church Association.

THE publication scheme lately announced by the Anti-state-church Association has our most hearty approval, and will, we hope, be carried out to a thoroughly successful issue.  Our school literature has long needed revision, and we know no better service that can be rendered to truth and liberty than the accomplishment of so desirable an end.  This has now, happily, been undertaken in good earnest, and we shall gladly avail ourselves of every opportunity which occurs to report our judgment on the progress made towards its accomplishment.  In the meantime, we are glad to introduce to our readers the two publications standing at the head of this notice.  The first, entitled 'Our State-church,' consists of four tracts, which embody a much larger amount of information respecting the revenues and administration of our State-churches than can elsewhere be found within similar limits.  The preparation of these tracts must have been a work of vast labor.  Their authors have evidently spared no pains to render them complete, while the marks of scrupulous exactness entitle them to confidence.  We strongly recommend their perusal to all classes.  Churchmen as well as Dissenters should examine them, and we are greatly mistaken if the former, equally with the latter, will not be much surprised at the disclosures they make.  They are published at the low price of one shilling, and contain the essence of many bulky folios.

The second is admirably suited to meet an inquiry frequently propounded.  'What is meant,' we are often asked, 'by a separation of the Church from the State, and how can it be effected?'  In reply, we point to the 'Model Law,' which, in fact, is nothing more nor less

than ' An A for      lishing Religious Freedom,        the
Assembly of Virginia (U.S.), in the year 1786.' This
brief, but its terms are clear, ar .      object is w   d
pose is obvious, and for that pi  ose it is com  ɛte.  .
entitled to thanks for having bro   .t this li      ug , i
mend our readers to obtain a      y of it, i  1   e:   e ii
prominent position so that it      serve
with the practicability of whi             niy        a oi
wish every one of our senatoi      ɪ   indi
over this ' Model Law.'  The si            '       v   ɣ pri
*Act* in a very neat style.  It is            on a r
so that it may be suspended        au
ninepence.

---

*The Kickleburys on the Rhine.* By M. A. Titmarsh. Second Edition.
London : Smith, Elder, and Co. 1851.

A PLEASANT book for a Christmas evening. It is a happy exposure of
the hollownesses and littlenesses which have been so prevalent among
our aristocracy, but are now, we would fain hope, going out of fashion.
Lady Kicklebury is a type of a class that still exists, though rapidly
disappearing, and soon to be numbered among the things that were. The
book abounds with sprightly passages and humorous sallies ; but, as a
whole, seems to be wanting in pith and point. The Prefatory Essay
on Thunder and Small Beer is very clever. There is a broader humour
and deeper wit in that preface than in the tale itself. The illustrations
are generally very spirited. The following passage will be read with a
truly sympathetic eye by many of our readers :—' The married Briton
on a tour is but a luggage overseer : his luggage is his morning thought
and his nightly terror. When he floats along the Rhine, he has one
eye on a ruin, and the other on his luggage. When he is in the railroad, he is always thinking, or ordered by his wife to think, " Is the
luggage safe ?" It clings round him. It never leaves him (except
when it *does* leave him, as a trunk or two will, and make him doubly
miserable). His carpet-bags lie on his chest at night, and his wife's
forgotten bandbox haunts his turbid dreams.'

---

*The King of the Golden River ; or, The Black Brothers : a Legend of
Styria.* Illustrated by Richard Doyle. Second Edition. London :
Smith, Elder, and Co. 1851.

A MOST fascinating fairy tale, beautifully got up, and characteristically
illustrated by Richard Doyle. We were almost content to become
children again, and read it with a child's unsuspecting faith in the actual existence of fairies, dwarfs, and river-kings. And this King of
the Golden River teaches lessons which a child cannot learn too early,
or feel too deeply. The moral of the tale is excellent. Selfishness is
shown to be its own greatest enemy, and self-sacrifice its own reward.
' And thus the treasure-valley became a garden again, and the inheritance, which had been lost by cruelty, was regained by love.'

*An Analysis and Summary of Thucydides, with a Chronological Table of Principal Events, Money, Distances, &c.—a Skeleton Outline of the Geography, Abstract of all the Speeches, &c.* By the Author of an Analysis and Summary of Herodotus. Oxford: Wheeler.

THIS title-page will sufficiently explain the sort of book we have here; a perfect messenger from the gods to gentlemen 'cramming' for their examinations, but capable of being used, and that with great advantage, by students of a higher class. It is clear, correct, complete; a full summary of all the aid needed in the study of the historian to whom it refers.

------

*Common Sense versus Common Law.* By William Massey, Barrister. London: Longman and Co.

MR. MASSEY seeks to reconcile the two terms of the portentous antithesis on his title-page; and his book will, no doubt, do something in aid of the rising movement for law reform. The author's great point is the system of special pleading, against which he wages war to the knife. The subject is an important one; and we recommend this volume as a clever, clear statement of the absurdities and vexations of our common law, in chronological order, from the writ of summons downwards.

------

# Review of the Month.

THE session of 1851 was opened, by her Majesty in person, on the 4th of last month. The royal speech, like all royal speeches, was vague and general. No reflecting man expected it to be otherwise. It was designed to conceal, rather than disclose, the intentions of its framers, and, so long as it is deemed expedient to maintain the appearance of unity where none really exists, such speeches cannot well do otherwise. In our simplicity, we imagine that it would be better—more dignified and truthful—to avoid all reference to disputed topics, or, at least, to restrict the *Address* to a simple expression of loyalty, coupled, it may be, with an opinion on points, if such there be, on which the House is agreed. We conclude, however—as in all duty bound—that there are reasons of State, which justify and call for this annual mystification. One thing is certain—no mortal is deceived by the illusion. Every one sees through it, while few have sagacity enough to discern a worthy end in all this delusive by-play. The reference contained in the royal speech to the recent measure of the Pope, and to the excitement it has occasioned, was similar to the replies given to many of the addresses which have been presented to the Queen. As matter of historic interest we give it entire :—

'The recent assumption of certain ecclesiastical titles conferred by a foreign power has excited strong feelings in this country, and large bodies of my subjects have presented addresses to me, expressing their attachment to the throne, and praying that such assumptions should be resisted. I have assured them of my resolution to maintain the rights of my crown and the independence of the nation against all encroachment, from whatever quarter it may proceed. I have, at the same time, expressed my earnest desire and firm determination, under God's blessing, to maintain unimpaired the religious liberty which is so justly prized by the people of this country.

'It will be for you to consider the measure which will be laid before you on this subject.'

To the Speech, from which this passage is taken, an *Address* in reply was moved in both Houses. That of the Commons was seconded by Mr. Peto, an open and avowed Dissenter. The fact is notable as a sign of the times—a pleasing indication of the progress of public sentiment. It forms, so far as our knowledge extends, the first instance of an avowed Dissenter occupying such a position, and in the present circumstances of the country was both expedient and praiseworthy. It is of more moment to remark, that the manner in which the member for Norwich discharged his trust was eminently honorable to himself, and to the Nonconformist body. It is not within our province to refer to the more general points of his speech. We have to do only with his allusion to ecclesiastical matters, than which it would be difficult to imagine anything more calm in its tone, more unobjectionable in the policy advocated, or more earnest in its spirit. Such as object *in toto* to Parliamentary interference, will, of course, take exception to Mr. Peto's speech, but those who advocate such interference will readily acknowledge that it avoided, on the one hand, the admission of legislative enactments in *spiritual* matters, and, on the other, an insensibility to the danger which threatens national freedom from the Papacy. For ourselves, we confess, this constituted the glory of the speech, and we shall be glad to find the same happy medium observed by other members, who are far more boastful of their allegiance to religious liberty. Of the speech of Mr. Roebuck, who instantly followed, we will say no more than that it is correctly described by ' Punch,' as ' a quibbling, crotchety, and disingenuous speech.' We would rather have the member for Sheffield as an opponent than a friend. In the former case he may snarl, vituperate, and falsify ; charge us with the worst possible motives, and magnify himself as the embodiment of patriotism and sagacity ; but in the latter he will offend by his spleen and vanity, will engender and foment division among friends, will irritate opponents by his waspish temper, and utterly fail to conciliate the ally whom it may be his avowed policy to serve. The *Address* was carried without a division, the real struggle being reserved till the Premier should introduce his promised measure.

This was done on the 7th,—at least the Premier then moved for leave to bring in a bill to prevent the assumption of certain ecclesiastical titles in respect of places in the United Kingdom. The debate on this preliminary vote was adjourned three times, but was at length concluded on the 14th, when leave was granted by a majority of 395 to

63. As the bill was not yet before the House, and its provisions were, in consequence, only partially known, it could not but happen that much of the talk of honorable members was irrelevant. The whole discussion was, in fact, premature, though under the exciting circumstances of the case we do not wonder at the course pursued. So far as the nature of the bill was gathered from the speech of Lord John Russell, it failed to satisfy the House. This was undoubted, and several members expressed surprise and regret. Messrs. Roebuck, Bright, and Gibson, condemned the measure as an abandonment of the course which had constituted the glory of the Premier's life; but others, who were equally alive to the protection of religious liberty, were disappointed at what they deemed the inadequacy of the measure to the case which had arisen. There was a want of proportion between his lordship's speech and bill, and of the two they preferred the former. In this preference we agree, unless, indeed, the subsequent explanation of the Attorney-General be admitted. There was a strange, and under the circumstances of the case, we must say, a suspicious, avoidance in his lordship's speech of reference to ' the mummeries of superstition' practised in his own Church, and which he had so emphatically condemned in his letter to the Bishop of Durham. For this omission we see no fair or honorable reason. If it were prompted by a desire to conciliate the Puseyite clergy, it will certainly fail—as it ought to do—for his lordship had already sinned beyond forgiveness. On the other hand, it involves his procedure in doubt, and must diminish the confidence of his countrymen in the purity of the Protestant zeal he has expressed. It is in vain to fulminate against the Popery of Rome, if that of the English Church be permitted. The latter is more dangerous than the former, and as the avowed champion of *Protestant England*, Lord John was under special obligation to denounce it. The silence of his speech contrasts singularly with the outspoken condemnation of his letter.

We are glad to find that his lordship at once admitted the inconsistency of his measure with some statements which he formerly made. It was manly and honorable to do so. ' I am not about,' he replied to the taunts of Mr. Disraeli, ' to say that these declarations, amounting to this, that I thought it childish and puerile to prevent the assumption of titles held by bishops of our own Church—I am not about to say that this is consistent with the opinions which I hold now. Whatever may have formerly been my confidence with respect to the conduct of the Roman Catholic ecclesiastics—whatever may have been my confidence with respect to the conduct of the people—I have found since that time that confidence was misplaced. And I have thought it better clearly and plainly to avow, that I was mistaken in the opinions I had formed.'

There was a discrepancy between the showing of the Premier and of the Attorney-General. The former limited his measure—such was the impression made—to a prohibition of the assumption by Roman Catholics of territorial titles within the United Kingdom, rendering null and void all acts done by any parties under such title, and declaring all bequests made to them to be forfeited to the Crown. The Attorney-General, on the other hand, affirmed that the bill, ' if, as he believed, it would effectually prevent persons from assuming these titles, it would as effectually *prevent the existence of any of these dioceses or sees.*' . . . 'It had been said,' he added, ' by the hon. member for Bucks, that the bill would not interfere with synodical action. He differed with the hon. gentleman on that point. He thought, on the contrary, *that interference with synodical action was the necessary consequence,* and that the hon. member himself would, on mature consideration, see that it was so. It was undoubtedly desirable, if they could, to effect that object in the most quiet way,' but *if it were done effectually,* that was all they ought to seek to do.' Which of these versions is the correct one? Are we to accept the Premier or the law-officer of the Crown as the exponent of the government measure? Thousands are perplexed by this inquiry, and something should be done promptly to clear away the mystery. The statements of Sir John Romilly are entitled to the more weight as they were formally introduced, with the avowed purpose of explaining ' the general scope and effect of the measure ;' and that, too, on the ground that the observations of the Premier ' had not been fully understood.' We have reason to believe that the Roman Catholic members were but slightly alarmed on the showing of his lordship, but that their case was very different after the speech of the Attorney-General. We are not surprised at this. It is just what we should have expected. The question, however, recurs—which version is to be received? We say not, that they are incompatible one with the other. They may be consistent; but if so, his lordship must have withheld a portion of the truth, and that the most important and interesting. The public press has generally sided with the Premier, and strong language has been used in denying the soundness of the view given by his colleague.

The bill is now before us. We have had an opportunity of examining it, and will attempt briefly to state the conclusion at which we have arrived. In doing this, we shall borrow assistance from Cardinal Wiseman's *Appeal.* In this pamphlet it is expressly declared that the ordinary form of Papal Government is ' by bishops with *local* titles, that is, by an ecclesiastical hierarchy;' that ' the canon law is inapplicable under vicars-apostolic;' and that 'without a metropolitan and suffragans, a provincial synod was out of the question.' In harmony with these views, it is subsequently stated that the main ground of the application made to the Pope was, ' the absolute necessity of the hierarchy for domestic organization and good government.' If, then, these positions are true—and they are those of Cardinal Wiseman—the explanation of the Attorney-General is not so manifestly erroneous as some have imagined. The Ministerial measure unquestionably prohibits the assumption of *local,* as opposed to *foreign* titles; but if so, then, on the showing of the Cardinal, it prevents the setting up of a Papal hierarchy ; and as, in such case, the canon law would, by the theory of the Romish Church, be inapplicable, and as a metropolitan and suffragans would not exist, synodical action could not ensue. The course of thought appears to be briefly this—without territorial or local titles there can be no bishops ; and without bishops, no canon law or synodical action. Hence, substantially, as we apprehend, the Attorney-

General concludes that the bill of Lord John will prevent the formation of sees, and *effectually*—for this is his term—interfere with synodical action. Such an operation of the bill does not, it is true, appear on its surface; but our view is confirmed by the remarkable sentence occuring at the close of the extract we have given from Sir J. Romilly's speech. The lawyer points out the tendency and operation of the bill; while the Premier contents himself with stating the direct and obvious import of its clauses.

Assuming, then, our interpretation to be in the main correct, will the measure, we ask, be efficacious? Can we hope by its machinery to compass the end contemplated? To these inquiries we are unable confidently to reply. We have our misgivings, and shall briefly indicate their source. The Attorney-General, it will be observed, speaks only of *interference*. It is true, he affirms that it will be *effectual*, and this, it may be argued, is tantamount to prohibition. But his view is inferential only, and a large door for misapprehension is thus opened. He may be perfectly honest in his conviction that such will be the working of the bill, but we have seen enough of the failure of past predictions, to be exceedingly doubtful on such a point. What has recently occurred in Ireland may well make us incredulous, and we fear, therefore, there is too much truth in the assertion of the *Times*, of the 18th, that ' It is not at all necessary to synodical action, that the bishops forming the synod should assume territorial titles. Witness the Synod of Thurles, in which, with the exception of Paul, Archbishop of Armagh, and John of Tuam, the Fathers were content to style themselves by their surnames.' If this was done in Ireland, what is to prevent a similar meeting in England; and if so, what becomes of the Attorney-General's doctrine of *effectual interference ?*

That there has been a violation of law, is clear. We have not been hasty to admit this, but the fact is now placed beyond doubt by Dr. Twiss, whose treatise we have noticed in a former article.* This illegality is not limited to Ireland, and the permissive sanction afforded renders us doubly suspicious of mere inferential legislation.

The subtilty of the Papal Court must also be taken into account in estimating the probabilities of the future. The system has been worked with inimitable skill in all ages. It has accommodated itself to all possible circumstances; has been at one time imperious, and at another supple; sometimes severe in its exactions, and at others most lax; now contending for a name or form, as if they were matters of life and death, and then treating them with neglect and apparent scorn. We cannot, therefore, doubt, but that some mode will be devised of securing synodical action, to a certain extent at least, though territorial titles may be forbidden to Papal dignitaries. Nor should we wish to prevent this. All we seek to guard against is the introduction of a hierarchy which would give to synods, and to the canon law, an authority and binding obligation, not otherwise possessed. Let the clergy of the Papal Church meet—if such be their pleasure—like those of the Free Church of Scotland, the Congregational, Wesleyan, or

---

* Ultramontanism.

Baptist-bodies, but let them have no hierarchical status which would enable them to work by means of a machinery, the growth of centuries, and which has always been the fatal enemy of freedom, whether

the pride and lust of power, already too dominant in the Episcopal State-church. But there is more than this involved. Such, at least, is our grave and solemn conviction, after close attention to the matter, with due regard to all that has been advanced on either side of the case. Let our people but acquiesce in the setting up of this hierarchy, and Rome, with its despot upholders, will triumph, while the friends of liberty throughout Europe, the Mazzinis and the Kossuths, will weep in very bitterness of heart at the prostration of their hopes, and the yet more distant prospect of their country's liberation. We smile at the charge of being unfaithful to religious liberty, because we refuse to Roman Catholics hierarchical power and action. It is the fact of our sworn allegiance to this good cause which compels such refusal. Let the adherents of the Papacy have the utmost liberty of conscience and worship; let there be no civil disqualification on the ground of religious opinions; let there be freedom of speech and the utmost latitude of spiritual action. For this we contend with an earnestness which yields to no man. What we claim for ourselves we readily cede to our Papal fellow-countrymen. But beyond this we cannot go. More especially are we averse to a hierarchy which, contributing to the power of the clergy, robs the laity of their rightful authority, and builds up a power subversive of national liberty and fiercely hostile to religious tolerance.

Neither must it be supposed that we have faith in legislation because we do not discard it altogether. There are two extremes in this matter, against both of which we would guard. 'Reliance on mere legislative devices' may be avoided, in perfect harmony with the employment of legislation within its legitimate province. We may refuse to *commit* ourselves to the State without proscribing its operation altogether. There are mixed cases, partly religious and partly political, in which conscience and the legislature has each a province, and in reference to which, therefore, both may act. Now, we believe the Roman Catholic to be one of these, and hence it is that we admit the interference of the legislature, so far as we deem the case political, while we sternly resist it in what we regard as the religious department.

Some of our friends are disposed to make light of the canon law, at which we much marvel. A more fearful instrument of tyranny was never framed. Let our countrymen know its character, and they will never permit its introduction. It is futile to allege that the canon law is the rule of the Papal Church, and ought, therefore, to be admitted on the ground of religious liberty. How far such a plea is sound may be learnt from the following description of this law, by the late Dr. Pye Smith, one of the largest-hearted and most candid men that ever lived, and whose conscientiousness and exact scholarship entitle his judgment to great weight :—

'Now that law decrees and enjoins that all heretics (and every person knows that Protestants are deemed to be eminently such) are to be punished, when it *can be done*, by every kind of suffering that the art of man can devise: non-intercourse in trade, or in any way disinheriting, expatriation, loss of property, imprisonment, tortures, death in any form, but chiefly the being burned alive, and barbarous indignities to the dead corpse; that kings or queens, princes, and all persons, even parents, brothers, and children, are held guilty and liable ultimately to the same punishments, if they do not their utmost for the execution of those penalties, or if they screen or support in any way the denounced heretics; that upon the excommunication and other sentence of the ecclesiastical authority being declared, the offenders are to be delivered over to the secular judge, that if the temporal authority refuse or neglect to inflict his part of the punishments, *he shall himself be excommunicated*, with the terrible consequences; and that informers, though accomplices, or convicted of perjury, shall be held valid witnesses.'*

It is of vast importance that the real character of the excitement recently awakened should be correctly understood. Many of the clergy are congratulating themselves on the evidence it affords of the attachment of the nation to the Episcopal Church. We believe nothing of the kind, and are confirmed in our view by the opinion of the Divinity Professor in King's College, London, who, in a recent work, avows his conviction, ' that the movement is entirely a national one; that neither the ecclesiastical nor the theological question occupies more than a very subordinate place indeed in the minds of those who are exclaiming against Papal aggression.'† Whatever may be the momentary effect, we cannot doubt the ultimate tendency, of what is passing before our eyes. Upon the Irish branch of the United Church, the storm will probably first burst. But its strength will not be exhausted there. The dark clouds which are gathering in the heavens portend calamity to institutions nearer home.

In the meantime, we repeat to Dissenters the counsel formerly given, ' to maintain their own distinctive principles in their opposition to the Papacy.' In this consists their safety and their strength. Let this counsel be complied with, and they will at once discharge the duty of the present hour, and be prepared for whatever may await them in the future. Their fidelity to Protestantism now will be a pledge of the faithful discharge of their duty in the coming struggle.

AGRICULTURAL DISTRESS has, of course, engaged the attention of Parliament. It was expected to do so; and, had it been considered without reference to party interests, on its own merits, and with a view, to the welfare of the community, every man would have approved its introduction. We need not say how far this was from being the case.

---

* Reasons for Protestantism, p. 45.
† Maurice's Church a Family.

It is impossible to read the debate without perceiving that the *nominal* was not the *real* matter at issue. The distress of the farmer is the pretext on which a defeated party is seeking its own reconstruction, and the recovery of the offices from which it was driven in 1846. That there is considerable distress amongst the occupiers of land is notorious. It was admitted in the Queen's speech, and ought to be fairly and thoroughly investigated. That such distress is attributable to our free-trade policy, and will continue so long as that policy is maintained, is the view of Mr. Disraeli and his supporters. Of this, however, they fail to adduce evidence; and Parliament, sustained by an overwhelming majority of the community, has refused to ratify their judgment. On the 11th of February, Mr. Disraeli, in conformity with the notice he had given, proceeded to move, ' That the severe distress which continues to exist in the United Kingdom among the owners and occupiers of land, renders it the duty of her Majesty's ministers to introduce without delay such measures as may be most effectual for the relief thereof.' The vagueness of this motion was paralleled by that of the mover's speech, which occupied three hours, and embraced every variety of topic that could be crowded into such an oration. Of the ability of the speech there is no question, and the tone which pervaded it was far more moderate than the usual declamations of the speaker. For both these qualities — the vagueness and the moderation — there are obvious reasons. The Papal question, it was well known, had, for a time, induced many Irish members to disavow allegiance to the Ministry; while the pecuniary interests of some landlords might prompt the support of a motion which talked only of relief to distress, though it really meant return to protection. The motion was designedly framed to catch all stragglers, to take advantage of the selfishness, and even to borrow support from the less discreditable interests of individuals. The master-speeches of the debate were those of Sir James Graham and Mr. Cobden. They were both good, the former pre-eminently. ' The motion implied,' said Sir James Graham, referring to commercial freedom, ' though it did not state, an approximation to the reversal of that policy. He objected to it on that ground; but he objected to it also that it was vague, illusory, and presented nothing tangible. . . He thought it his duty to vote against a proposal the certain extent and tendency of which he could not understand.' The numbers on the division were—For the motion, 267, and against it, 281, leaving Ministers with a majority of 14 only. We regret the smallness of this minority, not for the sake of Lord John's administration—for which we care little—but for the sake of the country, and for the farmers especially, among whom it will diffuse vague and most illusory hopes. We have no fear for the issue of the struggle, come when it may; but we are concerned that landlords and farmers should apply themselves at once, and vigorously, to the new state of things about them. Let it be borne in mind that Protection has made no real progress, notwithstanding the smallness of the Ministerial majority. Last year, Mr. Disraeli's motion was supported by 252 against 273, leaving to the Ministry a majority of 21, being only seven more than they had on the morning of the 14th. The defection of twenty-one Irish members, on

the ground of resentment, will much more than account for this difference.  The ‘ Morning Herald ’ affirms that ‘ the vote was taken on the
question of a re-enactment of import duties, which,’ it says, ‘ large or
small, would be a recognition of the rights of the agricultural classes.’
The division is consequently represented as having ‘ confirmed for the
hour the free-trade policy, which has thus received a victorious death-
blow.’   This exultation may befit the columns of a violent partisan
paper, but harmonizes very poorly with the exhibition subsequently
made in the Lords.   It is quite probable that we may have another
struggle.   The more violent of the Protectionists seem intent on this.
Well, let it be.   Belonging to the people, we have no fear for their interests ; but were we of the privileged order, we would whisper to our
compeers, that there may possibly be danger to our exclusive privileges
in arousing the British people to a defence of cheap food and fuller
employment.

Brief as the session has yet been, the Government has contrived to
destroy amongst earnest reformers all solicitude and zeal on its behalf.
With an infatuation for which it is difficult to account, they have
thrown from them the sympathies of the country, notwithstanding the
breakers that are a-head.   In reply to the question of Sir Joshua
Walmsley, Lord John stated that it was not his intention to propose
any extension of the suffrage ; and on the 20th, he stoutly opposed
Mr. Locke King’s motion for leave to bring in a ‘ bill to make the franchise in counties in England and Wales the same as that in boroughs.’
An opportunity was thus afforded, at the eleventh hour, to gain
strength and earnestness to his party—but he threw it recklessly from
him, and that, too, without advancing the plea of principle.   The expediency of reform was admitted ; a bill was promised next session ;
but the time was now inopportune, other measures claimed attention, and
the rights of the people and the good working of the Reform Bill were
therefore to be postponed.   His lordship deserved the defeat which
awaited him.   Last year his opposition was supported by 159 to 100,
but this year he could only muster 52, whilst the number of Mr. Locke
King’s supporters was still 100.   This defeat of Ministers by a majority
of 48 is a significant and instructive fact; and if the Premier be wise,
he will amend his policy, or retire from office.

The die, however, has been cast.   We write on the 22nd, and in
the knowledge of what occurred in the House last night.   The ill-
starred budget, which satisfied no one but the Chancellor of the
Exchequer, has brought things to a crisis.   We had intended to
analyze it, but this is no longer necessary.   The sooner it is forgotten
the better.   It is the last of a series of blunders which Sir Charles
Wood will ever have the opportunity of making.   The endurance of
the nation is exhausted, and the member for Halifax may retire—the
more speedily the better—to the ease and luxuries of private life.

Arrangements are in the course of being made for the census
of 1851, and we are especially desirous of calling attention to two
schedules, the importance of which cannot be over-rated.   We allude
to a return which is now proposed to be obtained of “ churches
and chapels belonging to the United Church of England and Ire-

land ;" and to another of " places of religious worship not belonging to the Established Church." In the former of these schedules will be shown in what parish or other ecclesiastical division, a church or chapel is situated ; when and under what circumstances it was consecrated or licensed ; if consecrated or licensed since the 1st of January, 1800 ; how and by whom erected—by parliamentary grant, parochial rate, subscription, or private benefaction, &c. ; how endowed, by land, tithe, glebe, pew-rents, fees, &c. ; the number of sittings, free and non-free ; the average number of attendants, and the estimated number on Sunday, March 30th ; also the number of pupils at the Sunday-school. In like manner, the second schedule will exhibit the local and denominational names of every religious building amongst Dissenters and Roman Catholics ; the parish and other district in which it is situated ; when erected ; whether a separate and entire building ; whether used exclusively as a place of worship ; the number of free and other sittings provided ; the average number of attendants on divine service ; and the estimated number on the last Sunday of March, together with the number of Sunday scholars.

We are glad to hear that the officers of the Congregational Union, the London Congregational Board, and the Baptist Congregational Union, heartily approve of this great scheme, and have promised their co-operation. It is also expected that the Wesleyan Methodists will cordially unite in promoting its object amongst their numerous churches.

It is moreover understood, 'that steps will be taken to obtain the educational statistics of the three kingdoms ; and we may confidently hope, that by official and private zeal directed to this great enterprise, a record of facts will be procured, gathered with care and digested with skill, illustrative of our physical, social, and religious condition, alike useful and interesting to the statesman, the financial reformer, the pastor, the moral instructor, and the private citizen, in a nation, and at an era, the greatest which the world ever beheld.

During the past month, the Nonconformist body has lost one of its brightest ornaments. The personal virtues, exact and profound scholarship, scientific eminence, and generous adherence to whatever was large-hearted and liberal, rendered the name of Dr. Pye Smith a household word amongst us. He has ceased from his labors, and his works follow him. We say no more at present, as we hope, in our next number, to present an ampler retrospect than our space now permits, of the life, principles, and labors of a man pre-eminently worthy of esteem and affection.

We have no heart to turn to foreign politics. In France, the President and the Assembly are still in collision. We have no sympathy with either, and see no hope for the country until other and better men are found to wield its powers. At Dresden, Absolutism is rampant, but as yet little has resulted from its consultations. The cloven-foot, however, is visible, and it becomes our country to be vigilant.

## Literary Intelligence.

*Just Published.*

Researches on Magnetism, Electricity, Heat, &c.; in their Relations to the Vital Force. By Karl Baron Von Reschenbach, P.D. Translated and edited at the express desire of the Author, with a Preface, Notes, and Appendix. by William Gregory, M.D., F.R.S.E. With three Plates, and twenty-three Woodcuts. Parts I. and II.

Letters on the Laws of Man's Nature and Development. By Henry G. Atkinson, F.G.S., and Harriet Martineau.

Two Lectures on the Poetry of Pope, and on his own Travels in America. By the Right Hon. the Earl of Carlisle. Delivered to the Leeds Mechanics Institution and Literary Society, December 5th and 6th, 1850. Revised and corrected by the Author.

The Introduction of the English Bible and its Consequences. Illustrative of the paramount duty and imperative obligation of British Christians to other Nations, in the present eventful period.

Domestic Fowl, and Ornamental Poultry. By H. D. Richardson.

Cautions for the Times; addressed to the Parishioners of a Parish in England. By their former Friend. To be published occasionally.

The Family Almanack, and Educational Register for 1851, containing a List of the Foundation and Grammar Schools in England and Wales, together with the Scholarships and Exhibitions attached to them. To be published annually.

Southey's Common Place Book. Fourth Series, Original Memoranda, &c. Edited by his Son-in-law, John Wood Warter, B.D.

Biblical Commentary on St. Paul's 1st and 2nd Epistles to the Corinthians. By Hermann Olshausen, D.D. Translated from the German; with Additional Notes. By the Rev. John Edmund Cox, M.A., F.S.A, Vicar of St. Helena, Bishopsgate, London.

Reflections arising out of the Papal Aggression for the Consideration of the Church, Laity, and Parliament. With Comments on the Dispute between the Rev. W. J. E. Bennett, and the Bishop of London. By a Simple Protestant.

The Poet of the Sanctuary. A Centenary Commemoration of the Labours and Services, Literary and Devotional, of the Rev. Isaac Watts, D.D. Preceded by Remarks on the Origin of Psalmody and Christian Hymnology in earlier times. By Josiah Conder.

Fragments of College and Pastoral Life. A Memoir of the late Rev. John Clark, of Glasgow; with Selections from his Essays, Lectures, and Sermons. By the Rev. John Cairns, A.M.

Comfortable Words for Christian Parents bereaved of Little Children. By John Brown, D.D., Edinburgh.

A Voice from the North. An Appeal to the Catholics of the Church of England, in behalf of their Church. By S. B. Harper, Priest. No. IV.

Dahomey and the Dahomans. Being the Journals of Two Missions to the King of Dahomey, and Residence at his Capital in the years 1849 and 1850. By Frederick E. Forbes, Commander R.N. 2 vols.

Parts I. and II. of the Pictorial Family Bible; with Original Notes. By Dr. Kitto.

Parts I. and II. of Leigh Hunt's Journal.

THE

# Eclectic Review.

## APRIL, 1851.

ART. I.—*The Science of Politics. Part I. The Theory of Human Progression, and Natural Probability of a Reign of Justice.* London: Johnstone and Hunter. 8vo. Pp. xii., 523. 1850.

IF our notice of this volume has been delayed, it is not because it has been overlooked by us, much less that we have been slow to appreciate, or reluctant to pronounce upon, its merits; but because we have been careful to do justice to three parties—the author, the public, and the truth. The subject of the volume is so important, and the pretensions of the author to have discovered a new method of discussing and practically applying it to the pressing wants of society are so high, that we could not satisfy ourselves with a cursory notice. If the 'Theory' here developed, and the views respecting political science founded on it, are correct, public attention cannot be too early or too earnestly directed to the fact; and if the discovery of what has so long been a desideratum is attributable to the author of this book, not even his obscuration under the anonymous should permit his claims on the gratitude of mankind to pass unrewarded. A proud thing, indeed, would it have been for England, could it have been said that, a second time in her history, Divine Providence has so distributed his gifts, that amongst her sons has arisen an instructor of the nations in what pertains to the certain advancement of learning, beyond all past, beyond all anticipated attainment; that after so many ages of all but fruitless speculation in the various departments of political inquiry—speculation which tasked so many great and noble minds; amongst the rest, Plato, Aristotle, Montesquieu, Bacon, Bodin, Hobbes, Grotius, Milton, and Locke—it was reserved for our age and country to produce the genius profound enough to discover the true scientific theory, and the understanding sufficiently informed to point the application of that theory to all the exigencies of social life.

We are compelled, however, and at the very outset, to express our conviction that the pretensions of the volume before us cannot in justice be conceded; but that, on the contrary, for all, or nearly all, that is substantially new to an ordinary English reader, it is indebted to a prior publication; and, further, that the theory propounded in it fails in that part precisely where it departs from the scheme developed in that prior publication. It is our intention to state the reasons which have necessitated this conviction. We regret that our limits will not admit of our attempting more. Had it been otherwise, we should gladly have devoted no inconsiderable space to features of the 'Theory of Human Progression' worthy of all praise :—the lucid arrangement and perspicuous style; the great beauty of occasional passages ; the admirable manner in which the main points of the argument are illustrated, by reference to past or passing events ; and, excepting the repetitions, not unfrequently occurring to the sixth or seventh degree, the interest thrown over the whole essay, which renders it, notwithstanding that this is the age of prize and other essays, one of the most readable of modern times. In addition, we should have been glad to have an opportunity of noticing the deep insight and philosophic generalizings, whether as exhibited in discursive passages or aphorismic sentences, that shine like constellations or sparkle like gems here and there, were it not that in too many instances these are borrowed lights. All these things, however, are really minor matters in a work that purports to unfold one continuous argument, the value of which depends not on the management of details, but upon the coherence and consistency of the whole. We proceed, therefore, at once to notice both the points adverted to, and in the order in which we have referred to them.

Before we come to the first of these—the question of originality of discovery—we must be permitted to make an observation or two in vindication of the course we are about to pursue.

It may be objected, that inasmuch as the present work is published anonymously, the author can scarcely be said to claim the merit of discovery, even supposing it can be proved that he has availed himself of the fruits of another man's genius. In reply, we remind such as may be inclined to entertain this objection, that authors always have a motive for assuming the anonymous, sometimes laudable, sometimes otherwise; and that, generally, an author retains a position of obscurity only so long as the public are uninterested in his productions. With the exception of Junius, we do not remember a single instance, in modern times, of one whose works have become famous being able permanently to conceal his name. Even the 'Great Unknown' was obliged perforce to become well known; and the mysterious 'Doctor Dove' at last revealed himself to his admiring pupils. If our present author, therefore, should find himself famous, it is more than probable that he will publish his name on the title-page of some future edition ; so that we cannot admit the plea founded on the fact of a present *incognito*. At the same time, we may be allowed to observe, while on this topic, that we have used our best endeavours to ascertain the author's name, without success ; neither have we 'the slightest suspicion respecting it. This avowal may, perhaps, screen us from any charge that might otherwise have been levelled against our strictures, as having been dictated by personal animus.

Indeed, it is on public grounds alone that we have determined to sift this question of originality, and lay the results before our readers. If the author of the 'Theory of Human Progression' has borrowed all that is essential to his argument from another man's writings, it is but right that the fact should be known ; and if he is careful to conceal that fact from his readers, by never once hinting at it—never once naming that other man or his works—it is all the more imperative on a reviewer who knows the truth to be as careful to give it ventilation. If, moreover, it so happens that the original discoverer is not an Englishman, but a foreigner, and, therefore, the less likely to learn that he is being robbed of his honours, or, knowing the fact, less able to vindicate his claims to originality ; then it becomes yet more clearly the duty of all who understand the merits of the case to adjudicate in the spirit of justice. Reputation is, surely, as sacred a thing as property ; neither is there any reason why the reputation arising from originality of discovery should not be held as inviolable, in the world of letters, as moral reputation in the world of men.

We have always admired the manner in which Southey laid down the rule for his own conduct in matters of this nature :— ' It has ever been a rule with me,' he writes in the preface to the first volume of his collected poems, ' when I have imitated a passage, or borrowed an expression, to acknowledge the specific obligation. Upon the present occasion, it behoves me to state the more general, and therefore more important obligations, which I am conscious of owing, either to my predecessors, or my contemporaries.' If our author had followed such a rule as this, in a department of literature where it is much more easy to ascertain one's obligations than in that of poetic influence and inspiration, we should have had no such unpleasant duty to discharge as that which now devolves upon us.

Neither does our author appear to be without a sense of what is due to the labours of those predecessors or coadjutors to whom he feels indebted. His essay, for example, is dedicated to M. Victor Cousin, as one who has 'laboured so earnestly and so well to give a correct system of ethical philosophy, and to communicate to Europe a scheme of natural morals which must ere long bear a rich and most beneficial harvest.' In the body of the work, also, he expresses his high appreciation of M. Cousin's 'History of the Moral Philosophy of the Eighteenth Century.' In a similar manner he acknowledges his obligations to Kant, whom he occasionally quotes; more especially in the Appendix, where he refers to him as 'the man to come,' on account of his discovery of the terminal method, and places him third in a series of which Aristotle and Bacon are the first two. Several lesser names are referred to in an honourable manner, in various parts of the volume. We should have had no cause for complaint if our author had followed the same course with the name we are about to mention—a name quite as distinguished, in the opinion of some, as that of Kant or Cousin, and to which he is equally, if not much more, indebted.

We refer to M. Auguste Comte, whose original genius and profound discoveries are sufficient, in our opinion—although from many points of his philosophy we strongly dissent—to justify the title that has been given him as the Bacon of the nineteenth century. The writings of this eminent philosopher are, we should imagine, but little known in England, and not much better in France. Indeed, he complains, in one of his latest volumes, of the neglect that has attended his publications in both countries; and states that, so far as he then knew (1842), no one had noticed his great work—the 'Philosophie Positive' —with the exception of Sir David Brewster, who reviewed the first two volumes in the 'Edinburgh Review,' in 1838. Although since then he has become better known by the references made to his philosophy in Mr. Mill's 'System of Logic,' and Mr. Lewes's 'Biographical History of Philosophy,' we infer that comparatively few have perused his voluminous work, from the fact that, although it is now more than twenty years since the first volume was published, it has not yet passed to a second edition. But we may have more to say upon this subject at a future period, when we hope to lay before our readers an extended notice of the whole of this remarkable production. At present, therefore, we shall confine ourselves, as strictly as may be, to the object we have before us, namely, to show that to M. Comte the author of the 'Theory of Human Progression' is

indebted for all that is essential to his argument.   If this is not
the case, we were never more mistaken in reference to a question
of literary obligation.

We have not made this statement lightly.   We have compared
the two authors, in all those respects to which our statement
relates, and have been *driven* to the conclusion—the word is not
too strong—that although the name and writings of M. Comte
are never once referred to in any way in the ' Theory of Human
Progression,' but for the former, the latter would never have
seen the light.   Let it be observed, however, that our statement
refers to the essentials and particulars of the argument, not to
the method and details of its exposition.   In the exposition of his
subject the author of the latter has adopted a method of his own,
and may be thought by some to have simplified, and even to
have improved upon M. Comte; while the illustrative matter
has been judiciously selected from facts or events calculated to
interest an English rather than a French reader.   What we
affirm is, that the basis and tenor of the argument, as such, are
derived from the writings of M. Comte ; and what we so much
regret is, that in a work abounding in many excellent qualities,
apart from the question of originality, the author should have
allowed any of his readers to attribute to him profound discoveries made at least twenty years ago.

In submitting the evidence that has led to this conclusion,
we shall first adduce the object and general plan of the volume
before us in the author's own words.   That object is, ' to exhibit
an argument to establish the possibility of a science of politics,
and to prove also the probability that such a science may
reasonably be expected to evolve at this period of man's progressive acquisition of knowledge.'

The nature of the argument is stated generally in the following words :—

' Our argument is based on the theory of progress, or the fact of
progress ; for it is a fact as well as a theory.   And the theory of progress is based on the principle, that there is an order in which man not
only *does* evolve the various branches of knowledge, but an order in
which man *must necessarily* evolve the various branches of knowledge.
And this necessity is based on the principle, that every science when
undergoing its process of discovery is *objective*, that is, the object of
contemplation ; but when discovered and reduced to ordination it
becomes *subjective*, that is, a means of operation for the discovery and
evolution of the science that lies logically beyond it, and next to it
in logical proximity.

' If this logical dependence of one science on another could be clearly
made out for the whole realm of knowledge, it would give the outline,
not only of the classification of the sciences, but of man's intellectual
history, of man's intellectual *development*—where the word development

means, not the alteration of man's *nature*, but the extension of his knowledge, and the consequent improvement of his mode of action, entailing with it the improvement of his condition.

' And if the law of this intellectual development can be made out for the branches of knowledge which have already been reduced to ordination, it may be carried into the future; and the future progress of mankind may be seen to evolve logically out of the past progress.'— *Theory of Human Progression*, pp. 23, 24.

Having thus stated the argument, a more precise account is given of the subject of the present volume, which is only the first part of a general system of politics.

' Let us, then, consider the aspects in which a science of politics may be viewed. 1. In the probability of its evolution based on the logical determination of its position in a scheme of classification. 2. In its constituent propositions, and the method it employs for their substantiation. 3. In the history of its doctrine (not the history of its *books*)—in the history of its theoretic principles in *practice*, and in the application of its principles to the present condition of society; thereby attempting to estimate what changes ought to be made, and what, in fact, ought to be the one definite form of political society. The present volume professes to treat of the first of these divisions.'—*Ib.* pp. 24, 25.

This, then, is the scope of the present volume : ' the probability of the evolution of a science of politics, based on the logical determination of its position in a scheme of classification.' Mixed up with this is another argument, perfectly distinct from the above, although based upon it; namely, an argument to prove the probability of a future reign of justice, or, as the author in several places expresses it, a political millennium, as antecedent to the millennium of Scripture.

The entire argument, then, of the volume, whether in its general or its more specific aspect, rests upon the theory respecting the development of the sciences. Apart from this there could have been no such argument as our author's in relation to human progression—no such argument as our author's in relation to the probability of a future reign of justice. Have we said too much in reference to the obligations of the author of the ' Theory of Human Progression' to M. Comte, if we show that the fundamental theory in question had been fully expounded and published by the latter at least twenty years ago ? The comparison, to which we now proceed, will set the question of originality in a clear and indisputable light.

In prosecuting this comparison we shall refer, in the first place, to the evolution and classification of the sciences, and then descend to a few details and other particulars of agreement between the two authors.

We have already quoted our author's words respecting his

argument as being based on ' the theory of progress.' Referring
the reader to that extract, we now turn to the section on 'the
order of the sciences,' for a more particular explanation of his
views on this subject. It is as follows :—

' The sciences are capable of being *classed* on a system which is not
arbitrary.

' The *discovery* of the sciences as a historical fact, is correlative with
the scheme of classification. The *classification* is a mere process of
the intellect, whereby the sciences are arranged in a certain order,
according to a principle. The *discovery* of the sciences is a historical
fact extending over many centuries. We assert that the order of discovery has been correlative with the order of classification.

' The sciences are classed *on their complexity*. To determine the
position of a science in the scheme of classification, we have only to
ask how many substantive concepts does it necessarily involve ; that is
with how many *nouns-substantive* can it be made and expressed.'—
*Theory of Human Progression*, pp. 168, 169.

We now turn to the first volume of the ' Cours de Philosophie
Positive,' published by M. Comte in 1830, and find in the
second *Leçon,* on 'the hierarchy of the positive sciences,' the
following passages :—

' The classification of objects should be determined by the real
affinities and the natural connexion which they present, in such a
manner that this classification may be in itself the expression of the
most general fact, manifested by a thorough comparison of the objects
which it embraces.

' Applying this fundamental rule to the actual case, it is then, according to the mutual dependence between the different positive sciences,
that we ought to proceed to their classification ; and this dependence,
to be real, can only result from that of the corresponding phenomena.'
— *Cours de Philosophie Positive*, tome i. pp. 60, 61.

' All science may be expounded according to two essentially distinct
methods, of which every other method can only be a combination—the
*historical* and the *dogmatical*. By the first process, we view the subjects of knowledge successively, in the same actual order in which the
human mind has really obtained them, and adopting, as far as possible,
the same views. By the second, we present the system of ideas such
as it might be conceived of at the present time by a single mind, when
placed at a convenient point of view, and provided with sufficient
knowledge, it is engaged in collecting the science into one whole. . . .

' The constant tendency of the human mind, in relation to the exposition of knowledge, is to substitute more and more for the historic
order the dogmatic, which alone accords with the perfected state of
our intelligence.'—*Ib.* 77—79.

' Nevertheless, although, after what has been said, we ought not to
take the historic order for the basis of our classification, I must not
omit to indicate beforehand, as an essential property of the encyclopædic scale I am about to propose, its general conformity with the
history of *science* as a whole ; in this sense, that, notwithstanding the

real and continued simultaneousness of the development of the different sciences, those which are classed first are in effect more ancient, and always more advanced, than those presented later in the scale. This is what ought inevitably to take place, if we really take as we should for the principle of our classification the natural logical connexion of the different sciences, the point of departure for the species being necessarily the same as for the individual.'—*Ib.* pp. 84, 85.

' Approaching this great question in a direct manner, let us recollect in the outset that to obtain a natural and positive classification of the fundamental sciences we should seek the principle in the comparison of the different orders of phenomena whose laws it is their object to discover. What we have to determine is the real dependence of the different scientific investigations (*études scientifiques*). But this dependence can only result from that of the corresponding phenomena. Considering all the observable phenomena under this point of view, we shall see that it is possible to class them in a small number of natural categories, disposed in such a manner, that the rational study of each category may be founded on the knowledge of the principal laws of the preceding category, and become the foundation of the study of the next. This order is determined by the degree of simplicity, or, which amounts to the same thing, by the degree of generality of the phenomena from which their successive dependence results, and, consequently, the greater or less facility of their investigation.'—*Ib.* pp. 86, 87.

Our readers, we think, will agree with us that there is no essential difference between M. Comte and the author of the ' Theory of Human Progression,' so far. We now proceed to the classification itself, as furnished by the two authors respectively.

The author of the ' Theory of Human Progression' shall speak first :—

'The order of the sciences is as follows :—1. The mathematical sciences. 2. The force sciences. 3. The inorganic physical sciences. 4. The sciences that treat of vegetable organization. 5. The sciences that treat of animal organization. 6. The sciences that treat of man and his functions.'—*Theory of Human Progression*, p. 169.

M. Comte shall speak next :—

' We have, then, exactly determined in this *leçon*, not following vain and arbitrary speculations, but regarding it as the subject of a veritable philosophic problem, the rational plan that ought constantly to guide us in the study of the positive philosophy. The following is the definite result: mathematics, astronomy, physics, chemistry, physiology, and social physics. Such is the encyclopædic formula which, amongst the very large number of classifications of which the six fundamental sciences are susceptible, is alone logically conformable to the natural and invariable hierarchy of the phenomena.'—*Philosophie Positive*, tome i. p. 115.

But neither of these classifications is complete. We shall,

therefore, submit the two tables of the respective authors, or, at least, so much of them as shall suffice to show the agreement between them when properly compared.

I.—*Classification of the sciences, by the author of ' The Theory of Human Progression.'*

1st. Primary knowledge, necessary and universal. Ontologic.
2nd. Science. Logic or Syllogistic. Mathematic. Dynamic. Physic —Mechanic, Magnetic, Chemic, Electro-galvanic. Organic—Botanic, Zoologic. Anthropologic, or Man-Science. Theologic.

---

II.—*Tableau Synoptique du Cours de Philosophie Positive de M. Auguste Comte.*

Préliminaires Généraux    Mathématiques—le calcul, la géométrie, la mécanique rationelle.    Astronomie — géométrique, mécanique. Physique—la barologie, la thermologie, l'acoustique, l'optique, l'électrologie.    Chimie—inorganique, organique.    Physiologie—végétale, animale.    Physique Sociale.    Résumé Général.

In comparing these two tables, it should be borne in mind that the latter is only a table of *leçons.* The *Préliminaires Généraux* discuss those portions of the general subject of knowledge which are classed in the first table under the heads of Ontologic and Logic; and the *Résumé Général* treats of the whole previous course, in its bearing on philosophy and theology. Some of the subdivisions of the sciences differ in the two tables, but not more than the author of the 'Theory of Human Progression' has made them to differ in the various classifications he has presented throughout his volume. There is still room for revision in this department of classification, on account of the imperfect advancement of the sciences themselves. Now, as M. Comte has shown, six sciences may be arranged in seven hundred and twenty different ways, and out of this number there is scarcely one for which some plausible reason might not be advanced. How is it, then, that the author of the 'Theory of Human Progression' has given the same classification as M. Comte? Let any one compare the classifications of other authors—say, for example, of Bacon, D'Alembert, Stewart, or one lately given in 'Man Primeval,' by Dr. Harris—and see how wide the contrariety. The question admits of but one answer—namely, that the author of the 'Theory of Human Progression' and M. Comte have followed the same principle. Let it be remembered, however, that although both that principle and the "Tableau Synoptique' were published in 1830, there is no reference to the fact in the volume before us.

But it may be asked, is it not possible that, conceding the prior publication of M. Comte, the author of the 'Theory of

Human Progression' may have made the same discovery independently? We do not deny the possibility, but we should be
glad to have proof of the fact. Our author has given too many
proofs of extensive acquaintance with both the French and
German schools of philosophy to admit of the supposition that
he has overlooked M. Comte; and although there is a marked
difference between the two authors in the method of developing
their respective views, it is evident, on reflection, that those
views could have been arrived at only in one way. Our author,
for example, proceeds synthetically, commencing with abstraction and proposition, and evolving the sciences one after the
other in logical order; while M. Comte proceeds analytically in
the first instance, showing in the second *Leçon* how the application of his principle of classification leads to a definite result, and
afterwards justifies and explains the preliminary analysis, in a
long course of *Leçons*, extending through six bulky volumes.
What we cannot help believing is, that M. Comte's analysis was
essentially antecedent to our author's synthesis.

Then, again, there is so much identity of view, if not of expression, between the two authors, not only in relation to the
logical development of the sciences, but also to other matters
bearing upon the general argument—the two minds seem to
travel so much in the same road—that we cannot doubt that the
one has acted the part of a pioneer, if not of a guide to the
other. We shall explain our meaning in a few particulars,
although necessarily in a very imperfect manner, on account of
our limited space.

We have seen how thoroughly identical are their views
respecting the *principle* of the scheme of classification, the
*scheme* itself, and the *correlation* of the logical and chronological
evolution of the sciences. We now state, in addition, that their
views accord more or less on most of the details of the scientific
analysis, where differences might have been expected to occur.
Where there is a difference, it arises from the use our author
has made of the results of ontological speculation, for which
M. Comte has a supreme contempt. But even on this part of the
subject it is not difficult to see the philosophic agreement between the two respecting the place which such ontological facts
ought to hold, if once admitted to be such. For example, our
author places ontology first in his scheme, designating it ' primary
knowledge;' M. Comte would give it the same place, could it
be received as a department of certain knowledge at all—as may
be seen by his remarks on the subject in his third *Leçon*. Proceeding downwards in the scale, we find essential agreement in
nearly every item. Our author observes in his Introduction :—
' With regard to the classification of the mathematical sciences,

we have not the slightest misgivings. We believe that the order in which they are presented will be found correct; and as logic has not usually been considered as the first and simplest of the mathematical sciences, we have said rather more on logic than might otherwise have been necessary.' M. Comte has the same views of logic in its relation to mathematics, and in his second *Leçon* describes the abstract portion of mathematics as 'nothing more than an immense and admirable extension of natural logic to a certain order of deductions;' while, a little before, he shows how both the science and art of logic are best to be learnt through the processes of positive science. 'Method,' he writes, 'is not capable of being studied separately from the researches in which it is employed.' Our author places arithmetic next to logic, and before algebra; so does M. Comte. Our author states, in a note, 'Quantity and number are frequently confounded with each other, and algebra has been termed universal arithmetic.' M. Comte says the same thing, but mentions the author of this misrepresentation. 'Even the celebrated definition,' he writes, in his third *Leçon*, 'given by Newton, when he characterised algebra as universal arithmetic, certainly gives a very false idea of the nature of algebra and of that of arithmetic.' Our author regards geometry as logically subsequent to algebra; so does M. Comte. Our author has some acute remarks on the 'preparatory analysis' of geometry; M. Comte has similar remarks, only more extended and complete, in his ninth *Leçon*.

On other points besides those relating to the details of the scheme of classification, we find substantial coincidence between the two authors. Both, for example, regard the scheme of classification as a test of the condition of the sciences generally; that is, of their advanced state, or otherwise. ('Theory of Human Progression,' pp. 206, 207; 'Philosophie Positive,' i. 101, 102.) Both regard the speculations of Philosophy or metaphysics as fruitless in comparison with the investigations of Positive Science. ('Theory of Human Progression,' pp. 110—113; 'Philosophie Positive,' i. 37, &c.) Both regard the historical method, or the natural history of a science, as chronologically antecedent to its logical or synthetic development. ('Theory of Human Progression,' pp. 326—328; 'Philosophie Positive,' i. p. 79, &c.) Both require new intellect, or new intellectual habits, to carry out their views of future progress. ('Theory of Human Progression,' p. 251; 'Philosophie Positive,' i. 106.)

But similar accordance is observable on topics of wider significance. Our author, for example, has some admirable remarks in his Appendix (also repeated in other parts of his volume), on the two methods of studying thought—the psychological and the critical. After characterising the psychological method, and the sceptical objections urged against it, he describes the critical method in the following terms:—'Far otherwise with the *critic*. The critic takes his stand on the immovable basis of *science*, and, leaving all questions of consciousness or of mental operation, he makes the whole range of the sciences objective, and asks, what thoughts they have posited, and what methods they have pursued? He leaves it to every science in particular to determine what is *true* and what is *false* in each region of inquiry; and when science has achieved her office, he culls the first and fundamental truths of each science, and says, "These are indisputable; and if you question them, you must fight your battle with the *world of science*, which has established and authenticated these propositions."'

These are admirably expressed views; but are, in fact, only a brief exposition of what M. Comte has insisted on throughout his work, and sketched out, even at greater length, in his first *Leçon*.

Then, again, our author has some profound remarks, in the third section of his first chapter, on the progress of the human mind in the knowledge of material nature, more particularly in reference to *causes*. Although this part of the 'Theory of Human Progression' is rather more confused than usual, in consequence of the author's mingling historical with dogmatical matters, it is plain that he traces that progress through three stages—the theological, or supernatural; the metaphysical, or scholastic; and that of positive science. Now this is one of M. Comte's discoveries, and referred to as such by Mr. Mill and Mr. Lewes, in their respective works already adverted to. This discovery is first announced in the first *Leçon* of the 'Philosophie Positive,' constantly adverted to and applied afterwards, and is fully expounded in the fifth volume.

Lastly—not to weary the patience of our readers with these parallelisms—the basis of our author's special argument respecting the probability of a future reign of justice is laid in the fact, that *credence*, or the diffusion of sound convictions amongst the people of any country, gives the law to social progress. This, under various forms, is the staple of our author's argument in all those portions of the volume where it is reproduced. Not only has M. Comte expounded the bearing of this fact on social progress (the fact has been long admitted, and is explicitly referred to by Stewart, Mill, and others); but he has distinctly, and for the first time, shown that when rightly viewed, it becomes the index of the political state. We are tempted to quote largely from M. Comte on this subject, but forbear. If any one wishes a critical exposition of his discoveries in this department of social science, by virtue of which it is already acquiring a new character and status, he will be amply rewarded by consulting the last book of Mr. Mill's ' System of Logic.'

We think we have now said enough respecting the correspondence between the two authors—a correspondence which we have found some difficulty in bringing within compass, on account of the many particulars it embraces. Are we not justified in the conclusion at which we have arrived, that the ' Theory of Human Progression ' is largely indebted to the ' Philosophie Positive ' for all that is really essential to it? Have we not also in fact made as many exceptions, in our preliminary statement respecting the amount of obligation, as are warranted by our brief review and comparison? We have not denied the ability of the volume before us, and we have given the author credit for suiting the arguments contained in it to the mental and political associations of English readers. But the fact remains, that the essentials of the argument have already been given to the world, yet without any acknowledgment on his part. It is this that we complain of. If, after all that we have said, it can be shown that the author of the ' Theory of Human Progression ' has arrived at results identical with those published in 1830 by M. Comte, yet without any knowledge of their prior discovery, not even the author will be more gratified than ourselves. But, after the many coincidences remarked upon, we think our readers will require irrefragable proof of so remarkable a fact, before they will feel disposed to alter the verdict we have pronounced. If, on the other hand, our author acknowledges his obligations to M. Comte, we then ask, where is the honesty of carefully withholding the acknowledgment from his readers ; especially after so many obligations of a far inferior, and, indeed, comparatively speaking, trivial nature, have been avowed in the course of his work?

Having disposed of the first branch of inquiry, as originally proposed, we now proceed to the second ; namely, the failure of the ' Theory of Human Progression,' at that point precisely where the author departs from the scheme of M. Comte.

In the two tables of the respective authors, as we have given them some pages back, there is a marked difference when we come to the last division. M. Comte terms this, *Physique Sociale*, or Social Physics ; but our author terms this, Man-science, or Mind-science. The former would have this division of science regarded as a branch of natural science, to be pursued on the wide induction of all that pertains to social phenomena, and on the basis of fact, or what *is* ; while the latter divides it into two distinct, and, as it seems to us, independent sciences— the first inductive in its method, and answering to Political

Economy; the second deductive, and designated Politics Proper. M. Comte classes Social Physics along with Physiology under the general head of the 'Science of Organized Bodies ;' while our author classes Vegetable and Animal Physiology only under this generic head, making a new and distinct division of Man-science, or Anthropology. This difference is one of some importance, as will appear in the course of our present inquiry.

On turning to our author's definition of the sphere of politics, we find him sufficiently specific, repeating and re-enforcing his views in several parts of his volume. The following passages will afford a complete view of the author's meaning :—

'We have, then, to ask, "What is the *matter* of political science ?" Of what does it treat? What are its substantives? what is the general character of the truths it professes to develop ? 1. It treats exclusively of *men*. 2. It treats exclusively of the *relations* between man and man. 3. It treats exclusively of the relations of men *in equity*. Equity, or justice, is the *object-noun* of the science of politics, as number is the object-noun of arithmetic ; quantity, of algebra ; space, of geometry ; or *value*, of political economy. *Politics, then, is the science of* EQUITY, *and treats of the relations of* MEN *in equity*. The fundamental fact from which its propositions derive a *practical* importance is the following :— "Men are capable of acting equitably or unequitably towards each other." To obliterate all unequitable (or unjust) action of one man towards another, or of one body of men towards another body of men, is therefore the *practical* ultimatum of the science of politics. Politics, then, professes to develop the *laws* by which human actions ought to be regulated, in so far as men *interfere* with each other.'—Pp. 14, 15.

' An evident distinction presents itself, which enables us to *classify* human action. We may ask, "What means will lead to a certain end?" and "What is the end that *ought* to be produced?" We have here *two* social sciences, in each of which there is the same stable truth that prevails in all the other sciences, if man can only discover it and reduce it to scientific ordination. . . . . . On the above distinction is grounded the division of social science into *non-moral* and *moral*—the one treating exclusively on the relation of means to an end, and the other exclusively on the end that *ought* to be the object of pursuit. In these new sciences *human* action is the element with which we have to reason ; and the *conditions of men* are the phenomena that result directly from that action. We have therefore—

'First. An inductive science of human action, which presents itself in the following form :—

'1. Given the actual *actions* of men in their social capacity. (This is the minor proposition of the syllogism.)

'2. Given the actual *conditions* of men. (This is the consequent or conclusion of the syllogism, the condition of men being the *effects* of their actions.)

'And the problem is to find "the general expression of the relation between the actions of men and their social condition." (When this general expression is found, it supplies the major proposition of the syllogism.)

'Second. A deductive science of human action. . . . . . The principles of this equity are abstract and universal convictions of the reason, and the problem presents itself in the following manner :—

'1. Given the general axioms of equity. (This is the major proposition.) And,

'2. Given the physical or non-moral characteristics of an action. (This is the minor proposition of the syllogism.)

'To find the moral character of that action, namely, whether it be a *duty* or a *crime*. (This is the conclusion of the syllogism.)

'The first of these sciences is political economy, which is purely inductive, and treats of the physical effects of human action so far as those effects are to be discovered in the condition of societies. The second is politics, the science of equity, which is purely abstract, and treats of the universal principles that ought to regulate human actions, so far as men can affect each other by their actions.'—Pp. 194—198.

From this exposition, it seems evident that political science is not ordinated logically *after* political economy, but on an independent basis of its own. Elsewhere the author treats of political economy as the science 'which furnishes the correct *mode* of action to politics.' This, of course, we can understand; it is nothing more than the utilitarian system, long since advocated by some of the first thinkers of our own country. But in the passages we have already cited, a wide distinction is drawn between the sciences of political economy, or social utility, and politics proper. The former is termed inductive, the latter deductive. The former is not supposed to have any logical connexion with the latter; since a case is supposed in which the results of the two processes may agree, while the processes are perfectly distinct. For example : 'By treating a question of interference by the rules of equity, we arrive at once at a conclusion; whereas, when it is treated by the rules of utility, it may require many years, many observations, and many disputations as to facts, before a conclusion can be drawn.' He then instances the case of the slave-trade, which he affirms *equity* might have settled in a few minutes, while *economy* required many years, and has not ' even now' settled it in the minds of all. Similar remarks are made, in continuation of the subject, to the effect that politics proper are perfectly distinct from political economy, and may even pronounce on any given case of political casuistry before political economy has commenced her career of utilitarian inquiry respecting it. Now what, we ask, does this amount to but an admission that politics proper, instead of receiving its *mode* of action from political economy, is altogether independent of its conclusions, and may even precede them? Our author has admitted as much as this in

saying: 'Where we can have a judgment in equity, no economical considerations whatever (even if it were *not* true that the
just coincides with the beneficial) can ever relieve man from the
imperative obligation.'—P. 238.

It appears to us very strange that the author should affirm
that political economy *necessarily* precedes politics after such
an admission as this. Can the same admission be made respecting any other two of the logically ordinated sciences? Can any
of the physical sciences give judgment without the aid of those
that are logically antecedent? Can animal physiology arrive at
just conclusions without the aid of vegetable physiology? Can
astronomy reveal the laws of the planetary system without
assistance from dynamics? Can geometry determine the relations of space apart from the conclusions of algebra, or algebra
determine the relations of quantity apart from the conclusions
of arithmetic?

In determining the position of politics as a science, he mentions three considerations, as leading to the required determination :—

'1. Man may act on the external world of matter, and we may
consider the laws of such actions without taking into consideration the
reflex effect on man.

'2. We may take into consideration the reflex effects on man, and in
them we find the laws of political economy.

'3. Man may act on man *directly* by interference. The laws which
prohibit, limit, or regulate those actions of interference constitute the
science of politics.

'We here proceed according to a regular progression, beginning at
the most simple forms of human action, and passing to those which are
more and more complex.'—P. 253.

We cannot admit the 'regular progression' in this series, in
reference to a system of logical and scientific ordination. We
can see a progression in the first two steps, since they both relate
to action on the external world, and the second is more complex
than the first. But the third is not related to the first two, of
necessity, in any way. It does not relate to the external world;
but to man. Then, as to the logical ordination, there is none
between the first two and the third of this series. Man might
be placed in another world differently constituted from the
present, and yet there might be an action of man on man directly
by interference, and laws prohibiting, limiting, or regulating
those acts of interference.

It seems evident to us that our author has arrived at a *fault*
in this part of his argument, which, unlike the fault in geological
phenomena, cannot be rectified, so long as he pursues his present

method of inquiry. He must seek the primordia of political science in some other direction.

But we have yet another objection to advance. He describes politics as ' a deductive science of human action, perfectly distinct from any deductions that might be made in the previous · science' (political economy); although there cannot be the slightest doubt that the two sciences, perfectly understood, would lead to the same identical conclusion.'—(P. 197.) We ask, then, if the one science be *perfectly distinct* from the other, yet both lead to the *same conclusion*, whether this is not sufficient to disprove the ordination of the one after the other? What reason can be given why the one science should be classed before the other? Especially why, if the one which our author has placed second, may pronounce judgment *first*, as in the case of the slave-trade, and other cases which he has mentioned? and what becomes in this case of our author's position respecting ' an order of discovery' according to a scheme of classification? Here is a deductive science, perfectly distinct from the conclusions of the inductive science—a science which may give its decisions before that inductive science ; that is, be discovered before it historically—and yet it is placed in the classification of the sciences after it! More than this, it is perfectly distinct, and arrives at its conclusions independently of that other science, yet is said to receive its mode of action from it! Can such an ordination as this be pointed out in any of the other sciences classified as logically antecedent and subsequent? It cannot. Where the inductive and deductive methods harmonize in their conclusions, we have a perfected science; but it is *one* science, and not two ; as in astronomy, where a perfect induction (if it could be made) would lead to the same results as by the deductive or dynamical method. But in the present case the deductive method is not only perfectly distinct from the inductive, but placed after it in our author's scheme of classification. It is precisely here that our author has departed from the true method of inquiry and progression, and vitiated the whole argument respecting the probability of a future reign of justice.

But, lastly, by making politics a deductive science, our author has removed it out of the series of the natural sciences altogether. ' The mind of man,' he observes, ' views actions not merely in their physical characteristics, but as being equitable or un-equitable, just or unjust ; and this *equity* gives an *à priori* boundary to action, and lays a moral restriction on man, which will prevent him from injuring his fellow even where he has no inductive evidence whatever. The principles of this equity are abstract and universal convictions of the reason, and the problem presents itself in the following manner :—1st, Given the general axioms of equity. (This is the major proposition.) And, 2nd, Given the physical or non-moral characteristics of an action. (This is the minor proposition of the syllogism.) To find the moral character of that action, namely, whether it be a *duty* or a *crime*. (This is ' the conclusion of the syllogism.')—Pp. 197, 198.

Without inquiring into the correctness of this syllogistic method of exhibiting the problem of politics, we ask if it is not evident that our author's mode of viewing political science places it out of the category of the natural sciences. As Mr. Mill justly observes, ' propositions of science assert a matter of fact ; an existence, a co-existence, a succession, or a resemblance. A proposition of which the predicate is expressed by the words *ought*, or *should be*, is generically different from one which is expressed by *is*, or *will be*.' But our author regards politics as the science of what *ought* to be. The axioms of equity are propositions of which the predicate is expressed by the words ought, or should be, and, whether regarded as abstract and universal convictions of the reason, or not, are essentially different from the propositions of science. Neither do we see any reason for placing political science, thus viewed, after political economy, or the physical sciences generally. If there be abstract and universal convictions of the reason, that is, convictions that do not depend on the discoveries of economical or physical science, but which are necessarily before them, and before all science, why may they not be applied deductively at once, and without any intervention of the minor premiss supplied by the author in the foregoing syllogism ? Thus: 1. Given the axioms of equity—2. Given the actions of men, whether in the matter of interference or not—to find the moral character of those actions, namely, whether they are *duties* or *crimes*. The minor of the author, according to his own showing, and as we have already seen, does not help, but rather delay, the just deduction. Why not, if this deductive method be the true method of political science, arrive at once at a conclusion, especially as by the rules of utility it may require ' many years, many observations, and many disputations as to facts, before a conclusion can be drawn?' Moreover, the physical or non-moral characteristics of an action cannot aid us in determining the moral characteristics of an action beyond what is indicated in the action itself. Indeed, the author has again and again asserted the same thing in his explanations respecting the difference between politics and political economy. The former is the science whose object-noun is *equity* ; the latter is the science whose object-noun is *value*, viewed under a certain aspect. The conclusions of the two sciences, he has told us, may be made to coincide, while the conclusions themselves are essentially and necessarily distinct from and independent of each other. Why, then, we ask, should the conclusions of the one be supposed to be necessary (as they are by being formed into a minor premiss) to the conclusions of the other?

On the whole, then, it appears to us that the author of the 'Theory of Human Progression' has failed to show that political science, as *he* regards it, is logically ordinated after political economy, and the physiological sciences. Nor is any cause shown, if *this* be the science of politics, why it should not have been perfected before any of the physiological or physical sciences were commenced; why it should not have been perfected as soon as men began to act by interference and to reason deductively. Before Bacon, before Euclid, such a science as this, if a science at all, might have been pursued to its conclusions and applied to practice. In a word, by making moral axioms of the reason the major of this science, the author has lifted it out of the sphere of natural science, and rendered it absolutely impossible to place it anywhere in the logically ordinated series of the natural sciences.

We have no room to enlarge on this subject, although many thoughts are suggested respecting the difference between the method of M. Comte and our author in this department of science. We hope to have an opportunity of expressing our views fully at some future period. Our present object is realized, if we have made good the position we assumed in the commencement of this article. As we have already said, there are many things in the volume before us worthy of all praise. Let the author, in future, adopt Southey's rule in reference to all matters of literary obligation; and his reviewers, freed from the necessity of tracing his opinions to their origin, will be enabled to dwell more fully upon those excellences which, whilst they are his own, will stand out all the more conspicuously on account of the care taken duly to acknowledge all that belongs to his predecessors.

---

ART. II.—*The Poetical Works of Joanna Baillie.*   8vo.   London: Longman and Co.

' POETICAL WORKS ' pour in upon us after ' poetical works ;' and the worst is, for captious critics at least, that the majority of them are, as Jacob Tonson would have said, from ' approved hands,' ' able pens,' ' persons of honour,' poets and poetesses whose names are household words, whose writings are already classical, and on whom there exist criticisms nearly as classical as the poems! But how long must we wait ere we see such a title as 'the *work*' of this or that distinguished author, his 'Iliad,' or his 'Paradise Lost?' Alas! we are in this age doomed to live upon fragments, although, sometimes, as a variety, these are presented to us in 'twelve' or two 'baskets,' or even in one. At least twenty real poets have written, or are writing still, during what has passed of the nineteenth century; and although all of them have left, or are leaving, 'poetical works,' yet where is the 'work' of any which fulfils the idea of the name? It is as if some such catastrophe as has shattered one stately planet of our system into Pallas, Vesta, and the rest, had visited the mind of this century, and split it up into disunited, although beautiful and centre-seeking, portions!

First, for the fact of this fragmentary tendency, and then for what seem to be the reasons which explain it. We may enumerate the following names as those of real poets, dead or alive, included in the first half of the nineteenth century in Britain:— Bloomfield, Wordsworth, Coleridge, Southey, Campbell, Moore, Byron, Shelley, Keats, Professor Wilson, Hogg, Croly, Maturin, Hunt, Scott, James Montgomery, Pollok, Tennyson, Aird, Mrs. Browning, Mrs. Hemans, Joanna Baillie, and the author of 'Festus.' We leave this list to be curtailed, or to be increased, at the pleasure of the reader. But, we ask, which of those twenty-three has produced a work uniquely and incontestably, or even, save in one or two instances, professedly GREAT? Most of those enumerated have displayed great powers; some of them have proved themselves fit to begin greatest works; but none of them, whether he has begun, or only thought of beginning, has been able to finish. Bloomfield, the tame, emasculate Burns of England, has written certain pleasing and genuine poems smelling of the soil, but the 'Farmer's Boy' remained what the Scotch poet would have called a 'haflin callant,' and never became a full-grown and brawny man. Wordsworth was equal to the epic of the age, but has only constructed the great porch leading up to the edifice, and one or two beautiful cottages lying around. Coleridge could have written a poem—whether didactic, or epic, or dramatic—equal in fire and force to the 'Iliad,' or the 'Hamlet,' or the 'De Rerum Natura,' and superior to any of the three in artistic finish and metaphysical truth and religious feeling—a work ranking immediately beside the 'Paradise Lost;' but he has, instead, shed on us a shower of plumes, as from the wing of a falling angel—beautiful, ethereal, scattered, and tantalizing. Southey's poems are large without being great—massive, without being majestic—they have rather the bulk of an unformed chaos than the order and beauty of a finished creation. Campbell, in many points 'the Virgil of his time, has, alas! written no Georgics; his odes and lesser poems are, 'atoms of the rainbow;' his larger, such as ' Gertrude of Wyoming,' may be compared to those segments of ' the showery arch we see in a disordered evening sky; but he has reared no complete ' bow of God.' Moore's ' Lalla Rookh' is an elegant and laborious composition—not a shapely building; it is put together by skilful art, not formed by plastic power. Byron's poems are, for the most part, disjointed but melodious groans, like those of Ariel from the centre of the cloven pine; ' Childe Harold' is his soliloquy when sober—' Don Juan' his soliloquy when half-drunk; the ' Corsair' would have made a splendid episode in an epic—but the epic, where is it? and 'Cain,' his most creative work, though a distinct and new world, is a bright and terrible abortion—a comet, instead of a sun. So, too, are the leading works of poor Shelley, which resemble Southey in size, Byron in power of language, and himself only in spirit and imagination, in beauties and faults. Keats, like Shelley, was arrested by death, as he was piling up enduring and monumental works. Professor Wilson has written ' *Noctes*' innumerable;

astards of his genius — and a great family of legitimate, chubby children of novels, bearing the image, but not reaching the full stature, of their parent's mind. Croly's poetry, like the wing of his own ' seraph kings,' standing beside the sleeping Jacob, has a ' lifted mighty plume,' and his eloquence is always as classical as it is sounding; but it is, probably, as much the public's fault as his that he has never equalled his first poem, ' Paris in 1815,' which now appears a basis without a building. Maturin has left a powerful passage or two, which may be compared to a feat performed by the victim of some strong disease, to imitate which no healthy or sane person would, could, or durst attempt. James Montgomery will live by his smaller poems—his larger are long lyrics—and when was a long lyric any other than tedious? Hunt has sung many a joyous carol, and many a pathetic ditty, but produced no high or lasting poem. Pollok has aimed at a higher object than almost any poet of his day; he has sought, like Milton, to enshrine religion in poetic form, and to attract to it poetic admirers: he did so in good faith, and he expended great talents, and a young life, in the execution; but, unfortunately, he confounded Christianity with one of its narrowest shapes, and hence the book, though eloquent in passages, and dear to a large party, is rather a long and powerful, though unequal and gloomy sermon, than a poem; he has shed the sunshine of his genius upon his own peculiar notions, far more strongly than on general truths; and the spirit of the whole performance may be expressed in the words of Burns, slightly altered—'Thunder-tidings of damnation.' *His* and *our* friend, Thomas Aird, has a much subtler, more original and genial mind than Pollok's, and had he enjoyed a tithe of the same recognition, he might have produced a Christian epic on a far grander scale; as it is, his poems are fragmentary and episodical, although Dante's 'Inferno' contains no pictures more tremendously distinct, yet ideal, than his 'Devil's Dream' upon Mount Acksbeck. Tennyson is a greater Calvinist in one sense than either of the Scotch poets we have named—he owes more to the general faith of others in his genius than to any special or strong works of his own: but let us be dumb, he is now Laureate—the crowned grasshopper of a summer day! Bailey of 'Festus' has a vast deal more power than Tennyson, who is only his delicate, consumptive brother; but 'Festus' seems either different from, or greater than, a *work*. We are reminded of one stage in the history of the nebular hypothesis, when Sir W. Herschel, seeing a central mass in the midst of a round burr of light, was almost driven to the conclusion that it was *something immensely greater than what we call a star*—a kind of monster sun. So with the prodigious birth men call 'Festus.' Our gifted young friend Yendys is more likely than any, if he live and avoid certain tendencies to diffusion and over-subtlety, to write a solid and undying POEM.

It were easy to extend the induction to our lady authors, and to show that Mrs. Hemans, Mrs. Browning, and Joanna Baillie, Mrs. Shelley, &c., have abounded rather in effusions or efforts, or tentative experiments, than in calm, complete, and perennial works.

And now for the reasons of this fragmentary phenomenon. These are various in various authors. In some it arises from the union of unlimited ambition with limited power—their energies, like the limbs of one running in a dream, sink below them; and they either relinquish the attempt as a bad job, or make a bad job of it by persevering. These betray a lack of mental foresight, and have not counted the intellectual cost. Others are stopt by sheer oddity and affectation. 'Is it not,' they say, 'characteristic of genius to be irregular—to veer and falter in its lofty aspirations? Are not all *asterisks stars*? Does not a bust give a more lively idea of the infinite than a finished statue?

'erish the slow, cumulative, gin-horse process which rears up
.ong elaborate works!' Others are injured by carelessness and
caprice. Each new day brings its new scheme, and no scheme
is ever permitted to consolidate or crystallize in its author's mind.
Thus, Coleridge once read to a friend, from his pocket-book, a
' list of eighteen different works which he had resolved to write,
and several of them in quarto, *not one* of which he ever effected.'
To this is often added a desire to pique and stimulate curiosity,
by ceasing ere they are well begun; and then they confound the
stare of astonishment which succeeds the abrupt close with
admiration. Others, again, stop short from the effect of those
cold damps, so incident to a high order of intellect, which
often fall, even in the noon of genius, to quench its ardour.
It requires the 'evening and the morning' to make the day—but
the poet has, perhaps, only the evening to dream of immortal
works; the morning has sterner duties. Sometimes he fails
from the want of encouragement held out by a public at once
fastidious and incompetent. And sometimes bad bitter criticism
kills at once the works he has produced and the capacity of
producing more.

While holding strong opinions on this subject, we must not
be understood to depreciate the quality or to deny the abundance
of the poetry of this age. Never since the world began was
there so much of the unconsolidated ether of genuine poetry
—never were so many beautiful verses wandering about our
literature, or so many minds thinking and speaking in a
poetical way. What we want, and the age wants, is to see
new Neptunes of song, separate poetic worlds, works of profound purpose, earnest tone, and high art, as well as of original
genius.

To pass to the subject of this review, it is with a certain awe
that we name the venerable Joanna Baillie. She belongs rather
indeed to the past than to the present—to history, not to us.
Living we almost think of her as dead, or as a spiritual presence
among us but not of us. Simple greatness is the leading feature
of Miss Baillie's character and of her intellect. She has no airs
—no artifices. Visit her, you find a plain, sensible woman, living
with her plain, sensible sisters, any one of whom you would
suspect as soon as her of the sin of authorship. Take up her
works, and you find yourself in conversation with a rich, full,
masculine, and yet womanly mind, conveying, through the
characters in her dramas, the clear, constant stream of her own
sentiments and feelings. It was the glory of Shakspere that
he never *was* himself—it is that of Joanna Baillie that, while
never an egotist, she never ceases to be herself—'a deep, majestical,
and high-souled woman.' She is no female Shakspere. Indeed,

a female Shakspere is an incongruous, and almost a ludicrous thought. The thorough identification with his characters, however atrocious or contemptible, which is Shakspere's peculiarity, is precisely that which woman cannot or dare not exemplify.

A far more striking resemblance exists between Miss Baillie and Sir Walter Scott. Health and solidity of mind, lyrical fire and enthusiasm, a love of legendary lore, and attachment to the manners and customs, to the hills and woods, of 'Auld Caledonia' —a tone of uniform respect for morality and religion—a clear, masculine, and unaffected eloquence, are qualities common to both. And although Miss Baillie, being less national in her subjects, and having chosen a less popular vehicle, has never obtained the same place or power in the literature of her country, her genius, on the whole, can hardly be pronounced much inferior. She stands up a sister of the Mighty Minstrel, holding his hand, exhibiting a milder form of the same poetic and patriotic ardour, along with greater subtlety of thought, and more delicate discrimination of character, than ever belonged to him.

Ere glancing at some of Miss Baillie's works—the complete copy of which now lies before us—we have some remarks to offer on the famous criticisms of Lord Jeffrey upon her ' Plays on the Passions.' These are certainly among the ablest and subtlest products of his pen. Some secret *animus*, it is said, had stung him into an unusual display of powerful and vindictive acumen. Some of his objections are, undoubtedly, as strong as they are well put. He has attacked the plan of her plays, as cramping her motions ; accused them of combining the faults of the French and of the English schools—the poverty of incident and uniformity of the one, with the irregularity and homeliness of the other ; cast wholesale contempt upon her comedies ; charged her plots with violent and systematic improbability, and her language with being a bad imitation of the Elizabethan dramatists ; called her versification heavy, lifeless, and cumbrous ; and seems to think that her genius is rather lyrical than dramatic.

Now her plan is, unquestionably, a yoke and trammel to her genius ; but, first, this should exalt our idea of her powers, which have gained, to say the least, a partial triumph over it ; and, secondly, her object in imposing on herself such trammels was commendable. She wished to lift up a strong protest, not only against the ' artificial stateliness and wearisome pomp ' of diction which prevailed in the tragedy of the time when her plays first appeared, but against its sacrifice of character and real passion ; to mere bustle, and incident, and stage effect. If she becomes too metaphysical and minute in her descriptive analysis of the passions, it is the opposite of a much worse extreme.

Lord Jeffrey charges her with monotony in her characters—

with having little sympathy with any but 'the cheerful, the sensible, and the good'—a charge which, to a lady, is a high compliment—a charge which is not, however, entirely true; since some of her most powerful pictures are of persons actuated by ambition, or burning with hatred, or foaming in frenzy. The creator of De Montfort, Basil, and Orra, goes, perhaps, as far as a lady gracefully can in sympathy with the fiercer and darker passions of human nature.

The critic, too, has subjected himself to the charge of inconsistency and self-contradiction. In his first paper he praises Miss Baillie for 'taking for her model the middle style of Shakspere;' and yet he afterwards speaks of the 'constrained and unnatural air produced by her affectation of antiquated phraseology.' He forgets, too, one reason she has for adopting many of the phrases of the old dramatists. Her *subjects* are generally as romantic and far-withdrawn as her language. When writing on 'an Election,' or a 'Country Inn,' her language is modern; but why should she not light up a 'Beacon' of the time of the crusades at Shakspere's torch, or describe the downfall of Constantinople in language reminding you of 'the large utterance of those early gods' of the stage? If, occasionally, too colloquial, it arises from the reaction of disgust at the buckram and conventional style which was the rage at the time when she 'arose,' the Deborah of the drama.

That her comedies are not equal to her tragedies is conceded; and to readers fresh from the incessant wit of Sheridan, or the bustling farce and riotous humour of Goldsmith, they may not seem comedies at all; but if they seldom provoke laughter, they never excite contempt—they are full of good sense, discrimination of character, a certain lady-like dignity, and are written in easy, vigorous, unaffected diction.

It is true that her genius was more lyrical than dramatic; but the dramatic quality in her was also strong. It is to be regretted that she had not written more 'lyrical dramas' like the 'Beacon,' and that she had not sprinkled lyrics with a more liberal hand through the rest of her plays.

But while Lord Jeffrey is right in desiderating in Miss Baillie's plays a greater freedom and play of passion, in thinking them stiffened by system, and paralyzed in part by the laborious anatomy she pursues; and in ridiculing the notion of a 'tragedy and a comedy on every passion' (somewhat like a poet who should write on 'the pains of hope, as well as its pleasures,' or on the pleasures of remorse instead of the pains); he has not dwelt with sufficient fidelity and fondness on her counter-balancing merits, which he acknowledges, indeed, but acknowledges with a grudge—her profound subtlety—her knowledge of human nature, alike in its fluctuating forms and its eternal essence—her touches of natural description, so sudden and so striking—the wild, legendary grandeur which surrounds her at times—the candour, charity, and womanliness of her nature—her freedom from every taint of the grossness of the early dramatists—and the strong, yet delicate imagery in which she enshrines her thoughts; like a star set in the trembling crystal of a summer-evening lake.

We propose to speak of some of Miss Baillie's plays individually, and then of her miscellaneous works. Her first play is 'Basil'—intended to illustrate the passion of love. The story is very simple. A noble, brave, and generous-hearted general, on his march to battle, falls into the toils of the fair daughter of a king who has an interest that he should delay his march. In a fatal hour, he consents to remain for a day, and does so, in opposition to the urgent counsels of a friend. He sees thus more of his inamorata, who dallies with his passion; but his soldiers are excited to a mutiny, which is with difficulty repressed; and toward evening the tidings arrive that a battle has been fought in Basil's absence, and his laurels tarnished. He resolves on suicide, flees, and is found bleeding to death in a cave. There his friend, his soldiers, and, ultimately, his beloved, find him, and, amid the wailings of their varied sorrow, he expires.

It will be seen, from this short analysis, that the play is rather an illustration of the power of infatuation than of the passion of love. It is a picture of the madness of love, rather than of the 'exalted portion of the pain.' Basil's passion is rather a 'nympholepsy' than a natural, probable, and powerful feeling. His taking refuge in suicide for such a slight cause as the gaining of a battle in his absence, is a weak baseness, unworthy of his character. Surely the desertion of his soldiers was a heavier blow than the success of his rival general. And yet, while he meets and quells the one with manly promptitude and triumphant success, he falls without a struggle before the other. Rossinberg is a mere *fidus* Achates. Victoria is a flirt of feeling; and although she talks of taking the veil after Basil's death, we leave her with the impression that in a year she will be singing, 'No, I won't be a nun—no, I shan't be a nun.' The rest of the characters are of no mark, with the exception of Mirando, the orphan, a sweet, sly, affectionate boy, of whom, however, more might have been made.

The power and beauty of 'Basil' lie not in the conception or execution of the whole, but in the excellence of particular scenes, and the beauty of individual sentences. The scene where Basil suppresses the mutiny of his soldiers is admirable. Miss Baillie has had, probably, in her eye, the story of Cromwell blowing out insurrection and its ringleader's brains at one and the same moment. So Basil, while he speaks, holds his pistol at a refractory soldier's head. The scene of the masks is managed with much graceful dexterity. The close of the play, around the dying Basil, is very harrowing, and has cost us tears, albeit not used to the melting mood. But the most subtle and successful scene is, we think, that between Victoria and Basil in the grove. Indeed, all love scenes show best by the light of nature. What to unimpassioned readers appears vulgar, ludicrous, or absurd, when described as passing in a parlour or drawing-room, assumes a very different aspect when shown amid the soft hush and spiritual beauties of an evening river-side, and in the light of an autumn moon. We feel, then, that the beautiful picture has received its proper setting—its ideal frame. Who has forgot, for example, the moonlit love-scene in the ' Merchant of Venice,' or the interview of Waverley and Flora near the waterfall ? Nature is the great asylum of lovers—shelters them from the laugh of the world—adopts them as her children—and seems to fondle them with all her woods, to accompany their low voices with all her waters, and to light their tender and music-measured steps with all her stars.

We quote a part of this fine scene.

> ' *Victoria.* But we must leave this grove—the birds fly low :
> This should forebode a storm, and yet o'er head
> The sky bespread with little downy clouds
> Of purest white, would seem to promise peace.
> How beautiful those pretty snowy clouds !
>
> ' *Basil.*   Of a most dazzling whiteness !
>
> ' *Vic.*   Nay, nay, a veil that tempers heaven's brightness,
> Of softest, purest white.
>
> ' *Bas.*   As though an angel, in his upward flight,
> Had left his mantle floating in mid-air.
>
> ' *Vic.*   But thou regard'st not !
>
> ' *Bas.*   Ah ! what should I regard, where should I gaze ?
> For in that far-shot glance, so keenly watched,
> That sweetly rising smile of admiration,
> Far better do I learn how fair heaven is,
> Than if I gazed upon the blue serene.'

Robert Burns visited the Caldron Linn, in company with Charlotte Hamilton, the ' fairest maid on Devon's banks.' She and the other ladies of the party wondered that he did not admire the scenery more. The fact was, he was too much occupied in admiring *them*. So, even after what we have said, we suspect that other lovers, besides Burns and Basil, love the reflection of nature in their mistress's eye rather than its direct vision.  Both, however, are, and are often felt to be, best.

Victoria's description of the circumstances in which she found the orphan Mirando is very beautiful and very touching.

> ' Perched in his nurse's arms, a rustic quean,
>   Ill suited to the lovely charge she bore ;
>   How stedfastly he fixed his looks upon me,
>   His dark eyes shining through forgotten tears—
>   Then stretched his little arms, and called me mother !
>   What could I do ?  I took the bantling home ;
>   I could not tell the imp he had no mother.'

' Shaksperian ' is an epithet we are sparing of, but we feel tempted to apply it to the above little picture.

Not so well do we like the incident of old maimed Geoffrey holding back his general from his purpose of ruin by his one remaining hand, while Basil turns round, looks on him with softness, and says,

> ' Two would not hold so well, old honoured veteran.'

Yet in a moment his fury returns, and he breaks violently from him, leaving the old man deploring that he has not another hand to stop him.  Surely this is grotesque to the brink of absolute farce.  It reminds us of a picture we have seen of a desperate lover springing over a precipice with the maiden—too late repentant—holding him back in vain by his coat-tails.

Altogether ' Basil' is full of interest, and abounds in lively and eloquent passages, if it be not in the highest or most powerful tragic vein.

' De Montfort' takes a darker and more daring flight.  In it, the poet seeks to sow the flowers of beauty upon the murk and haggard rocks of hatred.  Here, again, however, both the choice of the subject and the management of it are liable to certain objections.  In the first place, De Montfort's hatred, like Basil's love, is hardly a natural feeling.  It is exaggerated to frenzy.  It is neither demoniac nor human.  It is neither the warm and generous resentment of a noble nature, nor the slow, quiet, calm, deadly animosity of an Iago.  It unites fiendish intensity to maniac ferocity.  It is hatred without a cause.  No such feeling ever existed, or ever could, in such a breast as De Montfort's is represented to be.  And, secondly, Miss Baillie does not relieve the pressure of the improbability by tracing the gradual progress of the fell passion, by showing it slowly rising, often resisted, yet growing with Montfort's growth, and strengthening with his strength, till at last it towers beside him — of equal stature with himself, a dark, inseparable companion.  Instead of this, when De Montfort first appears on the stage his feeling to Rezenvelt is already fully formed.   Thirdly, we question much if even a more moderate degree of the horrid passion, unrelieved by a mixture of softer feelings, were susceptible of graceful or effective treatment.   Othello's real feeling to Cassio is not jealousy (jealousy is a transition state, and implies the existence of doubt), it is hatred ; but then there is blended with it a strong lingering affection for Desdemona ; and in the wavering balance, and fierce and swift interchange of those two passions, lies much of the power of the play.   But mere unmingled hatred cannot awaken much sympathy ; or though it do suck us in, by the eloquence with which it is accompanied, its suction is felt to be that of a Mahlstrom—crushing while it enthrals. And to this original difficulty, the author of ' De Montfort' has added another.   She has caricatured hatred, added ' blackness' to ' darkness,' made ' hell a murkier gloom'—and it is a proof of her powerful genius, that she has not utterly sickened and disgusted, but simply oppressed and overwhelmed us in the experiment.

The characters in ' De Montfort' are not strikingly original, nor is the poetry equal to that of ' Basil.'   The second duel between De Monfort and Rezenvelt is a clumsy expedient to hasten the catastrophe—clumsy, because an exact duplicate of the first.   Could he not have been irritated into murder in some other way than by being disarmed in single fight, a second time, by his deadly foe ?   The murder, its discovery, and the consequent remorse, are forcibly described—but without any remarkable felicity of thought or imagery.   The scenes succeeding De Montfort's death are—according to the author herself—superfluous.   They approach the face of the horror too closely, and keep the curtain suspended too long.   The imagery is less new or happy than in the rest of Miss Baillie's works.   We cannot admire the following :—

> ' O heavenly friendship,
> Thou dost exalt the sluggish souls of men,
> By thee conjoined, to great and glorious deeds ;
> As two dark-clouds, when mixed in middle air,
> With vivid lightnings flash, and roar sublime.'

This would better describe the collision of enemies than the conjunction of friends.   Milton employs precisely the same image to describe the impending strife of Death and the Devil ! Better far is the following :—

> ' Half-uttered praise is to the curious mind,
> As to the eye half-veiled beauty is,
> More precious than the whole.'

The power of ' De Montfort,' in short, lies in the strong, dark stream of the hero's passion—a stream from which tender and sensitive minds must ever shrink as from an arm of Acheron, nourishing but a few dusky flowers, receiving as it rolls on a tributary of blood, and over which droops the stately form of Jane De Montfort, in the dignity and majestic silence of a true sister's and heroine's woe !

' Orra ' is a play unfortunate in its subject ; the story is that of a young lady driven mad by the apprehension of ghosts, but it has some beautiful passages. We quote one which has been often quoted before :—

> ' Didst thou ne'er see the swallow's veering breast,
> Winging the air beneath some murky cloud,
> In the sunned glimpses of a stormy day,
>    Shiver in silvery brightness ;
> Or boatman's oar, as vivid lightning flash,
> In the faint gleam, that like a spirit's path
> Tracks the still waters of some sullen lake ;
> Or lonely tower, from its brown mass of woods,
> Give to the parting of a wintry sun
> One hasty glance in mockery of the night,
> Closing in darkness round it ? Gentle friend !
> Chide not her mirth, who was sad yesterday,
> And may be so to-morrow.'

We like to witness such splendid accumulations of imagery, so common in Shakspere and in Jeremy Taylor ; but which our modern criticism would explode as oriental, tasteless, and un-English. One critic lately asked, how we would like to see a ' midnight all stars.' Why, very well—once, like the inhabitants of Neptune, we were accustomed to it! They have a far more splendid firmament than ours, and would, doubtless, think ours somewhat cold and barren. So we beg leave to prefer the glory-sparkling and thick-studded pages of Jeremy Taylor and James Thomson—of Bacon and Burke—of Isaac Taylor and Christopher North—of Schiller and Jean Paul—to those of Tillotson and Atterbury, of Addison and Pope, of Lord Brougham, Sir John Herschel, and the ' Quarterly Review.'

The catastrophe of Orra is a powerful and harrowing picture of madness, and ranks Miss Baillie with those who have best depicted that sad calamity — with Crabbe, Richardson, Scott, and Shakspere themselves. But the last words of Orra are too horrible to be affecting, or to be quotable ; whereas the words of Lear, even at their wildest, never trespass the bounds of good taste ; they are worthy of one ' every inch a king,' and who is royal in his very rags and ravings.

We pass to speak, lastly, of the ' Beacon'—and with peculiar pleasure. It is certainly one of the most delicious dramatic *morceaux* in the language. Even Lord Jeffrey's fastidious, half-affected frown and sharp sneer relax over the beautiful flame of the ' Beacon,' and he looks and talks like a despot in love! We wish we had room to quote his analysis of the story—in our notion, the happiest of all his many happy outlines of the plots of poems, novels, and plays (in drawing up which he displayed, in general, consummate tact and liveliness); and free from the flippancy, and sad propensity to sneer, which disfigured many of them. But we cannot admit that the story has no merit, nor any 'pretensions to probability.' Surely it is at least as probable as that of the ' Lady of the Lake,' or of ' Gertrude of Wyoming,' or of any romantic love-story since the world began. What, indeed, can be more beautifully or poetically conceived than the figure of Aurora, whose lover is gone to the Holy Land, and reported to be slain; but who, hoping against hope, lights up, night after night, a beacon-flame, on the eastern cape of the island, to guide the vessel which is to restore him to her arms? Eve among her flowers, 'herself a fairer flower,' is not more fair than Aurora beside her fires, herself a purer and more celestial flame! The whole conception is one of pure and perfect genius—the time that of the crusades—the scene, an island in the Mediterranean; the beacon-light burning over the hallowed waves; and the high-born maiden, *Aurora* by name, bending over her love-lighted watch-fire, and looking eastward, with an eye soft with tremulous love and bright with high expectation. Surely she is, henceforth and for ever, the model-image of the passion of the play, which is Hope. Our readers will remember the issue. The ' Beacon' has not been lit in vain. Her lover, Ermingard, returns in disguise, is recognised and welcomed by Aurora, and, after overcoming some very ingeniously-constructed obstacles to their union, the play leaves them on the brink of having their mutual ' Hope ' realized.

We hardly know which of the scenes, or songs, or sentences in this lovely little drama we should quote, for all are so beautiful, and the most so well known. We take the following fine string of pleasant images, which might have been prefaced by the ' So have I seen,' of Jeremy Taylor. They refer to the beacon—

' *Viola.*                    Fie on such images!
Thou shouldst have likened it to things more seemly;
Thou mightst have said, the peasants' evening fire
That from his upland cot through winter gloom,
What time his wife their evening meal prepares,
Blinks on the traveller's eye, and cheers his heart;
Or signal torch, that from my lady's bower

Tells wandering knights their revels are begun;
Or blazing brand, that from the vintage house,
On long October nights, through the still air,
Looks rousingly.'

But the songs are the finest things in this drama. **They re-**
semble those little flourishes of flame we often see on the crest
of the evening fire—or they are the tresses of Hope's golden
hair.   Altogether the ' Beacon' shines Miss Baillie's least, but
loveliest play—and long shall warm-hearted admirers watch,
and dance and sing for gladness around, its unwaning light.
And, although she meant it not, yet to us it seems an unconscious
and mythic parable of the ' Old Hope' of the Church, lighted
up on the bleak rock of a stormy and infidel age—burning
towards the East, casting a beautiful, although dim, light upon
the troubled waters around it—fed by the midnight ministrations
of a few faithful hearts—and which is not always to burn in
vain.

' *The Absent will return, the long, long Lost be found.'*

Miss Baillie's miscellaneous works consist of metrical legends,
songs, and poems on general subjects.   In her metrical legends,
she likes best the weird and the terrible element, and wields it
with a potent hand.   Yet the grace and elegance are such that
we feel her to be a witch, not a sorceress; one who loves the
Terrible, but whom the Beautiful loves.   We prefer 'Lord John
of the East' to all the rest put together ; perhaps partly for the
reason that we met with it in childhood, and that it haunted us
like a veritable ghost, and has often since made the opening of an
outer door, in a dark evening, a somewhat tremulous experiment,
as we asked ouselves WHO or WHAT may be standing behind it
—between us and the stars?   ' Malcolm's Heir,' and the ' Elden
Tree,' are too manifestly imitations of 'Lord John'—far and
faint echoes of that tremendous knocking which shook the castle,
and made even fierce ' Donald the Red' aghast.   By the way,
what a subject for a poem in the words, ' Who knocks at the
midnight door?'  Is it the kind and dear friend, long absent? *or,*
the son returned from a far journey at sea? *or,* a messenger to
relate the tidings of a friend's deadly illness? *or,* a ghastly
maniac astray from his keepers? *or*—for imagination, awaked at
midnight, will have midnight fancies—the sheeted dead? *or,*
your own wraith? *or,* The Enemy? *or,* incarnate Death himself—
attired in some such fearful fashion as this—

' In reveller's plight he is bedight ;
   With a vest of cramoisie meet ;
But his mantle behind that streams to the wind
   Is a corse's bloody sheet?'

It is pleas    to        m                                  to
songs, which we hesitate no
Burns—superior to those of  r.            iv.       M
quite equal to those of Sir Wal      o    ar   oi   l  l.
we speak of ' The Gowan gli          sv    d,' '
coming?' 'Tam o' the Lin,'                        o
Scotchman in the world, w   ny  :        ne, k    t
heart—while, perhaps, thou   is                ;       t   v
Joanna Baillie.  We quote                  or a c
scription.

### SONG.

' What voice is this, thou evening gale!
That mingles with thy rising wail;
And as it passes, sadly seems
The faint return of youthful dreams?

' Though now its strain is wild and drear,
Blythe was it once as skylark's cheer—
Sweet as the night-bird's sweetest song,
Dear as the lisp of infant's tongue.

' It was the voice, at whose sweet flow
The heart did beat, and cheek did glow,
And lip did smile, and eye did weep,
And motioned love the measure keep.

' Oft be thy sound, soft gale of even,
Thus to my wistful fancy given;
And as I list the swelling strain,
The dead shall seem to live again.'

We may, by and bye, write a paper on the songs and song-writers of Britain, and hope, in this case, to do more justice to the merit of Miss Baillie's songs—to their dignified simplicity—their purity—their quiet, *pawky* humour—their pastoral tenderness, and all the other truly Doric qualities which distinguish them.

Her poems on general subjects are not, on the whole, equal to her others or to herself.  Some of her devotional strains are bald and tame, although here and there, as in the hymn at page 837, she rises on wings of worship soft as a dove's and strong as an eagle's.  But her muse is seldom a seraph.  Her poem—page 792—on the death of Sir Walter Scott, has many such prosaic lines as the first couplet:—

' Thou pleasant noble bard, of fame far spread,
Now art thou gathered to the mighty dead.'

Nor can we coincide with the criticism, any more than admire the poetry, of the following:—

' A tale like " Waverley " we yet may con,
But shall we read a lay like " Marmion?" '

That Scott's poems are superior to his novels, is a literary heresy of some magnitude. We grant, indeed, that parts of the 'Lay,' and of 'Marmion,' and the whole of the 'Lady of the Lake,' are quite worthy of his genius. But, in the first place, they reveal only a segment of Scott's mind—his minstrel spirit and fire; they contain little trace of his humour, strong insight into human nature, and power of personifying various characters. 2ndly. As artistic compositions, they are even more flimsily and hurriedly put together. 3rdly. By assuming the name of poems, they have subjected themselves to a much severer ordeal—we try them by such standards as the 'Iliad,' and the 'Odyssey;' whereas, where was the novel previous to Scott, except, 'Don Quixote,' which had risen into the region of lofty art at all? Richardson, Fielding, and Defoe, with all their merits, belonged to a far lower class. Goethe had only, as yet, written 'Werter.' So that, while Scott's poems are of a secondary order in their school, his novels are first in theirs. 4thly. Scott's poems are often centos—always imitative; his novels are a creation—a fact as new as the Flood, or the Reformation. And, 5thly, if we combine the consideration of quantity with quality, the poems of Scott sink like a driblet in the ocean. What are three clever metrical romances—the 'Lay of the Last Minstrel,' 'Marmion,' and the 'Lady of the Lake' (we drop at once the 'Lord of the Isles,' and more reluctantly 'Rokeby,' from the list, because confessedly inferior), to 'Waverley,' 'Guy Mannering,' the 'Antiquary,' 'Rob Roy,' 'Old Mortality,' 'Heart of Midlothian,' 'Ivanhoe,' 'Kenilworth,' 'Quentin Durward,' the 'Talisman,' and the 'Fair Maid of Perth,' with all the wondrous masses of description, dialogue, eloquent reflection, clear, easy writing, costume, character, historical information, and romantic interest, which they contain?

---

We were just preparing to bring this criticism to a close, when a newspaper arrived, containing the intelligence of Miss Baillie's death. This event, while it must affect all with sorrow, can take no one by surprise. She has died at the good old age of eighty-nine, full of years, of good deeds, and of well-deserved honours. She 'sleeps well,' although far in death from her beloved native manse of Bothwell. Peace to her ashes! In the circumstances in which her death has unexpectedly placed us, it is a pleasing thought that we were speaking of her in a reverent spirit, and that there is not a word in our critique which, on reflection, we feel inclined to alter. Nay, we are glad to leave it as it is—an estimate of the living, not a panegyric upon the dead. Yet we must now be permitted another sentence in addition to what we had written ere the painful tidings reached us.

Few writers have passed through
and penalties of an authorship tha
not intimately conversant with the particulars' of her life, nor
disposed to forestal the office of her biographer; but we speak in
this, we are certain, the general sentiment of the literary world.
She has had few literary feuds, and none of the disgraceful
notoriety of many of her contemporaries.   She has neither
fought nor puffed on
cumulative progress o
forgot the
dignity of the lady, that she might gain
poet.   Her course has been the quiet,
of a river, hid in woods; and speaking
                                          th
voice, or in the sheen of its waters.
general tone of her poetry, as well as
strains, done ample homage to the le
and religion, and is therein entitled
name of poet by itself usually justifies.

Thus do our great ones pass away!   Another splendid gem
on the circlet of our female authors, had but a few days before
dropped into the dust—Mrs. Shelley.   She, too, was a name to
' start a spirit '—a name interesting through many associations,
and from her own merits much and warmly admired.   But her
creed was cold—her mind was morbid—her works have a
gigantic, but abortive greatness—and we, for our part, had rather
have written one ' Beacon ' than one hundred ' Frankensteins.'
What meaneth, after all, this going out of our stars in clusters?
Is it because the day is near the breaking, and the SUN about
to arise ?

----

ART. III.—*The People's Dictionary of the Bible.*   2 vols.   8vo.
London: Simpkin and Marshall.

WHEN an unexpected parcel reaches us by coach or rail, we are
always impatient to inspect and explore it, to know whether we
have value received for the carriage.   It is a great relief to find
lying under the first packing a letter, stating that an absent
friend has herewith sent, and begs the acceptance of, so and so.
It may be a turkey and a goose, with *et cæteras* in abundance, or
a dozen or two of genuine champagne, or a set of books for
ourselves, with an elegant china tea-service for our wife, and

F F 2

it seems, with the general faith of the Christian
what is intended,
constructed to su                        ,
their defect most o



assault.'
But the people are the
opinions in religion,
especial design and purpose have in view the *more intelligent*
members of society.  If his Dictionary should gain them, then
his work may ultimately become, *perhaps,* what he has denominated it, ' *The People's Dictionary of the Bible.*'  We cannot,
however, augur for it very rapid success with either class, for
the reason just hinted—the reluctance of all classes of religious
persons to change their opinions; and for the additional
that the opinions herein recommended to supersede the
blished ones of the old dictionaries have already passed
trial, and, by the people, have been pronounced wanting.
may put on a new dress, and instead of coming forth in the
of criticism and theological controversy, may affect the impartiality
of a dictionary—develop themselves out of etymologies, manners
and customs, and, above all, history and antiquities; but they
are the same opinions still, striving to dislodge the established
opinions from the minds of the Christian people, and establish
themselves in their place.  Here it is obvious enough that the
author of this Dictionary is at war with the theology of the Christian Church; and it becomes us, as honest critics, just to make our
reader acquainted with this fact, by giving the author an opportunity of explaining his opinions on a few points that are considered important by all parties; and then the public, so far as
our pages extend, may judge for themselves whether this ought
to be, or is ever likely to be, ' The People's Dictionary of the
Bible.'  The excellence of dictionaries for particular authors consists in their being faithful keys to the recondite, obsolete, and
peculiar terms or diction of that author.  If he is an old author,
especially if a very old one, he may have used many terms that
require a dictionary.  This applies with more force to the Bible
than to any other book, because its authorship is various, and
extended through a period comprised in no other book; while
the whole volume, made up thus variously, terminates its authorship at a period which makes it to us a very ancient book.  Hence
much learning, the strictest impartiality, and the most transparent

a few trifles for the children, or anything else, no matter what;
but, at any rate, it is delightful to know all about it at once,
without the slow process of groping amidst dirty hay and straw,
mysterious wrappers, with pack-thread and brown paper, and
innumerable paddings and wedgings and stuffings, before we
can be sure that we have not been hoaxed, or exposed to the
explosion of some infernal machine.   Just so when we take up
a new book; we like to get at the secret at once, and come to
a clear understanding why it was written, and what it is intended
to prove or disprove.   The preface should honestly explain all
this.   Some prefaces do.   Others tell us nothing.   They keep
the secret.   You must unpack the whole, or a considerable
portion, before you can find it out; and then, it often proves
as worthless as if 'stuffed with brick-bats, earth, and stones.'
Other prefaces let out only a small part of the secret.   But 'if
you are a cat you may smell a rat.'   The purchasers of books
are like the receivers of parcels—they must pay the carriage at
least, generally something more, before they can know the
contents.   How much, then, are such parties indebted to us
purveyors of books, for telling them beforehand what every
parcel contains.   If, after fair warning, they pay for one that will
explode as soon as they lift the lid, or turn out mere rubbish,
they must take the consequences; we have done our duty.

Bible readers are very likely to be caught by the title of
'The People's Dictionary of the Bible.'   It is cleverly managed,
but the secret oozes out even in the preface.   Instead of candidly
admitting the excellences of former works of the kind, or, at
least, of some of them, they are all at once unceremoniously
condemned.   They needed correction, no doubt, as to various
matters of history, antiquities, philosophy, &c.; but these are
not, in this author's view, their greatest imperfections.   They
mostly exhibit the theological doctrines of the Bible in a form
that is offensive to the rationalism of a certain class of theologians
in the present age, and of our author in particular.   Behold, then,
his impeachment of them, and recommendation of himself:—

' The Dictionaries of the Bible—are either too much derived as to
their materials from the old, and, in the present state of biblical knowledge, in some measure antiquated dictionary of the celebrated Calmet,
or, *without exception, are too expressly designed and constructed in order
to support established opinions*, to appear to the author of the People's
Dictionary of the Bible altogether suitable to afford to the public,
especially to its more intelligent members, either such information as
they may need and may receive with confidence, or such views of the
nature and evidences of divine revelation as may in the present day be
least open to assault.'

The dictionaries thus described supply explanations in harmony,

what is intended, we presume, by the expression, 'designed and constructed to support established opinions.' Alleging this as their defect most offensive to this author, 'The People's Dictionary of the Bible' is confessedly not 'designed and constructed to support established opinions,' but something
stated, but yet described as 'information the
with confidence, or


and customs, and, above
are the same opinions still, striving to
opinions from the minds of the Christian people, and establish themselves in their place.   Here it is obvious enough that the author of this Dictionary is at war with the theology of the Christian Church ; and it becomes us, as honest critics, just to make our reader acquainted with this fact, by giving the author an opportunity of explaining his opinions on a few points that are considered important by all parties ; and then the public, so far as our pages extend, may judge for themselves whether this ought to be, or is ever likely to be, 'The People's Dictionary of the Bible.'  The excellence of dictionaries for particular authors consists in their being faithful keys to the recondite, obsolete, and peculiar terms or diction of that author.   If he is an old author, especially if a very old one, he may have used many terms that require a dictionary.   This applies with more force to the Bible than to any other book, because its authorship is various, and extended through a period comprised in no other book ; while the whole volume, made up thus variously, terminates its authorship at a period which makes it to us a very ancient book.  Hence much learning, the strictest impartiality, and the most transparent

candour are required in a dictionary-maker for the Bible. He must not be a mere analyzer of words, but an expounder of sentences. His business requires him to bring out of his subject nothing but what is in it, and to omit nothing that is there. The task is obviously a difficult and delicate one, demanding the utmost fairness and love of truth. The sacredness of the Bible as confessedly given by inspiration of God, adds an inexpressible weight of responsibility to these considerations. A Dictionary of the Bible might err, both by redundancy in some articles, and deficiency in others; but we should still not reject the work on this account, if it fairly exhibited the sense of the book itself. But if the lexicographer obviously perverts the teaching of the Bible to the support of his own opinions, if he conceals the meaning of words because it is offensive to himself, and 'throws off' considerable portions as mere verbiage, and resorts to ingenious artifices to convince his readers that the Bible contains no such doctrines as most men deem they find there; and, in fact, that the reader of it must sift out for himself the divine from the human; then it becomes all parties interested in the reputation of the Bible to look closely into this dictionary-process, and before they proceed to 'cast off' anything from the Bible, as the dictionary recommends, first 'cast off' from the dictionary whatever cannot stand the 'touchstone' of the Bible. Since this appears to us both the most reverential and the most rational mode of procedure, we mean to apply it to 'The People's Dictionary of the Bible.'

We are quite aware that this is reversing the process the author recommends.

Since we have found no sufficient reason for bringing the Bible to the standard of this Dictionary, we shall pursue the plan which, we are quite satisfied, is preferable, and which will appear so to our readers, of bringing this Dictionary to the 'touchstone' of the Bible.

We take the article '*Atonement*' because it is written more carefully and copiously than any other in the book, involving the same important doctrine. After a singularly undignified and inappropriate introduction, mixing up Shakspere, Tyndal, and Paul, the author thus proceeds to lay before his readers the scriptural idea of *atonement* :—

'The scriptural idea of atonement must be sought originally in the records of the Old Testament. The Hebrew word, in its radical meaning, signifies *to cover by means of some substance or thing*: for instance, the ark was ordered to be covered with pitch. But, if you cover, you obliterate, destroy, remove. Hence the term, when used of man, intended doing some act by which sin was covered or done away with; when used of God, it signified to blot out, to forgive. Accordingly, atonement is the means by which man obtains of God remission of sins. It is, in other words, God's method of pardoning his guilty creatures, and so receiving them into favour. As such, it is, in its very essence, an expression of mercy, not wrath. It is a divinely-originated expedient, by which man is enabled to prove his repentance, and God is pleased to manifest his grace. The idea of atonement is not to pacify, but to cover, and so to pardon sin. Further: sin it is which alienates man from God. "Your iniquities have separated between you and your God" (Isa. lix. 2). This is the general doctrine of Scripture. The fact of man's alienation necessitates atonement. Hence God appointed means by which sin should be covered and blotted out'—[*Why not tell us what these were? Why this dread of the command to shed the blood, and substitute the innocent for the guilty?*]—'so that, the intervening obstacle and disturbing cause being removed, man might be restored to God's favour, and, being at one with him, might perfect holiness and enjoy peace.

'Such is the general theory of revelation, commenced under the patriarchal dispensation, carried forward and enlarged by Moses, and completed and perfected by the Lord Jesus Christ. God's dealings with man have all been mediatorial; and their great aim has been to destroy sin, and to make the world happy by making it holy. The sin-offering has varied according to the moral and spiritual condition of each separate age. Now it was of the fruit of the ground, now of the firstlings of the flock. At another time it consisted of a portion of most of the objects used in the sustenance of human life.' [*Would any reader believe that from the first, and always, it was life itself—the life of animals, in the type; the life of Christ, in the antitype? Yet this is the account given of sin-offerings in the ' Dictionary of the Bible.'*] 'Finally, it was the death of Christ. But whatever the offering, regard was always had to the condition of the offerer, to consuetudinary observances, to spiritual progress, and spiritual impression and improvement; and equally, the entire system, in all its stages, was an expression of the Divine goodness, an adaptation to human weaknesses and wants; destined and fitted to act on the human soul, and so to reconcile it to the will of God. This is the grand leading idea of atonement in Scripture; and if any facts or words occur which seem to imply a change on the part of Deity, they are only partial and occasional; by no means essential elements of the system, but merely human views and representations of a great and divine instrumentality for the salvation of mankind.'—P. 107.

A more blundering, unscriptural, and sophistical explanation of atonement was assuredly never given in any biblical or theological dictionary. We doubt whether a worse could be raked out of the refuse of theological controversy. The atonement seems to be anything that anybody may be pleased to make of it; and appears, after all, so subtle, that, after slipping away half-a-dozen times from our grasp when we thought we had hold of a reality, it at last vanishes quite away under those cloudy phrases, 'consuetudinary observances'—'spiritual impression and improvement'—'an expression of the Divine goodness'—'an adaptation to human weaknesses and wants, destined and fitted to act on the human soul, and so to reconcile it to the will of God.' 'This,' says our author, 'is the grand leading idea of the atonement in the Scripture;' all other things, he says, are 'by no means essential elements of the system, but merely human views,' &c. But 'the grand leading idea of the atonement,' which, he says, he has given us, we cannot discover in any of his various phrases. The grain of gold does not even sparkle amidst the sand. To us it appears that he is substituting something else for the real atonement; and yet he tells us, 'finally, it was the death of Christ.' And that is all we learn of the matter, save that it had been previously many other things, all of which, it seems, answered the purpose equally well, for the only object of atonement was to produce a moral effect upon man. We ask, however, for the meaning of the death of Christ, and we cannot find it. In its place, we have references to *spiritual impression* and *improvement*, moral progress, repentance, sanctification, and various other things; but no real explanation of the relation in which the death of Christ stands to the salvation of sinful man.

In one passage we find the following words :—' It is a divinely-originated expedient, by which man is enabled to prove his re-pentance, and God is pleased to manifest his grace.' What can the proof of a sinner's repentance have to do with the death of Jesus Christ? Whether a sinner proves his repentance sincere or not—there stands the atonement, quite independent of him and his repentance. Surely repentance is not atonement, nor any of the proofs of repentance, else we make atonement for ourselves. But our author says the death of Christ was an atonement—and yet it was a divinely-originated expedient by which man is enabled to prove his repentance. Nothing can exceed this confusion of ideas; and yet this is the superior enlightenment of the nineteenth century, for which all the old dictionaries are to be sent to the cheesemongers' shops. There is not the slightest attempt made throughout the passage we have quoted to analyze the transactions called atonements. Attention is never once directed to the facts of substitution and punishment, which are prominent in all the accounts of atonement contained in the Bible. The import of the different parts of those transactions, even the Divine explanation, though obvious through both Testaments, this 'Dictionary' *ignores*, and substitutes the most confused, unscriptural, and fallacious explanation it was ever our lot to read. In fact, it is doubtful whether the author, fond as he is of *ideas*, had any idea which could be called a central one, around which this motley group of vague notions might cluster.

But this is not all. What will scripture readers say to the following?—'If any facts or words occur (*in Scripture*) which seem to imply a change on the part of the Deity, they are only partial and occasional, by no means essential elements of the system, but merely human views and representations of a great and divine instrumentality for the salvation of mankind.' Facts and words of Holy Scripture being thus coolly disposed of, we should like to know, on what authority, and then where, the process is to stop. For if one dictionary assumes the right of placing some facts and words to the score of erring humanity, without giving us any reason, another may place other facts and words under the same ban; and so we shall have neither facts nor words left to constitute any Bible. The breach already made in the citadel of Revelation appears a tolerably large one, by which our author turns out and lets in *ad libitum*.

For instance, let our readers just observe what a sweeping expulsion of scriptural facts and words this canon of interpretation authorizes. The facts of shedding the blood, offering it upon the altar, sprinkling it, &c. &c., all of which seem to imply a change, if not in the Deity, yet in his treatment of the sinner who stood to confess his sin, become thus utterly unmeaning. The Divine explanation, however, runs thus:—'The life of the flesh is in the blood, and I have given it to you upon the altar to make an atonement for your souls; *for it is the blood that maketh an atonement for your souls.*' Set that down as merely a human view, and then we should be puzzled to find a divine one: in short, the idea of an atonement would be lost altogether.

Again, in the gospel of Jesus Christ we meet with a distinct and special fact—the institution of the Lord's Supper; in the course of which he is recorded to have said, 'This is my blood which is shed for many for the remission of sins;' or, 'This cup is the new covenant in my blood, which is shed for you.' And, on another occasion, he said, 'Except ye eat the flesh and drink the blood of the Son of Man, ye have no life in you.' Are we to believe that these are only 'human views and representations,' to be 'thrown off' as 'by no means essential elements of the system,' because this 'Dictionary' says so? If this is the 'information' the people are to extract from this 'Dictionary,' and which 'the more intelligent may receive with confidence,' then we advise all parties to adhere to the *dicta* of Jesus Christ, and endeavour to penetrate into his meaning the best way they can, without any dictionary, but certainly without this.

We cannot, however, yet dismiss the single article which exhibits the author's notions of the atonement. There is in it still more illustration of the statement gleaned from the Preface, that this dictionary was designed to shake established opinions in the Church of Christ, and, if possible, establish new ones upon the most important doctrines of revelation. A few lines after the passage upon which we have commented, we find the following, which serves still further to obscure and nullify the scriptural idea of atonement :—

'We have intimated that the atonements of Scripture were divine. This requires some explanation. There is no record showing that offerings of any kind originated with God in primitive times. (*Compare this with what was said before about "a divinely-originated expedient," &c.*) Primarily, offerings had their origin on the part of man. They are the utterance of a human thought. (*Atonements, then, must be merely a human invention.*) They grew up in an oriental soil. In the East a sovereign is never approached without an offering. Hence, usage, as well as gratitude and piety, introduced offerings into religion. (*Cain and Abel's, for instance!*) But what arose thus naturally, bore the character of an appropriate expression of man's dependence on, and homage towards, the Almighty. Accordingly, that which existed as a practice, was adopted into Mosaism, and expanded and applied to the peculiar circumstances of the Hebrew people. . . . . Christianity, as developed out of Judaism, naturally partook of its system of atonement. Yet does it deserve especial notice, that sacrificial ideas are rarely found in the teachings of Christ. The existence of sin he does indeed distinctly recognise, and most feelingly deplore. The necessity of reconciliation to God, so that we may become one with the Father and the Son, he incessantly urges. But the means which he sets forth are moral and spiritual. Love is the great power which Jesus recommends as the instrument by which man may be brought to God. The central idea of his religion is the idea of the universal Father. The conception of a sovereign which Judaism enshrined, Jesus expanded into the noble and more attractive, and more refining conception of an infinitely wise and immeasurably good Parent. With such an idea, the pains and penalties of a system of satisfaction are wholly incompatible. The essence of the Saviour's doctrine is concentrated in the parable of the Prodigal Son, which thus becomes a picture of the Divine dealings with man. Here, then, we have love as the central doctrine of the gospel, as that *beau idéal* to which we should raise our conceptions, and by whose light we should try the spirits, discriminating the divine from the human in the scriptural record, in order that so we may find "the pearl of great price," become acquainted with the mind of God, and enjoy peace and rest in the broad and sure foundations of everlasting truth.

'We utter, then, no arbitrary assumption, but a truth which comes from the very centre of Christ's soul, when we declare, that, as the goodness of the Father is at the bottom of "the glad-tidings of great joy," proclaimed by the gospel; so, whatever is taught incompatible with this, whether by man or angel, by Paul or by Apollos, can have but a temporary import, must, in the lapse of time, be thrown off as an outer covering, and may, nay, will be laid aside by the mind as soon as it is pervaded and enlarged by the grand and ennobling conception of the divine paternity. Thus, the reader will see, does Christianity, as taught of Christ, throw out from its own essence an idea which, expanding into a system of spiritual truth, is fitted to purify and elevate the Church as in the nineteenth, so also in the first, century. Here, then, does Jesus present us with a standard by which to measure Christian doctrine, and a touchstone by which to discriminate between what is his and what is man's—what is from above and what is from below.

'While, however, it is declared that sacrificial language is found in the writings of the apostles, it does not follow that this language is necessarily the expression of sacrificial ideas. Terms last in a tongue long after the
away. Even
setting : error
ideas. And before
Paul, we must be
phraseology derived
put to an end.

'But one thing is
magnified the grace
human redemption. Paul taught, as did John—only in somewhat different terms—that, as "God is love," so "in this was manifested

grand essentials of the gospel.'—P. 108.

A complete exposure of the various misrepresentations, falsifications, and perversions of this passage, would occupy more space than we are disposed to give up to it. But a few of the salient points may be selected, and these will throw light upon the general speculations of the author, and the object of his dictionary.

Let us take the two following sentences—'It deserves especial notice, that sacrificial ideas are rarely found in the teachings of Christ'—and, 'While, however, it is declared that sacrificial language is found in the writings of the apostles, it does not follow that this language is necessarily the expression of sacrificial ideas.' It is admitted in the first sentence, that sacrificial *ideas* are found, though rarely, in the teachings of Christ; the apostles' sacrificial language, however, may be deprived of its sacrificial *ideas*. But if Christ taught sacrificial ideas, no matter how rarely, and therein taught truth, why should not Paul's language convey the same ideas? It could be no offence in Paul to teach the sacrificial ideas as well as his Master. Yet

Paul's words are to be deprived of their proper ideas to please
the author of this dictionary, without a single reason assigned
for it. Why, then, not extend this exsiccating process to the
words of Christ? Either allow sacrificial ideas to the words of
the servant as well as to those of the Master, or disallow them
to both. It would be more consistent to say, that, though it
cannot be denied that both Paul and Christ have used sacrificial
terms, yet neither of them intended to convey sacrificial ideas.
Herein the writer is signally inconsistent, conceding to the language of one what he denies to that of the other, yet covertly
intending the denial to extend *in effect* to both. It would have
appeared a somewhat startling assertion, to attribute to Jesus
Christ the use of language which conveyed no idea, or a false
one. The insinuation might be applied to Paul without shocking
so directly the feelings of a believer in the atonement, and it might
have the effect of inducing him to doubt whether the language
of Christ could have any more meaning than that of Paul. It
was similar to the Levitical language, represented only the customs of 'Mosaism,' which having passed away, have left nothing
real in Christianity to answer to them. Although these assertions would require strong proof to make us credit them, yet
they would have comported better with the honest statement that
the language both of Paul and Christ, though sacrificial, is void
of sacrificial ideas, than it now does with the divided and inconsistent statement we have noted. Moreover, the saving term,
'*rarely*,' as applied to the sacrificial ideas taught by Jesus Christ,
is neither true, nor of the slightest value; for if such ideas are
taught, whether rarely or frequently, the admission subverts the
whole speculation. It is not, however, true that such ideas are
rare in the teachings of Christ. He presents them in their
clearest forms, and with a vividness and prominence not equalled
by Paul or any of his apostles. It would require weightier
evidence than this dictionary supplies to convince us, that all this
sacrificial language, both of Paul and Christ, was utterly destitute of sacrificial ideas, and may now be laid aside.

The author of this dictionary evidently labours under the
consciousness that both Jesus Christ and Paul have employed a
phraseology in reference to the atonement, which conveys essentially the same ideas as were conveyed by the law of Moses;
and his attempts to 'throw off' the ideas while admitting the
language, is mere cajolery, neither respectful to the good sense
of his readers, nor reverential to the Saviour and his apostle.
What a piece of childish and transparent conjuration is attempted
in the following sentences: ' Terms last in a tongue long after
the realities which they at first represented have passed away.
Even to the present day, we speak of the sun's rising and

setting. Error can give to words a vitality which it cannot impart to ideas.' Let the pious reader think of the application of this whole passage to the words of Christ and Paul. But the philosophy is as rotten as the theology. 'Terms last in a tongue long after the realities which they at first represented have passed away.' And why should they not? They impart no vitality to error thereby. If the terms ever represented realities, though the realities may have ceased, the terms remain as true historical representatives of ideas, and are no more vacated of their meaning than when the reality was present. The true idea is in the word still.

But to apply this new philosophy to the case in hand. We have only to request the reader to recall the word *atonement*, and observe, it once represented a reality—a certain transaction, consisting in the infliction of death upon an animal, the collecting of its blood, presenting it on or before the altar of God, and even sprinkling it upon the ark, which was declared to be the symbol of the Divine presence. But 'the reality,' says this philosopher, 'has passed away,' and, therefore, you are to view the word as meaningless—a *vox et præterea nihil*. But, before we admit this sweeping conclusion, we should like to know where the author learned that the reality has passed away from the word *atonement*. He tells us that words 'last in a tongue long after the realities they represented have passed away;' but surely he would not have us vacate any word of its meaning while the reality lasts as well as the word. If the reality remains, then this piece of information avails us nothing. The question still remains,—What will you do with the reality represented by the word *atonement* under the gospel? The idea is in the teaching of Christ and Paul, as clearly as in the teaching of Moses. Don't tell us that the reality has forsaken the word, and left it like the shell from which the bird flew away; for that only tempts us to catch the bird if we can, and then we shall know what the egg contained, though then only in embryo. Neither Jesus Christ nor Paul tells us that the reality has passed away, nor anything that can possibly be construed into any such conclusion. This author informs us, but does not attempt to prove, that the word *atonement* remains, though the reality it once represented has passed away; but, on the contrary, Christ sets the reality before the disciples: ' 'This is my blood of the new *covenant*, which is shed for many for the remission of sins ' (Matt. xxvi. 28); and Paul expressly says, 'We have *now* received the *atonement* through Jesus Christ.' (Rom. v. 11.) The whole Epistle to the Hebrews, to say nothing of other portions, is expressly written to prove that, instead of the reality of atonement passing away, it remains in its perfected and permanent form under the new covenant, and that nothing has passed away but the shadow and the shell—the figures of the true ; that, in fact, the reality never was present till Christ died. What could the apostle mean by saying, 'He taketh away the first that he may establish the second. By the which will we are sanctified, *through the offering of the body of Jesus Christ once for all*'? And this in the very chapter where he is contrasting the imperfections of the Levitical sacrifices with the perfection of the real and final one made by Jesus Christ, concluding the comparison in these words : ' But this man, after he had offered *one sacrifice for sins* for ever, sat down at the right hand of God.' (Heb. x. 12.) We ask, then, where is the evidence that either Christ or Paul taught the passing away of the reality once signified by the word atonement? True, they refer to the passing away of the Levitical law ; but they tell us this is only the cessation of the shadow, by the coming of the reality—the ripening of the flower into the fruit. What, then, becomes of the learned author's philosophy and theology? His rule is irrelevant, and has no meaning here ; for both the word and the reality of atonement are shown to remain, and no artifice of criticism, or logic, or philology, or philosophy, can avail to empty the word *atonement* of its idea.

Moreover, the reference to the philosophy of the sun's rising and setting utterly fails to show a parallel case to that supposed, of words retaining no meaning though still in use; for the phrase is just as true as it ever was, and means at this day all it ever meant : it represents a fact as it appears to the senses of all men, and nothing more ; that was all it ever meant, and its use has not passed away, because the idea remains. So that the whole effort to dislodge from our minds all that the sacred writers teach concerning the reality of an atonement under the gospel, is a conspicuous failure, and that by a person making special pretensions to enlightenment, philological accuracy, pre-eminent love of truth, and emancipation from prejudices.

Through the whole article there appears, moreover, an evident distrust of the author's own reasoning. He does not write like one that feels confidence in his own exposition of the scriptural use of the word. Hence, after the whole disquisition, we are driven to the forlorn hope of bringing the sacred text itself to the bar of human reason. ' Whatever is taught incompatible with this, whether by man or angel, by Paul or Apollos, can have but a temporary import, must, in the lapse of time, be *thrown off* as an outer-covering, and may, nay will, be laid aside by the mind as soon as it is pervaded and enlarged by the grand and ennobling conception of the divine paternity.' ' This great scriptural truth, which has in its behalf the three-fold testimony of

Jesus (his word is itself sufficient), of Paul, and of John, will avail to *throw off* whatever uncongenial elements may at any time happen to gather around it, and eventually bring all disciples of Christ to acknowledge that the love of God and the love of man are the grand essentials of the gospel.' ' He who thoroughly enters into these views will find no serious difficulties, either in the exposition of particular passages of Holy Writ, in the interpretation of God's general providence, or in the reading and devout improvement of his own lot in life and his own opportunities.' This may be denominated the reading of the Bible made easy. What will our readers think of the attempt to limit the whole testimony of the sacred Scriptures to the parable of the Prodigal Son? That is the author's *beau ideal* of the gospel. Nothing that is dissimilar, or that qualifies that, though taught by Jesus, Paul, or John, can have any *reality*. The divine *paternity*, it seems, is the only idea we are to regard; for it is the only idea that will remain after this grand enlightenment which the mind is receiving in this nineteenth century, and when all other ideas are ' *thrown off;* ' and, consequently, it would be as well to *throw off* at once the whole New Testament, saving only this favourite parable of the Prodigal Son, for the author expressly says, ' Here, then, does Jesus present us (in this said parable) with *a standard by which to measure Christian doctrine, and a touchstone by which to discriminate between what is his and what is man's—what is from above and what is from below.*'

This is truly a new and ingenious use of the parable, such as we have never before seen hinted at by any commentator, ancient or modern. We are quite sure there is nothing in the Epistles of the Apostles, nor in all the teachings of Christ, indicating any such use. If it is never so used by any inspired writer, it would be a very perilous and presumptuous invalidation of other parts of the sacred volume for us so to use it. To make this a *touchstone* for other teachings of the same spirit—a *standard* by which all other Christian doctrine is to be measured, w obviously lead to the rejection of doctrines, quite as cl ly taught by the same authority, and would, therefore, be sistent as well as traitorous. Why not make other teachings the same authority touchstones of this? A why make a a- ble which is only a figure, a touchstone of t plainer and er explanations of Christian doctrine, where re is used? I sounder rule of criticism is, to interpret t literal and dogmatic. But the reason wny t means of getting rid of the obnoxi of s substitution, and atonement, is too obvi to re Yet it involves the author in the g y and tency of impeaching the authority of l, q of subverting even this portion of his teaching. If he is not to be accepted as infallible in the other passages, what evidence can show this to be the exception, and make it a rule *par excellence*, by which every other Christian doctrine is to be tried, and, if found wanting, rejected? The question must first be considered, whether this is a complete view of the whole scheme of man's redemption, or only a partial one, concisely representing rather the mercy of God towards the Gentiles, and the jealousy of the Jews who would exclude them, than any specific view of sal- vation. The use which this author would make of the parable is sufficiently reproved by the entire context. Let any one read the whole parable, and not take a portion of it, as is here done, and he will see clearly that nothing could be more perverse in itself, and inconsistent with the intentions of Jesus Christ, than to make it a standard or a test of anything. Every other parable might be exalted to the same honour; and why not every other statement coming from the same teacher? If so, they would cease to be touchstones of one another, and become simply separate *parts* of truth, among which, we may safely presume, the most perfect harmony must exist, and may be discovered. But to reject from a second parable what is not found in the first, or to give one a pre-eminence over another, is neither honest nor reasonable. Yet such is the rule laid down by this author. In the teachings of Jesus Christ he would reject a part and take a part. We say, reject all or receive all, and we can then understand you. But this new *touchstone-process* we can view in no other light than that of an artful manœuvre to sift out of the New Testament truths as certainly in it as the parable under consideration.

We have now said enough to indicate the worthlessness of this Dictionary, either in reference to its great subject, or in comparison with works of a similar nature. But a few more of its imperfections may show that we have not selected its only one. Who would have expected that so common a word as *salvation* should be omitted, while various words not in the Bible are explained at great length? Yet this is the case with the word *Agriculture*, occupying five columns, and *Antiochus* three. Under the word *Bible*, at page 171, the British and Foreign Bible Society is said to have been founded in 1780. Under the word *Ransom* we have only thirteen lines, and are referred to the notable articles *Atonement* and *Redeem*. Under the latter term, after a collection of various passages displaying different uses of the word, we are referred back to *Ransom*, from which the reader can learn nothing definite of the scriptural meaning of either word. *Satisfaction* is dismissed in fourteen lines with a reference to *Atonement* and *Salvation*—the latter not in the Dictionary; the former we have briefly analyzed. There it appears the chief dependence for the circumvention of established opinions was placed upon the very extraordinary explanation offered under the word *Atonement.*

One of the most prevailing and pervading heresies of the work is, the sanction given to every reader of the Bible to take what appears to him reasonable, and ' throw off' or nullify what appears otherwise. Inspiration is brought to the bar of reason. The ' touchstone' is assumed by fallible man.

the divine from the human is to be done by ev
enlightenment of the nineteenth century is to
portion of the Bible, emboldened by such
following, under the word *Adam*—' But there
tage afforded to the earnest and candid inquirer in the distinc-

as facts what the knowledge and expe
to have been nothing higher than the
points of view then prevalent. Thus the

formation of our opinions.'

This is the kind of reverence for the Bible manifested throughout this Dictionary. It appears on every occasion, and often when there was no occasion. If ' all scripture is given by inspiration of God,' then this author is wrong in treating it just as he would any uninspired book, as merely affording us materials out of which we may shape our opinions. He is constantly talking about *throwing off* from the Bible what is human. If he is right, the Scripture may be ' broken,' and is broken, though Jesus Christ says it ' *cannot be broken.*' The inspired writers *mean* the truth, no doubt, but were *mistaken.* We had marked many other articles for comment, but we cannot proceed further, and need not. Some subjects of an antiquarian and historical character are well enough, and the subject of Egyptian monuments, though fully treated with cuts and letter-press, is altogether disproportionate. Words of the utmost importance are dismissed in a few lines, while others of little interest are largely explained. As a whole, the thing is worthless, heretical, and sophistical. It professes to repudiate and answer Rationalism, but it prepares the way for it, and if credited by any one will lead to it. It assumes to be a dictionary for the people—but they must be the Socinian people. By the people at large it never can be accepted, it never ought to be; and while reverential submission to the Bible remains, or an honest love of tr   pervades the English mind, it never will be. ' To the la
to the testimony; if they speak not according to this word, because there is no light in them.' (Isaiah viii. 20.)

ART. IV.—*Lavengro; the Scholar—the Gypsy—the Priest.* By George Borrow, Author of 'The Bible in Spain,' and 'The Gypsies of Spain.' 3 vols. London: Murray. 1851.

MR. BORROW is one of the few writers of the present day, whose productions every one, as a matter of course, makes himself acquainted with. The scholar reads them because he is so distinguished a linguist; the novel-reader because they are as stimulating as Bulwer Lytton's romances; the religious public, because he translated the Bible into Mandtchu, and travelled in Spain to promote its circulation. Students of mankind pore over his pages, because they find in them rare and new aspects of 'human nature;' and the *fainéans* of society, because *ennui* is impossible as he hurries his readers through the strange scenes of gypsy-life, where farce and tragedy dwell side-by-side, but where (so our author has sketched it) the upshot of every movement accords with the most well-bred propriety. We could almost imagine those who belong to the orders of which Ainsworth and Sue are the hierophants, studying Mr. Borrow's books, to perfect themselves in 'gentle Rommany,' and in the manners and customs of those nomades of Europe in the nineteenth century amongst whom may be found, for aught we know to the contrary, as this 'matriculated chabo' supposes, the relics of the oldest human family, and the lawful descendants of the founders of Rome; for assuredly they have retained the habits of almost primitive barbarism, as far as police regulations would suffer them; and they are remarkable as comprising, even by Lavengro's admissions, the very elixir of the world's rogues and vagabonds.

All persons whatever, we may safely assume, will read the book before us; and we do not doubt that they who remember the author's former narratives will join with us in the desire to see, as speedily as possible, as many more volumes as will contain what yet remains untold of the wild adventures in our island and on the continent, in Spain, in Russia, and in distant Tartary, which have made up the 'dream, or drama,' which our philologist calls his 'Life.'

For ourselves, we confess to a long-standing prejudice in Mr. Borrow's favour. Amongst the treasured books of our latest schoolboy days, and ranking in our esteem with the 'Legends of Prince Arthur,' 'Percy's Reliques,' and ' Robin Hood's Garland,' was a poetical translation of certain ancient Danish Ballads, executed (as we learn from this autobiography), when the young scholar's attention ought to have been devoted to the mysteries of English law.  At the time when this thin octavo first fell into our hands, the translator was spoken of as one of the marvels of our native city; and we wish it were possible that our mention of it here should, in the *renaissance* now proceeding,

e are disposed to

place
state.
lubly
us at

country, would in foreign lands
what was new and piquant by
therefore least affected by the
English travellers.  Here is the
the ballad
has fused
*burden* to

> ' Svend Vonved binds his sword to his side,
> It lists him still further to ride—to ride ;
> His helm was blinking against the sun,
> His spurs were clinking his heels upon,
> His horse was springing, his bridle ringing,
> While sat the warrior wildly singing,
>     Look out !  Look out !  Svend Vonved !'

But we must turn to ' Lavengro.'  We have frankly acknow-ledged our ancient regard for the writer, not to weaken our commendation of his work, nor yet to apologize for certain remarks upon it which we shall afterwards make, but because such is the fact ; and being so, if we have read it with heartier sympathy than otherwise we should, we have been proportionably annoyed by those broad and numerous blots which Mr. Borrow's experience in literature should have spared us the trouble of pointing out.

This book belongs to the same class as Goethe's ' Dichtung und Wahrheit ;' and narrates the facts of the author's life till about his twenty-fifth year, as seen through the strongly-refracting and highly-colouring medium of a poet's mind.  There is a large infusion of the poetic element throughout the story ; and in the latter part of it especially, where no one can believe that more than the smallest proportion of the narrative is, in any sense of the word, *fact*. ' Lavengro,' it must be understood, signifies, in the language of the Gypsy race, *wordmaster*, and was bestowed upon the author by his instructor in that tongue, Mr. Jasper Petulengro, who is ' the Gypsy' of the title ; Borrow himself being ' the Scholar.' ' The Priest' is a sad specimen of humanity, and will not, we opine, find much favour with Englishmen ; although appointed emissary from the Roman See to this country because of two very marvellous fitnesses for labour here as a secret propagandist—he was a Briton born, and so could speak English, and ' bear a glass of something strong !' The most pleasing characters are the subordinate ones—the Welsh Methodist preacher and his wife; the eccentric gentleman who ' touched' to avert evil charms ; and a postilion, with whom Lavengro becomes accidentally acquainted whilst living in ' Mumpers' Dingle,' and with whose story the third volume concludes. We cannot doubt that these are sketches from the life ; for in all the portions of the tale which lie amongst scenes with which we are acquainted, we can perceive that, with the hand of a master, Mr. Borrow has drawn actual men and things.

The outline of the tale may be very briefly told. In about the year 1803—for the numerals of the century alone are given—the writer was born at a market-town of East Anglia, which we recognise as East Dereham. His father was a captain of militia, and the head-quarters of the corps happened to be in that town. With great assiduity Mr. Borrow maintains that, by his father's side, he was a *gentillâtre*, inasmuch as the said parent was of Cornish extraction, and the original family abode was a place named *Tredinnock*. With better grace, he insists on the honour of his maternal ancestry, who were Huguenots, that had taken refuge in this country when the Edict of Nantes was revoked. Until the disbanding of the militia, at the peace, when the old soldier settled down at Norwich with his little family, the circumstances of the autobiographer were in the highest degree favourable to the cultivation of one of his characteristic traits—love of rambling, as his mother accompanied her husband in all his changes of quarters ; and the boys were now at Dereham, now at Norman Cross, then at Hythe, anon at Edinburgh, and at last in the wild regions of the south of Ireland. The same passion was nurtured by the most reverent study of ' Robinson Crusoe,' to which book is ascribed the awakening of curiosity in his childish mind, and the impulse which aided him in mastering the difficulties in the art of reading. He was sent to one school after another in the different towns near the barracks ; and though such an interrupted course of culture secured for him but little academic lore, he acquired other kinds of information; some of which (did we not see that Mr. Borrow is a wonder unto himself, and therefore make the needful abatement) would smack of the miraculous; whilst others were of the kind most serviceable to such an errant genius as he has since been; and others were the contraband acquisitions of the Scotch and Irish tongues.

At the end of the war, as we said, his father settled at Norwich, and the wild-eyed boy was articled to a lawyer. But languages and adventures were still the objects of his affections; and, neglecting Blackstone, he devoutly made himself master of French, Italian, Spanish, Welsh, Danish, Hebrew, Arabic, German, Armenian, and, chiefest of all, of Rommany, the Gypsy tongue; his master being no other than the Pharaoh of the nation, whom he had met, when a child, at Norman Cross. In his earlier days he had acquired some skill in the blacksmith's art, and could both ride, and groom, and tame the horse he had shod; he now cultivated the science of ' self-defence,' as it is called, and became acquainted with those men of unenviable notoriety—the ' bruisers,' and their patrons. The description of the fine old city is admirable; and not less graphic are the sketches of Joseph John Gurney, the late eminent member of the Society of Friends; of William Taylor, the German scholar, and *bon-vivant*, and framer of absurd theories in all departments of theology; of Crome, the scarcely yet appreciated painter; of a certain magistrate, whose taste for boxing made his position and office a sad thraldom; of John Thurtell, and the heroes of the ring, who, once upon a time *dis*-graced Norwich with their presence; and of Mr. Petulengro, his Rommany brother. Few scenes have ever been more vividly pictured than the great prize-fight at a little village just within the borders of Suffolk, and the rush back to Norwich, through Bungay, when the crowds were dispersed by a storm.

At his father's death the autobiographer went to London, hoping to persuade some publisher of discernment and enterprise to bring out his translations of Ap Gwilym's poems, and the Danish ballads; and furnished with an introduction to the well-known Sir Richard Phillips. But his hopes were disappointed—his precious MSS. were not even looked at—he obtained mere hack-work, at worse than garretteer's pay—and having, at length, by a happy stroke, obtained sufficient cash to quit the flinty-hearted metropolis, he set forth on his adventures towards the south-west of England. At first he indulged himself in a pedestrian tour: but very soon purchasing a travelling tinker's equipment, he entered upon a life of ' savage freedom;' wandered far, met with many adventures, and not a few remark-

able characters ; and, finally, by virtue of his defeat of the rival
tradesman of the 'beat,' who bore the heroic epithet of 'the
Flaming Tinman,' became possessed of the sole right of camp-
ing in 'Mumpers' Dingle,' and gained as a partner of his
solitude one Isopel Berners, a young giantess, to whom he
teaches the declension of Armenian nouns; and with something
approaching to a demi-semi declaration of love from the *dilettante*
tinker to the fair tramp, which is not unhopefully received,
Lavengro's story ends.

Our space forbids our quotation of passages which would have
exhibited more than the literary execution of the work; but
for this purpose, the following will be sufficient.    The first is a
'picture' of Norwich, and its general fidelity will be recognised
by all who have ever taken their stand on the site of St.
Leonard's Priory, and looked down upon the city.

'A fine old city, truly, is that, view it from whatever side you will;
but it shows best from the east, where the ground, bold and elevated,
overlooks the fair and fertile valley in which it stands.  Gazing from
those heights, the eye beholds a scene which cannot fail to awaken,
even in the least sensitive bosom, feelings of pleasure and admiration.
At the foot of the heights flows a narrow and deep river, with an
antique bridge communicating with a long and narrow suburb, flanked
on either side by rich meadows of the brightest green, beyond which
spreads the city; the fine old city, perhaps the most curious specimen
at present extant of the genuine old English town.  Yes, there it
spreads from north to south, with its venerable houses, its numerous
gardens, its thrice twelve churches, its mighty mound, which, if
tradition speaks true, was raised by human hands to serve as the
grave-heap of an old heathen king, who sits deep within it, with his
sword in his hand, and his gold and silver treasures about him.
There is a grey old castle upon the top of that mighty mound; and
yonder, rising three hundred feet above the soil, from among those
noble forest-trees, behold that old Norman master-work, that cloud-
encircled cathedral spire, around which a garrulous army of rooks and
choughs continually wheel their flight. . . . Brave hearts in that old
town have borne witness against [idolatry], and sealed their testimony
with their heart's blood—most precious to the Lord is the blood of
his saints!  We are not far from hallowed ground.  Observe ye not yon
chalky precipice to the right of the Norman bridge?  On this side of the
stream, upon its brow, is a piece of ruined wall, the last relic of what
was of old a stately pile, whilst at its foot is a place called the
Lollards' Hole; and with good reason, for many a saint of God has
breathed his last beneath that white precipice, bearing witness against
popish idolatry, amidst flame and pitch; many a grisly procession has
advanced along that suburb, across the old bridge, towards the
Lollards' Hole; furious priests in front, a calm, pale martyr in the
midst, a pitying multitude behind.  It has had its martyrs, the venerable
old town.'—Vol. i. pp. 177—180.

In the following scenes, Mr. Borrow introduces his readers to an old woman who kept a fruit-stall in one of the alcoves of old London-bridge; he had observed her seated there when he walked upon that bridge on the first day after his arrival in town. Having watched the rush of water between the narrow arches for some time, he was about to climb upon the balustrade to look over into the river at a greater advantage, when he felt himself seized by the body, and, turning his head, saw the old fruit-woman :—

‘ “ Nay, dear! don't—don't!” said she. “ Don't fling yourself over —perhaps you may have better luck next time !”

‘ “ I was not going to fling myself over,” said I, dropping from the balustrade ; “how came you to think of such a thing ?”

‘ “ Why, seeing you clamber up so fiercely, I thought you might have had ill luck, and that you wished to make away with yourself.”

‘ “ Ill luck,” said I, going into the stone-bower, and sitting down ; “ what do you mean ? Ill luck in what ?”

‘ “ Why, no great harm, dear! cly-faking, perhaps.”

‘ “ Are you coming over me with dialects,” said I ; “ speaking unto me in fashions I wot nothing of ?”

‘ “ Nay, dear! don't look so strange with those eyes of your'n, nor talk so strangely ; I don't understand you.”

‘ “ Nor I you ; what do you mean by cly-faking ?”

‘ “ Lor, dear! no harm ; only taking a handkerchief now and then.”

‘ “ Do you take me for a thief ?”

‘ “ Nay, dear ; don't make use of bad language ; we never calls them thieves here, but prigs and fakers : to tell you the truth, dear, seeing you spring at that railing put me in mind of my own dear son, who is now in Bot'ny ; when he had bad luck, he always used to talk of flinging himself over the bridge, and sure enough, when the traps were after him, he did fling himself into the river, but that was off the bank ; nevertheless, the traps pulled him out, and he is now suffering his sentence ; so you see you may speak out, if you have done anything in the harmless line, for I am my son's own mother, I assure you.”

‘ “ So you think there is no harm in stealing ?”

‘ “ No harm in the world, dear! Do you think my own child would have been transported for it, if there had been any harm in it ? and, what's more, would the blessed woman in the book here have written her life as she has done, and given it to the world, if there had been any harm in faking ? She, too, was what they call a thief and a cut-purse ; ay, and was transported for it, like my dear son ; and do you think she would have told the world so, if there had been any harm in the thing ? Oh, it is a comfort to me that the blessed woman was transported, and came back—for come back she did, and rich, too—for it is an assurance to me that my dear son, who was transported too, will come back like her.”

‘ “ What was her name ?”

‘ “ Her name ; blessed Mary Flanders.”

‘ “ Will you let me look at the book ?”

' " Yes, dear, that I will, if you promise me not to run away
with it."

' I took the book from her hand; a short, thick volume, at least a
century old, bound with greasy black leather. I turned the yellow
and dog's-eared pages, reading here and there a sentence. Yes, and
no mistake ! *His* pen, his style, his spirit might be observed in every
line of the uncouth-looking old volume—the air, the style, the spirit
of the writer of the book which first taught me to read. I covered my
face with my hand, and thought of my childhood . . .

' " This is a singular book," said I at last ; " but it does not appear
to have been written to prove that thieving is no harm, but rather to
show the terrible consequences of crime ; it contains a deep moral."

' " A deep what, dear ? "

' " A ——, but no matter, I will give you a crown for this volume."

' " No, dear, I will not sell the volume for a crown."

' " I am poor," said I, " but I will give you two silver crowns for
your volume."

' " No, dear, I will not sell my volume for two silver crowns ; no,
nor for the golden one in the king's Tower down there ; without my
book I should mope and pine, and perhaps fling myself into the river ;
but I am glad you like it, which shows that I was right about you,
after all ; you are one of our party, and you have a flash about that
eye of yours, which puts me just in mind of my dear son. No,
dear, I won't sell you my book ; but, if you like, you may have a peep
into it whenever you come this way."—Vol. ii. pp. 28—32.

And on giving the old woman, at her request, ' a tanner to buy
a little baccy with,' Borrow departed, but often returned to the
' stone bower' and the life of the ' blessed Mary Flanders,' which,
however, the old fruit-seller at last exchanged for a Bible. And
this will serve to introduce some strictures upon ' Lavengro,'
which we are compelled to make, and which must be received
as defining, not contradicting, the general commendation we have
given above. The remarks made by the writer to the old woman,
although a somewhat flat and tame protest against thieving, are
nearly the only indications given of any moral disapprobation of
the proceedings of the denizens of that *imperium in imperio*—the
rascality of England. The oblique and insinuated apologies for
some distinguished members of this extensive community fill us
with wonder. At Edinburgh, he brings before the reader David
Haggart, as a newly-enlisted drummer, who, musing much upon
' Willie Wallace,' and emulating his renown, became a most
notorious robber, whose name and deeds were almost a terror in
all the three kingdoms. This man, it is added, crowned his
deeds of violence by homicide, and was executed, 'justly,' Mr.
Borrow says. And yet, by a comparison instituted between him
and (whom thinks the reader?) *Tamerlane*—although it is allowed
that no comparison is possible—and by an appeal *ad modestiam*,
for it is not to the consciences of his readers, a sort of shambling

defence is set up for this consummate villain! (Vol. i. pp. 115—
117.) Later, a yet more eminent criminal is introduced upon
the stage, John Thurtell, of whom it is needless to say one
word: his execution for murder in after years is hinted by the
Gypsy's pointing to a remarkable appearance in the clouds at
the prize-fight, which foretold, it is said, his bloody *dukkeripen*—
or fortune. ' I have nothing,' adds Mr. Borrow, ' to do with that
man's after life—he fulfilled his dukkeripen. " A bad, violent
man!" Softly, friend; when thou wouldst speak harshly of the
dead, remember that thou hast not yet fulfilled thy own dukkeripen!' (Vol. i. p. 340.) And it is so, that the most atrocious
scoundrels are, as it were, assoiled! We strongly suspect that
such slurring over of monstrous crimes is as hurtful to the interests of morality as the *apotheosis* of felony by Harrison Ainsworth. But startling as these and similar extenuations of guilt
are, there is a greater marvel. We have read the whole passage
again and again, and our astonishment at it increases rather than
lessens with our familiarity with the words. Mr. Borrow has
described, with wonderful skill and effect, a vast gathering of
prize-fighters at Norwich, on occasion of the battle for ' the belt,'
which we have alluded to above ; and he remarks, ' Let-no one
sneer at the bruisers of England—what were the gladiators of
Rome, or the bull-fighters of Spain, in its palmiest days, compared to England's bruisers? Pity that corruption should have
crept in amongst them ; but of that I wish not to talk; *let us
still hope that a spark of the old religion, of which they were the
priests, still lingers in the hearts of Englishmen!'* (Vol. i. pp.
328, 329.) In the following pages, he ascribes the corruption of
this ' old religion' to the Jews, who loved ' base lucre;' and says
of them, that they are ' endowed with every gift but one, and
that *the highest, genius divine—genius which can alone make of
men demi-gods. . . .'* The writer of these passages was engaged
by the Bible Society in circulating the Bible in Spain ; he has
even translated part, or the whole, into some rarely acquired
languages; and of the Jews, whose psalms and prophets he
must then have become acquainted with, he avers that they have
not genius divine! And that gift, be it well observed, is the *only*
deficiency noted in these knaves! Whilst the ' bruisers' of England, the brutality of whose pursuit he justly sets above that of
the Roman gladiators, and the Spanish bull-fighters, are ' *priests*'
of an ' *old religion!*' Nothing but silence seems a fitting comment on such an astounding statement. He might well say in
his preface, ' *Let no one think that irreligion is advocated in this
book.'**

---

* Perhaps Mr. Borrow's very extraordinary ethics may be explained by the
following passage, which contains counsel not only rigidly acted upon by the

The folly of such attempts to invest scoundrelism and brutality with something of a divine halo, is clearly seen when these
passages are put in contrast with those that darkly hint mysterious conflicts, through which the autobiographer says he
passed. As if one who could verily wrestle with the foe to
mankind, and triumphantly defeat him, would, or could, record
such judgments as these upon subjects which the merest smattering of morality must have utterly condemned! As if
supernatural agonies and prophetic throes are ever granted to
prepare for villanous revelations! Nor does this prate about
' dukkeripens ' and ' old religions ' appear less absurd when Mr.
Borrow proceeds in the third volume to utter, through the mask
of ' the priest,' his notions of the classes and parties of society
in the present day; the intent of which, as of many other parts
of the work, it is plain (although the conversation is alleged to
have happened before the passing of the Catholic Emancipation
Act), is to fan the anti-papal fervour of the country to a hotter
glow. His censures, his sneers, have no point; and however
hearty they may be, and however well they may be aimed (as,
for example, those against the Dissenters), they are powerless.
We think of the ' bruisers ' and their ' religion,' and smile at
the satirist. Nay, his very churchmanship, which he parades so
ostentatiously, loses its reality, and looks like a misfitting garment—of good cloth, and of the clerical cut, undoubtedly, but
not made for the wearer—second-hand—most unbecoming. It
is in the ' Newmarket cut ' alone (as he designates some queer
fashion in tailoring), that Mr. Borrow appears his proper self.

This, however, is not all that we have to object to. Connected
with what we have already said, we complain most earnestly of
the frequent adoption of the Hebraisms of our English Bible :
it is very offensive on every ground, and was quite unnecessary;
for nothing can be more flowing or graceful than the writer's
own style, as it appears in the latter part of the work; even his
imitations of the old standard novelists are better, and less
opposed to good taste. Of his sentimental passages, which in
the first volume abound, we can only say, that they show not
his depth of feeling, as they were intended, but his utter want
of it. Cold, strained, inappropriate, they, like his religious
observations, operate as a sort of counter-charm to the influence
of his vigorous graphic descriptions, and to the naturalness of

---

strict parent to whom it was given, but endorsed in an evasive way by Lavengro
himself :—' If you are anxious for *the success of your son in life*, for *the correctness of his conduct, and the soundness of his principles*, keep him to *Lilly's
grammar.* If you can by any means, *either fair or foul*, induce him to *get by
heart Lilly's Latin grammar*, you may set your heart at rest with respect to
him; I, myself, will be his warrant.'—Vol. i. p. 80.—' *Pro-digious !*'

his conversations, where he is not thinking about himself. And how inconsistent he is, what contradictions exist in him, seemingly unknown, many a page testifies. He will utter in one place, some one of the popular 'cries' against Dissenters, and in another, either commend them, or state what is an aspect of the principle of Dissent; or he sneers at 'Radicals,' and then shows that he knows the reality of the evils which Radicalism strives against. In only one thing is he fixed, his *political Protestantism;* and that is to be ascribed rather to the times than to himself.

We do not pretend to be word-masters ourselves, but *a Lavengro* should not have supposed the long, silky-furred cat to be named after *Angola* hosiery, instead of the goats of *Angora;* neither should he have called an Alpine lake, and a tidal river, *lagoons;* nor should he have spoken of 'not casting line and *angle* into river any more,' when he gave up fishing; nor have been guilty of many other linguistic solecisms. It would have been well, too, had he been a little more accurate *in minimis,* for it is in such matters that the great and truly powerful mind appears: 'rooks and choughs' do not fly about Norwich Cathedral spire—'cadders,' or jackdaws, alone haunt it; neither is the spire a *Norman* structure; the old clerk of East Dereham spelt his name *Philo,* not '*Philoh;*' and St. Withburga *called forth* the spring in the church-yard, but did not build the modern bath-house over it. The creature also that he captured without harm in his infancy, like a miniature Hercules, or Paul, was not a viper at all (if his gorgeous description present even the faintest image of the reptile), but an innocuous *snake;* the tints of the two animals being totally different. These may appear to be contemptible matters, but every part of the book in which we at all find ourselves at home, is *full* of them; and so we cannot doubt that where he wanders beyond our ken, there is the same inaccuracy, as well as the same graphic skill and power.

Against other things, too, we must needs protest. Thus we are distressed to see poor puns dragged in, in naked misery, at various parts of both narrative and conversation; and the 'contents' and 'running titles' are an unspeakable annoyance, being constructed by the selection of a word or two, seemingly at random, from the paragraphs, so as not to afford the slightest clue, in most instances, to the subject of the pages. This affectation is only one of the minor displays of the one great fault of the book, and it appears in the want of earnestness with which everything not of actual, every-day life is treated. Even the mysterious insinuations that the author has been admitted to look upon 'the night side of nature,' seem written to induce his readers to believe what he does not believe himself. And when he attempts to tell how his soul fared in these wanderings, it is more palpable, and yet more displeasing.

For the truth of the whole matter is, that no one but a man of unequalled self-complacency could, by any possibility, have produced such an autobiography. Nothing but the scenes from the life of the Pariahs of English society, and those of familiar places and persons, could counterbalance the effect of the almost sublime self-consciousness which nearly every page displays. Even in childhood he talks like a sage; he is never off his guard, according to this book; but, from his very boyhood, by word and deed, with a grand air of prompt and iron decision, proves himself equal to every emergency. His characters, whether in speaking to him or of him, flatter him grossly; at twenty, he says, he 'had made himself *master of the sum of human wisdom;*' and not the slightest crevice is overlooked by which he can thrust forward something about himself. *Intense self-appreciation*—this is the great, glaring defect of the book; or, rather, it *is the book itself.*

We are sorry to be compelled to seem to reduce our commendation of this work so greatly. We trust that Mr. Borrow will learn from this experiment that the charm of his writings does not lie in himself, but in the strange, unhacknied, unexplored regions which he, first in these days, opened to the gaze of civilized society, then longing for 'some new thing;' and that with the stores he has accumulated during his travels, he will construct another work, which shall, like 'the *Zincali*,' and 'the Bible in Spain,' tell us his adventures; but not pretend either to state, or to solve, the problem of life, by the detail of petty commonplaces, and of sentimentalities, which might have happened to, and been experienced by, any one in the world, as well as LAVENGRO.

———————

ART. V.—*Glimmerings in the Dark; or, Lights and Shadows of the Olden Time.* By F. Somner Merryweather, Author of 'Biblomania in the Middle Ages,' &c. London: Simpkin, Marshall, and Co. 1851.

THE science of history, constructed on philosophical principles, directing our inquiries, as it does, to the sources of human improvement, and to the impediments which ignorance, superstition, and tyranny present to its progress, is entitled to patient and persevering study. Though historical investigation may be regarded as only at present in its infancy, and as having accomplished but very partially its sublime ends, it has already bestowed many invaluable benefits on the world.   An endeavour to develop the events which have influenced the

the improvement of its people, forms a department of investigation that can never become useless or uninteresting.   Such inquiries, however, are surrounded with formidable difficulties, inasmuch

ancient times, are involved in obscurity; the early condition of all nations being necessarily blended with much of fable. National habits and peculiarities have, for the most part, originated in circumstances now buried in oblivion, and existing features of social excellence and political greatness may have taken their rise at a period so remote, or in events so minute, as to be entirely overlooked in the grandeur of their results. A multitude of influences and prejudices, of mistakes and misrepresentations, come in between us and the objects of our inquiries, and throw a mist of uncertainty and ignorance over the whole field of research ; so that we are compelled to grope our way with the aid of uncertain guides, and are frequently in danger of admitting as history what is little better than fiction, and of regarding the merest fables as undoubted facts.

Amidst the uncertainties which thus gather around all subjects connected with the history of the past, we welcome every guide who, with honesty of purpose, attempts to lead us up through the labyrinths of myth and error, to the temple of Truth. Highly as we prize such historic writers as Neibuhr and Arnold, Grote and Hallam, and thankfully as we walk in the light they assist to shed on our path, we are far from despising the 'glimmerings' of our author, who, in a lowlier path, but with kindred aim, seeks to bring out truthfully some of the lights and shadows of the olden time in England.   He has attempted to do with our Anglo-Saxon institutions and practices, and the mediæval society of Europe, what has been so well done by another modern author in the department of forensic eloquence.   We refer to the attractive historical sketch of the office and functions of an Advocate, by Mr. Forsyth, a barrister, who has, with great skill and ingenuity, interwoven a mass of interesting particulars with a narrative of legal oratory, as it has existed in the countries of Greece and Rome, France and England, from the time of Hortensius to the present day.   Such comparisons of the past with the present, joined with a description of the transition state from the one to the other, are of great value.   They serve to make us thankful for our existing privileges, and to moderate the strong complacency with which we are wont to regard the exclusive advantages of the times in which we live.   We know

of no book which, on the whole, is better fitted to promote these
objects than Mr. Merryweather's ' Lights and Shadows of the
Olden Time.' He has brought together a vast variety of curious
and interesting particulars, which lie scattered over volumes,
manuscripts, and inscriptions, inaccessible to the bulk of English
readers, and he has placed these in a portable and attractive
form. Without pretending to the dignity of history, or to a
continuous narrative, he has thrown together short dissertations
on a variety of subjects connected with our early annals, aiming
more especially at the illustration of the literary and social
character of our ancestors. These narrations are enlivened by
amusing anecdotes, by literary curiosities, and by flowers
gathered in paths but little trodden by the casual reader. It
would be easy to criticise each chapter, to show good reasons
for doubting many of our author's ' facts,' and to differ seriously
from some of his conclusions; but we are not in a mood to be
cynical; we have risen from the perusal of his book greatly
delighted, and we wish to make our readers acquainted with a
work which has refreshed our own memories, called up pleasure-
able recollections of by-gone times, and which, we doubt not,
will yield them mingled instruction and mirth, should they
become acquainted with its pages.

The contents of the book, as it may be supposed, are multifarious, and, to some extent, desultory; though they are all
bound together by an elastic thread. Some of these are much
less to our taste than others, and, therefore, while we shall indicate their general character and range, we shall linger over such
as are most in harmony with our own reveries and predilections.
The first chapter contains a description of monastic communities,
with an endeavour to estimate their influence on society and
civilization. The author refers to the manual labours of the
monks, to their cultivation of waste lands and vineyards, to their
preservation and protection of public roads, and to their extensive hospitality to the traveller, and to their neighbouring
poor. On these, and on other grounds, while fully admitting
the evils and corruptions of the monkish system, he concludes
that the influence of monastic institutions was much more favourable on European civilization than some modern writers, who
declaim eloquently on the evils of the dark ages, are willing to
allow. We incline to his opinion, for we believe that if they
did not originate or discover much, they conserved the knowledge which otherwise would have been lost, and that cloisters
and grated cells were the depositories of invaluable stores of
historic, and even scientific truth, the ripe fruits of which we
are privileged to enjoy. The picture of ' Bolton Abbey in the
Olden Time ' has given us a good idea of monkish love of rich

fare, and delight in well-filled larders and stored cellars; and this is justified by what we know from other sources of many individuals and communities of this extensive brotherhood. But there were among the monks of every age, some who pursued the even tenor of a literary life, or went about doing good, and some few who imbibed the spirit of the venerable Bede, who thus wrote:—' All my life I spent in the same monastery, giving my whole attention to the study of the Scriptures, and in the intervals, between the hours of discipline and singing in the church, I took delight in learning, or teaching, or writing something.' It is a curious fact that many of the monks reached an extreme old age. Mr. Merryweather has recorded the names and dwellings of several in England whose term of life extended from a hundred and fifteen to a hundred and sixty years of age. An historian of the old Saxon times records, without any expressions of surprise, the circumstance of five contemporary brethren of Croyland monastery having each braved the winters of nearly a century and a quarter. By some writers this longevity is attributed to the fact, that the monks were compelled to undergo the operation of bleeding at certain times in each year; but by others, and with much more reason, to the quiet seclusion of the cloister, in which the monkish author was uninterrupted by worldly cares, and seldom exposed to the vicissitudes of fortune; in which a provision was made for his daily bread, and where he might, free from earthly anxieties, indulge his soul in roaming through the golden treasures of ancient wisdom, or in adding, by his own writings, to the literature of his day.

Of all the monkish writers Roger Bacon is the most original and variously gifted. His works are singular, from the hints they convey of his capacious mind, and from the almost prescient spirit in which he, living in the thirteenth century, anticipated what science would perform under more auspicious circumstances. Many of his utterances, which excited sneers of contempt, or provoked ecclesiastical ire, have long since been verified; some have only recently been accomplished, and others possibly await their fulfilment. Our author says, remarking on the fact that Bacon received the appellation of a magician—

' We shall feel inclined to regard with a more favourable eye the experiments of the Franciscan, who, in his " Essay on the Works of Art, Nature, and Magic," describes with the prophetic pen of a seer some of the possibilities which science was destined to achieve. " It is possible," he writes, " to make engines to sail, so that a vessel may be guided by a single man, and with greater swiftness than others will which are full of men to help them." What would he have said to those mighty vessels which, by the aid of science, cross the Atlantic in less than a fortnight ?   These are results of experimental philosophy of which Bacon had no conception.   " It is possible," he continues, " to make a chariot move with an inestimable swiftness, and the motion to be without the help of any living creature."  Surely Roger Bacon was thinking of the locomotive, or dreaming of railways !  " It is possible to make an engine," he affirms, " by which a man may walk at the bottom of the sea without bodily danger."   Incredible as the assertion appeared to many in the thirteenth century, we now regard it without wonder ; we examine, by the aid of the diving-bell, vessels that have reposed for years beneath the waters, carry gunpowder to the bottom of the sea, and rescue from the deep the treasures which the tempestuous waves had swallowed up.   " It is possible," again writes this prophet of science, " to make engines for flying, so that a man, sitting in the midst, by merely turning an instrument that moves artificial wings, after the fashion of a bird's flight, may ascend into the air."   Where is he of this age of wonder and experiment, who, observing the vast things which science has accomplished, will have the hardihood to declare the impossibility of that which the Franciscan philosopher thus proclaims within her scope ?   Who can fathom the depths of science, or limit the progress of the spirit of invention ?'—Pp. 146—148.

Mr. Merryweather, however, in describing the monkish ages, dwells more on the lights than on the shadows which belonged to them ; and in order to understand their real character, we must remember that Bede and Bacon were exceptions to the men of their times—that ignorance, immorality, and superstition, were the characteristics of the monkish ages, and that much of the poetical light shed upon their institutions arises from the mellowing distance of time at which we behold them.   The monasteries themselves, at first the fantastic monuments of the superstitious devotion of monarchs, or of the purpled pride of fattened abbots, have gained, by the silent influence of antiquity, the power of impressing us with awe and veneration.   Even the stains and weather-tints upon the battlements of such buildings add, like the scars of a veteran, to the affecting impression.  Time has mouldered into beauty many an erection which was far less attractive, in its palmy days of completeness, than Netley or Tintern Abbey is now.   An intimate acquaintance with the inmates of such houses serves to dispel the illusion which often surrounds them in the historic page, and to reveal living men of sordid minds, of ambitious aims, and of ignorant devotion.   Several of the German monasteries, in the fifteenth century, had no public libraries for the monks ; and in some of them not a copy of the Scriptures could be found.   The original languages of the Scriptures were not only generally neglected, but the study of them was despised.   At the revival of learning in Europe, Conrad Heresbachius relates that he heard a monk declaiming in a church, who affirmed, ' A new language called Greek is discovered, and it is the parent of all heresy.  A book written in that language is everywhere got into the hands of persons, and is called the New Testament.  It is a book full of daggers and poison.  Another language has also sprung up called Hebrew, and those who learn it become Jews.'  Even Latin, the common language of their religious services, was so little understood by the monkish clergy, that the most ridiculous mistakes were made by them, both in the performance of their offices and in their writings.  The estimate which Wycliffe, that morning star of the Reformation, formed of the whole mendicant brotherhood, may be inferred from the fact, that when he was sick at Oxford, and expected to die, he was visited by a deputation from the body, who reminded him of the evil they had sustained from his attacks upon them, and urged him to recant.  He heard them in silence, and then beckoning his servants to raise him in his bed, and summoning all his remaining strength, exclaimed aloud, ' I shall not die, but live, and shall again declare the evil deeds of the friars !'  This incident is mentioned, with appropriate comments, by Dr. Vaughan, in his ' Life and Times of Wycliffe.'

The ignorance of the parochial clergy was equal to that of the monks, of which many amazing proofs are on record.  Aylmers, of Harborowe, tells us, that ' the vicar of Trumpington, in Cambridgeshire, reading the Passion on Palm Sunday, when he came to the place, " Eli, Eli, lama, zabatini," suddenly stopped, and calling the churchwardens aside, said, " Neighbours! this year must be altered.  Here is Eli twice in this book.  I assure you, if my lord (the bishop) of Ely come this way and see it, he will have the book.  Therefore, by mine advice we shall scrape it out, and put in our own towne's name, *Trumpington, Trumpington*, lama, zabatini."  They consented, and he did so, because he understood no Greek.'

Our author justly refers to the want of facilities for travelling in the middle ages, and to the difficulties of transmitting news by letter, as one great cause of the prevailing darkness.  He says :—

' The vast improvements in the modes of transmission have been so sudden, that we can scarcely credit the dangers and difficulties which impeded a journey in the olden time; even so recently as the seventeenth century the progress of news was so tardy, that the abdication of King James II. was not known in the Orkneys until three months after that important event had taken place.  But if the spread of news was slow then, at what a snail's pace must it have been diffused in the old times of monkish pilgrimage !  The massacre of the Jews in London, at the coronation of Richard I. was not known at Stamford, Norwich, or York, until several months had elapsed.  If a king died, and another sovereign sat upon the throne, the people beyond the vicinity of the metropolis were for days unconscious of the change.'—P. 41.

The badness of the roads, the lumbering construction of the vehicles, and the tolls exacted by the monks for passing over thoroughfares on their lands, all retarded that intercommunity of persons so essential to mental and moral advancement. The ignorance thus engendered became a fruitful source of error and fable. Monks recorded as historic truths, the floating, unsubstantiated reports wafted to them by pilgrims and travellers. The discoveries of science were magnified and distorted, while they were attributed to magic and satanic intervention, and the belief in witchcraft became all but universal. We have in the book before us an interesting, but defective, chapter on ' witchcraft and magic.' The perils incurred by the student in philosophy, from this popular superstition, were very numerous. The theologian might be revered, the poet might be praised, the historian might be honoured, but the philosopher was ever regarded with suspicion in the dark ages. Mr. Merryweather says :—

' Men were unable to understand how the effects which the philosophers produced by their experiments could be natural ; and phenomena which we now regard as the most simple results of science were looked upon as the fruits of magic. The effect observed through a crystal slightly convex was an illusion of necromancy. Arabic numerals were hieroglyphics of the arch-fiend ; alchemy was a suspicious study, and betokened some acquaintance with evil spirits and sorcery. The charge of witchcraft was a favourite means employed to excite prejudice against political foes. When the disciples of Peter Waldo had grown a numerous sect, the Church found it convenient to designate heresy by the more opprobrious name of witchcraft. It was an easy matter to excite suspicion ; the secret and midnight meetings of the Waldenses, for prayer and scripture reading, were said, by the priests, to be convocations for the purpose of entering into compacts with the devil ; their very forms of worship were pointed to as evidence of their witchcraft, and, without justice and without defence, they were hurried to the fire, amidst the hootings and execrations of a priest-ridden and superstitious populace. The belief in witchcraft was rampant even in the days of the Tudors, and almost universal in the days of the Stuarts. Senates, in grave consultation, framed laws, and judges passed condemnation upon old crazy women, and fanatic old men. The disease has not even yet worked itself out of the English mind ; we still have laws unrepealed to punish the witch, and we occasionally hear of votaries of the dubious craft in rustic districts.'—Pp. 80—83.

Doubtless, the history of witchcraft constitutes a very melancholy chapter in our national chronicles. Its palmy days are to be found, not in the mediæval ages, but in later times. In the year 1646, two hundred persons were tried, condemned, and executed for witchcraft, at the Suffolk and Essex assizes. Matthew Hopkins, the noted witch-finder, who was accustomed to weigh suspected women against the Church Bible, and to declare them guilty if they weighed it down, was the means of hanging sixty persons for this supposed crime in one year. Barrington, in his observations on the Statutes, says that thirty thousand persons were hanged or burned, in the United Kingdom, in twelve months. Mr. Merryweather is quite wrong in supposing that we have still unrepealed laws for punishing witches, and he will, we are sure, be thankful to be set right in this particular. By an act, passed in the ninth year of George II., our statute-book was purged of one of its darkest blots, by the following enactment—' No suit or proceeding shall be commenced or carried on against any person for witchcraft or enchantment, or for charging another with such an offence, in any court whatever.' The enlightened conduct of Lord Chief Justice Holt, who dismissed eight separate charges against supposed witches, and who eventually punished Richard Hathaway, as an impostor, for pretending to witchcraft, is worthy of all praise as leading to this result, and deserves to be honourably mentioned, and the more so, when it is remembered that Sir Matthew Hale, notwithstanding his learning and piety, actually passed the extreme sentence of the law on more than one convicted witch.

There are no chapters in these 'glimmerings in the dark' more inviting to us at the present moment than those on miracles and the history of relics. In the ages now passing under review, men believed in charms and miracles, regarded with reverential awe the jawbone of an ancient cœnobite, the tooth or toe-nail of a saint or martyr, and paid religious homage to every supposed relic that had been in any imaginable way connected with the author of our salvation. We cannot better illustrate the frauds connected with the manufacture and sale of relics than by a reference to the traditions once current concerning the Holy Cross. Helena, the mother of Constantine, undertook a pilgrimage to Jerusalem to rescue from oblivion the true cross. A vision, it is said, led to the discovery of the holy sepulchre and the cross. A church was erected on the spot, a part of the cross was gorgeously enshrined, and left on its altar; the remainder was sent to Constantine. Fragments of this precious relic, in process of time, were found all over Europe, and used as a charm against all evil. The way in which some natural doubts concerning these relics were set at rest, is thus described by our author :—

' When some more thoughtful than others began to wonder how pieces of the cross became so numerous, and yet the cross at Jerusalem diminished not, it was dexterously affirmed, by a grave authority of the Church, that the cross was no ordinary relic; it was true, that this sacred wood abounded; it was true, that had all the sacred fragments been collected together, there would have been sufficient timber to have built a ship of war. But, said an eminent saint, this is easily accounted for ; to supply the wants of Christendom, and to reward the zeal of pilgrims, this cross is allowed to grow and vegetate, so that the faithful may be fed, as Christ fed the multitude, with seven loaves and a few fishes. Thus, the holy cross, although every day divided into several parts, remained, as Paulinus testified, without any diminution in size.'—Pp. 149, 150.

As a pendent to this, we add a notice of a controversy between the monks, as related by William of Malmesbury, concerning the rival excellences of the bones of two saints—St. Martin and St. German. To solve the existing doubts as to the asserted supremacy of each, and to establish the reputation of their respective saints, the monks determined upon adopting the following experiment :—

'A leprous person, in the very last stage of disease, was placed in the church between the bones of the two saints, and left during the long night to their benevolence and mercy. The glory of St. Martin, it was said, was alone vigilant, for the next morning, the skin of that part of the leper's body on his side appeared clear; whilst that on the side of St. German was discoloured, as usual. The monks of the defeated saint demanded another trial. It was agreed on the following night to satisfy these scruples, by turning the yet diseased side to St. Martin. As soon as the morning began to dawn, the man was found by his anxious attendants with his skin smooth, and perfectly cured. Such wonders as these crowd the writings of the monks.'— P. 164.

And these are the times, the good old times, after which some are sighing; and these are the lying wonders which some would have the people of this country again believe in! But we have confidence in the sound-hearted attachment of this nation generally to the principles of the Great Protestant Reformation which shed light on the darkness, and in the fixed determination of the churches to stand fast in the liberty wherewith the gospel has made them free.

We have in this volume a section on the domestic habits and dwellings of the middle ages, which may instruct us in the great comfort and prosperity of the working-classes of the present day. There is a very interesting chapter on the history of the English Bible, and its dangers and triumphs in an age of gloom. There are some amusing exhibitions of the mirth and jocularity of the court and convent, and some touching illustrations of the rewards of literature in mediæval times ; but we must forbear to enlarge on these, and on some other topics we had marked for extract, contenting ourselves with the following citation on the origin of an office, which, in our times, appears somewhat likely to fall into disuse, though it is now gracefully filled by Alfred Tennyson, a true poet and genuine patriot, who has justly described our country, not as it was, but as it now happily is, as—

> 'The land where, girt with friends or foes,
>     A man may say the thing he will.'

'Cicero tells us,' says our author, 'that in his time the poet's name was sacred, *sanctum poetæ nomen;*' we may almost say the same in relation to the monkish days. The origin of the poet laureate may be traced to the royal versifiers and minstrels of the middle ages; they who pleased by their verses or their chivalrous ballads, found generous encouragement at the court of royalty, or in the halls of the barons. When William the Conqueror divided with his followers the fruits of his victory, he rewarded Berdie, his court minstrel, with the gift of several parishes in the county of Gloucester; and by the laws of Wales, the royal minstrel was allowed a horse for his use, clothing and maintenance, besides his salary. Geoffry Chaucer was the son of a vintner of London. He was generously encouraged by John of Gaunt, and married the daughter of Pain Röec, king-at-arms in France, and sister to the wife of his patron. Richard II. granted to the poet an income of twenty pounds per annum for life; this has been considered by some as the origin of the poet-laureate; it is probable, however, as we have remarked above, that an appointment similar to laureateship existed at an earlier period. Henry VI. confirmed the grant of Richard, in the year 1399; and, in addition to the salary, Chaucer received a cask of wine, which was ordered to be delivered to him every year during his life.

The following remarks on the hearths and homes, or household comforts, of Old England, strike us as remarkably correct, and will give a good idea of the author's style :—

'The history of Old England has never yet been written; monkish pens have chronicled the deeds of kings and nobles, have extolled the piety of prelates and priests, and related those triumphs of arms which formed the delight and soul of ancient chivalry; we have a Froissart to tell us of the minutiæ of a court life; a Joselin of Brokeland to gossip with us about the cares and deprivations that chequered a conventual existence; but we have no writer of the middle ages who thought it consistent with the dignity of his clerkly calling to tell us of the life and household manners of the English people. We deeply regret this, because we are convinced, by the few scraps of intelligence which are incidentally found in old authors, that if it were possible to describe the hearths and homes of mediæval life, we should observe a striking contrast between the inconveniences of that age and the manifold blessings of the present; we should observe in such a contrast the full triumph and glory which science has achieved, and our ideas of the splendour and rude gorgeousness of merry Old England would dwindle into the most worthless tawdriness before the substantial comforts of our present homes.'—P. 307.

Here we must end, thanking Mr. Merryweather for his book, which, if not very profound, is still very interesting, and which, while not supported by a long array of authorities, is yet usually accurate, and congratulating our readers that we live in better times than those in which learning dimly shone in solemn cloisters and baronial halls. The noon-day splendour of revealed truth now penetrates the cottage and the court, and guides the working-man, as the nobleman, into the path of life. Science sheds its certain and increasing beams on the world of nature, dissipates the darkness of spectral illusions, and consigns to the depths of oblivion those superstitious impressions which haunted the steps and broke the repose of our forefathers. And in such advancement in general knowledge we discern no necessary tendency to scepticism. On the contrary, we are convinced that the philosophy which separates truth from error, by defining physical influence and distinguishing it from spiritual agency, and which places the offspring of superstition at an immeasurable distance from divine operation, must tend to vindicate the moral government of the universe, and confirm the intelligent faith of mankind in the statements of a written revelation, supported by unquestionable miracles. Under the influence of these enlightened principles, our country has gradually risen to its present dignified and influential position amongst the nations of the earth. The history of the past, and especially those portions of it which we have now slightly reviewed, serves to endear to us the present attainments of our land. The eye reposes on many a storied spot, the recollections suggested by ancient chroniclers furnish many a legend of marvel, while fancy evokes images of tenderness and wild romance, from every dell, and cave, and ruined castle. The monuments of Druids and Romans, of Saxons and Danes, stand before us clothed with the grandeur, and mellowed by the shadowy tints, of a remote antiquity ; while anticipations of the future struggle in vain for adequate utterance, and we can but say of our country, *Esto perpetua!*

ART. VI.—*Dahomey and the Dahomans; being the Journals of Two Missions to the King of Dahomey, and residence at his Capital in the years* 1849 *and* 1850. By Frederick E. Forbes, Commander R.N., F.R.G.S. In 2 vols. London: Longman and Co.

MUCH interest attaches to these volumes. They are full of information respecting a people but little known, and whose very name was unheard till the beginning of the last century. They present us, moreover, with a phase of civilization not frequently looked upon, and carry with them irresistible evidence of truthfulness, and of the diligent use made by their author of unusual opportunities for observation. In examining many modern works of travel, we are painfully struck with the poverty of incident displayed, and are at a loss to discover any worthy reason for their publication. The little that is told is spread out after the most approved fashion of book-making, and the style of the narrative is rather that of a man who has two volumes to write, than of one who has some important and interesting facts to disclose. The vanity of authorship, or the hope of one of its prizes, is the only motive which even candor can suppose to have operated in such a case. Now nothing of this kind is suggested by Lieutenant Forbes's volumes. He has something to tell which is worth hearing, and which no other man has told before him, something interesting to various classes —to the politician, the philosopher, the naturalist, the philanthropist, and the Christian. His work may be deficient in artistic skill. It may suggest that the author is somewhat unpractised in the use of his pen; but this fact, so far from detracting from its value, serves rather to strengthen confidence, by being in obvious keeping with his position. Minute accuracy in matters of style would have savored more of professional authorship than of naval rank and occupation. The work—and this is its great commendation—is brimful of facts, which are recorded in an inartificial style, and in as few words as consists with the author's mental habits.

Dahomey now constitutes the most powerful kingdom of Western Africa. It lies inland on the Guinea coast, between the two rivers Niger and Volta. On the west it is bounded by Ashantee, on the east by Yarriba, and on the north it is supposed to extend to the Kong mountains. The small states which constitute its southern boundary, and lie between it and the Bight of Benim, are now practically included in it, as Dahomey ' domineers over, if it does not possess, the entire land that lies between the coast and the bases of the Kong mountains.' It is difficult to ascertain with exactness the limits of Dahomey, but, according to our author, it may be estimated ' at about 180 miles from east to west, and nearly 200 from the sea coast at Whydah to its most northern boundary.' At the beginning of the seventeenth century, the united provinces of Dahomey and Fohee formed a kingdom scarcely larger than the county of Rutland. But the territories of Dahomey have subsequently been increased by conquest, though its population has not advanced in the same proportion. The slave-hunts which have enriched its exchequer have depopulated the districts added to its territory. The population of Dahomey does not exceed 200,000, of whom nine-tenths are slaves. The regular army is about 12,000, of whom 5,000 are women, but, on special occasions, nearly one quarter of the whole population is summoned to arms.

The condition and policy of Dahomey are of more than ordinary importance from its connexion with the slave-trade, which is carried on to an immense extent by its people, and constitutes the chief source of the royal revenue. It was with a view of contributing to the extinction of this barbarous traffic that Lieutenant Forbes, in conjunction with the well-known African traveller, Mr. Duncan, visited the King of Dahomey in 1849. The recent death of his adviser, Da Souza, might leave him, it was hoped, more open to appeals for the suppression ' of the slave-trade in his dominions.' The supposition was natural, and the mission well advised. It did not, however, accomplish its object in persuading the king to substitute agriculture and commerce for the sale of his people, but we have confidence in its future influence. Failing in its immediate purpose, it may yet constitute a link in that chain which will conduct the African mind to the more enlightened and humane conclusions of our own country. In the meantime, we are thankful to our author for the assistance he renders us in estimating the effects of the present order of things on the social and political condition of the African people. ' It is the object of the author,' he says, ' in giving publicity to the following Journals, to illustrate the dreadful slave-hunts and ravages, the annihilations and exterminations, consequent on this trade; and to bring prominently before the British public the sacred service they are rendering their fellow-men, in prosecuting their increasing efforts to allay those fearful horrors.'

The first part of the work, constituting in fact its *Introduction*, is occupied with descriptive sketches of the Dahomans and their  labours, in which much interesting information is communi-
The nation is essentially military, and the king despotic. :mer has risen to its present extent and power by a

slave-hunts, which are
the conquest of the
inhabitants. A slave-
proclaimed yearly, and no guage can depict the
horrors it involves. The object being to enrich the royal
exchequer, an indiscriminate slaughter is made of all whom
age or infancy render valueless as subjects of merchandise.
Those only are saved who can be sold to the slave-merchant,
or are fit for the service of the Dahoman chiefs or army. The

and
Let the slave-markets of
military levies of Dahom
out on its unoffending and

' Industry and agriculture are not encouraged. On the contrary,

war. They are fed and partly clothed, but receive no pay, except at
the scramble at the Customs. Prisoners and heads are purchased

recipients of the royal bounty.'—Vol. i. p. 21.

One of the most singular institutions of the country is the
existence of a large female army. We know not the source
whence this institution has been derived. Our information is
not sufficiently ample to enable us to trace it back, but we may
note the fact, and readily draw conclusions from it. The happiness as well as the purity of social life are greatly dependent on
the *gentleness* of womanhood,—her soft and plastic nature as
opposed to the hard and rigid temperament of man. We are
far from meaning by this phraseology to attribute inferiority or
weakness to the female character. It may, and frequently does,
exhibit either or both of these; but this is the consequence of
individual infirmity or of false training, not of generic qualities.
Each sex has its superiority. Their attributes are entirely
distinct, and the perfection of both is found in the harmony of
their special qualities, with the general intelligence which
pertains to them as rational beings. Feminine softness is,
therefore, perfectly compatible with mental superiority, and
cannot be displaced by masculine qualities without involving
much discomfort and vice. What, then, must be the social
and moral condition of a people where the female population
are trained to arms, and are subjected to all the brutalizing
influences of a marauding soldiery!

' It is rarely,' says Lieutenant Forbes, ' that Europeans are called upon to believe in the existence of Amazons,—fighting women prepared to do battle on all around, the terror of the neighbouring tribes, dressed in the attire of male soldiers, armed with muskets and swords. These sable ladies perform prodigies of valour, and not unfrequently, by a fortunate charge, save the honour of the male soldiers, by bearing down all before them, discovering themselves to the astonished and abashed prisoners to be women, exceeding their male coadjutors in cruelty and all the stronger passions.

' Excited by the hopes of reward, the evil passions of man are fearfully developed in Dahomey. Blood-money is the sure reward of valour, the price of blood the only fee ; and it matters not if the prisoner is brought alive to the monarch, as his reeking head is almost equally valuable. Without a trophy, such as a prisoner or a head, the soldier had better have been killed ; disgrace, and often condign punishment, follow to the defaulters of either sex.

' There is not a more extraordinary army in the known world than that of the military nation of Dahomey. The nucleus of the national power, the throne, is occupied at the pleasure of the militant people, who claim an annual war as a birthright. If, from want of courage, or any other insufficient reason, the monarch dares to dispute the will of his people, he, who could by serving the vitiated appetites of his soldiers have taken the lives of any, high or low, is as surely dethroned and murdered.

' In speaking of the two armies, let not the sensualist imagine that a Dahoman campaign is disgraced by a freedom it would almost be natural to suppose to belong to so curiously disposed an army, half male half female. On the contrary, the latter are in charge of eunuchs, officered by their own sex, and scorn the softer allurements of their nature. To use their own words, " they are men, not women ! their nature is changed ! they will conquer or die !" Such expressions could not be openly used, even as mere boasts, by women standing in a jealous position, emulating the most daring acts and achievements of man, unless fundamentally true; and with the certainty of being openly contradicted, and brought to shame, by their fellow-soldiers of the opposite sex. Such, then, are the Amazons, in whose chastity we may believe, when we bear in mind that the extreme exercise of one passion will generally obliterate the very sense of the others. The Amazons, while indulging in the excitement of the most fearful cruelties, forget the other desires of our fallen nature.'—*Ib.* pp. 132—134.

The wars, or rather slave-hunts, of Dahomey are annual. It rests with the king to determine in what direction his forces shall move, though he defers much to the wishes of his people. The particular city or district marked out for destruction is usually unknown till its confines are reached, when the fierce passions of the soldiery—male and female—are allowed unbridled indulgence. These expeditions commence in November or December, and every artifice which can be devised is employed to lull their victims into false security. On the return of the army in January, the king ' sacrifices largely, and gives liberal presents to the Fetish people, and, at the same time, purchases the prisoners and heads from his soldiers : the slaves are then sold to the slave-merchants, and their blood-money wasted in the ensuing Custom, Hwae-nŏoeewha, as the great annual feast is entitled in Dahoman parlance.'

The following will, probably, startle some of our readers, and we should be glad to doubt its correctness. We cannot, how-ever, do this, as we fear that the fact to which it relates has a much wider and more pernicious influence than is generally imagined. British capital may be traced where British subjects dare not be seen.

' These wars are

its neighbouring parts ; have they no higher parties on whom to lay the blame of their actions ? are these, the agents of larger houses, the instruments in the hands of parties who have other means of disposing of their 'goods, to bear the whole blame ? Truth is strange, but a truth it is, that the slave-trade is

slave-dealers, by British if British goods were no

them.

' Thus the discontinuance of trading with the slave-ports would afford most important aid in the reduction of the horrors of the slave trade. Except with the natives for palm-oil or other native produce, the system of trading with the interior kingdoms is in pawns, or domestic slaves, saleable on the sea-coast to the highest bidder. But with these pawns a dawning of civilization has illustrated that the African is not even by nature the brute he is generally believed to be. Should the pawn become a parent, neither the parent nor the child can be forcibly expatriated.'—*Ib.* pp. 139, 140.

Mention is subsequently made of José Martins, ' the greatest slave-dealer in all Africa,' who is said to carry on ' a vast trade in British vessels.' English merchants also are reported to be deeply implicated in the guilt of perpetuating the slave-system, as the following brief extract will show :—

' The system of domestic slavery is by no means confined to the Liberian portion of civilized Africa. Pawns (as the fashion terms the slaves on the Gold Coast) are received and held by Englishmen in-directly, and are to all intents and purposes their slaves. The plan adopted is this; the merchant takes unto himself a *femme du pays*, and she manages his establishment. Nor does he inquire how she hires his servants. Her mode is to accept pawns, *i.e.* purchase slaves, by receiving man, woman, and child in liquidation of debt; in other words, selling goods to native merchants, who, for convenience, leave slaves in payment. These pawns are as directly slaves to their master as any slaves in the United States, but cannot be sold out of the country. I myself am aware of one *femme du pays* of a British merchant being the owner of forty pawns, who perform the household and other services of the master, and are, except in name, his slaves. His money purchased them, and they obey his commands on pain of corporal punishment, and draw him to and fro in his carriage when taking exercise. How far is this removed from actual slavery?'—*Ib.* pp. 149, 150.

The construction and internal arrangements of their houses, with their social habits, are thus described :—

' Dahoman houses, from the palace to the farm, all are similar. Walls, either of clay or palm branches, enclose, according to the number of inmates, courts and houses of all sizes, made of clay, and thatched with grass.

' A bamboo bedstead or a few mats, some country pots and agricultural implements, and weapons, a loom of coarse material, besides the insignia of office (if a caboocer or head man), are all the furniture. A store in each house is provided with cloths, grain, foreign goods, &c., according to the wealth of the owner. Within the enclosure are all domestic animals, and invariably a dog. The diet is simple, consisting chiefly of messes of meat and vegetable, mixed with palm oil and pepper, with which is eaten a corn cake called kankee, or dab-a-dab. There is very little variety. A mixture of beans, peppers, and palm oil, is made into a cake, and sold to travellers; yams and cassada form the staples of food. Foreign liquors are scarce and expensive; and as palm wine is forbidden by the king, the chief drinks are a very palatable malt called pitto, and a sort of burgoo called ah-kah-sar. Drunkenness is not allowed; nor is there, except in Whydah, much opportunity for it. As a public example, the king kept a drunkard and fed him on rum, and exhibited him at the Customs, that his emaciated and disgusting appearance might shame his people from making beasts of themselves: this terrible example is dead.'—*Ib.* pp. 29, 30.

The religion of the Dahomans is a strange compound of degrading and brutalizing superstitions. The Fetish men and women—its priests and priestesses—have great power, and, like their prototypes of all ages, are careful to employ it for their own advantage. ' The Fetish of Abomey is the leopard, that of Whydah the snake.' Human sacrifices form part of their religious rites, but are often perpetrated in mere deference to the savage passions of the soldiery. ' There are private sacrifices all the year round. If a rich man dies, a boy and a girl are sacrificed to attend him in the next world. Thus, when Da Souza died, a boy and a girl were decapitated and buried with him, besides three men who were sacrificed on the beach at Whydah.' The cruelty of Paganism is attested by a thousand facts.   Dreamers and sneering scoffers may depict scenes of Arcadian peace and brotherhood *without* the limits of

erected with a
ing for the blo
in flat baskets

ness so near death.   It did not seem real, yet it soon proved frightfully so.   One hellish monster placed his finger to the eyes of a victim who hung down his head, but, finding no moisture, drew upon himself the ridicule of his fiendish coadjutors.'

Our countrymen, of course, declined to be present at the sacrifice, and descending from the platform, heard the mob yelling fiercely, and calling upon the king to feed them—they were hungry?   What followed is thus described:

' As we reached our seats, a fearful yell rent the air.   The victims were held high above the heads of their bearers, and the naked ruffians thus acknowledged the munificence of their prince.   Silence again ruled, and the king made a speech, stating that of his prisoners he gave a portion to his soldiers, as his father and grandfather had done before.   These were Attahpahms.   Having called their names, the one nearest was divested of his clothes, the foot of the basket placed on the parapet, when the king gave the upper part an impetus, and the victim fell at once into the pit beneath.   A fall of upwards of twelve feet might have stunned him, and before sense could return the head was cut off, and the body thrown to the mob, who, now armed with clubs and branches, brutally mutilated and dragged it to a distant pit, where it was left as food for the beasts and birds of prey.   After the third victim had thus been sacrificed, the king retired, and the chiefs and slave-dealers completed the deed which the monarch blushed to finish.

' There was not even the poor excuse that these men had committed a crime, or even borne arms against the Dahomans,   No; they were murdered, innocent men, at least as far as their barbarous tyrant knew; and if not, may God forgive them in the world to come !

'As we descended the ladder, we came on another scene of this tragedy. Each in the basket in which the victim had sat a few moments before, lay the grizzly bleeding heads, five on one side, six on the other. We could not have expected any mercy would have been shown, and, therefore, were prepared for this spectacle.'—Vol. ii. pp. 52, 53.

We turn from these disgusting exhibitions, which we would gladly have passed over altogether, had we not felt that such things ought to be known, in order, amongst other reasons, to induce becoming gratitude for our own position. It is a sickly sentimentalism which refuses to look on what disgraces and pollutes large regions of our world, under the plea that such scenes are repulsive and demoralizing. There is nothing healthy and manful in this. Woe would have been to our world, had it been the temper of Paul, Peter, and James, of Luther and Zuinglius, of Whitefield and Wesley, or of the founders of modern missions. We must know the actual state of the world in order duly to feel the necessity which exists for exertion, and to adapt our measures to the condition and requirements of those whose benefit we seek. Such things as Lieut. Forbes recounts, are of daily occurrence in the pagan world, and we must view them in all their enormity in order duly to appreciate the mercies bestowed on ourselves. Still we gladly recur to other topics, which are supplied in ample measure by our author.

One of the singular customs of Dahomey, is the presentation of a *cane* as the symbol of good-will, or the assurance of protection. This is perpetually taking place, and though wearing an aspect somewhat ludicrous, is not more so, in reality, than some habits with which we are familiar. On the 10th October, 1849, our author, then at Whydah, received ' a gold-headed Malacca cane, which,' he tells us, ' was explained to be my protection;' the bearers of this mystical symbol, adding, ' that his Majesty commanded Mr. Duncan and myself to repair to Abomey at our earliest convenience.' Our two countrymen rode in hammocks, and had abundant opportunity of noticing the country through which they passed. ' In this forest,' says Lieutenant Forbes, referring to one of gigantic trees, abounding with monkeys, ' the absence of all birds by a freak of nature, was supplied by thousands of butterflies of every hue, and most pleasing to the eyes, whilst the air was redolent of the perfume of a thousand flowers as beautiful as they were fragrant.' At noon our travellers arrived at Alladah, a city twenty-four miles from Whydah, and immediately felt that they had entered Dahomey. Revolting memorials of the savage tyranny which prevailed were visible in the shape of human skulls and jaw-bones. ' With the shades of evening came flights of vampire bats that almost darkened the sky, and swarms of Turkey buzzards, so ravenous and daring that they almost fought with our servants in the court-yard for the entrails of the fowls. During the day the bats may be seen hanging in clusters on the tall cotton-trees, where the Turkey buzzards sit and sleep away their repletion, to which their active duties as the scavengers of town and country subject them. Not a scrap of animal remains escapes them, whether fresh or swarming with insect life.'

On the 14th, they proceeded towards the capital, through a beautiful park-like country, studded with magnificent sycamore trees 130 feet high. ' The variety of flowers was remarkable, and, together with the brilliant and varied colours of the butter-flies, rendered the scene at once fragrant and beautiful. No one that has not travelled in Dahomey will believe the beauty of its scenery.' The journey to Abomey was completed in something less than four days, and the account given of the city is far from flattering. No visitor, we are told, can enter it ' without a sensation of disappointment in the want of grandeur, and disgust at the ghastly ornaments of its gateway.'

' It is entered by six gates, which are simply clay walls crossing the road, with two apertures, one reserved for the king, the other a thoroughfare for his subjects. In each aperture are two human skulls; and on the inside a pile of skulls, human, and of all the beasts of the field, even to the elephant's. Besides these six gates, the ditch, which is of an oval form, branches off, at each side of the north-west gate, to the north and north-west, and over each branch is a similar gate-way, for one only purpose—to mislead an enemy in a night attack. In the centre of the city are the palaces of Dange-lah-cordeh and Agrim-gomeh, adjoining ; on the north stands the original palace of Dahomey ; about these, and to the south gate, are houses, the most conspicuous of which are those of the ministers. In front of Agrim-gomeh is an ex-tensive square, in which are the barracks and a high shed or palaver house, a saluting battery of fifteen guns, and a stagnant pond. Just inside the south-east gate (the Cannah) are a saluting battery and pond, and numerous blacksmiths' shops. The roads or streets are in good order ; and though there are not any shops, the want of them is sup-plied by two large markets—Ah-jah-ee, to the eastward of the central palace, at once a market, parade, and sacrificial ground ; and Hung-jooloh, just outside the south gate. Besides these are several smaller markets, the stalls of which are all owned, and are generally attended by women, the wives of all classes and orders, from the miegans to the blacksmiths. The fetish houses are numerous, and ridiculously orna-mented. Cloths are manufactured within the palaces and houses. The only other manufacture is in a pottery, which, with a dye-house, is a royal monopoly, inasmuch as the royal wives work them ; and none

may approach the factory.  Within the city are large waste lands and
many cultivated farms.   There are no regular streets, and it is difficult
for a European to imagine himself in the capital of a large country, as
all the houses are surrounded by high red clay walls, which enclose
large forest trees, besides orange, banana, and other fruit trees.  All the
houses are low and thatched, and one only, in the palace of Dange-lah-
cordeh, and one in that of Cumassee, can boast of two stories.  Leaving
the south gate, the traveller passes through the town of Beh-kon,
occupied principally by the palaces of Cumassee and Abgon-groo, and
the houses of the ministers ; whilst from the south-west gate the road
leads to another royal palace.  The Dahoman capital is, in fact,
entirely unprotected by its walls and gates, and built in the most ill-
judged of positions for so large a city.  For a distance of five miles on
every side there is no water.'—Vol. i. pp. 68—71.

Their reception by the king was strikingly illustrative of the
manners of the country.  Boh-peh, the governor of the capital,
first met them ' dressed in a country cloth wrapped round his
body, a slouched hat, necklaces of coral and other beads, and
armed with a handsome sword. . .  ' Arrived,' says Lieutenant
Forbes, ' in front of our position, he bowed, and then marched,
from right to left, round our seats three times, completing each
circuit with a low obeisance.  On his third round he discharged
three muskets and danced a short measure, then advanced and
shook hands, and seated himself on his stool of office, which its
bearer had placed on my right hand.'  These and other equally
graceful ceremonies having been performed, our countrymen
were presented to his Dahoman Majesty, in a style which Lieutenant Forbes thus describes :—

' The square of the palace was filled with armed people, seated on
their hams, the polished barrels of their Danish muskets standing up
like a forest.  Under a thatched gateway was the king, surrounded by
his immediate wives; while on each side sat the Amazons, all in
uniform, armed, and accoutred ; and in the centre of the square squatted
the males.   Hundreds of banners and umbrellas enlivened the scene,
and a constant firing from great guns and small arms increased the
excitement.

' When near the king's seat we came to a halt, while the caboceers
bowed down and kissed the dust.  Passing before the throne, we bowed
and made the circuit of the square three times, the caboceers pros-
trating, and ourselves repeating our obeisances each time that we passed
the royal seat.   On the third time, the ministers and caboceers formed
a line to the king's position ; and, as we stept from our hammocks, the
king, who had been reclining, rose, and forty discordant bands struck
up a quick step, whilst guns were fired, and all shouted except the
ministers and caboceers, who prostrated themselves and threw dirt on
their heads as we advanced and shook hands with the king.  His
Dahoman Majesty, King Gézo, is about forty-eight years of age, good-
looking, with nothing of the negro feature, his complexion wanting

several shades of being black ; his appearance commanding, and his countenance intellectual, though stern in the extreme. That he is proud there can be no doubt, for he treads the earth as if it were honoured by its burden. Were it not for a slight cast in his eye, he would be a handsome man. Contrasted with the gaudy attire of his ministers, wives, and cabooceers (of every hue, and laden with coral, gold, silver, and brass ornaments), the king was plainly dressed, in a loose robe of yellow silk slashed with satin stars and half-moons, Mandingo sandals, and a Spanish hat trimmed with-gold lace; the only ornament being a small gold chain of European manufacture.

'Taking our seats on chairs facing the royal mat, we entered into a complimentary conversation, the king asking many questions about our sovereign and England, and afterwards of Messrs. Freeman, Cruikshanks, and Wynniett, who had preceded us at his court. The ministers were then introduced by name, and we all drank together. Next, about forty cabooceers were similarly introduced.'—*Ib.* pp. 75—77.

'We now took leave ; the king, in compliment, seeing us on our road. As he stept forth, the whole crowd rose as a man, fired off their muskets, and shouted; the din and noise was consequently terrific. They then closed round the king, whilst the bands played a quick step. When we had arrived at the end of the square he took leave, shaking hands and snapping alternate fingers and thumbs thrice. The mayo's retinue continued firing, shouting, dancing, and singing all the way to our residence in the mayo's enclosure—a small neat house in a retired part, having two orange-trees and a kitchen enclosed in a yard, and hence private.

'No king could have been more civil or more condescending; yet, in all it was observable, that the visit of white men, and show of reception, amused his people and enhanced his own greatness in their ideas. In the journal of the customs the power of this king will be illustrated : suffice it here to say, as a military chief he is feared by all his neighbours, and the terror of his name is the strongest tie he has, and effects far more than the strength of his army ever could. Africans have but a poor means of counting; and, although their memory is retentive, cannot retain numbers, and beyond a thousand they have but little idea. These soldiers being yearly at war, have gained a fame that, if fairly tried, would soon be found wanting.'—*Ib.* pp. 79—81.

The *lions* of Whydah are the snake fetish house and the market. The former is, in fact, a temple built round a huge cotton-tree, in which many snakes of the boa species are allowed to disport themselves. If any of these wander to a distance, the services of a fetish man or woman are engaged to conduct them back, and so debased is the popular superstition that all who meet it bow down and kiss the dust. Morning and evening the people prostrate themselves before this snake temple, and we need not, therefore, wonder that their habitations are full of cruelty. This reference to the snake-worship of Whydah leads us to notice the account given of one of the most deadly of the reptile species. The statement confirms our general impression that, as the knowledge of natural phenomena extends, simple but most efficacious remedies will be discovered for the numerous ills under which humanity labors.

' Among the many species of reptiles, the cobra capella is the most dangerous. Yet, although we consider the bite of the cobra deadly, the native has an infallible cure for it, but those who are initiated are jealous of their knowledge. One of my hammock-men had been bitten three times, and his father was a doctor. Walking one day through some long grass, I pointed to his bare legs, and hinted at his danger. " None," said he ; " my father picks some grass, and if, on the same day as the bite, his decoction is applied, the wound heals at once." Strange as this may appear, it did not seem so to me, having witnessed the fights in India between the cobra and the mongoose. The cobra has always the advantage at first; and the mongoose, apparently vanquished by the deadly poison, is no sooner bitten than he retreats as far from his enemy as possible, but on devouring some small herb which grows wild, and is easily found, he revives, renews the attack, and conquers.'— *Ib.* pp. 164, 165.

There are many other points in the history and habits of the Dahoman people which might be illustrated from the volumes before us, but our space is exhausted. We must, therefore, refer our readers to the work itself, and if our extracts have not sufficed to induce the desire of further and more intimate acquaintance, we despair of producing that effect by anything we can say. It would be easy to suggest points on which Lieutenant Forbes might have been more explicit in his statements, or have borne more constantly in mind the ignorance of his readers touching the matters dealt with. We have no disposition, however, for this. So much is told, and the style of the narrative is so genuinely honest, that we tender him our best thanks, and shall be glad to meet him again on ground with which he is equally familiar.

ART. VII.—1. *Manchester Examiner and Times, Nov.* 2, 1850. *Conference at which the 'Lancashire Public School Association' was converted into the ' National Public School Association.'*

2. *Local Education. Instructions for the Draft of a Bill to Promote Education in the Municipal Boroughs of Manchester and Salford. Report of the Sub-Committee.*

3. *Westminster Review, January,* 1851.

4. *Manchester Guardian. Letters of Sir James P. Kay Shuttleworth, Bart., on the Plans of Secular and Local Education.*

5. *' Leeds Mercury.' ' The Secular Education Association,' Nov.* 9, 16, 23, 30; *Dec.* 14, 1850.

6. *The Economist. 'National Education,' Feb.* 1, 8, 22, 1851.

7. *Minutes of the Committee of Council on Education,* 1848-49-50. 2 *vols.*

THE intellectual activity and benevolence of the age are in nothing more conspicuous than in the zeal displayed for the extension of education. There is, perhaps, not a year of the present century that has not witnessed a considerable increase in the public institutions for the training of the young. Much has been done by enlightened individuals in the founding of schools; still more by the combined efforts of those who have organized themselves into societies. Every class has been benefited, from the highest, who avail themselves of the University and the College, to the very lowest, who are allured out of the streets into the Ragged School;—every age, from the lisping infant that receives instruction in the guise of amusement, to the young man preparing for the learned professions;—every religious community, from the Churchmen who have erected the vast structure of the National Society, to the humblest sect of Dissenters who support their own Sunday-schools, and combine with others to obtain the advantage of day-schools;—and each sex, not merely in regard to the elements of knowledge, but to some extent in the industrial qualifications that enable the man to win his family's bread, and the woman to keep her husband and children decently clad. Institutions are also continually rising up that carry on the means of instruction from childhood to youth and mature age; philosophical and literary societies, with the advantages of lectures, libraries, and museums,—Mechanics' Institutes, with lectures, libraries, reading-rooms, and evening classes,—and many other associations under different names, but of a like character. To improve the quality of education, Normal Schools have been established by most of the great educational societies, and a College of Preceptors by private schoolmasters. And at once to excite and gratify the intellectual appetite that has been created, cheap literature, in an endless variety of attractive forms, and with much substantial excellence, from the standard volume to the weekly tract, is presented, not merely by enterprising publishers, but by numerous societies, having in view either the general spread of knowledge or the still moré important interests of religion.

To all these efforts and enterprises we offer our heartiest welcome. Whether they spring from individual aspiration after improvement, or from parental anxiety for the welfare of children, or from the benevolent desire to do good, or from the self-interest of authors, publishers, schoolmasters, and lecturers, or from the zeal of Christian communities for the spread of truth, or from a sense of the civil and political advantages of popular education, they are all working together to ameliorate and elevate the condition of society. We do not say that there are no base elements mingled with the good. In the growth of knowledge, as in all human things, there are drawbacks that prevent the benefit from being unmixed. These incidental evils are serious enough to call for constant vigilance and activity on the part of the friends of truth. But it does not admit of a moment's doubt, that, on the whole, we have made prodigious advances during the nineteenth century, in every branch of true Christian civilization. The year 1851, when compared with the year 1801, is as the Palace of Glass when compared with the houses built under the *régime* of the window duty. The very creation of that palace for so magnificent a purpose is sufficient evidence of the improvement.

The best feature of the new institutions for promoting knowledge is, that (with slight exceptions) they have sprung spontaneously from the people themselves. They are the natural products of healthy seeds, as well as themselves the germ of more abundant harvests. They are the offspring of freedom, as well as destined to be the parents of a higher and better freedom. They are not conferred by the grace of enlightened despots ; or imposed by politic governments, which seek to retain under their own direction the intelligence they create; or dictated by legislatures, with the apparatus of coercion. They are *our own*. They are from us, and for us. As Englishmen, we have something of parental pride in them ; for our own blood circulates in their veins ; we have watched over their infancy, and guided their youth ; they are made in our image ;

they inherit our temper.　Free England has educated her free educators.　Nor is this only a matter of patriotic complacency. There are inestimable advantages in the natural and spontaneous action of the people for their own improvement; of which it may suffice here to mention two—namely, that, in the first place, it strengthens that self-reliance which is the main prop of a country's liberties; and next, that it promotes the exercise of a kindly influence by the more enlightened classes among those who are less enlightened: thus binding together the different strata of society by a living sympathy beyond the power of storms to separate them.

There are, however, educational projects brought forth in this

and of danger.　Impatient of that gradual progress which is according to nature, and eager to force a sudden development of education to the largest conceivable extent, many able and honest men are ready to call in the aid of legislative coercion, overlooking the evils that must necessarily attend the introduction of that element.　Our statesmen
the educational *cacoethes*.　On the
leather,' they think there is nothing
that a great part of the work of Re
the mis
religion
ment.
religion and trade, we are now in
education.　To our minds, ancient failures combine with modern successes to teach the great lesson of self-dependence.

We have frequently expressed our opinion, that the 'Minutes of Council' of 1846 and 1847, though certainly proceeding from sincere friends of education, were founded on false principles, and involved danger to liberty and a corrupting of the public sense of independence, as well as grievous injustice to Dissenters. It was made an indispensable condition of a grant of money to any school under those Minutes, that there should be *religious teaching* in that school.　By a Minute of 1847, special provision was made for grants to Roman Catholic schools.　The effect of the system is, that religious teaching of every kind is paid for by public money.　The Protestant and the Catholic, the Evangelical and the Tractarian, the Episcopalian, Presbyterian, Wesleyan, and Unitarian, are all at this moment deriving the means of propagating their respective doctrines from the same exchequer; and every man who pays taxes is thus made a contributor not only to religious teaching, but to the indiscriminate endowment of all sects.　It is superfluous to say that this is a violation of the principle of Nonconformists, which forbids them to receive money raised by taxation for the teaching of religion.* But it is equally a violation of the principle repeatedly asserted in the strongest terms by leading members of the Episcopalian, Wesleyan, and Presbyterian bodies, as well as by all Nonconformist sects, that the indiscriminate endowment by the State of all religions 'tends to destroy, in popular estimation, the difference between truth and error, and to degrade religion into a mere engine of political government.' Such were the words of a petition unanimously agreed upon at a meeting of twelve hundred Deputies from all parts of Great Britain and Ireland, including members of every Protestant sect, held in London on the first of May, 1845, to oppose the grant to Maynooth College; when the petitioners also declared that they 'objected to the measure and policy, not from any feelings of asperity and bigotry, but from a solemn and religious conviction that they cannot, without offending against Divine truth, consent to be thus made partakers in the teaching and spread of Roman Catholic doctrine.'

It was always, in our estimation, the greatest objection to the Minutes of Council, that they held out a perpetual bribe to the abandonment of sacred principles, and gently insinuated, through a measure of education, the system of universal religious endowment. Our fears have been too well justified by the result. The Presbyterian churches of Scotland and the leading Wesleyans of England, as well as the members of the Establishment, have been seduced by the grants of money; and from the moment that they received money themselves, they, of course, abandoned the opposition which they had so long and so earnestly given to the granting of public money to Roman Catholic schools. Accepting endowments themselves, they could not, with common decency, object to the endowment of any and every other form of religion. There are some even among professed Noncon-

---

* This principle was declared in the clearest and strongest manner, at one of the most important meetings ever held of Congregational ministers and laymen, more than three years before the Minutes of Council were published —namely, the meeting in the Congregational Library, on the 13th December, 1843. The resolution was drawn by that wise and able man, the late Rev. Algernon Wells, Secretary of the Congregational Union, and, after long and careful deliberation, was carried unanimously, as follows :—

' That this meeting, utterly repudiating, on the strongest grounds of Scripture and conscience, the receipt of money raised by taxation, and granted by Government, for sustaining the Christian religion, feels bound to apply this principle no less to the work of religious education; and considering that the education given by the Congregational churches must be religious education, advises most respectfully, but most earnestly, that no government aid be received by them for schools established in their own connexion; and that all funds confided to the disposal of the Central Committee in aid of schools be granted only to schools sustained entirely by voluntary contributions.'

formists, who have received public money for their schools. Yet nothing is more evident than that such conduct implies an abandonment, both of the principle that condemns the State-endowment of religion, and of that which condemns the indiscriminate endowment of all religions. We honour the conscientious stedfastness of those who continue to resist the golden seduction, even when the desertion of others aggravates the injustice they suffer; and we look upon them as the only consistent opponents of that continental policy which has made such inroads upon us. They alone can, with a good grace, oppose the endowment of the Roman Catholic priests in the United Kingdom and the colonies, and the taking of the clergy of every sect into State pay.

Whilst the Government system inflicts so much hardship upon Dissenters, whom it taxes for the schools of all other sects when they cannot accept money for their own, it is silently pervading the country with a governmental influence. School committees, masters, pupil apprentices, and stipendiary monitors, are taught to look up continually to Government inspectors, whose fiat decides whether or not they shall receive the grant which has become essential to them.* The system is manifestly liable to abuse, either on one side or the other; it may either become so lax as to be of no value for purposes of inspection, or it may be so stringent as to annoy the school committees, and rather to repress than to stimulate the zeal for education. It would be unreasonable, indeed, to suppose that a great amount of money can be dispensed yearly without doing any good. It is quite possible, in England as in Prussia, to conduct the

---

* It is the complaint of the 'Westminster Review' that the influence of the Church and the clergy over the National Schools is greatly increased, owing to the appointment of none but clerical inspectors, the power of the Archbishops over the inspectors, and the great concessions made by the Committee of Council to the Church in regard to the managers of the schools being church communicants. The 'Westminster' also shows, that the Committee of Council, in order to purchase the co-operation of the British and Foreign School Society, the Wesleyans and the Scotch Churches, (he might have added the Catholics,) have consented that no inspector of their schools shall be appointed without the 'full concurrence' of the committees of those respective bodies. It was distinctly pointed out, on the first publication of the Minutes of Council, that their working must necessarily increase the power of the clergy as well as of the Government. We are not surprised to find the 'Westminster' declaring that 'the Committee of Council has alienated many of its original supporters. It has spread the seeds of distrust of Government interference in education throughout the country; and the object for which it has sacrificed credit, character, and consistency—the hearty co-operation of the Church in the extension of secular instruction with religious has not been obtained.'—P. 408.

'The Committee have piled up obstruction upon obstruction to the cause of progress.'—P. 409.

whole education of the country under State management. This may certainly be done, and able officers may be employed to superintend the work. Whether the results would be equally conducive to the interests of liberty and religion, equally favourable to the spirit and character of the nation, or, in the end, equally advantageous to education itself, is, however, a very different question. To our judgment, it appears that there would be all the difference that there is between a nation trained under despotic, and under free, institutions.

We see little reason to believe that the Minutes of Council have worked so as to increase the number of schools or of scholars. In some cases, it is probable that a grant equal to a third or a fourth of the whole cost may have encouraged the building of schools; but the differences between the Committee of Council and the National Society must have had an opposite tendency; and perhaps nearly as many new schools would have been built if nothing had been granted from the public purse. The number of schools to which annual grants were 'conditionally awarded' in the year ending 31st October, 1850, in augmentation of the teachers' salaries and for apprentices, was 1,361; of which 973 were National or Church schools; 181 British, Wesleyan, or other schools not connected with the Church; 32 Roman Catholic schools; 82 Scotch Kirk schools; and 93 Free Church and other schools in Scotland. Of these schools, many may not receive the grants 'conditionally awarded,' owing to their non-fulfilment of 'conditions.' This statement does not appear to us to show great progress, considering the whole number of public schools. In England alone, the official return made by the National Society for 1846-7 shows that there were in that year 17,015 day-schools connected with the Church, of which 3,407 were dames' schools; the remainder, viz. 13,608, (so far as we can judge from the return,) were public schools. There are, also, some thousands of British and other schools not connected with the Church. The number of public day-schools in England can hardly be less than 17,000. Deducting 186 schools in Scotland from the 1,361 schools which last year had annual grants 'conditionally awarded' by the Committee of Council, there were 1,186 schools in England entitled to such grants; and this is a small proportion out of 17,000 schools.

From some cause or causes, the system is yet very far indeed from general; only about *one-fourteenth* of the whole number of public schools are in a condition to receive annual grants; and whatever the causes may be, they make the system a partial one and, of course, unfair in proportion as it is partial. We suspect that, if the system is to become general, it must be made more liberal in the pecuniary grants, and less troublesome to the school committees. But every step in that direction will increase the cost to the nation; and if the whole of the public schools should be brought into the receipt of grants, the Committee of Council will have to figure in the budget of the Chancellor of the Exchequer for between one and two millions sterling per annum.

Dissatisfied with the inefficient and unjust working of the Minutes of Council, a number of gentlemen in Manchester, about three years since, formed a project of their own for the county of Lancaster, and established an association called the ' Lancashire Public School Association.' At a conference, held in Manchester, on the 30th and 31st of October, 1850, it was determined to extend the objects of the association to the whole country, and to call it the ' National Public School Association.' The Lancashire Association put forth an elaborate plan; but the National Association, though forming branches in various places, has, as yet, cautiously abstained from entering into practical details, and has merely given to its members and the public a general definition of the objects, in the following resolution of committee :—

' BASIS OF THE ASSOCIATION.—The National Public School Association is formed to promote the establishment by law, in England and Wales, of a system of *free schools*, which, supported by *local rates*, and managed by *local committees*, especially elected for that purpose by the rate-payers, shall impart *secular instruction only*, leaving to parents, guardians, and religious teachers, the inculcation of doctrinal religion ; to afford opportunity for which, the schools shall be closed at stated times each week.'

Fallacy lurks in generals ; and until the details of the plan are published, it is as impossible to judge of the working of the system, as it would be to judge of a building from seeing the basement story. The above ' basis ' might have perfectly suited the bill introduced by Mr. W. J. Fox into the House of Commons last session ; but that bill, though professing to rest on local rates and management, gave such absolute power to the Committee of Council on Education over the local managers and over the rate-payers and their money, that Lord John Russell justly described it as follows (in the debate of the 17th of April, 1850) :—

' The bill was a measure *evidently despotic* in its mode of operation ; it was clearly opposed to all those principles which the English people had long been accustomed to enjoy.'

' The bill, in the face of all experience, would impose a new system upon the people of this country—a change which would have the effect of *destroying altogether the schools already existing.*'

'Here was a power given to the Committee of the Privy Council, in a few words, *to force upon people the establishment of a school according to this scheme and form, and to levy such rates and taxes as the Committee of the Privy Council might think it necessary to decide.* Why, here was a power, which, he must repeat, was a *despotic power,* and which he, for one, was unwilling to grant.'

'If Parliament did not make a grant, the power of the Privy Council ceased; but by this bill a power of taxation was given, which, if the calculation made by the noble lord (Ashley) were well-founded, amounted to 3,000,000*l.* If it were only 1,000,000*l.,* instead of 3,000,000*l.,* it was still *an enormous power of taxation,* and that for an object which might not be asked for by any parish, and *not desired by the people who would have to pay for it.*'

Such were the incredible invasions of liberty contemplated in the scheme of the honourable member for Oldham: invasions enough to make the hair of any true friend of freedom stand on end. Yet there were actually fifty-eight members of the House of Commons who voted for the second reading, including many who consider themselves Liberals of the first distinction. But it seems to be of the nature of the educational *cacoethes* to blind its subjects to the claims both of civil and religious liberty; for the plan of the Lancashire Association—the prototype of the National Public School Association—gave to a 'County Board' powers just as great as Mr. Fox proposed to give to the Committee of the Privy Council. It proposed that a County Board of twelve men, *nominated in the first instance by Parliament,* and of whom only the two worst attenders were to retire annually, should have the power of drawing up *a plan of education,* and *enforcing it in every school* in the county,—of *sanctioning all the school-books* to be used in *every* school,—if any parish should neglect to establish schools, *to do it of their own authority,* and *to levy rates on the parish for their support,*—to appoint three examiners, *without whose certificate no person should be employed as schoolmaster,*—and to appoint a commission of nine individuals, 'no two of whom should be members of the same religious denomination,' to make a selection of extracts from the Scriptures for the use of the schools, and *any one of whom should have power to exclude any passage to which he might object !*

If such a scheme had been drawn up in Austria or Prussia, under their most absolute sovereigns, or in France under Napoleon, it would have appeared in character. But that it should proceed from Lancashire Liberals in the middle of the nineteenth century, is what we could not possibly have believed, if we had not had the documents in our own hands. The intolerable quackery of enforcing one uniform system of education on the schools of a county comprising two millions of people, and of committing the supreme power over the education of such masses to twelve men appointed by Parliament, together with the power to establish as many schools as they please, and to levy as many rates as they please on every parish, without the consent of the rate-payers, or any check whatsoever, is absolutely astounding. Nor less alarming is the language of the agents employed to lecture on behalf of the ' *National* Public School Association.' For, on the 19th of November last, at a public meeting in the town of Bradford, Dr. Watts, of Manchester, an agent employed by the association, used the following expressions, unchecked, in the presence and company of the Rev. W. M'Kerrow, one of the original committee, who drew up the Lancashire plan, as reported in the ' Bradford Observer' :—

'If, in this matter of education, they could demonstrate which was the right road, the best way, if they wanted the unwilling to go along, was *to put them into the traces, and drive them along !*'

' They were trying to convince the public that the system was a right one ; and if they could prove that it was a right one, so that the majority obtained an enactment for it, *it would be right to thrust it down the throats of the minority by any and every means*' ! ! !

So strangely do extremes meet, that the language of this Socialist expounder of the scheme of secular education would, in spirit and principle, justify the conduct of the Holy Inquisition in its most naked tyranny over conscience. The rights of individuals, the rights of minorities, and the rights of conscience, are set at nought ; and a dragooning spirit is indulged, that would entirely destroy both civil and religious liberty.

The most distinguishing feature of the Lancashire plan, which is also adopted in the ' basis ' of the ' National Public School Association,' is, that the schools established under it are to ' *impart secular instruction only.*' The object of this restriction is, to avoid the two objections lying against the plan of the Minutes of Council, on the score of teaching religion, and of endowing all religions indiscriminately. But in avoiding one error, the secular plan falls into an opposite and still more objectionable error. It is an error for the civil magistrate to teach religion in our schools ; but the proper remedy is—*to exclude the agency of the magistrate,* not to exclude the teaching of religion.

By the common consent of all the religious bodies which have taken any interest in education, it has been declared to be the duty of those who give education to blend religious and moral with general instruction. Nothing can more clearly prove that this was the unanimous view of the Congregationalists in 1843, than the resolution we have quoted as passed at the educational conference held in the Congregational Library. The point was not argued as though any doubt could be entertained upon it ; but it was assumed as beyond controversy. ' Considering that *the education given by the Congregational churches* MUST *be* RELIGIOUS *education,*' are the words of Mr. Algernon Wells's resolution, unanimously passed. The National Society implies religious training in its title, which describes the society as being ' for promoting the education of the poor in the principles of the Established Church.' The British and Foreign School Society has always prominently defined its object to be ' scriptural education ;' and though it was required that no peculiar religious tenets should be taught, it was among its fundamental rules that ' the lessons for reading shall consist of extracts from the Holy Scriptures.' The more modern ' Home and Colonial Infant and Juvenile School Society' declares, in its second fundamental law, that its object was ' the improvement and general extension of the Infant-school system on Christian principles, as such principles are set forth and embodied in the doctrinal articles of the Church of England.' The Wesleyans laid a religious basis for their schools, stating that they were founded on ' an increased conviction of the paramount importance of giving a scriptural and decidedly religious education to young persons.' We scarcely need say, that the Church of Scotland and the Free Church require decided and distinct religious education, and universally teach the Westminster Assembly's Catechism. The ' Ragged Schools ' were established, among other ends, ' to encourage Bible-classes, and to assist the old as well as the young in the study of the word of God.' It may be remembered that Sir James Kay Shuttleworth, in his semi-official pamphlet, ' The School in its Relations to the State, the Church, and the Congregation,' said :—' According to the conscientious convictions of the religious bodies of this country, the school is a part of the machinery of a Christian congregation : . . . few or no schools were established on a purely secular basis : the whole elementary education of England tended towards a religious organization.' Lord John Russell and the Marquis of Lansdowne stated in Parliament, that they could not assent to any system of public grants which did not require religious teaching in the schools assisted.[*]

The *fact*, therefore, is undeniable, that the combination of

---

[*] Lord John Russell's declaration in his speech of the 19th April, 1847, alluding to Mr. Roebuck's argument for a plan of secular education, is memorable :—' To such a scheme I have the most decided objection. Under such a system the State would take cognizance, in schools set up by itself, of one-half only, and that not the most important half, of the instruction to be given to the children therein educated. I think myself that to omit any inculcation of the duties of religion—to omit instructing the children in the principles of love to God and love to their neighbour—would be a grave, a serious, and an irreparable fault.'

religious with secular instruction is *the rule of English education*, and is practised by all the societies hitherto formed for the educating of the poor. The reason of this rule seems to us clear and strong. Whether our object in training the children of the poor is to promote their welfare as individuals, or the welfare of the society of which they form the component parts, it is of unspeakably higher importance that they should grow up with sound moral and religious principles, than that they should possess the mere elements of secular knowledge. Now the chief training-place of the child during the period of life that mainly decides its character is the school. There it is for five or six hours of every week-day (except holidays); that is, nearly as long as it would be wise or practicable to tax the mind of a child for any serious object. If the whole of this precious time were to be devoted to the acquisition of letters, of grammar, of writing, arithmetic, and geography—and no attention were paid to the manifestation of character, and the development of passion—no lessons given for the government of the child's conduct to parents, to teachers, and to schoolfellows—no pains taken to inculcate the principles of truth, honesty, and kindness—and, above all, no instruction imparted in regard to the child's higher nature and paramount duty, his immortal destiny, the chief end of his existence, his Maker, his Saviour, the divine revelation given to guide him through his earthly pilgrimage—if such were to be the nature of his training, so inferior the things taught, and so vast and transcendant the things omitted to be taught, we should think it the saddest disproportion, and the utmost conceivable folly and injustice, on the part of those responsible for his education.

But the secular plan distinctly professes to give moral training, though with a peculiar limitation. In the words of Dr. Hodgson, at the Manchester Educational Conference, ' This association professes to qualify children for *the duties of this life ;* it professes to do *nothing beyond that.*' Mr. Holyoake, a lecturer and writer, whose leading object, avowed in the most open manner, is to establish the doctrine of atheism, said, at the same conference :—' George Combe had usefully defined " secular education" as being that kind of education, *the issues of which can be tested by the experience of this life* . . . . that education which was *simply useful to us here,* believing that it could not be ununseful to us in relation to *any hereafter.*'

Be it observed, then, the necessity of moral training is admitted ; and the plea sometimes made against the advocates of religious education, that there is no connexion between religion and the mechanical teaching of writing and figures, is shown to

be perfectly idle; for there is as little connexion between the
mechanical and the moral, as between the mechanical and the
religious.   But if there is to be moral training, we ask, first,
why should the lower part of morals be taught, and the higher
part be excluded?   Why should children be taught their duty
to man, and not be taught their duty to God?   Again, we ask,
*Can* any such severance be made, without taking away from
morals their only real authority and effective sanction, namely,
the Divine command contained in the Holy Scriptures?   Is the
morality taught in the secular schools to rest upon philosophy
and human reason, altogether independent of the law and the
gospel?   Will the Christians of England be content that their
children shall be taught a system of morals, all 'the issues of
which can be tested by the experience of *this life*,' without
'relation to *any hereafter?*'   In plain words, is it to be an
*Atheistic morality?*

Such is its character, as described by the authors of the system
themselves.   But will so mutilated, so wretched, a system of
heathen morals receive the sanction of the people of England?
Will they allow the living system of God's truth to be cut
asunder, as with the executioner's sword, and one bleeding half
given to the schoolmaster, and the other to the minister?   This
*must* be so; or else—Religion must be taught in the schools.
Proceed one step beyond heathen morality—inform the children
of a God that made them—of a Saviour that loved them—of a
Bible to guide them, or of any hereafter—and at once you come
upon the ground of religion, where the magistrate and the tax-
gatherer are forbidden to tread.

There are some advocates of secular education, who talk as if
the leading truths of religion might be taught in schools, whilst
all 'peculiar tenets' are forbidden.   And this seems to have
been the idea of the Lancashire plan, from the frequent introduction of those words in their publications, and from their
saying that '*doctrinal* religion' is left to parents, &c.   But what
would be the worth of that religious teaching which excluded
all controverted truths?   The existence of a divine revelation is
controverted.   The observance of the Christian Sabbath is controverted.   The doctrine of future punishment is controverted.
The depravity of human nature is controverted.   The divinity
of the Saviour is controverted.   The doctrine of the atonement
is controverted.   The very being of a personal God is controverted.   Then all these doctrines may be regarded as 'peculiar
tenets,' 'points of controversy,' and they must, consequently, be
excluded from the religion of the schools.   But, we ask again,
what would be the value of a religion thus stript of all the
truths that can animate or impress, allure or awe, the human

mind? It would be a sun without his beams—a heaven without its stars.

Independently, however, of this fatal objection, the consistent Nonconformist must have stopped at an earlier stage. As a man honestly jealous for his great principle of dissent from religious establishments, he will say—'Tell me distinctly whether the instruction in these schools is to be religious, or it is not to be religious. If *it is* to be religious, I cannot approve of putting the schools under the magistrate or supporting them by compulsory rates.' We think an enlightened Christian ought also to add—'If it is *not* to be religious, I cannot regard it as an adequate or proper education for the rising population of England.'

But the committee of the ' National Public School Association' think to evade these difficulties, by saying that they 'leave to parents, guardians, and religious teachers, the inculcation of doctrinal religion, to afford opportunity for which the schools shall be closed at stated times each week.' Now this is a palpable evasion. They shut out religion from the schools, and think to atone for the exclusion by allowing perhaps half a day per week, during which the children *may* receive religious instruction. One brief and sufficient answer is, that they *may not* receive it. In order that they should receive it, two things, at least, would be necessary—first, religious teachers must be willing and able to give the instruction at the particular time; and, secondly, the children must be willing to attend and receive it. The former would be difficult; the latter would be highly improbable. As the religious instruction could not be given at the school, it would be necessary that the children should disperse and re-assemble at other places. Unless the attendance on the minister were made *compulsory*, how many would attend? And *if* it were made *compulsory*, what would the Nonconformist say to it?

We regard this arrangement, therefore, as a poor attempt to evade a really insuperable difficulty. But if it were not so—if the plan could be conceived to work ever so well—would it not exceedingly aggravate the objection which is commonly made to religious schools, namely, that they train up children in *sectarian* feeling? Nothing could so forcibly draw the attention of the children to the religious differences of their parents, as telling them that they could not be taught religion together, but must separate, and go to their several churches and chapels for that purpose. Where religious instruction is combined with secular in the school, the mind of the children is seldom, if ever, drawn to the differences among the sects. By the proposed arrangement those differences would be constantly in view, and might become the subject of unhappy contention—the children of the more numerous or powerful sect boasting themselves, and disparaging those of the feebler sects.

There is still another objection, of the most serious kind, to the secular school system, namely, that it would take away the principal motive for attending to the religious character of the schoolmaster. If anything is important in education, it is that the schoolmaster should be a man of true Christian principles and character. His spirit, his temper, his whole discipline, the motives he presents to deter the children from what is wrong, and to encourage them in what is right, his mode of improving all the subjects of study, and all the events of the school, his references (for such must unavoidably be made) to the Author of nature, and to the rule and ends of life, will all be influenced by his own religious character. A truly pious teacher will inevitably produce an impression on the minds of the scholars *favourable* to religion; a merely worldly teacher will produce an impression that religion is a matter of *indifference*; an infidel teacher will leave an impression *hostile* to religion. But no system can be imagined so likely to cause the selection of pious teachers, and the pious training of teachers in normal schools, as the voluntary system, which leaves the schools, for the most part, under the influence of religious bodies. Nor can any system be *less* likely to produce pious teachers than that which avowedly excludes religion from the school instruction, and leaves the teachers to be selected by parish boards elected by the whole body of rate-payers. It is probable that any decided religious earnestness in the candidate for a school would excite the jealousies of those members of the board who belonged to other sects. At least, there would be a general consent to make no inquiry into the religious character of the candidates, as an irrelevant matter, and calculated to excite improper prejudice. In normal schools, not only could there be no religious instruction; but one distinct object in the training of the teacher would be, *that he should learn to shut out religion altogether from his instructions.*

But now let us suppose that the reasons we have urged in favour of a combined religious and secular education were invalid, still the notorious fact remains, that all the religious bodies and all the existing educational societies *think* this combination right and necessary. Of this we have given undeniable proof, by citing the fundamental rules and principles of the great educational associations. They not merely think a religious education admissible, or even the best—they think it *a positive and a religious duty* to give it. They would think it absolutely *impious to exclude religion* from the daily training of the young.

But the startling feature of the secular plan is, that *it would* FORBID AND PREVENT, *by force of law*, the teaching of religion in the schools to be provided by this system for *the whole country*, and to which *all would be compelled to pay!* Is it conceivable that any body of men should take up such a position? To establish secular schools by their own resources, would be right, if they think it their duty. But to force them upon *any* who *conscientiously disapprove* of them, and, still worse, to force them upon *the whole country, in direct opposition* to what (according to all present evidence) is *the conscientious view of every great Christian community*, would be A MONSTROUS VIOLATION OF CIVIL AND RELIGIOUS LIBERTY.

We feel certain that many of those who have approved of the secular plan have not looked at it in this light. They could not intend to wound and outrage the conscientious convictions of their countrymen. They could not intend to *compel any to pay* for what they thought *religiously wrong.* They have committed the common error of regarding the question as it appears to themselves, instead of regarding it—according to the rule in questions of religious liberty—in the light in which it appears to the minds and consciences of others. If it is wrong in a government to enforce any religious duty, it is still more wrong to forbid any religious duty. If it is bad to enforce religious education, it is much worse to forbid religious education. The interference with religion is as great in the latter case as in the former, and, therefore, the rule of the Voluntary is as much violated; only the violation is more objectionable, inasmuch as *any* religion is better than *no* religion.

We postpone the consideration of the question, whether it is desirable to establish a system of *free schools* in the whole country, till we have mentioned a more recent educational project brought out under most respectable patronage at Manchester, evidently as a competitor with the secular plan. In that project we find the same feature, that the schools are proposed to be free.

In the month of January of the present year, a printed paper was circulated to some extent in Manchester, and also published in some of the local newspapers, with the following endorsement:—'Local education. Suggestions and marginal notes for a bill to enable the inhabitants of the boroughs of Manchester and Salford, by means of local rates, to promote and stimulate education therein, and to render existing schools in the said boroughs more efficient, and to provide for the repair of school buildings therein, and effectually to supplement voluntary effort in the said boroughs, in the promotion of education. To show the practicability of constructing an effective system of local

education on the basis of plans now in operation. With a
preface, explaining the general principles of the scheme. Second
revise. By Rev. C. Richson, M.A.'

This project was laid before a private meeting summoned by
the Mayor of Manchester, Mr. John Potter, and consisting of
ministers and laymen of different denominations. The author
of the project, Mr. Richson, is one of the clergymen of the
Collegiate Church of Manchester, who has for some time taken
an interest in the subject of education, and with liberal views
towards Dissenters. It was stated that the plan had been laid
before Sir James Kay Shuttleworth, the former Secretary of
the Committee of Council on Education; and a letter from that
gentleman was read, expressing strong approbation of the plan,
and stating that it was in accordance with the principles on
which the great parties in Parliament had been able to agree,
and was a successful carrying out of those principles. The plan
met with the general, though not the unanimous, approbation
of the meeting; and a sub-committee, including ministers and
laymen of different denominations, was appointed to revise it.
The Report of the sub-committee has since been published, in
the form of 'Instructions for the draft of a bill to promote
education in the municipal boroughs of Manchester and Salford.'
The preamble of the bill sets forth that—

' Whereas in school buildings, erected within the respective municipal boroughs of Manchester and Salford, *there is a great amount of
unoccupied or unused school-room*, which it is desirable to make available for the children of the inhabitants; and whereas there is, notwithstanding, in some parts of the said boroughs, a want of conveniently
accessible school-room for such children, which it is necessary to supply; and whereas it is expedient to provide greater inducements than
heretofore, whereby the children aforesaid should be led in larger
numbers and with more regularity than at present to attend school;
and whereas it is expedient to provide, out of some public resource,
for the proper repair of school-buildings already erected, and for a
more effectual support of daily schools for the children aforesaid, than
voluntary liberality, aided by the payment of the children's pence, at
present furnishes.'

The bill then provides that a school committee shall be annually elected, by the municipal council of each of the boroughs
of Manchester and Salford, out of their own members;—that the
council shall have power, on the recommendation of the school
committee, to lay a rate on property, not exceeding sixpence in
the pound, in any year;—that any rate-payer may go to the
Town-hall, within three months after having paid the rate, and
require the secretary of the school committee to enter the class
of schools to which he wishes his rate to be appropriated—pro-

vided that if the amounts thus required to be appropriated shall exceed the amount of aid required by such schools, the surplus shall be applied to the general purposes of the act;—that all schools willing to submit to inspection shall be received into union;—that inspectors shall be appointed by the Committee of Council on Education, and that their certificates of the competency of the schoolmasters shall be indispensable;—that the schools shall continue under the direction of the present proprietors or managers;—that all the schools in the union shall be free schools;—that it shall not be lawful ' to compel children attending the schools either to learn any creed or formulary, or to attend any Sunday-school or place of religious worship, to which their parents, or persons having the care and maintenance of them, shall, in writing, object;'—that in all schools, except those which are now permitted or permissible, by any Minute in Council, to participate in the benefits of Parliamentary grants for educational purposes, it shall be required ' that the reading of the Holy Scriptures, in the Authorized Version, shall be a part of the daily instruction of the scholars;'—that parents may require free education for all their children above four years old, and may select the schools;—that the school committee may assist the managers or trustees of school-rooms not now used as day-schools, to open them for that purpose;—that schools in union may be assisted in repairs;—that the school committee shall pay to the managers of all the schools in union fivepence per week for every boy registered as attending the schools, and fourpence for every girl or infant under seven years of age;—that children of persons receiving out-door parochial relief, between four and twelve years of age, shall be required to attend school;—that new schools may be provided for necessitous districts, and placed under committees appointed by the municipal council;—and that in those schools, ' instruction in the daily reading of the Holy Scriptures is always to be provided for, but no distinctive religious creed or formulary to be taught;'—all expenses under the act to be paid out of the school-rate.

This scheme clearly indicates a reaction from the Lancashire secular plan. It is a return to the *universal-endowment* and *religious* character of the plan contained in the Minutes of Council. By the Rev. Mr. Richson's scheme all existing public schools would be received into the municipal school-union, on submitting to Government inspection, and having masters whom the inspectors considered competent. Of course all the public Church day-schools in Manchester and Salford, which, according to the Church School Return of 1846-7, were *ninety-six* in number, would come upon the borough-rates for support! The Roman Catholic Schools, which are extremely well conducted—the

... which is perhaps the best-conducted ... at Manchester—the Wesleyan schools—in short, the ... of every sect that would accept of public money and government inspection. We all certainly have a claim to support ... the extent of 6d. a week for every boy and 4d. for every girl, and ... assistance in ... repairs &c.

... therefore, we have the principle of *universal religious endowment* carried out to its full extent ... and it is no longer a small proportion of the cost of schools to be granted in aid of voluntary contributions as was done by the Minutes of Council, ... the pretence of stimulating voluntary liberality, but almost the whole expense of the schools is to be paid out of the borough rate. Such is the natural result of the system commenced by the Minutes of Council, which, by teaching the school committees to rely on Government aid, laid the sure foundation for ever-increasing demands on the government, and for an ultimate abandonment of the voluntary system. It is no breach of charity to suppose that Sir James Kay Shuttleworth, whom we now find a leading supporter of Mr. Richson's scheme, foresaw this result from the first and desired it.

We have now, then, before us, in full proportions, a scheme for establishing every form of religious teaching—to be applied, in the first place, to the manufacturing metropolis of England, but, if successful, there afterwards no doubt to be extended to other boroughs, and perhaps to the whole kingdom. It is clear, beyond all possible question, that the adoption of this plan would be an unexpected and practical adoption of the continental policy of the establishment of all religions. It would be at first confined to schools and schoolmasters: but there are exactly the same reasons for applying it to the support of places of worship and to pastors; and any sect or individual who would accept the provision for a school would accept it for a church or chapel.

A curious provision was inserted in the plan by the sub-committee, for the purpose of warding off this objection: but its insertion is only an acknowledgment of the objection, which the palpable inefficiency of the provision confirms and establishes. Every rate-payer, after paying his school-rate, is permitted to go to the Town-hall, and to require the secretary to put down his payment as to be appropriated to a certain class of schools. In ... place, it is altogether unlikely that any considerable ... of the rate-payers would take this trouble, even if it ... effectual for its purpose. The permission would soon ... entire disuse. But, unless the people of Manchester ... tely more obtuse than we suppose, they would not go ... so ridiculous a ceremony, when it is as clear as the day ... ould have no practical effect whatever. It is provided that *every* school shall have *a legal claim* to the allowance from the borough rates, just in proportion to the number of its scholars. Then where is the use of any apportionment? *No class of schools could be benefited by it : no class of schools could be excluded by it.* The man who cut two holes in the bottom of his stable door, of different sizes, one to admit his large dog, and the other to admit his little dog, was a wise man in comparison with those who should provide books and clerks for a yearly entry of all the sects in Manchester, when the law had provided that the schools of the smallest sect should have enough, and the schools of the largest sect should have nothing to spare! We do not remember to have ever seen so obviously futile a contrivance, or one which so effectually condemned the plan it was designed to save. If any persons should receive such an absurd contrivance as a salvo to their consciences, we really think their consciences not worth the salvo.

The effect of this plan on the schools of Dissenters would obviously be, *either to extinguish them, or to make their maintenance twice as expensive as at present.* Of course, no congregation of Dissenters, acting on the voluntary principle, and giving any religious instruction in its schools, could receive money for them from the borough-rate. They would be compelled to pay a new rate *far more oppressive than the church-rates ;* and to contribute to the teaching of the doctrines of the Church Catechism, of the Roman Catholics, of the Wesleyan Catechism, of Swedenborgians, possibly of Unitarians, in a hundred different schools ; but they could not receive a sixpence of the money towards the support of their own schools. Meanwhile their own schools would become doubly expensive. For when the other schools all around them were made free, it would be impossible to support pay schools any longer : all must be free alike, or the children would leave them. But the loss of the children's pence would double the cost of sustaining the schools ; and this would render it necessary to close the schools, especially as the subscribers would be likely to fall off, from the disinclination there is to subscribe to any object when the money can be obtained elsewhere for asking for.

It is, therefore, obvious that the effect of this plan on Dissenters would be in the highest degree unjust and oppressive. It would *tax them against their consciences, and at the same time destroy their schools ;* and the only alternative would be one far more malignant, namely, that they would, by the continual presentation of so strong a bribe, *be seduced into an abandonment of their principles.* So certain are these effects, that, if the object of the authors of this bill had been either to punish the Dissenters, or to drive them from their principles, a deeper or more effectual scheme could not have been devised for the purpose. Any Dissenter who should aid the plan would be helping to destroy the principles he has hitherto held sacred, and to oppress his more consistent brethren. If the Dissenters of Manchester do not at once give the strongest possible opposition to the proposed bill, they will be conniving at the ruin of their own cause, and at the open endowment by the State of all religions. The Factory Education Bill of Sir James Graham was a mere *bagatelle* in comparison with this measure of Mr. Richson's, so far as it affected Dissenters; and the Minutes of Council are but as the embryo in comparison with the grown giant.

Between this plan and the secular plan of the ' National Public School Association' there is an edifying reciprocation of intolerance. As the secular plan would shut out from participation in the school-rate all schools where religion is taught, so Mr. Richson's plan would equally shut out all schools where religion is *not* taught. The exclusion in each case is wrong—so wrong and so unjust that it ought to excite the lively indignation of every friend of justice or liberty. But it is exceedingly instructive. It shows how naturally, and even necessarily, unjust is any plan for supporting education by compulsory taxation; and how naturally men who speculate on the support of education at the public expense become blinded to considerations of justice and freedom. The supporters of each of these projects see clearly the injustice done by the other, but have no perception of the injustice done by their own project.

Under Mr. Richson's bill there would be a division of management and responsibility that must inevitably work ill. Each school would be under the general management of its own committee, consisting, perhaps, of a clergyman and his leading friends; but the funds would be chiefly derived from the school committee of the Town Council, which would have a superintending authority; and, after all, the Committee of Council on Education, which would furnish part of the funds, and appoint the inspectors, would have a power more substantial than all. Among these three authorities, it is quite certain that there would be either too much governing or too little. Conflict among them would be sure; and ultimate neglect—the usual effect of divided responsibility—would be highly probable. The expense of all this complicated machinery would be enormous, especially where the chief power is in one body, and the providing of the money in another.

The Committee of Council on Education, however, would have powers, which, if it chose to exercise them, would make it all but absolute. The bye-laws and regulations of the municipal school committee are not to take effect till sanctioned by the Committee of the Privy Council. The inspectors are to be Government inspectors. Their certificates are to be indispensable for every schoolmaster, and also to sanction every grant for repairs of premises. In case of a new school-trust being required, the Committee of Council must assent to the scheme. The mode of applying the funds in the payment of teachers and other expenses of the school, is to be subject to the approval of the same Committee of Council. And, lastly, the Committee of Council is the final court of appeal, in all complaints against the municipal school committee or the inspector. It is pretty evident that here are the means of bringing both the managers and the municipal school committee under complete subjection to the Committee of Council; and, when the number of schools and the amount of rates to be disposed of are considered, it will appear that the Committee of Council, representing the Government of the day, would (if the scheme should be extended to the whole country) acquire a tremendous amount of power and influence. This is surely a consideration that ought to arouse constitutional jealousy.

We now come briefly to consider a point in which the secular plan and Mr. Richson's plan concur, namely, the making of the schools *free*. The object of this provision is, of course, to induce a greater number of children to attend school, and to induce them to remain there longer. It is assumed that these would be the results, if the education cost nothing. We cannot take upon us to assert that no such results would ensue; but we should like to offer a few remarks, both on the practical working of the plan, and on its philosophy.

It might be that children would attend schools, off and on, for a greater length of time; but is it not according to all experience, that that which cost nothing would be lightly valued; and, also, that parents would be much more indifferent to the regular attendance of their children at school when they paid nothing, than when they paid a moderate sum for their children's schooling? It is shown by the Massachusetts reports of schools, that truancy prevails to a very great extent under that boasted system, and that, on the average, the children do not attend *one-third of the year*. When we are told that in Massachusetts there is one scholar to every four inhabitants, it is right that the mode of preparing their school statistics should be understood. It will be explained by the following sentences from the Massachusetts school reports for 1842-3:—

'There were only a little more than *one-half* of the children at school in the summer, and only eleven-seventeenths in the winter, in this State.' (p. 258.) 'In the most populous districts, the scholars are divided into two classes. All under nine or ten years of age attend the summer schools only, and all over that age attend the winter schools only; so that *the average attendance in these cases is only about* FIFTEEN WEEKS, *or less than one-third of the year;* hence *the apparent attendance is about* TWICE *as much as the actual attendance of any particular scholar.*'—P. 264.

The principal cause of the ampler education received by the children of New England is the vastly superior condition of their parents—there being no class that can be called poor in those states. The parents are, consequently, not under the necessity of so early taking their children from school to help in the support of the family. But the attendance of the children at school is more lax than in this country, and the fact is probably owing, in a great measure, to the schools being free. In England, the practice among the working-classes is to set their children to labour at an early age. That practice is not likely to be given up if the schools were free, because it brings in additional wages for the support of the family: it will only be gradually changed, as the sense of the value of education increases. On the whole, then, taking into account the value set upon education, which must be greater when it is paid for, the regularity of attendance at school, and the habit of employing children industrially at an early age, it is by no means certain that there would be any great or effective increase in the amount of education if all the schools were made free.

But what would be the influence on the quality of education, on the exertions of schoolmasters, and on the tendency to improvement in the methods of tuition, if the schools were supported by public rates? *The competition among schools and schoolmasters would be destroyed.* At present, the best schools secure the greatest number of scholars; the master and the committee have, therefore, a powerful and constant motive to exertion. There is a perpetual spur to improvement. But this would be gone, when the school was chiefly supported out of public funds. And if all the schools were to be taught on one uniform system, as proposed by the Lancashire secular plan, the educational dead level would be effectually attained.

It is obvious that free schools supported by public rates must *destroy all private schools*, as well as all schools which did not receive public money;—an enormous injustice on a numerous class of persons, no less than on several religious sects. The work of education must henceforth be wholly engrossed by public functionaries.

And this brings us to a general question, of the highest social importance, namely, Is it for the interest either of individuals or of society, that the great work of education should be taken out of the general law of *individual action and free competition*, and put under a system of *public superintendence and compulsory support ?* We know that the latter is the principle of *religious establishments ;* and it is also the principle of *Communism.* And it is curious to observe *how the Establishmentarians and the Communists agr*

Now the
portance.
freedom o
are we to
Fourier?

tending to destroy all man's energy and self-reliance, to suppress freedom, to stop improvement, and to revolutionize, by levelling, society. When applied to industry, it is the principle of Protection; when applied to religion, it is the principle of Establishments. The opposite principle gives us free-trade, and the voluntary support of religion and education. Are the people of Manchester, and, above all, are the Free-traders of Manchester, about to set up a principle the very antagonist of that which they so lately distinguished themselves by throwing down?

For ourselves, we have unbounded confidence in the volun-

ice. It taxes the energies of men, but only to give them a more masculine development. It leaves upon them all the burden of their duties, but only to give increased vigour to their virtues. It allows the conflict of competition, but only to sharpen and strengthen the faculties it calls into play. It leaves men free to combine wherever they can do it harmoniously and advantageously, but refrains from forcing them into unnatural and incongruous unions.

When we are told that society is deeply interested in the education of the masses, inasmuch as its welfare and safety depend upon their conduct, and that, therefore, society is justified in making education a matter of public provision, we reply, that society is far more interested in the moral and religious character of the masses, and yet there is not one word in the teaching of the Divine Author of our religion, or of his inspired apostles, that commits the charge of religious teaching to magistrates; but, on the contrary, everything to show that it was made, first, the duty of each individual to provide the means of his own religious edification; next, the duty of individual Christians and churches to promote the spiritual good of all within their influence; and, lastly, the special duty of parents to 'train up their children in the nurture and admonition of the Lord.' Christianity thus puts its seal on the great laws of nature, committing the charge of its own conservation and extension to individual conscience, to parental affection, and to the love and sympathy of universal brotherhood.  To supersede, or even to supplement, these laws, by calling in the authority of the civil magistrate, is admitted by Nonconformists—aye, and is beginning to be admitted by many others—to be presumptuous, unlawful, and practically mischievous.  And yet every argument for state education is used with great plausibility in defence of state-religion.  If the arguments should succeed in the former case, they will become unanswerable in the latter.   If the voluntary prin·ciple should be pronounced inadequate for education, it will be pronounced inadequate for religion.  The voluntary who labours to prove the necessity of state education is pulling down his own house ; and every establishmentarian sees it, and rejoices.

We urge another consideration. If the authority and wisdom of the magistrate are needful to support and guide education, they must be equally needful to support and guide *the press*.  There is quite as good reason why Government · should gratuitously supply every family with books and newspapers, as why it should gratuitously supply every family with education.  All that is said with regard to the interest of society, to the maintenance of order, to the present inferior quantity and quality of the intellectual food provided, to the difficulty which the poor have in obtaining a supply, and to the duty which property has to society, would justify a *book-rate* and *book-inspection*, with ' *certified' authors and editors*, to the full as much as a *school-rate* and *school-inspection*, with ' *certified' schoolmasters*. And what is this but another part of the same system, which, under the pretence of paternal government, keeps nations in a state of perpetual pupillage, puts every family under the regimen of the police, maintains *religious establishments, state-schools*, and a *censorship of the press* ?

Few things are more dangerous than the *impatience* which induces well-meaning men to adopt wrong means for securing right ends—to do evil that good may come.  It is the devout aspiration of the Christian, that heathen nations may be brought to the knowledge of the gospel ; but does any man lament that Government did not send out missionaries when the Protestant churches were neglecting their duty in this respect ?  It is now seen that Sunday-schools are one of the most invaluable institutions of our country ; but would it have been well for Government to establish them, before Robert Raikes began the work ?  In the eighteenth century, the periodical press of England was in a state of almost incredible inefficiency ; but would it have conduced to the public good, that Government should then have taken it under its charge? In all these matters we have seen a period, and that very recently, when it might have been said, with the greatest apparent reason, that if Government did not undertake the work, no other agency would or could. Yet our own eyes have witnessed the growth of mighty agencies, of the right kind, from among the people themselves, for all these purposes; and no man can doubt that it was better to wait for that spontaneous growth, than to trust matters so sacred and delicate to a governmental agency, that would have corrupted all it touched, that would have shackled the intellect it professed to nurse, and secularized the religion it patronized. If the Marquis of Lansdowne was right—as unquestionably he was—in saying, ' It is universally admitted that governments are the worst of cultivators, the worst of manufacturers, and the worst of traders;' the fact must be ascribed to causes which will apply at least as powerfully to the governmental direction of religion and education, as of industry.

If there ever was an age or a c
forth glorious energies for its ov
the nineteenth century. Tl
ment of duty or benevolence tl        1        n
fill. Since the century cam
ages of improvement; nor is
or decline. On the contrary,
accelerated speed. Our tow   a   :rov    w
public spirit and honourable   :erp   , of charity and p   '.
The triumphs of freedom are written in the largest characters on the face of our land. This is not the self-complacent boast of Englishmen: it is the well-remembered tribute of admiration publicly rendered to our voluntary system by one of the most celebrated statesmen of the age, himself identified with the opposite system—M. Guizot.

It would be very easy, and no less gratifying, to fill our pages with illustrations; but one fact speaks and sums up volumes. Mr. Sampson Low, jun., in his recent interesting work on ' The Charities of London,' fills 453 pages with an enumeration of those charities; and the summary of the whole is this—that in this metropolis, in addition to all congregational charities, there are 491 general charities, *of which 294 have been founded within the present century;* and that the annual income of those charities is as follows :—

| | | |
|---|---|---|
| Income from voluntary contributions | . . . . | £1,022,864 |
| ,,   funded property | . . . . . | 741,869 |
| Total income | . . . . . | £1,764,733 |

The increase in the number of schools and scholars within the half-century, and especially within the last thirty years, is an evidence which it is impossible to resist, of the power of a nation, awakened to the value of knowledge, to train its own juvenile population. On the day before these pages are issued, a census will have been taken, which, if carefully and accurately executed, will give us more exact educational and religious statistics than we have hitherto possessed. But as it may be some time before the results are drawn out and published, we can now only judge from former returns.

According to the educational returns obtained by a committee of the House of Commons, under Lord Brougham's chairmanship, in 1818, the number of day-scholars in England and Wales was in that year 674,883, and of Sunday-scholars, 447,225. According to the returns of Lord Kerry's committee in 1833, the number of day-scholars was 1,276,947, and of Sunday-scholars, 1,548,890 :—showing an increase, in fifteen years, of 602,064 day-scholars, and 1,101,665 Sunday-scholars. There are no general official returns later than 1833; but in the year 1846, when school statistics were much discussed, the number of day-scholars was supposed by Mr. E. Baines to have reached 1,876,947; by Professor Hoppus, 2,000,000; and by Mr. Charles Knight, 2,200,000. The number of Sunday-scholars was at the same time estimated at 2,000,000. If we take the medium estimate, Professor Hoppus's, and if we compare the scholars with the population in the three years, we shall have the following results :—

## ENGLAND AND WALES.

*Day-Scholars, Sunday-Scholars, and Population, in 1818, 1833, and 1846.*

| Years. | Population. | Day-Scholars. | Proportion of Day-Scholars to Population. | Sunday-Scholars. | Proportion of Sunday-Scholars to Population. |
|--------|-------------|---------------|-------------------------------------------|------------------|---------------------------------------------|
| 1818 | 11,398,167 | 674,883 | 1 to 17 | 447,225 | 1 to 24 |
| 1833 | 14,417,110 | 1,276,947 | 1 „ 11½ | 1,548,890 | 1 „ 9½ |
| 1846 | 17,026,024 | 2,000,000 | 1 „ 8½ | 2,000,000 | 1 „ 8½ |

Increase of Population from 1818 to 1846 . 50 per cent.
    Ditto    Day-Scholars    ditto    . 255 „
    Ditto    Sunday-Scholars    ditto    . 319 „

If these figures even approach to correctness (and we see no reason to doubt it), the results are so splendid as to justify the utmost confidence in the power of the Voluntary principle.

But in the city of Manchester, where this extraordinary fervour exists for new systems of education under legal compulsion, there is overwhelming evidence that the people can do what they please in the creation of schools. In the ' preface ' to the Rev. C. Richson's ' Suggestions,' he gives a table showing accommodation in *public* schools (Sunday and day-schools) in the parish of Manchester, for 66,000 children ; whilst the number of day-scholars in those schools is only 18,500 ; leaving *'redundant day-school-room (above what is used) for* 47,500 *children.'* It is a notorious fact that there is accommodation in the Church day-schools alone for 27,000 children, with an actual attendance of only 9,000. There are, or were lately, very noble schools belonging to other denominations, which were closed from want of scholars. It is an undeniable fact that *at this moment there is far more school accommodation in Manchester, than could by any possibility be used.* And how has all this accommodation been provided? *Nineteen-twentieths of it, we believe, by the voluntary contributions of religious bodies.* If secular schools are wanted, let them be provided ; the thing is nearly as soon done as said, in that wealthy and munificent city. If it is alleged that the working-classes cannot afford to send their children to school, but must have education given to them gratuitously, it is the most outrageous of delusions ; for there is not in England or in Europe a body of workmen better paid than those in Manchester. All the police returns of that city demonstrate moral and educational improvement, to a most gratifying extent. We extract the following from the ' Criminal and Miscellaneous Statistical Returns of the Manchester Police ' for 1849, printed in 1850 :—

| CRIME IN MANCHESTER, from 1840 to 1849. | | | | | |
| --- | --- | --- | --- | --- | --- |
| | | Prisoners Convicted. | | Uneducated. | |
| Years. | Population. | Number Convicted. | Proportion to Population. | Number Uneducated | Proportion to Population. |
| 1840 | 235,139 | 671 | ·28 per cent. | 368 | ·15 per cent. |
| 1845 | 295,277 | 535 | ·18 ,, | 189 | ·08 ,, |
| 1846 | 299,382 | 527 | ·17 ,, | 210 | ·07 ,, |
| 1847 | 299,445 | 654 | ·21 ,, | 235 | ·07 ,, |
| 1848 | 299,445 | 646 | ·21 ,, | 209 | ·06 ,, |
| 1849 | 302,182 | 527 | ·17 ,, | 171 | ·05 ,, |

Thus, in nine years, the population increased from **255,159** to 302,182; but in the same period the number of convicts diminished from 671 to 527, or from a proportion of ·28 per cent. to ·17 per cent. of the population; and the number of the uneducated convicts diminished from 368 to 171, or from a proportion of ·15 per cent. to ·05 per cent. of the population.

Facts such as these might be multiplied. But unless these can be impugned, there is unanswerable proof that the people are both able and willing to provide for their own education, without either government help or legislative compulsion.

We merely add the undeniable position, that never, at any period of English history, was there so great an amount of educational machinery in operation as in 1851. Not one of all the School Societies, so far as we are aware, has been abandoned, or has slackened its efforts. Not one of the means of popular instruction referred to in the commencement of this article has been withdrawn. On the contrary, all are on the increase. The Established Church is opening new National Schools in London, at Cheltenham, and in several of the dioceses. The Church of Scotland and the Free Church are vying with each other in activity. The Wesleyans have raised their great training institution in Westminster. It is true that in all these buildings a portion—a comparatively small portion—of the cost has been contributed by the Government; but we do not believe a single one of these efforts would have failed to be made, if the public purse had been closed. For we see that the Congregational Board of Education has purchased, without any such help, the buildings of Homerton College (already consecrated for such a purpose,) for its Normal Schools, and is carrying on its work with energy. The Voluntary School Association is also training teachers with unremitting zeal. And there is not a single feature so striking, in every suburb of this vast metropolis, or from all the railways that traverse the length and breadth of the provinces, as the number of churches, chapels, schools, and public institutions springing up in every seat of population.

We do not say the work is *done;* but it is *being done.* Immense progress has been made within our own day, and is now being made. We receive it as a decisive admission of increased intelligence, that Lord John Russell has announced another extension of the suffrage. We point out to our countrymen, that what has been done has been (with a comparatively slight exception) entirely by the people themselves, under a system of perfect freedom. To abandon that system for one of compulsion, of centralization, and of forced uniformity, and to purchase the new system at the expense of wounding the consciences and outraging the feelings of a large proportion of the people, including the bulk of religious men and many of the best friends of education, would be a false step and full of peril. Let us adhere to freedom, and we offend neither sect nor secular : all may put forth their zeal according to their own judgments ; and freedom will bear the fruits it has ever borne—intellectual and moral power, together with justice, truth, progress, and peace.

---

## Brief Notices.

*The Poet of the Sanctuary. A Centenary Commemoration of the Labours and Services, Literary and Devotional, of the Rev. Isaac Watts, D.D. Preceded by Remarks on the Origin of Psalmody and Christian Hymnology in Earlier Times.* By Josiah Conder. London : John Snow. 1851.

THIS elegant volume was origi
the last autumnal meeting of t
ton—the birth-place of Dr. W
was a happy one, and certainly to
been more fittingly assigned th
have done so much to enrich tl
The preliminary chapter on
Hymnology in earlier times, is ex          ly
information it conveys on a subject resp   ing wnich much ig   rance
prevails. Though brief, it is more than a mere compilation of dry
facts. Throughout, we feel that we are in the company of one whose
deepest sympathies are with his subject—one who is himself possessed
of the poet's soul. The tribute paid to Watts is graceful, just, and
discriminating. The remarks on the use of the Psalms as an element
in devotional worship will be useful in rebuking, on the one hand, that
superstitious reverence which is paid to the letter of the Psalms of
David, regardless of their spirit ; and, on the other hand, that reckless
innovation which would entirely destroy the separate character of the
Psalter. With all his warm admiration of Dr. Watts, as *the* poet of
the sanctuary, and with no measured acknowledgment of our obligations to him, yet we are glad to see that Mr. Conder is one of those
who advocate a revision of Dr. Watts's Psalms and Hymns, and such
a compression of their bulk by the omission of those portions which
are never used, that they might be incorporated into one book with
other hymns. We see by an announcement at the end of the volume
that he is already engaged in this work of revision. Surely the odious
two-book system cannot last much longer. Much, very much as we
owe to Dr. Watts, yet our collection of devotional hymns, of a distinctively spiritual character—expressive of the deeper thoughts and
aspirations of the soul, is meagre and defective. The author of this

volume has himself done much to supply the defect—but still the want
is not fully met. We hope that the attention which this volume will
draw to Dr. Watts, may inspire some of kindred spirit to take up his
lyre, and give forth strains which may express the thoughts and help
the devotions of many human hearts. Those who heard this paper
read at Southampton will be glad to renew their acquaintance with it
in its present attractive form, and those who heard it not, will find a
pleasant and profitable recreation in its perusal, and will unite with us
in thanking Mr. Conder for his truly interesting and able paper.

*Christianity and its Evidences: A Course of Six Lectures, delivered
at Newcastle-on-Tyne.* By the Rev. J. G. Rogers, B.A. London:
B. L. Green.

BEING in Newcastle one Sunday, during the last summer, our attention
was attracted to placards announcing a lecture to be delivered the
same day, in opposition to Christianity. In these bills, which stared on
the frequenters of public worship, as they passed to their several
sanctuaries, reference was made, in the most profane manner, to subjects which the pious of every denomination approach with awe and
affection, and which we believe the mass of the people venerate. On
inquiry, we learnt that strong efforts were being made by means of
lectures, and a cheap literature, to diffuse among the population of
that district the lessons of infidelity, and for a time, with so much
apparent success, that the sceptics raised the note of triumph. We
were glad to hear that Mr. Rogers intended to give, in a public room,
on week-day evenings, a course of Lectures on the Evidences, with a
special view to the attacks which had been made in the neighbourhood.
The course was delivered, and afterwards printed in the form of the
present volume. The lectures are six in number, and the titles, which
will give some idea of the mode in which the subject was treated, are—
1. The Ideal of Christianity. 2. The Oracles of Christianity. 3. The
Antecedents of Christianity. 4. The Records of Christianity. 5. The
Founder of Christianity. 6. The Antagonists of Christianity.
These subjects are discussed in a manner which displays a large
acquaintance with the general principles and facts which demonstrate
the Divine authority of the Scriptures, as well as study of the objections which in modern times have been brought forward to cast a doubt
on the genuineness of particular books. The great excellence of the
volume is its dealing with infidelity in those forms in which it is put
forth by its apostles of the present age. Mr. Rogers, with great intelligence and power, points out the baseless assumptions, and inconsequential reasonings, which abound in the writings of Strauss, Parker,
and others of that school. We think that the present publication may
do much service in guiding the thoughtful to such a view of the Christian evidences as will enable them to repel many of the objections
which some with little learning can very glibly put forth. Passages of
much eloquence and beauty abound in the volume, which indicate that
the writer is an accomplished lecturer, as well as an acute and vigorous
reasoner.

*Euphranor. A Dialogue on Youth.* London: William Pickering.

A CHARMING little volume, which we have read with much pleasure, and recommend to the early acquaintance of intelligent and inquisitive, young men. The interlocutors are, a young medical practitioner at Cambridge, and Euphranor, Lexilogus, Lycion, and Phidippus, four collegians; and the subjects of their discourse are accurately described by the first when he tells us:—'And so we went on, partly in jest, partly in earnest, drawing philosophers of all kinds into the same net in which we had entangled the poet and his critic—how the best histories had been written by those who had been busy actors in them —how the moralist who worked alone and dyspeptic in his closet was most apt to mismeasure humanity, and be very angry when his system would not fit; and so on a great deal more.' Such dialogues, amongst such speakers, must of course contain much which our gravity condemns. The wheat, however, far outweighs, and not only so, but exceeds in bulk, the chaff, and we recommend our readers to separate them for themselves.

---

*Lectures delivered at the Monthly United Service of the Nonconformist Churches in Nottingham, with other Discourses preached on Public Occasions.* By Samuel M'All. 12mo. London: J. Snow.

THIS volume furnishes a fair idea of our present Nonconformist preaching. We regard it as a creditable specimen of the preaching—less polished perhaps, and less carefully adjusted, but the same in substantial fulness and vigour of thought—that is weekly presented to a large portion of our Nonconformist congregations. Mr. M'All is a ' scribe well instructed in the kingdom of God;' and he is evidently solicitous that all who hear him shall be so too.

It is, however, but just to remark that these Lectures have been prepared with more than ordinary care; they are not the common Sabbath ministrations of their author, although experience proves that a man's productions, whether ordinary or special, will all bear the same general characteristics. The Nonconforming churches in Nottingham have a pleasant and wholesome practice of assembling together from time to time for fraternal association, and especially of uniting in a monthly service, at which the ministers preach in rotation upon some specified topic; and the sermons before us, with one or two exceptions, were preached on these occasions. They are, for the most part, simple and lucid in their arrangement—the author rightly estimating his *forte* and the end of pulpit ministrations, gives a studied prominence to the practical. The style is simple, chaste, elegant, and unassuming, with here and there a burr to make it stick—a vehicle for conveying the preacher's thoughts, and nothing more—his good taste rejecting the fineries and fopperies with which so many sermons are bestuck. The author abounds in felicitous quotations of Scripture, at the inlaying of which he is very skilful; occasionally quaintnesses occur, indicating something of dry humour, never, however, offending against the proprieties of sacred writing. And when events or characters are to be delineated, he succeeds well in a vivid picturing of them, as, for example, in the first Lecture, where Paul is described preaching in Antioch.

The Lectures are miscellaneous in their themes. The Aspects of Modern Infidelity—Revivals of Religion—the Gradation and Harmony of Religious Dispensations—Christian Churches, and their relationship to Christian Life—Christian Union, and the Means, True and False, adopted for promoting it—Human Responsibility, &c.—are the topics discussed; and the mode of treating them has suggested various thoughts which we had jotted down for remark, but must forbear.

We wish Mr. M'All had substituted some other subject for the Fourteenth Lecture. The topic selected is not the best fitted for his purpose, and the manner of its discussion is an exception to his success-ful treatment of the rest. The sermon is feeble and illogical in arrange-ment; and in the apprehension of the true character and connexion of the Transfiguration, is not what such a topic requires. On the whole, however, we commend this volume as one of the most intelligent and useful of its kind that we have latterly seen. We shall hope to meet Mr. M'All again.

---

*The Relation of Philosophy to Theology, and of Theology to Religion. Reprinted from the ' Eclectic Review.' January, 1851. Revised and extended. London: Ward and Co.*

As this is a reprint from our own Journal, we shall content ourselves with a simple announcement of its separate issue. It is printed in a neat and portable size, ' in the hope of promoting more widely the knowledge of the value of Coleridge's works, as a preliminary discipline to theological study.'

---

# Review of the Month.

---

THE Russell Cabinet has been reinstated in office, and the country has now had an opportunity of judging how far its future policy will justify and confirm its re-occupation of Downing-street. We are by no means sanguine. Were we to assume the province of a seer, we should say much on the loss of reputation and political status likely to accrue to Lord John and his associates from their return to the Treasury Benches. On account of the Whigs we regret this, for they have a historic name which we do not wish to see sullied; but on no other ground do we deplore it. The family coteries of Whiggery re-quire to be broken up; and what has just occurred will hasten this. Moreover, the stock of aristocratic legislators is shown to be greatly reduced, and though a desperate effort is being made to keep the mono-poly, we have no fear for the result. What we have witnessed is only one of many scenes which will be enacted before the common right of

Englishmen in the business of legislation is admitted. Both Whigs and Tories will struggle hard on this point. They will do everything, will submit to everything, will hazard everything, before their craft is surrendered. Yielded, however, it must be. The times for oligarchical rule are passed. Mere names have lost their spell, and our people, with all their folly, are wise enough to require that knowledge, integrity, and sympathy with their interests, should characterise their rulers. We have as yet seen only the initial struggle. The real contest is to come ; and, if we are not much mistaken, it will be brief and conclusive. The true Conservatism of the age is in giving to the people their due weight in the legislative and executive councils of the nation. We must secure talent and public virtue, by whomsoever exhibited, and in whatever class seen, without regard to the interested cliques which claim a monopoly of wisdom. We were on this ground— to say nothing of other considerations—sorry at the tone of Lord John's closing remarks on the evening of the 28th of February. We cannot go the length of the ' Daily News' in saying that they ' filled us with sad and supreme disgust;' but we do say, without hesitation, that they betokened great deficiency of judgment, and unaccountable ignorance of his real strength. He may not have meant it—we do not believe he did—but his words are understood to indicate an unalterable determination to maintain an aristocratic position, and will be referred to, in coming times, as marking out the line which separates his lordship from the people.

We need not now refer to the negotiations which have taken place. The Premier and Sir James Graham in the Commons, and Lords Stanley and Aberdeen in the Lords, have given their several versions. From the whole it appears that Lord Stanley shrunk from the responsibility of office as the leader of the Protectionist party, and that Sir James Graham declined to unite his fortunes with Lord John on account of ' The Ecclesiastical Titles Bill.' Some of our contemporaries appear to us to confound the resignation of the Russell Cabinet with the non-incorporation of the Peelites, when they refer the former to the Papal agitation. Nothing is more obvious than that the Government Bill would have passed both Houses with overwhelming majorities. We know no reason to suppose that the division which took place— 395 to 63—did not represent the comparative strength of parties. The only objection to the measure, from what may be termed the Ministerial and Protestant sections of the House, was, that it did not go far enough. Many thought and said this ; but none who were friendly to legislation refused to receive the instalment, though some affirmed that it was far less than ought to have been offered. So far, therefore, as the Papal question was concerned, there was no occasion for the resignation of Ministers ; nay, on the contrary, the Government would have been sustained by majorities far greater than have been known for years past. But though this question did not lead to the dissolution of the Cabinet, it doubtless prevented—such at least is the showing of the parties concerned—the formation of a coalition ministry, consisting of Whigs and Peelites. On this point we need not enlarge. The country is familiar with the statements made ; and the time is not yet come for our knowing the more private and individual aims of the policy pursued.

It is enough, at present, to note, that under the advice of the Duke of Wellington, her Majesty has called on her former Ministers to resume their posts, and that they have most dutifully complied with her summons. 'After what has occurred,' said Lord John, 'and the failure of the repeated attempts to form a Government, which have been detailed to the House, we thought we could not perform our duty to her Majesty and the public, otherwise than by accepting the offer her Majesty was pleased to make to us.' We do not impugn the integrity or high-mindedness of this decision. It may have been all it should be, but it is hard to persuade the country that a wise course has been pursued. The self-complacency of Ministers would, un-questionably, be diminished, if they realized the feeling with which the country witnessed their return to office. No bonfires were lighted, no bells were rung, no living man, as we believe—save those personally interested—rejoiced in the fact. The Administration had worn out the endurance of the nation ; not a particle of enthusiasm remained. Amongst its followers, a dull, dead, feeling of indifference prevailed; not, be it remembered, from any preference of their opponents, any liking of Lord Stanley or Mr. Disraeli, but simply from the conviction that they were a drag on the political wheel—so much dead weight, which broke down the strength and exhausted the energies of more active and earnest reformers. For a time the country was incredulous. They could not believe that the Ministry, *as a whole*, were reinstated. People had made up their minds to the return of Lord John and of a section of his Cabinet, but when assured that the *whole* were back in Downing-street, they rubbed their eyes, and looked incredulous, as if awaking from a dream. It never entered into their thoughts that Sir Charles Wood, or Sir John Cam Hobhouse, now Lord Broughton, or other mere nullities, could be returned upon their hands. But so it is. The Russell Cabinet, *intact*, is again in office, and, so far as the future can be seen, there is no improvement in their policy or measures.

When the first feeling of surprise had subsided, some began to speculate on coming events. Lord John, it was imagined, had resumed office with a view of carrying 'The Ecclesiastical Titles Bill,' and, having done so, would be joined by Sir James Graham and other Peelites. A compact and strong government it was alleged would, in such case, be formed, which would command the confidence of the country, and effectually resist a return to protection. Now we have no sympathy with all this. The *antecedents* of the Peelites are not of an order to permit our entertaining any such anticipations, neither are their numbers or their influence, so far as we can judge, likely to save a feeble and tottering Cabinet. Moreover, we have our misgiving on other points, especially since Sir James Graham and Mr. Disraeli walked out of the House, *arm in arm, to record their votes against the Government* on Lord Duncan's motion. One thing is clear. It was perfect madness for Lord John to resume the Govern-ment unless he was prepared to amend his policy, and, by more liberal and vigorous measures, to reunite the scattered members of the Liberal party. He had fallen into the rear, and having failed in negotiation with the Free-trade section of the Conservatives, there was no alternative apparently left him, but to recover the confidence of the more forward of the Liberals. Men looked for this, but have looked in vain, and their disappointment has confounded and bewildered them. Nearly two hundred members assembled in Downing-street on the 4th of March, and the general impression received was, that the Government would proceed with greater energy and more liberalism than it had done. Nothing of this, however, appeared in the explanations which the Premier gave to the Commons on the 7th, while the alterations which the Home Secretary proceeded to announce in ' The Ecclesiastical Titles Bill,' betrayed the old vacillation and infirmity of purpose, which are unhappily characteristic of the Whig Cabinet.* Sir R. Inglis correctly described the measure as

---

* While deeply regretting the course pursued by Lord John, we cannot express the disgust with which, in common with all honest men, we have witnessed the conduct of a portion of the London daily press. The ' Times' has maintained its usual character with a hardihood which has made us blush for the community which sustains it. Ready, like the Free Companies of a former age, to let itself to the highest bidder, it has forsworn itself, and now bitterly rails at the men whom only yesterday it lauded to the skies. Anything more shameless than the course pursued by this journal respecting the Durham letter, we have never witnessed. We are no worshippers of Lord John. We have freely, and on many occasions, animadverted on his policy, and should he continue in power shall do so, we doubt not, again and again. Yet we loathe from our very souls the warfare now waged against him. It is as un-English as it is mendacious—as insulting to the nation, as it is ungenerous and base to Lord John. ' We are as alive,' says the ' Daily News,' and we adopt its language, ' to his defects as to his merits. But when we recollect his long career, his early struggles, not for place, which was then hopeless, but for the achievement of those great measures of civil and religious liberty which for ever must attach to, and immortalize his name, we must own that we regard those flatterers who licked this great minister's plate, and who now, curs that they are, turn to bay and to bite at his heels, with a feeling of contempt indeed for them, but of indignant sorrow for the country whose character they stain.'

The ' Morning Chronicle' has labored hard to effect a junction of the Peelites with a section of the Russell Cabinet. The *animus* of this is sufficiently apparent. Many of the Peelites are Puseyites of the first water, who denounce all legislation on the Papal question. In this they are supported by Sir James Graham and Lord Aberdeen, and are known to be in harmony with the Grey section of the Cabinet. The ' Morning Chronicle' is their organ, and those who want to know what that party would do in ecclesiastical affairs have only to consult the leaders of this journal. Were it the property of Cardinal Wiseman it could not more thoroughly, or with more apparent zeal, advocate his cause. Truly there is a near relationship between Puseyism and Popery, and the abettors of the former readily learn the speech and adopt the policy of the latter. To compass their ecclesiastical purpose they advocate the abandonment of a colleague whose views are in obvious harmony with the great body of the community. We deeply regret that the Premier should give his opponents the advantage which they will not fail to reap from his own want of firmness and courage. There must be a *secret* history here which time only will disclose.

reminding him of ' the play of " Hamlet " with the part of Hamlet left out.' The second and third clauses of the bill are now omitted, and the measure purports, in consequence, to be a mere declaratory prohibition—under a specific penalty—of the assumption of certain ecclesiastical titles. This is the light in which it was exhibited by Sir George Grey, who, after expounding the views of the Cabinet, proceeded to meet the objections which were likely to be advanced against the measure ' as unworthy of the occasion, and not of a character to justify the expectations which had been excited.' We need not say that we join in these objections, and are at a loss to comprehend the process which has induced the Premier to submit his bill to such an emasculating process. As a mere question of titles, we care nothing about the matter. It lies, in such case, between the two rival hierarchies, and we would not cross the street to decide it one way or the other.

But it has a larger aspect, which engages somewhat of our interest, and which makes us tender of the bill even in its present enfeebled state. We are Englishmen, and, therefore, protest against a foreign potentate—be he Pope or King—assuming to divide our kingdom according to his pleasure, and assigning to his ministers the government thereof. We record our deliberate judgment against such an assumption, in ecclesiastical matters, even on the part of our own Sovereign, and are, therefore, more especially hostile to it in the case of a foreign ruler. All the objections which attach to the former case are applicable to the latter; while there are other and specific ones, of grave character, which apply to it exclusively. So far, therefore, and, *in this sense*, we concur with the Home Secretary in thinking there should be ' a national prohibition of the assumption of all such titles.'

But it is a vastly different thing to deem the measure, thus reduced and crippled, adequate to the occasion which has given it birth, and to the service for which it is proffered. On this ground we feel no hesitation. It is unworthy both of the Minister and of the nation. No ingenuity can reconcile it with the Durham Letter, or with the speech of the Premier on moving for leave to bring in his bill. It may admit of explanation, but, as at present advised, the policy of Lord John appears to be a compound of timidity, vacillation, and political subserviency, which gives a character of untruthfulness to his past professions, and is adapted to lower the reputation of public men. It would seem, though we hope it may prove otherwise, that, for the sake of retaining the votes of certain Irish members, he has consented to reduce his bill to its present enfeebled state. If such has been his object, he will realize disappointment only : for the Roman Catholic members have pronounced as vehemently against the present measure as against its predecessor.

We will not, however, hastily impute to Lord John a policy so short-sighted and discreditable. He has his faults, and we have never hesitated to denounce them ; but he has hitherto maintained a reputation infinitely above such suspicions. We wait to see what time will disclose. There is a revelation to be made we feel assured, and in the meantime we suspend our judgment on the personal question, simply recording our conviction of the inefficiency of the bill as it now stands.

There is a view of the matter to which we must briefly advert, and which, if sustained, would give a very equivocal character to the ministerial procedure. The case stands thus :—The bill in its original state, interfering, as was alleged, with certain spiritual acts of the Papal Church, ministers consented to abandon its second and third clauses. They did this as a concession to objectors, having no doubt previously consulted the law-officers of the Crown. Mr. M'Cullagh, however, reported to the House on the 14th that Mr. Bethell, of the Chancery bar, Mr. Bramwell, of the Common-law bar, and Mr. Surrage, of the Chancery bar. had been consulted respecting such omission, and had given their *Opinion* that it would be inoperative. This report was sufficiently startling, but we are bound to say that the subsequent statements of the Premier and of the Attorney-General constitute a satisfactory reply, while they triumphantly vindicate the ministerial measure from the charges of intolerance and persecution so freely lavished upon it. ' Gentlemen wishing to oppose this bill,' said the former, ' have represented it as one of persecution, and they say the first clause contains within itself the enactment of the second and third —that preserving the second and third, or omitting the second and third, will make no essential difference, for the first carries the same consequences. Now, without entering into a case of law, upon which many gentlemen of the long robe have already spoken, I will put this to you. If the first clause is so very persecuting a clause, how comes it that for one-and-twenty years the Roman Catholics of Ireland have been subject to that clause—and that we have hardly heard a murmur about it—that the only expression given was in the year 1830 by the Roman Catholic bishops, that that was an expression of acquiescence, and that, so far from having the table of this House loaded with petitions against it, the Roman Catholic clergy and laity have been silently submitting to it ?'

The Attorney-General spoke to the same effect, and as the point is of considerable importance we must be excused for quoting his words :—' It was undoubtedly the law,' he said, ' that any liability by a person calling himself Archbishop of Westminster—that any bond or any bill of exchange signed by such a person, and any contract entered into by him under such a title, could be enforced against him. No lawyer would dispute that. He was satisfied also that no lawyer would be found to dispute this, that a legacy left by will to a person styling himself Archbishop of Westminster would be quite valid and good. The only thing the Court of Chancery would look to would be as to who was meant as the Archbishop of Westminster. There was no question that the law would operate thus. Nor was there any doubt that it would be the same thing as regarded trusts made in favour of the Archbishop of Westminster for the time being. The right hon. baronet the Secretary for the Home Department had. on a former occasion, referred to a judgment of Sir E. Sugden, which had been carried out in a similar manner to what he had described. He admitted to this extent, to this only, that the second clause would be included in the first : if there were any act which was only proved by reason of the person who performed it being bishop of a territorial see holding a prohibited title—if it could only be efficiently done by persons holding these titles, then it would be void, and could not be founded in, or enforced in, any civil court.    That would be prevented by the first clause, and it might, to some extent, interfere with the action of synods, as far as it was necessary for civil courts to do so.    To no other extent could it have any effect.    The law had for the last twenty-one years been the same in Ireland as he was speaking of, and no inconvenience or oppression had been felt, or at least exclaimed against. The bishops had not felt that it was oppressive, and they had not been prevented from doing those acts which were necessary for the due carrying out of their religion.    In no court of law in Ireland had the Roman Catholic bishops suffered injury from this state of the law.'

After seven days' debate, the amendment of thé Earl of Arundel and Surrey was rejected by a majority of 438 to 95, which fully bears out what we have elsewhere said respecting the comparative strength of parties on this question.

The debate, though protracted to a wearisome extent, will be productive of good.    It inculcates many useful lessons, some of which are far from pleasing.    We are glad to observe that all parties concur in reprobating a return to penal legislation.    This is a great step onward, and shows beyond doubt the immense progress which has been made in the practice as well as the theory of religious liberty.    In 1829, it was otherwise ; and since then individuals belonging to one of our great political parties, have occasionally been heard denouncing the Emancipation Act, and calling for its repeal.    Nothing of this, however, has appeared in the recent debate.    All concurred in maintaining the integrity of the act of 1829.    The Ministers who propose ' The Ecclesiastical Titles Bill,' and the most zealous of their supporters, are, on this point, perfectly agreed with its opponents.    Strong terms have, no doubt, been used in describing the measure ; but every candid man will allow that its framers, equally with its opponents, have denounced the employment of pains and penalties in matters spiritual.    We regard this unanimity with unfeigned satisfaction.    It marks an epoch from which future legislation will date.

Again, the debate has placed beyond doubt the strong Protestant feeling of the community.    The Pope has evidently been misled in estimating the feeling of England.    The spread of Puseyism, and the conversions which have taken place to Rome, are now seen to have affected very slightly the general body of the nation.    They were symptoms of a fashion, not of a moral change—were the superficial attributes of a class, not the indications of a revolutionized national sentiment.    There never was a period when the British people were more resolved to maintain their Protestantism.

Again, the views of Puseyite politicians have been disclosed, and, if we mistake not, the disclosure has sealed their fate as public men. They were never very popular with the people, but they are now positively otherwise.    Their policy is not to be mistaken.    Papal in spirit, though Protestant in name, they possess the same general characteristics as those of the Laudean school, and are clearly without support in the country.   Prior to these debates they might have hoped for office, on the ground of their Free-trade policy ; but a wide gulf now intervenes between them and the English people.

Again, the philosophical Radicals are seen in their true colors.   We have never anticipated much from them ; but their bitterest foes may find matter for exultation in the position they have assumed, and the language they have uttered.   Infidelity was the dead weight which broke down the old Radical party ; and religious indifferentism—to use the mildest word—will be equally destructive to their successors.   The pertness and clever smattering of Mr. Roebuck are unhappily characteristic of his class, and a large section of the people are too earnest, and, we shrink not from saying, too enlightened, in their religious convictions, to commit their interests to such hands.   The past votes of these senators prove their ignorance of the real nature of religious liberty, and the contempt in which they hold the scruples of religious men.*

---

* As frequent mention was made of the Canon Law in the course of the debate, and as it is of the utmost importance that its operation, if introduced, should be correctly understood, we make no apology for presenting our readers with a brief extract from the speech of the Attorney-General in reference to this point.   We take occasion, in passing, to express our gratification at the view we gave last month of the bearing of Sir John Romilly's speech being borne out so thoroughly by his explanations of the 21st.   Mr. Roebuck, with much flippancy, having endeavoured to cast ridicule on the fear entertained of the Canon Law, which he strangely represented as ' nothing more or less than a system of spiritual direction for Roman Catholics,' the Attorney-General replied,—' He heard his hon. and learned friend the member for Sheffield state, that it was perfectly absurd to suppose that in any degree whatever the Canon Law could be of effect in this country—that the Canon Law was not the law of this country—but that the English law was the law of this land—and that it was absurd to suppose that the Pope could exercise the Canon Law in this country.   He thought his hon. and learned friend was mistaken in this view.   He held it to be a fact that could not be disputed by any person acquainted with Canon Law, that that Canon Law could only come into effect through bishops of territorial dioceses, in the common acceptation of that term.   He asserted that there might be in the Roman Catholic Church a person who should exercise episcopal functions within his district, and yet between whom and the bishop of a territorial diocese there was the broadest possible distinction, and that distinction was known to the Canon Law.   But a bishop territorial only could put the Canon Law into effect, in respect of the temporalities of persons inhabiting that diocese, and not by a bishop whose functions were purely episcopal. . . . So it followed that to take hold of matters temporal they were obliged to have bishops with defined districts, and by that means only were they able to carry into operation the Canon Law.   His hon. and learned friend said that this Canon Law was not the law of England.   He (the Attorney-General) admitted that—but that it was foreign law.   But the position was this : the law of England looked upon foreign law as a fact ; and, like other facts, was to be proved by witnesses of competent character, and, when once proved, the English law did not inquire whether the foreign law was fit and reasonable, but adopted the principle and acted upon it. . . The bishops of the Catholic Church claimed the right of appointing the priests for benefices.   But if simply bishops and not

Again, and we regret to make the statement, the debate has signally damaged the influence, on general politics, of the leading Free-trade members of the House. The course they have taken has shaken confidence in their judgment, as legislators, and would make the people pause before consenting to place the administration of affairs in their hands. We are far from advocating the substitution of expediency for principle: We honor rather the integrity which sacrifices popularity to duty. But in the present case we believe the course adopted to be wrong, and we bitterly, therefore, regret that by pursuing it, the men who achieved so much should have their power of future service seriously crippled. We are always glad to have Mr. Bright on our side. His talent, and earnestness, and public spirit, render him a most desirable ally, but we are compelled to regard his course on the pending question as one-sided, and to dissent from many of his views as wanting the breadth and largeness of a genuine statesman. Of Mr. Milner Gibson we say but little. On such subjects he is always superficial, and his tone, dogmatic and supercilious, betokens the *virus* which has led other and better men of his party to refer contemptuously to ' the Saints.' We are glad to see that our old friend Colonel Peyronnet Thompson—the father of the Free-trade movement—is of sounder mind, and we are glad to find the vote of the honorable member for Stockport in the majority on the 25th.

We say again to our friends, as we have said on former occasions, maintain your own position. Do not compromise your principles by entering into protestant associations with Churchmen. There is no common ground on which you can stand in such an alliance. It may wear a plausible air, it may look like a Christian brotherhood, it may be commended to you by your abhorrence of Popery, and may be urged by the entreaties of estimable and Christian men within the pale of the Establishment; but be sure you will find, sooner or later, that you are in an equivocal position, which will commit you to what you conscientiously disapprove, or will compel your secession. Let Dissenters and Churchmen take their own ground, and pursue their own measures. More will thus be done than by any compact which, founded on compromise, will cripple your powers, and exhibit you in a very questionable and suspicious light. We found our opposition to Papal aggression on principles, some of which cannot be made to square with the convictions of Churchmen, however pious or liberal.

TWO STRIKING ILLUSTRATIONS of some of the worst charges preferred against the Papal system have occurred in the course of this debate. One was the case of Mathurin Carré, a French emigrant, who has resided in this country more than half a century, a man of miserly habits, who, by dint of minute saving and self-sacrifice, had accumulated upwards of 10,000*l*. In 1847, being then 77 years old,

---

territorial bishops, they could not act upon that right. But the moment they were made territorial bishops, then, by the force of the Canon Law, they were immediately in a position to appoint persons to benefices, and if they came into the Court of Chancery, the court would enforce every one of the trusts. That was the effect of the Canon Law. The Court of Chancery would, in spite of any old practice previously existing, enforce the Canon Law.'

Carré resided with one Matthew Hamilton, in Somers-Town. At the end of February, 1847, he was seriously ill, and was attended by M. Gasquet, a Roman Catholic practitioner. Gasquet recommended nutritious food and wine, but expressed his fear that the circumstances of the sick man might not enable him to procure these. Hamilton replied, that the case was very different, for that the patient was in reality possessed of much property. The following morning, Gasquet informed a Catholic priest of the neighbourhood, Mr. James Holdstock, of the case, who instantly repaired to Carré, and required to see him *alone.* This was allowed, and the result was the execution of a deed, giving some 7,000*l.* for the benefit of schools in connexion with the chapel of which Holdstock was the priest. The details which have been elicited reveal one of the worst cases of Romish rapacity and unscrupulousness which we have met with for a long time past. As an illustration of the fearful power exercised by Papal priests over the dying members of their Church, it is eminently instructive, and as such, merits the gravest attention. The law has, happily, stept in to arrest the evil, by placing the property in safe keeping, until the decision of a competent tribunal is obtained.

The other illustration we refer to is that of the Hon. Miss Augusta Talbot, step-daughter of the Hon. Craven Fitzhardinge Berkeley, whose case is set forth in a petition from Mr. Berkeley to the House of Commons. Miss Talbot is entitled absolutely to 80,000*l.*, on attaining her majority, which will occur June 6th, 1852. On the death of her mother, in April, 1841, she was placed under the guardianship of her relatives, the Earl and Countess of Shrewsbury. What has followed is thus stated by Mr. Berkeley. 'The said Earl and Countess of Shrewsbury placed the said infant Augusta Talbot (notwithstanding she is a ward of court) at the convent called the Lodge, situate at Taunton, in the county of Somerset, *not as a pupil, or visitor, but as a postulant, with the avowed object of allowing the said Augusta Talbot to take the veil and become a nun.*' The prize, it must be confessed, was a tempting one, and the agents of Rome have played a bold stroke for it. We shall see whether English law will not meet the case; and in the meantime, our people will learn what they have to expect from the revival of Popish machinations and influence. We learn from the papers of the 22nd, that the member for Dublin has denied, in distinct terms, the truth of some of the most material of Mr. Berkeley's statements, founding his denial mainly on the authority of a Catholic priest and bishop. The matter, however, did not rest here. Mr. Reynolds was followed by Sir B. Hall, who fastened on him a charge of having suppressed a part of the evidence of the witness on whom he professed to rely. 'Mr. Craven Berkeley,' said Sir B. Hall, 'had declared, in his petition to the house, that his step-daughter was a postulant, and the hon. gentleman the member for Dublin had denied the allegation of the petition by a resolute assertion, declaring that it was altogether untrue. He now told him, that by the letter of one of his own bishops, which he had used as an authority, the statement in the petition was true.' The case has subsequently been brought before the Lord Chancellor, and the disclosures made give it a much worse appearance than it previously bore. It was bad enough when referred to in the Commons, but suspicions of the worst kind are now awakened. The Earl and Countess of Shrewsbury should lose no time in explaining their conduct in the matter.

THE WOODS AND FORESTS, after covering successive administrations with disgrace, have inflicted a defeat on the Russell Cabinet, which ought to have been foreseen and prevented. The mal-administration of the Crown lands has long been notorious. A Parliamentary Committee has brought this mystery of iniquity to light, and the case made out was so bad, that immediate reform was promised. As nothing, however, was done, or appeared likely to be done, Lord Duncan, on the 11th, moved a resolution, that all monies received from the royal forests, and other Crown lands, should be paid into the Exchequer, and that all expenses attendant on collecting the same should be voted by Parliament. This resolution was met, on the part of Government, by an amendment in the shape of motion for leave to bring in a bill to amend the management of the land revenues of the Crown; and, on a division, Ministers were left in a minority of one, the numbers being 120 to 119. The point of difference respected Parliamentary control, for which Lord Duncan contended, and we think rightly. Had this been conceded by Lord Seymour, the division need not have taken place; but as it was not, no other course, as it appears to us, was open to the honorable member for Bath, than that which he pursued. Ministers had ample time for preparation, and ought to have anticipated Lord Duncan, or have mustered their forces to defeat him. A curious incident, illustrative of party tactics, has come to our knowledge respecting this division. The Conservative members, Free-traders and Protectionists, remained immoveable on their seats until the Ministerial side of the House was completely emptied, when, seeing that the Government would have a considerable majority, they went out in a body to record their votes for Lord Duncan, the members for Ripon and Buckinghamshire, as we have already stated, walking out arm in arm. In the case of Mr. Locke King's motion, they abstained from voting, because a majority of the Liberals were against Ministers; but in this case they took part in the division, in order to insure a second defeat. The object of such a policy cannot be mistaken; but what shall we think of the probabilities of a junction between Lord John and Sir James Graham? If the former does not see the necessity of drawing the Liberal party into closer association with his Government, he furnishes an instance of infatuation which we cannot comprehend, and to which we know no parallel.

THE MARRIAGE AFFINITY BILL has been rejected by the Upper House, by a majority of fifty to sixteen. The Archbishops of Canterbury and York, with fifteen bishops, voted against it; and the ground on which this opposition was based befitted the lips of bishops much better than it accords with the common-sense of mankind. The Earl of St. Germans moved the second reading of the bill with moderation and ability, and was opposed by the Primate with an amendment that it be read that day six months. This was seconded by the Bishop of Exeter, in a characteristic speech, in which shrewdness and ability were blended with strange misapprehensions, and the violent prejudices of an ecclesiastic. The obligation of the Levitical code, and its application to the case of marriage with a deceased wife's sister, were strenuously insisted on. Indeed, Dr. Phillpotts 'asserted there was a direct repudiation of these marriages in the New Testament,' though the only case he referred to evinced his gross and most discreditable ignorance on a point with which a school-boy ought to be familiar. Lord Campbell expressed the strong prejudice of his country in opposing the measure, and was succeeded by Lord Brougham, who panegyrized his friend Lord Lyndhurst's Act of 1835. The result of their lordships' vote must have been anticipated, and constitutes another instance of discrepancy in the judgment of the two houses. The bill was passed in the Commons last session; and when we look at the feebleness of the argumentation now employed against it, we are reduced to the conclusion, either that our hereditary legislators are exceedingly prejudiced, or that their votes are swayed by very simple and foolish reasons. A page of our friend Mr. Binney's pamphlet contains more solid sense and sound scriptural interpretation than all the prosy speeches of the Primate and his brethren.* If these dignitaries would retain their seats in the Upper House, it would be advisable for them to refrain from frequently exhibiting themselves as expounders of Scripture, or of social economics and morals.

THE AFFAIRS OF CEYLON formed the subject of an episode on the 14th and 17th, which derived its interest from the special condition of the Government. Mr. Baillie, the member for Invernesshire, having given notice of a motion for the 25th, severely reflecting on the Government in the matter of Ceylon, the Premier stated that in consequence the Budget would not be proceeded with, as was previously intended. 'I do not think it right,' he remarked, 'when a vote of censure is hanging over our heads, that we should propose our financial arrangements for the year.' Mr. Baillie, on the 17th, complained of this, and at once withdrew his notice, on which a well-merited rebuke was administered by Lord John. Mr. Disraeli hastened to cover the retreat of his supporter, and the Home Secretary, Mr. Roebuck, and Sir B. Hall, followed, severely reflecting on the course pursued. The party character of the movement cannot be doubted, and we regret it the more, as the administration of Lord Torrington, and the sanction given to it by the Colonial Secretary, merit the reprobation of Parliament. There have been foul misdoings at Ceylon. The evidence obtained places this beyond doubt, and it is, therefore, deeply to be deplored that such a case should be mixed up with the strife of parties, or be polluted by the selfishness of aspiring ambition. Lord Torrington in the first place, Earl Grey in the second, and the Russell Cabinet in the third, are implicated in the charge; and our national character, as well as sense of justice, requires that it should be thoroughly sifted, and that the criminal, whether peer or commoner, should receive due punishment. Let the Ministry be judged by their own merits— and they are small enough—but let not the course of justice be stayed,

---

* 'An Argument in relation to the Levitical Marriage Law.'

or its waters be poisoned, by the animosities or malignity of faction. Lord Torrington has given notice of his intention to bring the matter before the Upper House on the day of our publication, when due justice, we trust, will be done both to the ex-Governor and to the colony over which he ruled.

ANOTHER CAFFRE WAR has, unhappily, broken out, and some of our journals are calling for the adoption of measures which remind us of the times of Pizarro and Cortez. *As yet we have heard only one side.* Let the British people remember this. The Cape authorities have spoken, the Cape journals have given their version, but the Caffre account is yet to come. *Audi alteram partem.* As we purpose entering largely into this subject next month, we will now only refer to the letter of the Rev. J. J. Freeman, in the ' Patriot,' of the 13th, and to the first article in ' The British Banner,' of the 19th. Judging from what we do know of the past, we fear that the revelation to be made will prove far from honorable to the character and policy of our country.

## Literary Intelligence.

### *Just Published.*

The Metamorphoses of Apuleius. A Romance of the Second Century. Translated from the Latin. By Sir George Head.

The Idolatry of the Church of Rome; proved from Cardinal Wiseman's Third Lecture on the Catholic Hierarchy. In a Lecture by George Barrow Kidd, Minister of Roe-street Chapel, Macclesfield.

Part II. of the Life and Epistles of St. Paul. By the Rev. W. J. Conybeare, M.A., and the Rev. J. S. Howson, M.A.

Christianity and its Evidences. A Course of Six Lectures, delivered in the Lecture-room, Nelson street, Newcastle-on-Tyne. By Rev. J. G. Rogers.

Rovings in the Pacific, from 1837 to 1849; with a Glance at California. By a Merchant, long resident at Tahiti; with four Illustrations, printed in colours. 2 vols.

The Passions of the Human Soul. By Charles Fourier. Translated from the French. By the Rev. John Reynell Morrell; with Critical Annotations. A Biography of Fourier, and a general Introduction. By Hugh Doherty. 2 vols.

Across the Atlantic. By the Author of ' Sketches of Cantabs.'

The Pye Smith Testimonial—Proceedings at a Public Breakfast in the London Tavern, Bishopsgate-street, January 8, 1851, on the Presentation of a Testimonial to the Rev. John Pye Smith, D.D., to which is added a List of Contributors.

Autobiography of the Rev. W. Walford. Edited (with a continuation) by John Stoughton.

Specimens of Translation and Versification. By Joseph Hambleton.

Lavengro; the Scholar, the Gypsy, the Priest. By George Borrow, Author of the Bible in Spain. In 3 vols.

Addresses and Charges of Edward Stanley, D.D., Lord Bishop of Norwich. With a Memoir by his Son, Arthur Penshyn Stanley, M.A.

The Cotton and Commerce of India considered in relation to the Interests of Great Britain. With Remarks on Railway Commerce in the Bombay Presidency. By John Chapman, Founder and late Manager of the Great Indian Peninsular Railway Company.

The Spanish Protestants, and their Persecution by Philip II. A historical work. By Senor Don Adolfo de Castro. Translated from the original Spanish by Thomas Parker.

Anti-Popery and all its Inroads. A Letter of Reply to a Tract of Mr. Edward Miall, of the Anti-state-church Association, entitled the Pope and the Prelates. By Joseph Judge.

Religion and Science; their Independence of each other, and their Mutual Relations. By a Physician.

The Pathway. A Monthly Religious Magazine. No. 1.

The Working-man's Friend and Family Instructor. Part XIII.

The Literature of Working-men. Being the Supplementary Numbers of the Working-man's Friend, from March, 1850, to February, 1851, inclusive. with an Introductory Essay. By Benjamin Parsons.

Bibliotheca Sacra, and American Biblical Repository. Conducted by B. B. Edwards, and E. A. Park. January, 1851.

The Pastor's Glory and Joy. A Sermon, Preached at the Independent Chapel, Kingston, January 12, 1851. By Laurence H. Brynes, B.A., on the occasion of the commencement of his stated ministry there.

The National Cyclopædia of Useful Knowledge. Part XLVIII. First half. V. — Wadham College.

The Pilgrim's Progress. With Forty Illustrations. By David Scott, R.S.A.

Discourses on some of the most Difficult Texts of Scripture. By Rev. James Cochrane, A.M.

The Family Sunday Book; or, Pleasant Pages for Sabbath Hours. Nos. I. and II.

A Voice from an Outpost. Two Discourses on the Papal Aggression. By W. Warwick, D.D.

A Tract for the Times. Not the Church, not the Pope, but the Bible. By William Thwaites.

Clara Eversham; or, the Life of a School-girl. A Narrative founded upon Fact. By Harriet D'Oyley Howe.

Lectures on the Scripture. Revelations respecting good and evil Angels. By a Country Pastor.

Familiar Things. No. I.

Borneo Revelations. A Series of Letters on the Serebas and Sakarran Dyaks, and the Rajah Brooke. By Scrutator.

Practical Sermons for Young Men. By J. A. James. I.—V.

Cuff the Negro Boy. Translated from the German of Dr. Barth.

Christmas Morning; or, the Little Ink Cask. Translated as above.

Reasons for Co-operation; a Lecture delivered at the Office for Promoting Working Men's Associations. To which is added, God and Mammon; a Sermon to Young Men: preached at St. John's District Church, St. Pancras. By F. D. Maurice, M.A.

The Mass. By William Anderson, LL.D.

Lectures to Young Men on various Important Subjects. By Rev. Henry Ward Beecher, Brooklyn, America. With an Introduction by Rev. O. J. Dobbin, LL.D.

Buds and Leaves. By Joseph Anthony, jun.

The History of Church Laws in England from A.D. 602 to A.D. 1850. By Edward Muscutt.

Rose Douglas ; or, Sketches of a Country Parish : being the Autobiography of a Scotch Minister's Daughter. By S. R. W. 2 vols.

The Geological Observer. By Sir Henry T. De La Beche, C.B., &c.

A Trip to Mexico; or, Recollections of a Ten Months' Ramble in 1849-50. By a Barrister.

A Week in the Isles of Scilly. By J. W. North, M.A., Chaplain.

The British Officer; his Position, Duties, Emoluments, and Privileges. By J. H. Stocqueler.

Military Memoir of Lieut.-Colonel James Skinner, C.B. Interspersed with Notices of several of the Principal Personages who distinguished themselves in the service of the Native Powers of India. By J. Baillie Fraser, Esq. 2 vols.

An Introduction to Neo-Hellenic, or Modern Greek ; containing a Guide to its Pronunciation, and an Epitome of its Grammar. By Henry Cape.

No. III. of Familiar Things.

Sketch of Mairwara. Giving a Brief Account of the Origin and Habits of the Mairs. With Descriptions of various Works of Irrigation in Mairwara and Aymeer. Illustrated with Maps, Plans, and Views. By Lieut.-Colonel C. G. Dixon, Bengal Artillery.

Man Natural and Spiritual. By Banks Farrand.

Rome ; its Temper and its Teachings. In Six Lectures. By George Henry Davis.

The Catholic Appeal, Don't burn us ; or, the State Church and the Catholics. By L. Tynman.

The Tenderness of Jesus Illustrated. By Rev. J. W. Richardson.

Correspondence betwixt the Hon. Lord Murray and the Rev. Dr. Candlish regarding the Interference of the Roman Catholic Priesthood with the Edinburgh Original Ragged and Industrial Schools, Ramsay Lane.

Remarks on the Influence of Tractarianism on Church Principles, so called, in promoting Secession to the Church of Rome. By Rev. Theyre T. Smith, M.A.

Lessons and Tales ; a Reading Book for the use of Children. Chiefly intended for the Junior Classes in Elementary Schools. Edited by Rev. Richard Dawes, M.A.

Sermons. By Rev. George Smith.

The Female Jesuit ; or, the Spy in the Family.

The Authority of God ; or, the True Barrier against Romish and Infidel Aggression. Four Discourses. By Rev. J. H. Merle D'Aubigné, D.D. With an Introduction written for this edition.

Scripture Light on Popish Darkness. Notes on Portions of Holy Writ perverted or neglected by the Papists. By Ingram Cobbin, M.A.

Lectures on the Characters of our Lord's Apostles ; and especially their Conduct at the Time of his Apprehension and Trial. By a Country Pastor.

The Creed of Christendom ; its Foundation and Superstructure. By William Rathbone Greg.

Notes, Explanatory and Practical, on the Gospels. Designed for Sabbath-school Teachers and Bible Classes. By Rev. Albert Barnes. Carefully Revised by Rev. Samuel Green.

A Pocket Volume on Punctuality. By Rev. James Kendall.

Maidens and Mothers ; or, the Christian Spinster and the Hebrew Wife. A Book for Young Women. By Rev. T. Binney.

Prayer. By Rev. C. G. Finney.

A Letter to the Right Hon. Lord Campbell on the Clause respecting Chloroform in the proposed Prevention of Offences Bill. By John Snow, M.D.

THE

# 𝔈clectic 𝔑eview.

MAY, 1851.

ART. I.—1. *Returns to an Address of the House of Commons, dated
19th May, 1840, for a Copy of the First and Second Charters of
the University of London—of the Minutes of the Senate of the
University, and of all Committees appointed by the Senate, &c., &c.
Ordered to be Printed, 5th Aug. 1840.*

2. *Third Report from the Select Committee of the House of Commons
on Medical Registration and Medical Law Amendment, with
Minutes of the Evidence and Appendix. Ordered to be Printed,
25th Aug. 1848.*

3. *Calendars of the University of London, Published Annually.
1843—51. London: R. and J. E. Taylor.*

WE have for some time contemplated laying before our readers
an account of the University of London. The successful stand
made by it in defence of its graduates against the assumptions of
the three great medical corporations—the annual number of
successful candidates which has at length justified the public
conferring of degrees—and still more recently the accession to
its senatorial ranks of men of such note as Sir James Graham,
Mr. Grote, Mr. Hallam, Mr. Cornewall Lewis, Mr. Macaulay,
Lord Monteagle, and Lord Overstone—sufficiently prove that the
university has made its position. Besides this, the pendency
even now of questions of vital import, makes us particularly
anxious to inform our readers fully as to its past career and

future prospects. Our limits enforce compression; but the subject fortunately admits selection of matter, and we shall return to it shortly.

Most of our readers will remember the circumstances to which the University of London owes its establishment. The project was first announced in 1825, and in a few months the funds received were sufficient to set it on foot. The proprietary contains a goodly list of names high in office and in rank. On the 30th of April, 1827, in the presence of upwards of two thousand persons, the Duke of Sussex laid the first stone of the building in Gower-street. On this occasion ' the patriot Duke' was supported by the Duke of Norfolk, the Earl of Carnarvon, the late Lord Auckland, the present Lord Brougham, Dr. Lushington, Mr. J. Smith, M.P., &c. &c. Early in 1828, the courses of instruction had been matured, and the necessary arrangements completed; and by November the institution was in full work in all the usual branches of academic learning, except theology.

In 1830 the founders applied for a Charter of Incorporation as an university. The opposition, at the last moment, of Oxford and Cambridge, prevented the grant; but in 1833 the application was renewed, backed by an address from the City of London. The matter was referred to the Privy Council, and the grant of the charter was here opposed not only by the old universities, but by the London Hospitals and the College of Surgeons. Sir Charles Wetherell led the attack for Oxford with his wonted energy; but the real difficulty arose from the medical opposition. It was felt that the power of granting medical degrees ought, if conferred at all, to be conceded to all alike, and not only to the new institution. Pending the discussion Sir Robert Peel succeeded Lord Melbourne as Prime Minister; and the question was then brought to a point by the carrying against Ministers of a motion, by Mr. Tooke, for an address to the Crown, praying for the University Charter. Almost immediately afterwards Lord Melbourne returned to office, and negotiations were actively carried on between Mr. Spring Rice on the part of the restored Government, and Mr. Romilly (the present Master of the Rolls), on behalf of the college.

The scheme proposed by the Government (which had been hinted at by Lord John Russell in the debate on Mr. Tooke's motion*) was a *tertium quid*—viz., to establish the Gower-street body and other educational institutions as *Colleges;* and to create a *University* of a distinct body, consisting of gentlemen

---

* Hansard, vol. xxxvii., 3d series.

eminent in literature and science. To this body was to be entrusted the function of examining candidates, and granting degrees; and to the Gower-street, and other *colleges*, was to belong the right of sending up their pupils as candidates. The fundamental principle was, that academical degrees were to be granted ' in London, to persons of all religious persuasions, without distinction, and without the imposition of any test or disqualification whatever.'

It will be seen that this plan avoided the difficulty started by the medical schools, and immensely widened the basis of the new university. All these bodies could now, if they chose, become colleges, and thus secure degrees for their students; while by confining the actual power of granting degrees to one body their value as a test was proportionably raised.

Some further explanations passed; the Chancellor of the Exchequer going somewhat out of his way to observe, that ' it should be always kept in mind that what is sought on the present occasion is, an equality in all respects with the ancient universities, freed from those exclusions and religious distinctions which abridge the usefulness of Oxford and Cambridge;' and, eventually, the Gower-street Council accepted the proposed arrangement, and, on the 28th of November, 1836, received the charter under

University of Londo

King's College had al

another charter, dated

by her present Majesty, a distinct body of gentlemen were incorporated as THE UNIVERSITY OF LONDON.[*] Henceforward, the history of the Gower-street Institution is that of University *College*, and our allusions to it will be in that character only.

The object of the University of London Charter was declared to be, ' for the advancement of religion and morality, and the promotion of useful knowledge, to hold forth to all classes and denominations of our faithful subjects, without any distinction whatsoever, an encouragement for pursuing a regular and liberal course of education.' The gentlemen we have referred to, whose names will be found in the Calendars, were incorporated as the University, and were further appointed to act as ' the Senate.' It provided for the nomination of a Chancellor by the Crown, to hold office for life; and of a Vice-Chancellor, annually, by the Senate. The Crown was to fill up vacancies or appoint additional members at pleasure; but the Senate was to complete its own numbers up to 36, if they should ever fall below 27.

---

[*] A charter had been granted by King William, on the same day with the University College charter, but owing to a technical inaccuracy, it expired with his life.

To the Senate was entrusted the 'entire management of, and superintendence over,' the affairs of the University. It was empowered to make all requisite bye-laws, subject to the approval of the Home Secretary; to hold examinations at least once a-year, and to appoint and remove examiners; to confer, 'after examination,' the degrees of B.A., M.A., LL.B., LL.D., M.B., and M.D.; and to charge fees for the degrees conferred, subject to the approval of the Treasury.

University and King's Colleges were empowered by the charter itself to send up candidates for examination; and provision was made for affiliating by sign-manual other educational institutions then or thereafter to be established within the United Kingdom. Medical schools and institutions were to be affiliated, on obtaining a report in their favour from the Senate, approved by the Home Secretary.

Candidates were to produce certificates from their respective colleges, stating that they had 'completed the course of instruction' determined by the regulations of the Senate in that behalf; and on being declared by the examiners entitled to their degree, they were to receive a certificate thereof under the university seal.

The university is not as yet in the enjoyment of a Senate House; and the apartments in Somerset House assigned to its use by the Government have for some time afforded very insufficient accommodation. The degrees were conferred last year in the hall of King's College. The first year's expenses, amounting to about 5,000l., were defrayed by the Government; and a promise was given of providing future assistance (until the fees should create an adequate income) from the 'votes.' Upon Sir Robert Peel's accession, Mr. Goulburn cut down the vote by 800l., with somewhat scant courtesy. The fees have steadily risen to nearly 2,000l. a-year, and are still rising.

Our inquiries will now be directed to ascertain what the Senate has done in discharge of the high trust committed to it; how far it has been met by the adhesion of public educational bodies; the number and character of its graduates; and the general result.

The regulations for graduating in each faculty may be found in the Calendar. Of what labours they are the result, we shall now endeavour to describe.

Almost at the first meeting of the Senate,* three committees were appointed (one in each faculty), with instructions 'to inquire and report on the departments of knowledge in which it is expedient for the Senate, in conferring degrees, to grant certificates of particular proficiency; on the course of instruction;

---

* This information is collected from a blue book, printed in 1840, by order of the House of Commons, on Mr. Hume's motion, containing an account of the entire proceedings of the University down to its date.

on the certificates which shall entitle candidates to examination for degrees in their several faculties; and also as to the expediency of requiring matriculation, and the time of doing so in each of these faculties.' The Committee in Arts consisted of the whole Senate; the Committee in Medicine, of the medical members, with the addition of the Chancellor, Vice-Chancellor, Bishop of Chichester, Mr. Amos, and Dr. Jerrard; the Committee in Laws, of the Chancellor and Vice-Chancellor, the Bishops of Durham, Chichester, and Norwich, and Messrs. Austin, Empson, Lefevre, Senior, and Warburton.

The Committees in Arts and Laws were ready with their reports in June, 1838; the Medical Committee did not conclude its labours until February, 1839. The manner of proceeding of the Arts Committee (to take one as a sample) was in this wise. It will be remembered that it consisted of the whole Senate. The whole body first determined—with the aid of a valuable letter from Dr. Arnold—upon the general subjects, a knowledge of which should be essential to the degree of B.A. The minutes printed by order of the House of Commons betoken an honourable anxiety on this important preliminary. When finally arranged, sub-committees were appointed ' to draw up a descriptive schedule of the particular subjects' to be included under the general heads of knowledge. Chemistry, and Animal and Vegetable Physiology, were entrusted to Mr. Faraday, Professor Henslow, and Dr. Roget; Mathematics and Natural Philosophy, to Mr. Airy, Dr. Arnott, and Mr. Lefevre; Logic and Moral Philosophy, to Mr. Empson, Mr. Senior, and Mr. Warburton; Classics, to the Bishop of Chichester, Dr. Arnold, and Dr. Jerrard. Their recommendations appear on the printed papers. They passed through the ordeal of an intermediate and more general sub-committee; and after a lengthened re-consideration, were substantially adopted by the Committee of the whole Senate. They involved examinations considerably more extensive and deeper than is now actually demanded; but it appears to have been since felt that it was possible to go too far in excess of what was made necessary elsewhere; modifications were, consequently, effected, reducing the Arts curriculum to its present shape.

We have been thus far specific, because the knowledge of such labours by the eminent persons named, continued almost *de die in diem* for a period of fourteen months, followed by constant revision by the light of further experience and actual working, must add materially to the weight of the LONDON UNIVERSITY CURRICULUM. The remark applies even more strongly to the regulations in Medicine.

A general sketch of the curriculum would convey no information as to the points we wish to illustrate; and to enter minutely into its details would much exceed our limits. We shall therefore, in as few words as possible, sum up what appear to be its general results.

I. The candidate for a London degree must prove a knowledge more general and more uniform than elsewhere, and not less deep than is required at other universities in the subjects of their especial encouragement.

We may easily illustrate this. Not less classics is required than would be sufficient at Oxford, and not less mathematics than would be sufficient at Cambridge; so that the amount of joint-knowledge, if we may so speak, is higher at London than at either Oxford or Cambridge. Again, Oxford and Cambridge have not regarded modern classics, nor modern history, nor simple physical science, unconnected, we mean, with mathematical development. At London, besides requiring the student to be as deep in logic and moral philosophy as elsewhere, he is led into animal physiology, English history to the end of the seventeenth century, and at least one modern language, an option being left him between French and German.

II. More complete provision is made than elsewhere for ensuring a continuance of study (and consequently real mental training) on the part of the candidate throughout the whole period of his course. The examinations, from first to last, are *bonâ fide*; they are placed sufficiently apart, and they are all accompanied by a further examination for honours.

What may be the absolute amount of improvement in these respects recently effected, or now in contemplation, at Oxford or Cambridge, we will not undertake precisely to say; but as there is avowedly no examination *after* the B.A. degree is taken, so we believe, practically, there is none of any real value before it; and that the examination for the degree itself is not such as to require any very extreme labour, or for any very long time. That the colleges have constant examinations (almost daily, we believe, some of them, as the struggle approaches), we are well aware; but this is not our point. They make provision for study, it may be conceded. They make none for *ensuring* it. Now at London, it is not impossible, certainly, but it is made as difficult as it well can be, to obtain a degree without continuous study. In the first place, matriculation is indispensable. The candidate for this must evince a knowledge (sound as far as it goes, and that not merely elementary) of the simpler problems of arithmetic and algebra, and the first book of Euclid, one Greek and one Latin book *melioris ævi et notæ*, and the grammatical structure, etymological as well as syntactic, of the English language,* and the history of England to the end of the seventeenth century. Besides these, he must be further prepared

---

* This examination is severe, requiring a knowledge of Saxon roots, and of the historical development of the language.

either in chemistry or in the usual branches of natural philosophy as popularly treated.

When we state further, that the candidate must have completed his sixteenth year, we have shown sufficient evidence of an intention that a London undergraduate shall need a sound school education to begin with. Our general readers are aware how far this is verified by the class of young men whom our schools send up to matriculate. It is further and very material evidence in its favour that the medical graduates find it sufficient without taking an Arts degree to place them in a position much superior to their professional brethren of the same length of standing, as regards the social consideration which a degree of literary acquirement always ensures.

We assume, therefore, that the London graduate must have a complete, sound, and, consequently, a lengthened school training before he begins his university course.[*]

The matriculated candidate for the B.A. degree must wait two years, and must then produce certificates of having, during that interval, been a well-conducted college student, before he can be admitted to the examination. After waiting two years longer, and completing his twentieth year of age, the B.A. will be admitted to try for the Master of Arts degree.

Not to overstate the case, we must here mention that it is a very small proportion of the candidates in Arts who have hitherto passed on to the final degree. An increase appears probable, but the number of M.A.'s does not yet reach forty out of more than four hundred bachelors. The course of training must, therefore, be taken as terminating at the same point with those of Oxford and Cambridge. The difference is, that it begins earlier and continues throughout. But the determination to insist on an examination for the M.A. degree speaks most strongly for the excellence of the London system. At Oxford and Cambridge, as is well known, the course of study ends with the B.A. degree. The M.A. is given of course to any graduate who chooses to pay for it. What is the object of retaining it at all, except to get money, we have no knowledge.

Another most valuable principle is acted upon in the arrangements for the Honours examination. It is not, as at Cambridge, left to the option of the candidate, whether to present himself for the mere degree, or for the Honours list; such Honours again being restricted to mathematics and classics. At London he is required first to pass; and thereby to give evidence of

---

[*] Let us not be misunderstood. A candidate for the Cambridge Wranglership begins his mathematics two, or even three years, before he enters the university. We are speaking of the provision for the mass, and showing that the London B.A., as such, must be a very different being from one of the Oxford or Cambridge οἱ πολλοι.

sound general training.  It being thus ascertained that all the faculties of his mind have had their due development, he is encouraged, by the variety of honours offered, to pursue his studies whithersoever his genius leads him.  At matriculation he may take Honours, not only in mathematics and classics, but also in natural history and chemistry; the former being understood to embrace botany and zoology.  The B.A. Honours include chemistry, animal and vegetable physiology, and structural botany. These latter Honours are not ranked so highly as the others, nor should they be; they are worthy, and they are treated as worthy, of special recognition where the taste for them exists.  A distinct branch of the M.A. examination is devoted to philosophy.

We are aware that numerous prizes await the freshman at the older universities.  Were they accompanied by a sound general examination, we should have nothing to say against them.  As it is, they lead to a warping of the student's mind at the very outset, by directing his attention inordinately to the subject in which he feels that he has already succeeded.  This partial, one-sided mode of study is the great evil (intellectually speaking) of the Oxford and Cambridge system; and one from which London has been hitherto, and we hope will ever remain, wholly free. The powers given by the recent supplementary charter, to grant certificates, without a previous degree, of proficiency in particular departments of study, such as navigation and civil engineering, seriously alarmed us.  These studies have no claim to an estimation which the university has so distinctly refused to even classics and mathematics, taken alone.  Fears were once entertained, looking to the known leanings of influential persons among the founders of University College, that its training would be formed too much in the 'Utilitarian' model.  Its conduct on the late certificate movement has entirely dissipated this fear; and, after what has passed, we hope that this most mistaken attempt will not be repeated.

III.  The faculties of law and medicine, elsewhere so long and so shamelessly neglected, are at London honourably recognised.

We have not heard that Oxford has done anything for MEDICINE since she sent up to the House of Commons Committee, as a specimen of her productions in that line, a doctor of Divinity ; nor if Oxford had, upon that occasion, taken any other course than that of insisting on the retention of her exclusive privileges, while avowedly doing no one thing for which they were given to her, would her inefficiency be much open to observation. Neither Oxford nor Cambridge have the means of providing medical teaching.  Even the strong evidence as to Cambridge, of the late Professor Haviland, fails to convince us that a solitary hospital, with not three hundred beds, can do as much for students as the thronged wards open to them all over London.

They may there see daily, and in every form and stage, diseases which they would only hear of throughout their whole courses at Oxford or Cambridge.

For their treatment of LAW, these learned bodies have not the same excuse. The great defect of the profession in this country is its want of scientific training. With a practical skill which distances all competition on this side of the Atlantic, yet to what that is to which their lives are devoted, they have never given a thought. Mr. Phillips leads you through two goodly octavos on the law of Evidence without once telling you what evidence is; while another learned writer proposes to supply the defect by informing you, with an amusing gravity, that it is *not* counsel's address to the jury. A 'debt' is defined by Mr. Serjeant Stephen as a 'predicament,' which it is. Now it is idle to say that universities—that Oxford and Cambridge, with their tutors, their libraries, their special and large endowments—cannot teach jurisprudence. It is disgraceful to say, that at one, if not both of these universities, the LL.B. or B.C.L. is a sort of back-door degree, sought for by those who dare not be plucked, and who are too idle or too ignorant for even the οἱ πολλοί.

In nothing has the London Senate displayed more admirable conduct than in meeting the great want of the medical profession. The old universities taught gentlemen, but not physicians; the London hospitals gave the education of surgeons and physicians, but not of gentlemen. The University of London does both. It expects of the mere student of literature that he shall be acquainted with the vital functions of the animal system; it expects of the medical student that his earlier life shall have been devoted to the *literæ humaniores,* and that at the close of his course he shall be read in moral philosophy and logic, and at least the elements of intellectual philosophy. With an exception, which rarely occurs in practice, the medical course is not concluded until the student has reached his twenty-fourth year, and involves, after matriculating, three examinations, the first and second alone of which carry the medical knowledge required through all the subjects involved in every department of practice, whether as a physician, surgeon, or apothecary, and carry it, too, to a higher point than is known at any other institution whatever. In Law, again, the LL.D. examination is equally severe. Indeed, the LL.D. medallist has attained the highest university honour which this country* has to bestow. An Arts degree is an essential preliminary; and then, after two years' legal study, the candidate for the mere LL.B. degree is required to prove his

---

* The Divinity degrees elsewhere are not an university honour. They require no examination, and are merely a recognition of what the public voice has already decided.

knowledge both of principle and practice by an examination in Blackstone and Bentham. But while the examinations display no lack of severity, there is a woful lack of encouragement. One scholarship and one medal are all the temptations of the law student. We see no reason why all the branches of jurisprudential learning should not have their appropriate *scholarship or exhibition* equally with the several divisions of medical study. The value of these stimulants cannot be doubted, when it is observed that all the candidates for law honours try for the jurisprudence scholarship, and rarely for anything else.

But the best prepared curriculum may become valueless, if care be not taken with the examinations. The London Senate confides this duty, in the first instance, to such of its own members as are willing to undertake it. Failing these, it attracts examiners of merit, by the offer of a position practically permanent, and a salary high in proportion to the duties. We cannot now discuss the relative advantages of this and the systems pursued elsewhere. Judging by the *results*, the London system has not hitherto failed to secure examiners of real and, what is hardly less important, of recognised ability.

For the examinations themselves there are two tests: one, universally recognised, is the proportion of plucked men; the other is the responsible expression of opinion by men of acknowledged position, respecting the standing of the graduates, or, still better, their relative success.

The proportion of plucked men, to get rid of the unpleasant test first, is shown by the following table,* giving the results from the first examination in 1838 to the last in 1850:—

| | No. of Candidates. | Passed. | Not passed. | Proportion plucked. |
|---|---|---|---|---|
| Matriculation . | 1,435 | 1,277 | 158 | 1 in 9 |
| B.A. . . . . | 480 | 415 | 65 | Over 1 „ 8 |
| M.A. . . . . | 40 | 37 | 3 | 1 „ 13 |
| LL.B. . . . . | 35 | 33 | 2 | 1 „ 18 |
| LL.D. . . . | 7 | 5 | 2 | 1 „ 4 |
| B.M., 1st. Exam. | 463 | 319 | 144 | Nearly 1 „ 3 |
| „ 2d. „ . | 229 | 200 | 29 | 1 „ 10 |
| M.D. . . . . | 102 | 95 | 7 | 1 „ 13 |
| Total . . | 2,751 | 2,381 | 410 | Over 1 in 7 |

* Constructed from an annual tabular statement, some results of which have already appeared elsewhere.

We think this table speaks for itself as to the good faith of the requirements of the curriculum.  With regard to the other tests, eleven years is a period fully short for the attainment of a ' position,' by any considerable number of the graduates ; yet we have seen a list of appointments, held by the London medical graduates, both numerous and important.  We may refer also to the partiality for London graduates as ministers, priests, and clergymen ; the proportion of ' reverends ' having, down to a recent period, been not less than one-sixth of the entire number

case in which the refusal
sidered to be worth not
in succession, in the first
don, and declined.
We had marked for extract
Report of the Committee on
hibiting, in strong relief, the
duates throughout the country,
disinterment.

London, therefore, has done what Oxford and Cambridge could not do.  It has extended, for all this country, the basis of a liberal education ; insomuch that Oxford and Cambridge are fain to follow in its track.  It has accorded their due rank to mental, moral, and political science, placing them at the end of the course, and attributing to them honours not less than equal to the continued pursuit of classics or mathematics.  In this, also, Oxford and Cambridge have been unable to disobey the lead.  Moreover, in a liberal education, London alone has embraced the studies of the liberal professions.

The financial condition of the university is somewhat as follows.  It has to provide for scholarships and other rewards, and examiners and other officers.  The estimates calculate nearly 1,100l. for scholarships, and nearly 2,500l. for examiners.  The registrar's salary is 500l., and the clerk receives 250l.  The remainder, consumed in incidentals, brings up the estimates to slightly under 5,000l.  To meet this, the amount of fees has reached 1,500l., leaving the remainder to be provided by the ' votes.'

THE LONDON UNIVERSITY:

Judging from the tabular statement below,[*] the income for fees is likely to increase. We should premise that the scale of fees is as follows:—2l. for matriculation, and 10l. for each degree in Arts; in Medicine, 5l. for each of the two bachelors' examinations, and 10l. for the M.D.; in Laws, 10l. for the LL.B., and 25l. for the LL.D. The table represents the amount of fees received upon all the examinations, year by year. It does not exactly represent the annual number of candidates, inasmuch as up to 1847-8 the fees were returned to unsuccessful competitors. In that year, the Senate, finding a loss of nearly 1,300l. already incurred by this system, determined on retaining the fees, admitting the candidates to re-examination without further payment.

| | 1838 | 1839 | 1840 | 1841 | 1842 | 1843 | 1844 | 1845 | 1846 | 1847 | 1848 | 1849 | 1850 |
|---|---|---|---|---|---|---|---|---|---|---|---|---|---|
| Matriculation £ | 44 | 60 | 138 | 128 | 132 | 160 | 158 | 206 | 198 | 306 | 322 | 362 | 400 |
| B.A. . . . . | — | 170 | 300 | 350 | 200 | 280 | 300 | 370 | 300 | 360 | 470 | 620 | 660 |
| M.A. . . . . | — | — | 30 | 10 | 30 | — | 30 | 10 | 20 | 30 | 40 | 70 | 100 |
| LL.B. . . . | — | 30 | 20 | 90 | 20 | 10 | 10 | 20 | 20 | 20 | 40 | 20 | 30 |
| LL.D. . . . | — | — | — | — | — | 25 | — | — | — | — | 50 | 25 | 25 |
| B.M. 1st Exam. | } 125 | | 190 | 250 | 125 | 105 | 130 | 125 | 130 | 120 | 135 | 160 | 140 |
| „ 2d „ | | | 95 | 90 | 95 | 105 | 100 | 80 | 65 | 100 | 120 | 75 | 80 |
| M.D. . . . . | — | 20 | 10 | 70 | 50 | 40 | 140 | 110 | 110 | 90 | 120 | 80 | 150 |
| Total . £ | 44 | 405 | 783 | 988 | 652 | 725 | 868 | 911 | 843 | 1026 | 1297 | 1412 | 1585 |

The extent to which those who had been excluded from Oxford and Cambridge have availed themselves of the facilities thus provided, will be judged of by the following statement. Colleges have been affiliated in connexion with the Independents, Baptists, Catholics, Church of England, and Wesleyans, besides colleges professedly open to all denominations. Of the latter, University College, to which is due the honour of our having an university at all, was affiliated at the outset. This was followed in 1840 and 1842 by the colleges at Manchester and Carmarthen. The Baptists and Independents affiliated their London colleges, Highbury, Homerton, and Stepney, in 1840. A technical point renders it necessary to affiliate New College afresh. Airedale, Bristol, Cheshunt, and Rotherham, joined in 1841; Huddersfield, and the Lancashire College, in 1844; Plymouth in 1848; and Taunton in 1849. The Roman Catholic

---

[*] Constructed partly from the tabular statement before mentioned, and as to part from direct information.

colleges at Carlow, Oscott, Prior Park, Stonyhurst, Ushaw, and Ware, all joined in 1840, followed by Downside in 1841, and by two Irish colleges in 1844 and 1849. The Church of England owns to King's, Queen's College, Birmingham (1846), and the universities of the United Kingdom. The Wesleyans, in 1844 and 1846, added their colleges at Sheffield and Taunton to the list.

The medical colleges and institutions defy specific mention. They are nearly one hundred in number. They are spread over England, Scotland, and Ireland. They are to be found in Calcutta, Montreal, Malta, and Ceylon. They include *all* the leading hospitals in London. And all of them have been admitted on their own application; many have submitted to rigid inquiry before being received; some of the best-reputed have expressed, in warm terms, their gratitude for the boon. It is uniformly the *élite* of their students who present themselves for the London degrees.

On the 7th July, 1849, the supplementary charter, to which we have alluded in connexion with the proposed certificate system, empowered the university to receive candidates from Oxford and Cambridge, and the other ancient universities in the three kingdoms. On this we postpone our judgment. The measure, which at best is far too slight an advance to call for any very warm expression of gratitude from us, *may* work in so many ways for which we should not be grateful, and had in its original proposal such* a *Timeo Danaos* look about it, that we must decline for the present expressing any opinion.

The above is a compressed statement of the past history of *the University* of London. A question is now pending, upon the right decision of which, it is not too much to say, depend its whole future fortunes.

We are not alluding to the admission of Dissenters at Oxford or Cambridge. If accorded, of which we see no present probability, the fate of London must still depend on itself. The question is,— *What a London graduate is to be?* It is traceable, by no means obscurely, in the foundation charter; it has been three times under the consideration of the Senate; and it is at this moment awaiting a further discussion by that body, as now constituted by the recent appointment of new members.

The demand was undoubtedly, in its full extent, equality with Oxford and Cambridge. Remembering what was deemed possible in those times, it would be an insult to common sense to infer anything less from the poured-out largess to found University College; the Guildhall address; the House of Commons resolutions; and the destruction of a Ministry. Now the graduate

* The debate was fully reported in the 'Patriot.'

of Oxford or Cambridge is a member of one of the most important public bodies in the country, wielding a commanding influence throughout the entire kingdom; an influence arising from the learning, station, and privileges* of its members. Its privilege and station belong to every graduate. The meanest graduate may, if he chooses, and often practically does, exercise an important influence on the affairs of his university, and holds a higher social position in consequence. The question of sending members to Parliament is beyond the present scope of our observations.

This is not the character of the degree now offered to the London students. The London graduates, as we have seen, *must* be, in respect of attainments, what the Oxford or Cambridge graduates *need not* be—but having ascertained this, the University of London has nothing more to do with him. He is not a member of the university at all. His entire connexion with it is a mere passing matter of bargain and sale. A fee is paid, an examination is passed, and a certificate is received, and this closes the transaction.

This state of things *may* have been at the outset the wisest course to pursue. But it could only have been intended to be temporary. As a point of common honesty between man and man it could not have been meant to last longer than was absolutely required. The very frame of the charter bespeaks a consciousness of this, or why the appointment of so many personages as 'the University,' and then the re-appointment of the self-same gentlemen over again as 'the *Senate* of the University,' with the 'entire management of, and supervision over,' the University, *i.e.*, themselves. Obviously a future modification was contemplated, in which the senatorial function was to be one, but not the sole essential element.

Such appears by the Blue Book to have been the view of the Senate. That body had no sooner disengaged itself from the important preliminaries we have been discussing, than, in 1840—as soon in fact as it had any graduates to think of—it began to consider their position. On the 25th March the Senate resolved itself into a committee of the whole body, 'to consider of any alteration it may be expedient to make in the charter.' The committee met seven times, and was attended on each occasion by from twelve to fifteen members. Those who appear to have given most attention to the subject, both by their regularity of attendance and the part taken by them in the discussions, were

---

* The large *income* commonly attributed to the old universities belongs not to them, but to the colleges connected with them. *We doubt much if it is larger than belongs to the institutions connected with London.*

Sir John Lubbock, Dr. Arnold, Dr. Billing, Sir James Clark, Sir Stephen Hammick, Dr. Hodgkin, Dr. Jerrard, Dr. Locock, Dr. Roget, Mr. Senior, and Mr. Warburton. Of the numerous resolutions come to we shall extract those which refer to our present point.

' 30th March. That as soon as the graduates of three years' standing shall amount in number to three hundred, it will be expedient to constitute the said graduates, and all future graduates of the same standing, together with the persons who then or thenceforth shall be or shall have been members of the Senate, the electoral body of this university. —Mr. Warburton. Carried *nem. con.*

'6th April. That the number of members of the Senate be limited to thirty-six, exclusive of the Chancellor and Vice-Chancellor.—Sir S. Hammick. *Aff.* 6 ; *neg.* 3.

' That until an Electoral Body be constituted, no appointment of any new member of the Senate shall take place by the Secretary of State, without one month's previous notice to the Senate, through the Chancellor or Vice-Chancellor, of the name of the individual proposed to be appointed.—Dr. Locock. Carried *nem. con.*

' 13th April. That it is expedient that as soon as the Electoral Body of the University shall be constituted, one-sixth part of the members of the Senate shall annually retire, those retiring not being re-eligible at the next ensuing election.—Mr. Warburton. *Aff.* 10 ; *neg.* 2.

' That the Electoral Body shall determine who shall be elected to the vacancies thus created.—Mr. Warburton.

' 15th April. That of the six retiring members of the Senate, three shall go out by rotation, and three in consequence of their having given the smallest amount of attendance during the last year.—Dr. Hodgkin. *Aff.* 4 ; *neg.* 1.

' 13th May. That not more than two persons belonging professionally to the same faculty shall be elected annually members of the Senate.— Mr. Warburton. *Aff.* 5 ; *neg.* 1.'

Such was the scheme proposed in 1840 by the whole Senate, sitting in committee, elaborated by the gentlemen we have named, and sanctioned by others of no less note, who were less frequently present. The above resolutions bear marks on the face of them of a full discussion and careful framing. However, on coming before the Senate, sitting senatorially, the resolution which stands first in order and importance received a variety of amendments, and was finally rejected.

After the subject had slept for eight years, it was again brought forward by the graduates. The alarm occasioned by the Medical Registration Bill, and the entire destitution of means in which the Senate found itself under its present constitution to pacify that alarm, led to the organization of the entire body of graduates —the other faculties joining their medical brethren rapidly and heartily. Communications were opened with the Senate in March, 1848; by June a full meeting of the graduates had been held at Freemasons' Tavern, at which a committee was appointed to protect their constitutional and medical interests. Their energy as to the latter has resulted, we may say at once, in an acknowledgment by the Government of the force of the arrangements of 1836 for ensuring to the London graduates equality in civil privileges with those of Oxford and Cambridge, and a promise to enforce it in any medical bill supported by the Government.

The more important measure—the admission of the graduates to a *de facto* existence—has proceeded much more slowly. In the first instance, the Senate did not do more than enable the graduates to state their wishes at the Home Office. This led to a request from Sir George Grey that the graduates would prepare a plan for effecting the incorporation desired. After much deliberation, this was drawn up; it was eventually referred to the Senate; and although that body declined to report in its favour, their resolution contained a declaration of their desire 'that the graduates should hereafter be admitted to a share in the government of the university.' This was on the 10th of June, 1849. Further communications have passed, and at the time we write the matter is under consideration, a special meeting of the Senate having been convened for the purpose.

We shall not anticipate their decision, anxiously as we *await* it; but while it is still pending, we propose to point out some circumstances favourable to the admission of the graduates.

The first, and most important, is the Metropolitan seat of the university. We doubt if the importance of this advantage can be over-estimated. It secures the constant presence in the immediate neighbourhood of the Senate of a large number of the most distinguished men. It is the great misfortune of Oxford and Cambridge that, with the exception of the necessarily few whom the highest university posts can detain, their best men all leave them as soon as they have completed their course—we might say *all* their men, for the number of residents is exceedingly few. They are at this moment suffering too severely from the inevitable consequences of power lodged in few hands, unchecked, except in special cases, and ignorant of the world without, to need enlargement upon it. The reverse is necessarily the case in London. There are the best men, and too many of them, to render it possible that if influenced by their energy, the University of London can lag behind the age; while the conservative feeling natural to professional classes will protect it equally from undue proneness to alteration.

Another important fact is the number of the graduates thus resident who are engaged in the liberal professions. The medical graduates of London find openings ready for them in all the principal towns; but London itself is the place where they 'most do congregate.'  The law graduates are few; but the graduates engaged in legal pursuits constitute probably the majority of the Arts men.  The considerable number engaged in tuition we have already alluded to.  Now we rank most highly this latter class, so nearly assimilating to our own; but a community of teachers only is not our notion of Utopia.  We have no doubt of the advantage to be derived from a very considerable infusion of the classes engaged in professional practice.  We are satisfied that their absence—their unavoidable absence—from Oxford and Cambridge, is one material cause of the acknowledged retrogression of those bodies.  London would have the best men, plenty of them, and of all classes.

No system can provide practically for every graduate.  Oxford and Cambridge have no means, we say advisedly *no* means, of enlisting in their active service more than a very small number. The only thing that enables them to effect an organization at all is their Parliamentary franchise.  In London, residence secures the co-operation of a full half, and the month of May brings a large proportion of the remainder annually to town.  These can be kept fully enough informed of what is intended, to decide upon it intelligently at the annual gathering.

But there are not only greater facilities, there is greater necessity.  At Oxford and Cambridge the governing body of the universities is composed (speaking generally) of the governing bodies of the colleges; and any nominal distinction is lost in the practical identity of interest and purpose permeating through the entire mass.  At London the Senate is carefully kept distinct from the colleges; and its individual members, with scarcely an exception, have, for all practical purposes, no acquaintance with the college authorities.  The connecting link is formed by the graduates, and they form a more efficient and safer connexion than any other—more efficient, because they are so nearly concerned; safer, because their organization connecting them collectively with all the colleges, precludes the narrowness and warping of view incidental to representatives isolated from each other, and charged with the peculiar interests of single institutions.

Nor would the result be confined to the colleges.  London has at present none of that influence which is so important an element in the value of an Oxford or Cambridge degree. During the twelve years of its existence many of the colleges have received even large public benefactions; the university not one. We believe that half the world is ignorant of its very locality. Not three days ago we saw the ' particulars' of a house in Gower-street described as ' near the London University.' In these economical times this influence is all important. Chancellors of the Exchequer have hitherto not refused assistance. But should a future Chancellor arise ' who knows not Joseph,' the first votes sacrificed to the pressure from without will be those granted to bodies having no hold on the country, and against which, as it happens, there is the recorded opinion of a select committee.* The incorporation of the graduates would effect a lodgment for the university in nearly every town in England. It would gratify thousands of families which never before had a graduate in their ranks. It would lead to substantial pecuniary aid; and would tell in any important struggle in the House of Commons itself.

We cannot overlook the fact that the graduates already are an organized body—that notwithstanding the difficulties of their unrecognised position, they have appointed a central committee, whose responsibility is secured by general meetings and periodical retirement. This committee, we are informed, is in communication with, allowing for deaths and absence abroad, about seven-eighths of the entire number of graduates. It has, as our readers have seen, been for the last three years in correspondence with the Senate and the Home Office. We were ourselves present at a meeting at one of the colleges at which their exertions in resistance to the certificate branch of the supplemental charter were recognised, and the college resolutions on the same point ordered to be forwarded to them.

Lastly, to look at the other side. What must be the effect of exclusion? Is it not as much as if the Senate were to say—' We were appointed twelve years ago on account of our acknowledged eminence in literature, science, and art, to train up a band of men who should rival the sons of the ancient universities? For twelve years we have devoted all our energies to this work. *But we have failed.* Our graduates, ourselves being judges, are not worthy even of our recognition, far less to hold that influential position in our university to which their zeal and activity, their collegiate and local influence, and the near neighbourhood to us of so many of their best men, seem peculiarly to entitle them; and would, but for that fatal objection which we thus painfully but thus unequivocally confess.'

* The committee appointed last session to inquire into reductions of expenditure expressly questioned the propriety of this vote.

ART. II.—*Autobiography of the Rev. William Walford.* Edited by John Stoughton. London: Jackson and Walford. Pp. 363.

be abundant in biographies. The
ed with this species of literature,
established custom with us, that

should use their Carrara
n—lest our writers should
condescend to be the biographers of those of whom candour could say this only, that they lived socially and harmlessly, and died peacefully. Now, if a book is to be made for every man who would like his ' Life' written, or who may have possessed estimable qualities, we shall speedily realize the literal and exact truth of that mournful predication of the Hebrew king, that ' Of making many books there is no end.' Of all the miserable books our imagination can picture, we know of none more completely so than a tedious biography. We look in it for life; we find death. We search for the record of glorious activities; we discern them not. We look for the ' human face divine,' sparkling with intelligence, and illumined by the kindliness of a constant charity; we find our hero entranced, or asleep. We seek for spirit-stirring thought; we hear the mumblings of a dreamer. We ask for bread; we receive a stone. Some biographies of recent issue among us justly called forth these lamentations on our part; not that the subjects of them were altogether worthless, but that they were of that class of easy,

virtuous citizens, who, though worthy to be remembered for many excellences, were altogether uninteresting as heroes. Every monk must not expect to be canonized. It is not every priest who is a Jerome or a St. Francis; and we hold it to be a mistaken kindness, the exuberance of a too fond affection, which prompts the survivors so often to write biographies of their departed kindred. These remarks are not in the least intended to apply censoriously to the volume before us; for in the subject of it there was much both to admire and to imitate. But by pointing out its folly, we would endeavour to rebuke the increasing practice of writing insignificant biographies.

As it was among the first which were successfully developed, so the historical is not the least among literary arts. A few only of the gifted of mankind have the faculty of narrating—that most simple power in which the great ' Father of History ' so much excelled; and among the almost innumerable historians and narrators whom every country has produced, but a few only have become renowned. He who is skilful in weaving the story of a nation's fame, may be utterly incapable of successfully delineating the life of an individual; just as a man may carve a statue like Thorwaldsen or Chantrey, who would be unable to execute a medallion. The historian has a vast field. Events are before him in masses; and he can hardly colour too darkly the baseness of tyrannous perfidy and the wickedness of political intrigue. Society is before him in huge outline; his groups are dense, and his figures colossal. In writing the history of an individual, however, there are needed the most accurate perception, a skilful exhibition of the minutest details, and the most careful colouring—a knowledge, not so much of the great principles which are motive in the cabinet and the field, as of the thought and purpose which sway the heart and influence the life. He who excels in landscape-painting is not always equally successful in miniature-drawing; and often the writer of the history of a nation would prove to be an indifferent biographer. But when a man takes it in hand to write ' memoirs of himself,' there is need of excessive caution, lest he should present to the world a too flattering likeness of himself. Not every one can depict himself with Hogarth's skill; nor is it among the least difficult of tasks for a man accurately to delineate his own character. The admonition of the ancient sage—' Know thyself,' must be well heeded, and a philosophical analysis of his own psychology must be completed by him who describes his own growth mentally and spiritually. In every autobiography, from the nature of the case, there must be, often perhaps unwittingly, a considerable *suppressio veri*. Self-love, and 'that last infirmity of noble minds,' a wish to be well-remembered by posterity, will compel the artist who attempts to portray himself, to be careful of his colouring, and prudent in the concealment of defects. What, however, with 'Confessions,' 'Recollections,' and those other works in which great minds have recorded their individual histories, autobiographical works are perhaps altogether both as interesting and as instructive as any historical writings whatso

traits, betokening

to enumerate the

not be completed till after his
friend, Mr. Stoughton. The
does not interest us so much
style sometimes reminds us of
there is an occasional repetition
of the peculiar technicalities of
tion might be made to the introduction of some matter which does not add to the grace of the narrative. We are too often assured of the piety of the deceased—whereas it had been better for the readers to have drawn their own conclusions in these matters from Mr. Walford's interesting Letters. There are, also, indications of the 'funeral-sermon' style of panegyric, which we do not admire. But we will not descend to minor criticisms. Doubtlessly, the editor did the best he could with the few materials he had at command; and on our part, while we commend the picture, we will not be angry at the flaws in the canvass.

William Walford was born in Bath, in 1773. Very early losing his father, he was taken by his mother to Nantwich, in Cheshire, her native town, where, at the age of nine years, he was sent to a grammar-school, to learn the rudiments of the Latin language. Like many others of the great and good of mankind, he delights to attribute his earliest and best instruction to his mother. The first lessons of religion, the first glimmering

ideas of the great truths of revelation, and the first knowledge of
duty, he received from her; acquiring from her teaching, as he
afterwards writes, when an old man, 'a respect for morality and
religion, which, in succeeding years of thoughtlessness and vicious
indulgence, was never entirely eradicated.'   The master of the
school was a clergyman—a stern Draconian pedagogue, as it
would seem, one of the principles of whose philosophy was, to
influence the mental through the physical.   So, if a boy's
faculties were dull, he beat him; if he was slow at receiving
such intellectual nutriment as was to be obtained from the
Eton Latin Grammar, and from Ovid's Metamorphoses, his pre-
ceptor inflicted frequent tortures upon his body; acting upon
the principle of counter-irritation, which, though no doubt an
excellent practice in soothing some of the 'ills which flesh is heir
to,' is in nowise remedial for the torpidity of mind.

We have much to object to in the general discipline of schools,
though perhaps, at present, there is less severity in such establishments than formerly; but we think even the present public-
school system altogether objectionable.  A number of lads, whose
features differ not more than their mental capacities, are collected
in one house from the four quarters of the kingdom.   For them
all—the gentle and the rude, the quick and the inert—the same
drilling system is made use of; though there may be differences
of disposition and of talent among them, as great as between
Carlo Dolce and Turner, Martin Luther and Titus Oates.   But
more serious objection lies against this system on account of its
tendency to demoralize the young; a tendency which William
Walford experienced to his ultimate sorrow.   In this school, the
learning and recital of religious formularies and creeds formed no
small part of education; the saints'-days were diligently observed,
'followed by a holiday in the afternoon;' and the Catechism—
that which the Episcopal Church glories in—was imprinted on
the memory of the young by those means which, if they are not
the best that could be adopted for the desired result, are nevertheless remembered with sorrow.   At the age of twelve years,
young Walford was removed to Birmingham, to be apprenticed
to an engraver for the term of seven years, and to live in a family
nearly all the members of which were notoriously profane and
immoral. In that busy town he was allured to vicious indulgence;
and then he learned how futile it is to compel schoolboys to an
acquaintance with religious truths.   All that he had acquired of
catechism and of creed had no power to restrain him from many of
those practices, so common in a large community, which enfeeble
the body and degrade the mind.   It happened, however, that
there were, in the house he lived in, a few volumes of the books
written by Mede, Shepherd, and others, in which one finds the

experiences of earth recorded in the completest assurance of their blissful issue; and in which the scenes in a good man's life are described more as an enchanted paradise, than as the scenes of pilgrimage and warfare. Such stimulating divinity was far too strong and pungent for young Walford; but an indirect benefit resulted to him from the perusal of it. He gradually became more thoughtful; began to question seriously as to the destiny of his soul; fretted under the bonds of his sin; and struggled after that freedom of soul which divine truth alone can effect. Gloomy apprehensions filled his mind: he groped after the light, if haply he might find it, and wept under that servitude from which he knew not how to be delivered.

No natural process is altogether more orderly and beautiful than the development of truth in the soul. The true seeker always finds. The lamp of the Lord sheds no delusive ray; and he who sought, in his anguish, for the solution of that which has ever been a great difficulty of mankind—'How shall man be just with God?' —came at length, after slow but certain processes, to the great central truth in the religious life, that he alone, who is 'Justified by faith,' has 'peace with God.' Very simply and charmingly is the instructive story of his spiritual development related in this volume. The governing disposition of his heart became changed; his entire moral constitution was transformed; and he, who sought counsel from on high, found at length that Truth, before which the brightest conceptions of an inquisitive philosophy of old grow utterly dark. The history of the 'great change' is unaffectedly told; and our readers will find that the narrator of it does not condescend to the enunciation of pious trivialities, nor to the use of a phraseology which grates upon the ear and pains the heart. He passed not at once 'from darkness to light,' for the path of the just is as the shining light, which grows more and more unto the perfect day; but the happy change of heart was wrought in strict accordance with those laws which govern the spiritual nature—that happy *becoming* which proceeds from stage to stage of its development, until the renewed heart is likened to its God. Concerning himself very little with the hair-splitting of dogmatic theology; inquiring but little as to the truth of those curious speculations which the schoolmen brought to bear upon religion, darkening its beautiful light and confusing its simplicity; and regardful rather to be right at heart, than distinctive in the niceties or particularities of a creed; young Walford threaded his way through those almost inextricable labyrinths with which the Reformed theology so often perplexes the catechumen, and reached the 'truth as it is in Jesus.' At the expiration of his apprenticeship, he formed the friendship of a Baptist minister in Birmingham—a man without education, and rather restricted in his opinions.  Of him Mr. Walford sought counsel; and, naturally enough, he advised the close and constant study of the works of Toplady—strange food for a young mind which had made so recent an affiance with Christ's simple truth —particularly his quaint treatise on Necessity, which was written not so much perhaps to recommend to the doubter that doctrine which gives emancipation to the enslaved soul, as to hold up to ridicule the positions taken in reference to this stern dogma by John Wesley and his followers.  Gladly he turned to the work of President Edwards on Free-will; in the perusal of which, while it was an athletic exercise to his mental powers, the particular opinions he had embraced on this subject became unalterably determined.  His Baptist friend advised him to enter ' the Christian ministry,' giving him no advice as to what sect he should join, but recommending him to study the distinctive principles of Nonconformity.

Mr. Walford began, accordingly, to investigate the causes of difference between the ministers in the Episcopal establishment and their Dissenting brethren.  In the New Testament he read of the poverty and humiliation of the Man of Galilee; that Peter was but a fisherman; that the eloquent Paul had no higher occupation than that of a tent-maker; and that the churches founded by him consisted, to some extent, of soldiers and slaves, or of men whose condition in life was but little superior to these, the poor and the lowly of mankind.  Struck with the primitive simplicity of the Christian Church, he compared it with that which was called, *par excellence*, the Church in England.  The successors of the apostles, as they boast themselves to be, he found surfeiting on the fat things of the richest country in Christendom.  They had forgotten the fisherman and tent-maker, the prison and the cross; but they could discourse with peculiar feeling on fair lands and prebendal stalls, on tithes and dues, and on the divine rights of covetousness and exclusiveness.  The astonished student found the apostolical overseers of the English Church telling their yearly income by thousands; lords of the land and powerful in the senate; unapproachable in immaculate lawn, and reverend in the dignity which wealth and arrogance confer.  He heard of Church laws which fretted the soul, and which, if need be, could manacle the body; of ecclesiastical courts and their dungeons; of widows' goods seized for tithes they could not pay, and of Nonconformists imprisoned for their breach of regulations which the Founder of Christianity forbad his followers to observe.  He saw that avarice and greed were the distinguishing characteristics of many of the professed ministers of Him who commanded his apostles to be indebted to no man, and to be humble in fare and lowly in mien; and that the faith of the apostles was held by men whose incomes were regulated by Act of Parliament, and collected by the civil power. He found that the clergy themselves were, in many instances, the most obsequious servants of the State—a sacred police, impeding human progress by maintaining restrictive laws. Some of their number broke their necks at the steeple-chase and in the hunting-field; some haunted the dens of vice, and betted vigorously at the cock-fight or on the race-ground; some flirted in the pump-room at Bath, or lisped amatory nothings in parks and saloons; some sat as magistrates in rigorous uprightness, to issue warrants to compel the payment of their own church-rates, or to commit the hungry for poaching, and the beggar for his poverty. A few only were preachers of righteousness, visitors of the poor, comforters of the mourner, and guides for the wandering; and all were attached to a system of which no trace was discoverable in that book which contains the history of the true Church, and the whole duty of man. The inquiring convert, seeking how best he might serve the God he loved, was not long in forming a conclusion, after comparing the English Church with that Church of whose origin the New Testament contains so simple and clear a history. To subscribe to all that the Prayer-book contained, was impossible to him; for he could not adopt the Jesuitical casuistry of putting a 'non-natural sense' on the dogmatical positions contained in that book. As an honest man, he conceived that that book meant what it expressed, and, with this understanding, he could not accord with all its propositions. As the Church system, therefore, is that which knows nothing of compromise, and, as its letter must be believed, or its entirety rejected, there was but one course open to Mr. Walford; and he determined forthwith to attach himself to the much-despised Nonconformists. After the formation of this resolution, he joined the Congregational Church in Carr's-lane, Birmingham, under the ministry of Dr. Edward Williams, whose name, for his learning and worth, will be held 'in everlasting remembrance.' By the advice of Dr. E. Williams, he obtained admission to Homerton College, then under the presidency of the Rev. John Fell. At that period, education was in much lower esteem among the Nonconformists than at present. The college discipline was loose and negligent; the instruction was of an inferior kind; and the attainments of the students generally insignificant. The whole system was bad; sound in the theory of it, but irremediably bad in practice.

The government of the Dissenting Colleges was in the hands of a promiscuous 'Committee,' composed of men who had really but little love for enlarged education, though they were laudably and peculiarly anxious, from the motive both of their piety and

542 AUTOBIOGRAPHY OF REV. W. WALFORD.

that the college might stand well with the public, that the students should become good preachers, and faithful in the discharge of their high trust. But the construction of this committee was objectionable. It consisted of a few of the ministers of the London Congregational Churches, and also of a number of persons who were engaged in city-business, as merchants, warehousemen, and shopkeepers. Excellent men as these latter were, they could not sympathize with their students in either their duties or their wants; and, therefore, at one time they allowed them to live almost without restraint, or they treated them as if they had been school-lads, and annoyed them by many silly, petty restrictions. Experience has shown that the system never worked well. The students and the committee were in constant collision. The matters in dispute between them were often utter trifles; but, as some ignorant and supercilious persons sat on this committee, their dicta were as authoritatively given forth and as despotically enforced as those of any conclave with their Pontiff, or of any council of ten with their Doge.

In referring slightly to Mr. Walford's subsequent history, we will observe that after concluding his studies at Homerton College, he became the pastor of the Congregational Church at Stowmarket; whence he removed to Yarmouth, in which town his memory is still fragrant. After some years' residence in Yarmouth, he was appointed Hebrew and Classical Tutor at Homerton College, having for his colleague the ever-beloved and lamented Dr. John Pye Smith, whose piety and scholarly renown will redeem Homerton Old College from that oblivion into which otherwise, perhaps, it would fall. Mr. Walford held this office for seventeen years. There a gloom fell upon his mind—that most terrible malady which can afflict humanity. Compelled to relinquish his office, after various endeavours to heal 'a mind diseased,' he retired to Uxbridge, in 1838; living there in health and ease on a small estate he had purchased, spending the kindly winter of his age in those pursuits which, while they give dignity to the mind, expand and mature it; and in preparation for that unbroken sabbath in which he will have an everlasting gladness. Putting off 'this muddy vesture of decay,' Mr. Walford entered into rest on June 22nd, 1850.

We commend this volume to the attention of our readers. Serious, thoughtful, and chaste, it contains much food for meditation. The doubter and the erring, the happy and the sad, will find in its pages that which will guide and console them in the narrative of his life, whose 'Manner of Prayer,' 'Book of Psalms,' and 'Curæ Romanæ' will cause him to be esteemed by posterity.

ART. III.—*The Planetary System; its Order and Physical Structure.* By J. P. Nichol, LL.D., Professor of Astronomy in the University of Glasgow. Edinburgh: James Nichol. 1850.

THE very title of an astronomical work, whether it be an original memoir, a systematic treatise, or a popular exposition, is fraught with the associations of sublimity and adoration. The hanging of the earth upon nothing, the sun and the moon in their courses, the planetary system and its manifold unity, the arrowy, yet obedient flight of comets, the classical, yet contemporary signs of the zodiac, the milky-way, the countless remainder of the starry firmaments, the unimaginable reach of space, are only a few of the external images called up in the modern mind by the word Astronomy. It always suggests to our remembrance one of the grandest and most expressive of the tropes of European poetry; a figure whose spirit came down upon the poet from the sacred heights of Hebrew lore. It occurs in a passage of the Dramatic Mystery of Faustus, in which Goethe speaks of Nature, in its relation to the Creator, as 'the garment thou seest him by;' and sings like a cherub, if not with all the love of the unquestioning seraphim, concerning that ever-unfolding robe, as 'still aweaving on the roaring loom of time.' What a wide-flowing, and what a gorgeous vesture is this, wherein the Ancient of Days 'reveals yet conceals' his eternal and incomprehensible lineaments! How clear in its outward sweep, and how mysterious in its interior ground! How beautiful and inviting, but also how sublime and spirit-quelling! Above all, how innumerable are its parts and its shows; yet how simple do science and the instinct of the soul perceive its principle to be! What a surpassing variety, along with what a still more surpassing unity! 'How manifold are thy works, O Lord; in wisdom hast thou made them all!' Alas! if one had fifty volumes to fill, instead of only a few pages in a monthly periodical, space would fail almost any man of reading in these days to tell his neighbour what he knows about the world we live in; and all that the best-read scholar in Christendom possesses is but a tittle of what is known; and all that is yet discovered is but a tittle to what is knowable; and all that is yet to be found out by created intellect were but a tittle of that immeasurable fulness of truth which is comprehended in the original and Divine Mind.

Perhaps the most wonderful thing about astronomy is its history. To the idealist indeed, the marvellous story of the origin, rise, and progress of that exulting science in the soul of man, its very substance and being. Even the materialist must consider the history of this (or any other) department of knowledge as both greater and more interesting than its objects, although these are no less glorious creatures than the stars of heaven. But the Christian philosopher, who organizes idealism and materialism into one living and altogether human frame of thought by means of the vital energy of a quickened conscience, must always take peculiar delight in tracing the footsteps whereby man has been led into the goodly tabernacle of Nature by his God. Partly under the influence of a theology too dishonouring to humanity, and partly, perhaps, owing to the mere love of antithesis, the works of the creature are too frequently put in injurious contrast with those of the Creator. 'God made the country, and man made the town.' So said Cowper, from a momentary and poetical point of view, or rather from a rhetorical one, for there is no poetry in it. But, as surely as he was at once a Christian and a poet, Cowper would never have insisted on so false a distinction except in one solitary and awful sphere —the sphere of moral good and evil. Apart from want of conformity to, or transgression of, the law of God—apart from self-assertion in the region of religious and moral duty—apart, in one word, from sin, it is rather to be said that the sinless works of man are the noblest of the works of God in nature. Is it not true that man draws his understanding from the inspiration of Heaven? Is it not God alone who can give us to will and to do according to his good pleasure, and that not only in the spiritual life which is hid with Christ in God, but also in the natural life of the soul? Are our whole substance and energy not created by him, sustained every moment by him, and operative in obedience to his physical, physiological, and psychological laws? Is a bird's nest, a rookery, or a beaver's settlement a work of God's, and not a palace, a cathedral, or a mighty city? Had the Creator more to do with the building of the octagonal cells of a beehive than with the orderly unfolding of the fabric of geometry, from the first problem in Euclid to the calculus of Leibnitz and Newton? But the argument is as obvious as it is cogent, and it needs not be prosecuted any farther. A landscape is greater than the scene, inasmuch as it required more cunning and complex powers of nature to produce it; and a landscape by Turner is also, in this view, a more beautiful, as well as a greater work than what it represents, for the true Creator of both is He whose is 'the earth and the fulness thereof.' A Madonna of Raphael's is fairer, purer, nobler than ever was woman born; and she is also a rarer work of the unseen Master, who held and guided the hand of the painter. Lear,

Macbeth, and Othello are more precious and enduring than the Susquehannah and the Atlantic, the Andes and the Himmaleh, the equatorial tropics and the poles. Astronomy is more wonderful than the stars, and God is the Author of them both ; so that the history or providential unrolling of the scroll, wherein the planetary system and the firmamental scheme are emblazoned for the view of all intelligent eyes, is still more wonderful than astronomy itself. All absolute sciences and all true poems, in so far as they are untainted by sin, are more divine than the things they severally interpret or symbolize, save when those things are themselves divine. But if such facts have to be affirmed of other genuine books of knowledge, of architectures, sculptures, paintings, and poetries of every kind, what shall be said of the Bible ? It is not only the greatest of literary performances, but, according to this view, the greatest of all phenomena.

The famous cumulative argument of design, from Cicero down to Paley and the Bridgewater Treatises, has generally been deduced from the phenomena of the material or sensible element of the universe ; but that is certainly the lowest, as undeniably as it is the easiest, source of the current proof. Chalmers did a great service in drawing it from the higher level of the nature of man himself. Not that the argument is logical and coercive upon the sheer intellect ; it is perfectly understood now-a-days that it is no such thing, for no amount of cumulation can ever reach immensity. The ' Bridgewater Treatises' were the unintentional means of putting an end to the idea that design demonstrates the undemonstrable, and thus theology proper gathered strength from their weakness. God is ' past finding out.' Infinitude of quality, and especially the infinitude of an infinite number of qualities, is insusceptible of definition ; and the indefinable cannot be proposed as a theorem, so that our GOD is, demonstrably by reason as well as assuredly to Christian faith, past finding out, and that in every available sense of these ever-memorable words. Although, however, this celebrated argument is as hollow as Paley's Christian Theology and Doctrine of Morals, in so far as the pure intellect or logical faculty is concerned with it, yet it tells with great force in a composite manner, partly through their intellect and partly through their conscience, upon the great majority of human thinkers. Along with a previous or simultaneous act of natural insight or common faith, in fact, the argument is irresistible to the half-logical, half-Christian, or even unatheistical mind. The philosopher perceives that it is naught as a demonstration ; the Christian is far above it by experience ; but the multitude of men are ready to second it with the still small voice of conscience, and so it is prevalent over them for good. It must also be remembered, that there are vast numbers

rise, and progress of that exulting science in the soul of man, its very substance and being. Even the materialist must consider the history of this (or any other) department of knowledge as both greater and more interesting than its objects, although these are no less glorious creatures than the stars of heaven. But the Christian philosopher, who organizes idealism and materialism into one living and altogether human body of thought by means of the vital energy of a quickened conscience, must always take peculiar delight in tracing the footsteps where man has been led into the goodly tabernacle of Nature's God. Partly under the influence of a theology too dishonest to humanity, and partly, perhaps, owing to the mere love of antithesis, the works of the creature are too frequently put in injurious contrast with those of the Creator. 'God made the country, and man made the town.' So said Cowper. From a momentary and poetical point of view, or rather from a rhetorical one, for there is no poetry in it. But, as surely as he was at once a Christian and a poet, Cowper would never have insisted on so false a distinction except in one solitary and awful sphere —the sphere of moral good and evil. Apart from want of conformity to, or transgression of, the law of God—apart from self-assertion in the region of religious and moral duty—apart, in one word, from sin, it is rather to be said that the sinless works of man are the noblest of the works of God in nature. Is it not true that man draws his understanding from the inspiration of Heaven? Is it not God alone who can give us to will and to do according to his good pleasure, and that not only in the spiritual life which is hid with Christ in God, but also in the natural life of the soul? Are our whole substance and energy not created by him, sustained every moment by him, and operative in obedience to his physical, physiological, and psychological laws? Is a bird's nest, a rookery, or a beaver's settlement a work of God's, and not a palace, a cathedral, or a mighty city? Had the Creator more to do with the building of the octagonal cells of a beehive than with the orderly unfolding of the fabric of geometry, from the first problem in Euclid to the calculus of Leibnitz and Newton? But the argument is as obvious as it is cogent, and it needs not be prosecuted any further. A landscape is greater than the scene, inasmuch as it required more cunning and complex powers of nature to produce it; and a landscape by Turner is also, in this view, a more beautiful, as well as a greater work than what it represents. But the true Creator of both is He whose is 'the earth and the fulness thereof.' A Madonna of Raphael's is fairer, purer, nobler than ever was woman born; and she is also a rarer work of the unseen Master, who held and guided the hand of the painter. It is

Macbeth, and Othello are more precious and enduring than the Susquehannah and the Atlantic, the Andes and the Himmaleh, the equatorial tropics and the poles. Astronomy is more wonderful than the stars, and God is the Author of them both; so that the history or providential unrolling of the scroll, wherein the planetary system and the firmamental scheme are emblazoned for the view of all intelligent eyes, is still more wonderful than astronomy itself. All absolute sciences and all true poems, in so far as they are untainted by sin, are more divine than the things they severally interpret or symbolize, save when those things are themselves divine. But if such facts have to be affirmed of other genuine books of knowledge, of architectures, sculptures, paintings, and poetries of every kind, what shall be said of the Bible? It is not only the greatest of literary performances, but, according to this view, the greatest of all phenomena.

The famous cumulative argument of design, from Cicero down to Paley and the Bridgewater Treatises, has generally been deduced from the phenomena of the material or sensible element of the universe; but that is certainly the lowest, as undeniably as it is the easiest, source of the current proof. Chalmers did a great service in drawing it from the higher level of the nature of man himself. Not that the argument is logical and coercive upon the sheer intellect; it is perfectly understood now-a-days that it is no such thing, for no amount of cumulation can ever reach immensity. The 'Bridgewater Treatises' were the unintentional means of putting an end to the idea that design demonstrates the undemonstrable, and thus theology proper gathered strength from their weakness. God is 'past finding out.' Infinitude of quality, and especially the infinitude of an infinite number of qualities, is insusceptible of definition; and the indefinable cannot be proposed as a theorem, so that our GOD is, demonstrably by reason as well as assuredly to Christian faith, past finding out, and that in every available sense of these ever-memorable words. Although, however, this celebrated argument is as hollow as Paley's Christian Theology and Doctrine of Morals, in so far as the pure intellect or logical faculty is concerned with it, yet it tells with great force in a composite manner, partly through their intellect and partly through their conscience, upon the great majority of human thinkers. Along with a previous or simultaneous act of natural insight or common faith, in fact, the argument is irresistible to the half-logical, half-Christian, or even unatheistical mind. The philosopher perceives that it is naught as a demonstration; the Christian is far above it by experience; but the multitude of men are ready to second it with the still small voice of conscience, and so it is prevalent over them for good. It must also be remembered, that there are vast numbers

rise, and progress of that exulting science in the soul of man: its very substance and being. Even the materialist must consider the history of this (or any other) department of knowledge as both greater and more interesting than its objects, although these are no less glorious creatures than the stars of heaven. But the Christian philosopher, who organizes idealism and materialism into one living and altogether human form of thought by means of the vital energy of a quickened conscience, must always take peculiar delight in tracing the footsteps whereby man has been led into the goodly tabernacle of Nature by his God. Partly under the influence of a theology too disdainful to humanity, and partly, perhaps, owing to the mere love of antithesis, the works of the creature are too frequently put in injurious contrast with those of the Creator. ‘God made the country, and man made the town.’ So said Cowper, from a momentary and poetical point of view, or rather from a rhetorical one, for there is no poetry in it. But, as surely as he was at once a Christian and a poet, Cowper would never have insisted on so false a distinction except in one solitary and awful sphere —the sphere of moral good and evil. Apart from want of conformity to, or transgression of, the law of God—apart from its assertion in the region of religious and moral duty—apart, in one word, from sin, it is rather to be said that the sinless works of man are the noblest of the works of God in nature. Is it not true that man draws his understanding from the inspiration of Heaven? Is it not God alone who can give us to will and to do according to his good pleasure, and that not only in the spiritual life which is hid with Christ in God, but also in the natural life of the soul? Are our whole substance and energy created by him, sustained every moment by him, and operative in obedience to his physical, physiological, and psychological laws? Is a bird's nest, a rookery, or a beaver's settlement a work of God's, and not a palace, a cathedral, or a mighty city? Had the Creator more to do with the building of the octagonal cells of a beehive than with the orderly unfolding of the fabric of geometry, from the first problem in Euclid to the calculus of Leibnitz and Newton? But the argument is as obvious as it is cogent, and it needs not be prosecuted any further. A landscape is greater than the scene, inasmuch as it required more cunning and complex powers of nature to produce it ; and a landscape by Turner is also, in this view, a more beautiful, as well as a greater work than what it represents, but the true Creator of both is He whose is ‘the earth and the fulness thereof.’ A Madonna of Raphael's is fairer, purer, nobler than ever was woman born ; and she is also a rarer work of the unseen Master, who held and guided the hand of the painter. I am

Macbeth, and Othello are more precious and enduring than the Susquehannah and the Atlantic, the Andes and the Himmaleh, the equatorial tropics and the poles. Astronomy is more wonderful than the stars, and God is the Author of them both ; so that the history or providential unrolling of the scroll, wherein the planetary system and the firmamental scheme are emblazoned for the view of all intelligent eyes, is still more wonderful than astronomy itself. All absolute sciences and all true poems, in so far as they are untainted by sin, are more divine than the things they severally interpret or symbolize, save when those things are themselves divine. But if such facts have to be affirmed of other genuine books of knowledge, of architectures, sculptures, paintings, and poetries of every kind, what shall be said of the Bible? It is not only the greatest of literary performances, but, according to this view, the greatest of all phenomena.

The famous cumulative argument of design, from Cicero down to Paley and the Bridgewater Treatises, has generally been deduced from the phenomena of the material or sensible element of the universe ; but that is certainly the lowest, as undeniably as it is the easiest, source of the current proof. Chalmers did a great service in drawing it from the higher level of the nature of man himself. Not that the argument is logical and coercive upon the sheer intellect ; it is perfectly understood now-a-days that it is no such thing, for no amount of cumulation can ever reach immensity. The 'Bridgewater Treatises' were the unintentional means of putting an end to the idea that design demonstrates the undemonstrable, and thus theology proper gathered strength from their weakness. God is 'past finding out.' Infinitude of quality, and especially the infinitude of an infinite number of qualities, is insusceptible of definition ; and the indefinable cannot be proposed as a theorem, so that our GOD is, demonstrably by reason as well as assuredly to Christian faith, past finding out, and that in every available sense of these ever-memorable words. Although, however, this celebrated argument is as hollow as Paley's Christian Theology and Doctrine of Morals, in so far as the pure intellect or logical faculty is concerned with it, yet it tells with great force in a composite manner, partly through their intellect and partly through their conscience, upon the great majority of human thinkers. Along with a previous or simultaneous act of natural insight or common faith, in fact, the argument is irresistible to the half-logical, half-Christian, or even unatheistical mind. The philosopher perceives that it is naught as a demonstration ; the Christian is far above it by experience ; but the multitude of men are ready to second it with the still small voice of conscience, and so it is prevalent over them for good. It must also be remembered, that there are vast numbers

rise, and progress of that exulting science in the soul of man is
its very substance and being.   Even the materialist must consider the history of this (or any other) department of knowledge
as both greater and more interesting than its objects, although
these are no less glorious creatures than the stars of heaven.
But the Christian philosopher, who organizes idealism and
materialism into one living and altogether human frame of
thought by means of the vital energy of a quickened conscience,
must always take peculiar delight in tracing the footsteps whereby
man has been led into the goodly tabernacle of Nature by his
God.   Partly under the influence of a theology too dishonouring
to humanity, and partly, perhaps, owing to the mere love of
antithesis, the works of the creature are too frequently put in
injurious contrast with those of the Creator.   'God made the
country, and man made the town.'   So said Cowper, from a
momentary and poetical point of view, or rather from a rhetorical
one, for there is no poetry in it.   But, as surely as he was at
once a Christian and a poet, Cowper would never have insisted
on so false a distinction except in one solitary and awful sphere
—the sphere of moral good and evil.   Apart from want of conformity to, or transgression of, the law of God—apart from self-
assertion in the region of religious and moral duty—apart, in
one word, from sin, it is rather to be said that the sinless works
of man are the noblest of the works of God in nature.   Is it
not true that man draws his understanding from the inspiration
of Heaven?   Is it not God alone who can give us to will and to
do according to his good pleasure, and that not only in the
spiritual life which is hid with Christ in God, but also in the
natural life of the soul?   Are our whole substance and energy not
created by him, sustained every moment by him, and operative
in obedience to his physical, physiological, and psychological
laws?   Is a bird's nest, a rookery, or a beaver's settlement a
work of God's, and not a palace, a cathedral, or a mighty
city?   Had the Creator more to do with the building of the
octagonal cells of a beehive than with the orderly unfolding of
the fabric of geometry, from the first problem in Euclid to the
calculus of Leibnitz and Newton?   But the argument is as
obvious as it is cogent, and it needs not be prosecuted any further.   A landscape is greater than the scene, inasmuch as it
required more cunning and complex powers of nature to produce
it ; and a landscape by Turner is also, in this view, a more
beautiful, as well as a greater work than what it represents, but
the true Creator of both is He whose is 'the earth and the fulness
thereof.'   A Madonna of Raphael's is fairer, purer, nobler than
ever was woman born ; and she is also a rarer work of the unseen
Master, who held and guided the hand of the painter.   Lear,

Macbeth, and Othello are more precious and enduring than the Susquehannah and the Atlantic, the Andes and the Himmaleh, the equatorial tropics and the poles.   Astronomy is more wonderful than the stars, and God is the Author of them both ; so that the history or providential unrolling of the scroll, wherein the
scheme are emblazoned
till more wonderful than
and all true poems, in so
re divine than the things
they severally interpret or symbolize, save when those things are themselves divine.   But if such facts have to be affirmed of other genuine books o
paintings, and poetries
Bible?   It is not only
according to this view,
   The famous


the univ
is the ea
service i
himself.


is no such thing,
immensity.   The


undemonstrable, and thus theology proper gathered strength from their weakness.   God is ' past finding out.'   Infinitude of quality, and especially the infinitude of an infinite number of qualities, is insusceptible of definition ; and the indefinable cannot be proposed as a theorem, so that our GOD is, demonstrably by reason as well as assuredly to Christian faith, past finding out, and that in every available sense of these ever-memorable words. Although, however, this celebrated argument is as hollow as Paley's Christian Theology and Doctrine of Morals, in so far as the pure intellect or logical faculty is concerned with it, yet it tells with great force in a composite manner, partly through their intellect and partly through their conscience, upon the great majority of human thinkers.   Along with a previous or simultaneous act of natural insight or common faith, in fact, the argument is irresistible to the half-logical, half-Christian, or even unatheistical mind.   The philosopher perceives that it is naught as a demonstration ; the Christian is far above it by experience ; but the multitude of men are ready to second it with the still small voice of conscience, and so it is prevalent over them for good.   It must also be remembered, that there are vast numbers

of the honest and professed disciples of our holy religion who
are Christians of only small attainments ; and the display of
divine wisdom, power, and goodness in creation is amazingly
encouraging and delightful to such children in grace.   They
may mount to the higher vision upon nature as on a ladder.
Nay, it is far from an unblessed, as it certainly is a most
pleasing, exercitation of the maturer scholar in the life and life's
lore of Christianity, to walk abroad betimes and behold the
beauty and exceeding goodness of his Father's transcending
ingenuity and boundless fertility of resources for the benefit and
delectation of his brethren and himself : the heirs of God, the
joint-heirs of Christ, one with the Father and the Son, the true
and indefeasible lords of the creation.   For although not worth
anything when considered as a merely intellectual or logical process, the argument of design is most glorious as a commentary
upon certain of the perfections of the Lord of life, his existence
and attributes (as those *a-posteriori* schoolmen are in the habit
of saying) being known to the faithful neither by arguments nor
by mathematics, but by faith, by participation, and enjoyment.
It is, therefore, highly desirable that this great argument should
be written anew.

It further appears that it could be urged far more effectively,
because more humanly, in connexion with the historical developments of the sciences.   Such a procedure would necessarily
bring forward all the capital and illustrious points of what is
called design, while it would present them in relation with the
hearts and minds and outward fortunes of the discoverers.   It
would drench the subject in flesh and blood ; to quote a homely
but powerful expression of Lord Bacon's, one of the quickeners
of science.   But, above all, it would show forth the excessive
and adorable wisdom of the Father of our spirits, in declaring
how the right man always came at the right time ; how specifically
he was in every instance qualified for his particular task ; and
how all things were made to open around him for the doing of
his work.   It would display before our sympathetic view in what
a providential manner the very superstitions and errors of his
age, the contradiction of sinners, the apathy of a light-hearted
world, and the faults of the new thinker's own character, were
all made to work together for the good of man, under the soft
compulsion of celestial forethought.   While the special providence and plan of God's government is as wonderfully manifested
in the experience of the lowliest of the sons of sorrow, as in that
of the greatest king, discoverer, or poet that ever lived ; yet it
is more conspicuously, and therefore visibly shown in the outward and relative life of the latter.   In the one case, it is private
and particular ; in the other, it is published and intended for the

world.   The history of science is the history of man considered

history ; it
is more certain and intelligible, for there is almost nothing to
vitiate the judgments of the historian.   The theologian, the poli-
tories more or

rally with man,
least, it has been such

the past.
   The history of as
preparation of the
great work, and
than that which

The
and
grad
by which it is over-canopied, is set forth with unsurpassable simplicity and beauty in the Old Testament; and especially in the
book of Job and in the Psalter.   'The heavens declare the glory
of God ; and the firmament showeth his handiwork. . . . . In
them hath he set a tabernacle for the sun, which is as a bride-
groom coming out of his chamber, and rejoiceth as a strong man
to run a race.   His going forth is from the end of the heaven,
and his circuit unto the ends of it ; and there is nothing hid from
the heat thereof.'   Such is a well-known example of scripture language concerning the more obvious phenomena of this science. The
grand and distinguishing thing about these descriptions, however,
is neither their truth to the appearance of things, nor yet their
poetic sublimity ; it is their invariable association with right
conclusions, their impenetration with right feelings ; it is their
moral thoughtfulness and spiritual power.   'For all the gods of
the nations are idols ; but the Lord made the heavens.'   'Bless
the Lord, O my soul.   O Lord, my God, thou art very great;
thou art clothed with honour and majesty.   Who coverest thyself with light as with a garment ; who stretchest out the heavens

like a curtain.' ' When I consider thy heavens, the work of
thy fingers, the moon and the stars, which thou hast ordained ;
what is man, that thou art mindful of him ? and the son of man,
that thou visitest him ?'

> While David, else his sire, 'tis all the same,
>     Lay long ago upon some purple hill,
>     To guard his sinless flock from nightly ill,
> The golden sun went home ; the pale moon came,
> A slender crescent wove of silver flame ;
>     And one by one, at first, then ten by ten,
>     The stars slipt out, and in, and out again,
> Until a thousand prankt the sapphire frame.
>     Some red, some blue, and others like the moon,
>     And also some like little suns at noon ;
> He knew them well, although unknown by name ;
> They shone all night for love, and not for fame.
>     Lord, what is man, he cried, that such a choir
>     Should overwatch him thus with eyes of fire !

But this is all according to the truth of appearance, not the
truth of reality; it is the language of perception, not that of
reflection ; it is common sense, not science. The sun only
appears to rise in the east, mount the zenith, and set in the west,
now more to the north, and now more to the south. Astronomy
discovers that, although rotating on its axis, and moving along
with both the earth and the moon, through a celestial space un-
dreamed of in the days of yore, the sun is fixed and immoveable
in relation to our globe; it is the earth that circles round the
sun from west to east, and therefore he seems to pass over our
sky from east to west. Science disabuses us of the seeming, and
finds us the real state of things. It is the very same in all
departments. There is everywhere a truth of appearance enveloping a truth of reality like a protecting fruit, and it is the
business of science to penetrate to the kernel. But it is a long
and laborious process, and it is little that one man can achieve :
*ars longa, vita brevis*, said Hippocrates, a great observer and
an eager, if not a successful disentangler of appearances. It has
frequently been little that even a whole great nation of men has
been able to do in this way. The Jewish people, for example,
from Abraham down to Habbakuk, cannot be said to have been
a scientific people. They put no new interpretations upon nature;
they were content with the poor fragments they brought away
from Egypt. Moses was doubtless accomplished in all the
learning of the court of the Pharaohs ; and the sacred literature
of his people is strewed with indications, for instance, of that
visceral physiology, in consequence of which the language of
Christendom speaks of the heart as the organ of love, the

spleen of malice, and the liver of blackbile or melancholy. 'Try my reins and my heart.' Solomon, indeed, is said to have. written many books upon the vegetable kingdom, from the hyssop that springeth on the wall to the cedars of Lebanon; but such botanical literature does not come under the category of science, as the discoverer and teacher of that greater reality which lies under the appearances of things. The Hebrews did not seek to penetrate beyond the surface of nature by the scientific organ, because they dived at once to its centre by the act of faith, and saw it to be but the manifesting forth of the glory of their God. Knowing its origin in Jehovah, they were content with the result, and neglected the process. Not that they were admirable in this respect; for, on the contrary, it was one of their wants; but humanity is unfolding by degrees. For the most part, one nation does only one thing; and the children of Abraham have most assuredly done the greatest, or rather the God of Abraham has done the greatest of the divine works in this world through their instrumentality.

But the great truth to be noticed with this connexion is as follows.

interior reality, is a matter of
view. The fair seemings
strange realities of science
What expressions

inspires, but the spirit to be inspired by it, that                red result; wherefore the biblical poets, with the minimum of scientific object, have absolutely produced the maximum of spiritual result. Yet it may also be set down as a most gracious ordination of the Supreme Mind, that mankind had by no means to await the slow evolution of science, before laying hold of the choicest of the healing fruits of nature. The outside of creation is more harmonious, and therefore more beautiful in fact, than the unequal, though magnificent sections of science; deeper and clearer here than there, more elaborated at one part than another, and altogether gloriously fragmentary rather than a living unit like the world itself. Moreover the sensuous and poetic, as well as probably the moral and spiritual, character of man is specifically adapted to receive the seraphic shining of the countenance of Nature, rather than to catch the cherubic light that comes from her secret heart when it is opened by the prayer of might, even the faithful labour of the true explorer. Love wants beauty and intellect wants truth. Doubtless the complete man wants both. Doubtless a nation or a world which shall be

as perceptive of holiness and the beauty of holiness as the
Hebrews ; as perceptive of beauty and the sacredness of beauty
as the Greeks ; as capable of being governed and of governing
as the Romans once were ; as sensible of the relations of outward
things, from starry firmaments and nebulæ down to chemical
atoms, as modern Christendom ; as firm of purpose as Great
Britain, and so forth through all the national virtues of history,
were something incomparably more excellent than them all put
together.   But in the meantime it is most exhilarating to see
how provision was made from the beginning for the voice of
Nature, still virgin from the touch of science, reaching and
arousing the conscience of man.   Science is good for godliness,
but godliness is independent of science.

For all popular and practical purposes, the history of astronomy may be said to have begun with the speculations of the
Greeks ; although, on one hand, the fundamental principles of
the Ptolemaic system (namely the standing still of the earth
and the circular revolution of its sky) were drawn from the
Chaldeans, probably by way of Egypt ; and, on the other, the
progress of positive astronomy is always to be dated from Copernicus, the contemporary, though the senior of Luther.   Beginning with the Oriental stellography, as rendered intellectually
clear by the Greek mind, the development of the science is
traced, with great precision of outline, felicity of illustration,
and gracefulness of feeling, in the book which has given rise to
this short dissertation ; and certainly no man, at present visible
within the literary horizon, could write the history of astronomy,
as a substantive and classical work for the study of the whole
world, so well as Professor Nichol.   It is a noble toil, in fact,
which we take this opportunity of recommending to his thoughts.
It would be a labour of love to write so illustrious a thing ; it
would be an exercise of love to read it ; and the scholar, who
shall accomplish the task with classical perfection, will certainly
live for ever in the affections of mankind.

It may be interesting and instructive, in the meantime, to
contrast the cosmographical conceptions of the Ptolemaic and the
Copernican Astronomies, taking them both in the greatest
fulness of their development ; the former in the time of Purbach,
' who succeeded in expressing the order and simplicity of the
solar system by a scheme of ninety-six spheres of crystal ;' and
the latter in our own day, the Augustan age of observation.   For
the narrative of revolution and growth, which should lead the
mind from the former to the latter of these extreme periods in
the life of the science, the reader must recur to any of the
accredited histories of astronomy.   He will probably content
himself with the free and slight, but eminently truthful indica-

tions in the popular works of our present author; awaiting the
coming of some altogether satisfactory record, learned in spirit
but popular in form, extensive, yet so well organized as not to be
large, at once scientific and humane.

The Ptolemaic conceived of the earth as a sphere, but without
either geometrical definition or positive knowledge.  A circular
sphere, of which the then known world was the upper surface, a
sort of solid crown upon the globe of waters, was his image of
the globe we live on.   This ocean-rounded ball was the centre
and the final cause of creation.   Hanging upon nothing, it lay
as still as silence in the midst of the universe, the vast metropolis of Nature.   Seven planets revolved around her in their
several planes of distance from her dismal centre.   First came
the Moon, the changeful star of mothers and the chase.   Next
came Mercury, the friend of genius.   Venus, the queen of
hearts, went round the earth outside of the Moon and Mercury.
The Sun, the king of day, the lord of the planets, Delios, the
star of wisdom, Apollo, the king and priest of beauty, Hercules,
the doer of wise and beautiful deeds, wove his dazzling sphere
around the world at a distance more remote than Venus,
Mercury, and the Moon.   Beyond him, on the other hand,
there revolved red Mars, great Jupiter, and old Saturn in their
order.   Such was the constitution of the planetary system; the
earth, or rather the universe, and its seven planets.   Each of
these planets was the Shekinah of a God to the priest or poet,
the seat of a divine power to the philosopher, the source of a
cosmical energy to the man of science.   They had a secret correspondence with the seven openings of the human head, that
globular microcosm, which corresponded with the great globe of
Nature herself; the two eyes, the two ears, the two nostrils, and
the mouth.   Francesco Sizzi argued, even in the days of Galileo,
that there could not possibly be more nor fewer than seven
planets in the sky, because there are only these seven windows in
the head of man, which is its antitype.   Each of the planets had
also a metal to itself, wherefore there could not exist more than
seven metals and seven planets.   Luna was silver, Mercurius
was quicksilver, Venus was copper, Sol was gold, Mars was iron,
Jupiter was tin, and Saturn was lead.   The days of the week were
likewise sacred to their respective planets, arranged, however,
not according to their local position in the scheme, but according
to their value as lights, beginning with Sunday and Monday;
but it was doubtless the mythological relations of that series that
gave it currency and reverence in the world.

The Ptolemaic furthermore conceived of this complicated, yet
simple scheme, of the earth with its greater and lesser lights, as
surrounded by a far-drawn and revolving sphere of constellations

and signs, composed of unwandering or fixed stars. This vast
astrorama was the outermost boundary and glorious enclosure of
creation proper.  Beyond it lay two starless spheres.  One of
these was the subject of a transcendental motion, the communi-
cator of movement, indeed, to the inner spheres (from the
constellations to the moon inclusive), and limited on both sides.
The other, enclosing the whole universe and its sources of power,
stretched athwart the immensity of space.  It knew no boundary
on the thither side.   It was as moveless as the world at the
centre of the system.   It was the empyrean, the heaven of ·
heavens, the boundless and ethereal antithesis of the hard little
earth; the dwelling-place of the Godhead, of the angelic hosts,
and of the spirits of just men made perfect.  The true opposite
of this all-expansive house of joy, or of 'serenity which is joy
fixed,' black hell lay crushed and crowded within the rock-built
depths of the central earth, 'far as the poles asunder.'  The dry
land, the abode of man, stretched between them; under the smile
of heaven and over the rage of hell, but more native to the
place of woe.
    The Ptolemaic was by no means content with this general
conception of the objective constitution of the universe. Unable
to measure distances, he made a vast number of useful observations, and constructed the most ingenious hypotheses for the
explanation of what he knew.  The reader of a review, published in the year 1851, is of course aware that the daily revolution of the whole heavens, moon, sun, constellations and all, is
nothing but a truth of appearance : it is owing to the diurnal
rotation, or spinning on its axis, of the earth, from which we look
into the sky.   But it was early noticed that individual stars in
the throng are constantly changing their places in reference to
others, say, in the course of a month or a year.  The sun, for
instance, does not go round so quickly as the sky in general.
Standing in one place (among the other stars) at noon one day,
he is somewhat to the east of that place at noon next day.  He
is later in coming round than the stars among which he stood
the day before.  This little difference in his apparent position
among the stars occurs every day, so that in the course of a
whole year the sun has actually seemed to travel through the
whole sky of stars.   The circle, along which this apparent
travelling of the sun through the signs of the Zodiac takes
place, is now called the Ecliptic.  Now this phenomenon, which
the Copernican refers with certainty to the annual revolution of
the earth around the sun, was attributed by the Ptolemaic to the
(supposed) fact that the sun goes round the earth with a velocity
rather less than that of the constellations ; a view which certainly
met all the wants of the case, to the extent that they were then

known. The same hypothesis was of course applied to the moon, only that her movement is still slower than that of the sun, for she traverses the whole sky of stars, always along her own ecliptic, in the course of a month; a phenomenon now-a-days explained by her periodical circumvolution of the earth.

The uninitiated may possibly be at a loss to understand how the position of the sun among the stars was observed, seeing his own radiance extinguishes their light. But the sky was well understood as regarded its mere appearances from very early ages. From the observations of the night, pursued year after year, the starry arrangements of the day could always be inferred. The procession of the sun through the twelve signs of the Zodiac was, therefore, a matter of easy recognition; the seasons of the year, and the year itself, were determined by it; while it furnished the mythologist with a framework for the stories of Osiris, Horus, Vishnu, Hercules, and their labours for man. Besides, it is to be remembered that the visibility of the stars by day, from the bottom of a deep pit, was a fact of immemorial notoriety. Hence Democritus the laughing philosopher, the first to perceive that the Milky-Way is a forest of stars so thickly strewn as to seem like one mass of light at the surface of the earth, was also the first to remark that ' truth is to be found at the bottom of a well.' It was the same Democritus, be it mentioned in passing, that first descried how sensible matter—a crystal or a plant, or any other figure—is just a sort of milky-way of atoms. Such is the unity of nature, and such the love of unity in the man of science!

The observation of the sky presented many a difficult problem to the old school of astronomy, but they were always resolved with ingenuity. One of them is illustrious on account of its general historical importance, as well as for its particular connexion with the admirable name of Plato. The planets were seen to wander from their relative places, not content with only going slower than the sphere of constellations. It is from this circumstance and truth of appearance, in fact, that they derive their name of planets, or wanderers, in contrast with the fixed stars; and not from their real and (now) known journeyings round the sun, as one might readily suppose. Several of the planets, then, such as Jupiter, were perceived to make their (apparent) revolutions round the earth in an irregular manner; sometimes going back a little, then forward again; sometimes making visible circles or loops, as they passed along the curve of their great and systematic circles round the world. It was the father of philosophical idealism that supplied the explanation of such (seemingly) eccentric movements. Let us use an illustration of Professor Nichol's :—

'If I walk along the circle of an amphitheatre with a lamp in my
hand, a spectator at the centre would of course perceive it passing
regularly around him in a circle. But suppose that I am likewise
turning on my heel all the while, how would the spectator then imagine
the lamp to be moving? In reality, there would be nothing here except regular circular motions; namely, my course around the amphitheatre, and my wheeling round on my heel. The spectator however,
looking at the lamp, would observe neither the one nor the other of
these separate regular motions, but their result, or rather the result of
their combination; and, although he would see that the course of the
lamp was still in the main through the entire circuit of the amphitheatre,
it could no longer be expected to move with any regularity. Nay, were
I moving swiftlier on my heel than I moved forward, the lamp must
ever and anon appear to go backwards for a little.'

This ingenious rationalè took root, germinated, and grew to such
an amplitude in the mind of Ptolemy of Alexandria, as to cover
the phenomena of the whole heavens, as then understood. It
was this idea and its application, in truth, that constituted the
essence of the Greek or Ptolemaic contribution to astronomy;
inasmuch as the general notion of the constitution and movement
of the universe, as conceived of until the coming of Copernicus,
was far more ancient than Greece and all her schools. The
secondary, or small and specific circles of the planets were called
their epicycles; their great circlings round the earth being their
respective cycles. The specific results of the several cyclical and
epicyclical movements of planets—that is to say, their wanderings
—were sought out and recorded with industry and care; and
proper epicycles were devised for the solution of each case.
When observations multiplied, the difficulty of this theory increased. Epicycles had in many cases to be put upon epicycles,
until the scheme became as wonderful for complexity, as for the
inventive talent displayed in its (imaginary) construction and its
adaptation to every new emergency. At length, the whole
mechanism was resolved into a system of ninety-six cyclical,
epicyclical and epi-epicyclical spheres, as has been mentioned
already. 'If God had asked my advice about creation,' said
Alphonso the Wise of Spain, 'I would have drawn up a simpler
and also a more reasonable plan.' But theories often make men
in love with complexity; drawing them on step by step, until
they are hopelessly lost in an inextricable jungle of appearances.

'Things bad begun make strong themselves by worse,'

whispers the voice of conscience in Macbeth. It is as true in
science as it is true in life. The later disciples of this Chaldæan
and Greek Astronomy proceeded to strange extremities in some
instances : abandoning the pure and abstract method of geometry,

they actually converted the planetary spheres and epispheres into hard realities of the material sort; and changed the heavens into a mechanical orrery of crystalline globes, with planets and stars flaming in their zeniths!

Such was the system of astronomy which satisfied the thought of man during the progress of more than fourteen hundred years. The whole mind of Christendom was subject to this conception of the universe. Poets, men of science, mathematicians, philosophers, all lavished their confidence, their knowledge, and their eloquence upon it. It had grown so slowly over the mind of those ages, that its hold was very firm; it bound the intellect of all observers with tremendous compulsion. No man was found strong enough to break its bands in sunder, till Kopernik saw and believed the truth. How great an organ is the intellectual eye of a seer! The phenomena of the heavens were the same

in
It
au
and
and devout belief of the thing God showed him;
the one wonderworker in the world. Few men are capable of belief in any sphere beyond the reach of sense. Everybody knows that fire burns, water drowns, or food fills; but very few people believe aught that is purely intellectual, and still fewer aught that is purely spiritual, with anything like the keen and close fidelity wherewith they put their trust in food, or water, or fire. Nobody would believe he might thrust his hand into the flames with impunity, even if all the rest of the world should go mad and swear loud oaths to the innocuousness of burning coals. It were easy to stand in a minority of one in that case; nay, the unconquerable difficulty would be the task of joining the majority; but so quick and vital a spirit of faith, extending to regions above the domain of the senses, is the attribute only of rare men. The mere courage, which braves the whole world, is a vulgar quality in comparison with this undivided, uncalculating, incorruptible, and perfect belief in the objects of moral, intellectual, or spiritual vision. Probably the man has not yet been born, endowed with an equal faithfulness of sight in all the spheres of human life. The saint lives and moves among spirituals with the same

irremissible certainty, as the man of his senses among the objects of sensation ; to the philosopher ideas are as real as general conceptions or laws to the man of science ; and so forth. But take the world as it is, and you will find very few men or women now on it who can trust a principle, as they cannot help trusting their food, so as to long for it, consider it with delight, eat it with confidence, digest it with gratitude, and live on it with comfort. Copernicus could and did.

Born in 1473, at Thorn, in Prussian Poland ; educated at Cracow ; he studied philosophy and medicine at Padua : whence he made excursions to Bologna, for the purpose of seeing the then illustrious Maria of Ferrara, whose assistant and friend he in good time became. On the 7th of the ides of March, in 1496, they observed an occultation of Aldebaran after the manner of the Greek astronomers. Dominic Maria recommended his young fellow-labourer to the chair of Astronomy in Rome itself, to which he was called in 1499. It is recorded how his eloquence drew so numerous and select an audience around him as to recall the splendid successes of Regiomontanus. It seems to have been while engaged in the exposition of the Ptolemaic doctrine that the sense of its insufficiency fell upon his soul. But old Rome in the reign of Pope Alexander VI., with his profligacies and his contests, was too troublous a dwelling-place for a rapt explorer like this teacher of astronomy ; and he returned to Cracow in 1502. If he had been a lover of money, he might have practised physic ; or of reputation, he might have lectured on astronomy :—but he was enamoured of the new thought that glowed and grew before the enchanted eye of his mind, and therefore he sought seclusion and repose. He entered into holy orders, and, upon the recommendation of his maternal uncle, the bishop of Warmia, became a canon at Frauenburg on the Vistula in 1510. Having thus retired from the world at thirty-seven years of age, he discharged the sacred duties of his office with piety and self-devotion, bestowed his great medical knowledge on the poor of the little city of his choice, and devoted all his leisure to the working out of the thought with which he had been visited during the free unhoused condition of his youth. A weary time he had of it for the most part. Those sad dogs and bastard sons of the Reformation, the knights of the Teutonic order, would let neither Frauenburg nor Copernicus alone. They harassed him with their summonsings, their accusations, and their inroads, for many a year. So great a tide of animosity rose against him at one period of his peaceable career, that he was mocked upon the stage, and hustled in the street. In fact, he was long exposed to all the paltry, yet spirit-breaking annoyances of public ingratitude and disfavour : and it is all the more vexing to think of such sufferings, that they were not incurred for his discoveries, for he had not yet made them known.

him.   The old observations of the science had to be repeated with more                                    new principle;
be undertaken;

amazing to
politan com
out a teles
jointed woo
noble life.

practised physi
fidelity the dut
commission of

and astronomers were pri

system, that another Ptolemy would come out of Prussia.   Nicholas Schomberg, the cardinal of Capua, was enthusiastically interested in his ideas, and sent a competent person to take copies of his commentaries and tables.   Rheticus, the young professor of mathematics at Wirtemburg, threw up his chair, and betook himself to the reformer of astronomy so early as 1539. Nor had he been two months in the society of Copernicus, when he wrote a letter to Schöner, a venerable mathematician then professing at Nurnberg, who had charged him to do so; a letter full of joy and admiration; in which the system of the Polish master was partially unfolded.   That letter forms a supplement to the *De Revolutionibus*, and it appears in the works of Kepler under the title of the *Narratio prima*, the first news of the victory.   In short, Rheticus was fascinated for life; his existence became absorbed in Copernicus and his work; and he was thenceforth and for ever the enlightened, obedient, and happy planet of the new sun that had risen on his soul.   He wrote letters of enthusiastic description and exposition to all his eminent friends in science, and more than one of them was published; so that the Copernican doctrine was widely known among the competent before it was formally made public.  He at length, in 1552 (thirteen years after his absorption), got a tract by Copernicus on Spherical Trigonometry published at Wittemberg; and this increased the zeal of the capable for our discoverer.  Doubtless this self-devotion and veneration of Rheticus, together with the enthusiastic regard of a scattered band of competent and eager disciples, must have proved a sweet compensation for the obstruction and enmity of the world at large.  Indeed such a man needed no compensation, perhaps, for discovery is its own exceeding great reward, and the conflict of the explorer strengthens his heart still more than it illuminates his mind.  At the time they were mocking him from city to city on the public stage, some of his friends endeavoured to stop the wretched buffoons, and cheat the people of their sport.  ' Let them alone,' said he : *Nunquam volui populo placere ; nam quæ ego scio, non probat populus, quæ probat populus, ego nescio.*  ' Let them enjoy themselves, for it is but fair, since I have never tried to please them ; they take no delight in the things I know, and I am quite ignorant of the things they take delight in ; therefore let them have their fun out of me in their own way !'

At length Gisius, the (Polish) Archbishop of Culm, backed by Cardinal Schomberg, persuaded Copernicus to complete the great work, which he had really finished in all but a few additional details many years before.  The manuscript was sent to Rheticus ; Rheticus chose Nurnberg for its publication; Schöner and Osiander lent him their aid ; Osiander wrote a timid and deprecatory preface; and after a world of difficulty it was actually published.  The first copy was sent with expedition to the author.  It was just in time.  Old age, toil, and adversity had brought him low at last.  A bloody flux and the paralysis of his right side had rendered him unfit for intellectual labour for some time.  His very memory was almost gone.  He was just dying when the printed copy of his work was brought him.  He looked at it, he caressed it with his hands; then put it from him like one who had something else to do, received the last offices of the Church, and expired.  It was on the 23rd of May, in the year 1543.  He was seventy years of age.  How original, industrious, effectual, beneficent, unostentatious, manly and pious a career! *Atque hujusmodi quidem vita, hujusmodi mors Copernici fuit*, says Gassendi, who seems to have been as deeply impressed by the consideration of the discoverer's piety, as by his vast originality and his Herculean success.  He died as he had lived.

All that concerns us at present in this epochal work, on the revolutions of the celestial orbs, is what is summed up in a passage, which we shall translate with close fidelity.  ' Of the wanderers (errantium) the first is Saturn, who completes his circuit in thirty years.    After him comes Jupiter, moving in a duodecennial revolution.    Then Mars, who goes round in a biennial one.    The annual revolution holds the fourth place ; in which we have said the earth is contained, together with the lunar orb somewhat like an epicyclical body.    In the fifth place Venus revolves within the space of nine months ; and, finally, Mercury takes the sixth place, running round in eighty days. In the true midst of all sits the Sun.    For who could place that lamp in another or a better place, within this fairest temple, than there whence it can illuminate the whole ?    Some, indeed, do

solar system in this the middle of the nineteenth century.    It will render us grateful to the industrious and conscientious men by whom the wondrous mechanism has been displayed and magnified ; grateful to the great interpreter, to whose virtue and genius we stand indebted for so glorious a new conception of our Father's house of many mansions ; and grateful to God, who is the true and original author of astronomy, as well as of the stars.

The earth is a huge oblate or orange-shaped sphere, spinning on its shorter axis like a humming-top, yet at such a rate of speed as to seem standing still ; it goes once round in twenty-four hours, its rotation being both the cause and the measure of day and night.    The highest mountains range from four to five miles in height ; the greatest depth of the ocean is probably little more than five miles, although Ross let down 27,000 feet of sounding-line in vain on one occasion.    So that the earth's surface is very irregular ; but its mountainous ridges and oceanic valleys are no greater things in proportion to its whole bulk, than the roughness of the rind of the orange it resembles in shape.    The geological crust—that is to say, the total depth to which geologists suppose themselves to have reached in the way of observation—is no thicker in proportion than a sheet of thin writing paper pasted on a globe two feet in diameter. The surface of the earth is some 148,500,000 of miles in extent; and only one-fourth of that large space is dry land, the rest being ocean and ice. The atmosphere rises all round to a height between forty-five and fifty miles above the sea-level. The solar radiance sends such heat as it brings no deeper anywhere than 100 feet into the surface or scurfskin of the dry land—from forty to a hundred feet, one-third of the sun's heat being absorbed by the air. Yet the deeper man digs beyond the hundred feet, the warmer he finds the earth, and that at a somewhat determinable rate of increase. Supposing that rate of increment to go on towards the centre, it is computable that the solid underwork of the world, say granite by way of conjecture, must be in a state of fusion at no vast depth from the ground on which we tread. Let the scientific imagination descend a little lower, and it will find the melted granite in the form of a fiery vapour or gas—the dry stream of a red-hot liquid, in which the rock-built foundations of ' the everlasting hills ' melt like icebergs. But this is conjectural and probable, not observable and proved.

Far away from this spinning and perilous globe of ours, at the distance of some 79,500,000 miles, stands the sun. A ray of light, starting from his surface at any given moment, takes eight minutes to reach us, although light runs at the speed of 195,000 miles in a second. The sun is 1,380,000 times as large as the earth, and 355,000 times as heavy; but the stuff of which he is made is just about a fourth part as dense as the average matter of this world. The sun is of as light a substance, taking his whole body, as coal; whereas the earth is twice as heavy as brimstone, striking the mean between the air, the ocean, the dry land, and the internal vapour. The sun has an atmosphere like the earth, or rather he has two. One of them, close upon his solid surface, seems to resemble our own; it bears cloudy bodies in its upper levels. The other is a sort of fiery gas, surrounding the former, kindled and sustained in the calorific and luminous state, no man knows or can conjecture how. Storms in the lower atmosphere are constantly blowing this phosphorescent airy envelope aside, so as to afford us glimpses down into the (comparatively) dark and black recesses beneath. These are the spots on the sun. Galileo inferred the rotation of the sun on his axis from the motions of those spots. The explanation of those spots, afforded by the discoveries of Wilson and Herschel, diminishes the value of the inference ; but no Copernican can doubt that the sun is for ever turning, and that with unimaginable swiftness and impetuosity.

At the distance, then, of more than seventy-nine millions of miles, this dim spot which men call earth, this great globe and all its dwellers, this ever-spinning planet revolves around the sun once every year, that revolution being both the cause and the measure of that space of time.   Its orbit is not a circle ; it is an ellipse, but not                                                                   ath.
The terrestrial axis is
were no seasons ; it
and yet uplifting description
and indeed for a singularly
yet systematic narrative of the
at large, the reader should h
           Professor Nichol.  It '

creation,  '

carrying an unresting sea in the
a soft gauze of air, going round

judgment.   I
told ; for the

the moon goes round the earth from month to month, and that at a distance of some 240,000 miles ; the same lunar side or hemisphere being always turned towards us, although that satellite turns upon her own axis as well as the earth and the sun.   The earth is in repose so far as the moon is concerned ; it is her sun.   The two combined, being as true a unity as any chemical molecule which is composed of two atoms, go round the sun as if they were one ; the earth carries her moon with her.   So that it is possible, if not probable in the first instance, that the sun, though in repose as to the earth and her moon (and, indeed, to all the planets yet to be mentioned) may be in motion on some vast orbit of his own ; an orbit along which he carries all his planetary adherents with him, just as the earth takes her moon round the sun, *tanquam epicyclo*, as Copernicus expresses it.   It is curious to perceive how, not only in the case of our own moon, but in the cases of the moons of Jupiter, Saturn and Uranus, and actually in those of all the planets considered as the moons of the sun, the Platonic epicycle really holds good.   The earth turns on her heel, with the moon held out at arm's length, while she goes round the amphitheatre before the solar eye; so do the other moon-bearers. So does the sun himself upon a vaster arena and before a greater spectator, like another Briareus; holding out his seventeen planets, and nobody knows how many comets, in his hundred hands. The moons, of those solar planets which have them, represent the epi-epicyclical orbits of the Ptolemaic theory. It is curious, and also touching, to notice how often the errors of man are thus the shadows of truth. Were it not for the preceding shadows, indeed, the substance would never arrive; and therefore the Ptolemaics of the world are second, in value and in merit, only to epochal discoverers like Copernicus.

Suppose the sun to be represented by a radiant little orb two feet in diameter, in order to bring it within the measure of our eye; then this great globe of ours, with all its stupendous histories, is no bigger than a full-sized pea in proportion, revolving at the distance of 215 feet. Neptune, the outermost and last discovered of the planets, would stand at the distance of a mile and a quarter from a sun of that imaginary size, and it would be no larger than a cherry. Another cherry at the distance of three-quarters of a mile would stand for Uranus. Saturn would be a small orange at two-fifths of a mile from our two-feet solar body. A middle-sized orange, at the distance of a quarter of a mile, would be his Jupiter. At some 500 feet the nine little planets, commonly called asteroids, probably enough the fragments of an exploded orb, and now moving in a sort of group, would be represented by as many grains of sand. A pin-head, at 327 feet, would do for Mars. Then comes the earth. Still nearer the sun, namely at 142 feet from our present model, revolves Venus, of the dimensions of a pea. And finally little Mercury wheels along his orbit, with a radius of 82 feet, and the dimensions of a mustard seed.*

Add the terrestrial moon, the four moons of Jupiter, the ring within ring that whirls round Saturn like an endless moon, the eight ordinary moons of that extraordinary planet, the moons of Uranus and Neptune (yet uncertain in their number), and it is impossible to say how many comets, not to forget the enormous groups or hosts of comparatively small stones or meteors, which are believed to be revolving round the solar centre like pigmy asteroids; and the Copernican conception of the mere constitution of the solar system, as developed by time and toil, is completed. The sun is 882,000 miles in diameter; the earth is 7,926; Juno is 79; Saturn, 79,160, and so forth. The earth is

---

* This diagram is an illustration of Sir John Herschel's. The nine asteroids, revolving in a group between Jupiter and Mars, are Flora, Vesta, Iris, Hebe, Astræa, Juno, Ceres, Pallas, Diana; five of them have been discovered since 1845, by Hencke, Hind, and Graham.

more than five tim
The earth rotates
earth revolves in

ater; Saturn is as light as cork.
hours; Jupiter in ten.  The

can apprehend
has become.
There can be no
Professor Nichol is
any language.  Its
illustration, its
enthusiastic
tone unite t

sidereal heavens, in a

---

ART. IV.—*Poems.*  By W. C. Bennett.  London: Chapman and Hall.  1850.

IF we have correctly read the characteristics of the age, there never was a time when true poetry was more desirable as an agent in human education, or more likely to be welcomed with general thankfulness and delight.  In every department of life, there is a growing pressure and a sustained excitement which not only task, to the verge of exhaustion, the intellectual energies, but tend to impair the health and impede the development of the emotional faculties.  Yet it is in this part of our nature that we must search for the springs of happiness; and here, when neglected or polluted, is the birth-place of life's least curable evils.  So far then as poetry addresses itself to the cultivation, and assumes the regency of the feelings, it demands our serious consideration; it is potent for evil as for good.  If, on the one hand, its influence be hurtful, it must not be overlooked as insignificant; and if, on the contrary, its sway over the affections be beneficial, we must reflect on its services with gratitude, and welcome its priesthood with reverence and love.

The exhausting character of human pursuits, to which we have alluded, may be illustrated by reference to the merchant, the mechanic, the votary of science; and to each of these classes, true poetry is at least a grateful beverage, and not seldom a healing balm.

Without disparaging their strenuous diligence, or doubting that their active world is one of the best schools for maturing manly virtues, and without any splenetic sentimentalism on the grovelling ambition of the wealth-seeker, we ask how much truth there is in the complaint of Wordsworth,

> The world is too much with us, late and soon
> Getting and spending we lay waste our powers.

Should not every source of refinement and every means of higher culture be carefully sought; everything that might help to replenish the heart which the excitements of life are so perpetually draining? Can we be unsafe, in promising the gratitude of those who, by the teaching of the poets, have been occasionally lifted above the din and perplexities of the world, into regions serene and spiritual, where their purer loves and loftier hopes may disport themselves with freedom?

But, in order to discharge the high functions we have assigned to it, poetry must be true. True to the artistic rules, by which its force and beauty are at once displayed and wisely husbanded; true to nature, whether in her physical or spiritual developments; true to the recognition and use of all that experience, science, and revelation, have added to the stores of human knowledge; and true, lastly, to the real necessities rather than the mere gallery-cry of the age.

Poetry, such as we have now described, will be embodied in works capable 'of enlarging the understanding, warming and purifying the heart, and placing in the centre of the whole being the germs of noble and manlike actions.'*

It is when such poems appear that we feel how premature is the sneer of the dissatisfied critic, who imagines that the day of poetry is gone. She is, indeed, no longer the hand-maiden to luxurious sloth, no longer the fury of war, no longer the sycophant of courts or the slave of fashion; so that she must needs cease from those ditties, amorous and adulatory, which were wont to awaken and nurse the lust and pride of the great; while, for the like reason, she must discard those themes which

---

* Coleridge.

long maddened and brutalized man. The voice of her harp is not silenced; though the notes may fall softly, they need not be dull; though we press not the flower for its harmful drug, it will continue to give its honey to the bee, and its perfume to the gentle air.

The ordinary life of earth, though deemed uneventful, abounds with difficulties; and is varied by defeats and victories, which the poet may predict, describe, or celebrate. The deeds of charity or the feats of patriotism, are not the less heroic in that they are bloodless; or because they clothe a life in light instead of kindling a funereal pile. And if we must have love-strains, the homely, modest love which God hath sanctioned, seeks through song, to tell its gladness and to utter its low call for solace. Simplicity of object and treatment, purity of passion and neatness of style, have happily replaced the worn gaudiness of a less natural age.

We do not introduce Mr. Bennett as one who either deserves or desires to be styled a master-poet; but we bespeak an interest in his book on the ground of its peculiar merits; and we notice it less to indicate its very apparent excellences than to protest against its imperfect exhibition of truth, and its lurking influences for evil. A considerable portion of its contents, to our knowledge, has met the public scrutiny elsewhere. The readers of ' Douglas Jerrold's Shilling Magazine,' ' Howitt's Journal,' and the ' Athenæum ' (if we mistake not), have been accustomed for some years, to peer through the list of contents, or glance cursorily through the pages, to ascertain if W. C. Bennett, of Blackheath, had uttered another musal response. Some of these periodical fugitives have not been honoured with a place in this volume; the reason of their omission does not lie on the surface. A sonnet to Colonel Thompson, breathing a healthy spirit, we would gladly have seen here; for, though inferior to the best, it is better than some, of the sonnets in the book; while another poem of the same kind, inscribed with the suggestive name of ' Wilderspin,' is, we submit, more in accordance with the spirit and canons of the sonnet, and richer in worthy sentiments, than any which this book has reclaimed from erratic life. Many of these lyrics, as we have remarked, have been floating amongst the bulrushes of periodical magazines, and it was time that a permanent, and somewhat attractive home should be provided for them, lest they should be seen no more. But, while confessing to the general opinion, that it is not good for one, born and reared in such lowly circumstances, to be suddenly arrayed in sumptuous purple and fine linen, we feel constrained to say a passing word to those who were entrusted with the arrangement

and getting up of this volume.  The print is large, and, what is
technically called, clean; but the margin is both cleaner and
larger ; and sometimes, when we reached the close of a song,
the graceful and pleasant swell set us a dreaming, and what was
the dream?  That we were attending a meeting, and signing a
petition that had some remote connexion with 'the repeal of the
taxes on knowledge ;' on awaking, we reflected that the practice
of leaving large marginal blanks has peculiar advantages in
these economical days; for it has a tendency to raise the *à priori*
estimate of the work, inasmuch as only a rich gem deserves an
ample setting ; as the result of subsequent and conclusive meditation on the subject, however, we remark that if the poetry
turn out bad, human nature grudges the setting, and if the
poetry prove good, English nature would have liked more of
the gem and less of the setting.

With these hints as to the mechanical, we pass to the poetical
character of the book.  The rythm and music of many pieces
will please the most delicate ear.  Some of the compositions will
pass muster with the most querulous censor, and, although the
critic, well versed in the mysteries of his art, may complain of
models neglected, rules violated, phraseology strained, and
license abused, the man who reads poetry for refreshment and
incitement, will steal through the pages with advantage and
pleasure.  It should not be approached as a task, but kept at
hand for perusal, when the head, or hands, or heart, or all alike,
are heavy and worn. It glitters with holiday fancies, and scarcely
less with the ore of working-day truths.

The book opens with ' A Tale of To-day,' professedly descriptive of a series of pictures, which illustrate the progress and
results of seduction.  Peaceful, indeed, and very pleasant is the
scene, and very loving are the characters first discovered amidst
that scene, but a shadow falls upon

> ' The vine-climbed cottage, redly-tiled,
> Deep-nooked within an orchard's green—

it is the approach of the lordly perjurer, it is the shadow of
earth's sorest, and also of her latest, grief; pollution, two broken-
hearts on the one hand, and on the other desertion, shame, self-
abandonment, and suicide, follow in succession, with truthful
rapidity.  When all is over, and the gas-lit eddies of the
mourning river have sunk with the ebbing tide, the old broken-
hearted love seeks for its ruined one ; and laying it in the tomb,
utters a lament of love, a low, sweet dirge, for a moment invest-
ing the suicide with the interest of a martyr, and the glory of
saintdom.  An ' unbreathed name ' is all that lives of the lovely
' Miller's Daughter ;' ' yet,' saith the poet—

'Yet ever in our thoughts she lies
  A memory all reproof above,
On whom reproach turns not its eyes,
    But only love—
Love with a misty gaze of gathering tears,
That no accusing word of chiding memory hears.'

This may be intended to describe, without approving, the actual
weakness of affectionate hearts in such a case; if so, we remark,
it is a weakness that should be hidden altogether, or should be
revealed only to be reproved.  Had she not sinned grievously
against man and God?  And does she even seem to repent?  If,
in the poet's esteem, she was only a victim, then woman is infinitely unworthy of the graceful idolatry of his muse; if, however,
his conscience does reproach her, and even condemn her, why,
we ask, does he purposely pass by the religion which God has
made for the penitent? why seek to hide the pollution of a soul,
so fearfully sinful, with the expressions of a love based on undiminished esteem, just as he robes the grave in living green, and
gems it with the flowers of spring.  Our thoughts revert, while
we write, to 'Poor Ellen;' a more touching story still, less startling and picturesque than the 'Tale of To-day;' (but pleading in
our weak hearts, still more strongly, for that pitying love which
cannot, or will not, think reprovingly of the fallen; for *she* was a
mother, and through sore trials did she pace the weary way
to death), but Wordsworth does not aim, unwarrantably, to excite, but proceeds, in Heaven's name and by Christ's example,
to demand from us, that love without reproach, when he says
of her:—

    'A rueful Magdalene,
To call her—for not only she bewailed
A mother's loss, but mourned in bitterness
Her own transgression—penitent sincere
As ever raised to heaven a streaming eye!'

When we bring back our wandering thoughts to the tale before
us, we can hardly bear the contrast it presents to the narrative in
the 'Excursion.'  The miller's daughter falls without sin; and
unprepared, according to any form of religious belief, she seeks,
through self-murder, her release from unmerited sufferings, in
the absolute quietude of the grave; which is all the repose the
atheist desires, and a fate which atheism alone would dare to
promise.
    Probably some explanation of this deficiency in our poet's
account of the life and death of the fallen one may be found in
the exquisite pleasure he derives from the contemplation of
innocent babyhood; he is willing to forget that innocence is a
mere accident of infancy, and, leaping over the chasm which

separates manhood from childhood, he regards the woman as still
morally beautiful, in precisely the same way as the little girl;
and regards the seducer of the one, much in the light he would
view a cruel nurse, or vicious dog, in reference to the other. At
any rate we turn with pleasure to his performances in the nursery.
To be born into this world—to be nursed, cherished, and petted
—are, undoubtedly, highly poetical items in our life's history;
and, therefore, babydom is very properly made the sphere of
poetical speculations and reveries.   We confess that of all things
small, we love babies ; and we derive more poetical inspiration
from baby-watchings and baby-nursings than from any other class
of *sub*-adorations; and we further confess, that we never met
with more truthful descriptions of them than we find in this
volume.   Memory itself is not so faithful, though it is capable of
appreciating the fidelity of the artist.   Our poet heartily wor-
ships infants ; and, doubtless, he has many idols in his shrine.
The very thought tempts a little waggery; but we refrain, and
will venture on a little philosophy instead.   We speculate
accordingly, that our sceptical author (for such we must of
necessity regard him), the philosopher—the enemy of all that is
superstitious, nonsensical, and bigoted—would be the likeliest
of Englishmen to bend the knee, finely-trousered, in the
greasy dirt of Rome, if he should chance to meet *Il Bambino* in
its close carriage, and under monkish guardiance, hastening to
administer the interesting assistance which Lucina was supposed
to render in the olden time.   We have not the seven ages of
man ; but we have several ages and stages of babyhood :—

> ' Hands all wants, and looks all wonder,
>   At all things the heavens under ;
>
>       *       *       *
>
>   Mischiefs done with such a winning
>   Archness, that we prize such sinning ;
>   Breakings dire of plates and glasses ;
>   Graspings small at all that passes ;
>
>       *       *       *
>
>   Silences—small meditations
>   Deep as thoughts of cares for nations ;
>   Breaking into wisest speeches,
>   In a tongue that nothing teaches ;
>
>       *       *       *
>
>   A rocker of dolls with staring eyes
>     That a thought of sleep disdain,
>   That with shouts of tiny lullabies
>     Are by'd and by'd in vain ;

A drawer of carts with baby noise,
  With strainings and pursed-up brow ;
Whose hopes are cakes and whose dreams are toys ;
  Ay, that's my baby now.

      *        *        *

  Love abundant, leaping out
  In thy lighted look and shout,
  In thy joy that sorrow dumbs,
  In thy bubbling laugh that comes
  Ever still with glad surprise
  When thy mother meets thine eyes ;
  Love is in thy eager watch
  Ever strained her form to catch,



  Dreaming eyes for ever raising
  Raptured gazes to her gazing—
  Gaze so blessed, sure we deem
  Heaven is in thy happy dream.'

It is in such instances as the above, that we perceive the advantage of the poet over the painter; they have the same image before them, and each looks out in his chosen line, for the best expression of the yet hidden thought; the one finds, ready to hand, the several parts of his intended composition, and proceeds straightway to assort and combine his miniatures, according to his best taste and skill, in order to make a representation of his *thoughts* as *he thinks it ;* but the other has, at the best, but rude materials which have of themselves no significance; and it is only by prolonged mechanical toil, by frequent trial and error, by line upon line, tint upon tint, and shade deeping shade, that he arrives at the point whence his brother started; so that the word-painter, in a few tasteful and well-considered stanzas, succeeds in conveying, with electric accuracy and speed, a serial picture, which must glide slowly from the brush of the colour-mixer, in a gallery of portraits but slightly differing from each other, and requiring for their production a lifetime of anxiety and labour at the easel.

We must not omit to notice the graceful fidelity of Mr. Bennett to his native tongue; seldom, indeed, have we read a book so pure from the words of the stranger, so proudly attesting the self-sufficiency of the English language, when needed to clothe great thoughts or to thrill cold hearts. To him, and to the poetical writers of his school, the prose writers

of this country are under great obligations, which will be most
suitably discharged, by pruning their works from all unnecessary
foreign words.

There are two poems in the book on the subject of popular
education; the one grave and stately, the other humorous and
satirical; both in their way good, and both somewhat fallacious.
The grave and stately cry for national education, is founded on
a survey of the more striking instances of the influence of culture—the sloe, by patient and skilful management, edified into
an Orleans plum; the violet, puffed out and deperfumed, till it
reach the grand, if not the sublime, in the pansy; and so forth;
suggesting to the poet's mind a complaint, that man alone has
been by man neglected; and awakening hopes, from a careful
culture of the general mind, which, though very luscious fruit to
look at, if we had no other means of reaching it than that pointed
out by our author, we should decidedly pronounce sour.

> 'Then were the terror of the exiling sword
>   From the lost Eden banished once again;
> Then bliss within creation's heart were cored,
>   And souls for love no more were made in vain;
> Shall not these golden days to man be brought?
>   Towards this goal do not the ages tend?
> Yea, take thou heart; not idly dreamest thou, thought;
>   Culture shall perfect souls, too, in the end.'

The satirical poem is entitled, 'The Cry of the lawful Lanterns.'

> 'A people dwelt in darkness,
>   In gloom and blinding night,
> Till some grew tired of candles,
>   And dared to long for light,
> When straight the established lanterns
>   Were stirred with hate of day,
> And loud the lawful rushlights
>   In wrath were heard to say,—
> Oh, have you not your lanterns,
>   Your little shining lanterns!
> What need have you of sunshine?
>   What do you want with day?'

We have only to remark, that we know no lanterns of this sort
at present, but are rather fearful that if a national system should
be adopted the lights which will be thus multiplied will also be
enlanterned; and further, that all this sentimentalism about national education is so much smoke. Show us the day-schools,
whether cheap or dear, as full on the week-day as they are on
the Sunday; let us see something like a desire for a higher education evinced in the earnest pursuit of the present means,

and then we may reasonably entertain liberal suggestions and patriotic schemes.

In a volume of lyrics, we look almost instinctively for the sonnets; if there be none we feel that the poet has not pretended to the mastery of his art; and if there be a few specimens, we search them for the indications and measure of his skill. The sonnet has been described as the test or touchstone of lyrical poetry; we feel disposed to say it is also the crown. So highly do we esteem it—this cabinet of one gem, this poem of one idea —that we would have each noble name, and every glorious thought, embalmed in its time-defying sweetness. It is a minia-ture; but it may, and should be, accurate; it is capable of the most fascinating beauty. Unknown to the ancients, and far surpassing their best epigrams in dignity and in power, its harmonious form was revealed to the romantic and lettered Provençeaux; soon won the love of the fervent Italian; and, under the auspices of our noble Surrey, found a palace-like home in English literature.

> ———————— ' with this key
> Shakspere unlocked his heart;'

and gave to the curiosity of wondering ages, some insight into the graver experiences and reflections of the model mind;

> 'A glow-worm lamp,
> In cheered mild Spencer—called from faery-land
> To struggle through dark ways;
> And when a damp
> Fell round the path of Milton, in his hands
> The thing became a trumpet whence he blew
> Soul-animating strains—alas, too few !'

In the perusal of Mr. Bennett's sonnets, we have been dis-appointed with the meagreness of the leading thought; and, notwithstanding the example of Shakspere and Milton, we have to protest against the rhyming couplet with which his sonnets conclude. We can believe or pardon anything in Milton or Shakspere; but we contend that the introduction of the rhymed couplet, at the close of a well-sustained sonnet, is out of place; it jars on the ear, it destroys the effect, and spoils the magnifi-cence of the poem; it is like the squeak of Punch on coronation-day.

Wordsworth, the prince of sonneteers, has indeed been guilty in one or two instances, on the count preferred against Mr. Bennett, in the poem from which we have quoted, and one or two others; but these exceptions are seemingly experiments; and they are suffered to remain, we might suppose, in order to warn less practised composers from the attempt, in which even

the master had failed.   We have described Mr. Bennett's book
as a pleasant companion for weary hours; as full of refreshing
scenes and joyous melodies; and as characterised by that minute
truthfulness of description which silently wins our interest, even
for the most ordinary objects, and renders us familiar and delighted with objects but seldom and slightly noticed before.   A
great portion of these pieces was evidently intended to cheer and
teach those who are too closely and constantly toiling, whether
for livelihood or wealth.   To such, he sings in blithesome measure, reproachfully or with pity, a welcome to the haunts of
vernal sweetness and May-day mirth.

> ' Come, hear the silver prattle
>     Of brooks that babbling run
> Through pastures green, where cattle
>     Lie happy in the sun;
> Where violets' hidden eyes
>     Are watching May's sweet coming,
> And gnats and burnished flies
>     Its welcome loud are humming.'

Such are the scenes which he would picture in the mind of
the toiling mass; and we need not look far for a very different
scene; that from which he would fain spirit them for a brief
while away.

> ' Close is the court and darkened,
>     On which her bare room looks,
> Whose only wealth is its walls' one print,
>     And its mantel's few old books,
> Her spare, cold bed in the corner,
>     Her single worn, worn chair,
> And the grate that looks so rusty and dull
>     As never a fire were there;
> And there, as she stitches and stitches,
>     She hears her caged thrush sing,
> Oh, would it never were May, green May,
>     It never were bright, bright Spring!'

So far, then, we accept the pleasant offering from Mr. Bennett's
muse with thanks; that special gratitude, which is defined 'a
lively sense of future favours.'

But we have intimated grave charges against him, and, though
with much reluctance, we feel bound, at least, to state the nature
of those charges.   They may be briefly comprised under an
expressive, though unauthorized term, 'religionless;' we do not
choose to employ the word 'irreligious.'   We do not insist on
the unseemly and forcible introduction of religious themes into
a work like the one before us; we are not now contending for
the doctrines of the gospel, as we discern and reverence them;

still less do we ask religiousness of form, merely as homage to general opinion; but we must pronounce a book religionless, in which we find the whole of our common Christianity shelved, and its very existence quietly ignored. We feel indignant when a tender recollection in surviving hearts, and an earth-home, decked with the flowers of the grass, are given to us as our meed of immortality; and, verily, this is the case here. Themes of touching interest, hopes of swelling import, desires large and clamorous, on every hand lead us to the very verge of religion, but never are we suffered to seek rest and joy, strength, or comfort, from its kindly influence.

We pronounce the book religionless, as we should call some religious book unpoetical; and just as there may be much in the religious book that resembles poetry, so there is (not much) but a little that resembles religion, in the poetical book before us; that little we will give :—

> ‘ I hear Him from the forest’s green,
>    From the swift light of stars above;
> From all the unnumbered forms of time,
>    His word is loud of power and love.
>
> Yea, unto all with open ears
>    By whom the circling earth is trod,
> The Eternal talketh as of old;
>    And all things are the tongues of God.’

And for a glimpse of a happy immortality—

> ‘ Nay, mother, mother, weep not so;
>    God judges for the best;
> And from a world of pain and woe,
>    He took her to his rest.
>
> Why should we wish her back again?
>    Oh, freed from sin and care,
> Let us the rather pray God’s love,
>    Ere long to join her there.’

We refuse the name of religion to this on the ground of its imperfection, its baldness, its starved and shivering poverty. On more serious grounds do we reprobate, what our author would doubtless call the religious experience of the doubter. His description of the sceptic, struggling towards the calm and perfect day of faith, awakens our tenderest sympathy; and if this description had stood by itself, we should have given it as it stood instead of any remarks of our own. But, appended to it, is one of those human remedies for the ailments of the soul, which sustain the same relation to the true, divine remedy, as quack medicines in the hands of quacks, to the same medicines mixed in different proportions, freed from injurious matters, and judiciously administered by a competent practitioner. Here follows the advertised remedy :—

> ' Work is worship; work for others;
> Toil in love, and doubt shall cease :
> On, for good—for men, thy brothers !
> Self-abjurement brings thee peace.'

Work and worship are not identical, though to a great degree inter-dependent. He who works on right principles and with due diligence, will not only appreciate the privilege of worship, but also engage in it with freedom; and again, the man who repairs the most frequently to the footstool of heaven, to seek forgiveness and blessedness, will have the wealthiest store of charity and good gifts for his brethren. We have no patience with the logic (all else apart) which teaches that a being who owes duty and service both to A and to B, may regard his zeal in the performance of the one service, as substantially a discharge from his obligations to the other. Man is bound to render love to his Maker, as well as to his neighbour ; to the one, the love of obedience and reverence and truth—spiritual sacrifices ; to the other, the love self-denying and forbearing and benevolent. How these two classes of love and duty have come to be identified or confounded ; or how men can think that either service can be properly rendered while the other is neglected; and by what strange delusion those men are possessed who think that loving man is loving God, and that loving man is all the love which God requires for himself; we confess ourselves unable to explain.

---

ART. V.—1. *The Pye Smith Testimonial.* London: J. Snow. 1851.

2. *Services occasioned by the Death of the Rev. John Pye Smith, D.D., LL.D., F.R.S., and F.G.S. Comprising the Oration at the Interment, by the Rev. George Clayton; and the Funeral Discourse, by the Rev. John Harris, D.D.* London: Jackson and Walford. 1851.

THE publications which suggest the topic of this paper have a value of their own, which we are not disposed to overlook, even in the sacredness of the memory to which they are consecrated. Each of them may be regarded as the sign of an amount of sentiment, honourable alike to the learning, the genius, the good taste, and the healthy Christian feeling, of a large body of English

Nonconformists. It was worthy of the men—of their history, and of their principles—that so holy and so richly-endowed an elder should receive from them, while yet on earth, such a graceful tribute of their veneration. The value of the ' Testimonial' (2,600*l.*); its appropriation—the founding of 'Pye Smith Divinity Scholarships' in the New College; and the manner in which it was presented; will be a perpetual record of the discernment, gratitude, and practical good sense, that are still to be found among the children of the Puritans. A month had not quite passed away, when the beloved man of God who had been thus honoured ascended to his eternal home. As devout men followed him to his grave, it was fitting that they should be spoken to in such words of ripened wisdom as those which were pronounced by the Rev. George Clayton. And when they met to worship in the ancient meeting-house wherein Dr. Smith had ministered for well nigh half a century, nothing could be more appropriate than the ornate and fascinating grandeur with which his eminent successor in the college preached the gospel to them, and portrayed, in brief but vivid touches, the character of their translated friend. Our readers are, we hope, already in possession of this ' Memorial,' and these ' Services:' any eulogy which could express our unfeigned thanks for the instruction and joy they have afforded us, would scarcely be in keeping with their success in calling our thoughts from the much honoured living to the more honoured dead.

' Dr. John Pye Smith was born at Sheffield, in 1774, and was the son of Mr. John Smith, a bookseller. Indications of piety, of great mental activity, and of an ardent thirst for learning, early distinguished him. Parental and family influences favoured the development of these qualities. In accordance with his desire for the Christian ministry, his education was early turned into a specific direction; and, at a suitable age, he became a student at Rotherham College, under the celebrated Dr. Edward Williams. When his own academical course was finished, his scholarship was so distinguished that he was at once chosen to assist in conducting the classical studies of the college. Soon after, he was invited by Coward's trustees to the classical tutorship of Wymondley College. And now appeared one of the qualities which characterised him through life—a readiness to sacrifice every temporal consideration to a sense of duty. He considered, whether he was right or wrong, that the mode of admission at that time to the advantages of the institution was not favourable to its ministerial efficiency; and, failing to obtain the change he desired, he unhesitatingly abandoned the tempting prospect. His exemplary discharge of his official duties at Rotherham College, and the marked excellence of his character, led to his being invited, at the early age of twenty-five, to become classical and resident tutor of Homerton College. In January, 1801, he entered on the duties of the office. Shortly after,

he was chosen to the theological chair, which he filled with untiring
devotedness and the highest efficiency for the long space of nearly fifty
years. In 1803, he opened the college-hall for religious services on
the Lord's-day. A little band of worshippers soon united in Christian
fellowship, and invited him to become their pastor. He was ordained
in 1804; and in 1811, the attendance was so much increased, that
larger accommodation became necessary. The use of *this* chapel—
which had been recently relinquished by the parties assembling in it
for a new one—was obtained. And thus a place in which Dr. Price,
Dr. Priestley, Mr. Belsham, and Mr. Aspland, had successfully ministered,
began to resound again with the doctrines of the proper divinity, and
the atoning sacrifice, of our Lord and Saviour Jesus Christ. At the
close of the year 1849, Dr. Smith returned into the hand of his church
the office of the pastoral oversight which, at their request, he had
assumed nearly forty-six years before. . . . Many of you will remember
his wasted but almost ethereal appearance on Wednesday, January 8th,
the day on which he received the "Testimonial" of our veneration and
affection. He had come to London the week before. During that
visit, he was expressing to some members of his family the extreme
difficulty which he felt in replying to his numerous correspondents.
And to show that he could scarcely guide the pen without the help of
his left hand, he traced some marks on a paper lying near. On subsequent examination, these marks proved to be portions of 1 John
iii. 2—"To be like him, to see him as he is."

'On Sunday, the 5th, he had joined here in the communion of the
Lord's Supper with the attached people of his former charge. After
the service, on returning to the vestry, he addressed the Rev. Mr.
Davies and the deacons, and said, "My dear brethren, this is the last
public service I shall enjoy on earth. Though I have not been able to
attend the public celebration of the Lord's Supper since I met you in
this place, I have observed it in my own house every Lord's-day."
Turning to the senior deacon, and taking his hand affectionately, he
said, "I bless God for your long and valued friendship; and (to the
next in order) for yours, my dear friend." Then addressing Mr.
Davies, he said, "I congratulate you, my dear sir, on your encouragements, and on the great success given to your ministry. I doubt not
that you will still prosper, and that here the cause of the Redeemer
will still flourish."

' During that short visit, he spoke to some affectionate relatives on
the design he had at one time formed of renewing his acquaintance
with the Greek poets. But adverting to his perusal of the Persæ of
Æschylus, and the picture of the woes produced by the invasion of
Xerxes, he added,—"How soon was I fatigued with the comparatively
feeble and puerile narrative, and eagerly turned to the Hebrew Scriptures; comparing with the Greek poet the majestic descriptions of
Jeremiah in his Lamentations. So unspeakably pathetic, powerful, and
satisfying is the inspired word."

' He deeply felt the kindness of his friends relative to the presentation of the testimonial, and the prospect of it almost overpowered him.
After the scene was over, however, though his deafness had prevented

him from hearing anything, he made no inquiry respecting what had been said, nor any specific reference to the meeting, except to express the pleasure of having recognised the countenances of so many old friends. Before going to rest, he pointed out the first chapter of the second epistle to Timothy for reading; and, in the course of the prayer which he then offered, he thanked God, with marked emphasis, for " the signal mercies—the unmerited favours of that day;" entreated " preparation for another and a more momentous day;" and after praying for his beloved children by name, added—"Though we part now, it is not for ever, nor can we ever part from Thee." On that day month he departed. No special disease invaded his frame. But, on returning to Guildford, the powers of life rapidly declined. "Thanks for your encourgement (he said, when a hope was expressed that he might yet revive); if so, well; if God order otherwise, I shall bless him in either, in every case." During the last six days, the only method of communication left to his sorrowing family was by writing, and offering to his eyes a few words of Scripture, for which he expressed hearty thanks.

' Looking intensely with his mild eyes in the faces of all who surrounded his dying bed, he made a last effort to bless them. "The Lord bless you all (said he); and he undoubtedly will." To a medical friend he articulated, with great difficulty, "Farewell, I am greatly obliged; the eternal God be thy refuge!" And, turning to his son— "The Lord be your portion for ever!" And thus (though he still lingered a short time), like his Divine Master, he may be said to have ascended in the act of blessing. . . . He was a man of the age; and faithfully did he serve it. In many respects he was in advance of the age; and served it by pioneering its way, and beckoning it onwards. At various points, he touched every great question of the century, so that his history, fully written, would be the history of the age. His life was spent pre-eminently in unfolding his ideal of truth and duty, and in carrying out their universal application, with the true earnestness of Christian devotion. And, by God's grace, he " kept the faith," and discharged his mission.'

We will not further quote, just now, from Dr. Harris's admirable ' Funeral Discourse,' but proceed to convey our own impressions of Dr. Smith, not only from personal acquaintance, and the study of his printed works, but also from private communications with which we have been favoured from those who knew him well, and greatly loved him.

From an early age to the end of life, he discovered a remarkable thirst for universal and accurate knowledge, and rare powers of acquisition. How far this thirst may have been excited by the profession of his father, it would be difficult to say. We are not believers in the creating power of outward circumstances. Yet all experience testifies that they have much to do with the particular direction which is taken by an energetic mind. It is certain that Pye Smith was, in an eminent degree, a *man of books.*

They seem to have been, at all times, a necessary of life to him. The quantity of volumes he had read, the eagerness with which he became absorbed in them, the variety of range which he took, and the accuracy with which he observed the literary, grammatical, and even typographical niceties of scholarship, are familiar matters. While engaged in his father's business, he had learnt the New Testament by heart, at the age of sixteen. He was so thoroughly versed in the Greek language, that he could repeat at any time a collection of short phrases, with Latin translations, containing the roots of the principal verbs. While a student at Rotherham, he was so scrupulously resolved to repair to the original sources of things, that even in studying Euclid he used the most correct edition he could procure of the Greek text of the ancient Geometer. The Rev. S. Thodey, of Stroud, formerly of Cambridge, has furnished us with a lively illustration of the minuteness of his learning, and the retentiveness of his memory, in this department. One morning, at lecture, a curious Greek verb occurred in reading. The Doctor remarked that this verb was used only *once* in Homer. A member of the class had just come from a Greek lecture on that poet, when, as he imagined, he had been translating the verb in question, and ventured to say that he thought this was another instance of Homer's use of it. 'Indeed, sir,' said the Doctor, slightly raising his brow, 'please to fetch the book.' He glanced at the book, and pushed it back into his young friend's hand, when he observed that it was another word, and said, to use our correspondent's language, with the indignant air of an injured ghost, dropping his voice, '*I should have been surprised if it had been possible to find a word in Homer I was not familiar with!*' This, probably, was the only instance in which any of his students knew him to refer to his own profound attainments with the smallest approach to self-complacency; and this escaped him only from a kind of disappointment in not adding to his knowledge of the use of a Greek verb.

Of his theological reading, not only in the ancient languages, and in the writings of the foreign reformers, as well as the great English divines of the Established Church, and among the Puritans, but in the philological, exegetic, and dogmatic treasures of the continental universities, he has left ample evidence, in the annotations and references of his great work—'The Scripture Testimony to the Messiah.' His appreciation of the value of such studies, and, indeed, of universal erudition, to a Christian minister, appears from an oration which he delivered at the anniversary of Rotherham College, in the year 1798—an oration which is very interesting, as the *first* of a series which has been continued at that college down to the present time, as the pro-

duction of a young man in his twenty-fourth year, as delivered
in Latin of remarkable purity and elegance, and, also, as containing the outline of the course of varied reading, to which his
long life was afterwards so assiduously devoted. In that oration,
now before us in his own neat and careful hand-writing, he
declares that the learning for which he pleads can never be a
substitute for Christian piety, and that it is not regarded by him
as necessary to the faithful and useful discharge of the office of
the holy ministry; while, with much intelligence and vigour, he
urges its great importance as *auxiliary* to higher qualifications.
He embraces the entire field of scholarship, the Hebrew, Greek,
and Latin languages; the fathers of the Church; the Greek and
Roman classic authors; the English language; (other modern
languages are omitted); history; natural philosophy; astronomy;
natural history; chemistry; dialectics; mathematics. In touching on chemistry, he introduces a tribute of veneration and
sorrow to the memory of Lavoisier, who had recently fallen a
victim, in the prime of life, to the ferocious tyranny of Robespierre. He, also, commemorates the discoveries of Priestley, of
whom he speaks as a minister among the Dissenters, ' *vir claris-
simus—sed quoad res divinas utinam felicior*—Josephus Priestley,
LL.D.'

The academic lectures of Dr. Smith, it is said by those who
have heard them, abound with the richest illustrations of his
vast acquirements in nearly every branch of knowledge; while
his Congregational Lectures on Scripture and Geology, and the
numerous notes illustrative of his investigations in all the collateral sciences, together with his occasional communications to
scientific journals, sufficiently evince the vivacity and promptitude with which he explored nearly every region of the world
of letters.

We must be allowed to remark, in this place, that, so far as
we know, Dr. Smith was the first theologian in our country who
gave attention to the bearing of geological discoveries on the
interpretation of the Bible, and that he boldly anticipated nearly
all that has been truly and wisely advanced on that subject, *in
the pages of this Review.* So long back as the year 1812, he
wrote a review of Dr. Hales's ' New Analysis of Chronology,'
containing a passage, which, as it contains the germ of his
'Congregational Lecture,' and is, besides, the most comprehensive
statement we have met with, of what we hold to be the truth on one
part of a very large question—the relations of science to the Holy
Scriptures—our readers will be glad to have placed before them.

' In the first volume, p. 321, compelled by astronomical reasons and
analogical argument, though not explicitly stated, Dr. Hales had said,
" Whether the host of fixed stars were all created and made at the same

time with our system, may reasonably be doubted." We lament that
he has not attended to this important subject in its proper place of the
present volume, and that, not only in relation to the suns and worlds
which we have reason to believe exist out of the limits of our solar
system, but with respect to that system itself, and the constitution and
structure of the earth.   Many modern geologists are daily confirming
themselves and others in infidelity, from the unfounded assumption
that the Mosaic cosmogony is contradicted by indubitable facts and
discoveries in mineralogical science.   We are sorry to say, that when
this objection was adverted to in the admirable lectures read by an
illustrious Professor at the Royal Institution, last year, the answer
which was produced was of that flimsy kind which could satisfy no man,
and must have left the objection to operate with more mischievous
force.   The false assumption rests on the idea that, according to the
Scriptures, the antiquity of the created universe does not much exceed
six or seven thousand years.   *From long and attentive consideration, we
are convinced that neither the Book of Genesis, nor any other part of the
Bible, authorizes any* such conclusion.   Certainly the Bible teaches that
the formation of man, and of the present species of organised beings
which people our planet, took place at the late date referred to; and
this fact is verified by the traditional testimony of all nations, by the
recent origin of the arts and improvements of life, and by all the
literary monuments of mankind.   But this by no means justifies the
inference, that the earth as a terrene body had not previously existed
for a period of duration not to be assigned.   The magnificent exordium
of the Hebrew prophet, and inspired teacher, is a simple declaration of
the fact, that the *whole* dependent universe did, at some period or other
in the retrospect of countless ages, *derive* its existence, form, and properties, from the Infinite and All-Perfect Intelligence which we deno-
minate God.   Moses, then, takes up the planet which was to be the
theatre of those great measures of Jehovah's moral government, the
history of which it was his immediate object to record; and the very
terms in which he describes it carry to our conviction the intimation of
a pre-existent state, and a dissolution from that state into a dark,
chaotic, decompounded mass.   We venture to give a translation of the
verse, submitting it to the candid judgment of those who study the
Hebrew language by the aid of its cognate dialects :—" Now the earth
was in a state of disorder and disarrangement, and darkness upon the
surface of the disordered mass; and the Spirit of God moved with
fostering influence upon the surface of the waters."   We would ask
the scientific geologist, whether he does not manifestly perceive, under
these expressions, the condition of a disorganized globe, its surface to
some depth in a state of watery solution and mixture, and its atmosphere
turbid and unpermeable to light?   The divine historian proceeds to
relate a series of phenomena, in which we may, without irreverence,
conceive that Almighty Wisdom acted by the operation of those physical laws which Itself had established—the attraction of gravitation,
and that of chemical affinity.   The atmosphere was cleared, and filled
with light on that hemisphere which was presented to the sun; but it
was not yet sufficiently purified to permit the heavenly bodies to be
seen, had a spectator existed on the earth; the diurnal motion of the

globe was established; the atmosphere was further cleared by the separation of watery vapour, and clouds were formed; the continents and mountains were heaved up, and, consequently, the waters subsided into the hollows; the agency of Creating Goodness covered the desiccated ground with vegetables; the atmosphere now became sufficiently pellucid to render the heavenly luminaries visible; fish and birds were created; then quadrupeds and reptiles; and, finally, man. We conceive, also, that the remarkable passage, 2 Pet. iii. 5, 6, is couched in terms which cannot be applied to the Noachic deluge, but which are fairly descriptive of the disintegration of our world from a former state, by solution of its external surface in water, reducing it to the very condition in which it becomes the subject of the Mosaic narrative.

' Our readers will not think that this digression requires an apology, when they consider the extensive popularity which geological studies have recently acquired; the impossibility that any person, who is really acquainted with mineralogical phenomena, can attribute an origin so recent as the creation of the present races of organized beings to the materials of the earth's structure, their deposition and arrangement; the importance of showing that the Holy Scriptures are in no respect impugned by the attribution of the remotest antiquity to the earth, under former constitutions of its existence; and that irreligion can derive no aid from the discoveries of geology and electro-chemistry. We return to Dr. Hales, again lamenting his total inattention to this great question.'

Dr. Smith was a member of several learned and scientific societies, and a constant attendant at their meetings, even after his almost total deafness rendered him incapable of reaping the full benefit of the communications and discussions which took place. We may mention particularly the Royal Society, the Geological Society, and the British Association for the advancement of Science, in whose geological sections his benignant and happy countenance was familiar, and where there were always those at hand who felt it an honour to assist him with notes which almost supplied to his quick perception the loss occasioned by his want of hearing.

The conscientious regulation of his literary and scientific powers was one of the most characteristic and constant manifestations of his character. While he loved knowledge for its own sake, as gratifying a noble instinct of his nature, his mind was too practical, too religious, to be insensible to the duties binding on him as a man, and especially as a teacher of aspirants to the ministerial office : it was most conspicuous, that he inquired for others even more than for himself, that his personal delights were heightened by sympathies with those whom he sought to raise to his own level, and that every book he read, and every scientific réunion at which he assisted, was most devoutly considered and employed with an habitual regard to his official

occupations.   He saw the latent harmonies of truths which the
superficial behold only in isolation or antagonism.   To him the
spiritual, the ethical, and the physical, were but varying phases
of one reality ; nature, science, philosophy, and revelation, were
the several rays of the eternal light; and he perceived their
relations, their appropriate developments, and their fundamental
unity, in the Infinite Mind, of which they are the mysterious
emanations.   It does not appear that abstract truth, whether in
the higher mathematics, or in purely metaphysical speculation,
had greatly occupied him ; nor are we acquainted with any
evidence that he worked out the analogies of the universe with
the power which imparts brilliancy to the imagination, and
clothes the intuitions of the soul in the burning words of the
poet or the orator : it is probable that his aptitudes for such forms
of intellectual life were not large or predominant : it is certain
that they were not strengthened and enlarged by exercise ; but
however this might be, he had a heart that was touched with the
grand or beautiful in nature, or in art, and had he been an
ostentatious man, or less rigidly guided in all his movements
by the stern yet cheerful sense of duty, we dare not say that,
with his sensibility, his amazing quickness of apprehension, his
entire command of language, his intense hatred of all evil, and
equally intense love of all good, he might not have been as distinguished for the splendour, as he really is for the transparency,
of his productions.
    We must not omit to notice Dr. Smith's pre-eminent facility in
communicating the knowledge which he was so constantly accumulating.   Though we believe not what is commonly understood
by being a popular preacher,—wanting, as he did, of some of the
rhetorical and elocutionary elements demanded for that purpose,
—those who listened to him as a Christian teacher, intent on
learning holy wisdom, preferred him to most others, even in the
pulpit.   If there were not striking originalities—dazzling images,
massive and overwhelming reasonings, pathetic and arousing
appeals to the common emotions, and the moral apprehensions of
human nature—there was always a serene and heavenly light, a
reverential seriousness, a gentle persuasion, a modest dignity, an
intellectual vivacity, an unaffected simplicity of manner, and a
chaste, perspicuous style.   These qualities of an instructor were
eminently beheld in his academic lectures.   That was his natural
orbit, where with steady equipoise he performed the tranquil
revolutions, girdled, like Saturn, with a ring, and followed, as
he moved along, by attendant orbs that caught and reflected
the radiations of his light.   It must not be inferred from this
description that there were no *librations*, no disturbing forces,
no play of mind amid the grave prelections of the theological

professor.  He would often pause, as a happy thought occurred
to him, and, by apt quotation, or felicitous allusion, or some
pleasant anecdote, would illustrate the theme in hand, or relieve
the listener—sometimes, perchance, the lecturer—by digressions
which have all the greater charm that they could be produced
only by a mind well ordered, and ever filling its expanding
receptivity from all fountains of intelligence.   According to
the testimony of all the ministers from Homerton, with whom it
has been our happiness to converse, the great objects of his constant anxiety were those so well expressed in the address which
accompanied the ' Testimonial :'—

' As a tutor, those only can estimate your worth who enjoyed the
privilege of your instruction.   Possessed yourself of matchless stores of
learning—literary, scientific, and theological,—all based upon accurate
classical scholarship,—you incessantly laboured to inculcate on your
pupils the importance of exact information, of large and liberal views,
and of profound and diligent research.   Your own example was a constant stimulus, and an ever-present encouragement.   Whilst you thus
endeavoured to lead them forward in the attainment of true knowledge,
you discountenanced all levity of mind, and love of idle speculation;
and, by your spirit, admonitions, and prayers, sought to impress them
with the feeling that learning must ever be subordinate to piety,—and
                                        and heavenly.mindedness are

foibles, your generous encouragement of their efforts, and your true
sympathy with them in their afflictions, made them look on you as a
father; nor will they, to their last hour, cease to rejoice that they were
allowed to call you tutor and friend.'

The largest and most permanent contributions to the instruction of mankind which Dr. Smith has given, are to be found in
his published writings, and in those manuscripts which, we
presume, will, ere long, be added to their number.   It is not
our purpose to review, even in a cursory manner, the printed
works of Dr. Smith, nor even to recapitulate their titles : we
purpose, rather, to seize the leading features of mind they
severally exhibit, and, from an examination of the writings, to
portray the man.   Some of his minor publications which have
long since been out of print, being on topics of a personal kind,
are not likely to be recovered from the oblivion into which he
himself permitted them to lie, but to those who, like ourselves,
remember to have read them, they long ago gave proof of that
conscious high-mindedness, that power of exposing misconception, that energy of meek rebuke, which were so beautifully matured by the discipline of reason and the mellowing

experiences of religion. It may be well for men of independent and enlarged minds to dwell on this portion of Dr. Smith's life. They may learn from it to be true to their own convictions, undismayed by the prejudices of less instructed minds, and calmly and meekly waiting for time, the great innovator, to bring about the triumph of *the* truth for the advocacy of which they must be content to suffer misconception and obloquy. It is also emphatically well for the impatient and stereotyped disciples of traditionary interpretations of revealed wisdom, to be reminded that there is some peril in resisting the progress of mind in any department of its operations. Prejudice is often very respectable, and attachment to the opinions of wise and good men is an amiable adjunct of reverence for Divine teaching; but convictions, based on evidence, are higher and mightier than any prejudices, and the mind of man is made for progress, and must advance in the path of real knowledge. Let Christian men have more faith in God than in man, in the Bible than in human explanations borrowed from imperfect knowledge; and let them know that there is a higher tribunal than the churches of any age or nation—the judgment of an independent public and of a better-informed posterity. Though we pass these compositions by with so very slight a reference, we cannot forget how deeply they impressed us, years ago, with admiration and affection for the writer. And, without awakening, in any quarter, recollections which are now too ancient to be accompanied with bitterness, we are unwilling that the present generation should be ignorant that few men have passed through severer tests of patience, of forbearance, of manly faith in his own personal integrity, and of filial confidence in the God of truth and righteousness, than the illustrious Christian, scholar, and divine, who has been so lately gathered, as a golden 'shock of corn,' into the garner of the Lord. It is neither by fate, nor chance, nor miracle, that *such* men are formed.

There are two practical discourses, separately published, we forget how long ago, by Dr. Smith, which we should be sorry to find unknown, for they are seasonable at all times, and the authority of his venerable name would attract towards them the attention of not a few minds, much needing sympathy and guidance — we refer to his judicious little publication entitled, 'Prudence and Piety recommended to Young Persons at their Entrance upon the Active Duties of Life;' and to a 'Sermon on the Means of obtaining Satisfaction with regard to the Truth of Religious Opinions.' This last, we fear, is not so well known as it deserves to be, for the gentle and judicious treatment of instances in mental history too much neglected or misunderstood by all, excepting such as have had to struggle hard and long for enlightened certitude, in those sacred regions which are divided, to an extent painful to contemplate, between the doubting and the dogmatic.

Many will remember the audacious attacks on Christianity by 'the Rev. Robert Taylor,' in 1826. A printed paper, issued by that person, entitled, 'Manifesto of the Christian Evidence Society,' induced the 'Society for Promoting Christian Instruction' to apply to Dr. Smith to draw up an 'Answer,' which was extensively circulated,
deep erudition, the

moral feelings of
sed, claim for it a


Religion to th
the 'Subjects at present
senters.' This Appendix
Dr. Smith and his eminen
To that controversy—du


Trinity College; and we can heartily c
given by Mr. Thodey, in his speech at
which the 'Memorial' was presented to

'I know that the regard of Professor Lee for Dr. Smith was wholly uninterrupted by the controversy in which they had been engaged. He has frequently said to me, "There is no man for whom I have a higher estimation than for Dr. Pye Smith. Our controversy was all upon paper, and before the world; but our mutual friendship is undisturbed. We were combatants in public, but the best of friends in private. I have always regarded him as one of the best of men."'

We understand that Dr. Lee has acknowledged, in very cordial terms, what he calls the 'acceptable service' rendered to himself by the manner in which his esteem for Dr. Smith had been represented.

Of Dr. Pye Smith's larger treatises, we gratefully cite the comprehensive panegyric of Dr. Harris, in a passage which describes the practical applications of his great intellectual activity:—

'It has been said that "to write is to act." Each of his books was an act; and an act designed to meet a want. Whether he architecturally built up the "Scripture Testimony to the Messiah," like the ancient Tabernacle of Witness, or rebuked the flippant attacks of Infidelity; whether he asserted the Sacrifice and Priesthood of Christ, exhibited the rules for the Interpretation of Prophecy, expounded the

experiences of religion.    It may be well for men of independent
and enlarged minds to dwell on this portion of Dr. Smith's life.
They may learn from it to be true to their own convictions,
undismayed by the prejudices of less instructed minds, and
calmly and meekly waiting for time, the great innovator, to
bring about the triumph of *the* truth for the advocacy of which
they must be content to suffer misconception and obloquy.    It
is also emphatically well for the impatient and stereotyped
disciples of traditionary interpretations of revealed wisdom, to
be reminded that there is some peril in resisting the progress
of mind in any department of its operations.    Prejudice is often
very respectable, and attachment to the opinions of wise and
good men is an amiable adjunct of reverence for Divine
teaching; but convictions, based on evidence, are higher and
mightier than any prejudices, and the mind of man is made for
progress, and must advance in the path of real knowledge.    Let
Christian men have more faith in God than in man, in the Bible
than in human explanations borrowed from imperfect knowledge; and let them know that there is a higher tribunal than
the churches of any age or nation—the judgment of an independent public and of a better-informed posterity.    Though we pass
these compositions by with so very slight a reference, we cannot
forget how deeply they impressed us, years ago, with admiration
and affection for the writer.    And, without awakening, in any
quarter, recollections which are now too ancient to be accompanied with bitterness, we are unwilling that the present generation should be ignorant that few men have passed through severer
tests of patience, of forbearance, of manly faith in his own personal integrity, and of filial confidence in the God of truth and
righteousness, than the illustrious Christian, scholar, and divine,
who has been so lately gathered, as a golden ' shock of corn,'
into the garner of the Lord.    It is neither by fate, nor chance,
nor miracle, that *such* men are formed.

  There are two practical discourses, separately published, we
forget how long ago, by Dr. Smith, which we should be sorry
to find unknown, for they are seasonable at all times, and the
authority of his venerable name would attract towards them
the attention of not a few minds, much needing sympathy
and guidance — we refer to his judicious little publication
entitled, ' Prudence and Piety recommended to Young Persons at their Entrance upon the Active Duties of Life;' and
to a ' Sermon on the Means of obtaining Satisfaction with
regard to the Truth of Religious Opinions.'    This last, we fear,
is not so well known as it deserves to be, for the gentle and
judicious treatment of instances in mental history too much
neglected or misunderstood by all, excepting such as have

tures. He does not make geology either supersede or contradict the Scriptures; neither does he make the Scriptures teach geology. The science he expounds by the legitimate methods of observation and comparison. The Scriptures he expounds according to the laws of grammatical and philological exegesis. Each department of truth is treated in its appropriate manner, independently of the other. And these separate and independent sources of truth are shown to harmonize. Other modes of exhibiting the harmony of geology with Scripture had been attempted. These are freely examined in the lectures: their errors pointed out, and their defects supplied. There are still not a few theologians to whom these lectures are distasteful; but we believe that, on the whole, they are highly satisfactory to the greater part of those who have studied geology in the free spirit of science, and the Bible in the equally free spirit of humble and teachable inquiry. For ourselves, we regard them as a precious contribution towards an end which will be more and more appreciated, both in its difficulties and in its solu-

the unity of method which embraces both as distinct, yet accordant, developments of the thought of the Infinite Revealer. The conviction is in our min

as unfettered by human
dition can attain, reflecting, as from
revealed mind of God, will b
gressive emancipations of the human mind from the accumulated errors of ages, whether in the interpretations of nature or in the interpretations of Scripture. We expect no physical science beyond the revelations of nature; neither do we look for any theological science beyond the revelations of Scripture. Both nature and written revelation have been *progressive* in their actual constitution; and as it agrees with these unquestionable facts, that human science respecting material nature is in a state of actual advancement to which it is not in our power to assign the limits, and that a similar advancement may be predicated of human science respecting man's intellectual, moral, and social constitution, it were more presumptuous to deny than to affirm that *human science respecting the spiritual truths imparted by the inspired messengers of heaven* is, in like manner, included within the range of the divine law of progression in the intellectual history of man. We are prepared, as we doubt not Dr. Smith was, to apply to every real discovery the human mind can make in psychical, ethical, or social investigations, not less than in the regions of abstract demonstration and of physical forces, the calm and confiding language in which the

Principles of the Reformation, or enforced the claims of Evangelical Nonconformity, his aim was usefulness of the highest order. His great work, the "Scripture Testimony," is universally acknowledged to be one of the greatest modern achievements of sanctified learning. I have long thought of him in this connexion, as the Lardner of Doctrinal Theology. The correspondence, indeed, is traceable in the inductive method which each has pursued, and in the extremely cautious and candid spirit in which their respective inquiries are conducted. The preponderance of learning and reasoning is decidedly in favour of Dr. Smith.'

In 1829, Dr. Smith published a discourse on the ' Principles of Interpretation as applied to the Prophecies of Holy Scripture.' There are many respects in which we have been accustomed to regard this discourse as the most valuable we have ever seen on the wide and difficult department of Biblical Theology which it embraces : it is so clear, so full, so admirably arranged, so richly pervaded by views at once broadly comprehensive and critically exact, and breathes at once so holy a frame of mind, such caution, such nice discrimination—such easy and well-wielded power in the destruction of theories based on misinterpretation, or on unwarranted conjectures, or on fanciful analogies—and such enlightened and practical reverence for the teaching of the Holy Spirit.

We have before adverted to the early and deep interest taken by Dr. Smith in the discoveries of geologists and their bearing on the interpretation of the Scriptures. We are told that his profound and far-reaching views of these discoveries, and these bearings, were given in his lecture-room at Homerton College, between thirty and forty years ago. When these antecedents are considered, it will be no matter of surprise that the Committee of the Congregational Library should have invited so competent a lecturer to discuss this momentous theme in the Congregational Lecture for 1839. In that interesting volume, what struck us most, when we first read it, was the familiarity of the lecturer with the entire field of geological science ; the simplicity, ease, and naturalness of his reference to facts, principles, theories, systems, and interpretations, with which even a moderate degree of acquaintance is the purchase of many years' devotion to such studies. We remember saying, at the time, to a well-educated and studious minister, now deceased, that these lectures formed an easy introduction to the fascinating study of geology; when he replied that, in his opinion, they required a considerable previous knowledge of that science to be able to comprehend them. Yet it is not as a professed teacher of geology that Dr. Smith brings forward his rich array of large and well-digested information, but as an expounder of the Scrip-

been reading, on the journey, a most spirited paper in the 'Eclectic Review,' exposing some abominations of the Church of England, and he spoke for a long time in the most serious and earnest strain of entire condemnation of that ecclesiastical system.  Some of the party were members of the Church which he had been so unsparingly cutting up.  A gentleman present, who knew this fact, and perceived that Dr. Smith did not, went to the side of the table on which the Doctor was sitting, and said to him, through his ear-trumpet, 'You are quite aware, Doctor, that some of us might very conscientiously hold different views on this subject from those which you have been now expressing, though it would be inconvenient, at present, to discuss them.'  He quickly replied, 'Certainly, sir; but the right must be on one side, and that side is taken by those who have thoroughly and fairly examined the whole question;' and then he proceeded, as before, to deliver himself in a style which would have delighted an assembly of sturdy Anti-state Church-men.  When the party had broken up, the worthy Doctor was told that some of the ladies who had listened to him were membe
a point
most el

his
unseasonableness of the
humility, to say that he was fully convinced of the truth, and the importance of what he had uttered.  It may be supposed that the ladies were greatly charmed with the simplicity, earnest-ness, and gentlemanly bearing of the learned divine; though, we believe, they continued to attend and to love their Church.

We cannot forbear alluding to the high-minded candour and fairness of Dr. Smith as a controversial writer.  Some of his ex-pressions might, indeed, be quoted, as having an appearance of conscious superiority in learning to his oppo    ιt; but it will scarcely be questioned by those who have stuaι    his writings that he displayed the attributes we have a    d    him in a pre-eminent degree.  It was in the regions oι        ce and scholarship, not in his peculiar province of theology, ι  t ap-parent, we believe *only* apparent, exceptions might be    ιnd. We refer, now, to that great work which he l                    - scribed as 'the work on which I rest my chief hope oι ness;' and

'It would be affectation to say, that I deem this bo    a feeble contribution to the cause of religious knowledge. ɾ    ι learned lecturer expounds the final result of his comparison of geology with Scripture.

'It follows, then, as a *universal* truth, that the Bible, faithfully interpreted, erects no bar against the most free and extensive investigation, the most comprehensive and searching induction. Let but the investigation be sufficient, and the induction honest. Let observation take its farthest flight; let experiment penetrate into *all* the recesses of of nature; let the veil of ages be lifted up from all that has been hitherto unknown, if such a course were possible; religion need not fear, Christianity is secure, and true science will always pay homage to the Divine Creator and Sovereign, "of whom, and through whom, and to whom are all things; and unto whom be glory for ever."'

While Dr. Smith was well known to be among the meekest and humblest of Christ's disciples, it deserves to be considered that these lovely qualities were guarded, so to speak, by the sterner virtues of unflinching integrity, the conscious dignity of a true man and a servant of God, the prompt antagonism of a well-ordered and fullyequipped championship of truth, righteousness, and freedom against all error, wickedness, and oppression. He was as strenuous an opponent of unequal, unwise, or unmerciful legislation, as if his whole life had been spent in clubs or parliaments. He was more orthodox than any of the scribes who assailed him for his sympathy with the heterodox in all questions of science or of civil freedom. He was a more thorough-going Dissenter than many who would not wish, or could not succeed, to live in terms of amity with ornaments and vindicators of the Established Church. In all matters of ecclesiastical or of general politics, he took what are sometimes spoken of, depreciatingly, as extreme views—a fact which may be accounted for partly by his early associations, and partly by his keen perception of principles, but still more by the transcendently religious and benevolent principle which ruled him, more than most men, in every action of his life. It was his abhorrence of sin, under all its guises, his deep feeling of brotherhood towards the whole human family, and, above all, his zeal for God, that made him the warm advocate for the reform of every abuse, and for the promotion of every scheme that contemplated the elevation and advancement of mankind; and in the advocacy of these reforms and meliorations he was as practically and self-denyingly earnest as though his formal and official occupations had not been those of the retired and laborious student.

We once spent a most pleasant day in his society, which afforded a singularly felicitous illustration of characteristics we have seldom seen combined. He had been travelling many miles the day before, and he told the company that he had

it such, I should have been highly culpable for troubling the public with it. In the subject which it treats, I was led by personal circumstances and connexions to take much interest, from an early period of life. Its composition and improvement, notwithstanding many interruptions, have been a *principal occupation* during many of my best years. It was begun with an apprehensiveness against irrational prepossessions, over-statement of premises, and excess in conclusions; amounting to a jealousy, and by some censured as a blameable timidity. Of this caution, however, even if it has been redundant, I do not repent. In proportion to the solicitude and tardiness of the process, has been the satisfactory character of the result. I should be faithless to the most serious convictions, were I not to profess my belief that these volumes contain a body of proof, not invented by an erring mortal, but elicited from the records of Divine Revelation, in favour of the ancient and common faith of Christians ; *a body of proof which can never be overthrown, and which time, so far from impairing, will but the more confirm and extend.'*

It is to this great life-labour of a great divine—his appropriate and imperishable monument—that we refer in illustration of our remark, to its *grand idea*—to its arrangement—to its skilful artistic execution—to its carefully-sifted reasonings—to its almost numberless proofs of assiduous and independent and multifarious readings in ancient and modern languages—to its serene and almost majestic sanctity of tone—to its entire structure, which reminds us of Newton in his ' Principia,' and to which we are at a loss to find any other parallel. In a special manner we call attention to the third chapter of the First Book on the ' Errors and Faults with respect to the present Controversy, which are especially chargeable on the Orthodox, but in part also on their Opponents.'

We conclude this genial, though most incomplete, labour of love by avowing our conviction that the name of JOHN PYE SMITH, instead of fading away with the generation which he has adorned by his genius, instructed by his learning, and edified by his beautiful and holy life, will acquire fresh lustre from the flight of years, and will be reverently pronounced in all the languages of men, as one of the most worthy in the highest rank of mortals—the ornaments of England, the lights of literature, the saints of Christendom, and the benefactors of that race of which ' THE MESSIAH' is ' THE PRIEST' and ' LORD.'

ART. VI.—*The Stones of Venice. Vol. I.—The Foundations.* By John Ruskin, Author of 'The Seven Lamps of Architecture,' 'Modern Painters,' &c. With Illustrations drawn by the Author. London: Smith, Elder, and Co.

MR. RUSKIN has fought his way, by his former works, against the most rooted prejudices of artists and architects, and through the most unflinching antagonism on his part, to a deservedly high reputation with the public. He has shown himself an earnest and honest thinker on all that concerns art, and for such men there will always be an audience, however much many of the auditors themselves may be startled by the enunciations made, and however impossible it may be for them to accord with the enunciator in all his views. There are points on which we are by no means prepared to agree with Mr. Ruskin, such as his wholesale admiration of the later paintings of J. M. W. Turner; his notion that such things as shops and railway stations, buildings for mere usefulness, should have no kind of ornament, and similar matters to which we shall point in the present volume. In the case of Turner's paintings we think that Mr. Ruskin, in his violent and undiscriminating admiration, departs from his usual good taste in a very extraordinary degree; and in the case of shops and railway stations, we think he errs in advocating no ornament instead of a *befitting* ornament. We can see no reason why our eyes should be offended with ugly dead walls wherever we turn, merely because shops and railway stations are things of every-day use. What wretched dreary objects would be the streets of our great towns on this principle—what huge revolting masses our railway stations! In these particulars Mr. Ruskin certainly departs from his own grand and correct rule, that we should make nature our guide in our architecture, for nature leaves no place without its appropriate embellishment. She clothes the poorest heath, and the most barren mountain, with vegetation, with flowers, and with colours, which are exquisite there, though they would be often out of place anywhere else.

But allowing these peculiarities to Mr. Ruskin, as we must allow for such exceptional points in all strong and original natures, we find him as a whole profoundly correct in his views of art. He has seized on the great principle that all art is 'the expression of man's delight in God's work.' That is his clue through the universe. Holding fast by that he can never get far wrong. There may be times when his attention is not so livingly excited, or when his imagination is too strong for his judgment, in which he admires or condemns in direct opposition to his own admitted axioms, and drags his clue to one side, instead of following it docilely; but in the main his pursuit of truth is as admirable for its clear-sightedness, as it is for its honesty. He follows nature with the ardour of a worshipper, and the stern obstinacy of a martyr. There is a profound sense of religion in his soul, one rare quality now-a-days in both art and science. He possesses a sublime idea of the great building and beautifying Spirit of all worlds, and this gives not only to his conceptions of artistic beauty a grandeur pre-eminent, but to his sentiments a fervid depth and an eloquence of expression, that pervade his work with an indescribable charm. Confident in the eternal truth of his system, he goes boldly battling his way through all the corruptions of art, knocking down false principles and false professors with a calm strength and fearlessness that astonish you. You see angry advocates and practisers of old errors assailing him on all sides, but with no more effect than arrows of stubble would have on the hide of the rhinosceros. The truth of nature triumphs in his person, and the heart and convictions of the public follow him and grow around him from day to day. There can be no question but that the works of Mr. Ruskin will produce the most decided and enduring revolution in every quarter of the world of art and architecture.

It will be only justice, however, to both author and reader, to state in the outset, that in the present volume there will be found few of those eloquent and detailed expressions of the author's views of art in general, which abounded in his two former ones, and which gave them so immediate a popularity. This volume is, for the most part, a simple and somewhat dry demonstration of the elementary laws of architecture. Had it been meant to stand alone it would have been only fair and proper to call it a treatise on architecture, on Mr. Ruskin's principles. It is not the stones of Venice, but the introduction to them, which we are led to expect in the next volume. Here we have the laws drawn from a severe study of the buildings of Venice. There we are to look for the exhibition of those laws in the description of the glorious erections themselves. It is evident, therefore, that this volume is intended rather for the student of architecture, than for the many. It cannot, by any means, gratify the general reader, but it will prove invaluable to the lover of art, whether he be acquainting himself with its principles for the purpose of future practice, or as an amateur in whom the love of art is the source of profound gratification. To such every line will be a line of light, leading on to the full development of the subject in the next volume, and will be studied with an enthusiasm of which the ordinary reader can have no conception.

Before speaking of the main topic of Mr. Ruskin's work, and the things in which we entirely agree with him, there are one or two dogmatic assertions, which it may be as well to deal with. They are just those particulars which startle his greatest admirers, and which raise especially an antagonist feeling.

'All European architecture,' he says, 'bad a
is derived from Greece through Rome, and
from the East. The history of architecture is
of the various modes and directions of this
and Corinthian orders are the roots, the one of

can name of the kind;
French, German, and Tuscan. Now observe

arch. The shaft and arch, the frame-work and strength of archi
are from the race of Japheth; the spirituality and sanctity of
Ishmael, Abraham, and Shem.
'There is high probability that the Greek received his shaft system from Egypt; but I do not care to keep this earlier derivation in the mind of the reader. It is only necessary that he should be able to refer to some fixed point of origin, when the form of the shaft was perfected. But it may be incidentally observed, that if the Greeks did receive their Doric from Egypt, then the three families of the earth have each contributed their part to its noblest architecture; and Ham, the servant of the others, furnishes the sustaining, or bearing member, the shaft; Japheth, the arch; Shem, the spiritualization of both. I have said that the two orders of Doric and Corinthian are the roots of all European architecture. You have, perhaps, heard of five orders; but there are only two real orders; and there never can be any more till doomsday.'—P. 13.

Now, we think that in this statement there are scarcely more lines than there are errors, and those delivered with a dogmatism that is astounding. In the first place, that there never can be more than two orders of architecture till doomsday, is at once to say that we have reached in art the extreme point of invention, and to limit the human intellect to the narrow bounds of our own accomplished knowledge. We are satisfied that the author will find but very few who will go along with him in so extraordinary an assertion. We also equally demur to the fact of there being only two real orders of architecture—Doric and Corinthian. That all orders hitherto known may be classified under those with a convex and those with a concave tendency of capital, may be true; but the essentials of a distinct order depend on other features than these; and we are persuaded that there would have been Gothic architecture as perfect, and as completely what it is at the present day, if there had never existed any Grecian architecture at all. The whole nature, essence, and character, of the

two styles of architecture, Greek and Gothic, are so utterly dissimilar, that they cannot be brought into question as to identity
of origin, or as to derivation of one from the other.   In fact, the
Greek architecture has conferred nothing on the Gothic, not
even the shaft; and Mr. Ruskin, indeed, partly recollects himself
and corrects himself, though reluctantly, in this respect.   He
admits that the Greeks derived the shaft from Egypt; a fact too
palpable to be denied.   That admitted, what, then, does Gothic
architecture derive from the Greeks?   The shaft is all that Mr.
Ruskin claims, and this he again gives up; the ornament and
spiritualization of both shaft and arch he properly ascribes to
Shem.

Gothic architecture, therefore, we re-assert, could and would
have existed as it does, had no Greece ever been.   In Egypt
existed the shaft before Greece was a nation; in India existed
the arch before Rome was heard of.   In fact, neither from Greece,
nor Egypt, nor India, do we derive the shaft or the Gothic arch.
The very first man who set up the stem of a tree to form a porch
for his forest shed, originated the pure shaft; and the next man
who joined two branches and two such stems with their upper
points meeting, originated the Gothic pointed arch.   The elements
of Gothic architecture descend from the earliest ages, independent
of the architecture of Greece or Rome; and the ornament of this
exquisite style of architecture has developed itself, through successive centuries, to its present affluent and most poetical existence.   Mr. Ruskin, indeed, sneers at the innumerable foolish
theories about the derivation of Gothic from trees and avenues,
' which have from time to time been brought forward by persons
ignorant of the history of architecture.'   But such dogmatic
sneers will not any the more set aside the belief in the origin of
Gothic architecture from such application of trees, and such observation of the sublime forms which they assume in nature.
Mr. Ruskin is well aware of the existence of the wooden churches
of the northern Goths, for he refers to them; and what so natural
as that the dwellers in the ancient forests, and especially in the
forests of the north of Europe, where the primitive rock was too
stubborn and resistant in its nature for the time and tools of the
inhabitants, should resort, as they did, to wood for their churches,
and should arrange their wood in the forms which the natural
sweep of branches and the striking grandeur of scenery so
palpably pointed out?   In the magnificent cathedral of Ulm, the
architect has recorded *his* conviction of this being the true origin
of that style which he was so noble a master of, by roofing his
porch with stone-work cut into the shape of branches, represented
with all their bark, their inequalities, and the lopping-off of side-
branches.

It is, at least, singular that Mr. Ruskin, while setting aside Grecian architecture as perfectly absurd and useless in this climate, and expending all his lore on the Gothic—which is, in truth, the only style in which all the ornaments whose direct derivation from nature he so ably recommends, can be employed in its endless variety—should have been at so much pains to draw the Gothic from the utterly incongruous Greek, and not from the genius of the ancient Gothic nations, where are found existing from the earliest times all its independent elements.

One more instance we may give of that waywardness, which affords so easy a handle to Mr. Ruskin's enemies.  We will not attempt to combat his positive declaration, to be found at page 44, that 'no man ever really enjoyed doing evil since God made the world;' for every person's experience, and the whole course of both sacred and profane history, must satisfy most people that there are tens of thousands who feel an intense pleasure in doing evil, in the exercise of malice, of despotism, and of destruction—or why do they do it?  The moral and religious philosophers can confute him so promptly and effectually, that to them we leave him.  But what of this passage?—

'A *builder*, not an architect; he may be a rough, artless, feelingless man, incapable of doing any one truly fine thing all his days.  I shall call upon you to despise him presently in a sort, but not as if he were a mere smoother of mortar; perhaps a great man, infinite in memory, indefatigable in labour, exhaustless in expedient, unsurpassable in quickness of thought.  Take good heed you understand him before you despise him.

'But why is he to be in any way despised?  By no means despise him, unless he happen to be without a soul, or at least to show no signs of it.'—P. 40.

Now if Mr. Ruskin's notion of architecture were no clearer than this passage, we should not expect much from it.  This man is to be despised and not to be despised.  We are called on to despise him, and then warned off from despising him.  In one place he is 'a great man, infinite in memory, indefatigable in labour, exhaustless in expedient, unsurpassable in quickness of thought.'  Surely such an architect cannot be a proper subject for contempt, unless, adds Mr. Ruskin, 'he happens to be without a soul.'  But how a man is to be a great man, infinite in memory, and exhaustless in expedient, and yet without a soul, is beyond the comprehension of ordinary mortals; or how 'a rough, artless, feelingless man, incapable of doing any one truly fine thing all his days,' can be a *great man*, as Mr. Ruskin seems to say that he may, is equally inconceivable.  We imagine that he means that a man may be a very clever builder and yet no original genius ; but just so many words could have expressed that idea, while this chaos of contradictory terms expresses nothing.

In the second half of the volume Mr. Ruskin steers more clear of these vagaries, though still they show themselves in occasional instances, but the bulk of the work is very soberly, methodically, and admirably occupied with demonstrating what is false and what is true in every department of the art. This demonstration is introduced in the second part by this sentence :—' I said that all noble ornamentation is the expression of man's delight in God's work. This implied that there was an ignoble ornamentation, which was the expression of man's delight in his *own*. There is a school, chiefly degraded classic and renaissance, in which the ornament is composed of imitations of things made by man. I think, before inquiring what we like best of God's work, we had better get rid of all this imitation of man's, and be quite sure that we do not like *that*.'—P. 205.

In this passage we have the test of whatever is true and beautiful in art. If we find there genuine and adequate imitation of the beautiful things of nature, applied in the same spirit and sense of beauty in which nature has been created, we may rest assured that we have true art before us. And Mr. Ruskin goes on through all the materials of architecture,—columns, with their bases and capitals, arches, with their tracery and spandrels, walls, windows, roofs, and all their decorations, showing us the true and the spurious by this unerring guide. When once our architects shall have come to embrace this principle, to take it fully and with a perfect love into their hearts, then we shall begin to see a new era arising, in which our present heavy monstrosities shall give way to fabrics, in which all the graceful forms of trees, flowers, animals, and the shadows and loveliest hues of nature shall be made to combine into a harmonious whole, charming us at once with their fitness and their grace. These teachings, as we have said, are for the careful student, and he must make himself perfectly master of these simple, but sublime elements of the art.

' These,' then continues the author, ' having been now defined, I do indeed leave my reader free to build ; and with what a freedom ! All the lovely forms of the universe set before him, whence to choose, and all the lovely lines that form their substance, or guide their motion ; and of all these lines—and there are myriads of myriads in every bank of grass, and every tuft of forest ; and groups of them divinely harmonized, in the bell of every flower, and in every several member of bird and beast—of all these lines, for the principal forms of the most important members of architecture, I have used but three ! What must, therefore, be the infinity of the treasure in them all ? There is material enough in a single flower for the ornament of a score of cathedrals; but suppose we were satisfied with less exhaustive appliance, and built a score of cathedrals each to illustrate a single flower? That would be better than trying to invent new styles, I think, There is quite difference of style enough between a violet and a harebell for all reasonable purposes.

' Perhaps, however, even more strange than the struggle of our architects to invent new styles, is the way they commonly speak of this treasure of natural infinity. Let us tax our patience for an instant, and hear one of them, not amongst the least intelligent :—

' " It is not true that all natural forms are beautiful. We may hardly be able to detect this in Nature herself; but when the forms are separated from the things, and exhibited alone (by sculpture or carving), we then see that they are not all fitted for ornamental purposes; and that, indeed, very few, perhaps none, are so fitted without correction. Yes, I say *correction;* for though it is the highest aim of every art to imitate Nature, this is not to be done by imitating any natural form, but by *criticising* and *correcting* it—criticising it by Nature's rules gathered from her own works, but never completely carried out by her in any one work—correcting it by rendering it more natural, *i. e.* more conformable to the general tendency of Nature, according to that noble maxim recorded of Raffaelle, ' that the artist's object was to make things not as Nature makes them, but as she *would* make them ;' as

be deduced from a comparison of her own efforts ; just as if a number of archers had aimed unsuccessfully at a mark upon a wall, and this mark were then removed, we could by the examination of their arrow-marks point out the most probable position of the spot aimed at, with a certainty of being nearer to it than any of their shots."*

' I had thought that by this time we had done with that stale, second-hand, one-sided, and misunderstood saying of Raffaelle's ; or that, at least, in these days of purer Christian light, men might have begun to get some insight into the meaning of it. Raffaelle was a painter of humanity; and, assuredly, there is something the matter with humanity—a few *dorrebbes* more or less wanting in it. We have most of us heard of original sin, and may, perhaps, in our modest moments, conjecture that we are not quite what God, or Nature, would have us to be. Raffaelle *had* something to mend in humanity ;—I should have liked to have seen him mending a daisy ! or a pease-blossom, or a moth, or a mustard-seed, or any other of God's slightest works. If he had accomplished that, one might have found him more respectable employment—to set the stars in better order, perhaps (they seem grievously scattered as they are, and to be of all shapes and sizes, except the ideal shape and the proper size) ; or to give us a more corrected view of the ocean—that, at least, seems a very irregular and improvable thing—the very fishermen do not know to this day how far it will reach, driven up before the west wind—perhaps some one else does, but that is not our business.'—Pp. 339—341.

Mr. Ruskin concludes his volume by giving us a sort of rapid

* Garbett on Design, p. 74.

journey from Padua to Venice, pointing out as he goes the true
and the false, till he introduces us into the latter city ; and with
the words, ' It is Venice,' he intimates that we are arrived at
the spot where in his next volume he intends to unfold before
us those architectural glories which shall vindicate the title he
has assumed.

But as it is said of ladies' letters, Mr. Ruskin puts almost the
most significant matter into his postscript—that is, an Appendix
of no less than sixty-four pages.   In this he opens his heart as
well as his intellect on various topics of peculiar interest.   Our
space forbids us indulging too much here, but there is one
section of the Appendix, the twelfth, which is of so much importance at the present moment, that we must give the substance of
it.   Mr. Ruskin is not only a sound architect, but a sound and
zealous Protestant, and, like every one who has visited Catholic
countries, he has seen everywhere with a proper indignation
the extraordinary manner in which Romanism debauches and
sensualizes the taste of its followers.   How, instead of leading
the popular mind to the great and noble spiritualities of the
Christian faith, withdrawing its contemplation from the mere
creature to the Creator, from the poorness of fallen humanity to
the sublime glory of Him whom ' the heaven of heavens cannot
contain,' and from the specious sanctity of saints and virgins to
the all-embracing love and divine purity of the Saviour, it
desecrates even the noblest specimens of ancient architecture, with
the most tawdry and trumpery of internal paraphernalia.   No contrast can be so striking, or so repulsive, as that presented by the
exquisite taste of many of the continental cathedrals, and the
execrable taste of their altars, their pictures, and their imagery.
In some few you have great works by great masters, but even
these are surrounded and almost lost in a crowd of paintings
or daubs, in which the most debasing objects are presented
to the eyes of the people.   Even in the images of the Saviour,
the wounds in the hands and feet are made swollen, fester-
ing and horrible, and from his side a wire nearly half-an-
inch thick is conveyed to the ground, painted red, to represent a stream of blood.   The architectural taste of their altars
is generally equally vile, and they are so loaded with articles
of tinsel, and things smacking of the toyshop, that you regard
them with equal wonder and disgust.

Whence comes this downward and unspiritualizing tendency ?
It is significant enough if we understand that this taste has grown
up since the Reformation.   It is part and parcel of the same
system which all over the Catholic world keeps down education,
discourages freedom of opinion, prohibits the Bible in the hands
of the people, and substitutes the confessional for the school, the

lecture-room, and the freedom of the press. It is but a portion of the system by which Catholicism seeks to keep the light out of the mind; and the mind, therefore, too poor and sensual to comprehend it, if it find its way in. But hear Mr. Ruskin's judgment of ' ROMANIST MODERN ART.'

'It is of the highest importance, in these days, that Romanism should be deprived of the miserable influence which its pomp and picturesqueness have given it over the weak sentimentalisms of the English people. I call it a miserable influence, for of all motives to sympathy with the Church of Rome, this I unhesitatingly class as the basest. I can, in some measure, respect the other feelings, which have been the beginnings of apostasy; I can respect the desire for unity, which would reclaim the Romanist by love, and the distrust of his own heart, which subjects the proselyte to priestly power. I say, I can respect these feelings, though I cannot pardon unprincipled submission to them, nor enough wonder at the infinite fatuity of the unhappy persons whom they have betrayed :—fatuity self-inflicted and stubborn in resistance to God's word and man's reason !—to talk of the authority of the Church, as if the Church were anything else than the whole company of Christian men, or ever were spoken of in the Scripture as other than a company to be taught and fed, not to feed and teach.

'Fatuity! to seek for the unity of a living body of truth and trust in God, with a dead body of lies and trust in wood, and thence to expect anything else than plague and consumption, by worms undying, for both. Blasphemy, as well as fatuity! to ask for any better interpreter of God's word than God, or to expect knowledge of it in any other way than the plainly ordered way: if any man will DO he shall KNOW. But of all these fatuities, the basest is the being lured into the Romanist church by the glitter of it, like larks into a trap by broken glass; to be blown into a change of religion by the whine of an organ-pipe, or stitched into a new creed by gold thread on priests' petticoats; jangled into a change of conscience by the chimes of a belfry. I know nothing in the shape of error so dark as this, no imbecility so absolute, no treachery so contemptible. I had hardly believed that it was a thing possible, though vague stories had been told me of the effect on some minds of merely scarlet and candles, until I came on this passage in Pugin's " Remarks on Articles in the Rambler:"—

'"Those who have lived in want and privation are the best qualified to appreciate the blessings of plenty: thus, to those who have been devout and sincere members of the separated portion of the English Church, who have prayed, and hoped, and loved, through all the poverty of the maimed rites which it has retained—to them does the realization of all their longing desires appear truly ravishing. . . . Oh! then, what delight! what joy unspeakable! when one of the solemn piles is presented to them, in all its pristine life and glory! The stoups are filled to the brim; the rood is raised on high; the screen glows with sacred imagery and rich device; the niches are filled; the altar is replaced, sustained by sculptural shafts, the relics of saints repose beneath, the body of our Lord is enshrined on its consecrated stone; the lamps of the sanctuary burn bright; the saintly portraitures in the glass windows shine all gloriously; and the albs hang in the oaken ambries, and the cope-chests are filled with the orphreyed baudekins; and pix and pax, and chrismatory are there, and thurible and cross." '

'One might have put this man under a pix, and left him there, one should have thought; but he has been brought forward and partly received as an example of the effect of ceremonial splendour on the mind of a great architect. It is very necessary, therefore, that all those who have felt sorrow at this, should know at once that he is not a great architect, but one of the smallest possible or conceivable architects.'—Pp. 272-3.

Mr. Ruskin quotes Mr. Pugin's own account of the building of St. George's, Southwark, the Catholic churches of Nottingham and Parkham, to prove his assertion.  He then adds:—

' I should have said, all that I have said above of artistical apostasy if Giotto had now been living in Florence, and if art were still doing all that it once did for Rome. But the grossness of the error becomes in-comprehensible as well as unpardonable, when we look to what level of degradation the human intellect has sunk at this instant in Italy. So far from Romanism now producing anything great in art, it cannot even preserve what has been given to its keeping.  I know no abuses of precious inheritance half so grievous as the abuse of all that is left in art wherever the Romish priesthood get possession of it.  It amounts to absolute infatuation.  The noblest pieces of midiæval sculpture in north Italy, the two griffins at the central (west) door of the cathedral of Verona, were daily permitted to be brought into service, when I was there, in the autumn of 1849, by a washerwoman living in the Piazza, who tied her clothes-lines to their beaks; and the shafts of St. Mark's, at Venice, were used by a salesman of common caricatures to fasten his prints upon, and this in the face of the continually passing priests: while the quantity of noble art annually destroyed in altar-pieces by candle-droppings, or perishing by pure brutality of neglect, passes all estimate.  I do not know, as I have repeatedly stated, how far the splendour of architecture, or other art, is compatible with the honesty and usefulness of religious service.  The longer I live, the more I incline to severe judgment in this matter, and the less I can trust the sentiments excited by painted glass and coloured tiles.  But if there be indeed value in such things, our plain duty is to direct our strength against the superstition which has dishonoured them: there are thousands who might possibly be benefited by them, to whom they are now merely an offence, owing to their association with idolatrous ceremonies.  I have but this exhortation to all who love them—not to regulate their creeds by their taste in colours, but to hold calmly to the right at whatever present cost to their imaginative enjoyment; sure that they will one day find in heavenly truth a brighter charm than in earthly imagery, and in striving to gather stones for the eternal building, whose walls are salvation, and whose gates are praise.'—Pp. 370—374.

The extracts we have made will, we think, satisfy the reader that the present work of Mr. Ruskin is well worthy of his reputation. If studied in the spirit in which it is written, it cannot fail of purifying public taste, and directing it into the right channel. In no department of art is this more necessary in this country than in architecture. Whenever the people at large shall have fully adopted our author's grand axiom, that ' all noble ornament is the expression of man's delight in God's work,' they will no longer tolerate erections which, indeed, astonish foreigners, but in a manner not flattering to our national pride. We shall look forward to the second volume of this truly important work with the anticipation of no ordinary pleasure.

---

Art. VII.—*Rovings in the Pacific, from* 1837 *to* 1849; *with a Glance at California.* By a Merchant long resident at Tahiti. 2 vols. London : Longman and Co.

Recent travellers have presented us with charming narratives of their strange adventures and hair-breadth escapes by flood and field. To travel has become the vogue. Men eagerly ask for new scenes for their adventure. They have wearied of the Grand Tour. Steam-locomotion gives the traveller great advantage in economizing both time and money ; so that, in these days of rapid transit, the snug citizen is not content to go only to Margate, or Brighton, or even to Boulogne, the *Ultima Thule* of holiday-tourists till a very recent period. Boulogne does not satisfy him ; Brussels becomes only the first resting-place on a very long journey. Even Paris is not an ultimate post ; and though the man who took breakfast in ' the city,' dines at his ease in the gay café, the appetite for sight-seeing is not satiated by the glories of the Louvre,—Switzerland and Naples must also be seen. For a long time, certain high-roads were followed by the Englishman in his travels. A hasty visitation to the quaint old towns of Flanders is not now enough for the dyspeptic barrister or the hard-worked citizen. The glories of the Rhine-banks, and the magnificent scenery of the Alps, have become familiar to many whose roving spirits are hardly satisfied by surveying Greece and Palestine. Of late, new fields of adventure have been sought and found. Not a few of our citizens have sojourned with the Dyaks, been scorched at Hong-Kong, or shivered off the Horn. Mr. Ruxton fascinates us by the glowing account of his Mexican rambles; and ' a Merchant long resident at Tahiti' makes it clear enough, in his two handsome volumes, that 'rovings in the Pacific' are both pleasant and profitable. His very interesting narrative is told with perfect English bluntness and heartiness; the reader is never allowed to become wearied. Our traveller graphically describes the lights and shadows of the southern isles; and, following him in imagination as he threads the perils of lagoons, scarcely escapes coral reefs, or scuds before the driving sea-wind, we almost hear the roar of the breakers, the lashing of surges, and the howling of storms. The author informs us, he has ' passed his days not in the idealities of life, but in its downright rough realities; and he is not without hope that these volumes, the simple record of his experience, may stimulate many a youth, whose energies are lying dormant for want of a field for their exertion in this densely-peopled country, to seek, in the Isles of the Pacific, the home and the adventurous career which he is sure to find there, if he faint not.'

Our worthy rover's tale is a very simple one. Rejected by the lady of his love—though whether merely 'refused,' or cruelly jilted by that fair sovereign-personage, deponent doth not say— he determines to seek peace for his distracted heart, if not fortune for his pocket, in foreign lands. Thus sternly resolving, he joins a ship at Deptford, which was chartered not merely to take out emigrants, but also to carry to penal settlements those children of vice and crime whom society first neglects, and then makes outcasts from her pale. The description given of the prison-ship is graphic enough; though the 310 convicts on board her appear, on the whole, a harmless, though a motley assemblage. The truant esquire, *perculsus amore*, seems not to have carried the envenomed barb long in his heart, or, at least, it did not rankle there. *Haud ignarus mali*, one wishes not to 'jest at scars;' but we cannot think that our hero's wounds were either sore or deep—for, what with his amusing experiences in the boatswain's mess, his night-phenomena, and many daily occurrences of a ludicrous tendency, he must have had an exciting time of it in the prison-ship, and have been altogether a most entertaining messmate. After a not disagreeable voyage, the good ship anchors in the harbour of Sydney, a city ' in every respect so completely English, that having made up one's mind to become a foreigner, you are rather surprised to discover that you have travelled so many thousands of miles to no purpose.' Our rambler is not contented to abide in Sydney; and he goes out to see life in the bush, and, narrating his fortunes there, he gives a frightful story of the whip-snake, as it is termed in the Australian vernacular, a small but deadly reptile. The aborigines, ' the ugliest race of beings conceivable,' are not more physically than morally hideous. In them we behold, perhaps, the lowest grade of humanity. Their religious instinct is exceedingly faint; and though we cannot believe with Bougainville, that there is any tribe on the face of the earth, however savage, in which this instinct has not place; in the Australian tribes the religious idea has certainly its least possible development. They fear, but they do not reverence; they have certain brutal and disgusting customs connected with superstition, but they know not what it is to worship. With a rude and bare language of their own, they learn the English tongue with amazing facility. Without settled abode—for all the native tribes appear to be more or less nomadic—they neither sow nor reap. Snakes, opossums, grubs, and iguanas, furnish them with food. That scourge of the savage, alcohol, has been abundantly introduced among them, and will, doubtless, ere many years, commit ravages as frightful among the Australian tribes, as formerly among the savage inhabitants of the American forest and prairie. Our romantic adventurer found nothing attractive in the aboriginal society of New Holland; and without a great increase in his worldly wealth, after a sojourn of two years and a half, he proceeded to New Zealand. Thither our emigrants, of late years, have rushed, expecting either to make rapid fortunes, or to find a paradise among the Maoris; but nothing can be more wretched than the townships, nothing more humiliating than the disappointment of the unfortunate emigrants, the 'victims,' in New Zealand phraseology. The market is glutted with goods; there are far more settlers than houses; and the traveller, on reaching the commercial town of Kororarika, found himself 'a disappointed man.' On visiting Pihea, the episcopal missionary-settlement, he observed that the missionaries lay claim to vast tracts of the best land, which they have ingeniously termed 'Church property;' having, no doubt, a calculating thought in reference to the future, when the Anglo-Saxon perseverance shall have turned the New Zealand wilderness into a fruitful field. It is curious to observe how the priest, in whatever circumstances he may be, never belies the distinctive peculiarities of his order. From that evil hour in which Constantine folded the imperial purple around the cross, and graciously took the religion of Jesus Christ under his protection; it has always happened—accidentally, no doubt —that in every land it has entered, the ecclesiastical genius has quickly discovered and possessed itself of whatever treasures the land contained, either in the soil, the mountain, or the stream. So the gentlemen, who have made spiritual excursions to the savage New Zealand, may possibly find those excursions in every sense profitable. It is noteworthy how the episcopal

offensiveness and greed, which have been, many ages, so glar-
ingly manifested at home, have gradually, but very astutely,
been developed in the colonies.

We commend these volumes to the serious attention of those
persons who have hastily determined to emigrate ; not that there
is aught in them which should altogether dissuade the emigrant
from his excursion ; but they contain many excellent observations and suggestions, which will be found very useful by all
who essay to find a home among the Maoris and their pahs.
In reference to the natives themselves, we indulge a hope
that the better influence of European society may be exerted
upon them, and that English intrusion may not lead, as in
other regions, to the complete extermination of the aboriginal
inhabitants. The young traveller was agreeably surprised
by the noble appearance of the native people—fine, strongly-
built men, possessed of no little intelligence and activity.
The women did not ' captivate' the love-exile. No doubt,
he contrasted them with his capricious Miranda in London ; but, alas, for the comparison ! Their movements were
ungraceful, and ' they walked with the waddle of a duck.' It
is, perhaps, to the unreflecting a strange fact, that in the
dominions of heathen barbarity — and we believe the fact
obtains universally among savage tribes—how attractive soever
the younger people may appear to the eye of a European, the
old are generally hideous to a great degree. The elder.Maori-
people possess this disgusting quality to a vast extent. The
elder women especially are wrinkled ' like animated mummies.'
Their senile condition may be attributed either to the positive
hardships of their youth and maturity, or to the wretched nutriment they obtain for the sustenance of life, or perhaps to both
these causes. Till within a very few years, the Maori was a
filthy and bloody savage, eating his prisoners, restrained by no
law from the gross excesses of heathenism, hateful and hating.
Now, though his civilization is in only an incipient state, it
is in actual existence, and in a certain, though, it may be, slow
progress. The European has introduced many evils, but he has
also conferred upon the land some benefits ; and though the
white man may rob the islander of his land and its fruits, though
he may overthrow his rude shrines, and demolish his pahs ; he
will, nevertheless, indirectly introduce that religion which ever
proves to be a blessing and not a curse. Already, as we find,
some light has broken in on the dense darkness of the tribes.
The greater number of them can read and write, and there
are few who have not some correct notions of duty and of
responsibility. At one of the native settlements, near Hicke's
bay, the Maoris had appointed one of their own people to be

their minister, and he offered daily prayer among them, with great regularity and decorum in its observance at morning, noon, and evening. The people join in the services of devotion with much attention and seriousness. Every hut contained a Bible or a Prayer-book; wars have almost ceased; and the Sabbath-day is observed with a strictness and decency which would put to shame the English metropolis. It is beautiful—amid all the errors, real or exaggerated, of the episcopal missionaries, and it is possible those errors may have been considerably magnified —to see the holy and serene light of the true faith breaking upon the land once so notorious for its heathenism, ignorance, and barbarity. Our traveller may be taken as a safe authority in all matters relative to New Zealand, as he spent much time there, and as he became thoroughly familiar with the habits of the natives. Starting from New Zealand, he visited various islands in the Pacific, obtaining, by his rovings, much knowledge, which will be very useful, in its publication, both to geographer and to mariner. In one excursion, he chanced upon Norfolk Island, the doleful spot to which the English Government transports its worst malefactors, escape from which could be effected only by miracle—an island, which shows on the main like a desolate rock. Indeed, its very appearance from the sea indicates that hope can have no place in the breasts of its doomed inhabitants, estranged to the world and the world's law, except in the penalty of it. A sentinel forbade our traveller to approach; but having obtained the necessary permission to land, he was surprised to find the island to be about twenty miles in length and from three to six in breadth, with a rich and fertile soil, producing many tropical fruits. To quote from his narrative—

' On waiting upon the commandant, he received me with evident alarm ; and so far from gratifying me with any vegetables, he told me they were short themselves of everything, and begged me to leave the island, as he should not feel happy until he heard that I was gone. The commandant, I was informed, had been attempting a legislation different from that practised by any of his predecessors. Many of the prisoners had been freed from their manacles, and greater liberty had been granted to them than they had ever before experienced under their penal circumstances. The return they made for this clemency was to treat with insolence those placed over them, and several attempted to effect their escape. One party, only a few days previous to my visit, seized a boat belonging to a brig that touched for refreshments, and got clean off with it; but as a heavy gale sprang up that same night, it is supposed they must have perished ; and before this event, another party, who had been engaged building a boat for the authorities, so soon as it was completed, succeeded in launching it, and in getting away. Some time after, the master of a whaler out of

Sydney landed at a barren island in a north-westerly direction, and picked up seven human skulls; and as they tallied with the number of those who made their escape, it is not improbable that they reached this spot to die a miserable death from hunger and exhaustion. The commandant admitted that the island was in a very disorganized state, which will account for his anxiety to cut our acquaintance short. The island was formerly a place of banishment for double-convicted felons only, desperadoes of the blackest dye, on whom ordinary punishment had no effect. But since transportation to New South Wales has been done away with, several shipments of prisoners have been consigned to Norfolk Island direct; and this may have had some effect in causing the commandant to ameliorate the condition of the prisoners generally; but the common opinion seemed to be that they were allowed by far too free scope, and from what I observed I should think so too. Many appeared to be seeking their own pleasure, some were lolling about in apathetic idleness, and others were strolling apparently unrestrained; and long before the sun had made his *congé*, we could distinguish parties of eight and ten assembled on the rocks fishing with rod and line. Now, as there are 1,800 prisoners on the island, and only 160 soldiers, including officers, I should be inclined to doubt the policy of allowing them such liberty. With the exception of the wives of the officers, and those of a few of the soldiers, there are no women on the island, which tends to brutalize the prisoners to a frightful extent, and they are guilty of more *monstrosities* than probably they ever contemplated in the land they have been expelled from *to correct them of their crimes*. The accounts furnished me by an overseer, in tones of cool indifference, were so revolting that my blood ran chill with horror.'
—Vol. i. pp. 153—155.

During all his rovings, there was no island which so much delighted our traveller as Tahiti, which he does not hesitate to name ' Queen of the Islands in the Pacific.' Tahiti does not show well from the sea; but, so soon as one has landed, he finds himself in a vale of level land, fertile and beautiful exceedingly. Well-watered, abundant in the tropical fruits and vegetables, prolific in soil and in the production of fragrant flowers, shrubs, and noble trees, the island provides its inhabitants not only with the necessaries, but also with many of the comforts of life. The scenery of the island is that of fairy-land. The inhabitants, both male and female, are, perhaps, the most graceful and well-proportioned of all the savage tribes; the women endowed with beautiful hair, which they keep scrupulously clean and neat; and the whole race are decidedly handsome people. We are very sorry to find that our author describes them as ' the most sensual people under heaven.' He informs us that the missionaries, with laudable zeal, have endeavoured to check prostitution by making it, when discoverable and brought home to the guilty parties, punishable by a fine of so many dollars; but, he adds, ' this system of punishment is eluded and laughed at, or, if the parties are detected, the paramour pays the fine, and the crime continues.' We are disposed to take this writer as an authority upon many matters connected with the island of Tahiti, because he has lived many years upon it—because it is his home — and because he gives the missionaries there a very high character for zeal and earnestness in their noble work. Of course, missionaries have the frailties which are common to humanity, as they cannot lay claim to apostolical infallibility; and they may sometimes have erred in judgment by taking too prominent a position in the economical or political affairs of the island; but we must be permitted altogether to dissent from the opinion expressed in vol. i. p. 223—and we are astonished such an opinion should have found expression in these otherwise credible volumes — 'that he conscientiously believes the character of the 'natives has not been improved by missionary intercourse;' that 'fear and not religious restraint is the governing principle' among the natives; and that 'there have been as many wolves as shepherds amongst the folds.' These opinions, though formed and written on the spot by an intelligent, dispassionate, and philanthropic man, are directly contradictory to numerous other credible witnesses, and, indeed, to many of his own subsequent statements. That the English public have expected too much from the missionaries, whose exertions—though they may be foolishly supposed by the ignorant to be capable of almost miraculous success among the heathen—are constantly thwarted by the evil influence of the European vessels touching at the island; and that the halo of a ridiculous romance has been cast around the evangelist's labours in the southern isles, we are bound to believe;—but that those labours have been productive of other than good—and that not a physical, but a spiritual benefit to the natives—to say nothing of the direct advantage conferred upon them by the introduction of European civilization—is a statement we cannot, and will not, receive. At the time of the 'Merchant's' first visit to the island, Pomare was queen, and high is the tribute which he repeatedly pays to her great worth, and to her forbearance and Christian fortitude under her many sorrows. She took but little part, however, in the government, which was carried on by seven supreme judges. The natives have a law in force something similar to that of curfew, which obtained in this country, after the Norman invasion and conquest; by the provisions of which all persons, dwelling in the island, found walking abroad, after the hour of eight in the evening, are fined. Native constables keep a strict watch during the entire night. Drunkenness is severely fined. In almost every village there is a place of worship. The old superstitions have, with but one or two excep-

tions, fallen almost into oblivion. The power of the missionaries
is very great in the island, and, on the whole, we must believe
their power has been well used. The natives meet, it appears,
in larger or smaller numbers, for divine worship, every morning,
when the 'reading-desk' is occupied by some native teacher.
The natives sing with peculiar sweetness. Some of the women
especially have voices of silvery sweetness and delicacy;—and
long may they attune them to those divine melodies which the
missionaries have introduced! The Church of Rome has
been, for some years, very busy in the islands of the Pacific;
and we must be allowed to present to our readers the author's
graphic description of the French priests and their establishments
on the island of Mangarava.

'Within the last seven years, three French missionaries, of the Papal
persuasion, have established themselves upon the island; and the control they have contrived to acquire over the simple inhabitants must be
seen to be believed : it is so absolute, that their very movements appear
to be guided by what the missionaries would think of them. They
have churches erected on every island; and that on Pearl Island would
not disgrace any civilized country. It is built of stone ; the roof supported by two rows of massive stone pillars, nine in each row, forming
an aisle on either side ; the ceiling in the centre of the building being
dome-shaped, arching over from the pillars. . . . So much scenic
display, and the mysterious ceremonies used in the Romish Church,
are well calculated to dazzle the senses, and instil awe into the minds
of the ignorant heathen, as in their own practices they invariably used
emblems to appeal to the senses ; and, short as is the time that it has
taken to effect it, and few the labourers, the natives are completely
enslaved, body and soul. The wonders that have arisen before their
eyes, through the instrumentality of these priests, have inspired them
with fear as much as any other emotion : they are full of amazement
at their resources and their power; and their displeasure is dreaded in
proportion to the extent that this feeling can be excited. What filled
me with the greatest astonishment was, *that the priests have actually
established a nunnery*, in which they have contrived to immerse, at this
present writing, NINETY NATIVE WOMEN. The building is on a bare
shoulder of Mount Duff, *so that no one can approach or leave it without
the priest's knowledge.* The women on the island are instructed to
conceal themselves on the approach of a man, and during my rambles
every woman that I saw at a distance made her escape to some place
of retirement on my meeting her observation. With the exception of
two withered old women, I had no opportunity of judging of the
features of any of the females on the islands. I only saw two of the
" fathers "—jolly, portly-built fellows, with such rotundity of paunch
that one is irresistibly led to the conclusion, that *such* could only be
obtained by the fasting, vigils, and denying penances of Robin Hood's
friar. I wonder if their visits to the nunnery are frequent ; it strikes
me that the harem of the Grand Turk is more excusable than such a
system of Church government '—Vol. i. pp. 283—285.

' Two French priests have recently obtained footing on the island, agents of the Propagandist Society, and their eagerness to gain proselytes persuades me that they belong to a body who will scruple at no means to establish themselves. At present, they are living with the natives, and conforming to their modes and habits, with Jesuitical skill preparing the way for a future display, by a contrast of their power. It is surmised that they belong to a strong party in France, who are endeavouring to effect a revolution in the religious world, and to gain for their Church power equal to that once possessed by the head of the Papal Church. *Attached to their mission they have a trading store*, similar to the store belonging to the same society in Tahiti. Louis Philippe, it is said, is in some way connected with the society; and from his accredited trading propensities, it is not unlikely. The society is supported by shareholders; and what a field seems open! and what a speculation—*the trade for souls, and worldly wealth and power!*'— Vol. ii. p. 157.

his 'rovings' in Pacific; but we concern ourselves with his account principally of Tahiti, as any authentic intelligence of that island and its people must be interesting to our readers. On his second visit to this beautiful island that Captain Du Petit and by the terror of hi the 'protection' of the some Frenchmen, who on the most unhappily advised to for the reason that she wished her people to have but one religious faith. This was done by virtue of a law, the scope of which was not confined to religious teachers. As an abstract principle, the French had an equal right with the English to introduce their doctrines into the island; and this error of their expulsion lay at the foundation of all the subsequent evils. The French captain, who only wanted a pretext to seize the island—at the instance of a hungry Belgian, who wished, in any manner, to better his circumstances—armed with great force, and, by way of compensation, extorted 2,000 dollars from the queen; and, as a reward for his honourable services, the Belgian beggar was nominated Consul de France. At length the French seized the island; and M. D'Aubigny, a fantastical coxcomb, was appointed Commandant-particular of the island. This is the worthy who—in violation of the law of the civilized world —seized and imprisoned 'one Pritchard,' at that time the British Consul there. After this outrage, the French carried matters with a high hand in the island—violating the native women, destroying the bread-fruit trees, and turning the smiling Eden of those seas either into a desert, or into that moral pest-house, a military settlement. Our author gives full and graphic accounts of the successive defeats of the marauding Gaul by the heroic islanders, with whom, and with their excellent missionary-teachers, his sympathies are entirely enlisted. He furnishes us with many details which, if we remember rightly, the public journals of the time ignored. The murder of poor Mr. M'Kean, the pious missionary, who, as our readers will remember, was shot in his own house, is very touchingly told.

No one, with a good heart, and with a clear, discriminating sense of justice, can read these volumes, which so clearly and with so much right feeling describe the cruelties of the French brigands, and the sufferings of the heroic natives and their queen, without attesting how true it is, that the French character generally, so far as military and political events have developed it, combines the cunning artifice of the monkey, with the cruelty and bloodthirstiness of the tiger. Until our perusal of these volumes, we had but a very faint idea of the atrocious proceedings of the French in the Pacific—proceedings, indeed, which differ but little from the villanies of the bucaniers; and of the utter perfidy of King Louis Philippe, and of his faithful servant, the Huguenot-Jesuit, M. Guizot. European discipline, it is true, triumphed over savage valour; the Bourbon-banner supplanted the rude flag of the helpless island-queen; her brave subjects were forced into subjection; and the shorn and pursy priests of the Italian Church have a wide field for preaching the charities of Christianity to the people whom their compatriots endeavoured to destroy; —but they, who wrought these evils, have verily reaped according to their own sowing. It is instructive to him who would trace effects to their causes in the economy of the world, to observe how, after all, justice establishes herself against the wrong-doer. Violence and fraud, cruelty and perfidy, go not for ever unpunished; and to the careful discerner of the principles on which the Great Ruler of all conducts his government, it will generally be clear that the injury which falls upon the transgressor is like in kind to that which he himself has inflicted upon others. Retribution is one of the grand principles in the Divine administration of human affairs; and that requital is imperceptible only to the wilfully unobservant. So the French king, wealthy, powerful, and astute beyond compare, approved of the cruelties and atrocities done by his servants upon a poor, ignorant, and half-savage woman, the mistress of an insignificant island; and after a very few summers, frantic-stricken by the cries of a mob, the refuse of the cellars and gutters of Paris, this same king is driven from his throne, a fugitive, whom none in his dominions truly loved, and whom few of mankind have ever really pitied. Thus we see the working of the everlasting law of requital—man always gets as he gives.

We invite the special attention of the public to these volumes. They are exceedingly instructive, amusing, and gratifying. The writer is a man of correct taste and feeling ; and he has done not a little to instruct the English people on many subjects relating to the South Seas, of which, till our author's advent, they possessed no means of information. Ardent young men who have but scanty resources, and who long for some new field for enterprise and fortune, will do well to acquaint themselves with these very interesting and instructive ' Rovings in the Pacific.' It were needless to praise the beautiful style in which the volumes are published, because their appearing under the patronage of Messrs. Longman and Co. is a guarantee for their admirable execution.

---

Art. VIII.—1. *Correspondence with the Governor of the Cape of Good Hope respecting the Caffre Tribes; and the Recent Outbreak on the Eastern Frontier of the Colony. Presented to both Houses of Parliament by command of Her Majesty,* 20th March, 1851.

2. *The Caffre War: a Letter to Earl Grey on the Causes of the Present War, and the Payment of its Expenses; with Means of Preventing Future Discontents Within and Beyond the Frontiers of the Cape Colony.* By J. J. Freeman, recently returned to England from Caffreland and the Cape of Good Hope. 8vo. London : Trelawney Saunders. 1851.

3. *The Book of the Cape; or, Past and Future Emigration.* By Lieut.-Colonel E. Napier. Edited by Mrs. Ward, Author of ' Five Years in Caffreland.' 8vo. London. 1851.

4. *Petitions from the Colonists of the Cape of Good Hope to Her Majesty the Queen, and to both Houses of Parliament.* 8vo. London. 1851.

No apology will be required for entering fully into the subject of this paper ; seeing that questions of the highest importance respecting it must be re-opened, and that great interests, British, colonial, and aboriginal, depend on the sober and prompt settlement of those questions.

It is pretty well known who sowed tares, in olden times, when *the good man slept* on his charge ; nor is it ever disputed, that

when, in the terms of the ancient fable, dragons' teeth are
scattered in an apt soil, armed men spring up plentifully.  In
South Africa the armed men are fearfully come upon us —
that at least is certain.  It is likewise but too true, that the *good
man* has for years been sleeping out a deep sleep ; and the issue
to be tried hereupon in this country, and in South Africa, is,
whether these armed men—this fifth Caffre war and all its awful
accompaniments—with the official ignorance and apathy that
preceded it, are signs of the rash sowing of dragons' teeth—the
tares of a policy of force and oppression ; and whether we are
not entitled to say that the time is ripe for earnestly repudiating
that bad policy, and for substituting for it a well-considered
system of conciliation, intelligence, and vigour.

The recent facts of the case are few and striking: they are
known, too, upon the highest authority ; inasmuch as Ministers,
being disappointed in their promised measures of colonial
economy, are compelled to justify the very unwelcome call of a
large sum of money from our Exchequer, by laying the worst
news before Parliament up to the latest date.  It thus appears
that the Governor of the Cape Colony was, lately, shut up in a
fort in British Caffraria, eight hundred miles from the seat of
government, and forty miles from the sea.  The colonists, both
Dutch and English, refused to enrol themselves ; whilst the
frontier Hottentots, hitherto most faithful, and the Caffre police,
are gone over in large bodies to the enemy.  That enemy is not,
as the Governor a little while ago said, a few discontented chiefs,
deprived of power to oppress their people, who are happy to be
freed from their rule by becoming British subjects ; but the
whole Caffre nation, chiefs and people together, with the exception of some weaker tribes.

This astonishing refusal of the *colonists* to march to the frontier, proves irresistibly that this is not a war of races.  The
fact would be incredible, if not stated on the best evidence.  ' I
regret to add,' said the Cape Colonial Secretary, on the 31st of
January last, writing for the absent Governor, ' that a second
difficulty, and a very serious and *unprecedented* one, with which
the Governor has to contend is, the determined and dogged in-
activity of the farmers, *principally* the Dutch, who, notwithstanding the proclamation of martial law in the eastern districts,
cannot be induced to move to the frontier.  When I last heard
from General Somerset, on the 24th of January, *not one* had
joined him ; and the accounts I receive from all quarters confirm
me in the opinion that no assistance of this kind can be reckoned
upon.  This is most serious, and cannot fail to add greatly to the
duration and expense of the war.'  Some have since turned out .

By great efforts, the authorities at Cape Town had induced

2,000 Hottentots in that quarter of the colony, and 700 others, to volunteer for the governor's rescue, at the cost of 2*l.* a-head bounty for six months, and rations for their families in their absence. The undertakers to get volunteers were also paid 10*s.* a-head each. What sort of a bill we shall have to pay for these items and their accompaniments, will be readily conjectured by those who know what a Cape commissariat account is. In addition to these poor, despised Hottentots, the governor has himself sent for 3,000 Zoolies from Natal to attack the Caffres in the rear! These allies set out, but were recalled to meet danger at home.

A glance at a map of South Africa will show the bearing of these events. *British* Caffreland, thus at war with us, has the discontented colonists on one side, to the west and north-west; various tribes, of doubtful attachment to us, to the north-east and east; and, further north, eagerly alive to all that is passing, some ten thousand emigrant Cape Dutch colonists, with whom already we have fought several pitched battles, and who are a terror to all about them, natives and missionaries, but who might be ruled by justice.

There is no rashness in asserting that the system of government which produces such a state of things, must deserve condemnation ; and proof is producible that Ministers have been warned, over and over again, against coming calamities. Ministers, however, are by no means the only parties who are open to reproach on this point. After years of struggle in Parliament on behalf of the claims of common humanity towards the native tribes of South Africa, the *philanthropists* succeeded in putting a curb upon colonial cupidity, in giving a wholesome stimulus to official indolence, and in imposing a check upon false principles. Some better views of colonial administration were recognised—one great fact, the *restoration of an unjust conquest,* brought peace, and several excellent measures to secure its continuance were established on the Caffre frontier. If all was not done that the occasion called for, what was effected was in the right direction, and even bold. By a great oversight the philanthropists suffered themselves to be diverted from their duty ; and the good efforts of 1835, 6, and 7, in Parliament and in the colonies, soon gave way. The result is before us; and it will be convenient to show, from our own former pages, that before the mischief happened the measures were recommended which the Government must now institute, along with other steps proposed by higher authority; most especially, and forthwith, a commission of local inquiry, and at once a free elective constitution for the Cape colonists, with whose aid the frontier-administration must of necessity be carried on;—and then their elective representation, with other colonists, in Parliament, where the supreme power of the empire must, of equal necessity, reside, with all its responsibilities. A mere official government, either at home or in the Cape colony, is no longer endurable.

In December, 1847, we remarked respecting the accession of the Governor of the Cape, whose administration is now so prominently before the world—

'The appointment of Sir Harry Smith to succeed Sir Henry Pottinger in the government of the Cape of Good Hope, announced in the "Gazette" of the 10th of September, 1847, carries back the affairs of South Africa exactly to the position in which they stood eleven years ago. This fact is well worth attention, in all its bearings. It is nothing less than the open abandonment of a great endeavour to reconcile the progress of British power with the principles of a humane system, successful as far as that system was fairly carried; *and not completely successful, only because it was long ago shaken to its very foundations by the gross neglect of the Colonial Office.* It is, moreover, a formal return to the system of simple force and conquest, hitherto always costly and cruel, and often unsuccessful.

'The humane system thus formally abandoned, originated with a committee of the House of Commons, which devoted three sessions almost exclusively to the consideration of aboriginal, and especially Caffre affairs—namely, in 1835, 6, and 7.'

'The best hopes of African civilization ever conceived, and the wisest measures for its advancement ever planned, were disappointed in that quarter through official ignorance in Downing-street.'

Our statements, though repeated by other journalists, had no effect. From time to time the system denounced produced scenes of violence, and strange, fantastic acts on the part of the Governor selected by Earl Grey to carry it out, which outraged public good feeling despite of the general indifference to such subjects. '*The deeds of blood*' done under this system in South Africa, since 1847, excited deep sympathy in that land for the sufferers; and some of those deeds were of frightful atrocity; but, it must be added with remorse, that, in England none cried shame upon them!

At length, however, events have produced something stronger than words of remonstrance against the system so rashly sanctioned by the Colonial Office; and, as usual, the day of trial has brought out the men equal to its difficulties. A faithful missionary of the good old stock—a successor of *Vanderkemp,* before whose image the Caffre and the Hottentot have been seen to shed tears of grateful affection, and one who has been almost brought up under the able and aged Dr. Philip in the very scene of these disasters—the Rev. Joseph John Freeman—

speaks out upon this occasion with the boldness that becomes his character, and the force that belongs to his experience and station. His letter to Earl Grey on the causes of this war—on the payment of the expense and the disaffection of tribes once friendly—and *on measures of immediate urgency*, scarcely admits of abridgment. It will have been seen by our readers, before these pages reach them; and will have brought something of the authority of a sworn witness to the issue about to be settled in Parliament.

Mr. Freeman asserts, with great probability of being in the right, that the deposition of the chief of the Gaika tribes, Sandilla, by our Governor, and the attempt to take that chief prisoner, were the immediate causes of the war. It had been more than whispered that he ' *ought to be hanged ;* ' and it is well known, that a powerful party on the frontier have advocated the policy of *destroying* the Caffre chiefs, and seizing Caffreland at any price, to be divided among British settlers. That land was already largely appropriated by us without scruple, and the greatest chiefs were, not long ago, treated with extraordinary indignity by the present Governor in person. One of the worst treated was Macomo, who in his ripe manhood used to grieve that he could not write *a book* to tell of the wrongs his people had experienced at our hands, and whose old age is degraded by vices we have encouraged, and broken by sufferings and sorrows we have inflicted and aggravated, when we might have taught the noble barbarian to become a civilized, Christian man. It was not necessary the maxim of European history, *that the step is a short one from a prince's prison to his grave*, should be known to Sandilla, to make him, at all hazards, shun an English gaol. His Father Gaika—for half his life ridiculously our pet—was watched for in the same manner ; the other half to be put into that gaol, and mulcted of territory too. The topic is a familiar one upon both sides of the frontier. Sir Harry Smith was emboldened to attempt Sandilla's seizure, by supposing his policy had destroyed the affections of the Caffre people for their chiefs. He forgot that he had given to that people literally nothing in exchange for their accustomed feelings. Making all due allowance for some puny efforts to educate a few hundred Caffre children, in which the Cape Governor was 'beaten-hollow' by any one of our various denominations of missionaries, facts prove that he altogether miscalculated the moral and political effect of his work, the severe as well as the beneficial. The dethronement of the chiefs, and the confiscation of their lands—his severe works—have not yet stricken terror into our neighbours ; the education of their children—his work of beneficence—has not bribed those neighbours to put up with political ruin.

Mr. Freeman makes a very strong statement in one part of the case in this respect :—

' I cannot refrain from saying that *all* the border tribes are in a state of comparative discontent and alienation, and that, too, against their own deliberate wishes and judgment. They are most anxious for peace and friendship. They are ready to meet our fair demands on all occasions; to part with portions of their territory for our convenience, on adequate compensation ; and to observe with all fidelity the treaties we make with them. I affirm this on my personal knowledge of them, and their own deliberate and reiterated assurances. But I have, nevertheless, seen that, with all their wishes for peace and friendship, and all their own deepest conviction that their very existence depends on their friendship with us, they were suffering extreme vexation and disgust, and repressed resentment. They looked to Sir H. Smith in vain for relief from his oppressive measures, and on this ground they entreated and charged me to lift up a voice on their behalf, as on behalf of an oppressed people, too impotent to defend themselves. I failed not to bring these matters under your Lordship's attention as early as I could, and I hesitated not to intimate then, that I was sure it was essential to the peace and welfare of the colony that the border tribes should be in a state of friendship with us, and not of restless dissatisfaction and sullen enmity. What I feared as a result has now overtaken us, and more rapidly and terribly than I had supposed.'

On the 20th of December last, Sir Harry Smith wrote to Earl Grey that ' it was evident that Sandilla and other chiefs had endeavoured to excite the people against the present rule, while it is equally evident they have signally failed. The people see the advantages they derive from the present state of things ; and as they have generally, throughout the country, remained tranquil, and expressed their happiness, I feel warranted,' he says, ' in anticipating that the system so successful for three years, and which has tended to the mutual advantages of Caffres and colonists, will be perpetuated.'

On the 26th of the same month, only six days later, he wrote again that he had sent a strong patrol (of 19 officers and 568 men !) *to seize Sandilla,* ' having been led to believe, from every source of information, that if a patrol shows itself, he would either surrender or fly the country.'[*] He goes on—' *This movement has been the signal of a* GENERAL *rising. . . . . The state of affairs in British Caffreland is critical.*[†] *. . . . No people can evince more determined, reckless, and savage hostility than do the Caffres at this moment. What is ultimately to be done with them remains a problem.*'[‡]

But it is not alone the Caffres, people and chiefs, that Sir

---

* Despatch from Fort Cox, in British Caffreland, Correspondence, p. 72.
† Ibid.                                                    ‡ Ibid.

Harry Smith has fearfully misunderstood and alienated.  Mr.
Freeman states, and more recent accounts from the spot confirm
the statement, that the hitherto devoted Hottentots have in
great numbers turned against us.  This is a grave fact, if true.
This new hostility is aggravated by these men having been
driven mad, as Mr. Freeman shows, by new oppressions under
Sir Harry Smith.  The charge is a heavy one, indeed, to
have forced these remarkable people back from civilization into
the arms of barbarism—from the use of Christian ordinances
during *three* generations, and from frequent sacrifices in our
defence, into a desperate rebellion!  The wholesale discontent of
the colonists, English as well as Dutch, completes this tale of
mal-administration, and strange ignorance of the feelings of the
people he governs.

In a despatch of the 7th of January last, Sir Harry Smith informs Earl Grey that ' the spirit of enthusiastic loyalty which
pervades all classes of burghers within the colony, bids him calculate on their vigorous aid.'*

And what has been the response to this call for instant enrol-
ment?

a ' lingering irresolution on the part of the burghers ' to march
to the frontier; but he fears this springs from motives of deep
and lasting disaffection, unless a radical change takes place in
ou                                        The Colonial
Secretary, writing for the Governor, who can no longer communicate with England, being shut up in an isolated fort in
British Caffreland, says that *not a colonist* will join the army.
General Somerset, from the frontier, says the same thing.  And
another frontier functionary put forth a notice, on the 29th of
January, to the effect that the colony was threatened with a more
determined combination than was ever known before.  The
Caffres were resolved to exterminate the whites, as the Governor
was determined to crush them.  ' To do the last,' says this
frontier magistrate, ' *the colony must unite.  Never was delay so
dangerous.  Divisions among colonists now, or even a few days'
delay, may bring on a great portion of the colony unheard-of
calamities.*'

Thus Sir Harry Smith has proved himself as little acquainted
with the disposition of the colonists of all classes, as with the
feelings of the Caffre people.

The pecuniary part of this matter is boldly put forward by Mr.
Freeman as a clear *British* treasury item.  The occasion of war
is *British* Caffreland : a new jewel in Queen Victoria's imperial

---

* Despatch from Fort Cox, in British Caffreland, Correspondence, p. 76.

diadem.  The declarer of the war is not the **Governor of the**
*Cape Colony ;* he is the High Commissioner of a region where
the Cape authorities have no jurisdiction.  If the facts of the
case are correctly stated by Mr. Freeman, his conclusions would
seem to be irresistible.  Earl Grey reserved the point, which,
however, is already settled in favour of the colonists by Parliament and the public with acclamation.  It deserves one remark,
moreover, now—which is, that, pay the bill who may, Sir Harry
Smith and Earl Grey are the very costly providers of this national
banquet of horrors.  Such a result will, undoubtedly, be looked
upon by the people of England as a very serious argument
against their system of conquest and coercion.

Mr. Freeman is not the only person who has warned Earl Grey
not to delay doing right in South Africa at the risk of convulsions.  Even stronger warnings than his have come from a more
experienced pen.  It is sixteen years since Sir Andries Stockenstrom was called upon for advice upon these very Caffre frontier
and interior affairs.  He then spoke out boldly, and he traced
clearly the only policy that could possibly prevent the multitudinous disasters caused by the neglect of his advice by *the Colonial Office* which sought that advice.  Last year, called upon
again, he spoke out once more ; and Earl Grey, with fatal fatuity,
read his earnest, burning African denouncement of the *evil that
has been recently doing*, and termed his statesmanlike, honest
letter 'IMPROPER'!!  As Mr. Freeman's letter to Earl Grey is
doubtless already in the hands of most of our readers, we have
given a very brief view of its contents.  Sir Andries Stockenstrom's letter to the Secretary of State is printed only in a Blue
Book, so that it will be acceptable with only the abridgment of
portions not essential to the meaning.

'If the Right Honourable the Secretary of State for the Colonies,'
he says, 'had seen fit to promote the inquiry which I felt it my duty
to urge upon him, he would have seen, and if he would be pleased to
examine the records of his office for 1835, 6, and 7, he might still see.
that the tract of country, now the subject of contention between the
Boers and the Tambookies, lying between the old colonial boundary
and the Great or White Kei, was in the possession of the Tambookies
when the Caffre war of 1835 broke out, that although the Tambookies
had taken no part in that war, and had, indeed, more favoured the
colony than the Caffres, Sir Benjamin D'Urban annexed to the colony
the said tract of country, together with part of Caffreland ; and that, in
consequence of Lord Glenelg's instructions, it was restored to the
independent possession of the Tambookies.

'Thus stood matters when the Caffre war of 1846 broke out ; and
when the present Governor arrived, at the close of 1847, the colonists
were still limited to the right or western bank of the Klaas Smit's
River—mark this, if you please.

'Towards the close of last year, 1849, in November, I believe, Mr. Zacharias Pretorius suddenly appeared at this place ; I had seen this man once during the war of 1846 as a private individual. He informed me that he had since then been appointed field-cornet, and that he had resorted to me for advice and assistance in obtaining from the Governor the execution of his own promise, whereby he had given the said Tambookie territory to the farmers. When I naturally expressed my astonishment at such a promise, Pretorius produced a copy of a memorial which the said farmers had presented to the Governor, the details of which I cannot now give, but which in substance prayed for the annexation of the said territory to the colony, and the reply to which, written and signed by the Governor's own hand, which Pretorius likewise produced, granted the prayer, subject only to this exception; viz., that the Caffre chief, Kama, and his followers, were not to be expelled, because the former was a Christian, and the latter would make good servants for the farmers.

'Now, I leave to the British Government to judge, whether if the Governor had intended to set the Boers and Tambookies at mutual slaughter, he could possibly have hit upon a more effectual contrivance to produce such a result than this reply; and it is a positive fact that part of the said territory was forthwith measured out for some of the said Boers, under the Governor's authority, and by way of climax it so happened that the lands thus measured out, did not belong to the followers of the chief, Mapassa, who had joined the Caffres in the last war, but to those of Umtirara, whom we considered our ally. . . . . . I am well aware how convenient it would be for certain parties to trace these Tambookie disturbances to some Glenelg or Stockenstrom system of interference, or to the Boers exclusively; but, for once at least, they shall not succeed. The cause is palpable. There is the Governor's fiat written in a plain round-hand, independent of any system on earth but his own, and capable of no other construction to the Boer but this : viz., provided you do not molest the Christian Kama, you may expel the heathen Tambookie as fast as you please; and in order that there be no mistake as to the meaning of this document, the surveyor shall forthwith measure out for you part of the land of that heathen. That the Boers should act up to this view of the matter is natural enough, and that the Tambookies should resist, is not less so. Hence the conflict ; and it is supererogation to search deeper for the solution.

Here, then, we have on the *north-east* one part of the present frontier system working to admiration, whilst on the *north* we have, at an enormous expense of blood and treasure, just removed ' rebellion' from the further back of the Orange River to that of the Vaal River, and rendered all parties more discontented than ever. And how is it in the *east?* All perfection, of course ! But having been led to the discussion of these matters, I do not think that I have the right of withholding from the Government the fact that I have, within the last twelve months, been visited by at least half a dozen of Caffre deputations with the most doleful prayers that I might intercede so as to bring about the peace which the Governor promised them, and for which the chiefs kissed his foot, as the nation is tired of the war, and that all my explanations that I had nothing to do with the matter, having failed of ridding me of these painful intrusions, I was only able to put a stop to them by refusing either to see the messengers, or to give them a mouthful to eat.

'I tell the Government, once more, that by injustice and oppression, by the violation of treaties, and the abuse of superior knowledge, granted by Heaven for better ends, we have half ruined ourselves, and completely ruined a nation. I have in my own service men whom, not long since, I knew as opulent farmers, one, indeed, who sat in council with me when I represented British majesty, now reduced to labour for me, naked, and hungry for the crumbs which fall from my table, or rather, for what I choose to give them, and to whose physical condition, therefore, slavery itself would be an improvement. Of these there are thousands brooding over their misfortunes, and looking, as we have just seen, upon our happy peace and glorious working system, as a state of war of which they are tired.

'That precaution is not visionary I shall show by a brief rehearsal of what must still be fresh in the memory of every man acquainted with the recent history of this colony.

'It was long generally believed, and is still credited by some few, that during the war of 1835 we slaughtered "four thousand Kafir warriors," and so completely crushed the enemy that he called for "Mercy," "Mercy;" "Peace," "Peace"!!! which we granted; that upon this, the Governor, Sir B. D'Urban, established a frontier system, which was so successfully worked by Lieut.-Colonel (now Sir Harry) Smith, as to restore tranquillity to the country, and give perfect satisfaction to all parties, including colonists as well as Caffres; that this happy state of affairs was destroyed by the reversal of the said system by order of the then Colonial Minister, and the introduction of the so-called "Glenelg policy," which produced general discontent on both sides of the frontier, led to the emigration of the Boers beyond the Orange River, and resulted in all the calamities which have since both disgraced and half-ruined South Africa! So deeply rooted became the faith inspired by the above allegations, that the idea of the condition which Lieut.-Colonel Smith had created and left on the frontier produced an irregular vote of the local Legislature in his favour of a considerable sum of the public money, as well as a long protracted species of idolatry towards himself and his chief; every man who dared to dissent from an implicit reliance on the above creed became, together with the supreme Government and some of the most virtuous men in the kingdom, the objects of the most virulent denunciations and libellous personalities in prints under high auspices; even respectable publications in the mother-country, though incapable of stooping to the local vulgar scurrilities, contributed for a time to give currency to the fallacies which were sometimes reiterated even in Parliament, and remained uncontradicted through the ignorance of those who ought to have known better.

'Now what are the facts? So far from 4,000 Caffre warriors having fallen in the war of 1835, we fortunately did not kill one-half of 400, including even the unhappy wretch whose ears we cut off and salted!

So far from the Caffres being crushed and calling out for mercy or peace, *we had to send out officers into the bush, at the peril of their lives, to sue for peace from the Caffre chiefs,* who were so thoroughly convinced that they had the best of the conflict, that they laughed to scorn our demand of the restoration of the colonial property which they had taken, whereon we did not dare to insist further, although we had made it a positive stipulation that all the fire-arms in Kaffreland should be delivered up to us before the treaty of peace should be ratified. The Caffre set us at defiance; and, although Sir B. D'Urban had issued a peremptory order that the ratification should not take place before the fulfilment of the stipulation, Lieut.-Colonel Smith was so embarrassed with the question that he was too glad to ratify the treaty, and left the Caffre nation better armed than it had been since its creation! So far was the D'Urban system from being satisfactorily worked, or being reversed by order of Lord Glenelg, that Sir B. D'Urban himself, with his own hand, gave it the death-blow, and rendered it a mere self-evident impossibility, by revoking martial law, which Lieut.-Colonel Smith himself knew and declared to be the foundation upon which the whole fabric rested. So far was any party whatever, except such as had profited by the war, and hoped to profit more, from being satisfied, that the Caffres were organizing a regular plan for the renewal of the war, which was only prevented by the reversal of the said system. The Boers who had begun to emigrate by families long before they heard the names " Glenelg," " D'Urban," " Smith," now began to leave in crowds before they could dream of any " Glenelg policy," furiously irritated at and openly denouncing the conduct of the war, the terms of the peace, and the state of insecurity existing under the system. The auxiliary or provincial troops left to defend the frontier were in a state bordering on open mutiny; and even the officer in command of the forces, after the retirement of Colonel Smith, complained of the unsafe posture of affairs!! Satisfactory issue indeed!!!!'

This letter is dated 1st July, 1850.

In this melancholy condition of things, we have to look to the responsibility of Earl Grey for our redress. Unfortunately for his character as a colonial minister—unhappily for his prospect of holding the high station in our colonial history, he has toiled long to merit—he has acted in every matter concerning the Cape of Good Hope so as to be himself open to the heaviest of all charges against a minister—utter incapacity and wilful ignorance. He has been told of all that must come upon us, and that is come upon us. He has refused to hear what he has been told; and he has failed to reflect upon the inevitable result of a course of proceedings on the part of his nominee, Sir Harry Smith, in which proceeding there is nothing really new in measures or principles, or in their consequences.

The House of Commons meets the startling news of this Caffre, *Hottentot, and Tambookie* war with a committee, obtained after

some difficulty, by a vote of 128 to 60; and not without the imputation of a parliamentary cloak being sought for ministerial defaults. The aborigines' committee of 1835-6-7 was granted to Sir Thomas Fowell Buxton with acclamation by an applauding House, and received by the public with universal satisfaction. It was a step in harmony with the recent peaceful victory of negro emancipation, for which her bitterest opponents gave England honourable credit; and it evinced a progress in philanthropic legislation, which is surely, although slowly, characterising the age in both hemispheres. Whilst these lines are being written the spirit of that great change is influencing our American friends, who have summoned a congress of Indians to settle terms of peace, and a system of civilization in the far west—*the local commission* which Mr. Adderley will by perseverance obtain, by-and-bye, for South Africa.

The chief points of the South-African case were discussed in the debates; and, whatever may be the secret motive for the committee, no reserve was used by Lord John Russell in proposing it. Its members will, undoubtedly, be in fault, if the whole case be not now brought out; and the debates themselves are already useful feelers to the committee's coming work, by showing the opinions probably prevalent on the subject. Lord John Russell declared that he and his colleagues wish to deal with the Caffre question as one belonging to our common humanity, and involving the performance of the highest duties of empire, at once to the British people, to the Cape colonists, and to our barbarous neighbours. This sound view of the case redeems grave errors in fact and in judgment, respecting the Caffre frontier; and it may help to correct those errors by facilitating the proof that they have wofully influenced the policy of the Government, and grievously misled public opinion. The manner in which the proceedings shall be conducted on the part of Government, will soon test its sincerity in appointing the committee, and its good faith and ability in this branch of colonial administration.

Lord John Russell limited the various Cape-frontier systems to three :—

The first is, conciliation of the natives, with a restricted colonial frontier, commonly called Lord Glenelg's system.

The second is, coercion of the natives, with the seizure of their lands, attributed to Sir Benjamin D'Urban.

Both of these systems are at the cost of the British treasury.

The third is, the abandonment of the frontier administration to the colonists under a popular constitution; and at their cost.

His Lordship asserted that the first system failed upon trial: and that the third is a disgraceful repudiation of the noblest task of a civilized people like ourselves, namely, the task of gradually suppressing inhuman practices among our barbarous neighbours, and of labouring perseveringly for their improvement. He insists that the second system has had this good tendency; and, therefore, it is to be adhered to, unless the committee now appointed shall discover cause for its rejection or modification. He admits that the wars it has already produced justify much anxiety on the subject; so that *other* measures that ' *might* be devised to improve it, ought to be dispassionately considered.'

Giving conditional credit to ministers for honesty of purpose, common sense carries us, on their own ground, to a very simple solution of the great difficulties of this momentous question. If proof be adduced before the committee—plain and solemn proof—that the system of *force did not succeed*, and rival system of conciliation did not fail *so far as it*

fusing t
mises.
and for
the bad
Govern
under its continu
due vigour, the
policy, which are

The first business of the committee        the whole truth respecting the system of conciliation promulgated in 1836-7 —in what it consisted—how it was established—what it effected —and, above all, what became of it.

These points can be settled to the minutest particular; and they ought to have had a parliamentary record long ago. All the secretaries and under-secretaries of state, numerous as they have been—all the governors and lieutenant-governors, except Sir B. D'Urban and Sir J. Hare—all other chief functionaries, civil, military, and *medical*—all the colonists of note, all the missionaries, and even the poor writers on the subject, once heedfully listened to—all of these, except the chief of them all, the lamented Thomas Pringle; in short, all who have in any shape meddled with the subject, are living, and most of them are within reach. Lord John Russell is certainly correct in the remark, that ' there are numerous persons in England qualified to give the necessary information.'

Especially there must be produced the important despatches on the subject written since 1837, of which Parliament will now hear for the first time, and the secretaries of state, to whom they were addressed, probably read for the first time—so mischievous has been the practice of delegating their most delicate duties to their subordinates in the Colonial Office. Nor will commentators upon these unread, or these read, despatches be wanting.

Lord J. Russell has discovered satisfactory circumstances in the character of this war as compared with former ones. The attentive consideration of the histories of both will convince him of his mistake.

Mr. Gladstone, too, made a notable discovery from colonial history upon a capital topic in this case. It is universally agreed, that, as things are now managed, the cost of Caffre wars must be borne by us in England, because England governs the Caffre frontier. If, on the other hand, its rule be passed over to the Cape colonists, they will be delighted, as is believed by the credulous, to accept it even burdened with Caffre war disbursements. 'Strike this bargain forthwith,' says Mr. Gladstone; and so say others who do not always follow him, as, for instance, Mr. Hume and Sir William Molesworth. To enforce this bargain, its propriety is asserted by Mr. Gladstone to be demonstrable by experience. 'The *old* colonists,' says he, 'would in their fearful wars with the Indians have scorned aid from England!'

Now the committee will be the place for fitting details to refute this historical blunder, which is sure to be reproduced there. It is enough here to set two or three examples against the assertion. In the few years before the revolutionary war of 1776, and after the French lost Canada, not only were many British troops employed in North America, but the *provincial* corps received and pressed for British pay. Even the noble provincial officer, Washington, was proud of British military rank as another of nature's nobles, the Cape provincial Stockenstrom, is now proud of a British baronetcy.

But a famous example is in every schoolboy's hand, in which a colony sought help from England against a handful of aborigines. This was St. Vincent's, to which British soldiers were under orders of sailing, in obedience to that call, to hunt down the Caribbs, when Granville Sharp, *a philanthropist*, stayed the expedition, although he spent a life in vain efforts to check the official corruptions which rendered such an expedition possible. It is a still stranger misapprehension of Mr. Gladstone's, that if colonial affairs are to be administered in England, they belong to the Crown exclusive of Parliament; so far otherwise, that, for more than two hundred years, the Journals of Parliament are full of evidences to the contrary.

Mr. Gladstone and Mr. Vernon Smith voted against the committee; but as both were in the Colonial Office in stirring Cape times, they are entitled to the benefit of a full disclosure of what they did themselves to make things better.

Mr. Gladstone must go to his books again before he ventures to talk of colonial affairs, which, indeed, he should have understood better before accepting the Colonial seals.

Mr. Roebuck adopted these blunders; and he added an especial one of his own, when he said that the Caffres are *hunters* who take up wastefully an extent of ground which it will be *useful*, and therefore just, to conquer at any cost, and give to Anglo-Saxon husbandmen! Never did utilitarianism put on so miserable a rag of philosophy. If the electors of Sheffield do not call their member to account for these slips in colonial history and ethnography, and, more severely, for the scandalous doctrine he would introduce into our colonial practice, they will prove themselves very ill learners of the lesson taught him at Bath on topics not more serious. These Cape debates, however, offer compensation for such *escapades*.

Mr. Bell gravely denounced the illogical brutality of Mr. Roebuck, whose doctrine, that to destroy the Caffres is a providential necessity in favour of civilization, is, after all, stolen from Earl Grey's and Lord Stanley's rash despatches. Its audacious promulgation, however, on this occasion, proves how urgent is the duty of philanthropists in Parliament and out of it, to declare themselves earnestly in defence of the aborigines whom Providence has placed in our hands, and at once to accept a challenge which would never have been so rudely proffered if they had not long deserted their post. Colonel Thompson, indeed, was not now wanting with apt reminiscences of older tyrannies, fatal to the tyrants who inflicted them; and he wisely appealed to the eternal Avenger of national crimes, in order to deter us from repeating their commission. Sir Edward Buxton, too, struck right in reproving the vulgar error, that the justice done to the Caffres in 1837 failed; and the committee will do excellent service in producing the documents and proofs which are capable of refuting this reiterated, enormous falsehood.

There is one topic belonging to the subject, not alluded to in the remotest degree by any of the speakers in these debates, but which was brought formally before Parliament in the discussions of the Reform Bill. More than once, this topic has been mentioned in the pages of the *Eclectic Review*, and the time is come for its full examination; for that purpose it should be proposed to the committee. It is, *the elective representation of the Cape, along with other colonies, in the House of Commons.* Intimate local knowledge is confessedly wanted in order to the due settlement of local questions. It is felt strongly, and it will soon be declared clearly, that Parliament cannot abdicate its duty, as

supreme head of the empire, duly to control all great colonial
administrations.   Let Parliament, then, take the steps—as old
as the constitution—of calling within itself the men capable of
contributing to the proper discharge of that duty.   The details
of the measure may be arranged by no great effort; its effect
may be anticipated from the vast advantage attending a similar
measure in the parliament at Washington, which is enlightened
and strengthened by the presence of elected members, the
delegates from the *territories* of the United States, which are
nothing more nor less than our colonies under another name,
and furnished with better constitutions.

This important subject was first discussed by the late Baron
Maseres, Attorney-General in Canada in 1763—1766.   When
the measure was proposed to Franklin in 1775, he said it was *too
late*.   In 1782 it was pressed in Parliament by very able men;
but ' too late,' unquestionably, then.   Occasionally it has been
discussed, in the last twenty years, as well worth adoption; and
in 1832 Mr. Hume moved it in the House of Commons, when
Sir John Malcolm, and other eminent men, spoke for it.   The
Colonial Reform Society could not spend *one hundred pounds*
of their funds more wisely, than by republishing the essays and
debates from 1766 to the present day on this question of colonial
representation in Parliament.

That society deserves well of the country for insisting upon
good constitutions for all its colonies; but it will make a woful
mistake in leaving even free colonists *exclusively* masters of a
field in which the violent passions and the unreasoning cupidity
of actors have hitherto always overcome their sense of duty.
Disastrous as our defeats must be, and inglorious as are our
victories in Caffreland, there is hope that the bitter lesson will
at no distant day rouse a high-minded Parliament, and an impartial, intelligent people at home, to compel the execution of a
wise and humane policy, to make our progress prosperous and
peaceful, without the frightful alternations now inflicted upon
our colonial world, so replete with elements of good perverted
to evil solely for want of a rational system of government.

Let Ministers, and Parliament, and the public, but consider
the scenes presented to the world in South Africa.   Caffreland,
dotted over with British forts, and covered with slaughter;
the Cape colony, a despotism, and rife with disaffection from one
end to the other; Natal, so much a smothered volcano, that,
however willing, it cannot spare a handful of men to save
Governor Smith from disgrace; and the whole interior full of
danger.   And this is a land so valuable by nature, that, in one
article alone, *fine wool, the increase* of 1849 over the export of
former years was beyond a million of pounds weight; and there

is reason to believe that the country will grow cotton for 1,500 miles from Cape Town to Delagoa Bay. The whole of South Africa, too, is eminently healthy—a capital point in reference to the grand object of native African civilization—here the best agents of civilization, the missionaries, are never prematurely cut off in their work by the climate.

But it is not to missionaries *alone* that the civilization of barbarians connected with us is to be left. Fifteen years ago, a Committee of the House of Commons reported that it would not be difficult to devise a good system of frontier-government. The suggestion was unskilfully followed up; and we have now to resume the inquiry, with the immense advantage of those fifteen years' experience, during which the ablest men have practically examined the subject in several colonies. In India, also, we possess excellent examples to follow from Mr. Cleveland's triumph in Rajemal, in 1786, to Major Hall's among the Bheels, and the Indian law of 1822 for the Garrows, and many more analogous to the South African cases. At the same time, other civilized states in the Old World and the New, have work on their hands like our own—Russia, over all her frontiers; France, in Algiers; America, North and *South*, too, with millions of Indians—and all are seeking the better system, that is, to save civilized men from the disgrace of being as savage in the coercion of their barbarous neighbours, as they might be beneficent in considerately helping their difficult progress to civilization.

---

## Brief Notices.

*Madam Dorrington of the Dene; the Story of a Life.* By William Howitt. In 3 vols. London: Henry Colburn.

WE have read these volumes with very considerable pleasure, and should any of our readers object *in toto* to the class to which they belong, we advise them to follow our example, and if we are not much mistaken, their doing so will greatly modify, if it do not wholly reverse, their judgment. It is the scandal of religious men that our lighter literature—our poetry and works of fiction especially—has been abandoned to the unbeliever, or the immoral, and has received in consequence the impress of their creed and character. Such has been too commonly the case, but its origin is to be found, not in the nature of either of these species of composition, but in the erroneous conceptions prevalent in the Christian world, and the consequent abandonment of a province which ought to have been occupied for good. Mr. Howitt has honorably distinguished himself in this walk of literature, and is specially entitled to a warm greeting on the present occasion. 'Madam Dorrington' is one of the best books of its class. No reader who commences its perusal will fail to proceed to its close, or to regret when the last leaf is turned over that the end of the tale is gained. There is a fresh and healthy feeling throughout, a hearty sympathy with natural beauty under all its varied aspects, whether seen in a glowing sky, the rich foliage of the wood, the calm deep waters of the silent stream, the 'human countenance divine,' or the yet more exquisite charm of Virtue in her generous and divine moods. We shall not forestall the tale by detailing the course of the narrative, or pointing out the influence of the principal actors on each other. It is enough to say that they are sketched with much skill; that the evolution of the plot is highly creditable to the author's powers; and that the sentiments which pervade the work are in keeping with the higher and more generous sympathies of our nature. Every page of the three volumes may be read aloud in the family circle, and yet there is nothing dull in the tale—nothing approaching to the sermonic prosiness of the so-called religious novel.

The characters introduced are varied, and the individuality of each is well sustained. Madam Dorrington is somewhat too perfect for real life, and with the solitary exception of complaining to Mr. Bathurst of her husband's injustice to their youngest son, Vincent, is a picture of what our nature might be rather than of what it is. Vincent himself is a fine-hearted, talented, and generous youth; while his two brothers, Buckley and Delmey, are specimens of very different, yet distinct classes. Sally Horobin, the old and favoured servant, who loved the absent Vincent as a foster-mother, and availed herself of the privilege of her position to speak the truth which others feared to utter; the simple-hearted and benignant vicar, Jeremiah Gould, who forgot himself in seeking the happiness of others; Farmer Greatorex, with his large heart, practical sagacity, and exuberant kindliness; Mr. Khesteven, the London merchant, and his daughter, Mrs. Hetty Harrison, 'that creature of sweetness and love;' together with Elizabeth Arden, and her aunt Nelly, have interested us deeply, and cannot well fail to fascinate all classes of readers.

The general impression of the work is so pleasing that we are not inclined to note minor defects. Amongst such, however, we may just mention the character of Mrs. Delmey, the mother of Madam Dorrington, which is surely overdrawn; the death of Mr. Delmey, which is unnatural in the extreme; and the apparition of Hinchliffe in the chamber of his sister. These are, in our judgment, blemishes; but they weigh so little against the sterling excellence of the work, that it is enough to name them. Indeed, we should be content to pass them by, were we not solicitous to justify our impartiality in the praise we have awarded.

*An Address to the Students of Chesham College.* Delivered by the
Rev. W. H. Stowell, D.D., at his public recognition as the President
of that Institution, November 6th, 1850. 8vo. Pp. 24. London:
John Snow.

WE cannot speak of this *Address* as we should like to do, for reasons
which will be obvious to our readers. It is one of the best of its class,
full of sober, solid, enlightened counsel, just such an *Address* as young
men would be likely to listen to with respectful interest, and from
which a large measure of wisdom may be drawn. Its style is that of
the gentleman and scholar, while the spirit it breathes, and the lessons
it inculcates, are well suited to the grave and onerous labors of the
President of a ministerial institution. More we will not say, lest our
commendation be misunderstood; but less would not satisfy our sense
of justice, or convey an adequate conception of the worth of this
charge.

---

*The Bath Fables; or, Morals, Manners, and Faith. With Illustrations
in Prose, from many Writers of Celebrity.* By Sheridan Wilson,
F.S.A. Second Edition. London: Longman and Co. 1850.

THE 'Fables' in this volume, which is most elegantly printed, and
illustrated with an ingenious Punch-like frontispiece, appeared, for the
most part, in the 'Bath Journal,' for which reason the name of that

writer, and will do more to commend the volume than any elabo-
rate examination or eulogy of ours. The following are a few of them.
They are fifty-three. I. The Gazelles and the Giraffe. For our
beloved Queen. Prose from *Goldsmith and Dryden.* II. The Maid
and the Eggs. For Castle-builders. *Addison and Steele.* III. The
Eagle and the Bats. For Artists. *Eustace, Lady Morgan, &c.* IV. The
Jackdaw and the Rook. For Lovers. *Addison.* V. Time and his
Clients. For Triflers. *Ackermann and Dr. Young.* VI. Punch and
Judy. For Husbands. *Budgell, Steele, &c.* VII. Jonathan and
Sambo. For Slaveholders. *Legh Richmond.* VIII. The Robin and
the Trout. For Protectionists. *Disraeli.* IX. The Oak and the
Holly. For Sufferers. *Ackermann.* X. Judy and Punch. For
Wives. *Steele.* XI. The Lark and the Rook. For Zealots. *Acker-
mann, and New Monthly.* There are fables thus adapted to Churches,
the Quarrelsome, Jurists, Youngsters, Parents, the Stingy, Senators,
Fops and Flirts, all Good People, Duellists, Place-hunters, the Proud,
Landlords, Sneerers, Preachers, Sceptics, Braggarts, Liberals, Vestries,
Pilgrims, Impostors, Tipplers, Belligerents, Maidens, 1849, the Pope,
Improvidents, Egotists, Universities, Sentimentalists, Sectarians, His
*Grace* of Exeter (wrong title—ask Lord John), Cardinals, Sluggards,
Thinkers, Rulers, Husband-hunters, Flats.

The versification of the Fables is refined. The thoughts are often original. The wit sparkles, but wounds not. The illustrations are well selected, suggestive, and very entertaining, as well as instructive. We have no space for any one of the Fables. Extracts would scarcely be just, and descriptions would be too dull for our reputation, as well as that of the author. We wish him success in a novel undertaking, and assure our readers that they will find his book a most pleasant companion.

---

*Hebrew Records : an Historical Inquiry concerning the Age, Authorship, and Authenticity of the Old Testament.* By the Rev. Dr. Giles, 8vo. London: J. Chapman.

THE object of this work is 'to prove the Old Testament, in its actual form, to be a thousand years later than the date to which it is generally referred.' The detail of this 'proof' exhibits much industry. But the writer appears to be little conversant with the works of Hengstenberg and Hävernick, by whose learned, critical, and candid researches, his principal objections to the genuineness of the Old Testament writings are anticipated and thoroughly refuted. To biblical scholars, these Hebrew Records can appear to be no more than the feeble dogmatism of a writer, whose range of reading is narrow, whose critical powers are slight—a compiler rather than an author—an amateur printer, laborious enough, and more than enough, confiding in his own judgment, but with too small an amount of biblical learning, and too little *reverence* for the sacred writings, to be a safe guide. On many topics, especially the thirtieth chapter, on 'the Style of the Old Testament,' the writer is manifestly out of his depth, and betrays an entire unacquaintedness with the genius and spirit of the Hebrew literature. While professing that his work is 'historical, and not theological,' the whole drift of the volume shows that his object is theological, and that he aims at undermining the belief of Christians in 'the *doctrinal* parts of the Christian scheme,' by shaking their confidence in the *authority* of the Old Testament, which he declares to be 'essential to the existence of our own creed.' To expose the fallacies, mistakes, and foregone conclusions of such a work, is scarcely the business of one who writes so brief a notice as the present. It appears to us, however, that the circulation of works of this character is a fact not to be overlooked, and our chief design in noticing it as we have done, is to suggest the desirableness of some popular treatise, by a well-furnished and vigorous writer, on the whole question of these multiform attacks on Christianity, by writers who, if we are to take them at their word, have no idea of the tendency of what they publish!

---

*Maidens and Mothers; or, the Christian Spinster and the Hebrew Wife. A Book for Young Women.* By the Rev. T. Binney. London: J. Paul.

THE eminent preacher of the Weigh-house has done himself much honour, and the public good service, by permitting these ingenious, instructive, and highly characteristic discourses to be published. We understand that Mr. Binney gave away large numbers of them to the females of his own congregation. We have been much struck with one observation at the close of the 'Hebrew Wife,' which seems to explain the preacher's design in both : 'such young men and women as the Bible would form, as its writers approve, and its pages depict, would constitute the happiness of two generations—they would bless their parents who would rejoice in the promise of their early goodness— they would bless their children, who would be sheltered and nourished by its mature expansion and ripened fruits. They themselves would be a glory and defence to the nation they adorned ; would find that religion is not only no enemy to the comfort, business, virtues, and accomplishments belonging to the scene of their temporary pilgrimage, but that true *godliness is profitable for all things—for the life that now is, and for that which is to come.'*

---

*The Family Almanack and Educational Register for the Year of our Lord* 1851. *Containing, in addition to the usual contents of an almanack, a List of the Foundation of Grammar Schools in England and Wales, together with an Account of Scholarships and Exhibitions attached to them.* To be published annually. London : John W. Parker, Strand. 1851.

IT is somewhat late in the year to introduce to our readers a new almanack; but as the chief value of the one before us consists in matters of permanent interest, it cannot be unreasonable to recommend it even now. It seems generally accurate, and is remarkably full and complete. We have noticed, however, what seems to be a small error in page 80, where the President of the Board of Trade is represented as enjoying a salary of 35,000*l.* a year. We presume that there is a cipher too many.

---

*The Pictorial Family Bible. With copious Original Notes.* By J. Kitto, D.D. Parts I.—III. London : Orr and Co.

THE Pictorial Bible needs no commendation. Its value has been very generally admitted, and the work is now so extensively known as to supersede the necessity of one word being uttered in its praise. We shall, therefore, merely describe the present edition, which, in point of cheapness, equals, if it do not exceed, any of the productions of the day. The work is to be completed in one hundred and twenty weekly numbers, of twenty pages each, quarto, price threepence, or in thirty monthly parts, at one shilling each. It will, therefore, consist of 2,400 quarto pages, with innumerable engravings, and may be obtained at the very low price of thirty shillings. The original work was published about twelve years since, and the character of the present edition will be best understood from the following extract from the announcement of the proprietors. For our own use, we greatly prefer the Standard edition, but the cheapness of the present issue fits it for a much larger class of readers, while it furnishes, in truth, all which such readers ordinarily require. 'Although the sale of the original work continues to be very large from year to year, a new edition, more suitable to the critical scholar and student, was demanded, in conse-

quence of the immense stores of Biblical information acquired within a
few years after its first appearance.   This want was supplied by the
Standard edition of the " Pictorial Bible ;" a large amount of Biblical
and theological knowledge, drawn from the habits, natural history, and
archæology of Eastern countries, being added.   To admit of this new
matter, which comprised nearly one-third of the whole work, it was
found necessary, besides increasing the work from three to four
volumes, to divest it of some of the more popular but imaginative
illustrations, such as pictures from paintings of the old masters, and
confine the engravings strictly to matter-of-fact illustrations, thus producing what the Standard edition professes to be—a Bible for the
student; which edition will steadily be kept up to the current standard
of Biblical knowledge.   To meet, however, the wants of a more extended class of readers, a new edition of the original and more popular
work is considered desirable ; and to that class is addressed the Pictorial Family Bible.'

---

*The National Cyclopædia of Useful Knowledge.*   Vol. XII.    8vo.
London : Charles Knight.

THE concluding volume of an admirable work, which, in comparatively
narrow limit, and at a very reduced price, places the results of modern
science, literature, and travels, within the reach of the great majority
of intelligent readers.  We have watched the progress of ' The National
Cyclopædia' with much interest.   Mr. Knight has honorably fulfilled
his engagement, and we trust that the public will duly appreciate his
labors by giving to this work an extensive, and, thereby, a remunerative
circulation.   If any man has merited success, it is certainly Mr. Knight,
who has probably done more than any other individual in supplying to
the people a sound and cheap literature.

---

## Review of the Month.

---

No progress has been made in ' The Ecclesiastical Titles Bill ' during
the past month.    This is matter of regret, and has somewhat damaged
the reputation of the Ministry.    On such a subject, and after such
professions, so much delay was not anticipated.   The interval which
has elapsed since the second reading of the bill, has allowed time
for reflection, but has not elicited, so far as our knowledge extends,
any reversal of the decision formerly pronounced.   There is less
passion, it may be, and consequently fewer words, but the more the
matter is reflected on, the deeper, as it seems to us, becomes the
feeling of the rightfulness and the expediency of rebuking the assumption of the Papacy, and of thus guarding future times from the
appeal which might otherwise be made to our acquiescence in the
present policy of Rome.   We yield to none as advocates of the *right*

of every man to worship God according to the dictate of his conscience; but such right is not to be confounded with the ecclesiastical
platform of a body owing allegiance to a foreign power, partly secular
and partly spiritual. We plead for the religious liberty of the Roman
Catholic, but we object to the introduction of a hierarchy which gives
fearful power to priestism, and would degrade by enslaving the nation.

The former has been possessed by our Catholic countrymen for many
years; the latter is now attempted for the first time in a tone of insolent assumption, which reminds us of the days of Hildebrand. We
have already seen how this attempt has been met, and the unanimity
and earnestness of the opposition has astonished probably both friends
and foes. The government measure is to be proceeded with on
Monday, the 5th instant, and we confess to some anxiety as to the
form which may be impressed on it in Committee. We trust its future
progress will redeem the Ministry from suspicion, and speedily destroy
all hopes founded on 'the chapter of accidents.'

The celebrated Durham Letter made special reference to 'the
mummeries of superstition' practised by members of the Church of
England. It answered a party purpose to apply these words to the
services of Roman Catholics, but this device was too obvious to succeed with intelligent and impartial readers. The Premier's allusion
was clearly to the 'histrionic arrangements' now made in many English
churches, and by which it is sought to assimilate their form of worship
to that of the Papacy. We are sorry that the subsequent proceedings
of Lord John have evinced no intention to deal with this master and
primary evil. His bill makes no allusion to it, and from his speech
it was cautiously excluded. There is something suspicious in this.
Whether his lordship trembles, as most Whig statesmen have done,
at the thought of dealing with Church matters, or whether there are
difficulties in the way unknown to the public, but visible to him,
we know not. Of one thing, however, we are certain. His silence is
regarded with mistrust and disapproval by an overwhelming majority
of the people, whether Churchmen or Dissenters. It gives an air of
insincerity to much which he says and does, and keeps open the fountain of evil, one of whose poisoned streams he is seeking to turn back.
'Can it be,' it is frequently asked, 'that his lordship, while courageous in
resisting foreign priestism, timidly succumbs to that which is domestic?
Is his Protestantism a thing of name rather than of principle, or is
the policy of his administration controlled by clerical influence, rather
than dependent on the will of the people, and the obligations of a large
and far-seeing statesmanship?' Whatever reply may be given to such
queries, one thing is certain,—his lordship has been silent as the grave,
and the great evil which invited the aggression of Rome has remained,
so far as government action is concerned, not only untouched, but un-
threatened.

In such circumstances we are glad to find that other members of the
Church have been truer to their convictions than his lordship. As
Dissenters we should of course decline to appeal to the sovereign in
religious matters. But the case is different with members of the
Establishment. They admit the *headship* of the Crown, and may

therefore be expected, in consistency, to betake themselves to it when danger threatens. Such course has been pursued by a large number of Churchmen, who have presented an *Address* to her Majesty signed by 63 peers, 108 members of the lower House, and 821,240 other lay members of the Church of England, in which, after expressing themselves strongly on the recent aggression of Rome, they say, 'But we desire also humbly to represent to your Majesty our conviction, confirmed by the recent testimony of several bishops of our Church, that the court of Rome would never have attempted such an act of aggression, had not encouragements been held out to that encroaching power by many of the clergy of our own Church, who have, for several years past, shown a desire to assimilate the doctrines and services of the Church of England to those of the Roman communion. While we would cheerfully contend for the principles of the Reformation against all open enemies, we have to lament that our most dangerous foes are those of our own household; and hence we feel that it is to little purpose to repel the aggressions of the foreigner, unless those principles and practices, which have tempted him to such aggressions, be publicly and universally repudiated.

'We are conscious that the evils to which we allude are deeply seated, and have been the growth of a series of years, and hence we entertain no expectation that they can be suddenly eradicated. But we humbly entreat your Majesty, in the exercise of your royal prerogative, to direct the attention of the primates and bishops of the Church to the necessity of using all fit and lawful means to purify it from the infection of false doctrine; and, as respects external and visible observances, in which many novelties have been introduced, to take care that measures may be promptly adopted for the repression of all such practices.'

This *Address* has been forwarded by her Majesty, through the Home Secretary, to the Primate, with a request that he would lay it before the Archbishop of York, and the suffragan bishops in England and Wales.

'Her Majesty,' says Sir George Grey, 'places full confidence in your Grace's desire to use such means as are within your power to maintain the purity of the doctrines taught by the clergy of the Established Church, and to discourage and prevent innovations in the modes of conducting the services of the Church not sanctioned by law or general usage, and calculated to create dissatisfaction and alarm among a numerous body of its members.'

The tone of this communication was indicative of earnestness without assumption. No Churchman could fairly take exception to it, for there was no parade of authority. Supremacy, indeed, was assumed: it lay at the basis of what was done, and might have justified the use of more peremptory language. But her Majesty knew her strength, and her words were, therefore, mild and conciliatory.

An *Address* to the clergy has subsequently appeared, signed by the two archbishops, and twenty-two bishops, of which we may truly say that it is about as pointless a production as can well be imagined. This should not perhaps be matter of surprise, when it is remembered that the *Address* itself was evidently a compromise. It bears the signatures of the bishops of London and Oxford, and we need scarcely say these could not have appeared had the evils deprecated been honestly and radically dealt with. ' Peace, peace,' say the archbishops and their brethren, when God's truth and the convulsive throes of the Church herself declare there is no peace. Four bishops, those of Exeter, Bath and

about him which we admire. He is an outspoken and honest man, so far at least as his Church principles are concerned; and it would be well for his brethren of London and Oxford if as much could be said of them. He has now brought the matter to an issue, and we wait to see whether the Premier is equal to the crisis which impends. The Bishop of Exeter treats the decision of the Privy Council in the Gorham case with
heresy, denies the
compel an early an
—a provincial
such matters a
be permitted? If
men have yet to
clerical bondage.
much of his former
think he will. He
that i
ecclesiastical t

CHANCERY REFORM has for some time stood prominently before the public, and is now warmly supported even by the Chancery bar. The most eminent persons connected with the Courts, including the late Lord Chancellor, the present Master of the Rolls, and the new Vice-Chancellor, have all committed themselves to nothing less than an entire reconstruction of the system of Chancery procedure. Our present business, however, is with Lord John Russell's measure of the 28th of March. It has the title of a ' Bill for the better Administration of Justice in the Court of Chancery;' but, judging by the noble lord's speech, it should rather have been entitled a bill for the better enabling the Lord Chancellor to attend to his political functions. The great argument in its behalf rested on the inadequacy of Lord Cottenham's assistance in the Cabinet; and the measure itself professes simply to assist the Lord Chancellor in his Chancery duties, by associating with him on the bench the Master of the Rolls and a Common Law Judge. The bill makes no other alteration. For reasons not stated, the ecclesiastical patronage is to be taken away; and, for reasons which are stated, and in which we cannot be supposed to acquiesce, it is to be vested in the Treasury. This arrangement has nothing to do with the main object of the bill. Its presence betokens a pre-formed purpose, fulfilled at the first convenient opportunity.

We do not think that in its present shape Lord John's bill will pass; and as Chancery Reform has obtained a position not dependent upon the success or failure of the measure, we cannot say that we shall regret its rejection. It is open to precisely the objections which proved fatal to Lord Redesdale's proposal in Lord Eldon's time, and more recently to the measure of Lord Cottenham; and it is not attended by the counterbalancing advantages which were ensured by Lord Cottenham's bill. It shuts up the Rolls Court; it deprives Chancery of the great weight derived from the presidency of the Lord Chancellor; it seriously lessens the authority of the House of Lords as a final court of appeal; and it makes no provision for colonial litigants before the Privy Council. The first and the last of these results were avoided by Lord Cottenham; the second and third alone were sufficient to prove fatal to his measure.

That the second is an inherent defect in Lord John Russell's scheme is obvious on a little reflection, though the measure seems framed to disguise it. The Lord Chancellor is still to 'sit' as Chief Judge in Chancery; but if he is to attend there as heretofore, how will he be more able than at present to attend to his political duties? It is agreed on all hands, that nothing will suffice for this object short of an entire release from his Chancery engagements. The only question has been, whether this is not too great a price to pay for the advantage. So far as the Court of Chancery is concerned, the effect of the measure will be to place the Great Seal always in commission.

The third objection is involved in the second. The present Chief Judge in Equity has his mind continually engaged in the mastery of numerous diverse and complicated matters of litigation, creating an amount of mental power in judicial development for which Mackintosh could find no other epithet than 'prodigious,' but very largely dependent, it is obvious, upon its continual exercise. Departing from Chancery and retiring to the Lords, the infallible consequence will be speedily felt in a loss of judicial power, and consequently of authority in the Court. Sir Samuel Romilly forcibly insisted on this objection, in answer to Lord Redesdale's measure, and Lord Lyndhurst did little more than repeat it in defeating that of Lord Cottenham.

MR. LOCKE KING's BILL for the Extension of the County Franchise has been cast out on the second reading. We are not surprised at this. The result, indeed, appeared so certain, that we greatly regret the motion having been pressed to a division. A very serious responsibility rests on those to whom this is attributable. They have damaged a good cause which they intended to serve, and have furnished additional evidence—not certainly needed—of the want of practical skill, which operates so fatally on the movements of our most onward reformers. When will the men with whose principles we accord, do those principles justice by a sagacious observance of times and seasons? The first reading of the bill was carried by a majority of 100 to 52. This was a great point gained; it placed the question on new and most advantageous ground. A Parliamentary sanction was thus given to the principle of the measure, which ought not to have been trifled with, much less should an opportunity have been afforded for its reversal. Government had declared its adoption of the principle ; and Mr. Fox Maule had reiterated and strengthened the pledges of Lord John. It was right to test the Commons in the first instance ; but what has subsequently occurred ought to have made the friends of the measure pause, more especially when it was evident, from the state of the House on the 2nd, that an adverse vote would be given. Several Liberal members counselled a postponement of the measure, and its best friends must now regret that such counsel was not adopted. A division, however, was called for, and the bill was rejected by a majority of 299 to 83. We have thus lost the vantage ground on which we previously stood, and that, too, through the folly and recklessness of our own friends. We do not wonder at the mistrust evinced by some Liberals. Lord John has recently done very little to warrant confidence, and had it been possible to carry the measure, we should have counselled perseverance. But as this clearly was not the case, as Mr. Locke King was sure to be defeated, and as Mr. Bright himself 'had listened with considerable gratification to the speech of the right hon. Secretary at War,' who spoke as the mouth-piece of Government, it was cruelty to a noble cause, the merest folly which could be enacted, to force the matter to a division, and thus tear down the popular flag from the high ground on which it had been planted. Until our onward men learn more wisdom, they will do but little in advancing the people's cause.

JEWISH DISABILITIES have again formed the topic of Parliamentary discussion. The subject was introduced by the Premier on the 3rd, who moved 'That the House resolve itself into a Committee of the whole House to take into consideration the mode of administering the oath of abjuration to persons professing the Jewish religion.' The debate, which was brief, was not characterised by any novel or striking features. Sir Robert Inglis, Mr. Plumptre, and Mr. Newdegate, spoke against the motion, while Mr. Milner Gibson expressed a hope that if the measure ' were rejected a third time in another place, some decided measures would be taken by Government to prevent so important a principle of civil and religious liberty being set aside.' The motion of Lord John was carried by a majority of 166 to 98. We need not say we are glad that such a measure has been introduced, while 'The Ecclesiastical Titles' bill is before the House. It constitutes a practical answer to many of the charges preferred against the spirit and policy of the framers of that bill. An enlightened attachment to religious liberty is perfectly consistent, nay, seems to us imperatively to require earnest opposition to the aggressive policy of the Papacy. The more we reflect on the subject, the deeper becomes our conviction that the Papacy is not to be dealt with as a purely spiritual or ecclesiastical institution. The second reading of the bill is fixed for the 1st of May.

SIR CHARLES WOOD SUBMITTED HIS AMENDED BUDGET to the House on the 4th, and partially succeeded in regaining its good feeling. His budget, though substantially like its predecessor, has received some modifications which entitle it to a more favorable reception. The feeling of the House was, no doubt, also influenced by what has recently occurred. The effect of a hostile vote is more clearly seen than formerly, and honorable members are, therefore, probably in a mood to be satisfied with little rather than risk another ministerial crisis. Calculating on the same surplus, 1,892,000*l.*, as in his former budget, the Chancellor devotes it principally to the *extinction* of the window-tax. The present produce of this tax is 1,856,000*l.*, for which he proposes a partial substitute in a house-duty, chargeable on houses of an annual rental exceeding 20*l.* This tax it is calculated will produce 720,000*l.*, being 1,136,000*l.* less than the window-tax. So much, therefore, will be remitted to the public, while all objections grounded on sanitary considerations will be got rid of. By the former budget the rates of duty were 1*s.* and 9*d.* in the pound on the rental which was chargeable on 500,000 houses, but this is now lowered to 9*d.* in the pound on dwelling-houses, and 6*d.* on houses having shops. The number of houses chargeable with the tax is also reduced to 400,000. These features of the budget constitute a material improvement on the Chancellor's first project, and ought to be received as such. The duties on coffee and foreign timber are also to be reduced, and a further reduction of the sugar duties takes place this year. The whole saving to the public will therefore be—

| | |
|---|---:|
| On Windows    .    .    .    . | £1,136,000 |
| On Sugar  .    .    .    .    . | 330,000 |
| On Coffee  .    .    .    .    . | 176,000 |
| On Foreign Timber  .    .    . | 286,000 |
| | £1,928,000 |

This sum exceeds the surplus on which the Chancellor calculates, but the loss will be partly met by increased consumption, while a half year's window-tax, now due, amounting to 568,000*l.*, will go to the credit of the year's account. An excess of income over expenditure, amounting to 924,000*l.*, is therefore anticipated. Would that this could be applied to the reduction of the national debt: but we much fear that our misgovernment at the Cape will involve a larger sacrifice than the surrender of this surplus. The agricultural interest has gained nothing by the reconstruction of the budget. The boon proffered has been withdrawn, at which we are not much surprised, considering the scorn with which it was treated. 'Another proposal,' said the Chancellor, 'which I made to the house, of minor importance certainly, and one which I submitted in accordance with the recommendation of the House of Lords, was to undertake a portion of the charge of maintenance of lunatic asylums, to be paid out of the consolidated fund, as also to abolish the duty on clover and grass seeds. Well, I have heard many objections to both, and not a single word in their favour, and, therefore, whatever my own opinion may be as to the merits of these proposals, I am certainly most unwilling to press it upon the House.'

The income-tax is to be renewed without modification, or improvement, which is much to be regretted on many accounts, and not the least so on account of the Government. All parties admit the inequitable and inquisitorial nature of the tax. It was first imposed to meet a temporary urgency, as the Chancellor himself admits. The danger then impending inclined men to submit to any evil as the means of sustaining national credit. They did not, therefore, look narrowly into the practical injustice of the scheme, or, to whatever extent they did so, they deemed it better to submit to temporary wrong, than to hazard the other evils which threatened. The case, however, is different now. Instead of a deficiency there is a surplus; and the time, therefore, is surely come for a reconsideration of the matter, so far, at least, as the distinction of property and income are concerned. But Sir Charles Wood thinks otherwise, and his budget evinces the class-policy of our rulers. The tendency of our recent legislation has been to relieve the great masses of our countrymen from the disproportioned share of taxes formerly pressing on them. In this we rejoice; but, on the other hand, we are equally opposed to the middle class being made a scape-goat for their richer neighbours. Such is the policy now in vogue, and it should be watched and steadily opposed by all lovers of fair-play. To tax the produce of a man's labor,—the salary of a clerk, the profit of a merchant, the income of a lawyer, physician, or clergyman, in the same way, and to the same extent, as the interest or other produce of realized capital, is manifestly inequitable. It confounds things which differ so notoriously, that one word need not be added in proof of its injustice. Such is the proposition of Government, and the House will no doubt adopt it.

ON THE 7TH MR. HERRIES submitted a resolution, the effect of which would be, to substitute for the repeal of the window-tax, and the other reductions proposed by the Chancellor, a diminution of two-sevenths of the income-tax. He did not attempt to obviate the objections which lie specially against the tax; it was to remain—five-sevenths of it, at least—as inquisitorial and unrighteous as ever. The essential injustice of the impost, in confounding income and property, making what is variable and contingent on labor and anxiety yield the same revenue as what is fixed and absolute, was not in the slightest degree diminished by Mr. Herries' resolution. The tax was to continue, though its amount was altered, as alien as ever to the habits of our countrymen, and unpopular in the very highest degree. We are, therefore, glad that the House rejected his resolution by a majority of 278 to 230. It was a pitiful attempt at popularity, which utterly failed, and would reconcile us— were reconciliation needed—to the loss of Lord Stanley's financial measures. On one point only Mr. Herries' speech was effective. He made free use of ' Hansard;' and we do not envy the feelings with which some of her Majesty's Ministers must have listened to the extracts he read. The second reading of the Income Tax Bill is to be taken on Monday, the 28th, and we shall not, of course, be able to announce the result.

IT WAS NOT TO BE EXPECTED that the Country party would allow the occasion to pass without calling attention to the subject of agricultural distress. The Chancellor possessed a surplus; taxes were to be reduced; and Mr. Disraeli, therefore, on the 11th, moved as an amendment to the motion for going into committee on the Assessed Taxes Act, ' That in any relief to be granted by the remission

640      REVIEW OF THE MONTH.

or adjustment of taxation, due regard ought to be paid to the distressed condition of the owners and occupiers of land.' To these words no reasonable objection could be taken, and had they expressed all that was intended, the House would probably have affirmed them by an overwhelming majority. But it was well known that they did not do so. Mr. Disraeli had modified his amendment with the obvious design of catching as many votes as possible, and notwithstanding the strange assertion of Mr. Reynolds, there was not, we apprehend, a single member who did not regard it as a Protectionist amendment, and did not vote, for or against it, under the full conviction that it was so. If the commercial policy of Sir Robert Peel's government is to be rescinded, let it be done openly and after an English fashion. Those who deem it injurious to our national interests, or see reason to believe that it presses unequally or with injustice on the landed interest, are fully entitled to state their case and to claim redress. If their reasonings cannot be met, or their alleged facts disproved, in the name of common justice, let them have the redress they claim. At any rate, a fair and open field is their due, and in such case we should respect their integrity, whatever we might think of their statesmanship. But the affair is vastly otherwise when they propose one thing and mean another—when their speeches and resolutions avoid the obnoxious terms, while their policy evidently contemplates the re-establishment of protection. We say with Mr. Gladstone, 'If hon. gentlemen are going to restore protection, let them not talk of the alleviation of local burdens.' Mr. Disraeli, as was remarked by Mr. Labouchere, deprecated discussion on the policy of the late Government, yet that evidently lay at the basis of all he did. 'If the hon. gentleman,' said Mr. Labouchere, 'had not struck out of his amendment the words, "in the first instance," he could have understood his proposition ; but as it stood at present, it amounted to a truism.' Whatever qualities Mr. Disraeli may possess as an able rhetorician, however skilfully he can avail himself of the weaknesses of an adversary or of the prejudices of his heterogeneous followers, he has yet failed to exhibit any one characteristic of English statesmanship, or to carry himself a whit nearer the confidence of his countrymen. On a division, the Irish members acted as in a former instance, and the Government obtained only the small majority of thirteen : the numbers being—for the amendment, 250 ; and against it, 263. We regret this issue of the debate on account of the parties most immediately concerned. It will keep up their delusion, and thus aggravate the evils they are suffering. As a mere party division, the smallness of the majority is no doubt gratifying to Lord Stanley and Mr. Disraeli, but it does not advance the return of protection one inch. That is doomed, and is past recovery, whatever the vengeance of Irish members may prompt, or the subtilty of their English allies attempt. ' The question of protection,' as Mr. Bright observed, ' is one which has been finally and irrevocably settled.'

THE SUBJECT OF CHURCH-RATES has again been introduced to the Commons' House. For some time past it has been in abeyance, and the reason of its being so is very obvious. The Administration has been

seeking favor with the Church, and has, therefore, shrunk from under-taking it, while the energies of the more earnest and active Dissenters have been directed against the alliance of Church and State, rather than the practical grieva
has
sele
the
the assessment
to the House.'
motion was di
ably seconded
promise. We
Treasury requesting the attendance of its supporters in order to pre-vent the motion from being out-voted. This was wise on the part of Lord John, and may be taken, we trust, as an indication of return to his fut
at the
followed with one of his
which he triumphantly vin
representation preferred by
minded, member for the
at the surprise of Sir R.
similar feeling ourse
gave no promise of
two years since that
he could *gravely* do


we are glad to find that adversity has not been without its good effect. ' It is never,' as the ' Daily News' remarks, ' too late to mend ;' and we shall be glad to find that what was ceded promptly, is honestly carried out. The committee, we presume, will be chosen immediately after the re-assembling of Parliament, and its composition will enable us to judge of the good-faith or otherwise of the Premier. If it consists of impartial men we are satisfied. Let the case be thoroughly sifted and an honest judgment be given. If so constituted it may answer a very important end; but if otherwise it will only form another instance of the manner in which trickery and fraud are confounded with statesmanship by many politicians. We will not, however, anticipate this. Time, the great revealer, will speedily disclose the truth, and we wait for its instruction. In the meantime we are desirous of offering two remarks.

First. We must go to the *extinction* of the rate. Nothing short of this will meet the justice of the case. It is not a question of money, but of principle, and as such it must be presented by all our witnesses.

Secondly. An organization should immediately be effected with a view of presenting to the committee a list of witnesses competent to speak to the law of Church-rates, the grounds of our objection, the religious and social evils which flow from them, the pecuniary outlay of Dissenters in the erection and support of their own religious edifices, and in general the marvellous achievements of the Voluntary principle wherever it has had fair play.   Gentlemen should be brought up from various parts of the country, and the records of Parliament and the reports of Church-rate meetings should be examined, in order to present the case fully to the legislature.   We are glad to hear that the London Deputies have taken the matter up, and we trust that their proceedings will be prompt and generous.   The question respects the whole country, and an immediate application should therefore be made to our friends throughout the kingdom for such pecuniary aid as is needed. There is not a moment to lose.   Our opponents will bestir themselves, and we must not sleep at our post.

## Literary Intelligence.

### *Just Published.*

Yeast: A Problem.   Reprinted, with Corrections and Additions, from ' Frazer's Magazine.'

Inauguration of the New College of the Free Church, Edinburgh, November, 1850. With Introductory Lectures on Theology, Philosophy, and Natural Science.

Local Self-Government and Centralization: the Characteristics of each; and its Practical Tendencies as affecting Social, Moral, and Political Welfare and Progress: including comprehensive Outlines of the English Constitution. By J. Toulmin Smith, Esq.

The Caffre War: A Letter addressed to the Right Hon. Earl Grey, containing Remarks on the Causes of the present War, and the Payment of its Expenses; the means of Prevention, &c.   By J. J. Freeman.

Madam Dorrington of the Dene: the Story of a Life.   By William Howitt.   3 vols.

A Funeral Discourse on the Decease of Rev. Algernon Wells.   By Rev. T. Binney. To which is prefixed, the Funeral Address, by Rev. H. F. Burder, D.D.

On the Great Exhibition.   A Lecture delivered to the Literary and Scientific Society in the Town Hall, Woburn, Beds, on Thursday Evening, December 19, 1850.   By Rev. J. Andrews.

Funeral Services occasioned by the Death of the Rev. John Pye Smith, D.D.

The Stones of Venice.   Vol. I.   The Foundations.   By John Ruskin. With Illustrations drawn by the Author.

Notes on the Construction of Sheep-folds.   By John Ruskin, M.A.

Ceylon and the Government of Lord Torrington.

The Chronicle of Battel Abbey, from 1066 to 1176. Now first Translated; with Notes and an Abstract of the subsequent History of the Establishment. By Mark Anthony Lower, M.A.

Christian Socialism and its Opponents. A Lecture delivered at the Office of the Society for Promoting Working Men's Associations, 76, Charlotte-street, Fitzroy-square, on Wednesday, 12th February, 1851, by J. M. Ludlow, Esq.

A Letter to the Right Hon. Lord Ashley, M.P., being Reflections at the expiration of fifty years spent in the Anglican Ministry, including Remarks on the present Crisis of the Protestant Cause. By John Riland, M.A.

The Huntyng and Fyndyng out of the Romish Fox, whiche more than seven yeares hath bene hyd among the Byshoppes of England, after the Kynges Hyghnes Henry VIII. had commanded him to be dryven out of his Realme. Written by Wyllyam Turner, Doctore of Physicke, and formerly Fellow of Pembroke College in Cambridge. Amended and curtailed, with a Short Account of the Author prefixed, by Robert Potts, M.A., Trinity College, Cambridge.

Nineveh and the Tigris.

Lives of the Popes, from the Rise of the Roman Church to the Age of Gregory VII. A.D. 100—1046. Part I.

Maidens and Mothers; or, the Christian Spinster and the Hebrew Wife. A Book for Young Women. By Rev. T. Binney.

Paul the Apostle, or Sketches from his Life. By Rev. Henry J. Gamble.

The Genius of Popery opposed to the Principles of Civil and Religious Liberty.

Eight Lectures, delivered before the Young Men's Christian Association in the Rotunda.

The Primitive Christian. An interesting Narrative having reference to the Early Persecutions in Provence. By Rev. Cæsar Malan.

The History of John Birgan, a blind boy, a native of Ireland, who was converted from the errors of Romanism to true Christianity, as related by Himself. With a Memoir by Rev. Thos. H. C. Finney.

A Brief History of the Wesleyan Missions on the Western Coast of Africa; including Biographical Sketches of all the Missionaries who have died in that important field of labour. With some Account of the European Settlements and of the Slave Trade. By William Fox, upwards of teh years Missionary on the Gambia.

Romanism and Congregationalism contrasted; or, the relative Aspects of their Polity, Teachings, and Tendencies. By R. G. Milne, M.A.

The Western Coast of Africa; comprising Suggestions on the best Means of Exterminating the Slave Trade, &c. By William Fox.

Favourite Song Birds. Being a Popular Description of the Feathered Songsters of Britain. Parts 9, 10, 11, and 12.

The Three Trials of Loide, Sunshine and Shadow, The Phantasmal Reproof, and other Poems. By Calder Campbell.

The Parents' Great Commission; or, Essays on subjects connected with the higher part of Education. Second Edition.

Christian Aspects of Faith and Duty. Discourses by John James Tayler, B.A.

Odes of Petrarch. Translated into English Verse, by Captain R. G. Macgregor.

A Text-Book of Zoology, for Schools. By Philip Henry Gosse, A.L.S.

The Law of Moses, its Character and Design. By David Duncan.

Emilie the Peacemaker. By Mrs. Thomas Geldart.

Collegiate Addresses. Being Counsels to Students on their Literary Pursuits and Future Life. By Rev. Jonathan Maxey, D.D. With a Biographical Introduction, by Romeo Elton, D.D.

The Infallibility of the Church of Rome. A Correspondence between the Right Rev. Bishop Brown, of Chepstow, and the Rev. Joseph Baylee, M.A., Principal of St. Arden's College, Birkenhead.

Thoughts on Electricity, with Notes of Experiments. By Charles Chalmers.

Bibliotheca Sacra, and American Biblical Repository, conducted by E. B. Edwards and E. A. Park, April, 1851.

The Inquisition; its History, Influence, and Effects, from its first Establishment to the present Time, including its recent Proceedings relative to Dr. Achilli, Father Ventura, &c. &c.

The History of the Church of Rome, to the end of the Episcopate of Damasus, A.D. 384. By Edward John Shepherd, A.M.

Historical Sketch of Logic, from the Earliest Times to the Present Day. By Robert Blakeley.

Gregory of Nazianzum. A Contradiction to the Ecclesiastical History of the Fourth Century. By Dr. Carl Ullmann. Translated by G. B. Cox, M.A.

State Education self-defeating. A Chapter from Social Statics: on the Conditions essential to Human Happiness specified, and the first of them developed. By Herbert Spencer.

A Text-Book of Popery, comprising a Brief History of the Council of Trent, and a complete View of Roman Catholic Theology. By J. M. Cramp, D.D. Third Edition.

The Life and Epistles of St. Paul. Part XII. By Revs. W. J. Conybear and Howson.

The Supremacy of the Pope: the Monthly United Lecture delivered in Cannon-street Chapel, March 10, 1851. By Rev. J. Edwards.

Protestant Christianity :] how it is to be maintained and propagated in opposition to the Church of Rome. A Discourse, delivered by W. M. Thompson, December 1st, 1850, on occasion of the recent Papal Aggression.

Historical Memorials of Broad-street Chapel, Reading; being Sketches of its Pastors and its Progress. By W. Legg, B.A., Pastor.

The Pictorial Family Bible, with copious Original Notes. By J. Kitto, D.D. Part III.

National Cyclopædia of Useful Knowledge. Part XLVIII. Second Half. Completing the Work.

The Journal of Sacred Literature. No. XIV. By John Kitto, D.D.

The National Cyclopædia of Useful Knowledge. Vol. XII.

Popery: its Character and its Crimes. By W. Elfe Tayler. Second Edition—revised and enlarged.

THE

# 𝔈clectic 𝔑eview.

JUNE, 1851.

Art. I.—1. *The Life and Poems of Hartley Coleridge.* Two vols. London : Moxon.

2. *Essays and Marginalia.* By the same Author. Two vols. London : Moxon.

Let no one say, that although fairies trip it no more—that although Robin Goodfellow no more reclines his 'hairy strength' by our firesides—that although ghosts and witches are fast 'wearing awa to the land o' the leal '—that Nature's FREAKS are for ever over and gone ! Still, as we contemplate the varied multitudes of mankind, were it not for the sublime and serious aspects in which Christianity has taught us to regard *all* our race, we might be tempted to suppose that many of them were made in the haste, or in the mirth, or in the transient caprice of the Mighty Mother. Looking back, especially, along our literary annals, what strange and grotesque combinations do we perceive ! The most ample and magnificent of all minds, living in the revelry of a playhouse, and departing, according to uniform tradition, in the midst of a fever caught from a debauch of ale— the most superb of our early artistic poets, engaged in endless squabbles, compelled to write lewd and stupid plays for a liveli- hood, nay, to change his religion for a piece of bread ;—the most acute of thinkers, the most profound of satirists, the most energetic of homespun English writers, transforming himself, through the indulgence of malevolent feelings and bestial prac- tices, and manifold betrayals of the female heart, into a Yahoo, the reality of his own detestable creation—the finest and subtlest

N. S.—VOL. I.          U U

wit of the world, married to a crooked body, and a more crooked temper and soul—the most powerful painter of Nature, in her external aspects, becoming, through sensuous and lazy habits, little else than a sloth of genius—the noblest lyrist of England living drunk and dying mad—one of the finest of humorists, and truest of poets, gaining justly the title of an ' inspired idiot' —our great lexicographer and moralist, blasted with hypochondria from his cradle, and bearing about a body of death as bulky as his own giant soul—the most powerful, save one, of Christian poets spending half of his days under medical surveillance, and departing in darkness—the bard of a country, and who might have been the second bard of a world, dying of a combination of mean sins and mean miseries as an exciseman in a third-rate Scottish town—and, to crown all, the Apollo of modern song, one

> ' At home where angels bashful look,'

the most daring and one of the most sublime of poets, dying, a degraded name, on a foreign shore, and with hardly a brother Englishman to receive his last sigh, or cover his burning eyes with the veil of death—such are only a few specimens of the ' aberrations of British genius ;' and yet they almost tempt us to exclaim, ' These be thy gods, O Israel !'  If these be the elegant extracts from the volume, what must be the volume itself?

Things are mending, doubtless, with our literary men.  They are now, as a class, respectable members of society ; and if still often eccentric, are better able to *manage* and to *disguise* their eccentricities.  And yet, when the veil shall have gradually dropt from the history of some of our living, or recently dead authors, it will be found that there have been, or are among us, no unworthy representatives of the Savages, Swifts, and Collinses of the past—that, in the composition of many men of genius, the ' ounce of mother wit' is still too often forgotten ; or that they have taken special care, by imprudence or indulgence, to extinguish it themselves.

One of this class of belated unfortunates was William Thom, of Inverury, the Weaver Poet ; a man of great natural powers, of strong sense, keen wit, much observation ; whose little poem, ' The Mitherless Bairn,' is the finest thing in the Scottish language since Burns, but whose history was a sad tissue of misfortune and imprudence.  Such another was Edgar Poe, of America, who for subtlety and originality had scarcely his match in the Western World ; who was no mocking-bird of British authors, but whose note was wild and native as that of his own ' Raven' (one of the strangest, dreariest, most unique, and powerful things in poetry, rising at once upon you from the great sea of imagination, like the cloud which was like unto a man's hand, and covering all your sky with a weird darkness); but who was a dissipated wanderer, and died in a poorhouse. And a third like unto these was Hartley Coleridge—heir to a portion of his father's genius, and a double share of his frailties—the simplest and most amiable of human beings; and yet we were told by one of the most eminent of his friends that he latterly ceased to call on him on the Lakes—' It was so ridiculous and pitiable to find the poor, harmless creature, amid the finest scenery in the world, and in beautiful summer weather, *dead drunk at ten o'clock in the morning.*'

Ere proceeding to speak of poor Hartley Coleridge's life and poems, we propose to make a few general remarks on the infirmities and aberrations of genius; a theme for which his history furnishes us with a text but too appropriate.

We must, then, in the first place, deny that there is any *necessary* connexion between genius and vice, or madness, or eccentricity. Genius is a ray from heaven; and is naturally akin to all those things on earth ' which are lovely and pure, and of a good report.' Its very name shows its connexion with the *genial* nature; its main moral element is love. Men are now in their hearts so conscious of this, that when they hear of instances of disconnexion between genius and virtue, it is with a start of surprise and horror; and we believe that though all the men of genius who ever lived had been tainted with vice, still the *thoughtful* would have been slow of drawing the horrible inference, that the brightest and most divine-seeming power in the human mind was a fiend in the garb of a radiant angel, and would have sought elsewhere for the real solution of the problem. But when we remember that so many of this gifted order *have* been true to themselves and to their mission, the belief is strengthened, that the instances of a contrary kind can be accounted for upon principles or facts which leave intact alike the sanity, the health, and the morality, of genius *per se*.

Such principles and facts there do exist; and we now proceed to enumerate some of them. And first, some of the most flagrantly bad of literary men have had no real pretensions to genius. Savage, for example, Boyce, and Dermody, were men of tolerable talent, and intolerable impudence, conceit, and profligacy. Churchill was of a higher order, but has been ridiculously overrated by whoever it was that wrote a paper on him, not long since, in the ' Edinburgh Review '—a disgraceful apology for a disgraceful and disgusting life. Swift and Chatterton, with all their vast talents, wanted, we think, the fine differentia, and the genial element of real poetic genius. And time would fail us to enumerate the hundreds of lesser spirits who have employed their small modica of light, which they mistook for genius, as lamps allowing them to see their way more clearly down to the chambers of death.  Talent, however great, is not genius.  Wit, however refined, is not genius.  Learning, however profound, is not genius.  But genius has been confounded not only with these respectable and valuable powers, but with glibness of speech, a knack of rhyming, the faculty of echoing others, elegance of language, fury of excitation, and a hundred other qualities, either mechanical or morbid, and then the faults of such feeble or diseased pretenders have been gravely laid down at the door of the insulted genius of poetry.

Secondly, real genius has not always received its due meed from the world.  Like real religion, it has found itself in an enemy's land.  Resisted, as it has often been, at every step, it has not been able uniformly to maintain the dignity, or to enjoy the repose, to which it was entitled.  Men of genius have occasionally soured in temper, and this has bred now the savage satisfaction with which Dr. Johnson wrote and printed, in large capitals, the line in his 'London'—

'Slow rises worth by poverty depressed;'

and now feelings still fiercer, more aggressive, and more destructive to the moral balance of the soul.  It is a painful predicament in which the man of genius has often felt himself. Willing to give to all men a portion of the bread of life, and unable to obtain the bread that perisheth—balked in completing the unequal bargain of light from heaven with earthly pelf— carrying about fragments of God's great general book of truth from reluctant or contemptuous bookseller to bookseller—subject even after his generous and noble thoughts are issued to the world, to the faint praise, or chilly silence, or abusive fury of oracular dunces—to the spurn of any mean slave who can find an assassin's cloak in the 'Anonymous,' and who does not even, it may be, take the trouble of looking at the divine thing he stabs, but strikes in blind and brutal fury; such has been and is the experience of many of whom the world is not worthy and can it be wondered at, that some of them sink in the strife, and that others, even while triumphing, do so at the expense of much of the bloom, the expansive generosity, the all-embracing sympathy which were their original inheritance?  Think of Byron's first volume, trampled like a weed in the dust—of Shelley's magnificent 'Revolt of Islam,' insulted and chased out of public view—of Keats's first volume and its judicial murder—of other attempts, less successful, such as the treatment of Carlyle's 'French Revolution,' at its first appearance, by a weekly journal (the 'Athenæum'), which now follows his proud path with its feeble and unaccepted adulation, and then speak with more pity of the aberrations into which the weaker sons of the muse have been hurried, and with more respect of the stern insulation and growing indifference to opinion and firmness of antagonistic determination which characterise her stronger children.

Thirdly, the aberrations of genius are often unduly magnified. The spots in a star are invisible—those in a sun are marked by every telescope. No man is a hero to his *valet de chambre*. And the reason often is, the valet is an observant but malicious and near-sighted fool. He sees the spots without seeing their small proportion to the magnitude of the orb. Nay, he creates spots if he cannot see them. The servants of Mrs. Siddons, while she was giving her famous private readings from Milton and Shakspere, thought their mistress mad, and used to say, 'There's the old lady making as much noise as ever.' Many and microscopic are the eyes which follow the steps of genius; and, too often, while they mark the mistakes, they are blind to the motives, to the palliations, to the resistance, and to the remorse. The world first idolizes genius—rates it even beyond its true worth—calls it perfect—remembers its divine derivation, but forgets that it must shine on us through earthly vessels, and then avenges on the earthly vessels the disappointment of its own exaggerated expectations. Hence each careless look, or word, or action of the hapless son of publicity, is noted, and, if possible, misinterpreted; his occasional high spirits are traced to physical excitement; his occasional stupidity voted a sin; his rapture and the reaction from it are both called in to witness against him: nay, an entire class of creatures arises, whose instinct it is to discover, and whose trade it is to tell his faults as a writer, and his failings as a man. It is under such a broad and searching glare, like that of a stage, that many men of warm temperament, strong passions, and sensitive feelings, have been obliged to play their part. And can we wonder that—sometimes sickened at the excessive and unnatural heat, sometimes dazzled by the overbearing and insolent light, and often disgusted at the falsehood of their position, and the cruelty or incompetence of their self-constituted judges—they have played it ludicrously or woefully ill?

But again, till of late, the moral nature, and moral culture of genius, were things ignored by general opinion, by critics, and even by men of genius themselves. Milton and a few others were thought lucky and strange exceptions to the general rule. The general rule was understood to be that the gifted were MOST apt to go astray—that the very light that was in them was darkness—that aberration, in a word, was the law of their goings. One of their own number said that

> 'The light that led astray,
> Was light from heaven.'

Critics, such as Hazlitt, *too* well qualified to speak of the errors
of the genius which they criticised, were not content to palliate
those by circumstances, but defended them on the dangerous
principle of necessary connexion.   The powers of high intellect
were magnified—its errors excused—and its solemn duties and
responsibilities passed over in silence.  The text, 'Where much is
given, much also shall be required,' was seldom quoted.   Genius
was regarded as a chartered libertine—not as a child of divine law
—guided, indeed, rather by the spirit than the letter, but still in
accordance with law, as well as with liberty,—as a capricious
comet, not a planet, brighter and swifter than its fellows.   Now,
we think all this is changing, and that the true judges and
friends of the poet, while admitting his fallibility, condemning
his faults, and forewarning him of his dangers, are ever ready to
contend that his gift is moral, that his power is conferred for
holy purposes, that he is a missionary of God, in a lower yet
lofty sense—and that if he desecrate his powers, he is a traitor
to their original purposes, and shall share in the condemnation
of that servant who 'was beaten with many stripes.'   But must
not the long—the written—the sung, the enacted prevalence of
a contrary opinion—of a false and low idea of genius, as a mere
minister of enjoyment, or child of impulse, irresponsible as the
wind, have tended to perpetuate the evils it extenuated, and to
render the gifted an easier prey to the temptations by which
they were begirt, and infinitely less sensible to the mischiefs
which their careless or vicious neglect of their high stewardship
was certain to produce?   Must THEY bear the whole blame?
Must not a large portion of it accrue to the age in which they
lived, and to that public opinion which they breathed like an
atmosphere?

We attribute the higher and purer efforts which genius is
*beginning* to make, both in art and in life, to the growing prevalence of a purer opinion, and of a more severe, yet charitable
criticism.   The *public*, indeed, has, as we have intimated above,
much to learn yet, in its treatment of its gifted children; but
the wiser and better among the critics have certainly been taught
a lesson by the past.   Into the judgment of literary works the
consideration of their moral purpose has now entered as an irresistible element.   And the same measure is also fast being
applied, mercifully, yet sternly, to our literary men.

Finally, it follows from these remarks, that we expect every
year to hear less and less of the aberrations of genius.   And
that for various reasons.   First, fewer and fewer will, under our
present state of culture, claim to be considered as men of genius,
and the public is less likely to be troubled with the affected
oddities of pretenders, and the *niaiseries* of monkeys run desperate.   Then, again, the profession of letters is now less likely

to be chosen by men of gifts, it is so completely overdone ; and need we say, that as a profession, its exceeding precariousness and the indefinite position it gives to the literary man have been very pernicious to his morals and his peace. Then

' The old world *is* coming right,'

and as it rights, is learning more to respect the literary character, to understand its peculiar claims, and to allow for its SINLESS infirmities. Lastly—and chief of all, men of letters are *beginning* to awaken—are feeling the strong inspiration of common sense— are using literature less as a cripple's crutch and more as a man's staff—are becoming more charitable to each other, and are sensible with a profounder conviction that literature, as well as life, is a serious thing, and that for all its ' idle words' they must give an account at the day of judgment. May this process be perfected in due time. And may all, however humble, who write, feel that they have each his special part to play in this work of perfectionment!

We are very far from being blind worshippers of Thomas Carlyle. We disapprove of much that he has written. We think, that unintentionally, he has done deep damage to the realities of faith, as well as to the ' shams' of hypocrisy. He has gone out from the one ark and has not returned like the dove with the olive leaf—but rather like the raven strayed and croaked hopelessly over the carcasses of this weltering age. And our grief, at reading one or two of his recent pamphlets (which posterity will rank with such sins of power, as the wilder works of Swift and Byron), resembled that of a son whose father had disgraced his grey hairs by a crime or outrage. But even in the depth of this undiminished feeling of sorrow, we must acknowledge that no writer, save Milton and Words- worth, has done so much in our country to restore the genuine respectability, and to proclaim the true mission of literature. In his hands and on his eloquent tongue it appears no idle toy for the amusement of the lovesick or the trifling—no mere excite- ment—but a profound, as well as beautiful reality—to be attested, if necessary, by a martyr's tears and blood, and at all events by the life and conversation of an honest and virtuous man. And he has himself so attested it. With Scott, literature was a great money-making machine. With Byron it was the trunk of a mad elephant, through which he squirted out his spite at man, his enmity at God, and his rage at even his own shadow. Carlyle has held his genius as a trust—has sought to unite it to his religion (whatever *that* may be)—has expressed it in the language of a determined life—and has made, by the power of his example, many to go and do likewise. If he has not pro-

of feeble or false defence, steeped in Germanism, and suspected of infidelity, with a name that had become, through the unbelief of one who bore it, a symbol of infamy, and with a style which deliberately and fiercely set common criticism at defiance, has waxed into one of the most influential and energetic rulers of the intellect of the nineteenth century.

While reading Hartley Coleridge's life, we have been often grieved, but never for a moment have been tempted to anger. There is so much bonhomie, so much unaffected oddity, he is such a queer being, such a *character*, in short, that you laugh more than you cry, and wonder more than you laugh. The judge would be a severe one who could keep his gravity while trying him. One mischief, too, which often attends faulty men of genius is wanting in him. He has not turned his ' diseases into commodities'—paraded his vices as if they were virtues, nor sought to circulate their virus. He is, as the old divines were wont to say, a ' *sensible* sinner,' and lies so prostrate that none will have the heart to trample on him. His vices, too, were so peculiarly interwoven with his idiosyncrasy, which was to the last degree peculiar, that they can find no imitators. When vice seems ludicrous and contemptible, few follow it : it is only when covered with the gauzy veil of sentimentalism, or when deliberately used as a foil to set off brilliant powers, that it exerts an attraction dangerously compounded of its native charm, and the splendours which shine beside it. Men who are disposed to copy the sins of a gifted, popular, and noble poet like Byron, and who, gazing at his sun-like beams, absorb his spots into their darkened and swimming eyes, can only look with mockery, pity, and avoidance upon the slips of an odd little man, drivelling amid the hedgerows and ditches of the lake country, even although his accomplishments were great, his genius undoubted, and his name Coleridge.

His nature was, indeed, intensely singular. One might fancy him extracted from his father's side, while he slept, and *dreamed*. He was like an embodied dream of that mighty wizard. He had not the breadth, the length, or the height of S. T. Coleridge's mind, but he had much of his subtlety, his learning, his occasional sweetness, and his tremulous tenderness. He was never, and yet always a child. The precocity he displayed was amazing —and precocious, and nothing more, he continued to the end. His life was a perpetual promise to *be*—a rich unexpanded bud —while his father's was a perpetual promise to *do*—a flower without adequate fruit. It was no wonder that when the father first saw his child his far-stretching eye was clouded with sorrow as he thought, If I—a whole, such as has seldom been created, have had difficulty in standing alone, how can this part of myself ?

of feeble or false defence, steeped in Germanism, and suspected of infidelity, with a name that had become, through the unbelief of one who bore it, a symbol of infamy, and with a style which deliberately and fiercely set common criticism at defiance, has waxed into one of the most influential and energetic rulers of the intellect of the nineteenth century.

While reading Hartley Coleridge's life, we have been often grieved, but never for a moment have been tempted to anger. There is so much bonhomie, so much unaffected oddity, he is such a queer being, such a *character*, in short, that you laugh more than you cry, and wonder more than you laugh. The judge would be a severe one who could keep his gravity while trying him. One mischief, too, which often attends faulty men of genius is wanting in him. He has not turned his 'diseases into commodities'—paraded his vices as if they were virtues, nor sought to circulate their virus. He is, as the old divines were wont to say, a '*sensible* sinner,' and lies so prostrate that none will have the heart to trample on him. His vices, too, were so peculiarly interwoven with his idiosyncrasy, which was to the last degree peculiar, that they can find no imitators. When vice seems ludicrous and contemptible, few follow it: it is only when covered with the gauzy veil of sentimentalism, or when deliberately used as a foil to set off brilliant powers, that it exerts an attraction dangerously compounded of its native charm, and the splendours which shine beside it. Men who are disposed to copy the sins of a gifted, popular, and noble poet like Byron, and who, gazing at his sun-like beams, absorb his spots into their darkened and swimming eyes, can only look with mockery, pity, and avoidance upon the slips of an odd little man, drivelling amid the hedgerows and ditches of the lake country, even although his accomplishments were great, his genius undoubted, and his name Coleridge.

His nature was, indeed, intensely singular. One might fancy him extracted from his father's side, while he slept, and *dreamed*. He was like an embodied dream of that mighty wizard. He had not the breadth, the length, or the height of S. T. Coleridge's mind, but he had much of his subtlety, his learning, his occasional sweetness, and his tremulous tenderness. He was never, and yet always a child. The precocity he displayed was amazing —and precocious, and nothing more, he continued to the end. His life was a perpetual promise to *be*—a rich unexpanded bud —while his father's was a perpetual promise to *do*—a flower without adequate fruit. It was no wonder that when the father first saw his child his far-stretching eye was clouded with sorrow as he thought, If I—a whole, such as has seldom been created, have had difficulty in standing alone, how can this part of myself?

of feeble or false defence, steeped in Germanism, and suspected of infidelity, with a name that had become, through the unbelief of one who bore it, a symbol of infamy, and with a style which deliberately and fiercely set common criticism at defiance, has waxed into one of the most influential and energetic rulers of the intellect of the nineteenth century.

While reading Hartley Coleridge's life, we have been often grieved, but never for a moment have been tempted to anger. There is so much bonhomie, so much unaffected oddity, he is such a queer being, such a *character*, in short, that you laugh more than you cry, and wonder more than you laugh. The judge would be a severe one who could keep his gravity while trying him. One mischief, too, which often attends faulty men of genius is wanting in him. He has not turned his ' diseases into commodities'—paraded his vices as if they were virtues, nor sought to circulate their virus. He is, as the old divines were wont to say, a ' *sensible* sinner,' and lies so prostrate that none will have the heart to trample on him. His vices, too, were so peculiarly interwoven with his idiosyncrasy, which was to the last degree peculiar, that they can find no imitators. When vice seems ludicrous and contemptible, few follow it: it is only when covered with the gauzy veil of sentimentalism, or when deliberately used as a foil to set off brilliant powers, that it exerts an attraction dangerously compounded of its native charm, and the splendours which shine beside it. Men who are disposed to copy the sins of a gifted, popular, and noble poet like Byron, and who, gazing at his sun-like beams, absorb his spots into their darkened and swimming eyes, can only look with mockery, pity, and avoidance upon the slips of an odd little man, drivelling amid the hedgerows and ditches of the lake country, even although his accomplishments were great, his genius undoubted, and his name Coleridge.

His nature was, indeed, intensely singular. One might fancy him extracted from his father's side, while he slept, and *dreamed*. He was like an embodied dream of that mighty wizard. He had not the breadth, the length, or the height of S. T. Coleridge's mind, but he had much of his subtlety, his learning, his occasional sweetness, and his tremulous tenderness. He was never, and yet always a child. The precocity he displayed was amazing —and precocious, and nothing more, he continued to the end. His life was a perpetual promise to *be*—a rich unexpanded bud —while his father's was a perpetual promise to *do*—a flower without adequate fruit. It was no wonder that when the father first saw his child his far-stretching eye was clouded with sorrow as he thought, If I—a whole, such as has seldom been created, have had difficulty in standing alone, how can this part of myself?

duced a yet broader and more permanent effect—if Carlylism, as a system, is fast weakening and dying away—if the young minds of the age are beginning to crave something better than a creed with no articles, a gospel of negations, a faith with no forms, a hope with no foundations, a Christianity without facts, (like a man with life and blood, but without limbs!) the fault lies in the system, and not in the author of it. Although, to this also we are tempted to attribute his well-known disgust *latterly* at literature. He has tried to form his own sincere love and prosecution of it into a religion, and has failed. And why? Literature is only a subjective, and not an objective reality. It is made to adorn and explain religion—but no sincerity of prosecution, or depth of insight, can change it into a religion itself. *That* must have not only an inward significance, but an outward sign, more vital and lasting than the Nature of the Poet. This the Christian finds in Jesus, and the glorious facts connected with him. But Carlyle, with all his deep earnestness, and purity of life, has become, we fear, a worshipper without a God, a devotee with the object of the devotion extinct—a strong swimmer in a Dead Sea, where no arm can cleave the salt and sluggish waters—and although he seems to despise the mere adorer of beauty, yet nothing else does he adore, and nothing else has he hitherto taught, but this, that one may worship no distinctly objective Deity, and be, nevertheless, a sincere, worthy, and high-minded man. But he has left the questions unanswered: Will such a faith produce results on the generality of men—will it *stand?* and, although it may so far satisfy the conscience as to produce in one man, or a few like unto him, the satisfaction of sincerity, can it produce the perseverance of action, the patience of hope, and the energy of faith, which have worked, and are working, in thousands and millions of Christian men—alike high and humble, rich and poor, ignorant and refined? Still, great should be the praise of a man who has redeemed literature from degradation, and changed it into a noble, if not a thoroughly religious thing, by the sheer force of genius, and rugged sincerity.

From Carlyle, thus casually, but not irrelevantly introduced, to Hartley Coleridge, is a steep descent, not so much in point of mind, as in point of manhood, will, conduct, and fortune. We must not pursue the comparison of two persons who do not stand on the same plane, farther than to notice how the son of a poet, the inheritor of his genius, early patronized, and endowed with a fellowship, from an infantine weakness and want of self-control became a wreck, while the son of an obscure mason in an obscure Scottish village, without patronage, without any gift that might be called popular, early the object of abusive attack, and

of feeble or false defence, steeped in Germanism, and suspected
of infidelity, with a name that had become, through the unbelief
of one who bore it, a symbol of infamy, and with a style which
deliberately and fiercely set common criticism at defiance, has
waxed into one of the most influential and energetic rulers of
the intellect of the nineteenth century.

While reading Hartley Coleridge's life, we have been often
grieved, but never for a moment have been tempted to anger.
There is so much bonhomie, so much unaffected oddity, he is
such a queer being, such a *character*, in short, ·that you laugh
more than you cry, and wonder more than you laugh.   The
judge would be a severe one who could keep his gravity while
trying him.   One mischief, too, which often attends faulty men
of genius is wanting in him.   He has not turned his ' diseases
into commodities'—paraded his vices as if they were virtues,
nor sought to circulate their virus.   He is, as the old divines
were wont to say, a ' *sensible* sinner,' and lies so prostrate that
none will have the heart to trample on him.   His vices, too,
were so peculiarly interwoven with his idiosyncrasy, which was
to the last degree peculiar, that they can find no imitators.
When vice seems ludicrous and contemptible, few follow it : it
is only when covered with the gauzy veil of sentimentalism, or
when deliberately used as a foil to set off brilliant powers, that
it exerts an attraction dangerously compounded of its native
charm, and the splendours which shine beside it.   Men who are
disposed to copy the sins of a gifted, popular, and noble poet
like Byron, and who, gazing at his sun-like beams, absorb his
spots into their darkened and swimming eyes, can only look
with mockery, pity, and avoidance upon the slips of an odd
little man, drivelling amid the hedgerows and ditches of the lake
country, even although his accomplishments were great, his
genius undoubted, and his name Coleridge.

His nature was, indeed, intensely singular.   One might fancy
him extracted from his father's side, while he slept, and *dreamed*.
He was like an embodied dream of that mighty wizard.   He
had not the breadth, the length, or the height of S. T. Coleridge's
mind, but he had much of his subtlety, his learning, his occasional sweetness, and his tremulous tenderness.   He was never,
and yet always a child.   The precocity he displayed was amazing
—and precocious, and nothing more, he continued to the end.
His life was a perpetual promise to *be*—a rich unexpanded bud
—while his father's was a perpetual promise to *do*—a flower
without adequate fruit.   It was no wonder that when the father
first saw his child his far-stretching eye was clouded with sorrow as
he thought, If I—a whole, such as has seldom been created, have
had difficulty in standing alone, how can this part of myself ?

If a frail tendency, running across my being, has damaged me, what is to become of one whose name is Frailty?'  Some such thought was apparently in his prophetic mind when he wrote the sonnet beginning with

'Charles, my slow heart was only sad,' &c.

Nor did the future history of the child belie the augury of this poetic sigh of a fond, yet fearing parent, over the extracted, embodied frailty and fineness of his own being.

Indeed, a circle of evil auguries surrounded the childhood of little Hartley.   The calm, quiet eye of Wordsworth surveyed the sports of the child, and finding them those of no common infant, he wrote the poem to ' H. C., six years old,' where he says—

'Thou art a dew-drop which the morn brings forth,
Ill-fitted to sustain unkindly shocks,
Or to be trailed along the soiling earth.'

His power of youthful fancy and language was wonderful. Not even Scott's story-telling faculty was equal to his.  He delighted in recounting to his brother and companions, not a series of tales, but ' one continuous tale, regularly evolved, and possessing a real unity, enchaining the attention of his auditors for a space of years.'  ' This enormous romance, far exceeding in length the compositions of Calprenede, Scudery, or Richardson, though delivered without premeditation, had a progressive story with many turns and complications, with salient points recurring at intervals, with a suspended interest varying in intensity, and occasionally wrought up to a very high pitch, and at length a final catastrophe and conclusion.'  While constructing this he was little more than twelve years of age.

A *curiosity*, Hartley Coleridge commenced life by being—and a curiosity, somewhat battered and soiled, he continued to the end.   His peculiarity lay in such a combination of wonderful powers and wonderful weaknesses, of the mind of a man, the heart of a child, and the body of a dwarf, of purposes proud and high, and habits mean and low—as has seldom been witnessed. The wild disorganization produced by such a medley of contradictory qualities, no discipline, no fortunate conjuncture of circumstances, nothing, perhaps, but death or miracle could have reconciled.   He was not *deranged*—but he was *disarranged* in the most extraordinary degree.   And such dark disarrangements are sometimes more hopeless than madness itself.   There is nothing for them but that they be taken down, and cast into the new mould of the grave.

This original tendency and formation are thus described by his brother: ' He had a certain infirmity of will—the specific evil of his life.   His sensibility was intense, and he had not wherewithal to control it. He could not open a letter without trembling. He shrank from mental pain—he was beyond measure impatient of constraint. He was liable to paroxysms of rage, often the disguise of pity, self-accusation, or other painful emotion—anger it could hardly be called—during which he bit his arm or finger violently. He yielded, as it were unconsciously, to slight temptations, slight in themselves, and slight to him, as if swayed by a mechanical impulse apart from his own volition. It looked like an organic defect—a congenital imperfection.'

'Of such materials wretched men are made.'

And so it fared with poor Hartley Coleridge. Up, indeed, to the time (1814) when he left school, he seems to have been as happy as most schoolboys are—nay, happier than most, in constant intercourse with Mr. Wordsworth, carrying on his English studies in his library at Allanbank, in the vale of Grasmere, and having become acquainted with John Wilson, then residing at his beautiful seat, Elleray, on the banks of Windermere, who became from that time, and continued to the last, one of his kindest friends. Through Mr. Southey's active intervention, he was sent to Merton College, Oxford. His curriculum there was at first distinguished. If inferior in scholarship to many, he yielded to none in general knowledge, in genius, and, above all, in conversation. Ultimately he gained a fellowship in Oriel, with high distinction. But his powers of table-talk became snares to him, and at the close of his probationary year he ' was judged to have forfeited his fellowship on the ground mainly of intemperance.' Great efforts were made by his father and others to reverse the sentence—but in vain. His ruin was now only a question of time. He repaired to London, but the precarious life of a man of letters was fitted to nurse instead of checking his morbid tendencies and unhappy habits. He next returned to the Lake country, commenced a school in conjunction with another gentleman, and even talked of entering into holy orders. But nothing would prosper with him. His school dwindled away, and he was reduced to make a scrambling livelihood by contributing to periodicals; domesticated the while at Grasmere, in the house of a farmer's widow. Various attempts were made, ever and anon, to make him useful—by taking him to Leeds to edit a biographical work; assisting a friend in teaching a school at Ledbergh, &c.; but all in vain. To Grasmere he as uniformly found his way back, to resume his erratic existence. In 1845, his mother's death brought him in an annuity, which placed him on a footing of complete independence. During all this time he was employed fitfully in literary effort, wrote poems, contributed papers to 'Blackwood's Magazine,' and delivered occasional addresses to literary societies. He was gentle, amiable, frank ; and, notwithstanding his oddities and errors, was a great favourite with all classes in Cumberland. He was, as a Churchman and politician, liberal, almost radical, in his opinions. He was a daily reader of his Bible. To the last, he struggled sore to unloose the accursed bands of indolence and sensualism which bound him; but to little purpose.

At length, in the beginning of 1849, he departed this life, after giving various evidences of a penitent spirit. He lies now in a spot, beside which, in little more than a year, the dust of one—alike, but oh, how different!—Wordsworth, was to be consigned. He was in his fifty-second year. His 'coffin, at the funeral, was light as that of a child.' 'It was,' says his brother, 'a winter's day when he was carried to his last earthly home, cold, but fine, with a few slight scuds of sleet and gleams of sunshine, one of which greeted us as we entered Grasmere, and another smiled brightly through the church-window. May it rest upon his memory!'

Many and melancholy are the reflections which crowd on us as we close this sad and mysterious page in the history of genius, but we will indulge in only a word. We are far from being disposed entirely to palliate the conduct of the departed : he was deeply to blame. In passionate language, in burning tears, he often owned this while on earth ; and who can conceive in what terms he would own it *now ?* But if we are to form a fair judgment of the whole case, we must remember that he had no father during the most critical portion of his opening years, which synchronized with the very depth of S. T. Coleridge's eclipse in the cloud of opium—that his father's example, probably, proved rather a pattern than a beacon—that the son was constitutionally morbid—that his precarious and dependent position, his tenderness of character, his very face and figure, debarred him from what seems to have been the warmest wish of his heart, a suitable female companion, and thus, as his brother expressly states, increased his native melancholy—that the proceedings against him at Oriel seem to have been sufficiently summary—that he did, though in vain, conscientiously struggle against his foe—and that, amid all his lamentable excesses in one respect, his heart, and temper, and purity, and simplicity, as well as his intellect and genius, continued to live, if not to bring forth their proper amount of fruit. Had he succeeded in his contest, with such a temperament as he possessed, and such circumstances as begirt him, he had been one of the greatest of moral heroes : as it is, we deem him hardly an offender like his father, whose constitution originally was of a far more powerful and manlike mould, although his errors were less glaring and ruinous ; and think that more truly than Byron might he tell any one of his severe judges,—

'All my faults perchance thou knowest ;
All my *madness none can know.*'

But we pass from the ungrateful, though necessary, task of recording the faults, to look to the literary results of his life. His prose works have but newly appeared. We cannot speak of them as a whole. We remember two papers in ' Blackwood ;' one on the character of Hamlet, which struck us at the time as much more *true* than that famous passage of Goethe's (where, as in the well-known story, the Hamlet is 'omitted by special desire') ; but we have forgotten Hartley Coleridge's theory. The other was entitled, ' Shakspere a Tory and a Gentleman ;' which might easily have been answered, and that, too, best by poor Hartley himself, in another on ' Shakspere a Radical and a Man.' But it is with his poems that we have now briefly to deal.

Now these certainly do not constitute that fine whole, for which, in our paper on Joanna Baillie, we were seeking through our recent poetical literature in vain. They are the orts of fragments. They consist of all kinds of occasional poetry, such as ' album verses,' ' Valentines,' thoughts and fancies, impromptus, miscellaneous ' pieces,' and sonnets thickening upon sonnets. The largest and most peculiar of them is ' Prometheus ;' but it, too, is only a larger fragment. And not only are they fragmentary, but most of them are imitative. ' Lines suggested by —— ' is a title which would suit almost every poem in the volume. We trace, especially, the shadow of his neighbour Wordsworth, at once provoking and overwhelming rivalry. We have seen a Highlandman talking, walking, and swelling beside his favourite Ben, till he seemed strutting in emulation of the mountain, and we could not choose but laugh. Thus, in many of his sonnets, Hartley subjects himself to mortifying comparisons. He seems even *literally* to have ' Wordsworth in his eye,' as if from his window he saw the bard in the distance ' murmuring to the running brooks a music sweeter than their own,' and must try to shape the language of his inarticulate lips into song ! Prometheus, too, was unquestionably suggested by Shelley's poem. His biographer, indeed, says that Shelley *afterwards* took up the subject, but what are the facts ? H. Coleridge's ' Prometheus ' was written in 1820 ; Shelley's was written and published in 1819.

But while no one of his poems can be counted either great or, in the highest sense, creative, they abound in beauties of thought and language. One is astonished at the cheerful and sunny

spirit shed over many of them.   And even when sad, their grief
is chastened, manly, and subdued.   He never pines, or whines,
or cries out, 'I do well to be angry;' but knowing right certainly
that he has been the 'careful pilot of his proper woe,' is equally
careful how he expresses it.   We feel, had he but possessed a
grain or two of self-control, what a happy chirrupping songster
he had been—another Herrick, or Suckling, or Walton.   Of all
the various series of poems bundled up in his two volumes, we
prefer that 'on birds, insects, and flowers.'   The conception is
his most original one; the execution is, throughout, of sustained
excellence, and there was something in the subject very congenial to his better nature.   He retained to the last, as Wordsworth had predicted—

> ' A young lamb's-heart among the full-grown flocks.'

And in these little poems we hear a young lamb's voice, too,
bleating out praise and love to such small creatures of the
Almighty as crickets and larks, nightingales and cuckoos!   His
sonnet on this last mysterious bird ranks with the poem attributed
to Logan, and with that by Wordsworth.   Logan, or Bruce, has
beautifully expressed this bird's everlasting connexion with the
spring.   'Old Pan' has, with a deeper penetration, uttered the
mystery and terror which surround her to the youthful fancy, as
he asks—

> ' O, cuckoo, shall I call thee bird,
>     Or but a wandering voice?'

And Hartley Coleridge translates her limited note into poetry—

> ' Methinks thou art a type of some recluse,
>     Whose notes of adoration never vary;
> Who of the gift of speech will make no use,
>     But ever to repeat her Ave Mary.
> Two syllables alone to thee are given,
> What mean they in the dialect of heaven?'

None of the three is the cuckoo of the others; and between
them they exhaust the poetry of the bird.   We are tempted to
add a sentence from a journal kept by Dr. Thomas Brown.   'The
name of the cuckoo has generally been considered as a very
pure instance of imitative appellation.   But in giving that name,
we have most unjustly defrauded the poor bird of its very small
variety of sound.   The second syllable is not a mere echo of the
first; it is the sound reversed, like the reading of a sotadic line;
and, to preserve the strictness of imitation, we should give it
the name of Ook-koo.'   A lady to whom we quoted this remark
of Dr. Brown's, assured us that the real sound is 'ku-hu'—the
second syllable being pronounced by the bird softer.   So much
for this bird of April.

Next to this series of sweet lamb-like bleatings to the kindred creatures around him in the wilderness, we may specify as among his best his verses ' to a Nautilus,' ' a Brother's Love to his Sister ' (a poem with a beautiful train of ' virgin ' thought, imperfectly adorned); ' Address to certain Gold-fishes' (which beats with the genuine ' lamb's heart,' as the eye of the perpetual child contemplates the gambols of those genii of gold); and ' To a very young Nun,' from which, as suited to the times, we beg leave to quote the following lines :—

> ' Yes, yes ! thy face, thine eyes, thy closed lips, prove
> Thou wert intended to be loved and love.
> Poor maiden ! victim of the *vilest craft*,
> At which e'er Moloch grinned or Belial laughed,
> May all thy aimless wishes be forgiven,
> And all thy sighs be registered in heaven,
> And God his mercy and his love impart,
> To what thou shouldst have been, and what thou art.'

Whether in any circumstances H. Coleridge could have elaborated a great original poem, is very questionable. His ' Prometheus ' furnishes no adequate base for the solution of the problem. It is a brilliant, but broken-off, misty, and unequal production ; nor does the author seem to have thrown his *heart* into it ; and hence a frosted Prometheus among eternal snows ! It is very different with the passionate and half-insane production of Shelley, who says Derwent Coleridge justly ' brought to it vehement impulse, exhaustless fancy, the music of the spheres, and a diction glittering as sunlight in the mist of a waterfall.' But he adds, with like truth, ' he did *not* bring a clear insight, or a sane judgment, and his conception or adaptation of the *mythus*, stripped of its gorgeous dress, may be called vulgar, at once false and obvious.' We refer our readers, for more information, if not light, on this grand Promethean mystery, to two recent papers, one in the (unhappily defunct) ' Palladium ' for January, 1851, and another in the ' Éclectic ' for October, 1850.

We cannot then be justified in predicting immortality, or even long life, or even the prosperity of a few years, to the poetical works of Hartley Coleridge. They have beauties ; but they are hardly of the perennial sort. The strange story and character of the man, supply at present an odd and curious frontispiece. But the poems themselves have neither the vitality of absolute origination, nor that of strong purpose, nor that of a unique and indivisible structure, nor that of consummate art and elaborate polish. They are neither more nor less than the elegant amusements of an accomplished and unhappy man, and, as such, are destined to slow and certain oblivion ; or if they escape this fate, it will be mainly owing to the interest posterity must attach

to every thing and person connected with S. T. Coleridge—one
of the great spiritual potentates of the age.   The day of bishops
and of popes is well-nigh over, but it may be drowned in the
glory of a better day, when the memory of the kings of thought
—who rule us from their urns—shall be preserved with jealous
care, and worshipped with almost Popish veneration ; and when
this noble feeling shall, in its wide sweep, extend, perhaps, to
all their works, however inferior, and to all their sons, although
but the shadows more strongly, or more faintly described, of
their giant parents.

Nor, while Hartley Coleridge was unquestionably an inheritor
of a portion of his father's mind, can the author of this biography,
prefixed to the poems, be deemed unworthy of the world-
famous name he bears.   It is, in all respects, highly creditable
to him—to his judgment—to his taste—to his learning—to his
power of writing his mother tongue—to his comprehension and
sagacity of thought—to his reverence for his father's memory,
and to his regardful pity and sorrowing respect for his ill-fated
brother.   And we shall wait, with considerable interest, for the
conclusion of the truly fraternal task, which he purposes in ' a
collection of the author's miscellaneous writings,' as well as in a
new edition of the ' Northern Worthies, with additional notes,
some of them from the pen of S. T. Coleridge.'

---

Since this Review was in proof, we have received, and read,
most of the ' Essays and Marginalia.'   They are far more interesting than the poems—less suggested by others, and more
suggestive to us.   We see in them the riches of an irregular,
but extensive learning—great critical sagacity—a refreshing independence of thought—and all his usual vividness of fancy.
The constant *healthiness* of taste, mind, and morality, is, considering his life and habits, the most curious characteristic of the
whole.   His essay on Hamlet develops a view which is, in a
great measure, our own, which we had formed on independent
grounds, and hope soon to develop in another place.   His paper
is written with great power and mastery.   But, perhaps, the most
interesting portion of the book is the Marginalia—those slipshod
sentences which he was in the habit of inscribing on his books.
These ' fly-leaves,' in his case—would it had been so with all his
father's still more profuse and precious deposits—have been
arrested, and are here fixed in a permanent form.   The best are
those on Shakspere and on good old John Brown of Hadding-
ton's Dictionary of the Bible.   A copy of this rather obsolete
work came, somehow or other, into poor Hartley's possession—
and it is almost ludicrous to find him, with great gravity and

occasional wrath, refuting opinions of the excellent old Burgher, which all Biblical scholars had abandoned fifty years before. Still the notes are full of interest and learning—although there occur expressions, now and then, which would have made honest John aghast. The notes on Shakspere are remarkably ingenious. The work altogether is a characteristic and readable one—and, as such, we cordially commend it.

Art. II.—1. *The New York Independent, November and December,* 1850; *January,* 1851.

2. *The New York Weekly Tribune, April,* 1851.

3. *The Anti-Slavery Reporter, January to April,* 1851.

4. *Opinions of American Ministers on Slavery and the Fugitive Slave Bill.* Selected from recent American Publications.

THE United States Congress of 1850 promises to acquire a posthumous fame in more ways than one. Protracted to an inordinate length by the mutual recriminations of contending parties, who would not, or could not, agree on the terms of the Clay Compromise, it was abruptly ended by the virtual acceptance, both in the House of Representatives and in the Senate, of all the substantial measures contemplated in that Compromise. Among these, are the admission of the free-soil California as the thirty-first state of the Union; the admission of New Mexico and Utah as independent territories; the abolition of the slave traffic in the district of Columbia; and, on the other hand, in the so-called 'adjustment' is the settlement of the boundary of Texas, the surrender of 95,000 square miles of free territory, and the grant of 10,000,000 dollars to that state in compensation for a confessedly unfounded claim preferred by it to the territory of New Mexico; and last of all is the Fugitive Slave Act.

President Fillmore, in his message at the opening of the present Congress, set his seal of approval to the passing of this series of measures. He considers them ' as a settlement in principle and substance—a final settlement of the dangerous and exciting subjects which they embraced;' and maintains that, ' in their mutual dependence and connexion, they formed a system of compromise the most conciliatory and best for the entire country that could be obtained from conflicting sectional interests and opinions;' a system viewed by him ' as the best, if not the only, means of restoring peace and quiet to the country, and maintaining inviolate the integrity of the Union.' It appears, however, that such peaceful results as President Fillmore and his Cabinet contemplate are not likely to ensue.   California has, indeed, been admitted as a *free state*, and the Union is not dissolved, notwithstanding all the blustering threats of Mr. Foote and other Southern men ; and by this admission the balance of power in the Senate between the slave and the free states has been destroyed.   The *slave-trade* has been abolished in Columbia ; though the very mention of such a thing, a few years ago, was forbidden in Congress.   The free states have shown much forbearance, to say the least—if, indeed, they have not compromised their principles as honest citizens, in respect of the Texan measures—and they have seen their will overruled in respect of the territories which, so far as federal action is concerned, are laid open to the inroads of slavery.   But the Fugitive Slave Bill contains principles so outrageous in themselves, and so opposed both to the letter and spirit of the constitution, that the man can scarcely be in his sane mind who expects that *that* measure will conduce to peace.   This bill, hurried through all its stages during the last days of a protracted session, is confessedly designed to allay the choler of Southern planters, boiling over at the admission of *free* California.   If, however, it is fitted to appease the South, it must needs exasperate the North, by compelling all citizens to form an organized press-gang to hunt down runaway slaves, and to hand over all *alleged* to be such to the men who claim them for their own.

We were not, therefore, surprised to hear that when the tidings of the passing of this bill first reached Boston, a league of freedom was organized, and the most intense feeling of sympathy manifested for the oppressed race, coupled with the resolution to shelter them, and obtain a fair trial until the law itself should be repealed.   Connecticut, Vermont, and other free States, have spoken with emphasis at the meeting of the State Conventions.   We may instance the *third* resolution adopted by the Democratic State Convention of Vermont : — ' 3. That we hereby express our unqualified disapprobation of the Fugitive from Service Bill, recently passed by Congress ; because we hold that, in some of its features, it is clearly unconstitutional, and, if not, that it is grossly tyrannical in its provisions, and tramples down all those safeguards of personal liberty which have borne the sanction of ages, and have been the chief glory of Anglo-Saxon legislation from time immemorial.'   The Northern States generally have evinced hostility to this bill, and a determination to resist its application to the utmost. On the other hand, the slave-states, seeing the excitement and opposition created by this question in the North, have threatened disunion, and even war.  Governor Floyd recommends the State Legislature of Virginia to lay 'a tax of ten per cent. upon all the products of the non-slave-holding States offered for sale within our territory,' and also, 'a tax upon foreign goods imported through non-slave-holding states, such as will offer effectual encouragement to direct importation into our own ports.'  The Georgian Convention repudiates the ordinance of 1787, claims the perpetuation of slavery in Columbia, and demands abstinence in the North from the agitation of the question of slavery.

The Mississipi Legislature has appointed a committee of fourteen members of the House, and seven of the Senate, to take such steps as may be necessary.  The governor has sent in a message asking for the immediate organization of the militia.  The Senate of South Carolina has passed a bill for a convention, and given 300,000 dollars to be applied to military purposes. It is the avowed sentiment of the Southern States 'that the repeal of the law, or any essential modification of it, is a virtual repeal of the Union.'

We confess ourselves not sorry that the professed philanthropy of the Free States will now be fully put to the test. The anomaly of their position must thus force itself prominently on their notice, the general question of slavery will be more fully discussed, and, even should the obnoxious bill not be speedily repealed, it will, ere long, become a dead letter in the statute book from the practical difficulties attending its execution.

A strong Union party has originated with these measures of compromise, headed by the President, Messrs. Webster, Cass, Dickinson, Buchanan, and Clay, backed by the entire South, and by the mercantile interest of the North.  They have agitated with much effect in large cities like Boston and New York, and have even succeeded, for a time, in diverting popular resentment from themselves, and in bringing it to bear against the abolitionists, as though they were traitors to the Constitution. On thanksgiving day, many ministers of religion made themselves notorious by preaching sermons on the duty of implicit obedience to the powers that be, thus virtually endorsing the compromise measures, and tacitly condemning the conscientious deference paid by multitudes of enlightened and patriotic citizens to the higher law of heaven.  The 'Journal of Commerce,' the 'New York Herald,' and a large portion of the press in the Free States, have re-echoed these sentiments, and, *for a time*, the cries of Union and Federalism succeed in drowning those of Justice, Liberty, Equality, Fraternity; and, it is hoped, even by such statesmen as Daniel Webster and Henry Clay, that the Compromise will stand.  We are strangely mistaken, however, if the feelings thus attempted to be smothered, do not burst

x x 2

forth with redoubled energy when the question comes to be discussed, as it cannot but be, in Congress, and we are persuaded that every instance in which the law is sought to be enforced will tend to hasten the abolition of the entire system of slavery. It may be worth our while to consider the Fugitive Slave Act, *first* in its origin and general bearing on the constitution of the Federal Union, and, *secondly*, in the principles on which it is based, and the mode of its operation.

I. It is well known, that, in the original formation of the Union, the question of slavery was got over by a compromise, each state agreeing not to interfere with the institutions which might be prevailing at the time in the others.   The question of slavery, in the district of Columbia, over which alone the federal government had control, was left unsettled.   The debates of the Federal Convention of 1787, and the spirit of the constitution then finally adopted, indicate, however, with sufficient distinctness, that slavery was regarded, as a system, exceptional, local, and destined gradually to be abolished; at the same time, it was agreed that the question, thus excluded from national politics, was not within the province of the federal government.

As the loss by runaways from the slave-plantations was found to be very considerable, the Southerners forced a law through Congress in 1793, enacting that the master, or his agent, should be permitted to pursue, retake, and carry back his slave.   This law was, however, very inoperative in practice.

The Hon. Josiah Quincy, one of the oldest and most reputable citizens of Massachusetts declared, not long ago, that in that state no person has ever been delivered to his master under the law of 1793; and it appears, from a statement of Lord Carlisle, in his lecture at the Leeds Mechanics' Institute, that Pennsylvania and other Free States had granted a trial by jury to the retaken fugitives, until it was ruled by the Supreme Court of Justice in 1842, that the Free States were not empowered so to do. This appears to us an infringement on the independent action of the States, and has not, we believe, been submitted to. It may be well imagined that individual citizens of the Free and Slave States were constantly coming into collision on the question. The Southerners were contented with nothing less than complete silence on the subject of slavery in Congress — all petitions and memorials relating to the slave-trade in Columbia were ordered to be laid on the table unread, and never recurred to. Ministerial sanction was given to the detention of abolition papers at Charleston, and Mr. Calhoun's Gag Bill, prohibiting all postmasters from receiving or forwarding such papers, was only thrown out on the third reading. The Compromise was surely enough in itself to satisfy the South, and humiliate the North, without additional exactions and exceptions. Slavery was avowedly admitted in that Compromise as a basis for direct taxation and representation, and, according to its provisions, the slaveholders are actually entitled to send to Congress sixty representatives more than is allowed to an equal number of citizens in the North, the property in human flesh giving to those States the voice which they would have if their slaves were free citizens. We can only blush for those Free States that could thus culpably commit themselves to so iniquitous a compact. And even now, when, in spite of governments and presidents favourable to slavery, the voice of abolition has made itself heard and respected in the halls of Congress, and when, as the result, the district of Columbia is free, there is yet, on the part of the Free States, an extraordinary, and, as it appears to us, most shameful and suicidal deference shown to the bullyings of the South. We comprehend the distinction between the acts of the federal government and those of the several States. We do not implicate Maine or Vermont in the direct upholding of slavery, nor do we condemn the Republic, as a whole, for the threatened repudiations of Pennsylvania and Alabama, and the actual repudiation of Mississipi. We are aware of the plausible reason alleged for the Free States not pressing the federal government to legislate on the general question of slavery, that the commercial and social interests of the States at large are not to be put in jeopardy by a threatened dismemberment of the Union, which the agitation of this particular question might induce; but still we must aver that, where a moral principle is at stake, mere political considerations should give place. Besides, the rule has been already broken through: the federal government has taken action on the slavery question, once and again, in authorizing the operation of the Fugitive Slave Bill, which acts prospectively, be it remembered, and involves all States hereafter to be formed in the responsibility of upholding the system. The government was acting in its legitimate province to legislate, as it has wisely and well done, in the district of Columbia, but it stepped out of its proper province in sanctioning the introduction and operation of a bill which must compromise and embarrass the whole Union. In the enactment of this law, therefore, we conceive that the pact between the States in the Convention of 1787 has been palpably broken, and that the action of Congress in this case is a violation of the Constitution.

The decision of the Supreme Court of Justice in the United States, above referred to, must go for nothing with those *true* descendants of the Puritans who remember that the Court of King's Bench decided that Charles I. was authorized to levy taxes without the consent of the House of Commons,—and that it was ruled in the highest tribunal of England that Parliament had the right, in all cases whatever, to tax the colonies, without being represented.

2. Let us now inquire whether the provisions of the Fugitive Slave Act can stand the test of constitutional law.

The Act of 1793, being found, in a great degree, inoperative, the present act provides for ' the appointment by district judges of *commissioners* in each county of the several States, whose duty it shall be to issue process for the arrest of slaves, and of *assistant commissioners,* whose duty it shall be to arrest such slave. The deputy-marshal in each county is also authorized and required to serve such process. And any of the said commissioners or marshal, holding such process, may call to his aid every citizen of the county, and if such citizen shall refuse when called on, he will forfeit five hundred dollars, and if the deputy-marshal or commissioners shall fail to arrest such slave, when he has power to do so, he will forfeit one thousand dollars.' The commissioner is to receive ten dollars if a certificate is granted in favour of the claimant, and five dollars if the fugitive is discharged.

In the sixth section of the act are the words, 'And by taking, or causing such person to be taken, forthwith, before such court, judge, or commissioners, whose duty it shall be to hear and determine the case in a *summary manner.*'

This sixth section is enough in itself to condemn the whole act, and is a palpable violation of the fifth article of the Constitution, which avers that no person shall ' be deprived of life, liberty, or property, *without due process of law.*' It is equally a violation of the constitution of each free state, which guarantees personal liberty to all, unless deprived of it by ' *due course of law,*' and maintains that ' the right of trial by jury shall be inviolate.' The affidavit and bare testimony of the slaveholder arc received as sufficient evidence, and the alleged fugitive is not allowed to procure and to produce evidence to establish his freedom.*

---

* At Detroit a negro was brought before the commissioner as a fugitive slave from Tennessee. The counsel for the negro presented an affidavit, duly sworn by the former, that he was manumitted by the deed of the present claimant for 700 dollars, which the latter had received for the same, and that the deed is now in the hands of the negro's friends in Cincinnati. On this affidavit the counsel for the prisoner moves that the case be continued until the deed of emancipation can be procured, and used as evidence. The commissioner decides that the deed would be inadmissible if produced; that he has no power to inquire into any defence the negro may have against the claim, but only to determine whether the case presented, on the part of the claimant, is sufficient to entitle him to a certificate for the removal of the negro. The ' Buffalo Express' comments with reason, ' If this decision

THE FUGITIVE SLAVE ACT.

The virtual bribe, and the liability to a forfeit equivalent to the value of the fugitive, are likely to prove too much for the integrity of ordinary men. The parts of the act, however, most revolting to the feelings of Northern men, are the clauses which require all *good citizens* to aid and assist in the prompt and efficient execution of this law, whenever their services may be required, ' under heavy penalties, and those in section seven, by which it is enacted that any person who shall, in any way, directly or indirectly,' aid the fugitive in his flight, shall incur a penalty of two thousand dollars, and suffer six months' imprisonment.

monwealth to be petty informers, and to form a constabulary of slave-hunters, contrary to their most sacred convictions, and contrary to the laws of Christ. Will the Act prove to be a dead letter, or will its provisions be carried out? Time alone

justice of G
the heads of
the fugitives
charged with
it to pass th

in the New York
case in the proper light    en he says :—

' No citizen is bound to obey a law which commands *him* to INFLICT injury upon another. We must *endure*, but never *commit* wrong. . . . A law which enjoins upon a citizen the commission of a crime, and, still more, of an open, disgraceful, and flagitious crime, has violated the confidence of the citizen, and is dissolved in the court of God the moment it is enacted. . . . Liberty of conscience is but another name for liberty of resistance to legal invasions of conscience. . . . A law to make citizens the inflicters of wrongs the most fatal, for which, once committed, no patience can bring a remedy, is such an insult to moral sense and common sense that the Christianity of a land which

---

sustained, no coloured man north can be safe for a day. If the deed of freedom is annulled by the act, there will be perjuries enough to send into slavery every coloured man and woman north of Mason and Dixon's line.' Another glaring case is that of Adam Gibson, a free citizen of New Jersey, arrested, on a false pretence and without legal warrant, in Philadelphia, and hurried off to slavery in defiance of positive evidence of his freedom. At Government expense he was conveyed to Wm. Knight, of Elkton, Maryland, his alleged master, who disavowed the ownership which had been affirmed by the commissioner. But for the honesty of this planter, this free citizen would have remained a slave for life.

should tamely obey it would be a solemn mockery. What are we asked to do? To keep the compromise of the constitution by violating the fundamental declaration of the Bill of Rights.'

This strikes us as sound doctrine, and we are glad to think that such avowals are a fair expression of the feeling of a large body in the Free States. We trust that the bugbear of federalism will not succeed in overlaying the honest convictions of the freemen of the North. A *Christian*, who sends his *Christian* brother back to slavery, severing him from his domestic relations, consigning him to a savage, godless, taskmaster; to a serfdom worse to him than that of Siberia—to banishment from the sanctuary of law, from religious privileges, from the Church of which he is a member, barring from him the word of God—such a Christian, we say, belies his name, or else is Christ leagued with Belial. Would a Roman Christian betray his brother, and consign him to the lions? Let American professors judge and act accordingly. That the anti-slavery cause has received, and will yet receive, an immense impetus by the enactment of the Fugitive Slave Bill, we have not the shadow of a doubt. In the meantime, the spleen of the pro-slavery party vents itself forth with envenomed bitterness upon the friends of abolition. The 'New York Herald' has always been notorious for its hatred to the coloured race. In a number of that print, published soon after the enactment of this bill, after referring to the intense excitement of the coloured people at Detroit, and other places on the Canadian frontier, thus occasioned, it is remarked—

' We would not be at all surprised to hear of a war of extermination breaking out between the races, which will not be confined to the West, but which will spread throughout the whole of the Free States. After an agitation of twenty years, the slavery question has reached a crisis, the only crisis that could follow, and the scenes which the abolition fanatics laboured to produce in the South between the black and the white races, these are now in danger of being enacted in the Free States.'

This is significant enough from the print which on August 30, 1845, pronounced as follows:—

' That the whole of the Southern States will one day be peopled solely by a white race, and that the African races will disappear, is just as certain as that the red race which formerly occupied the States of New England, New York, and their sister communities, have faded and disappeared before the Anglo-Saxon millions who now occupy the soil. They will disappear *in the same way*, and *by a similar process** as that by which the red races have disappeared.'

---

* The italics are ours.

Compare these sentiments—'look on this picture, and on that,' and say whether the atrocious libeller is not condemned by his own mouth. Surely the guilt of Southern slave-owners is black enough already, without the infusion of this yet deeper dye. The 'Herald' is not alone, unhappily, in its ideas of the black race 'disappearing' and 'fading away,' but we cannot do such injustice to the Northern States as to believe that they would connive at such a result. The extermination of the Indian races does not surely sit so lightly on the nation's conscience that it would willingly see enacted such another scene. Then, indeed, would liberty wail for her lost children—then would the stars on the national escutcheon be emblazonments of infamy, and its stripes be darkly stained with the blood of millions of human beings. As things are now, in many Southern States, men calling themselves civilized and free, are coolly and systematically consigning millions of their fellow-creatures to a living death. We do not profess to *pronounce*, like the 'New York Herald,' on the future destinies of the coloured race, but we cannot help drawing a parallel between the bond-slaves of Egypt and the slaves of these Southern United States. 'Let my people go that they may serve me,' was the command of God to the Egyptian taskmasters, but the more his messengers remonstrated, the more galling was the yoke of bondage made. The heaviest charge that we have to bring against the slaveholders of the Southern States is, that they will not let these millions serve their God; they will not let them know, if they can help it, that they have immortal souls. They withhold from them education, and then say, How ignorant! how much below the white man in the scale of being! They bar out religion, and exclaim, How wanting they are in natural affection and moral principle! If they longer delay to do what justice, and what the God of justice, demands, these bond-slaves may have their exodus—their cruel oppressions may, at length, exceed the limits of endurance, and, as a nation, encouraged by the sympathies of all true sons of freedom, they may unite to throw off the yoke, and seek a settlement elsewhere; of their own free will, they may go forth, guided by Divine Providence, to found a noble community, and to testify, it may be, to all the nations, How their intellectual and moral capacities have been belied. The soundest policy of the several States is to prepare at once for an event which *must* sooner or later transpire—the complete emancipation of the negro race—and thus to preserve the Republic from the danger of sudden outbreaks, if not from a Helot war.

The question of emancipation is not so simple as might at first sight be imagined. It is possible that the negroes themselves would suffer by immediate emancipation, if some other measures which the case requires, and which justice enforces, were not contemporaneously adopted. Even in the tropical climates of Alabama and Louisiana, the labour of the whites is found to be the most profitable. In these states labour constitutes the wealth, and they would probably be greatly and speedily enriched by the improvement of the *quality* of labour which the abolition of slavery would induce. The blacks have, at present, nearly the monopoly of labour; and it appears that in several states, Virginia for instance, frequent strikes occur among the white workmen, who insist on the discharge of all (free) coloured people in their master's employ. To such a pitch has this jealousy been raised in Georgia, that, by positive statute of the State, coloured mechanics and masons, slave or free, are prohibited from making contracts for the erection or repairs of buildings. It would thus appear that immediate emancipation might create new miseries for the blacks, unless protected for a while from white competition. It seems, from recent accounts, that the Southern States are preparing to get rid of the difficulty occasioned by the presence of *free* coloured people, in a very summary manner. In the recent Convention of Virginia, it was formally proposed to expel the free people of colour from the State; and Governor Seabrook, in his message to the legislature of South Carolina, recommends a similar course. We should entertain more sanguine hopes for the speedy advent of emancipation, were it not for the extraordinary prejudice which prevails even in the Free States against all people of colour. The slightest taint of African blood suffices to ostracise a man. This repugnance is shown not only in their exclusion from public offices, and the commonest rights of citizenship, but in social life. They must dine at separate tables, travel in separate conveyances, worship in separate conventicles; and now, by the operation of the Fugitive Slave Act, are liable to be arrested on mere suspicion, on the bare statement of two interested pursuivants, without the benefit of Habeas Corpus or trial by jury. Coloured children are taught in separate schools from those of the privileged class, as if to perpetuate the distinction between the races in every succeeding generation. It is the fear of amalgamation which accounts, in great measure, for the inferior social position of the blacks. The repugnance to intermarriage can scarcely be exaggerated. 'They shrink from it,' says Sir Charles Lyell, 'as a European noble would do if told that his grandchild would intermarry with the direct descendant of one of his menial servants. . . . That the attainder of blood should outlast all trace of African features betrays a feeling allied to the most extravagant aristocratic pride of the feudal age.' Under such circumstances it is no wonder that the Colonization scheme has been revived. In the Session of the United States Senate, on the 15th of January last, Mr. Clay presented three petitions from Indiana, praying that Congress would adopt some steps to remove all those free coloured people in the States who were willing to go to Africa, and that provision be made for their support for one year after their arrival there. The honourable gentleman, in supporting the petitions, expressed his conviction that there was no project of the age equal to this, and that ' nothing could be done for their relief, except to transport them to the home of their ancestors.' *Nothing, indeed?* A philanthropy more mawkish and flimsy than that of this Colonization scheme can hardly be conceived, for not only have former attempts of the kind proved utter failures, but experience attests that negro families removed to Liberia are cut off by fever almost as rapidly as Europeans. And as to Mr. Clay's other proposal to put down the African slave-trade, let him first shut up the *home* markets of Virginia and Carolina. All such legislation is wide of the mark. Why not grapple boldly with the evil, and deal *justly* by the coloured race, whether slave or free ; for we do maintain, that these proscribed millions have as good a foothold on the soil, and as good a title to the name and privileges of *Americans,* as white men sprung from a European stock.

It seems by the latest accounts that the Union party are, for the present, carrying all before them in the Northern States ; and that the dread of disunion is so great, that even the enormity of the Fugitive Slave Act is overlooked. The position is a very grave one, it must be owned ; but if union can be purchased at no less dear a rate than by perpetuating slavery as a *national* institution, we can see but one alternative for an honourable state to follow. One principal result of pandering to Southern views is that of the spirit of aggrandisement ; the craving for extended territory and glory has taken strong possession of the national mind. This suits well the cupidity and duplicity of the slave-breeders and slave-owners. Why was Florida purchased, if not mainly to subserve the objects of slavery—that so ready a refuge might be withheld from the fugitives? Why was Texas overrun and forcibly possessed, except as a convenient field for the extension and perpetuation of slavery? It will be, indeed, a melancholy instance of the selfishness of man in the most favourable circumstances of enlightenment and civilization, if this worship of territory, of gold, and of glory, should, when weighed in the scales with a union of smaller dimensions, but purer principles, be found to prevail. But this we cannot bring ourselves to believe. Under present circumstances, we cannot understand with what justice the United States can be called a

Free Republic, while abolitionists dare not tread the soil of Southern States, and while mobs of *gentlemen* can be found to pack anti-slavery meetings in the Northern States, and to enact such scenes as Faneuil Hall has witnessed in August, 1835, and November, 1850. In the cradle of American liberty, that sacred name has been grossly outraged by her perjured sons. We believe most firmly that the Federal Union cannot be maintained but with the extinction of slavery; and when the public mind of the Free States shall be brought calmly to consider the case, we think that this conviction will gain rapid ground.

When the abolition movement attains to such a head that an emancipation bill shall be introduced, and strongly backed in Congress, the last desperate cry of the Slave States will be for compensation. The slave-planting States will scarcely need it, if free white labour is really more profitable than that of slaves; and the slave-breeding States, so flagrant is their guilt, surely do not deserve it. No doubt, however, to perpetuate the Federal Union, compensation would be made; and in the national treasury are funds available for the purpose, which can be indefinitely increased by a slight addition of rental on the immense public lands. Matters of detail could be adjusted, were the principle once recognised—that after such a date, ' all slaves and all children of slaves shall be free.'

A fearful responsibility rests upon the churches of America. Whatever may be said by their apologists, their supineness constitutes the strength of the slave system. They might bring it to a speedy termination, and nothing prevents their doing so but the corrupting influence of the associations in which they stand. They have yielded to the power which they ought to have controlled. Public opinion, which they should have moulded, has, unhappily, moulded them. The salt has lost its savour—the light has been hid under a bushel; and it has resulted, in consequence, that the rankest vice of American society finds an asylum within precincts which ought to have been too hallowed even for its momentary presence. It is in vain for Americans to tell us that we do not understand the matter; that we are ignorant of the peculiarities of their political institutions, and see not the tendency of the measures we advocate. We deny all this. There is no such mystery in the case as their assertions imply; and the acrimony with which these assertions are frequently made, betray their own mistrust and conscious weakness. The case is no further difficult than a thousand others in which secular interests are apparently opposed to moral principle. Apart from such interests, the matter would not admit of a moment's doubt. It would be clear, simple, and easily-determined —a case in which the rule of Christian duty would be instantly

discerned, and where all the energies of the Christian Church would combine for its enforcement. That such is not the fact, constitutes one of the most mournful incidents in the chequered page of the Church's history. We need not wonder at the sale of Indulgences being defended by the Papacy, at Calvin concurring in the martyrdom of Servetus, at Cranmer urging the youthful Edward to consign Joan of Kent to the flames, at Bonner and Gardiner making havoc amongst the saints of their day, or at the prisons of England being filled by Puritan confessors under the relentless and licentious rule of the Stuarts, if, in these more enlightened times, and amongst a people boastful of their liberty, Christian ministers can be found dishonoring the book of God, and defaming the name they bear, by pleading the sanction of religion for a system of gigantic wrong. Such, however, is the fact. We write it in sorrow, and with a feeling of humiliation which no language can express. We should be unfaithful to
professors
what we bitterly
slavery is mainly

'Let all evangelical denominations,' says the American commentator, Albert Barnes, 'but follow the example of the Quakers in this country, and slavery would soon come to an end. There is not vital energy enough—there is not power of influence and numbers enough, *out of the Church*, to sustain it. Let every religious denomination in the land *detach itself* from all connexion with slavery, without saying a word against others ; let the time come when in all the mighty demonstrations of Christians it can be announced that *the evil has ceased with them for ever ;* and let the voice of each denomination be lifted up in kind but firm and solemn testimony against the system—with no "mealy words," with no attempt at apology ; with no effort to throw the sacred shield of religion over so great an evil, *and the work is done.* There is no public sentiment in this land—there could be none created —that would resist such a testimony ; there is no power *out* of the Church that could sustain slavery an hour, if it were not sustained *in* it.'

Unhappily, the various denominations referred to by Mr. Barnes are criminally implicated in the system. Their members have a large pecuniary stake in it ; and others are either silenced, or made actively concurrent, by sympathy with them. By the most exact information which can be obtained, it appears that the Methodists hold 219,563 slaves ; the Baptists, including the Campbellites, 226,000 ; the Episcopalians, 88,000 ; the Presbyterians, 77,000 ; and other denominations, 50,000.

With such facts before us, we need not wonder at the opinions which have been expressed by many American ministers of eminent name on the subject of slavery in general, and of the Fugitive Slave Law in particular. We must quote a few lest we be thought to misrepresent the class; and in doing so, we avail ourselves of the third publication at the head of this article, which, though issued anonymously, is entitled to the fullest confidence. We select the following as belonging to various bodies :—

'The Rev. Dr. Gardiner Spring, an eminent Presbyterian clergyman of New York, lately declared from the pulpit that, " if by one prayer he could liberate every slave in the world, he would not dare to offer it."

' The Rev. Dr. Parker, of Philadelphia, affirms in a recent Thanksgiving sermon,—"That there were no evils in slavery but such as were inseparable from any other relation in civil and social life."

' The Rev. Moses Stuart, D.D., well known in this country by his works on the exigesis and criticism of the Bible, in his vindication of the Fugitive Slave Law, reminds his readers that, " though we may *pity* the fugitive, yet the Mosaic Law does not authorize the rejection of the claims of the slaveholders to their stolen or strayed *property*."

' The Rev. Dr. Spencer, of Brooklyn, New York, has published a sermon entitled the " Religious Duty of Obedience to the Laws," in support of the " Fugitive Slave Bill," which has elicited the highest encomiums from Dr. Samuel H. Cox, the Presbyterian minister of Brooklyn (notorious both in this country and America for his sympathy with the slaveholder), and also from the Hon. Daniel Webster, who says that " it is quite refreshing to read a production which, founding itself upon the express injunctions of the Holy Scriptures. goes back from theory to commandment,—from human hypothesis and speculation, to the declared will of God."

' The Rev. W. M. Rogers, an orthodox minister of Boston, delivered on the last thanksgiving-day a sermon, in which he says, " when the slave asks me to stand between him and his master, what does he ask? He asks me to murder a nation's life; and I will not do it, because I have a conscience,—because there is a God." He proceeds to affirm that if this resistance to the carrying out of the " Fugitive Slave Law" should lead the magistracy to call the citizens to arms, their duty was to obey, and " if ordered to take human life, in the name of God to take it; " and he concludes by admonishing the fugitives to " hearken to the word of God, and to count their own masters worthy of all honour."

' The Right Rev. Bishop Hopkins, of Vermont, in a lecture at Lockport, on the 13th of January last, while admitting that slavery. from *its inherent nature*, had in every age been a curse and a blight to the nation which cherished it, throws the sacred mantle of the Scriptures over it. He says, " It was warranted by the Old Testament; " and inquires, " What effect had the gospel in doing away with slavery? None whatever." Therefore, he argues, as it is expressly permitted by the Bible, it does not in itself involve any sin ; but that every Christian is authorized by divine law to own slaves, provided they were not treated with unnecessary cruelty.

' The Rev. Orville Dewey, D.D., of the Unitarian connexion, declares that, for his part, he would send his own brother or child into slavery, if needed to preserve the union between the free and slaveholding States ; and, counselling the slave to similar magnanimity, thus exhorts him :— " *Your right to be free is not absolute, unqualified, irrespective of all consequences.* If my espousal of your claim is likely to involve your race and mine together in disasters infinitely greater than your personal servitude, then you ought not to be free. In such a case, personal rights ought to be sacrificed to the general good. You yourself ought to see this, and be willing to suffer for a while—one for many." '

It must not be supposed that the ministers of America are all chargeable with the opinions we have adduced. There are noble exceptions, and they are daily becoming more numerous. Large numbers of our transatlantic brethren feel deeply the
the perpe-
ing with national
energy to bring it to a speedy termination. May the God of mercy sustain and bless them, guide their counsels by his wisdom, enable them to endure the reproach with which they are assailed, and give them speedily to hear the joyful shout of an enfranchised people, whose prison doors they are seeking to open ! To such laborers in the field of Christian philanthropy, the religious people of this country are bound to render every aid in their power. We rejoice to believe that they will do so, and shall devote our brief remaining space to an exhibition of the steps which have been taken with a view to this end. A large number of Americans are now visiting our country, many of whom will probably seek the fellowship of our churches. We have already expounded to them what we deem the law of Christian rectitude in this matter; we have expostulated, warned, and entreated them, and nothing now remains, but that we enforce, with honesty, yet with kindness, what we deem the discipline of the Church to such of them as continue to uphold the ' accursed thing.' We are glad to see that this course is being widely adopted, and shall still more rejoice if it prove the means of awakening the attention, and of changing the course, of any of our visitors. The first impression probably will be to irritate, but a time of thoughtfulness will succeed, when the lesson will be conned over, and conversion may ensue. At any rate, we owe it to ourselves to separate between the faithful and the faithless, and we have strong confidence in the upright discharge of this duty. ' The British and Foreign Anti-Slavery Society' was early in the field, and by adopting the following resolution, on the 21st of April, gave an unmistakeable indication of its spirit and views :—

' That this Committee, in view of the anticipated large influx of

American citizens into this country, of various religious denominations, feel it to be their solemn duty to call upon every section of the Christian Church in the United Kingdom to discriminate, in acts of Christian fellowship, either in respect of church communion, occupation of pulpits, or other intercourse, between those who are either directly implicated in the system of American slavery, which mercilessly consigns upwards of three millions of human beings to hopeless degradation and misery, or who by their guilty silence or apologies indirectly sustain it; and those faithful brethren who, in the spirit of the gospel, are earnestly labouring to remove, from the churches and from their country, the guilt and reproach of this atrocious iniquity. And, further, this Committee would respectfully but urgently recommend to British Christians to unite in a solemn protest against American slavery; and to press upon American visitors, as they have opportunity, the obligation of promoting, by all the means in their power, its immediate and complete abolition.'

Four days afterwards, the annual meeting of the 'Baptist Union' was held in London, and those who are acquainted with its past proceedings on the slave question will not be surprised that its views were embodied in language like the following:—

'That this Union, having heretofore faithfully and affectionately remonstrated with their brethren of the Baptist denomination in the United States, on the degree of support unhappily given, both by churches and ministers, to the system of slavery, deem it an imperative duty at the present season, both on account of the enactment of the recent Fugitive Slave Law, and more especially on account of the large number of persons from the United States, whom the Industrial Exhibition may be expected to draw to this country, to renew its protest against this essentially criminal and abominable system. They call to remembrance the fact, that a large number of the Baptist churches in England have formally and publicly resolved not to allow ecclesiastical fellowship to slaveholders; and they sincerely hope that the spirit which dictated these resolutions will operate universally, both towards professors and ministers, in such a manner as shall unequivocally show that British Christians cherish an imperishable hatred towards slavery, and are ever ready to show double honour to those who reprobate it and seek its extinction.'

This resolution is clearly intended to have practical effect. The men who adopted it do not regard it as a thing of words merely. They know what slavery is. They struggled hard in our own abolition contests, took part with Knibb and Burchell when those devoted missionaries appealed to British justice on behalf of the negroes of Jamaica, and are not disposed to shrink back now. This was shown on the 29th of April, when fifty-one ministers educated at the Baptist Colleges of Stepney, Bristol, and Bradford, resolved:—

'That they unite in expressing their abhorrence of the American

Fugitive Slave Law, as opposed alike to every feeling of humanity, and to the principles of religion; and that they deem it right to avow their detestation of this enactment, and of the support which it has received from many of the ministers of the gospel in America, by declaring their resolution not to receive into their pulpits any minister from America who is known to support this most cruel and iniquitous measure.'

The Congregational Union, also, at its annual meeting in London, adopted the following resolution on the 16th of May :—

'That this Assembly, while most anxious to reciprocate sentiments of fraternal regard and unity towards the pastors and churches in the United States of the same faith and order as the churches in connexion with this Union—more especially to the descendants of the venerated Pilgrim Fathers in the New England States—deem it their duty to renew their solemn and indignant protest against slavery as still existing among the American churches; and, in particular, to express their great surprise and deep regret at the conduct of those ministers of various denominations, who have given either their direct countenance or their tacit support to the Fugitive Slave Law recently passed by the American Legislature; inasmuch as they cannot but regard that wicked and accursed statute as being, in the language of the eminent patriot and philanthropist, Judge Jay, "a palpable violation of the principles of justice, the rights of humanity, and the religion of Jesus Christ;' a statute to which no one who would obey God rather than man can consistently or righteously submit. And this assembly earnestly pray, that it may please the Divine Head of the Church, in whom there is neither bond nor free, to open the eyes of the ministers and churches in the United States to the aggravated guilt of participating in the sin of man-stealing, or holding their brethren in unjust and cruel bondage, which creates, in the judgment of this Union, an insuperable barrier to Christian fellowship with them on the part of all who reverence the authority of God and respect the inalienable rights of their fellow-men.'

The ministers and other deputies of the Bristol and Gloucestershire Congregational Union, at their recent half-yearly meeting, recorded their sentiments in an equally unequivocal manner, and we place their resolution on record as alike honorable to themselves and worthy of imitation :—

'That the grief and shame,' say the deputies, 'which we have long felt on account of the slavery which prevails in several of the United States of North America are greatly aggravated by the fact, that not a few Christian churches and Christian ministers, so called, plead for the continuance of that wretched system; that our sorrow has been recently still further deepened by the atrocious " Fugitive Slave Law," which the Legislature of the United States has enacted; that while it would give us pain to do anything that should even seem to be inconsistent with international and Christian hospitality, especially towards our transatlantic kinsfolk, during the approaching Congress in London, *we deem it right to express our unanimous determination not to welcome to our pulpits any minister of religion*, whatever may be his reputation in the States, who hesitates to avow his abhorrence of slavery, and his earnest desire for its speedy abolition ; but that, on the other hand, we regard those American ministers and others who, in their own country, boldly declare their anti-slavery principles, to be worthy of " double honour." '

A like feeling prevailed in the council of the ' Evangelical Alliance ' at its meeting at Torquay, in November last.  Some differences of opinion on minor points of the case probably prevailed.  The wording of the preamble of their resolution— and this is our only authority for the surmise—seems to indicate this.  But the resolution itself is clear and simple, and we rejoice in adding it to the other testimonies adduced.  We give it entire as due to the body from which it emanates, and trust that the conclusion arrived at will awaken serious consideration in the parties concerned.  The constitution of the Evangelical Alliance, and the temper in which its proceedings have been conducted, preclude the supposition of any other motive having swayed its decision than that of an overwhelming sense of duty.  The resolution runs thus :—

' That, while there is an important difference between the admission of persons as members of the British organization and their admission simply as visitors, and we, therefore, do not consider the resolution adopted at Birmingham (read *Manchester*), in 1846, in regard to the non-admission of slaveholders to the British organization as positively deciding questions in regard to visitors ; and, while there is a difficulty of principle in admitting as visitors professing Christians, some of whose views and practices we may strongly disapprove of, and yet excluding other professing Christians because we consider them in certain matters to be faulty ; yet the slavery of America presents special features which warrant and demand a distinctive resolution on the subject.  If the intercourse which might be held with slaveholders from America should assume such an amicable aspect as to bear the interpretation that we look with a qualified indignation on American slavery, and more particularly on the Fugitive Slave Bill which has recently come into force, the responsibility which would thus be entailed would be very dreadful, and which we ought not to incur ; and, on the other hand, any attempt to deal faithfully on this matter with American slave-holders, would, too probably, terminate in angry and mischievous collision.

' Resolved, therefore, that slaveholders shall not be admissible as visitors to the proposed Conference.'

One more example, and we close.  We take it designedly, not from a society or association, but from the proceedings of a single ' Congregation of Faithful Men.'  The church meeting in Bloomsbury Chapel, London, under the pastoral charge of the Rev. William Brock, adopted, May 2nd, the following resolution, on the motion of S. Morton Peto, Esq., M.P. :—

'That this church cannot admit to the fellowship of the Lord's supper any person whatever, who either sympathizes with or supports the Fugitive Slave Law of the United States, or who withholds his influence from the efforts which are being made to restore to the coloured population of the United States the rights of which they have been so wickedly deprived.'

Our case is complete; we need say nothing to sustain it. The decision of the evangelical bodies of this country—so far at least as Dissenters are concerned—is taken, and we do not doubt but that it will be faithfully adhered to. They have no inducement to this course beyond the dictate of duty. So far from wishing to disparage the religious profession of America, all their tendencies are in an opposite direction. They would gladly think otherwise than they are compelled to do. It is with bitter mortification they reflect on the existence of an evil which shades the lustre of the transatlantic Church, and mantles their face with a blush when they point to America as the land of the pilgrim-fathers, and the special sphere of religious voluntaryism. Our appeals are thus nullified—our boasting is proved vain. ' Physician, heal thyself,' is the taunting rejoinder of our opponents, when we adduce the example of America in support of the efficiency of our principles, to maintain the purity and widen the domains of the Church. That this rejoinder may be met, we know; but it would be far better, infinitely more satisfactory, if we could deny its truth, or speak of it as a thing of the past. The spirit of the gospel ought to have sufficed to work the extinction of slavery; but as it has failed to do so, we are driven to the use of other weapons. We recur to these reluctantly, and only in the last resort; and shall hail, with joy which no words can express, the signs of penitence and reformation on the part of American professors. We know their sensitiveness; we are prepared for their resentment; we shall not be surprised if they reply in terms of indignant defiance. All this, and more than this, may be; but if there is truth in Christianity, or power in moral principle, the time will come when they will lie prostrate before their Master, and, in language of the deepest penitence, will make confession of their sin. In the meantime, by the course our churches are now taking, we vindicate the Christian faith from the foulest of all aspersions, and rebuke the triumph of the ungodly as they tauntingly exclaim, ' So would we have it.'

ART. III.—1. *Address of the Synod of Thurles.* Dublin. 1850.
2. *The Tablet Newspaper.* Dublin. 1851.

As Ireland has proved the great difficulty with Ministers in their attempts to legislate on the subject of the Papal aggression, it may not be useless to trace the difficulty to its source, and to inquire how far it has been diminished or aggravated by the policy of Lord Clarendon in dealing with the Roman Catholic hierarchy. It will be found that a concatenation of causes has involved our rulers in their present dilemma; and that the first link of the chain is the Irish Church Establishment—a fact which is now admitted by the 'Dublin Evening Post,' the organ of Dublin Castle and of the Irish Whigs. The existence of the Establishment in that country is incompatible with social and political equity. The absence of these led to disaffection and insurrection, for the suppression of which the Government entered into an alliance with the priesthood, and coquetted with the Pope; and now, when they would repel an aggression upon the sovereignty of England, their hands are tied up by their own past policy, in which principle gave way to expediency.

England, with an empire the most extended, resources the most ample, a framework of society the most solid and stable, the best constitution and the strongest government, found it desirable, some years ago, to establish, by act of Parliament, three colleges for the education of the middle classes, in one of the worst governed of her provinces. These institutions were greatly needed in order to cultivate the abundant, but wasted, talent of that country, and give it a practical direction. It was essential to their utility that they should be open to all parties, without any religious tests. This was felt by the Government; and on this principle they were founded—a principle which had already been recognised in the national system of education, after parliamentary committees and commissions had again and again declared that the opposite principle, persisted in for ages, had utterly failed, and had frustrated all the good intentions of the Legislature. Many were gratified with this entrance on what they deemed the right path. But the two extreme parties into which misgovernment had marshalled a portion of the Irish people raised a factious outcry against the new colleges, and, with unprecedented harmony, united in calling them 'godless.'

One party called them so, because they excluded from their teaching the Thirty-nine Articles, for which provision more ample than ever priesthood enjoyed since the beginning of the world had been already made by the State. The other called them so, because they excluded the Creed of Pope Pius IV., for which Parliament had just voted to Maynooth College a very large endowment, to be paid out of the Consolidated Fund, without any real responsibility for the right or honest use of it. This cry was only what Government had reason to expect, and what it was bound to disregard. It was to render such factious cries unavailing—to raise up an instructed, independent middle class, who would laugh down such preposterous bigotry, and rebuke the fomentors of discord—that the Queen's Colleges were devised and established. It happened, however, that certain Roman Catholic prelates in Ireland, who had proved themselves bitterly hostile to united education, to a legal provision for the poor, and to every other measure of utility which threatened to weaken their own authority by elevating the people, appealed to Rome against the decision of the Legislature—to the Pope against Cæsar. Government had undertaken to afford a literary and secular education only, and to impart it in such a manner as not to obstruct, in the slightest degree, the action of religious instruction, but rather to afford it every possible facility. The appeal was carried to Rome by Drs. M'Hale and Higgins, two of the most intolerant and ultramontane of the prelates, who, however, managed to get on their side a majority of their brethren, though opposed by the two Primates, Crolly and Murray, as well as the most enlightened portion of the laity. They owed their success to the influence of the late Mr. O'Connell, and the ignorant democracy which he wielded.

The Government, instead of ignoring this foreign tribunal, as it was bound in law to do, actually condescended to plead before it; and ere an act could be hurried through Parliament, to render this conduct legal, they sent a Cabinet Minister, Lord Minto, to circumvent Dr. M'Hale with the Pope. The Lord-Lieutenant of Ireland, with the approbation of the Cabinet, sent extracts of the College Statutes to the see of Rome for its sanction, stating at the same time, in terms of abject homage, that they had been revised to meet its requirements; this revision involving the exclusion of the essential principle of religious freedom on which the colleges were founded. Never did Government so truckle to the bigoted behests of a contemptible foreign power; and never was departure from the right path more ignominiously punished! Vain was the diplomacy of the Earl of Minto—vain the eulogy and unbounded confidence of the Viceroy—and vain all the efforts of the ' Castle bishops,' Crolly and Murray. The statutes, amended so as to make the colleges promote and inculcate the Roman Catholic religion, and for its sake to place every Protestant professor under a jealous *surveillance*, were pronounced full of ' intrusive and grievous dangers' to the ' sensitive faith' of the youth of Ireland. Sensitive indeed it must be, since it fades in the free air, and is blighted by sunshine—flourishing, like the cholera, on whatever is most unfavourable to the health of the human mind!

The Pope, who trembles for the existence of his authority, which has little weight with the nations nearest his throne, and least of all among his own subjects, had decided, against the earnest request of England, that his holiness would be graciously pleased to sanction one of the acts of her Parliament. England had a right to expect a favourable answer, for she had done much to propitiate the Pope, to sustain him in his usurped position as the pretended sovereign of the human mind—the worst of all pretenders, since he seats himself on the throne of Christ—the worst of all tyrants, since he would reign over conscience. But the appeal of proud Protestant England was spurned from the Pope's footstool! Wherefore have we been subjected to this national humiliation? Wherefore has England become a *defendant* before this shadow of a pope, whose jurisdiction the very mob of Rome treats with contempt, simply because England persisted in keeping up in Ireland a system of most unrighteous inequality? She refused to put an end to the ecclesiastical ascendency of a small minority by relieving the majority from the support of a creed which they reject; and their clergy from a social degradation, which galls them to the heart. She refused to open the national University in order that merit, in whatever Church found, might win its honours and enjoy its privileges; and she tried to atone for this exasperating injustice by boons to the hostile Church, which neither obliterate the memory of past oppression, nor remove the sense of present inferiority. Dr. M'Hale and his party are well aware that a main object with the Government in wishing them to receive a State provision is to reconcile them to the existence of the Protestant Establishment and the domination of an unsympathizing aristocracy, to wean them from agitation, and to get the priesthood to ride the Celtic democracy, not as its master, but as the hired jockey of England. They know that in this case that hard-mouthed animal which even famine cannot tame would become altogether unmanageable, and would fling its rider into the mire.

They had some significant hints of this danger in 1848. In the agitation of the Young Ireland party, the religious element was quite subordinate. Nationality was their all-absorbing passion. They were tolerant of everything that did not interfere with that. Protestantism was even dearer to them than Catholicism, if it came under their revolutionary colours. So far as intelligence and education had spread among the people before the famine, wherever patronage could not corrupt, or landlordism intimidate, love of national independence was the ruling passion. Hence the success of the Young Ireland party, and hence the fact urged in Parliament as a reason for endowing Irish Romanism,—that the priests were *people-ridden,* whipped, spurned, and driven whither they would not go, if they could otherwise have their daily bread. This certainly was a strange and anomalous state of things—an infallible priesthood dominated over by an erring multitude, a people bound to implicit obedience, and yet ruling their spiritual lords with a rod of iron !

The priests, however, though bending for a reason to the popular storm, were resolved to be revenged on the first opportunity. Some of them, indeed, whether sincerely or not, had written and preached the rankest sedition. A dignitary named Hughes, in the west, had laid down the plan of a rebel campaign, and publicly submitted to the Prime Minister the method by which the power of England in Ireland might be destroyed, in the winter of 1848. One of his prescriptions was, that the police throughout the kingdom should be all seized and disarmed in one hour! And Dr. Miley, O'Connell's confessor, a priest who officiated in Archbishop Murray's metropolitan church, declared, amidst the shouts of a warlike multitude, that if matters came to be decided by the sword, the priests would be found, as in the rest of revolutionary Europe, by the side of the people.

But it must be recollected that the *Pope* was *then* by the side of the people, and so revolution was a holy thing in sacerdotal eyes. They soon learned to curse bitterly what they had so fervently blessed, for the priests are the sworn subjects of their bishops, and the bishops are the sworn subjects of the Pope. To disobey the supreme Pontiff would be to abjure their faith, and to give a triumph to its mortal enemy. The Pope was in difficulties, his very existence in jeopardy, and by a singular fatality, Protestant England had it in her power to tame him for a while. In doing this, Lord Clarendon thought he could seize the rudder of the Irish hierarchy, and make even the M'Hales submissive to his power. It was hoped that the Diplomatic Relations Bill would enable the Government to accomplish this purpose. Having done without the Pope for three centuries—having no commercial intercourse with his States, which a consul is not adequate to protect—yet in the moment when his power as a temporal prince was on the brink of perdition, his office was recognised by our sovereign in order to make the government of Ireland *practicable on principles of injustice !* So far as the Pope's power operates in this country, the Queen can have to do with him only in his spiritual capacity. It is not as sovereign of a few petty Italian states, but as 'Ruler of the Faithful,' and 'Vicar of the Redeemer,' that he presumes to parcel England into dioceses, and to convert towns into ' *cities.*'

With the Queen of England thus reconciled to the Pope—with a large establishment supported by the State for the free educa· tion of Irish priests—with the prospect of having three other colleges completely under their control—with an ampler endow· ment of their Church in the colonies—and with every prospect of increasing power and pelf, founded on confidential communica· tions with Dublin Castle—the Irish hierarchy could not do less than assist the Government in putting down the rebellion of Smith O'Brien.  The state of feeling among the laity at that time may be seen from the following letters, written by observers on the spot.  The first appeared in ' Saunders's Newsletter,' a Dublin daily paper, and was copied, without comment, by the ' Tablet.'  It was written at the time when the Habeas Corpus Act was suspended, and 10,000 warrants had been ordered to be printed, in order to arrest the leaders and the members of the clubs.

' The priests get the credit of placing them in their present ridicu· lous position, and many individuals of the lowest orders speak out their minds plainly about their clergy having urged them on against law and authority, by every means open and covert in their power, and then when the time came, and they found that themselves and their own interests might be endangered, they cunningly discountenanced the movement, and consigned the confederates and clubbists to what· ever might be their fate ; but, while the people generally are most indignant at the conduct of the priests, they, on the other hand, take credit to themselves for the part they have acted, and are, doubtless, delighted at the prospect of four or five millions from Government. Notwithstanding the number of arms that have been seized by the police, it is said by those who are acquainted with the rural districts, that a vast quantity are still in the possession of the peasantry, con· cealed, but ready for use.'

The correspondent of the ' Times,' writing from Thurles, in Tipperary, said :—

' The attitude of the people still continues decidedly and unmis· takeably hostile.  I should even say that this feeling is on the increase within the last few days, for the impression of terror created by the first appearance of a large military force has sensibly diminished, and by a thousand slight but undoubted signs, one is hourly reminded that one is living in an enemy's country.  An overwhelming rebelliousness of spirit has seized upon the people, and it is not the sacrifice of a few lives, in an obscure struggle with the constabulary, which will stifle the gigantic growth of so many years' agitation.  They believe that " the war," as they call it, has only been postponed, and that when the priests are won over to the popular cause its triumph is secure.'

The priests had been won over, not to, but from the popular cause.— Matters were arranged between the bishops and the Government, and then the word of command went forth to the parishes, and General M'Donald's flying column did not move more quickly than it was obeyed. The effects are candidly and truthfully detailed in the narrative which poor young Meagher has sent from the place where he now suffers for his folly in trusting sacerdotal patriotism. The priests instantly changed sides, everywhere preaching vehemently against the rebellion they had fomented, and denouncing its leaders as insane. The Memorial of the Tuam priests to the Lord-Lieutenant was the most impudent thing of the kind on record. The lowest Jesuitical cunning is manifest in its concoction. They sought, at the same time, to win a character for loyalty, to secure the confidence of their flocks, and to blast the reputation of the leaders whom they had encouraged to lift up the standard of revolt, and to disarm the constabulary in one hour throughout Ireland. This sudden outburst of sacerdotal loyalty was as prudent as it was profitable. The strength of the rebellion lay in the towns, and they were disarmed at the cannon's mouth. Government was prepared to go to all lengths in crushing the insurgents. Knowing these things, and dreading the consequences, the priests made a merit of necessity ; and then their cries became loudest in the chorus of execration, by which the defeated confederates were covered with infamy.

This was not the first occasion on which the Irish bishops betrayed their dupes, and sold the cause of sedition to the Government, when they had it worked up to marketable value, and could put the price in the Church's treasury. Nor will it be the last. But it is time for the people of Great Britain, and the Protestants of the Empire, to ask whether Government has not given too much for the whistle, and to see that such bargains are not again struck at their expense. The consequences of such barterings are now before us.

Since that time the Government has stopped at no sacrifice of principle to uphold the declining influence of the priests. First, they encourage it by putting a premium on agitation. Every measure of justice must be extorted from them. The *Encumbered Estates Act*, which has worked so well, is an instance in point. It was repeatedly before Parliament, ere the Government took it up in earnest. It would have passed the first year, but for the opposition of the money-lenders in London, who were some of the Premier's most influential constituents. This fact we have on the authority of one well acquainted with their tenets, Sir C. E. Trevelyan, who tells us, in his 'Irish Cities,' reprinted from the 'Edinburgh Review,' that ' this bill passed the House of Lords, but was withdrawn in the Commons, owing to the opposition of some of the Irish proprietors, and to the objections entertained by the great Insurance Companies, who are the principal lenders on Irish mortgages, to have their investments

disturbed.   Lord John Russell, who could have made the bill
law by speaking the word, then truckled to those parties, and his
doing so, Sir C. E. Trevelyan said, was a 'national misfortune.'
An attempt was made to remedy the misfortune early in the next
session.   On the 24th of February, 1848, the bill was read a
second time in the Lords without a division.   There it slept for
nearly three months, but as soon as a real rebellion seemed
imminent, it was hurried through the Commons much improved.
It is not strange that the organ of the priests should thus express
the *Rationale* of Irish agitation.   The 'Tablet' said on that
occasion :—

'Every body knows that without a rebellion, actual or proximate,
the opposition of Lord John's political patrons, the money-lenders,
would never have been overcome; that the delay originating in
London—not in Ireland—has been overcome solely by the disposition
to rebel; and that when next the people of Ireland can contrive to
terrify these Whigs, to whom, for our sins, we are subjected, they will
get other instalments in exact proportion to the severity of the "pressure from without."'

*Ex uno disce omnes.*   Every good measure has been thus
extorted, after all the arts of state policy have been used
to stave off a just claim.   The Irish want to see in the Government an example of straightforwardness—of upright principle, and they see subserviency, trickery, violation of promises,
underhand dealings, and slippery intrigue.   Our rulers swear
against Popery and then endow it.   They believe that the
influence of the priests is a bad influence, that it is the influence
of ignorance, prejudice, tyranny, and yet they sacrifice all that
ought to be most dear to men and Christians in order to uphold
that influence.   It ought to be the main object of government
to enlighten the people, and by the force of truth, justice, and
education, to emancipate them.   But instead of treating priests
like other subjects who violate the law, they send off to Rome
and beg the Pope to call them to order—to make the rebellious
loyal, the ignorant intelligent, and the vulgar genteel.   This
is actually what the 'Times,' some time ago, desired that the
Pope should do, but that was before the Papal aggression made
it politic in Printing-house Square to thunder against the
Vatican.   There ought to have been some assurance that his
Holiness was able to effect such metamorphosis at Rome, before
he was invoked to work miracles in Ireland.   It was owing to
a crooked policy like this that Roman Catholic prelates were
*ennobled* in the *Royal Gazette*, and got precedence before dukes
at the viceregal levees, and were permitted to smuggle their
titles and jurisdictions into private bills, as in the case of Archbishop Murray.   But such conduct on the part of a government
never escapes with impunity.   Retribution will come as surely

as the crop corresponds to the seed sown. It has come upon the Whigs in its worst form, and there is none to pity them.

One of the most singular results of the Papal aggression is the position into which it has forced Lord John Russell, as the execrated antagonist of 'Catholic claims.' Who could imagine that the great Parliamentary leader in the contest for emancipation, the historic champion of religious liberty, should live to write the letter to the Bishop of Durham, or to introduce the Ecclesiastical Titles Bill? His tenure of office was so precarious, that without the Roman Catholic members, he could scarcely hope to stand. Assailed by the Protectionists on the one side, and the Financial Reformers on the other, he could not escape defeats in Parliament, except by the aid of his friends or the Irish members. The New Franchise Bill made it more important than ever to secure this party by every possible concession that English patience would endure. With what pain must such a high-minded, obstinate Minister have brought himself to avow that he had been deceived by the professions of the Irish hierarchy! Such an avowal, and the position which constrained it, must have been forced upon him by uncontrollable circumstances. What are we to infer from all this? That the mightiest statesmen are mere straws on the stream of Providence. What can the Whig leader do against the course of events? He is helpless as a child. All his experience and sagacity did not enable him to forecast the future for a few brief years. When he wished to restore the Pope in 1848, he little imagined the relations he would have to sustain to the 'Holy See' in 1851. There was a power in England which he despised, which he said should not hinder his endowing the Irish hierarchy, and whose voice one of his colleagues contemptuously called 'the bray of Exeter Hall.' It protested against the Maynooth Endowment Bill, but it was disregarded as fanatical; yet, in a few years, that voice reaches the throne in thunder peals, and is hailed as the resistless public opinion of England.

A much greater fact brought prominently out in this agitation, is the amazing progress of Ultramontanism. We did not require the authority of its organ in these islands, the 'Tablet,' to inform us that the Gallican liberty — the *Church constitutionalism,* which would put the restraint of law upon the power of the Pope, is fast diappearing from Catholic Christendom. Revolution had long time broken all the local and national bonds of the French Church, deprived it of all coherence other than its attachment to Peter's chair—flung it back violently on the *infallibility of the Pope,* and thus, in half a century, made France nearly as Ultramontane as Italy. The 'Tablet' assures us that neither English nor Irish Catholics shall ever have the power of choosing their own bishops. Ireland had that power till the appearance of Primate Cullen, in whose case the free choice of the parish priests was arbitrarily set aside, and Pius IX. gave them a taste of his prerogative. The reason of this distrust of local authority is thus frankly given by the Ultramontane organ—it is very suggestive :—

' A weak and easy priest, chosen at this moment to fill up a vacant diocese in Ireland, might give a vote to the Castle on the side of the colleges, and turn a " minority of thirteen " into something very like a majority. Accordingly, we may be sure that in Ireland, no less than in England, vacancies will not be filled up without the fullest assurance that the new bishop can be depended on to go all prudent and necessary lengths in opposition to Government intrigues. If the election of the clergy does not give this security, some other method of attaining it must and will be found out in Rome ; and if Lord John Russell has small fancy for Dr. Cullen's appointment to Armagh, perhaps he may have just as little occasion to rejoice in the appointment that will follow.'

Here is something for the laity and the inferior clergy to reflect upon. The Pope thinks that if the election of a bishop were left in the hands of the clergy, they would chose 'a weak and easy priest to fill up a vacant diocese,' one whom the Government could make the tool of their policy. On the contrary, we believe they have been in the habit of selecting the ablest of their number to wear the mitre. But, lest the bishops should retain a spark of nationality, or of patriotism, or loyalty to the civil government, lest a single instinct of his nature should be likely to revolt against the policy of the Propaganda, the right of election is abolished, and the appointment made absolutely by a foreign power. When the Pope trembled for his life a few years ago, the ' Tablet' proposed that he should have a body-guard of English, Scotch, or Irish. Now, it seems, the interests of the Church are not safe even in the hands of the Irish priests.

We do not need the vision of a seer to discern in this policy a true sign of the speedy downfal of the Papacy. The climax of centralization, whether ecclesiastical or political, is the signal of destruction. The last step in that perilous course is a step over the precipice. When all the roots of national and local self-government in the Church of Rome are torn up, the main root will not long survive. At the present time there seems something like the infatuation of the foredoomed, in binding all the vitality of Catholicism to the Pontifical throne, when we consider how recently its occupant had to fly into exile, and how soon the holy city may be again in the hands of men who execrate the name and office of the Pope. The tendency of this policy is to give all the Roman Catholic Churches in Christendom but *one neck*, that Infidelity may lay it on the block.

The most disheartening thing connected with this centralizing movement, this all-grasping absolutism of the Vatican, is, that there is no Roman Catholic voice raised up against it. Priests and people tamely and silently suffer themselves to be denuded of every right by a foreign power, and not only quietly suffer themselves to be bound, but glory in their bonds. They fancy, in their blindness, that Rome is the safest guardian of their ecclesiastical independence. There never was a greater mistake. A document, directly bearing upon this subject, appears in the Appendix of the second volume of Mr. John O'Connell's Memoirs of his Father. The Rev. — Hayes, an Irish priest, was appointed as a deputation to Rome, to protest against the *veto* in the name of the Irish priesthood, and to secure the domestic nomination of the bishops. The document to which we have referred is a narrative of what occurred at Rome in connexion with his mission, and it is so instructive and so *apropos* at the present moment, that we will give some extracts.

'On the 16th of September, 1815,' writes the Rev. Mr. Hayes, 'the remonstrance of the Irish Catholics was confided to me. Reaching Rome on the 25th of October, I lost no time in waiting on Cardinal Litta, and disclosing my mission. His Eminence honoured me with assurances of support—denied that the Genoese letter conceded the veto, and gave me a copy to send to Ireland. I found at once that my mission had to meet the implacable resistance of Cardinal Gonsalvi, Secretary of State. He much complained at my not having selected him for my communication. I did not conceive myself warranted to submit, contrary to all practice, our religious concerns to the political cabinet. On the 9th of November, I had my first audience of his Holiness, who received me and my documents in the most gracious manner. I had the satisfaction of removing some erroneous impressions, and hearing his declaration, that he had never granted the veto to the British Crown. The influence of his minister was, however, too visible—his Holiness expressing a desire that I should place the papers in the hands of Cardinal Gonsalvi: but he accompanied the request with the warmest assurances of his personal care, and a promise to refer them to a congregation of Cardinals. For some time I was engaged in arrangements, and was also much occupied in removing the effect of the extravagant misrepresentations of the vetoistical faction, aided by the public press, which was under the control of my opponents. Cardinal Litta's official deputation to the Austrian Emperor at Milan, increased my difficulties. Scarcely was he gone, *when the Secretary evaded the promised reference.* However, after many efforts, I prevailed on two of the most venerable Cardinals, Pietro and Somaglier, to interpose with the holy Father, who was not aware of the evasion of his orders, and subsequently obtained another interview. I found *his mind had been practised upon, and I had to put into his hands a strong protest against the arts and the whole conduct of the minister.* I expostulated with the latter; and, after much discussion, succeeded in inducing him to admit the injustice of the representation he had allowed to be made to the Pope.'

Mr. Hayes laid before the Cardinal Secretary of State the plan of domestic nomination 'of which he affected to approve, but evaded by every means the giving it any aid.' On every occasion he found the adviser of the Pope false in his professions, and entirely in the interest of the British minister, to whose aims he made the Pope's authority subservient. 'I was now satisfied,' wrote Mr. Hayes, 'that the measure of domestic nomination was the only one which could substantially prevent the veto; for *it was manifest that if the appointment of our prelates was to rest in Rome, that the Cardinal Secretary would place it at the disposal of the British Crown.* The upshot of these negotiations is thus described in the words of the honest Irish priest:—

'The plan of domestic nomination had been printed by Propaganda three weeks before, and distributed among the Cardinals who were to attend. I hold a correct copy of this plan, and propose to include it in my future narrative. Several reasons, in favour of domestic nomination, are adduced in the Penenza, or printed case, laid before their Eminences, who unanimously approved of it, including the aged Cardinal Quarantotte, whose prominent zeal I would deem it injustice to overlook, as I found his Eminence a most earnest supporter, and apparently anxious to compensate thereby for the *mischievous rescript with which, in an inconsiderate moment, under the influence of the grossest misrepresentation, he suffered his venerable name to be associated.* The divisions in the Catholic Association gave new life to the vetoists. However, all the Cardinals voted for the decree, *except Cardinal Fontana; and he prevailed on Cardinal Litta to postpone it.* Thus was lost domestic nomination, though the pending appointments in Ireland had been decided on its principle. The triumphant vetoists laboured for my expulsion. Two months were gone since my letter, in the Irish papers, had been known, and the sensation in Rome, on the subject, had died away. However, as I seemed abandoned by the Dublin Association, it was thought a favourable opportunity to drive me from Rome; and *I was accordingly ordered to leave that city in twenty-four hours, and the States in three days. I remonstrated in vain. Fever then attacked me; yet my persecutors did not desist. They broke into my bed-room, placed guards over my person, and continued them to the day of my deportation—a period of eight weeks. On the 16th of July, I was conveyed, by a military escort, to the frontiers of the Roman States;* and, having remained some days at Florence to recruit my health, reached home finally on the 24th September.'

As Mr. John O'Connell published this narrative in his Memoirs of his father, and as he professes to be the champion of the independence of his Church, we would ask him a simple question: What assurance has he that the present Cardinal Secretary of State who has got the appointment of the Irish bishops in his hands, will not place it at the disposal of the British minister, should the interest of the Papal court seem to require it ? The political secretary, Cardinal Gonsalvi, ruled the Pope in those days; and the political secretary Antonelli rules the Pope now. Why should infallibility be less flexible in one case than the other? The truth is, that the Papal policy has often been involved in strange and almost inexplicable complications in consequence of the mixture of the spiritual and temporal powers. The exigencies of the prince have modified the theology of the pontiff. Spiritual claims have yielded to State necessities. The cardinals sat in conclave, deliberating on matters of solemn import, affecting the eternal interests of men, and have deferred their decisions, until, by crafty intrigue, they obtained the *ultimata* from foreign powers; then they pronounced accordingly, declaring that they were guided by the Holy Ghost. When Pius IX. ascended the throne, he put his hand to a document in which the principles and missionary proceedings of Protestants were vehemently anathematized. In a few months he was obliged to look to England, the first of Protestant powers, to defend him against the aggressions of Austria, the first of Catholic powers. Then the Pope was the champion of popular rights, the patron of self-government, the idol of Reformers. Vainly would he have preached—vainly would he have blessed or cursed, as the tool of the Emperor of Austria, or the successor of St. Peter. The ominous murmurs of sullen discontent would have been the only response. Oppressive taxes, tyrannical and peculating officials, fettering and impoverishing restrictions, the galling chains of national degradation, would have appealed to the multitude with a far more powerful voice. It is always painful when truth and nature are at war with authority and law. But when these happen to be in harmony—when might takes counsel with right—when religion sanctifies the struggles of freedom—then is invoked for heroic conflict all that is noble in the heart of man, and even base natures are inspired for the time with an elevating and purifying enthusiasm.

Such was the enthusiasm that attended the present Pope at the commencement of his career. But despotism with her wily blandishments soon deprived the spiritual Samson of his strength. Panic-stricken by the French revolution, he forswore his liberalism, and fled into the arms of the bloodstained tyranny of Naples, and he now exists a miserable dependent on France and Austria. His aggressions on England and Ireland are the natural results of these political relations. The Papacy was never a self-sustaining power. It has seldom attempted anything even in its missions, from the days of Augustine down, without seeking an alliance with the civil power, and having the sword of the magistrate for its precursor. Even infallibility can part with some of its prerogatives for a consideration, nor has it

refused a *concordat* with heretical or infidel·powers. Mr. Pugin,
in his 'Earnest Address on the Establishment of the Hierarchy,' states his conviction that state and temporal power have,
in every age, 'crushed the free action of the Church, enslaving
its ministers in worse than Egyptian bondage" (p. 2); that in
England 'the true and lawful bishops and clergy,' by a vile
surrender, sacrificed the Church and people; that the bishops
were generally royal nominees, the antipodes of what the Holy
Ghost would have chosen ; that the Cardinals have been the
tyrants and betrayers of the Church, and that there never was a
hierarchy founded on free principles under a monarchy, before
that which the Pope has now founded in England; a thing,
however, which he could not have ventured to do in any other
kingdom, because no other has so fully established ' the noblest
of all noble principles, perfect religious freedom.' So intelligent
a Catholic as Mr. Pugin ought to ask himself the questions—
why freedom can flourish only under a Protestant Government—
and how long the new Hierarchy would remain free itself or
suffer freedom in others ?

Recent events have made it obvious to all that the Papal
power in Ireland is now absolute, and that it is in the highest
degree dangerous.   In England it can do little mischief.   The
old national spirit that repelled the aggressions of Rome before
the Reformation still lives in the hearts of English Catholics.
There are few of them so fanatical as to sacrifice their loyalty to
gratify the ambition of popes and cardinals.   If there were a
contest with some Catholic power on the continent, the great
body of them would be true to their sovereign.   But if not, their
traitorism would not signify much, as they are but a small fraction
of the population.   But it is not so in Ireland.   The population,
which hates the English yoke, and gives unlimited allegiance to a
foreign despot, amounts there to six millions.   Suppose Austria
and France at war with England, while the Pope blessed their
arms and instigated the fanaticism of his followers, and that
Ireland were encouraged by the priests to revolt, in order to
resist what is called persecution, the consequences might be very
calamitous.

Nothing can be more preposterous than the conduct of the
Government in forbidding the use of titles in Ireland, or in any
other way checking the progress of Popery, while Maynooth is
endowed and maintained as it is.   Maynooth is the nursery of a
vast number of priests, intensely anti-English and anti-Protestant
in their spirit, ultra-Montanists of the first water, trained up in
passive obedience, serving a seven-years' apprenticeship to
tyranny, and going forth in all our colonies to disseminate their
principles and spirit in the rising nations of the new world.
Setting aside for a moment the doctrines they teach, the supreme

worship of the Virgin, which is now the great vital force of Romanism, and which Protestants must regard as downright idolatry, and looking merely at the crushing despotism which is the essence of the Papal government, it is marvellous that Protestants are content to support such a seminary.

The endowment of Maynooth should, then, be withdrawn. As the hierarchy are able to erect a Catholic university in opposition to the Queen's University for the education of the laity, they ought to be able to educate their own priests. Why should not this be done? There is no persecution in withholding an endowment. The reason why the Government will not do it, and why even the high Protestant party in Ireland will not urge them to do it, is, that if it were done, a tremendous agitation would arise against the Protestant Establishment. This agitation would be just. It is not fair to withdraw or withhold endowments from the majority, while so small a minority enjoys such an enormous amount of public funds.

There is, therefore, but one honest and consistent course open to the Dissenters of England, and to all true Protestants. The Maynooth grant must be withdrawn; but, in order to this, the Irish Establishment must be abolished. Any Dissenters who join a ' Protestant league,' which would strip the Romanists of their endowments and spare that Establishment, would not only stultify themselves, but insure their own defeat. The sole way of getting rid of these quarrels with the Roman hierarchy in Ireland, and with Irish Roman Catholics in all the British colonies, is to leave religion to the voluntary system at home and abroad. Without dealing thus impartially with religionists in Ireland, the Government cannot escape the charge of intolerance and injustice. The Establishment question could now be carried with the aid of Churchmen, so far as Ireland and the colonies are concerned, if this opportunity were well and wisely used. This would be an immense victory gained for Protestantism and religious freedom. It is only by keeping the Papacy totally separate from the State that its persecuting fangs can be extracted. The moment it has pecuniary relations with the State, the Government becomes involved in a network of intrigues, and importunities, and threats, from which it is almost impossible to escape without loss of strength and honour. Nothing can be more humiliating to men of spirit than the position of the Whig Government towards the Irish hierarchy. The Synod of Thurles met under a foreign prelate, arbitrarily appointed, and poured contempt on the Queen's Colleges, in obedience to a rescript from Rome, which the new Primate held in his hand, and in which the whole question was prejudged and predetermined. It was under such circumstances that the

British sovereign was advised to gazette that same Primate, and Dr. M'Hale, and some more of their brethren, as visitors of the Queen's University, without asking their consent. But these proud prelates spurned the honour! How humiliating is all this to such a nation as England! How can Englishmen bear to have their sovereign so treated? How can they endure the policy which has caused the British lion to crouch at the feet of the Pope?

There can be no peace in these realms till the State is wholly rid of Popery, and has resolved to know Roman Catholics only as British subjects. The price that *must* be paid for this riddance is the separation of Protestantism from the State in Ireland and the colonies. Enlightened, earnest, and just men, would not hesitate to pay this price, if they had a government to carry out their wishes; for Protestantism would gain by the change as much as the State.

---

ART. IV.—*The Burden of the Bell, and other Lyrics.* By T. Westwood. London: Lumley. 1850.

MR. WESTWOOD has, at least, one rich element of poetical genius —an intense sympathy with nature. It may truly be said that his fancy 'finds tongues in trees, books in the running brooks.' As a poet, his chief tendency is to personify; to implant a voice and a sentiment in every department of the creation. That this taste has its dangers might be illustrated by a reference to not a few poets of distinguished name, who, in indulging it, have fallen into vapidness and puerility. Mr. Westwood is, we think, safe from such a fate. He estimates aright the narrowness of that interval which lies between the sublime and the ridiculous. While he approaches, in some respects, to the school of poets to whom we have alluded, he shows himself untainted with the fanaticism of their dogma, that every object is a fitting theme for the muse. Thus, while he never exhibits himself in foppish finery, he never exposes himself in rags. He finds syllables in the murmur of the brook, and chimes in the harebells and wild hyacinths, but is unconscious of any inspirations from old clothes; he can find 'sermons in stones,' but not the hint of a homily in the stores of a pedlar.

But this is not the only vice of modern schools from which the author before us has kept himself free. It is still more to his credit, that, though he has evidently imbued himself almost to imitation with the writings of contemporary poets, he sees and avoids their capital defect, that of obscurity and mysticism. We have thoughtfully examined passages even in Tennyson's poems, to which we believe that the writer himself did not, when he penned them, attach the faintest shadow of a meaning; while some who would fain belong to the same class, appear frequently to be practising some such a hoax on their readers as Dr. Johnson played on one occasion upon a company, when he read aloud a poem for their approbation, omitting every alternate line. The courageous good sense with which Mr. Westwood exposes this contemptible sham, deserves to be exhibited by the citation of his own words. We quote from a piece entitled, 'Mummy-wrapping,' whose merits, as a composition, are those of the epigram rather than of the poem, of Peter Pindar rather than of his ancient name-sake.

> 'What! you would speak out your thought—
> Out, quite plainly—sore distraught
> You must be, young Poet;—know
> Now-a-days bards sing not so.
> What! espouse that worn-out style,
> Spenser's, Chaucer's—flowing bright
> As the full, clear morning light,
> With no symptom in the air
> Of the least fog anywhere;
> Pshaw! the world would only smile
> At your folly—folks have grown
> All too wise to spend their praises
> On such antiquated graces.
> No, the plan by which alone
> Bards win honour for their verse
> Now, is the complete reverse
> Of your own, and lies in *hiding*
> All their thoughts and all their meanings,
> So that not the smallest gleanings,
> High or low, be found abiding;
> So that men may read and read
> This way, that way, up and down;
> And when the obscure has grown
> Into a conglomeration,
> Past all human extrication,
> May cry, "Very fine, indeed!"'

After a humorous description of the design and process of Egyptian embalming, which has suggested the idea of the satire, he continues:—

> 'Poets, in these latter days,
> Go ahead of such trite ways;
> Let their bodies seek the goals
> Natural to them—life once ended,

z z 2

But meanwhile make wonderful
Mummies of their sentient souls;
Wrap them round with strange devices,
And embalm with mystic spices,
So that when the oracle
To set speech hath condescended,
Seems it, that whate'er he says
Hath had very far to travel,
And the labyrinth unravel
Of a thousand bandages.

\*          \*

Go, ask famous Emerson,
How his crowns and palms are won,
And he'll tell you, it may be—
Partly by the verity
And the luminous discourse,
That my soul *would* utter by
Right of its nobility.
And that men approved, perforce;
But far more, young bard, I deem,
By my new, fine-writing scheme,
That the age greets with such clapping;
Or, to use a figure, screening
An immensity of meaning—
By my skill in mummy-wrapping.'

This for a *debutant* is a bold stroke. In a note on the above passage he brings his charge home :—' Mr. Emerson himself,' he says, ' in his " Representative Men," accepts the axiom that every thought clearly conceived may also be clearly expressed, and, therefore, either condemns his own practice, or reflects on the lucidity of his thinking. Would it be too much to ask of him and of his English friend, Mr. Carlyle also, vehement declaimers as they both are against the " shams" and the " cants" of the day, to think a little of this " sham" also, and, for the sake of their consistency, to " put it down?" '

After this the reader will not be surprised to hear that Mr. Westwood's poems have, at least, the merit of being intelligible, and that, as times go, is no small praise; but, in addition to this, they are fresh and vivid in their conceptions, cheerful in their tone, and genial and healthful in their tendency. Poetic fancy has too often been made the handmaid of scepticism, and the pander to vice. In these cardinal respects our author, we believe, has not written in the lightest hours of his life a line which at its most solemn season he would desire to erase. To say of him that in perusing his writings we meet with a profusion of ' fairy fiction,' very disproportionate to the amount of ' truth severe,' and that we are inclined to desiderate a little

more bread, and a little less sack, is only to affirm, either that
Mr. Westwood is not endowed with the highest order of poetic
genius, or that the fugitive character of his pieces does not
admit of its complete manifestation.   Still we see, or think we
see, in this volume some marks of a fancy and a feeling which,
with a subject favourable to their full development, would win
for the author a high place among modern poets.   He has no
weakness that he cares to disguise, and is distinguished from
many of his contemporaries, by scorning the apish mystification
which would impose it on the vulgar, if he had it, as a misunderstood and hidden power.

Mr. Westwood, though free from mannerism, betrays the
company which he has kept as favourites, if not as models ; and
we cannot help thinking they must have been somewhat too
exclusively of modern date.   'The Poet's Flower-gathering,'
and 'Effie's Secret,' and perhaps 'A Vision of Old Fames,' but
for its excellent anti-martial moral, will remind the reader of
Tennyson ; 'Love her still' will suggest the recollection of
Hood's 'Bridge of Sighs ;' and the poem entitled 'A Justification' more closely resembles the 'Poete Mourant' of M. de
Lamartine than is perhaps quite safe in one who would resolutely avoid the fault of plagiarism.   A comparison of the two
following passages will, we think, justify our conclusion :—

> ' *Then wherefore dare to sing ?* you ask.   Go out
> Into the orchard closes, good my friend,
> And ask the bee and ask the grasshopper,
> Why *they* sing, they, frail creatures of an hour ;—
> Ask why, beneath the same soft loving sky,
> The artist nightingale woos time to stay
> With witchery of subtlest cadences,
> And the poor sparrow twitters overhead
> In self-asserted insignificance.'

The parallel passage from the French poet is as follows :—

> ' Mais pourquoi chantais tu ?   Demande a Philomèle
> Pourquoi durant les nuits, sa douce voix se mêle
> Au doux bruit des ruisseaux sous l'ombrage roulant ;
> Je chantais, mes amis comme, l'homme respire,
> Comme l'oiseau gémit, comme le vent soupire,
>     Comme l'eau murmure en coulant.'

This is the only close imitation we have detected, and even this
may have been accidental ; and if not, may be sheltered under
the example of some of our greatest poets.   Our author, indeed,
never even reminds us of any but masters, and of these he is
anything but a servile copyist.

With the exception of a brief passage introduced for the

purpose of criticism, we have only suffered our author to exhibit
himself as a satirist.    It is only doing him justice to place before
the reader, in conclusion, a specimen of his talent and taste as a
poet.    Some extracts which we should have preferred are too
extended for our limits ; and from the piece we select, entitled
' The White Angel,' we are, from the same reason, compelled to
cite a single scene :—

> ' Ah, Luigi ! how we lived in those old days !
> How we *felt* life !—you, in your studio, perched
> High up amongst the roofs, on the shady side
> Of the great grass-grown court—working betimes
> In the cool morning ;—in my idlesse, I,
> Loitering and looking on, or listening
> To the glad under-current of the song
> That seemed to float your fancies into life,
> With magical impulsion.    How you sang,
> The day you finished my white angel there !
> Some snatches of that pleasant melody
> Ring in mine ears e'en yet—a dulcet strain,
> A love-lay for two voices, was it not?
> For little Bice, poor Arlotto's child,
> Who came that morning from the farm, with grapes
> And water-melons for our thirsty noon,
> Blent her clear tones with yours, and unawares,
> It may be, left some record of herself
> In the rare cunning of your handiwork.
> Dear little Bice ! how she stared, the while
> She watched your chisel tripping lightly o'er
> The exquisite fair face—coaxing a smile
> To hover round the lips—outshedding calm
> On the high forehead—waving the broad stream
> Of floating hair, or adding, plume on plume,
> To the white glory of the folded wings,
> Drooped meekly, earthward.    We all sang . . ay, *all*,
> When, the last touch bestowed, your statue stood
> In its perfected grace :—we sang till walls
> And windows thrilled, and Bice's childish voice,
> Swelling, exulting, like a lark's up-borne
> Over the topmost cloud beneath the sky,
> Poured its sweet silver treble through the storm,
> Till it seemed to stir the down on the snowy vans
> Of the immaculate angel, and uplift
> The light transparent folds of drapery.'

If we must take one exception against a work, the perusal of
which has afforded us much pleasure, it will refer to the *book* as
distinguished from its contents.    It is, altogether, too pretensive,
and reminds us unpleasantly of the hot-pressed dilettanti whose

names have long been forgotten, and whose writings which have escaped the more ignoble uses of trade are only found among the ' and twelve others' at the close of an auction-catalogue. The rivulet of type in the meadow of margin is too unsuited to the utilitarian tendencies of the age even for poetry, and is certainly the only feature in Mr. Westwood's book which reminds us of an inferior portrait in a very gorgeous frame.

---

ART. V.—*Report of the Debate in the House of Commons on the English Universities.* July 10, 1850.

WHAT form of education would really meet the wants of the present time—what habits, what tastes, what tone of feeling it is desirable to develop in young men to enable them to play a healthy and a manly part in the professions or other employments into which modern life distributes them—is a question very often asked, and very hard to answer. That it is not supplied in the universities, as they work at present, is generally agreed; but the agreement ends in the negative, and the loudest fault-finders are most at a loss when asked what they would substitute. Some clamour for professional education, some for more physical science; some to be rid of the religious discipline, some to make it more stringent; and those who see with any distinctness that the business of a university is the education of the man rather than the professional man, know just as little what the man is to be when he is educated, or how to set about making him what he ought to be. It is rather, therefore, from the vague feeling that something is wrong, than from any decided knowledge of what is to be changed, that the present stir has arisen about the education of Oxford and Cambridge; and it has taken the form of a commission of inquiry, under the pressure of public opinion, which has been leading recently to many other wholesome inquiries. People are asking why the expenses of an education there are so enormous; why, whether it is good or bad, it costs more than four times what the best education costs in France or Germany; and that when there is so good reason to suspect that the endowments and other resources of our two great universities (beyond what is received from the students themselves) exceeds those of all the twenty universities in Germany put together. They have borne the infliction for a long time without complaining, but the longest patience and the longest purse become at last exhausted. The evil has been growing worse and worse, and a few very bad cases of young men in the Insolvent Court, with the exposure of the university life, which took place in the investigation, have brought the thing to a crisis. A commission has now been sitting for five months, receiving such evidence as would voluntarily offer itself, and (it is said) with so much success, that in a short time we are to expect at least a proximately fair account of the resources of the colleges and of the universities, of the proportion in which they are distributed, and of the work which is done for them. A financial agitation has succeeded when agitation on a higher principle has failed again and again, and we will not quarrel with the motive of the reform, provided we can be once satisfied that reform is really to begin.

We are on the way to acting on high principle when we can get to right action upon any principle. And this financial reform, which is spreading through the whole of our legislation, is found, when rightly considered, to involve reform throughout our administration from end to end. We have been a long time talking of our duties to the poor, of the disgrace of leaving them to rot in their filth, and in their ignorance; but it is the pressure of the rates which has worked conviction. A filthy and ignorant population is found more expensive than a decent and educated one ; and, as a prudent outlay, we are in consequence bestirring ourselves. So famine-rates framed the Encumbered Estates Bill, and began the moral reformation of Ireland. We cannot afford the Colonial Office the luxury of an empire on which the sun never sets; and the colonies are obtaining a justice from us, for which, as justice, they might have pleaded long enough. Let us not quarrel with the old proverb, that 'Honesty is the best policy.' Coleridge says that the proverb is true, but that he is not an honest man who acts upon it, but he may be on the way to become an honest man, and, at any rate, he is a much pleasanter neighbour. Whatever it be in the estimation of desponding satirists, it is a strong practical principle. This world is so well constituted, that, on the whole, the prudent is the right, and the right the prudent. A man's account-book, if kept faithfully, is an index of his character; and, in the long run, the outlay which will bring in most market profit conduces largely to higher objects of human endeavour. It is the fact of our constitution, with only rare exceptions. Our experience of individuals largely proves it. Our experience of generations invariably proves it. And, at any rate, in bringing so many questions to so definite an issue, we may congratulate ourselves on having cleared the ground of infinite noise and insincere cant—on having something positive and distinct to deal with—

on being able to put the sincerity of loud profession to that keen money-test which has silenced utterly so many such.

And so the Commission is sitting—the University accounts are passing an audit—and in a few months we are to know all about them. *One fact among the rest at which the English people will open their eyes rather widely, is, that at Oxford alone some 120,000l. annually is paid away in fellowships, to which no duty whatever is attached, except that of residence and study at the university; and that by a convenient evasion of the statutes, some 70,000l. goes to eke out the income of poor curates and young barristers, whose residence consists in presenting themselves once a year inside the college walls to take out new leave of absence.* But for our comments on facts such as this we must wait till they are officially revealed. In the meantime, we may as well say that we cannot look on this present move as more than the first, when many will have to be taken—one leaf turned over of a long document. The evidence is voluntary, and therefore suspicious. The heads of houses are making difficulties; and without them, or even with them, the accounts of the colleges, like those of all ecclesiastical corporations, are so complicated, from the system of fines, which prevails so largely, that it will be a matter of very great difficulty to get at the real value of their properties. Moreover, the Commissions are constructed in a spirit of kindness rather than of severe scrutiny; they will shrink from broadly exposing the faults of the homes in which their members have all been nurtured; and we fear that there will be an endeavour to distract the attention of the public towards general questions of university education —an endless subject, on which it is scarcely possible to speak a reasonable word. However, there can be no doubt something will come out, enough to stimulate further inquiry, and if that is all, we shall be satisfied that at least a beginning has been made.

But the university finance is but one point which will require searching into. There is another far deeper, far more difficult one with which the present commission does not offer to deal, but with which hereafter some commission must deal before any real improvement can be looked for. Not the university and college expenditure, but the students' own expenditure, their habits, their taste, their lives, which are, in part, an index of the value of the education which they receive, and as young men so largely influence each other, form the one important moral element in the education itself. Considering the claims of the Church of England, considering that the ground on which she demands a control over the education of the whole country, is, that other bodies may teach, but that she only can train—she only can form the character—it cannot be thought unjust to try her by her own works.    Yet, alas, this unhappy leaf is the last she will dare to turn—the moral condition of her children at school or college, is the very last feature to which she will be compelled to admit the public eye.   This is not, in the least, a pleasant business to bring under discussion ; yet it is one which, for the Church's sake, for all our sakes, must be looked into, and that speedily.   These are not times when we can shut our eyes and be willingly ignorant; we must have the veil lifted off from the institutions, where, so long as she has existed, she has had her own way without let or hindrance; and it is this subject with which we shall principally occupy the following pages, while we wait for the Report from Downing-street.   We shall follow it up, as the Commission must one day follow it, to the public schools ; for it is there that the fountain of the mischief is perennially flowing, and it is as idle to attempt to purify the universities while these corrupted streams remain in their pollution, as to filter the water of a river in the centre of its course, so long as filthy sewers are draining into its current.

Sir Charles Napier, in taking leave of the Indian army, touched the core of the disease.   He had found the mess-rooms utterly disorganized by immorality, and he charged the vicious habits of the young officers, in large part, on the false notions of manliness which they had brought with them from the English schools.   It has never been supposed that a very high morality is necessary for the healthy working of army discipline, and things must be bad indeed when they force such a protest from a commanding-officer.   Dr. Arnold, who, alone of modern school-masters, did anything to improve the moral tone of his school, deplores, in language almost piteous, the barrenness of his labour.   He speaks in one of his sermons as if the boys only met together to corrupt each other, and invokes the holy influences of home to counteract in the vacation the pernicious lessons which they learn at the scene of their education.   The inter-pretation which he offers of the evil is the most mournful satire on his own position, and, if it were true, would be conclusive against schools altogether as fatally and necessarily poisonous. He saw that young boys came there innocent, that, when their education was over, and they returned to the world, they recovered themselves, and became, at least, tolerably decent; and he supposed, in his despair, that there was something imprac-ticable in the school period of life, when the boy was passing into the young man, and the passions had outgrown their under-standing.

But, whatever is the cause, the fact is, beyond question ; things are so bad that we are afraid to look them in the face.   We pass them by as necessary evils for which silence is the best remedy; we varnish over the surface and say nothing, and allow nothing to be said; or if ever (as from time to time will happen) the crust breaks and discloses what is below, we smother it up in haste and horror, as if it was the exception and not the rule. A few months ago there was an exposure of the kind at one of the dependencies of Woolwich, and there has been seldom any larger piece of injustice than in the mode in which the authorities dealt with it. It was unjust alike to the boys and to the public; for the boys ought not to have been held up to gaze as if they had been involved in some extraordinary badness, when their fault was shared by the mass of boys in every school in England, and the public were cheated into supposing that the uncommon severity of the punishment was a proof of the uncommonness of the fault.

Unhappily it is much easier to see why the schools are in such a state than to suggest a remedy. We do not give it up in despair, and accept Arnold's libel upon boys' natures; we believe them naturally to be high-minded and generous; more easily stirred to feel and act in a really noble way than by-and-bye they will be in their older and cooler life, if only the right means be taken to stir them; but, perhaps, there is something in this whole system of modern life into which we have passed making just means more hard to come by than it has yet been in any past period of history. Boys *may* be *taught to learn*, they *cannot be taught to live.* They learn by method, they live by example. They form their rule of action, not by what they know, but by what they admire; by what seems to them to be noble and manly; and unless a high ideal is given them, they will and must form a bad one of their own. There is this misfortune in the present state of things, that the virtues of grown men are not such as boys understand; they cannot enter into them, and, therefore, the master's *lives* are no pattern to them. The masters do not excel them in any points in which their sympathies are enlisted strongly, and are, therefore, looked up to as scholars, but despised as men. There is a strong animal nature in boys and in young men which requires direction—which requires a noble direction; with noble examples before it, with danger to be ventured and honour to be gained—such as the Olympic games furnished in old Greece, or the discipline of chivalry in the middle ages; and we have nothing, nor is it easy to see what we could or should have. But the resulting evil it is, unhappily, too easy to see: all that side of our boys' natures (and it is by far the largest), is left to run to waste; and of all waste places in this world the devil, it is said, is not slow to take possession. He has persuaded the poor boys, wherever

they get together, to accept a standard of manliness as deplorable
as ever human nature went astray after.   Debt is manly, as Sir
Charles Napier had to say; so is swearing, so is drinking, so is
filthy talking ;  and something else there is more manly than
either debt, or drunkenness, or swearing, or filthy language,
which they look upon as the inauguration of manhood—a
mystery which sheds a *nimbus* round the initiated, and makes
them objects of admiring wonder to the poor aspiring proselytes
of the gate.   It is no use to blame the boys, they are unguided,
and they do but repeat the phenomena which human nature has
many times exhibited.   They are unguided ; the guidance by
which boys can profit is not to be found in catechizing and
in chapel-going, but in strong healthy action, and there is none
provided for them.  Still less is it desirable to keep it all so secret ;
there is no surer way to make a bad wound mortal, than to skin
it over before it is healed.   The world puts it aside with a foolish
hope that things are better than they were ; that ten years ago,
or twenty years ago, it might have been as we describe, but that
there has been some great marked improvement since their
time.   Ten or twenty years hence it will be the same story, for
it means no more than that the speakers themselves are improved,
they and their own contemporaries ; and, as they no longer see
any more of their old schools than the outside, and the outside
is kept decent, they try to persuade themselves that there has
been a change.

   The masters know better ; they know it, but they cannot help
it.   They console themselves, as Arnold did (though, indeed,
he could not console himself), partly with supposing it inevitable,
partly with the few exceptions, which of course there are.   In
all schools there are a few boys of really high principle—there
are a few more whose constitutions are animally defective.   Out
of these are formed the scholars, the distinguished of school and
college, who, afterwards, as they grow up, become the after
teachers and masters in the same institutions.   But the evil repro-
duces itself, even through them ; for, as a rule, they shrink from
contact with the other boys in the schools.   They cultivate their
minds and discipline their consciences, but they grow up by a
sort of fatal necessity again defective in the one side of the
character which would give them a commanding influence as
men, and so the old mischief repeats itself.  The same causes and
the same effect, the same mass of evil—the same small exception
of imperfect good.   We are quite ready to acknowledge the
difficulty of finding the real remedy for so deep an evil.   It will
come, but it will be of long, slow growth.

' Penitusque necesse est
Multa diu concreta modis inolescere miris.'

We do not blame the masters ; we do not absolutely blame the system which we cannot see the way to mend. There is only one decisive corollary which we at once and surely draw from it—that the claims of the Church of England to a monopoly of the education of the country, with such witnesses against her in her own institutions, is little less than monstrous. The point on which she rests her claim is precisely that on which she herself decisively and ignominiously fails.

Well, with such ideas and with such preparation as one of these schools will furnish him with, a boy of eighteen comes up to college. He is installed in his own rooms. He is his own master, free to choose his own society, with large command of ready money, with fawning tradesmen pressing upon him un-limited credit; in the heart of temptation, and yet without experience; as far as his habits of life are concerned, utterly without control; and with his time (with the exception of chapel once a day, and three hours in the morning, when he must be at lecture) at his own disposal. Every day of his life, from noon till midnight, he is his own, to do what he will with : he may go where he pleases, do what he pleases, and no inquiry is made after him. His time is his garden, to which his will is gardener; and none but he claims any interest in the virtues or the vices which he shall choose to plant there. Such is the inestimable ' college discipline,' of which we hear so much. It may not be easy to insist on anything more stringent; but it should not be called discipline. And now can any one doubt what sort of life a boy so circumstanced, so trained, and so tempted, will lead? It seems really as if the universities go on the principle that ex-perience is the best teacher; and expose their children to every temptation, that their falls and their sufferings may be a lesson to them.

But we will follow the clue of an undergraduate's expenses, and the items of his account-book shall be the index of the moral atmosphere about him. A low average of the cost of Oxford to each student—including entrance-fees, dues, degree-fees, and other university charges—cannot be taken as less than 200*l.* for each year of residence ; or for the four years, 800*l.* We say, a low average. There are a few, a very few, cautious, well-trained young men, who get through for a smaller sum, but they are rare, and exceptive—men who have a genius for managing money, which, like all other genius, is uncommon. The common man, who is tolerably pliant to circumstances, is the test of the strength of the circumstances about him ; and, therefore, not taking the actual average of the expenditure of commoners at the university (which is above 300*l.* a year), and setting against the few econo-mists the considerably larger number of excessive spendthrifts,

we keep well under the mark when we
sum for which, with average care and
education can be obtained at the pres
remember that seven-tenths of these y
educated for holy orders. They are to go
and maintain themselves at their curaci
lucky if they earn 100*l.* a year. Yet at
where they are sent to fit them for th
taught how to live—they spend in six m
period of each year's residence), more
and-bye must feed, clothe, lodge them, ar
for charity, for a whole long year. And
this money is got rid of, there is only on
habits of self-indulgence, which it will
labour of years to unlearn again.

Who is to blame, then? Surely someb
other matters in this world, it is difficult t
*some* into a particular, each party concerne
share of blame for themselves. More
authorities obtrude their own part of the l
control reaches, everything they declare
the most rigid economy; and if the stude
least, they will have it, it is no fault of th
over and over again, and so seldom ques
believe what they say;—we mean to qu
that very seriously.

On looking round, the first morning
wakes into his new life, the young fresh
are far from disagreeable. He finds hi
rooms better furnished, in most cases, tl
accustomed to in his father's house—sofas
elegant tables, luxuriate about him; and
friends, no other creature except himself c
in them. They are his: such as the cu
gards as necessary for a boy of his age to
a gentleman, and for which he will be
average, perhaps 60*l.* The annual rent wh
from 12*l.* to 16*l.*: a sufficiently small sum a
lect that the Oxford year is only six mont
more considerable figure of 10*s.* a week.
his furniture, at the end of three years
return, setting the wear and tear at 20*l.* fo
or something over 5*s.* a week; add for c
battery, bread, cheese, beer, &c.), 18*s.*;
there is the grocer's bill for tea, sugar, co
bill, at the end of term, for milk, egg

breakfast or tea necessaries ; wear and tear of plate and linen, of glass and crockery, candles, and washing of sheets and towels ; and putting all these items together, the lowest weekly average of expense for *board and lodging,* as it would be furnished by contract at a boarding-house, is at least 2*l.* 10*s.* a week ; and that at the colleges where the large wholesale dealing offers every facility for cheapness.

It is absolutely enormous ! Contractors would be found who would gladly undertake the
fortune into the bargain. We do not
graduates do not get their money's worth (such as it is). They do get it—it would be better if they did not. They get it in a style and in a luxury which, with few exceptions, they have never known before, and most likely will never know again ; and which they will one day count it their worst misfortune to have ever known at all. Surely the authorities are responsible for this—surely it is not a sufficient excuse for them to say that the boy is under no obligation to take the handsome furniture, that he may turn it out if he likes, and live with drugget and rush chairs, as he will do afterwards, whether he likes or not, when he gets to his curacy. But who can expect the courage or the sense to do it from an inexperienced boy ? The temptation ought not to be thrown in his way under the sanction of the authority which he is taught to respect ; and if he choose to be luxurious and foolish, it should be through his own seeking. As it is, he is not slow to follow on the road on which he is thus happily started. He finds himself launched among a number of young men of his own age ; and if he go into society at all, he must live as the rest, do as the rest—and, of course, he will. If he go to parties, he must return them, and entertain as he is entertained. The school ideal is carried out to its fulness ; unhappily at college there is every facility for carrying it out. As an illustration of the life which results, let us look at a wine party, at its best, at a quiet man's room (and most men either give or accept such parties every night of their residence). Hall-dinners are at five ; at about six, the party will be found, collected in numbers varying from ten to twenty, before a table piled with luxuries, such as once a year, perhaps, find their way to their *home* dinner-table ; in summer, large basins of ice ; in summer and winter, chipped orange-peel, and sponge-cake, fruit, and preserves, often bad enough, but always expensive enough. For each dish, and often there are dozens of them (for it is left commonly to the pastry-cook's discretion), the unwise host (or rather his father, when he settles *the bills*), pays eighteen-pence —and they say they are never eaten. The pastry-cook contracts with the scout, and the same trash appears and re-appears

we keep well under the mark when we fix 200*l.* a year as the sum for which, with average care and prudence, an Oxford education can be obtained at the present day. Now, let us remember that seven-tenths of these young men are being educated for holy orders. They are to go down into the country and maintain themselves at their curacies, where they will be lucky if they earn 100*l.* a year. Yet at college—at the places where they are sent to fit them for their duties, and to be taught how to live—they spend in six months (for that is the period of each year's residence), more than double what by-and-bye must feed, clothe, lodge them, and leave them a surplus for charity, for a whole long year. And when we ask, how all this money is got rid of, there is only one answer—in learning habits of self-indulgence, which it will cost them the bitter labour of years to unlearn again.

Who is to blame, then? Surely somebody! Yet, as in many other matters in this world, it is difficult to convert that indefinite *some* into a particular, each party concerned refuses to accept any share of blame for themselves. More particularly the college authorities obtrude their own part of the business ; as far as their control reaches, everything they declare to be conducted with the most rigid economy ; and if the students are extravagant, at least, they will have it, it is no fault of theirs. This is repeated over and over again, and so seldom questioned that they really believe what they say ;—we mean to question it, however, and that very seriously.

On looking round, the first morning of residence, when he wakes into his new life, the young freshman's first impressions are far from disagreeable. He finds himself in possession of rooms better furnished, in most cases, than what he has been accustomed to in his father's house—sofas and settees, arm-chairs, elegant tables, luxuriate about him ; and all for himself and his friends, no other creature except himself claiming part or interest in them. They are his ; such as the custom of the college regards as necessary for a boy of his age to enable him to live like a gentleman, and for which he will be required to pay, at an average, perhaps 60*l.* The annual rent which he will pay will be from 12*l.* to 16*l.* ; a sufficiently small sum apparently, till we recollect that the Oxford year is only six months, when it assumes the more considerable figure of 10*s.* a week. If he has paid 60*l.* for his furniture, at the end of three years he will receive 40*l.* in return, setting the wear and tear at 20*l.* for the eighteen months, or something over 5*s.* a week ; add for coals, 4*s.* ; kitchen and buttery (bread, cheese, beer, &c.), 18*s.* ; in all 1*l.* 17*s.* Then there is the grocer's bill for tea, sugar, coffee, &c. ; the servants' bill, at the end of term, for milk, eggs, and other ordinary breakfast or tea necessaries; wear and tear of plate and linen, of glass and crockery, candles, and washing of sheets and towels; and putting all these items together, the lowest weekly average of expense for *board and lodging*, as it would be furnished by contract at a boarding-house, is at least 2*l.* 10*s.* a week; and that at the colleges where the large wholesale dealing offers every facility for cheapness.

It is absolutely enormous! Contractors would be found who would gladly undertake the business at half-price, and make a fortune into the bargain. We do not mean that the under-graduates do not get their money's worth (such as it is). They do get it—it would be better if they did not. They get it in a style and in a luxury which, with few exceptions, they have never known before, and most likely will never know again; and which they will one day count it their worst misfortune to have ever known at all. Surely the authorities are responsible for this—surely it is not a sufficient excuse for them to say that the boy is under no obligation to take the handsome furniture, that he may turn it out if he likes, and live with drugget and rush chairs, as he will do afterwards, whether he likes or not, when he gets to his curacy. But who can expect the courage or the sense to do it from an inexperienced boy? The temptation ought not to be thrown in his way under the sanction of the authority which he is taught to respect; and if he choose to be luxurious and foolish, it should be through his own seeking. As it is, he is not slow to follow on the road on which he is thus happily started. He finds himself launched among a number of young men of his own age; and if he go into society at all, he must live as the rest, do as the rest—and, of course, he will. If he go to parties, he must return them, and entertain as he is entertained. The school ideal is carried out to its fulness; unhappily at college there is every facility for carrying it out. As an illustration of the life which results, let us look at a wine party, at its best, at a quiet man's room (and most men either give or accept such parties every night of their residence). Hall-dinners are at five; at about six, the party will be found, collected in numbers varying from ten to twenty, before a table piled with luxuries, such as once a year, perhaps, find their way to their *home* dinner-table; in summer, large basins of ice; in summer and winter, chipped orange-peel, and sponge-cake, fruit, and preserves, often bad enough, but always expensive enough. For each dish, and often there are dozens of them (for it is left commonly to the pastry-cook's discretion), the unwise host (or rather his father, when he settles *the bills*), pays eighteen-pence —and they say they are never eaten. The pastry-cook con-tracts with the scout, and the same trash appears and re-appears

till it is putrid. Then there is wine, plenty of it, profusion of
it; and if quiet men don't drink much, at least they drink a
great deal more than they need; but the quiet men do not
number above a third of the university; and of late years, it has
been found necessary, at most colleges, to fix the hour of evening
chapel before hall-dinner, instead of at seven, which used to be
the hour. The wild eyes and unsteady steps had become a
scandal. Let us go on with the evening in what is called a fast
man's room—a vague term—but which, between its extreme
limits, comprehends the large majority. Among the others, the
conversation is, at least, decent, if not wise; but here, full of
wine and folly, the poor unwise fellows talk of things and listen
to things which it will be the shame of their after lives to have
uttered or endured. Here, amidst the thick rolling tobacco-
clouds, they arrange their hunting parties, tandem drives, steeple
chases. Here they display the trash of their tailor, their
jeweller, and their haberdasher: boys dressing for boys as if
Oxford was the Court. So flows away the money, so flows the
time. More than half of them are to be clergymen by-and-bye.
They make hay while the sun shines. They make haste to enjoy
themselves ere yet the evil days come, and the hour in which
they shall say, 'We have no pleasure therein.' The evenings
after such an introduction are of little service for any reasonable
purpose. A lounge to the billiard-room, or to the tobacconist's,
or worse, a lounge in the streets, follows the break up of the
party, and then, perhaps, back to supper, to more wine, more
evil talk, more trash, or else cards or novels. Such is the
evening of the larger portion of the Oxford students. The
mischief of it all struck us so forcibly that we used to urge on
the college authorities the desirableness of choosing an earlier
hour for the hall-dinner, which would put an end to wine parties,
and save each undergraduate at least thirty pounds a year, and
three hours each day of reasonable possession of himself. But
what stopped the wine party would have been equally fatal to
the fellows' common room party; and the proposal was scouted
as a disturbance of established usage.

It is here that the reform must commence, if Oxford and
Cambridge are to be ever accessible to poorer men—with the
habits of the undergraduates themselves. Something must be
done to put an end to all this absurd self-indulgence—self-
indulgence on which they themselves, as their better judgment
ripens, will look back upon with disgust and shame. Even those
who live vicious lives are not vicious; very few of them, indeed,
are so; but corrupted by school, and without opportunities of
wiser knowledge, they fall, as a matter of course, into the habits
of the circle into which they are thrown. When they get away,

with few exceptions, they right themselves; but what a satire is it on educational discipline! What waste of precious years! And how many home struggles, what family unhappiness, what alienation between child and parent, what broken friendship, what forfeited respect, what domestic tragedies, may not lie in the unseen history of many a young man, germinating up out of these woeful years at college — of young men, otherwise well-meaning, who did well enough before, and will, in the end, come back to be what they were, but on whom the miserable influences of their education worked like a fatal spell. Surely it is a hard thing to force them into such temptation, yet as things are they are forced into it. There is no escape—they cannot help it. They must enter at some one of the colleges. All the colleges are in the same state, and they must either forego all society, which it is ridiculous to expect, or they must enter what they find, with the chances, of course, infinitely against them. No matter what a man is, whether he is rich or whether he is poor, the average level of expenses is not suited as it ought to be to the means of the poorest, but of the wealthiest; and the son of the poor clergyman, who is denying himself and his family the most ordinary conveniences to give him the 'benefit of a university education,' can only obtain it at the cost of being maintained for three or four years in a ridiculous luxury, which unnerves and unmans him. Wherever the untamed spirits of young men get together, there will be temptation; but woe to those who might check them, and who do not; who pass them by, if they do not foster them; woe to those who make that a necessity which might be no more than a chance.

We shall offer a few suggestions presently on what we believe to be the best present practical remedy; but we must first insist that it is *not* what now offers itself as the only one to the minds of the authorities—'the establishment of poor colleges.' They cling to their system like ivy to a decayed old tree, and cannot conceive any good to be possible without it. But when it has once failed, and still fails so utterly, why should we expect any better from it in a new foundation? The existing colleges are poor colleges; they are founded for poor men. The statutes are never weary of repeating it. If, with the existing machinery, a college can be conducted more cheaply, if board and lodging and teaching can be furnished on easier terms, it ought to be done now. Either such colleges would slide away into the ruts, and become as the rest; or if they did not, it could only be prevented by arbitrary distinctions of a wounding and degrading kind. Because men are poor we have no right to set a public mark upon them, and stamp them so. It would inflict a deeper and more dangerous hurt on their self-respect than would be compensated by the previous college discipline. The way, as we see it, to amendment lies through another serious charge, which we have to bring against the present system.

The duties attached to fellowships by the statutes of the various foundations are simply residence and study. They were intended as the support of a leisured class—as literary pensions for services too substantial to meet a ready recompense from the world. And this was all. Fellows of colleges were not supposed to teach; the teaching was carried on in unendowed halls, and the colleges had nothing to do with it. At the Reformation, however, from various causes, the halls declined; the colleges changed their character and took in students, and in the end revolutionized the system. The meaning of fellowships changed from its first intention, and they fell to those whose business was to be educating others rather than reading and writing themselves. But the 'close foundations' produced inequality in the attainments of the fellows. In each college there would be only a few really qualified to teach; and these, therefore, it grew the practice to select as tutors, to give them a definite salary (for which the students paid), and to leave the remainder to live idly, to go away into the country or into other professions, and to have nothing more to do with their colleges than to receive their annual dividends. The small number left to fill the tutorships has, of late years, been even more reduced by the religious animosities. The Heads of Houses, with whom the appointments rest, have considered themselves bound to protect the undergraduates from what they severally consider heterodox. If the Head is a Low Churchman, he cannot conscientiously make a tutor of a Puseyite; if he is himself Puseyite, he looks jealously on the liberal Protestant; and hence the disproportion in the number of tutors to their pupils has become so great as to render them ineffectual for any real service. The number is ridiculously too small; the quality often inferior—the unable man being often more near in opinion to the Head of his college than the able: and the result is, that as the college tutor superseded the professor, he, in his turn, is superseded by the private tutor, to whom more and more all the real work is falling, while the college tutor becomes a cipher. But, alas! for all these changes the undergraduate must pay. The private tutor is a clear extra expense. Most men read with one for a year, at least. At the rate of 17 guineas a term, or for the year 51 guineas; add for the very frequent long vacation, 30 guineas; and there are 81 guineas laid on upon the other inordinate extravagances as a consequence of the jealousies, the follies, and inefficiencies, of the colleges. So ludicrously, too, does this religious jealousy revenge itself, that the student who may not have the ablest man in his college to teach him officially, for fear of dangerous doctrine, may go where he will for his own inofficial private tutor, over whom no authority whatever is, or can be, exercised.

Of the sort of fruits which occasionally result from such proceeding, take the following for an illustration. We allow it to be an extreme case; but it serves all the better to show what things may come to. A few years ago (it may be so now for all we know), the favourite private tutor in Oxford—the 'crack coach' in all desperate cases, to whose assistance it would be dangerous to say how many country gentlemen's sons do not owe their present possession of the family living—*used to teach the Bible, the Early Church History, the Heresies, the Thirty-nine Articles, and whatever subjects enter into the Divinity Examination, with a Memoria Technica of blasphemy and obscenity*: with no specimen of which have we any intention of defiling these pages. An hour a day is the time usually given by the private tutor; but this gentleman's pupils used to club their hours and form a class, to secure more of his instruction. A supply of cigars and beer, which usually added to his eloquence, was provided alternately at their several rooms, while they sat round him with their note-books. Yet, in spite of such abominable abuse, the private-tutor system is the healthiest part of the present working institution. It is the healthiest because it is the most efficient—because whatever work is done at all is done through it. Even this divinity tutor was the ablest for his purpose; and the fault lay rather in the foolish inefficiency of the examination, the requirements of which such teaching would satisfy. Scholarship could not be taught so, nor philosophy, nor history, nor mathematics; the imposture would be detected in an instant. And surely his existence is no more than a *reductio ad absurdum* of the existing divinity schools. The severe examinations are severely met. Whatever it be which he wants, the undergraduate's necessities are an unerring guide to him. Reading for high honours, he cannot afford to choose his private friend to teach him, or the man with whose opinions he sympathizes; he chooses whoever is best able to give him what he wants; and, consequently, by far the ablest men in both universities are, or have been, employed in private tuition. Here we see the free working of the free principle of *competition*. When competition has its scope, there is at least work done. When there is monopoly, there is idleness and worthlessness. By all means, therefore, let private tuition have its full way; it is the natural growth of the necessities of the place. Let the undergraduate choose his own tutor, and he will surely best choose him. The present problem is rather to leave his choice free, and yet, by some better distribution of the enormous misapplied education fund, to relieve him, at least partially, of a burden of extra payment which he has no right to have inflicted on him. The tutor of largest popularity, if the work required be what it should be, will be the best man for tutor, the man who ought to be employed; let him therefore be recognised and paid.

It is through this same principle of competition, too, that we see a way out through those far more painful moral difficulties with which we were perplexed above. We cannot do more in this place than merely indicate what we mean. But we ought not to press the evil into prominence without suggesting at least a possible remedy. Our universities were free under the Edwards; and the college restrictive system, which was an innovation, has as notoriously failed. Let them go back to what they were. Leave the colleges as they are, with their grand rooms, their extravagance, and their ineffectual discipline, for such parents as believe that they are both good and effectual. Leave them alone—do not meddle with them—only do not leave them their monopoly. Do not force a young man wishing to be educated, into a circle of expense and temptation. If he is thrown into it, let it be his own fault, or the fault of his friends.

The colleges will not reform themselves, their habits are too confirmed and too inveterate; but there can be no reason why students should not be allowed to come up as they used to do in the early days of the university, to live not in the colleges, but in such lodgings as they pleased to provide for themselves. As a matter of course boarding-houses would spring up, where contractors would supply whatever was necessary at half the present cost; and rich and poor would find their separate levels, as they do in the world. Each would take his own place without injury to either, and the poor man's self-respect would never be wounded by any vexatious or arbitrary distinctions. It is easy to bear the humblest position when we voluntarily choose it—when it is but a simple condition which our circumstances require of us; but what in itself is trifling becomes intolerable when it is forced to wear a public livery of shame. Whether or no such boarding-houses should be subject to any internal discipline would be a matter of after consideration. To work well it must be their own natural growth, which, beforehand, it is impossible to anticipate. The only discipline which at present is the least effective in repressing vice is that of the proctors and university police; and to this, of course, all residents, whether in college or out of it, would be alike subject. Thus competition would have its free way. The necessary expenses would be kept down by the competing boarding-houses. The colleges, when they saw a new growth rising up beside them, might, perhaps, be shamed into rivalry; but for this the new growth must have free scope, and free room ; the life must not be strangled out of it by forcing it into a strained obedience to a system which experience proves to be in the offensive sense of that expressive term, good for nothing.

And now to pass on to a higher region. It is said that the teaching at the universities does not meet the present demand, that it is behind the age—and it is true. The man of business scarcely finds it worth his while to send his son there. Lawyers and statesmen, perhaps even clergymen, are as fit for their work without a university education as with one ; at least the facts of the day appear to say so. Oxford and Cambridge do not lead the present English mind. As a rule they drag painfully behind it, and except in the Tract movement, which was against the spirit of the age, and which has failed, they have exercised, of late years, but little influence; and that little is growing daily less. Their wise men, their heads of houses, professors, tutors, are adequate only to working the institutions as they are. Once they were celebrated through Europe ; now their names are not known beyond their own walls. The thinkers, the poets, the men of science, with rare exceptions, are not university men. Even in Parliament, another order of statesmen is striding forward, and will soon be in the first place, to whom these learned schools seem mouldered as the walls of their colleges. It is true, and there is no remedy for it. There is none now, and there can be none till England herself better understands her own position, and her own wants. It is she who must solve this difficulty, for the interests which are at issue in it are only hers. If we suggest anything, it is not now what the change should be, but how to put ourselves on the road towards learning what it should be. Nor is this more than a suggestion, one out of many which will have to be offered from many sides, and weighed and digested before any active stir is made. And, meanwhile, the universities may smile at the present assault upon them. They need not struggle against change. They may rest passive in their own inertness, for there is no party above the political horizon which will dare to lay rough hands on them. In proposing the free boarding-houses we said the present colleges might be left as they are, but we meant only in their working order, and not in their superfluity of useless fellowships. The work, as is proved by their actual condition, can be done by less than half the present staff of fellows. Cut down the number to what is necessary, and sixty or seventy thousand pounds a year will be set free for some better purpose. Out of this might be provided the salaries of the private tutors, funds for scholarships, for prizes in new branches of science, and for endowments of fresh professorships. And there is one more purpose to which a large sum, we think, should be set apart; in more strict harmony with the spirit of the old founders' wills than the modern non-residence, though it may clash more loudly with the letter:—if the universities are to lead the age, it can only be by the presence among them of the leading men of the age. At each of them let there be some twenty considerable salaries to be given as pensions to such men as have best deserved of the country, by important literary and scientific services. Of course they should be required to reside, but without any definite duties assigned to them. They should be men (the value of them would consist in their being so) who could be trusted to make their own duties, and work as occasion called. It has long been the discredit of England that services of such a kind are not publicly recognised among us. There are no rewards for merit, no honourable distinctions—nothing to mark the difference between real greatness and the sham greatness, which to day is in its zenith and to-morrow is gone and forgotten; and men of high gifts either choose a less barren profession, or fall under the temptation of selling themselves for present popularity; or, at best, if they persevere to the end in a really noble self-culture, yet find themselves without a position, without opportunity of usefulness, with powers developed to their very best, and with nothing which they can do with them. In old times, all Europe supplied Oxford and Cambridge with its learned men. If we cannot any longer sift Europe, we can at least sift England. And it is impossible to measure the benefit to the country, to themselves, or to the universities, which with such a home, and such a position provided for them, they might be able to realize. Consider what it might be! Twenty of the picked men of the day really and permanently settled there—men picked for their firm and simple greatness—picked out of all ranks, and, therefore, not with narrow but with broad, national sympathies—a council of the wisest living English men. We should have no fear then for the universities: they would soon take their old place, and lead Europe again. Only if the wisest could be once got chosen—but who shall choose?—there seems the fatal difficulty. A difficulty which if fatal is sad indeed, for it means that there is no man, or body of men, in England who may be trusted with such a patronage without danger of their abusing it. It is not that they are so hard to find. The few greatest men do really stand out upon their pedestals; and if we will be honest with ourselves, we know who they are. If we were to take the suffrage of all the educated men in England, it would be found so. In the names of second-rate men there would be infinite variety; in a few great ones there would be an instinctive agreement. It would be perhaps as it was with those old Greeks who fought at

Salamis: to find the one among them who had best deserved of his country, they took the suffrages of the several states, and it was discovered that each state gave the first place to its own leader, but the second all gave to Themistocles.

And so with us, the first names might be our own party leaders, Whig or Tory, Protestant or Catholic; our second, the few whose greatness, whatever they are, forces us to acknowledge it. But we are not proposing an election of the wisest by universal suffrage, or by any suffrage; at present we suppose them found, and suggest the position which should be given them. And with the hope that it is not impossible that one day the minds which do the real work shall openly hold the first place— that the education of the country shall fall at last into the hands of those who best see into the age and into its wants, we leave this matter, not expecting to find it recommended by any present Commission, royal or parliamentary, but expecting that in some form or other it will be found, generations hence, perhaps, among the happy influences which are giving back to the old seats of English learning their old worth and nobleness.

But whatever the value of this or other suggestions, before we venture on change of any kind, it is indispensable for us to know at least something of what we want. In all large systems there must be short-comings; and to be quarrelling with the universities, and picking them in pieces for this or that superficial fault, without any wide idea to guide us, without asking ourselves for what purpose they exist, and without assuring ourselves that they are not even proximately fulfilling it, is a form of the same culpable rashness, which will tear in pieces political institutions, on account of some small hardships or inconveniences in detail— which it is a dream to suppose anything human on this side the grave can be without. The reformers have been unfortunate hitherto in their parliamentary representatives; what folly was it to waste session after session in vague declamations against Puseyism. Would, indeed, that there were nothing worse! Puseyism is the birth not of the universities, but of the constitution of the Church of England; and of the form in which at the Reformation, its formularies were determined by a compromise. Puseyism at the universities (even at Oxford), was never more than an insignificant sect. Its strength was in the country. Still more ineffectual were those small personalities which were introduced into the debate. Wretched scandal of college elections, inherited by Mr. Heywood from his predecessor, and worn threadbare with repetition, so false and groundless that those who knew the facts passed them by with no answer, but contemptuous silence—Oxford might well laugh to scorn attacks upon her which hinged on such and such a college having elected a fellow because ' he was the nephew of a baronet.'

But we will hope that the cause will pass up into the hands of wiser men, who will henceforth rather look straight into the root of the matter, than stay pointing and picking at a few withered leaves. What is the meaning of education? That is the question. What is it for? What is it to do? Is it not to impart information? Men are sent into this world *to do*, not *to know ;* and knowledge is only valuable as it is convertible into noble activity. The Puseyites are right enough so far, in declaring against an education which will give new powers, and sharpen the wits, without determining them into any positive direction. Talent is not goodness, nor is knowledge, nor do either of them at all necessarily lead to it. The worst crimes of late years have been perpetrated by men of more than rudimentary education—of the sort which we call education—and profligacy, so far from being checked by the best education extant of such sort, is nowhere stronger than in the public schools and colleges where it is conducted. Why should we expect the art of life to be more easily learnt than any other art? We cannot teach music, or drawing, or language, or mechanics, or physical science, by information, but by enforcing a perpetual application of it. The artist must go to his instrument or his pencil, the scholar to his grammar and his translations, the artisan to his tools, the philosopher to his experiments or his facts. Every step in knowledge, as it is imparted, must be carried out into practice, or it is not gained; the higher knowledge cannot be imparted at all till the rudiments are mastered ; and the art of all arts. the art of life, is like the rest, only, as it is the highest, requiring a more patient and more constant discipline. People seem to suppose that they have only to teach what is right in words, and that right action will follow as a matter of course ; as well they might expect that it was enough to teach the law of perspective and of colours, and that the pupil's eye would at once follow the mind and the hand obey the eye.

The present collegiate institutions were founded by men who knew well enough what they wanted; but the wants of the fourteenth century are not the wants of the nineteenth. We have outgrown the old idea. We have burst the livery of monasticism, the rent fragments of which are still clinging about us, but, as yet, without sign of any new garment forming below them. As the old monks looked out at the world, they could see in the rude, rough, lawless, sensual life of it, little more than a devil's service ; and the business of the ecclesiastical training-schools was, not to fit men to fill any part *there*, but rather keeping altogether clear of it, to live not for this world, or in this world, but in retirement from the world to live for another, to live with the incessant thought of death present to them, and to discipline themselves for it by unwearied prayer, by watching and fasting, by pain and sorrow, by silent study of sacred things. And it is this idea, the echoes of which linger in the chapel bells, and in those mournful lamentations, in which, on each succeeding Ash Wednesday, the Church deplores the degeneracy of the modern age. But we are not degenerate— we are rather in an unhappy moulting season—and we are sick and faint till it is over.

The problem for us is to unite what the monks divided; not to cultivate any more that ' fugitive and cloistered virtue,' but to carry out our knowledge into the world, into strong divine activity in it, and to live out our natures nobly as becomes men who fear God. But to see our duty will be to see our present nakedness ; and when we do see it we shall be for a time like him of old who hid himself in the trees of the garden. Such a feeling was that of Puseyism, which saw it, and grasped in her shame at the rags which fluttered about her, and piecing them together, and wrapping her shivering limbs in them, would crawl back into the past. But the spirit of the age has been too strong: They are again rent, and Puseyism is gone, or fast going ; in a few years more it will have ceased, and have become a name. But woe to us if we have asserted our liberty only to turn it to license ! There is a critical period in the lives of all of us, when we pass out from all restraints, when we put on our manhood, and cannot be held any longer under the strong external authority which controlled us as children. We cannot stay our growth. There is no putting back the clock of life. Ready or unready, the time must come, and we must meet it. We must pass under new conditions, and thenceforth take charge of ourselves in other and wider scenes. As the phrase says, we become our own masters ; and it is well for us if we really are so, for we can be nothing better—passing at once under that perfect law of liberty in which restraint has ceased to be because there is nothing to restrain, and we are completely free because we completely obey. But the change is seldom so happy or so easy ; usually it is painful and distorted, full of errors, sorrow, suffering, and shame.

Through some analogous transition period Europe has for some time past been struggling. The struggle lasts longer, unhappily, with nations than with persons ; and to judge by the progress which we have made as yet towards understanding our position, we can have scarcely entered upon its really serious difficulties.

ART. VI.—*The Bards of the Bible.* By George Gilfillan, A.M. 8vo. Pp. 346. Edinburgh: J. Hogg.

IN contemplating the wonderful world on which we live, the inadequate faculties of man have been compelled to the expedient by which he had already subjugated the ruder difficulties of existence.

'Divide et impera' is the canon at once of labour and of science. We are all sectaries in knowledge; botanists, zoologists, geologists, geometrists, geographists; and must be content to learn each to the uttermost his single part of the terrestrial whole. All actors in the great drama of wisdom, but none knowing it throughout; all soldiers in the grand contest of light with darkness, but neither commanding a view of the complete order of march or the broad combinations of the field. Alas! that each too often mistakes his single feature for the wondrous face, his separate scene for the argument of the sublime tragedy, his own particular hillock of enveloping smoke—haply of blood and horrors, of dismay and defeat—for the whole wide battle-ground of genius and of victory. Now and then a Humboldt arises, to whom, having passed a life in every glen and deep place of the earth, it is given before death to ascend the Pisgah of science and behold the unity of his complex world. As with the ' Kosmos,' so with the Microcosm. So much less laborious is consciousness than understanding, that we deliberately divide among our philosophers the investigation of powers and passions, of which, nevertheless, the daily life of each is encylopædic. Different authors have treated of ' imagination,' ' memory,' and ' hope,' though each of them at once hoped, remembered, and imagined.

Moreover, so inefficient is simple consciousness to produce without the intervention of another faculty such a mental representation as shall subserve reason and admit of communication, that the most violent sufferers are often vague in conception, poor in wisdom, and scant in testimony on the very subject of their experience; and so insufficient are the feebler perceptions of particular minds to undergo whatever is the necessary antecedent of an idea, that he who will rise to poetry in a peculiar mental province is often hopelessly barren in the adjoining districts of life. The rustic who fell down yesterday convulsed with rage, what does he know of anger compared with him who drew the wrath of Achilles? There are spiritual monoptotes whom a single song has immortalized.

And this specific character, which mortal weakness and an undeveloped organization have left upon the majority of human minds, has been encouraged and perpetuated by our national and individual habits till we find everywhere indurated callings, personified crafts, incarnate creeds; or (in another phase of specialty) embodied affections, palpable 'ruling passions,' and single faculties done in flesh and blood.

Here and there only we meet with *a man* :—one in whom the complement of human sensations and the plenitude of human passions subserve a commensurate system of adjusted intellect, and the ample frame of a thoroughly furnished mind, knit by adequate sinews and fed by the pulsations of all-circulating energies, is filled by the adit of an unfailing reverence with the vitalizing Spirit of God: one in whose capacity the provinces of intellect lie out green and broad in spacious and well-ordered fertility :—in whom philosophy has not straitened religion, nor religion disorganized philosophy; poetry has not inundated science, nor science undermined poetry; but in whom the federal empire, watered by mingled streams and fragrant with winds rich in united odours, brings the multiform stores of her garnered wealth, and the variegated produce of her teeming fields, to the footstool of an invisible King. For such a man there is in every age a great work to do. The men who make up an age are at best the miniatures of its totality, the ultimate atoms which repeat the shape of the whole; the men by whom an age is *made* are those whose capacity can contain its total as a mere element in a grander combination. The servant of an age may be its natural fruit; the ruler of an age must be begotten of it by God. In every age there are webs of destiny to weave of which the separate threads are to be drawn from the four corners of the spiritual world, and for which every human faculty must spin its filament: elf-cups to mingle, and, alas! hell-broths to boil, wherein the failure of an ingredient breaks the spell; composite structures—chryselephantine statues of thought—for which he is not sufficient artist whose craft is in a single tool, though he handle it never so wisely; systems to be constructed, theories to be absorbed and resolved, general views to be obtained, and universal ideas to be conceived, which require the presence of a consciousness co-extensive with human knowledge, and the assistance of powers representative of the whole nature of man.

Above any epoch that the earth has yet seen, the present generation demands, in whomsoever assumes its spiritual government, the possession of such encyclical powers and acquisitions. The mental phenomena of the period are distinguished not so much for magnitude as multiformity; the complex human soul is roused in every faculty, profoundly exercised in none. Pre-eminently an age of smatterers, this lively time of ours is at once especially unwilling to expect a master, and peculiarly fitted to acknowledge him when he appears. An age of smatterers will yield no subjection to any denizen of smatterdom—no, though he be very prince of smatter. But let the real universalist come forth, and its submission is in the ratio of its sciolism. Every scar of knowledge is tender to his touch, every opened faculty is an avenue of influence, and every ill-governed province of learning rises in irrepressible testimony to its rightful lord.

To all the ordinary forms of leadership such an age is and must be invincibly insubordinate. From the theologian it takes refuge in universal truths; from the philosopher it retreats to special afflatus; from the intuitions of genius it turns to the sobriety of induction; and from the severity of reason to the ardours of popular inspirations. From the solemn face of learning it finds relief in the ready leer of the charlatan, and discards him at length from a dim belief in the possibilities of the unfathomable; for the devotee it has learned the titter of the sceptic, but burns the atheist to satisfy the cravings of its reverence; to the moralist it will recommend a plurality of wives, and turn to write *Mort aux voleurs !* upon the banners of anarchy. It reads Jean Jacques in the ear of civilization, and throws him aside for a pamphlet upon progress: confutes the ' Citizen' in a sonnet on a snowdrop; and answers the ' Ode to Mont Blanc' by a ticket for the Palace of Glass. The statesman is rebuffed by its democracy, the democrat by its omniarchs and ' Cæsars ;' heroes rule in the hearts of its millions, and rot in the bowels of its deserts and dungeons; and the patriot and the exile despoil tyranny of its Schoenbruns and Siberias, by making them the hermit's wilderness and the martyr's cell. Communism defies its accumulated wealth; and a family of money-changers command its politics. Romish aggression is met by British intolerance, and the interdict of the Protestant bigot is answered by the genial Mussulman with the freedom of St. Sophia; Anglican Episcopacy kisses toes from which the Barnabite cries 'Aloof !' and creeps into the discarded confessional of Papal priesthood for the absolution which monkery itself has put to scorn. Peace congresses reply to physical force; barricades and Russian legions laugh sulphu-rously at the pacificator; Sicilian insurrection begets French freedom, which, in turn, assassinates Italian liberty; and the representative of absolute power stands a dictator among the kings of that Europe whose patriots are already banded, whose sternest spirits are already sworn, and whose strongest hand-are already armed to the realization of 'liberty, equality, and association on this earth.'

This strange world-wide arabesque—this grand kaleidoscope of interminable transformation—this age of infinite external and internal confusion, with its chameleon body and unstable soul, its harlequin faces and wear of motley—offers the noblest of enterprises to the powers, the sympathies, the benevolence, the ambition, of the man we have essayed to describe.

It must be approached by no petrified fraction of humanity, by no statuesque countenance of marble uniformity, no ding-dong voice of monotonous dogmatism: still less by him whose facile temper or cartilaginous skeleton cannot resist the example of the antics he would reduce, who sways the mummers by leading the morris, and is content to surpass his fellows by the excess of fellowship—the height of a greasier pole and the breadth of a ghastlier grin.

The multiformity of that                                     age must be the multiformity of Nature—incalculable complexity, but absolute unity; or the multiplicity of an Indian deity—many faces, but one god. With the firm step and genial eye of self-acknowledged purpose, he must advance to this changing time which stands before him mutable and iridescent; its mono-

the 'great white throne.' His relation to
of succession, but co-existence. It must behold in him *at once* so much of all its features as to despair of escaping by a new metamorphosis. He must subdue the Proteus by being superior to *every one* of its shapes.

With all these constitutionally his own, but modified, idealized, and in harmonized subjection to a directing masterdom, an overruling *Ich*, a sovereign individuality, he must advance even to contact with the whole body of his day, seize upon every separate characteristic by virtue of the specific affinity in himself, and at the pace and in the path of his own progress draw the great whole up the hill Excelsior, 'at the pace and in the path of his own progress.'

Of angels speaking to it from heaven, and gnomish subterranean warnings heaving the earth beneath it, this poor age has had, and will yet have, no dearth; what it looks for (consciously or not) is one of those cosmical *men* of whom we speak; coming to it with the outspread arms of a brother, lifting it from its slough into his bosom, resuming his onward path with energies renewed by the burthen, and making his own journey the measure of our advancement. If it were possible that a man should come

to us in greyheaded perfection, equipped in ripe accomplishments, and everywhere developed into final and polished completion, the spectacle would be noble indeed, but comparatively
useless to the moving age.  We want some one to live with us
on a nobler scale the life of all; an elder brother, a head of
the class, a prizeman of the college, a spiritual tribune, a citizen
king :—One who needs small dependence on information from
without—no weatherglass, few soundings, little news, and less
commentary ; who requires neither to collect symptoms, nor to
hold consultations, nor to build observatories, nor to rectify the
globes ; because his own heart is the Ephemeris of his time ;
because he discerns his brother's ailment in his own ; learns its
fluctuations by his own pathology, repeats for our enchantment
the spell that has charmed his proper life, and of the balm which
has healed his own stripes ministers in confidence to the wounds
of the world.

Upon all that the eye sees, and the ear hears, there will be no
lack of commentators in a loquacious time : voluble critics and
popular philosophers, who look up to the starry host of truth in
a sublime superiority to parallax, and to whom, since they
speak only of apparent places, the multitude are likely to give
heed.  The sooner these are silenced, the more distinctly we
shall hear the true voices.  Let them stand aside, that we may
look out intently for that which it is just now our highest interest
to behold.  We require to see enacted before us the genesis,
development, and experience of some great nineteenth century
souls ; ideal minds, the very amplest possible humanity, who, by
virtue of their grade, shall keep in front of the multitudinous
age, but who, refusing to be called the sons of Pharaoh's daughter,
shall remember their brethren in the palaces of Egypt, and
making our dull veins tingle with their fraternity, go before us
(before, but with reverted face) in our exode from this troublous
generation into the milk and honey of the better land.  For
these men, wherever they are, how many and how great are the
problems that be waiting to be solved, and towards the solution
of which the mental and physical warfares of the last half
century have done no more than provide the data and clear
away that dust of ages which hid us from the postulates.  To
point authoritatively to the axioms still remains for him who
shall vindicate his right to apply them.  These subjects are
of a scope and importance to satisfy the loftiest ambition, and
involve such novel elements, such indefinite possibilities, and
such unlimited rewards, as might stimulate to the uttermost the
most accomplished capacity among men : subjects which we do
not require to hear debated, but which it would be unspeakably
well for us to see calmly and elaborately passed through the

broad extent of such a mind as we have described; submitted as a whole, with their crude accumulations of centuries, to the slow and sure resolution of that all assimilating alkahest.

Among them there are some so especially *secular*, so peculiarly eminent in theoretic interest, practical usefulness, and urgent opportunity, as to make it a safe prediction that when the intellect appears which is really competent to its day and generation, it will proceed to deal directly or indirectly with one or all of the five following difficulties. If you are grandiloquent, good reader, you may call them the FIVE HEROIC THEMES. *Accipe hæc.*

An inquiry as to the changes in the theory and practice of society made necessary by the physical and mental transmutations of modern Europe :—

A harmony of religion and philosophy; involving a synopsis expurgatorial of metaphysical and other science, and of the pure deductions from the Scripture records of revelation :—

A hypothesis from psychology, and a demonstration from universal history, touching the capability of the human being to the task of human government:—With the necessary inferences:—

A discrimination and harmonious exhibition of the genuine instincts, intuitions, and inferences in things moral and spiritual, of humanity everywhere, after tracing and abstracting whatever disturbances *ab extra* may fairly be concluded, according to established or establishable laws of intellectual dynamics, from such (and no greater) central force of revelation as the Bible history records :—An exposition of the collateral evidence for the divine authority of the Bible, as the repository of a peculiar revelation from God.

Of this last all-important subject there are four principal departments, each in itself a labour. I. The tendencies of the universal human soul as evidenced in the prevailing literatures, politics, and popularities of Europe; II. The ethical wisdom of the Scriptures exemplified by an analysis of all religions, ancient and modern; III. The prophetic foresight, as evinced in the past history, present state, and probable future of the world; IV. The literary superiority and poetic pre-eminence.

It is precisely this last division of the subject that has been chosen by the gifted author of the noble book before us. Mr. Gilfillan's name is already well known to our literature. As the earnest and elaborate critic of forty or fifty of the 'representative men' of our age and country, he has given evidence of powers discursive of every province of intellect, and sympathies conversant with the whole human heart.

But wonderful as those 'first and second Galleries' were for their glowing poetry, fervid eloquence, many-sided universality and varied accomplishment, there was a spiritual movement through the whole, which showed them to be the productions of a mind still on its lees. They are not the man so much as the outcries of his growing pains—not the flesh and blood, but the flush upon the labouring face. You felt that the light they gave was the luminous track of a passage through great deeps. You laid down the last book with a hope and expectation for the next: a keen interest in the succeeding scene of a mental drama which evidently must open and widen as it goes. This book, 'the Bards,' is a worthy successor to those noble volumes, and will be highly satisfactory to those who inferred from the former works of the author the gradual and unfaltering development of his genius.

We are not surprised at the district of his subject which he has chosen. It was an unploughed field, and one for which he was alike fitted by temperament and experience. We should rather wonder that he has so long withstood its manifold temptations. With him it must have been a natural and irresistible impulse to walk into the midst of those grand old Hebrews who still, like chiefs on a day of battle, stand clustered and regardful on their hill, among, yet above, the conflicts of this world. Apart from the peculiarities of their inspiration, there are features in their old-world humanity, towards which, the lusty manhood of our author must needs yearn audibly. Primeval strength, larger pulses, the unmingled wine of existence, riot together in the superabundant power of their utterance. Our modern Boanerges — our Dantes, Miltons, and Goethes — seem the children of weaker sunshine, shorter seasons, and a diminished humanity. Matched with the hot creations of those ancients, the creatures of their genius seem clammy and *contained*. The warmth of life does not exhale from them. They come and go as ghosts, filling and displacing nothing. We neither quail under their presence nor feel the wind of their passing by.

Go into the heaven of these princes of modern magic; behold their niggard angels, starveling saints, and material gods. Enter the enchanted palaces of their earth. See buskinned heroes— mortal and otherwise—heaving with human sinews to move the limbs of Hercules. Even the author of 'Hyperion,' though, in that one poem of his, his speech be that of a Colossus to Colossi, lacks the rude health of these Hebrews. Compared with them, his phlegmatic giants, albeit among the grandest in profane literature, are pale and marble cold. Their great bulk lacks vital energy; the frame of Olympus is feeble with the soul of a man. Their best godhead is

> 'A fallen divinity,
> Casting a shade '

Over the whole literature of modern times there is a feeling
reduced inspiration, milder possession, relaxed orgasmus,
bescent vitality, spiritual collapse.    The Hebrew bards, on
ιe contrary, heave with an exuberant life, that reminds us of
ιose pre-Adamite days when the fern-bank was a forest, and
arsh-weeds and mosses surpassed the oaks and palms of to-day.
: this great earth cried out to us, or some irrepressible message
)ened the lips of one of the silent congregation of the stars,
ιeir afflatus would be sufficient for it.    There are words of
ιaiah and Ezekiel which would sound worthily, though they
ιme up through the volcanoes of the world, or shone down to
ι from the divine faces which look by night from heaven.
Small wonder, therefore, that succeeding poets have been the
ery heliotropes of these ancient lights; that the best radiance
·e have received in later times has been flushed with reflections
om their warmer illumination; and that our author has been
ιle in his seventeenth chapter to show that the most glorious
ιtellects of Europe have turned, when they sang devoutly,
ιwards the East.  Small marvel, too, that they have found their
.test and ablest panegyrist in a writer whose burly strength
ιight almost claim to be of their posterity, and whose

> ' Thunders, like demon lions with their mates,'

ιve already shaken more than one prim northern studio from
ι critical propriety.    It is a dangerous thing to disturb the
ιsty equilibrium of the up-piled table of a critic; and if Mr.
ιilfillan thinks to have endured the whole consequences of his
terary tornados he has a happy constitution.
Maugre the Cyclopean architecture of his eloquence, despite
is

> ' Firmament over firmament, and firmaments
> 'Neath firmaments, untold, unseen, unthought,
> Unspeakable,'

·e could pause to point *in limine* to an omission which will
ring the structure about his ears.    While professing to indicate
ιe poetic element in the Holy Scriptures, has he not started
·ithout an attempt at a theory of poetry?
Pilate said, ' What is truth?' and washed his hands of it; and
·e predict that the question, ' What is poetry?' will be the first
nd last greeting of Dryasdust, and others, to this magnificent
anegyric on the poetry of the Bible.
For ourselves, we have long given up all hope of a definition
f poetry, from a consciousness of what previous definitions are
ιvolved in it.    Is he who demands such a definition prepared
ιr its preliminary exercises?    Will you follow us, Dogmaticus,
ι much as through the lesser mysteries?

When looking steadfastly on this unspeakable universe, we touch it with the finger of science, and behold its rainbow and adamant dissolve into thick vapours, and them also, by new resolutions, disappear, and leave space no visible tenant; and, still gazing, we see that the inane is void, but know that it is full of all things, the soul is perplexed and abashed before its work, but upheld, nevertheless, by a flattering imagination of power. Ask of it, *What is nature?* and you are bidden to wait, indeed, but it is in a voice of hope.

Doubtless, Philosophy is on the trail of the Salamander. She has not yet toiled the Phœnix, but behold the warm ashes! She has not seen the sun, but, lo! the west red with his recent down-going! Another day's journey, and he is surely won!

And yet what have you done, Sir Sciolist? You have analysed the great toy as it was arranged to come to pieces; following the routine of illusion, you do not break it. You open the doors prepared for you, pursue the ways beflowered for you, and run the round of the labyrinth in unconscious compulsion.

Look now, we prithee, with other eyes upon your universe. Seek not to divide, but to know—not to translate, but to comprehend. Turn your soul loose for truth in the inner and outer world. Find that the last analysis of science deals no less with phenomena than the first. Aside from the path. Think of that *quæsitum* which is not phenomenal; long to ask for it; and inquire of your soul with which faculty it would be recognised. Where is your capacity to know what *is?* Beat about bewildered among the infinite variety of things; stretch your hands for ever in the vain attempt to touch them; journey hopeless of a resting-place; start, sun by sun, after a new mirage. Press, as a sleeper, in directions from which you shall of necessity diverge; ever beguiled by human landmarks from a road on which they are not, or passing inevitably the golden turning that can never be regained, or keeping, as in dreams, the path apparent to the senses while seeking a goal of which they have no cognizance; always fainting when endurance would have won; coming up to breathe when the depth was almost gained; for ever thwarted by human incapacities; able to communicate less than you can declare, and to declare less than you can know, and to know less than you can believe; for ever hearing 'the sound of a going;' perpetually conscious of the neighbourhood of truths which you have no eyes to see, and, whenever you follow the track of the greatest, coming to the borders of an element you have no powers to traverse, standing at last gasping as one who walks by dark among pit-falls, doubting all appearance, and groping blindly for anything that is more; forced to accept inconsequential sequences for lack of the sense which should have preserved the legitimate succession of events, and to arrive at conclusions which you cannot admit, but may not deny, because they stand in the place of truth. The soul is sick and unsatisfied—buffeted, oppressed, and overridden, by the mysteries of nature and of life. Alarmed, you shrink towards the inner self, to find the boundary which separates the apparent from the absolute. You go back frightened from sense to sense, and find each transfer reality to the next, till the tradition ends only because you cannot follow it; or, beginning from within, and advancing from the inexplicable Shekineh of existence, feel down the line of consciousness, and find it cease with the round of your skull. Condense to that area your vast superfluous universe, which, if it exists *per se*, exists for you only in so much as it exists in you; and if it exists in you, may as well not exist *per se*. Learn that you can know nothing beyond yourself; that, in the star-filled space which dissolved at the touch of your science, and in the great truths and mysteries that oppressed and overrode you, you chronicled a mental experience, and no more; that sun and moon, and the unspeakable beauty of the world, the incalculable bulk of unnumbered stars, and all hard rocks, and indestructible gold, and intolerable fire, have become an intangible, existing how and where. Twenty-three inches by sixteen really contain heaven and earth, and all of past, present, and future, that exists for you; the whole a fashion, a complexion—if you will, a skin-rash—of the mind, a wear of motley for the soul. And this meagre area you concede, not from any likelihood of its reality, but from the failure of your consciousness to know if there be evidence for it or not.

We have seen enough of the fallacy of our perceptions to doubt if they be ever true, and, consequently, to give grounds to doubt the existence of truth itself; while the implanted impulse *to believe* within us proclaims the existence of the believable and the absolute, and reduces us once again, by a new route, to the conclusion, that we have as yet no organs to know it.

You shall now impartially spread out the soul and the universe together—a web of one tissue for ever weaving. You shall abdicate our strong egotisms; you shall make no false centres; you shall no more expect the soul to prove the universe, than the universe the soul. The fibre shall not deny the fabric because the fabric is not in the fibre. You shall see all things as a great thought passing through the mind of the Eternal, real throughout as the Divine Spirit, homogeneous as the One God. You shall see in the successions of the material and spiritual world—the infinite complexity of cause and effect, motive and action, virtue and reward, crime and punishment, the progressive move-

ment of the Infinite Spirit, the development of the Eternal
Thought. You shall see the great consentaneous existence passing in its multiform unity; in which no part has relation to the
other, but everything to the great Author; in which neither is
proof of the other, but all are co-witnesses of him. In this
re-organization of all our knowledge we find but little difficulty
with the outward world, advancing from the things we name
inanimate, through the more deceptive individuality of the
brutes, even up to the souls of our fellow-men. Nay, entering
the arcanum of self, we can surrender it step by step; stripping
off at every intenser moment of attention some nearer passion,
more intimate faculty, more central intelligence. But, after the
last most subtle decortication, there remains a consciousness which
we do not touch; and here, for the most part, we give up in
despair. And for the majority of us this must remain intangible,
for in attempting to remove it we are essaying a manifest impossibility—the *I* is trying to *be conscious* that it is not. They who
have been at the point of death know, however, that it is tangible,
and have been sensible of a state of mind wholly unique and
incommunicable, in which the last consciousness was surrender-
ing—with no remainder.*

We have now dissipated our personality, have reached the
widest generalization of philosophy, and our nature recoils again
at conclusions to which our best faculties have no choice but to
come. We feel that there is yet another theory for which we
are created, to which our involuntary beliefs bear partial testimony, but at which the noblest efforts of all men have been
unable to arrive; and we reach again, by yet another road, the
conclusion that we are born blind; the conviction that the
liveliest of our perceptions bears, perhaps, less relation to spiritual vision than our sense of hearing to that of sight. Nay,
that in applying our best powers to the universe we have been
attempting to solve the problem of divinity as it were by touch.

Retiring, then, from the attempt upon external nature, and
relinquishing even an effort to reach the essence of the mind,
but turning our attention inward, content to deal only with
appearances, we shall find no less in this humblest sphere that
all satisfactory definition is impossible. In strictness, we can
speak only by a poor synecdoche of any noble quality of a mind
which is destined to an immortality of growth. What the
unknown remainder may be, and in what relation our present
given quantity stands to it, God and eternity only can unfold.
Even of that present quantity, that small surface of mental
observation which is open to us, how little can we say, how

---

* In this world.

much less it is becoming possible to say—how, as in giddy dreams, our standing-ground already swims below us, and the palpitating landscape now expands into the skies, and now collapses to a point, now heaves up towards heaven, and now opens the abyss beneath our feet—now shows us pictures which make us proud to be human, and now whirls round in such hopeless vertigo that we are fain, with closed eyes, to fall upon the breast of God.

Therefore, to the questions, ' What is nature? ' and ' What is mind? ' we who live amidst the one, and possess the other, can give no answer. We know no more of either than if they were not. We draw near to the soul and the universe to find them recede as we approach. We seek truth in her well, indeed, but descend only to deeper and yet deeper darkness, and lose the last glimpse of the very stones that bruise and support us to behold her smiling overhead from the fair-seeming of unapproachable stars.

But, till we have solved the problems of nature and mind, let no man dare to answer ' *What is poetry?* ' Let us have no theory rather than a wrong one. Every *fact* is in harmony with an unseen system of facts, is of value of itself, and can never need to be unlearned, and will take its place one day in the great machine of which it is, perhaps, an unrecognised part. Even a false theory, as a *fact*, has its use, beauty, and place in the great system of human error. But a false theorem, in the connexion into which it is forced, in the commerce with the honest facts of palpable experience—as an intellectual engine, an organization of knowledge—is an unmitigated evil, an interpolation upon the text of this world : a discord, and of endless reverberation. Let us, therefore, know nothing as a whole, unless it be as that divine whole in which it was created. Let us be content to deal with the existence of poetry, and to say of it that it is, and was, and will be. Sufficient for us that man has known it always and everywhere :—that man has breathed of it everywhere since he came upon the earth ; that it has soothed him by its zephyrs, stirred him by its gales, and uprooted him by its storms ; swelled the sails of his prosperity, and heaped the waves over his wreck ; played amid the locks of his childhood, and driven the last snowdrift about his hoary head ; roared among the forests of his power, sung through the myrtles of his love and joy, and sighed over the sweetness of his violet beauty—

——— ' Stealing and giving odours.'

In the saddest, the grandest, and the holiest moments of his history it has been no less above and around him. In it flew the dove of the Deluge; it bare the pillar of cloud through the Wilderness, and on it the chariot of Elijah rose to heaven. Like the great globe itself, whereof every man has portion, and no man possession, it is at once in the enjoyment of either antipodes, the desire and satisfaction of all nations, the delight and sustenance of every age and people; and, though there be no human stature so sublime as to behold the round completion of the planet, neither is there any variety of humanity so poor that it has not ministered to its life and blossomed over its grave. 'Day unto day uttereth speech, and night unto night showeth knowledge, but there is no speech nor language where its voice is not heard.' But such simple philosophy is too humble for the sciolist. Therefore, every age and literature has had its own definition of poetry, and Brahma has been represented in the form of each of his incarnations. Everywhere, the undistributed term has been taken for the whole generality, the integer has stood for the unknown sum, the member for an incalculable architecture, the verse for the inexhaustible epic:—

Seeing, then, that poetry is everywhere present upon the earth, that it is useful and essential to man, but that it is amenable to no scientific formula or passport portraiture, can neither be cried in the market-place nor mathematically described; seeing that the best efforts of pure reason are insufficient to decide its nature, to determine its limits, or adjudicate upon its identity, we may fairly infer that we are conversant with it by virtue of other faculties than the simply rational. Instinct, within its own province, is always superior to reason; and that philosopher would not show his wisdom who should argue with the hound on the direction of the fox, instruct the raven in the diagnosis of death, dispute the spring evangel of the cuckoo, or reprove the swallow

———— 'Flying from the golden woods.'

Instinct, in a higher sphere of action, is a principal element of genius. The instinct of the poet is the natural provision for the infallible identification of subjective and objective poetry. Among the crowd of images in his thoughtful soul, this instinct recognises, with unerring and involuntary emotion, a certain divine few, which he afterwards exhibits to the world as poetry. To apply the same intuition to the thoughts of other men, to enact for them objectively the internal process of the poet, is the only unfailing test for the poetic element they contain. From the results of this discrimination there is an appeal in the ascending order of poets. From your arch-poet, when you have found him, no appeal. To him, in matters poetical, but in no other, the world is bound to listen in absolute faith; towards him, in these affairs, it has the one duty of unquestioning and unmitigated acceptance. The high-priest of that phasis of God which we behold in Nature, his dictum in things natural is divine. Endowed with mysterious consciousness of divine attributes, stirred at the beautiful, bowed and shaken at the sublime, his soul the very Urim and Thummim of inspiration, in him the visible and the audible are made flesh, and at him the mind and the universe convert. Ποιητης is a large genus, and the characteristics of its archetype are partaken, in varying measure, by all its individuals. To this group of men, therefore, is committed the whole poetic ministry—the evolution, exposition, discovery, and authentication of poetry on this earth. And, in the proportion in which these functions are confined to this priesthood, will be the purity and divinity of our poetic literatures, and their efficacy as conduits through which the fertilizing spirit of all things is poured into the general mind of man.

Among these sons of the prophets the author of the book before us has been so frequently and formally recognised, has been baptized and re-baptized by such indubitable apostleship, that any further consideration of his claims would be, to say the least, out of taste. That title is already questioned which receives the unhappy homage of demonstration. Throughout Mr. Gilfillan's literary career, while evincing a very high order of creative power, he has chosen to employ his genius in that useful department of poetic exercise which has to do with the discovery and authentication of the poetry of other men. The profound, subtle, and reverent critic of the great masters of our literature, the quicksighted, fearless, and enthusiastic herald of rising powers, the generous, patient, and catholic counsellor of strange diversities of aspiring talent,—we have seen him walking as a discerner of spirits among the monuments of the dead and the world of the living. Having trodden the wide circle of humanity, we can sympathize with the beautiful and natural necessity by which he approaches the higher grounds of the mount of vision. He has been familiar for years with the streets of the holy city, has worshipped in the outer court of the Gentiles, and drunk of

'——— Siloa's brook that flowed
Fast by the oracles;'

he would now, at length, strong in knowledge, rich in experience, purified by penance, disciplined by labour, his zeal attested by forbearance, his citizenship confirmed by habitation, ascend the steps of the temple of God.

'Twas a fine impulse; and, in itself, eminently poetic. We equally appreciate the delicate sense of propriety and keeping with which, in leaving all other poets for 'the Bards of the Bible,' he has left the air and garb he had worn among them—has put the critic's shoes from off his feet as he drew near the sacred ground. To enter upon the consideration of the inspired writers apart from their divine authentication, to investigate the literary merits of the supernatural, was, we confess, a bold task in these unfaithful days. We can hardly imagine a more pitiable enterprise to an author of ordinary powers, or a more offensive imbroglio, than the results of his best efforts. Genius simplifies the whole business. It goes into the world of spirit as into the world of matter, content only to *bear witness*. Not to question the incomprehensible scheme of the universe, but to cry out at the glories it is gifted to see ; not to sit in plenary judgment on inspiration, neither bound to explain or renounce, justify or condemn, but to confess the spontaneous emotions of an intellect whose emotions are the oracles of our intellectual life. Genius is an infallible censor, but to ban is the lowest of its offices. For the repellant powers of genius are only protective (the nervous outworks which defend the upturned eye of the soul), but the seraphic and cherubic it must exercise or die. Though it can cry with terrible vehemence of those things which offend, it could not exist long in an exclusive atmosphere of offence. To wonder and to adore are the daily necessities of its existence. Praise is the exponent of its happiest intuition ; its normal gesture is the attitude of reverence, and its natural music is the *lobgesang*. In dealing, therefore, with a subject of such indefinite limits and uncertain character as the literature of the Scriptures, the man of genius will lay aside the censorial function altogether, conscious that his temperament has jurisdiction over but a single province of the unknown empire he has entered. He will be silent where he cannot praise. He will speak only as he is moved by the sight of the divine. He will set his heart like a harp among the music and the thunder, and be content to chronicle the sympathetic notes that tremble from its involuntary strings.

In such a spirit has Mr. Gilfillan undertaken the consideration of the poetry of the Bible ; and we were relieved from whatever anxiety might have accompanied the perusal of his title-page, by the first few lines of his preface. 'In order that the book may be tried by its own pretensions, the author deems it necessary to premise that its main ambition is to be a prose poem or hymn, IN HONOUR of the poets and poetry of the inspired volume.'

But of what avail, it may be asked, is this laborious exposition

of a poetical element in books, to which we refer as our
authorities, not in art, literature, or science, but in the stern
theories of duty, and the homely practice of life? Why expend
in an elaborate declaration of so much or so little ornament in
the garments of the prophet the time, talents, and learning which
might have enlightened us upon his person? Why give us a
dissertation on poetry, when we might have had a disquisition
on Hebrew particles, an essay on Greek flexions, or a new
theory of the Apocalypse? Above all, why employ above three
hundred pages upon demonstrating the presence of that which
is confessedly undefinable? These questions, we doubt not, will
arise in the mind of many a well-meaning reader; and we answer
them in justice to the high place and warm eulogy which we feel
it our duty to give the book under review. Doubtless, we cannot
define poetry as a whole, and must be content with ignorance as
to the *rationale* of its effects; but the existence of those effects
no man calls in question. The abstract idea of poetry we cannot
form, but the concrete fact of poetry we all recognise; and
though the majority of us are liable to mistake in the attempt to
identify it, there are always a class of men, as we have before
said, to whom the recognition of it is a natural function. We
have placed the literary excellence of the Bible among those
indirect evidences of its authenticity, which it is competent to
certain minds among us to expound. Let us briefly show that
there are recognisable qualities in poetry which make the demonstration of the poetic element the one important *quæsitum*
in the establishment of that excellence.

When the Greeks said, αειδω, *I sing*—α intensive, and
ειδω, *I see*—they expressed in a word one vital secret of the
poet. When Carlyle calls for a generation which should learn
only from experience, he is unconsciously demanding an age
whose life and literature should be poetry. For every poet
speaks only from experience—from the things seen, heard, and
felt. Therefore, his sayings take place among the works of
nature. Therefore, they contain truths of which himself is not
conscious, and which, as fresh centuries and circumstances arise
to elicit them, will go on developing to the end of time. For
every stone we tread upon has petrified truths in it of which
philosophers have hardly begun to dream; and every true poem
is in harmony with all the secrets of the universe. Whatever
explains man or the world is the key also of, or to, its deeper
meaning, its sweeter beauty, its more divine intelligence; every
discovery of history makes it older, and every fresh experience
of life renews its youth. Therefore, it furnishes maxims for
ranks, conditions, epochs, and occasions, which the poet neither
knew nor foreknew; and often appears aimed at evils which

the poet never saw, full of intentions which never troubled his
singleness of eye, and significant of logical conclusions, at which
possibly his incompetent reason would have recoiled.  Nature
is never silent, and no man can direct his gifts.  The very brand
in the hand of the first fratricide prophesied against him while he
smote.  Poetry, the transcript of Nature, is, like her, a perpetual
teacher; and there is no worthy saying of a true poet that will
not some day to some man become golden.  Happy he against
whom his own words bear not unconscious but terrible witness;
who, having raised the inexorable spirit, stands not trembling
and guilty before the accuser he has invoked.  Happy the poet
who can live up to his poetry; he who, having the genius to
speak with tongues, has the gift also to interpret; to learn of
the inspiration to which he has been voice, and drink of that
living water of which he is else but the painful conduit to the
world.

Every other writer and speaker writes and speaks upon a
recognised plan, and his speech and writing are means to an
end.  To the poet only, as the agent not of calculation but of
instinct, to write and to speak are in themselves the end.  To
the most of men, the moral duties and Christian graces are the
fruit of heavy labour and hard self-sacrifice; here and there we
find that moral genius, to whose exquisite organization virtue is
its own and exceeding great reward.  In the same relation stands
the poet to the *intellect* of his day.  In him only, duty repays
itself, and to know, and to utter, are the necessities of existence.
Every other author is flattered with some appearance of independence, seems to be the originator of the purposes he obeys,
lord at once of his objects and their execution; the poet only
is, by *appearance* and reality, the involuntary instrument in the
hands of overruling power.  Every other author, standing, as it
were, above his work, takes up, at his own choice, his task from
among the labours of the world; only the poet and the prophet
are doomed to bear a 'burden' coming upon them from above,
and of which, be it heavy or light, it is enough that it is 'the
burden of the Lord.'  To be a declarer of mysteries, to give
form to independent and impersonal truths—truths so impartial
that they condemn him, so high that himself sits a learner at
their feet—to be the only infallible witness to realities, the living
chronicle of God, are, therefore, among the vocations of the
poet.

We are perpetually confounding speech with language.  Speech
varies with stirps and geography, era and circumstance; but,
strictly speaking, the whole human race are as much of one
language as if Babel had never been.  The universe, our infinite
vocabulary, is spread out before us, and every dialect of the

earth is but the different index by which we point to the desired living word. There, O linguist, lies, and will yet lie, the perennial dictionary, patent to the earliest and the latest of mankind; and whether it be in the *tongues* of men or of angels, doubt not the last man will speak the *language* of the first. Audible speech is that arbitrary invention, that system of numerals, by which we single out the words of the everlasting language, and indicate the *order* in which creation is to speak to us.

Now to have in his soul a fair transcript of the universal Lexicon, to mirror heaven and earth within him, is confessedly one of the great characteristics of the poet.

Nature is consistent in her gifts, and from him whom she has endowed with the central language of mankind we may fairly expect a message similarly universal. We are too apt to confound knowledge with wisdom, and to forget that the principle evolved from a thousand facts might be as certainly learnt from one of them, if we had but the detective power to apprehend it. Now it is the part of the poet to deal with wisdom rather than knowledge. He waits so reverently upon nature, and his mind is so mysteriously attuned to her fashion that he learns involuntarily to move in her step, and when imagination swings him beyond reality, he still preserves (so to speak,) the orbit of truth. It has happened, therefore, to the poet to anticipate, by centuries, the discoveries of the philosopher; and the progress or retrogression of science can no more change the place of poetry than the motions of this globe of ours can show parallax in the furthest of the stars.

Speech, as speech, as a pure system of significant sounds, is, of course, unable to convey anything new to the mind; and its province, therefore, is necessarily limited to whatever knowledge is mutual to the speakers. Strictly, the province of pure speech would be confined to the outward world, because any other mutual knowledge would only be possible through modes of communication which are beyond simple speech. Two men may agree that a certain sound shall stand for any objective thing, because their mutual cognizance commences with the thing and succeeds to the sound, the sound being in this case representative of a pre-existing knowledge; but when we come to such subjects of knowledge as are, by the nature of them, exclusive and individual, and out of the range of community of experience, pure speech, which never *is*, no longer *seems* to be, language. Sound is a useful memorandum, and but little more. A invents a new (uncompounded) sound for his new thought, but B is uninstructed by it. We may, therefore, throw audible speech altogether aside in reflecting upon real language, and on the necessary conditions under which mind affects the condition of mind.  Not to adopt the technicalities of philosophy, the ideas which we receive by communication are principally of two kinds —progressive and reactionary.  The progressive are, when we combine two known images to produce a third, as a horse and a man for a centaur ; or when we call up a known image to induce the appearance of another, which, by the nature or habit of the mind, is usually its sequent—as spring to induce the idea of flowers, or snow-drops the idea of spring, or clouds that of rain, a bellying sail that of wind, a look of terror an approaching enemy, or the statue of ' the eagle-slayer,' with uplifted bow, the image of the discharged and invisible arrow.  This power to produce and combine images, and the instinct to foreknow infallibly their necessary sequents, is, by common consent, one of the characteristics of the poet.  The reactionary ideas are when the presence of a mental feeling—or the excitement of it— elicits such an idea as would have produced it.  As from the presence of those feelings which ordinarily result from ideas of power, goodness, greatness, and the unknown, we pass to a resulting indescribed consciousness which is as near an idea of God as we may come.  For there is a constant action and re-action between ideas and sensations, by which not only certain ideas produce corresponding sensations, but sensations taking place in the absence of ideas, call up the ideas which would have begotten them.  And there are ideas which can only be produced worthily as the reactionary result of these sensations.  Such is the idea of God of which the worthiness is destroyed directly we attempt to procure it by direct description.  Such the idea of infinity which the Druids approached more closely, perhaps, than ever before or since an abstraction has been neared, when they covered the moor with disordered stones, *which it was unlucky to count.*  In addition to the powers and simplicity of the visible elements employed, the exquisite nicety which substituted super-stition for commandment, an indefinite fear for a definite penalty, made it not so much unlawful as *unfortunate* to count—supplaced ' I *may* not,' by ' I *cannot*,' and bound the will while appearing to leave it free, completed an instrument for mental sensations whose reaction in idea must have been wonderfully true.  Either wholly or in part of this reactionary kind are many of the best ideas we receive.  In fact, images that are generated are superior to those that are, as it were, transplanted, inasmuch as being less connected with imperfect language, and as being formed in each case according to the mode of movement peculiar to the indi-vidual mind, they are purer and more natural.  Now these reactionary images may occur subjectively from the spontaneous action of the emotions and sensations ; but if we would produce such images in another, we must first evoke the feelings of which they are the reaction. This power over the feelings, and the instinct to use it infallibly, is, as we all know, one of the characteristics of the poet.

Thus powerful over man, poetry has also essential and peculiar relations to God. We are apt to look upon music as a sister among the arts; we should rather consider her their mother. Perhaps (in a high sense), it may be found that music is the one art; and the highest form of music is poetry, or, *the music of things*. In it there is such an association of the accordant and discordant, as may produce in the soul the consciousness and effects of harmony. And harmony? We only know of it that it is the manner of God in the universe. God has created us with involuntary tendencies towards all his perfections, and the poet is that man in whom towards certain of those perfections that tendency is stronger than in his fellows.

The Balaam of genius can only prophesy in virtue of this nature within him, and by a necessity of his being he is, therefore, in the maddest aberration of his will, and the wildest rebellion of his reason, so far involuntarily true to the divine.

In these recognitions of some characteristics of poetry and poets, although we have by no means exhausted the discoverable poetic attributes, we have done enough to conclude, with satisfaction, that, as confessedly the representative of the quality of insight, as habitually an unresisting servant of some kind of afflatus, as the only possessor of the universal language, as the chief repository of persecular wisdom, as the acknowledged master of the human heart, and as the intellectual echo of a portion of the Divine nature, the poet fills so central a place in the moral machinery of the world, that he is, by position, the natural adit of whatever motive force may be communicated to it from above; and that, assuming the advent of a direct and universal revelation from God, such a revelation, in making itself apparent to human senses, would be clothed in the universal language which God had prepared, and taking the appearance and neighbourhood of that which in quality was most nearly allied to itself would descend among a companionship of poetry.

Inverting the order of the Enthymeme, let us show the Bible to be poetry, and we not only substantiate its claim to those advantages which are inherent in that fact, but we have established a probability for its divine authority; we have determined the lode of the gold, and attained to that baptism in which Messiah will appear. In the words of our gifted author, ' Perhaps this subject may not be found altogether unsuited to the wants of the age. If properly treated, it may induce some to pause before they seek any longer to pull at the roots of a thing so beautiful.  It may teach others to prize that book somewhat more for its literature, which they have all along loved for its truth, its holiness, and its adaptation to their nature.  It may strengthen some faltering convictions, and tend to withdraw enthusiasts from the exclusive study of imperfect modern and morbid models to those great ancient masters.  It may, possibly, through the lesson of infinite beauty, successfully insinuate that of eternal truth into some souls hitherto shut against one or both; and as thousands have been led to regard the Bible as a book of genius, from having first thought of it as a book of God, so in thousands may the process be inverted.'  So says that noble ' Introduction,' which for calm, wide, massive, dignified elo-quence it would be difficult to parallel in English prose.

We have no intention to supersede an *in extenso* study of the book before us by any attempt at an analysis or a summary. That the book is not the best the author will write we frankly tell him; but we are at a loss to lay our finger upon the name of any other living writer who could attain to its peculiar kind of excellence.  Who, on such a subject, could combine with the high poetic spirit, which is, of course, the main feature and most important element of the work, such stalwart faith, such warm benevolence, such vital charity, such wide experience, such genial learning; a power of argument so trenchant, of criticism so varied; such terrible vigour of conception, and a gift of expression so singularly happy?  Who, moreover, in the consciousness of these great powers, could define with so much abstinence the legitimate provinces of genius, turn so inexorable an ear to the plea of intellectual pride and standing—a scholar and a poet—beside the herdsmen of Bashan, and the fishermen of Galilee, honour so watchfully, above the rapt genius of the one and the idyllic instinct of the other, the scar of the ' burning coal,' and ' tongues of fire;' and proclaim, with so faithful and distinct a voice, the divine superiority and immutable differentia of their inspiration?—We had marked many passages for extract, and are sorry that space forbids us to present them.  Especially we regret to pass over those noble and peculiar outpourings of fraternal sympathy with the doubt and soul-distraction of this transition time, which are, perhaps, among the most characteristic in the book.

If we had space for a single excerpt, we should hesitate between the ' Paul of the present'—certainly among the most magnificent portraits ever drawn—and the glowing poetry of the ' vision ' in the chapter on the ' Destiny of the Bible.'

The ' vision ' would have been far too long for our pages, and we would not mutilate the ' Paul.'  Let that great picture remain in its majestic completeness, and among the youthful intellects of this strange time let whoso is ambitious resort to it and try if it be the prophetic portrait of himself. Such stirring passages run like a torrent through the sterner literature of this remarkable book. And whether it shake with the waves of a terrible eloquence, or murmur in tributary streams of tenderest poetry, or settle into broad and placid deeps of thought, the spirit of God moves upon the surface of the waters.

---

ART. VII.—*Official Catalogue of the Great Exhibition of the Works of Industry of all Nations*, 1851. London: Spicer Brothers, and W. Clowes.

IT is difficult to arrive at the true estimate of a matter as to which the whole world is stirred into wondering admiration. Things really great and noteworthy, are so seldom greeted by universal attention, or instant reception, that one is a little confused by the deafening and unanimous plaudits raised on the present occasion. The earth offers up its incense in honour. And whether it be destined, as heavenly halo, imperishably to hang around the undertaking, or, to subside like mere terrestrial vapour; it is at present thick enough to be an obscuring veil between the object of so wide gratulation, and those who would see it in a more definite aspect, in its wider, more enduring relations. The exhibition of the world's Industry is undoubtedly a significant and suggestive fact. The project was a noble one, cognate to the Time, and characteristic of its tendencies. Yet, hitherto, the organ of wonder has been the faculty chiefly excited—a condition not favourable to exact or conclusive enquiries.

It stands alone, for the universality of the interest aroused. A strange phenomenon is presented. All persons, all classes, from the meanest to the highest, from the least instructed to the most, in all quarters, have been more or less vividly affected by the influence. The comprehensiveness of the scheme is one cause of this; leaving nothing sectarian or exclusive in its appeal. It is brought home to the business and bosoms of people, the most widely differing in their sympathies. All meet here, as on common ground, though arriving by various routes. Its colossal scale is another. *Size* is a powerful lever of the masses. Those who would never have visited a Birmingham or Manchester Exhibition, will visit the same multiplied by

fifty.   In its magnitude and internationality, we have imposing
attributes—a great idea made tangible.   As a realised *thought*,
the enterprise is a sublimation of the average capacity—the
ideal of the average calibre of aspiration.   *Therefore,* does it
meet with ready and universal apprehension.

Amid the green country solitudes, one is led, on reflection, to
tremble lest the noisy event of to-day be destined to shrink a little
in the estimation of the coming days; lest that is, it be not quite
as intrinsically as extrinsically notable.   Startling is the ebullition
of sentimentality rising to the popular mouth; from poets down to
journalists, and from them to village gossips: a before uncalcu-
lated reserve-fund—called into play by the sparkling superficies
of the business.   A world-wide clamour of enthusiasm is raised,
already greater in volume, than during half a century has
celebrated the printing-press and steam-engine; certainly, more
vociferous than the first announcement of the former fact.   A
portion must of necessity be found to signify little.   The conjectural views now afloat on the ultimate mission of the great
show, lack in weight what they supply in fervour and credulity.
Pœans are prospectively sung, of doubtful appositeness.   Borne
on the wings of prophecy, their eyes in a fine frenzy rolling,
poetasters and newspaper editors foretel the end of war and
commencement of universal fraternity, to spring from this memorable industrial convocation, as oak from acorn.

Why should it run so perversely in our head? that strange
incident in the drama of the French Revolution, that lull in the
gathering storm, when the ghastly, sickly sunbeams shot through
the black thunder-clouds into the murky air?   The ' Federation
of the Universe' was proclaimed.   And from all corners of the
land, nay, of the earth, thronged a jubilant multitude: every
breast glowing with fraternal love, and renewed loyalty.   Democracy and Despotism ' kissed each other.'   Young anarchy, and
decrepit feudalism, like the lion and the lamb, ' lay down
together.'   All hands helped to dig the festal amphitheatre.
Noblesse and sansculottes worked cheek by jowl.   Women
wheeled the barrows; fine ladies prepared the tinsel flags and
banners.   But the sunbeams vanished; the fraternal love committed suicide; and loyalty grew so enthusiastic, it sent its king
' to heaven.'   Grim death put on the crown.   Universal and
absolute monarch became he.   The ' tears of joy' were turned
to tears of blood, and with their plentifulness watered the earth.
A great farce proved the opening scene of a great tragedy.

We mean not to suggest like terrors as now imminent.   But is
not a sudden, universal efflorescence of rose-pink at the surface,
a grotesque if not ominous contrast to the stern facts weltering
unheeded beneath?

Gladly as we hail this novel demonstration of Industry's—of 'tired labour resting on his anvil,' and showing his strength and anew, in *play*, for a world's amusement and profit; high as we rate its actual and potential influence, we do not think swords are about to be 'converted into ploughshares,' and war unpremeditatedly to 'loose his grisly steeds for aye.' Before we may look for these desirable consummations, many a hard lesson has to be reluctantly learned by struggling humanity. The throes of great social revolution have to be endured; many a problem to be solved—problems whose solution is needful to the continued vitality of modern nations. A Great Industrial Exhibition is only a link in the ever lengthening chain of history, though a sufficiently important and interesting one, and one which cannot fail to be productive of good.

Let us not flounder in a deluge of sentimentalities about the great fact of 1851, nor lose strength in airy speculations about the unseen, but try and really grasp the results which we see. All men are possessed by a high idea of the advantages to accrue; but have scarcely made up their minds what they are to be. Our people have been roused to an almost Oriental tone. The general speech has been coloured with novel, felicitously grandiloquent expressions, of common origin and acceptance— the 'Crystal Palace,' the 'Festival of Industry.' All point to a sense of the importance of the occasion, which, if open to question in the specific forms assumed, is right in substance. The full results of any event are not beforehand to be fathomed. The indirect will ever be of more permanent import than the direct and obvious. But these simple, tangible bearings of an uncompleted fact are all we may hope to apprehend.

Two generally-recognized aspects of the Exhibition, appear peculiarly definite and incontrovertible: the unexampled facilities it affords for the general information about the productive capabilities, activities, and appliances of our time; and the tribute of honour to industry. It has been happily designated a *school*. It is such, on the largest scale, in the most practical sense. In the proportion of this, its enlightening influence, must be its catholic and civilizing one. The industry and the arts of all nations are approximately represented for the practical benefit of the manufacturer and designer, the edification of all—the *superficial* edification that is. Of course, as to look at a thing is not always to see it; 'to *see* we must first know;' the intelligence generally conveyed by much that is here, is more apparent than actual. The heart of the manufacturing and mechanical mysteries remains untouched. How show *this* by ever so much *exhibiting*, or appeals to the *eye?* Industry can only make believe to be thus comprehensively communicative.

Still, over and above the surface-interest, the spectacle has a specific pertinence in some one part or another for every member of the industrious and practically intelligent classes. In some one thing or another, or class of things, every such visitor can take a more intelligent interest, derive information of the kind and amount for which his occupation and training have fitted him.

Still more really significant is its bearing on industry ; its representation of the working bees of the world's hive ; its tacit reflection on the drones. Were we asked what lesson most unmistakably and vividly we read, stamped in indelible characters on the face of the Exhibition, we should without hesitation reply, *this*, its popular tendency. Directly, and indirectly, its teaching is, in this sense, a democratic one. Tradesmen may exhibit, princes patronize, the aristocracy have their private and public views ; but it is to the actual *producers*, the grand display straightway leads the mind—to those real sources of the world's wealth, with which land and specie, and things extraneous used to be confounded. Honour to the working-man, honour to the canvass cap and fustian coat : this is the message it speaks—honour to the brains and sinews which were employed, the hands that wrought, with noble strain and effort, on the works around ; from the most utilitarian to those of finest use ; from a brass lock to Kiss's poetic bronze. Intellect and energy pervade the arena, on the topmost range of which stands Art, the crown of the many-sided life. The workers stand forth as the really great men.

The details of the great show are being given on all hands— in newspapers, catalogues, and shilling volumes. We would here attempt general views. But it is not easy to reduce so colossal a 'miscellany of facts' into the order and harmony of thoughtful arrangement. Yet, seeming chaos though it be, a cosmos *is* to be shaped out ; is already *there*, awaiting the grasp of the adequately-comprehensive capacity. Where might such be found ?

The Exhibition was proved to be a result of the age—an undertaking it was prepared for—by the hearty way in which the nation and the world at once closed with the proposal it is honourable to a *prince* to have made. In its completed state, it is, above all, characteristic of the Age ; of its positive attainments, its industry, its material resources, its material energies ; its science, pure and applied ; its mechanical triumphs. The realities of the day are represented ; and also, its shams. On the one hand, are illustrated, as never before, the whole range of its ever-perfecting machinery, its stupendous locomotives, complex power-looms, spinning-jennies, printing-machines — inanimate witnesses of animate intelligence, embodied symbols of intellect and power; the activity of its textile manufacture, the variety of its pottery and glass, its multiplied material everywhere. On the other hand, is exemplified, thousandfold, the archæologicalness run wild and rampant of its *art ;* the helter-skelter chase after classic, Gothic, Moresque, and almost every other excellence hitherto attained. Smallest attempt at a new one of our own we have, in unguided, unsystematized, *naturalistic*, design—design, that is, too closely mimicking nature, not·adequately conventionalizing, in other words, *adaptive* of natural forms to its specific purpose—or, in such puerile anomalies, and base, as *rustic-work* stiffened into cast-iron—a singularly eloquent witness to our opulence in decorative resources. While this humiliating text is enforced through the whole range of manufacturing design, nineteenth-century perfection of copyism, in one characteristic branch, is witnessed in bran-new Gothic crosses and altar-pieces, in mechanical Gothic wood-carving, in more or less tolerable stained glass, and in the ' Mediæval(*izing*) Court' of Pugin, Hardman, Crace, and Minton. The latter, in the strikingly-harmonious combination of its stained glass, hardware, wood-carving, hangings, encaustic tiles—all successful repetitions of Gothic models—will at least have the merit of suggesting to many, who would not otherwise have heard of such facts, the fulness of beauty and character, and the homo-geneousness, of mediæval design, however applied, to domestic as to ecclesiastic purposes.

We have a running commentary on the age, its attainments, and shortcomings; and also on the Nations. Here, the change-less *East*, the conditions of whose petrified civilization have pre-served the excellences as well as the imperfections of youth, contrasts with changeful Europe. China, India, Turkey, Persia, and their natural decorative ally, Tunis, present a group, judi-ciously disposed in the centre of the building, the most æsthetically interesting and satisfying of any. It is a perfect study for true principles in decorative art: whether it be the refined, yet characteristic, outline of a China vase that arrests attention; the sober fulness of colour, and effectively-conven-tional design, of a Persian or Turkey carpet, or Indian shawl; the contenting simplicity of a piece of matting; the delicate grace of a wall-decoration ; unaffected truth and fitness of design generally, to whatever material applied; or earnest beauty of hue, within whatever limits confined, to whatever extent developed. Costly as are many of the articles exhibited in the Indian and Chinese stalls, their splendour of mere material is always the least part of their real effectiveness. It is the har-mony of hue however profuse, the homogeneous of design though golden or gilded throughout, which lend them a charm

and value quite beyond that of precious ore and stones, and
which the crude splendours of Sèvres or Gobelins have not.
How definite are the results of human *labour* in the achievement
of real value, and development from the earth's scattered raw
material, of things of beauty and significance, is in no section
of the Exhibition more strikingly evinced than in the Indian
and Chinese. Yes, the Exhibition has its meaning for the poor
stunted 'skilled labourer' of Cathay, could it but reach him.
It is to be observed both of China and India how little favourable have been European influences on their design. Where
independent of them, there, only, is it wholly consistent and true.
Imitation of European *picture*-design forms a strange alloy in
some recent works. The finest samples of Oriental design all
belong to the last or previous centuries.

Great credit is due to the East India Company for its very
magnificent and copious display of Indian productions. Truly
'*Honourable*' has been its activity in setting before us, by proxy,
the manufacturing and natural resources of its vast empire;
and in doing justice to Indian felicity and fulness of design.

In startling contrast to the nations of the East, stands
*France;* with its versatile activity, its nimble apprehension,
its ready adaptiveness of intellect. In design, what is wanting
in highest excellences, simplicity and consistent fitness, is
adroitly masked by an efflorescence of ornament, by naturalistic
luxuriance, by clever audacity of imitativeness, and expert-
ness of *finish*, at once the Frenchman's strength and weakness in art. As to *colour*, a surviving refinement and grace,
in blending and treatment and delicacy of hue—harmony, however, in a weaker key than that of the East—gives to some
French manufactures a position exceptional to that of Europe
generally. These qualities are best manifested in paper-hangings
and ribbons. In French, as in German, porcelain, we have
gaudy masses of colour, wanting alike in richness and sobriety.
In carpets, conjoined with effects imposing to the vulgar eye,
are harsh discords of colour and inappropriate sprawling pattern;
defects not to be atoned for by technic perfection, attained in false
tracks. Similar inappositeness disfigures the otherwise artist-like
design of French silks. In shawls, more or less of well-blended
colour, and successful originality of pattern, whether in departure from, or obedience to, the literal routine of the admirable
Oriental models, are the result of earnest, practical devotion to
the study of design as an art. In the metals, in cutlery, in
weapons, design, sometimes copied from bygone styles, sometimes original, prevails, where the English have little or
nothing of the kind to show. In small bronzes, with their
excellent modelling, and technic beauty, the French workman's

artistic superiority is triumphantly manifest. Taken generally, in French manufactures, the *picture* system triumphs at the expense of purity of design and real harmony of hue. In such elaborately difficult achievements as the Royal portraits in Sèvres, and the other reproductions of pictures—in porcelain, carpets, and tapestry, we have simply the more glaring samples of a current mistake, that of mimicking the appropriate effects of one form of art, in another more limited, and totally opposed in its aims and governing conditions.

*Switzerland* brings much unqualified pleasure to the lover of harmonious colour and unsophisticated design. In its muslins, laces, &c., the true canons of textile design are often illustrated: in smallness of pattern, simplicity of effect, and homogeneousness. For graceful truth and purity of colour, single or blended, its humbler manufactures bear away the bell.

*Germany,* like France, makes a varied display of manufacturing power. In the higher departments of art, it rises supreme. Its group in the nave, of bronzes and other sculpture, forms one of the most attractive points of the Exhibition. Kiss's grand Amazon, of which we have a zinc cast, coloured bronze—why the illegitimate deceptive simulation of *another* material?—is one of those unmistakable works of true mastery which command the appreciation of all. Simple in treatment, broad in effect, and *real*, it is undoubtedly one of the noblest works of art the world has at any time seen. The vitality of the feeling makes amends for the irrelevant classicism of subject. With earnest self-command sits the heroic rider, and while the supple foe fastens on the affrighted steed, whose sides quiver, and eyes glisten with terror, her womanly countenance glows divine resolve, serene assurance, her whole womanly form breathes unshrinking power; and we *know* that the uplifted arm will not fail of its purpose. Informing energy, truth, moderation, such as are here put forth—speech so definite and full, do not fail to raise a work of art into the highest region of the poetic. The technic qualities of the execution are of parallel merit to the conception. One cannot but look forward with sorrow to a removal of this sample of sovereign art, from its present felicitous position; and to the cast which now glows in the sunbeam unhurt, being doomed to lose its present harmonious and clear effect, the natural attribute of the *protected* statue, amid the blackening and blunting influences of the open air, always, in a northern climate, an unpropitious fate for sculpture. The smaller zinc casts are of great interest, finely modelled, and illustrative of the capabilities of the material. The bronzes are of high mark, æsthetic and technic. The colossal lion loses its significance and effect detached from the group of which it properly forms a component. In textile and fictile manufacture, Germany manifests notable activity. The magnificent array of Bohemian glass, in deep and vivid beauty of hue, affords a parallel, yet an individual one, to oriental decorative glories. In some branches of pottery and metal work, the Zollverein has realized a development of naturalistic design, more living and original than its anti-types in France and England. As regards some of the more dazzling contributions, it would be well if the admiring visitor would recollect that costliness and ingenuity are not *art*. Austria, by the way, would fain confuse current geographical notions; by taking the sculpture and other delicate productions of enslaved Milan under its paternal wing. Milan is not a part of Italy but of Austria, according to the latter's statement of the case.

Of the Spanish and Portuguese stalls, the most noticeable features are the characteristic natural products of those southern latitudes, and the very interesting collection of elaborately and beautifully ornamented weapons.

Belgium and Holland make a miscellaneous and striking display. The former, more especially in its design, partakes of the character of the French school. Considerable activity in wood-carving, metal-work, carpets, &c., is evinced. And, as in France, the reigning gods are expert archæologicalness—copyism, that is, of past styles, on the one hand; the naturalistic tendency on the other. Exuberance of ornament prevails in either case.

Italy is significantly represented by the dilettant tenor of most of its contributions; Greece by marbles out of which a Phidias *once* hewed divinities which the world has not yet let die; also, by costume and textile goods allied to the neighbouring Oriental productions, in their well-harmonized splendour. Malta, an English dependence, but Italian affinity, contributes articles ranking under the ' Fine Arts' head, evidencing considerable refinement of workmanship. Norway, Sweden, and Denmark, present interesting types of their natural resources, and some good sculpture. Russia and the United States come out greater in raw material, than in manufactured products;—or rather, in blank spaces. The Exhibition is but too suggestive of the attainments the latter great, yet adolescent, country, still lacks. It is a pity our transatlantic cousins should have made this fact so conspicuous, by applying for twice as much space as they could fairly or instructively occupy. ' Vaulting ambition has o'erleaped itself!' And though ' the prairie of the Exhibition' be very characteristic of the vast, but as yet only partially-developed, resources of the Infant Hercules, a tithe of the Exhibition's space and the sacrifice of other more substantial claims were not needed to gain this piece of significance. The æsthetic barrenness in this quarter is agreeably relieved by a series of good daguerreotypes. Some of these are exceedingly forcible and individual, bold in their light and shade, strongly marked in outline, and faithful to living character. A host in itself, also, is Hiram Power's well-known sculpture, the 'Greek Slave.' Significant enough is this subject, as attracting an American's sympathies, and as the artistic representative of the 'States.' The piece is rightly popular, thoughtful in conception, eloquent in feeling, masterly in *language*—the technic execution. The copies abroad give this work the slenderest justice. The sacrifice of the æsthetic beauty of fulness and softness of outline, the legitimate aim of a sculptor's rendering of the feminine form, is in them prominent, at the expense of that which justifies, and in this particular instance necessitates, it—the sentiment and living 'motive' of the original. Certainly, next to the 'Amazon,' this is the most poetic and earnest achievement of the sculptor's art to be found in the Exhibition.

England, though fully, is not always consistently represented, Minor irrelevant departments, such as wigs, artificial teeth, boots and shoes, were especially calculated to profit by the advertising capabilities of the Exhibition, and, therefore, assume some of the space and consequence which might well have belonged to the grand staple manufactures. Exhibitors of the latter class, make a much more disinterested sacrifice to the public. On the whole, however, our country makes a noble industrial figure, with its magnificent and suggestive array of powerful and delicate machinery, its similarly unequalled muster of carriages, and agricultural implements, its hardware, its cottons, woollens, silks, and other textile goods, its versatile pottery and colossal triumphs in glass. The machinery in *motion* is, above all, a suggestive sight; nor least of all the intelligent-looking operatives that attend it. Earnest labour in their persons makes holiday, gains the privilege of *recognition*, of seeing and being seen by the world at large. Not penned in obscure corners, but in the light of open day, before fine ladies and idle gentlemen, the Manchester factory-girl, or London printer's boy, goes through his accustomed task. Suggestive and noble histrionics these, representing that earnest work-a-day life which makes the world what it is, and not a den of savages. Certainly, as we gaze and listen to these imposing machines, performing their unerring evolutions, it is only of their thoughtful, hard-working inventors, and the hard-working operatives, we think. Or, perhaps, some reflections arise, on the natural blessing machinery was destined to bring the world, in the lightening of labour and facilitation of production, and the large share that has been wrested to a curse, to keeping up *Class*-laws, paying for legitimist wars, and doubling the importance of landed and other labour-proprietors. And fair, indeed, seems that day when labour shall at last reap the harvest which it sows.

For design, the 'Mediæval Court' already mentioned is, perhaps, the most noticeable feature, in the beauty accruing from well-directed, felicitous copyism. To the same class belong Mr. Chubb's locks, with their successful Gothic design; certainly an amendment on no design at all, as used to be the case in such things. Living, self-reliant design, where, indeed, shall we find? The happiest imitation of such original vitality, is but a poor succedaneum. The prevalence of favourite styles of copyism, Gothic, Elizabethan, Louis-Quatorze, which, in decorative art, as in architecture, is the fruit of modern lethargy and corruptions in æsthetics, of our having forgotten to maintain an artistic language of our own, is especially prominent on the British side; in its undisguised literalness, unrelieved by continental fancy and vivacity. It is the normal fact, however, among all modern European nations. In textile design, there is most to content, both in originality, and adherence to true decorative principles. In furniture, iron-castings, carvings of all kinds, elaborateness but too often takes the place, to some eyes the aspect, of *design*; and essential poverty in the latter, is veiled by costliness of material and execution. Compare one of the giant locomotives, where intrinsic necessities have shaped external form, resulting in apparent and essential coherence with nature and fact, with one of those numerous objects wherein a pretence or specious show of art has been made a *mask* in the place of an embodiment of Purpose. How superior æsthetically are the mere reality of the former, the power, the eloquence, the fitness, the simple outlines and harmonious combinations, utility has developed; to the poor meretricious make-believe, of your rococo side-board with its false outlines, incongruous ornament, or to the dead mechanicalness of the barefaced copy of a Gothic screen.

In sculpture—that formative art in which England has, on the whole, least of all distinguished herself, in which she is even less independent and less technically-proficient than the rest of modern Europe—the stand we take is low indeed. The imposing array of German works of high excellence throws into the shade the wavering attempts of English sculptors. They have now had a fair trial, plenty of space, light, and notice: and must be pronounced scarcely *worth* it. The blame has long been laid on the poverty of exhibition-accommodation: just as if the great man could be hidden from us by a mean residence, or shabby clothes. We fear the fault is an essential one, of the sculptor's own; lack of purpose and reality; an unreality tainting the whole range of his working. French and German attempts are often as puerile in '*motive*,' as empty of meaning, as idle in their classicism; but the sculptor more uniformly attains the end he had proposed to himself. The English sculptor's fulfilment halts in the rear even of his very slender ideal.

As especially conspicuous examples of ineptitude, may be noticed Wyatt's pitiably-bad equestrian statues of the Queen and Prince, with their vulgarity, their low style of art, their cabbage-leaf-veined horses; hideous masses of plaster and bronze, like those colossal abominations purporting to represent Lords Stowell and Eldon, and Dr. Jenner, types of a class but too familiar to us all; and that black agglomeration of prospective 'warming-pans' cast into the semblance of a wizen face and contorted form, bearing at its base the label '*Rutland*.' The statues of Hampden and Falkland, which once looked so plausible in Westminster Hall, shrink into mere pseudo-significance on reappearance in their original plaster; with their studied prettiness, their theatric and anatomically-questionable attitudes, and mere costume effectiveness. Character, force, idealization, but too evidently centre in this latter quite extraneous department of loose breeches and creased boots. Mr. Bell re-exhibits also an elaborately-pretty figure of a 'gentleman' of the Elizabethan day —judging by doublet and hose—with a smooth face and bald head, a kind of idealized Pinch, which he would fain persuade us is the ' Bard of all Time;' and which certainly *does* persuade us he knows less than nothing of what manner of man *Shakspere* was. As redeeming features, however, we have several bronze casts of the same sculptor's really fine work, informed with energy, character, power, and ably modelled—the ' Eagle-slayer.' Plaster casts, also, of the two happiest flights of the English Sculptor's fancy, of late years — Bell's Dorothea, and Foley's Ino and Bacchus—are exhibited. Could not our sculptors have got up a subscription among their friends for a small supply of *marble*, even if to be sold, at the Exhibition's close, as ' old material?' Continental liberality in this respect of itself gives the foreign side the advantage. Inexpressibly poor and disagreeable is the effect of the wilderness of plaster the English side presents. Thorneycroft deserves our thanks for relieving it with the Vauxhall sham of a coat of bronze paint, whose temporary splendours illuminate his wreath-extending and, of course, equestrian, Victoria.

For the reputation of the English school, 'tis pity, that as sculpture fell within the scope of the Exhibition, the principle was not carried out consistently, and painting included also.

ng a testimony to our resources as a manufacturing nation, so admirably consistent as a (possibly) temporary building, and one erected within the briefest space of time; so appropriate to its purpose, and expressive of it. It obeys Mr. Fergusson's canon for a modern building, that it should be constructed fit for its purpose, and trust for æsthetic effect to honesty and fidelity, to unaffected avowal of the ruling conditions of its existence. Certainly, it is the only architectural reality of modern times— the *truest* word spoken in architecture since the days of fourteenth century Gothic. There is no pretence or disguise. The resources of the material, and of the occasion, are alone relied on. And what a world of commendation is bound up in that one word *Truth*, considering what architecture and nearly all art have so long degenerated into. As whole volumes of falsehood cannot be set at the value of one word of truth, so a whole truthless palace of Westminster is less than a reality like Paxton's. Yet consider the *cost* of falsehood, the cost in superfine material and mechanical ornament, it takes, to conceal the want of art and truth; the inexpensiveness of truth itself. Falsehood costs a nation 2,000,000*l*.; truth, 150,000*l*. The one thing is just 150,000*l*. better than nothing; the other, two millions *less*, or *worse*, than nothing.

It has been the fashion with its decriers to call the building a 'great greenhouse:' as if this proved anything, except to Mr. Paxton's honour. All had seen, and many built, green-houses; but none had before thought to get architecture out of them. No professed architect, notwithstanding its great natural capabilities of grace and lightness of effect, had constructed a greenhouse proper, even, moderately æsthetic in outline and proportion. Not one of the thousands of designs, for a *temporary* building, sent in on this occasion, contained a suggestion of the kind. Officialism and professionalism characteristically enough opposed their dead-weight at first, and slight the unprofessional architect with mere passing mention now. But it is Mr. Paxton's rare merit to have seen the latent capabilities of a thing living under his eye, and to have developed them. It is ever thus new realities arise. 'It is but a step from a truism to a great truth;' from a common-place to a poem. But few see where or how to take that step; or that it *can* be taken. In the present case, we have been saved from a hideous and costly mass of brick and mortar, and have a graceful and beautiful creation in its stead; and a new and suggestive *fact*,—a step taken along a fresh track. By fresh tracks alone can we hope to arrive at anything true in an art which has become so flat and stale, as far as the old tracks are concerned; has fallen so helplessly into the hands of quacks, as architecture. It was quite in keeping with the present state

Here, English art would have assumed a better position. The Exhibition would then have comprehended that one item now wanting to make it complete. It would have been really an illustration of the industry *and arts* of all nations; not, as at present, of their industry, and, very partially, of their arts. Much additional instruction and interest, and popular benefit, would have attended this liberal reunion of the modern schools of England, Germany, France, Belgium. Each would have thrown light on the other; and a comparative summary been presented of their strongly-marked individualities. The Chinese limners themselves would have had interest for us; as also the attempts of less civilized nations, with their instinctively pure and vivid colour. It would have been instructive, also, to have seen how far our transatlantic brethren have advanced. The artists and the people of different countries would, for the first time, have had an opportunity of mutual acquaintanceship in art. It would have removed much ignorance, and many prejudices, on all sides. The interest of the Exhibition would have wanted nothing to its universality. As it is, in the æsthetic province, the leading part is omitted; since it is painting which, contrary to ancient and mediæval example, is, in modern Europe, *art* in any prominent or living sense. The projectors of the Exhibition were apparently *afraid* of this so legitimate feature in their undertaking—afraid of the adverse 'interests' of the exhibitions; above all, of that venerable trading monopoly, the Academy. It was dangerous ground for dillettant commissioners. Consider also the ' *rights* of British painters!' a class that tremulously demands the strictest 'protection'—a protection not needed; and were it needed, false and unjust. English painters have fought their way against a much more formidable enemy than any continental competition, namely, that unanimous election of the 'old masters' as sole conceivable producers of pictures worth buying, once so tyrannously the *mode*. It is to be regretted private enterprise should not have supplied the missing link, by an independent exhibition of the best works of the best living and recent painters of the world, or, failing that, of Europe. Meanwhile, we may call attention to a small exhibition of Mr. Wass's, now open in Bond-street, which affords the fulfilment of one part in the scheme; in a very choice selection from the modern English painters, including none but works of excellence, and many of highest mark, from the hands of Etty, Leslie, Turner, Maclise, Linnell, Poole, Herbert, Müller, Eastlake, &c.: an instructive supplement to the Vernon Gallery, and in its purified æsthetic atmosphere quite the ideal of an exhibition.

After all, whether, as a work of art, or of industry, the most agreeable English contribution, is the building itself; so imposing a testimony to our resources as a manufacturing nation, so admirably consistent as a (possibly) temporary building, and one erected within the briefest space of time; so appropriate to its purpose, and expressive of it. It obeys Mr. Fergusson's canon for a modern building, that it should be constructed fit for its purpose, and trust for æsthetic effect to honesty and fidelity, to unaffected avowal of the ruling conditions of its existence.

the *truest* word spoken in architecture since the days of fourteenth century Gothic. There is no pretence or disguise. The resources of the material, and of the occasion, are alone relied on.

mechanical ornament, it

2,000,000*l.* ; truth, 150,000*l.*
better than nothing; the other, nothing.

No professed architect, notwithstanding its great natural capabilities of grace and lightness of effect, had constructed a greenhouse proper, even, moderately æsthetic in outline and proportion. Not one of the thousands of designs, for a *temporary* building, sent in on this occasion, contained a suggestion of the kind. Officialism and professionalism characteristically enough opposed their dead-weight at first, and slight the unprofessional architect with mere passing mention now. But it is Mr. Paxton's rare merit to have seen the latent capabilities of a thing living under his eye, and to have developed them. It is ever thus new realities arise. ' It is but a step from a truism to a great truth ;' from a common-place to a poem. But few see where or how to take that step ; or that it *can* be taken. In the present case, we have been saved from a hideous and costly mass of brick and mortar, and have a graceful and beautiful creation in its stead ; and a new and suggestive *fact,*—a step taken along a fresh track. By fresh tracks alone can we hope to arrive at anything true in an art which has become so flat and stale, as far as the old tracks are concerned ; has fallen so helplessly into the hands of quacks, as architecture. It was quite in keeping with the present state of architecture, that the only man in our day to do anything architectural really satisfactory, should *not* be an architect by calling. Architecture had to wait for help from a botanist. Quite in keeping is the building, too, with the age. It is the æsthetic blossom of its practical character, and of the practical tendency of the English nation. It was just such a practical man as Mr. Paxton that was calculated for the emergency; to rescue the degraded art from lies, and enable it to do something consistent with the time. It is such an attainment as the time was capable of, and *no more ;* turns to account its manufacturing facilities, its mechanical advances, and expresses its realities, as far as they go : material rather than spiritual, but coherent and definite.

A new material, imperatively suggesting a new *style*, frees us from the ordinary common-places and pretences of professors, at once ; gives us a chance. We do not say that a really architectural new style has been developed, only that a beginning has been made, a lesson given. The loss entailed by glass, of such important architectural attributes as strong light and shade, and resultant emphatic definement of form, are severe drawbacks; though possibly attractive to the unthinking, as novelties. But the graceful characteristics of the materials their faithful treatment has educed, are some compensations ; not to mention again the charms of that now rare virtue, (architectural) veracity. Always, too, in estimating the merits of the building we must bear in mind its purpose. Calm examination, then, bears out the popular decision in its favour : a decision, however irreflective and indiscriminate, instinctively right, having unconscious reason. Of course, a structure of this size, erected with so much celerity, cannot possess in its details and individual parts the thought and feeling animating almost every square inch of a mediæval cathedral. Moreover, the result cannot be greater than the cause. The motive-power being a material and utilitarian one, however catholic and intelligent, the significance attained must be utilitarian, purely intellectual, rather than spiritual. They know very little of architecture who think masses of glass can be architectural in the sense in which a Parthenon or Westminster Abbey are ; can speak the same full, deep-toned speech. But when we say the building is not architecture in the old sense, it does not follow that it is not architecture at all. To be such in a new, that is to say in these days, *any* sense, it of course must forsake the old.

It is in the work, as a whole, architectural character must be sought ; in its bounding lines, its grand perspectives, the coherence of every separate part with the rest. Simplicity and unity preside ; multiplicity of parts without complexity. These *motives,* combined with vastness, cannot fail of their effect. Nature-wise, a *whole* is developed by the consistent application of a few simple principles. A work in harmony with, not as are ordinary modern buildings in defiance of, nature, is produced, an embellishment, not a scar on her fair face; one making the smallest possible professions, fulfilling what few it does make. Few things in art perform thus much now-a-days.

That condition, at once such a building's possible capability and possible stumbling-block, its colossal size is made the most of. Compare the squandering of a similar capability in the river-front of the New Houses of Parliament, and the fulness of power, the power of simplicity and truth, with which this noble chord is struck both in the exterior and interior of the Palace of Industry. No one, as he stands in the centre of the transept, and glances to either end, along each aisle, and up to gallery or truss, can well escape feeling the imposing general effect, and the satisfactoriness of the individual constituents, unalloyed by a single one among the many jarring or meretricious architectural influences of the day. He is impressed, perhaps, without knowing why, by the good faith and coherence which are the key-notes of the piece; and tacitly recognizes that here is an architectural reality of its kind.

Such a palace, it is plain, must *not* come down. To remove it would be to efface the only yet existing structure wherein we have manifested our ability to do other than disfigure the earth and annihilate the legacies of past art. There are not wanting purposes to which such a building might be applied.

It remains to be added, great credit is due to much of the moulding and ornament of the iron-work throughout, always simple, often novel, and true to the material. It is consistent and effective, down to the pallisade outside. For once in a way, this is artistic, which that of many a new gothic pretence, all archæologicalness and ornament elsewhere, is not. The attempt is usually dropped as hopeless here, at the outposts, where we approach something real, therefore intractable.

Polychromy was of course an essential feature in a building constructed of wood, iron, and glass; as more or less it is rightly of all buildings. Owen Jones's simple endeavour is eminently effective. His blue and yellow, with incidental reds, are as felicitous in their harmonious combination, as appropriate. A fuller development of decorative effect might well have been adopted. But, considering the present crude state of public taste, no inexcusable timidity has been evinced. It is to be regretted that certain arbitrarily-chosen colours were not employed in invariable connexion with certain materials, so as to become distinctively suggestive to eye and mind. On this plan, one material does not simulate another, but, telling truly its own tale, contributes to the general intelligence of the whole building. This is an essential principle, not usually recognized in all architectural decoration of various materials. It might readily be subordinated to general harmony, were adequate thought and trouble expended. These conventional limitations might be transmuted, as are those of certain forms of verse, into the means of a more perfect success. In the present instance, iron and wood are mutually confounded. The mind is prevented from recognizing that, especially demanding expression,—the conditions of material supplying at once the fabric's stability and grace. In the exterior, the ugly brown of the wooden panels on the ground tier is the most serious blemish of the building, easily to be rectified by substitution of another hue.

We had purposed developing a more determinate and satisfactory comparative view of the Industry and Arts of all Nations, as illustrated by the present Exhibition. Here are assembled the data for such a summary, ordinarily scattered abroad, unmethodized and disjunct, and to be apprehended in their natural relationships and mutual bearings, only by an effort of thought. The survey would not have been unattended with interest and profit. The characteristic excellences, and short-comings, and individualities of each nation would have appeared. But we cannot compliment the Executive Committee on the spirit in which they forwarded our design. On and after the opening day we were excluded. No provision had been made for literary men employed on the subject, if without the pale of the newspaper-press. The latter is respected because *feared;* because formidable at the moment. Literature is for its own sake held cheap enough. We may here mention that some who were entrusted by the Commission with dispensing the free admissions, inclined at first to ostracise the religious portion of the press; but, in the end, abandoned so illiberal and absurd an exception. Such a fact is little creditable to the subalterns in question.

The Commission itself has manifested that practical wisdom which an undertaking of the kind was likely to call forth in England. It has been steadied in its course by the intelligence from without brought to bear upon it, and by the assistance so many capable men have volunteered. In the talent it has *educed* rests its happiest success. The Building Committee was once on the brink of a fatal error, by its award of prizes to plausible professional feats of architectural ambition in the 'grand style,' altogether beside the mark, when Mr. Paxton came forward and rescued it. By a single felicitous idea, he enabled the Commission at once to engage the interest and sympathies of the world on its side. Throughout, other powers besides the Commission have assisted to make things feasible. Had not the manufacturers and tradesmen of all countries stepped forward so energetically and nobly, where would have been the Exhibition ? Where the representation of the world's industry, with its new facilities for the world's instruction? It is, in substance, to the capitalists who supplied the sinews of war; to the exhibitors; to Mr. Paxton, the architect; to Messrs. Fox and Henderson, the able contractors ; that the present edifying manifestation of industrial skill and power is due. They have been the main-springs of the work—the creators.

The *Executive Committee*, that body entrusted with the practical control of the Exhibition, and in the working of it, the more really though not ostensibly prominent, is altogether separate from the Commission in character and claims. Credit is due to it as a body, for its industry and energy. But a stronger infusion of men of business would, in any after undertaking of the kind, be desirable. Its performance of its duties has been of mixed merit. Neither has it failed to indulge in some of the more orthodox failings of the official genus. It would be too much to expect from officialism, even on an occasion like the present, that it should forget to be itself. There have not been wanting signs, in fact, of these minor ruling heads growing giddy with their elevation.

However well the plan may have answered on the present occasion, assisted by the general intelligence and public spirit, and by the earnest efforts of exhibitors *en masse*, the conduct of a second great industrial exhibition, whether national or universal, will require to be placed on a broader and more popular basis. In it a due proportion of the exhibitors' representatives must have their just and natural share. We believe that no future enterprise of the kind will command their confidence, or be responded to as the present has been, if its government be similarly constituted to the present.

Both the Commission and its executive have naturally enough but indistinct perceptions on some subjects : their true relations to the public, and the exhibitors, for example. They do not, perhaps, with sufficient clearness, bear in mind that *they* are not the Alpha and Omega of the exhibition. Exhibitors, as the virtual authors of the exhibition, have surely their *rights* as well as their duties ; and we should have been glad, had it been deemed possible and expedient, to give them as a class free admission. This has been done, we are aware, to a large extent in the case of foreign exhibitors, and several hundreds of our own countrymen made early application for season tickets. The number of exhibitors, therefore, affected by the regulation of the Commissioners, is comparatively small; and we are not ignorant of, nor do we underrate the objections which attach to an indiscriminate issue of free tickets to such. Still it would have been matter for gratulation, if some plan could have been devised, by which the wishes of such exhibitors might have been harmonized with the responsibilities of the Commission. Contributors to every other kind of exhibition hitherto known, that of the Academy included, are untaxed visitants. True, the exhibitors have not been formally charged for the space occupied. But, be it remembered, it is *their* contributions the public go to see, and which will thus pay for the building, and the official expenses. A few thousand pounds are gained, but the good will of many of the exhibitors is endangered, and a future occasion may show whether it be a profitable exchange.

We trust the good cause of industrial exhibitions, local, national, or universal, with their enlightening influence, and, as yet, undefined capabilities, may not suffer by this merely incidental hitch. Means may be discovered to avoid like drawbacks in coming times. The present exhibition is sure to prove a self-paying one.* This should supply the manufacturers and tradesmen of England with a hint. Let them study the words *co-operation* and *voluntary*. They must be reminded that those who wait to be helped by another get the help on that other's terms. They who cannot stand alone, complain to little purpose that the crutch galls them. High patronage has lent an *éclat* and impetus to the Exhibition, has riveted the attention of fashionables, and respectables, as of the people at large; made it popular among those who once decried as among those who always steadily apprehended the value of that which is now a

---

* The number of Season Tickets issued to the 24th inclusive, is 24,787; and the amount paid on them, 65,776l. 4s. The daily receipts paid on entrance are as follows; and we rejoice to find, what we have previously anticipated, that the reduction of the fee from 20s. to 5s., instead of diminishing the receipts, has served largely to increase them:—

| | £ | s. | d. | | | £ | s. | d. |
|---|---|---|---|---|---|---|---|---|
| May 2 | 560 | 0 | 0 | | May 14 | 2064 | 15 | 0 |
| „ 3 | 482 | 0 | 0 | | „ 15 | 2426 | 0 | 0 |
| „ 5 | 1362 | 19 | 0 | | „ 16 | 2556 | 10 | 0 |
| „ 6 | 1458 | 10 | 0 | | „ 17 | 2472 | 5 | 0 |
| „ 7 | 1790 | 15 | 0 | | „ 19 | 2345 | 0 | 0 |
| „ 8 | 2018 | 0 | 0 | | „ 20 | 3360 | 15 | 0 |
| „ 9 | 1824 | 10 | 0 | | „ 21 | 3512 | 5 | 0 |
| „ 10 | 1843 | 15 | 0 | | „ 22 | 3797 | 11 | 0 |
| „ 12 | 1597 | 10 | 0 | | „ 23 | 4095 | 10 | 0 |
| „ 13 | 2229 | 10 | 0 | | „ 24 | 5078 | 0 | 0 |

realized fact. This aid has filled the exchequer. And all praise is due to liberal-minded high personages for interesting themselves in matters ordinarily so beside the aims and sympathies of their order. But such influence has its drawbacks. Realities cannot, in the long run, profit by dilettant encouragement, however enlightened. It casts suspicion on them. They had better stand on their own basis. Attracting an interest in kind and amount not naturally their own, they take an unreal position, and lose by the alliance. There comes a reaction. The exaggerated brightness of the theatre at evening spoils us for the sober light of morning. All things considered, it were better that Industry should learn to be independent. We hope one day to see equally important exhibitions with the present set on foot, and governed by manufacturers and traders themselves; appealing to the public for support in the legitimate way, without resort to eleemosynary aid.

After all deductions, notwithstanding the too apparent presence in its origin and management of the hand of dilettantism; notwithstanding some appearance of injustice to exhibitors, and a false system of relations between them and the governing powers; notwithstanding an anomalous tinge of the old Adam, and a Commission which has sometimes needed an omnipotent press to keep it right; despite executive committee-men and secretaries, whose failing is not an inadequate sense of their own importance; the enterprise has been a prosperous one. The Exhibition itself is a marvel of the day; and, for once, rightly so. As a mere gala-'sight' it is the most imposing and brilliant the modern world has seen. In its more essential bearings it is a work fruitful in good; calculated to help on many a good cause —that of manufacturing design, of popular education, of practical realities in every kind. The people's day has just set in. The shilling visitor's turn is come. Happily, his is intrinsically the best. He sees the Exhibition at its fairest, really opened, not disordered and incomplete. They for whom the Exhibition has so pregnant meaning; they who by their strong arms fashioned its rich contents, are now admitted. All along, the real import of the Exhibition is the same. In every sense of the word, it is a *people's* exhibition. From the people it springs; for the people, most of all, it has a mission. The operative's triumph, conscious or unconscious, will be great.

We can scarcely hope to see, in this world, a sight to be compared with the majestic and joyous ceremony of opening the Crystal Palace on the First of May. To describe the particular facts, even in the most dry detail, would be no easy task—they were so numerous, so diversified, so widely apart, so singular in themselves, and so harmonious in their effect. To signify by words the emotions of the mind in a scene so vast, so gorgeous, so solemn, yet so gay, is utterly impossible. Our own experiences, we confess, were, in most respects, different from what we had expected. The occasion was entirely novel. Its whole character was unique. The first feeling was that of being overwhelmed with a sense of vastness; our next, an unusual ruffle of delight at being surrounded with such radiations of dazzling beauty, and such masses of artistic grandeur; then came a dizzy admiration of the fairy-like enchantment, which seemed to endow one with a power familiar to our dreams, of gliding smoothly and rapidly over continents, islands, mountains, seas, blending in fantastic groups the ages of the past with the day that was passing, and mingling the spirit of the times gone by with the higher and broader hopes of the times that are drawing on. The perfect solitude of whole regions of the building was in almost petrifying contrast with the marvellous crowds of both sexes, and of remote nations, that were pressing and thronging near the transept and down the front of the nave to witness the inauguration and the royal procession. As the hour of noon approached, the whole multitudinous assembly appeared to have settled down into a quiet, but intense, consciousness, of being about to see something, for the first and for the last time, in the heart and crisis of the world's civilization. Then the distant hum of the hundreds of thousands of good-humoured people forming the larger company outside; the boom of the cannon; the blast of the trumpets; the full swell of pealing organs, and a thousand voices in sweet yet thundering harmony. Then a hush—a solemn prayer. Then the Queen, leaning on the arm of Prince Albert, each of them leading one of their children; and the gentle and courteous loyalty with which the endless rows of elegantly-dressed ladies and gentlemen smiled and wept, and waved their hats and handkerchiefs, as the beautiful pageant passed before them, while organ after organ took up the National Anthem. We scarcely think there was one person in that wonderful congregation that did not feel, for a while, that he was in a temple rather than a palace. Such was our own case. Such was the case with all with whom we have compared remembrances. In one short sentence we may say—The *opening* of the Exhibition was worthy of the *Exhibition* itself.

## Review of the Month.

THE ECCLESIASTICAL TITLES BILL has made but little progress during the past month. We are not much surprised at this, and have no disposition to join in the contemptuous and indiscriminate censures passed on its opponents by some of our contemporaries. We make no allowance for the partizanship of Mr. Disraeli, the personal resentments of Mr. Urquhart, or the vanity of some other members who often figure in the debate. But the case is different with Mr. Reynolds, Mr. Keogh, and other Roman Catholics. Their position entitles them to forbearance. There is at least the semblance of a principle in their procedure; and much, therefore, as we differ from them—though we deem their reasoning illogical, their language intemperate, their threats absurd, and the course of some of them most factious—yet we are prepared to bear with much. They view the bill as one 'of pains and penalties,' and denounce it, with an intensity of vituperation to which we are not accustomed, as an insult to their religion, and a wrong to their country. Knowing what we do of Ireland and of Irish members, we are not surprised at this. It is characteristic, and was to be looked for. The expectations of the Premier have probably been somewhat exceeded; but he must have calculated on much of this sort of thing. It is true, that the forms of the House are being pressed to the utmost, to the serious detriment of the public service, and that a change will be necessitated, if the present policy be persisted in. We shall much regret this, and hope the Irish members will yet restrain their resentment and their volubility. The forms of the House cannot be altered, to meet the case which has arisen, without furnishing a precedent which may be injurious hereafter to the freedom of Parliamentary discussion.

The case is vastly different with the principal performers in the scene which was enacted on the 9th. On the question being put, that the Speaker do leave the chair, Mr. Urquhart moved:—' That the recent act of the Pope, in dividing England into dioceses, and appointing bishops thereto, was encouraged by the conduct and declarations of her Majesty's Government. That the publication by Lord John Russell of his letter to the Bishop of Durham, which contained expressions calculated to wound the religious feelings of many of her Majesty's subjects, produced large expectations of legislative remedies which have been disappointed by the provisions contained in the measure now submitted to the House.'

We need not say that we agree with both these resolutions. To do so would only be to repeat what we have frequently stated. The fourth article in our present number is clearly expository of our views as to the encouragement given by our rulers to the Papal Court. Had the propositions, therefore, been submitted in good faith, and on their own merits, they would have been entitled to the support of the Commons. But they were not so submitted. The mover himself did not hesitate to avow that his object was to ' get rid of an inconvenient bill ;'

that the effect of his amendment would be ' a vote of censure upon the past conduct of the Government ;' and that, as the Premier would only ' resign on a direct vote of want of confidence, there was no reason for urging against this proposition that it would occasion the resignation of Ministers and the inconvenience and agitation of a general election.' A more contemptible move we never witnessed. The genuine party spirit is capable of stooping to any artifice, of resorting to any trick, by which its purpose may be served. It has no sense of honor—it regards no rule of right. True or false, useful or pernicious, generous or base-minded, it resorts to any expedient, assumes any form, utters any language, by which it can hope to compass its own selfish end. But even in this depth there is a deeper still; and that is found when personal resentment and ungratified vanity come to the aid of the partizan. Of these evils combined Mr. Urquhart's amendment furnishes a pregnant example. Lord John rightly described it as a ' paltry and shabby pretence,' and laid bare, in his best style, the hollowness of the plea under which it was sought to obtain an anti-ministerial vote. ' As it is at present,' said the Premier, ' they bring forward a substantive motion. As it is at present, they are taking the chance that those who are opposed to the bill will vote with them for the purpose of getting rid of it, though at the same time they wish to make it more stringent, or to introduce another bill with severer provisions. If they choose to take that course, undoubtedly it is in their power to do so ; but I don't think it is such a course as the people of England expect.'

Mr. Disraeli followed in a speech of considerable power ; the caustic declamation of which must have been severely felt. He had truth on his side, and he availed himself of it for a party purpose. He inflicted on the Whig Cabinet, with merciless exultation, a chastisement which they richly deserved; though he made no progress in vindicating his own course  He delivered himself of a damaging party-speech, without raising his reputation with the country, or evidencing one quality of genuine statesmanship. On a division the Government had a majority of 79, the numbers being 201 to 280. Considering all the circumstances of the case, this majority was large, and we are not therefore surprised at being informed that its announcement ' was received with loud cheers by the ministerialists.'

On the following Monday, the 12th, a different course was pursued. The bill, it was argued, related to ' laws affecting religion,' and ought to have been submitted to a committee of the whole House. This, however, not having been done, a preliminary objection was taken by Mr. Moore, which he contended was fatal to the measure. The Speaker gave a different opinion ; but notwithstanding this, much time was occupied in discussing the question, which was not, however, pressed to a division. The member for Dublin moved the adjournment of the debate, which being negatived by 179 to 53, another Irish member immediately moved the adjournment of the House. This motion was rejected by 145 to 36, and was rendered memorable by a piece of secret history which it elicited from the Premier. ' The House,' said Lord John, ' having decided that they would not adjourn the debate, it was now proposed that the House should adjourn, in order to get rid of the bill. This proposition made him suspect that that resolution which hon. members told him they had come to some time ago—not to make any factious opposition to the bill—a resolution he very much admired—he was afraid they had faltered in that resolution now. The House had heard the opinions of the Speaker and some competent members; and were matters now to be reversed because there were some Roman Catholics in Ireland who might suppose that they had a better opinion of order than the Speaker'?

The adjournment of the debate was again moved, and again rejected by an increasing majority, the numbers being 365 to 54; but Lord John ultimately gave way, deprecating the course pursued by the Irish members. 'After they had been,' he remarked, 'four nights discussing the introduction of the bill, and seven nights more upon the second reading, he thought they might now fairly go into committee. He did not, however, wish to keep the House there all night, and he would therefore consent to the adjournment of the subject until Thursday.'

The debate on Thursday, the 15th, terminated in a similar manner, and was distinguished, on the one side, by the speeches of the Lord Advocate and of Mr. Whiteside, in defence of the ministerial measure, and on the other by the violence of Mr. Reynolds, who appeared concerned lest Mr. Keogh should be regarded as more genuinely Irish than himself.

On the following day, the House divided without debate on the question of going into committee; and the affirmative was carried by 116 to 35. Mr. Disraeli's speech, in the after part of the evening, was that of a trickster rather than of a politician. There is no making out what he meant, or what he will do. He had evidently in view two parties, hostile to each other, both of whom he wanted to secure. One eye was turned to the Roman Catholic opponents of the ministerial measure, while the other was fixed on Conservative members, who would make it something more than ' an unhappy semblance of petty religious persecution.' Ultimately, it was agreed that the bill should be re-committed on Monday the 19th; and that, in the meantime, it should be printed as amended.

When the House met on Monday, the bill was presented in its amended form, its preamble slightly enlarged, to include the title of dean with those of archbishop and bishop, and the following enactment inserted as its first clause:—'The said brief, rescript, or letters-apostolical, and all and every the jurisdiction, authority, pre-eminence, or title, conferred or pretended to be conferred thereby, are and shall be and be deemed unlawful and void.'

Its former first clause is now the second; and a third is added, excepting Scotch bishops from the operation of the measure.

To the first clause we raise no objection. On the contrary, we deem it an improvement of the bill, and, as such, urged its adoption in our journal for February last.* We are therefore glad that Lord John has

* P. 252.

incorporated this amendment of Mr. Walpole, and are not surprised that those who have repeatedly asserted his wish to fritter away the measure should be irritated at the adoption of so stringent a provision.

Immediately that the House went into committee on the amended bill, Mr. Reynolds moved that the chairman report progress. Three divisions subsequently took place; and a fourth having been called for, the member for Dublin expressed a hope ' that the Irish members would stand firm in their resistance to a tyrant majority that sought to force upon them a bill of pains and penalties. They would get nothing by political gentility, or by bowing and scraping to the Treasury bench. He could tell them that, if only half-a-dozen members stood together, the Government should not go on with the clause that night; and the sooner they were made acquainted with that fact the better.' Such a system of tactics cannot fail to accomplish its purpose for a time. Its temporary success, however, is dearly purchased, and nothing short of the most absolute necessity can justify a resort to it. Ministers, of course, gave way, and further progress was deferred till Friday.

On that day, the 23rd, three divisions took place on amendments proposed by Mr. T. Duncombe, the Earl of Arundel and Surrey, and Mr. Sadlier, in which the views of Government were affirmed by majorities of 172, 155, and 160. The chairman then reported progress, with leave to sit on the 26th. When the House met accordingly on the 26th, the same course was pursued. Four divisions took place on amendments substantially similar, and on its being moved that the chairmain report progress, the Premier gave way, remarking that, ' It was now sufficiently clear that hon. members had been making the same motion over and over again. That when they had gone into the lobby, finding themselves in a small minority, they had framed motions at the moment which had been before rejected, and brought them before the committee in a different shape. That being sufficiently obvious, he thought it as well they should have time to reflect on this conduct.'

THE OATH OF ABJURATION BILL was read a second time on the 1st, and the majority in its favor was, we doubt not, considerably diminished by the august ceremony enacted in Hyde-park on the same day. The debate—if it may be called such—was insipid and unimproving. Mr. Newdegate was the hero of opposition, and the views he broached were sadly out of date. They might have done for the good old Tory days of Lord Liverpool, but we wonder where such men have been living during the last thirty years. ' The Almighty,' said the hon. member, and this is a fair specimen of his logic and theology, ' had decided by his providence that Jews should not legislate for themselves, and he could not conceive, therefore, how they were qualified to legislate for a Christian country. For a thousand years this had been a Christian country, with a Christian legislature.' If the members of the Commons House are to be influenced by such balderdash, their intellect must be far inferior to the average intellect of the community. Sir R. Inglis was, of course, prominent in opposition. This was to be expected, but we did not look for the gratuitous insults which the consistently bigoted member for Oxford University is reported to have uttered. One can scarcely help smiling, at the

same time that one is indignant, at such language as the following:—
' He asked what right had the Jews now residing in England to claim
anything except protection and freedom in the exercise of their religious
opinions? What right had they to expect admission into municipal
offices in this country? Who asked the Jews to come into this
country?' On a division the numbers were 202 for the bill, and 177
against it, leaving in its favor a majority of 25 only. We fear the
fate of the measure in the Upper House.

THE INCOME TAX has been proposed for renewal without improvement, or even modification. All parties—Ministerialists, Conservatives,
Peelites, Free Traders, Radicals—unite in admitting the inequalities
and injustice of the impost, and yet our rulers, with a folly for which
no reasonable excuse can be found, have sought to re-enact it for three
years, without even attempting to diminish the force of a single objection. It afforded them a noble opportunity of recovering popular
favor. It was just such an occasion as a first-class statesman would
have seized, in order to repossess himself of the heart of a people.
The administration needed it; but, alas! for themselves and the
country they rule, they were not equal to the opportunity. Had they
advocated the renewal of the tax for a limited period on the distinct
ground that it is incomparably preferable to a duty on corn, and had
they at the same time sought to remove, or at least to diminish some
of its most objectionable features, they would have carried with them
the concurrence and the thanks of all reflecting men. But they did
not do this. On the contrary, they demanded the tax with all its
manifold and admitted inequities for three years, and gave no very
doubtful intimation of its being regarded, substantially, as a permanent
impost. The folly of their proposition was great, but that of the
Chancellor's speech was greater still. Ultimately, Mr. Hume's amendment, limiting the tax to one year, with a view to inquiry by a select
committee into the mode of assessing and collecting it, was carried by
244 to 230. This division, as ' The Daily News ' remarks, ' is in more
respects than one a remarkable one. The insurgent liberals who have
been enabled by ' foreign aid ' to place Ministers in a minority, are not
mere flash Radicals, neither are they the most stern of the middle-class
financial reformers, who profess to vote on all questions regardless of
the consequences to the Ministry. The Wakleys and O'Connors were
absent from the division, and the Manchester school was found, *en
masse,* in the ministerial ranks. The Liberals who backed Mr. Hume
are the quiet, steady representatives of mercantile communities, who
are in general extremely chary of extremes—the Mowatts, Dukes,
Duncans, and Hasties. If the accession of the Manchester party to
the list of the minority deprives it of the character of a mere Whig
catalogue, the list of Liberals in the majority is one that cannot be
said to consist of reckless or impracticable men.' The Cabinet wisely
bowed to the decision of the House, and a committee is, in consequence, to be appointed.

ON THE MOTION OF LORD NAAS respecting *Home-made Spirits in
Bond,* Ministers were again in a minority on the 6th. The numbers
being equal (159), the Speaker, according to custom, gave a casting-

vote for the motion. The only circumstance of general interest was the hasty and most unseasonable appeal of Mr. Roebuck to the Premier, and the manly and somewhat caustic rejoinder of Lord John. Some persons attach great importance to these ministerial defeats ; we do not do so. They are, no doubt, undesirable, and very damaging ; but their recurrence is, we apprehend, one of the results of the Reform Bill. The old state of parties is broken up, and for a time, at least, we must be content with the inconveniences of a transition state.

THE PROTECTIONISTS have had a great field-day, of which their party loudly boast. Druly-lane Theatre and St. Martin's Hall were crowded, the former to overflowing. The Duke of Richmond presided in the one place, and Earl Stanhope in the other. The speaking, we need scarcely say, was not to our mind. It was earnest even to passion, and dealt in threats which wise men would have withheld. The Chairmen, the Earl of Winchelsea, Mr. Butt (an Irish barrister), Mr. G. F. Young, and Colonel Sibthorp, were not likely to make any large contributions to our knowledge ; while the absence of Lord Stanley and Mr. Disraeli was an ominous fact, which the country will understand. That much suffering is involved in the great commercial change which has been introduced cannot fairly be denied, and we do not, therefore, wonder that landlords and many tenant-farmers loudly condemn it. They are entitled to commiseration, and should be aided in every possible way. The fictitious state of things under which they flourished having been suddenly annulled, they are left without artificial props to contend against the productiveness of the world. A new order has arisen, for which they are unprepared, and their lamentations are loud and grievous. If they were wise, they would see that protection cannot be restored ; but, like another Quixote, they have gone forth on a mission which can only cover them with derision, and must end in failure. They should be thankful for the monopoly they enjoyed so long, instead of deluding themselves with the hope of reviving it. The Drury-lane demonstration was emphatically a class movement. It betokens no strength of will, no earnestness of purpose, no resolve of unceasing labor on the part of the general public. Every one feels that it was the movement of a few whose interests clash with those of the many, and no sane man, therefore, expects much from it. In the event of a general election, it may influence some county, and a few borough, returns, but protection will be no nearer on that account. Even were a majority obtained in the next Parliament, that majority would be more dangerous to the landed aristocracy than to free trade. The people have tasted cheap bread, and will never again permit its price to be raised in order to replenish the exchequer of a class. It would be wiser and far better to employ their energies in manfully contending with the crisis which has arisen, than in calling spirits from the 'vasty deep.'

Two things are suggested by the Drury-lane demonstration. The Protectionists must henceforth be silent respecting the arts and violence of agitators. Having adopted, in its fiercest mood, the calling of the agitator, they must not complain of those who wield it with more effect on behalf of the rights of labor, and the wants of the poor. Again, the advocates of free trade—the Thompsons, the Villierses, the Cobdens, and the Brights—must prepare for another, a brief it may be, but a severe and final struggle. Their opponents are marshalling their forces, and determined, apparently, on another trial of strength. Let not the country be taken unawares. The press and the platform, and the floor of St. Stephen's, should be vigorously worked in elucidation of the *real* working of unrestricted commerce. The people want *facts*. Let these be supplied, and we fear not the result, whenever the contest may come. We are not sure that our leaders are fully alive to the requirements of the hour, or to the responsibilities of their position.

THE MALT-TAX was brought before the House on the 8th, by Mr. Cayley, who moved the appointment of a committee to consider the tax, 'with a view to the introduction of a bill for its repeal.' Many of the agricultural and Irish members were absent; and the majority which divided against the motion was doubtless increased by the vote previously taken to renew the income-tax for one year only. Very little interest characterised the debate; and on a division, the motion of the hon. member for the North Riding was lost by a majority of 136—the numbers being, 122 for, and 258 against it. We are not surprised at this result, though it ought surely to open the eyes of agriculturists to the manner in which they are duped.
affecting them, from which they ente
relief, and about which their would-be
to discourse on the hustings and at c
topic only 122

tax Bill being brought up on the 9th, the Chancellor of the Exchequer announced his intention to introduce a clause, by which a right of appeal would be given to tenant-farmers rated under Schedule B. We have nothing to say against the concession, save that, if right now, it was right when the bill was framed, and ought then to have been incorporated in it. Our Ministers, however, are men of expediency rather than of principle. They seem to have no settled purpose, no fixed rule. They move hither and thither according to the force put upon them;—are content to stave off the difficulty of the hour, instead of forecasting events, and of taking large, broad, views of things. This defect has been specially visible in their financial arrangements.

THE RAILWAY AUDIT BILL, introduced by Mr. Locke, has been advanced a stage, notwithstanding the unfriendly feeling with which it is regarded by the Government. On the order for going into committee, on the 7th, the President of the Board of Trade, though not dividing against the bill, did all in his power to damage it, by declaring that 'the country would be deluded did it suppose that any additional security to the audits of railway accounts would result from the operation of the bill.' The centralizing policy of the Whig Government is perpetually showing itself, and constitutes one of their worst features. It is obviously a system, and ought to be steadily opposed by every lover of freedom. What we have already witnessed in the matters of

education, interments, and Smithfield, are but samples of a monster
evil.   Hitherto, Englishmen have relied on themselves, but the
Government is now proffering to do everything for them ; and this
lies at the basis of Mr. Labouchere's opposition to the Audit Bill, prepared by forty gentlemen who represented 120,000,000*l*. sterling.
Mr. Hume took the sound position, and put the case in a light which
could scarcely fail to have influence on impartial men.    He held ' that
the present bill *was based on a sound principle;* and that the Government had no right to interfere with joint-stock companies further than
to give them the power to carry out their own affairs.    Suppose any
such company acted improperly, who suffered ?   The shareholders.    It
therefore appeared wonderful to him that Government should seek to
take the measure out of the hands of those forty gentlemen ; and he
should protest against Government interference with joint-stock companies.'    An amendment, ' That the bill be committed that day six
months,' having been moved, a division took place, when the original
motion was carried by a majority of 23 : the numbers being, 72 for, and
49 against it.    We rejoice in this decision as accordant with sound
principle ; and hope that, in other matters, the House will equally refuse to sanction the continental policy of our rulers.    The bill was
subsequently proceeded with to the 8th clause, when the chairman
reported progress, and had leave to sit again on Wednesday, the 28th.

IN THE MATTER OF CHURCH-RATES, the following gentlemen have
been appointed as a select committee :—Mr. Trelawney, Sir Robert
Harry Inglis, Mr. Henley, Sir David Dundas, Mr. Bright, Mr. Pole
Carew, Mr. Alexander Hope, Mr. Horsman, Sir Charles Douglas, Mr.
Hardcastle, Mr. John Ellis, Sir John Duckworth, Mr. John George
Smythe, Mr. Littleton, and Mr. Heyworth.    It remains to be seen
whether the constitution of the committee is such as to secure a
thorough investigation of the subject.   We have our doubts ; but
feel such confidence in the strength of our case, as to be comparatively
indifferent respecting the *material* of the committee.   One thing certainly
forces itself on our notice.   With the exception of Mr. Bright, there
is no Dissenter, so far as our knowledge extends, on the committee.
This ought not, we think, to have been, more especially as Sir R. Inglis
is amongst the number chosen.

We have reason to believe that diligent efforts are being made to
collect and arrange evidence for the committee.    Mr. Offor, Mr.
Courtauld, and Mr. Pritchard, have been already examined ; and
Mr. Edward Baines, Mr. Joseph Sturge, the Rev. J. A. Goulty, and
others, are prepared to follow.   We have little doubt, whatever the
report of the committee may be, that a body of evidence will be collected which will go far with the country to settle the question.    We
again repeat, that nothing short of the entire extinction of the rate
can meet the claims of justice, or satisfy the demands of enlightened men.

PARLIAMENTARY REFORM has made little way ; or rather, its more
prominent advocates have done themselves little credit during the past
month.   Mr. Hume's annual motion for Parliamentary Reform stood
for the 13th ; but as only twenty-one members were present, no House
was constituted.   Comment on such an occurrence is needless.   The
country understands it, and we are sorry to acknowledge that it confirms

our prior misgivings. We never had much faith in what is termed, 'the People's Party.' There are names in the list which awaken suspicion rather than confidence; and if the whole thing were known, we have a notion that the country would turn away disgusted with the sham. Sir George Grey, we doubt not, gave the true cause of the absence of many when he said, 'that as her Majesty's Government had announced their intention of bringing in a bill on this subject in the next session of Parliament, the members of the House generally felt indisposed to enter upon a discussion which could lead to no practical result, the more especially after having been obliged to sit up to a very late hour on the preceding night.'

This was, no doubt, the case; and it satisfactorily accounts for the absence of mere Whig members, and of many others, who are more or less inclined to put faith in Lord John. The fact alluded to may also have been a good reason—it would have been so to ourselves—why Mr. Hume's motion should not be pressed to a division. But it is no reason—it tells, on the contrary, the other way—why there should not have been a strong muster of Reformers, and such an exposition of their views as would prepare the country for the demonstration which may be needful next year. A display of intelligent earnestness just now, would have done much to facilitate success hereafter. But no such earnestness was seen. Nay, we do not believe it exists; or, if it do exist, it is warped and hand-bound by personal vanities or rivalship. Mr. Hume's explanation was straightforward and satisfactory; and Mr. Williams will do well in future to abstain from such splenetic exhibitions as he made on the 14th. We should be glad to believe that the course of some others was as upright and free from censure as that of the Nestor of Reform.

THE RELIGIOUS HOUSES BILL was rejected on the second reading, by 123 to 91. The mover, Mr. Lacy, stated to the House, on the 14th, in his explanation of the measure, that there were fifty-three Roman Catholic nunneries in England and Wales, and that the number was greatly on the increase. The object and scope of the bill will be best understood from Mr. Lacy's own words, who, in moving the second reading, remarked, 'that he had been informed that it was not Roman Catholic houses only which would be affected by this bill, as there were some Protestant houses of the same description. The word "vows," inserted in this bill, would, he believed, include both. His intention certainly was, that all houses in which ladies resided who were under monastic or religious vows, should be registered—that magistrates should be appointed at quarter sessions to visit them without notice—and that if any persons were found in them who wished to come out, the magistrates should have the power of releasing them. That was the sum and substance of the bill.' Various members spoke against the bill, and Sir George Grey announced that it 'was not a measure which ought to receive the support of Government.' The details of the bill appear to be open to serious objection, while no evidence was adduced in proof of the existence of the evil which it was sought to prevent. The Solicitor-General put these objections in a strong light, when he said, referring to the bill, 'It brought a very grave indictment against a large body of our fellow-subjects without any case whatever being established.  He expected to have heard some cases which would justify the House in accusing the Roman Catholics of forcible detention, because to bring in a bill to prevent that which probably did not exist was not the proper way to proceed. . . . Unless the hon. member for Bodmin could show that there was forcible detention, how could he expect the House to pass a measure which would brand with infamy and crime the whole of our Roman Catholic subjects? because it was a great crime forcibly to detain any person.  The house had been told that because there was suspicion in the public mind, an act of the present kind ought to be passed.  Inquiry was not asked for, but the passing of the bill without inquiry was the object solicited.  It was worthy of remark that not one hon. member had got up in support of the bill who had not said he disapproved of its provisions, although he approved of its principle.'

MR. FOX'S ANNUAL MOTION, in favor of a system of national secular education, to be provided for by local rates, and managed by the rate-payers, was submitted to the House on the 22nd, and rejected by 139 to 49.  As we have so recently entered into this question at considerable length,* we will not dwell upon it further now than to say, that no new feature was elicited in the debate, and that we are more confirmed than ever in the conviction that the cause in which the hon. member for Oldham has embarked is utterly hopeless.  Individuals may do as they please, but the time is yet far distant when the English people will regard with favor such a system as Mr. Fox proposes.  We are glad to find Mr. Heyworth opposing the motion ' as destructive of the voluntary principle, which had already effected so much good.  It was a farce,' he said, ' to talk of giving the people a free education if a rate was to be levied for the purpose.  He subscribed 200*l*. a year to education, and should be sorry if such streams of voluntary contribution were closed up by the substitute of a tax.'

WE TURN FROM OTHER TOPICS, in order briefly to notice the various missionary anniversaries which have been held during the past month.  These are now characteristic of our day and country, and will not be overlooked by any intelligent observer who is desirous of noticing the features of our times.

With but one exception, we believe, that of the Wesleyan Missionary Society, all these institutions exhibit a condition of financial improvement.  The Wesleyan Society only, from causes well known, announces a diminution in its receipts, to the amount of more than 9,000*l*.  But this decrease must not be regarded as in any sense an indication of the loss of interest in the great work of heathen evangelization, but rather as a testimony against the autocratic spirit by which all Conference affairs are pervaded.

One general feature may be said to characterise the present position of missionary labors.  Successes have everywhere attended the efforts put forth, and in numerous cases they are the cause of embarrassment.  Converts multiply; but their great numbers render past and present plans in some cases useless, in others unsuitable.  Neither European agency, nor funds, is sufficient to meet the require-

* The Rival Educational Projects.

ments of the numerous populations now accessible to the messenger of divine mercy, or to provide men of European civilization or habits to form the native churches. All the societies are, therefore, turning their most anxious attention to the preparation of a native ministry, that shall take up the work where the European is constrained to leave it, and secure permanent possession of the ground at present occupied. We rejoice in this. The evangelization of the heathen has been made to rest on the hands of European laborers too long. Too little confidence has been placed in the Christian character of the converts. Their assumed feebleness has been made a reason for keeping them feeble; their supposed inability to go alone, the ground of withholding from them the opportunity of effort. As if the nestling would ever fly without running the risk of a fall, or be prevented by its careful parent from the attempt, until on a strong pinion it could mount aloft, and battle with the wind and storm.

correlative obligations. And we have every confidence in the power of that divine truth they have received, to render them worthy of the Christian name, and to sustain them amidst the moral dangers of their position.

But while evangelical laborers toil
the gospel to the heathen, the enemy

dissensions, strifes, recriminations, and heresies.
immature convert is perplexed by the various and adverse claims of the contending parties. The party spirit of the apostolic age is revived, and errors as gross are promulgated among the lately converted heathen by men in the garb of Christianity. The source of many of these lamentable events is at home, and their counteraction is to be sought in an increasing evangelism brought to bear on the people of this country, and the cessation of that State support, which gives to Puseyite and Papist so large a part of the means of injury and annoyance, to which our missionary operations are exposed.

We must confess to some regret at the small number of episcopal visitants and speakers on some of the platforms. A more manifest protest could not have been given against the Tractarian heresy, or a more decisive proof exhibited of the earnestness of the heads of the Establishment to maintain evangelic and Protestant truth, than a numerous and manly support of the Bible and Church Missionary Societies. Their absence indicates hesitation or indifference. In either case it justifies the most painful forebodings from the pious Churchman, and the anticipated early triumph of the Establishment's opponent. With such leaders and defenders as the Church of England now possesses, its doom is certain, nor can it be long delayed.

It is an especially cheering feature of the times, and one that should quicken the steps of every true disciple of Christ, that all heathen nations are open to the preaching of the gospel. Since apostolic days, never were there so many tribes and peoples accessible to the messengers of mercy. Almost every land may be traversed by the missionary without danger, and to an unwonted extent men listen with attention to the word of God. India seems to be on the eve of a mighty change. Its idolatries are giving way before the progress of the gospel. All its tribes are evincing a wavering attachment to their ancient creeds, and a wide sentiment is prevailing among every class, and is often expressed, that that glorious land must soon bow to the sceptre of the Prince of the kings of the earth.

### Note on Art. VII. of the May Number.

The gentleman who reviewed the work entitled 'Rovings in the Pacific,' in the last number of this journal, has been at the pains, since the publication of that number, to make strict inquiries—and which he could not make at an earlier period—in reference to the author's allegations as to the character of the missionaries, and the partial failure of their operations in the island of Tahiti. The Reviewer has sought information on these subjects from a gentleman of the highest respectability, who has been for more than twelve years resident on the island, is intimately acquainted with all the missionaries and their labours, and but recently returned therefrom; and the Reviewer begs to inform the readers of the *Eclectic* that those allegations are *utterly without foundation*, as the author, from his inability to enter into the spirit of the missionary work, is unqualified to take a just and proper estimate of its success or failure. The Reviewer, therefore, earnestly begs to retract all that part of his article which is in the least commendatory of the author as a witness in the matters referred to; as his testimony in those matters is not that which a truth-loving public ought to receive.

## Literary Intelligence.

### Just Published.

Essays and Marginalia. By Hartley Coleridge. Edited by his Brother. 2 vols.

Caleb Field: A Tale of the Puritans. By the Author of 'Passages in the Life of Mrs. Margaret Maitland,' &c.

On the Publication of School Books by Government, at the public expense. A Correspondence with the Right Honourable Lord John Russell, M.P., &c.

Lectures on Systematic Theology; embracing Moral Government, the Atonement, Moral and Physical Depravity, Natural, Moral, and Gracious Ability, Repentance, Faith, Justification, Sanctification, &c. By Rev. Charles G. Finney. Edited and Revised, with an Introduction, by the Rev. George Redford, D.D., LL.D., of Worcester.

Floreat Ecclesia. A Manual of Church Poesy. By Miss Rosa Raine.

The Honour and the Sanctity of the Christian Ministry. Being the Substance of a Charge at the Public Setting Apart of the Rev. Alfred Crisp to the Pastoral Office at Longdon, Salop, November 21, 1850. By Edmund Crisp.

St. Paul's Epistles to the Corinthians. An Attempt to convey their Spirit and Significance. By John Hamilton Thom.

Letters to a Candid Inquirer on Animal Magnetism. By William Gregory, M.D.

Autumnal Rambles among the Scottish Mountains; or, Pedestrian Tourist's Friend. By Rev. Thos. Grierson, A.M.

The Poems of Schiller, complete; including all his early suppressed Pieces, attempted in English. By Edgar Alfred Bowring.

The Family of Iona, and other Poems; with Historical Notes.

A Grammar of the German Language, on Dr. Becker's System, with copious Examples, Exercises, and Explanations, for the use of Schools, and for Self-Tuition. By H. Assel. Third Edition.

Tracts for the Times. The Church of England in the Reigns of Henry VIII., Edward VI., and Mary. Vol. I. Part I.

The Talbot Case. An Authoritative and Succinct Account, from 1839 to the Lord Chancellor's Judgment, with Notes and Observations, and a Preface. By Rev. M. Hobart Seymour, M.A.

Logic for the Million. A Familiar Exposition of the Art of Reasoning. By a Fellow of the Royal Society.

Gospel Reminiscences in the West Indies. By Leonard Strong.

The Land of Promise; or, a Topographic Description of the principal Places in Palestine, and of the Country eastward of the Jordan, embracing the Researches of the most recent Travellers. By John Kitto, D.D.

Mines and Mining.

London in the Seventeenth and Eighteenth Century.

A Treatise of Equivocation, wherein is largely discussed the Question, whether a Catholic, or any other person before a magistrate, being demanded upon his oath whether a Prieste were in such a place, may (notwithstanding his perfect knowledge to the contrary) without perjury, and securely in conscience, answere, No, with this secret meaninge reserved in his mynde, that he was not there, so that any man is bound to detect it. Edited by David Jardine, Esq., Middle Temple.

Tryphina, and other Poems. By John William Fletcher.

Romanism versus Protestantism; or, the inevitable result of the Present Crisis in the World's History. Part I., the Chart. On Penance and the Confessional, as unscriptural and immoral. By Rev. J. Ross.

The Greek Septuagint Version of the Old Testament, according to the Vatican Edition: together with the real Septuagint Version of Daniel and the Apochrypha, including the Fourth Book of Maccabees, and an Historical Introduction.

The Christian Visitor's Hand-Book to London; comprising a Guide to Churches and Chapels, &c.

The Educator; or, Home, the School, and the Teacher. A Quarterly Journal of Education. No. I.

The New Testament. 'The Received Text,' with selected various readings from Griesbach, Scholz, Lachmann, and Tischendorf, and references to parallel passages.

Traveller's Library: Warren Hastings. By Thomas Babington Macaulay. Reprinted from Mr. Macaulay's 'Critical and Historical Essays.'

Traveller's Library: Lord Clive. By Thomas Babington Macaulay, from ditto.

Traveller's Library: London in 1850, 1851. From the Geographical Dictionary of J. R. M'Culloch.

An Analytical Arrangement of the Holy Scriptures, according to the Principles developed under the name of Parallelisms, in the Writings of Bishop Lowth, Bishop Jebb, and Rev. Thomas Boys. With an Appendix and Notes. By Richard Baillie Roe, B.A. 2 vols.

The Telescope and Microscope. By Thomas Dick, LL.D.

The Great Exhibition, suggestive and anticipative. By Rev. John Cumming, D.D.

Marie Madeleine. Translated by Lady Mary Fox. With Illustrations by M. Lesselle De Bois Gallais.

Voices of the Day. By Rev. John Cumming, D.D.

Great Sights. A Discourse delivered in Kingsland Chapel, on the Sabbath preceding the opening of the Great Exhibition. By Rev. Thomas Aveling.

Christ and Christianity. A Lecture delivered to the Working Classes, at the request of the Committee of the Christian Instruction Society. By Rev. Thomas Aveling, Kingsland Chapel.

Sketches of the Poetical Literature of the Past Half-century, in Six Lectures, delivered at the Edinburgh Philosophical Association. By D. M. Moir.

Violenzia. A Tragedy.

The Hymn Book prepared from Dr. Watts's Psalms and Hymns, and other Authors. With some originals.

Popular Treatise on the Sacrifice of Christ, its nature and extent. By John Paul.

Soft Spring Water from the Surrey Sands. By Hon. William Napier.

Baptismal Regeneration tested by the Scriptures, ancient Fathers of the Church, the Sentiments of the Reformers, and the Confessions and Standards of the Reformed Churches. By a Clergyman of the Church of Scotland.

The Convict Ship and England's Exiles. By Colin Arnott Browning, M.D. R.N. Fifth Edition. Containing an Account of the Convict Ship 'Hashemy,' long detained at the Motherbank by Cholera, and Notices of Prisoners in former Ships.

The Cross and the Crucifix; or, Popery, what it is, and how to repress it. A Lecture delivered before the Members and Friends of the Lincoln Young Men's Improvement Society. By Rev. R. S. Short, Lincoln.

A Word to the Wise; or Hints on the current Improprieties of Expression in Writing and Speaking. By Parry Gwynne. Second Edition.

A Commentary on the Acts of the Apostles. By C. M. Du Veil, D.D. Edited for the Hanserd Knollys Society, with an Historical Introduction, by Rev. F. A. Cox, D.D., LL.D.

Faith and Order. Hints to Candidates for Church Fellowship. By Rev. J. S. Pearsall.

Infants in Heaven; or, the probable Future State of deceased Children. By Rev. R. Edleston, Minister of Albion Chapel, Leeds.

Skeleton Themes, intended to assist in teaching and acquiring the Art of Composition. By Margaret Thornley.

Notes and Reflections on the Epistle to the Romans. By Arthur Pridham.

Desolation of the Sanctuary, and Time of Restitution. A Course of Lectures, designed to show that the first Christian Church has come to its end, and that a new Church is now being established. By Rev. Robert Abbott, Minister of the New Church, Norwich.

Divine Socialism; or, 'The Man Christ Jesus.' By Newman Hall, B.A.

Thoughts on the Death of Moses, Aaron, and Miriam, in three Letters to a Sister.

Papal Errors, their Rise and Progress.

The Way of Peace. An Easter Plea. A Sermon preached before the University of Oxford, on Easter Sunday, 1851. By Rev. S. J. Bernays, M.A.

An Appeal from Earl Grey and Sir William Denison to British Justice and Humanity, against the proposed continuance of Transportation to Van Dieman's Land. In a Letter to the Liberal Press of the Nation (with Petitions and Appendix). By C. G. Stevens, Member of the Anti-transportation Committee, Van Dieman's Land.

# INDEX.

VOL. I. NEW SERIES.

*Alton Locke : Tailor and Poet*, 85; his character, 88; *conduct of the Clergy to the working classes*, 89; *his Socialistic tendencies*, 90; *the author's opinion of the Charter*, 93; the Chartist demonstration 10th April, 94; Alton Locke's death, 94; mixture of truth and error, 95.
Anderson, Dr. J., *The Course of Creation*, 116.
*Annotated Paragraph Bible*, 118.
Astronomy : the Ptolemaic and Copernican systems compared, 543; history of astronomy, 543; Ptolemaic astronomy, 551; history of Copernicus, 556; system of, 558; facts of astronomy, 561.

Baillie, J., *Poetical Works of*, 407; fragmentary tendency of our present poets, 408; the reasons, 410; character of Joanna Baillie, 411; Lord Jeffrey's criticisms, 412; her plays, 414; her miscellaneous works, 420.
Bell, E. and A., *Wuthering Heights and Agnes Grey*, 222; biographical notice, 223.
Bennett, W. C., *Poems*, 563; object of poetry, 564; poetical character of the book, 566; *stages of babyhood*, 568; *popular education*, 570; want of religion in the book, 572.
Binney, Rev. T., *Maidens and Mothers*, 630.
Bloomfield, Rev. Dr., *Additional Annotations on the New Testament*, 239.
Borrow, G., *Lavengro : the Scholar—the Gypsy—the Priest*, 438; out-

line of the narrative, 440; *picture of Norwich*, 442; strictures on the work, 444.
*Bourdaloue, Works of*, 276.
Brown, Dr. J., *Discourses and Sayings of our Lord*, 33; *interests of vital godliness best served*, 33; moral condition of the people, 35, 36; duty of Christian churches, 37, 38; exposition of the Scriptures, 39, 40.
Brown, J. B., *Priest, the essence of Pope*, 98.
Browning, E. P., *Poems*, 295; *the Drama of Exile*, 297; *Lady Geraldine's Courtship*, 300; *Runaway Slave*, 302.

Caffre War, 611; causes of the war, 612; Mr. Freeman's letter to Earl Grey, 615; *Sir Andrew Stockenstrom's letter to the Secretary of State*, 618; points to be settled by the Parliamentary committee, 622.
Calvin, J., *Antidote to the Popish Articles of Faith*, 97.
Capper, S., *The acknowledged doctrines of the Church of Rome*, 97.
Carlile, Dr. J., *The Papal Invasion : how to defeat it*, 97.
Carlisle, Lord, *A Lecture on the 'Genius of Pope,'* 191; lecture on America, 192; estimation of Pope, 194; the rank of a poet, 195; Pope's genius, 195; his culture, 197; his special faculties, 199; his works, 200.
Cartwright, Rev. J. B., *No Popery*, 228.

*Cautions for the Times*, 347, 357.
*Christian Socialism*, 66 ; state of the
working classes, 66 ; union of working tailors, 70; *meaning of socialism,*
73 ; how is it to be established, 75 ;
its effect, 76 ; success of working-
men's associations, 79 ; necessity of
self-reliance. 81.
*Chronological New Testament,* 241.
Cochrane, A. B., *Young Italy,* 204.
Coleridge, H., *Life, Poems, and
Essays of,* 645 ; aberrations of
genius, 647 ; influence of Carlyle
on literature, 651 ; characteristics
of H. Coleridge, 653 ; biography
of, 655 ; character of poetry, 657 ;
Essays and Marginalia, 660.
Coleridge, S. T., *Works of,* 1 ; religion not exempted from change,
1, 2 ; development of, 3, 4 ; relation of philosophy to theology, 5 ;
theology a science, 5 ; relation of
theology to religion, 8, 9 ; distinction between theology and religion,
8 ; charge of plagiarism, 10 ; *influence of philosophy on religion,*
13 ; *view of the evidences of Christianity,* 18 ; *original sin,* 19 ; Shakspere, 21.
Collette, C. H., *Romanism in England
exposed,* 98.
*Colonial Land and Emigration Com-
missioners, Tenth Report of,* 179 ;
distribution and fluctuation of emigrants, 181 ; causes of the same,
183 ; interior settlements, 187 ;
means to be used, 188.
Conder, Rev. G. W., *Protestantism
for* 1850, 228, 238.
Conder, J., *The Poet of the Sanctuary,*
499.
*Congregational Year-Book for* 1850,
243.
Crompton, J. B., *Excise Duty on
Paper considered as affecting the
employment of the Poor, the grievance of the Manufacturer, and the
injury to the Consumer,* 360.
Cumming, Dr. J., *Lectures on Cardinal
Wiseman,* 97; *Prophetic Studies,*
228, 234.

Dennistoun, J., *Memoirs of the Dukes
of Urbino, from* 1440 *to* 1630, 257 ;
Influence of Italy on the world,
258; on religious art, 260 ; condition of Urbino, 262 ; state of

Italy in 1444, 263 ; Urbino the
retreat of the learned, 266.
*Duty of England. A Protestant
Layman's Reply to Cardinal Wiseman's ' Appeal,'* 347, 357.

Education, Rival Projects of, 471 ;
state of education, 471 ; working
of the Minutes of Council of 1846
and 1847, 473 ; remarks on the
Lancashire and National Public
School Associations, 477 ; also on
the Manchester School Association,
485 ; ought admission to schools to
be free ? 491 ; is education to be
supported by voluntary efforts or
by compulsion ? 492 ; results of
voluntary efforts, 495.
Ellis, Rev. W., *Village Lectures on
Popery,* 228, 237.
*Euphranor : A Dialogue on Youth,*
501.
Exhibition, The Great, 739 ; universal
interest of, 739 ; what it indicates,
740 ; a school, 741 ; bearing on
industry, 742 ; commentary on the
age, 743 ; productions of France,
744 ; Switzerland, 745 ; Germany,
745 ; Spain, Portugal, Belgium,
Holland, and Italy, 746 ; England,
747 ; the building, 750 ; merits of
the Commission, 754 ; the Executive Committee, 755 ; success of
Exhibition, 756 ; future tendency,
757 ; opening of, 758.

*Family Almanack for* 1851, 631.
Fison, Mrs. W., *Hints for the Earnest
Student,* 247.
Fleming, R., *The Rise and Fall of
the Papacy,* 97.
Fletcher, Rev. Dr., *Lectures on the
Principles and Institutions of the
Roman Catholic Religion,* 228, 238.
Forbes, F. E., *Dahomey and the
Dahomans,* 459 ; the locality of
Dahomey, 459 ; its connexion with
the slave-trade, 460 ; *its army,* 462;
*the social habits of the people,* 464 ;
*their religion,* 465 ; *description of
the city,* 467 ; *reception by the king,*
468.
Forster, Rev. W., *Plain Words to
Plain People,* 98.
Freeman, J. J., The Caffre War, 611.
French Pulpit, 278 ; Bourdaloue and
Bossuet, 278 ; Massillon, 285.

Fugitive Slave Law, 661 ; passing of, 662; history of, 664; repugnance to constitutional law, 666; *Mr. Beecher's opinion on*, 667; obstructions to emancipation, 669; slavery upheld by the Church, 672; *opinions of various ministers*, 674; *position taken up by British Churches, &c*, 675—679

Geldart, Mrs. T., *Thoughts for Home*, 118.

Giles, Rev. Dr., *Hebrew Records*, 630.

Gilfillan, G., *Bards of the Bible*, 718; division of human knowledge, 718; complete man, 719; anomalous character of the age, 720; want of the age, 721; characteristics of author, 723; characteristics of the Hebrew poets, 725; nature of poetry, 729; spirit of the work, 732; distinction between speech and language, 734; specific inspiration of the Bible, 738.

Green, Rev. S. G., *The Working Classes of Great Britain*. 115.

Hall, Newman, *Dissent and the Papal Bull*, 98.

Hall, Dr. C., *The Effects of Civilization on the People in European States*, 118.

Halliwell, J. O., *Popular Rhymes and Nursery Tales*, 172; similarity of nursery literature in several countries, 173; superstitions connected with animals, 175; *supposed efficacy of certain herbs and ceremonies*, 176; dairymaids' charms, 178.

Hogan, W., *Auricular Confession and Popish Nunneries*, 97.

Holland, Lord, *Foreign Reminiscences of*, 335; hospitality of Holland House, 336; *sketch of Mirabeau*, 338; *of Lafayette*, 339; *of Marie Antoinette*, 340; *of M. de Talleyrand*, and Fouché, 342; of Napoleon, 344.

Howitt, W., *The Year Book of the Country*, 245; *Madam Dorrington of the Dene*, 627.

*Illustrated Year Book*, 244.

*Imperial Cyclopædia, Parts* i. to v., 114.

Irish Church, 680, the great difficulty in dealing with the Papacy, 680; tampering with Papacy, 681; policy of Irish priests, 684; position of Lord John, 687; policy of Papal Court, 688; Maynooth, 692; abolition of Irish Church security of Protestantism, 693.

James, J. A., *The Papal Aggression and Popery contemplated Religiously*, 347, 357.

*Journal de St. Petersbourg de* 1849 *et* 1850, 41; Designs of Russia, 41; state of Central Asia, 41; and of its tribes, 45, 53.

*King of the Golden River: or, The Black Brothers: a Legend of Styria*, 377.

Kitto, Dr., *Journal of Sacred Literature*, 242; *The Pictorial Family Bible. Parts* i.—iii., 631.

Knight, C., *The Case of the Authors as regards the Paper Duty*, 360.

Knox, A. E., *Game Birds and Wild Fowls : their friends and their foes*, 55; *poachers' method of catching partridges*, 57; *breeding of pheasants*, 58; *asylum for the same*, 60; *on peregrines*, 61; *affection of the falcon*, 64; *defence of the badger*, weasel, and squirrel, 65.

Legge, George, *Christianity in harmony with Man's Nature*, 117.

*Literary Intelligence*, 126, 255, 388, 514, 642, 770.

London University, 517; its establishment, 518; its object, 519; labours of its Senate, 520; its curriculum, 521; its finances, 527; its prospects, 529; position of its graduates, 530.

Massey, W., *Common Sense v. Common Law*. 378.

*Massillon, Works of*, 276.

Mazzini, J., *Royalty and Republicanism in Italy*, 204; Mr. A. B. Cochrane as an historian, 206; *state of feeling in Italy*, 211; part taken by England, 212; *Mr. Cochrane's Libel on the Italian Republic*, 213; character of Mazzini, 219; *his account of the Roman army*, 220.

M'All, S., *Lectures delivered at the*

*Monthly United Service of the Nonconformist Churches in Nottingham*, 501.

M'Crie, Dr. T., *Memoirs of Sir Andrew Agnew*, 145; the leader of the Sabbath cause in Parliament, 145; election to Parliament, 149; his motion for the better observance of the Lord's-day, 151; *report of the committee*, 152; loses his seat, 157; his death, 158; his Parliamentary career, 159.

M'Cahe, W.B., *Bertha : A Romance*, 241.

Menteath, Mrs. A. S., *Lays of the Kirk and Covenant*, 22; punctuation, 23; duty of an immature poet, 27; paucity of religious poets, 29; *persecution of Covenanters*, 30; *Peden at the grave of Cameron*, 32.

Merryweather, F. S., *Glimmerings in the Dark ; or, Lights and Shadows of the Olden Time*, 448; description of monastic communities, 450; *works of Roger Bacon*, 451; ignorance of the monks, 452; *want of facilities for travelling*, 453; on *witchcraft and magic*, 454; on miracles and the history of relics, 455; origin of the office of poet-laureatship, 457; *on the household comforts of Old England*, 457.

Morison, Dr. J., *The Present Aspects of Protestantism in Great Britain*, 97.

Morgan, Lady, *Letter to Cardinal Wiseman*, 228, 235.

*Museum of Classical Antiquities*, No. 1, 246.

Napier, Lieut.-Col., *The Book of the Cape*, 611.

*National Cyclopædia of Useful Knowledge, Vol.* xii., 632.

*Nature's Wonders*, 245.

Neander, A., *Light in Dark Places*, 117.

Nichol, LL.D., J. P., The Planetary System; its order and Physical Structure, 543.

Payne, G., *A Manual Explanatory of Congregational Principles*, 118.

*Peeps at Nature*, 245.

*People's Dictionary of the Bible*, 423; on *Atonement*, 426; other subjects,

436; dangerous tendency of the work, 437.

*Politics, the Science of, Part* i.: *The Theory of Human Progression, and Natural Probability of a Reign of Justice*, 389; question of originality, 390; failure of the Theory of Human Progression, 401; sphere of politics, 402; *position of politics as a science*, 404.

Popery, Papal controversy, 98; gradual decay of interest, 99; causes of, 100; truths of the gospel not to be modified by transient speculation, 102; *number of Tractarians*, 103; Papal principles in the Anglican Church, 105; weapons to be used in combating Popery, 107; Power of Romanism, 228; a Power, 228; its many-sidedness, 229; real element of its power, 230; Ultramontanism, 347; *Dr. Twiss on the Roman Catholic Church in Belgium*, 349; *on the recognition of Roman Catholic Bishops in the Colonies*, 352; *the late act of the Pope opposed to the Law of Europe*, 353; *case of Ireland*, 355.

Reed, Dr. A., *The Pope, and his Pretensions*, 97.

*Reflections arising out of the Popish Aggression*, 347, 357.

Review of the Month, 119, 247, 378, 502, 632, 759; Papal question, 119, 247, 379, 505, 632, 759; the budget, 252; Rev. A. Wells and Mr. R. Norris, 252; crisis in France, 253; Schleswig-Holstein contest, 254; agricultural distress, 384; vote on the suffrage, 386; the census, 386; Dr. Pye Smith, 387; position of ministers, 502; Parliamentary business, 512; chancery reform, 635; County Franchise Extension Bill, 636; Jewish disabilities, 637; the amended budget, 637; Church-rates, 640, 766; abjuration bill, 762; income-tax, 763; home-made spirits, 763; protection, 764; malt-tax, 765; railway audit bill, 765; Parliamentary reform, 766; religious houses bill, 767; national education, 768; May anniversaries, 768.

Richards, A. B., *Britain Redeemed and Canada preserved*, 179.

Rogers, J., *Roman Catholicism and Protestant Christianity contrasted*, 347, 359.

Rogers, Rev. J. G., *Christianity and its Evidences*, 500.

Rohner, G. W., *A Practical Treatise on Musical Composition*, 328; system of teaching, 328; works on the subject, 333.

*Rovings in the Pacific, from 1837 to 1849*, 601, 770; the present taste for travel, 601; state of New Zealand, 603; *account of Norfolk Island*, 605; Tahiti and the French invasion, 606.

Ruskin, J., *The Stones of Venice*, Vol. i., 591; derivation of European architecture, 593; ornamental architecture, 596; *Romanist Modern Art*, 599.

Seymour, Rev. M. H., *Mornings among the Jesuits at Rome*, 115.

Smith, Rev. G., *The Protestant Reformation*, 347; 358.

Smith, Dr. J. P., *The Reasons of the Protestant Religion*, 98. Notice of. The Pye Smith Testimonial, 574; *Funeral Discourse*, 575; Dr.Smith's theological engagements, 578; his writings, 583; his controversies, 585; his character, 588.

Smith, Rev. T., *South Africa Delineated*, 247.

Smith, J. S., *Social Aspects*, 161; imitation of Carlyle, 162; social and domestic changes of the age, 163; education and position of English women, 164; Mammonworship, 167; literature, 169; the Spiritual, 170; author's theological sentiments, 170.

Snow, W. P., *Voyage of the 'Prince Albert' in Search of Sir John Franklin*, 315; description of scenery, 317; interview with the Esquimaux, 322; the store-house prepared for Sir John Franklin, 325.

*State Church: in England, Ireland, Scotland, and Wales*, 376.

Stafford, C. T., *Compendium of Universal History*, 246.

Stowell, Dr., *An Address to the Students of Cheshunt College*, 629.

Strange, R., *An Inquiry into the Establishment of the Royal Academy of Arts*, 129; its monopoly, 129; its institution, 129; claims of men of genius not admitted, 134; necessity of a National Academy, 135; its offences, 135; condition of art in England, 137; sculptors, 139; painters, 141.

Stratten, Rev. T., *The Heavenly Supremacy*, 228, 236.

*Taxes on Knowledge*, 360; effect of the impost, 361; its inequality, 363; cost of production of a large octavo volume, 364; its influence on paper manufacture, 366; its unfairness to the honest trader, 367; the mode of assessment, 370; hindrance to enterprise, 373; its injurious effect on other trades, 374.

Thom, Adam, *Chronology of Prophecy*, 243.

Thomas, Rev. D, *The Core of Creeds*, 246.

*Thucydides, an Analysis and Summary of*, 378.

Thwaites, W., *A Tract for the Times*, 347, 359.

Tidmarsh, M. A., *The Kickelburys on the Rhine*, 377.

Timbs, John, *Wonders, Events, and Discoveries* of 1830, 244.

*Trial of Antichrist*, 97.

Turnley, J., *Popery in power, or, The Spirit of the Vatican*, 97.

Twiss, Dr., *The Letters Apostolical of Pope Pius IX., considered with Reference to the Law of England and the Law of Europe*, 346, 347.

University Commission, 699; popular feeling on the necessity for University reform, 699; expense of University education, 701, 705; moral character of public schools, 702; habits of gownsmen, 708; reforms needed—not the establishment of poor colleges, 709; fellowships, 710; private tutors, 711; curriculum, 713; adaptation of colleges to the age, 716.

Urwick, W., *A voice from an Outpost*, 347, 358.

Walford, Rev. W., Autobiography of,

535; number and characteristics of biography, 535; early life of W. Walford, 537; college life, 540.

Warren, S., *The Queen or the Pope*, 346, 356.

Watts, A. A., *Lyrics of the Heart*, 240.

Weiss, B., *A Christian Jew on the Old Testament Scriptures*, 118.

Westwood, T., *Burden of the Bell*, 694; characteristics of Mr. Westwood. 694; *mummy-wrapping*, 695; *The White Angel*, 698.

Wilson, S., *The Bath Fables: or, Morals, Manners, and Faith*, 629.

Wilson, F. A., *Britain redeemed, and Canada preserved*, 179.

Winckelmann, J., *History of Ancient art among the Greeks*, 303; eminence of the Greeks in Sculpture, 303; account of the life of Winckelmann, 306; *influence of the climate on the Greek Artists*, 311; *corporeal beauty of the ancient Greeks*, 312; *honour and respect paid to the Greek Artists*, 313.

LONDON:
MIALL AND COCKSHAW, HORSE-SHOE COURT, LUDGATE-HILL.

Lightning Source UK Ltd.
Milton Keynes UK
UKHW021826190219
337363UK00005BB/947/P